MindTap

MindTap is an online learning solution available with this Philosophy title.

Tap into engagement

MindTap empowers you to produce your best work—consistently. MindTap is designed to help you master the material. Interactive videos, animations, and activities create a learning path designed by your instructor to guide you through the course and focus on what's important.

- With MindTap, everything is in one place—the eBook, activities, flashcards, quizzes, dictionary, and more—making study time more efficient.

- Students will improve their comprehension of course topics and their critical thinking and test-taking skills with interactive activities and quizzes.

- Videos offer concepts from the text in another medium and format, and check student understanding with short quizzes.

- The KnowNow Philosophy Blog, updated weekly by a philosophy instructor, connects philosophical questions with real-world events.

- Instructors can fully customize their MindTap course, organizing and assigning the content and adding videos, links, and their own materials. MindTap can be used on its own or integrated seamlessly with most learning management systems.

Visit us online for complete information or to explore a demo at

www.cengage.com/demo/mindtap or call us at **1-800-423-0563**

MindTap

1. To get started, navigate to www.cengagebrain.com and select "Register a Product."

A new screen will appear prompting you to add a Course Key. A Course Key is a code given to you by your instructor — this is the first of two codes you will need to access MindTap. Every student in your course section should have the same Course Key.

2. Enter the Course Key and click "Register."

If you are accessing MindTap through your school's Learning Management System, such as BlackBoard or Desire2Learn, you may be redirected to use your Course Key/Access Code there. Follow the prompts you are given and feel free to contact support if you need assistance.

3. Confirm your course information above and proceed to the log in portion below.

If you have a CengageBrain username and password, enter it under "Returning Students" and click "Login." If this is your first time, register under "New Students" and click "Create a New Account."

4. Now that you are logged in, you can access the course for free by selecting "Start Free Trial" for 20 days or enter in your Access Code.

Your Access Code is unique to you and acts as payment for MindTap. You may have received it with your book or purchased separately in the bookstore or at www.cengagebrain.com. Enter it and click "Register."

NEED HELP?

PHILOSOPHY

A Text with Readings

PHILOSOPHY
A Text with Readings
THIRTEENTH EDITION

Manuel Velasquez

The Charles Dirksen Professor

Santa Clara University

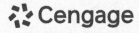 Cengage

Australia • Brazil • Canada • Mexico • Singapore • United Kingdom • United States

Philosophy: A Text with Readings,
Thirteenth Edition
Manuel Velasquez

Product Director: Paul Banks

Product Manager: Debra Matteson

Senior Content Developer: Anais Wheeler

Product Assistant: Michelle Forbes

Media Developer: Amanda Sullivan

Marketing Manager: Sean Ketchem

Content Project Manager: Dan Saabye

Art Director: Marissa Falco

Manufacturing Planner: Julio Esperas

IP Analyst: Alex Ricciardi

IP Project Manager: Betsy Hathaway

Production Service: MPS Limited

Compositor: MPS Limited

Text Designer: Diane Beasley

Cover Designer: Anne Bell Carter

Cover Image: Peter Adams/Photolibrary/
Getty Images

For product information and technology assistance, contact us at
Cengage Customer & Sales Support, 1-800-354-9706
or support.cengage.com.

For permission to use material from this text or product, submit all requests online at **www.copyright.com.**

Library of Congress Control Number: 2015955777

Student Edition:
ISBN: 978-1-305-41047-3

Loose-leaf Edition:
ISBN: 978-1-305-87545-6

Cengage
200 Pier 4 Boulevard
Boston, MA 02210
USA

Cengage is a leading provider of customized learning solutions with employees residing in nearly 40 different countries and sales in more than 125 countries around the world. Find your local representative at: **www.cengage.com.**

To learn more about Cengage platforms and services, register or access your online learning solution, or purchase materials for your course, visit **www.cengage.com.**

Printed in the United States of America
Print Number: 09   Print Year: 2022

For my sons, Brian, Kevin, and Daniel

Contents

CHAPTER 8   Social and Political Philosophy 578

CHAPTER

9

Postscript: The Meaning of Life   666

Preface

When the early Greek philosopher Heraclitus declared "Everything changes!" he could have been speaking of our own era. What word could characterize our time better than the world "change"? New fashions, fads, styles, technologies, and philosophies now supplant each other in ever shorter periods of time. Many believe that the increasing pace of change has profound implications for philosophy. Whether or not this is so, rapid change forces revisions of a more mundane kind in textbooks on philosophy such as this. So although *Philosophy: A Text with Readings* continues to excite readers about philosophy, changes in philosophy and in the world we inhabit necessitate revising the text. I have tried to retain what users have said they like best about this book: that it provides depth and rigor yet is easy to read, fun to use, and manages to cover all the traditional issues with a unique combination of attention to the history of philosophy, regard for interesting contemporary concerns, and substantial selections from classical and contemporary texts. I have worked hard to explain the difficult concepts and texts of philosophy in a way that is technically rigorous and accurate, yet uses language and style that make it easy for a beginning college student with modest reading skills to understand. I have also worked hard at making philosophy interesting and relevant to contemporary undergraduates by showing how it is directly related to their real-life concerns and preoccupations. In addition, a series of sections on critical thinking provide the tools that will enable students to develop their thinking and logical reasoning skills.

I should emphasize what a quick glance at the table of contents will confirm: this text is designed to cover more than most instructors would want to cover in a single course. The coverage is intentionally broad so that the instructor can select those topics that he or she believes are most important and is not limited by the choice of topics that someone else has made. To make it easier for an instructor to choose what his or her course will cover, the chapters are largely independent of one another so that reading a later chapter will not require reading an earlier one. Moreover, the materials within each chapter are arranged so that the most basic or fundamental topics are at the beginning of the chapter, while later sections in the chapter address aspects of the topic that are less fundamental but that probe more deeply or more broadly into the topic. This arrangement gives the instructor the option of either having students study only the basic issues in a chapter by assigning only the early sections or pursuing the subject matter of the chapter more in depth by also assigning the later sections. Some instructors may want to cover the basics in class, and then assign students (or groups of students) the later sections as special projects. There are many different ways of teaching the materials in the book and many different courses that can be put together from these materials.

I have always found that working to revise this text is an enormously satisfying and exciting experience because of the new perspectives and ideas it leads me to confront. I hope that readers will be just as excited by their own explorations of the many visions philosophy offers of what it is to be a human being in today's changing world.

Changes in the Thirteenth Edition

The most important change in this edition is one that affects all of the chapters. I have gone through the text sentence by sentence and have rewritten every sentence whose construction was too complex to be easily understood. I have simplified the syntax of each complex sentence, eliminated any jargon or abstruse vocabulary, and shortened any long or convoluted sentences. I believe the text now can be easily comprehended by any reader, including one with poor reading skills.

A second set of changes that affects every chapter is the introduction of two new types of small "boxes" containing questions designed to help students understand the numerous excerpts from primary sources. Each box contains two or three questions about the excerpt and is positioned next to or immediately after the excerpt. Some of the boxes are entitled Analyzing the Reading. These contain questions that help the student focus on the important philosophical claims made in the excerpt, and to understand and evaluate those claims and the arguments on which they are based. A second type of boxed feature is entitled Thinking Like a Philosopher. These contain questions that ask the student to apply the ideas expressed in the excerpts to his or her own life. Virtually every reading selection has at least one box of questions associated with it. Because these boxes now offer a wealth of questions that are directly related to the readings, I have not felt it was necessary to include the end-of-chapter questions that were in previous editions. However, readers who would like to have such questions can go to the text's website where such questions are provided for each chapter.

As in the previous edition the text includes sixteen modules entitled Thinking Critically that are spread out over several chapters. Each Thinking Critically module not only teaches important reasoning skills, but also helps the reader apply these skills to the philosophical topics discussed in the text. Beginning with the introduction to critical thinking in Chapter 1, the aim of these logic modules is to teach students, step by step, how to critically evaluate their own philosophical thinking and reasoning, as well as the philosophical thoughts and arguments of others. Because critical thinking skills are so important to doing philosophy, most of the Thinking Critically modules occur in the earlier chapters of the book (most, in fact, are in Chapters 1–4).

Five new end-of-chapter readings, some from works of fiction, have also been added to this edition, while numerous new or expanded excerpts from classical and contemporary texts have been incorporated into the chapters.

In addition to hundreds of minor or stylistic revisions, the more substantive changes in specific chapters are as follows:

Chapter 1

- In Section 1.3 the excerpts from Socrates' *Apology* and from the *Crito* have been expanded.

Chapter 2

- In Section 2.2 the excerpts from Plato's *Republic*, the *Phaedrus*, and the *Phaedo*, and the excerpts from St. Augustine's *Confessions*, have been expanded.

- The previous edition's short excerpt from Sartre's *Being and Nothingness*, in Section 2.2, has been replaced with several much longer excerpts from his *Existentialism and Humanism* and the accompanying discussion has been revised.

- New excerpts from Descartes' *Discourse on Method*, new excerpts from two of Smart's articles on the identity theory of the mind, and several new excerpts from Ryle's *The Concept of Mind* have been added to Section 2.2. New discussions of these materials have also been added.

- A new extended excerpt from one of Armstrong's articles on functionalism and a new extended excerpt from an article by Churchland on eliminative materialism also have been added to Section 2.2, and the accompanying discussions have been revised.

- New excerpts from Hume's *Treatise* have been added to Section 2.4 and the discussion has been revised.

- The end-of-chapter readings that accompanied the previous edition have been removed and replaced with three new readings on female identity: Kate Chopin's "The Story of an Hour"; Janice M. Steil's "Contemporary Marriage: Still an Unequal Partnership"; and Jean Grimshaw's "Women's Identity in Feminist Thinking."

Chapter 3

- New excerpts from the writings of the Indian Charvaka philosophers have been added to Section 3.2.

- New excerpts from de La Mettrie's *Man a Machine* have been added to Section 3.2 together with new accompanying discussions.

- Several new excerpts from Berkeley's *Principles of Human Knowledge* have been added to Section 3.2 and the excerpts from the previous edition have been expanded, while discussions of these additions have also been added.

- The Critical Thinking module in Section 3.2 now discusses only conditional arguments and not disjunctive arguments.

- The discussions of pragmatism in Section 3.3 have been revised, and new excerpts from the writings of Pierce and James have been added, while the James excerpts from the previous edition have been expanded.

- In Section 3.6 the discussions of Husserl and Heidegger that were in the previous edition have been removed, while most of the discussion of Kierkegaard has been moved into Chapter 4 and much of the discussion of Sartre has been moved into the discussion of determinism and freedom that now occupies Section 3.6.

- The discussions of determinism and freedom in Section 3.6 have been revised, and several extended excerpts from the writings of Laplace, Sartre, and Stace have been added.

- The end-of-chapter readings in the previous edition have been removed and replaced with two new readings: Sophocles' *Oedipus the King*, and Robert Solomon's "Fate."

Chapter 4

- In Section 4.3 the excerpt from Mackie's article on the problem of evil has been expanded, and new excerpts from Rowe's article on the problem of evil and from Augustine's discussion of the nature of evil, have been added, together with new or revised accompanying discussions.

- The excerpt from James' "The Will to Believe" in Section 4.4 has been substantially expanded, an extended excerpt from Clifford's "The Ethics of Belief" has been added, and the accompanying discussions have been revised.

- In Section 4.5 new excerpts from Kierkegaard's writings on religion and the "leap of faith" have been added, as well as new excerpts from Tillich's writings on attempts to prove that God exists, and new excerpts from the *Bhagavad-Gita*. The discussions accompanying each of these have been revised.

Chapter 5

- New excerpts from Descartes' *Discourse on the Method* have been added to Section 5.2 along with a fuller discussion of his views.

- In Section 5.3 several new excerpts from Locke's *An Essay Concerning Human Understanding* and from Hume's *Treatise* and his *Enquiry* have been added.

- In Section 5.4 the excerpts from Kant's *Critique of Pure Reason* have been expanded and several new excerpts have been added. In addition the text's discussion of his transcendental idealism has been revised.

Chapter 6

- Section 6.1, the introduction to the chapter, has been considerably shortened and simplified by eliminating the discussion of basic and nonbasic beliefs, of foundationalism, and of coherentism. A new brief discussion of truth-bearers has been added.

- The discussion of the correspondence theory of truth in Section 6.2 has been simplified and shortened and the discussion of Tarski's definition of truth has been removed.

- The discussion of the coherence theory of truth in Section 6.2 has been completely revised, and several extended excerpts from Blanshard's *The Nature of Thought* have been added.

- In the discussion of the pragmatic theory of truth in Section 6.2 the excerpts from James' *Pragmatism* have been expanded and the discussion has been revised.

- A new discussion of "pluralist" views of truth has been added to Section 6.2.

Chapter 7

- The discussion of ethical relativism in Section 7.2 has been revised.

- The discussion of utilitarianism in Section 7.3 has also been revised.

- In Section 7.4, the discussion of the "principle of double effect" has been revised as well as the discussions of Kant and of Buddhist ethics.

- The discussion of Aristotle's theory of virtue in Section 7.5 has been revised, the excerpts from his *Nicomachean Ethics* have been expanded, and new excerpts from the writings of Gilligan and Noddings have been added.

- In Section 7.6, a new discussion of the implications of the principle of double effect has been added, along with a new excerpt from Aquinas' *Summa*.

Chapter 8

- The introduction, Section 8.1, has a new short discussion of power and authority.

- In Section 8.2 a new excerpt from Plato's *Republic* has been added, and the excerpts from Hobbes' *Leviathan* and Locke's *Second Treatise* have been expanded and the accompanying discussion has been revised. The short discussion of Rousseau in the previous edition has been removed.

- The excerpts from Mill's *Utilitarianism* in Section 8.3 have been expanded, and new excerpts from Rawls' writings have been added, and the discussion of these has been revised.

- The excerpts from Mill's *On Liberty* in Section 8.4 have been substantially expanded, along with the discussion of his views.

Chapter 9

- In Section 9.1 the excerpt from Tolstoy's *My Confession* has been expanded and a new excerpt from Ayer's writings has been added.

- In Section 9.2 the excerpt from Tolstoy's *My Confession* has been expanded, and a new excerpt from Baier's writings has been added.

- The excerpt from Taylor's *The Meaning of Life* in Section 9.4 has been expanded and the supporting discussion has been revised.

- The excerpts from the writings of Kierkegaard and Sartre in Section 9.5 have been expanded.

- The aesthetics section entitled "What Is Art?" that was formerly part of this chapter is now available in the MindTap, and instructors who wish to use it may have it custom-published with the text.

Organization

Self-discovery and autonomy remain the central notions around which this edition is organized (although these notions are critically discussed in Chapter 2). Each chapter repeatedly returns to these notions and links the materials discussed to the reader's growth in self-knowledge and intellectual autonomy. The ultimate aim of the text is to empower and encourage self-discovery and autonomy in the reader, in part by developing his or her critical thinking skills.

Although the text is organized by topics, the chapters have been arranged in a roughly historical order. The book opens with an introductory chapter on the nature of philosophy that focuses on Socrates as the exemplar of philosophy and includes substantial selections from the Socratic dialogues. Because of the book's focus on the self and the intrinsic importance of the topic, and because human nature was an important concern from the earliest time of philosophy, I turn immediately in Chapter 2 to the discussion of human nature, a discussion that raises several issues more fully treated in later chapters. Then, because Chapter 2 raises many metaphysical and religious issues, I turn to metaphysical issues in Chapter 3 and then to discussions of God and religion in Chapter 4. These issues, of course, were of passionate concern during the medieval and early modern periods of philosophy. Chapters 5 and 6 focus on questions of epistemology, interest in which historically followed the medieval and early modern interest in metaphysical issues. Chapters 7 and 8 are devoted respectively to ethics and social and political philosophy, topics that have preoccupied many philosophers during the late modern and contemporary periods. Chapter 9 focuses on the meaning of life, an issue that is particularly important for many of us today.

Yet no historical period has a monopoly on any of these topics. Consequently, each chapter moves back and forth from classic historical discussions of issues to contemporary discussions of the same or related issues. The chapter on metaphysics, for example, moves from the early modern controversy between materialism and idealism to current discussions of antirealism, some of which hark back to idealism.

Special Features

This text is unique in many ways and includes the following special features:

Learning Objectives. The first page of each chapter outlines the chapter contents and describes the pedagogical objectives of each section of the chapter.

Extended Selections from Primary Sources. Substantial excerpts from primary source materials are introduced in the main text, where they are always carefully explained. To make these materials accessible to beginning undergraduates, new and simplified translations of several texts (by Plato, Aristotle, Aquinas, and others) have been prepared, and several standard translations (such as Max Mueller's translation of Kant) have been simplified and edited. In addition, full versions of many of the excerpts are linked to the eBook in the MindTap for *Philosophy*, via the Questia database. These Questia versions of the readings are also collected in a folder so that instructors and students can see all the supplemental Questia readings in a single location.

Analyzing the Reading Boxes. These boxed features appear alongside each primary source excerpt and contain questions designed to help the student understand the source text and the arguments it advances.

Thinking Like a Philosopher Boxes. These boxed features are also associated with each excerpt and contain questions that apply the concepts in the excerpts to the student's personal life.

Marginal Quick Reviews. These summaries, which appear alongside the text they summarize, help readers identify the main contents of the chapter and give them an easy way to review the materials they have read.

Thinking Critically Modules. A sequence of sixteen modules entitled Thinking Critically, designed to develop the critical thinking and reasoning skills of the reader, is integrated into the text.

Philosophy and Life Boxes. These inserts throughout the text show the impact of philosophy on everyday life or its connections to current issues such as medical dilemmas, sociobiology, psychology, and science. Each box ends with a set of questions designed to spark further thought on the subject.

Color Illustrations. Color photos and art reproductions are used throughout the text to provide visual illustrations of the people and ideas discussed in the text and to stimulate student interest.

Glossary of Terms. Unfamiliar philosophical terminology is explained and defined in the text and highlighted in bold. These highlighted terms are defined again in an alphabetized glossary at the end of the book for easy reference.

Philosophy at the Movies. At the end of each section of the text is a short paragraph that summarizes a film that addresses the topics treated in that section, along with questions that link the film to those topics.

Chapter Summary. The main text of each chapter ends with a summary of the major points that have been covered, organized according to the chapter's main headings and learning objectives (initially laid out at the chapter opening), making them particularly helpful as an overall review.

Readings by Philosophers. Near the end of each chapter are highly accessible readings examining a philosophical question raised in the text. These questions are as diverse as "Does the existence of evil prove God does not exist?" and "Is war morally justified?"

Literature Readings. At the end of each chapter is a short literature selection that raises the issues discussed in the chapter. These readings provide a friendly entry into philosophy for readers who are unaccustomed to traditional philosophical style.

Historical Showcases. Substantial summaries of the life and thought of major philosophers, including female and non-Western philosophers, are placed at the end of each chapter. These historical discussions feature large selections from the works of philosophers who have addressed the issues treated in the chapter. Arranged in chronological order, the Historical Showcases provide a clear and readable overview of the history of philosophy and enable students to see philosophy as a "great conversation" across centuries.

Historical Timeline. Inside the front and back covers is a timeline that locates each philosopher in his or her historical context.

Ancillaries

MindTap. Available for this edition is MindTap for *Philosophy: A Text with Readings*. A fully online, personalized learning experience built upon Cengage Learning content, MindTap combines student learning tools—readings, videos, and activities supporting critical thinking—into a singular Learning Path that guides students through their course. Each chapter contains a wealth of activities written to support student learning. Critical thinking exercises help guide students through complex topics, extended and related readings are integrated with the ebook via the Questia database, and video activators spark connections to the real world, while video lectures reinforce the complex topics presented in the text.

MindTap provides students with ample opportunities to check their understanding, while also providing a clear way to measure and assess student progress for faculty and students alike. Faculty can use MindTap as a turnkey solution or customize by adding their own content, such as YouTube videos or documents, directly into the eBook or within each chapter's Learning Path. The product can be used fully online with the eBook for *Philosophy*, or in conjunction with the printed text.

The Examined Life Video Series. A series of videos has been produced to accompany *Philosophy: A Text with Readings*. Entitled *The Examined Life*, the 26 half-hour videos cover most (but not all) of the topics treated in this edition and move in sequence through each section of each chapter. Each video consists of interviews with contemporary philosophers, dramatizations, historical footage of well-known philosophers, discussions of classical philosophical texts, and visual interpretations of key philosophical concepts. Among the philosophers specially interviewed for this video series are W. V. O. Quine, Hilary Putnam, John Searle, James Rachels, Martha Nussbaum, Marilyn Friedman, Hans Gadamer, Gary Watson, Susan Wolf, Peter Singer, Michael Sandel, Daniel Dennet, Ronald Dworkin, and many others.

Instructor's Manual and Test Bank. This extensive manual contains many suggestions to help instructors highlight and promote further thought on philosophical issues. It also comes with a comprehensive Test Bank featuring multiple-choice, true/false, fill-in-the-blank, and essay questions for each chapter.

Acknowledgments

For their helpful comments and suggestions on this 13th edition revision, I offer sincere thanks to Femi Bogle-Assegai, Capital Community College; Jessica Danos, Merrimack College; Christy Flanagan-Feddon, University of Central Florida; Douglas Hill, Saddleback College and Golden West College; Theresa Jeffries, Gateway Community College; Sharon Kaye, John Carroll University; Richard Kelso, Pellissippi State Community College; Thi Lam, San Jacinto College Central; Bradley Lipinski, Cuyahoga Community College; Ananda Spike, MiraCosta College; Michele Svatos, Eastfield College; and Paul Tipton, Glendale Community College. The members of the Introduction to Philosophy Technology Advisory Board also provided insight into their classrooms that contributed to the development of the MindTap for *Philosophy: A Text with Readings*. Thank you to Kent Anderson, Clarke University; Tara Blaser, Lake Land College; David Burris, Arizona Western College; Dan Dutkofski, Valencia College; Bryan Hilliard, Mississippi University for Women; Sharon Kaye, John Carroll University; Terry Sader, Butler Community College; Julio Torres, Los Angeles City College; Jere Vincent, Great Bay Community College; and Timothy Weldon, University of St. Francis. For their helpful comments and suggestions on earlier editions of the text, I offer sincere thanks to Cathryn Bailey, Minnesota State University; Teresa Cantrell, University of Louisville; A. Keith Carreiro, Bristol Community College at Attleboro; Michael Clifford, Mississippi State University; Christina Conroy, Morehead State University; Stephen Daniel, Texas A&M University; Janice Daurio, Moorpark College; Scott Davison, Morehead State University; Dennis Earl, Coastal Carolina University; Miguel Endara, Los Angeles Pierce College; Philip M. Fortier, Florida Community College at Jacksonville; Paul Gass, Coppin State University; Nathaniel Goldberg, Washington and Lee University; Khalil Habib, Salve Regina University; Randy Haney, Mount San Antonio College; William S. Jamison, University of Alaska Anchorage; Jonathan Katz, Kwantlen Polytechnic University; Stephen Kenzig, Cuyahoga Community College; Hye-Kyung Kim, University of Wisconsin–Green Bay; Emily Kul-backi, Green River Community College; Thi Lam, San Jacinto College Central; David Lane, Mt. San Antonio College and California State University, Long Beach; Mary Latela, Sacred Heart University, Post University; Matthew Daude Laurents, Austin Community College; George J. Lujan, Mission College; Darryl Mehring, University of Colorado at Boulder; Scott Merlino, California State University Sacramento; Mark Michael, Austin Peay State University; Jonathan Miles, Quincy University; John C. Modschiedler, College of DuPage; Michael Monge, Long Beach City College; Jeremy Morris, Ohio University; Patrice Nango, Mesa Community College; Joseph Pak, Los Angeles City College; William Payne, Bellevue College; Steven Pena, San Jacinto College, Central Campus; Alexandra Perry, Bergen Community College; Michael Petri, South Coast College; James Petrik, Ohio University; Michael T. Prahl, Hawkeye Community College and University of Northern Iowa; Randy Ramal, Mt. San Antonio College; Matthew Schuh, Miami Dade College; Ted Shigematsu, Santa Ana College; Karen Sieben, Ocean County College; Paula J. Smithka, University of Southern Mississippi; Doran Smolkin, Kwantlen Polytechnic University; Tim Snead, East Los Angeles College; Mark Storey, Bellevue College; Matthew W. Turner, Francis Marion University; Frank Waters, Los Angeles Valley College; Diane S. Wilkinson, Alabama A&M University; Holly L. Wilson, University of Louisiana at Monroe; and Paul Wilson, Texas State University–San Marcos.

1 The Nature of Philosophy

The feeling of wonder is the mark of the philosopher,
for all philosophy has its origins in wonder.

PLATO

1.1 What Is Philosophy?

LEARNING OBJECTIVES: When finished, you'll be able to:

- Explain how Plato's Allegory of the Cave shows that philosophy is a freeing activity.
- thinking critically Explain what critical thinking is and how it is related to philosophy.
- Explain the importance of the philosophical perspectives of women and non-Western cultures.
- thinking critically Define reasoning and its role in critical thinking.

1.2 The Traditional Divisions of Philosophy

LEARNING OBJECTIVES: When finished, you'll be able to:

- Define epistemology, metaphysics, and ethics, and explain the kinds of questions each asks.
- thinking critically Recognize and avoid vague or ambiguous claims.
- thinking critically Identify an argument, its conclusion, and its supporting reasons.

1.3 A Philosopher in Action: Socrates

LEARNING OBJECTIVES: When finished, you'll be able to:

- Explain how Socrates' unrelenting questioning of conventional beliefs exemplifies the quest for philosophical wisdom.
- thinking critically Identify the main premises and conclusions of an argument, and its missing premises or assumptions.

1.4 The Value of Philosophy

LEARNING OBJECTIVES: When finished, you'll be able to:

- Compare Plato's and Buddha's claims that philosophical wisdom is related to freedom.
- State how philosophy can help you build your outlook on life, be more mindful, and become a critical thinker.

Chapter Summary

1.5 Reading

Voltaire, "Story of a Good Brahman"

1.6 Historical Showcase: The First Philosophers

> **MindTap** MindTap for *Philosophy: A Text with Readings* includes:
> - Activator videos that spark connections to the real world
> - Critical thinking exercises that help guide student understanding
> - Extended versions of the readings excerpted in the text via the Questia database, linked directly from the eBook text
> - Video lectures that reinforce complex topics
> - Assignable essays and chapter quizzes

1.1 What Is Philosophy?

Philosophy begins with wonder. Although many of us know very little about the jargon and history of philosophy, we have all been touched by the wonder with which philosophy begins. We wonder about why we are here; about who we really are; about whether God exists and what She or He is like; why pain, evil, sorrow, and separation exist; whether there is life after death; what true love and friendship are; what the proper balance is between serving others and serving ourselves; whether moral right and wrong are based on personal opinion or on some objective standard; and whether suicide, abortion, or euthanasia is ever justified.

This wondering and questioning begin early in our lives. Almost as soon as children learn to talk, they ask: Where did I come from? Where do people go when they die? How did the world start? Who made God? From the very beginning of our lives, we start to seek answers to questions that make up philosophy.

In fact, the word *philosophy* comes from the Greek words *philein*, meaning "to love," and *sophia*, meaning "wisdom." Philosophy is thus the love and pursuit of wisdom. It includes the search for wisdom about many basic issues: what it means to be a human being; what the fundamental nature of reality is; what the sources and limits of our knowledge are; and what is good and right in our lives and in our societies.

Although philosophy begins with wonder and questions, it does not end there. Philosophy tries to go beyond the answers that we received when we were too young to seek our own answers. The goal of philosophy is to answer these questions for ourselves and to make up our own minds about our self, life, knowledge, society, religion, and morality.

We accepted many of our religious, political, and moral beliefs when we were children and could not yet think for ourselves. Philosophy examines these beliefs. The aim is not to reject them but to learn why we hold them and to ask whether we have good reasons to continue holding them. By doing this we make our basic beliefs about reality and life our own. We accept them because we have thought them through on our own, not because our parents, peers, and society have conditioned us to believe them. In this way, we gain a kind of independence and freedom, or what some modern philosophers call *autonomy*. An important goal of philosophy, then, is **autonomy**, which is the freedom and ability to decide for yourself what you will believe in, by using your own reasoning powers.

Plato's Allegory of the Cave

Plato is one of the earliest and greatest Western philosophers. He illustrated how philosophy aims at freedom with a famous parable called the Allegory of the Cave. The Allegory of the Cave is a story Plato tells in *The Republic*, his classic philosophical work on justice. Here is an edited translation of the Allegory of the Cave, which Plato wrote in his native Greek:

> **QUICK REVIEW**
> Philosophy begins when we start to wonder about and question our basic beliefs.

> **QUICK REVIEW**
> The goal of philosophy is to answer these questions for ourselves and achieve autonomy.

> **QUICK REVIEW**
> In Plato's Allegory of the Cave, chained prisoners watch shadows cast on a cave wall by objects passing in front of a fire. They mistake the shadows for reality.

Walking with his student Aristotle, Plato points upward: "And the climb upward out of the cave into the upper world is the ascent of the mind into the domain of true knowledge."

School of Athens, from the Stanza della Segnatura, 1510–1511 (fresco), Raphael (Raffaello Sanzio of Urbino) (1483–1520)/© Vatican Museums and Galleries, Vatican City, Italy, Giraudon/The Bridgeman Art Library International

Now let me describe the human situation in a parable about ignorance and learning. Imagine men live at the bottom of an underground cave. The entrance to the cave is a long passageway that rises upward through the ground to the light outside. They have been there since childhood and have their legs and necks chained so they cannot move. The chains hold their heads so they must sit facing the back wall of the cave. They cannot turn their heads to look up through the entrance behind them. At some distance behind them, up nearer the entrance to the cave, a fire is burning. Objects pass in front of the fire so that they cast their shadows on the back wall of the cave. The prisoners see the moving shadows on the cave wall as if projected on a screen. All kinds of objects parade before the fire including statues of men and animals. As they move past the fire their shadows dance on the wall in front of the prisoners.

Those prisoners are like ourselves. The prisoners cannot see themselves or each other except for the shadows each prisoner's body casts on the back wall of the cave. They also cannot see the objects behind them, except for the shadows the objects cast on the wall.

Now imagine the prisoners could talk with each other. Suppose their voices echoed off the wall so that the voices seem to come from their own shadows. Then wouldn't they talk about these shadows as if the shadows were real? For the prisoners, reality would consist of nothing but shadows.

Next imagine that someone freed one of the prisoners from his chains. Suppose he forced the prisoner to stand up and turn toward the entrance of the cave and then forced him to walk up toward the burning fire. The movement would be painful. The glare from the fire would blind the prisoner so that he could hardly see the real objects whose shadows he used to watch. What would he think if someone explained that everything he had seen before was an illusion? Would he realize that now he was nearer to reality and that his vision was actually clearer?

Imagine that now someone showed him the objects that had cast their shadows on the wall and asked the prisoner to name each one. Wouldn't the prisoner be at a complete loss? Wouldn't he think the shadows he saw earlier were truer than these objects?

Next imagine someone forced the prisoner to look straight at the burning light. His eyes would hurt. The pain would make him turn away and try to return to the shadows he could see more easily. He would think that those shadows were more real than the new objects shown to him.

But suppose that once more someone takes him and drags him up the steep and rugged ascent from the cave. Suppose someone forces him out into the full light of the sun. Won't he suffer greatly and be furious at being dragged upward? The light will so dazzle his eyes as he approaches it that he won't be able to see any of this world we ourselves call reality. Little by little he will have to get used to looking at the upper world. At first he will see shadows on the ground best. Next perhaps he will be able to look at the reflections of men and other objects in water, and then maybe the objects themselves. After this, he would find it easier to gaze at the light of the moon and the stars in the night sky than to look at the daylight sun and its light. Last of all, he will be able to look at the sun and contemplate its nature. He will not just look at its reflection in water but will see it as it is in itself and in its own domain. He would come to the conclusion that the sun produces the seasons and the years and that it controls everything in the visible world. He will understand that it is, in a way, the cause of everything he and his fellow prisoners used to see.

MindTap To read more from Plato's *The Republic*, click the link in the MindTap Reader or go to the Questia Readings folder in MindTap.

✓ QUICK REVIEW
If a prisoner is freed and forced to see the fire and objects, he will have difficulty seeing and will think the shadows are more real than the objects.

✓ QUICK REVIEW
If the prisoner were to be dragged out of the cave to the light of the sun, he would be blinded, and he would look first at shadows, then reflections, then objects, then the moon, and then the sun, which controls everything in the visible world.

ANALYZING THE READING

1. At the end of his allegory Plato says the journey up to the sunlight represents the mind acquiring knowledge. What does the sunlight represent? What does the darkness of the cave represent? What do the shadows on the wall of the dark cave represent? Who do the people who stay in the darkness of the cave represent? Who does the person who guides the prisoner out of the dark cave represent? Read the allegory again and indicate what you think other things in the Allegory are supposed to represent.

2. What is Plato trying to say when he writes that a person who sees the real sunlit world and then returns to the dark cave will seem "ridiculous" to those who have stayed in the dark? Do you think Plato is right?

3. What is Plato trying to say when he writes that a person who sees the real sunlit world will "feel happy" and will "endure anything rather than go back to thinking and living like" those who stay in the dark? Is Plato right?

4. Is Plato assuming that knowledge is always better than ignorance? Is it ever true that "Ignorance is bliss"? So do you think Plato is right or not?

QUICK REVIEW
If he returns to the cave, he would be unable to see and would be laughed at.

MindTap In Plato's Allegory of the Cave, the prisoners perceive the cave as the whole world. How can we trust our senses? Go to MindTap to watch a video about what philosophers have thought about this.

QUICK REVIEW
The climb out of the cave is the ascent of the mind to true knowledge.

Suppose the released prisoner now recalled the cave and what passed for wisdom among his friends there. Wouldn't he be happy about his new situation and feel sorry for them? Perhaps the prisoners would honor those who were quickest to make out the shadows. Or perhaps they honored those who could remember the order in which the shadows appeared and were best at predicting the course of the shadows. Would he care about such honors and glories or would he envy those who won them? Wouldn't he rather endure anything than go back to thinking and living like they did?

Finally, imagine that someone led the released prisoner away from the light and back down into the cave to his old seat. His eyes would be full of darkness. But even though his eyes were still dim, he would have to compete in discerning the shadows with the prisoners who had never left the cave. Wouldn't he appear ridiculous? Men would say of him that he had gone up and had come back down with his eyesight ruined and that it was better not to even think of ascending. In fact, if they caught anyone trying to free them and lead them up to the light, they would try to kill him.

I tell you now, that the prison is the world we see with our eyes; the light of the fire is like the power of our sun. The climb upward out of the cave into the upper world is the ascent of the mind into the domain of true knowledge.[1]

Plato's Allegory and "Doing" Philosophy

Plato wrote this intriguing allegory more than two thousand years ago. It is important for us because we can interpret it as an explanation of what philosophy is.

Philosophy as an Activity. First, in the allegory, the activity of journeying upward from the dark cave to the light can be seen as what philosophy is. That is, philosophy is an activity. In this respect, it differs from other academic subjects. Unlike some other subjects, philosophy does not consist of a lot of information or theories. True, philosophers have developed many theories and views. However, philosophical theories are the *products* of philosophy, not philosophy itself. While studying philosophy, of course, you will study the theories of several important philosophers. But the point of studying them is not just to memorize them. You will study them, instead, as an aid to help you learn how to "do" philosophy. By seeing how the best philosophers have "done" philosophy and by considering their views you will better understand what philosophizing is. More importantly, you can use their insights to shed light on your own philosophical journey. It's the journey—the activity—that's important, not the products you bring back from your journey.

Philosophy Is Hard Work. Second, as Plato made clear in the allegory, philosophy can be a difficult activity. The journey upward is hard because it involves questioning the most basic beliefs that each of us has about ourselves and the world around us. As the allegory suggests, your philosophical journey sometimes may lead your thinking in directions that society does not support. It may lead you toward views that others around you reject. Philosophy is also hard because it requires us to think critically, consistently, and carefully about our fundamental beliefs. We may rebel against being asked to systematically and logically question and criticize views that we have always accepted. Yet the journey out of the darkness of the cave requires intellectual discipline and the hard work

---

[1]   Plato, *The Republic*, from bk. 7. This translation copyright © 1987 by Manuel Velasquez.

of reasoning as carefully and logically as we can. That is why someone taking the first steps in philosophy can be helped by a teacher. As Plato says, the teacher must "take him and drag him up the steep and rugged ascent from the cave and force him out into the full light of the sun." The teacher does this by getting the student to ask the hard questions that the student is reluctant to ask on his or her own.

The Aim of Philosophy Is Freedom. Third, as Plato indicates and as we have already suggested, the aim of philosophy is freedom. Philosophy breaks chains that imprison and hold us down, chains we often do not even know we are wearing. Like the prisoners in the cave, we uncritically accept the beliefs and opinions of those around us. This unthinking conformity leads us to see the world in narrow, rigid ways. Philosophy aims at breaking us free of the prejudices and unthinking assumptions we have long absorbed from those around us. Once free, we can move toward more reflective views that are truly our own.

Philosophy Examines Our Most Basic Assumptions. Fourth, Plato's allegory suggests that philosophy examines our beliefs about the most basic issues of human existence. These include many assumptions we are not even aware of although they play a crucial role in our thinking and our actions. We are like the prisoner who is forced to look at the real objects whose shadows he had always assumed were real. In a similar way, doing philosophy means questioning the most basic assumptions we make about ourselves and the universe around us. The word *philosophy* itself suggests this, for, as we noted earlier, it means "the love of wisdom." To do philosophy is to love wisdom. Wisdom is a true understanding of the most fundamental aspects of human living. So the love of wisdom is the desire to understand the fundamental assumptions we have about ourselves and our world.

The view that philosophy examines our beliefs about the most fundamental issues of life was perhaps most clearly expressed not by Plato, but by Perictione. Perictione was a woman philosopher who lived around the time of Plato. She wrote:

 THINKING LIKE A PHILOSOPHER

1. What does wisdom mean to you?
2. Who are the people in your life who you think are truly wise? What qualities do they have that make you think they are wise? How do you think they became wise? How has their wisdom affected you?
3. Would you describe yourself as a person who is wise? Would you describe yourself as a person who loves wisdom? Why?
4. What kind of wisdom would you most want to have? What kinds of things would you most want to be wise about? Why is it important to you to have wisdom about those things?

> Humanity came into being and exists in order to contemplate the principle of the nature of the whole. The function of wisdom is to gain possession of this very thing, and to contemplate the purpose of the things that are. Geometry, of course, and arithmetic, and the other theoretical studies and sciences are also concerned with the things that are. But wisdom is concerned with the most basic of these. Wisdom is concerned with all that is, just as sight is concerned with all that is visible and hearing with all that is audible. . . . Therefore, whoever is able to analyze all the kinds of being by reference to one and the same basic principle, and, in turn, from this principle can synthesize and enumerate the different kinds, this person seems to be the wisest and most true and, moreover, to have discovered a noble height from which he will be able to catch sight of God and all the things separated from God in serial rank and order.[2]

---

2   Quoted in A *History of Women Philosophers*, ed. Mary Ellen Waithe (Boston: Martinus Nijhoff, 1987), 56.

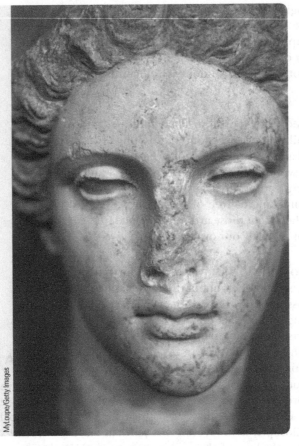

A woman philosopher who lived about the time of Plato, Perictione saw philosophy as a search for understanding: "Humanity came into being and exists in order to contemplate the principle of the nature of the whole."

MyLoupe/Getty Images

Perictione is saying that the search for wisdom is a search for an understanding of the ultimate truths about ourselves and our universe. It is a search for a kind of understanding that goes beyond mathematics and the other sciences. These—mathematics and the other sciences—look only at particular aspects of our world. Philosophy, on the other hand, desires to know the ultimate truth about all aspects of our world. It desires to understand the assumptions that underlie the sciences as well as everything we think and do.

For example, philosophy examines the basic assumptions that underlie religion when it asks: Is there a God? Is there an afterlife? What truth is there in religious experience? Philosophy examines the basic assumptions that underlie science when it asks: Can science tell us what our universe is really like? Are scientific theories merely useful approximations, or do they impart real truths about the universe? Is there such a thing as truth in science? Philosophy examines the basic values that underlie our relations with one another when it asks: Is there really such a thing as justice? What, if anything, do we truly owe each other? Is true love really possible or are all our activities based on self-interest? And it examines the basic notions that underlie our views about reality. For example, it asks: Are we truly in control of the choices we think we make, or is everything we do determined by forces we do not control? Are the ordinary objects we experience all that reality contains, or does another kind of reality exist beyond the world that appears around us? Philosophy, then, examines the basic assumptions that underlie everything we do and believe. In fact, we can define **philosophy**—the love and pursuit of wisdom—as critically and carefully examining the reasons behind our most fundamental assumptions about ourselves and the world around us.

 thinking critically • Assumptions and Critical Thinking

Doing philosophy, then, often involves trying to discover the assumptions we are making or that others are making. Assumptions are beliefs we take for granted and that would have to be true if the other things we believe and say are true, or if what we do makes sense. For example, most of our religious beliefs and activities assume that God exists. If it were not true that God exists, then most traditional religious beliefs could not be true and traditional religious activities would make little sense. In a similar way, most of us assume that what we perceive with our five senses is real. If it were not true that what we see is real, then most of our beliefs about what we know about reality would not be true. And most of us assume that what we are doing is worth doing, for otherwise it would make little sense for us to continue doing it. It is important to be aware of the assumptions we and others make. Otherwise we risk becoming like the prisoners in Plato's cave who unthinkingly assume the shadows they see are real objects. To help you identify assumptions in the readings, the boxes entitled Analyzing the Reading will sometimes point out an assumption the author may be making. An example is the fourth question in the Analyzing the Reading box you saw at the end of Plato's Allegory of the Cave. Read it now and see what you think. Later we will look more closely at the process of identifying assumptions.

QUICK REVIEW
Identifying assumptions—beliefs we take for granted and that have to be true if other beliefs are to be true and actions are to make sense—is part of critical thinking, which is essential to philosophy.

Doing this kind of thinking—trying to discover our own and others' assumptions—is an important part of what is called critical thinking. What is critical thinking? We are always thinking, of course, and we use our thinking any time we decide what we should do or believe. But our thinking can be illogical, biased, close-minded, or based on mistaken assumptions, unsupported beliefs, false generalizations, and fallacious reasoning. Such thinking risks leading us astray. **Critical thinking** is the opposite of this kind of risky undisciplined thinking. Critical thinking is the kind of disciplined thinking we do when we base our beliefs and actions on unbiased and valid reasoning that uses well-founded evidence, that avoids false generalizations and unrecognized assumptions, and that considers opposing viewpoints. Using this kind of disciplined critical thinking to examine an issue involves seven steps: (1) identify and state your own views on the issue, (2) clarify your views by defining key words or terms your views contain, getting rid of ambiguities, and providing examples of what your views involve, (3) identify the important assumptions on which your views depend, (4) determine the reasons or evidence that support your views and make sure these reasons support your views with sound and valid reasoning and are not false generalizations, (5) consider other views people may have about the same issue and the reasons they have for their views, (6) come to a conclusion about whether your own view or one of the other views makes the most sense, and (7) determine the consequences of your conclusion. Don't worry if these steps are not completely clear to you yet. As you move through this book, the meaning of each should become clear.

Obviously, critical thinking is important in every aspect of life. But it is especially essential in philosophy because, as we have said, philosophy is the activity of thinking through the most basic beliefs we have accepted about ourselves and our world, and trying to form our own views about these. If such philosophical thinking is not to go wrong, it has to be critical thinking. Because critical thinking is so important in philosophy, this book contains several sections, like this one, entitled Thinking Critically. Each of these sections explains some aspect of critical thinking and applies critical thinking to the philosophy discussed in the book. The aim of these sections is to enable you to learn, step by step, how to evaluate your own philosophical thinking, as well as the philosophical thinking of others. It is sometimes said that philosophy "Teaches you how to think." This is absolutely true. To learn philosophy is, at the same time, to learn to think critically.

The Diversity of Philosophy

Both Plato and Perictione are representatives of so-called Western philosophy. Western philosophy is a part of the cultural tradition that began in ancient Greece and eventually spread to Europe, England, and the United States. Yet the search for wisdom has been a concern of all races and cultures. The study of Western philosophy is important for us because it has had a profound and direct influence on our society. And it continues to influence and shape the thinking of each of us today.

Yet, non-Western philosophical traditions have had equally profound impacts on our planet's civilizations. Moreover, the world's nations have become so interdependent that non-Western philosophies now directly influence our own thinking. So learning about those other philosophical traditions is as vital as learning about the Western traditions that have shaped us and our society.

We will spend a good deal of time discussing the views of Western philosophers. But we will not ignore the contributions of non-Western philosophers, such as Indian, African, and Asian philosophers. By looking at their contributions, you can expand your horizons. These perspectives provide new ways of looking at yourself and reality. By looking at worlds that are different from the one you live in, you can understand what your world is really like. More important, perhaps, you can envision ways of making it better.

We will also not ignore the contributions of a group of people who are sometimes overlooked in philosophy courses. This is the group of people that make up 50 percent of the human race: women. For many historical reasons (including subtle and overt sexism), the major contributors to Western philosophy have been males. Nevertheless, several important women philosophers, like Perictione, have made significant philosophical contributions. Therefore, this book includes discussions of an approach to philosophy that tries to capture the special philosophical insights of female philosophers. This approach is what is generally referred to as "feminist philosophy." Feminist philosophy attempts to look at philosophical issues from the perspectives of women. The pages that follow, then, do not ignore the contributions of feminist philosophy. Instead they include numerous discussions of the views of important feminist philosophers.

QUICK REVIEW
It is important to also look at philosophy from the perspective of non-Western cultures and of women.

MindTap Visit MindTap to do critical thinking exercises on logic and reasoning, where you'll learn to recognize and evaluate arguments.

thinking critically • Reasoning

We said earlier that philosophy "requires us to think critically" and that thinking critically requires "valid reasoning." So reasoning is an essential component of philosophical thinking. Reasoning is the process of thinking by which we draw conclusions from the information, knowledge, or beliefs we have about something. We call the information from which we draw a conclusion the "reasons" or the "premises" or the "evidence" for the conclusion. We are reasoning, for example, when we use the information we have about the universe to try to figure out whether we should believe that God exists. We also use reasoning when we use our knowledge of a person to try to figure out whether we should marry that person, or when we use the information we have about a college to figure out whether we want to go to that college. In fact, reasoning pervades our whole life since we use reasoning every time we rely on the knowledge or information we have about something, to figure out what we should believe or do about it.

Although reasoning pervades our lives, it plays an especially important role in philosophy because when we philosophize we are always engaged in reasoning. In fact, so essential is reasoning in philosophy, that you could almost say that philosophizing *is* reasoning: It is reasoning about our most fundamental beliefs and assumptions.

But philosophers do not engage in just any kind of reasoning. Philosophers want their reasoning to be good reasoning. Good reasoning is reasoning in which the reasons we have for a conclusion provide sound and valid evidence for that conclusion. Consequently, a lot of the work of philosophizing involves trying to figure out or evaluate whether the reasons or evidence for a conclusion provide sound and valid support for that conclusion. Because we all use reasoning when we make important decisions in life, learning to evaluate reasoning will help you throughout your life. Good reasoning is not only a key to philosophy, it is also a key to success in getting whatever it is that you want out of life.

PHILOSOPHY AT THE MOVIES

Watch *The Matrix* (1999) in which the leader of a rebel group shows Neo, a computer hacker, that the "reality" around him is actually a computer simulation called the "Matrix." How is the Matrix like Plato's cave, and how is Neo like Plato's released prisoner? How do they differ? Is your situation today in any way like that of the people in the Matrix? How do you know? While savoring a steak in a restaurant in the Matrix, one of the rebels, Cypher, agrees to betray the rebels to Agent Smith and says, "Ignorance is bliss." What does he mean? Would Plato agree with Cypher? Why or why not? Would you agree? Why or why not?

Other movies with related themes: *The Animatrix* (2003); *Equilibrium* (2002); *Vanilla Sky* (2001); *Mulholland Dr.* (2001); some related older classics: *eXistenZ* (1999) and *The Thirteenth Floor* (1999).

© Pictorial Press Ltd/Alamy

1.2 The Traditional Divisions of Philosophy

Another way of understanding what philosophy means is to look at the kinds of questions it has traditionally asked. Philosophy has been generally concerned with three broad questions: What is knowledge? What is real? What is right and good? These questions are related and the distinction among them is sometimes blurred. Nevertheless, philosophers have traditionally seen most philosophical questions as parts of these three inquiries.

These three questions suggest the three topics to which most philosophical questions are related. These are knowledge, reality, and values. Philosophers call the fields of philosophy that explore these topics *epistemology, metaphysics,* and *ethics.*

Epistemology: The Study of Knowledge

Epistemology literally means "the study of knowledge." Some of the problems discussed in epistemology include: What is the structure, reliability, extent, and kinds of knowledge we have? What is truth? What is logical reasoning? How do words refer to reality? What is meaning? What is the foundation of knowledge? Is real knowledge even possible?

To get a better idea of what epistemology is, and its importance, consider the interesting views of Gail Stenstad. Stenstad is a contemporary feminist philosopher. She argues that male approaches to knowledge assume that there is only one truth—one correct theory. This male approach holds, she claims, that all other conflicting insights must be wrong. Stenstad calls this male approach to knowledge *theoretical thinking.* She contrasts this approach to knowledge with a feminist approach that she calls *anarchic thinking.* Feminist anarchic thinking, she says, recognizes that there is not just one "objective" truth. Feminist thinking recognizes there are many different truths, and that none should be ruled out as "incorrect."

> **QUICK REVIEW**
> Epistemology looks at the extent and reliability of our knowledge, truth, and logic, and whether knowledge is possible.

> **QUICK REVIEW**
> Stenstad claims that there are many different truths and that differing views can be accepted as equally valid and true.

In some ways the difference between theoretical thinking and anarchic thinking is analogous to the difference between monotheism [belief in one God] and polytheism [belief in many gods]. Theoretical thinking and monotheism both tend toward "the one." Monotheism, obviously, is oriented toward one god; historically, many monotheistic religions have also been very concerned with oneness in doctrine, with arriving at doctrine that can be taken to be the only true or correct one. "One lord, one faith, one baptism." This sort of focus creates an in-group and an out-group: the saved and the damned. While none but the most rigid theorists would go so far in demarcating an in-group and an out-group, accusations of "incorrectness" have been used to silence disagreement. Further, in its very structure, any claim to possess the truth, or the correct account of reality or the good, creates an out-group, whether we like it or not. The out-group is all those whose truth or reality or values are different from those posited in the theory. . . . [But] polytheism has room to include a monotheistic perspective (though the reverse is not the case). A belief in many gods, or in many possibilities or sacred manifestations, can allow for an individual's preference for any one (or more) of those manifestations. Likewise, anarchic thinking does not abandon or exclude or negate the insights achieved by theoretical thinking, but rather demotes "the theory" to a situational analysis, useful and accurate within limits clearly demarcated in each case. Other, very different analyses, based on other women's situations and experiences, are not ruled out.[3]

In this passage, Stenstad is comparing male or theoretical thinking with monotheism. **Monotheism** is the belief that there is just one God and all beliefs in other gods should be rejected. In a similar way, she says, male "theoretical thinking" assumes there is only one true view of reality and all opposing ("different") views must be rejected. Her point appears to be that theoretical thinking, the male view of truth, assumes that if several views of reality conflict (are inconsistent), then only one can be true. We must reject such male approaches to knowledge and truth, she seems to imply. Instead, she is apparently saying, we should accept the anarchic view of truth. The anarchic view holds that truth is many and that several opposing insights can be equally valid and equally true. This approach to truth and knowledge, she believes, can give women the power to break free of male theories that deny the equal validity of opposing views. Moreover, the male approach creates an in-group that has the truth and an out-group that does not. The anarchist approach, however, does not divide people into a group that knows the truth and a group that does not. Instead it embraces the many truths of people with different experiences and different insights.

Is truth many or one? Is there a male approach to knowledge and truth that is intolerant and exclusive? Should we embrace the view that truth is many and that there is no single correct truth about what the world is like? Are the conflicting insights of people with different experiences of the world all equally valid and equally true? Out of these kinds of puzzling questions arises the field of epistemology, the attempt to determine what knowledge and truth are. As this short discussion of Stenstad suggests, the answers to these questions may even influence how we relate to each other as male and female.

 thinking critically • Avoiding Vague and Ambiguous Claims

The quotation of Stenstad above contains several claims. A claim is a statement or sentence or proposition that can be true or false. Stenstad makes the claim, for example, that there are two kinds of thinking: theoretical thinking and anarchic thinking. Earlier, we saw that Plato made the claim that the person who acquires "true knowledge" is like a prisoner who is freed from his chains. And Perictione made the claim that to have wisdom is to understand "the purpose of the things that are." The point is that philosophers proceed by making claims.

Like all claims, the claims of a philosopher can be clear or they can be vague or ambiguous. Vague claims are those that do not have a precise meaning. Ambiguous claims are those that have several possible meanings. Some of Stenstad's claims about anarchic

---

3   Gail Stenstad, "Anarchic Thinking: Breaking the Hold of Monotheistic Ideology on Feminist Philosophy," in *Women, Knowledge, and Reality: Explorations in Feminist Philosophy*, ed. Ann Garry and Marilyn Pearsall (Boston: Unwin Hyman, 1989), 333.

thinking, for example, seem ambiguous. She says that theoretical thinking holds that if one view about reality is "correct," then any "different" view has to be "incorrect." And anarchic thinking holds that if one view is correct, another view that is "very different" is "not ruled out." But what does she mean by a "very different" view? Does her claim mean that in anarchic thinking views that *contradict* each other can both be true? Is she saying, for example, that if one person says God exists and another says God does not exist, anarchic thinking can accept both statements as true? Or does her claim just mean that anarchic thinking accepts views that are dissimilar but that do not contradict each other? For example, is she saying that if one person says God is loving and another says God is just, anarchic thinking can accept both views as true? The trouble is that we don't know exactly what her claim is because it is ambiguous: It could have at least two different meanings. There are, of course, times when vagueness or ambiguity is appropriate. If your wife asks you what you think of her mother, it may be best to be vague. But there is usually something wrong with philosophical claims that are vague or ambiguous. Since we are not even sure what they mean, we cannot really reason about whether they are true or false.

One of the most important ways of evaluating the claim of a philosopher (or any-one else), then, is by asking whether his or her claim is clear or ambiguous. If the claim is too vague or ambiguous we may not be able to figure out exactly what it means. Vague and ambiguous philosophical claims are defective and should be avoided. We will discuss numerous philosophical claims in the pages that follow. As you read and think about these claims, you should evaluate them. Ask whether they have the most fundamental charac-teristic of an adequate claim: Is the meaning of the claim clear, or is it vague or ambiguous?

Metaphysics: The Study of Reality or Existence

Metaphysics is the second major area of philosophy. Metaphysics is the study of the most general or ultimate characteristics of reality or existence. Some questions that belong to metaphysics are: What is the purpose and nature of reality? What is real? What am I? What is the mind? Is God real? Is my soul real? Can my soul survive death?

To get a clearer idea of what metaphysics is about, consider one of the core questions of metaphysics. Is everything I do determined by outside causes, or am I free to choose for myself what I will do? By looking at how some philosophers have treated this issue we can get a better understanding of metaphysics.

One important theory in metaphysics is **determinism**. **Determinism** is the claim that all things and all human beings are unfree because everything that occurs hap-pens in accordance with some regular pattern or law. Paul Henri d'Holbach, who wrote in the eighteenth century, made such a claim:

> In whatever manner man is considered, he is connected to universal nature, and submitted to the necessary and immutable laws that she imposes on all beings she contains. . . . He is born without his own consent; his [physical and mental] organization does in no way depend on himself; his ideas come to him involuntarily; and his habits are in the power of those who cause him to have them. He is unceasingly modified by causes, whether visible or concealed, over which he has no control and which necessarily regulate his existence, color his way of thinking, and determine his manner of acting. . . .
>
> In short, the actions of man are never free; they are always the necessary conse-quence of his temperament, of the ideas he has received, including his true or false notions of happiness, and of those opinions that are strengthened by example, by edu-cation, and by daily experience. . . . Man is not a free agent in any instant of his life.[4]

QUICK REVIEW
Metaphysics looks at ultimate characteristics of reality or existence.

QUICK REVIEW
D'Holbach claimed everything is determined by causes we do not control, so we are not free.

---

[4] Baron Paul Henri d'Holbach, *System of Nature* (London: Dearsley, 1797).

Yet many other philosophers deny these deterministic claims about reality. One of them is Viktor Frankl, a twentieth-century Jewish psychologist and existentialist philosopher who lived through World War II. Frankl suffered terrible degradations while imprisoned by the Nazis after they murdered his entire family. There, in the terror-filled German prison camps, he was struck by how often people responded to their situation with generosity and selflessness. He said that his experiences proved to him that human beings are ultimately free and that each of us has the freedom to make of ourselves whatever kind of person we choose to be:

> Man is not fully conditioned and determined; he determines himself whether to give in to conditions or stand up to them. In other words, man is ultimately self-determining. Man does not simply exist, but always decides what his existence will be, what he will become in the next moment. By the same token, every human being has the freedom to change at any instant. . . .
>
> A human being is not one thing among others. *Things* determine each other, but man is ultimately self-determining. What he becomes—within the limits of endowment and environment—he has made out of himself. In the concentration camps, for example, in this living laboratory and on this testing ground, we watched and witnessed some of our comrades behave like swine while others behaved like saints. Man has both potentialities within himself. Which one is actualized depends on decisions but not on conditions.[5]

Some Eastern philosophers have turned to the Hindu idea of **karma** to claim that humans can be both free and determined. *Karma* literally means "action" or "deed," and consists of the accumulation of a person's past deeds. For the Hindu, everything we have done in our past (possibly including past lives) determines our present selves. That is, the past determines who and what we now are. Some Hindu philosophers have argued that although this seems to imply that we are not free, the idea of karma allows us to combine both determinism and freedom. Our past actions—our karma—they claim, determine the kind of being we have become, but we are still free to choose within the limits of what we have become. Freedom is choosing now within a situation that is determined by our past. As the Hindu philosopher Sarvepalli Radhakrishnan writes,

> Freedom is not caprice, nor is Karma necessity. . . . Freedom is not caprice since we carry our past with us. Our character, at any given point, is the condensation of our previous history. What we have been enters into the "me" which is now active and choosing. The range of one's natural freedom of action is limited. No man has the universal field of possibilities for himself. . . . Only the possible is the sphere of freedom. We have a good deal of present constraint and previous necessity in human life. But necessity is not to be mistaken for destiny which we can neither defy nor delude. Though the self is not free from the bonds of determination, it can subjugate the past to a certain extent and turn it into a new course. Choice is the assertion of freedom over necessity by which it converts necessity to its own use and thus frees itself from it.[6]

Which of these views is supported by the strongest reasons? Is it true that all reality (including ourselves) is causally determined? Or is the truth that we humans, at least, are free to choose what we will do? Or is the real truth that we are determined but free to choose within the constraints set by our past? This is but one example of the fundamental questions that metaphysics asks.

---

[5]   Viktor Frankl, *Man's Search for Meaning* (New York: Washington Square Press, 1963), 206, 213.

[6]   Sarvepalli Radhakrishnan, *An Idealist View of Life* (London: George Allen & Unwin, 1932), 220–221.

PHILOSOPHY AND LIFE

Philosophical Issues

Virtually every activity and every profession raises philosophical issues.

Science, psychology, the practice of law and medicine, and even taxation all involve questions that more or less directly force us to address philosophical issues.

Mark Woodhouse invites us to consider the following examples:

1. *A neurophysiologist, while establishing correlations between certain brain functions and the feeling of pain, begins to wonder whether the "mind" is distinct from the brain.*

2. *A nuclear physicist, having determined that matter is mostly empty space containing colorless energy transformations, begins to wonder to what extent the solid, extended, colored world we perceive corresponds to what actually exists and which world is more "real."*

3. *A behavioral psychologist, having increasing success in predicting human behavior, questions whether any human actions can be called "free."*

4. *Supreme Court justices, when framing a law to distinguish obscene and non-obscene art forms, are drawn into questions about the nature and function of art.*

5. *An IRS director, in determining which (religious) organizations should be exempted from tax, is forced to define what counts as a "religion" or "religious group."*

And, as Woodhouse also suggests, philosophical questions are continually raised in our everyday life and conversations. Consider, for example, the following statements, which all involve philosophical issues: Sociology is not a science. Drugs reveal new levels of reality. History never repeats itself. Every religion has the same core of truth. We should all be left free to do our own thing, as long as we don't hurt anyone else. All truth depends on your point of view. The most important thing you can do is find out who you are. This could all be a dream.

QUESTIONS

1. Identify other areas of life that involve philosophical issues and explain the issues they raise.

2. What are your views on the issues that Woodhouse lists? Can you give any good reasons to support your views on these issues, or is it all "just a matter of opinion"?

Source: From WOODHOUSE. *A Preface to Philosophy,* 8E. © 2007 Wadsworth, a part of Cengage Learning, Inc. Reproduced by permission. www.cengage.com/permissions

thinking critically • Supporting Claims with Reasons and Arguments

Notice that the metaphysical claims of the philosophers we quoted earlier are not isolated statements. The philosophers accompany their claims with reasons in support of those claims. D'Holbach, for example, claims that humans are not free *because* every person "is unceasingly modified by causes . . . over which he has no control and which necessarily . . . determine his manner of action." On the other hand, Frankl claims that external conditions do not determine what people do *because* in the concentration camps he saw some "comrades behave like swine while others behaved like saints" yet all of them were subject to the same external conditions.

As these examples suggest, in philosophy our claims should not only be clear, they should also be supported by reasons. Philosophy is not mere speculation. When we speculate we dream up grand ideas and visions about how things might be. We might speculate, for example, that "The world around us is a dream!" But philosophy is more than speculation. Philosophy has to show its claims are true, so philosophers must give reasons for the claims they make. Without reasons, there is no philosophy, only speculation. Unsupported philosophical claims are inadequate. They are inadequate because without reasons to back them up, we cannot know whether they are true or false, or whether we should accept or reject them.

A claim together with its supporting reasons is called an argument. An argument in philosophy is not a heated quarrel accompanied by shouting. Instead, an argument consists of a group of reasons or "premises" plus a claim or "conclusion" that the reasons are supposed to prove or support. So every argument has two parts: (1) a group of premises

> **✓ QUICK REVIEW**
> Philosophical claims should be supported by reasons; a claim or conclusion together with its supporting reasons or premises is an argument.

which provide reasons or evidence for a conclusion, and (2) a conclusion which is the claim that those premises are supposed to establish. Take the argument that d'Holbach gives, for example. His premises include the statement that every person "is unceasingly modified by causes . . . over which he has no control and which necessarily . . . determine his manner of action." His conclusion is the claim that "the actions of man are never free." Or consider the argument that Frankl gives us. The premises include the statement that in the concentration camps some "comrades behaved like swine while others behaved like saints" although all were subjected to the same external conditions. His conclusion is the claim that "man is not fully . . . determined" by external conditions.

The first step in evaluating a philosopher's argument is to figure out his conclusion and the reasons or premises he gives to support his or her conclusion. After we know his premises and conclusion, we can move on to the second step which is to evaluate whether the premises provide adequate support for the conclusion. For example, now that we know d'Holbach's premises and conclusion, we can ask: Are his premises true? And if we find his premises are false, then we know his argument does not give us a good basis for accepting his claims about human freedom. But the first step in this process of evaluating a philosopher's claim is crucial. We have to begin by identifying the philosopher's conclusion, and the reasons or premises he gives to support his conclusion.

Ethics: The Study of Values

Ethics, the third major area of philosophy, refers to the study of morality. It is the attempt to understand and critically evaluate our moral values and moral principles and to see how these relate to our conduct and our social institutions. Ethics includes questions like the following about the nature of moral virtue and moral obligation: What are the moral principles we should follow? What is moral virtue? What are my obligations as a friend? Are abortion, suicide, and euthanasia ever morally right? Is capitalism or communism a better form of life? Should our society permit or prohibit adultery, pornography, capital punishment, or homosexuality? Is our society a just one? What is justice? Are there any human rights? Do I have an obligation to obey the law? Can a war be just? Is it just to use torture against terrorists?

Again, some examples may make these questions a bit clearer. Consider a statement Mahatma Gandhi once made. Gandhi was the great twentieth-century Indian statesman who used nonviolent political resistance to defeat the British rulers of India. Gandhi devoted his life to breaking down racial and religious forms of discrimination. He campaigned for equality of respect for all human beings. In doing this, he advocated and practiced *ahimsa*, or nonviolence. In Gandhi's view, we should harm no living thing. Nevertheless, we should resist evil. The greatest evil that faced India, he believed,

Gandhi: "The highest love is wherein man lays down his life for his fellow-men. That highest love is thus *Ahimsa."*

was its occupation by the British. He therefore believed he must oppose and defeat their rule. His method of opposition was to stand in the path of the violence of the British military, letting their blows fall on him while passively resisting their oppressive policies. Gandhi lived the philosophy that service toward others is our primary moral duty:

> To proceed a little further, sacrifice means laying down one's life so that others may live. Let us suffer so that others may be happy, and the highest service and the highest love is wherein man lays down his life for his fellow-men. That highest love is thus *Ahimsa* which is the highest service. . . . Learn to be generous towards each other. To be generous means having no hatred for those whom we consider to be at fault, and loving and serving them. It is not generosity or love, if we have goodwill for others only as long as they and we are united in thought and action. That should be called merely friendship or mutual affection.
>
> The application of the term "love" is wrong in such cases. "Love" means feeling friendship for the enemy.[7]

Yet not everyone agrees with such lofty sentiments. Many philosophers, in fact, have reasoned that ethics is a sham. For example, Harry Browne concludes that morality is really a kind of trap if we take it to mean that people should put the happiness of others ahead of their own. Selfishness, he holds, is and should be everyone's policy:

> Everyone is selfish; everyone is doing what he believes will make himself happier. The recognition of that can take most of the sting out of accusations that you're being "selfish." Why should you feel guilty for seeking your own happiness when that's what everyone else is doing, too? . . .
>
> To find constant, profound happiness requires that you be free to seek the gratification of your own desires.[8]

Browne believes that we should never put the happiness of others before our own. His main premise for this claim is that everyone's actions always aim at achieving their own happiness. This shows, he concludes, that everyone is selfish. Since everyone else is selfish, he claims, we should be selfish too.

The contemporary philosopher James Rachels strongly questions Browne's premise. Rachels explains his reasons for rejecting Browne's main premise in the following passage:

> Why should we think that merely because someone derives satisfaction from helping others this makes him selfish? Isn't the unselfish man precisely the one who does derive satisfaction from helping others, while the selfish man does not? Similarly, it is nothing more than shabby sophistry to say, because Smith takes satisfaction in

THINKING LIKE A PHILOSOPHER

We all have philosophical views. Our philosophical views include our beliefs about God, religion, an afterlife, morality, what is most valuable in life, whether life has any meaning, whether our choices are free, whether all people have basic human rights, whether we live in a just society, whether we should ever accept anything "on faith," whether we have a soul, whether life begins at birth or at conception, whether the rich have an obligation to help the poor, whether it is wrong to inflict pain on animals, whether people always act out of self-interest. Take any one of these topics and try to identify your own philosophical views about that topic. Try to explain your view by defining your terms and giving examples of the difference it makes in your life. What reasons or evidence do you have for your view? How did you come to hold this view? How hard would it be for you to question, criticize, change, or even give up this view?

✓ QUICK REVIEW
Browne says selfishness is and ought to be everyone's policy.

✓ QUICK REVIEW
Rachels claims that finding satisfaction in helping others is not selfishness.

---

7   Mahatma Gandhi, *Gita—My Mother*, quoted in *Beyond the Western Tradition*, ed. Daniel Bonevac, William Boon, and Stephen Phillips (Mountain View, CA: Mayfield, 1992), 243.

8   Harry Browne, *How I Found Freedom in an Unfree World* (New York: Macmillan, 1937).

helping his friend, that he is behaving selfishly. If we say this rapidly, while thinking about something else, perhaps it will sound all right; but if we speak slowly, and pay attention to what we are saying, it sounds plain silly.[9]

Which of these views is correct—that everyone is selfish so we should also be selfish? Or that we have a duty to love and serve even our enemies? These kinds of inquiries form the subject matter of ethics, the third major area of philosophy.

Other Philosophical Inquiries

Finally, there is a wide range of philosophical inquiries that we usually refer to as "the philosophy of ..." or, simply, "philosophy and ..." These include the philosophy of science, the philosophy of art, and philosophy and the meaning of life. Each of these areas of philosophy attempts to question and analyze the basic or fundamental assumptions of the subject. For example, the philosophy of science asks what the scientific method is, whether it is valid, and whether the theories it produces are merely useful mental constructs or objective descriptions of reality. The philosophy of art asks what art is and whether we can judge art with objective standards or whether judging art is merely a matter of personal tastes. An inquiry into philosophy and the meaning of life is an attempt to look carefully at the question of whether life has meaning and, if so, what that meaning might be.

The list of topics about which we can philosophize is in fact endless. Consider the titles of several books that have appeared mostly during the last few years: *Food and Philosophy, Beer and Philosophy, Philosophy Looks at Chess, Coffee and Philosophy, Green Lantern and Philosophy, The Philosophy of Tolkien, Running and Philosophy, South Park and Philosophy, The Daily Show and Philosophy, The Matrix and Philosophy, Physics and Philosophy, Batman and Philosophy, Bullshit and Philosophy, X-Men and Philosophy, iPod and Philosophy, The Beatles and Philosophy, The Philosophy of Martin Scorsese, Jimmy Buffett and Philosophy, The Philosophy of Science Fiction Film, Metallica and Philosophy, The Philosophy of Andy Warhol,* and even *The Philosophy of Philosophy.* In short, beyond the traditional areas of philosophy—epistemology, metaphysics, and ethics—lies an entire universe of topics about which we can philosophize, or which raise interesting philosophical questions.

PHILOSOPHY AT THE MOVIES

Watch *Examined Life* (2008) which looks at some of today's leading philosophers addressing a variety of philosophical questions. Identify some of the questions of epistemology, metaphysics, and ethics that the movie raises in these conversations. Which of these questions interests you the most? Does the movie seem to give any answers to the questions? Have you arrived at any—perhaps tentative—answers to these questions? Are there any issues discussed in the movie that are not philosophical?

Other movies with related themes: *Waking Life* (2001); *Mindwalk* (1990); *My Dinner with Andre* (1981).

---

[9]   James Rachels, "Egoism and Moral Skepticism," in *A New Introduction to Philosophy*, ed. Steven M. Cahn (New York: Harper & Row, 1971).

1.3 A Philosopher in Action: Socrates

The best way to understand the nature of philosophy is to consider a philosopher in action. And the best place to begin is with the Greek thinker Socrates, who is sometimes called the father of Western philosophy. However, we should note that Socrates was not the first Western philosopher. A group of philosophers called the pre-Socratics preceded him. The **pre-Socratics** were the first thinkers in the West who questioned religious authority and tried to provide nonreligious explanations of nature. (For more information, see the Historical Showcase about the first philosophers at the end of this chapter.) Nevertheless, Socrates' life and views exemplify the meaning of philosophy, so we will look at his work.

Socrates was born in 469 BCE in Athens, Greece, a flourishing and vigorous city-state. The Greek theater had already produced the noted dramatist Aeschylus. It would soon see the comedies of Aristophanes and the tragedies of Sophocles and Euripides. The Greek armies had defeated those of the much larger nation of Persia, and Athens was on the verge of attaining naval control of the Aegean Sea.

As he grew older, Socrates began to question the conventional beliefs of his fellow Athenians. He would haunt the streets of Athens, buttonholing powerful men and questioning them about their knowledge. To a person who pretended to know about justice, for example, he would ask, "What is justice? What do all just acts have in common?" In the same way he might examine another person's ideas about virtue, knowledge, morality, or religion. His questions would probe and test the person's beliefs, deflating the person's cherished certainties. Inevitably he would show that the person did not know what he thought he knew. Socrates' persistent questioning of people's traditional beliefs intrigued many and he gathered several young followers. But many others reacted with anger, especially when he exposed their ignorance.

Socrates saw Athens rise to glory under the great leader Pericles. Under his leadership Athens enjoyed a splendid golden age of democracy. Athens also experienced great architectural, artistic, and literary advances. The golden age of Athens, however, depended on the powerful military and economic forces that Athens commanded. The golden age ended when Athens was defeated in war and then became embroiled in a disastrous thirty-year civil war. Plague broke out and inflation struck the economy. Then intense class struggles erupted between the rich old aristocratic families and their poorer fellow citizens. In the end, the defeated, desperate, and frustrated Athenians searched for scapegoats to blame. They settled on Socrates. With his habit of questioning everything, they said, he had weakened the traditional values and beliefs that had once made Athens strong. So they sentenced Socrates to death.

Because Socrates left no writings, most of what we know about him comes from the *Dialogues*, written by Socrates' disciple Plato. The *Dialogues* are short dramas in which the character of Socrates plays a major role. There is

MindTap Go to MindTap to watch a video about Socrates, his ideas and life.

© Vatican Museums and Galleries, Vatican City, Italy, Giraudon/The Bridgeman Art Library International

Socrates (right center) questioned almost to the point of irritation.

some controversy over how accurately Plato's *Dialogues* reflect the real conversations of Socrates. Nevertheless, most experts today agree that the first dialogues Plato wrote (for example, *Euthyphro, The Apology,* and *Crito*) are faithful to Socrates' views, although they may not contain Socrates' actual words.

Euthyphro: Do We Know What Holiness Is?

One of these early dialogues, *Euthyphro,* presents a marvelous example of how Socrates questioned people almost to the point of irritation. In fact, as you read through the dialogue, you will probably start feeling irritated yourself. You may begin asking why Socrates doesn't get past the questions and start giving answers. He gives no answers because he wants you to realize that you, too, do not have any good answers to his questions.

The dialogue takes place at the court of the king. Socrates is there to learn more about an indictment for "unholiness" brought against him for questioning traditional beliefs. He sees an old friend arrive, a priest named Euthyphro. Here, in an edited translation, is Plato's dialogue about their meeting:

QUICK REVIEW
In *Euthyphro,* Socrates questions a priest's knowledge of what holiness is.

EUTHYPHRO: Socrates! What are you doing here at the court of the King?

SOCRATES: I am being charged, Euthyphro, by a young man I hardly know named Meletus. He accuses me of making up new gods and denying the existence of the old ones.

EUTHYPHRO: I am sure you will win your case, Socrates, just like I expect to win mine.

SOCRATES: But what is your case, Euthyphro?

EUTHYPHRO: I am charging my father with murder, Socrates. One of my slaves in a drunken fit killed a fellow slave. My father chained up the culprit and left him in a ditch unattended for several days to wait the judgment of a priest. But the cold, the hunger, and the chains killed him. So now I am charging my father with murder, against the ignorant wishes of my family who do not know what true holiness requires of a priest like me.

SOCRATES: Good heavens, Euthyphro! Do you have such a clear knowledge of what holiness is that you are not afraid you might be doing something unholy in charging your own father with murder?

EUTHYPHRO: My most valued possession, Socrates, is the exact knowledge I have of these matters.

SOCRATES: You are a rare friend, Euthyphro. I can do no better than take you as my teacher so that I can defend myself against Meletus who is accusing me of being unholy. Tell me, then, what is holiness and what is unholiness?

EUTHYPHRO: Holiness is doing what I am doing: prosecuting anyone who is guilty of murder, sacrilege, or of any similar crime—whether he is your father or mother, or whoever, it makes no difference—and not to prosecute them is unholiness.

SOCRATES: But wouldn't you say, Euthyphro, that there are many other holy acts?

EUTHYPHRO: There are.

SOCRATES: I was not asking you to give me examples of holiness, Euthyphro, but to identify the characteristic which makes all holy things holy. There must be some characteristic that all holy things have in common, and one which makes unholy things unholy. Tell me what this characteristic itself is, so that I can tell which actions are holy, and which unholy.

EUTHYPHRO: Well, then, holiness is what is loved by the gods and what they hate is unholy.

QUICK REVIEW
Socrates wants not examples, but the characteristic that all, and only, holy things have in common.

QUICK REVIEW
Euthyphro says that whatever the gods love is holy.

SOCRATES: Very good, Euthyphro! Now you have given me the sort of answer I wanted. Let us examine it. A thing or a person that the gods love is holy, and a thing or a person that the gods hate is unholy. And the holy is the opposite of the unholy. Does that summarize what you said?

EUTHYPHRO: It does.

SOCRATES: But you admit, Euthyphro, that the gods have disagreements. So some things are hated by some gods and loved by other gods.

EUTHYPHRO: True.

SOCRATES: Then upon your view the same things, Euthyphro, will be both holy and unholy.

EUTHYPHRO: Well, I suppose so.

SOCRATES: Then, my friend, you have not really answered my question. I did not ask you to tell me which actions were both holy and unholy; yet that is the outcome of your view. In punishing your father, Euthyphro, you might be doing what is loved by the god Zeus, but is hated by the god Cronos.

EUTHYPHRO: But, Socrates, surely none of the gods would disagree about the rightness of punishing an injustice.

SOCRATES: Both men and gods would certainly agree on the general point that unjust acts should be punished. But men and gods might disagree about whether this particular act is unjust. Is that not true?

EUTHYPHRO: Quite true.

SOCRATES: So tell me, my friend: How do you know that all the gods agree on this particular act: that it is just for a son to prosecute his father for chaining a slave who was guilty of murder and who died in chains before the religious authorities said what should be done with him? How do you know that all the gods love this act?

EUTHYPHRO: I could make the matter quite clear to you, Socrates, although it would take me some time.

SOCRATES: Euthyphro, I will not insist on it. I will assume, if you like, that all the gods here agree. The point I really want to understand is this: Do the gods love what is holy because it is holy, or is it holy because the gods love it? What do you say, Euthyphro? On your definition whatever is holy is loved by all the gods, is it not?

EUTHYPHRO: Yes.

SOCRATES: Because it is holy? Or for some other reason?

EUTHYPHRO: No, that is the reason.

SOCRATES: Then what is holy is loved by the gods because it is holy? It is not holy because the gods love it?

EUTHYPHRO: Yes.

SOCRATES: Then, Euthyphro, to be loved by the gods cannot be the same as to be holy. And to be holy cannot be the same as to be to be loved by the gods.

EUTHYPHRO: But why, Socrates?

ANALYZING THE READING

Socrates asks Euthyphro: "(a) Do the gods love what is holy because it is holy, or (b) is it holy because the gods love it?" This puts Euthyphro in a dilemma. If (a) the gods love what is holy because it is holy, then the gods do not make things holy; instead, holy things are holy even before the gods love them. On the other hand, if (b) holy things are holy because the gods love them, then the gods make things holy; that is, things are not holy until after the gods love them. But then holiness is completely arbitrary since the gods could make anything holy by choosing to love it.

1. Euthyphro takes option (a): He agrees that "what is holy is loved by the gods because it is holy." But Socrates replies "you gave me only a quality that accompanies holiness, the quality of being loved by the gods. But you have not told me what holiness itself is, the quality that leads the gods to love holy things." Can you explain what Socrates means?

2. If Euthyphro takes option (b), what problem will that option lead him into?

3. Substitute "morally right" for "holy," "command" for "love," and "God" for "the gods." What dilemma will Socrates' question now create for religious people?

SOCRATES: Because, Euthyphro, when I asked you for the essence of holiness, you gave me only a quality that accompanies holiness: the quality of being loved by the gods. But you have not yet told me what holiness itself is [that quality that leads the gods to love whatever has the quality]. So please, Euthyphro, do not hide your treasure from me. Start again from the beginning and tell me what holiness itself is.

EUTHYPHRO: I really do not know, Socrates, how to express what I mean. Somehow or other our arguments seem to turn around in circles and walk away from us.

SOCRATES: Then I will help you instruct me, Euthyphro. Tell me—is it not true that everything that is holy is also just?

EUTHYPHRO: Yes.

SOCRATES: Does it follow that everything that is just is also holy? Or is it rather the case that whatever is holy is just, but only some just things are holy while others are not? For justice is the larger notion of which holiness is only a part. Do you agree in that?

EUTHYPHRO: Yes, that, I think, is correct.

SOCRATES: Then, since holiness is a part of justice, let us ask what part.

EUTHYPHRO: I know, Socrates! Holiness is that part of justice which involves service to the gods, while the other part of justice involves service to our fellow men.

SOCRATES: Very good, Euthyphro. But there is still one small point on which I need your help: What do you mean by "service"? Is not service always designed to benefit or improve those who are served?

EUTHYPHRO: True.

QUICK REVIEW
Euthyphro next says that holiness is serving the gods with acts they love.

SOCRATES: So does holiness, which is a kind of service, benefit or improve the gods? Would you say that when you do a holy act you make the gods better?

EUTHYPHRO: Good heavens, no!

SOCRATES: Then what is this service to the gods that is called holiness?

EUTHYPHRO: It is the kind that slaves show their masters.

SOCRATES: I understand. A sort of ministering to the gods.

EUTHYPHRO: Exactly.

SOCRATES: And now tell me, my good friend, about this ministering to the gods: What activities does it involve?

EUTHYPHRO: It would be difficult to learn them all, Socrates. Let me simply say that holiness is learning how to please the gods by prayers and sacrifices.

SOCRATES: And sacrificing is giving to the gods, while prayer is asking of the gods?

EUTHYPHRO: Exactly, Socrates.

SOCRATES: But real giving involves giving them something they want from us, does it not? For surely it would be pointless to give someone what they do not want.

EUTHYPHRO: Very true, Socrates.

SOCRATES: But then tell me, what benefit comes to the gods from our gifts? Clearly they are the givers of every good thing we have. So it puzzles me how we can give them any good thing in return.

EUTHYPHRO: But Socrates, you do not imagine that the gods benefit from the gifts we give them?

SOCRATES: If not, Euthyphro, then what sort of gifts can these be?

EUTHYPHRO: What else but praise and honor and whatever the gods love.

SOCRATES: Holiness, then, is doing what is loved by the gods and not what is beneficial to them?

EUTHYPHRO: I would say that holiness, above all, is doing what is loved by the gods.

SOCRATES: Does it surprise you our arguments go in circles? Surely you must remember that a few moments ago we concluded that to be holy is not the same as loved by the gods?

EUTHYPHRO: I do.

SOCRATES: Then either we were wrong in that admission or we are wrong now.

EUTHYPHRO: Hmm. I suppose that is the case.

SOCRATES: Then we must begin again and ask, "What is holiness?" If any man knows, you must. For if you did not know the nature of holiness and unholiness I am sure you would never have charged your aged father with murder and run the risk of doing wrong in the sight of the gods. Speak, then, my dear Euthyphro, and do not hide your knowledge from me.

EUTHYPHRO: Perhaps some other time, Socrates. Right now I am in a hurry to be off somewhere.

SOCRATES: My friend! Will you leave me in despair? And here I had hoped that you could teach me what holiness itself is.[10]

 THINKING LIKE A PHILOSOPHER

Euthyphro wants and has tried to devote his life to being a priest. Perhaps the most important service of a priest is explaining what is holy (what God wants) and what is unholy (what God does not want). But Socrates shows Euthyphro does not really understand what these are. Ask yourself: Do you understand the things that are most important to you in your own life? For example, are you religious? Then do you understand why God seems to want some things but not others? Is it important to you to be a good parent, or good son, or good daughter, or good husband, or good wife, or good boyfriend, or good girlfriend? If so, do you really understand what it is to be these things? Do you really understand those things that you think are most important to you and to the way you want to live your life? Write down those things that are most important to you. Now write down what you think you know about these things and what you think you do not understand. How can you get a better understanding of those?

In this dialogue, Socrates is doing the kind of critical questioning that characterizes philosophy. With careful reasoning he probes the religious beliefs on which Euthyphro bases his life and actions.

Socrates brings critical reason to bear on those beliefs that are most important both to Euthyphro and to himself. For Socrates himself is being accused of acting against religion and so of not being holy.

Moreover, Socrates' method reveals that Euthyphro does not really understand the basic things he assumes he knows. Socrates questions Euthyphro's easy assumption that he knows what his religious duty is, that he knows what it means for something to be just, and that he knows what it is to serve the gods and why the gods want to be served through certain acts and not others. At every turn, Euthyphro finds that he does not really understand the conventional beliefs he has been brought up to hold. He does not even know what makes an action pleasing to the gods. All he can say is that he believes the gods approve of certain acts, but he has no idea why they approve of those acts and not others.

[10] Plato, *Euthyphro*. This edited translation copyright © 1987 by Manuel Velasquez.

thinking critically • Evaluating Arguments

We said earlier that to evaluate a philosopher's claim we need to identify the premises and conclusion of his argument. So what is Socrates' argument in *Euthyphro*? Well, at the beginning of their dialogue Euthyphro brags to Socrates that he has an "exact knowledge" of what holiness is. Socrates then says that since Euthyphro knows exactly what holiness is, he must know what characteristic(s) a thing must have in order for it to qualify as something holy. But in the end Euthyphro cannot say what characteristics a thing must have in order for it to be holy.

Although Socrates does not explicitly say so, it is clear what his conclusion is: *Euthyphro does not know what holiness is.* And the reasons or premises that support this conclusion are also pretty clear: *If Euthyphro knew what holiness is, he would know what characteristics a thing must have in order for it to be holy, but Euthyphro does not know what characteristics a thing must have in order for it to be holy.* We can summarize Socrates' argument by putting the premises and conclusion in a numbered list, with the conclusion at the bottom, and the premises above it, like this:

1. If Euthyphro knew what holiness is, then he would know what characteristics a thing must have in order for it to be holy.
2. But Euthyphro does not know what characteristics a thing must have in order for it to be holy.
3. Therefore, Euthyphro does not know what holiness is.

Listing the premises and conclusion of an argument in this way is the standard way of stating an argument. Now that we know exactly what Socrates' argument is, we can begin to evaluate it by asking whether the premises are true. You will probably agree that premise (2) is true since in the dialogue Euthyphro clearly cannot say what characteristics qualify a thing as holy. But is premise (1) true? Is it true that if a person knows what something is, then he or she must know what characteristics a thing must have in order to be that kind of thing? Think about a specific example: Is it true that if you know what a dog is, then you must know what characteristics a thing must have in order for it to be a dog? Is it possible for a person to know what a dog is, without being able to say exactly what characteristics make it a dog? In other words, can you know what a thing is, even though you cannot define it?

QUICK REVIEW
The standard way of stating an argument is to put the premises and conclusion in a list with the conclusion at the bottom and the premises above it; the premises can then be evaluated.

Euthyphro might be you or me. Are you so sure about your own most basic religious beliefs? Do those of us who believe in God really know why God approves and commands certain acts and not others? If Socrates' method of questioning without arriving at answers seems frustrating, it is partly because it exposes our own lack of wisdom.

QUICK REVIEW
Socrates' questioning gave him the reputation of an irritating "gadfly."

The Republic: Is Justice Whatever Benefits the Powerful?

Perhaps it is not surprising to learn that Socrates' habit of showing people that they were ignorant of what they thought they knew angered many of them. In fact, Socrates quickly got a reputation for being a "gadfly." Many saw him as just an irritating person who picked away at people's confident assertions. And in the end he left them with nothing more than the embarrassing realization of their ignorance. Here, for example, in a selection from *The Republic,* we see Socrates questioning Thrasymachus, a cynical teacher. Socrates shows that Thrasymachus does not know what he is talking about. We see how Socrates used irony to poke fun at pretentious people like Thrasymachus. We can see also how Socrates never pretended to know something he didn't. In this dialogue, Socrates has been sitting with his friends and followers and asking them if they know what justice is. No one seems to have a good answer. Then Thrasymachus gets into the discussion. Thrasymachus is proud of his own knowledge and is fed up with Socrates' questions:

THRASYMACHUS: What nonsense are you talking about, Socrates? Why does everyone always give in to you? If you really want to know what justice is, Socrates, then don't just keep asking your questions and showing that everyone else's answers are wrong. As you know, of course, it's easier to ask a lot of questions than to provide answers. So why don't you try giving us some answers yourself? Tell us what you think justice is, Socrates. And don't give us a simple-minded answer like "justice is what ought to be," or "justice is what benefits us," or "justice is what profits us," or "justice is what is useful to us." Tell us clearly and in detail what you think, and don't just give us some simplistic stupidity.

SOCRATES: Don't be so hard on us, Thrasymachus. If my friends and I have made a mistake in our discussions, I assure you we didn't do it on purpose. . . . We are searching for justice and that is more precious than gold. We don't want to spoil our chances of finding it by being easy on each other and not giving it our best efforts. As you see, we haven't been able to discover what it is. So a clever man like you shouldn't be angry with us. You should feel sorry for us.

THRASYMACHUS: Oh, God! That's a great example of your well-known irony, Socrates. I knew you would do this. In fact, I warned everyone here before you came that you wouldn't answer any questions yourself, but would pretend to be ignorant. I told them you'd do anything rather than answer someone else's questions.

SOCRATES: So you are very wise, Thrasymachus . . .

THRASYMACHUS: Well, what if I said that I'm willing to answer your questions about justice anyway and that I can give you better answers than anyone else has given? . . .

SOCRATES: Well, then, it would be best if an ignorant man like myself tried to learn from someone like you who has knowledge.

THRASYMACHUS: Oh, yes, of course! That way Socrates can again avoid giving any answers and can cross-examine others and refute them.

SOCRATES: But look, my friend, how can someone like myself answer a question if, to begin with, he doesn't know the answer and doesn't claim to know it? . . . Isn't it more reasonable for you to answer since you say you know and can tell us? Don't be so stubborn. Do us a favor by giving us your answer and stop being so selfish with your wisdom . . .

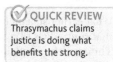

QUICK REVIEW
Thrasymachus claims justice is doing what benefits the strong.

✓ QUICK REVIEW

And the strong are rulers who make the laws, so justice is following their laws.

THRASYMACHUS:	Listen up, then. I say that justice is nothing more than whatever is advantageous to the stronger. [Pause.] Well, why don't you praise me? But no, you'd never do that!
SOCRATES:	Well, first I have to understand what you mean, for I don't quite get your point yet. You say justice is whatever is advantageous to the stronger. What exactly do you mean by this?
THRASYMACHUS:	As you must know, Socrates, some nations are ruled by tyrants, others are ruled by a democratic majority, and still others are ruled by a small aristocracy. . . . Whoever rules—the ruling party—is the stronger in each nation. . . . And in each nation, whoever rules passes laws that are to their own—the rulers'—advantage. After they pass these laws, they say that justice is obeying the law. Whoever fails to keep the law is punished as unjust and a lawbreaker. So that, my good man, is what I say justice is. Justice is the same in all nations: whatever is to the advantage of the ruling group. The ruling group, you must admit, is the stronger. So if one reasons correctly, one will conclude that everywhere justice is the same: It is whatever is advantageous to the stronger.
SOCRATES:	Now I think I know what you mean. But now we have to figure out whether you are right or not. You say that justice is something advantageous, but you add that it is what is advantageous to the stronger.
THRASYMACHUS:	Perhaps you think that's only a small point?
SOCRATES:	That's not clear yet. We need to see whether what you say is true. For I too think that justice is something advantageous. But you say that it is what is advantageous to the stronger, while I don't claim to know this. So we need to inquire.
THRASYMACHUS:	Inquire away.
SOCRATES:	First tell me, do you admit that it is just for citizens to obey their rulers?
THRASYMACHUS:	I do.
SOCRATES:	But are the rulers of a nation absolutely infallible, or do they sometimes make mistakes?
THRASYMACHUS:	Of course, they sometimes make mistakes.
SOCRATES:	So when they pass laws, they sometimes pass the right laws, and sometimes they mistakenly pass the wrong laws?
THRASYMACHUS:	True.
SOCRATES:	When they pass the right laws, they pass laws that are advantageous to their own interests, but when they make mistakes they pass laws that are contrary to their own interests. Is this your view?
THRASYMACHUS:	Yes.

ANALYZING THE READING

Socrates says that according to the statements Thrasymachus made earlier, "justice is sometimes what is not in the interests of the stronger." When Thrasymachus asks which earlier statements Socrates is talking about, Socrates says: "Didn't you just admit that the rulers might mistakenly pass laws that are not in their own interests, but that obeying such laws is still justice?" Why does the statement that:

1. Rulers sometimes mistakenly pass laws that are not in their own interests.

and the statement that:

2. Obeying such laws is still justice.

show that:

3. Justice is sometimes what is not in the interests of the stronger?

What earlier statement did Thrasymachus make that contradicts (3)? So the view of justice that Thrasymachus explains leads to a contradiction. What does that show about his view of justice?

SOCRATES:	But whatever laws they pass must be obeyed by their subjects, and that is what you say justice is.
THRASYMACHUS:	Of course.
SOCRATES:	Then justice, according to you, is sometimes what is not in the interests of the stronger, but something contrary to the interests of the stronger?
THRASYMACHUS:	What's that you just said?
SOCRATES:	Didn't you just admit that the rulers might mistakenly pass laws that are not in their own interests, but that obeying such laws is still justice?
THRASYMACHUS:	Why, yes, I think so.
SOCRATES:	Then you must also acknowledge that justice is not what is in the interests of the stronger when the rulers unintentionally pass laws that are contrary to their own interests! . . .
THRASYMACHUS:	Well, I hope that you have been completely entertained, Socrates, since today is a holiday for feasting.
SOCRATES:	And it is you who furnished the feast for us, Thrasymachus.[11]

QUICK REVIEW
Sometimes rulers mistakenly pass laws that do not benefit themselves; in such cases, if justice is following their laws, then justice would be following laws that do not benefit the rulers. But this contradicts what Thrasymachus said justice was.

Thrasymachus is a cynical philosopher. His view is that might makes right. Justice is obeying the rules of society, and these rules, he claims, always favor the interests of whatever group happens to hold power in that society. For example, Thrasymachus might have said that in a society ruled by white people, right and wrong will be defined in terms of what benefits white people. But is this cynical view of justice true? Socrates shows easily that it leads to a contradiction, and in so doing, he makes Thrasymachus look foolish.

The Apology: Socrates' Trial

Socrates' relentless and, to some people, infuriating questioning of his fellow citizens eventually led to his death. Shortly after the scene described in *Euthyphro,* Meletus and others indicted Socrates and brought him to trial. In his brilliant work *The Apology,* Plato summarized the speech Socrates delivered in his defense. The speech is especially fascinating because it provides a summary of Socrates' life and of his devotion to philosophical questioning. Socrates is standing in court, facing the jury composed of five hundred Athenian citizens. Those citizens have just heard the testimony of his accusers. They charge him with corrupting the youth of Athens and with not believing in the gods of the state, that is, with being an atheist:

QUICK REVIEW
The Apology is Socrates' speech at his trial on charges of being an atheist and of corrupting youth.

QUICK REVIEW
Socrates says it was his mission to find if the oracle was right when it said he was the wisest man alive.

SOCRATES:	I do not know, my fellow Athenians, how you were affected by my accusers whom you just heard. They spoke so persuasively they almost made me forget who I was. Yet they hardly uttered a word of truth. I am older than seventy now, and come to this court of law for the first time. So excuse my manner of speaking, which may or may not be correct. Consider only whether what I say is just.
	I will defend myself, Athenians, first against my old accusers, and then against the later ones, those who are my new accusers.
	First, then, there are many who have accused me falsely for many years. Let me sum up the accusation in their indictment: "Socrates is

---

[11] From *The Republic,* bk. I, lines 336c–339e, translated by Manuel Velasquez, © 1998 by Manuel Velasquez.

guilty of wrongdoing in that he searches into things under the earth and in the sky, and he teaches others how to speak so that the worse cause appears to be the better one."

Now the simple truth is, Athenians, that I have nothing to do with speculations about the earth or sky. Many of you who are present here have witnessed my conversations. Testify now if you have ever heard me talk about such matters.

There is as little basis for the claim that I am a teacher and take money. This accusation is as false as the other one. If a man has knowledge I think it would be fine for him to teach it to people for a fee. I would be proud myself if I had knowledge. The truth is, I have no knowledge to teach.

But many of you are thinking, "Then what is the origin of these accusations, Socrates?" That is a fair question. Let me explain their origins.

Some of you know my good friend Chaerephon. Before he died he went to Delphi and asked the religious oracle there to tell him who the wisest man in the world is. The oracle answered that there was no man wiser than Socrates.

When I learned this, I asked myself, "What can the god's oracle mean?" For I knew I had no wisdom. After thinking it over for a long time, I decided that I had to find a man wiser than myself so I could go back to the god's oracle with this evidence. So I went to see a politician who was famous for his wisdom. But when I questioned him, I realized he really was not wise, although many people—he especially—thought he was. So I tried to explain to him that although he thought himself wise, he really was not. But all that happened was that he came to hate me. And so did many of his supporters who overheard us. So I left him, thinking to myself as I left that although neither of us really knew anything about what is noble and good, still I was better off. For he knows nothing, and thinks that he knows, while I neither know nor think that I know. And in this I think I have a slight advantage.

Then I went to another person who had even greater pretensions to wisdom. The result was exactly the same: I made another enemy. In this way I went to one man after another and made more and more enemies. I felt bad about this and it frightened me. But I was compelled to do it because I felt that investigating god's oracle came first. I said to myself, I must go to everyone who seems to be wise so I can find out what the oracle means.

My hearers imagine that I myself possess the wisdom which I find lacking in others. But the truth is, Men of Athens, that only god is wise. And by his oracle he wanted to show us that the wisdom of men is worth little or nothing. It is as if he was telling us, "The wisest man is the one who, like Socrates, knows that his wisdom is in truth worth nothing." And so I go about the world obedient to god. I search and question the wisdom of anyone who seems to be wise. And if he is not wise, then to clarify the meaning of the oracle I show him that he is not wise. My occupation completely absorbs me and I have no time for anything else. My devotion to the god has reduced me to utter poverty.

There is something more. Young men of the richer classes, who do not have much to do, follow me around of their own accord. They like to hear pretenders exposed. And sometimes they imitate me by examining others themselves. They quickly discover that there are plenty of people who think they know something but who really

QUICK REVIEW
So he searched for a wiser man by questioning everyone's knowledge.

QUICK REVIEW
He made enemies but learned the wisest man is he who knows he does not know.

QUICK REVIEW
His young followers did the same kind of questioning.

know nothing at all. Then those people also get angry at me. "This damnable Socrates is corrupting our young people!" they say. And if somebody asks them, "How? What evil things does he do or teach them?" they cannot say. But in order not to appear at a loss, these people repeat the charges used against all philosophers: that we teach obscure things up in the clouds, that we teach atheism, and that we make the worst views appear to be the better. For people do not like to admit that their pretensions to knowledge have been exposed. And that, fellow Athenians, is the origin of these old accusations against me.

I have said enough about the indictment of my old accusers. I turn now to my new accusers who are led by Meletus who calls himself a true lover of his country. The sworn indictment of my new accusers says this: "Socrates is guilty of corrupting our young people and he does not believe in the gods of the state, but in other new divinities of his own." That is their charge against me. But come here, Meletus, and let me question you.

Meletus, have you thought a great deal about how our young people might be made as good as possible?

MELETUS: Yes, I have.

SOCRATES: Tell the court, then, who improves them. You must know since you accuse me of the opposite.

MELETUS: The judges, Socrates, those who are present here in this court.

SOCRATES: That is good news! There are plenty of improvers then. And what about the audience here, do they improve them?

MELETUS: Yes, they do.

SOCRATES: And the senators?

MELETUS: Yes, the senators improve them.

SOCRATES: And what about the members of the assembly?

MELETUS: They improve them, too.

SOCRATES: Then every Athenian improves them, except myself. Let me ask you a question. Consider horses. Aren't horses improved only by one man—the trainer who is an expert in horses? While if horses were put in the care of any of the others, they would be injured? Is that not the truth, Meletus, about horses or any other animals? Well, that is the truth even if you will not answer me, Meletus. I think our young people would be very lucky if only one person corrupts them while the many others improve them.

But let me ask you another question: Is it better to live among bad citizens, or among good ones? Don't good citizens do good to their neighbors, while the bad inflict evils on their neighbors?

MELETUS: Yes.

SOCRATES: Well Meletus, am I so ignorant that I do not know that if I intentionally corrupt those with whom I have to live, they will later do me evil? Would I intentionally inflict such damage on myself? So either I have not corrupted

ANALYZING THE READING

1. Why do you think that Meletus says that everyone present in the court improves young people?

2. Socrates says that horses are improved by only the one (or the few) people who know what they are doing, while the many others will injure them. What is he implying about Meletus' claim that everyone improves young people? Do you think what Socrates says is right?

3. Socrates states: "So either I have not corrupted them or I have done so unintentionally." Can you explain his reasons for that statement? Do you think those reasons are true?

4. Socrates comes to the conclusion that Meletus' indictment contains a contradiction (i.e., Socrates believes in gods and does not believe in gods). How does Meletus' indictment lead to this contradiction?

them or I have done so unintentionally which the law excuses. In either case, I am not guilty of your accusation that I corrupt our young people.

But tell us, Meletus, what is the teaching by which I am supposed to corrupt our young people? Your indictment of me swears that I teach them not to believe in the gods of the state, but in some new divine agents instead. Is that right?

MELETUS: Yes, exactly.

SOCRATES: Do you mean that I believe in some gods but not those of the state, or that I do not believe in any gods whatsoever?

MELETUS: I mean the latter, that you are a complete atheist.

SOCRATES: So you say I do not believe in any gods. Now according to your own sworn indictment, I believe in divine agents. But if a person believes in divine agents, then they must believe in divine beings, no Meletus?

MELETUS: That is right.

SOCRATES: And what are divine beings but gods or beings who come from gods? Isn't that right, Meletus? I will take your silence as agreement.

So you seem to have invented a facetious riddle for us, Meletus. You say, first, that I do not believe in any gods. And then you say that I believe in divine beings, and divine beings are gods or come from gods. So I must believe in gods. This is nonsense. You made up this indictment, Meletus, because you had nothing real to accuse me of. No one with a particle of understanding will believe you when you claim that a man who believes in divine beings is an atheist. That's enough, Meletus, I am done questioning you. I think I have refuted your charges.

But some of you will ask, "Don't you regret what you did since now it might mean your death?" To these I answer, "You are mistaken. A good man should not calculate his chances of living or dying. He should only ask himself whether he is doing right or wrong—whether his inner self is that of a good man or of an evil one."

And if you say to me, "Socrates, we will let you go free but only on condition that you stop your questioning," then I will reply, "Men of Athens, I honor and love you. But I must obey god rather than you, and while I have life and strength I will never stop doing philosophy." For my aim is to persuade you all, young and old alike, not to think about your lives or your properties, but first and foremost to care about your inner self. I tell you that wealth does not make you good within, but that from inner goodness comes wealth and every other benefit to man. This is my teaching, and if it corrupts youth, then I suppose I am their corrupter.

Well, my fellow Athenians, you must now decide whether to acquit me or not. But whichever you do, understand that I will never change my ways, not even if I have to die many times. To talk daily about what makes us good, and to question myself and others, is the greatest thing man can do. For the unexamined life is not worth living.

[At this point, Socrates rested his case. The jury debated among themselves and then, in a split vote, they reached their final verdict.]

Men of Athens, you have condemned me to death. To those of you who are my friends and who voted to acquit me let me say that death may be a good thing. Either it is a state of nothingness and utter unconsciousness, or, as some people say, it is merely a migration from this world to another. If it is complete unconsciousness—like a sleep undisturbed even by dreams—then death will be an unspeakable gain. And if it is a journey to another world where all the dead live, then it will also be a great good. For then I can continue my search into true and false knowledge: In the next world, as in this one, I can continue questioning the great people of the past to find out who is wise and who merely pretends to be. So do not be saddened by death. No evil can happen to a good man either in this life or in death.

Well, the hour of departure has arrived, and we must each go our ways. I to die, and you to live. Which is better only god knows.[12]

Again, Socrates' speech provides a remarkable example of what philosophy is. Philosophy is the quest for wisdom: an unrelenting devotion to uncover the truth about what matters most in one's life. This quest is undertaken in the conviction that a life based on an easy uncritical acceptance of conventional beliefs is an empty life. As Socrates puts it, "The unexamined life is not worth living." Philosophy is a quest that is difficult. It is difficult not only because it requires hard thinking but also because it sometimes requires taking positions that are unacceptable to those around us. Taking such positions may offend others. In Socrates' case, his fellow citizens were so offended by what he said and did that they condemned him to death.

Crito: Do We Have an Obligation to Obey the Law?

Socrates was jailed immediately after his trial. While awaiting his execution, he continued his avid questioning. But his questions now focused more on his own beliefs about right and wrong, good and evil. In one of his final conversations, Socrates considered whether he had the courage to face death for his beliefs. Plato recorded these conversations in the dialogue *Crito.* It takes place the day before Socrates' execution when he awakes to find his close friend Crito sitting in his jail cell next to him:

 THINKING LIKE A PHILOSOPHER

When he is asked whether he regrets his actions since now he might have to die for them, Socrates says: "A good man should not calculate his chances of living or dying. He should only ask himself whether he is doing right or wrong—whether his inner self is that of a good man or of an evil one." Socrates believed he was doing the right thing when he questioned people because he thought that was what the Oracle wanted him to do. And doing this was more important to him than "living or dying." Ask yourself: Is there anything or anyone that is so important to you that you would be willing to die for it or for them? Or do you think staying alive is so valuable that you would be willing to do anything, or give up anything or anyone just to stay alive? In either case, indicate what is most important to you right now, more important than the other things in your life. What is it and why is it important to you? How much of what you have would you be willing to give up just to be able to keep that which is most important to you?

SOCRATES:	Crito! What are you doing here at this hour? It must be quite early.
CRITO:	Yes, it is.
SOCRATES:	What time is it?
CRITO:	The dawn is breaking.
SOCRATES:	I am surprised the jailer let you in. Did you just get here?
CRITO:	No, I came some time ago.
SOCRATES:	Why didn't you wake me up?

MindTap™ To read more from Plato's *Crito*, click the link in the MindTap Reader or go to the Questia Readings folder in MindTap.

---

[12] Plato, *The Apology*. This edited translation copyright © 1987 by Manuel Velasquez.

✅ QUICK REVIEW
In *Crito*, Socrates' friend urges him to escape from prison as "the many" would advise.

CRITO:	I saw how peacefully you were sleeping, so I didn't want to disturb you. I've often thought you are lucky to be able to remain so peaceful even at a time like this.
SOCRATES:	So why did you come here so early?
CRITO:	Oh my dear friend, Socrates! Let me beg you once again to take my advice and escape from here. If you die, I will not only lose a friend who can never be replaced, but people who do not know us will think that I could have saved you but was not willing to pay the necessary bribes. And that would be a shameful reputation to have.
SOCRATES:	But why do you care about the opinions of other people?
CRITO:	Because their opinions can lead them to inflict great evil on us, as your situation right now proves.
SOCRATES:	Crito, they can't inflict the greatest evil on us, nor give us the greatest good, since they cannot make us wise or foolish.
CRITO:	Let that be, then. But listen to me, Socrates. You are going to betray your own sons if you die and abandon them. They are sure to meet the unhappy fate of orphans.
SOCRATES:	Dear Crito, your zeal is invaluable, if it is right. But if wrong, the greater the zeal, the greater the evil. I have always been guided by reason. I cannot turn away now from the principles I have always tried to honor. So let us look carefully at the issues before us. Shall we begin with your views about what people will think? Tell me, were we right long ago when we said that not all the opinions of men should be valued? Or was that just a lot of hot air? Didn't we conclude that we should listen to people's good opinions and not the worthless ones.
CRITO:	Yes, that's right.
SOCRATES:	Aren't the good opinions those of the wise, while the worthless ones come from the ignorant? Think about the athlete in training. Should he follow the advice and opinions of every man? Or should he listen to one man only—his doctor or trainer?
CRITO:	He should follow the one man's advice.
SOCRATES:	He should train in the way that seems best to the man who has knowledge rather than listen to the opinions of the many?
CRITO:	True.
SOCRATES:	And if he doesn't listen to the man with knowledge, but instead listens to the many who are ignorant, won't he harm and destroy his body?
CRITO:	He would have to.
SOCRATES:	Doesn't the same principle hold, Crito, in the matter we are discussing: which course of action is right and good and which is wrong and evil? In this kind of matter should we follow the opinions of the many or of one who has knowledge? If we do not listen to one who has knowledge about right and wrong, we will destroy that inner self that is improved by doing what is right and destroyed by doing what is wrong. Don't you agree?
CRITO:	I certainly do, Socrates.
SOCRATES:	If the athlete follows the advice of men who have no knowledge, he will destroy his body. Is life worth living when the body has been ruined and destroyed?
CRITO:	Not at all.
SOCRATES:	What about that inner part of us that improves by doing what is right and is destroyed by doing what is wrong? Is life worth living when that part of us has been destroyed? Or is the body better than that inner

✅ QUICK REVIEW
Socrates replies that we should not listen to the opinions of the many but do what is truly right.

part of ourselves that is concerned with right and wrong?

CRITO: Certainly not.

SOCRATES: Then, Crito, you are wrong to suggest that we should listen to what the many will say. We should, instead, listen to one who has knowledge about right and wrong. The values you bring up—money, loss of reputation, and educating children—are based on the opinions of the many. They do not concern the only real issue before us: Is it right or wrong for me to escape against the wishes of the Athenians? So follow me now in my questioning.

CRITO: I will do my best, Socrates.

SOCRATES: Is it true that we should never intentionally do wrong?

CRITO: It certainly is.

SOCRATES: And what about returning evil for evil—which is the morality of the many—is that right or not?

CRITO: It is not right.

SOCRATES: But in leaving this prison against the will of the Athenians, am I doing evil to anyone?

CRITO: I am not sure, Socrates.

SOCRATES: Well, imagine that just as I was about to escape, the laws of our government arrived and asked me, "Socrates, what are you trying to do? Do you want to destroy us? Won't government fall if its law has no power and if private citizens can set the law aside whenever they want?" How will I answer them, Crito? Perhaps I could respond, "Yes, but the government injured me: It sentenced me unjustly." Is that what I should say?

CRITO: Definitely, Socrates!

SOCRATES: Then what if the laws reply, "But didn't you agree to obey our judgments, Socrates?"

             And if I show astonishment at this reply, the laws might add, "Do not be surprised, Socrates. You, who are always asking questions, answer us now. Long ago we gave you birth when your father married your mother by our laws so they could conceive you. Do you object to our marriage laws?"

             "No," I would have to reply.

             "Then do you object to the laws under which you were raised and which provided for your education?"

             "They were fine," I would say.

             "Well, then," they would conclude, "we brought you into the world. And we raised and then educated you. Can you deny then that you are like our son and should obey us? Is it right to strike back at your father when he punishes you?

             "Moreover, after we brought you into the world, and after we educated and provided you with many benefits, we proclaimed that you and all Athenians were free to leave us with all your goods when you

ANALYZING THE READNG

1. Socrates says that if an athlete "doesn't listen to the man with knowledge, but instead listens to the many who are ignorant," he will "harm and destroy his body." What is Socrates trying to say in this statement? Is he right?

2. After saying an athlete will destroy his body if he does not listen to the man with knowledge, Socrates says "the same principle holds" when trying to figure out "which course of action is right… and which is wrong." So he concludes: "If we do not listen to one who has knowledge about right and wrong, we will destroy that inner self that is improved by doing what is right and destroyed by doing what is wrong." What is Socrates saying here? What is his reason for saying it? Do you think he's right?

3. After saying an athlete should care for his body by following only the advice of one who has knowledge, he asks: "Is the body better than that inner part of ourselves that is concerned with right and wrong?" What is Socrates implying here? Do you think he's right?

QUICK REVIEW
The government will collapse if its laws are not followed, so laws should be obeyed.

QUICK REVIEW
Moreover, citizens should obey their government because it is like a parent, because it gave them many benefits, and because they agreed to obey by freely choosing to stay. So it is wrong to escape the judgment of the government.

came of age. But he who has experienced how we administer our society and freely chooses to stay, enters into an implied contract that he will obey us.

"So he who disobeys us, we maintain, does wrong in three ways: First, because in disobeying us he is disobeying his parents [since our marriage laws united his parents so they could bring him into the world]; second, because in disobeying us he is disobeying those who gave him all the benefits involved with raising and educating him; third, because he agreed to obey us and now he neither obeys nor does he show us where we were wrong. But are we right in saying that you agreed to be governed by us?"

How shall I answer that question, Crito? Must I not agree?

CRITO: There is no other way, Socrates.

SOCRATES: Then the laws will say, "Then, Socrates, in escaping you are breaking the agreement you made with us. So listen to us and not to Crito. Think not of life and children first and of justice afterwards. Put justice first." This, Crito, is the voice I seem to hear quietly murmuring nearby, like a mystic who thinks he hears a flute playing in his ears. That voice is humming in my ears, and it prevents me from hearing any other. Still, if you have anything more to add, Crito, speak up.

CRITO: I have nothing more to say, Socrates.

SOCRATES: Then, Crito, let me do what I must, since it is the will of god.[13]

The next morning, after saying farewell to his family and friends, Socrates drank the poison hemlock and died.

Here again, then, on the evening of his death, we find Socrates doing philosophy. But now he aims his philosophical questions at his own assumptions and his own life. He reasons that where morality is concerned, he should disregard the "opinions of the many." In other words moral right and wrong do not depend on whatever most people in our society believe is right or wrong. Instead, to determine what is right and wrong, we should rely on those who have knowledge and can reason correctly about these matters. And to reason correctly about right and wrong one must ask whether one's actions inflict evil on others. So Socrates turns to the task of trying to reason correctly about whether escaping from prison as Crito suggests would inflict evil on anyone. Socrates' reasoning leads him to the conclusion that if he escaped, he would inflict evil on his government—the "laws"—because he has an obligation to obey it. He says he has this obligation, first, because his government is like a parent that gave him birth. Second, he has the obligation to obey because as he grew up the government bestowed important benefits on him. And third, he has the obligation to obey because he has agreed to obey the government. Other considerations,

c.1650 [oil on canvas], Dufresnoy, Charles Alphonse (1611–68)/Galleria degli Uffizi, Florence, Italy/Alinari/The Bridgeman Art Library

The Death of Socrates

[13] Plato, *Crito*. This translation copyright © 1987 by Manuel Velasquez.

PHILOSOPHY AND LIFE
Breaking the Law for the Sake of Justice

In March 2014 hundreds of college students were arrested for breaking the law by trespassing at the White House in protest of the Keystone oil pipeline project that could increase global warming by increasing the supply of oil. The previous year hundreds more had been arrested in similar protests. During 2011 in New York, "Occupy Wall Street" demonstrators illegally occupied a park near Wall Street to protest unjust economic inequalities that benefit the richest "1 percent" at the expense of the other "99 percent." Within days, the movement spread to Boston, Los Angeles, San Francisco, Washington, D.C., Salt Lake City, Philadelphia, Sacramento, Portland, Houston, Dallas, Tampa, New Orleans, Cleveland, Denver, Seattle, Berkeley, and more than a hundred other U.S. cities where demonstrators also illegally took over private property in protest of rising inequality.

These were not the first times Americans deliberately broke the law to protest something they felt was morally wrong. During the 1960s, thousands of black people illegally sat in "white-only" sections of restaurants, theaters, buses, and other segregated businesses to protest unjust segregation laws. During the 1970s, tens of thousands of people broke the law to protest the U.S. war in Vietnam, occupying

government property, refusing to pay taxes that would support the war, and trespassing on the private property of companies that made military weapons. In the 1990s, thousands broke the law to protest the Gulf War, and in 2003, thousands more did so to protest the war in Iraq. And during the past decade numerous groups have illegally occupied power plants, illegally blocked logging operations, illegally prevented construction workers from building new coal plants, and staged illegal sit-ins, all in protest of the ongoing destruction of the environment. When arrested, protesters have inevitably said that their actions are a matter of conscience and that they are obligated to obey their conscience rather than the law.

QUESTIONS

1. Is it morally wrong to break the law in the situations just described? Is it wrong when a demonstrator breaks only those specific laws the demonstrator believes are unjust? Explain your answers.
2. How would Socrates respond to the civil disobedience of these various groups of protesters? Who is right, Socrates or the demonstrators?

---

he claims, are irrelevant. What matters is that these three arguments prove that he has an obligation to obey the government. And so, Socrates concludes, it is wrong for him to escape.

thinking critically • Identifying Premises, Conclusions, and Assumptions

How good are Socrates' arguments? To answer this question, we need first to figure out exactly what those arguments are. Let us focus on the three arguments he gives Crito at the very end of their conversation, since these state the fundamental reasons why Socrates refuses to leave his prison. Socrates summarizes these arguments when he tells Crito that "the laws" (the government) will say:

> So he who disobeys us, we maintain, does wrong in three ways: First, because in disobeying us he is disobeying his parents [since our marriage laws united his parents so they would bring him into the world]; second, because in disobeying us he is disobeying those who gave him all the benefits involved with raising and educating him; third, because he has agreed to obey us and now he neither obeys nor does he show us where we were wrong.

QUICK REVIEW
The conclusion of an argument is the basic claim the argument is trying to prove and is often indicated with the words: *so, therefore, consequently, hence, accordingly, which shows that, as a result, we may infer that, we may conclude that, which shows that.*

To figure out what Socrates' three arguments are, we need to identify the premises and the conclusion of each of the three arguments. The conclusion of an argument is the basic claim or assertion that the argument is trying to prove. Here the conclusion of the arguments is fairly easy to figure out since the three arguments are all supposed to prove that it is wrong to disobey "the laws." "The laws" here refers to the government. So the conclusion of the three arguments seems to be: "He who disobeys his government, does wrong," or, more simply: "It is wrong to disobey the government." How do we know that we have correctly identified the conclusion? When people state an argument, they often (but not always) use certain words to indicate what their conclusion is. Those words are *so, therefore, consequently, hence, accordingly, which shows that, as a result, we may infer that, we may conclude that, which shows that.* Notice that in the earlier quote, Socrates uses the word "so": "*So* he who disobeys us, we maintain, does wrong in three ways." The use of the word "so" indicates that the sentence that follows is in fact the conclusion of the arguments.

So what are the premises of the arguments? The premises are the reasons or evidence given to support the conclusion. People tend to use certain words to indicate their premises. In particular, people often (but not always) use the following words to identify their premises: *because, inasmuch as, since, for, otherwise, in view of the fact that, for the reason that, on account of the fact that, in view of the fact that, considering that.* In the earlier quote, notice that Socrates uses the word "because" at the beginning of three sentences. That indicates that each of those sentences is the premise of an argument. So let's put each argument's premises and conclusion in a list, with the premises first and the conclusion last:

1st Argument: In disobeying the government, one is disobeying his parents. So: It is wrong to disobey the government.

2nd Argument: In disobeying the government, one is disobeying those who gave him all the benefits involved with raising and educating him. So: It is wrong to disobey the government.

3rd Argument: One has agreed to obey the government and now he neither obeys nor does he show us where we went wrong. So: It is wrong to disobey the government.

If you read over each of these arguments, you will notice that something seems to be missing in each: the arguments don't have a clear connection between what the premise says, and what the conclusion says. In each argument, the premise indicates what disobeying the government involves, but the premise does not say anything about the wrongness of this. Yet the conclusion jumps to a claim about the wrongness of disobeying. How does the argument move from a premise that says nothing about wrongness to a conclusion about wrongness? What is the connection between the premise and the conclusion?

Well, Socrates does not tell us what that connection is: It is an unstated assumption that he leaves for you to figure out. But this is not unusual. You will see a lot of arguments that jump from a premise to a conclusion without a clear connection between them. And when an argument does this, it is up to you to figure out what the unstated connection is, that is, to figure out the unstated assumption that connects the premise to the conclusion.

Fortunately, in this case, the connecting assumptions are not hard to figure out. Let's take the first argument. The argument begins with the premise that disobeying the government is the same as disobeying a parent, and the argument concludes from this that disobeying the government is wrong. Obviously, the premise that disobeying the government is the same as disobeying a parent proves that disobeying the government is wrong *only if it is wrong to disobey a parent*. So the argument as stated in (1) earlier is missing an unstated premise, that is, a premise that is assumed but not stated and that is needed if the premises are to support or prove the conclusion. If we add the missing or assumed premise to the argument, and we get rid of unnecessary words, we can restate the complete argument like this:

1st Argument: Disobeying one's government is the same as disobeying
                 one's parents.
                 But disobeying one's parents is wrong.
                 Therefore, disobeying one's government is wrong.

The second argument is similar. The second argument begins with the premise that disobeying one's government is the same as disobeying someone who gives one the benefits of being raised and educated. How would this premise prove that disobeying one's government is wrong? Obviously, disobeying one's government would be wrong *only if it is wrong to disobey someone who gives one the benefits of being raised and educated*. So the second argument can be restated with the assumed premise like this:

2nd Argument: Disobeying one's government is the same as disobeying some-
                 one who gives one the benefits of being raised and educated.
                 But disobeying someone who gives one the benefits of
                 being raised and educated is wrong.
                 Therefore, disobeying one's government is wrong.

The third argument begins with the premise that everyone makes an agreement to obey their government. Then it concludes that it is wrong to disobey the government. How can this premise and conclusion be connected? Well clearly, making an agreement to obey the government would make disobeying the government wrong, *only if not doing what you agree to do is wrong*. So inserting this assumed premise into the third argument leaves us with this:

3rd Argument: One makes an agreement to obey one's government.
                 If one makes an agreement to obey one's government, then
                 not obeying one's government is wrong.
                 Therefore, not obeying (or disobeying) one's government is
                 wrong.

Now that we have complete statements of Socrates' three arguments, we can see if they are acceptable. To do this, you need to ask whether the premises are true. Take the first argument: Is it true that the government is like a parent to you, and is it true that it is wrong to disobey a parent? Or take the second argument: Is it true that government has given you the benefits of helping to raise you and educate you, and is it true that if your government bestows such benefits on you, then you should repay it by obeying its laws? And take the third argument: Is it true, as Socrates suggests, that an adult who "has experienced how we administer our society and freely chooses to stay, enters into an implied contract that he will obey" the government? And is it true that if you make an agreement, then not doing what you agreed to do is wrong?

We will not answer these questions for you, but I think you will agree that their answers are significant, so we must return to them in a later chapter. At this point, what is important is the realization that stating arguments clearly and then pondering the questions they raise is crucial to philosophy. Socrates' own willingness to struggle with these questions even in the face of death gives us a priceless and still powerful example of what philosophy is.

PHILOSOPHY AT THE MOVIES

AF archive/Alamy

Watch *Hunger* (2009), a film about 27-year-old Bobby Sands who, in prison for his activities as a member of the PIRA (a paramilitary group battling against British rule of Northern Ireland), joins other PIRA prisoners who seek "prisoner of war" status and more humane treatment through protests such as refusing to wear prisoner garb, refusing to wash themselves, smearing their cells with excrement, and, finally, organizing a hunger strike in which Sands is the first to die. In what ways is Bobby Sands' commitment to what he believes is "right" similar to Socrates' commitment to what he believes is right? Is their commitment different in any important ways?

Another movie with related themes: *Into the Wild* (2007).

✓ QUICK REVIEW
For Plato, philosophical knowledge makes us free.

1.4 The Value of Philosophy

A person studying philosophy for the first time might ask a question: Why devote all this time and effort to study philosophy?

Achieving Freedom

✓ QUICK REVIEW
For Buddha, philosophical knowledge frees us from the cycle of birth, suffering, death, and rebirth.

We have seen that Plato, in the Allegory of the Cave, suggested an answer: The value of philosophy is that through it we achieve freedom—freedom from assumptions we have unquestioningly accepted from others, and freedom to decide for ourselves what we believe about ourselves and our place in the world around us.

Other philosophical traditions have also suggested that philosophical wisdom will lead to personal freedom, but to a different, more profound kind of freedom than Plato had in mind. For example, Buddhism holds that when we have dispelled our philosophical ignorance and have understood the true nature of the universe, we will be freed from the otherwise unending wheel of birth, suffering, death, and rebirth to which all living creatures are bound. In this view, each living thing, when it dies, is reincarnated in another living thing, its new condition determined by its past action, or *karma*. Yet by dispelling ignorance and acquiring wisdom we are each able to break out of the wheel. For example, Buddhist writings of the second century CE describe a vision experienced by the great Eastern sage, Buddha:

> In the first watch of the night he recalled his previous births. He remembered thousands of births as if he was living them all over again. "There I was so and so and my name was such and such; I died and from there I came here." Upon recalling his many births and deaths in these lives, he was filled with compassion for all living things: "Again and again they tear themselves away from their family in one life, and must go on to live another. And they must do this endlessly. This world is truly helpless as it turns round and round like a wheel." Without flinching, he continued recalling his past and began to realize that this world of endless turning must be as insubstantial as the hollow core of a banana tree. In the second watch of the night . . . he saw the entire world as though reflected in a spotless mirror. He saw that the death and rebirth of each creature is determined by how inferior or superior its previous actions have been. This is the law of *karma*. And his compassion grew even greater. He saw there was no resting place in the river of endless rebirth and death . . . . Then, as the third watch of that night approached, he meditated on the nature of this world: "How sad that living beings wear themselves out for nothing! Over and over again they are born, grow old, die, pass on, and are reborn! What is more, desire and illusion blind them so that they have no knowledge of how to end this suffering." . . . He looked at the processes by which one thing leads to another, and saw that it is

ultimately because we lack knowledge that we end up subject to old age and death, and that ending this ignorance can lead to the end of rebirth, old age, death and suffering. The great seer realized that if our ignorance is overcome, then even the law of *karma* will stop. At that moment he achieved a true knowledge of all there is to be known, and he stood out in the world as a Buddha.... For seven days he dwelt there.... He thought, "Here I have found freedom."[14]

In the Buddhist perspective, then, **philosophy** can lead to the ultimate freedom: an understanding of the universe that will allow us to escape from the endless cycles of birth, suffering, death, and rebirth to which we are condemned by our past. From this perspective, then, the value of philosophical wisdom is great indeed!

Building Your View of Life

Still, the value that Plato and the Buddha attribute to philosophical wisdom may not be enough for you. Everyday tasks and social preoccupations crowd our lives and leave us little time for anything else. Why should we spend the time and effort to study philosophy when so many more practical needs are pressing in on us? For example, it is clear why we should spend time studying those subjects that will provide the knowledge and skills needed to get a job or succeed in a career. We each need a job or a career to get along, to earn our living and meet our basic needs. But why should we spend time studying philosophy?

Consider, first, that we all seek to make sense of the world we live in and to understand our place in that world. We seek to do this in a variety of ways: through allegiance to religious beliefs, adherence to political parties, commitments to causes. Such loyalties and behaviors reveal the human need to put order in our world and to make sense of things. One goal of philosophy is to develop a unified, coherent view of yourself and your life in the world. Studying philosophy will expose you to different ways of making sense of the world. It also will show you how various philosophers have conceived of the universe around us and of their place in that universe. Seeing all this will help you develop a view of life that can enable you, too, to make sense of yourself and your place in the world around you.

What's more, philosophy will expose you to the history of thought. By portraying humanity's intellectual achievements, philosophy provides a perspective on the continuing development of human thought. As we confront the thoughts and views of various philosophers, we realize that there are many different ways of understanding the universe. A merit of this exposure is that it breeds humility. We realize that the way we have always thought about ourselves and our universe is but one way among many. As a result, we become more tolerant, more receptive, and more sympathetic to views that conflict with our own. We're less biased, provincial, ingrown; we're more open-minded and cosmopolitan.

Cultivating Awareness

Something else that makes philosophy worthwhile is the mindfulness or awareness that it can help us cultivate. Consider the importance of awareness. Personal freedom depends to a large extent on one's awareness of the self and

---

[14] This translation is based in part on the translation in *Sacred Texts of the World*, ed. Ninian Smart and Richard D. Hecht (New York: Crossroad, 1982), 234–235, and in part on the translation of the same passages in E. H. Johnston, trans., *The Buddhacarita or Acts of the Buddha* (Delhi, India: Motilal Banarsidass, 1972), 203–204, 208–209, and 213. I have further edited the text to simplify and clarify it and to modernize the language.

PHILOSOPHY AND LIFE

Albert Ellis and Rational Emotive Behavior Therapy

Dr. Albert Ellis is a well-known clinical psychologist who has developed a form of therapy based on the idea that neurotic symptoms and psychological problems spring from an irrational philosophy: irrational beliefs that are the result of "philosophical conditioning." According to Ellis, our emotions and behaviors are the result of the beliefs and assumptions we have about ourselves, other people, and the world in general. It is what people *believe* about the situations they face—not the situations themselves—that determines how they feel and behave. According to Ellis, this idea was first stated by Epictetus, a Roman stoic philosopher who, in the first century CE, said that people are disturbed not by things but by the views they take of them. To eliminate the disturbance, we need merely change our views. In his book *The Essence of Rational Emotive Behavior Therapy* (1994), Ellis states that although many irrational philosophical beliefs exist, the three main ones that affect our happiness are:

1. *"I must do well and get approval, or I am worthless."*
2. *"You must treat me reasonably, considerately, and lovingly, or else you're no good."*
3. *"Life must be fair, easy, and hassle-free, or else it's awful."*

If a person is to be happy, he or she must change these irrational philosophical beliefs, which are the source of anxiety, depression, hopelessness, resentment, hostility, and violence. The person can change these irrational ideas by asking questions: "Is there any evidence for this belief?" "What is the evidence against this belief?" "What is the worst that can happen if I give up this belief?" "What is the best that can happen?" We can be happy only when the irrational beliefs that underlie our neuroses and other psychological problems are replaced by a more rational philosophy.

QUESTIONS

1. Do you agree that a person's philosophical assumptions can have the significant psychological impacts that Ellis' theory claims? If Ellis is right, what are the implications for philosophy?

2. Consider Ellis' three main irrational beliefs and determine whether they belong to the field of epistemology, metaphysics, or ethics.

3. Can you think of any other "philosophical beliefs" that can produce the kinds of psychological problems that Ellis describes?

4. What if Ellis' three beliefs are true? Could they be true? Explain.

how our actions and thoughts are being influenced by the world around us. To a large degree, we are free only to the extent that we are aware of these many significant influences. In helping us deepen our awareness of these, philosophy will give you the ability to deal with and perhaps throw off the blinders that keep you unaware and unfree.

Learning to Think Critically

Finally, we should note that the study of philosophy will help you refine your ability to reason well, and this ability will help you get ahead in every area of your life and education. Philosophy can teach you to think critically, to reason, and to evaluate how adequate is your own reasoning or the reasoning of others. As we said earlier, such skills are the tools of philosophy. Pondering the great ideas and arguments of extraordinary thinkers will hone your powers of analysis and give you reasoning skills that you will be able to use in every area of your life: your job, your other classes, your close relationships, and your political and social activities.

In fact, the importance and value of good reasoning and critical thinking cannot be exaggerated. Every day we are bombarded by advertisements, political controversies, claims about climate change, arguments about the morality of abortion, assertions about the evils of immigration, and countless other claims and counterclaims, arguments and counterarguments. Politicians tell us what they think our country needs and try to convince us to vote for them. Companies try to persuade us to buy their products. News commentators, bloggers, and editorials try to influence our thinking. Every day we hear some people issue dire warnings about the future, while others argue that the warnings are exaggerated. Without the ability to think critically, to reason well, and to evaluate the reasoning of others, we are vulnerable to all these different interests and their constant clamor to have us do what they tell us to do, and think what they tell us to think. If we are to be able to defend ourselves against the countless attempts at persuasion that surround us every moment of every day, we must learn how to evaluate the many claims and arguments they hurl at us. Philosophy, with its ability to instill good reasoning skills, will be of invaluable help as you try to navigate your way through these numerous attempts to sway your thinking and your decisions.

The Theme of This Text

In the pages ahead, as we consider many enduring philosophical questions and hone our reasoning skills, uppermost in each of our minds will be this question: Who and what am I? We could call this the unifying theme that draws together what may seem disparate philosophical concerns. We'll see that the study of philosophy can help us in answering this question, for ultimately a human being is many things: a real existing being; a moral, social, and political animal; a perceiver and knower; a scientist; a religionist; and a pilgrim in search of meaning. All these aspects of humanity and self are areas of intense philosophical concern and speculation. Therefore, our adventure into the world of philosophy is more than an encounter with great ideas, thinkers, systems, and movements. It's a voyage into ourselves, a quest for self-definition and understanding.

PHILOSOPHY AT THE MOVIES

Watch *Pleasantville* (1998), an older classic about a young man, David, and his twin sister, Jennifer, who are sucked through their television into a 1950s black-and-white sitcom where it is always a pleasant 72 degrees, books have no words, there is no sex, and everyone accepts rigid conventional lives. Does the use of color in *Pleasantville* indicate enlightenment? What do black and white indicate? What role, if any, do you see autonomy, knowledge, rationality, freedom, and choice playing in the movie? What does the library represent?

Another movie with related themes: *Revolutionary Road* (2008); a related older classic: *A Clockwork Orange* (1971).

Chapter Summary

This opening chapter tries to communicate some of the interest and importance of philosophy and to show that philosophy is not to be feared but rather to be cultivated and relished. We began by observing that everyone philosophizes in daily life, and we saw how Plato pictured philosophy as a climb from darkness to light in the pursuit of wisdom. We cited the three main fields of philosophy and then turned to watch the philosopher Socrates at work. We saw the value of studying philosophy: Nevertheless, we noted that some feminists have charged that up to now philosophy has had a male bias.

The main points of this chapter are:

1.1   What Is Philosophy?

● Philosophy, which literally means the love of wisdom, begins with wonder about our most basic beliefs. Its goal is to help us achieve autonomy by making us more aware of our own beliefs and encouraging us to reason and think through issues for ourselves.

● The Allegory of the Cave is one of the best-known passages in *The Republic*, a work of the Greek philosopher Plato. The allegory describes the philosopher's climb from the dark cave of philosophical ignorance up into the light of philosophical wisdom.

● thinking critically Philosophy is the critical and rational examination of the most fundamental assumptions that underlie our lives, an activity of concern to men and women of all cultures and races.

● thinking critically Reasoning is the process of thinking by which we draw a conclusion from the reasons or evidence that support or prove the conclusion. Critical thinking is disciplined thinking that bases beliefs and actions on well-founded evidence and unbiased and valid reasoning, that avoids false generalizations and unrecognized assumptions, and that considers opposing viewpoints.

1.2   The Traditional Divisions of Philosophy

● The three main fields of philosophy are epistemology, metaphysics, and ethics.

● Epistemology deals with questions of knowledge (including the structure, reliability, extent, and kinds of knowledge); truth, validity, and logic; and a variety of linguistic concerns. An example is the question of whether truth is relative.

● Metaphysics addresses questions of reality (including the meaning and nature of being); the nature of mind, self, and human freedom; and some topics that overlap with religion, such as the existence of God, the destiny of the universe, and the immortality of the soul. An example is the question of whether human behavior is free or determined.

● Ethics is the study of our values and moral principles and how they relate to human conduct and to our social and political institutions. For example, do we have a moral obligation to love and serve others, or is our only obligation to ourselves?

● Philosophy also includes several fields usually referred to as "the philosophy of …," including the philosophy of science, the philosophy of art, and the philosophical meaning of life. These fields of philosophy examine the basic assumptions underlying particular areas of human knowledge or activity.

● thinking critically Philosophical claims should be clear and neither vague nor ambiguous.

● thinking critically Philosophical claims, unlike speculation, must be supported by arguments. Arguments consist of (1) premises, which provide reasons or evidence for a conclusion, and (2) the conclusion, which is the claim that those premises support.

1.3   A Philosopher in Action: Socrates

- Socrates is usually considered the father of Western philosophy, although he was preceded by a group of earlier Greek philosophers, the pre-Socratics. Socrates was put to death for persistently examining the unquestioned assumptions of his fellow Athenians. Plato, a disciple of Socrates, preserved his views in dialogues, including *Euthyphro, The Republic, The Apology,* and *Crito.*

- *Euthyphro* shows Socrates questioning traditional religious beliefs; *The Republic* shows Socrates inquiring into the meaning of justice; *The Apology* shows Socrates at his trial explaining his lifelong commitment to philosophy; *Crito* shows Socrates awaiting death and questioning his own beliefs about the authority of the state.

- thinking critically To evaluate a philosopher's claims, like those of Socrates, we must identify the premises and conclusions of his or her arguments. Premises are reasons or evidence given to support a conclusion and are often indicated by words such as *because, inasmuch as, since, for, otherwise, in view of the fact that, for the reason that, on account of the fact that, in view of the fact that, considering that.* The conclusion is the main point or claim the argument is trying to prove or establish and is often indicated by words such as *so, therefore, consequently, hence, accordingly, which shows that, as a result, we may infer that, we may conclude that, which shows that.*

- thinking critically Sometimes arguments, like some in the *Crito,* are missing an assumed premise. To identify the missing premise or unstated assumption of an argument, we must ask: What claim(s) is (are) needed if the premises are to support or prove the conclusion? Once the premises and the conclusion of an argument are identified and organized into a list in which the premises are first and the conclusion is last, the argument can be assessed by figuring out whether the premises are true or false.

1.4   The Value of Philosophy

- Both Plato and Buddha claim that philosophy can help us achieve freedom

- Philosophy can also make us more tolerant and enable us to think critically and reason well, skills that can help us in almost every area of our lives.

1.5 Reading

Why study philosophy? In his short story, the eighteenth-century French philosopher Voltaire suggests that even though an ignorant person may be much happier than a learned philosopher, we nevertheless "madly" prefer the despair of philosophy to the happy contentment of ignorance. Is this true? And if it is, why do we prefer knowledge to happiness?

VOLTAIRE

Story of a Good Brahmin

While I was traveling I once met an old Brahmin who was very wise and prudent, and very learned. He was also rich, which made him even wiser because, lacking nothing, he had no need to defraud anyone. His household was very well managed by three beautiful wives who endeavored to please him; and when he was not amusing himself with his women, he occupied himself with philosophy.

Near his house, which was beautiful, well furnished, and surrounded with some delightful gardens, lived an old Indian woman. She was very bigoted, ignorant, and rather poor.

One day the Brahmin said to me: "I wish I had never been born."

I asked him why.

"Because," he answered, "I have been studying for some forty years, and those forty years have been wasted. I teach others, and I myself am ignorant about everything. The realization of my condition fills my soul with such humiliation and disgust that life is unbearable to me. I was born and exist in time, yet I do not know what time is. I am standing, as our wise men say, between two eternities, yet I do not have the faintest idea what eternity is. I am made of matter, I think, but I have never been able to learn how it produces thought. I do not know whether my understanding is a simple faculty in me like that of walking or of digesting, or whether I think with my head in the same way I grasp things with my hands. I am not only ignorant of the source of my thinking, but even the source of my bodily movements is just as hidden from me. I do not know why I exist. Yet every day people ask me questions about all these matters. I have to answer them, but I have nothing worthwhile to tell them. I talk a lot but I am confounded and ashamed of myself after I have spoken.

"It is even worse when someone asks me if Brahma was produced by Vishnu or if they are both eternal. God is my witness that I know nothing about these matters, and this is clear from my answers. 'Oh! Reverend Father,' one will say to me, 'please tell us how evil came to flood the whole world.' I am as much at a loss about this as the one who asks the question. Sometimes I tell them that everything that happens is for the best. But those who have been ruined or mutilated by war, don't believe that; and I don't either. I return to my house filled with curiosity and my ignorance. I read the writings of our ancient sages, but they only increase my darkness. When I talk with my friends about this, some tell me we ought to just enjoy life and laugh at mankind. Others think they know something, and lose themselves in absurd theories. Every effort I make to solve these mysteries just increases the burden I feel. Sometimes I am ready to fall into despair, when I think that after all my study I know neither where I came from, nor what I am, nor where I will go, nor what will become of me."

The condition of this good man made me feel very bad. No one could have been as reasonable nor as open and honest as he was. It seemed to me that his intelligence and sensitive heart were the causes of his misery.

That same day I saw the old woman who was his neighbor. I asked her if she had ever been distressed at not knowing how her soul was made. She did not even understand my question. Not for a moment in her entire life had she thought about a single one of the questions that tormented the good Brahmin. She believed with all her heart in the many manifestations of her god Vishnu. And if she could just have a bit of sacred water from the Ganges river to wash herself, she thought she was the most fortunate woman in the world.

Struck by the happiness of this poor creature, I returned to my philosopher and said to him:

"Aren't you ashamed to be so miserable when all this time right at your door there is an old automaton who thinks of nothing yet lives contentedly?"

"You are right," he replied. "I have told myself a thousand times that I would be happy if I was as ignorant as my old neighbor, and yet that is a happiness I do not want."

This answer of the Brahmin made a greater impression on me than anything else he had said. I thought about myself and realized that I myself would not want to be happy on condition of being stupid.

I brought this up to some philosophers, and they agreed with me.

"Yet," I said, "there is a tremendous contradiction in this way of thinking. For after all, what is the point? Isn't it to be happy? What does it matter whether we are wise or stupid? And consider the fact that those who are content with their condition know for sure that they are content; but those who try to reason things out are not always sure that they have reasoned correctly. "So it seems clear," I continued, "that we should not choose wisdom, if wisdom is what makes us miserable."

Everyone agreed with me, and yet none of them wanted to accept the bargain of becoming ignorant in order to be happy. From this I concluded that although we value happiness, we value reason even more.

But, after more reflection upon this subject, I still thought that it makes no sense to prefer reason over happiness. How can this contradiction be explained? Like all other things, there is a great deal more that can be said about this.

Source: Translated by Manuel Velasquez from "Histoire d'un Bon Bramin," [1759] in *Oeuvres Completes de Voltaire*, WikiSource, la bibliotheque libre, accessed February 5, 2015, at http://fr.wikisource.org/wiki/Histoire_d%E2%80%99un_bon_Bramin.
Translation copyright 2015 by Manuel Velasquez.

1.6 HISTORICAL SHOWCASE

The First Philosophers

Because so much material is, and must be, covered in any introduction to philosophy, the overall treatment may lack focus and leave the student confused or with a superficial understanding. Although there is no easy solution to this problem, one useful device is to take a more in-depth look at important figures in the material being covered. This book will use this strategy. Because the purpose of this technique is to exhibit the writings and thoughts of philosophers, an appropriate term for it is *showcase*. Each showcase includes both an overview of the philosophy of important figures and edited selections from their writings so that you can read each philosopher's own words. Moreover, taken together, the showcases are intended to provide a feeling for the history of philosophy. Consequently, for the most part they are in historical order.

Because we are beginning philosophy, our first showcase spotlights the earliest Western and Eastern philosophers. Examining these will provide a better idea of the historical significance of philosophy. These first philosophers had a remarkable impact on how we view reality and ourselves today, an impact that philosophy continues to have through the ages.

Pre-Socratic Western Philosophers

THALES: EXPLAINING REALITY

Western philosophy began with a question the Greek thinker Thales asked around 585 BCE: What is the ultimate reality of which everything is made? Thales' answer will strike you as a bit funny and prosaic. He answered, "Everything ultimately is made of water!"

But the factual correctness of Thales' answer isn't really important. What is significant is that he was the first to take a radically new "philosophical" approach to reality. Thinkers before Thales were content to explain reality as the whimsical work of mythical gods. For example, the Greek poet Hesiod (circa 776 BCE) explains how the sky came to rain on the earth by describing the sky as a male god who was castrated by his son while sleeping with goddess Earth:

> Great Heaven came at night longing for love.
> He lay on Earth spreading himself full on her.
> Then from an ambush, his own son stretched out
>   his left hand.
> And wielding a long sharp sickle in his right, He
>   swiftly sliced and cut his father's genitals.
> Earth received the bloody drops that all gushed
>   forth.
> And she gave birth to the great Furies and mighty
>   giants.
> Now when chaste Heaven desires to penetrate the
>   Earth,
> And Earth is filled with longing for this union, Rain
>   falling from her lover, Heaven, impregnates her,
> And she brings forth wheat for men and pastures
>   for their flocks.[1]

Thales departed in three ways from this mythological and poetic approach to reality. First, he had the idea that although reality is complex, it should be explainable in terms of one or a few basic elements. Second, he decided that reality should be explained in terms of natural, observable things

---

[1] Hesiod, *The Theogony*, pt. 11, lines 177–185. This translation copyright © 1987 by Manuel Velasquez.

(such as water) and not by poetic appeals to unobservable gods. Third, he rejected the idea that reality should be explained through the authority of religious myths from the past, which could neither be proved nor disproved. Instead, he tried to provide a literal and factual explanation that others could evaluate for themselves through reasoning and observation.

Thales' theory—that water is the basic stuff out of which everything is made—may seem naive. Yet he was the first to break away from religious myth and strike out on a path that uses human reason and observation to explore the universe. That he took this momentous and daring step marks him as a genius. In fact, today we continue to travel the path Thales opened for us. Much of our basic scientific research is still devoted to finding the simplest elemental forces out of which everything in the universe is made, and we still proceed by proposing theories or *hypotheses* that can be proved or disproved through reason and observation. It took the genius of Thales to set Western civilization on this amazingly fruitful path of discovery.

But two other early Greek philosophers, Heraclitus (circa 554–484 BCE) and Parmenides (circa 480–430 BCE), proposed the most interesting and radical of the early philosophical views of reality. Both philosophers left the question of what things are made of and turned their attention to the problem of *change*—whether change is a basic reality or a mere illusion, real or merely appearance.

HERACLITUS: REALITY IS CHANGE

Heraclitus, in a remarkable series of sayings, proposed that change is the fundamental reality. He asserted that like a fire's flame, "All reality is changing." Like a flowing river, everything in the universe changes from moment to moment, so we can never touch or perceive the same thing in two different moments. The only enduring realities are the recurring patterns (like the seasons) of change itself:

> In the same rivers we step and yet we do not step; we ourselves are the same and yet we are not. You cannot step in the same river twice, for other waters are ever flowing on. The sun is new every day. The living and the dead, the waking and sleeping, the young and the old, these are changing into each other; the former are moved about and become the latter, the latter in turn become the former. Neither god nor man shaped this universe, but it ever was and ever shall be a living Fire that

flames up and dies in measured patterns. There is a continual exchange: all things are exchanged for Fire and Fire for all things. Fire steers the universe. God changes like Fire.[2]

PARMENIDES AND ZENO: CHANGE IS AN ILLUSION

Parmenides, convinced that Heraclitus was completely mistaken, proposed a theory that was the exact opposite. Parmenides held that change is an illusion and that the universe in reality is a frozen, unchanging object: "We can speak and think only of what exists. And what exists is uncreated and imperishable, for what exists is completely what it is and so long as it continues to exist it must remain what it is. It was not nor shall be different since it is now, all at once, the same and continuous."[3] How was Parmenides led to this view? He argued that nothingness or "nonbeing" cannot be a real thing, for if it was something real then it would no longer be nothingness but would instead be something. In fact, we cannot even think of nothingness. Nonbeing, therefore, cannot exist. Yet change requires nonbeing or nothingness. For if something changes, it must change into something that did not exist before: Something would have to come into being out of nonbeing. But nonbeing does not exist. So a thing could not have come from nonbeing. Therefore, change is impossible and so change cannot be real. The changing world we seem to see around us has to be an illusion. The universe could not have had a beginning nor can it have an end, for nothing in it can ever change:

> For what beginning of the universe could you search for? From what could it come? I will not let you say or think "From what was not" because you cannot even conceive of "what is not." Nor will true thinking allow that, besides what exists, new things could also arise from something that does not exist. How could what exists pass into what does not exist? And how can what does not exist come into existence? For if it came into existence, then it earlier was nothingness. And nothingness is unthinkable and not real.[4]

Parmenides' strange view received support from one of his students, Zeno. Zeno argued that "a runner cannot move from one point to another. For to

---

2   Diels-Kranz, *Fragments of the Presocratics,* Heraclitus, fragments 49, 12, 6, 88, 30, 90, 64, 67, trans. Manuel Velasquez.
3   Ibid., Parmenides, 7.
4   Ibid., 8.

do so, he must first get to a point half-way across, and to do this, he must get half-way to the half-way point, and to do this he must get half-way to that point, and so on for an infinite number of spaces."[5] Because an infinite number of spaces cannot be crossed (at least not in a finite length of time), Zeno concluded that no object moves: Motion is an illusion of our senses!

CONTRIBUTIONS OF THE PRE-SOCRATIC PHILOSOPHERS

In spite of—or perhaps because of—their unusual views, the pre-Socratic philosophers made several crucial contributions to our thinking. They got us to rely on our reason and to search for new ways of looking at reality instead of relying on the authority of the past. They introduced us to the problem of the one and the many: Can the many things of our experience be explained in terms of one or a few fundamental constituents? They introduced the problem of appearance and reality: Does a more basic reality underlie the changing world that appears before us? Moreover, the views they proposed continue even today to have followers. Modern "process philosophers," for example, hold that change or "process" is the fundamental reality, a view that has much in common with Heraclitus' view. Moreover, some modern British philosophers have held, like Parmenides, that change is an illusion.

Eastern Philosophers

THE VEDAS

But even before Thales, Parmenides, and Heraclitus had developed their fresh nonmythical approaches to knowledge, the great visionaries of India had put Eastern philosophy (the systems of thought, belief, and action espoused by many in the Near and Far East) on a similar path to discovery. However, the path they opened up would take Eastern philosophy in a very different direction.

Between 1500 and 700 BCE, the first of a long line of Indian thinkers composed the Vedas, poetic hymns that contain the beginnings of Indian wisdom and that were meant to be chanted in religious ceremonies. The authors of many of these hymns are unknown, and many of the hymns describe "visions" of "seers." These writings, steeped in myth and symbolism, nevertheless also contain early attempts to find a new nonmythical understanding of the universe. Here is how one of the greatest of these hymns, the Rig Veda, describes the origin of the universe in the mythical terms of the seers, while at the same time wondering whether the seers' myths are adequate:

> Neither being nor non-being then existed
> There was no air or sky beyond it
> What was concealed? Where was it? What
>   sheltered it?
> And was there deep unfathomable water?
> There was neither death nor anything immortal,
> Nothing indicating it was day or night.
> By its own force, the breathless ONE breathed.
> Apart from that there was nothing.
> There was darkness hidden in darkness,
> All undifferentiated chaos.
> Everything was void and formless.
> Then by the power of heat that ONE was born.
> In that beginning there was love,
> The primal seed and source of spirit.
> Sages who searched with the wisdom of the heart
> Have seen the bond between being and non-being.
> A crosswise line divided being and non-being.
> What was above it and what was below?
> There were fertile powers and mighty forces,
> Pushing from below and pulling from above.
> Who really knows and who here now can say
> When the world was born and where it came from?
> The gods were born after its creation,
> So who can know its origin?
> From where it came,
> And whether he produced it,
> Only He who sees it from the highest heaven
>   knows
> And maybe even He does not.[6]

Although the author of this hymn is still groping for a nonmythical way of understanding the universe, he nevertheless succeeds in expressing a great insight: There is a fundamental reality that underlies all the distinctions and objects our language draws for us, and that fundamental reality is the ultimate source of the universe. That reality, which we can only point to as "That One," is neither "existence nor nonexistence," it is "neither the world nor the sky beyond," it is "undifferentiated," and it was there before even God or the gods existed. This great idea of the Vedas posed a basic question for Eastern philosophy: What is the nature of the ultimate reality from which everything we perceive arises?

---

[5]   Aristotle, *Physics*, 239b11, trans. Manuel Velasquez.

[6]   Based on the translation of A. A. MacDonell, *Hymns from the Rigveda* (London: Oxford University Press, 1922), 19–20.

THE UPANISHADS

In the Upanishads, writings later added to the Vedas, we find the first attempts of Indian thinkers to understand this ultimate reality in philosophical terms. The Upanishads refer to the ultimate reality as **Brahman** and describe it in negative terms:

> Invisible, incomprehensible, without genealogy, colorless, without eye or ear, without hands or feet, unending, pervading all and omnipresent, that is the unchangeable one whom the wise regard as the source of beings.[7]

Thus, Brahman cannot be seen, smelled, felt, or heard. It cannot be imagined, and words cannot describe it. But it is the ultimate reality that must be present behind everything in the universe, causing everything to be, while itself being unlimited and greater than any specific knowable thing.

At this point, the philosophers of the Upanishads took a momentous step that was destined to forever change the course of Eastern philosophy. Seeking to understand Brahman, the deepest reality that underlies the universe, they thought to ask, "What am I?" The self, after all, is part of reality. By understanding the self, one could perhaps also understand ultimate reality. The Upanishad philosophers thus turned to understand **atman**, or the deepest self.

The Upanishad philosophers argued that atman is the *me* that lies behind all my living, sensing, and thinking activities; it is the *me* that lies behind my waking experiences, my dreaming experiences, and my deep-sleeping experiences; it is the *me* that directs everything I do but that is not seen or heard or imagined. This deepest self, which can be known only by enlightened inner self-consciousness, the philosophers of the Upanishad concluded, is identical with Brahman, ultimate reality. This profound idea is the foundation of Indian philosophy.

These ideas—that one ultimate reality underlies everything in the universe and that the self is identical with this reality—are beautifully expressed in an Upanishad parable. The parable is about a proud young man, Svetaketu, who returns from the Hindu equivalent of college only to find that his father is wiser than all his teachers:

Now, there was Svetaketu Aruneya. To him his father said: "Live the life of a student of sacred knowledge. Truly, my dear, from our family there is no one unlearned. . . ."

He then, having become a pupil at the age of twelve, having studied all the Vedas, returned at the age of twenty-four, conceited, thinking himself learned, proud.

Then his father said to him: "Svetaketu, my dear, since now you are conceited, think yourself learned, and are proud, did you also ask for that teaching whereby what has not been heard of becomes heard of, what has not been thought of becomes thought of, what has not been understood becomes understood?"

"What, pray, sir, is that teaching?"

"Just as, my dear, by one piece of clay everything made of clay may be known—the modification is merely a verbal distinction, a name; the reality is just 'clay'—

"Just as, my dear, by one copper ornament everything made of copper may be known—the modification is merely a verbal distinction, a name; the reality is just 'copper'—

"Just as, my dear, by one nail-scissors everything made of iron may be known—the modification is merely a verbal distinction, a name; the reality is just 'iron'—so, my dear, is that teaching."

"Truly, those honored men did not know this; for if they had known it, why would they not have told me? But do, sir, tell me it."

"So be it, my dear," said he. . . .

"Understand that this [body] is a sprout which has sprung up. It cannot be without a root.

"Where else could its root be than in water? With water, my dear, as a sprout, look for heat as the root. With heat, my dear, as a sprout, look for Being as the root. All creatures here, my dear, have Being as their root, have Being as their abode, have Being as their support. . . .

"When a person here is deceasing, my dear, his voice goes into his mind; his mind, into his breath; his breath into heat; the heat into the highest divinity. That which is the finest essence—this whole world has that as its soul. That is Reality. That is Atman. That art thou, Svetaketu."[8]

Svetaketu's father is here explaining that everything in the universe arises out of the same ultimate

---

[7]   Mundaka Upanishad, 1.1.6, in *Oriental Philosophies,* 28.

[8]   Chandogya Upanishad, in Daniel Bonevac, William Boon, and Stephen Phillips, *Beyond the Western Tradition* (Mountain View, CA: Mayfield, 1992), 151.

reality. We say there are many different things in the universe, but the differences we see are of our own making: They are mere "verbal distinctions." Underlying the variety of objects is a single unified reality, Brahman. And Brahman is identical with atman—your deepest self. In short, you are the ultimate reality behind the universe!

The Upanishad philosophers did for the East what the pre-Socratics did for the West. Like the pre-Socratics, the Upanishad philosophers taught the need to inquire carefully into the nature of reality instead of merely accepting the authority of the past. And like the pre-Socratics, the Upanishad philosophers showed the need to look behind appearances to the one ultimate reality.

But the Upanishad philosophers took a further step that fundamentally distinguished the thought of the East from that of the West. The pre-Socratics taught the West that to find the ultimate constituents of reality, one must analyze the outer, physical world. The Upanishad philosophers, on the other hand, taught that the way to discover the ultimate reality of the universe is to look within ourselves.

QUESTIONS

1. Explain why Thales is so important to Western philosophy.

2. How would Heraclitus have responded to the following statement? "Heraclitus is wrong because the objects we see around us continue to endure through time; although a person, an animal, or a plant may change its superficial qualities, it still remains essentially the same person, animal, or plant throughout these changes. In fact, we recognize change only by contrasting it to the underlying permanence of things. So permanence, not change, is the essential reality."

3. How would you answer Zeno's proof that no object moves?

4. Are there any similarities between the views of Parmenides and those of the Upanishads? Are there essential differences? Explain.

5. In the Upanishads, Svetaketu's father says, "That art thou, Svetaketu." What does "that" refer to? What does "thou" refer to? Do you see any problem with saying that these two (what "that" refers to and what "thou" refers to) are identical—in other words, that they are exactly one and the same thing? Explain.

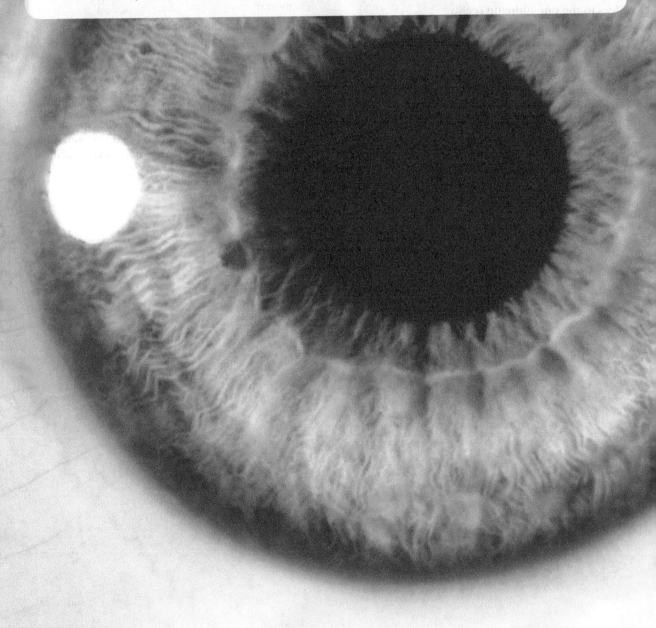

2 Human Nature

*Indeed it is of the essence of man ... that he can lose
himself in the jungle of his existence, within himself,
and thanks to his sensation of being lost can react by
setting energetically to work to find himself again.*

JOSÉ ORTEGA Y GASSET

2.1 Why Does Your View of Human Nature Matter?

LEARNING OBJECTIVES: When finished, you'll be able to:

- Define "human nature" and "psychological egoism."
- **thinking critically** Define what deductive and inductive arguments are, explain what validity and soundness are, and apply these notions to arguments.
- Explain how your views of human nature influence your relationships with other people, the universe, and your society.

2.2 What Is Human Nature?

LEARNING OBJECTIVES: When finished, you'll be able to:

- Describe and critically evaluate the Greek rationalistic and Judeo-Christian versions of the Traditional Western view of human nature.
- Explain how Darwinism challenged these views.
- **thinking critically** Define what an inference to the best explanation is, explain what constitutes a "best explanation," and apply these notions to an argument.
- Explain how existentialism and feminism have challenged the Traditional Western view of human nature.

2.3 The Mind–Body Problem: How Do Your Mind and Your Body Relate?

LEARNING OBJECTIVES: When finished, you'll be able to:

- Explain why dualism is so influential a view of human nature, even though it leads to the mind–body problem.
- **thinking critically** Explain how to evaluate whether the premises of an argument are true.
- Explain and critically evaluate the way materialism, identity theory, behaviorism, functionalism, the computer view of human nature, eliminative materialism, and property dualism each tries to solve the mind–body problem.

2.4 Is There an Enduring Self?

LEARNING OBJECTIVES: When finished, you'll be able to:

- Explain the role an "enduring self" plays in human life and how it leads to the problem of personal identity.
- Explain and criticize attempts to solve the problem of personal identity by appealing to the body, the soul, the memory, and the no-self view.

2.5 Are We Independent and Self-Sufficient Individuals?

LEARNING OBJECTIVES: When finished, you'll be able to:

- Describe the idea of an independent and self-sufficient individual and explain the role it plays in our lives.
- Compare how Aristotle, Hegel, and Taylor challenge that idea.

MindTap Explore MindTap for *Philosophy* for interactive activities, essay and discussion topics, videos, additional readings, and study tools.

Chapter Summary

2.6 Readings

2.7 Historical Showcase: Plato, Aristotle, and Confucius

2.1 Why Does Your View of Human Nature Matter?

Imagine walking down the streets of a city on a wintry day. You see an old unshaven man in ragged clothes sitting cross-legged on the sidewalk. In front of him is a sign that reads "I am blind and deaf. Please help me." Almost immediately you reach into your pocket for a couple of dollar bills, which you put into his cardboard box. Then, feeling good, you walk on.

Why did you give him the money? You might respond with the easy answer that you wanted to help relieve some of his obvious need. Yet was this your real motive for helping? Is it possible that your actual motive was self-interest? That you wanted the good feeling you knew you would get from helping him and wanted to avoid the guilt you would feel if you didn't? Are human beings, yourself included, moved ultimately and always by a desire for self-gratification and the avoidance of pain? Is self-interest an inescapable and pervasive part of being human? Does it drive even those actions that seem to arise out of love for others? Or do we human beings at least sometimes act unselfishly?

The most basic philosophical question you can ask is this: What am I? Your understanding of what you are—what a human being is—affects how you see yourself, how you see others, and how you live. A view about what you are is a view about **human nature**. That is, it is a view about what it is to be a human being. We'll look now at what some psychologists and philosophers have said about human nature. Understanding their views will help you see how profoundly your view of human nature can affect you.

For centuries thinkers have wondered whether human nature is motivated solely by self-interest. Many psychologists have thought it is. Some have even claimed that humans are not only selfish, but aggressively and cruelly so. Take, for example, the father of modern psychology, Sigmund Freud (1856–1939). Freud argued that if we look at ourselves and the history of humanity we cannot dispute the "aggressive cruelty of human nature." Here is what he said in his book *Civilization and Its Discontents:*

Sigmund Freud:
"Men are not gentle, friendly creatures wishing for love, but [possess] a powerful measure of desire for aggressiveness."

© Pictorial Press Ltd / Alamy

MindTap™ To read more from Sigmund Freud's *Civilization and Its Discontents*, click the link in the MindTap Reader or go to the Questia Readings folder in MindTap.

Men are not gentle, friendly creatures wishing for love, who simply defend themselves if they are attacked, but … a powerful measure of desire for aggressiveness has to be reckoned as part of their instinctual endowment. The result is that their neighbor is to them not only a possible helper or sexual object, but also a temptation to them to gratify their aggressiveness on him, to exploit his capacity for work without recompense, to use him sexually without his consent, to seize his possessions, to humiliate him, to cause him pain, to torture and to kill him.

[Who can] dispute it in the face of all the evidence in his own life and in history? This aggressive cruelty usually lies in wait for some provocation. ... When those forces in the mind which ordinarily inhibit it cease to operate, it also manifests itself spontaneously and reveals men as savage beasts to whom the thought of sparing their own kind is alien. Anyone who calls to mind the atrocities of the early migrations, of the invasion of the Hun or the so-called Mongols under Genghis Khan and Tamerlane, of the sacks of Jerusalem by the pious crusaders, even indeed the horrors of the last world war, will have to bow his head humbly before the truth of this view of man.[1]

Many philosophers have agreed with Freud that human beings are essentially selfish and aggressive. Long before Freud, the philosopher Thomas Hobbes (1588–1679) argued for a view called **psychological egoism.** This theory says that human beings are made so that they act only out of self-interest. Hobbes was a materialist. He held that everything in "the Universe, that is the whole mass of things that are, is corporeal, that is to say body."[2] Humans, too, are material bodies, and we can explain their activities much like those of a biological machine. The mechanism of desire moves human beings to act. So whenever human beings do something, they are seeking satisfaction of their own mechanistic desires. In fact, Hobbes anticipated Freud. Hobbes argued that the antisocial desire for power over others is what mainly motivates human beings. "In the first place," he wrote, "I put for a general inclination of all mankind, a perpetual and restless desire of power after power, that ceases only in death."[3]

Closer to our own time, the Canadian philosopher Mark Mercer (1957–) argued that humans always seek "self-regarding ends." He wrote: "behind any action ... an agent performs intentionally ... there lies the agent's expectation of realizing one or more of her self-regarding ends." If the agent did not expect to get a self-regarding end, "the agent would not have performed the action."[4] A "self-regarding end" is something that rewards or benefits one's own self. Self-regarding ends include getting pleasure, being happy, avoiding pain, gaining power or possessions, having self-respect, being loved, feeling good about oneself, or having others think well of oneself. Mercer says that when we do something and look inside ourselves we always find some self-regarding goal. He uses the word "introspection" to refer to looking inside oneself:

> Introspection reveals to me that whatever I decide to do, indeed I do expect that, should I meet with success in doing it, I will realize one of my self-regarding ends. Further, when I ask myself before acting on my decision to perform some particular action whether I would still do what I have decided to do were I to lack any expectation of realizing thereby a self-regarding end, I find that I answer no, I would not still

ANALYZING THE READING

1. According to Freud people have a desire for aggression that leads them to enslave, rape, steal, humiliate, injure, torture, and kill each other. What reasons does he give to support this view? Do you agree with his reasons? Why?

2. What does Freud mean when he says anyone can find "evidence in his own life" supporting Freud's view? What does he mean by "when those forces in the mind which ordinarily inhibit it cease to operate"? What "forces" do you think he's talking about? When would they "cease to operate"?

3. Do you see any evidence in history to support the view that people are really "gentle, friendly creatures wishing for love, who simply defend themselves if they are attacked"? Do you see such evidence in your own life?

QUICK REVIEW
Psychologists such as Freud claimed humans are cruel, aggressive, and selfish.

QUICK REVIEW
Hobbes claimed that humans act only out of self-interest and are material bodies.

QUICK REVIEW
Mark Mercer claims that when people act intentionally they always expect a self-regarding benefit or reward; introspection reveals this and we could not understand their actions as intentional unless we attributed such a motive to them.

---

1   Sigmund Freud, *Civilization and Its Discontents* (London: Hogarth, 1930), 85–86.
2   Thomas Hobbes, *Hobbes's Leviathan* (Oxford: Clarendon, 1909; original work published 1651), 524.
3   Ibid., 86.
4   Mark Mercer, "In Defense of Weak Psychological Egoism," *Erkenntnis*, vol. 55 (2001), no. 2, (pp. 217–237), p. 221.

do what I have decided to do. Were I not to expect to realize some self-regarding end in or through my action, I would find myself losing the desire to perform that action. I would, I think, cease to find important or attractive the goal I intend to achieve through that action ... I now note that I am a typical agent in the world, not ... different from other agents. This fact enables me to generalize from my own case to the case of all agents and actions. I conclude, then, that all actions are performed in expectation of reward.[5]

In fact, Mercer says, when anyone does something, we cannot fully understand what he did until we know what he wanted. That is, until we know what motivated him. And unless we see "an expectation of realizing some self-regarding end, we cannot see in any consideration we attribute to an agent, a motivation to act."[6] So the only kind of human motivation we can even understand is "the expectation of some self-regarding end." In short, humans always act out of self-interest and we can only understand their actions in terms of self-interest.

The views just described, then, say that human nature is aggressive, selfish, and cruel (Freud). Human nature is material, selfish, and desirous of power over others (Hobbes). And human nature is motivated always by self-interest (Mercer). Apart from their intrinsic interest, these views have profound and highly personal implications for each of us. But before we look at those implications, let's look more closely at the reasons that support—or fail to support—these views.

 MindTap Is Freud, Hobbes, or Mercer correct about human nature? Go to MindTap to watch a video about the relationship between human nature and morality.

thinking critically • Deductive Arguments, Validity, and Soundness

How good are the arguments given for the views about human nature that we have just seen? Let's focus on the views of the Canadian philosopher Mercer, for example. Mercer concludes that when people act intentionally they always expect to get a self-regarding end. What are his reasons for this conclusion? This seems to be his key argument:

1. I always expect a self-regarding end when I act intentionally.
2. If I always expect a self-regarding end when I act intentionally, then everyone always expects a self-regarding end when they act intentionally.
3. Therefore, everyone always expects a self-regarding end when they act intentionally.

Mercer says that we know premise (1) is true by "introspection" (i.e., by looking into myself at my own motives). Moreover, he says, we know premise (2) is true because I am "not different from other agents." So Mercer also gives us reasons for each of his premises, which means you should be able to turn those reasons into arguments for each premise.

Is Mercer's argument a good one? We saw in the last chapter that one requirement of a good argument is that the premises must be true. But true premises are not the only requirement of a good argument. In a good argument, the premises, if true, must prove or provide strong support for the conclusion. Assuming Mercer's premises are true, do they prove or strongly support his conclusion? To answer this question, we need to understand that there are two main kinds of arguments. Some arguments are deductive arguments

---

5   Ibid., 229–230.
6   Ibid., 231.

and others are inductive (or probable) arguments. A **deductive argument** is one that is supposed to show that if its premises are true then its conclusion *necessarily has to* be true. An **inductive argument** is one that is supposed to show that if its premises are true then its conclusion is *probably* true. We'll discuss inductive or probable arguments later because Mercer's argument is deductive. Mercer wants to show us that if his premises are true then it *necessarily has to* be true that everyone's actions are always motivated by self-regarding ends. So his argument is deductive.

So, do the premises of Mercer's deductive argument prove or support his conclusion? The premises of a deductive argument prove or support its conclusion if in every possible situation in which the premises are true, the conclusion also must be true. We say a deductive argument is **valid** when in every possible situation in which its premises are true, its conclusion also must be true. Another way of saying the same thing is this: A deductive argument is valid when it is such that if its premises are true, then its conclusion must also be true. If a deductive argument is not valid, then we say it is **invalid**. Notice this *extremely* important point: The premises and conclusion of a valid argument *do not have to be true*. All that a valid deductive argument guarantees is that *if* its premises are true, then the conclusion must also be true.

Some examples might make this clearer. Here is a valid argument whose premises are true:

1. If Socrates is human, then he's a mammal.
2. Socrates is human.
3. Therefore, Socrates is a mammal.

Because this is a valid argument and its premises are true, we know its conclusion must also be true. That is, in every situation in which premises (1) and (2) are true, the conclusion, (3), must also be true. An argument that is *both* valid and has true premises like this one is called a **sound argument**.

Consider, next, this valid argument whose premises and conclusion are false:

1. If Arnold Schwarzenegger is president of the United States, he is 10 years old.
2. Arnold Schwarzenegger is president of the United States.
3. Therefore, Arnold Schwarzenegger is 10 years old.

In this valid argument, premise (1) and premise (2) are false, and so is the conclusion (3). But we said this argument is valid. So we know that *if there ever were* a situation in which premises (1) and (2) were true, then in that situation conclusion (3) would also have to be true. To test this, try to imagine a situation in which premises (1) and (2) are true, and see if in that situation conclusion (3) would also be true. Imagine, for example, the following situation. Suppose the Constitution of the United States said the president *was required to be* exactly 10 years old (remember this is an imaginary situation!) and suppose Arnold was elected president (use your imagination!). In that imaginary situation, premise (1) would be true and premise (2) would be true. Could conclusion (3) be false in that specific situation? No, (3) would have to be true in that situation, because in that situation Arnold would be president and the president would be required to be 10 years old! In fact, no matter how much you try, you won't be able to come up with a situation in which premises (1) and (2) are true and conclusion (3) is false. That is why we know that this argument is valid. But although the argument is valid, its premises are false. So the argument is not a *sound* argument.

How can we tell whether a deductive argument is valid? One answer to that question should now be clear. If we can think up a situation in which the premises of the argument are true and its conclusion is false, then we know the argument is not valid. So read to the end of this next argument, and then stop reading and try to figure out whether this argument is valid. Figure out whether it's valid by trying to think of a situation in which the premises would be true, but the conclusion false:

1. If you get an "A" on the final, then you will get an "A" for the course.
2. You did not get an "A" on the final.
3. Therefore, you will not get an "A" for the course.

I'm sure you quickly figured out a bunch of ways in which premises (1) and (2) could be true and conclusion (3) false. For example, imagine you could get an "A" for the course by getting *either* an "A" or a "B" on the final. And imagine you got a "B" on the final. In that situation, premises (1) and (2) would be true, but conclusion (3) would be false. So we now know the argument is invalid.

So what about the argument that Mercer gives us to prove that when we act we are always motivated by a self-regarding end, that is, by self-interest? His argument is complicated and uses complex abstract concepts. So it will be hard to think up a situation in which its premises are true but the conclusion is false. But the main reason it will be hard for you to come up with such situations is because the argument is valid so there are no such situations.

So Mercer's argument meets at least one of the two essential characteristics of a good argument: It is valid. But is it also sound? It is sound if the premises are true. So think hard now about the two premises. Take the first premise of the argument: Is it true that when you do something intentionally and look carefully at your own motives, you always find that there is some benefit or reward you expect to get from doing it? Or take the second premise: Is it true that if you are self-interested then everyone else must be self-interested? It's your job as a philosopher to try to figure out whether Mercer's premises are true.

The Importance of Understanding Human Nature

Views of human nature—like Mercer's view that humans are driven by self-interest—can have a profound influence on you. For example, if you accept that humans always act out of self-interest, this belief can shape your relationships with other people. If a person thinks that human beings are basically unselfish, won't that person instinctively relate to other people with trust and openness? Won't such a person accept the kind gestures of strangers as natural and not feel surprised that others help simply because they want to? But if a person believes that human beings are basically self-interested, won't that person mistrust others? Won't that person be suspicious of kindness and continually wonder what people are trying to get from her? Won't she feel that the only way to get help from others is by offering them something in return? Won't she believe that true altruism—actions that seek only the good of others—does not exist in this world?

Your views about human nature also influence your beliefs about your place in the universe. If a person believes that human beings are spiritual as well as material, he or she may be more open to religious experience. Such a person can see himself

THINKING LIKE A PHILOSOPHER

1. Do you think you always act out of self-interest? What about your friends and the people in your family? Do you think you've ever loved someone for his or her own sake and not for what you got from that person?
2. How do you think people you know would act if there were no social restraints—like laws and police? Would most tend to take advantage of each other? Or would most tend to cooperate and help each other? Why do you think that?
3. Whatever you think people are—self-interested or loving or both—how do you think they got that way? Do you think you were born self-interested (or loving or both)? Did society make you the way you are? Did you make yourself what you are?
4. Make a list of the things that you think define a human being. Your list should let you distinguish humans from other kinds of creatures.

PHILOSOPHY AND LIFE

Is Selflessness Real?

Several contemporary biologists have argued that apparently selfless human behavior is actually a kind of selfish activity that our genes impel us to carry out. For example, Desmond Morris suggests that when a man rushes into a burning house to save his daughter—or if an old friend or even a complete stranger rescues the child—he is actually saving an organism that contains or, in the case of the friend or stranger, may contain his own genes. We have evolved these protective behaviors so that our genes can survive and be passed on to future generations. Thus, helping behaviors are genetically selfish: They are mechanisms that our genes have evolved to ensure their own survival.

The man who risks death to save his small daughter from a fire is in reality saving his own genes in their new body-package. And in saving his genes, his act becomes biologically selfish, rather than altruistic.

But supposing the man leaping into the fire is trying to save, not his daughter, but an old friend? How can this be selfish? The answer here lies in the ancient history of mankind. For more than a million years, man was a simple tribal being. ... [T]he chances were that every member of your own tribe was a relative of

some kind.... [In saving your old friend] you would be helping copies of your own genes. ... Again ... genetic selfishness.

[Moreover, when man] was tribal, ... any inborn urge to help his fellow men would have meant automatically that he was helping gene-sharing relatives. ... But with the urban explosion, man rapidly found himself in huge communities, surrounded by strangers, and with no time for his genetic constitution to alter to fit the startlingly new circumstances. So his altruism inevitably spread to include [complete strangers].

QUESTIONS

1. Suppose Morris is right. Does the fact that a man's genes have evolved so that they now make him want to save his daughter show that he is not altruistic?

2. What do you think theories of evolution like Morris proposes say about our human nature?

3. Could a "selfish gene" make humans altruistic?

Source: Desmond *Morris, Manwatching: A Field Guide to Human Behavior* (New York: Harry N. Abrams, 1977), 153–154.

---

or herself as having a spiritual aspect that makes him or her different from the material universe. He or she can see his or her life in this material universe as a kind of preparation for a spiritual life in another world. On the other hand, a person may feel that a human being is a purely physical creature. A person may feel that a human has a highly developed brain, to be sure, but not one fundamentally different from other animals. Such a person will believe that death is the end of a human existence. Won't such a person feel that this material universe is all there is and all that anyone can have?

Your perception of human nature determines even how you think we should set up our society. Ask yourself this, for example: Should our society be based on capitalism or socialism? Well, suppose that humans are essentially self-interested. Then, wouldn't the best way to get people to work be to allow every individual to keep whatever benefits he or she produces and to not support those who don't work? Won't self-interest then lead every person to work hard and to produce as much as he or she can? This is, in fact, the basic idea behind capitalist societies, with their free markets and support for individualism. And if people are basically self-interested, then shouldn't we spend more on police and prisons? Shouldn't we be more willing to support the military, and other institutions we use to protect people from one another? On the other hand, what if humans are not self-interested, but cooperative and able to act for unselfish motives? Then, wouldn't it make sense to inspire people to work for one another's good and to share whatever each produces? Socialist institutions, such as welfare programs and redistributive taxes, are based on the idea that humans are social and can and should share with one another? If people

QUICK REVIEW
Beliefs about our nature influence our relationships, our view of our place in the universe and our view of how society should be arranged.

are social then the huge sum of money we spend on prisons, police, and the military should be put to better use helping meet human needs. Which of these two options is more realistic? How far should our society go in pursuing either one? Ultimately your answer will depend on what you think human beings are.

It is clear, then, that a lot hangs on how you answer the question "What am I? "In this chapter, you begin your philosophical journey by looking at how several philosophers have tried to answer this question. By examining what they say in support of their views, you will be in a better position to form your own answer. You can make up your own mind, for example, about whether we are unselfish and spiritual beings, or self-interested and material beings. The aim is not to get you to believe any of the arguments about human nature presented here. The aim is to help you use your own reasoning powers to decide for yourself what it means to be a human being.

PHILOSOPHY AT THE MOVIES

Watch *The Blind Side* (2009), a dramatization of the true story of Michael Oher, a professional football player in the NFL who began playing for the Carolina Panthers in 2015. Homeless during high school, Oher was taken in and then adopted by the Thohy family. Are Leigh Anne's actions consistent with your view of human nature? Was she motivated by self-interest? Does the movie support or undermine the views of Freud, Hobbes, and Mercer? How do you think each of the three would explain her actions?

Other movies with related themes: *Seven Pounds* (2008); *Schindler's List* (1993); *River's Edge* (1986).

AF archive/Alamy

2.2 What Is Human Nature?

Several years ago, a man who was revived after his heart stopped while he was in a hospital operating room described his experience as follows:

> I knew I was dying and that there was nothing I could do about it, because no one could hear me. . . . I was out of my body, there's no doubt about it, because I could see my own body there on the operating room table. My soul was out! All this made me feel very bad at first, but then, this really bright light came. It did seem that it was a little dim at first, but then it was this huge beam. It was just a tremendous amount of light, nothing like a big bright flashlight, it was just too much light. . . . It seemed that it covered everything, yet it didn't prevent me from seeing everything around me—the operating room, the doctors and nurses, everything. . . . The love which came from it is just unimaginable, indescribable.[7]

This startling account is one of many similar stories told by people who have suffered near-death experiences. Many people whose hearts have stopped and then started again report similar experiences. At the moment of "death" they left their body and hovered over the scene of their death. Then they encountered an "unimaginable, indescribable" bright white light that came for them. Convinced that they have experienced life after death, such people lose all fear of death. They never again doubt that they have a soul that will survive death. They are convinced that human life has a purpose: that humans have a destiny related to life after death.

---

[7] Raymond Moody Jr., *Life After Life* (New York: Bantam, 1979), 63–64.

Notice that all these accounts of life after death ask us to make several assumptions about human nature. First, and most obviously, they ask us to believe that all human beings have a **self.** This self is the ego or "I" that exists in a physical body and that is conscious and rational. That is, this self can think, reason, and perceive. Often tied to this is the idea that this thinking self can have a purpose: Its life can have a destiny. Second, they ask us to believe that this self is different from, but related to, the body. The body is a material entity, whereas the self is an immaterial entity—a spiritual "soul"—that survives the death of its body. Third, they ask us to believe that this self endures through time. That is, not only does the self remain the same self throughout its life, but it continues to be the same self after death. Finally, they ask us to believe that the self is an independent individual. It exists separate from other things and people, with an independent identity.

✓ QUICK REVIEW
The belief in life after death assumes that the self is conscious, has a purpose, and is distinct from its material body.

Many of us today embrace this complex view about human beings. It is also a view that many Western philosophers and thinkers have espoused. As we will see, it is a view with ancient roots. We will call this view the "Traditional Western" view of human nature because it has influenced Western thinkers since ancient times. The Traditional view holds, then, that humans have a rational spiritual self. This self is distinct from its body, has a purpose, endures over time, and exists as a separate individual.

Not everyone accepts the Traditional view. As we will see, many thinkers have rejected the view that humans have a rational nature that has a purpose. Others deny that the self is a kind of immaterial entity that is different from our physical body. Still others have rejected the assumption that humans have an enduring self. Still others quarrel with the idea that the self is an independent individual.

We continue our journey of self-exploration by looking at the Western Traditional view of human nature. We will consider two of the most influential versions of this Traditional view. The first is what we call the "rationalistic" view of human nature, which says that reason is our highest power. We can call the second view the "Judeo-Christian religious" view. We will then look at several challenges to the Traditional Western view. By examining these views of ourselves, we can understand how they affect the way we see ourselves, the way we interact with others, and the way we live our lives.

The Rationalistic Version of the Traditional Western View of Human Nature

Reason: Humanity's Highest Power. One influential version of the Traditional view holds that our most important feature is our ability to reason. We can see this rationalistic view in the writings of the Greek philosopher Plato (427–347 BCE), a man many people believe was the greatest philosopher. Plato did not think that reason is the only constituent of human nature, but he did hold that it was the most superior part. Plato presents this view in his work *The Republic.* There he presents Socrates and Glaucon discussing the question: What is the self? Notice in the following passage the use of the word "soul," a common translation of Plato's Greek term *psyche.* But Plato did not intend all the theological meanings that we give the word *soul.* So you might want to substitute *inner self* for the word *soul.*

SOCRATES: Isn't it sometimes true that the thirsty person also, for some reason, may not want to drink?

GLAUCON: Yes, often.

SOCRATES: What can we say, then, if not that in his soul there is a part that desires drink and another part that restrains him? This latter part is distinct from desire and usually can control desire.

GLAUCON: I agree.

SOCRATES: And isn't it true in such cases that such control originates in reason, while the urge to drink originates in some other part of us?

GLAUCON: Yes, it seems that way.

SOCRATES: Then we can conclude that there are in us two distinct parts. The first we call "reason," and the second the nonrational "appetites." This second part hungers, thirsts, desires sex, and is subject to other desires, no?

GLAUCON: Yes, that is the logical conclusion.

SOCRATES: But what about our emotional or spirited element: the part in us that feels anger and aggression? ... Anger sometimes opposes our appetites so it is something distinct from them. ... Yet this emotional part of ourselves is [also] distinct from reason.[8]

> **QUICK REVIEW**
> Plato claimed that reason often conflicts with our appetites or our aggressiveness, and our appetites can conflict with our aggressiveness.

THINKING LIKE A PHILOSOPHER

1. Describe some of the times you felt conflicts among your reason, appetites, or aggressions. Did you feel as though these were different parts of you pulling you in different directions? Did your reason win out in these conflicts?
2. Do you think your own reason can always rule over your own appetites and aggressions? Do you think your reason should rule over your appetites and aggressions?

To understand Plato's view, consider this illustration. Suppose you are extremely thirsty. Before you is a glass you know contains polluted water. One part of yourself, what Plato calls *appetite* (which he located in the abdomen), wants you to drink. *Appetite* is the part of you that feels thirst and hunger, as well as sexual and other desires of the body. But a second part of yourself, reason, tells you not to drink. By *reason*, Plato meant that part of you that can think, reason, and draw conclusions. It is the part of your mind that can move from one thought to another in a logical and rational way. This rational part of the self, Plato thought, has its center in the brain. So as you see the glass of polluted water, a conflict arises between your appetite and your reason. According to Plato this conflict shows that your reason is a part of you that is distinct from your appetite.

But Plato claimed that you also experience a different kind of conflict. This is the conflict between your reason and the part of you that we might call your aggressive side. Suppose that someone cuts you off on the highway while you are driving. You get angry. You begin to blow your horn and shake your fist at the other driver. Your anger even tells you to tailgate him for a few miles just to show him. Yet your reason tells you that would not be rational. Besides being illegal it would endanger your life. Plato would say that the conflict here is not between reason and appetite. The conflict is between reason and our aggressions or what he calls "spirit," or the "spirited element." The spirited part of ourselves is what we would call our aggressive or self-assertive side. Plato suggested that it resides in the chest and we display it in war, in fighting, and in anger. While reason seeks what is rational and good, our aggressive part wants to surpass others and assert itself. Plato described these conflicts among reason, appetite, and aggression in a striking image. He compares reason to a charioteer pulled by the two horses of appetite and spirit:

> **QUICK REVIEW**
> Plato concluded that reason, appetite, and aggression are the three main parts of human nature.

> Let me speak briefly about the nature of the soul by using an image. And let the image have three parts: two winged horses and a charioteer.... One of the charioteer's horses is of noble breed, the other ignoble. The charioteer controls them but with great difficulty.... The vicious steed—when it has not been thoroughly trained—goes heavily, pulling the charioteer down to the earth. And this is a time of great agony and extreme conflict for the soul....

---

8   Plato, *Republic*, from bk. 4. This edited translation copyright © 1987 by Manuel Velasquez.

Above them, in the heaven above heaven, … there exists the true reality with which real knowledge is concerned. This is the world of the Forms which are visible only to the mind, the pilot of the soul, and have no color, shape, or hardness. … The souls that are most like the gods are carried up there by their charioteer,… although troubled by their two steeds and only with great difficulty reaching high enough to behold true being. … Other souls rise only to fall again, some barely glimpsing the world that is truly real, and then seeing it no longer because their steeds are too unruly. The other souls also long for the upper world and strive to reach it. But being too weak their steeds remain below it, plunging and trampling on each other, each trying to be the first. There is great confusion and they sweat and toil from their extreme efforts. Many of the horses are lamed, some have their wings broken because of the poor driving of the charioteers. But after all their fruitless toil they do not reach the mysteries of true being. They go away and feed on mere opinions.[9]

ANALYZING THE READING

1. Plato claims that reason can oppose our appetites and our aggressions can oppose both. He concludes that our reason is different from our appetites, and both are different from our aggressions. What assumption does Plato make to get from what he claims to what he concludes? Is his assumption right? Why?

2. When Plato compares the three parts of the self (or "soul") to a charioteer and two steeds, he says reason is the charioteer. What is the noble steed and what is the ignoble one? What does the comparison tell you about each of the three parts of the self? Do you agree? Why?

Notice Plato's use of the word *Forms*. For Plato, the forms are eternal and perfect ideals that exist in an unchanging heavenly world. They are like concepts or ideas that serve as the models or patterns according to which all material objects are made. Things here on earth, then, are nothing more than imperfect copies of the perfect Forms. The things around us here on earth are like the shadows in the Allegory of the Cave that we discussed in the first chapter. The purpose or destiny of the soul is to be free of its body and ascend to this heavenly world. There it can exist with the true reality of these perfect forms. But the soul can do this only if it has trained its appetites and aggressive impulses so it can control them and so both obey reason.

In Plato's view, then, reason, appetite, and aggression are the three defining parts of our human nature or "soul." Depending on which part dominates, we get three kinds of people. These three are those whose main desires are for knowledge, for wealth, or for power, respectively. Yet Plato leaves no doubt about which element can and should dominate. Reason must rule. Each element is an essential part of us, of course. But appetite and aggression have no knowledge with which to order themselves. So we must bring them under the control of reason. By using our reason we can discover the truth about how we ought to live. So when our reason controls our appetites and aggressions, we can live according to this knowledge. True knowledge, Plato held, is knowledge of the ideal Forms that exist in another world only reason can apprehend. After death, the person will be free from his or her body. The person whose desires and aggressions are under the control of his or her reason will then be capable of ascending to this world. (For a fuller discussion of Plato's views, see the Historical Showcase at the end of this chapter.)

In Plato's rationalistic view, then, humans can control their appetites and aggressive impulses by using their reason. They are not necessarily moved only by their self-interested bodily appetites, as Hobbes claimed. However, Plato holds that reason's ability to control appetite and aggression depends on a person's past choices. If a person always gives in to his or her aggressive impulses or appetites, he or she will lose the ability to

> **QUICK REVIEW**
> Plato concluded that reason, appetite, and aggression are the three main parts of human nature.

> **QUICK REVIEW**
> Because reason can know how we ought to live, it should rule appetites and aggressions.

---

9   Plato, *Phaedrus*, selections from 246a–247e. This translation by Manuel Velasquez.

PHILOSOPHY AND LIFE

Is Human Nature Irrational?

Many social psychologists who have studied the choices and behaviors of people have concluded that humans do not behave rationally. For example, Max Bazerman, in his book *Judgment in Managerial Decision Making*, cites numerous studies that show that humans rely on irrational beliefs and rules of thumb when making important decisions. For instance, people rely on a nonexistent "law of averages" that they believe influences the risks they take. People believe they can control purely chance events. People regularly underestimate the risk of dying in familiar but highly risky activities such as driving, smoking, or eating fried foods, and overestimate the risks of unlikely but memorable events such as dying in a plane crash or being attacked by a grizzly bear in a national park.

Robert Cialdini notes in his book *Influence* that he found people's choices can be manipulated by appealing to six nonrational norms or rules that we generally follow:

Reciprocity. I should do this for you because you did something for me.
Commitment and Consistency. I should do this because it is consistent with something I already committed myself to doing.

Liking. I should do this because I know and like you.
Authority. I should do this because an authority says I should.
Scarcity. I should do this because there's only a few chances left and I may not get a chance later.

QUESTIONS

1. Suppose that social psychologists are right in claiming that human beings behave irrationally. Does this show that human nature itself is not rational? Why or why not?

2. Can a psychological study of how people often—or even usually—behave disprove a philosophical theory of human nature? Why or why not?

3. Many advertisers, sellers, and promoters believe that Cialdini is right and that his theory provides the key for manipulating people into buying their products or doing what they want. Is there anything wrong with giving people the knowledge about human nature that will enable them to manipulate others?

QUICK REVIEW
If a person always gives in to his appetites or aggressive impulses, these will enslave him and reason can no longer rule them.

control them. Such people become slaves of their appetites or their aggressive impulses. When something makes them angry, they give in to their anger. When something arouses one of their appetites, they must satisfy it. But by practicing self-control, a person can learn eventually to restrain and control his or her appetites and aggressive impulses. The person can thereby gain the ability to do what his or her reason says is best.

For Plato's student Aristotle (circa 384–322 BCE), reason is also a human being's highest power. In some ways, however, Aristotle's views differed from Plato's. Aristotle agreed that human reason can discover the truth about human nature and how we ought to live. But Plato held that the truth about human nature involved knowledge of another world of reality. Aristotle, on the other hand, held that the truth about human nature and human life required only knowledge of our own world. Nevertheless, Aristotle agreed with Plato's basic point that reason is the characteristic that sets the human self apart from all other creatures of nature. (For a fuller discussion of Aristotle's views, see the Historical Showcase at the end of this chapter.)

QUICK REVIEW
For Aristotle, reason is our highest power and what distinguishes human nature.

The Human Purpose. Aristotle emphasized even more than Plato that humans have a purpose. Aristotle claimed that each of our parts has a purpose. For example, it is clear that the purpose of the eye is to see, and of the ears to hear. So, he concluded, the person as a whole must have a purpose. As he put it in a work entitled *Nicomachean Ethics*:

> Surely, just as each part of man—the eye, the hand, the foot—has a purpose, so also man as a whole must have a purpose. What is this purpose? Our biological functions we share in common even with plants. So these cannot be the purpose

of man, since we are looking for something specific to man. The activities of our senses we also plainly share with other things: horses, cattle, and other animals. So there remain only the activities that belong to the rational part of man. ... The specific purpose or function of man must involve the activities of that part of his soul that belongs to reason.[10]

Both Plato and Aristotle, then, stress reason as the most important feature of our human nature, certainly as more important than our desires and emotions. Reason is what is unique in humans—what makes us unique and different from all other animals. In addition, both see the exercise of reason as the purpose of human nature. That is, the purpose of human beings is to be rational: to use their reason well, both in thought and in action. And for both Plato and Aristotle, reason should control our desires and emotions. As Aristotle wrote, "human virtue consists of dealing with our feelings, [desires], and actions in such a way that we attain in them the kind of moderation that reason determines is right."

The Immaterial and Immortal Soul.   Plato also claimed that human nature has a spiritual aspect. In one of his dialogues, *Phaedo,* Plato has Socrates argue that the self—the soul—is immaterial and so is immortal. It can survive the death of its body. Plato argues that our mental abilities provide the clearest evidence of the immaterial nature of the soul. That is, our ability to grasp perfect abstract ideals is evidence of our immaterial nature. Plato held that when our mind has and uses ideas of perfect things it is doing something that a material body cannot do. In particular, our ability to think about ideally perfect things that do not exist in this material world is evidence that we have an immaterial soul. We can think, for example, about a perfectly straight line, a perfect circle, or a perfect horse. But in this world lines are only approximately straight, all circles are slightly imperfect, and every horse has flaws. So our minds can apprehend what does not exist in the material world around us. Notice in the following passage how Plato contrasts the changing material objects around us with the unchanging nature of the ideal Forms. He argues that the soul or mind must be like these ideal immaterial concepts:

SOCRATES: Consider perfect equality or perfect beauty or any other perfect ideal. Doesn't each of these, considered in themselves, always remain what it is, unchanging and not varying in any way from one moment to the next?

CEBES: They always remain the same, Socrates.

SOCRATES: And what about the many material instances of ideals like beauty, such as beautiful individual people, horses, dresses or what have you; or what about material instances of equality, or any other material instances of an ideal. Do these always remain the same or do we see them changing constantly and becoming something else?

CEBES: They are continually changing, Socrates.

SOCRATES: These changing material objects can be seen and touched and perceived with our bodily senses. But the unchanging Ideals you can know only with the mind and they are not visible to the body's senses.... So shouldn't we say that there are two kinds of entities: those which are

ANALYZING THE READING

1. Aristotle claims that each part of a person has a purpose. He concludes that a person as a whole must have a purpose. What assumption does Aristotle make to move from what he claims to what he concludes?

2. Aristotle says that the purpose of a human being has to be some activity that no other animal can engage in. Do you think that is true? Why?

QUICK REVIEW
For Aristotle, all living things have a purpose. The purpose of humans is to use their reason to think and to control desires and aggressions.

QUICK REVIEW
In *Phaedo*, Plato argues that the soul is immaterial and immortal because it can perceive nonmaterial ideals that do not exist in this world.

---

[10]   Aristotle, *Nicomachean Ethics*, bk. 1, ch. 7. This translation by Manuel Velasquez.

visible and those which are not? ... And the visible are changing while the invisible are unchanging?

CEBES: That seems to be true. ...

SOCRATES: Now which of these two kinds of things is our body like?

CEBES: Clearly it is like the visible things. ...

SOCRATES: And what do we say of the soul? Is it visible or not?

CEBES: It is not visible to us, Socrates.

SOCRATES: Then the soul is more like the invisible things and the body like the visible ones?

CEBES: That is most certain, Socrates.

SOCRATES: ... [W]hen the soul withdraws within itself and begins to think, she passes into the realm of pure ideas that are unchanging and eternal. These are her kindred. She would stay there forever if she was not hindered. She would no longer stray but would stay there in contact with what is most like herself, that is, what is eternal, constant, and unchanging . We would say that such a soul possesses wisdom.

CEBES: That is a fine description, Socrates! And it is completely true.

SOCRATES: Very well, then. And to which of the two kinds of things is the soul most closely related and most similar?

CEBES: It's clear, Socrates, that the soul most resembles the unchanging things and the body those things that change constantly.

SOCRATES: Now when the soul and body are united the soul rules the body. Isn't it the nature of the divine to rule and the mortal to serve? And if so isn't the soul like something divine?

CEBES: Yes, Socrates.

SOCRATES: So, Cebes, mustn't we conclude that the soul most resembles something divine, immortal, intelligible, uniform, indissoluble, and unchangeable? While the body is like what is mortal, unintelligible, multiform, dissoluble, and changeable? Can anyone argue against this?

CEBES: No one could, Socrates.

SOCRATES: I say, then, that the soul, which is invisible, departs at death to a world that is, like itself, glorious, pure, and invisible, the world of the good and wise God. ... She goes to a world that is divine and immortal and rational. Arriving there, the soul is secure in its happiness and is released from the error and folly of men. It is free of their fears and wild passions and all other human ills. It will forever dwell, as they say at ritual initiations, in the company of the gods.[11]

ANALYZING THE READING

Plato claims that the human soul or mind can know, think about, and mentally deal with ideal concepts that are not material, not visible, unchanging, and eternal. He concludes that the soul or mind must therefore have these same characteristics. What assumption does Plato make to move from what he claims to what he concludes? Do you think this assumption is true? Why?

Plato thought, then, that the body and soul are two different entities. That is, the soul is one thing and the body is a separate thing, although the soul is connected to the body. The body is like a host within which the soul lives and which the soul controls. The soul, Plato claimed, is the real human self, not the body. Moreover, the soul can grasp or comprehend the immaterial Forms. So the soul must be immaterial, unlike the body which is material. The immaterial soul, then, can go on living after its material body dies.

---

[11] Plato, *Phaedo*. This edited translation copyright © 1987 by Manuel Velasquez.

Plato's student, Aristotle, agreed that a human being has a soul. But Aristotle's view of the soul differed drastically from Plato's. Aristotle did not believe the soul and the body were two separate entities. For Aristotle the soul is just the structure or organization of the materials the body is made of. That is, a person is just physical material that has a certain structure or organization. Just as a vase consists of clay that has a certain shape or form, a person consists of physical matter that has a certain arrangement or form. That structure or form is the soul. When physical matter is arranged into the form of a person, it can live, move, and think. So the soul or arrangement is what turns physical matter into a living thing. In Aristotle's view, then, death occurs when a body looses its structure. So death is the end of both the soul—the body's structure—and the body. Yet Aristotle did think that the *rational part* of a person somehow survived death. He agreed with Plato that reason can grasp immaterial concepts so it must be immaterial. But for Aristotle reason is not the person. Reason is just a part of the person and the rest of the person ends at death.

In this traditional rationalistic view of human nature, then, we are creatures of reason, appetite, and emotion. We are, however, distinct from the material world because our reason enables us to stand apart from our material environment and grasp immaterial ideas. Plato held that at death, if we have learned to control our passions and appetites, we can escape the confines of our material body and rise to the realm of these perfect, eternal, and unchanging ideas. We gain such self-mastery by learning to control our passions and appetites with our reason during life. To attain such self-mastery through the exercise of reason is the ultimate purpose of human beings. Aristotle agreed with much of Plato's view of human nature. But for Aristotle only a part of the person—his reason—survives death. Although reason is only part of the person, however, it is this rational part that defines human nature. Humans are rational animals. And their rationality makes them different from all other animals.

Implications of the Traditional Rationalistic View. This view of human nature looks innocent and optimistic in the role it gives to reason. Yet is it? Let's consider one conclusion Aristotle drew from his theory of human nature. To be human, he had argued, is to be rational. So, he claimed, if a group of people is less rational than the Greeks, they would be less human: They would be "barbarians." Since "barbarians" are not fully human, then, people who are more rational and more human (like the Greeks) can enslave them. As Aristotle wrote, "The lower sort are by nature slaves, and it is better for them as for all inferiors that they should be under the rule of a master." This view of human nature, then, could be, and was, used to justify enslaving those who did not live up to its standards.

Several centuries after Plato and Aristotle, for example, Spain paid for the voyage of Christopher Columbus. Columbus, as you know, discovered the New World of the Americas. But the New World was already populated by millions of "Indian" natives. This was a problem for the Spanish who wanted to colonize the New World and exploit its resources. And for this they needed laborers. Several Spanish scholars found a solution to this problem: Enslave the natives. To justify their proposal they quoted Aristotle. Juan Gines de Sepulveda, for example, was a Spanish professor. He argued that "one part of mankind is set aside by nature to be slaves in the service of masters [who are] born for a life of virtue free of manual labor." The men of "virtue," of course, were the Spaniards, and those "set aside by nature to be slaves" were the American natives. Sepulveda, and others like him, convinced many that Aristotle's view justified treating the natives of the New World as slaves. That view led to much of the suffering the Spanish and other Europeans inflicted on the New World's natives.

QUICK REVIEW
Aristotle claimed that because barbarians were less rational than Greeks, they were less human and so could be ruled and enslaved by the Greeks.

But perhaps we should not be surprised. Racism and ethnic discrimination are often, perhaps always, based on the idea that other races are not as human as one's own people. Your view about what human beings are influences your views about who counts as a full human being. It is crucial, therefore, to be aware of your view of human nature. Your view of what a full human being is, will affect the judgments you make about people who are different from you.

Whatever its problems, the rationalistic view of human nature is one of the most influential theories of Western civilization. Many people still accept it. And it has shaped a second important version of the Traditional view: the Judeo-Christian religious view of human nature.

The Judeo-Christian Version of the Traditional Western View of Human Nature

According to the Judeo-Christian tradition, humans are made in the image of God and they are made to love God and one's neighbor. For example, the Jewish scriptures portray God as saying, "And God said, let us make man in our image, after our likeness." And according to the Christian scriptures Jesus of Nazareth said, "The most important commandment is this: Love the lord your God with all your heart and with all your soul and with all your mind and with all your strength. The second is this: Love your neighbor as yourself." This notion of a loving God in whose image humans are made and whose love they should emulate changed the rationalistic view. Nevertheless, a large part of the Greek rationalistic view of human nature has been incorporated into the Judeo-Christian view.

Plato, in particular, influenced Christian thought through thinkers such as Saint Augustine (354–430 CE). Augustine was familiar with Platonist views and adapted many of Plato's doctrines to Christianity. For example, Plato had said that after death the souls of those who love the "perfect, eternal" ideal Forms would rise to heaven. There they would be united with those eternal Forms that serve as models or patterns for material objects. Augustine adopted this idea but modified it. He argued that the souls that will rise to heaven are those that know and love the perfect, eternal *God*. Moreover, Augustine claimed that the eternal ideal Forms exist in the mind of God. They are the ideas God has of the things He creates. Here is how he expresses this view:

> Ideas are certain original forms, or permanent and unchanging archetypes of things that are not themselves formed by anything else. That is, they are eternal and always exist and remain the same within the mind of God. They themselves do not come into being nor do they decay. But everything is made by God according to these ideas. Everything that can or has come into being or decayed is formed according to these ideas.[12]

From Plato, Augustine also took the doctrine that the human self is a rational immaterial self. It is a soul that can think and reason and is immaterial and immortal. And he borrowed, too, the idea that the rational self should rule over its appetites and emotions.

Unlike Plato, however, Augustine emphasized the notion of a will and not just that of reason. The will, Augustine held, is the mind's ability to choose between

---

12   Augustine, *De Diversis Quaestionibus Octoginta Tribus*, [On Eighty-Three Different Questions], Q. XLVI [46], quoted in Aquinas, *Summa Theologica*, Q. 15, a1.

good and evil. This mental ability is the seat of the most significant Christian virtue: love. For the Christian, as for the Jew, the fundamental religious duty is to freely choose to love God and neighbor. The human will, the power to decide what we will do, allows human beings to make this choice. Still, the will is a two-edged sword. Although it enables people to choose the good, it also enables them to choose evil. Evil is chosen when people choose lesser goods in preference to God or the good of other persons. Augustine claimed that every person experiences three basic disorderly desires: the desire for the pleasures of the body; a craving for new experiences; and the desire for others' approval, love, or fear. He summarized these as "lust, curiosity, and pride." Because of these, Augustine held, people are constantly attracted to evil and away from God. He describes an event in his boyhood that illustrates this:

THINKING LIKE A PHILOSOPHER

Did you ever do something wrong with friends like Augustine's theft of pears from a neighboring orchard? What did you feel when you did it? Were you and your friends able to laugh about it afterward like Augustine and his friends did? Did you get a sense of power when you got away with it? What do you think motivated you to do it? Did your motives fit Augustine's three basic desires? Did your motives in any way resemble Augustine's claim that he stole not for the pears but just to do something forbidden with friends? To what extent do you think Augustine's motivations in stealing the pears resemble many people's motivations to engage in more serious wrongdoing?

> Near our vineyard there was a pear tree, loaded with fruit. ... I and some other low-minded fellows got the idea to shake the pears off this tree and get away with a load of them. We set out late at night ... and stole all the fruit we could carry. And this was not to feed ourselves. We may have tasted a few, but then we threw the rest to the pigs. Our real pleasure was simply in doing something that was forbidden. ... I did wrong for nothing, with no reason for the wrongdoing except the wrongdoing itself. ... I loved the sin, not the thing for which I had committed the sin, but the sin itself. ... Yet sin is committed because we have an inordinate desire for goods of a lower order and turn away from the better and higher good. ... So what was it in that theft of mine that I desired? ... Pride disguises itself as high-spiritedness ... and curiosity as the desire for knowledge. ... So did I want to be like God in some disguised way? Did I want to rebel against God even though I had no real power to do so? Was I trying to achieve some kind of false freedom by doing what God had forbidden so I could feel a false omnipotence? ... But I clearly remember that by myself alone I would not have committed the theft. So I also did it because I enjoyed doing pranks with my friends. ... We laughed uproariously because our hearts were tickled by the thought that we had deceived the owners of the orchard. They had no clue what we were doing and would have vehemently objected if they had. ... So the pleasure I got from the theft was not from what I stole, but from the stealing itself and the enjoyment I got from doing it with my friends.[13]

Of course, Augustine did not think that stealing pears from someone was hugely sinful. But he did think that this incident of his boyhood reveals something about the real sins of adulthood. Like Plato, Augustine held that humans have within them powerful desires that, like unruly "steeds," drag us down to the earth and away from "heaven above." His boyhood attraction for "the sin itself," for a false sense of "omnipotence," and for doing forbidden things with friends, were small examples of the powerful desires that lead adults away from God. It is with our will, of course, that we master our desires. But Augustine felt that without God's help our will cannot master our desires. We are then like he was in his boyhood: possessed of a will

---

[13] Augustine, *The Confessions of St. Augustine,* excerpts from bk. II, chs. 4, 5, 6, 8, and 9. Translated by Manuel Velasquez.

that is attracted to evil and unable to stop itself from wronging his neighbor for little reason "except the wrongdoing itself."

The human being, then, has both reason and will: the ability to know the truth about God and the ability to love God and other people. Thus, the Judeo-Christian view agrees with the classic rationalistic view, that human nature is not basically self-interested. Humans, with the help of God, can rise above their self-interested desires and genuinely love both God and neighbor.

The Judeo-Christian tradition adopted and also modified another key part of the rationalistic tradition. Aristotle argues that like all living things, human beings have a purpose. The purpose of humans is to achieve happiness by using their reason. The influential Christian thinker Saint Thomas Aquinas (1225–1274 CE) agreed. Aquinas borrowed from Aristotle the view that humans and all other creatures have a purpose. However, he claimed, the purpose of humans is to achieve happiness by using their reason to know God:

> The heavenly bodies cause the generation of all things here below. So the purpose of their motion is the generation of things below. Now [here below] ... the simplest elements exist for the sake of compound minerals; these latter exist for the sake of living bodies, among which plants exist for animals, and animals for humans. So humans are the purpose of the whole order of generation.... Now humans naturally desire, as their ultimate purpose, to know the first cause of things. But the first cause of all things is God. So the ultimate purpose of humans is to know God.[14]

Interestingly, Aquinas also accepted much of Aristotle's view of the soul and rejected Plato's view. Like Aristotle, Aquinas held that the soul is the structure or organization of the physical materials humans are made of. And Aquinas also accepted Aristotle's view that part of the person—reason—survived death. But Aquinas also held that the person's soul gives its reason whatever organization or structure reason has. That is, the soul or structure of the physical materials of the body is also the soul or structure of the person's reason. There is not one structure or soul for a person's body and another structure or soul for its reason. So if the structure of the person's reason survives death, so must the rest of the person's structure or soul. So Aquinas rejected Aristotle's view that only reason survives death. Aquinas argued that the whole soul that gives reason its structure has to survive along with its reason. However, Aquinas agreed that the soul and reason are not the whole person. To be a complete person the soul must be united to its body. Nevertheless, the person's whole soul in some way survives death. And, Aquinas claimed, Christians believe that at some point in history, the resurrection of the body will reunite the person's soul with its body.

Saints Augustine and Aquinas are key figures in the development of the Judeo-Christian view of human nature. Today, in fact, almost all Christian denominations accept some aspect of their views. But some have leaned more toward Augustine's adaptation of Plato, while others have leaned more toward Aquinas' adaptation of Aristotle.

Many other people have found both the rationalistic and the Judeo-Christian views of human nature appealing. These two versions of the Traditional Western view of human nature seem to describe something that we all experience: the conflict between what our desires want and what our reason tells us is good for us. It seems to provide an uplifting picture of human beings as fundamentally spiritual and capable of surviving death. Reason sets us off from other creatures, making us "unique" in the classical rationalistic version, and "like God" in the Judeo-Christian version, while in both we humans are capable of choosing between good and evil.

---

[14] Aquinas, *Summa Contra Gentiles*, bk. III, ch. 22, paras. 5, 7, 8; ch. 25, para. 11. Translated by Manuel Velasquez.

All these are familiar ideas about ourselves: the idea that we have an immortal soul that can survive death; the idea that humans are unique and different from other creatures; the idea that reason is what makes us different and that reason should rule over our appetites; and the idea that human beings have a purpose and that this purpose is related to the soul and its reason. As we noted, these views of ourselves have been among the most influential in Western civilization and beyond.

Yet these views of ourselves have been challenged from several directions. Perhaps the most serious challenge to these ideas has come from science. As we will see, the theory of evolution, in particular, challenges key aspects of the Traditional Western views of what we are, and raises significant philosophical issues. In fact, numerous leading contemporary philosophers have recently written several book-length works addressing the philosophical implications that Darwin's theory of evolution has for human nature, including Daniel Dennet, Elliott Sober, Mary Midgley, Michael Ruse, Marjorie Grene, Richard Richards, Francisco Ayala, Alex Rosenberg, Janet Richards, Peter Singer, James Rachels, Alvin Plantinga, Jerry Fodor, and Stefan Linquist.[15] In addition, contemporary philosophers have written numerous articles on evolution and its philosophical implications, and *Biology and Philosophy* is an entire journal devoted to the topic. This large and growing philosophical interest in the impact of evolutionary ideas on our contemporary views of human nature points to the major importance that Darwin and his theories have for us as we inquire into who and what we are.

THINKING LIKE A PHILOSOPHER

1. Do you agree with the claims made by the Judeo-Christian view of human nature? For example, do you agree that you have a soul that will survive death? Do you think your most important goal should be to try to love God with all your mind and strength and your neighbor as yourself?
2. Do you think it should matter to a Christian that many of Christianity's beliefs were taken from Plato and Aristotle who were not Christian?

Adam and Eve. In his idealized figures of the first man and woman being tempted by Satan, the fifteenth-century Christian artist Albrecht Dürer (1471–1528) attempted to portray humans as rational loving beings made in the image of God but capable of great good and evil.

---

15 Daniel Dennett, *Darwin's Dangerous Idea: Evolution and the Meanings of Life* (London: Penguin Books, 1995); Elliott Sober, *Did Darwin Write the Origin Backwards: Philosophical Essays on Darwin's Theory* (New York: Prometheus Books, 2010); Mary Midgley, *The Solitary Self: Darwin and the Selfish Gene* (London: Acumen Publishers, Ltd., 2010); Michael Ruse, *The Philosophy of Human Evolution* (Cambridge: Cambridge University Press, 2012); Marjorie Grene, *The Philosophy of Biology: An Episodic History* (Cambridge: Cambridge University Press, 2004); Richard A. Richards, *The Species Problem: A Philosophical Analysis* (Cambridge: Cambridge University Press, 2010); Francisco J. Ayala, *Am I a Monkey? Six Big Questions About Evolution,* (Baltimore, MD: Johns Hopkins University Press, 2010); Alexander Rosenberg, *Darwinism in Philosophy, Social Science and Policy,* (Cambridge: Cambridge University Press, 2000); Janet Radcliffe Richards, *Human Nature After Darwin: A Philosophical Introduction* (London: Routledge, 2001); Peter Singer, *The Expanding Circle: Ethics, Evolution, and Moral Progress* (Princeton, NJ: Princeton University Press, 2011); James Rachels, *Created from Animals: The Moral Implications of Darwinism* (New York: Oxford University Press, 1999); Alvin Plantinga, *Where the Conflict Really Lies: Science, Religion, and Naturalism* (Oxford: Oxford University Press, 2011); Jerry Fodor and Massimo Piattelli-Palmarini, *What Darwin Got Wrong* (New York: Farrar, Straus and Giroux, 2011); Stefan Linquist, *Philosophy of Evolutionary Biology* (London: Ashgate, 2010).

We will look now at the challenge evolutionary theory has posed for the Traditional Western view of human nature by looking at the ideas of Charles Darwin. It was Darwin who forced us to take the theory of evolution seriously and thereby forever affected our view of ourselves.

The Darwinian Challenge

Variation, the Struggle for Existence, and Natural Selection. Darwin proposed three key ideas. The first is the idea that animals and plants are sometimes born with features that are different from those of their parents but that they can pass on to their own offspring. Darwin called these differences "variations." For example, a giraffe may be born with a longer neck than its parents. When mature, that giraffe can pass on this "variation" to its own offspring.

Charles Darwin:
"Natural selection is daily and hourly scrutinizing, throughout the world, the slightest variations; rejecting those that are bad, preserving and adding up all that are good; silently and insensibly working at the improvement of each organic being.

Charles Darwin (1809–82) (photo), Cameron, Julia Margaret (1815–79)/Private Collection/The Stapleton Collection/The Bridgeman Art Library International

MindTap To read more from Charles Darwin's *The Origin of Species*, click the link in the MindTap Reader or go to the Questia Readings folder in MindTap.

The second key idea Darwin proposed is that living creatures are in a great "struggle for existence." That is, they must continuously compete with one another to stay alive. They must compete because living creatures produce more offspring than can survive.

> A struggle for existence inevitably follows from the high rate at which all organic beings tend to increase. Every being, which during its natural lifetime produces several eggs or seeds, must suffer destruction during some period of its life, and during some season or occasional year, otherwise, on the principle of geometrical increase, its numbers would quickly become so inordinately great that no country could support the product. Hence, as more individuals are produced than can possibly survive, there must in every case be a struggle for existence, either one individual with another of the same species, or with the individuals of distinct species, or with the physical conditions of life.[16]

A newborn bobcat, for example, starts life having to compete with its many brothers and sisters as they all struggle to suck from their mother's few nipples. Later, the bobcat has to compete with other bobcats for mates and food. Throughout its life, it struggles to keep away from wolves and other predators. Always it must struggle against heat and cold, sun and snow, droughts and storms.

The third key idea was "natural selection or survival of the fittest." Darwin pointed out that some variations give a creature an advantage over other members of its species in the struggle for existence. Such variations give the creature a better chance of surviving. By surviving it can have offspring, and pass the variation on to its descendants. A giraffe with a longer neck can feed itself better and so live longer. It can then mate more often, and leave more offspring with longer necks than other giraffes. So the struggle for existence "selects" organisms with advantageous variations and lets them survive and multiply. At the same time, the struggle for existence weeds out animals and plants that lack advantageous variations and lets them die. After many generations, all the members of the species

---

16   Charles Darwin, *On the Origin of Species by Natural Selection* (London: John Murray, 1859), ch. 4.

will have the new advantageous variation, and those lacking the variation will have died out:

> [C]an we doubt (remembering that many more individuals are born than can possibly survive) that individuals having any advantage, however slight, over others, would have the best chance of surviving and of procreating their kind? On the other hand, we may feel sure that any variation in the least degree injurious would be rigidly destroyed. This preservation of favorable individual differences and variations, and the destruction of those which are injurious, I have called Natural Selection, or the Survival of the Fittest. . . .
>
> Let us take the case of a wolf, which preys on various animals, securing some by craft, some by strength, and some by fleetness; and let us suppose that the fleetest prey, a deer for instance, had from any change in the country increased in numbers, or that other prey had decreased in numbers, during that season of the year when the wolf was hardest pressed for food. Under such circumstances the swiftest and slimmest wolves would have the best chance of surviving and so be preserved or selected.[17]

After millions of years, so many advantageous variations can mark the members of a species that they will be very different from earlier members. If they become sufficiently different, they will be a new species. A species of fish over millions of years may evolve into a species of amphibians that can take advantage of life on land. The amphibian species may evolve into a hardy dinosaur species that is better able to fight for its survival on land. And the dinosaur species may evolve into a bird species that has the advantage of flight:

> It may metaphorically be said that natural selection is daily and hourly scrutinizing, throughout the world, the slightest variations; rejecting those that are bad, preserving and adding up all that are good; silently and insensibly working, whenever and wherever opportunity offers, at the improvement of each organic being in relation to its organic and inorganic conditions of life. We see nothing of these slow changes in progress, until the hand of time has marked the lapse of ages, and then so imperfect is our view into long-past geological ages, that we see only that the forms of life are now different from what they formerly were.[18]

We are so used to the idea of evolution that it is hard for us to understand how incredible Darwin's theory was to people of his time. The idea that natural processes might make any species evolve into a new species disturbed many people. It meant the living world around us had not been created as it was, but was the result of a still continuously changing nature.

Yet as disturbing as Darwin's ideas about the evolution of species were, his ideas were even more disturbing when he applied them to human beings. For humans are animals. So if Darwin's theory applied to animals, then humans also must have evolved from earlier nonhuman ancestors! Darwin himself made the point in *The Descent of Man,* a book that aroused a flurry of angry controversy:

> Thus we can understand how it has come to pass that man and all other vertebrate animals have been constructed on the same general model, why they pass through the same early stages of development, and why they retain certain rudiments in common. Consequently we ought frankly to admit their community of descent: to take any other view, is to admit that our own structure, and that of all the animals around us, is a mere snare laid to entrap our judgment. . . . It is only our natural prejudice, and that arrogance which made our forefathers declare that they were descended from demigods, which leads us to demur to this conclusion.[19]

QUICK REVIEW

Darwin said that some creatures have variations that can be inherited by offspring, and those with advantageous variations can better survive and pass them on, while those with injurious variations are destroyed, a process he called "natural selection" or "survival of the fittest." Descendants of a species can be so different that they are a new species.

QUICK REVIEW

Darwin's theory applies to humans. But if all human abilities evolved from lower animals, reason is not unique but just a more developed animal ability.

---

[17] Ibid.
[18] Ibid.
[19] Charles Darwin, *The Descent of Man,* 2nd ed. (New York: A.L. Burt, 1874), ch. 1.

Implications for the Traditional View. Think of the implications of Darwin's theory for the Traditional view of human nature. Take, first, what the Traditional view says about the differences between humans and animals. The Traditional view says that although humans are animals, they have a power that makes them unique. This power is the ability to reason. Humans are rational animals, and our ability to reason and think are beyond the abilities of any other animal. Reason is not just a more developed and more powerful version of the same kinds of abilities that other animals have. The Traditional view says reason is a completely different kind of ability than the abilities of other animals.

Darwin denied this. If humans evolved from nonhuman animals, then human abilities evolved from those of our nonhuman ancestors. That means human abilities, including reason, are just more developed variations of the abilities of nonhuman animals. Darwin wrote: "[T]here is no fundamental difference between man and the higher mammals in their mental faculties."[20] Yet the Traditional view holds that reason is unique, and is what makes us like God. In Darwin's view, though, reason is no different in kind from the mental powers of nonhuman primates. Humans are made, not in the image of God, but in the image of the primates that came before them.

Second, and even more important, the Traditional view holds that human beings are designed for a purpose. Aristotle had noted that human organs, such as "the eye, the hand, and the foot," were clearly designed for a specific purpose. The eye is designed to see, the hand to grasp, and the foot to walk. Since each part of us is designed for a specific purpose, Aristotle argued, a human being as a whole must also have a purpose. Just as the purpose of the eye is to do what our other organs cannot do, the purpose of a human being is to do what no other creature can do. Aristotle concluded that the purpose of humans is to exercise their reason since only humans can reason. Christian philosophers such as Augustine and Aquinas added that the purpose of humans is to use their reason and will to love God and neighbor.

Darwin's theory of evolution, however, undermined the idea that living things and their parts are designed for a purpose. Animal organs, such as the eye, the heart, and the foot, Darwin held, were not made to serve a specific purpose. Instead each developed bit by bit through the accumulation of countless tiny variations and the blind process of natural selection. It is true, as Aristotle and others had noted, that the eye and all our other organs seem to be specially designed to serve a specific purpose. But this apparent design and purpose are an illusion. The eye is simply the accumulated outcome of numerous chance variations that survived because each gave a slight advantage to an animal. As the outcome of this process of natural selection, the eye is adapted to seeing because that adaptation is an advantage in the struggle for survival. The blind processes of natural selection, not purposeful design, resulted in the eye and each of its intricate parts. Neither did humans as a whole have a purpose. The evolution of a species, like the evolution of each of their organs, Darwin argued, is the result of blind natural selection, not of purposeful design.

> **✓ QUICK REVIEW**
> Darwin's theory undermined the idea that living things and humans are designed for a purpose.

Darwin's Evidence. Because Darwin's theory has such important implications for our view of human nature, we should look at the arguments he gave in support of his theory. Darwin pointed to several kinds of evidence for his theory.

One piece of evidence was the fact that animals of different species can share similar characteristics. For example, chimpanzees, gorillas, and orangutans share

---

[20] Ibid., ch. 3.

similar characteristics. These shared characteristics are easily explained by his theory of evolution, Darwin claimed. His theory says that variations and natural selection will split an earlier species into several distinct later species. Some of those later species will split into several more distinct species. And some of those in turn will split into other distinct species. The result is like a branching tree that continually grows new branches, which in turn develop new branches. This branching of species, Darwin argued, was the best explanation of the fact that species can be classified into groups that share similar characteristics. According to his theory, species (like monkeys and gorillas) share common characteristics because they descended from a common ancestor. The fact that different species of animals can share similar characteristics, Darwin added, could not be explained by the view that each was independently created. If that had happened each species would be unrelated to other species:

> It is a truly wonderful fact—the wonder of which we are apt to overlook from familiarity—that all animals and all plants throughout all time and space should be related to each other in groups subordinate to groups, in the manner which we everywhere behold—namely, varieties of the same species most closely related, species of the same genus less closely ... related, ... species of distinct genera much less closely related, ... forming sub-families, families, orders, sub-classes, and classes. ... If species had been independently created, no explanation would have been possible of this kind of classification; but it is explained through inheritance [from common ancestors] and the complex action of natural selection, entailing extinction and divergence of character.[21]

Another piece of evidence for his theory, Darwin argued, was the way that species are distributed over the earth. The distribution, he claimed, was easily explained by his theory. But it could not be explained by the view that each species had been independently created. If his theory was right, he said, each species would have originated in a single location. Its members would then spread out from there, evolving into additional species as they moved. But they would have to stop wherever they encountered barriers. So barriers, like oceans, that a species could not cross would confine them to one side of the barrier. But species that could cross the barrier would cross and continue to evolve on the other side of the barrier. This, he claimed, is what we see:

> We see the full meaning of the wonderful fact, which has struck every traveler, namely, that on the same continent, under the most diverse conditions, ... most of the inhabitants within each great class are plainly related; for they are the descendants of the same progenitors. ... We clearly see why species belonging to those groups of animals which cannot cross wide spaces of the ocean, as frogs and terrestrial mammals, do not inhabit oceanic islands; and why, on the other hand, new and peculiar species of bats, animals which can traverse the ocean, are often found on islands far distant from any continent. Such cases as the presence of peculiar species of bats on oceanic islands and the absence of all other terrestrial mammals are facts utterly inexplicable on the theory of independent acts of creation.[22]

Darwin also argued that the body parts of animals are also evidence that they evolved from common ancestors. Bone structures, embryos, and useless rudimentary organs, he claimed, are best explained by his theory of evolution. They could not be explained by the view that each species was separately created:

QUICK REVIEW
Darwin argued that his theory that "variations and natural selection" had caused species to evolve from earlier species explained numerous facts better than the view that each species was "independently created," including: the similarities between distinct species, their geographical distribution, the similar bones and embryos of different species, rudimentary organs, and the fossil record.

---

[21] *Origin of Species*, 104.
[22] Ibid., 418–419.

The similar framework of bones in the hand of a man, wing of a bat, fin of a porpoise, and leg of the horse; the same number of vertebrae forming the neck of the giraffe and of the elephant; and innumerable other such facts, at once explain themselves on the theory of descent [from a common ancestor] with slow and slight successive modifications. The similarity of pattern in the wing and in the leg of a bat, though used for such different purpose, in the jaws and legs of a crab, in the petals, stamens, and pistils of a flower is likewise, to a large extent, intelligible on the view of the gradual modification of parts or organs, which were originally alike in an early progenitor in each of these] classes. [My theory also explains] why the embryos of mammals, birds, reptiles, and fishes [that descended from a common ancestor] should be so closely similar, and so unlike the adult forms. ... [We can also see how] disuse, aided sometimes by natural selection, will often have reduced organs when rendered useless under changed habits or conditions of life; and we can understand on this view the meaning of rudimentary organs [organs that are useless to an animal].... On the view of each organism with all its separate parts having been specially created, how utterly inexplicable is it that organs bearing the plain stamp of inutility, such as the teeth in the embryonic calf or the shriveled wings under the soldered wing-covers of many beetles, should so frequently occur. ... It can hardly be supposed that a false theory would explain, in so satisfactory a manner as does the theory of natural selection, the several large classes of facts above specified.[23]

ANALYZING THE READING

1. Darwin said that we should accept his theory of evolution because it is the best explanation there is for several facts such as the fact that different species of animals can share similar characteristics, the fact that species spread out over continents but not over oceans, the fact that the bones of related species are similar, and so on. Do you think that if a theory is the best explanation for many facts it is probably true? Can you think of other reasonable explanations for the facts that Darwin points to?

2. Descartes and others have claimed that our ability to use language shows that the human ability to reason is unique. Who do you think is right, Darwin or Descartes? Why?

But the most important evidence Darwin pointed to were the fossilized skeletons of ancient animals and plants found in layers of rocks under the earth. The oldest fossils found in the lowest layers of rock, he pointed out, were less like today's plants and animals than the more recent ones in higher layers of rock. Darwin claimed this fossil record was best explained by his theory that species living today had descended from different earlier species. And those in turn had descended from yet earlier species. All of this could be explained by the gradual modifications his theory proposed:

If we admit that the geological record is imperfect to an extreme degree, then the facts, which the record does give, strongly support the theory of descent with modification.... The fact of the fossil remains of each formation [layer of rock] being in some degree intermediate in character between the fossils in the formations above and below is simply explained by their intermediate position in the chain of descent. The grand fact that all extinct beings can be classed with all recent beings naturally follows from the living and the extinct being the offspring of common parents.[24]

So Darwin pointed to a large number of facts as evidence for his theory. In every case, his argument came down to the same claim. His theory was the best

---

[23]   Ibid., 420–421.
[24]   Ibid., 417.

explanation for the facts—particularly when compared to the popular view that each species had been independently created.

Responses to Darwin. In view of all the evidence that Darwin offered for his theory, is the Traditional view of human nature dead? Hardly. Supporters of the Traditional view have responded to Darwin's challenge. Some have pointed to problems in the evidence he gave for his theory. Others have argued that Darwin was wrong in his belief that his theory disproved the idea that human nature has a purpose. Still others claimed that, in spite of Darwin's theory, human reason is uniquely human.

First, and most controversially, some have argued that fossils do not support Darwin's view that species gradually evolve into other species. When we examine fossils, recent critics have claimed, we find that most new species seem to appear suddenly. They appear without earlier, gradually different forms leading up to them. They seem to appear in the layers of rock almost as if they were suddenly created. There are sudden jumps from one completely formed species in one layer of rock, to another completely formed species in a later layer of rock. Missing, in most cases, are the gradual changes and many intermediate steps that should be there if new species evolved by gradual steps as Darwin claimed. As the well-known biologist Stephen Jay Gould writes,

> The history of most fossil species includes two features inconsistent with [Darwinian] gradualism: 1. Stasis. Most species exhibit no directional change during their tenure on earth. They appear in the fossil record looking much the same as when they disappear.... 2. Sudden Appearance. In any local area, a species does not arise gradually by the steady transformation of its ancestors; it appears [in the fossil record] all at once and "fully formed."[25]

Gould, however, does not conclude that the large gaps in the fossil record disprove evolution. Gould claims that the gaps show only that evolution generally occurs by rapid "jumps" or "saltations" from one species to another. The evolution of one species into another takes place so quickly that it leaves few if any fossils. Some critics of Darwin insist that the gaps prove that Darwin was wrong. But Gould argues that the "gaps" are due to not yet having found all the fossils to fill in the gaps, or perhaps, due to evolution working much faster than Darwin thought.

A second group of critics have argued that even if Darwin's theory is correct, it is a mistake to conclude that human nature is not designed for a purpose. For example, philosopher George Mavrodes suggests that there are two ways of understanding evolution. A "naturalistic" understanding of evolution holds that evolution is "explicable entirely in terms of natural laws without reference to a divine intention or intervention." But a "theistic" understanding of evolution holds that "there was a divine teleology in this process, a divine direction at each crucial stage in accordance with divine plan or intention."[26] In other words, a theistic understanding of evolution holds that evolution occurred, but God directed evolution. On this view, God, through evolution, designed human beings for a purpose.

A third group of critics attack Darwin's claim that the power to reason is not unique to humans. Darwin claimed that since the human ability to reason evolved from the mental abilities of our nonhuman ancestors, the difference between them is one of degree. It is not a difference in kind.

QUICK REVIEW
Critics of Darwin claim that gaps in the fossil record disprove his theory, that a "theistic" view of evolution allows for purposeful design, and that reason does make us unique.

MindTap To read more from Stephen Jay Gould's *The Panda's Thumb*, click the link in the MindTap Reader or go to the Questia Readings folder in MindTap.

---

[25] Stephen Jay Gould, *The Panda's Thumb* (New York: Norton, 1980), 182.
[26] George Mavrodes, "Creation Science and Evolution," *Chronicle of Higher Education,* January 7, 1987, 43.

THINKING LIKE A PHILOSOPHER

Darwin claimed that the human ability to reason is not unique but is just a more developed version of the mental abilities other animals have. Do you think this claim of Darwin should matter to a Christian? Why? Does it matter to you? Are there others to whom you think it might matter?

But critics of Darwin have argued that human reason is unique in all of nature. The major difference between human mental capacities and those of all other animals, critics claim, is our ability to use language in our reasoning. In fact, before Darwin was even born, the French philosopher René Descartes made a similar point. He declared that what distinguishes humans from the "brutes" is the ability to "arrange different words together, forming of them a statement by which they make known their thoughts; while, on the other hand, there is no other animal, however perfect and fortunately circumscribed it may be, which can do the same."[27] Of course, many animals can communicate by using simple signs. But only humans seem able to communicate and think using complex languages. Human language can produce an infinite number of new sentences expressing ideas that have never before been expressed. The ability to use such languages seems unique to human beings. Many scientists have tried to show that nonhumans can be taught to "speak" and understand human languages. But these attempts have proven frustratingly inconclusive.

Perhaps, then, we can think of human reason as the ability to think linguistically. Perhaps reason can be seen as the ability to create, understand, and engage in complex chains of reasoning about thoughts embodied in language. If that is what reason is, then it may indeed be unique to humans. It may even be qualitatively different from anything found in other animals.

thinking critically • Inference to the Best Explanation

Part of the reason why Darwin's theory is still looked at with suspicion by many people is perhaps due to the kind of argument that he gave for his theory. Darwin argued, as we have seen, that his theory was true because it was the best explanation for the facts he described. This is not a deductive argument. Many different explanations can be given for any fact, including explanations that no one has yet thought of. So even if an explanation of a fact is the best one we currently have, there may be a better explanation that we have not yet discovered. Until the early seventeenth century, for example, the rising and setting of the sun were explained by the view that the sun rotates around the earth. Only later in that century did people realize that those facts are better explained by the theory that the earth rotates while moving around the sun. So there is always at least a possibility that a theory is wrong even if it is the best explanation we have today. Darwin's argument, then, cannot show that if his evidence is correct, then his theory must be true. His argument can only conclude that his theory is probably true. His argument, then, is an inductive or probable argument.

Darwin's argument is a kind of argument called an "inference to the best explanation." An **inference to the best explanation** is an argument that assumes that the theory that best explains a large set of facts is probably true. We can describe the form of such an argument in the following way. Suppose we use the letters "p, q, r, s, ..." as symbols for the many different kinds of facts a theory explains. And suppose we use the letter "T" to stand for the theory that is supposed to explain these facts. Then we can say that an inference to the best explanation has the following form:

1. Theory T is the best explanation we currently have for the facts p, q, r, s, ...
2. If a theory is the best explanation for all the facts, then it is true.
3. Therefore, theory T is probably true.

---

27 René Descartes, *Discourse on Method*, pt. 5, in *Philosophical Works*, trans. E. Haldane and G. Ross (Cambridge: Cambridge University Press, 1911), vol. 1, 116–117.

Although this form of argument looks like it could be deductive, it is not. Premise (1) says that theory T is merely the best explanation we *currently* have. But premise (2) is talking about the absolutely best explanation there is, not just the best we currently have. As we've seen, the best explanation we currently have might be surpassed by a better one tomorrow. So it is possible that theory T may not be the absolutely best explanation there is and may actually be false.

We rely on this kind of argument every day. For example, suppose you walk outdoors and find that the ground and vegetation are wet all over the neighborhood. You may conclude that it probably rained because that is the best explanation for all the wet things you see. Many, perhaps most, criminal trials rely on an inference to the best explanation. Suppose these were the facts: The fingerprints of the accused were found on the murder weapon. He had a motive for killing the victim. Witnesses saw him fleeing the scene of the crime immediately after they heard a shot. And he has no alibi. Then although the accused says someone else did it, the jury may conclude that the best explanation for all the facts is that the accused murdered the victim. Inferences to the best explanation are also common in science. We have already mentioned, for example, that before the seventeenth century people accepted the theory that the sun revolves around the earth. That theory was rejected during the seventeenth century in favor of the better explanation that the earth revolves as it moves around the sun. In fact, virtually all scientific theories are based on an inference to the best explanation. This includes the theory that light consists of waves, the theory of relativity, the theory of atoms, Newton's laws of motion, and so on.

An inference to the best explanation, we said, is an inductive or probable argument. Good inductive or probable arguments are not said to be valid or invalid. Instead, we say they are either strong or weak. An inductive argument is strong when there's a high probability its conclusion is true. It is weak when there's a low probability its conclusion is true.

So when is an inference to the best explanation a strong argument? That is, what conditions does such an argument have to meet to be a strong argument? We can start to answer this question by looking first at premise (1) above and asking when is it true? In other words, when is a theory the "best explanation" of a set of facts? To begin with, we say a theory "explains" a set of facts when we know that if the theory were true, then all the facts would turn out like they did.

Still, there are usually a lot of different theories that can explain a set of facts. For example, a lot of different theories could explain why all the vegetation we saw this morning was wet. So how do we decide which of these theories is the "best explanation" of the facts as premise (1) requires? Here are several criteria that are used to determine whether a theory is the "best" explanation for a set of facts:

1. The theory that is the best explanation should be judged best only *after all serious alternative theories have been considered*. Obviously we don't have to consider preposterous theories. But it is not always easy to draw the line between a serious and a preposterous theory.
2. Other things being equal, the theory that is the best explanation *should be consistent with our other well-established beliefs*. The words "other things being equal" are important. For many theories we accept today overthrew beliefs we once thought were well established. So if the evidence for a theory is more convincing than the evidence for a "well-established" belief, we should be willing to change that belief and accept the theory.
3. The theory that is the best explanation *should explain more kinds of facts* (including new facts it predicts that turn out to be true) than other competing theories do. In other words compared to the other theories, the best explanation explains more facts about distinct phenomena that seemed unrelated before.
4. The theory that is the best explanation *should provide more information about the mechanisms that led to the facts* than the other theories do. In other words, the best explanation will describe how the facts were brought about in greater detail than

✓ QUICK REVIEW
Darwin's argument was an inference to the best explanation, which assumes the best explanation is probably true. The best explanation: is determined after considering all serious alternatives; harmonizes with well-established beliefs; accounts for more kinds of facts; provides more information about the causal mechanisms; and is simplest. However, we can't say why best explanations are probably true.

other theories. And it will identify the specific causes, conditions, processes, and relationships that brought the facts about.

5. Other things being equal, the theory that is the best explanation *should be simpler* than the competing theories. That is, it will make fewer unsupported assumptions and refer to fewer unobservable entities (such as aliens or fairies or unseen agents). The words "other things being equal" are important. They are important because sometimes we may have to accept a very complicated theory if it is the only one that can explain all the facts.

Premise (1) of an inference to the best explanation is true, then, to the extent that the theory T that it is talking about, meets these five requirements. The better it meets requirements 1–5, the stronger the case that it is the best explanation.

Now let us look at premise (2) of an inference to the best explanation. Premise (2) says "If a theory is the best explanation for all the facts, then it is true." Is this premise correct? In other words, does a theory that provides the best explanation for a set of facts have to be true? One answer to this question was suggested by Darwin himself. He wrote: "It can hardly be supposed that a false theory would explain, in so satisfactory a manner as does the theory of natural selection, the several large classes of facts [I described]." Darwin's suggestion is similar to one made by the American philosopher Hilary Putnam. Putnam claimed that it would be "a miracle" if a theory was false yet was able to successfully explain all the facts (including the new facts predicted by the theory). But critics have pointed out that the suggestions of Darwin and Putnam are themselves based on an inference to the best explanation! Both claim that the best explanation of why theories that explain all the facts are true is because the best explanation of why they explain all the facts is that they are true! But then Darwin and Putnam are arguing in a circle. They rely on premise (2) to prove premise (2). The truth of the matter is that nobody has yet come up with an argument for premise (2) that everyone is willing to accept. We all assume premise (2) is true. We use premise (2) every day of our lives. And our most basic scientific theories rely on premise (2). But we just don't know exactly why premise (2) is true.

Since we are forced to assume that premise (2) is true, the only premise that we should worry about in an inference to the best explanation is premise (1). So long as premise (1) meets the five requirements we discussed above, then conclusion (3) will follow. So the strength of an inference to the best explanation ultimately depends on how probable premise (1) is. And that, as we said, will depend on how well it meets the five requirements above.

So, is Darwin's argument for his theory of evolution a strong one? That is, does Darwin's theory of evolution meet the five requirements of an inference to the best explanation? You must decide the answer to that large question yourself. However you answer that question, it is clear that your view of yourself, and of the kind of creature you are, ultimately depends on the answer you give.

The Existentialist Challenge

In the middle of the twentieth century, another view of human nature challenged the Traditional view. This view, called **existentialism,** holds there is no such thing as human nature because humans are whatever they make themselves. Existentialism denies any essential human nature in the traditional sense, insisting that individuals create their own nature through their free choices and actions.

The chief proponent of existentialism is Jean-Paul Sartre (1905–1980). Sartre claimed that there are no true universal statements about what human nature is. Nevertheless we can say what the human condition is. His most important claim about the human condition is that people have the freedom to create their own human nature. When we choose, nothing forces us to choose what we choose. And through the actions we choose we create what we are.

In *Existentialism and Humanism,* Sartre vigorously defends this existential view of human nature. He points out that when an artisan makes something, he knows ahead of time the nature of the object he will make. So its "essence"—its nature or what it is—is determined before it even exists. Similarly, if God is seen as an artisan that creates each person, then what a person is will be determined ahead of time by what God decides that person will be. But in the existentialist view, Sartre claims, a person's nature or "essence" is not determined ahead of time by God nor anything else. For "atheistic existentialism," this view is based on the fact that atheism denies God exists. But Sartre says there are also Christian existentialists, and they too believe that human nature is not determined ahead of time. In the view of all existentialists, Sartre says, humans first begin to exist in the world, and only after they exist do they become what they are.

The key to Sartre's view is the idea that humans, unlike things, are defined by their actions. So humans are nothing more than the sum total of what they have done. You are what you do. Since you had not yet done anything when you were first born into the world, at that point you existed but were not yet any kind of person. But as you grow up, you begin to determine what you are—what your nature is—by the actions you choose. Sartre combines these ideas with his claim that we are free. Since you are free to choose your actions, and since your actions define what you are, you alone are responsible for what you are, that is, for what you have become.

If one considers an article of manufacture as, for example, a book or a paper-knife, one sees that it has been made by an artisan who had [in mind] a conception of [what it would be]. ... Let us say, then, of the paper-knife that its essence ... precedes its existence ...

When we think of God as the creator, we are thinking of him, most of the time, as a supernatural artisan.... Thus, the concept of man in the mind of God is comparable to that of the paper-knife in the mind of the artisan: God makes man according to a procedure and a concept, exactly as the artisan manufactures a paper-knife, following a definition and a formula [he had in mind]. Thus each individual man is the realization of a certain concept that dwells in the divine understanding. ... Here, then, the essence of man [would] precede that historic existence [of a man] which we confront in experience.

Atheistic existentialism, of which I am a representative, declares ... that if God does not exist there is at least one being whose existence comes before its essence, a being which exists before it can be defined by any concept of it. That being is man. ... What do we mean by saying that existence precedes essence? We mean that man first of all exists, encounters himself, surges up in the world—and defines himself afterwards. If man as the existentialist sees him is not definable, it is because to begin with he is nothing. He will not be anything until later, and then he will be what he makes of himself. Thus, there is no human nature, because there is no God to have a concept of it. Man simply is. Not that he is simply what he conceives himself to be, but he is what he wills [himself to be]. ...

If it is true that [human] existence is prior to essence, [then] man is responsible for what he is. Thus, the first effect of existentialism is that it puts every man in possession of himself as he is, and places the entire responsibility for his existence squarely upon his own shoulders.... The doctrine I am presenting before you ... declares that there is no reality except in action. It goes further, indeed, and adds, "Man is nothing else but what he proposes, he exists only in so far as he realizes himself, he is therefore nothing else but the sum of his actions, nothing else but what his life is."[28]

MindTap To read more from Jean Paul Sartre's *Existentialism and Human Emotions,* click the link in the MindTap Reader or go to the Questia Readings folder in MindTap.

QUICK REVIEW
"Existence is prior to essence" means humans are first born (exist) and then define their nature (essence) by acting.

---

28 Jean-Paul Sartre, *Existentialism and Humanism,* trans. Philip Mairet (London: Methuen, 1949), 85.

Clearly, existentialism provides an important challenge to the Traditional view of human nature. If Sartre is correct, then there is no universal human nature shared by all people. Instead, Sartre claims, we each create our own nature. If Sartre is right, then, we cannot say that humans are defined by their rationality. Ahead of time, we cannot say what will define a person. Only the choices the person makes through his life can define what he is. Moreover, if Sartre is right, we cannot say that humans have a purpose. Humans are not made for anything. We simply exist, and each of us must decide for ourselves what purpose, if any, our existence will serve. Finally, people do not have immaterial souls that will live on after death. In Sartre's view there is no God to provide a heaven for us.

Sartre emphasizes that because we each create our own nature, we are completely responsible for what we become. But Sartre also argues that when we choose the acts that define what we become, we imply that everyone should choose them. So we are responsible not only for what we become, but for what we imply everyone should be. If we realize our responsibility, Sartre argues, we will feel anguish. And since God does not exist we are alone and it is useless to hope God will "adapt the world" to what we want. So we will also feel abandonment and despair.

> When we say man chooses his own self ... we also mean that in making this choice he also chooses all men. In fact, in creating the man that we want to be, [we] at the same time create an image of man as we think he ought to be. To choose to be this or that is to affirm at the same time the value of what we choose ... and nothing can be good for us without being good for all.
>
> Thus, our responsibility ... involves all mankind. If I am a workingman and choose to join a Christian trade-union rather than be a communist, and if by being a member I want to show that the best thing for man is resignation, that the kingdom of man is not of this world, I am not only involving my own case ..., my action has involved all humanity. ... Therefore, I am responsible for myself and for everyone else. ...
>
> This helps us understand ... words [existentialist use] such as anguish, abandonment, and despair. ...
>
> First, what is meant by anguish? ... What this means is this: the man who realizes that he is ... at the same time, choosing all mankind as well as himself, can not help escape the feeling of his total and deep responsibility. ... So every man ought to ask himself, "Am I really the kind of man who has the right to act in such a way that humanity might guide itself by my actions?" And if he does not say that to himself, he is masking his anguish.
>
> When we speak of abandonment ... we mean only that God does not exist and we have to face all the consequences of this. The existentialist is strongly opposed to a ... secular ethics which would like to abolish God ... [yet believe] that values exist all the same ... The existentialist, on the contrary, thinks it very distressing that God does not exist, because all possibility of finding values in a heaven of ideas disappeared with Him; there can no longer be an a priori Good, since there is no infinite and perfect consciousness to think it. Nowhere is it

ANALYZING THE READING

1. Sartre claims that God does not exist. His conclusion is that there can be no "concept" or "essence" or "human nature" that defines what all men are. Does Sartre's conclusion follow from his claim? Why or why not?

2. Sartre claims that each specific human being is "nothing else but the sum of his actions." Do you think this is a good way of looking at specific human beings? Why?

3. Suppose Sartre is right when he says that a specific human being is "nothing else but the sum of his actions." Does it follow that we cannot provide a definition of what human beings are in general? Can you give a general definition of human beings that can distinguish them from all other kinds of animals and objects?

4. According to Sartre, every human being "defines himself" or "makes himself" or is "what he wills." Do you think this is true? Do you think it is completely true or only partially true? Why?

written that the Good exists, that we must be honest, that we must not lie. ... Indeed, everything is permitted if God does not exist, and as a result man feels abandoned, because neither within him nor without does he find anything to cling to. ... If God does not exist, we find no values or commands to turn to which legitimize our conduct. ... We are alone, with no excuses. ...

As for despair, the term has a very simple meaning. It means that we shall confine ourselves to reckoning only with what depends upon our will. ... No God, no scheme, can adapt the world and its possibilities to what I want. When Descartes said, "You must conquer yourself rather than the world," he meant essentially the same thing.[29]

For Sartre, the most troubling thought of all is the realization that we alone are totally responsible for what we make ourselves. We can try to escape the feelings of anguish, abandonment, and despair that this realization produces by pretending that our choices have been forced on us. We have many ways of doing this. We may try to convince ourselves that outside influences have shaped our nature. Or that forces beyond our control have shaped us. Or we may pretend that our family or our genes or our environment is the cause of what we are. But Sartre claims that these are all attempts to hide the truth from ourselves. They are what Sartre called forms of "bad faith." In the end, he holds, if we are honest with ourselves, we must accept that we bear full responsibility for what we are.

A human being in Sartre's view, then, is not necessarily rational, or material, nor does she have a purpose. A person is instead a "project" that possesses a subjective life. A person is the sum, not of everything that happens to her, but of everything she has done. In the end, according to Sartre, our nature is what our choices make it. To be human is to create one's own nature.

Yet do we have the kind of control over ourselves that Sartre assumes people always have? Doesn't our unconscious mind—the unconscious motivations and desires that psychologists say operate within us without our knowledge—control much of what we are and do? For example, doesn't our unconscious mind heavily influence the choices we make and the actions we engage in? Doesn't the kind of conditioning we have received in the past shape our behavior in the present? If so, then what I am depends not so much on what I freely choose but on psychological forces I do not control. So do we really have the kind of absolute freedom to create our nature that Sartre attributes to us? Are we fully responsible for the nature we have? Are you wholly to blame for who and what you are today? Yet if you deny that you are free and responsible, are you in fact using this very denial as an excuse to escape your responsibility? Is your denial of your responsibility for yourself nothing more than a kind of dishonesty, a form of "bad faith"?

> **QUICK REVIEW**
> Bad faith is deceiving ourselves by pretending we are not free and so not responsible.

> **QUICK REVIEW**
> The self has no rational nature but is the sum total of all its actions.

> 💬 **THINKING LIKE A PHILOSOPHER**
>
> Sartre says you are ultimately responsible for all your choices and for what you are and what you will be. Do you think he's right? Do you find the idea that you alone are completely responsible for what you are and what you are troubling or freeing? Explain. Does it make you feel any anguish, abandonment, or despair? Should it? Do you experience your life as free as Sartre describes? Explain.

> **QUICK REVIEW**
> Existentialism says there is no universal human nature, no rational human nature, no purpose for human nature.

The Feminist Challenge

The most troubling challenge to the Traditional view of human nature is that it is fundamentally sexist. It is sexist because it discriminates against women. Many—but not all—feminist philosophers have raised this objection. The objection clearly

---

[29] Jean-Paul Sartre, *The Humanism of Existentialism*, trans. Bernard Frechtman in Wade Baskin, ed., *Essays in Existentialism* (Secaucus, NJ: The Citadel Press, 1965), excerpts from 37, 38, 40, 41, 45, 46, and 48.

strikes at the center of the Traditional view, and to understand it, we must go back to Plato and Aristotle.

Recall that in the Traditional view of human nature, humans are rational beings whose reason should rule over the body and its desires. Plato explains this idea in the dialogue *Phaedo*, part of which we saw earlier. In this dialogue Plato puts his own view into the mouth of Socrates:

QUICK REVIEW
Some feminists claim the Traditional view of human nature is sexist.

SOCRATES: Now when the soul and body are united the soul rules the body. Isn't it the nature of the divine to rule and the mortal to serve? And if so isn't the soul like something divine?

CEBES: Yes, Socrates.

SOCRATES: So, Cebes, mustn't we conclude that the soul most resembles something divine, immortal, intelligible, uniform, indissoluble, and unchangeable? While the body is like what is mortal, unintelligible, multiform, dissoluble, and changeable? Can anyone argue against this?

CEBES: No one could, Socrates.

SOCRATES: I say, then, that the soul, which is invisible, departs at death to a world that is, like itself, glorious, pure, and invisible, the world of the good and wise God. … She goes to a world that is divine and immortal and rational. Arriving there, the soul is secure in its happiness and is released from the error and folly of men. It is free of their fears and wild passions and all other human ills. It will forever dwell, as they say at ritual initiations, in the company of the gods. Isn't that right, Cebes?

CEBES: Yes, beyond a doubt.

SOCRATES: But the soul which has been polluted, and is impure at the time of death, and is the companion and servant of the body always, and is in love with and fascinated by the body and by the desires and pleasures of the body, until it is led to believe that the truth only exists in a bodily form, which a man may touch and see and taste, and use for the purposes of his lusts—the soul, I mean, which is accustomed to hate and fear and avoids the intellectual principle, which to the bodily eye is dark and invisible, and can be attained only by philosophy;—do you suppose that such a soul will depart pure and unalloyed?

CEBES: Impossible.

SOCRATES: Such a soul is held fast by the corporeal, which the continual association and constant care of the body have wrought into its nature.

CEBES: Very true.

SOCRATES: And this corporeal element, my friend, is heavy and weighty and earthy, and is that element of sight by which a soul is depressed and dragged down again into the visible world, because it is afraid of the invisible and of the world below—prowling about tombs and sepulchres … and these must be the souls, not of the good, but of the evil, which are compelled to wander about such places in payment of the penalty of their former evil way of life.[30]

Plato associates the soul with reason and opposes these two to the body and its earthy desires. The "pure" soul is supposed to rule over the "impure" body and

---

[30] Plato, *Phaedo, in Dialogues of Plato*, trans. Benjamin Jowett and ed. Justin D. Kaplan (New York: Simon & Schuster, 1950), 103–106.

to turn away from the "desires and pleasures of the body." If the soul controls the body and turns away from its desires and "wild passions" or emotions, it will be "good." Such a pure soul can rise up to the higher level of true knowledge and even join the gods. But if the soul becomes the "companion and servant" of its body and bodily desires and pleasures, it will become "polluted" and "evil." It is doomed to be dragged down to earth to wander in error among "tombs and sepulchres."

Although Plato thought men and women were more or less equal, his student Aristotle next made a move that would forever give the rationalistic view of human nature a sexist bias. Aristotle associated men with reason and claimed that women do not share fully in reason. Consequently, men should rule over women:

> QUICK REVIEW
> Plato said reason is superior to and should rule our desires and emotions; Aristotle then associated women with desires and emotions and men with rationality and concluded that men should rule over women.

> There are three elements of household rule, the first being the rule of the master over slaves …the second that of the father over his children, and the third that of the husband over his wife. … For the male is naturally more qualified to lead than the female, unless something unnatural happens, and the older and more complete adult is more qualified to rule than the younger and incomplete child. … For in the soul there is by nature an element that rules and also an element that is ruled; and in these elements we recognize different virtues, the virtue, to wit, of that which possesses reason, and the virtue of that which lacks reason [but which should obey reason]. It is clear, then, that the same rule holds good in other cases also, so that most things in the world by nature are rulers or are ruled. But it is in different ways that the free man rules the slave, the male rules the female, and the adult rules the child. Although in each of these there is present an appropriate share of soul, it is present in each in a different manner. For the slave, speaking generally, does not have a reasoning faculty; the woman has it but without the power to be effective; and the child has it, but in an incomplete degree.[31]

Aristotle claims that reason characterizes the essential nature of humans. But it is fully present only in adult males. Women, like children, are not fully rational. So, women should obey males, who are fully rational, just as our bodily appetites and emotions should obey reason.

Thus, from the beginning, some feminist critics say, the rationalistic view associated men with reason and women with the bodily appetites and emotions. And then that view claimed that reason must control the appetites and emotions. Reason is male and should rule, whereas feelings and desires are female and must be ruled. And, finally, reason is pure, good, and raises us to heaven and true knowledge, while bodily desires and emotions are impure, bad, and drag us down to earth and illusion.

Centuries later the religious version of the Traditional view came on the scene. And it adopted this association of reason with men and the idea that men should rule. For example, in the *Confessions*, the Christian philosopher Saint Augustine wrote the following in a prayer to God:

> Then You took man's mind, which is subject to none but you and needs to imitate no human authority, and renewed it in Your own image and likeness. You made rational action subject to the rule of the intellect, as woman is subject to man.[32]

---

[31] Aristotle, *Politics*, quoted in *Philosophy of Woman: Classical to Current Concepts*, ed. Mary Briody Mahowald (Indianapolis: Hackett, 1978), 68.

[32] Augustine, *Confessions*, quoted in Genevieve Lloyd, "The Man of Reason," in *Women, Knowledge, and Reality: Explorations in Feminist Philosophy*, ed. Ann Garry and Marilyn Pearsall (Boston: Unwin Hyman, 1989), 111–128.

Somewhat earlier, the Jewish philosopher Philo also accepted the rationalistic view of human nature. He made it part of Judaic thinking, along with its sexist bias:

> The male is more complete, more dominant than the female, closer akin to causal activity, for the female is incomplete and in subjection and belongs to the category of the passive rather than the active. So too with the two ingredients which constitute our life-principle, the rational and the irrational; the rational which belongs to mind and reason is of the masculine gender, the irrational, the province of sense, is of the feminine. Mind belongs to a genus wholly superior to sense as man is to woman.[33]

This brief look at the history of the rationalistic view of human nature clarifies the objections of feminist critics. They claim the rationalistic and the Judeo-Christian religious view based on it are both sexist. The rationalistic and the Judeo-Christian religious views of human nature are biased against women. The rationalistic view says reason is the essential characteristic of human nature. But full reason belongs only to adult males. As a result, the rationalistic view allows only men to be fully human because only men are fully rational. Women are not fully rational. Instead they are driven by their emotions and desires. And emotions and desires are "earthy," "impure," and "polluting," while reason is pure and uplifting. Moreover, the rationalistic view asserts that reason must rule. So it implies that men should rule over women.

THINKING LIKE A PHILOSOPHER

1. Describe some of the times you were treated, or saw a woman being treated, in a sexist way. What effect do you think sexist treatment has on women? On men?
2. What are some ways of thinking about women that are usually not seen as sexist but that seem sexist when examined closely?
3. The rationalistic view of human nature suggests that men are more rational and women are more emotional. Have you ever thought of men or women in this way? Do you think other people think of men and women in this way? If you did think of men and women in this way, would that necessarily be bad?

These views about reason and emotion, men and women, ruler and ruled, pure and impure, etc., matter because they affect the way we think today. Many of us today unconsciously continue to think of women as emotional and of men as rational. Many today still think that our bodily desires tempt us into evil and impurity, while reason prompts us to do what is right and pure. Many today think that while reason seeks to be objective, the emotions get in the way and lead us into being subjective. Many today think that men make better leaders than women. And today, feminist critics claim, the rationalistic view has justified the oppression of women.

The feminist claims about the rationalistic view of human nature are related to the way that the rationalist view was used to subjugate the Indian natives of the New World. As we saw earlier, when Columbus discovered the New World it was populated by millions of natives. Some Europeans declared that the natives of the New World were less rational than Europeans. They quoted Aristotle's claim that those who are less rational are "barbarians" who may be enslaved by those who are more rational. So they therefore looked upon the New World natives as "barbarians" whom they could justifiably treat like slaves.

[33] Philo, *Special Laws*, in *Philo*, vol. 1, trans. F. H. Colson and G. H. Whitaker, Loeb Classical Library (London: Heinemann, 1929), 125.

Many philosophers, however, do not accept these objections to the rationalistic and religious views of human nature. Many others, male and female, have accepted the objections but have looked for ways to get around them.

Can We Think Differently?   Are sexist views that assume the inferiority of women to men essential to the Traditional view of human nature? Can we talk about reason and emotion, body and spirit, knowledge and desire without covertly assuming sexist views? Many people continue to think of rationality as a "male" trait and emotion as a "female" trait. Some thinkers have asked: Can't we learn to think differently? Granted, many people still feel that emotion is an obstacle to the attainment of the true knowledge that reason seeks. But can't we create new ways of thinking about the emotions and the search for knowledge? Granted, many people still believe that if we are to be moral and righteous, we should restrain our bodily appetites. But can't we start to think differently about the value of our body and its appetites? And granted many religious people still feel that our bodily desires "pollute" us and prevent us from attaining eternal salvation. But can't we create new forms of religion and spirituality that look at our bodily desires from a different perspective? In short, is the sexist picture of human nature such a deep part of our way of thinking about ourselves that we can't change?

Consider a more radical proposal. Why don't we simply throw out the rationalistic view of human nature if it is sexist? Genevieve Lloyd, a feminist philosopher, argues that this is not as easy to do as it may first appear:

> It is a natural response to the discovery of unfair discrimination to affirm the positive value of what has been downgraded. But with the kind of bias we are confronting here the situation is complicated by the fact that femininity, as we have it, has been partly formed by relation to, and differentiation from, a male norm. We may, for example, want to insist against past philosophers that the sexes are equal in possession of Reason; and that women must now be admitted to full participation in its cultural manifestations. But ... this approach is fraught with difficulty.... For it seems implicitly to accept the downgrading of the excluded character traits traditionally associated with femininity, and to endorse the assumption that the only human excellences and virtues which deserve to be taken seriously are those exemplified in the range of activities and concerns that have been associated with maleness.
>
> However, alternative responses are no less beset by conceptual complexities. For example, it may seem easy to affirm the value and strengths of distinctively "feminine" traits.... Thus, it is an understandable reaction ... to stress ... the warmth of feeling as against the chillingly abstract character of Reason. But ... subtle accommodations have been incorporated into the social organization of sexual division which allow "feminine" traits and activities to be both preserved and downgraded. There has been no lack of male affirmation of the importance and attractiveness of "feminine" traits—in women—or of gallant acknowledgement of the impoverishment of male Reason. Making good the lacks in male consciousness, providing it with a necessary complementation by the "feminine," is a large part of what the suppression ... of "womankind" has been all about.[34]

Lloyd seems to be saying that one way of rejecting the rationalistic view is to insist that women have as much reason as men. Yet, she points out, insisting on this implies

QUICK REVIEW
So, the rationalistic view implies that reason is good, is male, and should rule, whereas feelings and desires are bad, are female, and should be ruled. This is sexist.

QUICK REVIEW
Insisting women are as rational as men still assumes that "male reason" is better than female desires and emotions; saying desires and emotions are as good as reason still allows that because males have reason they should rule females, who have emotions and desires.

---

[34]   Genevieve Lloyd, *The Man of Reason: "Male" and "Female" in Western Philosophy* (Minneapolis: University of Minnesota Press, 1984), 104.

that reason—the "male" trait—really is superior. A second way of rejecting the ratio-nalistic view, she suggests, is to insist that the "female" traits of feeling and emotion are as valuable as the "male" trait of reason. Yet males have always "gallantly" said that these "female" traits are valuable, Lloyd says. But this gallant admission implies that women should be content with their role in society. And their role is to provide males the feminine warmth males lack because males have only cold (but ruling!) reason.

Do the concepts that the rationalistic view developed—reason and desire, body and mind, rational and emotional—have such deep roots in us that we can't get rid of them? Do the very meanings of these words assume that women are inferior to men? When we use these notions, are we forced into seeing women as inferior to men? Is it possible for us to stop using the notions of reason and desire, body and mind, and rational and emotional? In fact, is it possible for us to reject the rational-istic view of human nature, which seems to be built into our very notions of what men and women are?

PHILOSOPHY AT THE MOVIES

Watch *Control* (2007), a dramatization of the life of Ian Curtis, lead singer for Joy Division, a highly successful post-punk band. At 19 Ian married Debbie, a girl of 18, and a year later joined the band that became Joy Division; after singing with the band for four years he committed suicide. Are the character and actions of Ian Curtis, as portrayed in this movie, consistent with the Traditional view of human nature? How would Plato use his three-part theory of the soul to explain Ian's life? What would Sartre say about the many pressures Ian felt and the choices he made? Is Sartre right?

Another movie with related themes: *24 Hour Party People* (2002).

2.3 The Mind–Body Problem: How Do Your Mind and Your Body Relate?

It's obvious to each of us that we have a mind and a body. We spend much of our time fretting and fussing over our body. We exercise to keep it healthy. We diet to keep its weight down. We comb its hair and paint its face to make it more alluring. We lift weights to inflate its muscles and jog to keep its stamina up. We adorn it with clothes and jewelry to make it aesthetically pleasing. We hire doctors to cure its illnesses.

We are each also well aware of the properties of our bodies. We know our body has a certain weight. We know it has spatial dimensions. It has a definite color, odor, and shape. It can be seen and touched and measured. In short, we know it is a material or physical entity with the properties that are characteristic of all physical objects.

Your mind, too, gets its share of attention. We study and learn to increase its knowledge. We travel to expand its experiences. We read or watch movies to keep it entertained. We spend many hours daydreaming to while its time away. We hire psychiatrists to cure it of its illnesses. And we sleep to keep it rested.

Our mind, we feel, is the source of our creativity and all deepest feelings. It is with the mind that we experience the ordinary and the unusual, feel desires and emotions, belief or doubt. It is with our mind that we feel hope, fear, love, hate, disgust, shame, pride, amusement. Strangely, and unlike the body, the features of the mind seem to have no observable color, size, or shape. It makes no sense, for example, to say that our mind's beliefs, desires, sensations, emotions, or ideas are colored. Or that they are so many inches long, or shaped like a square or a sphere. In fact, the properties of the mind, and the mind itself, seem to lack the properties that all physical bodies have.

Most puzzling of all is the most characteristic feature of the human mind: its consciousness. What is consciousness? Suppose you are sleeping, or sleepwalking, or anesthetized, or knocked out. Then, you are unconscious and have no consciousness. As you wake up in the morning, and as you gradually become aware of yourself and the world around you, as you become aware that you see your bedroom, become aware that you feel the wrinkled sheets beneath you, become aware that you smell the musty odors of your closed room, and become aware of the dry stale taste in your mouth, you are becoming conscious. Consciousness is this awareness you have of your sensing, feeling, and thinking when you are awake. For example, when I am awake and thinking, I am aware of the thoughts I am thinking; when I perceive, I am aware of my perceptions; when I feel pain, I am aware of the pain I am feeling; and in general, when I am experiencing something, I am aware of my experience. This awareness is consciousness.

Consciousness is subjective. This means, first, that it exists only to the extent that it is being experienced by someone. Consciousness is always the consciousness of someone, and it is present in that person only so long as the person experiences it. And, second, it means that I am directly aware of my own consciousness in a way that you and others are not. Because of this subjectivity, consciousness is sometimes said to have a "first-person" nature. That is, consciousness is something I am directly aware of "from the inside" in a way that you and others cannot be aware of "from the outside."

Finally, consciousness, like the other features of the mind, seems to lack all physical properties. Consciousness appears to have no weight, color, taste, mass, or physical dimensions.

In short, once you think about your mind and its mental properties, it seems to be completely different from your body and its physical properties. It seems as if the mind is not the same kind of physical object that your body is.

The idea that we consist of a mind and body that are completely different from each other has given rise to profound problems. Philosophers, like each of us, have long pondered our nature. And the feature of human nature that has most troubled them is this apparent dual or double nature of human beings. How can the mind and body be so different from each other? And what are they?

Some have rejected the idea that the mind is something completely different from its physical body. Nothing exists beyond the physical, they have argued. So somehow the conscious mind must be a part of, or a property of, the physical body and its brain. But this approach, we will see, faces some important problems. Others have simply accepted the common view that humans consist of two different kinds of things. They accept that we consist of a physical body and a nonphysical or immaterial mind. But those who accept this view also have a major problem on their hands. We will look at these problems after we look more closely at the common view that our minds are different from our bodies. We can note here, however, that the problems that surround this issue are not just problems about human nature. As we will see in the next chapter, these problems also touch on the views we have about the entire universe!

QUICK REVIEW
To many, it is obvious that humans have both a mind and a body and that they are completely different from each other.

The Dualist View of Human Nature: You Are an Immaterial Mind with a Material Body

The view that human beings have immaterial minds and material bodies is an ancient one. As we saw it is a view that many adherents of the Traditional view of human nature adopted, including Plato and Saint Augustine. But they often explained the view using metaphors, such as Plato's metaphor of the charioteer. And many of the arguments they gave to support the view that humans have immaterial minds seem weak.

The seventeenth century thinker René Descartes (1596–1650) was the first great philosopher of the modern age. He proposed a much clearer version of the view that our minds are different from our bodies. Not only was his version of the view more precise, it was also supported by arguments that seemed more convincing. In fact Descartes' version of the view set the terms of the great philosophical debate over human nature that still rages today.

Descartes lived during the great scientific revolutions of the seventeenth century. New discoveries in astronomy, physics, chemistry, and biology were shaking people's views of themselves and their place in the universe. Scholars, for example, had taught that the sun revolved around the earth. But Nicolaus Copernicus argued in 1543 that the earth revolved around the sun. Scholars had accepted the view of the Greek physician Galen that the liver continuously produced blood and pushed it out through the veins to the body. William Harvey argued in 1628 that the heart pumped the blood, and the same blood circulated repeatedly through the body. Scholars had long held that heavy bodies fall to the earth faster than light bodies as Aristotle had taught. Galileo demonstrated that heavy bodies and light bodies fall to earth at the same speed. Scholars had taught that the heavens are perfect and unchanging and planets are stars fixed on crystal spheres. With his telescope Galileo discovered that Venus was a ball with changing phases like our moon, that Jupiter had moons revolving around it, and that our own moon had mountains and craters. These and other new discoveries gave rise to major controversies and strident debates. The Church argued that many of the new claims had to be wrong because they contradicted what scriptures said. Others argued that the new claims had to be wrong because they conflicted with what Aristotle or ancient texts had said.

All these claims and counterclaims and the questioning of long-accepted theories affected Descartes. The ongoing disputes left him disillusioned with science and philosophy. While yet a young man he resolved to try to work out the truth for himself by trusting only those claims he was absolutely certain were true. To guide him in this quest he developed four "rules":

 MindTap Descartes' views concerning the relationship between the soul and the body—or the mind and the body—are still influential today. Go to MindTap to watch a video outlining Descartes' views on the mind-body problem.

THINKING LIKE A PHILOSOPHER

1. Do you think you could continue to live your everyday life if you decided "to accept nothing as true which I did not clearly recognize to be so"? What, if anything, would you have to change? As an experiment, try doing this for an hour.
2. Descartes says that he will "avoid haste and prejudice in judgments." Do you think this rule is a good idea? Do you think this is something you yourself can do? How, if at all, do you think your life would have to change if you always tried to stick to the rule that you would "avoid haste and prejudice in judgments"?

The first of these was to accept nothing as true which I did not clearly recognize to be so: that is to say, carefully to avoid haste and prejudice in judgments, and to accept in them nothing more than what was presented to my mind so clearly and distinctly that I could have no occasion to doubt it.

The second was to divide up each of the difficulties which I examined into as many parts as possible, and as seemed requisite in order that it might be resolved in the best manner possible.

The third was to carry on my reflections in due order, commencing with objects that were the most simple and easy to understand, in order to rise little by little, or by degrees, to knowledge of the most complex....

The last was in all cases to make enumerations so complete and reviews so general that I should be certain of having omitted nothing.[35]

With these rules in mind, Descartes resolved to investigate whether any ideas his mind were so clear and distinct manner he could not doubt it. On November 10, 1619, to escape the cold, Descartes shut himself up in a small room with a small wood stove. There he began thinking about what truths, if any, he might find within his own consciousness. Here is one of his accounts of what happened.

Because I wished to give myself entirely to the search after Truth, I thought that it was necessary for me to take an apparently opposite course, and to reject as absolutely false everything as to which I could imagine the least ground of doubt, in order to see if afterwards there remained anything in my belief that was entirely certain. Thus, because our senses sometimes deceive us, I wished to suppose that nothing is just as they cause us to imagine it to be; and because there are men who deceive themselves in their reasoning and fall into fallacies, even concerning the simplest matters of geometry, and judging that I was as subject to error as was any other, I rejected as false all the reasons formerly accepted by me as demonstrations. And since all the same thoughts and conceptions which we have while awake may also come to us in sleep without any of them being at that time true, I resolved to assume that everything that ever entered into my mind was no more true than the illusions of my dreams.

But immediately afterwards I noticed that while I thus wished to think all things false, it was absolutely essential that the "I" who thought this should be something, and remarking that this truth, "I think, therefore I am" was so certain and so assured that all the most extravagant suppositions brought forward by the skeptics were incapable of shaking it, I came to the conclusion that I could receive it without scruple as the first principle of the Philosophy which I was seeking.

And then, examining attentively that which I was, I saw that I could conceive that I had no body, and that there was no world nor place where I might be; but yet that I could not conceive that I did not exist. On the contrary, I saw from the very fact that I thought of doubting the truth of other things, it very evidently and certainly followed that I existed. On the other hand, if I had only ceased from thinking, even if all the rest of what I had ever imagined had really existed, I should have no reason for thinking that I existed. From that I knew that I was a substance [a thing] the whole essence or nature

ANALYZING THE READING

1. Descartes says the idea "I think, therefore I am" is so clearly true that even if he "wished to think all things false," he cannot think that this idea is false. Is Descartes right? Why? Do you agree with him?

2. Suppose that Descartes was having a dream. Could he think in his dream that something was clearly true although it was really false? Could he think in his dream that "I think therefore I am" was clearly true when in fact it was false? Why?

3. The idea "I think, therefore I am" seems to say: if (1) the activity of thinking is going on, then (2) a thing must exist that is doing the thinking. Does (2) really follow from (1)? Can an activity exist by itself even if nothing is "doing" that activity? Why?

4. Descartes says he can conceive of himself without a body, but he cannot conceive of himself without a thinking mind. He concludes he is not a body but he is a thinking mind. What assumption is Descartes making? Is it true? Why?

---

[35] René Descartes, *Discourse on Method*, in *The Philosophical Works of Descartes*, vol. 1, trans. and ed. Elizabeth S. Haldane and G. R. T. Ross (Cambridge: Cambridge University Press, 1911), 92.

of which is to think and that for its existence there is no need of any place, nor does it depend on any material thing; so that this "me," that is to say, the soul [or mind] by which I am what I am, is entirely distinct from the body, and is even more easy to know than is the latter; and even if the body did not exist, the soul [or mind] would not cease to be what it is.[36]

THINKING LIKE A PHILOSOPHER

Descartes says that he resolved that anything he thought of was just something that was happening in a dream. Can you do what Descartes says he did? That is, can you convince yourself that right now you are having a dream and that everything you are doing or thinking at this moment is just part of your dream? Is there any way that you can figure out for sure that you are not having a dream right now?

Notice two important points Descartes makes that we must return to in a later chapter. First is Descartes' famous "method of doubt." His method is to see if any truths remain after he sweeps away every belief that is the least bit doubtful. Second is his equally famous discovery of the absolutely certain truth that "I think, therefore I am." Since I am thinking I must exist. We will return to these two vitally important points and discuss them fully in Chapter 5. Here we will focus on what Descartes' discovery tells him about what he is: that is, about what his—and your—nature is.

In the passage above Descartes not only has no doubt that he exists, he is also certain that he is an immaterial mind that is distinct from his body. Descartes points out that we can conceive of ourselves as existing without a body. He then makes a crucial assumption: If we can conceive of one thing without the other, then those two things are different; if we can't, then one must be an essential part of the other. Because we can conceive of the self as not having a body, he claims, the self is not a body—that is, it is not a physical thing. On the other hand, I cannot think of myself without thinking. So, thinking is necessary for the self. Thinking is part of the **essence** (the defining characteristics that make a thing what it is) of my self. All humans, then, are selves that are immaterial thinking minds or "souls." Moreover, the existence of this immaterial thinking self does not depend on any material thing. In other words, its existence does not depend on the body. But what is the body? Descartes describes the body thus:

> **QUICK REVIEW**
> Descartes said we can think of the self without a body, so it is not a body; we cannot think of the self without thinking, which is not a material act. So, the self must be a thinking, immaterial mind with a material body.

By the body I understand all that which can be defined by a specific shape: something which can be confined in a certain place, and which can fill a given space in such a way that every other body will be excluded from it; which can be perceived either by touch, or by sight, or by hearing, or by taste, or by smell: which can be moved in many ways not, in truth, by itself, but by something different, by which it is touched.[37]

Descartes' view of human nature, then, says that a human consists of two distinct things. A human has a material body that is extended in space and an immaterial mind, or "soul," that thinks or is conscious. Philosophers call this view **dualism** because it claims that humans are made up of dual (meaning "two") substances. However, although a person has a body, the person is not his body. The person is his mind. You are your conscious thinking mind; you are not your breathing, extended, body. The two are connected, of course. If your body is injured,

---

[36] Ibid., 101. I have replaced the word *conceive* with the word *think*, and in some places the word *is* with the word *exists* to make the meaning clearer.

[37] René Descartes, *Meditations*, "Meditation ii", in *The Philosophical Works of Descartes*, vol. 1, trans. and ed. Elizabeth S. Haldane and G. R. T. Ross (Cambridge: Cambridge University Press, 1911), 151.

for example, you become aware of pain in your mind. And if your mind directs your body to stand up and walk, your body will do what your mind directs it to do. But although they interact, you are, strictly speaking, only your thinking conscious mind.

To many people, dualism seems obvious. As we noted earlier, our bodies have physical characteristics (such as color, size, and shape) that our minds do not seem to have. When people's bodies weaken, their minds can remain strong. And the mind can deteriorate even though the body remains vigorous. Such differences suggest that the mind and the body are distinct entities. Dualism is also important to many because it suggests that the self can survive death. Such a separation of the mind from the body is especially important for religions that say that after the body dies, the mind or soul can live on in an afterlife.

But this dualist view—that the mind and body are two entities each made of a different kind of stuff—raises a hard problem. How can an immaterial mind control a physical body, and how can a body made of heavy, dense, spatial matter affect an immaterial mind? If the mind is immaterial, it is not part of the physical world. How then can something like the mind reach into the physical world to control its physical body? If it did so, then the mind would somehow have to introduce new energy and force into the physical world. But scientists tell us that this is impossible because it would violate the principle of the conservation of matter and energy.

Descartes recognized the problems created by saying that we have an immaterial mind that somehow interacts with a material body. Since the mind and body obviously interact, he said, there must be some point of contact between the two. He suggested that perhaps the mind interacts with the body through the pineal gland, a tiny gland at the base of the brain. Descartes apparently believed that this gland is so tiny and so sensitive that even the immaterial mind could move it. Yet Descartes' own contemporaries ridiculed the idea that the immaterial mind and the material body interact at the pineal gland. No matter how small and sensitive the pineal gland might be, it is still a physical entity. So the problem still remains: How can a nonphysical entity produce effects in the physical world?

Descartes' theory of the mind and body, however, convinced many philosophers of his day. They therefore tried to come up with an explanation of how the mind can influence—indeed, control—the body. The philosopher Gottfried Leibniz (1646–1716) suggested that the mind and body don't interact at all, but just seem to. The mind and body run in parallel order, Leibniz said, like two synchronized clocks that keep time in lockstep with each other. So they seem to be connected yet they operate independently. When the mind issues a command, the body moves, and when the body is affected, the mind is affected also. But the two never really interact. Other philosophers said that this was as ridiculous as Descartes' pineal gland theory. For example, the philosopher Nicolas Malebranche (1638–1715) agreed with Leibniz that the immaterial mind could not interact with a material body. Still, he refused to believe that by some incredible coincidence the mind and body were perfectly synchronized. What happens instead, he said, is that God steps in to synchronize the body and the mind. When something affects the body, God obligingly comes forward to cause a corresponding feeling in the mind. When the mind commands the body to move, God again obligingly steps forward to move the body for the mind.

THINKING LIKE A PHILOSOPHER

1. Do you think of yourself as a thinking mind; that is, do you think that the real "you" is that part of you that right now is thinking, feeling, perceiving, and is aware of what is going on around you and in you? Or do you think that the real you includes your body?
2. Do you think there is an afterlife? If you do, will the real "you" survive? Would this mean the real you is your mind and not your body?

QUICK REVIEW
But how can something that has no physical dimensions act on or be acted on by something that does?

QUICK REVIEW
Leibniz agreed that mind and body can't interact but said they run in parallel order like two synchronized clocks. Malebranche also agreed that mind and body can't interact, but he said that God obligingly moves the body for the mind and affects the mind for the body.

Yet don't the contorted explanations of Descartes, Leibniz, and Malebranche suggest that dualism has gone wrong somewhere? Wouldn't it make more sense to reject dualism? This is the approach that many other philosophers have taken to the mind–body problem. Before we look at those philosophers' arguments, however, we'll look at some more critical thinking tools you can use to help you evaluate their arguments.

thinking critically • Evaluating an Argument's Premises

The arguments that Descartes, Leibniz, and Malebranche give us are interesting and perhaps valid. But even if they are valid, are they sound? That is, are the premises or reasons they give for their conclusions true? We've said several times that "You will have to decide for yourself" whether this or that claim a philosopher makes is true. But how do you do this? Are there any rules or guidelines that can help you evaluate whether a philosopher's claims are true?

In a sense there are no step-by-step procedures that will always let us determine whether a claim is true. If there were such procedures, then we could use them to answer any question we had. But obviously, it takes a lot of investigation, thinking, ingenuity, and time to discover the truth about most important questions. For example, it took centuries to discover that genetic DNA controls how our cells and bodies function. And it took almost as long to discover that the heat of the sun is produced by atomic fusion. Nevertheless, there are some guidelines that can help guide your thinking when evaluating the premises of arguments. Before you use those guidelines, however, you should make sure you understand the claim you are trying to evaluate. To check your understanding of the claim, restate it in your own words or give examples of what it is talking about. Once you are sure you understand the claim, you can use the following guidelines to help you evaluate whether it is true.

First, ask yourself whether the claim fits with your own experience. Generally speaking, your own past experience is your best source of information about the world. And it is your best starting point when evaluating a claim someone makes. But there are two questions you need to ask when you rely on your own experience to evaluate a claim. First, your experience is not a reliable source of information if your memory of what you experienced is mistaken. Nor is it reliable if your senses weren't working right when you had the experience. And it is also not reliable if you weren't being sufficiently observant at the time. So when you rely on your experience to evaluate a claim, you should ask yourself the following question. (1) Is there any reason for me to doubt the reliability of that particular experience? Second, your experience is not a reliable source of information if you are confusing *what you experienced* with a *conclusion you drew* from what you experienced or an *assumption you made* about what you experienced. For example, if I heard someone walking around in the bedroom next to mine, I may conclude or assume that it is my brother. Afterwards I might claim that I heard my brother walking around in his bedroom. But that claim about my brother would be a *conclusion* or *assumption* about what I experienced. It would be a conclusion or assumption because what I experienced were only sounds. I did not actually see or experience my brother in his bedroom. So when relying on your experience, you also need to ask the following question. (2) Is this what I actually experienced, or is this a *conclusion* or *assumption* about what I experienced? Both points (1) and (2) raise important philosophical questions about our experience. For example, is experience generally a reliable source of knowledge? And can we completely separate what we experience from conclusions and assumptions about what we experience? We will examine these questions later. For now your experience should always be your starting point when you ask whether a philosopher's premises are true.

Second, when evaluating a philosopher's claim you should ask whether the claim fits the information you accept and believe but got from someone else. Most of your information doesn't come from your own experience. Most of your information you get from others. You get your information from what friends and family tell you, from books and articles you read, from people you hear on radio or television, from what you find on the Internet. When the information you are using to evaluate a claim is from someone else, you should ask the following questions. (1) Is the source of the information known to be trustworthy? (2) Is the source an expert on the subject? (3) Are the memory, senses, and powers of observation of the source reliable? (4) Does the source have any motive to mislead?"

Third, if the claim you are evaluating is a generalization, then you should ask whether there are any counterexamples to the generalization. Most claims philosophers make, and many that others make, are generalizations. That is, they are claims about *ALL* the phenomena being discussed, or claims about what is *ALWAYS* the case. For example, we earlier saw that Aristotle claimed that *every* organ has a purpose. Generalizations are claims that say all the members of a group of things have some characteristic. This means that the generalization is false if *just one* of those things do not have the characteristic. That is, the generalization is false if there are one or more exceptions to the generalization. So, one way to determine whether a generalization is false is by checking to see if there is an exception to the generalization. Such exceptions are called counterexamples to the generalization.

Fourth, when evaluating a philosophical claim or premise, you should also ask the following question. Does it imply or require other claims that are absurd, false, impossible, or inconsistent with other well-established knowledge. For example, is it inconsistent with well-established scientific laws? We have seen that Descartes claims that humans consist of a nonphysical mind and a physical body. Descartes' claim implies that a nonphysical entity can interact with a physical entity. But such interactions, some argue, are impossible. Others claim that such interactions are inconsistent with the well-established scientific law of the conservation of matter and energy. Still others claim that such interactions require some absurd theory to explain them. It would require Descartes' pineal gland theory, or Leibniz's synchronization theory, or Malebranche's theory that God steps in and does it. So if a claim implies other claims that are absurd, false, impossible, or inconsistent with well-established knowledge, it usually should be rejected.

Finally, when evaluating a philosophical premise or claim, you should ask whether there are good arguments that support the claim, or good objections against that claim (besides those you found by using these guidelines). For example, we saw earlier that Mercer provided arguments to support the premises of his main argument. And we've seen several objections against the claims of the rationalistic view of human nature. But sometimes a philosopher does not provide evidence to support the premises of his argument. And sometimes you will not find ready-made objections to those premises. In those cases you will have to try to think up such evidence or objections on your own.

To evaluate the premise of an argument, then, begin by asking whether it is consistent with your own experience (and whether your experience is reliable). Second, ask whether it is consistent with information you believe but got from others (and whether they are reliable sources of that information). Third, if the claim is a generalization, ask yourself if there are, or you can think up, counterexamples. Fourth, ask if the claim implies other claims that are absurd, false, impossible, or inconsistent with well-established knowledge. And fifth, ask if the claim can be supported by good arguments or attacked by good objections (besides those you found earlier).

We will now look at several arguments philosophers have given to support an alternative to Descartes' views. The main alternative to Descartes' dualism is the claim that only the material body exists and that what we call the mind is in some sense reducible to this material body. We will look at several philosophers who take this "materialist" approach. We begin with Thomas Hobbes who was one of the pioneers of this approach. As we look at his arguments and those of other philosophers, you should use the guidelines we just discussed to evaluate the premises of their arguments.

The Materialist View of Human Nature:
You Are Your Physical Body

The problem with Descartes' dualism, Hobbes said, is that it says there are two things in human nature. Instead, let us say there is only one: the material body that we observe with our senses. Let us agree, he argued, that only physical or material things exist. If so, then the activities we attribute to the mind are really activities of our material body. So we should be able to explain the operations of the mind in terms of the working of the body. Thomas Hobbes was a *materialist* who felt that we can explain all human activities, including our mental activities, as working much like those of a machine:

> For seeing life is but a motion of limbs, the beginning whereof is in some principal part within; why may we not say, that all *automata* (engines that move themselves by springs and wheels as does a watch) have an artificial life? For what is the *heart,* but a *spring;* and the *nerves,* but so many *strings;* and the *joints,* but so many *wheels,* giving motion to the whole body, such as was intended by the artificer?[38]

This kind of view—that mental processes are really just physical processes—is a kind of **reductionism.** Reductionism is the idea that we can fully understand or explain one kind of reality in terms of another kind, or that one kind of reality is actually a different kind of reality. Reductionists take what seems to be one kind of thing and argue that it is really some other kind of thing. Hobbes, in particular, argues that what seem to be immaterial mental processes are really nothing more than physical processes. In other words we can reduce mental processes to physical processes. That way there is no need to postulate the existence of "immaterial substances." Instead, we acknowledge that only material things exist.

What led Hobbes to embrace materialism? In part, he accepted materialism because he felt he had shown that mental processes could be conceived as material processes. In part he accepted it because he thought that the very idea of an "immaterial substance" was a contradiction. The very word "substance," he claimed, implied something material. But Hobbes was also motivated by the many advances that science was making at his time. As we noted earlier, Copernicus, Galileo, Kepler, and others had made gigantic strides in understanding the universe. Their scientific advances seemed to be based on what they could observe with their senses and measure quantitatively. Hobbes seems to have concluded that a scientific view of the universe required accepting as real only what we can observe and measure. Because we can observe and measure only material or physical bodies, Hobbes came to his famous conclusion: "The Universe, that is the whole mass of things that are, is corporeal, that is to say body; and has the dimensions of magnitude, namely length, breadth, and depth ... and that which is not body is no part of the Universe." As we will see, Hobbes was not the only philosopher who believed that science requires a materialist view of the universe

Still, Hobbes' theory failed to convince many of his contemporaries. Although he claimed that the operations of the mind could be explained as physical processes, his explanations did not persuade everyone. Many objected that his kind of reductionism was not possible. How can a physical system, even a very complicated one, produce mental processes that seem to have no physical characteristics?

QUICK REVIEW
The materialist Hobbes said the mind could be reduced to the physical actions of a material body, so there is no need to believe that immaterial things exist. He was influenced by the science of his day.

---

[38]   Thomas Hobbes, *Hobbes's Leviathan* (Oxford: Clarendon, 1909; original work published 1651), 23.

The Mind/Brain Identity Theory of Human Nature: Your Mind Is Your Brain

If materialist views like those of Hobbes are to be acceptable, they must explain how the conscious mind is supposed to be related to the material body. A contemporary materialist view that attempts to provide such an explanation is what we now call the **identity theory** of the mind.

Several philosophers developed the identity theory including the Australian philosopher J. J. C. Smart (1920–2012). The identity theory claims that mental states like thinking or feeling a pain are identical with states of the brain. Since the brain is a physical or material organ, mental states and processes are physical states and processes. When we have a mental experience like an ache or an after-image, it is nothing more than the material brain working. The same is true of any other conscious experience, such as dreaming, hoping, and feeling. Smart emphasized that identity theory does not say that words for mental states *mean the same* as words for brain states. Instead, the theory says that science will someday *discover* which mental states are identical to which brain states. Here is how Smart explained his identity theory:

> Let me first try to state more accurately the thesis that sensations are brain processes. It is not the thesis that, for example, "after-image" or "ache" means the same as "brain process of sort X" (where "X" is replaced by a description of a certain sort of brain process). It is that, in so far as "after-image" or "ache" is a report of a process, it is a report of a process that happens to be a brain process. It follows that the thesis does not claim that sensation statements can be translated into statements about brain processes. … All it claims is that in so far as a sensation statement is a report of something, that something is in fact a brain process. Sensations are nothing over and above brain processes.[39]

MindTap To read more from J. J. C. Smart's "Sensations and Brain Processes," click the link in the MindTap Reader or go to the Questia Readings folder in MindTap.

The identity of mental states and brain states, Smart explained, is a "contingent" relationship. For example, we now know that water and H_2O are identical. But science had to discover this. In the same way, science will someday discover which brain states are identical to the mental states of desiring, seeing, feeling pain, being happy, and being sad. But just thinking about the meanings of the words, "desiring," "seeing," etc., will not reveal the brain state to which each is identical.

What reasons does Smart give to support his view that mental states are nothing more than brain processes? One reason is that he does not think that mental states are "something irreducibly psychical." That is, he does not think that mental states are some kind of special "psychical" stuff that cannot be reduced to something physical. Mental states, he thinks, must be reducible to physical processes. Why must mental states be reducible to physical processes? Because science has been so successful in reducing everything else to physical processes:

> The suggestion I wish if possible to avoid is … that to say "I have a yellowish orange after-image" is to report something irreducibly psychical. Why do I wish to resist this suggestion? Mainly because … it seems to me that science is increasingly giving us a viewpoint whereby organisms are able to be seen as physicochemical mechanisms: it seems that even the behavior of man himself will one day be explicable in mechanistic

---

[39] J. J. C. Smart, "Sensations and Brain Processes," *The Philosophical Review*, vol. 68, no. 2 (April 1959), 144–145.

1. At one point Smart argues that "states of consciousness" are physical because the opposite is "frankly unbelievable." Why is this not a good argument? Can you think of things you yourself could prove because the opposite was "frankly unbelievable"?

2. According to Smart a nonphysical entity could not arise or evolve from a physical entity. Do you agree? Why?

terms. There does seem to be, so far as science is concerned, nothing in the world but increasingly complex arrangements of physical constituents. All except for one place: in consciousness. That is, for a full description of what is going on in a man you would have to mention not only the physical processes in his tissue, glands, nervous system, and so forth, but also his states of consciousness: his visual, auditory, and tactual sensations, his aches and pains. … So sensations, states of consciousness, do seem to be the one sort of thing left outside the physicalist picture, and for various reasons I just cannot believe that this can be so. That everything should be explicable in terms of physics … except the occurrence of sensations seems to me to be frankly unbelievable.[40]

Like Hobbes, Smart believes that science requires a materialistic or "physicalist" view of the universe. Smart argues that mental processes are not material because that "seems … frankly unbelievable." Smart's argument may not seem to you to be a very good one. Why should we accept Smart's view of what is believable? But Smart provides another argument for his identity theory. Smart's other argument is based on the claim that a nonphysical property or nonphysical entity could not "suddenly arise in the course of animal evolution."

It may be asked why I should demand of a tenable philosophy of mind that it should be compatible with materialism. ….. One reason is as follows. How could a nonphysical property or entity suddenly arise in the course of animal evolution? A change in a gene is a change in a complex molecule which causes a change in the biochemistry of the cell. This may lead to changes in the shape or organization of the developing embryo. But what sort of chemical process could lead to the springing into existence of something nonphysical ? No enzyme can catalyze the production of a spook![41]

Here Smart is arguing that all human capacities evolved from the physical capacities of our animal ancestors through biochemical processes. But biochemical processes cannot produce a nonphysical thing from a physical thing. So human capacities all have to be physical.

Smart claims, then, that thinking and other activities or states of the mind are identical with processes or states of our physical brain. We do not yet know which brain state is identical with a specific mental state like feeling a pain. But he is confident that science will someday discover this.

Yet such attempts to identify conscious experiences with brain states quickly ran into problems. Consider, for example, that whereas brain states are publicly observable, our conscious experiences are not. If a surgeon exposes the brain, she can observe its brain states, such as the reaction of a ganglion. She could pinpoint the brain state's precise location, describe its color and shape, and truthfully say that anyone can literally *see* it. On the other hand, only you can have your conscious experiences. So no one else can literally see or be directly aware of the conscious experiences in your mind right now. Moreover, an experience such as thinking has no precise location, no color, and no shape. So brain

---

40   Ibid., 142–143.
41   J. J. C. Smart, "Materialism, *The Journal of Philosophy*, vol. 60, no. 22 (October 24, 1963), 660.

states and conscious experiences seem to be two very different things, with very different qualities.

The problem with identity theory is that if two things are identical, then both must have exactly the same properties. For example, George Washington is identical with the first president of the United States. So George Washington must have had exactly the same properties as the first president of the United States. We know that George Washington did have exactly the same properties that the first president of the United States had. So we can say truthfully that they are identical. But if mental activities are identical to brain processes, then brain processes must have exactly the same properties that mental activities have. But mental activities do not seem to have the properties that brain processes have. So it seems that they cannot be identical.

However, such objections have not led philosophers to abandon the search for a materialist understanding of the mind. Many remain firmly convinced that, as Smart put it, dualism is "frankly unbelievable." Objections to Smart's kind of materialism have therefore spurred efforts to find other, more defensible materialist theories of the mind.

QUICK REVIEW
Critics of Smart's analysis say that mental states have no location in space but that brain states do, and that thoughts require surroundings such as practices, agreements, and assumptions but that brain events don't. Thus, mental states are not identical to brain states.

The Behaviorist View of Human Nature: Your Mind Is How You Behave

Many philosophers have turned to another materialist view of human nature called "behaviorism." **Behaviorism** began as a school of psychology that restricted the study of humans to what can be observed—namely, their external behavior. Psychological behaviorists argued that they could not observe internal states of consciousness, so psychology should not be concerned with them. Several philosophers agreed with this idea. They argued that when explaining human nature, we should restrict ourselves to what is publicly observable: the outward physical behavior of human beings. But how, then, do we explain interior mental processes that do not seem to be physically observable, such as thinking, feeling, knowing, loving, hating, desiring, and imagining?

Behaviorist philosophers argued that it is possible to explain people's mental states in terms of their behaviors and their *dispositions* to behave in certain ways. The British philosopher Gilbert Ryle (1900–1976) was the major advocate of this behaviorist approach to the mind.

Ryle argued that Descartes' view of the mind was utterly mistaken and we must abandon it. He ridiculed Descartes' view by describing it as "the dogma of the Ghost in the Machine." Descartes' "dogma" says that minds are entities or substances just like physical bodies are entities or substances. The mind is an immaterial thing inside a physical thing. But this would mean, says Ryle, that minds and bodies belong to the same "category." That is, it would mean that both bodies and minds belong to the category of individual entities. In other words, they are both individual entities or things. But this is a "category mistake," Ryle argues. It is a mistake because the word "mind" does not refer to an individual entity; it does not refer to some kind of immaterial object. In fact, the word "mind" does not refer to any object at all. What Descartes did not realize, Ryle argued, is that words like "mind," "thought," "consciousness," or "feeling" are just labels we use for certain behaviors or dispositions to behave in certain ways. Here is how Ryle describes the "category mistake" Descartes made with his "dogma of the Ghost in the Machine":

> When two terms belong to the same category, it is proper to construct conjunctive prop-
> ositions embodying them. Thus a purchaser may say that he bought a left-hand glove
> and a right-hand glove, but not that he bought a left-hand glove, a right-hand glove and
> a pair of gloves. "She came home in a flood of tears and a sedan-chair" is a well-known
> joke based on the absurdity of conjoining terms of different types [or categories]. . . .
> Now the dogma of the Ghost in the Machine does just this. It maintains that there exist
> both bodies and minds; that there occur physical processes and mental processes; that
> there are mechanical causes of corporeal movements and mental causes of corporeal
> movements. I shall argue that these and other analogous conjunctions are absurd.[42]

Ryle is saying that statements that put "bodies" and "minds" on the same level
are "absurd." They are absurd because bodies are physical things, while minds are
not things; minds are dispositions to behave in certain ways. Ryle argued that we can
explain the mind and all mental states in terms of externally observable behaviors
and dispositions related to those behaviors. For example, "John knows what chairs
are" could be taken as meaning something like "When a chair is present, and given
certain other conditions, John is disposed to engage in certain specific behaviors
with the chair." In other words, to say that a person *knows* what a chair is, is to say
that the person is *disposed to behave* in certain ways when a chair is present (sit on it,
for example). Similarly, to say that a person *loves* someone is to say that she is *disposed
to behave* in certain ways toward that person. Or, as Ryle wrote: "To say that this
sleeper knows French, is to say that if, for example, he is ever addressed in French,
or shown any French newspaper, he responds pertinently in French, acts appropriately or translates it correctly into his own tongue." For Ryle, then, the mind is nothing more than a label for the dispositions to engage in observable behaviors that we
have. Moreover, for Ryle a disposition seems to be a person's tendency, inclination,
ability, or proneness to engage in such behaviors.

> To say a person knows something, or aspires to be something, is not to say that he is
> at a particular moment in the process of doing or undergoing anything, but that he is
> able to do certain things when the need arises, or that he is prone to do and feel certain
> things in situations of certain sorts. Abandonment of [Descartes's] two world legend
> involves the abandonment of the idea that there is a locked door and a still to be discov-
> ered key [to the mind]. Those human actions and reactions, those spoken and unspoken
> utterances, those tones of voice, facial expressions and gestures, which have always
> been the data of all the other students of men, have, after all, been the right and the
> only manifestations to study [i.e., to study thoughts, feelings, etc.]. They and they alone
> have merited but fortunately not received, the grandiose title "mental phenomena."[43]

Ryle uses a key argument to support his claim that "mental phenomena" are
just observable actions or dispositions to act. His argument is based on the idea
that we generally know when people are in pain or are thinking. But we could
never know these things if all mental states were inside minds that we could not
observe. So they must be something observable. In the following passage he uses
this argument by comparing two ways of understanding what the mental motive of
"vanity" is. The first way is to see vanity as something in a person's mind that causes
the person to boast. The second is to understand vanity as a person's disposition
to behave in ways that will make others admire or envy him. Ryle argues that the
second is correct.

---

[42] Gilbert Ryle, *The Concept of Mind* (New York: Routledge, 2009), 11.
[43] Ibid., 100, 293–294.

The present issue is this. The statement "he boasted from vanity" ought, on one view, to be construed as saying that "he boasted and the cause of his boasting was the occurrence in him of a particular feeling or impulse of vanity." On the other view, it is to be construed as saying "he boasted on meeting the stranger and his doing so satisfies the law-like proposition that whenever he finds a chance of securing the admiration and envy of others, he does whatever he thinks will produce this admiration and envy."

My ... argument in favor of the second way of construing such statements is that no one could ever know or even, usually, reasonably conjecture that the cause of someone else's overt action was the occurrence in him of a feeling. Even if the agent reported, what people never do report, that he had experienced a vanity itch just before he boasted, this would be very weak evidence that the itch caused the action, since for all we know, the cause was any one of a thousand other synchronous happenings. On this view the imputation of motives would be incapable of any direct testing and no reasonable person would put any reliance on any such imputation.[44]

> ## ANALYZING THE READING
>
> 1. According to Ryle we could not know people's thoughts, feelings, beliefs, pains, or intentions if these were inside people's minds where we could not observe them. We could not even know what people were talking about when they talked about their thoughts, feelings, beliefs, etc. But we generally know people's thoughts, feelings, etc., by observing their actions. So their thoughts, feelings, etc., must just be those actions or dispositions to engage in those actions. Do you think Ryle's argument is sound?
>
> 2. Is Ryle right when he says that we know people's thoughts, etc., by observing their actions? Is he right that we could not know people's thoughts, etc., if they were hidden inside people's minds?

Ryle's point is simple. If motives were inside minds where we could not observe them, then we could never know other people's motives. We could never know what another person meant by the word "vanity" because we could not see what he was talking about. But we do know when a person is motivated by vanity. We know a person is motivated by vanity when we observe the person behaving like vain people behave. In other words, we know people's motives, thoughts, feelings, pains, etc. by observing their actions. So mental words, Ryle concludes, must be words for observable behaviors or for dispositions to engage in observable behaviors.

Still, are all thoughts and feelings reducible to observable behavior or dispositions to engage in such behavior? Can't you keep a certain very personal thought or feeling in your mind without ever betraying it in your exterior behavior? The contemporary philosopher Hilary Putnam (1926–) has argued that it is easy to come up with examples that show behaviorism is wrong. Imagine a "superactor" who often gives a perfect imitation of the behavior of someone in pain. Behaviorism says such a "superactor" is feeling pain, even if in fact the superactor is conscious of no pain whatsoever. Or imagine a "superspartan" who endures pain without ever giving any external sign in his or her behavior of the pain the superspartan feels. Behaviorism says such a "superspartan" feels no pain even if the superspartan is conscious of excruciating pain.

> **✓ QUICK REVIEW**
> But critics like Putnam say we can have an idea in mind without any externally observable behavior.

In behaviorism, our interior consciousness has been eliminated. But there is something odd with the approach behaviorism takes. In spite of what the behaviorist says, we seem to be directly aware of what is in our consciousness. We seem to be directly aware of our thoughts, feelings, and sensations in a way that others are not directly aware of them. For example, I can directly feel a pain I have and so am directly aware of it. But you cannot feel my pain, so you cannot be aware of it like I am. Yet behaviorism says that all feelings are dispositions or behaviors that others

---

[44] Ibid., 75.

can observe. So behaviorism says others who observe my behavior should know my feelings just like I do—perhaps before I do. This seems wrong. In fact, behaviorism inspired a famous joke. Two behaviorist philosophers have just finished making love. So, the first behaviorist says to the second: "It was great for you. How was it for me?"

The problem, then, is that behaviorism reduces the mind to dispositions toward observable behaviors. So it leaves out anything about the mind that is not necessarily related to our outer behaviors. In doing this, it seems to leave out our interior conscious states.

The Functionalist View of Human Nature: Your Mind Is Like a Computer

A contemporary materialist view that grew out of behaviorism is a theory of the mind called *functionalism*. During the twentieth century, scientists and engineers made great strides in developing computers that could calculate and manipulate bits of information at an amazing speed. When we give a computer certain "inputs," such as a math problem, the computer calculates, then provides an "output," such as the answer to the problem. Many philosophers began to think that the computer could provide a useful model of the mind. Some thought the computer model suggested a way of revising behaviorism that would avoid the problems it had run into. The theory that emerged was functionalism.

Functionalism was developed by several philosophers including the Americans Hilary Putnam and Jerry Fodor (1935–), and the Australian David M. Armstrong (1926–2014). **Functionalism** holds that we can explain mental activities and mental states in terms of sensory inputs and behavioral outputs and other mental states. The inputs of the human mind are the stimulations that affect our nervous system through our senses. That is, the inputs are what we see, hear, taste, smell, etc. The outputs of the human mind are the external behaviors that result: running, walking, sitting, standing, etc. Then, we can think of a mental state such as a *belief* as a connection the brain makes between certain inputs and certain outputs. For example, suppose that when a certain man sees a dog (the input), he runs off (the output). And suppose we explain this behavior by saying that he ran "because he believes that dogs bite people." Then, we can say that the man's *belief that dogs bite people* is just something in his brain that linked his sensory input (seeing a dog) to his behavior (running away). In other words, we can explain mental states in terms of the functions they serve in the processes that connect our sensory inputs to our behavioral outputs. Here is how Armstrong explained his functionalist theory of the mind:

> What is it to have a mind? … I think the best clue … is furnished by … modern science. … One view … bids fair to become established scientific doctrine. This is the view that we can give a complete account of man in purely physico-chemical terms. … [Therefore] we must try to work out an account of the nature of mind which is compatible with the view that man is nothing but a physico-chemical mechanism. … What reason have I … for taking my stand on science? … If we consider the search for truth, in all fields, we find it is only in science that men versed in their subject can, … reach substantial agreement. … [Only] science has provided us with a method of deciding disputed questions.

ANALYZING THE READING

1. Armstrong, Smart, and Hobbes all believe that science requires the view that only physical things exist. Do you think they are right?

2. Suppose they are right and science does require the view that only physical things exist. Would that show that only physical things exist? Why?

Now there is one account of mental processes that is ... sympathetic to a materialist view of man: this is Behaviorism. ... [Behaviorism claims that] the mind is not an inner arena, it is outward act. It is clear that such a view of mind fits in very well with a completely Materialistic or Physicalist view of man. ... [But] behaviorism is a profoundly unnatural account of mental processes. If somebody speaks and acts in certain ways it is natural to speak of this speech and action as the expression of his thought. It is not at all natural to speak of his speech and action as identical with his thought. We naturally think of the thought as something quite distinct from the speech and action, something which, under suitable circumstances, brings the speech and action about...

This suggests a very interesting line of thought about the mind. ... Perhaps the Behaviorists are wrong in identifying the mind and mental occurrences with behavior, but perhaps they are right in thinking that our notion of a mind and of individual mental states is logically tied to behavior. Perhaps mind can be defined not as behavior, but rather as the inner cause of certain behavior. Thought is ... something within the person which, in suitable circumstances brings about speech. ... I believe that this is the true account ... of what we mean by a mental state.

[Moreover] we can think of perceptions as inner states or events apt for the production of certain sorts of selective behavior towards our environment. To perceive is like acquiring a key to a door ... The blind man is a man who does not acquire certain keys and, as a result, is not able to operate in his environment in the way that somebody who has his sight can operate. It seems, then, a very promising view to take of perceptions that they are inner states defined by the sorts of selective behavior that they enable the perceiver to exhibit.[45]

✓ QUICK REVIEW
Functionalists like Armstrong say mental states can be explained in terms of perceptual inputs and behavioral outputs; some mental states can be explained in terms of other mental states but ultimately must be connected to sense inputs and behavior outputs.

We said earlier that according to functionalism mental states can be explained in terms of the connections among sensory inputs, behavioral outputs, and *other mental states*. So far we have ignored what "other mental states" means. Functionalism does not say that the only function of mental states is to connect sensory inputs with behavioral outputs. The theory of functionalism claims that mental states can have the function of causing or being caused by *other mental states*. That is, functionalism holds that the function of a mental state might be to cause other mental states. For example, a pain is a mental state caused by a bodily injury. But a pain is more than that. A pain is also something that causes feelings of distress and the desire to get rid of it as well as the belief that something is wrong with one's body. Pain then is a mental state that has the function of being caused by an injury and of causing the mental states of distress, of certain desires, and of certain beliefs.

ANALYZING THE READING

Some functionalists say that anything can have a mind so long as it connects sensory inputs, mental states, and behaviors the way humans do. So could you be a functionalist and still believe you have an immaterial soul? Could you believe that the soul will survive death? Why?

For the functionalist, then, the mind is just a group of complex functions within the body and its brain. That is, the mind consists of all those complex connections that our brain makes between its sensory inputs, its mental states, and its behaviors. Many functionalists say whatever connects sensory inputs to mental states and behaviors in the same way we do has the same mental states and the same mind we do. Some functionalists (but not Armstrong) believe that it does not matter what an object is made of. So long as it connects sensory inputs, mental states, and behaviors like we do, anything can have a mind like ours. If it makes such connections, even something made of Play-Doh or a cloud of particles floating out in space could have a mind. Some functionalists, like Hilary Putnam, suggested that even immaterial creatures could have minds and mental states, if any existed.

---

45   David M. Armstrong, "The Nature of Mind," in *The Nature of Mind and Other Essays* (St. Lucia: University of Queensland Press, 1980).

But critics claim that functionalism, too, seems to leave something out. Critics argue that functionalism leaves out the inner conscious states we are directly aware of. Some critics have argued as follows: Imagine two people who experience colors differently. When one sees a red object, she has the kind of visual experience that the other person has when the other person sees a green object. The color red has the appearance to her that green has to the other person. And the color green has the appearance to her that red has to the other person. Otherwise, the two people are exactly the same. In fact, they don't even know that colors appear differently to them. How could they? Each can't get into the other's mind to see how colors appear. Now, suppose we ask them to look at some colored objects (the "input") and to sort them into different piles (the "output"). Each person will sort colors exactly like the other: Green objects will go into one pile, red ones into another. Now, functionalism says that if two people in the same environment respond with the same behaviors to the same input, those two people have the same mental state. So, functionalism says that the conscious states of the two people must be exactly the same. But this seems wrong. What one person consciously experiences is different from what the other person consciously experiences. The problem is that functionalism wants to reduce mental states to nothing more than the connections between inputs, outputs, and mental states. But all this seems to leave out what is most important to us: our inner consciousness.

QUICK REVIEW

Critics argue that if two people experience colors differently, they may link the same behavior outputs to the same sense inputs, yet they don't have the same mental states, as functionalism asserts.

From its beginnings functionalism was associated with the view that the human brain is *like* a computer. Some functionalists later went on to claim that the brain *is* a computer. It is a computer that processes inputs (our sense observations), causes certain mental states, and produces certain outputs (our behaviors). In short, we humans are sophisticated computers. Some philosophers believe that very soon real computers will be able to imitate the input-output processing of the human brain. Some have argued that when computers can process inputs and outputs like the human brain does, we will have to admit they have minds and can think. For example, the British mathematician Alan Turing (1912–1954) suggested what we now call the "Turing Test."[46] Imagine that you are in a room where there are two computer keyboards and two printers. One keyboard and a printer are connected to a computer somewhere outside the room. The other keyboard and printer are connected to a human being who is also somewhere outside the room. You do not know which keyboard and printer are connected to the computer and which are connected to the human being. You can type questions on the keyboards, which the computer or human on the other end will respond to by printing out the answer on the printer. Your job is to figure out which answers are coming from the computer and which are coming from the human being. According to Turing, when a computer is so powerful that we cannot tell the difference between its answers and the answers of a human being, that computer has a mind. That is, if the outputs a computer generates in response to its inputs are the same as those a human mind would generate, the computer has the equivalent of a human mind.

QUICK REVIEW

Turing said the mind is a computer following a program that generates certain outputs when given certain inputs. The Turing Test says that if the outputs a computer program gives to certain inputs cannot be distinguished from the outputs a human would make to the same inputs, the computer program is equivalent to the human mind.

Many computer experts, including Turing himself, have predicted that it is only a matter of time before computers pass the Turing Test. Then, we must say that those computers think and have minds. We will then know that materialism is right. For if a machine which is completely physical can have a mind, then the mind is not something nonphysical. It is the workings of a sophisticated physical contraption.

---

[46] A. M. Turing, "Computing Machinery and Intelligence," *Mind* LIX, no. 236 (1950).

Several philosophers hotly contest this computer theory of human nature. One of the most influential opponents of the theory is the American philosopher John Searle. Searle has pointed out that a computer is nothing more than a machine that follows the instructions in its program. But the instructions that a computer follows can also be followed by a human being. So, if following a certain program can produce mental states in a machine, a human following the same program should have the same mental states. However, says Searle, when a person follows a program that is supposed to give a computer certain mental states, the person will not have those states.

Searle gives a simple example of what he means. Suppose a computer had a program that let it pass the Turing Test in Chinese. Then, supposedly, the computer could think in Chinese. Now suppose that a human being, such as yourself, followed the same program the computer was using. Then, according to the Turing Test, you should now be able to think and understand Chinese. But in reality, says Searle, following a program will not put Chinese thoughts into your head:

Suppose that we write a computer program to simulate the understanding of Chinese so that, for example, if the computer is asked questions in Chinese, the program enables it to give answers in Chinese; if asked to summarize stories in Chinese, it can give such summaries; if asked questions about the stories it has been given, it will answer such questions.

Now suppose that I, who understand no Chinese at all and can't even distinguish Chinese symbols from some other kinds of symbols, am locked in a room with a number of cardboard boxes full of Chinese symbols. Suppose that I am given a book of rules in English that instruct me how to match these Chinese symbols with each other. The rules say such things as that the "squiggle-squiggle" sign is to be followed by the "squoggle-squoggle" sign. Suppose that people outside the room pass in more Chinese symbols and that following the instructions in the book I pass Chinese symbols back to them. Suppose that unknown to me the people who pass me the symbols call them "questions" and the book of instructions that I work from they call "the program." The symbols I give back to them they call "answers to the questions" and me they call "the computer." Suppose that after a while the writers of my program get so good at writing programs and I get so good at manipulating the symbols that my answers are indistinguishable from those of native Chinese speakers. I can then pass the Turing test for understanding Chinese. But all the same I still don't understand a word of Chinese. And neither does any other digital computer because all the computer has is what I have: a formal program that attaches no meaning, interpretation, or content to any of the symbols.[47]

ANALYZING THE READING

1. Searle claims that inside his "Chinese room," with his program and his symbols, he would not understand Chinese. So a computer with its program and symbols could not understand Chinese. But critics say that the room as a whole (with Searle, program, and symbols inside it) does understand Chinese. In the same way, a computer as a whole could understand Chinese. Who do you think is right, Searle or his critics?

2. How does Searle's "Chinese room" example show that there is a problem with the Turing Test?

QUICK REVIEW

Searle objects that a computer following a program is not conscious. His "Chinese Room" example is a person in a room who follows a program that outputs the right Chinese characters when given certain Chinese inputs. This passes the Turing Test, yet the person is not conscious of knowing Chinese.

Searle claims his argument shows that human minds have something a computer following a program does not have. What does the computer lack? Consciousness. Consciousness, argues Searle, is essential to the human mind. And a computer following a program does not have consciousness.

Even so, Searle is not a dualist. Nor does he think that humans have nonphysical minds. Searle claims that humans are physical creatures in whom only physical, chemical, and biological processes occur. These processes, he claims, cause or produce all our mental states or activities. These mental states or activities themselves are not reducible to physical things. But what produces them—namely, our brain—is a physical thing.

---

[47] John Searle, "The Myth of the Computer," *The New York Review of Books*, vol. 29, no. 7, April 29, 1982.

Eliminative Materialism: You Have No Mind

The identity theory, behaviorism, and functionalism have all encountered difficulties. These have led philosophers to look for other ways of dealing with the problem of the mind. Some have adopted a view called "eliminative materialism." They claim that the everyday commonsense views we have about the mind are profoundly mistaken. Moreover, the ordinary words we use to talk about our minds—"desire," "belief," "fear," "intention"—do not refer to anything real. Paul Churchland, for example, calls our ordinary views about human minds "folk psychology." "Folk psychology," he argues, is an antiquated "theory" of the mind. This antiquated theory uses terms like "desire," "belief," etc. The theory also includes several rough "laws." For example, our folk psychology includes the law that when a person fears that something will happen, he will feel the desire that it not happen. And if a person hopes that something will happen, then he will feel pleased if it does happen. According to Churchland, this folk psychology theory "is a radically inadequate account of our internal activities."[48]

Eliminative materialism is the thesis that our commonsense conception of psychological phenomena constitutes a radically false theory, a theory so fundamentally defective that ... [it] will eventually be displaced, rather than smoothly reduced, by completed neuroscience.

The average person is able to explain, and even predict, the behavior of other persons with a facility and success that is remarkable. Such explanations and predictions standardly make reference to desires, beliefs, fears, intentions, perceptions, and [other mental states] ... Each of us understands others, as well as we do, because we share a tacit command of an integrated body of lore concerning the law-like relations holding among external circumstances, internal states [like beliefs and intentions], and overt behavior. Given its nature and functions, this body of lore may quite aptly be called "folk psychology." [FP]

When one centers one's attention ... on what FP ... cannot explain or fails even to address, one discovers that there is a very great deal. As examples of central and important mental phenomena that remain largely or wholly mysterious within the framework of FP, consider the nature and dynamics of mental illness, the faculty of creative imagination, or the ground of intelligence differences between individuals. Consider our utter ignorance of the nature and psychological functions of sleep, ... Reflect on the common ability to catch an outfield fly ball on the run, or hit a moving car with a snowball. ... Consider the rich variety of perceptual illusions. ... Or consider the miracle of memory .... On these and many other mental phenomena, FP sheds negligible light.

FP's explanatory impotence and long stagnation inspire little faith that its categories will find themselves neatly reflected in the framework of neuroscience. On the contrary, one is reminded of how alchemy must have looked as elemental chemistry was taking form, how Aristotelian cosmology must have looked as classical

ANALYZING THE READING

1. According to Churchland our ordinary everyday way of talking about our desires, beliefs, fears, intentions, etc., is really a "theory of the mind." So it must be judged by the standards we use to judge any scientific theory. By those standards, he concludes, it is a "radically false" theory so we have to eliminate it. Do you think that our ordinary way of talking about our desires, beliefs, etc. is really a "theory"? Do you agree it is a false theory?

2. Suppose Churchland is right and it is a theory. Does the fact that it does not explain mental illness, creativity, intelligence, sleep, etc., show that it must be a "radically false" theory? Why?

---

[48]   Paul Churchland, "Eliminative Materialism and the Propositional Attitudes," *Journal of Philosophy*, vol. 78 (1981).

mechanics was being articulated, or how the vitalist conception of life must have looked as organic chemistry marched forward. ... What we must say is that FP suffers explanatory failures on an epic scale, that it has been stagnant for at least twenty-five centuries, and that its categories appear (so far) to be incommensurable with ... the categories of the physical science whose long-term claim to explain human behavior seems undeniable. Any theory that meets this description must be allowed a serious candidate for outright elimination.

For the eliminative materialist the folk psychology concepts of desires, beliefs, and intentions are like the ancient concept of demons. Folk theories about demon possession were once used to explain mental illness. But modern science has found other explanations for mental illness. Today's science-based theories of mental illness have eliminated the notion of demons, and most people today no longer believe that demons exist.

The eliminative materialist claims that advances of science will eliminate the concepts of desires, beliefs, and intentions just like demons have been eliminated. When that happens, folk psychology will be replaced with a better scientific theory based on neuroscience, a theory that no longer refers to desires, beliefs, and intentions. According to William Ramsey and others, the eliminative materialist is suggesting that mental states and the mind as we ordinarily talk about them do not really exist. And future science will allow us to eliminate such notions from our scientific theories.

Eliminative materialism does seems a bit extreme to many. One critic, Jerry Fodor, has said that "if commonsense psychology were to collapse, that would be, beyond comparison, the greatest intellectual catastrophe in the history of our species." Other critics argue that eliminative materialism denies what we seem to experience directly. We seem directly aware of our desires, beliefs, intentions, and other conscious states. How can they not be real?

Some critics of eliminative materialism have argued that if eliminative materialism were true, then no one could believe it is true. The philosopher, Lynn Baker, wrote: "Obviously, if the common-sense conception [of belief] is eliminated, no one is justified in believing anything; indeed, no one believes anything, justifiably or not."[49] Other critics have argued that the eliminative materialist herself relies on the mental states she says are not real. The eliminative materialist asserts that her claims are true. But a person cannot genuinely assert something unless the person believes it. Therefore the eliminative materialist has to believe what she asserts. So the eliminative materialist has to rely on beliefs when she asserts her claims. But if she relies on beliefs, then she has to assume beliefs are real. So the eliminative materialist is involved in a kind of contradiction: She asserts that beliefs are not real, yet in making that assertion she assumes that beliefs are real. So, the critics conclude, the eliminative materialist must be wrong.

The New Dualism: Your Mind Has Nonphysical Properties

The difficulties that have plagued materialist views of human nature have prompted some philosophers to return to dualism. But this new dualism is not quite the dualism of Descartes. The new dualists do not hold that there are two kinds of

---

[49] Lynne Rudder Baker, "Cognitive Suicide," in John Heil, ed., *Philosophy of Mind: A Guide and Anthology* (Oxford: Oxford University Press, 2004), 402.

substances—that is, two kinds of entities or things—in the universe. Instead, they hold that there are two different kinds of *properties* in the universe. For example, the American philosopher David J. Chalmers is a kind of dualist. In his book *The Conscious Mind,* he writes the following:

> [M]aterialism is false: there are features of the world over and above [its] physical features.... The character of our world is not exhausted by the character supplied by the physical facts; there is an extra character due to the presence of consciousness. This failure of materialism leads to a kind of dualism.... The arguments do not lead us to a dualism such as that of Descartes, with a separate realm of mental substance that exerts its own influence on physical processes.... The dualism implied here is instead a kind of property dualism: conscious experience involves properties of an individual that are not entailed by the physical properties of that individual, although they may depend lawfully on those properties.[50]

Chalmers argues for these claims by saying that we can conceive of a world that is physically identical to ours but whose people lack consciousness. Such a world would contain "zombies" that look and act exactly like we look and act in our world. But those zombies would not be conscious. Clearly we can conceive or imagine such a zombie world, Chalmers claims. So a zombie world physically identical to ours but without consciousness is at least possible. But if consciousness is a physical feature of our world, then a world that contains all the physical features of our world would have to contain consciousness. Yet it is possible for a zombie world to contain all the physical features of our world without containing consciousness. So consciousness is not a physical feature of our world. In other words, consciousness must be a nonphysical property of our world.

QUICK REVIEW
Critics say that eliminative materialism denies the existence of what we all know we experience, and so gets rid of the very thing that has to be explained.

In a way, we have come full circle. Most philosophers are not willing to return to Descartes' idea that the mind is a special kind of nonphysical substance. Yet the various materialist views of human nature appear to leave out what seems familiar to us: our consciousness. This has now led philosophers like Chalmers to the view that although there are no nonphysical substances, there are nonphysical properties. Interestingly, Chalmers uses an argument that is similar to Descartes'. Descartes argued that our mind is not a physical body because we can conceive of our mind existing without a physical body. Chalmers argues that consciousness is not a physical property because we can conceive a world that is physically exactly like ours but without consciousness.

So, is the mind something unique that cannot be reduced to something physical? Does consciousness reveal that the mind is some kind of immaterial stuff? Or does science require that we embrace the view that the mind is material, a kind of process in the brain? Or is the whole idea of a mind based on a false folk psychology we must eliminate?

The answers to these questions have tremendous implications. If the mind is a physical thing, or a physical feature of the world, then you and I are wholly material. There is no spiritual realm. We have no souls. We do not survive death.

But perhaps we are immaterial minds with material bodies. Perhaps there is a spiritual realm and we will survive death as conscious selves? But then how do mind and body relate? How can my weightless, intangible, unobservable, immaterial consciousness affect my heavy, solid, observable, physical body?

---

50   David Chalmers, *The Conscious Mind* (New York: Oxford University Press, 1996), 123, 124, 125.

PHILOSOPHY AT THE MOVIES

Watch *Chappie* (2015) in which the maker of a robot named "Chappie" enables it to become conscious and to feel and think; Chappie eventually transfers the consciousness of a human being into a robot. What would the dualist, the materialist, the identity theorist, the behaviorist, the functionalist, and computer views each say both about Chappie and the transfer of human consciousness into a robot? Do you agree with Roger Ebert, a movie critic who once said of a robot in a movie that since it is a machine "it does not genuinely love. It genuinely only seems to love. We are expert at projecting human emotions into non-human subjects, from animals to clouds to computer games, but the emotions reside only in our minds"? How would the behaviorist and functionalist answer Ebert?

Other movies with similar themes: *Transcendence* (2014); *Artificial Intelligence: A.I.* (2001); *I, Robot* (2004); *Bicentennial Man* (1999); *Blade Runner* (1982).

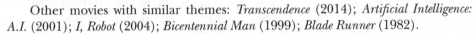

2.4 Is There an Enduring Self?

The Traditional Western view of human nature makes an assumption that may seem so obvious to you that you feel it would be foolhardy to question it. This view assumes that you are today the same person you were earlier in your life. In other words, it assumes that we humans are selves that endure through time. This simple obvious "fact" has enormous and profound consequences for you. Yet, as we see when we explore this assumption, it is not as obvious as it initially appears.

Consider, first, how obvious it seems that you are now the same self you were yesterday. Of course you have changed a bit. You're a day older. Maybe you weigh a bit more than you did yesterday. Maybe you've lost some of your tan. Your hair might be combed differently. And, no doubt, you're not wearing the same clothes. Yet though you've changed in these ways, you can't say you're not basically the same person you were yesterday. In fact, you're going to insist that you are the same person today that you were yesterday. For example, suppose that yesterday you promised a friend that today you'd go to the movies with her. Then, it wouldn't make sense for you to say: "It wasn't *me* who made that promise. It was the person I was yesterday who made the promise. But today I'm not *that* person. So *I'm* not the one who has to keep that promise!" Wouldn't you admit, instead, that, yes, you are today the same person you were yesterday?

We each carry with us, then, this belief that we remain the same person—one and the same self—throughout our lives. And we remain the same person even though we may change in many small and many large and dramatic ways. When you were born, for example, you were only one and a half feet tall, weighed only eight pounds, and had no hair. Now you are five and a half feet tall, weigh one hundred and sixty pounds, and have hair over many parts of your body. When you were born, you knew nothing. Now you are a brilliant brain surgeon. Yet for all these changes, you are still the same person.

This continuity of yourself through time is a basic part of your nature as a human being. In fact, maybe it is the most important part of your human nature. Think of how our lives would fall apart if we did not remain the same person from one moment to the next. No job or task or project would ever be completed because the person who began it yesterday would not be here today to finish it. You could not have any personal relationships because the person you liked and loved yesterday would not be here for you today. Nor would you be here today for the person who loved you yesterday. There could be no personal commitments because the person who committed herself yesterday would not be the same person today. You could have no personal history, no full story of your life. Your life would not be the life of one continuous person through the years. Instead it would consist of many different lives of many different persons, each succeeding the other for a brief period of time. Almost everything about yourself, everything about what you think you are, everything about who you think you are, everything you are trying to do, everything you plan or have planned for yourself—all these depend on your being a self that endures and remains the same self through time.

Yet sometimes people say that this or that person has not remained the same person through time, and we accept it. For example, suppose that Susan, a good friend of yours, has Alzheimer's disease. Or suppose she was in a terrible accident that caused some serious brain damage. As a result, her personality has changed. She used to like going for walks, but now she doesn't. She used to talk rapidly, but now she talks slowly. She used to joke a lot, but now she tends to be serious and quiet. Suppose that she also has complete amnesia and no longer remembers anything before the accident (or before she was afflicted with Alzheimer's). She does not remember who she was, who you or her other friends or family members are, what her life was like, where she lived, what her name was. Then, you might want to say, "Susan isn't the same person she used to be."

Still, these are unusual cases. There are more normal situations in which we are still willing to take someone's word that he is not the same person he used to be. For example, consider when people have changed so much that we are willing to say that they are no longer the same people they used to be. Suppose that your parents, John and Lisa, have been married for twenty years and have two teenage children—you and your sister. Then, one day you hear your mom talking to your dad: "John, I'm leaving you and the kids. I just don't love you anymore, and I don't think I have any feelings for the children. When we got married, I probably loved you, and maybe wanted to be a mother. But now I want out." To this, your dad responds in anguish that your mother can't leave him. When she married him, he pleads, she promised she would stay with him "till death do us part." But to all this, your mother answers: "John, you aren't the person I married. And I'm not the person you married. I was young and naive and dumb when we married. But since then I've come to realize what I really want, and figured out who I really am. I've grown up and changed. You've changed, too. You used to like to do new things all the time; you used to like to go out dancing with me; you used to be energetic, young, and exciting. Now look at you! You've got a beer belly, you sit around all evening watching television. And we never go anywhere. So, I don't feel I have to stay tied down by a commitment two other people made." True to her word, your mom abandons the three of you and starts a new life as the new person she's become.

The fact that we change raises another interesting question: Do we ever truly remain the same person? Obviously, we change enormously as we go through life. In fact, doesn't everything about us eventually change completely? How, then, can we say that most of us, most of the time, remain the same person?

THINKING LIKE A PHILOSOPHER

Have you ever known anyone who changed so much that you felt he or she was no longer the same person? Have you known someone as a child or young boy or girl, then not seen them for 10 or 15 years until they were a grown man or woman? Have you felt that they had changed so much that you could say they were not the same person you once knew?

The ancient Greek philosopher Plato was also puzzled by how we could remain the same person when everything about us changes. In his dialogue *The Symposium*, he gives a sympathetic account of the views of the philosopher Diotima. She argued, he says, that people do not remain the same person as time passes, so they "long for immortality":

> Although we speak of an individual as being the same so long as he continues to exist in the same form, and therefore assume that a man is the same person in his old age as in his infancy, yet although we call him the same, every bit of him is different, and every day he is becoming a new man, while the old man is ceasing to exist, as you can see from his hair, his flesh, his bones, his blood, and all the rest of his body. And not only his body, for the same thing happens to his soul. And neither his manners, nor his dispositions, nor his thoughts, nor his desires, nor his pleasures, nor his sufferings, nor his fears are the same throughout his life, for some of them grow, while others disappear.... Thus, unlike the gods, a mortal creature cannot remain the same throughout eternity; it can only leave behind new life to fill the vacancy that is left as it passes away.... And so it is no wonder that every creature prizes its own offspring, since everything is inspired by this love, this passion for immortality.[51]

Obviously, we do change significantly as we go through our lives. How, then, can anyone ever say that he or she has remained the same person? In what sense am I today the same person I was when I was born? Philosophers call this the "problem of personal identity." What makes a person be the same person from one moment to the next?

Perhaps what makes you the same person today that you were ten years ago is your body. Many philosophers have suggested as much. Even the ancient philosopher Diotima suggests in the passage above that "we speak of an individual as being the same as long as he continues to exist in the same form." It is true that the body changes dramatically as we grow older. Cells in different parts of the body die, and new ones are born. Yet the body never changes completely from one day to the next. Perhaps what makes us the same person today that we were ten years ago, then, is this bodily continuity between each succeeding period of our life. I am the person I was when I was born because during each day of my life, most of my body continues the same as it was the previous day. And most of it continues the same into the next succeeding day. Our body is like a ship sailing on the ocean, a ship made up of hundreds of wooden boards. If each day we remove one or two of the boards and replace them with new ones, eventually we will change all of the boards that make up the ship. Still, because most of the boards remain the same from one day to the next, we say it is the same ship from the beginning to the end of its voyage.

Moreover, think about how often we use a person's body to establish that a certain person today is the same as a person who did something earlier. For example, suppose that some person committed a crime. Suppose that at the scene of the crime the person's body left fingerprints, blood, and hair. Suppose that a hidden camera took pictures and that someone witnessed the crime from a distance. Afterward, the authorities link all this evidence to your body. The fingerprints match those of your body. The blood and hair match those of your body. The pictures are of your body. And the witness points to your body as that of the criminal. Wouldn't

---

[51] Plato, *Symposium*, trans. Michael Joyce, in *The Collected Dialogues of Plato*, ed. Edith Hamilton and Huntington Cairns (Princeton, NJ: Princeton University Press, 1961), 559–560.

✅ QUICK REVIEW

Some philosophers say that what makes us the same person today that we were ten years ago is the continuity of our body.

✅ QUICK REVIEW

But critics point out that sometimes we say that a person with brain damage has the same bodily continuity but is not the same person as before.

✅ QUICK REVIEW

Also, if bodily continuity was required to make a person the same from one moment to another, then the idea of life after death should be incomprehensible.

we decide that you and the person who earlier committed the crime are one and the same? Doesn't this show that bodily continuity is what makes you now the same person you were earlier?

However, there are many problems with the view that bodily continuity is what makes us remain the same person from one day to the next. First, if bodily continuity makes us the same person throughout our lives, then we could never become totally new persons. We would have to say that people with total amnesia or Alzheimer's disease are "really" still the same persons they always were. We would have to say that the woman who wants to abandon her marriage and family commitments because she feels that she is no longer the same person is mistaken. The woman is "really" still the same person she always was. Yet in at least some of these cases we believe that a person may no longer be the person she used to be even though she has the same body. So, perhaps bodily continuity is not what makes a person remain the same person from one moment to the next.

Consider, second, that if bodily continuity makes us remain the same person from one moment to the next, then our ideas about a life after death should not make any sense. For example, some religions claim that after the death of the body, a person will continue to live in some kind of "afterlife." Such claims may be false. Nevertheless, even if they are false, they seem to make sense. That is, we seem to be able to understand or at least imagine the possibility they describe, even if we do not think that it will really happen. Yet if bodily continuity is what makes us remain the same persons, such claims should not make sense. We should not even be able to understand the possibility they describe. For if bodily continuity makes us remain the same person, how could we even understand what it means to say that a person remains the same where there is no bodily continuity? Because such claims at least make sense, bodily continuity is not what makes us remain the same person from one moment to the next.

Consider, third, a kind of "thought experiment." Imagine a brilliant but mad brain surgeon who kidnaps Manny, a man, and his best female friend, Maryann. In his secret laboratory, the mad surgeon succeeds in extracting Manny's brain and implanting it inside Maryann's skull. And he implants her brain into Manny's skull. When Manny awakes from the operation, he finds himself "in" Maryann's body. He looks at the body lying on the bed next to him and is horrified to discover himself looking at what was previously his own body. Yet when that body—or the person "in" that body—speaks, he/she identifies himself/herself as Maryann and is just as horrified to find himself/herself with this new body.

ANALYZING THE READING

1. Would a materialist have to say that in some way bodily continuity is what makes us remain the same person from one moment to the next?

2. Could a materialist answer the criticisms of the view that bodily continuity is what makes us remain the same person from one moment to the next? If so, how? If not, why not?

This thought experiment is fictional, of course. But the question we need to ask is this: What do the ideas you and I have about what makes a person remain the same person over time say about this fictional example? Wouldn't we say that the person Manny used to be is now the person in Maryann's body? Wouldn't we say that the person Maryann used to be is now in Manny's body? But if so, then bodily continuity is not what makes a person at one time the same as a person at another time. For in this imaginary case, Manny and Maryann's bodies continue to be the same, yet we say the person "in" the body is not the same. There is something else, something "in" the body that makes a person continue to be the same person even if his or her body changes completely.

Such considerations have led some philosophers to conclude that what makes a person remain the same person over time is not the body. Instead, there is something

✅ QUICK REVIEW

In thought experiments where a mind is put in a new body, we say the body is now the person whose mind was transferred, not the person whose body was used. So, bodily continuity does not make someone the same person over time.

"in" the body—an immaterial "soul" or "mind"—that remains the same even as the body changes.

The Soul Is the Enduring Self

The Traditional Western view says that in each living human body is a soul. This soul is not made out of physical stuff like the body. Instead, the soul is "immaterial" or spiritual. This soul, in fact, is the self: the "me" who lives inside my body. This soul remains the same as the body changes. Yet as long as the soul remains in my body, I remain the same person.

René Descartes characterized this view of the enduring self. He wrote that the self is a "thinking thing" and that if "I should wholly cease to think, then I should at the same time altogether cease to be." For Descartes, it is the continuity of the thinking mind or soul that makes a person endure as the same person over time. Here is how he puts it in the *Meditations:*

> Thinking is another attribute of the soul; and here I discover what properly belongs to myself. This alone is inseparable from me. I am—I exist: this is certain; but how often? As often as I think; for perhaps it would even happen, if I should wholly cease to think, that I should at the same time altogether cease to be.[52]

Descartes implies that it is the continuity of his thinking mind that makes him remain the same person "as often as" he exists. If his thinking mind or thinking soul did not continue to be the same, then "he" would no longer continue even to exist.

This Traditional view—that the soul or mind is what makes a person continue to be the same person through time—makes life after death understandable. Because a person is a nonphysical mind or soul, the person can continue to exist after the body dies. The Traditional view also accounts for the fact that we can imagine someone waking up with a different body, as in our "mad surgeon" mind experiment. In such cases, the mind has been transferred to a different body. Since the person is the mind, the person continues but in a different body.

Yet there are also many problems with Descartes' view. For example, how are we supposed to know that a person's mind continues to be the same over time? For instance, I know that you today are the same person you were when I talked with you yesterday. Nevertheless, I certainly do not see or perceive your mind or soul. So, I know you are the same person today that you were yesterday without observing your mind or soul. This seems to suggest that it is not your soul or mind that makes you the same.

Consciousness as the Source of the Enduring Self

The English philosopher John Locke (1632–1704) also objected to Descartes' view that it is people's immaterial souls or spirits that make them the same person over time:

> Let anyone reflect upon himself, and conclude that he has in himself an immaterial spirit, which is that which thinks in him, and, in the constant change of his body keeps him the same, and is that which he calls himself. Let him also suppose it to be the same soul that was in Nestor or Thersites at the siege of Troy. (For souls being as far as we

---

[52] Descartes, *Meditations*, 151–152.

know anything of them, in their nature indifferent to any parcel of matter, the supposition has no apparent absurdity in it.) ... But [suppose] he now ... [has] no consciousness of any of the actions of Nestor or Thersites. Does or can he conceive himself the same person with either of them? Can he be concerned in either of their actions? Attribute them to himself or think them his own? [53]

Locke here is suggesting another "thought experiment." Suppose that people do have immaterial souls. And suppose that the soul of someone who lived a long time ago named "Nestor" (or "Thersites") somehow got into the body of someone living today. Then, that person living today should be the same as the person Nestor who lived long ago. But suppose that the person is not conscious of being Nestor. He has no awareness of himself as Nestor. Then, claims Locke, the person would not think he was the same person as Nestor, even if he has the same soul that Nestor had.

Locke concludes that what makes a person at one time the same person later is not that the person has the same immaterial spirit. Instead, suggests Locke, what makes a person at one time the same as a person at another time is his *consciousness*. By consciousness Locke means a person's awareness. Locke thinks that it is the continuity of "consciousness" that makes me today the same person I was yesterday. Here is what he says in *An Essay Concerning Human Understanding*:

Since consciousness always accompanies thinking, and it is that which makes every one to be what he calls "self," in this alone consists personal identity, i.e. the sameness of a rational being. And as far as this consciousness can be extended backwards to any past action or thought, so far reaches the identity of that person; it is the same self now it was then. ... If the same Socrates waking and sleeping do not partake of the same consciousness, Socrates waking and sleeping is not the same person. And to punish Socrates waking for what sleeping Socrates thought, and waking Socrates was never conscious of, would be no more right, than to punish one twin for what his brother-twin did.[54]

> **QUICK REVIEW**
> Locke proposed that what makes a person remain the same person from one time to another is her memory of those times.

Locke's view is straightforward. What makes me be the same person I was ten years ago is that I am conscious of being that person ten years ago. My consciousness of my experiences of the past is what makes me today the same person I was then.

Locke's view has seemed correct to many people. Consider the example of a woman who has a serious automobile accident. Years later a friend finds her living in a town somewhere. She is not conscious of any experiences before the accident. A man who says he is her husband shows up at her door. He has many pictures and witnesses to prove that this woman's body, at least, is the same as the body of the woman to whom he was married. After talking with her, the man feels that her very soul is that of the woman he once married. She has the same mannerisms, the same voice, the same character, the same desires, likes, dislikes, values, and attitudes. Because he is now convinced that he was once married to this woman, he says she must return with him now and again live with him as his wife. But must she go with him? Wouldn't we

ANALYZING THE READING

1. Locke objects to Descartes' view that the soul or mind is what makes a person the same person from one moment to the next. Instead, Locke says, it is "consciousness" that makes a person the same person from one moment to the next. Do you think there is a real difference between Descartes' view and Locke's view? Is there a difference between a person's mind and the person's consciousness?

2. How do you think that Descartes might answer Locke's "Nestor" objection?

---

[53] Locke, *An Essay Concerning Human Understanding*, (Oxford: Clarendon Press, 1894), bk. 2, ch. 27, sec. 14.
[54] Ibid.

want to say that this woman is no longer the same person as the one who was once married to this man? Wouldn't we say this even if she has the same body and even if, somehow, we know she has the same soul? Wouldn't we want to say that if she has no consciousness of being the man's wife, then she is now simply no longer that same person?

Or take the case of a man whom police accuse of robbing a bank. Suppose that he honestly has no awareness of ever having done so. He remembers all events on the day before the robbery. But he has no consciousness of himself robbing a bank the next day, or of planning to rob a bank, or of ever even considering robbing a bank. Then, should police hold him responsible for robbing the bank? Many of us would say no: A person who has no awareness of ever doing something cannot be responsible for doing that thing.

Yet there are some troubling objections to Locke's view. For example, the British philosopher Thomas Reid (1710–1796) suggested that Locke's view produces contradictions.[55] Suppose that Tom is now 30. Suppose that when Tom was 20, he used to be conscious of many things that happened to him when he was 10. So, in Locke's view, Tom at age 10 is the same person as Tom at age 20. Suppose also that Tom, now in his 30s, is aware of many things that happened to him when he was 20. So, in Locke's view, Tom at age 20 is the same person as Tom at age 30. But then in Locke's view, because Tom at age 10 is the same person as Tom at age 20, and Tom at age 20 is the same person as Tom at age 30, it follows that Tom at age 10 is the same person as Tom at age 30. Yet suppose, finally, that Tom at age 30 no longer has any awareness of himself as a boy of 10. Then, by Locke's view, Tom at age 10 is not the same person as Tom at age 30. So, we have a contradiction! In Locke's view, Tom at age 10 is the same person as Tom at age 30. At the same time, in Locke's view, Tom at age 10 is not the same person as Tom at age 30—a contradiction.

There are other problems with Locke's idea. For example, what about the fact that I am no longer conscious of everything that I ever did? There are many activities from my earlier life that I have just forgotten. Does this mean that some "other" person did those things? And what about the insane person who "remembers" that he was once Napoleon? Does this mean that he must be the same person as Napoleon because he is conscious of having been Napoleon?

If the body, the soul, and consciousness do not make a person the same person he or she was in the past, what does? Some philosophers have suggested that there is a mistaken assumption in this question. The mistaken assumption is the assumption with which we began. We assumed that there is something called the "self" or the "person" that endures through time. Perhaps humans have no self. Could it be that there is no such thing as a "person" who stays the same throughout a human life?

The No-Self View

Perhaps the most radical views of human nature are those that completely deny the existence of an enduring self. With few exceptions, Western thinkers have assumed that even if nothing else exists, I can be sure that I—my individual self—exist. The existence and significance of the individual self are, in fact, the foundation of most Western thought. Westerners tend to believe that the private self is all-important and that individuality should be praised. We are each taught we should become

> **◯ QUICK REVIEW**
> Reid objected: Suppose at age 20 I remember myself at 10, and at 30 I remember myself at 20 but not at 10. Then on Locke's view at 20 I am the same person I was at 10, and at 30 I am the same person I was at 20. So at 30 I must be the same person I was at 10. Yet Locke's view also says at 30 I am not the person I was at 10!

---

[55] See Thomas Reid, "Mr. Locke's Account of Our Personal Identity," in *Personal Identity*, ed. John Perry (Berkeley: University of California Press, 1975).

aware of "who we really are." And we each feel that our inner self is a unique being of immeasurable dignity and worth.

Yet not all people are convinced of the significance, or even the existence, of the self. Much of Eastern philosophy, in fact, is based on the notion that the individual self does not exist. Eastern philosophy holds that the delusion that the self exists is the source of all pain and suffering. When we speak of Eastern philosophy, we refer to those systems of thought, belief, and action espoused by many peoples in southwestern and eastern Asia. Because Eastern thought offers many views of human nature, it is impossible to mention them all.

QUICK REVIEW
The no-self view gets rid of the self altogether.

Buddhism. Here we briefly examine one Eastern philosophy, Buddhism, and its view of human nature. (Chapters 4 and 7 continue the discussion of Buddhism in more detail.) Our intention is to provide a transcultural perspective on our subject and see what people of other cultures have to say about our self.

Siddhartha Gautama (circa 563–483 BCE), the founder of Buddhism, was the son of a king or chief of a tribal kingdom in what is now Nepal. Tradition indicates that Prince Siddhartha was raised in great luxury and sensuality. In his father's palace he was completely shielded from the sight of suffering, old age, and death. But when, at 29, Siddhartha ventured out of his palace he saw an old man. He became upset when told that everyone grows old. He became more upset when he saw a diseased man and then a dead man and learned that these, too, are part of human life. The distraught Siddhartha now gave up his life of luxury to become an ascetic. He hoped to find a way to overcome the suffering of age, sickness, and death. After many years of great deprivation and meditation, Siddhartha realized that extreme asceticism would not achieve his goal. He became the leader of a small group of followers who practiced a "middle way" between extreme asceticism and an indulgent life of pleasure. As we saw in the last chapter, Siddhartha finally gained enlightenment and became the Buddha. While meditating under a banana tree at Bihar, he understood the Wheel of Life. And he discovered how to escape the cycle of birth, suffering, death, and rebirth. The Buddha devoted the rest of his life to teaching these truths to his followers. He died at the age of 80 in the fifth century BCE.

About a century after his death, the Buddha's followers split into two groups. One was a group of dissenters named the Mahasanghikas. The other was the Theravada, who claimed to remain true to the original teachings of the Buddha's first followers. No one knows how many of the legends and sermons attributed to the Buddha by the Theravada are really his and how many are the later work of his followers. But for our purposes we can accept the doctrines of the Theravada as the core doctrines of traditional Buddhism.

Central to Buddhist thought is the belief that all things are composite and transient, the key idea behind the Wheel of Life. All things are aggregates of elements that time inevitably breaks apart, separates, and scatters. Thus, no

The Buddha: "It is simply the mind clouded over by impure desires and impervious to wisdom, that obstinately persists in thinking of 'me' and 'mine.'"

Vani/iStockphoto.com

individual thing abides permanently. Constant change and dissolution characterize everything, including the gods and all living things.

Every person, like everything else, then, is in a state of constant disintegration. Each of us is nothing more than a fleeting momentary composite of constantly changing elements. Our body, our feelings, our perceptions, our motives, and our mind all dissolve away. These are never the same from moment to moment and they remain together only fleetingly. What we call the self, then, either considered as the body or considered as the mind, is utterly transient. It is a changing aggregate from one moment to the next that cannot even control its own dissolving states. So there is no enduring self. The individual self does not exist.

In the Theravada writings, the Buddha argues that the idea of an enduring individual self is an illusory belief. To show this, the Buddha argues that if there was a thing that was truly the self, then one should be able to control that thing. For the self should be able to control itself. But, the Buddha argues, there is nothing over which we have full control.

> **QUICK REVIEW**
> Buddhism holds that nothing in the universe, not even the self, remains the same from one moment to the next. Everything consists of aggregates of elements that are in constant flux.

If the body were the self, it could do this and that as it would determine. [But] a king ... becomes ill despite his intent and desire, he comes to old age unwillingly, and his wishes and the course his life takes often have little to do with each other. If the mind were the self it could do this and that as it would determine, but the mind often flies from what it knows is right and chases after evil unwillingly.

If a man believes that such an impermanent thing [as the body], so changeable and replete with suffering, is the self, he makes a serious mistake. The human mind is also impermanent and suffering; it also has nothing that can be called the self.

Therefore, both body and mind ... are far apart from the conceptions of "me" and "mine." It is simply the mind clouded over by impure desires and impervious to wisdom, that obstinately persists in thinking of "me" and "mine."[56]

ANALYZING THE READING

The Buddha argues that if the body or the mind was the self, then they should be able to control what they do and what happens to them. But neither the body nor the mind can control what they do or what happens to them. So neither can be the self. Are the premises of this argument true?

Permanence and an enduring self do not exist. And the inevitable result of thinking they do is the cause of the suffering that fills human life. For suffering comes from collecting and clinging to things for the sake of the self. Yet there is no self. The illusion of the self is the source of suffering, then. It is an illusion that produces damaging thoughts of selfish possessiveness, of "me," "mine," desire, vanity, egoism, and ill will.

Unless we accept that everything, including our so-called self, is momentary and fleeting, we are doomed to suffer. If we desire things to last, including our self and what we love, we desire what cannot be. If we try to hold on to people, things, or even our self, we will suffer the endlessly repeating pain of loss and grief, disappointment and frustration.

David Hume. The view that humans have no self is characteristic of Buddhist thought. But some Western philosophers have made similar claims.

 THINKING LIKE A PHILOSOPHER

1. Does the Buddhist no-self view make sense to you? What do you think it would feel like to really believe that you have no self? What do you think would change in your life if you believed that? As an experiment, try this: Sit in a quiet place and try to truly believe that you have no self. Were you able to do it?

2. Do you agree that the idea that we have a self is the main reason why we are possessive, selfish, and egotistical? If you could rid yourself of the idea of the self, do you think you would be less possessive, less selfish, and less egotistical?

---

56   *The Teachings of Buddha* (Tokyo: Bukkyo Deudo Kyokai, 1976).

The Scottish philosopher David Hume (1711–1776) offered some strong arguments for his claim that humans have no enduring self. In his book *A Treatise of Human Nature*, Hume argues that all real knowledge is based on what we can perceive with our senses. Knowledge is based on what we can see, hear, touch, smell, taste, and feel, or what we experience within ourselves. Because genuine knowledge depends on experience, assertions that are not based on experience cannot be genuine knowledge. With this in mind, Hume points out that we have never experienced the self. So we have no real knowledge of a self and no justification for claiming that we have a self. What we perceive within ourselves is an ever changing display of sensations. The notion of an enduring unified self, then, is a fiction philosophers made up:

> There are some philosophers who imagine we are every moment intimately conscious of what we call our SELF; that we feel its existence and its continuance in existence; and are certain, beyond the evidence of a demonstration, both of its perfect identity and simplicity. ...
>
> Unluckily all these positive assertions are contrary to that very experience which is pleaded for them, nor have we any idea of *self*. ... For from what impression could this idea be derived? ... [There] must be some one impression that gives rise to every real idea. But self or person is not any one impression, but that to which our several impressions and ideas are supposed to have a reference. If any impression gives rise to the idea of self, that impression must continue invariably the same, through the whole course of our lives; since self is supposed to exist after that manner. But there is no impression constant and invariable [that we perceive in the mind]. Pain and pleasure, grief and joy, passions and sensations succeed each other, and never all exist at the same time. It cannot, therefore, be from any of these impressions, or from any other, that the idea of self is derived; and consequently there is no such idea.
>
> For my part, when I enter most intimately into what I call *myself* I always stumble on some particular perception or other, of heat or cold, light or shade, love or hatred, pain or pleasure. I never can catch *myself* at any time without a perception, and never can observe anything but the perception....
>
> Setting aside some metaphysicians ..., I may venture to affirm of the rest of mankind, that they are nothing but a bundle or collection of different perceptions, which succeed each other with an inconceivable rapidity, and are in a perpetual flux and movement.... The mind is a kind of theatre, where several perceptions successively make their appearance, pass, re-pass, glide away, and mingle in an infinite variety of postures and situations. There is properly no simplicity in it at one time, nor identity in different [times]; whatever natural propensity we may have to imagine that simplicity and identity [are there]. ... The identity which we ascribe to the mind of man is only a fictitious one.[57]

According to Hume, then, we never perceive among our sensations an enduring object we can call the *self*. All we can say, Hume claims, is that we are "a bundle or collection of different perceptions" that are all continuously changing. Not only are there no enduring things in the Humean and Buddhist views, but because absolutely everything is in flux, there can be no enduring self.

Thus there is an important similarity between Hume's argument for the claim that there is no self and Buddhism's argument for the same claim. For both Hume and the Buddhist, our experience is one of unceasing change without

---

[57] David Hume, *A Treatise of Human Nature*, ed. L. A. Selby-Bigge (Oxford: Clarendon, 1896), bk. I, pt. iv, sec. 6.

permanence. In our world nothing has a contin-uous existence. So there can be no continuous self. For both Hume and the Buddhist then, the impermanent nature of things provides the basic reason for rejecting a self that would be more or less permanent.

Despite their similarities, Hume's view about how we should deal with the absence of the self differs in important ways from the Buddhist's. Buddhism believes that we can give up the idea that we have an individual self. Buddhism sug-gests, in fact, that salvation is achievable only by giving up the craving for self-identity and the striving for personal success and self-fulfillment. However, Hume did not believe that we can give up the idea of the self. Hume believed that we have a powerful instinct to continue to hold on to our everyday beliefs about the self and other commonsense beliefs. This powerful instinct of nature makes it impossible for us to permanently accept the "specula-tions" of our reason:

> Most fortunately it happens, that … nature herself … cures me of this philosophical … delirium, either by relaxing this bent of mind, or by some avocation, and lively impres-sion of my senses, which obliterate all these chimeras. I dine, I play a game of back-gammon, I converse, and am merry with my friends; and when after three or four hours' amusement, I would return to these speculations, they appear so cold, and strained, and ridiculous, that I cannot find it in my heart to enter into them any farther. Here then I find myself absolutely and necessarily determined to live, and talk, and act like other people in the common affairs of life.

We are left, then, with a mystery. We assume in virtually everything we do that we have an enduring self—in other words, that we remain the same person from day to day. So does everyone else. Every day, every hour, every moment we are engaged in caring for this individual self. Yet when we probe this ordinary assumption, it seems that there is little to support it. Neither the body, nor the soul, nor even our consciousness seems to provide a sound basis for our belief that we have a self that endures through time. Yet giving up the idea of an endur-ing self is also profoundly unsatisfying. Perhaps we should look more closely at the idea of individuality itself.

THINKING LIKE A PHILOSOPHER

1. Hume says that if he looks outside and within himself, he cannot perceive any object that could be the self. He can see momentary shapes and colors, sounds and tastes, etc. But he cannot see, hear, taste, feel, or smell a permanent object that could be an enduring self. Do you think Hume is right? If you try to look inside yourself, can you catch any sight of your own self? Do you agree that this means that you do not have an enduring self? Why?

2. Do you think the view of no self has anything to offer you? That is, do you think you would be a better person if you really accepted the no-self view?

> QUICK REVIEW
> But if there is no enduring self, then all the care we take for our future makes no sense.

PHILOSOPHY AT THE MOVIES

Watch *Before I Go to Sleep* (2014) in which a vicious attack inflicts a kind of amnesia on Christine that makes her unable to form new memories. Every morning she must become reacquainted with her husband, doctor, and everything else in her life. She keeps a journal and video diary that one day lead her to question everything about herself and her situation. Do you think Christine has an enduring self? Why? Which of the theories of the enduring self does this movie support?

Other movies with related themes: *Memento* (2000); *Unbreakable* (2000); *Total Recall* (1990); *Persona* (1966); *The Bourne Identity* (2002); *Eternal Sunshine of the Spotless Mind* (2004); *50 First Dates* (2004).

2.5 Are We Independent and Self-Sufficient Individuals?

Isn't it obvious that parents should help their children achieve independence and self-sufficiency? Isn't it obvious that one of the worst things parents can do is to raise their children to become and remain dependent on others? Parents teach their children to value and develop self-reliance so they will become independent individuals. Parents also try to teach their children how to think on their own, how to make judgments on their own, how to choose and explore on their own. They try to teach children independence of thought and action.

Or consider some things parents teach children to avoid. One is conformity. Most parents don't feel that it is good to teach a child to want to conform. They advise children not to follow their friends or peer groups blindly. They teach children that it is not good to always submit to the expectations of others. Parents advise children, instead, to think for themselves. They urge their children to learn to judge and evaluate for themselves whether what others tell them is true.

Parents also teach their children to try to be true to themselves. Parents teach their children the importance of being in touch with their real individual nature and inner feelings and needs. They should not try to change themselves to please others.

Finally, think about some things we value that support these parental ideals. Take privacy, for example. Don't we feel that we should allow people to live their own lives? Don't we feel that something is wrong when society forces its values on private individuals? Or consider how we value creativity in people, or how we enjoy novelty, excitement, and challenge in life. Consider how much we prize freedom, being able to "do your own thing." How we praise individual achievement and ambition. How we cherish individual freedom. How we believe that choosing a path that is her own is all-important for a person, rather than choosing one that others impose on her.

The Atomistic Self

All these views about how we should raise children, and assumptions about what we should value, are part of a pattern. They are based on a certain view of the self: the view that the self is and should be independent of others and self-sufficient. This view has deep roots in our culture and in our ways of thinking and feeling. It is a view that some philosophers call the *atomistic view of the self*. On this view, the self is like an atom that is self-contained and independent of other atoms. The self is an autonomous individual with its own unique inner qualities. The things I go through, the people I meet, and the things I witness can touch me and move me. They can injure and hurt me. Yet the real me, the core of my self, can always rise above these and remain independent and different from all that it meets. The great American poet Walt Whitman perhaps expressed this idea best in his well-known poem "Song of Myself":

> *I celebrate myself, and sing myself. . . .*
> *Trippers and askers surround me,*
> *People I meet, the effect upon me of my early life or the ward and city I live in, or the nation,*
> *The latest dates, discoveries, inventions, societies, authors old and new,*
> *My dinner, dress, associates, looks, compliments, dues,*
> *The real or fancied indifference of some man or woman I love,*
> *The sickness of one of my folks or of myself, or ill-doing or loss or lack of money, or depressions or exaltations,*

✓ QUICK REVIEW
Many hold the view that the self is and should be independent of others and self-sufficient.

Battles, the horrors of fratricidal war, the fever of doubtful news, the fitful events;
These come to me days and nights and go from me again,
But they are not the Me myself.

Apart from the pulling and hauling stands what I am,
Stands amused, complacent, compassionating idle, unitary,
Looks down, is erect, or bends an arm on an impalpable certain rest,
Looking with side-curved head curious what will come next,
Both in and out of the game and watching and wondering at it.[58]

To see how powerful this atomistic view of the self is, think for a moment about your "real self." How do you get at the "real" you? Not the "you" that tries to live up to the expectations of others, not the face that the world sees, but the real and genuine "you." Don't you find this real you by withdrawing into yourself and contemplating the you that lies within?

This is what many philosophers have also thought. Consider the example of Descartes. He tells us that one day he resolved to understand himself better. So he withdrew from the company of others to discover within himself the truth about himself:

> After I had employed several years studying the book of the world and trying to acquire some experience, I one day formed the resolution of also making myself an object of study.... Winter detained me in a place where I found no society to divert me and no cares or passions to trouble me. I remained there the whole day shut up alone in a stove-heated room, where I had complete leisure to occupy myself with my own thoughts.[59]

Alone, apart from others, Descartes could search for his inner real self and could decide for himself what is true and what is false:

> I shall now close my eyes, I shall stop my ears, I shall call away all my senses, I shall efface even from my thoughts all the images of corporeal things, or at least (for that is hardly possible) I shall esteem them as vain and false; and thus holding converse only with myself and considering my own nature, I shall try little by little to reach a better knowledge of and a more familiar acquaintanceship with myself. I am a thing that thinks, that is to say, that doubts, affirms, denies, that knows a few things, that is ignorant of many, that loves, that hates, that wills, that desires, that also imagines and perceives. ...
>
> In order to try to extend my knowledge further, I shall now look around more carefully and see whether I cannot still discover in myself some other things which I have not hitherto perceived. I am certain that I am a thing which thinks; but do I not then likewise know what is requisite to render me certain of a truth? Certainly in this first knowledge there is nothing that assures me of its truth, excepting the clear and distinct perception of that which I state. ... And accordingly it seems to me that already I can establish as a general rule that all things which I perceive very clearly and very distinctly are true.[60]

Notice what Descartes is saying. First, he says that the real me exists within myself. Second, he claims that this real me and its qualities—my desires, fears, hopes, loves, hatreds—exist there inside me independently of others. Third, he claims that I, by myself, can discover this real me by withdrawing or separating from others. Fourth, he claims that only I can be the judge of what the truth about myself is.

QUICK REVIEW
Descartes said the self exists and can be known independently of others and that only the self can judge the truth about what it is.

---

[58] Walt Whitman, *Leaves of Grass* (New York: Eakins Press, 1855), 13, 15.
[59] Descartes, *Discourse on Method*, 87.
[60] Descartes, *Meditations*, 157–158.

In short, Descartes gives us a picture of the independent and self-sufficient individual. I do not need others to be who I really am. Of course, I may need others to help me live. For example, I depend on others for food, housing, and the many other material things I need. Still, I do not need others to have the inner qualities that make me who I am. My desires, fears, hopes, loves, and hatreds are all there inside me, whether or not anyone knows or sees them. These do not depend on others but come from within me. They are me. My real self and my inner qualities are there, and are independent of others. Moreover, a key aspect of the real me is my ability to decide for myself. That is, I have the ability to judge the truth of things for myself without relying on others.

Some philosophers have gone even further than Descartes in emphasizing the importance of this ability to judge things for oneself. For example, the German philosopher Immanuel Kant (1724–1804) argued that the core of the real self is the ability to choose for oneself. In particular, it is the ability to choose the moral laws and moral principles by which one will live one's life:

> The [moral] laws to which man is subject are only those that he himself makes.... [This is] the principle of autonomy of the will, that is, the principle of self-imposed law.... The will's autonomy consists in its capacity to be its own law, without being influenced by the objects it chooses.... The will is a causal power that living beings have if they are rational. We say such a causal power has freedom if its acts are not determined by causal influences other than itself.[61]

✓ QUICK REVIEW
Kant argued that the core of the real self is the ability to choose for oneself.

ANALYZING THE READING

Descartes claimed that the self can find the truth without depending on others; Kant claimed that the self can determine right and wrong without depending on others. Are their claims true?

Notice here how Kant claims that the real me is a being who can choose or will for himself. The real me can choose without having to conform to what external forces impose on him.

We see in Descartes and in Kant some sources of a view of the individual self that is very familiar to us. It is the view that who I am exists here inside me, independent of others and able to freely choose independently of others. As suggested earlier, we value this view of self. We try to raise our children to become independent individuals who will be true to their inner self. We want them to be individuals who will not merely conform to what external society demands, and who will exercise independent and free choice.

The Relational Self

Still, now let us ask ourselves this question. Is there such a thing as the independent and self-sufficient individual we have been discussing? Is it possible for children, or adults, to be independent and self-sufficient individuals? The twentieth-century Canadian philosopher Charles Taylor (1931–) does not believe so:

> In the twentieth century, we may no longer believe, like Descartes, in the soul or mind as an inner space open to transparent introspection ... but we retain the idea that self-understanding is getting a clear view of the desires, aversions, fears, hopes, aspirations that are within us. To know oneself is to get clear on what is within.
>
> This seems so normal and inescapable to us, that we can hardly imagine an alternative. But let us try. If I can only understand myself as part of a larger order;

---

[61]   Immanuel Kant, *Foundations of the Metaphysics of Reason*, quoted in M. Velasquez and C. Rostankowski, *Ethics: Theory and Practice* (Englewood Cliffs, NJ: Prentice Hall, 1985), 90–91.

indeed, if man as the rational animal is just the one who is rationally aware of this order; then I only am really aware of myself, and understand myself, when I see myself against this background, fitting into this whole. I must acknowledge my belonging before I can understand myself. Engaged in an attempt to cut myself off, to consider myself quite on my own, autonomously, I should be in confusion, self-delusion, in the dark.[62]

QUICK REVIEW
Taylor objects that we depend on others for our very self because we need others to define for us who our real self is.

Taylor suggests that there is another way of understanding who the real me is besides that of getting in touch with what is within me apart from others. This other way is to see that who I am—the real inner me—depends on my relationships to others.

We saw earlier that we depend on others for the material things we need to survive. Still, this is not what Taylor has in mind. Taylor suggests that we also depend on others for our very self. I need others to define for me who the real me is. Philosophers sometimes express this by saying that the self is "constituted" by its relations to others.

Yet, surprisingly, the traditional view of the self that most of us share is the atomistic view. It is the view that says you are who you are independently of your relationships with other people. We feel that we can know ourselves by withdrawing from others and looking deep within ourselves to find the real me or my real "self."

Not all views of the self assume that the self is independent of others. For example, Aristotle declared that humans are "social animals" who are not self-sufficient:

> The individual, when isolated, is not self-sufficing; and therefore he is like a part in relation to the whole. But he who is unable to live in society, or who has no need because he is sufficient for himself, must be either a beast or a god.... social instinct is implanted in all men by nature.[63]

QUICK REVIEW
Aristotle argued that I depend on others not just to exist but to be the human that I am.

Aristotle is not just saying that we need others to survive. He is arguing that what a human being is, the person I am and the qualities I have, arise from my relationships with others. Without these relationships, which make me the human that I am, I would be an animal, or a god. The self is a relational self.

But it was the philosopher Hegel who most forcefully challenged the idea of the independent, self-sufficient individual. He argued instead for the idea of a relational self. Hegel claimed that my own identity—who I really am—depends on my relationships with others. So I cannot be who I am apart from my relationships with others:

> Every self wants to be united with and recognized by another self [as a free being]. Yet at the same time, each self remains an independent individual and so an alien object to the other. The life of the self thus becomes a struggle for recognition.... Each self is in a struggle to convince the other that he is [a free being] worthy of the other's respect and recognition. This mutual struggle for recognition by the other is mixed with feelings of mistrust and uncertainty. The struggle carries with it all the dangers and risks that the self faces when it dares to lay itself open to the other. This life-and-death struggle can degenerate into a bloody fight in which one of the combatants is killed. But then the

---

[62] Charles Taylor, "Legitimation Crisis?" in Charles Taylor, *Philosophy and the Human Sciences*, vol. 2 (New York: Cambridge University Press, 1985), 257.

[63] Aristotle, *Politics*, bk. 1, ch. 2. This translation by Manuel Velasquez.

whole issue of recognition will be missed. Recognition requires the survival of the other as a condition and sign of one's freedom.

The struggle of the self is essentially a struggle for freedom. Historically, this struggle is the basis of the rise of masters and slaves.... Preferring survival to freedom, the slave gives up his attempt to be recognized as free. The master, on the other hand, is recognized as free. The master sees in the slave the very sign of his freedom.

Independent masters and dependent slaves together form a community. The concern of the master becomes to preserve and protect the life of his workers.... The slave learns to work. He acquires habits and skills. At the same time he disciplines himself. In making objects [for the master] he also makes himself. In working together with others he overcomes his isolation and is recognized for his excellence. In this process, the relation of dependence and independence is reversed. The independent master becomes dependent on the skills and virtues of the servant.[64]

Georg W. F. Hegel:
"Each self is in a struggle to convince the other that he is a free being worthy of the other's respect and recognition. This struggle is the basis of the rise of masters and slaves. The slave gives up his attempt to be recognized as free. The master sees in the slave the very sign of his freedom."

Portrait of Georg Wilhelm Friedrich Hegel (1770–1831), 1825, Jacob Schlesinger (1792–1855)/Nationalgalerie, Berlin, Germany/© The Bridgeman Art Library International

Hegel claims that each of us can know we have certain human qualities only when others recognize those qualities in us. In particular, each of us can know that we are free and independent persons only if we see that others recognize us as free and independent persons. A free and independent person is one who is not a slave to his desires or to some external force. A free and independent person is one who is able to choose for himself what course his life will take. So Hegel is saying that we cannot develop the capacity to choose for ourselves independently of others. Others must develop this capacity in us by recognizing and affirming our freedom and self-mastery.

✓ QUICK REVIEW
Hegel denied the independent self, arguing that who one is depends on one's relationships with others and that we can know we are free and independent only if others recognize us as such.

✓ QUICK REVIEW
Everyone struggles to get from others the recognition each needs to be independent and free. Some emerge as slaves, others as masters, yet the master becomes dependent on the slave, and the slave comes to see himself as more competent than the master.

Power and Hegel

Moreover, in the passage above, Hegel claims that each of us is continually involved in a struggle with others. We each struggle to get the recognition from others that we need to exist as truly independent, free persons. We realize that to be free and competent, we need others to acknowledge that we are worthy of being respected as free and competent persons. So, we try to force others to respect us, even as they struggle to force us to respect them. In this struggle—a life-and-death struggle—some people emerge as dominant and others as submissive. In Hegel's words some emerge as "masters" and others as "slaves." The dominant ones are those who get the respect they demand. The submissive ones are those who give up the struggle for respect and settle for merely being allowed to live. Thus arise the two great social classes: masters and slaves—those who command and those who submit. Yet though the slave appears to have lost the battle to the master, eventually, slowly, the tables are turned. For as the slave serves the master, the master recognizes the capability of the slave. The slave then becomes more confident of himself. He sees himself as a capable competent supporter of the master. Meanwhile, the master gradually becomes dependent on the slave. Both come to recognize the master as incapable and incompetent.

---

[64]   Wilhelm Hegel, *Encyclopedia of Philosophy*, trans. Gustav E. Mueller (New York: Philosophical Library, 1959), 215–217.

The key idea, then, is that who you are ultimately depends on your relationships to others. The slave who identifies himself as a slave is such because he defines himself through his relationship to the master. The master who sees himself as free and independent is such only to the extent that others recognize him as such.

The implications of Hegel's idea are profound. In every society there are powerless and powerful, strong and weak, dominant and submissive. Hegel is suggesting that these classifications are not there ahead of time. Instead, we create them by the qualities we are willing to recognize in others. The same is true of social classes. Some groups in society—perhaps some minority groups, for example—may exhibit submissive characteristics. Yet we are the ones who make them submissive. We make them submissive by failing to show them the respect and recognition that alone can empower them to be assertive and independent.

Charles Taylor is a leading authority on Hegel. In the following passage he explains the importance of Hegel's notion of recognition:

> The thesis is that our identity is partly shaped by recognition or its absence, [or] by the misrecognition of others. And so a person or a group of people can suffer real damage, real distortion, if the people or society around them mirror back to them a confining or demeaning or contemptible picture of themselves....
>
> Thus some feminists have argued that women in patriarchal societies have been induced to adopt a depreciatory image of themselves. They have internalized a picture of their own inferiority.... An analogous point has been made in relation to blacks: that white society has for generations projected a demeaning image of them, which some of them have been unable to resist adopting. Their own self-depreciation, on this view, becomes one of the most potent instruments of their own oppression.
>
> ...Recently, a similar point has been made in relation to indigenous and colonized people in general. It is held that since 1492 Europeans have projected an image of such people as somehow inferior, "uncivilized," and through the force of conquest have often been able to impose this image on the conquered.[65]

THINKING LIKE A PHILOSOPHER

1. Suppose Hegel's views about the master–slave relationship are right. What do you think his view means for workers in our society?
2. Think about jobs you have had. Do you feel that the employer–employee or the boss–worker relationships in those jobs were like Hegel's master–slave relationship? Why?

QUICK REVIEW
Thus, the slave is slave because that is what others see him as being, and the master is master because others recognize him as such.

QUICK REVIEW
Hegel implies that the powerful and powerless classes in society are created by the qualities we are willing to recognize in them.

ANALYZING THE READING

1. According to Hegel you can have the ability to be independent, the ability to choose for yourself, and the ability to not be submissive, only if others recognize that you have these abilities. Is Hegel right?

2. Is Taylor right when he claims that a person or group will see themselves as inferior if others see them as inferior?

3. Suppose that Hegel and Taylor are right in these claims. Is there any way that a person who belongs to a group that is seen as servile, submissive, and inferior can overcome this?

Culture and Self-Identity

There is another important implication of Hegel's view. Consider that every person has a culture. A culture consists of the traditions, symbols, and language of a group of people. It includes their arts, literature, ideas, and outlooks, and their practices, customs, morals, and beliefs. Hegel argues that a person's culture is the mirror through which society shows the person who and what she is. It is, in fact, through

---

[65] Charles Taylor, "The Politics of Recognition," in *Multiculturalism and the Politics of Recognition*, ed. Amy Gutman (Princeton, NJ: Princeton University Press, 1992), 25.

her culture that a person gets the recognition that makes her a free person. Recognition comes through culture.

What this means is that who I am, the qualities that define me, depends on my culture as well as my relationships to the people in my life. There is, then, no "real me" that I can find inside myself apart from others. Instead, I am who others tell me I am in the language and symbols that culture gives me. Again, Taylor expresses the idea best:

> In order to understand the close connection between identity and recognition, we have to take into account a crucial feature of the human condition.... This crucial feature of human life is its fundamentally dialogical character. We become full human agents, capable of understanding ourselves, and hence of defining our identity, through our acquisition of rich human languages of expression. For my purposes here, I want to take language in a broad sense, covering not only the words we speak, but also other modes of expression whereby we define ourselves, including the "languages" of art, of gesture, of love, and the like. But we learn these modes of expression through exchanges with others. People do not acquire the languages needed for self-definition on their own. Rather, we are introduced to them through interaction with others who matter to us. ...
>
> Moreover, this is not just a fact about genesis, which can be ignored later on. We don't just learn the languages in dialogue and then go on to use them for our own purposes.
>
> ... We define our identity always in dialogue with, sometimes in struggle against, the things our significant others want to see in us. Even after we outgrow some of these others—our parents, for instance—and they disappear from our lives, the conversation with them continues within us as long as we live. Thus, the contribution of significant others, even when it is provided at the beginning of our lives, continues indefinitely.[66]

To understand what Taylor means, consider how you think of who you are, your self-identity. Don't you identify who you are by your relationships to others, particularly to the groups to which you belong? You identify yourself as the son or daughter of your parents. Your name identifies you by the family to which you belong. You identify yourself as an American, a Canadian, a German, or a Mexican. You are a member of a racial or ethnic group: white or black, Indian or Asian. Consider the wants that make you who you are. The culture you were raised in determines the foods, the clothes, and the music you prefer. In fact, all your wants are shaped by what your culture teaches you to want. From your culture you also draw all your ideas about the kind of person you might be. You use those ideas to understand yourself: lover, loner, kindly, coward, punk, stoner, preppy, hipster, jock, troll, beautiful, ugly, popular, unpopular, nerd, thug, jogger, drama queen, selfish, compassionate, animal, chick, rocket scientist, intellectual, creative, mother, father, son, daughter. Consider the most basic tools and products you know and use every day: your watch, phone, tablet, car, computer, apps, television, movies, skateboard, knives, forks, plates, glasses, shoes, clothes, comb, toothbrush. Each of them is the result of the discoveries, inventions, and work of countless humans. And they each shape and make possible all of your everyday actions. Your religious ideas all come from the traditions of a church into which you were socialized. The language and concepts you use to express your thoughts to yourself and others are a gift of your culture. Thus, we depend not only on the recognition of others to be who we are. We depend also on our culture to give us the words and ideas we use to define who we are.

---

[66] Ibid., 32–33.

Search for the Real Self

Who is right, then? Is Descartes right when he claims that the real you is discovered within yourself and is independent of others? Or are Hegel and Taylor right when they claim that the real you is relational. In other words, when they say the real you is found only in relationship to others?

Think about it. From childhood and from every side we hear the constant refrains: "Be true to yourself and not to what others expect you to be," "Think for yourself and don't just follow the crowd," and "Take responsibility for yourself and don't blame others for what you are." Yet, if Hegel and Taylor are right, then all these ideas are completely wrong. The real me is not there inside, independent of others and waiting to be discovered. The real me is something that exists in my relationships with others and with my culture. Who I am depends on how the people I love see me and what those who matter to me recognize in me. Who I am depends on the people whose views of me I accept and on those ideas and beliefs of my culture that define me. It is to them I must turn to find myself. So I cannot be true to myself unless I am true to what such people and my culture make me. And I cannot think for myself unless I use the ideas that they and my culture give me. In a very real sense I am what they make me.

But are Hegel and Taylor right? Perhaps not. If who and what you are depends on others, then you are not responsible for what you are. Neither are you responsible for what you do. But surely that is not right. Surely, in some way and to some extent, you are responsible for who you have become and what you are. As we saw earlier, Sartre argues that you alone make yourself who you are. Doesn't it seem that to some extent at least Sartre is right?

There is a deeper problem with the idea that who I am depends on my relationships with others. For my relationships with others are many. Are there many "me's"? For example, one "me" for each person to whom I am related? Hegel says that what I am depends on what others recognize in me. Still, suppose that different people recognize different things in me. This person recognizes me as loving, that one as mean, that other one as wise, and this one as stupid. Which is the real me? Which of these different things constitute the real me? Are there many me's? The pragmatic philosopher William James was not afraid to accept this conclusion:

> Properly speaking, a man has as many social selves as there are individuals who recognize him ... We may practically say that he has as many social selves as there are distinct groups of persons about whose opinion he cares.[67]

Yet this seems an odd conclusion. How can I be many me's? Are we, without realizing it, multiple personalities? Do we turn a different face to each person depending on what that person sees in us? Perhaps we do. But which of these many faces would really be me?

Moreover, don't you have many qualities that are not dependent on others? Take, for example, your basic physical qualities: your height, your weight, your hair color, your skin color, your facial features, your musculature, your health. Surely, these are a basic part of who you are and do not depend on your relationships with others. Or take your basic mental qualities, such as your I.Q. and your ability to feel pain, to hate, to love, to think. Even if *what* you feel, hate, love, think, or choose depends on others, surely your *ability* to feel, hate, love, think, or choose does not depend on others. To some extent, at least, the ability to think and choose

QUICK REVIEW
So, the self is not independent and self-sufficient, but depends on others for his or her existence as the kind of person he or she is.

QUICK REVIEW
But if one has many relationships with others, does this mean one has many selves?

QUICK REVIEW
And aren't many of our basic physical, mental, and personality traits independent of others?

---

[67] William James, *Psychology (Briefer Course)* (New York: Collier, 1962), 192.

for yourself seems natural and not something created by others. Or take your basic personality traits, such as your tendency to feel cheerful or depressed, your willingness to take risks, and your disposition. We inherit many of these kinds of personality traits, scientists tell us. Such personality traits depend on the genes you are born with. And surely such traits are part of who you are.

We have, then, a dilemma. On the one hand, we are told we are only what others make us. We are what the significant people in our lives make us and what society through its culture makes us. On the other hand, we are told we are or can be independent selves. And we seem to have many qualities that do not depend on others. In particular the ability to choose and think for ourselves to some extent at least does not seem to depend on others. So we seem to face two options: others make us who we are, or who we are depends on ourselves and the real self within. Which of these two options is right? The choice between them is important.

Clearly, if others make us, then we in turn make others. If so then the way we raise our children, the money we spend on schools, the kinds of social environments we create, the respect or lack of respect we give others, the way our culture talks about different races—all these become tremendously important. For all these arrangements will make the young members of our society the kind of people they turn out to be. They will make young people become powerful or powerless, capable or incapable, assertive or submissive, masters or slaves.

On the other hand, if we are independent selves with the ability to choose and think for ourselves, then these externals are not so important. More important is that we get young people to use their own ability to choose and think for themselves. More important is that young people learn to look into themselves for their own inner power and strength. More important is that young people learn to rely on themselves and find in themselves who they really are.

The challenge for each of us, perhaps, is to find what comes from within and what comes from without. The challenge is to learn what comes from others and what comes from inside ourselves. A great deal hangs on this.

PHILOSOPHY AT THE MOVIES

Watch *The Long Walk Home* (1990), which takes place in the South during the 1955–1956 civil rights bus boycott led by Martin Luther King and tells of the relationship between Miriam Thompson, the rich white wife of a narrow-minded businessman, and Odessa Cotter, their black maid who is struggling to raise her family and whose participation in the boycott makes her arrive so late and tired that Miriam begins to drive her to work. Explain whether the movie supports or undermines Hegel's ideas about "recognition" and the origins of the master–slave relationship.

Other movies with related themes: *Bend It Like Beckham* (2002); *My Big Fat Greek Wedding* (2002); *Borat* (2006).

Chapter Summary

This chapter opens by raising the issue of human nature: What am I? How we see ourselves has been profoundly influenced by Traditional Western theories of human nature: the rationalistic view and the Western religious view. These Traditional views have been challenged on a number of fronts. Darwinian evolution challenges the ideas of uniqueness and purpose. Existentialism challenges the idea of a universal human nature. Feminists raise questions about the role of gender in forming our identities. The Traditional view also favors dualism, which was most clearly articulated by Descartes. Dualism has in turn been challenged by various forms of materialism including identity theory, behaviorism, functionalism, and eliminative materialism. The Traditional view also assumes that humans are enduring selves and that humans can and should be independent and self-sufficient, and these, too, are contested.

The main points of this chapter are:

2.1 Why Does Your View of Human Nature Matter?

- *Human nature* refers to what a human is. An important issue about what humans are concerns whether humans are aggressive, material, and self-interested.

- thinking critically Arguments can be deductive or inductive; in a valid deductive argument, if the premises are true then the conclusion must also be true; that is, a deductive argument is valid if in every situation in which its premises are true, the conclusion is also true. A deductive argument is sound if it is both valid and has true premises.

2.2 What Is Human Nature?

- Traditional Western views of human nature claim humans are rational selves, who are immaterial, have a purpose, endure through time, and exist independently of others.

- One important version of the Traditional Western view of human nature is the rationalistic view that sees humans as rational immaterial beings with a purpose, in whom reason should rule over passions and desires. The Judeo-Christian religious view claims that humans are made in the image of God, who has endowed them with reason and an ability to love; the self is immaterial and its purpose is to know and love God.

- Darwin argued that all living organisms evolved from earlier species through variations, a struggle for existence, and natural selection. Darwin's view has been taken to imply that humans have no purpose and are not unique.

- Existentialist views deny that there is a fixed human nature and claim that each human creates his or her own nature, and so human existence precedes essence. Existentialism asserts people are responsible for what they are: the sum total of their actions.

- Many feminists have argued that in the Traditional Western view of human nature, our concepts of reason, appetites, emotions, mind, and body are biased against women.

- thinking critically Darwin's argument, which claimed that his theory was the best explanation for many different phenomena, is called an inference to the best explanation. Criteria for "best explanation" include a consideration of all the alternatives, harmony with well-established beliefs, an ability to account for many different kinds of facts, information about causal mechanisms, and simplicity.

2.3 The Mind–Body Problem: How Do Your Mind and Your Body Relate?

- Descartes' dualist view of human nature says that humans are immaterial thinking beings different from, but connected to, material bodies. It is unclear how immaterial minds can interact with material bodies.

- **thinking critically** To evaluate a premise ask: (1) Is it consistent with your experience and is your experience reliable? (2) Is it consistent with information you believe but learned from others, and are they reliable sources of that information? (3) Is it a generalization that has counterexamples? (4) Does it imply claims that are absurd, false, impossible, or inconsistent with other well-established claims? (5) Can it be supported by good arguments or undermined by good objections?

- Materialist views say we are solely material bodies. Identity theory holds that mental states are identical with brain states. Behaviorism says that mental states are labels for observable behaviors or dispositions to engage in observable behaviors. Functionalism says that mental states refer to the connections the body makes among its sensory inputs, other mental states, and its behavioral outputs. The computer view says that computers running programs can have minds, and the human brain is itself a computer. Searle uses the "Chinese Room" argument to show the mind is not a computer program. Eliminative materialism says beliefs, desires, and intentions are terms of a "folk psychology" and must be eliminated. Chalmers uses a "zombie argument" to support property dualism, a view that claims mental properties are not physical properties.

2.4   Is There an Enduring Self?

- The Traditional view of human nature and our ordinary thinking assume that humans have a self that endures through time.

- Bodily continuity does not seem to be the basis of the enduring self. Descartes claims that the enduring self is a soul. Locke argues that consciousness is the basis of the enduring self. Buddhism and Hume suggest that there is no enduring self.

2.5   Are We Independent and Self-Sufficient Individuals?

- Many people believe that the human self can and should be independent of others, self-sufficient, and capable of thinking and choosing for itself, which is how Descartes seems to have conceived of human beings.

- Hegel argues that who we are depends on the recognition of others and on our culture.

2.6 Readings

The first reading, Kate Chopin's well-known "The Story of an Hour" has been called "one of feminism's sacred texts." Chopin wrote her story during the Victorian era when men and women were seen as destined for marriage, a relationship in which women were defined as homemakers and mothers and men as providers. Chopin's story is about the oppressive constraints that such definitions of men and women can create. The question her story should lead us to think about is how we ourselves define male and female selves and the consequences our definitions have, particularly on how men and women relate to each other.

The second reading is a short excerpt from a much longer article by Janice Steil that summarizes recent research on today's marriage ideals and the reality. As her title indicates, marriage is "still an unequal partnership." She suggests that one of the causes of this "unequal partnership" between men and women is the way we define men and women today and the expectations those identities create. Her article raises the question whether our definitions of men and women today are really that much different from those in Chopin's story.

Jean Grimshaw, an internationally known British philosopher, discusses feminist views of women in the third reading. She argues that many feminists see women as victims so indoctrinated and brutalized by men that they no longer are in touch with their "real selves." These feminists believe that women can become their real selves if they throw off the effects of male domination. But Grimshaw suggests that the very idea of a "real self" waiting to be discovered is questionable. Grimshaw's article may make you reflect on whether your views of the natures of men and women are influenced by men's power over women, whether women, as a result, lose their "real selves" both in and outside of marriage; and whether the nature of men is accurately described by the feminists she discusses.

KATE CHOPIN

The Story of an Hour

Knowing that Mrs. Mallard was afflicted with a heart trouble, great care was taken to break to her as gently as possible the news of her husband's death.

It was her sister Josephine who told her, in broken sentences; veiled hints that revealed in half concealing. Her husband's friend Richards was there, too, near her. It was he who had been in the newspaper office when intelligence of the railroad disaster was received, with Brently Mallard's name leading the list of "killed." He had only taken the time to assure himself of its truth by a second telegram, and had hastened to forestall any less careful, less tender friend in bearing the sad message.

She did not hear the story as many women have heard the same, with a paralyzed inability to accept its significance. She wept at once, with sudden, wild abandonment, in her sister's arms. When the storm of grief had spent itself she went away to her room alone. She would have no one follow her.

There stood, facing the open window, a comfortable, roomy armchair. Into this she sank, pressed down by a physical exhaustion that haunted her body and seemed to reach into her soul.

She could see in the open square before her house the tops of trees that were all aquiver with the new spring life. The delicious breath of rain was in the air. In the street below a peddler was crying his wares. The notes of a distant song which some one was singing reached her faintly, and countless sparrows were twittering in the eaves.

There were patches of blue sky showing here and there through the clouds that had met and piled one above the other in the west facing her window.

She sat with her head thrown back upon the cushion of the chair, quite motionless, except when a sob came up into her throat and shook her, as a child who has cried itself to sleep continues to sob in its dreams.

She was young, with a fair, calm face, whose lines bespoke repression and even a certain strength. But now there was a dull stare in her eyes, whose gaze was fixed away off yonder on one of those patches of blue sky. It was not a glance of reflection, but rather indicated a suspension of intelligent thought.

There was something coming to her and she was waiting for it, fearfully. What was it? She did not know; it was too subtle and elusive to name. But she felt it, creeping out of the sky, reaching toward her through the sounds, the scents, the color that filled the air.

Now her bosom rose and fell tumultuously. She was beginning to recognize this thing that was approaching to possess her, and she was striving to beat it back with her will—as powerless as her two white slender hands would have been.

When she abandoned herself a little whispered word escaped her slightly parted lips. She said it over and over under her breath: "free, free, free!" The vacant stare and the look of terror that had followed it went from her eyes. They stayed keen and bright. Her pulses beat fast, and the coursing blood warmed and relaxed every inch of her body.

She did not stop to ask if it were or were not a monstrous joy that held her. A clear and exalted perception enabled her to dismiss the suggestion as trivial.

She knew that she would weep again when she saw the kind, tender hands folded in death; the face that had never looked save with love upon her, fixed and gray and dead. But she saw beyond that bitter moment a long procession of years to come that would belong to her absolutely. And she opened and spread her arms out to them in welcome.

There would be no one to live for her during those coming years; she would live for herself. There would be no powerful will bending hers in that blind persistence with which men and women believe they have a right to impose a private will upon a fellow creature. A kind intention or a cruel intention make the act seem no less a crime as she looked upon it in that brief moment of illumination.

And yet she had loved him—sometimes. Often she had not. What did it matter! What could love, the unsolved mystery, count for in face of this possession of self-assertion which she suddenly recognized as the strongest impulse of her being!

"Free! Body and soul free!" she kept whispering.

Josephine was kneeling before the closed door with her lips to the keyhole, imploring for admission. "Louise, open the door! I beg; open the door—you will make yourself ill. What are you doing, Louise? For heaven's sake open the door."

"Go away. I am not making myself ill." No; she was drinking in a very elixir of life through that open window.

Her fancy was running riot along those days ahead of her. Spring days, and summer days, and all sorts of days that would be her own. She breathed a quick prayer that life might be long. It was only yesterday she had thought with a shudder that life might be long.

She arose at length and opened the door to her sister's importunities. There was a feverish triumph in her eyes, and she carried herself unwittingly like a goddess of Victory. She clasped her sister's waist, and together they descended the stairs. Richards stood waiting for them at the bottom.

Some one was opening the front door with a latchkey. It was Brently Mallard who entered, a little travel-stained, composedly carrying his grip-sack and umbrella. He had been far from the scene of accident, and did not even know there had been one. He stood amazed at Josephine's piercing cry; at Richards' quick motion to screen him from the view of his wife.

But Richards was too late.

When the doctors came they said she had died of heart disease—of joy that kills.

Source: From Kate Chopin, "The Story of an Hour," *Vogue*, December 6, 1894.

JANICE M. STEIL

Contemporary Marriage: Still an Unequal Partnership

Egalitarian marriages are endorsed by increasing numbers of the population. Yet, contemporary marriages remain unequal. But why?

[The research summarized here shows] husbands still are more likely ... to be in higher status positions compared to their wives. Indeed, even when wives hold high-status positions, the husbands' careers still are likely to be considered more important than the wives' careers. Furthermore, wives, despite their involvement in the paid labor force, still are more likely to do a disproportionate share of the work in their homes and relationships. ...

Employed wives continue to do nearly twice as much housework as do their husbands, including 80% of the repetitive, routine, and time-consuming tasks such as cooking, cleaning, and laundry. Wives also do from one-quarter to two-thirds more child care than do their husbands.

Wives also do much more of the emotional and interactional work that relationships require. Fishman, in a detailed analysis of the conversations of white professional couples at home, effectively illustrated the gender differences in the work of relationships. An analysis of 52 hours of taped conversations showed that wives were three times more likely than husbands to ask questions as means of initiating and maintaining interaction. Wives used minimal responses such as "yeah" and "umm" to demonstrate interest, whereas husbands more often used these same minimal responses to display a *lack* of interest. ...

[A study of dual-career couples showed that] although 17% of the women earned more than their husbands, none of the wives' careers was considered primary. Indeed, despite the fact that the men and women had comparable careers, more than half (51%) of the male and female respondents considered the wives' careers to be less important than those of the husbands, and 65% of women and 43% of men reported that wives retained the primary responsibility for homemaking tasks. ...

Despite respondents' endorsement of marital equality as ideal ... fewer than 28% were in relationships in which homemaking tasks were equally shared and careers were equally valued. ... Why is equality so difficult to achieve?

Dual-career couples, it seems, "build life structures with one foot in the past, mimicking traditional marriages of their parents' generation, and one foot in the feminist-influenced present." (Silberstein.) They hold not only "consciously altered expectations (about gender roles, work, family, and marriage) but also deeply socialized, internalized and probably change resistant experiences, emotional needs, and entrenched patterns of behavior." The result of the foot in the past is that work is considered more important to men than to women, and family is considered more important to women than to men. Similarly, we expect that men's self-worth will be more closely tied to paid work than will women's and that women's self-worth will be more closely tied to motherhood than men's will be to fatherhood. ... [T]hese entrenched identities influence the numerous large and small decisions and acts that make up everyday life, limiting conscious choice, ... and impeding the achievement of more equally sharing relationships.

Source: From Janice M. Steil, "Contemporary Marriage: Still an Unequal Partnership," in Clyde Hendrick and Susan S. Hendrick (Eds.), *Close Relationships: A Sourcebook* (Thousand Oaks, CA: Sage, 2000), 125–136. Excerpts from pp. 125, 126, 127, 131, 132, 133.

JEAN GRIMSHAW

Women's Identity in Feminist Thinking

Feminist writers have wanted ... to indict the various forms of brutality and coercion from which women have suffered. But this brutality and coercion has been seen not merely as ... physical or "external" coercion or constraint; the force of subjection has also been seen as a psychic one, invading women's very selves.

The language of "conditioning," "brainwashing," "indoctrination," and so forth, has been used to describe this force. The female self, under male domination, is [said to be] riddled through and through with false or conditioned desires. But set against this conditioned, non-autonomous female self are various images of a female self that would be authentic, that would transcend or shatter this conditioning. I want now to look at some of these images of the female self in feminist discourse: my particular examples are from the work of Mary Daly, Marilyn Frye and Kate Millett.

Daly, Frye and Millett all stress the way in which women have been subject to the power of men. Much of Daly's book, *Gyn/Ecology*, is an account of the barbarities inflicted on women such as suttee, clitorectomy, foot-binding and other forms of mutilation. Millett in [her book], *Sexual Politics*, sees patriarchal power as something so historically all-embracing that it has totally dominated women's lives. Frye, in her *The Politics of Reality*, uses the situation of a young girl sold into sexual slavery and then systematically brutalized and brainwashed into a life of service to her captors as an analogy for the situation of all women. And all three writers stress the way in which they see the female self as 'invaded' by patriarchal conditioning. Millett writes:

> When, in any group of persons, the ego is subjected to such invidious versions of itself through social beliefs, ideology and tradition, the effect is bound to be pernicious. This should make it no very special cause for surprise that women develop group characteristics common to those who suffer minority status and a marginal existence.

Women, she argues, are deprived of all but the most trivial sources of dignity or self-respect. In her discussion of Lawrence's depiction of Connie in *Lady Chatterley's Lover*, what she sees Connie as relinquishing is "self; ego, will, individuality," all those things which, Millett argues, women had but recently achieved (and for which Lawrence had a profound distaste).

Mary Daly's picture of the way in which women's selves are invaded by patriarchal conditioning is even more striking. She describes women, for example, as "moronized," "robotized," "lobotomized," as "the puppets of Papa." At times she seems to see women as so "brainwashed" that they are scarcely human; thus she describes them as "fembots," even as "mutants." In Millett, Daly and Frye, women are seen primarily as victims: the monolithic brutality and psychological pressures of male power have reduced women almost to the state of being "non-persons." And indeed, as Daly sees women as having become "mutants" or "fembots," so Millett sees them as not having been allowed to participate in fully "human" activities (which she characterizes as those that are most remote from the biological contingencies of life), and Frye sees them as simply "broken" and then "remade" in the way that suits their masters.

But behind this victimized female self, whose actions and desires are assumed to be not truly "her own," since they derive from processes of force, conditioning or psychological manipulation, there is seen to be an authentic female self, whose recovery or discovery it is one of the aims of feminism to achieve. The spatial metaphor implicit in the word "behind" is not accidental, since this model of self is premised on the possibility of making a distinction between an "inner" and an "outer" self. Ibsen's Peer Gynt compared his quest for identity to the process of peeling layers off an onion; but after shedding all the "false selves," he found that there was nothing inside, no "core." The sort of spatial metaphor implicit in Peer Gynt's account of himself is also apt in the accounts of self given by Daly, Millett and Frye, except that there is assumed to be a "core." This is clearest in the work of Daly. In *Gyn/Ecology*, discovering or recovering one's own self is seen as akin to a process of salvation or religious rebirth, and Daly writes of what she calls the unveiling or unwinding of the "shrouds" of patriarchy to reveal the authentic female Spirit-Self underneath. And this Self is seen as a unitary and harmonious one. Splits and barriers within the psyche, she argues, as well as those between Selves, are the result of patriarchal conditioning. In the unitary and harmonious female Spirit-Self there will be no such splits.

Millett's picture of the authentic female self is rather different from that of Daly. It does not draw, as Daly's does, on religious metaphors of salvation and rebirth. It derives, rather, from a picture of the self as fundamentally a unitary, conscious and rational thing, a picture which, in Western philosophy, can be traced back to Descartes. It emerges most clearly in her discussion of Freud. She describes Freud's theory of the Unconscious as a major contribution to human understanding, but her account of the self owes, in fact, scarcely anything to Freud. She is scathingly critical of Freud's theory of penis envy: Freud, she argued, "did not accept his patient's symptoms as evidence of a justified dissatisfaction with the limiting circumstances imposed on them by society, but as symptomatic of an independent and universal feminine tendency." He made a major (and foolish) confusion between biology and culture. Girls, Millett argues, are fully cognizant of male supremacy long before they see their brother's penis; and what they envy is not the penis, but the things to which having a penis gives the boy access—power, status and rewards. Freud ignored the more likely "social" hypothesis for feminine dissatisfaction, preferring to ascribe it to a biologically based female nature. What we should be studying, Millett argues, are the effects of male-supremacist culture on the female

ego. And what will undo these effects, she writes in the Postscript, is altered consciousness, and a process of "human growth and true re-education."

The "social" factors of which Millett writes are here [in her writings] seen as pressures which are "external" to the self, and which have the effect of thwarting the conscious and unitary rationality of female individuality, or the female ego. And the task is that of removing their influence. If, in *Lady Chatterley's Lover*, the scales were to fall from Connie's eyes and she were to see the worship of Mellor's phallus for what it is, a means of subordinating and oppressing women, she could free herself and develop her authentic will, ego and individuality.

The paradigm of coercion, writes Frye, is not the direct application of physical force. Rather, it is a situation in which choice and action do take place, and in which the victim acts under her own perception and judgment. Hence, what the exploiter needs is that

> the will and intelligence of the victim be disengaged from the projects of resistance and escape but that they not be simply broken or destroyed. Ideally, the disintegration and misintegration of the victim should accomplish the detachment of the victim's will and intelligence from the victim's own interests and their attachment to the interests of the exploiter. This will effect a displacement or dissolution of self-respect and will undermine the victim's intolerance of coercion. With that, the situation transcends the initial paradigmatic form or structure of coercion; for if people don't mind doing what you want them to do, you can't really be making them do it.

And, she writes:

> The health and integrity of an organism is a matter of its being organized largely towards its own interests and welfare. She is healthy and "working right" when her substance is organized primarily on principles which align it to her interests and welfare. Co-operation is essential of course, but it will not do—that I arrange everything so that you get enough exercise; for me to be healthy, I must get enough exercise. My being adequately exercised is logically independent of your being so.

Frye is writing here as if it were possible to distinguish the interests of one self sharply from those of another, and as if, were the effects of male domination to be undone, it would not be too much of a problem for the self to know what its interests were. In various ways then, underlying much of the work of these three writers is a set of assumptions about the self. First, that it is, at least potentially, a unitary, rational thing, aware of its interests. Second, that "splits" within the psyche should be seen as resulting from the interference of patriarchal or male-dominated socialization or conditioning. Third, that the task of undoing this conditioning is one that can be achieved solely by a rational process of learning to understand and fight against the social and institutional effects of male domination. . . .

But one cannot assume that an everyday 'coherent' sense of self is readily available. One reason, for this is that women (and men, of course) are often faced with the problem of negotiating contradictory or conflicting conceptions of themselves. Women may, for example, be required to be both sexually exciting and available, and modest and chaste. And gender relationships may be subject to the problems that can arise from conflicting discourses about femininity or masculinity. Men may, for example, both see themselves as "stronger" than women and tend to see women as more weak and passive, but also see women as having a power over

them that can seem to engulf the man in forms of emotional dependence by which he may feel threatened. Discourse about femininity and masculinity is by no means a homogeneous or stable thing. . . .

There is no authentic or unified "original" self which can simply be recovered or discovered as the source of "autonomous" actions. But we are often faced with the experienced need to make "sense" of our lives and our feelings and goals to relate confused fragments of ourselves into something that seems more coherent and of which we feel more in control. We are often also faced, however, with the need to tolerate contradictions, not to strive for an illusory or impossible ideal, and to avoid self-punishing forms of anxiety, defense and guilt (and feminist guilt can be as punishing as any other kind).

Source: From Jean Grimshaw, "Autonomy and Identity in Feminist Thinking," in Morwenna Griffiths and Margaret Whitford (Eds.), *Feminist Perspectives in Philosophy* (Bloomington, IL: Indiana University Press, 1988), 90–108. Excerpts from pp. 91, 92, 93, 94, 102, and 106.

2.7 HISTORICAL SHOWCASE

Plato, Aristotle, and Confucius

The discussion of human nature was intended to provide an array of overviews of what it is to be human. Thus, it has certain pitfalls. One might conclude from the discussion that philosophy is merely a catalogue of diverse opinions, that when engaging an issue such as human nature, philosophy ultimately does little more than serve up a smorgasbord of opinions. Moreover, focusing on a single issue as we have just done inevitably dislodges the portion from the mosaic of interrelated pieces that, taken together, make up a full-scale philosophy. In fact, one cannot fully appreciate a position on an issue without understanding how it fits in with an entire outlook. To avoid these pitfalls and give the preceding material a sharper focus, we now take a more in-depth look at three philosophers: Plato, Aristotle, and Confucius.

Plato

Plato was born in 427 BCE into a wealthy family of the nobility of Athens, Greece. As a teenager, he met and became well acquainted with Socrates, eventually adopting him as an informal teacher. Plato admired

School of Athens, from the Stanza della Segnatura, 1510–1511 (fresco), Raphael (Raffaello Sanzio of Urbino) (1483–1520)/© Vatican Museums and Galleries, Vatican City, Italy, Giraudon/The Bridgeman Art Library International

Plato: "If, as we say, perfect beauty and goodness and every ideal exist, then it is a necessary inference that just as these ideals exist, so our souls existed before we were born."

Socrates deeply, feeling that Socrates' reliance on reason was the key to the solution of the many political and cultural problems that then plagued Athens. Since the death of the great Athenian statesman Pericles, Athens had been engaged in an unending series of wars that Pericles himself had initiated and that ended with the defeat of Athens at the hands of the city-state of Sparta. After peace was restored, the Athenians condemned Socrates to death, accusing him of undermining Athenian culture and thus being responsible for its many troubles. Shocked and disillusioned by Socrates' execution, Plato withdrew from public life and devoted himself to philosophy until his death in 347.

In his philosophical theories, Plato fashioned a distinctive view of human nature, a view that has had a crucial formative influence on all subsequent theories of human nature. In fact, an important twentieth-century philosopher, Alfred North Whitehead, asserted that "all philosophy is nothing more than a footnote to Plato." Whitehead was referring to the fact that Plato was the first philosopher to develop philosophical notions of human nature, human knowledge, and metaphysics. He was also the first to pose the basic questions about these topics that all subsequent philosophers have continued to ask. Plato's views on human nature are important, then, not only for themselves but also because of their enduring influence.

Most of what we know about Plato's philosophy is based on the many dialogues he wrote in which the character of Socrates is the major speaker. In his early dialogues, Plato more or less faithfully reported Socrates' views. But as Plato grew older and his own theories began to develop, the character of Socrates increasingly became the mouthpiece for Plato's own views. In what are called the middle and late dialogues, in fact, the views expressed by the character Socrates are entirely those of Plato.

Plato's most fundamental contribution to philosophy was the distinction he drew between the changing physical objects we perceive with our senses and the unchanging ideals we can know with our minds. One of his clearest examples of this distinction is drawn from the science of geometry. Plato pointed out that we use our minds in geometry to discover unchanging truths about ideally perfect lines, squares, and circles. Yet the physical objects in the visible world are never perfectly straight, square, or circular, and they are continually changing. At best, physical objects are imperfect replicas of the ideal objects we contemplate in geometry.

As Plato put it, "Those who study geometry use visible figures and reason about them. But they are not thinking of these, but of the ideals which they resemble. They are thinking of a perfect square or a perfect line, and so on, and not of the imperfect figures they draw.... The visible figures they draw are merely replicas and what they are seeking is to understand the ideals which can be known only by the mind."[1]

Plato pointed out that this distinction between a perfect ideal and its imperfect replicas also applies to art and morality. With our minds we are able to think about the ideal of perfect beauty and perfect goodness. But the many physical objects we see with our senses are only imperfectly beautiful and imperfectly good. The following dialogue, in which Plato put his own ideas into the mouth of Socrates, expresses the matter in this way:

SOCRATES: We say there are many objects that are beautiful and many objects that are good and similarly many objects that are instances of something specific.

GLAUCON: Yes, indeed.

SOCRATES: And, in addition, we say there is perfect beauty itself and perfect goodness itself. And a similar thing may be said about any definite ideal which has many instances. Each of the many instances is related to its perfect ideal insofar as each shares in that ideal and each gets its name from that ideal.

GLAUCON: Very true.

SOCRATES: The many objects are visible but they are not the objects we know [with our minds], while the ideals are the objects we know [with our minds] but they are not visible to the eye.[2]

As this passage suggests, Plato realized that his distinction between a perfect ideal and its many imperfect physical replicas actually extended to every class of things "of which there are many instances." The many human beings we see, the many oak trees, and the many tables are more or less imperfect replicas of what we think of as the ideal human being, the

---

[1]   Plato, *Republic*, from bk.6. This translation copyright © 1987 by Manuel Velasquez.
[2]   Ibid.

ideal oak tree, and the ideal table. Again, in Plato's words as expressed by Socrates in dialogue:

SOCRATES: Don't we usually assume that when there are many things that have the same name, there is also an ideal that corresponds to them? You understand, don't you?

GLAUCON: I do.

SOCRATES: Consider any such group of many things. For example, there are many things we call beds and many tables.

GLAUCON: Yes, there are.

SOCRATES: And these have ideals corresponding to them. Two, in fact: one of the bed and one of the table.[3]

To these ideals, Plato gave the name *forms*. He came eventually to hold that a separate form exists for each kind of thing. For example, for things that are good, there is the form of goodness; for things that are human, there is the form of humanness; for things that are triangular, there is the form of triangle. The form of a certain class of objects consists of those characteristics that make those objects the kind of objects they are. For example, the form of horse consists of those characteristics that make each horse a horse.

The visible objects in our world never perfectly embody their forms: visible objects are only imperfect and changing reflections of the invisible, perfect, and unchanging forms. For example, each of the many horses in our world is an imperfect duplicate or copy of the one perfect form of horse, just as each human is a replica of the one perfect form of human being.

To a large extent, Plato's theory of forms was inspired by the questioning of his teacher Socrates. Socrates, you may recall, would ask his hearers for the characteristic that makes a thing what it is. For example, in the dialogue *Euthyphro*, Socrates says, "I was not asking you to give me *examples* of holiness, Euthyphro, but to identify the characteristic that makes all holy things holy. There must be some characteristic that all holy things have in common, and one which makes unholy things unholy. Tell me what this characteristic itself is." In a similar manner, Socrates searched for the characteristic that makes a thing just and the characteristic that makes a thing

beautiful. Plato believed that his forms were the characteristics for which Socrates had been searching because the form of a thing is what makes it what it is. Thus, Plato felt that in discovering the forms he had discovered the objects for which Socrates had searched all his life.

All sciences, Plato said, must be based on these ideals we know with our minds and not on their visible, changing, and imperfect replicas. As geometry is about ideal figures, and morality is about ideal goodness, so also each science is about the ideal forms that pertain to a certain class of things. For example, the science of medicine is based on the doctor's knowledge of the ideally perfect human body. Because visible objects are continually changing and imperfect, they cannot be what a science studies—for science, like geometry, tries to state laws and truths that are exact and do not change from moment to moment.

However, Plato's discovery that the mind knows perfect ideals that are not found in the visible world created a problem. Because they do not exist in the visible world, are those perfect ideals merely arbitrary creations of the mind? Are they mental figments that have no reality outside the mind? Plato saw that if the ideals that make up geometry, morality, and the sciences had no reality, then all of these sciences would be worthless, because they would be about unreal objects.

Plato had a passionate faith that our scientific and moral knowledge is concerned with reality, so he drew the only conclusion possible: The perfect ideals with which geometry, morality, and the sciences are concerned must be real. That is, these perfect ideals, or forms, really exist outside the mind. Because they do not exist in the visible world, they must exist in a world that is not visible to us. Plato concluded that there are two real worlds: the nonvisible world of unchanging perfect forms and the visible world that contains their many changing replicas. In fact, Plato held, the forms are *more* real than their replicas, for somehow (Plato suggested that God was responsible) the forms are the basic models according to which their imperfect replicas are made. As he put it, "These ideals are like patterns that are fixed into the nature of things. Each of the many things is made in the image of its ideal and is a likeness to it. The many replicas share in the ideal insofar as they are made in its image."[4]

---

3   Ibid., from bk. 10.

4   Plato, *Parmenides*. This translation copyright © 1987 by Manuel Velasquez.

But how do we acquire our knowledge of the perfect ideals if they do not exist in the visible world? Plato's solution to this problem was ingenious. He argued that because we do not see the perfect ideals in our present world and because we obviously have knowledge of these ideals and investigate them in the sciences, we must have acquired this knowledge in a previous life. This shows, he held, that we have souls and that our souls must be immortal. Thus, Plato's theory of forms directly influenced his views on human nature, as Plato's own words, expressed by the character Socrates, reveal:

SOCRATES: Tell me, Simmias, do we think that there is such a thing as perfect justice?

SIMMIAS: We certainly do.

SOCRATES: And perfect beauty as well as perfect goodness?

SIMMIAS: Of course.

SOCRATES: Well, did you ever see these with your eyes?

SIMMIAS: Certainly not ...

SOCRATES: And do we say there is such a thing as perfect equality? I do not mean the imperfect equality of two lengths of wood or two stones, but something more than that: absolute equality.

SIMMIAS: We most certainly say there is ...

SOCRATES: But when did we come to think about perfect equality? Didn't we do so when we saw the imperfect equality of stones and pieces of wood and this brought to mind something else, namely perfect equality?

SIMMIAS: Certainly.

SOCRATES: Now when we see one thing and it brings to mind something else, that is what we call remembering, is it not?

SIMMIAS: Surely ...

SOCRATES: Do we agree, then, that when someone sees something that he recognizes as an imperfect instance of some other thing he must have had previous knowledge of that other thing? ...

SIMMIAS: We must agree ...

SOCRATES: Then we must have had a previous knowledge of perfect equality before we first saw the imperfect equality of physical objects and recognized it fell short of perfect equality ...

SIMMIAS: Yes.

SOCRATES: Then before we began to see or hear or use the other senses, we must somewhere have gained a knowledge of perfect equality ...

SIMMIAS: That follows necessarily from what we have said before, Socrates.

SOCRATES: And we saw and heard and had the other senses as soon as we were born?

SIMMIAS: Certainly.

SOCRATES: Then it appears that we must have acquired our knowledge of perfect equality before we were born.

SIMMIAS: It does.

SOCRATES: Now if we acquired that knowledge before we were born, and ... lost it at birth, but afterwards by the use of our senses regained the knowledge which we had previously possessed, would not the process which we call learning really be recovering knowledge which we had? And shouldn't we call this recollection?

SIMMIAS: Assuredly.

SOCRATES: Then, Simmias, the soul existed previously, before it was in a human body. It existed apart from the body and had knowledge. ... If, as we say, perfect beauty and goodness and every ideal exists, and if we compare to these whatever objects we see, then it is a necessary inference that just as these ideals exist, so our souls existed before we were born ...

SIMMIAS: Yes, Socrates. You have convinced me that the soul existed before birth. ... But perhaps Cebes here still has doubts ...

SOCRATES: Well, these ideals of Forms, which are true reality, are they always the same? Consider perfect equality or perfect beauty or any other ideal. Does each of these always remain the same perfect form, unchanging and not varying from moment to moment?

CEBES: They always have to be the same, Socrates.

SOCRATES: And what about the many individual objects around us—people or horses or dresses or what have you—which we say are equal to each other or are beautiful? Do these always remain the same or are they changing constantly and becoming something else?

CEBES: They are continually changing, Socrates.

SOCRATES: These changing objects can be seen and touched and perceived with the senses. But the unchanging Forms can be known only with the mind and are not visible to the senses. ... So there are two kinds of existing things: those which are visible and those which are not. ... The visible are changing and the invisible are unchanging.

CEBES: That seems to be the case ...

SOCRATES: Now which of these two kinds of things is our body like?

CEBES: Clearly it is like visible things ...

SOCRATES: And what do we say of the soul? Is it visible or not?

CEBES: It is not visible.

SOCRATES: Then the soul is more like the invisible and the body like the visible?

CEBES: That is most certain, Socrates.

SOCRATES: Recall that we said long ago that when the soul relies on its bodily senses—like sight or hearing or the other senses—it is dragged by the body toward what is always changing. Then the soul goes astray and is confused as it staggers around drunkenly among these changing things.

CEBES: Very true.

SOCRATES: But when the soul turns within and reflects upon what lies in herself [knowledge of the Forms], she finds there the perfect, eternal, immortal, and unchanging realm that is most like herself. She would stay there forever if it were possible, resting from her confused wanderings. So long as she continues to reflect upon the unchanging [Forms], she herself is unchanging and has what we call wisdom.

CEBES: That is well and truly said, Socrates.

SOCRATES: So which kind of thing is the soul most like?

CEBES: The soul is infinitely more like what is unchanging ...

SOCRATES: And the body is more like the changing?

CEBES: Yes.

SOCRATES: One more thing: When soul and body are united, it is the nature of the soul to rule and govern and of the body to obey and serve. Which of these two functions is like god and which is like a mortal? Is it not true that what rules is like god and what is ruled is like a mortal?

CEBES: True ...

SOCRATES: Then, Cebes, does it not follow that the soul is most akin to what is divine, immortal, intellectual, perfect, indissoluble, and unchanging, while the body is most like what is mortal, unintellectual, indissoluble, and ever changing?

CEBES: That cannot be denied.[5]

Plato's view of human nature, then, is a direct consequence of his theory of forms. Because we know the forms, it follows that we have souls and that our souls existed apart from our bodies before we were born into this world. Although our bodies are visible, changing, and subject to decay, our souls are like the forms, so they are invisible, eternal, immortal, and godlike.

Having come to the conclusion that our souls—our inner selves—existed before we were born and will continue to exist after our deaths, Plato felt that it is imperative to care for our souls. He held that the soul consists of three parts that sometimes struggle against one another:

SOCRATES: But does our soul contain ... three elements or not? ... Do we gain knowledge with one part, feel anger with another, and with yet a third desire food, sex, drink, and so on? This is a difficult question.

GLAUCON: I quite agree.

SOCRATES: Let us approach the question in this way. It is clear that the same parts of a single thing cannot move in two

5   Plato, *Phaedo*. This edited translation copyright © 1987 by Manuel Velasquez.

GLAUCON: opposing directions. So if we find that these three elements oppose each other, we shall know that they are distinct parts of ourselves.

GLAUCON: Very well …

SOCRATES: Now consider a thirsty man. Insofar as he is thirsty, his soul craves drink and seeks it.

GLAUCON: That is clear …

SOCRATES: Yet isn't it sometimes true that the thirsty person [who wants to drink] also, for some reason, may *not* want to drink?

GLAUCON: Yes, often.

SOCRATES: In his soul there is a part that desires drink and another part that restrains him. This latter part then is distinct from desire and usually can control desire. … Doesn't such control originate in reason, while the urge to drink originates in something else? …

GLAUCON: So it seems.

SOCRATES: Then we can conclude that there are in us two distinct parts. One is what we call "reason," and the other we call the nonrational "appetites." The latter hungers, thirsts, desires sex, and is subject to other desires …

GLAUCON: Yes, that is the logical conclusion.

SOCRATES: So there are at least two distinct elements in us. But what about our emotional or spirited part: the part in us that feels anger and indignation?

GLAUCON: Perhaps we should say that it is part of our appetites.

SOCRATES: Maybe. But think about this story which I think is true. Leontius was walking up from Piraeus one day when he noticed the bodies of some executed criminals on the ground. Part of him was overcome with a desire to run over and look at the bodies, while another part felt angry at himself and tried to turn away. He struggled with himself and shut his eyes, but at last the desire was too much for him. Running up to the bodies, he opened his eyes wide and cried, "There, damn you! Feast yourselves on that lovely sight!"

GLAUCON: I'm familiar with that story.

SOCRATES: The point of the story is that anger sometimes opposes our appetites as if it is something distinct from them. And we often find that when our appetites oppose our reason, we become angry at our appetites. In the struggle between appetite and reason, our anger sides with reason …

GLAUCON: That is true …

SOCRATES: Yet this emotional part of ourselves is distinct from reason. The poet Homer, for example, … describes people whose reason inclines them to choose the better course, contrary to the impulses of anger.

GLAUCON: I entirely agree.

SOCRATES: So … the soul has three distinct parts.[6]

Plato thought that his discovery of the three-part soul provided the key to happiness and virtue. Personal happiness and virtue, Plato held, can be achieved only when the three parts of our soul are in harmony with one another and are properly subordinated to one another. Happiness is possible only if reason rules the emotions and desires and both the emotions and desires have been trained to be led harmoniously by reason.

We become unhappy when the three parts of ourselves are constantly fighting against one another so that we lack inner harmony, and we fall victim to vice when we are ruled by our emotions or desires:

SOCRATES: A man is just when … each part within him does what is proper for it to do …

GLAUCON: Indeed.

SOCRATES: Isn't it proper for reason to rule since it can acquire knowledge and so can know how to care for the whole soul; and isn't it proper that the emotions should obey and support reason?

GLAUCON: Certainly …

SOCRATES: When reason and the emotions have been trained and each has learned its proper function, they should stand guard over the appetites … lest the

6   Plato, *Republic*. This translation copyright © 1987 by Manuel Velasquez.

appetites grow so strong that they try to enslave and overthrow them.

GLAUCON: Very true. ...

SOCRATES: In truth, justice is present in a man ... when each part in him plays its proper role. The just man does not allow one part of his soul to usurp the function proper to another. Indeed, the just man is one who sets his house in order, by self-mastery and discipline coming to be at peace with himself, and bringing these three parts into tune like the tones in a musical scale. ... Only when he has linked these parts together in well-tempered harmony and has made himself one man instead of many will he be ready to go about whatever he may have to do, whether it be making money, satisfying his bodily needs, or engaging in affairs of state ...

GLAUCON: That is perfectly true, Socrates ...

SOCRATES: Next we must consider injustice. That must surely be a kind of war among the three elements, whereby they usurp and encroach upon one another's functions. ... Such turmoil and aberration we shall, I think, identify with injustice, intemperance, cowardliness, or the other vices.

GLAUCON: Exactly ...

SOCRATES: Virtue, then, seems to be a kind of health and beauty and strength of the soul, while vice is like a kind of disease and ugliness and weakness in the soul.[7]

To train the emotions and appetites so that they will readily obey reason was crucial for Plato. He likened our emotions and appetites to two winged steeds that can either drag our reason downward into the confusions and illusions of the visible changing world or help carry our reason upward to contemplate the world of unchanging perfect forms through the study of the sciences and the acquisition of wisdom. In a beautiful image, Plato compared the three-part soul to a chariot, with the charioteer driving a white-winged horse and a black-winged horse:

Let me speak briefly about the nature of the soul by using an image. And let the image have three parts: two winged horses and a charioteer.... One of the charioteer's horses is of a noble breed, the other ignoble. The charioteer controls them but with great difficulty. ... The vicious steed—when it has not been thoroughly trained—goes heavily, pulling the charioteer down to the earth.... Above them ... in the heaven above heaven ... there exists the true reality with which real knowledge is concerned. This is the world of the Forms which are visible only to the mind ... and have no color, shape, or hardness. ... It is the place of true knowledge ... where every soul which is rightly nourished feeds upon pure knowledge, rejoicing at once again beholding true reality. ... There souls can behold perfect justice and temperance ... not in things which change, but in themselves. The souls that are most like the gods are carried up there by their charioteer ... although troubled by their two steeds and only with great difficulty reaching high enough to behold true being. ... Other souls rise only to fall again, some barely glimpsing the world that is truly real and then seeing it no longer because their two steeds are too unruly.[8]

As this passage suggests, Plato held that we can be completely virtuous only if our reason knows the forms. In particular, our reason must know the form of the good because only by grasping what goodness is can we know what the three parts of the soul must do to be good. Thus, for Plato, complete virtue can be achieved only by coming to have knowledge of the form of the good, which exists unchanging in a world of forms separate from ours.

Plato held that the best ruler, the perfect king, would be a person—male or female—whose soul was self-disciplined enough to enable him or her to contemplate true being in the perfect forms. Such a person, Plato wrote, would be a true *philosopher,* which in Greek means "lover of wisdom":

SOCRATES: If a man believes there are many things which are beautiful but does not know beauty itself ... is he awake or is his life nothing but a dream?

GLAUCON: I would say he is dreaming.

SOCRATES: And if a man knows beauty itself and can distinguish it from its many replicas, and does not confuse beautiful things with beauty itself ... is he dreaming or awake?

---

[7] Ibid.

[8] Plato, *Phaedrus.* This edited translation copyright © 1987 by Manuel Velasquez.

GLAUCON:	He is awake ...
SOCRATES:	If people look at the many visible things which are beautiful, but do not know beauty itself, ... and similarly see things which are just but do not know justice itself, then they merely have opinions and do not have real knowledge of these things. ... While those who know the real unchanging [Forms] have true knowledge ... and are philosophers ...
GLAUCON:	By all means.
SOCRATES:	Well, are those who have no knowledge of true being any better than blind men? They have no true models in their souls to illuminate things. They cannot fix their eyes on true reality nor can they refer to it when they lay down their laws regarding what is beautiful, just and good.... So should we make them rulers? Or should we establish as rulers those who know true reality and who are virtuous?
GLAUCON:	Obviously the latter.[9]

Thus, rulers, even more than ordinary citizens, must keep their minds fixed on the unchanging ideals or forms—especially the form of the good—and their emotions and appetites under the control of reason. Only in this way will they rule states in such a way that, like the virtuous individual, they will have harmony and happiness.

Plato's theory of forms, which he developed under the influence of Socrates' teaching, was the basis for his influential view of human nature. All future philosophers would struggle with Plato's problem: How can we account for the fact that our mind comprehends perfect ideals that this world only imperfectly duplicates? Many twentieth-century philosophers (such as Kurt Gödel, John McTaggart, Alfred North Whitehead, and Bertrand Russell) have agreed that only Plato's theory of forms can adequately account for our knowledge of certain ideals, especially mathematical ideals. And many philosophers who have rejected Plato's theory of forms have agreed, nevertheless, with Plato's claims concerning the soul and the body. Plato's philosophy remains very much alive today.

Aristotle

Although Aristotle was a student of Plato, his approach to human nature was very different. Son of a physician of a Macedonian king, Aristotle was born in 384 BCE at Stagira in northern Greece. When he was 17, his father sent him to Athens to study in Plato's Academy, the ancient equivalent of a modern-day university. There he found in Plato an inspiring teacher whom he later described as a man "whom bad men have not even the right to praise, and who showed in his life and teachings how to be happy and good at the same time." Aristotle stayed on as a teacher at the academy until Plato's death twenty years later. After leaving the academy, Aristotle was asked by King Philip II of Macedonia, the new conqueror of the Greeks, to tutor his young son, the future Alexander the Great. Three years later, when his pupil ascended the throne, Aristotle returned to Athens to set up his own school, the Lyceum. There he taught and wrote for twelve years until the death of Alexander, his protector, released a wave of pent-up anger the Greeks had long harbored toward their Macedonian conquerors and their friends. Under threat of death, Aristotle fled Athens and took refuge in a Macedonian fort, saying that he did not want the Athenians to "sin twice against philosophy" by killing him as they had killed Socrates. He died there one year later.

Aristotle: "In all our activities there is an end which we seek for its own sake, and everything else is a means to this end. ... Happiness is [this] ultimate end. It is the end we seek in all that we do."

---

9   Plato, *Republic*.

As a young man, Aristotle seems to have been a close follower of Plato, but as he grew older, he came to have increasing doubts about Plato's views. Aristotle agreed that each class of things has certain essential characteristics—its form. But unlike Plato, Aristotle did not believe that forms exist in some separate world apart from the visible things around us. Instead, he held, the forms of visible things exist in the visible things themselves. How is this possible?

According to Aristotle, those characteristics that make a thing what it is and that all things of that kind have in common are the form of a thing. For example, the form of roundness consists of those characteristics that all round things have in common and that make a thing round. The form of a horse consists of those characteristics that all horses have in common and that make a thing a horse and not, say, a cow. Although we can distinguish *in our minds* between roundness and visible round things, this does not mean that, besides the visible round things around us, there also exists *in reality* a *separate* ideal object called roundness. Roundness exists only in round things, and horseness exists only in actual horses.

Once Aristotle realized that the world could be explained without a separate world of ideal forms, he began to develop a new view of reality that was much closer to common sense than Plato's. Aristotle explained the changing world by using his new concept of form together with three other kinds of causes: the material cause, or the stuff out of which things are made; the efficient cause, or the agent who brings about a change; and the final cause, or the purpose of the change.

Consider, for example, how a block of marble can be changed into a statue of Socrates by a sculptor. If we ask *why* the marble changed as it did, we can give four kinds of explanations. First, we can explain why the marble statue came to have some of its characteristics by identifying its form, or *formal cause.* Because it has the form of a statue of Socrates, it came to be shaped like Socrates. Second, we can explain why the statue has other characteristics by identifying the matter out of which it is made, or the *material cause.* Because it is made out of marble, it is hard and white. Third, we can explain why the marble changed as it did by identifying the agent who made the statue, or the *efficient cause.* Because the artist chiseled the marble, it gradually came to be shaped like Socrates. And fourth, we can explain why the statue came to be by identifying the purpose for which it was made, or the *final cause.* The artist made the statue because he was trying to please a

patron. Thus, things can be explained completely in terms of their causes in this world without having to theorize forms from some other world, as Plato did. Aristotle explained his four causes in these words:

> Next we must examine explanations or "causes," and state clearly the number and kinds of explanations there are. For we are seeking knowledge of things and we know a thing only when we can explain why it is as it is. And we explain something by identifying its basic causes. So, obviously, if our aim is to know the changing and perishing objects of nature, we will have to know their basic causes and use them to explain things.
>
> One kind of explanation [the material cause] is provided by identifying the material of which a thing is made and which remains present in the thing. For example, the bronze of which a statue is made or the silver of a bowl ...
>
> A second kind of explanation [the formal cause] is provided by identifying the form or plan of a thing, that is, by stating the essential characteristics that define a thing ...
>
> A third kind of explanation [the efficient cause] is provided by identifying the agent who produced or changed something. For example, an advisor is the efficient cause of the changes he advises, a father is the efficient cause of the children he produced, and generally whatever produces or changes anything is the efficient cause of what is produced or changed.
>
> Finally, a kind of explanation [the final cause] is also provided when we give the end or purpose of a thing. For example, health can explain taking a walk, as when we ask, "Why is he taking a walk?" and reply, "For the sake of his health" and thereby feel that we have given an explanation.[10]

Aristotle held, then, that everything in the universe has a certain form, is made out of a certain matter, is produced by certain efficient causes, and is made to serve a certain purpose or function. The purpose of science is to explain the many things in the universe by identifying their four causes. Science should study the individual things in *this* world to identify their various causes, Aristotle held, instead of spending time thinking about an invisible world of forms.

Besides rejecting Plato's views on a separate world of unchanging forms, Aristotle also rejected his views on the soul. Plato had argued that the soul can exist apart from the body and that in an

---

10 Aristotle, *Physics*, bk. 2, ch. 3. This edited translation copyright © 1987 by Manuel Velasquez.

earlier existence it had acquired knowledge of the forms, which it remembered in this life. Aristotle thought that here, too, we must adhere to the four causes, which involve our experience in this world only. Therefore, he noted, to say that something has a soul is to say that it is alive. Consequently, the human soul is nothing more than those characteristics that distinguish a living human from a dead one. This means that the soul cannot exist apart from the body and cannot survive death.[11] The soul is merely the form of a living human—those essential characteristics that make each of us a living human being—and like other forms, it cannot exist apart from the visible things in this world:

> Let us leave behind, then, the theories of the soul that have come down to us from our predecessors and let us make a fresh start by trying to define what the soul is. . . .
>
> As I have said, the individual things in the world are composed in part of the matter [out of which they are made] . . ., and in part of a form which makes them be the kind of thing that they are. . . .
>
> The most common individual things are physical bodies, especially the natural physical bodies from which everything else is made. Now some physical bodies have life, and some do not. . . . Every natural physical body that has life is an individual thing and so it, too, must be composed of matter and form. . . . Now a physical body itself, when it has life, cannot be a soul. For the body is what *has* attributes [such as life or soul] and is not itself an attribute. The body is rather the matter [of which the living being is made]. The soul, therefore, must be the form of a physical body that has the power of living. . . .
>
> It is as pointless, therefore, to ask whether the body and the soul are identical, as to ask whether the wax and its shape are identical, or, in general, to ask whether the matter of a thing is identical with its form. . . .
>
> So we now have the definition of the soul. The soul is the form or the essential characteristics of a body that has the power of living. . . . Clearly, then, the soul is not separable from the body.[12]

But if the soul does not preexist (as Plato had suggested), how then do we come to have knowledge of the forms of things? Aristotle's answer to this question was straightforward. We know the forms of things—their essential characteristics—because through repeated experience, our minds come to know the essential characteristics of physical things and can consider them apart from these physical things. For example, after seeing many round things, we become capable of thinking about the characteristic of roundness itself, and after studying many horses, we become capable of thinking about horseness. In this way, our minds are able to abstract or mentally separate the form of a thing from the thing itself. Through this process of abstraction, the mind forms the ideal concepts with which the sciences deal. For instance, by considering many imperfect circles, lines, and squares, we abstract the idea of the perfect circle, the perfect line, and the perfect square, and reason about these in the science of geometry. The sciences deal with these ideal essences of things. Thus, Aristotle concluded, although the sciences deal with ideal forms, this does not require us to posit a separate world where these ideal forms exist. The forms of things are real enough because the real objects in our visible world embody these forms. And the sciences deal with these forms when our minds abstract them and consider them as ideals separate from the visible objects in our world. But although we *think* of them as separate, they do not *exist* as separate.

Aristotle also departed from Plato's views on happiness and virtue. Plato held that we could achieve full happiness and virtue only by coming to know the perfect forms that exist in another world. Aristotle rejected this view and held, instead, that happiness and goodness had to be found in *this* world: "Even if there were a perfect Good that existed apart from the many things in our world which are good, it is evident that this good would not be anything that we humans can realize or attain. But it is an attainable good that we are now seeking."[13]

To discover what kind of goodness is attainable in this life, Aristotle examined the various pursuits and activities in which we actually engage. In doing this, he was following the method required by his theory of the four causes: Everything is to be explained in terms of its cause in *this* world. Aristotle began by pointing out that when we do something, we are usually trying to achieve some other

---

[11]   However, Aristotle may have thought that *part* of the soul—what he called the active intellect—survived death. In some passages he seems to hint at this, but scholars still debate his meaning.

[12]   Aristotle, *De Anima*, bk. 2, ch. 1. This edited translation copyright © 1987 by Manuel Velasquez.

[13]   Aristotle, *Nicomachean Ethics*, bk. 1, ch. 6. This translation by Manuel Velasquez.

aim or good. Our "highest good" or "highest end," then, would be whatever we are ultimately seeking in everything we do:

> Every art and every inquiry, and likewise every activity, seems to aim at some good. This is why the good is defined as that at which everything aims.
>
> But sometimes the end at which we are aiming is the activity itself while other times the end is something else that we are trying to achieve by means of that activity. When we are aiming at some end to which the activity is a means, the end is clearly a higher good than the activity ...
>
> Now if in all our activities there is some end which we seek for its own sake, and if everything else is a means to this same end, it obviously will be our highest and best end. Clearly there must be some such end since everything cannot be a means to something else since then there would be nothing for which we ultimately do anything and everything would be pointless. Surely from a practical point of view it is important for us to know what this ultimate end is so that, like archers shooting at a definite mark, we will be more likely to attain what we are seeking [in all our actions].[14]

Because human beings are in continual search of something, it is obviously important for us to be clear about what this "something" is. This "something," of course, would be the "final cause" that explains *why* we humans do what we do. Aristotle tries to identify this "highest end," or "final cause," in the following passage, in which he remains true to his view that we must look for the causes of things by examining what happens in *this* world:

> Some people think our highest end is something material and obvious, like pleasure or money or fame. One thinks it is this, and another thinks it is that. Often the same person changes his mind: When he is sick, it is health; when he is poor, it is wealth. And realizing they are really ignorant, such men express great admiration for anyone who says deep-sounding things that are beyond their comprehension ...
>
> Most people think the highest end is pleasure and so they seek nothing higher than a life of pleasure.... They reveal their utter slavishness in this for they prefer [as their highest end] a life that is attainable by any animal.... Capable and practical men think the highest end is fame, which is the goal of a public life. But this is too superficial to be the

good we are seeking since fame depends on those who give it. ... Moreover, men who pursue fame do so in order to be assured of their own value.... Finally, some men devote their lives to making money in a way that is quite unnatural. But wealth clearly is not the good we are seeking since it is merely useful as a means to something else. ... What, then, is our highest end?

> As we have seen, there are many ends. But some of them are chosen only as a means to other things, for example, wealth, musical instruments, and tools [are ends we choose only because they are means to other things]. So it is clear that not all ends are ultimate ends. But our highest and best end would have to be something ultimate ...
>
> Notice that an end that we desire for itself is more ultimate than something we want only as a means to something else. And an end that is never a means to something else is more ultimate than an end that is sometimes a means. And the most ultimate end would be something that we always choose for itself and never as a means to something else.
>
> Now happiness seems more than anything else to answer to this description. For happiness is something we always choose for its own sake and never as a means to something else. But fame, pleasure, ... and so on, are chosen partly for themselves but partly also as a means to happiness, since we believe that they will bring us happiness. Only happiness, then, is never chosen for the sake of these things or as a means to any other thing.
>
> We will be led to the same conclusion if we start from the fact that our ultimate end would have to be completely sufficient by itself. ... By this I mean that by itself it must make life worth living and lacking in nothing. But happiness by itself answers this description. It is what we most desire even apart from all other things ...
>
> So, it appears that happiness is the ultimate end and completely sufficient by itself. It is the end we seek in all that we do.[15]

Having concluded that in everything we do we are seeking happiness, Aristotle then turned to this question: What must we do to achieve happiness? Plato had said that we will be happy only if we achieve knowledge of those forms that exist in another world. Aristotle rejected this suggestion. Human happiness must be achievable in this life, through our activities in this world. Aristotle felt that before

---

14 Ibid., bk. 1, chs. 1–2.

15 Ibid., bk. 1, chs. 4–5, 7.

we can discover the path to happiness, we must first know what the specific purpose of humanity is: What is it that human nature is meant to do and that nothing else can do? Here is Aristotle's answer:

> The reader may think that in saying that happiness is our ultimate end we are merely stating a platitude. So we must be more precise about what happiness involves.
>
> Perhaps the best approach is to ask what the specific purpose or function of man is. For the good and the excellence of all beings that have a purpose—such as musicians, sculptors, or craftsmen—depend on their purpose. So if man has a purpose, his good will be related to this purpose. And how could man not have a natural purpose when even cobblers and carpenters have a purpose? Surely, just as each part of man—the eye, the hand, the foot—has a purpose, so also man as a whole must have a purpose. What is this purpose?
>
> Our biological activities we share in common even with plants. So these cannot be the purpose or function of man since we are looking for something specific to man. The activities of our senses we also plainly share with other things: horses, cattle, and other animals. So there remain only the activities that belong to the rational part of man.... So the specific purpose or function of man involves the activities of that part of his soul that belongs to reason, or that at least is obedient to reason...
>
> Now the function of a thing is basic, and its good is something added to this function. For example, the function of a musician is to play music, and the good musician is one who also plays music but who in addition does it well. So, the good for man would have to be something added to his function of carrying on the activities of reason; it would be carrying on the activities of reason but doing so well or with excellence. But a thing carries out its proper functions well when it has the proper virtues. So the good for man is carrying out those activities of his soul [which belong to reason] and doing so with the proper virtue or excellence.[16]

Human happiness, then, is to be found by doing well what humans are best able to do: live their lives with reason. And to do something well is to act with virtue. So human happiness is achieved by acquiring the virtues that will enable us to use our reason well in living our lives. But what is human virtue? What does it mean to have the "virtue" of using our reason well in living our lives? Aristotle replies that human virtue requires learning to achieve "the mean" in our feelings and actions, learning to avoid both excess and deficiency. We have virtue when our reason knows what the mean is and when we live according to this knowledge:

> Since our happiness, then, is to be found in carrying out the activities of the soul [that belong to reason], and doing so with virtue or excellence, we will now have to inquire into virtue, for this will help us in our inquiry into happiness ...
>
> To have virtue or excellence, a thing (1) must be good and (2) must be able to carry out its function well. For example, if the eye has virtue, then it must be a good eye and must be able to see well. Similarly, if a horse has its virtue, then it must be all that it should be and must be good at running, carrying a rider, and charging. Consequently, the proper virtue or excellence of man will consist of those habits or acquired abilities that (1) make him a good man and (2) enable him to carry out his activities well ...
>
> Now the expert in any field is the one who avoids what is excessive as well as what is deficient. Instead he seeks to hit the mean and chooses it.... Acting well in every field is achieved by looking to the mean and bringing one's actions into line with this standard of moderation. For example, people say of a good work of art that nothing could be taken from it or added to it, implying that excellence is destroyed through excess or deficiency but achieved by observing the mean. The good artist, in fact, keeps his eyes fixed on the mean in everything he does ...
>
> Virtue, therefore, must also aim at the mean. For human virtue deals with our feelings and actions, and in these we can go to excess or we fall short or we can hit the mean. For example, it is possible to feel fear, confidence, desire, anger, pity, pleasure, ... and so on, either too much or too little—both of which extremes are bad. But to feel these at the right times, and on the right occasions, and toward the right persons, and with the right object, and in the right fashion, is the mean between the extremes and is the best state, and is the mark of virtue. In the same way, our actions can also be excessive or can fall short or can hit the mean.
>
> Virtue, then, deals with those feelings and actions in which it is wrong to go too far and wrong to fall short but in which hitting the mean is praiseworthy and good.... It is a habit or acquired ability to choose ... what is moderate or what hits the mean as determined by reason.[17]

---

16   Ibid., bk. 1, ch. 7.

17   Ibid., bk. 1, ch. 13; bk. 2, ch. 6.

The path to human happiness, then, is by living according to the moderation that our reason discovers. By using our reason, Aristotle is saying, we can know what it means not to go to excess in our feelings and actions. To the extent that we live according to his knowledge, we have virtue and will be happy in this world. Aristotle provides several specific examples of what virtue is:

> But it is not enough to speak in generalities. We must apply this to particular virtues and vices. Consider, then, the following examples.
>
> Take the feelings of fear and confidence. To be able to hit the mean [by having just enough fear and just enough confidence] is to have the virtue of courage. … But he who exceeds in confidence has the vice of rashness, while he who has too much fear and not enough confidence has the vice of cowardliness.
>
> The mean where pleasure … is concerned is achieved by the virtue of temperance. But to go to excess is to have the vice of profligacy, while to fall short is to have the vice of insensitivity …
>
> Or take the action of giving or receiving money. Here the mean is the virtue of generosity. … But the man who gives to excess and is deficient in receiving has the vice of prodigality, while the man who is deficient in giving and excessive in taking has the vice of stinginess …
>
> Or take one's feelings about the opinion of others. Here the mean is the virtue of proper self-respect, while the excess is the vice of vanity, and the deficiency is the vice of small-mindedness …
>
> The feeling of anger can also be excessive, deficient, or moderate. The man who occupies the middle state is said to have the virtue of gentleness, while the one who exceeds in anger has the vice of irascibility, while the one who is deficient in anger has the vice of apathy.[18]

Our human nature, then, is capable of achieving happiness in this world. Although we do not have an immortal soul as Plato argued, we do have reason and can use our reason to control our feelings and actions. To live according to reason by being moderate in our feelings and actions is to acquire human virtue. And this kind of virtue will produce the happiness that our human nature seeks in everything we do.

Thus, although Aristotle's views of human nature grew from the views of his teacher Plato (much as Plato's views grew from those of his teacher Socrates), Aristotle's final theories were quite different from Plato's (as different as Plato's were from Socrates'). Where Plato looked to another world of unchanging forms to explain human nature, Aristotle looked for the "four causes" of things completely within this world. As a result, Aristotle looked only to this world to explain how our human nature can achieve knowledge and happiness. Although Plato said that human knowledge was acquired in some earlier life when the soul existed without the body, Aristotle held that we acquire all our knowledge in this life and that the soul cannot exist apart from the body. And although Plato believed that happiness is acquired by coming to know the forms that exist in another world, Aristotle held that happiness is acquired by being moderate in our feelings and actions in this world.

Confucius

About a century before Plato and Aristotle set the path for Western philosophy by their reasoned inquiries into the nature of reality and the soul, a very different approach to philosophy was being developed in China. Confucius, who was destined to become the most influential thinker in the history of China, fashioned a philosophy the method and concerns of which were quite unlike those of Plato and Aristotle.

Confucius was born about 551 BCE and died about 479 BCE. China at the time was a feudal nation ruled by the Chou dynasty and characterized by war, violence, intrigue, and a general breakdown of morality. The Chou kings were often mere puppets of whatever group of feudal lords managed to take power through force or trickery. Political upheavals, poverty, strife, suffering, and the constant threat of death were the order of the day. Confucius emerged in this context as a reformer who believed that the problems of China derived from

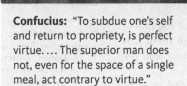

Confucius: "To subdue one's self and return to propriety, is perfect virtue. … The superior man does not, even for the space of a single meal, act contrary to virtue."

© Gautier Willaume/iStockphoto.com

---

[18] Ibid., bk. 2, ch. 7.

the immorality of its rulers and its citizens. Throughout his life he argued that China would emerge from its crisis only when both rulers and subjects lived up to the highest standards of moral integrity.

Although a member of the nobility, Confucius lost his father when he was 3 and grew up in poverty, learning firsthand about the hardships to which the ordinary people of China were being subjected. Self-educated, Confucius entered government service in his early twenties, where he gained some experience in practical politics and a keen interest in contributing something to his afflicted society. The central question he soon set himself was this: How can the happiness of society be achieved? His answer was simple: through widespread adherence to humanistic principles of morality.

Confucius' views are expressed in his main work, *The Analects,* a collection of sayings recorded by his disciples and students. Although it is unclear to what extent *The Analects* are exact renditions of the words of Confucius, they have for centuries been accepted as more or less faithful expressions of his key ideas.

Unlike the lengthy reasonings that became characteristic of Western philosophy in general and of Plato and Aristotle in particular, the method of philosophizing that Confucius used was epigrammatic. *The Analects,* in fact, contains virtually no passages of lengthy, sustained reasoning. Instead, it sets forth pithy sayings that summarize Confucius' views in a highly compressed and intuitive manner.

The philosophy of Confucius in *The Analects* also contrasts starkly with that of Plato and Aristotle in the issues it discusses. Plato and Aristotle were keenly interested in metaphysical issues, including, for example, questions relating to the nature of the gods, the immortality of the soul, and the nature of humankind. However, Confucius counseled his followers to turn away from such inquiries. For Confucius, the only significant questions related to how one ought to behave. *The Analects* recounts the following sayings of Confucius:

2:16—The Master said, "The study of strange doctrines is injurious indeed!"

5:12—Tsze-kung said, "The Master's personal displays of his principles and ordinary descriptions of them may be heard. His discourses about man's nature and the way of Heaven cannot be heard."

6:20—Fan Ch'ih asked what constituted wisdom. The Master said, "To give one's self earnestly to the duties due to men, and, while respecting spiritual beings, to keep aloof from them, may be called wisdom."

11:11—Chi Lu asked about serving the spirits of the dead. The Master said, "While you are not able to serve men, how can you serve their spirits? " Chi Lu added, "I venture to ask about death?" He was answered, "While you do not know life, how can you know about death?"[19]

Confucius' philosophy, then, turned away from supernatural matters and focused entirely on ethics and humanity. His philosophy, in fact, is often characterized as an "ethical humanism." That is, his ethics is not based on religion but on human nature. This basic idea is the unifying principle behind all his philosophy:

4:15—The Master said, "Shan, my doctrine is that of an all-pervading unity." The disciple Tsang replied, "Yes."

The Master went out, and the other disciples asked, saying, "What do his words mean?" Tsang said, "The doctrine of our master is to be true to the principles of our nature and the benevolent exercise of them to others,—this and nothing more."[20]

What are these "principles of our nature"? Confucius insisted that to develop our human nature, we must develop *jen,* or virtue. By virtue, Confucius meant those uniquely human qualities of benevolence and humanity that form the foundation for all human relationships. This sense of love for humanity is, Confucius claimed, the basis of all morality and the quality that distinguishes humans from animals. Without it, life is not worth living. Virtue, according to Confucius, should be our ultimate value, and we should forsake even riches or honor rather than act contrary to virtue:

4:5—The Master said, "Riches and honors are what men desire. If they cannot be obtained in the proper way, they should not be held. Poverty and meanness are what men dislike. If they cannot be obtained in the proper way, they should not be avoided.

"The superior man does not, even for the space of a single meal, act contrary to virtue. In moments of haste, he cleaves to it. In seasons of danger, he cleaves to it."[21]

But what, exactly, is virtue? For Confucius the heart of virtue is reciprocity, the firm resolve to treat others as you would like others to treat you:

---

[19] From Confucius, *The Analects,* in *The Chinese Classics,* vol. 1, ed. and trans. James Legge (Oxford: Clarendon, 1893), reprinted in Daniel Bonevac, William Boon, and Stephen Phillips, *Beyond the Western Tradition* (Mountain View, CA: Mayfield, 1992), 256, 257, 259. The numbers preceding the excerpts refer to the numbering of the paragraphs in the Oxford edition.

[20] Ibid., 257.

[21] Ibid., 256.

12:2—Chung-kung asked about perfect virtue. The Master said, "It is, when you go abroad, to behave to everyone as if you were receiving a great guest; to employ the people as if you were assisting at a great sacrifice; not to do to others as you would not wish done to yourself; to have no murmuring against you in the country and none in the family." Chung-kung said, "Though I am deficient in intelligence and vigor, I will make it my business to practice this lesson."

15:23—Tsze-kung asked, saying, "Is there one word which may serve as a rule of practice for all one's life?" The Master said, "Is not RECIPROCITY such a word? What you do not want done to yourself, do not do to others."[22]

Such virtue, Confucius held, is the key to inner peace and tranquility. It is also the basis of true feelings toward others and the source of right behavior:

4:2—The Master said, "Those who are without virtue cannot abide long either in a condition of poverty and hardship, or in a condition of enjoyment. The virtuous rest in virtue; the wise desire virtue."

4:3—The Master said, "It is only the truly virtuous man who can love or who can hate others."

4:4—The Master said, "If the will be set on virtue, there will be no practice of wickedness."[23]

Achieving virtue is not an easy matter. Virtue requires self-restraint in the use of one's senses and in one's conduct. It requires that we channel our selfish impulses into civilized behavior. Such self-control, Confucius warned, is something that each individual must achieve for himself or herself; it is not something that others can do for one:

1:14—The Master said, "He who aims to be a man of complete virtue in his food does not seek to gratify his appetite, nor in his dwelling place does he seek the appliances of ease."

12:1—Yen Yuan asked about perfect virtue. The Master said, "To subdue one's self and return to propriety, is perfect virtue. If a man can for one day subdue himself and return to propriety, all under heaven will ascribe perfect virtue to him. Is the practice of perfect virtue then from a man himself or is it from others?"

Yen Yuan said, "I beg to ask the steps of that process." The Master replied, "Look not at what is contrary to propriety; listen not to what is contrary to propriety; speak not what is contrary to propriety; make no movement which is contrary to propriety." Yen Yuan then said, "Though I am deficient in intelligence and vigor, I will make it my business to practice this lesson."[24]

Although reciprocity in general should guide our actions, we need to know just what reciprocity requires in specific circumstances. Confucius held that *li,* the "rules of propriety" or the moral customs of one's society, provide this specific and concrete guidance. Reciprocity is attained, then, by restraining oneself in accordance with the moral customs of one's society, which spell out the proper behavior for specific situations:

2:5—The Master said, "Mang-sun asked me what filial piety was, and I answered him, "Not being disobedient.""

Fan Ch'ih said, "What did you mean?" The Master replied, "That parents, when alive, should be served according to propriety; that, when dead, they should be buried according to propriety; and that they should be sacrificed to according to propriety."

6:25—The Master said, "The superior man, extensively studying all learning and keeping himself under the restraint of the rules of propriety, may thus likewise not overstep what is right."[25]

Confucius held that virtue should serve not only as the basis of personal behavior but also as the foundation of political authority. If the ruler exercised virtue, Confucius claimed, then citizens would eagerly follow his leadership. Moreover, if the ruler appointed virtuous ministers, social unrest would end. Thus, virtue is the foundation of a well-ordered society and the key to peace within the state:

2:1—The Master said, "He who exercises government by means of his virtue may be compared to the north polar star, which keeps its place and all the stars turn towards it."

2:19—The duke Ai asked, saying, "What should be done in order to secure the submission of the people?" Confucius replied, "Advance the upright and set aside the crooked, then the people will submit. Advance the crooked and set aside the upright, then the people will not submit."[26]

Confucius also believed that one of the functions of the ruler was to help make people virtuous. Government is not established merely to keep the peace or to raise taxes and fund public enterprises. The virtue of the ruler, Confucius held, affects the virtue of his subjects. For example, the ruler who attempted to instill order through laws and punishments would find that his subjects would be dependent upon external motivations and would not become virtuous. But the ruler who attempted to

---

[22] Ibid., 259.
[23] Ibid., 256.
[24] Ibid., 255, 259.

[25] Ibid., 255, 258.
[26] Ibid., 255, 256.

rule by setting a virtuous example and by enacting laws that were consistent with the rules of propriety would find that his subjects would be motivated by their own internal desire to do what is right and would in time become virtuous:

2:3—The Master said, "If the people be led by laws, and uniformity sought to be given them by punishments, they will try to avoid the punishment, but have no sense of shame.

"If they be led by virtue, and uniformity sought to be given them by the rules of propriety, they will have the sense of shame, and moreover will become good."

12:17—Chi K'ang asked Confucius about government. Confucius replied, "To govern means to rectify. If you lead on the people with correctness, who will dare not to be correct?"

13:6—The Master said, "When a prince's personal conduct is correct, his government is effective without the issuing of orders. If his personal conduct is not correct, he may issue orders, but they will not be followed."

13:13—The Master said, "If a minister make his own conduct correct, what difficulty will he have in assisting in government? If he cannot rectify himself, what has he to do with rectifying others?"[27]

Thus, for Confucius the key to overcoming the political strife and unrest that had held China in their grip for so many centuries was personal virtue. Virtue should not only be the primary concern of the individual; it should also be the basic concern of the ruler. When rulers and citizens behave virtuously in all their social relationships, political strife ends. These ideas are succinctly stated in *The Great Learning*, another work attributed to Confucius:

3. Things have their root and their branches. Affairs have their end and their beginning. To know what is first and what is last will lead near to what is taught in the Great Learning.

4. The ancients who wished to illustrate illustrious virtue throughout the kingdom, first ordered well their own states. Wishing to order well their states, they first regulated their families. Wishing to regulate their families, they first cultivated their persons. Wishing to cultivate their persons, they first rectified their hearts. Wishing to rectify their hearts, they first sought to be sincere in their thoughts. Wishing to be sincere in their thoughts, they first extended to the utmost their knowledge. Such extension of knowledge lay in the investigation of things.

5. Things being investigated, knowledge became complete. Their knowledge being complete, their thoughts were sincere. Their thoughts being sincere, their hearts were then rectified. Their hearts being rectified, their persons were cultivated. Their persons being cultivated, their families were regulated. Their families being regulated, their states were rightly governed. Their states being rightly governed, the whole kingdom was made tranquil and happy.

6. From the Son of Heaven [the ruler] down to the mass of the people, all must consider the cultivation of the person the root of everything besides.[28]

Confucius devoted his life to living and propagating these views. He spent numerous years traveling through China, teaching his views to more than three thousand disciples and students. Although during his lifetime most political rulers were uninterested in his views, his teachings eventually became part of the official philosophy of China.

QUESTIONS

1. Why is Plato's philosophy sometimes said to be poetic? Is this a good or bad quality for philosophy?

2. Mathematicians often make statements such as "There exist two primes between the numbers 4 and 10." What kind of existence do you think they are talking about? How does Plato explain this kind of existence?

3. What do you think is the source of the ideas we have about ideals that we do not see in our physical world (such as beauty, justice, goodness)?

4. "If each person derived her ideas of mathematics by generalizing from her personal experience, then the laws of mathematics would differ from person to person: for one person, 2 plus 2 would equal 4, and for another, it would not. If mathematical ideas were constructed by society, then the laws of mathematics would differ from society to society: in America, 2 plus 2 would equal 4, but in other societies, it might not. The fact that the laws of mathematics must be the same for every person and every society proves that numbers and their laws exist independently of any person or society. And this shows that Plato was right." Evaluate this argument.

5. Compare Plato's theory of the soul to Freud's view that the human psyche contains three parts—an irrational id, a conscious ego, and an unconscious superego, each of which can be distinguished from the others by the psychological conflicts that arise among them.

27   Ibid., 255, 259, 260.

28   Ibid., 263

6. Do you agree with Plato's view that appetite and emotion (at least anger) must be subject to reason? Why or why not?

7. Aristotle's theory of abstraction says each person "abstracts" his own concepts of things from his own knowledge of the particular concrete things around us. But mathematical concepts have to be the same for all persons and all societies. So does Aristotle's theory of abstraction account for our knowledge of mathematical concepts? (See question 4.) Who do you think best accounts for our knowledge of mathematics and our knowledge of ideals such as beauty, goodness, and justice, Aristotle or Plato?

8. Do you agree with Aristotle's view that all moral virtue is a mean between the extremes of excess and deficiency? What about honesty and love? Can you be too honest so that your honesty becomes a vice? Can you love too much so that your love becomes a vice?

9. Does Aristotle's theory imply that only a virtuous person can be happy? Do you agree that happiness without virtue is impossible? Explain.

10. Is there any difference between doing what is morally right and doing what will make one happy?

11. Compare how Aristotle and Confucius each deal with virtue. In what ways are they similar, and in what ways do they differ?

12. What is reciprocity for Confucius? What role does reciprocity play in his philosophy?

13. Do you agree with Confucius' view that government should make people good? Explain your answer.

3 Reality and Being

The true lover of knowledge is always striving after being. . . . He will not rest at those multitudinous phenomena whose existence is appearance only.

PLATO

OUTLINE AND LEARNING OBJECTIVES

3.1 What Is Real?

LEARNING OBJECTIVES: When finished, you'll be able to:

- State why our assumptions about what is real are vitally important.

3.2 Reality: Material or Nonmaterial?

LEARNING OBJECTIVES: When finished, you'll be able to:

- Explain what materialism is and why consciousness is difficult for materialism to explain.
- Explain what idealism is and why some philosophers have objected to it.
- thinking critically Determine the validity of conditional or "if-then" arguments by examining their logical form.

3.3 Reality in Pragmatism

LEARNING OBJECTIVES: When finished, you'll be able to:

- Explain and critically evaluate pragmatism's approach to philosophy, its method for determining what reality is, and James' views on "sub-universes."

3.4 Reality and Logical Positivism

LEARNING OBJECTIVES: When finished, you'll be able to:

- Explain why logical positivists such as Ayer hold that metaphysical claims about reality are meaningless.
- Explain why critics have said that the logical positivists are wrong.
- thinking critically Determine the validity of categorical syllogisms.

3.5 Antirealism: The Heir of Pragmatism and Idealism

LEARNING OBJECTIVES: When finished, you'll be able to:

- Explain what realism and antirealism are and why antirealists say that there is no reality independent of our language or concepts.
- Explain why some feminists object to antirealism and how realists like Searle have tried to prove realism.

3.6 Is Freedom Real?

LEARNING OBJECTIVES: When finished, you'll be able to:

- Explain and evaluate determinism, libertarianism, and compatibilism.

3.7 Is Time Real?

LEARNING OBJECTIVES: When finished, you'll be able to:

- Explain the difference between objective and subjective time and why some philosophers have argued that subjective time is not real and others argue that objective time is unreal.

©Judson Castro/Shutterstock.com

Chapter Summary

3.8 Readings

3.9 Historical Showcase: Hobbes and Berkeley

3.1 What Is Real?

One night you're awakened by a frightened scream. Even though you're groggy with sleep, you recognize your little brother's cry and quickly stumble out of bed. Apparently, your brother's cry did not awaken anyone else. You make your way through the darkness to his bedroom, where you find him shivering with his head hidden under his blanket. "What's the matter?" you ask.

"I'm scared."

"Of what?"

"I don't know. Something's here in my room."

"There's nothing here," you tell him as you flip on a small night-light: "See for yourself."

Your brother looks around the empty room but isn't convinced. "I *saw* them," he insists. "They're here. They're big, with big mouths and staring eyes. They were coming to get me."

"You were only dreaming," you assure him. "It wasn't real. What you saw was only a dream, and dreams aren't real."

"They're real!" he persists.

"No," you say. "If they were real, then why can't you see them now? Where did they go?"

"Sometimes you can see them and sometimes you can't," he replies. "They're here right now in the house, but you can't see them. They're spirits! They're waiting for the dark. They're waiting to get me alone again."

"Shush!" you say. "You're just scaring yourself. I'm going back to bed."

"Don't leave me alone!" he wails. "They'll get me!"

"Just tell yourself that they aren't real," you say as you turn off the light. You don't tell him, but for some reason you feel a little uneasy as you make your way back to your bed through the dark. You hear small creaking noises and faint rustling sounds behind you. So you tell yourself, "They aren't real. Spirits aren't real!" But how do you know? Recall the line in Shakespeare's *Hamlet:* "There are more things in heaven and earth, Horatio, / Than are dreamed of in your philosophy." Why *can't* spirits be real? Why does your philosophy reject the reality of spirits?

Metaphysics is the attempt to answer the question: What is real? A child trembling in the dark may be fearful because he believes that reality is more than the hard material objects

ANALYZING THE READING

In his book *The Examined Life,* philosopher Robert Nozick writes: "The notion of reality has various aspects or dimensions. To be more intense and vivid is to be more real, to be more valuable is to be more real, and so on." Provide some examples of things you think are part of reality and that you think matter to you. Do you agree that some things have "more reality" than others? Would you say some of your examples have more reality than the others? What would you yourself mean when you say something has "more reality" than something else? How would you explain the difference between something that is part of reality and something that is not part of reality?

around him. Reality for him also includes an unseen spiritual realm. You may defend yourself against these fears by insisting that such a realm cannot be a part of reality. Reality consists only of the hard enduring objects around you that can be seen, heard, touched, and smelled. But what grounds do you have for this belief? In fact, many intelligent and thoughtful people have concluded that reality includes more than material objects. And many people—perhaps even you—have suspected that spirits are very real. What reasons can you give for saying that they are wrong? Don't virtually all religions declare that reality is more than the material world around us? Can a person even claim to be religious without believing that there is more to reality than the material world around us? Doesn't God or "the gods" have to constitute a kind of reality that is utterly different from material reality?

But it isn't just spirits and gods that raise troubling metaphysical questions about what we admit to be real. For example, what are we to say about most of the things for which people are willing to live and die? Consider justice, or goodness, or liberty, or truth, or beauty, or love. Are these material? Can they be seen, touched, smelled, or heard? Do they have a size, a shape, or even a place? Are these real? Haven't millions of people died for these ideals? Don't millions of people devote their entire lives to the pursuit of ideals such as these? Doesn't such devotion imply that they are real?

QUICK REVIEW
For many, reality consists only of physical objects and excludes nonphysical entities. But then how real are God, economic forces, subatomic quarks, numbers, and laws?

Perhaps to a practical person these notions seem too soft-minded to be real. So, consider some tougher notions. Economists regularly discuss "inflationary pressures" and the "forces" of supply and demand. Has anyone ever heard, seen, or physically felt these pressures and forces? Yet surely they are real; indeed, their reality creates the wealth of the rich and the impoverishment of the poor. But in what sense are these pressures and forces real? What does it mean to say that these are real? And if these unseen entities are real, then why can't spirits be admitted into the realm of reality? Or consider the physicist's force fields, electrons, protons, neutrons, quarks, and other subatomic particles; the mathematician's numbers, formulas, roots, and equations; and the astronomer's laws, curved spaces, black holes, and compressed or stretched intervals of time. Do we admit these odd entities into our notion of "reality"? Yet none of these are like the hard, visible, colored objects that make up our material world. What, then, is reality? What does it include?

These questions are puzzling. But are they important? Let's see. Think about what you imply when you say that something is not part of reality. For example, consider what you imply when you tell your little brother that "spirits aren't real." Isn't the point of saying this to convince him that he should pay no attention to so-called spirits? Aren't you telling him that spirits can exert no causal influence on him? That they cannot act on him or on anything else and so can neither hurt nor harm (nor even help) him? That they do not matter and cannot matter? Aren't you saying that they have no importance, no power, no actuality, no significance? That they should be disregarded, paid no heed, dismissed?

If these are some of the implications of saying something is unreal, then the implications of saying something is part of reality are great indeed. For in saying that something is part of reality, are we not saying that it has importance, significance, actuality, power? Are we not saying that it is something that should not be dismissed, something that can make a difference to our lives, something to which we need to be attentive? As the philosopher Robert Nozick has said, to say something is real is to say it has "value, meaning, importance, and weight."

QUICK REVIEW
For many, what is real is important, significant, actual, makes a difference, matters, and must be attended to. For Nozick, what is real has "value, meaning, importance, and weight."

PHILOSOPHY AND LIFE

The Experience Machine, or Does Reality Matter?

In his book *The Examined Life,* philosopher Robert Nozick suggests the following "thought experiment":

> Imagine a machine that could give you any experience (or sequence of experiences) you might desire. When connected to this experience machine, you can have the experience of writing a great poem or bringing about world peace or loving someone and being loved in return. You can experience the felt pleasures of these things, how they feel "from the inside." You can program your experiences for tomorrow, or this week, or this year, or even for the rest of your life. If your imagination is impoverished, you can use the library of suggestions extracted from biographies and enhanced by novelists and psychologists. You can live your fondest dreams "from the inside." Would you choose to do this for the rest of your life? If not, why not?... The question is not whether to try the machine temporarily, but whether to enter it for the rest of your life. Upon entering, you will not remember having done this; so no pleasures will get ruined by realizing they are machine produced.

Nozick suggests that at least the first instinctive impulse of most of us would be to choose not to enter the machine where we would live forever in a dream world that, unknown to us, was not real.

QUESTIONS

1. Would you enter the experience machine? Why or why not?

2. Nozick claims that the reason most of us would not enter the experience machine forever is because we don't just care about the feelings and sensations we experience but also want our lives to be based on reality and not on illusion. Do you agree? Is it enough to spend your life just thinking that you are accomplishing great things, are engaged in fulfilling and worthwhile activities, and are loved by, say, your children and a wonderful spouse? Or would these things have to be real to be worth devoting your life to them? Explain.

3. If a person in the experience machine thinks his experiences are real, then are they real? Is reality whatever you experience and think is real?

Source: Robert Nozick, *The Examined Life* (New York: Simon and Schuster, 1989), 104–105.

Metaphysical Questions of Reality

Metaphysical questions about what reality is, then, are among the most significant questions we can ask. They are intimately linked to what is important to us, what we need to pay attention to, what has significance, what matters. If ghosts are not real, then ghosts don't matter. If God is not real, then God doesn't matter. If the spiritual realm is not real, then it can make no difference in our lives. If only the material exists, then only the material is important. Clearly, our beliefs about reality will profoundly affect what we do with our lives and what we strive for, what we respect and what we ridicule, what we dismiss and what we are willing to live and die for. Only what is real (in some sense) can matter.

In Chapter 2, we raised the question of whether human nature is material or spiritual. But we did not directly

The Persistence of Memory, Salvador Dali. The critical study of the nature of reality is called metaphysics. But perhaps we can never say what reality ultimately is; perhaps the question and any subsequent theories are meaningless.

Digital Images © The Museum of Modern Art/Licensed by SCALA/Art Resource, NY Copyright ARS,NY.

examine the more fundamental issue underlying this question: Is matter all there is, or is there another kind of reality besides matter? In this chapter, we focus directly on this question of what is ultimately real, what the essence of all being, including our own, is. The critical study of the nature of reality is called *metaphysics*.

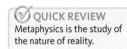

The Search for Reality

Perhaps, however, we can never say definitely what reality is; perhaps both the question and the theoretical answers are meaningless. Perhaps the search for reality is meaningless. As we will see, some people believe that it is meaningless. If so, we cannot even ask what aspects of ourselves and of the universe around us are real and ultimately matter to us. Or if we can ask the question, perhaps the answer will forever remain beyond our grasp. We must wait and see.

We begin this chapter with what many still see as the most fundamental question in metaphysics: Is reality purely material, or does reality also include a nonmaterial element? We look first at the case for materialism and next consider its opposite, idealism.

PHILOSOPHY AT THE MOVIES

Watch *Buddy Boy* (1999) in which Francis, a reclusive, guilt-ridden young man who has suffered brutality and misfortune and who now cares for his abusive ill mother, spies obsessively on a beautiful young woman even after they become romantically involved, and eventually spirals into a bizarre world of suspicion, violence, and death. How much of what Francis sees is real? What distinguishes reality from unreality in this movie? How do you try to distinguish what could be real from what could not be real in this movie?

Other movies with related themes: *Stranger Than Fiction* (2006), *Mulholland Drive* (2001), *The Sixth Sense* (1999), *The Machinist* (2004).

3.2 Reality: Material or Nonmaterial?

Saint Augustine (354–430), one of the greatest of the early Christian theologians, did not find it difficult to believe that spirits are real. Augustine held that reality—the real existing universe—contains within itself every possible kind of being. Beings in the universe range from the "lowest" kind of inert matter to the "highest" kind of spirit. God is all-powerful and wanted to fill reality with goodness, Augustine reasoned. So God created every possible kind of creature that had within itself some degree of reality and so some degree of goodness:

> So great is the variety of earthly things that we can conceive of nothing which belongs to the form of the earth in its full extent which God, the Creator of all things, has not already created. . . . There can exist in nature things which your reason is incapable of conceiving. It cannot be, however, that what you conceive with true reasoning cannot exist. You cannot conceive of anything better in creation which has escaped the Maker of the creation.[1]

Where are human beings in the order of Augustine's universe? Augustine placed us somewhere in the middle of his hierarchy of reality. Humans have material

---

[1] Saint Augustine, *On Free Choice of the Will*, trans. Anna S. Benjamin and L. H. Hackstaff (New York: Bobbs-Merrill, 1964), 96–97.

bodies, so we belong to the lower material world. But we also have spirits, or **souls,** making us part of the higher spiritual world. Humans are both matter and spirit: We straddle two realms of reality.

But can Augustine's view of reality make sense to a person in the modern world? Has modern science's success in explaining the universe in material terms made such beliefs impossible for us? True, much of the world continues to believe that spiritual beings inhabit the universe and that humans are partly spirit. But does it make more sense now for us to believe that matter is all that exists in the universe? Many people today are in fact materialists, who deny that spirit can be real.

ANALYZING THE READING

Look up the meanings of *material* and *materialism* in a dictionary. Do the words have more than one distinct meaning? If so, what are the main distinct meanings of these words? How do you think these distinct meanings are related to each other? This chapter of your textbook uses both words. Do any dictionary meanings of these words seem to be the same as the meanings that these words have in this chapter? Which of the dictionary meanings of these words seem closest to the meanings of these words as they are used in this chapter?

ANALYZING THE READING

The Charvaka philosophers claimed that generalizations are always unreliable because they always go beyond what you observe. How does a generalization go beyond what you observe? Why is a generalization "unreliable" if it goes beyond what you observe? Do you think there is any way of making sure your own generalizations are not "unreliable" in this way?

Materialism: Reality as Matter

Materialism, the view that matter is the ultimate constituent of reality, is as old as philosophy itself. Both Eastern and Western philosophers have argued for the view that only material things are real. A school of materialism flourished even in India, a land that has long celebrated spiritual values. In the West, many ancient Greeks thought everything was made out of the four material substances: water, fire, air, and earth. Others, such as the Greek atomists, had more sophisticated theories but still held that the ultimate stuff of the universe was material.

Eastern Materialism: The Charvaka Philosophers of India.

The "Charvaka" school of Indian philosophers flourished from around 600 BC to the twelfth century AD when it died out. The original works of the Charvaka philosophers have all been lost. What we know about them is what other ancient and medieval Indian philosophers said about them in their own works. The most important of these works was written by Madhava Acharya in the fourteenth century AD.

According to Acharva, the Charvaka philosophers argued that we have only one reliable source of knowledge about the world around us. That one reliable source of knowledge is sense perception. Other possible sources of knowledge, such as inductive or deductive reasoning, they argued, are unreliable. **Inductive reasoning** is generalizing about what we observe. The Charvaka philosophers gave the example of smoke and fire as an example of inductive reasoning. After observing many cases of smoke accompanied by fire, we may generalize that "wherever there's smoke, there's always fire." The problem with inductive reasoning, they argued, is that generalizations always go beyond what we observe. So it is unreliable. **Deductive reasoning** is also unreliable. Deductive reasoning must use general statements to reach its logical conclusions. So deductive reasoning ultimately depends on the generalizations that inductive reasoning produces. Deductive reasoning, then, is as unreliable as the inductive reasoning on which it depends. Therefore, all reasoning—inductive or deductive—about the world around us is unreliable. Our only reliable source of knowledge about the world, then, are our senses.

Once the Charvaka philosophers concluded that we can know only what we can perceive with our senses, they used that conclusion to argue for materialism. Whatever we perceive with our senses is physical and material. But all we know is what we can perceive with our senses. So everything we know is physical and material.

Therefore the soul is nothing more than the body exercising the attribute of intelligence. For there is no evidence for any soul distinct from the body, and the existence of an immaterial soul cannot be proved, since . . . perception is the only source of knowledge. . . . It follows, also, that there is no hell except this world's pains which have mundane causes such as thorns, and so forth. And the only supreme being is the earthly king whose existence anyone can prove by using his senses. The only Liberation is the dissolution of the body. Nor does fate, destiny, and all the rest exist, since these can only be proved by deduction [which is unreliable]. But someone may object that if there are no immaterial powers, then the world would have no creator. But this objection is invalid since all the phenomena of the world could be produced spontaneously from their own inherent natures.[2]

The Charvaka became famous for heaping ridicule on the spiritualism of their religious countrymen. They came to be called "Lokyata" which means "those who go the worldly way." They earned that name because they urged people to turn away from religion and its delusions and to indulge themselves in worldly pleasures. Religious stories and rituals, they said, were made up by the Brahmin priests for their own benefit. And the Vedas, the scriptures of Hinduism, were frauds. We should seek our happiness in this material world and its physical pleasures. Beyond this world there is nothing:

There is no heaven, no final liberation, nor any soul in another world,
Nor do the actions of the castes, orders, or priesthoods, have any real effect.
The three Vedas, the ascetic's three staves, and smearing one's self with ashes,
These are but means of livelihood for those who have no manliness nor sense.
While life remains live happily, feed on butter even if you run up debts.
When once the body becomes ashes, how can it ever return again?
It is only for their own benefit that Brahmins have established
so many ceremonies for the dead—these have no other benefit.
The authors of the Vedas were buffoons, knaves, and demons.[3]

In short, the Caravaka argued, the only world that is real is the finite material world around us. Anything we cannot perceive with our senses—souls, god, or any spiritual

THINKING LIKE A PHILOSOPHER

According to the Charvaka philosophers, generalizations are unreliable because they go beyond what you observe. Give some examples of generalizations you have made. How do you think these generalizations of yours went beyond what you observed? Give some examples of difficulties you have run into because you made some generalizations that later turned out to be wrong. Explain how you try to make sure your own generalizations will not turn out to be wrong. How do you think racial, sexual, ethnic, or other kinds of prejudices are related to generalizations?

ANALYZING THE READING

The Charvaka philosophers said that since sense perception is our only reliable source of knowledge, there is no soul, no hell, no God. Explain how they used the fact that sense perception is our only reliable source of knowledge to show that there is no soul, hell, or God. Does the fact that we cannot perceive something with our senses prove that it does not exist? Why?

---

2   Madhava Acharya, *The Sarva-Darsana-Samgraha, or Review of the Different Sysems of Hindu Philosophy* [c. 1330], trans. E. B. Cowell and A. E. Gough (London: Trubner & Co., Ludgate Hill, 1882), excerpts from 3, 4, and 9.

3   Ibid., excerpt from 10.

QUICK REVIEW
The Indian Charvaka philosophers said that only what the senses perceive is real, so only the physical material world is real.

"realities"—cannot be said to exist at all. Beyond the material world, as far as we know, there is nothing. So religious worship is a pointless waste and priests are charlatans anyway. There is no soul that leaves the body after death, no heavenly rewards, no punishments of hell, no afterlife at all. Human life begins in this world and ends in this world. So "the only end of man is the enjoyment of sensual pleasures," they declared.

Western Materialism. The Greek philosopher Democritus (460–370 BCE) also believed that reality consisted only of matter. The smallest bits of matter he called *atoms*. He described atoms as solid, indivisible, indestructible, eternal, and uncreated. Atoms were not qualitatively distinguishable from one another. And they constantly moved through space, where they combined to form the recognizable physical objects of the universe. According to Democritus, the universe consisted of material atoms and empty space. He believed that even the soul, which he equated with **reason**, consisted of atoms. In this atomic universe, "all things happen by virtue of necessity, the vortex being the cause of the creation of all things."[4]

QUICK REVIEW
The ancient Greek philosopher Democritus said all real objects are made up of material atoms.

But Democritus' theory never became popular. For people soon became disenchanted with philosophers' many attempts to explain the cosmos. Their interest turned to more personal concerns, such as how to lead a happy life. Although their interests reached much further than such questions, the Greek philosophers Socrates, Plato, and Aristotle were also interested in questions about the good life. They argued that moral virtue was the road to a good and happy life. The rise of Christianity fanned this interest in personal moral conduct, which predominated throughout the Middle Ages. As we saw in the last chapter, the idea of an afterlife and the soul gave the medieval view of reality a distinctly nonmaterial bias.

In the seventeenth century, however, a growing interest in the world and the rise of **scientific method** and scientific discovery turned minds once again to materialism. Awakened by the discoveries of Copernicus, Kepler, Galileo, and Newton, people watched science cultivate a full-blown materialism. Committed to the belief that the world could be quantified by scientists, several philosophers made the claim that only matter is real.

We briefly discussed the philosophy of Thomas Hobbes (1588–1679) in the previous chapter. In Hobbes we see Democritus' belief in matter presented as the view that everything consists of measurable matter. Hobbes held that ultimately we can know nothing about the real world other than its measurable aspects:

According to Hobbes,: "The universe, that is the whole mass of things that are, is corporeal, that is to say body." But according to Berkeley, "All of the choir of heaven and furniture of the earth, in a word all those bodies which compose the mighty frame of the world, have no substance without a mind.... [S]o long as they are not actually perceived ..., they have no existence at all."

> Every object is either a part of the whole world, or an aggregate of parts. The greatest of all bodies, or sensible objects, is the world itself; which we behold when we look round about us from this point . . . which we call the earth. Concerning the world, as it is one aggregate of many parts, the things that fall under inquiry are but few; and those we can determine, none. Of the whole world we may inquire what is its magnitude, what its duration, and how many there be, but nothing else.[5]

4   Quoted in Diogenes Laërtius, *Lives and Opinions of Eminent Philosophers*, vol. 2, trans. R. D. Hicks (Cambridge, MA: Harvard University Press, 1925), 455.
5   Thomas Hobbes, "Elements of Philosophy," in *The English Works of Thomas Hobbes*, vol. 1, ed. Sir W. Molesworth (London: J. Bohn, 1839), ch. 1, sec. 8.

Hobbes concluded that measurable matter is all there is. Only measurable matter is real:

> The universe, that is the whole mass of things that are, is corporeal, that is to say body; and has the dimensions of magnitude, namely, length, breadth, and depth. Also every part of body is likewise body, and has the like dimensions. And, consequently, every part of the Universe is body, and that which is not body is no part of the Universe. And because the Universe is all, that which is no part of it is nothing, and, consequently, nowhere.[6]

QUICK REVIEW
Influenced by science, Hobbes held that we can know only the measurable aspects of objects, so we can say only that measurable material objects exist.

Hobbes suggested that our mental states (sensations, thoughts, and emotions) are "motions" in our material "brain and heart." Moreover, a "general inclination all mankind" possess is "a perpetual and restless desire of power after power." (For a fuller discussion of Hobbes' views, see the Historical Showcase at the end of this chapter.)

Julien Offray de La Mettrie carried Hobbes' materialism one step further. In 1748 he published *Man a Machine,* a book that argues that humans are nothing more than complex machines.

> Experience and observation should . . . be our only guides. Both are to be found throughout the records of the physicians . . . and not in the works of the philosophers who were not physicians. Only physicians have traveled through and illuminated the labyrinth of man. . . . Thus, only the physicians have a right to speak on this subject. . . . Man is so complicated a machine that it is impossible to get a clear idea of the machine beforehand. . . . For this reason, all those investigations have been vain, which the greatest philosophers have made *à priori,* [reasoning without relying on experience and observation]. That is to say, in so far as they have used, as it were, the wings of the spirit.
>
> Thus it is only *à posteriori* [by relying on observation and experience], . . . that one can reach the highest probability concerning man's own nature. . . . Let us then take in our hands the staff of experience, paying no heed to the accounts of all the idle theories of the philosophers. To be blind and to think one can do without this staff is the worst kind of blindness. . . . The human body is a machine which winds its own springs. It is the living image of perpetual movement. Nourishment keeps up the movement which fever excites. . . . [Moreover,] since all the faculties of the soul depend to such a degree on the proper organization of the brain and of the whole body, that apparently they are but this organization itself, the soul [also] is clearly an enlightened machine. . . . Let us conclude boldly that [the whole] man is a machine and that in the whole universe there is but a single substance differently modified.[7]

ANALYZING THE READING

La Mettrie says we should rely only on "experience and observation" and concludes that matter is the only "substance" that exists. How does this view of his compare to the views of the Charvaka philosophers? Do you agree with La Mettrie? Why?

MindTap To read more from La Mettrie's *Man a Machine,* click the link in the MindTap Reader or go to the Questia Readings folder in MindTap.

In La Mettrie, materialism came into full bloom. Notice how La Mettrie urges us to rely on "experience and observation" and on those scientists who have relied on experience and observation. Notice, also, that once La Mettrie has satisfied himself that the whole "man is a machine," he concludes that "there is but a single

---

6 Thomas Hobbes, *Hobbes's Leviathan* (Oxford: Clarendon, 1909; original work published 1651), 524.
7 Julien Offray de La Mettrie, *Man a Machine,* [1748], W. Calkins, trans. (La Salle, IL: Open Court, 1912), excerpts from 88, 89, 93, 128, and 148.

substance." That "single substance," of course, is physical or material substance. Showing that even human beings are material, he believes, entitles him to conclude that everything in the universe must be material. The soul itself is just a machine in the head that runs the rest of the machine that is our body.

What had happened to the religious doctrine of the soul? What remained of the creature supposedly made in the image of God and possessed of an eternal destiny? So much medieval superstition! declared the new materialists.

But these early materialists' optimistic faith that humanity would soon explain the universe in terms of matter in motion gave way to doubt.

Objections to Materialism

One fundamental objection to materialism we have already seen. This is its difficulty in accounting for human consciousness—that is, for our conscious mental activities such as thinking, wishing, experiencing, hoping, dreaming, loving, and hating. Hobbes and other traditional materialists like La Mettrie say these mental activities can be explained as the activities of our physical or material bodies. For traditional materialists a material thing is simply a physical object, at rest in a specific location or moving, that takes up space and has a specific mass. So, traditional materialists like Hobbes hold that human consciousness can be explained in terms of things that have these specifiable material qualities. Yet consciousness does not seem to have such material qualities.

What do we mean by "consciousness"? We saw in Chapter 2 that consciousness is the kind of awareness we have when we are awake but not when we are sleeping, sleepwalking, anesthetized, or knocked out. Consciousness is this awareness of our sensing, feeling, and thinking that we have when we are awake. Consciousness has no apparent location, no volume, no mass. Consciousness is subjective in the sense that it exists only if it is being experienced by someone and that person is directly aware of it in a way that others are not. An interesting aspect of consciousness we have not yet noted is what philosophers call its *intensionality*. Intensionality refers to the fact that consciousness and many other mental states must have an *object*. That is, when I am conscious, I must be conscious of *something*. When I see, I must see *something*. When I believe, I must believe *something*. And when I love or hate, I must love or hate *something or someone*. What is interesting is that the objects of which one is conscious need not exist. For example, I can think of a golden mountain or a unicorn, even though they do not exist. I can feel fear of things that aren't real. I can hallucinate and see or hear things that aren't there.

Philosophers have long noted how different the qualities of consciousness are from those of matter. Many believe those differences show there are two different kinds of entities. There are immaterial entities that can be conscious, and material or physical entities that cannot be conscious. Materialists, however, have insisted that all entities are material entities. We saw in the last chapter, for example, that some materialists claim that states of consciousness are states of the brain. The brain, of course, is a physical or material organ. When we experience a thought, this experience is supposed to be our physical brain functioning in a certain way. But the claim that a conscious experience is identical to a brain state runs into a significant obstacle. Brain states can be seen, felt, and touched. But our conscious experiences cannot. For example, a brain surgeon can observe the condition of a ganglion in your brain and identify its location, color, and shape. Yet no one can know what your inner conscious experience is like. No one can know what it is like to consciously see and experience the world as you do. And your conscious experience has no location, color, or shape, while your brain has all of these. The materialist has a hard time explaining, then, how the features of consciousness can be identical to the features of a material brain.

The debate about the implications and significance of consciousness has arisen in the midst of some startling discoveries in atomic physics. For a long time we have known that matter consists of molecules. Molecules, in turn, are composed of a little more than a hundred types of atoms. Until the early twentieth century, no one believed that atoms could be split into smaller components. Today we know that several sub-atomic particles make up the atom including the electron, the proton, and the neutron. These in turn can be broken down into yet more elementary particles. Physicists have discovered more than two hundred of these so-called elementary particles. And these have turned out to be made up of still more elementary entities called *quarks*. The point is that modern scientists are showing reality to be ever more complex.

But, even more important, these elementary bits of stuff do not seem to be matter as traditionally conceived. They are more like energy, or fields, or, perhaps, probability waves. Matter as it was traditionally conceived may depend on interactions of elementary particles. But the particles themselves do not seem to be composed of matter in the traditional sense. That is, they are not made of a hard, solid, perceptible stuff that occupies a definite volume of space and has a specific location and motion. In his article "The De-materialization of Matter," philosopher-scientist N. R. Hanson states the implications:

> Matter has been dematerialized, not just as a concept of the philosophically real, but now as an idea of modern physics. Matter can be analyzed down to the level of fundamental particles. But at that depth the direction of analysis changes, and this constitutes a major conceptual surprise in the history of science. The things which for Newton typified matter—e.g., an exactly determinable state, a point shape, absolute solidity—these are now the properties electrons do not, because theoretically they cannot, have . . .
>
> The dematerialization of matter . . . rocked mechanics at its foundations. . . . The 20th century's dematerialization of matter has made it conceptually impossible to accept a Newtonian picture of the properties of matter and still do a consistent physics.[8]

Materialists have been able to adjust to these new conceptions of elementary particles by expanding their definition of matter. Matter can be redefined to include anything that has observable effects. If this is done then the materialist can accommodate these new conceptions into his or her theory of the universe.

Yet there is another aspect of the discoveries Hanson describes that is not so easily accommodated by simply expanding our definition of matter. During the early 1930s, the German physicist Werner Heisenberg (1901–1976) made a surprising discovery. He found that we cannot observe a subatomic particle's specific location and its momentum at the same instant of time. (Momentum is the mass of a particle multiplied by its velocity.) If we observe a particle's precise location at some instant, we cannot observe its precise momentum at that instant. And if we observe its precise momentum at some instant, we cannot observe its precise location at that instant. Heisenberg called this the "principle of indeterminacy." This principle implied, he said, that at its most basic level—the level of the subatomic—the world is intertwined with the mind. Heisenberg drew this conclusion because he interpreted his principle in a startling way. He claimed that at the subatomic level, things do not even exist at specific locations and are not moving with any specific momentum until they are

---

8   N. R. Hanson, "The Dematerialization of Matter," in *The Concept of Matter*, ed. Ernan McMillin (Notre Dame, IN: University of Notre Dame Press, 1963), 556–557.

observed. And even when they are observed, the more specific the location at which a particle exists, the less specific the momentum at which it is moving, and vice versa. In other words, looking for, and observing, the location of a subatomic particle brings the particle into existence at a specific location. But the particle will exist without any similarly specific momentum; that is, it will have an indefinite velocity or an indefinite mass. And looking for and observing the momentum of a subatomic particle brings it into existence with a specific momentum. But it will not exist in a similarly specific location; that is, it will exist "smeared out" over an area, not at a specific point. Physicist Pascual Jordan (1902–1980), a colleague of Heisenberg, expressed these astonishing conclusions with these words: "Observations not only disturb what has to be measured, they produce it. . . . We compel [the electron] to assume a definite position. . . . We ourselves produce the results of measurements."[9]

Subatomic particles could no longer be thought of as tiny permanently existing points of matter. Instead, they are areas or "waves" of probabilities. That is, they are areas over which there is a greater or lesser probability that the subatomic particle, when observed, will pop into existence. And when it appears, the more specific its location is, the more indefinite its momentum will be. And the more specific its momentum is, the more indefinite its location. As a result, many scientists, including Heisenberg, have concluded that we live in an idealistic universe, one whose reality depends on the mind. At its most fundamental level, the universe is made of

PHILOSOPHY AND LIFE

The Neutrino

The neutrino is perhaps the most bewildering of all the elementary particles known to physics and among the most philosophically provocative. It has no physical properties—no mass, no electric charge, and no magnetic field. It is neither attracted nor repelled by the electric and magnetic fields of passing particles. Thus, a neutrino originating in the Milky Way or in some other galaxy and traveling at the speed of light can pass through the earth as if it were so much empty space. Can it be stopped? Only by a direct, head-on collision with another elementary particle. The chances of that are infinitesimally small. Fortunately, there are so many neutrinos that collisions do occur. Otherwise, physicists would never have detected them. Just think, even as you read this sentence, billions of neutrinos coming from the sun and other stars are passing through your skull and brain. And how would the universe appear to a neutrino? Eminent astronomer V. A. Firsoff provides a picture:

The universe as seen by a neutrino eye would wear a very unfamiliar look. Our earth and other planets simply would not be there, or might at best appear as thin patches of mist. The sun and other stars may be dimly visible,

in as much as they emit some neutrinos. . . . A neutrino brain might suspect our existence from certain secondary effects, but would find it very difficult to prove, as we would elude the neutrino instruments at his disposal.

Our universe is no truer than that of the neutrinos—they exist, but they exist in a different kind of space, governed by different laws. . . . The neutrino. . . is subject neither to gravitational nor to electromagnetic field. . . . It might be able to travel faster than light, which would make it relativistically recede in our time scale.

QUESTIONS

1. What impact does the presence of neutrinos have on your view of reality?

2. Arthur Koestler writes: "To the unprejudiced mind, neutrinos have indeed a certain affinity with ghosts—which does not prevent them from existing." What does this mean?

Sources: V. A. Firsoff, *Life, Mind and Galaxies* (New York: W. A. Benjamin, 1967); Arthur Koestler, *The Roots of Coincidence* (New York: Random House, 1972), 63.

---

9   Pascual Jordan, quoted in Marcelo Gleiser, *The Island of Knowledge: The Limits of Science and the Search for Meaning,* (New York: Basic Books, 2014), 189.

mind-dependent stuff! At the subatomic level, mind-independent matter seems to have disappeared. All that is left are "probability fields" of potential entities that do not become definitely real until they interact with a mind. And even then, some of their features will only have a kind of strange indefinite or nonspecific existence.

To better understand what an idealistic universe is, we will now look at some traditional idealist views. This will also enable us to understand how an idealist universe differs from a materialistic one.

PHILOSOPHY AT THE MOVIES

Watch *Bicentennial Man* (1999) in which Andrew, a domestic robot purchased by the Martin family, gradually comes to display characteristics of a human being— such as creativity, compassion, love, and desire. He is eventually freed by the Martin family and many years later petitions to be legally recognized as a human being. Does this movie imply that Hobbes was right when he wrote: "The universe, that is the whole mass of things that are, is corporeal, that is to say body"? Do you think it is possible for a material creation like Andrew to really be conscious and "feel" compassion, love, and desire, or does Andrew merely act *as if* it experienced these? How would you tell the difference? Should Andrew be legally recognized as a human being?

Other movies with related themes: *Robert and Frank* (2012); *A.I. Artificial Intelligence* (2001); *Blade Runner* (1982); *I, Robot* (2004).

Idealism: Reality as Nonmatter

As we noted, modern atomic theory has led some philosophers to claim that reality consists of something other than matter as traditionally conceived. They claim that the most fundamental particles that make up the universe depend on the mind in some strange way. Historically, several philosophers reached the same conclusion for very different reasons. These philosophers are called idealists.

The Development of Western Idealism. Although idealists differ, we can define **idealism** as the claim that reality is essentially composed of minds and their ideas rather than matter. Whether idealists believe that there is a single absolute mind or many minds, they all emphasize the mental or spiritual, not the material. This is the view that the great English playwright William Shakespeare expressed toward the end of his life in his final play, *The Tempest*. There he characterized the universe around us as "this vision" that exists only in our minds just like a dream:

> Our revels now are ended. These our actors,
> As I foretold you, were all spirits and
> Are melted into air, into thin air:
> And, like the baseless fabric of this vision,
> The cloud-capp'd towers, the gorgeous palaces,
> The solemn temples, that great globe itself,
> Yea, all which it inherit, shall dissolve
> And, like this insubstantial pageant [play] faded,
> Leave not a rack behind. We are such stuff
> As dreams are made on, and our little life
> Is rounded with a sleep.[10]

---

[10] William Shakespeare, *The Tempest*, Act 4, Scene 1, lines 148–158.

In the West, the belief that the reality we see around us exists only in our minds is at least as old as the ancient Greek philosopher Pythagoras (about 600 BCE). However, Plato formalized one of the first versions of this belief. He held that the individual entities we perceive around us are merely shadows of reality. Behind each material entity in our experience is a perfect form or ideal that is truly real in a way material entities are not. This absolutely real form or ideal is what accounts for the lesser and derivative reality of the objects we see around us. Individual entities around us come and go, but the ideal forms are everlasting and indestructible.

We have seen that such thinking fit in well with the Christian thought developed by the Christian bishop, Saint Augustine. In *The City of God*, Augustine warned us to beware of the world and the flesh because they cannot last and so are not fully real. What is fully real is the enduring spiritual world, the world without matter. Although we are citizens of the physical world, we are ultimately destined to be citizens of the spiritual and fully real world of God.

But the founder of modern idealism is another Christian bishop, George Berkeley (1685–1753). Berkeley reacted strongly against the materialist philosophies of Hobbes and other philosophers of his era. As a Christian leader, Berkeley was dismayed at the implications of their new materialist philosophies. By eliminating spirit, he felt, they had eliminated the foundations of Christianity. For Christianity, he felt, was built on the premise that a nonmaterial God exists and that the human soul itself is nonmaterial. Idealism, he felt, was the perfect antidote to the deceptions of materialism. For idealism not only recognizes a spiritual reality, it claims that there is no other reality except spirit and its ideas!

Berkeley claimed that conscious minds and their ideas or perceptions make up the whole of reality. He did not deny the reality of the world we perceive. He denied only that this world is an external material world that is independent of the mind. Berkeley reasoned that all we perceive of the world around us are the sensations and perceptions that stream into our minds through our senses. So, Berkeley concluded, the world consists of nothing more than these sensations and perceptions, together with the minds that experience them. Since sensations and perceptions are but ideas in the mind, the world itself consists of the stuff that ideas are made of. (For a fuller explanation of Berkeley's views, see the Historical Showcase at the end of this chapter.)

To appreciate Berkeley's idealism, it's helpful to distinguish between two kinds of idealism: subjective idealism and objective idealism. Every type of idealism claims that the world around us is ultimately mental, or mind-dependent. But this mind-dependency can be viewed as dependent on my mind, which is subjective idealism. Or it may be viewed as dependent on some other mind, such as God's, which will result in an objective idealism. Berkeley's version of idealism seems to include elements of both.[11] At least in its initial stages, Berkeley's argument presents idealism as the view that the ideas that make up the world are my ideas. This is subjective, or "me-dependent" idealism. But in its later stages Berkeley's argument claims that the ideas that make up the world actually depend on God's mind. And at that point his idealism becomes objective idealism.

Berkeley said that we find out about the things of the world through the perceptions and sensations our senses present to us. That is, we learn of trees, rocks, houses, cats, and dogs through the perceptions of our senses of sight, touch, taste, smell, and hearing. When we use our senses, we see light or color; feel hardness or softness, smoothness or roughness; smell sweetness or decay. These are all sensations or perceptions in our minds. We have no other experience of a world beyond these perceptions. So, Berkeley concludes, all the things that we perceive are nothing more than collections of these perceptions and sensations in our minds. In

MindTap We normally think that the world around us is made up of material stuff. George Berkeley challenged this idea, holding that it is contrary both to our experiences and to common sense. Go to MindTap to watch a video introducing his revolutionary views.

✓ QUICK REVIEW
Subjective idealism says that reality consists of my mind (and perhaps other human minds) and its ideas; objective idealism says that, in addition, reality includes a supreme mind that produces an **objective** world of ideas that does not depend on my own mind, although it does depend on a mind—God's.

---

[11] See Elmer Sprague, *Metaphysical Thinking* (New York: Oxford University Press, 1978), 93–103.

other words all the things we perceive around us are just ideas in our minds. Here is how he expresses his argument:

It is evident to any one who takes a survey of the objects of human knowledge, that they are either ideas actually imprinted on the senses, or else such as are perceived by attending to the passions and operations of the mind. . . . By sight I have the ideas of light and colors. . . . By touch I perceive hard and soft, heat and cold, motion and resistance. . . . Smelling furnishes me with odors, the palate with tastes, and hearing conveys sounds. . . . As several of these are observed to accompany each other, they come to be marked by one name and so to be reputed as one thing. Thus, for example, a certain color, taste, smell, figure and consistency having been observed to go together, are accounted one distinct thing, signified by the name *apple*. Other collections of ideas constitute a stone, a tree, a book, and the like sensible things. . . .

But besides all that endless variety of ideas or objects of knowledge, there is likewise something which knows or perceives them. . . . This perceiving, active being is what I call *mind, spirit, soul* or *myself.*

It seems . . . evident that the various sensations or ideas imprinted on the sense, however blended or combined together (that is, whatever objects they compose), cannot exist otherwise than in a mind perceiving them. The Table I write on, I say, "exists," that is, I [actually] see and feel it; and if I were out of my Study I should say "it existed," meaning thereby that if I was in my Study I would perceive it, or that some other Spirit actually does perceive it. There was an Odor, that is, it was smelled. There was a Sound, that is to say, it was heard. [There was a] color or shape, and it was perceived by sight or touch. This is all that I can understand by these and the like expressions. For as to what is said about the absolute existence of unthinking things without any relation to their being perceived, that seems perfectly unintelligible. Their *esse* [existence] is *percipi* [to be perceived]. Nor is it possible they should have any existence out of the minds or thinking things which perceive them.

It is indeed an opinion strangely prevailing among men that houses, mountains, rivers, and, in a word, all sensible objects have an existence, natural or real, distinct from their being perceived by the understanding. But with however great an assurance . . . this principle may be entertained in the world, yet whoever shall find in his heart to call it into question will, if I mistake not, perceive it to involve a manifest contradiction. For what are these objects but the things we perceive by sense? And what do we perceive besides our own ideas or sensations? And is it not plainly repugnant [contradictory] that any one of these or any combination of them should exist unperceived? . . .

Some Truths there are so near and obvious to the mind, that a man need only open his eyes to see them. Such I take this important one to be, to wit, that all of the choir of heaven and furniture of the earth, in a word all those bodies which compose the mighty frame of the world, have no substance without a mind. Their being is to be perceived. Consequently, so long as they are not actually perceived by me or other created spirits, they must either have no existence at all or else exist in the mind of some eternal spirit. It is perfectly unintelligible . . . to attribute to any single part of them an existence independent of a spirit. To be convinced of which, the reader need only reflect and try to separate in his own thoughts the being of a sensible thing from its being perceived.

ANALYZING THE READING

1. According to critics Berkeley says that what we perceive are our own ideas or sensations of things; that is, that we perceive our perceptions of things. But, critics say, we never perceive our own sensations or ideas. Instead, they say, we perceive things in the world around us, not perceptions or ideas in our head. Do you think the critics are right? Read the selection from Berkeley again, and see if you can find any statements that support or disprove what the critics say.

2. Suppose the critics are right. That is, suppose Berkeley says we perceive ideas or sensations in our head but actually we perceive things and not our sensations or ideas of things. Would this make any difference to Berkeley's argument for idealism? That is, if the critics are right would that demolish Berkeley's argument for his claim that nothing exists "without the mind" (in other words, that everything exists in the mind)? Or would it make no difference?

3. Some critics claim that Berkeley is wrong to say we perceive our sensations and perceptions of things. These critics say we perceive things *by means of* our sensations and perceptions, but we do not perceive sensations and perceptions themselves. Would you agree with these critics? If these critics are right, would this make any difference to Berkeley's argument for idealism?

QUICK REVIEW
Berkeley argued that all objects are bundles of perceptions; since perceptions can exist only in a mind, all objects exist only in the mind, and there is no independent material reality outside the mind.

THINKING LIKE A PHILOSOPHER

1. Berkeley says that "heaven and . . . earth" have no existence outside the mind. Can you force yourself to believe that all the universe around you exists only in your mind?
2. Suppose that everything you see exists only in your mind like Berkeley says. Then your friends and the people you see around you would exist only in your mind. If that was true, do you think it would still be wrong to kill one of them?
3. If your friends existed only in your mind, who would you be talking to when you have a conversation with a friend? What do you think Berkeley would say?
4. If Berkeley is right about everything he says, would you have any way of knowing there was anyone else in the universe besides yourself?

But for the fuller proof of this Point, let it be considered that the sensible Qualities are Color, Figure, Motion, Smell, Taste, and such like. That is, [these are] the Ideas perceived by sense. Now for an idea to exist in an unperceiving thing, is a manifest contradiction; for to have an idea is . . . to perceive it. [So] that in which color, figure, and the like qualities exist, must perceive them. Hence it is clear [that] no unthinking substance or substratum [can be that in which] those ideas [exist].

But say you, though the ideas themselves do not exist without the mind, yet there may be things like them of which [our perceptions] are copies or resemblances. [And what our perceptions represent] may exist [outside] the Mind, in an unthinking substance. I answer [you thus]: an idea can be like nothing but an idea. A color or shape can be like nothing but another color or shape. If we look but ever so little into our thoughts, we shall find it impossible for us to conceive a likeness [between an idea and something else] except only [other] ideas. Again, I ask whether those supposed originals or external qualities, of which our ideas are [supposed to be] pictures or representations, are themselves perceivable or not? If they are, then they are ideas, and we have gained our point. But if you say they are not, I appeal to any one [to say] if it makes sense to assert that a color is like something [external] which is not visible. Or that Hard or Soft, are like something which is not tangible? And the same may be said of the rest of the qualities.

But . . . [even if] it were possible that solid. . . . Substances may exist without the mind, . . . yet how is it possible for us to know this? Either we must know it by sense, or by reason. As for our senses, by them we have knowledge only of our sensations [and] ideas. . . . But they do not inform us that things exist without the Mind. . . . Therefore if we have any knowledge at all of external things, it must be by reason inferring their existence from what is immediately perceived by Sense. But what reason can induce us to believe the existence of bodies without the mind from what we perceive? . . . It is granted by all . . . (and what happens in dreams, hallucinations, and the like, puts it beyond dispute) that it is possible we might be affected with all the ideas we have now, though no Bodies existed. . . . In short, if there were external bodies, it is impossible we should ever come to know it. And if there were not, we might have the very same reasons to think there were that we have now. Suppose . . . an intelligence, without the help of external bodies, was affected with the same train of sensations or ideas that you are. . . . I ask whether that Intelligence has not all the reason to believe [in] the existence of corporeal substances . . . that you can possibly have for believing the same thing? Of this there can be no Question. . . . [This] one Consideration is enough to make any reasonable person [doubt] . . . whatever arguments he may think he has for the existence of bodies without the mind.[12]

MindTap To read more from Berkeley's *A Treatise Concerning the Principles of Human Knowledge*, click the link in the MindTap Reader or go to the Questia Readings folder in MindTap.

Berkeley here seems to be arguing as follows. Suppose we carefully examine the knowledge we have of the objects around us. Then we will see that our only knowledge of such objects consists of knowing the perceptions and sensations of them that we have in our minds. Objects as we know them, then, consist of their perceptions and sensations in our minds. But perceptions and sensations can exist only in the mind. So it follows that every object we perceive must exist only in the mind.

---

[12] George Berkeley, *Principles of Human Knowledge* (1710), part I, excerpts from paras. 1–4, 6–7, and 18–20. Spelling, punctuation, and obsolete words have been modernized.

That is, every object that we think of as existing in an external material world outside the mind is actually a bundle of perceptions and sensations in the mind. Or, to put it in different words: The objects we see around us are just sensations and ideas in our minds. Moreover, if some things did exist outside our minds, we would have no way of knowing them or knowing that they were there.

Berkeley suggests that you may still insist that our perceptions and sensations are at least copies or likenesses of the qualities of external objects. But Berkeley rejects this idea. Consider a color sensation, like a sensation of blue. A color sensation that you perceive in your mind, he points out, can only resemble or be like another similar color sensation. A sensation of a color like blue can only be similar to another sensation of a blue color. And that second color sensation would also have to exist in a mind. Or suppose you try to match a shape you perceive with something like it. Then you can only match it with another shape you perceive. And that second perception of shape would also have to exist in a mind. So the only things that our sensations and perceptions can resemble are other similar sensations and perceptions. And such sensations and perceptions cannot exist in mindless material objects outside us.

Up to this point in his argument, Berkeley seems to be saying that the world I perceive consists of ideas that are dependent on my own mind. If we stop Berkeley's analysis right here, then, we would be left with **subjective idealism**. This is the position that the world consists only of my own mind and things that are dependent on my mind. But Berkeley went further and introduced an objective dimension.

Berkeley pointed out that there are two very different kinds of ideas in my mind. Some I produce and these are short-lived, changeable, and within my control. For example, I can, if I choose, imagine a red horse with purple wings flying through a green sky and can easily control these imaginings. Other ideas, however, I do not produce; instead they come into my mind through my senses. These are more orderly, regular, enduring, and not within my control. Consider, for instance, the perceptions you have on your usual route to class. You experience the same landmarks each time—perhaps the library, the gym, and the student union. When you look up at the night sky you see the stars wheeling across the sky in the same circular pattern they had the previous night. You see the seasons come and go with predictable regularity. Unlike the imaginings of winged horses that you control, perceptions that enter your mind through your senses have a regularity you do not produce. But what is the source of those sense perceptions if they are not from you? This can only be explained as the work of another supreme mind: the mind of God. God must produce in our minds the display of orderly perceptions that we call the world. And it must be God that gives this display its regularity and stability.

ANALYZING THE READING

Some critics have said that Berkeley's idealism encourages a withdrawal from the real world, a retreat from secular problems, and an immersion in otherworldly concerns. As a result, they claim, the idealism of Berkeley will lead us to neglect real and pressing social concerns. Do you think this is a legitimate criticism of Berkeley's view? Explain why or why not.

QUICK REVIEW

Berkeley also argued that because our orderly perceptions of the world are not controlled by our minds, they must be produced by God's divine mind. This is an objective idealism.

I find I can excite some ideas in my mind at pleasure, and vary and shift the scene as often as I think fit. It is no more than willing, and straightway this or that idea arises in my imagination. And by my same power it is obliterated, and makes way for another idea.

But whatever power I may have over my own thoughts, I find that the ideas actually perceived by my senses have not a like dependence on my will. When in broad daylight I open my eyes, it is not in my power to choose whether I shall see or not, or to determine what particular objects shall present themselves to my view. And so likewise as to hearing and other senses, the ideas imprinted on them are not creations of my will. There is therefore some other will or spirit that produces them.

[Moreover,] these ideas of sense are more strong, lively, and distinct than those of [my] imagination. They have a steadiness, order, and coherence, and are not excited at random, like those which are the effects of [my] will, but [they arise] in a regular train or series, the admirable connection of which sufficiently testifies to the wisdom and benevolence of its author.[13]

PHILOSOPHY AND LIFE

Our Knowledge of the World

What kind of world do we live in? Some physicists today describe it as a flux of energy that exists in different forms at different levels. Because of the limitations of our sense organs, our brains cannot know directly about all of the world's energy. Indeed, a relatively small part of the electromagnetic spectrum—that is, of the entire range of radiation—can stimulate our eyes. In other words, although we can hear or feel parts of it, we can't see a large portion of the spectrum. Electromagnetic energy covers a wide range of wavelengths, from extremely short gamma rays, having wavelengths of about a billionth of an inch, to the extremely long radio waves, which have wavelengths that are miles long. In fact, we can see very little of the electromagnetic spectrum.

Our ears also sense a limited range of the mechanical vibrations transmitted through the air. Similarly, although we can smell and taste certain chemical substances and feel the presence of some objects in contact with our skin, most of what occurs in our environment cannot be perceived by these senses either. In effect, the great flux of energy that physicists say exists is largely lost to our senses. We know about it only indirectly, through specially devised instruments that can detect radio waves, X-rays, infrared rays, and other energy forms that we can't directly experience.

What implications do these facts hold for our view of reality? If nothing else, they should make us wonder just how complete a picture of reality we have and how accurate our interpretation of it is. In *New Pathways in Science*, Sir Arthur Eddington addresses this issue:

As a conscious being I am involved in a story. The perceiving part of my mind tells me a story of a world around me. The story tells of familiar objects.

It tells of colors, sounds, scents belonging to these objects; of boundless space in which they have their existence, and of an ever-rolling stream of time bringing change and incident. It tells of other life than mine busy about its own purposes.

As a scientist I have become mistrustful of this story. In many instances it has become clear that things are not what they seem to be. According to the storyteller I have now in front of me a substantial desk; but I have learned from physics that the desk is not at all the continuous substance that it is supposed to be in the story. It is a host of tiny electric charges darting hither and thither with inconceivable velocity. Instead of being solid substance my desk is more like a swarm of gnats.

So I have come to realize that I must not put overmuch confidence in the storyteller who lives in my mind.

QUESTIONS

1. Undoubtedly, things are often not what they appear to be. But to say that is to imply another experience of things. Can we be sure that alternative experiences are any closer to how things are?

2. If a desk is indeed more like "a swarm of gnats" than a solid substance, what practical difference does that make in the way you live? Or is such a question irrelevant?

Source: Sir Arthur Eddington, *New Pathways in Science* (Ann Arbor: University of Michigan Press, 1959), 11.

---

[13]   Ibid., excerpts from paras. 28–30.

This second stage of Berkeley's idealism is an *objective* kind of idealism. It claims that the world of my perceptions does not depend on my mind, but on something external to my mind, that is, on God. The perceptions of the world that enter my mind through my senses are produced in me by God. The advantages of **objective idealism** are that it can account for the fact that the world I experience is not wholly in my control. Yet it allows the world to be viewed as an ultimately intelligible system because it is the product of mind. It explains also why, for example, when I shut my eyes and open them again, the world I see before me is the same world that was there before I shut my eyes. It is the same world because God makes sure it is.

> It will be objected that from [my] Principles it follows that things are every moment being annihilated and then created anew. [For I said that] the objects of sense exist only when they are perceived. The trees therefore are in the Garden, or the Chairs in the Parlor, [only] while there is somebody [there] to perceive them. Upon shutting my eyes all the furniture in the room is reduced to nothing, and barely upon opening them it is again created.
>
> [Our answer to this objection is that] although we hold indeed that the objects of sense are nothing else but ideas which cannot exist unperceived, yet we may not conclude that they have no existence except while they are perceived by us. For there may be some other Spirit that perceives them, though we do not. Wherever bodies are said to have no existence without the mind, I should not be understood to mean this or that particular mind, but all minds whatsoever. It does not therefore follow from [my] Principles, that bodies are annihilated and created every moment, or exist not at all during the intervals between our perception of them.[14]

In other words, God keeps the world and all its contents in existence when no one is perceiving them. He keeps them in existence by keeping the ideas that make up the world in His own mind. There's a famous limerick about Berkeley's philosophy that expresses exactly what Berkeley is getting at in the passage above. The limerick is about the continued existence of a tree in a quad, that is, in a courtyard:

> *I have always thought that God*
> *Must find it exceedingly odd*
> *To think that his tree*
> *Won't continue to be*
> *When there's no one about in the quad.*
>
> *Dear Sir:*
> *Your astonishment's odd.*
> *For I am always about in the quad.*
> *And so my tree will continue to be,*
> *Since observed by*
> *Yours faithfully,*
> *God.*

Many people found Berkeley's views difficult to accept. A major stumbling block for many was that they thought he was saying that the world we see around us is unreal. Moreover, his views seemed to imply that the sun, the moon, and even the stars were all in our heads when it was obvious that they were quite distant from us. But Berkeley did not think his "Principles" had these implications and he was

---

14 Ibid., excerpts from paras. 45 and 48.

anxious to show that they did not. In the following passage he tries to answer these objections:

> It will be objected that by [my] Principles, all that is real and substantial in nature is banished out of the world.... All things that exist, exist only in the mind.... What therefore becomes of the Sun, Moon, and Stars? What must we think of Houses, Rivers, Mountains, Trees, Stones; nay, even of our own Bodies? Are all these but so many fantasies and illusions of the imagination?
>
> To all [this] ... I answer that by [my] Principles ... we are not deprived of any one thing in Nature. Whatever we see, feel, [and] hear, ... remains ... as real as ever.
>
> I do not argue against the existence of anything that we can apprehend.... That the things I see with my eyes and touch with my hands do exist, really exist, I do not in the least question....
>
> Ideas ...[that] we perceive by sense ... are not fictions of the mind that perceives them. And in this sense, the sun that I see by day is the real sun.... In the sense here given of reality, it is evident that every vegetable, star, mineral, and in general each part of the world system, is as much a real being by our Principles as by any other.[15]

ANALYZING THE READING

1. Berkeley claims that even if nothing existed outside the mind, we would still perceive everything exactly as we perceive everything right now. As proof he points to dreams and hallucinations where we can perceive things that do not exist outside our minds. Suppose Berkeley's claim is right. Would this claim be enough to prove that nothing exists outside the mind? Why?

2. Berkeley says that even if all his claims are right, "whatever we see, feel, [and] hear remains as real as ever." Do you agree that if he's right, everything remains as "real" as it was before? Is there any sense in which things do not remain "real" if he's right?

But Berkeley seems to be trying to have his cake and eat it too. He seems to want to say that his views change nothing and do not make reality any different from what we always thought it was. Yet it is clear that Berkeley felt his "Principles" made a huge difference in the way we thought and looked at reality. They were supposed to show that the universe is made out of a stuff that is completely different from the stuff we thought it was made of. In the passage above he seems to want to correct the view that "all things that exist, exist only in the mind." Yet that view seems to be exactly the view he holds.

To many people Berkeley's idealism seems outrageous. Yet many philosophers have agreed with the kind of idealist metaphysics that Berkeley put forward. Idealism, in fact, became the dominant philosophy in the English-speaking world during the early twentieth century. It was promoted by numerous philosophers including F.H. Bradley (1846–1924), J.M.E. McTaggart (1866–1925), Josiah Royce (1855–1916), and Bernard Bosanquet (1848–1923). In fact, idealism continues to have adherents today. The Canadian philosopher John Leslie (1940–), for example, proposes a kind of objective idealism. He claims that all the things in our universe are but thoughts in the mind of God:

> [T]he structures of galaxies, planets, and continents, of mice and of elephants, and of you and me, as well as of the houses, fields, and streams with which we interact, are nothing but the structures of various thoughts in the divine mind. The divine mind does not contemplate any universe that exists outside it. Its thinking about our universe is what our universe *is*.[16]

---

15 Ibid., excerpts from paras 34–36.
16 John Leslie, *Infinite Minds* (Oxford: Clarendon Press, 2001), 8.

As you can no doubt guess, idealist views like Berkeley's have been intensely controversial. But before we look at some of the objections his opponents raised, let's look briefly at a non-Western version of idealism.

Eastern Idealism. Idealism has not been confined to Western philosophy. Indian philosophy, in particular, has been home to a number of idealist philosophers. In fact, Vasubandhu, an Indian philosopher who lived in the fourth century CE, held views similar to those of Berkeley. Vasubandhu is usually regarded as the greatest member of the "Yogacarin" or "Vijnanavada" school of Buddhist philosophy. This is one of the four great philosophical "schools" of India that interpreted the views of Buddha after his death. *Yogacarin* means "truth through the practice of meditation," and *Vijnanavada* means "the mind-only doctrine."

Vasubandhu argued that we do not directly perceive objects in the world around us. Instead, when we think that we are perceiving something, we are experiencing nothing more than a sensation in our minds. When we see colors, hear sounds, or smell odors, we infer that these sensations must represent or be correlated with external objects that cause these sensations in us. But, Vasubandhu claimed, we are not justified in drawing such conclusions about the **existence** of external objects. All we ever perceive are sensations within us, so we have no basis for concluding that external objects cause these sensations.

To make his point, Vasubandhu draws attention to the way that many of us seem to see fine hairs drifting across our vision or are sometimes afflicted with double vision. We do not conclude that these fine hairs exist in the air around us or that everything in the world has suddenly doubled. Exactly the same can be said about all of our sensations, Vasubandhu argued. Just because we have sensations that seem to represent external physical objects, we cannot conclude that any external objects exist. Everything that is experienced is all in the mind. As Vasubandhu put it in one of his key works, *Twenty Verses and Their Commentary*,

> Reality consists only of consciousness. There are no objects outside of consciousness. It is true that when inner sensations arise in consciousness, they have the appearance of being correlated with external non-mental objects. But this is no different from situations when persons who have eye disorders see hairs, moons, and other objects that do not exist.[17]

But there's an important objection against Vasubandhu's view that the world is nothing but consciousness and sensations unrelated to external objects. The objection is this. Suppose all the events we perceive were just sensations dancing in our mind. Then why does everything happen in a specific position in space and at a specific point in time? That is, why do events seem to occur in a spatial and temporal world outside of us? And why do the objects in that world physically affect us? Surely perceptions or sensations can exist only in the mind, not in a spatial and temporal world outside us. And surely our sensations or perceptions cannot physically affect us. In short, perceptions can exist only in the mind, yet the objects we perceive seem to exist in a world outside of our minds. And perceptions cannot have physical effects, yet the objects we perceive do physically affect us. So, we might object, the objects we perceive cannot be mere perceptions in our mind.

<aside>
QUICK REVIEW

The Indian philosopher Vasubandhu held that all our experiences of things consist of nothing more than sensations in our minds, which does not show that external objects exist. The apparent existence of an external world is an illusion as in a dream. When meditation "awakens" us, we will see that the "external world" is an illusion just as we know a dream is an illusion when we awaken from sleep.
</aside>

---

[17] Excerpt from S. Radhakrishnan and C. Moore, eds., *A Source Book in Indian Philosophy* (Princeton, NJ: Princeton University Press, 1957), 328.

Vasubandhu had an answer to this objection. He pointed to what happens in our dreams:

> The place and time of the objects we perceive around us is determined just like in a dream. . . . And dreams can physically affect us by, for example, sexually arousing us. . . .
>
> In a dream although there are no real objects, we nevertheless see things—like a village, a garden, a man or a woman—as if they exist in a specific place in the world. We do not see them as if they are in no specific place. And we see these things—a village, a garden, etc.—as if they exist at a specific time, not as if they exist at no specific time at all. . . . Again, although the objects we see in a dream are unreal, they nevertheless can have a physical effect on us, such as sexually arousing us.[18]

ANALYZING THE READING

In what ways are Vasubandhu's arguments for idealism similar to Berkeley's arguments for idealism? In what ways are they different from Berkeley's arguments?

Vasubandhu is pointing out that in our dreams we see, hear, feel, touch, and smell "things" that exist only in our minds. Yet in our dreams things happen in specific places and at specific times. So also in the world we perceive when awake, things happen at specific times and specific places. But like our dreams, it too exists only in our minds. Things in our dreams can also physically affect us even though they are not real. In the same way the unreality of the world we perceive does not prevent it from physically affecting us.

But you might raise another objection to Vasubandhu's view. Somehow, we can naturally tell that our dreams are not real. If the material world we see is also not real, then why can't we just as naturally tell that the material world we see around us is unreal? Vasubandhu's answer is quite simple: We can in fact tell that the world is unreal. Consider, he says, that we know a dream is unreal only after we have awakened from the dream. During the time of the dream, we think the dream is real. In the same way, most of us think the world we perceive around us is real because we live out our lives in a kind of dream. While we are in this illusory dream world, we think it is real. But by practicing meditation, we can awaken our mind from its slumber and attain a true, pure, and enlightened understanding of reality. When we have thus awakened, we will understand perfectly that the external world we thought was so real was, in truth, nothing more than a dream:

> It may be asked: if, when we are awake as well as when we are dreaming, perceptions may arise although there are no real objects, then, just as everyone naturally knows that dream objects are non-existent, why is the same not naturally known of the objects we perceive when we are awake? I reply: Before we have awakened we cannot know that what is seen in the dream does not exist. In the same way it is only afterwards, when the purified knowledge of the world is obtained and one awakes, that this knowledge will take precedence. Then we can know according to the truth and clearly understand that those objects we perceived were unreal. The principle is the same.[19]

Vasubandhu summarized his views in a famous statement that "only mind exists." But he did more. Vasubandhu also tried to teach his followers a method by which they could come to understand and accept that the world around us is just a dream in our minds. This method is the method of meditation and ethical living. Meditation and an ethical life, he claimed, are the keys to waking up from our dream and seeing reality as it actually is.

---

18   Ibid., 328–329.
19   Ibid., 329.

thinking critically • Conditional Arguments

Here is one of the arguments Berkeley uses to support his objective idealism:

> If we have perceptions of things whose uniformity, consistency, and continuity do not come from us, then they must come from a supreme mind.
> We have perceptions of things whose uniformity, consistency, and continuity do not come from us.
> So they must come from a supreme mind.

Is this argument valid? We explained earlier that to determine the validity of a deductive argument we see if we can imagine a situation in which its premises are true and its conclusion false. We could use that method to evaluate Berkeley's argument. But this method is time consuming, so we'll now look at a shorter way to determine the validity of deductive arguments, one that uses the notion of a "logical form."

To explain what the logical form of an argument is, we begin by noticing that most arguments contain compound claims. A compound claim consists of sentences joined together by a connective like "if-then." For example:

> **If** Tom went, **then** Susan went.   **If** the ground is wet, **then** Tom went.
>
> **If** it's raining, **then** Susan went.   **If** it's raining, **then** the ground is wet.

Claims that use the connective "if-then" can be "translated" into their "logical form" by replacing their sentences with lowercase letters that we assign to represent those sentences. For example, we can assign letters to represent the sentences of the compound claims above in this way:

> t: Tom went.   r: It's raining.
> s: Susan went.   w: The ground is wet.

Then if we use these assignments to translate the compound claims above into their logical forms, we get:

> If t then s   If w then t
> If r then s   If r then w

Arguments can also contain negative claims like "Tom did not go" or "It's not raining." To translate negative claims into their logical form, we attach "Not-" in front of the letter assigned to the *positive version* of the claim:

> "Not-t" is the logical form of "Tom did not go."
> "Not-r" is the logical form of "It's not raining."

Whole arguments, like their claims, also have a logical form. The logical form of an argument is what we get when we translate all of its claims into their proper logical forms. For example, here are two arguments, (1) and (2):

> (1) If it's raining, then the ground is wet.   (2) If it's raining, then the ground is wet.
>   It's not raining.   The ground is not wet
>   So the ground is not wet   So it's not raining.

If we translate the claims of these arguments into their logical form, using the letters we assigned earlier, then the logical form of argument (1) is (1*), and the logical form of argument (2) is (2*):

> (1*) If r then w   (2*) If r then w
>   Not-r   Not-w
>   So Not-w   So Not-r

Notice that when you write down the logical form of an argument, you need to keep using the same letter to represent the same sentence through the whole argument.

Of course, you don't have to use "r" and "w." We could have used "p" and "q" by making these assignments:

p: It's raining.   q: The ground is wet.

And then we would have written the logical forms of (1) and (2) like this:

(1**) If p then q   (2**) If p then q
      Not-p   Not-q
      So Not-q   So Not-p

Although they use different letters, (1*) and (1**) are exactly the same logical form, and (2*) and (2**) are also the same logical form. It doesn't matter which letters you use to write down a logical form; if the connectives of two logical forms are the same and both the connectives and letters are arranged in the same way, then the two forms are the same regardless of the letters you used.

Now we can explain the shorter method of figuring out if an argument is valid. Here is the basic idea: If an argument is valid, then every other argument with the *same logical form* is also valid; if an argument is invalid, then every other argument with the *same logical form* is also invalid. So you don't need to test the validity of every new argument that comes along. All you need to do is, first, translate the new argument into its logical form. Then, if you earlier found that another argument with the same form was *valid (or invalid)*, you know without having to test the new one, that it, too, is *valid (or invalid)*.

For example, take argument (1). To test whether it is valid, try to imagine a situation in which its premises are true but its conclusion is false. Here is one such situation: Suppose it's true that when it rains the ground gets wet, but today the ground got wet because the sprinklers were on although it was not raining. In that situation, the first two premises of argument (1) are true, but the conclusion is false. So argument (1) is invalid. But the logical form of argument (1) is (1*). So any argument with logical form (1*) will also be invalid. For example, these arguments have the same logical form, so they are invalid:

If it's raining, then John went.   If the ground is wet, then Susan went.

It's not raining.   The ground is not wet.

So John did not go.   So Susan did not go.

Next, take argument (2). No matter how much you try, you will not be able to come up with a situation in which the premises of (2) are true but its conclusion is false. Argument (2) is valid. But (2*) is the logical form of argument (2). So any other argument with logical form (2*) is also valid. For example, these arguments have the same logical form, so they are valid:

If it's raining, then Susan went.   If the ground is wet, then John went.

Susan did not go.   John did not go.

So it's not raining.   So the ground is not wet.

Being able to use an argument's logical form to evaluate its validity is extremely useful, especially if you have memorized the logical forms of the most common type of valid arguments and of the most common types of invalid arguments. Here, then, are the logical forms of the most common kind of *VALID* arguments that use the "if-then" connective in their premises. You should memorize these logical forms so that you can use them to quickly check whether an "if-then" argument is valid. *Any argument with one of these forms*

✓ QUICK REVIEW

If an argument is valid, then any argument with the same logical form is also valid; if an argument is invalid, then any argument with the same logical form is also invalid. So to determine a new argument's validity, translate it into its logical form; if its logical form is that of a valid argument, then the new argument is valid; if its logical form is that of an invalid argument, it is invalid.

✓ QUICK REVIEW

The logical forms of the most common *valid* "if-then" arguments are: "If p then q; p; So q," and "If p then q; Not-q, So Not-p." The logical forms of the most common *invalid* "if-then" arguments are: "If p then q; q; So p" and "If p then q; Not-p; So Not-q."

has to be VALID. The first of these two forms of *VALID* arguments is called "Affirming the Antecedent" and the second is "Denying the Consequent."

If p then q	If p then q
p	Not-q
So q	So Not-p

And here are the logical forms of the two most common *INVALID* arguments that use the "if-then" connective. *Any argument that has one of these forms has to be INVALID*. The first of these two forms of *INVALID* arguments is called "Affirming the Consequent" and the second is "Denying the Antecedent."

If p then q	If p then q
q	Not-p
So p	So Not-q

The main difficulty you will have when using these logical forms to evaluate arguments will be trying to translate the premises and conclusions of English arguments into their proper logical forms. To help you, here are some of the kinds of English expressions that students often have trouble translating into their proper logical form. The letters we assign to each sentence are in parentheses, and the troublesome expressions are underlined; the correct logical form of each statement is at the right in bold:

John gets to school (s) <u>only if</u> his alarm rings (r): **If s then r**
John gets to school (s) <u>only when</u> his alarm rings (r): **If s then r**
You'll die (d) <u>unless</u> you jump (j): **If not-j then d**
<u>Unless</u> you jump (j), you'll die (d): **If not-j then d**

We're now ready to use an argument's logical form to evaluate Berkeley's argument for objective idealism; the letters we assign to each sentence are in parentheses:

If we have perceptions of things whose uniformity, consistency, and continuity do not come from us (p), then they must come from a supreme mind (m).
We have perceptions of things whose uniformity, consistency, and continuity do not come from us (p).
So they must come from a supreme mind (m).

The logical form of this argument is:

If p then m
p
So m

A quick glance at our list of the forms of valid arguments shows that this form is on that list, so Berkeley's argument is valid. You, of course, will have to decide for yourself whether its premises are true. To help you we'll look at some objections to Berkeley's idealism next.

Objections to Idealism

An important problem for idealists is this: Don't idealists commit the fallacy of **anthropomorphism?** That is, don't they project a human power—the mind and its contents—onto the nonhuman universe? The claim that the universe is a mind and things are ideas seems to be an attempt to describe in human terms something that is just not human. It is one thing to speak of people as having "minds" with "ideas." But it seems mistaken to take those terms out of the human context, and apply them to the universe and its contents. It amounts to trying to understand something unfamiliar and mysterious (the universe) by giving it the familiar qualities of human beings. Children's fairytales do the same thing. They describe animals, for example, as if they could talk like humans. Idealism seems to be nothing more than a fairytale.

Consider, also, whether you or anyone else has ever experienced mind, idea, or spirit independent of a material biological system. All the minds and ideas we know about seem to require the wet hardware of the living brain. For once the brain dies, then the mind and its ideas seem to vanish. These thoughts suggest further problems, which require a closer look at subjective and objective idealism.

Objections to Subjective Idealism. Subjective idealism claims that whatever I perceive is merely one of my perceptions or a collection of perceptions. But this is at least puzzling and suggests that subjective idealism is based on a mistake. The mistake is failing to distinguish between my *perception* of a thing and the *thing* that I perceive. If I'm looking at a tree, for example, isn't there a difference between my *seeing* the tree and *the tree* that I see? Can subjective idealism make such a distinction? In saying that all we perceive are our own perceptions, isn't Berkeley mistakenly saying that there is no difference between my perception of a tree and the tree I perceive?

But the subjective idealist may have an answer to this objection. If I say that there is more to perceiving the tree than my perception of the tree, the subjective idealist can ask me how I know about this "more"? The subjective idealist can say that when I perceive a tree I can know nothing more about it than what is contained in my perception of the tree. Thus, if I claim that there's more to the tree than my perception of it, I am postulating the existence of something that I cannot know. And how can I be justified in claiming that something is real when I can't even know it?

"But," as philosopher Elmer Sprague points out, "it still seems odd to say that I perceive my perceptions, and not that I perceive something out there to be perceived. It seems odd to say that to perceive the [tree] is but to perceive my own mind. It is all very well for the Subjective Immaterialist to say 'That's just the way it is.' Less hardy mortals still wonder if we might not say something else instead."[20] Sprague suggests that what subjective idealists say cannot be disproved because their theories cannot be falsified. But we can still ask them how they know that their claim is true. Ultimately, the claim seems to hinge on the assumption that perceptible *things* are mere collections of our *perceptions* of them. But why make this assumption? Why not make the more commonsensical distinction between perceptions and the objects of perception?

Subjective idealism's claim that things are collections of perceptible qualities is essential to its arguments. This claim requires that we not make a distinction between the things we perceive and our perceptions of them. If we don't make that distinction then we cannot say that there is a distinction between our perceptions and reality. Since subjective idealism does not make that distinction, it cannot talk about objective reality. It can only talk about our subjective perceptions. Subjective idealism, then, does not really answer the question of what reality is objectively like. Instead it seems to dissolve the question by making it impossible to ask what reality is like apart from our subjective perceptions. Moreover, in saying that what I perceive are my own perceptions, subjective idealism is saying that things are exactly as I

QUICK REVIEW
Critics of idealism claim that idealists wrongly project human characteristics onto nonhuman parts of the universe.

QUICK REVIEW
Critics of subjective idealism propose that it mistakenly claims that our perceptions are what we perceive.

[20]   Sprague, *Metaphysical Thinking*, 98.

perceive them. So subjective idealism also rules out the possibility of being mistaken about what we perceive. For how can my perceptions ever be wrong about reality if there is no reality beyond my perceptions?

Objections to Objective Idealism. As for objective idealism, we observed two apparent strengths. It explains why perceptible things seem to be independent of the mind, and why the universe seems to have an ultimately intelligible and rational order. However, neither of these aspects may be as significant as they may appear to be.

Recall your classroom experience. You perceive the classroom anew each day exactly as it was the day before because some other mind, call it God, perceives it all the time. God thus holds the classroom in place each time you happen to stop perceiving it. But do we really need such an explanation? Won't the existence of an enduring external physical world account for the constancy of the classroom as well as the things that you pass on your way to it? And should they one day disappear, can't materialism also account for that eventuality. For example, the realist can point out that the physical buildings fell down, were torn down, or were blown up while you were not looking? Why do you need to involve the mind of God?

Objective idealists seek an ultimate explanation of the order and permanence of the world. Thus, "God does it" is the ultimate explanation of the objective idealist. But what does that tell us? If the classroom stands, God does it. When it lies in ruins, it does so because God does it. What does "God does it" add to a commonsensical account of the classroom or of its destruction?

Objective idealists also claim that the world is intelligible because it's a product of God's mind or of some sort of cosmic intelligence. But simply because our own mind may be intelligible, does that mean God's is? How are we to know God's mind? How can we distinguish between our own perceptions, which by strict idealistic principles we can never get beyond, and God's perceptions? Shouldn't idealism answer these questions before it can be considered a compelling explanation of ultimate reality?

But what is the alternative to idealism? Many philosophers believe that materialism is just as inadequate. Is perhaps the most viable option to admit that the universe contains both nonmaterial spirit and physical matter? As we saw in Chapter 2, this is the view of dualism. Dualism holds that reality contains two different kinds of things: immaterial spirits and material objects. Yet, as we saw in our earlier discussion of dualism, this view raises an almost insoluble question: How can an immaterial spirit or mind interact with a material universe? If a nonphysical entity moved or affected an object in the physical universe, it would violate the most basic law of science. Science is based on the law of the conservation of energy (sometimes called the first law of thermodynamics) discovered in the nineteenth century. This law states that the total energy contained in a closed physical system can change its forms, but can neither increase nor decrease in total quantity. For example, energy in the form of motion may be changed into heat, which is another form of energy (the motion of rubbing your hands together rapidly will produce heat). But the total amount of energy in the physical universe can neither increase nor decrease. Yet if an immaterial spirit changed or altered some physical object in any way, this would introduce additional energy into the physical universe. This would violate the basic law of the conservation of energy. Similarly, if a physical object somehow moved or changed an immaterial spirit, this would in effect take energy out of the physical universe. Again this would violate the law of the conservation of energy. If nonmaterial spirits coexist with material objects, then neither should be able to affect each other in the slightest way. Neither should even be able to perceive the existence of the other!

> **QUICK REVIEW**
> Critics of objective idealism say that materialism, not God, provides the best explanation of the order and permanence of the world we perceive.

So, dualism seems as improbable as materialism and idealism. What, then, is left? Perhaps a different approach is needed. Pragmatism offers another approach to reality, one that rejects the entire materialism/idealism debate.

PHILOSOPHY AT THE MOVIES

Watch *The Thirteenth Floor* (1999) in which Douglas Hall, accused of murdering a friend who invented a virtual reality simulation of 1937 Los Angeles, enters the simulation and there is almost killed by an angry man who has discovered he is only an artificial simulation. This leads Hall to quickly exit the simulation and return to our own world—only to discover that our world, too, is a simulation. According to this movie, how many worlds are there? According to idealism, is our world "real" in this movie? Does this movie imply an acceptance or rejection of idealism? Explain. Does the movie imply there is no reality? Is this possible?

Other movies with related themes: *Inception* (2010), *eXistenZ* (1999), *Matrix* (1999), *Matrix Reloaded* (2003), *Matrix Revolutions* (2003), *Vanilla Sky* (2001), and *Total Recall* (1990).

3.3 Reality in Pragmatism

To many people, the debate between materialism and idealism seems to be meaningless. Nothing will change, they claim, if we decide that all reality is matter. For example, people who believe in an afterlife will continue to believe in an afterlife. But the afterlife will be in a material world. And similarly, they insist, nothing will change if we decide that all reality is immaterial. The things around us will still feel hard, will still smell, will still have shapes, colors, positions, and motions. None of this will change if we decide everything consists of ideas in the mind. Since the debate between materialism and idealism has no practical consequences, many come to the conclusion it is meaningless. Their conclusion assumes our beliefs about reality are meaningful only if they have practical consequences. This assumption is the cornerstone of a particularly American approach to reality called *pragmatism*.

ANALYZING THE READING

Look up the meaning of "pragmatist" in a dictionary. What meanings seem to match the meaning of pragmatist used in the textbook's discussion of philosophical pragmatism? How would you say the other meanings of pragmatist in the dictionary are related to the meaning of pragmatist in the textbook?

Pragmatism as a philosophical movement developed and grew in the United States during the last century. It began in the writings of Charles S. Peirce (1839–1914), William James (1842–1910), and John Dewey (1859–1952). Of these three, Charles Peirce is the accepted founder of the movement.

Peirce defined pragmatism as:

> The opinion that metaphysics is to be largely cleared up by the application of the following maxim for attaining clearness of apprehension: Consider what effects, that might conceivably have practical bearings, we conceive the object of our conception to have. Then, our conception of these effects is the whole of our conception of the object.[21]

---

[21] Charles S. Peirce, "Pragmatic and Pragmatism," in *Dictionary of Philosophy and Psychology*, vol. II, 321–323 (London: Macmillan and Co., 1902).

Peirce explained that this "pragmatic maxim" provided a method to figure out the real information a concept contains. The method, he once wrote, was to "trace out in the imagination the conceivable practical consequences—that is, the consequences for deliberate, self-controlled conduct—of the affirmation or denial of the concept."[22] Thus, for Peirce, the concepts we use contain no information unless they make a practical difference in our actions, at least in our deliberate and thoughtful actions. And those practical differences are the real information the concept contains. In other words, when a philosopher uses a concept, we should always ask: "What practical difference does it make?" And if it makes no practical difference in our lives, then the concept is empty.

THINKING LIKE A PHILOSOPHER

Peirce said that to figure out whether our ideas have any real meaning we have to "trace out in the imagination their conceivable practical consequences." Think of the ideas that are most important to you at this point in your life. For example, for some people such ideas might include God, Justice, Friendship, Church, Christianity, Art, etc. Now using your imagination, try to describe the "conceivable practical consequences" that these ideas have in your life. Can you think of any ideas that you believe are important yet have no "conceivable practical consequences"?

William James accepted Peirce's views, but defined **pragmatism** more informally as "the attitude of looking away from first things, principles, 'categories,' supposed necessities; and of looking towards last things, fruits, consequences, facts."[23] Pragmatism was a reaction to traditional systems of philosophy, such as materialism and idealism. The concepts used in these traditional systems of philosophy, they argued, were largely empty. That is, they made no practical difference in people's lives. These systems, claimed the pragmatists, erred in looking for absolutes. Reality is hardly a single thing: It is pluralistic. And we are part of it. Using intelligence and reason, we can understand and exercise some control over reality. We thereby help create its immense variety.

✓ QUICK REVIEW
James held that philosophy should not lose its connection to personal and social problems.

Pragmatism's Approach to Philosophy

Pragmatism is decidedly humanistic.[24] Peirce, James, and Dewey tried to bring the insights of psychology, sociology, scientific method, and the arts into philosophy. They opposed philosophers' failure to view philosophy in its larger human and social context.[25] Philosophy, they felt, is not just a self-contained discipline with its own cluster of specialized problems. It is an instrument used by living individuals who are wrestling with personal and social problems. It is part of our common struggle to clarify our standards, directions, and goals. In his book, *Reconstruction in Philosophy*, John Dewey argued that all philosophy arises out of the struggle to deal with our social and moral problems. Philosophy cannot be allowed to remain a merely intellectual debate about esoteric matters that do not touch people's real concerns.

Hulton Archive/Getty Images

John Dewey: "Philosophy originated not out of intellectual material, but out of social and emotional material."

22 Charles S. Peirce, "A Draft of a Review of Herbert Nichols' A Treatise on Cosmology," manuscript in Charles S. Peirce Collected Papers, accessed April 10, 2015, at http://www.commens.org/bibliography/manuscript/peirce-charles-s-1904-c-draft-review-herbert-nichols-treatise-cosmology-vol.
23 William James, *Pragmatism: A New Name for Some Old Ways of Thinking* (New York: Longmans, Green, 1907), 54–55.
24 The following discussion is indebted to Charles Frankel, *The Golden Age of American Philosophy* (New York: George Braziller, 1960), 1–17.
25 See Frankel, *Golden Age*, 3.

This is the trait which, in my opinion, has affected most deeply the classic notion about the nature of philosophy. Philosophy has arrogated to itself the office of demonstrating the existence of a transcendent, absolute or inner reality and of revealing to man the nature and features of this ultimate and higher reality. It has therefore claimed that it was in possession of a higher organ of knowledge than is employed by positive science and ordinary practical experience, and that it is marked by a superior dignity and importance—a claim which is undeniable *if* philosophy leads man to proof and intuition of a Reality beyond that open to day-by-day life and the special sciences.

Various philosophers have of course, denied this claim at various times. But for the most part these denials have been agnostic and skeptical. They have contented themselves with asserting that absolute and ultimate reality is beyond human ken. . . . Only comparatively recently has another conception of the proper office of philosophy arisen. This course of lectures will be devoted to setting forth this different conception of philosophy. . . . At this point, it can be referred to only by anticipation and in cursory fashion . . .

If this lecture succeeds in leaving in your minds as a reasonable hypothesis the idea that philosophy originated not out of intellectual material, but out of social and emotional material, it will also succeed in leaving with you a changed attitude toward traditional philosophies. They will be viewed from a new angle and placed in a new light. New questions about them will be aroused and new standards for judging them will be suggested.[26]

MindTap To read more from Dewey's *Reconstruction in Philosophy*, click the link in the MindTap Reader or go to the Questia Readings folder in MindTap.

✓ QUICK REVIEW
According to Dewey, philosophy arises out of social and emotional material.

Dewey's "conception" that philosophy arises out of our "social and emotional" lives arose from his view of the nature of thinking. Dewey believed that all thinking is related to people's interests and their conscious or unconscious desires. All thinking aims at strengthening or securing some human interest or desire. Rather than compromising human ideals, this notion shows that ideals have a natural home in the world. The purpose of thinking is to discover new and better ways of realizing these ideals.

The pragmatists denied sharp distinctions between matter and mind, science and morals, and experience and reason. They held that we must examine all distinctions and ideas from the biological and social points of view. We should treat ideas as instruments for making sense of our experience. We must judge any idea or distinction by its consequences within its human context. Its value depends, then, on its problem-solving capacity. If distinctions like matter and mind, science and morals, or experience and reason do not solve any real human problem, they are distinctions between things that do not differ in any practical sense. These views lie at the heart of the pragmatic method.

ANALYZING THE READING

1. According to Dewey all knowledge "arises out of social and emotional material." What do you think he means by this statement? Is his statement ambiguous? If so, what are some of the various meanings his statement could have?

2. Suppose James' statement that all knowledge "arises out of social and emotional material" means that all knowledge arises out of the knower's own social and emotional needs. Would you agree with his statement? Would his statement still be ambiguous? Explain why.

The Pragmatic Method

The *pragmatic method* is a way to discover what our ideas mean by studying their consequences in actual experience. It is, in other words, the working out of what Peirce's "pragmatic maxim" meant. Pragmatists expanded on Peirce's core idea

---

[26] John Dewey, *Reconstruction in Philosophy* (New York: Henry Holt, 1920), 406–407.

that concepts must make a difference in people's lives (their deliberate actions) or be judged empty of any real content. Pragmatists like William James expanded this idea by applying it to several philosophical questions. Any metaphysical claims about reality, he held, must be based on facts and real consequences and not on abstract theories alone. We cannot base judgments by whether they are connected to some supposed ultimate reality. Any judgment must be rooted in real experiences that are meaningful to humans. In effect, we must set aside ultimate principles and self-evident values. In fact, pragmatism allows few certainties. The test of an idea, James suggested, is simply its capacity to make a difference in solving the real problems that it addresses. Both materialism and idealism are metaphysical theories that would probably fail this test. Here is how William James expresses the point in his important work *Pragmatism* (1907):

William James: "Pragmatism is the attitude of looking away from first things, principles, 'categories,' supposed necessities; and of looking towards last things, fruits, consequences, facts."

© Bettmann/CORBIS

> The pragmatic method is primarily a method of settling metaphysical disputes that otherwise might be interminable. Is the world one or many? Fated or free? Material or spiritual? Here are notions either of which may or may not hold good of the world; and disputes over such notions are unending. The pragmatic method in such cases is to try to interpret each notion by tracing its respective practical consequences. What difference would it practically make to anyone if this notion rather than that notion were true? If no practical difference whatever can be traced, then the alternatives mean practically the same thing, and all dispute is idle. Whenever a dispute is serious, we ought to be able to show some practical difference that must follow from one side or the other's being right.[27]

> **✓ QUICK REVIEW**
> For James, the pragmatic method interprets an idea in terms of its practical consequences and asks what difference it would make if it were true.

Pragmatists differ—understandably, for pragmatism is not a monolithic system of thought. For example, Charles S. Peirce was more concerned with the logical implications of ideas, not their psychological effects. He focused on the scientific function of ideas—their role in fostering reasoned consensus. In contrast, William James, a physiologist and psychologist, was interested in ideas as events in personal experience. He viewed ideas as instruments of will and desire. And John Dewey was neither a student of logic nor a psychologist. His main interest was social criticism. He used the pragmatic method to reassess the functions of education, logic, the arts, and philosophy in human civilization. Still, the observations about pragmatism that we have so far presented underlie the thoughts of all three American philosophers. And the pragmatic method outlined above guided the thinking of all of them. We will turn now to

ANALYZING THE READING

According to James, if "no practical differences whatever can be traced" between two opposing ideas, then they "mean practically the same thing, and all dispute is idle." Can you think of any important opposing ideas that make no real "practical difference"? For example, is there a real practical difference between being a Lutheran and being a Catholic? Between being a Democrat and being a Republican? Think of some opposing ideas similar to these but that you think have no real "practical differences." Even if opposing ideas have no real "practical differences," does it follow that they must "mean" the same? Why?

---

[27] William James, *Pragmatism*, 46.

focus, however, on the writings of one of these influential thinkers. We focus on the views of William James who is often seen as the main exponent of pragmatism.

Applied to metaphysical questions, the pragmatic method indicates certain criteria for determining what's real. Many materialists had relied on sense observation and scientific method. Many idealists (although not Berkeley) relied primarily on reason. In contrast, James accepted neither of these as the final determinant of reality. According to James, we determine whether something is real by its relation to "our emotional and active life." In particular, he wrote, "whatever excites and stimulates our interest is real." But several different systems of ideas or objects might excite a person's interests. So, he argued, a person will recognize several different "sub-universes" or "worlds" as real. Among them are the worlds of sense experience; of science; of abstract truth; of prejudices; of the supernatural; of personal opinion; and of madness. According to James, each of us selects the world or worlds that are most personally meaningful to us, and these, for us, are "reality":

> Really there are more than two sub-universes of which we take account, some of us of this one, and others of that. . . . The most important sub-universes commonly discriminated from each other and recognized by most of us as existing, each with its own special and separate style of existence, are the following:

ANALYZING THE READING

1. James claims that each of us is convinced that one of the seven worlds he describes is the world of real things or "the world of ultimate realities," and that the things of the other worlds are not truly real. Is James' claim correct? What would you think it means to say that things are "real" in the world you accept as real, but "not real" in the other worlds?

2. James seems to claim that we cannot say any world is the true reality independent of what anyone believes. All are equally real and for each of us reality is what "excites and stimulates our interest." Do you agree? Why?

3. If James is saying that every world is equally real, then does he have to accept that contradictory sentences are equally true? Suppose for example that in the world of science "God does not exist" is true, but in a supernatural world "God exists" is true. Then must James accept that God both exists and doesn't exist? Would this make any sense?

4. Critics say James assumes that saying someone *believes* a thing is real is the same as saying that thing *is* real. Do you agree? When James says that for each person one of the worlds is real, is he saying that each person *believes* one of the worlds is real, or is he saying that one of the worlds *is* real when a person accepts it as real? Which of these two interpretations of James makes most sense to you? Which of these two interpretations of James do you think was his real meaning?

1. The world of sense, or of physical "things" as we instinctively apprehend them, with such qualities as heat, color, and sound, and such "forces" as life, chemical affinity, gravity, electricity, all existing as such within or on the surface of the things.

2. The world of science, or of physical things as the learned conceive them, with secondary qualities and "forces" (in the popular sense) excluded, and nothing real but solids and fluids and their "laws" (i.e., customs) of motion.

3. The world of ideal relations, or abstract truths believed or believable by all, and expressed in logical, mathematical, metaphysical, ethical, or aesthetic propositions.

4. The world of "idols of the tribe," illusions or prejudices common to the race. All educated people recognize these as forming one sub-universe. The [belief in the] motion of the sky round the earth, for example, belongs to this world . . .

5. The various supernatural worlds, the Christian heaven and hell, the world of the Hindoo mythology. . . . The various worlds of deliberate fable may be ranked with these worlds of faith—the world of the Iliad, that of King Lear, of the Pickwick Papers, etc.

6. The various worlds of individual opinion, as numerous as men are.

7. The worlds of sheer madness and vagary, also indefinitely numerous.

Every object we think of gets at last referred to one world or another of this or of some similar list. It settles into our belief as a common-sense object, a scientific object, an abstract object, a mythological object, an object of some one's mistaken conception, or a madman's object; and it reaches this state sometimes immediately, but often only after being hustled and bandied about amongst other objects until it finds some which will tolerate its presence and stand in relations to it which nothing contradicts. The molecules and ether-waves of the scientific world, for example, simply kick the object's warmth and color out, they refuse to have any relations with them. But the world of "idols of the tribe" stands ready to take them in. . . . Each world while it is attended to is real after its own fashion; only the reality lapses with the attention. . . . Each thinker, however, has dominant habits of attention; and these practically elect from among the various worlds some one to be for him the world of ultimate realities. . . . For most men, as we shall immediately see, the "things of sense" hold this prerogative. . . . [But in] the sense in which we contrast reality with simple unreality, and in which one thing is said to have more reality than another, and to be more believed, reality means simply relation to our emotional and active life. . . . In this sense, whatever excites and stimulates our interest is real; whenever an object so appeals to us that we turn to it, accept it, fill our mind with it, or practically take account of it, so far it is real for us, and we believe it. Whenever, on the contrary, we ignore it, fail to consider it or act upon it, despise it, reject it, forget it, so far it is unreal for us and disbelieved.[28]

James is saying that in effect we choose our own reality by the criterion of its meaningful relation to our emotions and actions. Some philosophers may insist one world is more real than another, for example, the world of "matter" or the world of "mind." But James interpreted such views as indicating the world that was real to such philosophers because of its relation to their emotional and active lives. Simply put, reality is whatever stimulates and interests us, and these interests ultimately determine what is real. A newly perceived object becomes part of a "real world" when we can bring it into a consistent relationship with the other objects already in that particular world. In this way, we gradually build up and increase what we recognize as reality.

James rejected the idea that the scientific method is the exclusive determinant of reality. He himself was willing to use science to learn the secrets of one particular reality and the self that was part of that reality. Still, science alone, he felt, does not determine what all reality is. But James also did not think there was some cosmic mind or intellect that defined all reality as some idealists have thought.

 THINKING LIKE A PHILOSOPHER

James lists seven different kind of "sub-universes" or "worlds." Which of these worlds would you say is for you "the world of ultimate realities"? For example, for almost all of us the contents of the world of "illusions or prejudices common to the race" are not real. Most of us think the apparent motion of the sky around the earth is not real but is only an unreal illusion that results from the earth spinning on its axis. So which of James' seven worlds contains the things that you are most convinced are "real"? Do you agree with James that the things in your world (or worlds) are not just real but that they "stimulate your interest," you "accept" them, and you "believe" in them? Is he right that the things in the other worlds are things you "ignore," "fail to consider or act upon," "despise," "reject," "forget," and "disbelieve"?

Objections to Pragmatism

Is pragmatism an acceptable way of getting beyond the disputes between materialism and idealism? Or is it muddled thinking? Does pragmatism give us a clear notion of what it understands to be real? Some pragmatists have claimed to know only their experiences, which critics argue is a claim of idealism. Peirce, in fact, eventually adopted a version of idealism. But if we know only our experiences don't we have to reject all belief in an objective physical reality?

---

[28] William James, "The Perception of Reality," in *The Principles of Psychology* (New York: Henry Holt, 1890), selections from 291–294.

Are pragmatists correct, also, in holding that the mind and its ideas are only instruments for the pursuit of interests? Can't we create disinterested mathematical theories or try to understand the universe in a dispassionate way? And don't we sometimes try to investigate philosophical questions in an objective way that is not distorted by our interests and emotions? The mind and its ideas, say the pragmatists, exist to fulfill desires and interests. Then how do we explain the commitment to dispassionate scientific inquiry? Why do we place such a stress on impartiality when seeking truth and less reliance on the interests that may affect us?

And consider the implications that pragmatism has for its own views. Wouldn't a pragmatist have to say that pragmatism itself is true only in relation to people's interests and desires? Would a pragmatist be willing to accept the view that pragmatic philosophy is not an objective and disinterested search for the truth? Would James have to agree that pragmatism itself is nothing more than a theory that he proposes because he thinks it will advance his own interests?

Pragmatism also seems to erase the distinction between our knowledge of facts and the independent existence of facts apart from our knowledge.[29] James emphasizes that many realities exist each related to our interests. This seems to imply that there is no reality independent of our mind As James says, reality is what "excites and stimulates our interest," or what "so appeals to us that we turn to it, accept it, fill our mind with it or practically take account of it." This seems to mean that nothing is real apart from our beliefs and desires. Of course, pragmatists do not completely deny the existence of a world independent of the presence of human beings. Yet they do deny that anything counts as "real" unless it is related to human interests, emotions, and what we "accept." We will explore some of the implications of these ideas when we look at the views of recent pragmatic "antirealists."

PHILOSOPHY AT THE MOVIES

Watch *Hilary and Jackie* (1998), the true story of a brilliant musician, Jacqueline du Pré, who gives up everything to pursue her career only to succumb to a fatal disease, and her sister, Hilary, who pursues a domestic life with husband, Kiffer Finzi, and children and witnesses her sister's decline. The movie is divided into three parts: The first, labeled "Hilary and Jackie" shows reality from the point of view of both Hilary and Jackie; the second, marked "Hilary," shows reality from Hilary's point of view; and the third, marked "Jackie" shows much of the same reality as "Hilary," but now from the point of view of Jackie. At three points these realities diverge: when Kiffer first visits the du Pré home, when Hilary tells Jackie in a darkened bedroom that she is engaged to Kiffer, and when Kiffer has sex with Jackie. To what extent does this movie illustrate the pragmatic view of what reality is?

3.4 Reality and Logical Positivism

We saw that pragmatism understands reality in terms of pragmatic consequences. But another influential modern philosophy rejects all metaphysical attempts to understand reality. This is the outlook of **logical positivism**, which is based on a certain view of language and meaning.

Like pragmatism, logical positivism began as a reaction to the idealist and materialist disputes. Pragmatism reacted by arguing that these disputes wrongly failed to

---

[29] See Frankel, *Golden Age*, 7.

consider "fruits, consequences, facts." But logical positivists argued that the disputes arose from a failure to consider language and its meaning. They said an understanding of language and meaning shows all metaphysical claims about reality are meaningless. Metaphysics, logical positivists claim, is literal nonsense.

The most influential logical positivist was the British philosopher Alfred J. Ayer (1910–1989). According to Ayer, many philosophical claims are meaningless. Metaphysical claims, in particular, are mere nonsense. To make his point, Ayer offered "a criterion by which it can be determined whether or not a sentence is literally meaningful":

> I divide all genuine [meaningful] propositions into two classes: those which, in this terminology, concern "relations of ideas," and those which concern "matters of fact." The former class comprises the *a priori* propositions of logic and pure mathematics, and these I allow to be necessary and certain only because they are analytic. That is, I maintain that the reason why these propositions cannot be confuted in experience is that they do not make any assertion about the empirical world, but simply record our determination to use symbols in a certain fashion. Propositions concerning empirical matters of fact, on the other hand, I hold to be hypotheses, which can be probable but never certain. . . . I require of an empirical hypothesis . . . that some possible sense-experience should be relevant to the determination of its truth or falsehood. If a putative proposition fails to satisfy this principle, and is not a tautology, then I hold that it . . . is neither true nor false, but literally senseless.[30]

Ayer's point is that there are only two kinds of meaningful statements. These are (1) tautologies, or "relations of ideas," and (2) empirical hypotheses, or "statements of fact." Tautologies are true by definition. For example, "All bachelors are unmarried," "His sister is a female," and "Triangles have three sides." Tautologies are statements in which the meaning of the predicate is part of the meaning of the subject. Tautologies, which are sometimes called analytic statements, do not give us any real information about the world. They only tell us about the meanings of words. On the other hand, statements of fact are those that, at least in theory, can be verified by some possible observation of the world around us. That is, we can determine whether they are true by making some observations of the world. Examples are "It's raining," "California is about three thousand miles from New York," and "A spirochete causes syphilis." Statements of fact, which are sometimes called *synthetic* or *empirical statements,* do give us information about the world. They tell us something about what the world is like.

If a statement is neither a tautology nor a statement of fact, Ayer argued, then it is meaningless. Statements that are not in one of these two groups are nonsense. That is, they have no sense. Since metaphysical statements are not tautologies nor statements of fact, Ayer concluded, they are meaningless. Look at how he argues for this point:

ANALYZING THE READING

Earlier we saw that Peirce provided a "pragmatic maxim" that gave us a pragmatist "method" to figure out the information a concept contains. In what ways is Peirce's pragmatist method similar to Ayer's "criterion of meaning"? In what ways is it different?

> The criterion which we [will] use to test the genuineness of apparent statements of fact [such as those of metaphysics] is the criterion of verifiability. We say that a sentence is factually significant to any given person if, and only if, he knows how to verify the proposition which it purports to express—that is, if he knows what

---

[30] Alfred J. Ayer, *Language, Truth, and Logic,* 2nd ed. (New York: Dover, 1952), 31.

observations would lead him, . . . to accept the proposition as being true, or reject it as being false. If, on the other hand, the putative proposition is of such a character that the assumption of its truth, or falsehood, is consistent with any assumption whatsoever concerning the nature of his future experience, then, as far as he is concerned, it is, if not a tautology, a mere pseudo proposition. The sentence expressing it may be emotionally significant to him; but it is not literally significant. . . .

In the first place, it is necessary to draw a distinction between practical verifiability and verifiability in principle. Plainly we all understand, in many cases believe, propositions which we have not in fact taken steps to verify. Many of these are propositions which we could verify if we took enough trouble. But there remain a number of significant propositions concerning matters of fact which we could not verify even if we chose, simply because we lack the practical means of placing ourselves in the situation where the relevant observations could be made. A simple and familiar example of such a proposition [in 1936] is the proposition that there are mountains on the further side of the moon. No rocket has yet [in 1936] been invented which would enable me to go and look at the further side of the moon, so that I am unable to decide the matter by actual observation. But I do know what observations would decide it for me, if, as is theoretically conceivable, I were once in a position to make them. And therefore I say that the proposition is verifiable in principle, if not in practice, and is accordingly significant. On the other hand, such a metaphysical pseudo-proposition as "the Absolute enters into, but is itself incapable of, evolution and progress," is not even in principle verifiable. For one cannot conceive of an observation which would enable one to determine whether the Absolute did, or did not, enter into evolution and progress. Of course it is possible that the author of such a remark is using English words in a way in which they are not commonly used by English-speaking people, and that he does, in fact, intend to assert something which could be empirically verified. But until he makes us understand how the proposition that he wishes to express would be verified, he fails to communicate anything to us. And if he admits, as I think the author of the remark in question would have admitted, that his words were not intended to express either a tautology or a proposition which was capable, at least in principle, of being verified, then it follows that he has made an utterance which has no literal significance even for himself.[31]

 THINKING LIKE A PHILOSOPHER

According to Ayer statements are meaningless unless they are "tautologies" (they are true by definition) or "statements of fact" (they can be proved by sense observation). Think of some true statements that express beliefs that you have at this point in your life about what should matter most in human life, or what you think the purpose of human life should be. Write down those statements in a list making sure they are declarative sentences. Using Ayer's criterion of meaning, figure out whether each of your statements is a "tautology" or a "statement of fact." Are any of your statements neither of these? If so, would you say those statements are meaningless? Why? Carnap suggests that when statements are neither tautologies nor statements of fact, they might express feelings like a poem would. Would you say any of the statements on your list just express your feelings? If not, can you think of any statements that you believe, and that would express feelings like Carnap suggests?

Metaphysical statements are not the only kind of statements logical positivists like Ayer rejected as meaningless. They also claimed that most ethical and religious statements are not tautologies nor statements of fact. So they would say the following statements are all meaningless. "God exists," "God doesn't exist," "Lying is wrong," "Lying is right," and "Democracy is the best form of government." The fact that very few people consider such statements meaningless raises a question. How can such statements be rejected as meaningless when so many people believe that they are filled with meaning?

---

[31] Ibid., 33–36.

PHILOSOPHY AND LIFE
Parallel Universes

Max Tegmark, a physicist/astronomer highly respected as an international expert on the nature of the universe, has argued that there must be parallel universes: other areas of space that are about the size of the universe that is visible to us and that are exact replicas of own visible universe. (The "visible universe" consists of a sphere around us with the earth at its center and whose farthest point is the longest distance from us that light has been able to travel during the 14 billion years since the Big Bang began everything.) Such a replica of our visible universe would have to contain "a person who is not you but who lives on a planet called earth, with misty mountains, fertile fields and sprawling cities.... The life of this person has been identical to yours in every respect."

The idea that there must be another area of space that is an exact copy of our visible universe—and that contains an exact copy of you—is required by the fact that astronomers have concluded that the entire cosmos—that is, everything that extends beyond our visible universe—is infinite and is uniformly filled with galaxies, stars, and planets like our own visible universe. A volume of space the size of own visible universe, if it were fully packed with matter, could contain only up to 10^{118} protons. In a different volume of space the same size, each of these protons may or may not, in fact, be present. Hence there are, at most, only 2 to the 10^{118} different possible arrangements of protons in a volume of space the size of our own visible universe. That means that, in a volume of space larger than 2 to the 10^{118} times the volume of our own visible universe,

the arrangements of protons would have to start repeating. Beyond that huge volume, then, there would have to be a volume of space the size of our own visible universe that was, proton for proton, an exact copy of our own visible universe. Because observations of the cosmos indicate that it is infinite in volume, this means that somewhere in that infinite volume there must be an area of space the size of our own visible universe that is an exact replica of the volume of space we call our "visible universe" and that therefore includes an exact replica of you.

QUESTIONS

1. Tegmark makes assumptions about what lies beyond the visible universe (the part of the universe that we cannot perceive with even the most powerful telescopes or any other instruments we could possibly invent). In what sense do you think such parallel universes are "real"?

2. What would a materialist, an idealist, a pragmatist, a phenomenologist, or a logical positivist probably have to say about the reality of these parallel universes?

3. Tegmark says his parallel universes are not part of the "domain of metaphysics" but belong to the "frontiers of physics." What do you think he means by this? Do you agree?

Source: Max Tegmark, "Parallel Universes," *Scientific American*, April 14, 2003; see also Joel Achenbach, "The Multiuniverse," *National Geographic*, August 2003.

Logical positivists had an answer to this question. True, metaphysical statements are not literally meaningful. But they have another nonliteral kind of meaning. They express emotion. Lyrical poets use words to express feelings and emotions. Metaphysicians, they said, do the same. They use words to express feelings and not to represent facts about the world. Here is how the point is made by Rudolf Carnap (1891–1970), who was also a logical positivist:

> Now many linguistic utterances are analogous to laughing in that they have only an expressive function, no representative function. Examples of this are cries like "Oh, Oh" or, on a higher level, lyrical verses. The aim of a lyrical poem in which occur the words "sunshine" and "clouds" is not to inform us of certain meteorological facts, but to express certain feelings of the poet and to excite similar feelings in us. A lyrical poem has no assertive sense, no theoretical sense, it does not contain knowledge.

The meaning of our anti-metaphysical thesis may now be more clearly explained. This thesis asserts that metaphysical statements—like lyrical verses— have only an expressive function, but no representative function. Metaphysical statements are neither true nor false, because they assert nothing, they contain neither knowledge nor error, they lie completely outside the field of knowledge, of theory, outside the discussion of truth or falsehood. But they are like laughing, lyrics, and music, expressive. They express not so much temporary feelings as permanent emotional or volitional dispositions. Thus, for instance, a metaphysical system of **monism** [the view that reality is only one kind of thing—either matter or spirit, but not both] may be an expression of an even and harmonious mode of life, a dualistic system [the view that reality is made up of two kinds of things, matter and spirit] may be an expression of the emotional state of someone who takes life as an eternal struggle.... Realism [materialism] is often a symptom of the type of constitution called by psychologists extroverted, which is characterized by easily forming connections with men and things; idealism, of an opposite constitution, the so-called introverted type, which has a tendency to withdraw from the unfriendly world and to live within its own thoughts and fancies.

Thus we find a great similarity between metaphysics and lyrics. But there is one decisive difference between them. Both have no representative function, no theoretical content. A metaphysical statement, however—as distinguished from a lyrical verse—seems to have such a content, and by this not only is the reader deceived, but the metaphysician himself. He believes that in his metaphysical treatise he has asserted something, and is led by this into argument and polemics against the statements of some other metaphysician. A poet, however, does not assert that the verses of another are wrong or erroneous; he usually contents himself with calling them bad.

The non-theoretical character of metaphysics would not be in itself a defect; all arts have this non-theoretical character without thereby losing their high value for personal as well as for social life. The danger lies in the *deceptive* character of metaphysics; it gives the illusion of knowledge without actually giving any knowledge. This is the reason why we reject it.[32]

Metaphysical statements about reality, then, are meaningless. They only express our feelings about reality.

thinking critically • Categorical Syllogism Arguments

The key argument Ayer earlier makes is this:

All meaningful statements are tautologies or empirically verifiable.
Metaphysical statements are not tautologies or empirically verifiable.
Therefore, metaphysical statements are not meaningful.

This is an interesting argument but it does not fit into any of the logical forms we studied earlier, so we don't yet have a way of testing whether it is valid or not. Ayer's argument is what we call a "categorical argument," and we'll turn now to explaining how to determine whether a categorical argument is valid.

Categorical arguments are made up of categorical claims. A **categorical claim** is a claim that has a subject and a predicate and that uses the connectives "all," "some," "no," "not," "is," and "are." For example: "All dogs are small mammals" and "Some of the apples in this box are not edible." A categorical claim says that all or some of a general category

32   Rudolph Carnap, "The Rejection of Metaphysics" (1935), in *Twentieth-Century Philosophy: The Analytic Tradition*, ed. Morris Weitz (New York: Free Press, 1966), 215–216.

of things (like "dogs") is included in another general category of things (like "small mammals"), or that some or all of a general category of things (like "apples in this box") is excluded from another general category of things (like "edible things"). Categorical claims always have exactly two terms, one for the subject and one for the predicate. The following statements are all categorical claims; in parentheses are explanations of how the claim should be interpreted:

(1) *All religious statements are meaningful.* (The whole category of religious state-ments is a part of the category of meaningful statements.)

(2) *No religious statements are meaningful.* (The whole category of religious state-ments is excluded from the whole category of meaningful statements.)

(3) *Some religious statements are meaningful.* (A part of the category of religious statements is a part of the category of meaningful statements.)

(4) *Some religious statements are not meaningful.* (A part of the category of religious statements is excluded from the whole category of meaningful statements.)

There are only four kinds of categorical claims, and the preceding four statements are examples of those four. If we use capital letters in place of the terms of the four statements mentioned (R for "religious statements" and M for "meaningful state-ments"), we can see that these four kinds of categorical claims have the following four logical forms:

(1*) All *R* are *M*. (The whole category of R is a part of the category of M.)

(2*) No *R* are *M*. (The whole category of R is excluded from the whole category of M.)

(3*) Some *R* are *M*. (A part of the category of R is a part of the category of M.)

(4*) Some *R* are not *M*. (A part of the category of R is excluded from the whole category of M.)

Notice that the explanations in parentheses indicate whether the terms refer to a whole category or to only part of a category. This is important, as we'll see in a moment.

Now we can explain what a "categorical argument" is. A categorical argument is one that consists entirely of some combination of the four categorical claims. The most important kind of categorical argument is called the **categorical syllogism**. The categori-cal syllogism contains exactly *two premises* and *a conclusion*. In addition, a categorical syl-logism contains only *three terms*. For example, here is a categorical syllogism that is based on Berkeley's argument for idealism:

(5) All ideas exist in the mind.

(6) All of the things we perceive are ideas.

(7) Therefore, all of the things we perceive exist in the mind.

Suppose we assign the following letters to represent the three terms of this syllogism:

I = ideas
M = things that exist in the mind
P = things we perceive

Then this syllogism has the following form:

(5*) All *I* are *M*. (The whole category of I is a part of the category of M.)

(6*) All *P* are *I*. (The whole category of P is a part of the category of I.)

(7*) Therefore, all *P* are *M*. (The whole category of P is a part of the category of M.)

As we will see, a syllogism with this form is valid. Notice that one of the terms, I, occurs in both of the premises but not in the conclusion. This term is called the "middle term" because it relates the other two terms to each other. In the categorical form men-tioned earlier, premise (5*) relates M to I and premise (6*) relates I to P, so the conclusion (7*) says M must be related to P.

QUICK REVIEW
The logical form of a categorical claim is the result of replacing both of its terms with capital letters. There are four kinds of categorical claims and they have these four logical forms: "All R are M," "No R are M," "Some R are M," and "Some R are not M."

QUICK REVIEW
A categorical syllogism has two premises and a conclusion that are a combination of the four categorical claims, and that contain three terms.

How can we figure out whether a categorical syllogism is invalid? One way is to use the method we've seen before: Try to imagine a situation in which the premises are true, but the conclusion is false. But this method, as we've seen, has some drawbacks.

Fortunately, logicians have developed four rules for determining whether or not a categorical syllogism is valid. But to understand the rules, you need to keep two things in mind. First, categorical claims can be affirmative or negative; that is, they can say that one category *is* included in another, or that it is *not* (i.e., that it is *excluded* from the other). For example: "All *A* are B" (e.g., "all abortions are bad") is affirmative, and "No *A* are B" (e.g., "no abortions are bad") is negative. Second, as we mentioned earlier, the *terms* in a categorical statement can refer to a whole category of things or to a part of the category. When we say "All X," we are referring to the whole category of X. When we say "No X is Y" we are saying that the whole category of X is excluded from the whole category of Y, so both X and Y refer to a whole category. When we say "Some X are not Y," we are saying that a part of the category of X is excluded from the whole category of Y's, so only the Y term refers to a whole category. And when we say "Some X are Y," we are saying that a part of the category of X is a part of the category of Y, so neither X nor Y refer to a whole category. *As a rule, a term that occurs immediately after "all," or a term that occurs anywhere in a claim after "no" or "not" refers to a whole category.* In the following summary, the terms that refer to a whole category are in underlined bold italics:

All **_A_** are B   Some A are B
No **_A_** are **_B_**   Some A are not **_B_**

Now here are the four rules that a valid categorical syllogism must follow. If a categorical syllogism breaks one or more of these rules, it is invalid:

1. The middle term (the term that is present in both premises but absent from the conclusion) must refer to a whole category in at least one premise.
2. If a term in the conclusion refers to a whole category, it must also refer to the whole category in one of the premises.
3. Both premises must not be negative.
4. If one of the premises is negative, then the conclusion must be negative.

You can see more clearly why syllogisms that break these rules are invalid by testing each rule. Just find an argument that breaks the rule and then imagine a situation in which the premises are true and the conclusion is false. Here, for example, is an argument that breaks rule 1:

Some Men in this town are Barbers.
Some Men in this town are Tall.
Therefore, some Barbers in this town are Tall.

Now imagine a situation in which all the barbers in town are short men, and all nonbarbers are tall men. Then the premises would be true, but the conclusion false; so the argument, which breaks rule 1, is not valid. You should test the other rules on your own.

One more thing: As with other kinds of arguments, if you know a certain categorical argument is valid (or invalid), then any other argument *with the same logical form* will also be valid (or invalid). So if you memorize the logical forms of the common kinds of categorical arguments, and know which are valid and which are invalid, then you can easily tell whether other arguments with the same form are valid or not.

Now let's return to Ayer's argument:

All meaningful statements are tautologies or empirically verifiable.
Metaphysical statements are not tautologies or empirically verifiable.
Therefore, metaphysical statements are not meaningful statements.

QUICK REVIEW
Categorical claims can be negative or positive, and their terms can refer to a whole category or to a part of a category. A term that occurs immediately after "all," or a term that occurs anywhere in a claim after "no" or "not" refers to a whole category.

QUICK REVIEW
A categorical argument is valid when and only when: (1) The middle term refers to a whole category in a premise; (2) If a term in the conclusion refers to a whole category, it also refers to the whole category in a premise; (3) Both premises are not negative; (4) If a premise is negative, the conclusion must be negative.

Let's assign these letters to the three terms of Ayer's argument:

M: Meaningful statements
T: Statements that are tautologies or empirically verifiable
E: Metaphysical statements.

Here is the logical form of Ayer's categorical syllogism:

All M is T
No E are T
So: No E are M

You should now be able to check whether this argument is valid by using the four preceding rules.

Categorical arguments are combinations of the four main forms of categorical claims: "All A are B," "No A are B," "Some A are B," and "Some A are not B." It is not always easy to translate the claims of an ordinary English argument into one of these four forms. So here are some suggestions to help you.

First, when translating English sentences into their logical forms, keep in mind that terms have to refer to *categories of things*. This means that when an English sentence consists of a subject and a verb, both the subject and the verb have to be interpreted as categories of things. You can do this by adding "things that are. . ." or "things that. . ." to the subject and verb. For example, you should interpret "All wolves run in a pack" as meaning "All things that are wolves are things that run in a pack," and interpret "Some of the sheep hid from the wolf" as meaning "Some of the things that are sheep are things that hid from the wolf."

Second, here are some English expressions you should translate as "All X are Y":

Every X is Y   Only Y's are X's
Whatever is X is Y   Nothing is X without being Y
If something is X then it is Y   Nothing is X unless it is Y

Here are some English expressions that should be translated as "No X are Y":

X's are not Y's   Not a single X is Y
Each X is not Y   Not any X is Y
Whatever is X is not Y   If something is X, then it isn't Y

These English expressions should be translated as "Some X are Y":

One or more X's are Y's   X's are sometimes Y's
There are X's that are Y's   A few X's are Y's

And here are some English expressions you should translate as "Some X's are not Y's":

One or more X's are not Y's   Sometimes X's are not Y's
There are X's that are not Y's   Not all X's are Y's

Now that we've seen what kind of argument Ayer has given us, and how to figure out whether this kind of argument is valid, let's examine some objections to the premises of Ayer's argument.

Objections to Logical Positivism

During the twentieth century many philosophers, especially in the United States and England, embraced the views of the logical positivists. Others argued that their views were simply wrong. One of the fundamental objections to the views of the logical positivists is that their basic "criterion of meaning" is an unproved assumption. Logical positivists like Ayer argue in this way:[33]

> All meaningful statements are tautologies or empirically verifiable.
>
> Metaphysical statements are not tautologies or empirically verifiable.
>
> Therefore, metaphysical statements are not meaningful statements.

But, say critics, the logical positivists do not prove that the first premise in this argument is true. In fact, critics claim, the premise is meaningless according to the logical positivists themselves! Their criterion of meaning says "all *meaningful statements are either tautologies or empirically verifiable.*" But this statement itself is not a tautology. For the dictionary does not define *meaningful statements* as "either tautologies or empirically verifiable statements." Nor is the criterion of meaning empirically verifiable. For we cannot verify it by observing the world around us. So, critics say, by its own standards the criterion of meaning is meaningless. It is just the logical positivist's own "expression of emotion."

Other critics argue against the positivist's refusal to discuss metaphysical questions about reality. They refuse to discuss metaphysical claims because they do not meet their own unproved assumptions about meaning. But by doing this the logical positivists have in effect pretended that our real human questions and problems do not exist. The logical positivists have avoided the hard questions raised by materialists, idealists, and pragmatists. But that is playing ostrich. The problems, critics contend, are still there, and people still continue to think about them. But by failing to deal with these problems, logical positivists have ignored some of the most profound and significant issues that human beings face. This, critics claim, is one of the most disappointing aspects of logical positivism: its failure to discuss questions that really matter.

Some philosophers who were once sympathetic to logical positivism have agreed with the critics. Some have come to recognize as legitimate not just one or two but many kinds of meaning, including those related to questions of metaphysics. Most now agree that philosophers need to discuss questions not just of metaphysics, but those of morality, religion, politics, and education. Certainly, any inquiry into ourselves, any search for what we are, that ignores these aspects of our experience seems incomplete.

✓ QUICK REVIEW
Critics of logical positivism say that its criterion of meaning is unprovable and that if it is applied to itself, it implies that it is itself meaningless.

PHILOSOPHY AT THE MOVIES

Watch *Contact* (1997) in which scientist Ellie Arroway discovers a radio signal coming from the star Vega that has to have been transmitted by nonterrestrial intelligent beings and that when deciphered includes plans for a machine to transport a human to Vega, a journey that Ellie undertakes although few later believe she did so. To what extent are Ellie's beliefs and outlook on the world consistent with the logical positivist view of what is real; to what extent do they diverge? In what ways does the logical positivist view of reality conflict with Palmer Joss's view of reality? How would a logical positivist respond to the events Ellie experiences on her "journey"? How would a logical positivist respond to Ellie's views at the very end of the movie?

---

[33] Ayer, ibid., 34.

3.5 Antirealism: The Heir of Pragmatism and Idealism

For much of the last century pragmatism and logical positivism managed to clear away the earlier debates between idealists and materialists. But recently some philosophers have rejected the existence of an independent external reality much like idealism did. And some have returned to pragmatism's view that there are many "realities." These views, as we will see, are "postmodern" in the sense that they reject the "modern" belief in a single reality. We will examine these "new" views about reality. As we will see they have critically important implications about the relations between men and women. These views of reality have been labeled *antirealist* by many contemporary philosophers. The label indicates that, like Berkeley, they reject the view that there is an external reality that is independent of our minds. There are, however, many different kinds of antirealist views. Here we will focus on the kind of antirealism that denies the existence of an external physical world that is independent of the mind.

The opposite of antirealism is realism. And, as there are many antirealisms, there are many realisms. The kind of realism we will discuss is the kind that claims that there is an external world that is independent of our minds. More precisely, **realism** is the view that a real world exists independent of our language, thoughts, perceptions, and beliefs.[34] Realism says our world would be the same even if no one ever perceived it, thought about it, or described it. Take, for example, the object in our sky that we refer to as the moon and that we describe as the largest satellite orbiting the earth. The realist holds that the moon would exist and continue to be the largest object orbiting the earth even if no one ever described it, perceived it, or thought of it.

The realist says, then, that an external world exists, a world whose existence and features don't depend on how anyone describes it, perceives it, or thinks about it. The antirealist, on the other hand, denies that such a world exists. **Antirealism**, as we use the term here, claims that the world and its features depend on how they are described, perceived, and thought about.

Unlike Berkeley, modern antirealists do not argue that all we know are our own perceptions or ideas. Instead, the new antirealists base their views on language. They argue, in effect, that all we know are our own linguistic creations. Contemporary antirealists say that when we think about or talk about reality, we have to use a particular language. But different languages will describe the same reality in different ways. Antirealists claim that each of these different descriptions may describe the world as having different features. So, they conclude, we cannot say that reality has features that are independent of our language.

"**If a tree** falls in the forest and no one is around to hear it, does it make a sound?"

---

[34] My account here follows the discussion of realism by philosopher John Searle in his unpublished paper "Is There a Problem About Realism?" presented on February 28, 1992, at Santa Clara University.

The features of reality depend on the language or system of concepts we use to describe or think about reality. For example, the antirealist might say the moon exists because our language and way of thinking mark off a part of the sky as the moon. But our language did not have to mark off the sky in this particular way. In fact, if our language had partitioned the sky in a different way, we might not have counted the moon as the largest satellite orbiting the earth.

Proponents of Antirealism

For the antirealist, then, no reality is completely independent of the particular language or system of concepts we use. Moreover, our different languages and systems of concepts create different realities. Many contemporary philosophers have held this antirealist view. They include Paul Feyerabend, Richard Rorty, Jacques Derrida, Liz Stanley, Sue Wise, Ruth Hubbard, Nelson Goodman, Hilary Putnam, Dale Spender, and many others. We will concentrate on the arguments of Goodman, Putnam, and Spender.

Nelson Goodman was one of the first contemporary philosophers to argue that there is no reality independent of the categories we construct to describe the world. All reality, he argued, depends on the way we humans have chosen to describe the world. Goodman asserts that we "make" reality or "worlds" by choosing a particular way of describing, or drawing boundaries around things:

> Now as we thus make constellations by picking out and putting together certain stars rather than others, so we make stars by drawing certain boundaries rather than others. Nothing dictates whether the sky shall be marked off into constellations or other objects. We have to make what we find, be it the Great Dipper, Sirius, food, fuel, or a stereo system.[35]

Goodman suggests, further, that we humans construct and live in many different worlds. Each is created by different and overlapping languages and systems of thought and each is equally real. Artists, poets, and novelists create new and pleasing worlds by fashioning new languages and ways of thinking. But many of us also create our own more or less pleasing, more or less successful worlds, each of them as "real" as the others. Goodman's theories, like those of other antirealists, echo those we saw the pragmatist William James express.

Hilary Putnam is another important antirealist (although Putnam has now changed his mind about some antirealist claims). Putnam has said that he accepts some of the claims of pragmatism but rejects others. He makes an argument, however, that is similar to Goodman's.[36] Consider, he suggests, objects such as in Figure 3.1. Our ordinary system of counting would say there are three

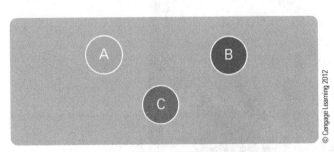

Figure 3.1   Hilary Putnam's circles—how many objects do *you* count?

© Cengage Learning 2012

---

[35]   Nelson Goodman, *Of Mind and Other Matters* (Cambridge, MA: Harvard University Press, 1984), 36.

[36]   Hilary Putnam discusses how his views are related to the "inheritance of pragmatism" in his book *Words and Life* (Cambridge, MA: Harvard University Press, 1994); see especially 152 where he summarizes the "theses" of pragmatism that he accepts. Putnam gives his counting argument in several places, including his book *The Many Faces of Realism* (LaSalle, IL: Open Court Publishing, 1987), 18–20.

objects in Figure 3.1. But certain nonstandard systems of counting would say there are seven objects. Besides the three objects A, B, and C, these nonstandard systems would "see" the object that consists of A and B together, the object that consists of B and C together, the object that consists of A and C together, and the object that consists of A, B, and C together. There is, Putnam asserts, no single correct answer to the question: How many objects are there really in Figure 3.1? So what reality is depends on the system of concepts we use to describe it.

The antirealist position has been especially important to several feminist philosophers. For example, the American philosopher Dale Spender has also argued that there is no reality independent of our language:

> Language is not neutral. It is not merely a vehicle which carries ideas. It is itself a shaper of ideas, it is the program for mental activity. In this context it is nothing short of ludicrous to conceive of human beings as capable of grasping things as they really are, of being impartial recorders of their world. For they themselves, or some of them, at least, have created or constructed that world and they have reflected themselves within it.
>
> Human beings cannot impartially describe the universe because in order to describe it they must first have a classification system. But, paradoxically, once they have that classification system, once they have a language, *they can see only certain arbitrary things.*[37]

The antirealist view is important for feminists such as Dale Spender because it explains why the world that women are forced to accept is often sexist. Often the language we use to describe women is demeaning. Male experiences are taken as the norm for thinking about and describing the experiences of women. Women, for example, have long been referred to by the supposedly generic word *man.* If language creates reality, then it is not surprising that our common reality is focused on males:

> Given that language is such an influential force in shaping our world, it is obvious that those who have the power to make the symbols and their meanings are in a privileged and highly advantageous position. They have, at least, the potential to order the world to suit their own ends, the potential to construct a language, a

ANALYZING THE READING

Putnam says that the same reality can be described as three objects or as seven objects. Is he assuming that reality is there to be described even before we describe it? If he is, then is he also assuming that reality exists independently of our descriptions and our language, just as the realist says it does? In other words, is he assuming that reality and its features exist even before we describe them with our language?

✓ QUICK REVIEW

Spender argues that we cannot know "things as they really are" because the classification system of the language we use "shapes" the reality we see. By creating our language, men have shaped our reality "to suit their own ends." But there are many other equally true realities and not just one true "objective" male reality.

ANALYZING THE READING

1. Spender seems to be saying the following: Every language makes us see reality in a certain way, so each language creates the reality that people who use that language see. Men shaped the languages we use and thereby created a reality that benefits them and oppresses women. Yet some women have created new realities. All realities—including women's new realities—are equally valid. Let's assume this is what Spender is saying.

2. Do you think what she is saying is true? Do you think some of the things she says are true, but some are wrong? Explain.

3. Assume what Spender says is all true. And suppose that the languages men and women use are different. (Suppose they both use English, but their words don't quite mean the same thing.) Then would men live in one reality and women in a different one? If men and women live in different realities could they ever really understand each other; that is, would they always end up talking about two different realities? Explain.

---

[37] Dale Spender, *Man Made Language,* 2nd ed. (Boston: Routledge & Kegan Paul, 1985), 139.

reality, a body of knowledge in which they are the central figures, the potential to legitimate their own primacy and to create a system of beliefs which is beyond challenge. . . .

In the patriarchal order this potential has been realized. . . .

Males, as the dominant group, have produced language, thought and reality. Historically it has been the structures, the categories and the meanings which have been invented by males—though not of course by all males—and they have been validated by reference to other males. In this process women have played little or no part.[38]

Like Nelson Goodman, Dale Spender suggests that we have to recognize that there are different female worlds or realities. And these are just as real as the male world that women are usually forced to inhabit:

Most women within the women's movement are developing their skills at handling more than one reality. The pluralism of the movement is itself both a source and a manifestation of the ability to function in a multidimensional frame of reference. There are numerous "truths" available within feminism and it is falling into male defined (and false) patterns to try and insist that only one is correct. Accepting the validity of multidimensional reality predisposes women to accept multiple meanings and explanations without feeling that something is fundamentally wrong. . . .

The concept of multidimensional reality is necessary, for it allows sufficient flexibility to accommodate the concept of equality. Multiple reality is a necessary condition for the acceptance of the experience of all individuals as equally valuable and viable. Only within a multidimensional framework is it possible for the analysis and explanation of everyone to avoid the pitfalls of being rejected, of being classified as wrong.[39]

THINKING LIKE A PHILOSOPHER

1. Describe times that it seemed to you that someone was living in a world or reality that was different from the one you live in. Think about an important misunderstanding you have had with another person. Explain that misunderstanding in terms of the idea that you and the other person were living in different realities or different worlds; describe the two realities and how they were different.

2. Explain how the idea that people may live in different realities can help you understand why people often "see" things differently from the way you do? Explain how that idea can help you understand why it is sometimes difficult for someone else to accept your own view about something.

3. Spender suggests that the languages we use create the reality and world we know. She also suggests that men have had the power to shape language so that it has created a world that favors them and oppresses women. Can you think of some examples of what Spender seems to be talking about? That is, can you think of words, phrases, or expressions we use that either favor men or that denigrate or disparage women without our realizing it? For example, many of us use the word "chick" to refer to a woman yet we are completely unaware of what that implies about women.

The new antirealists, then, do more than deny that there is one external real world independent of our thought and language. Many new antirealists claim there are many different real worlds. Each world is created by different, but perhaps overlapping, languages and ways of thinking. Moreover, each of these worlds is as real and valid as the others.

The views of such antirealists are sometimes described as "postmodern" views. **Postmodernism** is a movement that rejects the view that there is only one reality and that we are progressing toward a more accurate scientific

---

38 Ibid., 142–143.
39 Ibid., 102–103.

understanding of that one reality. The world of the eighteenth to the early twentieth century believed in such a single reality. But our own postmodern world recognizes a Babel of different and contradictory accounts of many distinct and equally valid realities. These are created by people from many different cultures and subcultures and from many different times and places. Postmodernism, then, is the view that there are many realities constructed by the many languages of the different cultures and subcultures that now swirl around us.

Objections to Antirealism

Not everyone has been convinced by the postmodern arguments of the antirealists. And several feminists have voiced concern over the implications of some antirealist claims. We must consider the objections they raise.

The antirealist claims that the worlds created by different languages and ways of thinking are equally real and valid. According to the antirealist there is no reality apart from our language and thought. Yet if all worlds are equally valid, then isn't the oppressive world created by sexist male language as valid a reality as any other? Moreover most men do not see women as oppressed. So in most men's reality women are not oppressed. But then doesn't the antirealist have to admit that the reality of such men is entirely valid? And if such men's reality is every bit as valid as women's reality, then shouldn't we stop criticizing men? As the British feminist philosopher Jean Grimshaw writes,

> This highlights what is perhaps the most central problem of all in the theory of "multiple realities," all of which are equally "valid." Theories, ideas and ideologies are not only ways of "making sense" of the world. They may also be means by which one group of people may dominate or exercise control over another. And the fact that one group has power over or exploits another, cannot be reduced to anyone's belief that this is so; nor does the fact that someone does not understand their own experience in terms of oppression or exploitation necessarily mean that they are *not* oppressed or exploited. . . . [T]he assumption of multiple female "realities," all of which are "valid" and none of which have any claim to be regarded as more adequate than any other, cannot provide a way of conceptualizing things such as oppression, exploitation, the domination of one social group by another.[40]

QUICK REVIEW

Critics of Spender point out that if language created multiple realities that were all equally true, then the supposedly sexist reality created by sexist male language would be as true and acceptable as any other; sexism would not be an objective reality because there would be no one true objective reality.

Grimshaw is pointing to a fundamental problem in antirealism. For the antirealist, something is real if and only if it is part of someone's language or way of thinking; otherwise, it is not real. But this means that if women do not believe they are exploited, oppressed, or dominated, then in reality they are not exploited, oppressed, or dominated. And if women speak and think in a male language that sees them as inferior, weak, and contemptible, then in reality they are inferior, weak, and contemptible. And if men think and speak as if

---

[40] Jean Grimshaw, *Philosophy and Feminist Thinking* (Minneapolis: University of Minnesota Press, 1986), 100, 102.

nothing they do is domineering and oppressive, then this too is as real and as valid as the view that some male actions are oppressive and domineering.

Antirealism seems to imply, then, that sexism or oppression is not an objective reality because there is no objective reality. Sexism and the oppression of women cannot be real if men think otherwise in their worlds. And if men or women believe there is no sexism, then this belief is as valid and real as the feminist belief that sexism exists. Antirealism, then, does not let the feminist say that sexism is objectively real so long as men or women think otherwise. Nor does it let the feminist say that the oppression of women is an objective reality so long as some men or women think and speak otherwise. Antirealism only lets the feminist say that sexism and oppression are real in her own world. Thus, antirealism seems to explode some of the basic claims of feminism.

Some contemporary philosophers have argued that antirealism is mistaken. American philosopher John Searle is an example. He agrees that there are many different languages or systems for describing or "seeing" reality. But he claims that although the descriptions we give of reality depend on our language, the reality we are describing does not. Searle argues that Putnam and Goodman confuse our descriptions of reality with the reality we are describing:

> From the fact that the *description* of any fact can only be made relative to a set of categories, it does not follow that the facts themselves only *exist* relative to a set of categories. . . . What counts as a correct application of the term "cat" . . . is up to us to decide and is to that extent arbitrary. But once we have fixed the meaning of such terms in our vocabulary by arbitrary definitions, it is no longer a matter of any kind of relativism or arbitrariness whether actual features of the world satisfy those definitions. We arbitrarily define the word "cat" in such and such a way; and only relative to such definitions can we say, "That's a cat." But once we have made the definitions and once we have applied the concepts relative to the system of definitions, whether or not something satisfies our definition is no longer arbitrary or relative.[41]

To understand Searle's point, let us return to Putnam's example of the three objects. In our ordinary system of counting objects, Figure 3.1 must be described as showing three objects. And in the proposed nonstandard system of counting objects, the figure must be described as seven objects. But in either case the objects—the reality—in the figure remain the same and do not change. So our *description* of the figure depends on the system of concepts we use. But the *reality* of the figure does not depend on either system because it remains unchanged whichever system we use.

Is it possible to *prove* that the real world exists, as the realist says it does? Searle believes that a kind of proof is possible. To understand his argument, it will help if we first consider a point that Searle makes about Berkeley's idealism. Searle points out that "Berkeley saw that it was a problem for his account that if each person refers only to his own ideas when he speaks, then there is a question about how we succeed in communicating with other people." Searle's point is this: If idealists like Berkeley were correct, then each of us would know only his or her own particular ideas. If so, people could never talk to one another about the same thing. For each of us would be talking about our own personal ideas, while others would

---

[41]   Searle, "Is There a Problem About Realism?" 10.

be talking about their personal ideas. Since people would never be talking about the same thing, they could never really communicate with and understand one another. But we do sometimes succeed in communicating with and understanding one another. So, Berkeley's idealism must be wrong: Sometimes, at least, we must be talking about the same external reality.

Searle makes a similar argument against the new antirealism of Putnam, Goodman, and Spender. If people at least sometimes understand one another, Searle claims, then sometimes they must refer to an independent reality. For two people to understand each other's statements, their statements must mean the same thing to both of them. That is, they must be talking about the same facts. But for a statement to mean the same thing to two people, both must see their statements as having the same "conditions of satisfaction." That is, both people must take the same facts as making their statement true. This means that the two people must take their statements as expressing the same facts about the same reality. So, if people understand one another, they must assume the existence of an independent reality—an external world—that they are all talking about:

> The person who denies metaphysical realism presupposes the existence of a public language, a language in which he or she communicates with other people. But what are the conditions of possibility of communication in a public language? What do I have to assume when I ask a question or make a claim that is supposed to be understood by others? At least this much: if we are using words to talk about something, in a way that we expect to be understood by others, then there must be at least the possibility of something those words can be used to talk about. Consider any claim, from particular statements such as "my dog has fleas," to theoretical claims such as "water is made of hydrogen and oxygen," to grand theories such as evolution or relativity, and you will see that they presuppose for their intelligibility that we are taking metaphysical realism for granted.
>
> I am not claiming that one can prove metaphysical realism to be true from some standpoint that exists apart from our human linguistic practices. What I am arguing, rather, is that those practices themselves presuppose metaphysical realism. So one cannot within those practices intelligibly deny metaphysical realism, because the meaningfulness of our public utterances already presupposes an independently existing reality to which expressions in those utterances can refer.[42]

Notice that Searle assumes that, sometimes at least, we understand and communicate with one another. But is it possible that we never really succeed in understanding one another? Perhaps we never really know what others are talking about because we live in different worlds created by our different ways of thinking and speaking? For example, do men and women live in different worlds and therefore always misunderstand one another? Are all worlds equally real and valid, even those that deny the reality of sexism and oppression? Or is there only one real world in which we all live and about which we all talk and think? Is it possible to say that sexism, for example, is an objective reality for all women, even those who believe otherwise?

The debate between the realists and the antirealists has intensified during these last few years and has not yet been resolved. However, it is clear that a great deal hangs on this debate's resolution.

MindTap To read more from Searle's "The Storm Over the University," click the link in the MindTap Reader or go to the Questia Readings folder in MindTap.

QUICK REVIEW
Searle argues that if people successfully communicate, they must assume there is one independent external reality because for people to understand each other's statements, they must be talking about the same independent external reality. So, our ability to communicate implies that antirealism is false.

---

[42] John Searle, "The Storm over the University," *New York Review of Books*, December 6, 1990, 40.

PHILOSOPHY AT THE MOVIES

Watch *He Said, She Said* (1991) in which Dan and Lorie are journalists who write columns with opposing views on issues and who eventually launch a TV program in which they do the same, and in which key events in their lives are replayed twice, once from Dan's perspective and once from Lorie's. Does this movie accept or reject the antirealist views of Goodman, Putnam, and Spender? Does it confirm or disconfirm Searle's argument against antirealism? Do men and women live in the kind of different worlds this movie suggests? Is there a "real" reality according to this movie?

3.6 Is Freedom Real?

No other metaphysical issue is as debated as the question of freedom. It has given rise to a controversy that still rages in our society. Consider the case of Leopold and Loeb.

Nathan Leopold and Richard Loeb, both 18-year-olds, were wealthy and brilliant. They had just graduated from college when they brutally murdered a 14-year-old boy in a rented automobile in Chicago's south side on May 21, 1924. During college, the two had been addicted to reading crime magazines and novels. They had experimented in petty theft and arson. Then, together they came up with the idea of committing the "perfect crime." The challenge of planning, executing, and getting away with a murder intrigued and fascinated them. For what they later described as the "intellectual thrill" of it, they kidnapped young Bobbie Franks. They beat him on the head with a chisel, suffocated him by stuffing a gag in his mouth, and then phoned his wealthy parents to demand $10,000 in ransom. The family alerted police investigators, who soon found the boy's bloody body half-buried in a railway culvert. Lying next to the body were Leopold's eyeglasses. When confronted, the two quickly confessed and were subsequently tried for murder, punishable by death.

Their lawyer was the famous defense attorney Clarence Darrow. At trial before Judge John R. Caverly, for thirty-three days in July and August 1924, Darrow argued

Nathan Leopold (left), and Richard Loeb, who were convicted for the kidnapping and murder of Loeb's distant cousin, 14 year-old Bobby Franks.

© Hulton Archive/Getty Images

that the boys, who had already pleaded guilty, should not be executed. Science has proved, Darrow suggested, that everything in the universe is governed by rigid laws of causality. These laws ensure that everything that happens has to happen. Therefore, no one is responsible for his or her actions. The real causes of our actions lie outside us, in the events and conditions that caused us to act as we did and in the laws that govern our acts. In particular, Darrow claimed, Leopold and Loeb's murderous act was caused by their heredity and the way they were raised. Speaking in defense of "Dickie" Loeb, Darrow said this at the trial:

> I do not claim to know how it happened. I know that something or some combination of things is responsible for this mad act. I know that there are not accidents in nature. I know that effect follows cause. What had this boy to do with it? He was not his own father. All this was handed to him. He did not make himself. . . . Do you mean to tell me that Dickie Loeb had any more to do with his making than any other product of heredity that is born upon the earth?. . . And yet there are men who seriously say that for what nature has done, for what life has done, for what training has done, you should hang these boys. . . . [But] to believe that any boy is responsible for himself or his early training is an absurdity that no lawyer or judge should be guilty of today. . . . I know that if this boy had been understood and properly trained . . . he would not be in this courtroom today with the noose above his head. If there is responsibility anywhere, it is back of him; somewhere in the infinite number of his ancestors, or in his surroundings, or in both. And I submit, your Honor, that under every principle of natural justice, under every principle of conscience, of right, and of law, he should not be made responsible for the acts of someone else . . .[43]

QUICK REVIEW
Darrow argued that their heredity and upbringing together with the laws of causality made Leopold and Loeb do what they did, so they were not morally responsible for killing Bobbie Franks.

In the end, Judge Caverly agreed with Darrow and refused to impose the death penalty. Instead, he sentenced the two boys to life in prison, the only other option available to him. His decision raised a public outcry. Darrow was simply wrong, the public claimed. Leopold and Loeb acted freely and deliberately. They were fully responsible for what they did and deserved the maximum penalty.

Although the case of Leopold and Loeb is an old one, the issues it raised are still argued in courtrooms today. For example, in December 2002, Thomas Koskovich was put on trial for a murder that he and a friend had committed in 1997. They had lured two pizza delivery men into driving to a deserted rural house to bring them a pizza they had ordered as a ruse. When the two delivery men drove up with their order, Koskovich and his friend walked up to the car. They pulled out pistols, and shot both of them dead through the car windows. Eleven days before, they had stolen the guns and practiced to prepare for the killings. Earlier, Koskovich had told a girlfriend he was planning a murder so that he could see "what it felt like" to kill someone. After emptying the pockets of their victims, the leader, Koskovich, hugged his friend excitedly. He was thrilled with what they had just done. "I love you, man," his friend said. Returning home, the two changed out of their bloody clothing and went to church. The following day, Koskovich said to a friend who stopped by the house, "How does it feel to shake the hand of a killer?"

During Koskovich's trial, his defense lawyers argued that the crime was caused by his environment. Koskovich grew up neglected and unloved in a household plagued by violence, drugs, alcoholism, abuse, abandonment, and suicide attempts. A local newspaper reporter wrote the following:

QUICK REVIEW
Darrow's view often shows up in murder trials today.

> Citing her client's "horrific, depraved, tragic" family life, a lawyer asked a jury Thursday to spare the life of convicted killer Thomas Koskovich, but the prosecution demanded the ultimate penalty for "murder done for the thrill of it." . . . [Koskovich's lawyer] said defense witnesses will show that the murder . . . was the product of mitigating factors—immaturity, drug use, stunted emotional development, mental

---

[43] Clarence Darrow, "Leopold and Loeb," quoted in G. L. Bowie, M. W. Michaels, and R. C. Solomon, *Twenty Questions: An Introduction to Philosophy* (New York: Harcourt Brace, 1988), 688, 691.

and psychological disorders, family abandonment and rejection, and a home life rife with infidelity, gambling, psychological abuse, and criminal activity.[44]

During the trial, witnesses stated that his father abandoned his mother and went to live with another woman when Koskovich was 9. He told the boy as he walked away that he "loved him the least" of any of the children. The house became a noisy, chaotic place where stray cats, dogs, and a goat wandered freely. His mother took on lovers, his brother became a hardened criminal hooked on drugs and alcohol, and his sister several times attempted suicide. An assortment of cousins, nieces, nephews, an uncle who was in and out of jail, and several acquaintances slept on the floors and the couches of the small littered house. In the sometimes violent, chaotic household, Koskovich was neglected. Nobody cared if he didn't get to school, and neither did anyone notice if he failed to come home. His addicted uncle sometimes had Koskovich cut up lines of cocaine for him. When Koskovich was 12, his mother abandoned him to go live with a boyfriend. She took his younger brother with her but left him in the house with his grandmother, Bertha Lippincott. Bertha had been raped by her father, was a convicted robber and drug abuser, and was now living with her lesbian lover because her husband had left her for her aunt. Like his parents, his grandmother neglected him emotionally. Koskovich grew into a depressed, barbiturate-addicted teenager.

On December 5, 2002, the jury reached a decision. They found that the criminal activity of his family, abandonment by his parents during his adolescence, family infidelity, domestic violence, substance abuse, gambling, criminal activity, and suicide attempts were so pervasive in his household that they "mitigated" his responsibility for the killings. So Koskovich, they had decided, should not be sentenced to die. Thomas Koskovich, instead, was sentenced to life in prison.

Koskovich's lawyers obviously felt that his crime was the predictable outcome of the violent life that had preceded it. So they agreed he should not be held fully morally responsible for his acts. It was therefore right that he not receive the death penalty. Others, like the sister of one of the victims, strongly disagreed. People are morally responsible for what they do. No matter how we are brought up, we have the power to choose what we will do. Believing that Koskovich freely chose to kill and so should have received a fitting punishment, the victim's sister reacted bitterly after hearing Koskovich had avoided the death penalty. "Is this justice?" she asked. "No. This is not justice."

Determinism

There is, perhaps, no more controversial question in metaphysics than the one raised in the preceding cases. Is human freedom a reality? Or are human actions completely determined by what we are and what the laws of nature cause us to do? Many philosophers believe that our actions are not free. Human actions are events, they point out. And every event is caused or "determined" by previous conditions and events and the physical, biological, and psychological laws that govern reality. In such a view of reality there can be no freedom. A person's action is free if that person controls what he or she does and so has the ability to do something else. Freedom is the ability to choose something other than what we actually choose. So our choices are not free if they are completely determined by previous events and conditions and the scientific laws that determine what those events and conditions produce. They are not free because we would not have the ability to choose anything other than what we actually choose. That was the basis of the arguments of the

---

[44] John Cichowski, "New Penalty Trial Opens in Thrill Killing," *The Record* (Bergen County, NJ), November 1, 2002.

lawyers of both Leopold and Loeb and of Koskovich. Both lawyers argued that previous events and conditions had made their clients what they were. Given the events and conditions in which they were raised, and the psychological laws that govern us, they could not have chosen to do anything else the day of the murders. So they were not free when they murdered their victims.

Freedom is related to moral responsibility. What is moral responsibility? To say a person is morally responsible for an action is to say that action originated in the person so he or she is accountable for that action and its consequences. That is, the action and its consequences can be blamed on, or credited to, the person in whom the action originated. If an action is bad, we blame the person who was morally responsible for it. If the action is good then we credit it to the person who was morally responsible for it. Suppose, for example, that I get mad at another driver while he and I are driving on a freeway. So I purposely ram his car with mine, causing his to skid and crash. Then I am morally responsible for ramming his car, for the crash, and for any injuries the driver suffered. Or suppose that while walking in the park I see a child in a lake and hear him calling for help. When I realize the child is drowning, I jump into the lake, swim out to him, and save his life. Then, I am morally responsible for saving the child's life. And doing so is to my credit and deserves praise.

Moral responsibility is related to freedom because a person is morally responsible only for what he or she does freely. If a person's action was not freely chosen, then the person is not morally responsible for it. Suppose, for example, that I am walking down a crowded stairway and you are standing in front of me when someone pushes me from behind. And suppose the push makes me bump against you so hard that you fall down the stairs and break a leg. Then, although I caused your injury, I am not morally responsible for it. I am not morally responsible for it because I was not free to prevent myself from doing what I did. The action that led to your broken leg did not originate in me, but in the person who pushed me. So I cannot be blamed for your injury. So if a person's actions are not free, then the person is not morally responsible for what he did. That, again, was a basic claim in both the Leopold and Loeb and the Koskovich trials. Their lawyers argued that since their clients did not act freely, they were not morally responsible for murdering their victims.

The view that human actions are completely determined is called *determinism*. **Determinism** is the view that every event is causally determined by previous conditions and events operating in accordance with the laws of nature. So each event is at least theoretically predictable if we know all its previous conditions and events and the laws that determine what those events and conditions will cause. Determinists argue that human actions are events and so they are part of this causal chain of nature. That is, all human actions are determined. Stated in another way, determinists hold that there is only one path leading from the past through the present and into the future. It is not possible for the future to take any path other than the one that prior events and conditions and the laws of nature force it to take.

Materialism and determinism have been close allies. Materialism holds, we saw, that our decisions and choices are caused by the brain or are events in the brain. But these brain processes are physical processes. So they have to be caused by prior physical events that are governed by scientific laws, like any other physical process.

The discoveries of the great British scientist Sir Isaac Newton (1642–1727) tended to support determinism. Newton showed that the movements of all material bodies in the universe, from the smallest atoms to the largest planets and comets, follow three universal laws of motion. He described those laws in his amazing work *Principia Mathematica Philosophia Naturalis.* Newton's three laws were incredibly simple. His first says that all bodies continue to move in the same direction and speed unless acted on by an external force. His second law is called the law of universal gravitation. This law states that all bodies in the universe attract all other bodies with a force proportional to their masses and their distances from one another. And his third law says that every action has an equal and opposite reaction. Newton's three simple laws implied that it is possible to predict the future location and motion of any body in the universe. Suppose we knew the locations, masses, speeds, and directions of motion of a set of bodies at some moment in the past. Then using Newton's laws we could determine their exact locations, speeds, and directions of motion at any moment in the future. Astronomers could now predict the future positions and motions of planets and comets. Determinists now began to argue that the activities of human beings are also caught up in the mechanical workings of the universe. Because people have physical bodies, they, too, must be subject to the universal laws of nature.

These ideas were brilliantly expressed by the French mathematician Pierre Simon, Marquis de Laplace. Laplace, who was a determinist, wrote the following in 1812:

> **MindTap** To read more from Laplace's *Philosophical Essay on Probability* in Dennis Richard Danielson's *The Book of the Cosmos,* click the link in the MindTap Reader or go to the Questia Readings folder in MindTap.

All events, even those which are so insignificant that they do not seem to follow the great laws of nature, are the result of those laws just as necessarily as the revolutions of the sun.... Present events have a connection with previous ones that is based on the self-evident principle that a thing cannot occur without a cause that produces it. This axiom, known as the *principle of sufficient reason*, extends even to actions about which people may feel indifferent. For even the freest will is unable to give birth to an action without a determining motive.... The contrary opinion is an illusion of the mind, which, being unaware of the elusive motives that move its will when choosing among indifferent matters, believes that its choices are determined by itself and not by its motives.

ANALYZING THE READING

Laplace claims that people's motives cause their actions in accordance with the laws of nature. Critics have said, however, that motives by themselves do not cause any actions. At any given moment, critics argue, we have a bunch of different motives for doing a bunch of different things. For example, I might have a motive to study, to play a video game, to go to a movie, and so on. So my mind has to decide which of these motives I will act on. My motives will not lead to any action until my mind makes that decision. According to the critics, my mind's ability to select the motive that I will act on is what makes me free. How do you think Laplace would answer this objection of the critics?

We ought to regard the present state of the universe as the effect of its earlier state and as the cause of the one which is to follow. If a great intelligence could comprehend in an instant all the forces which move the natural world, and the situations of all the beings that make it up, and if that intelligence was powerful enough to analyze all the data it would have, then it would be able to produce a detailed description of all the future movements in the universe from those of the largest bodies in the universe to those of the lightest atom. For such an intelligence nothing would be uncertain and the future, like the past, would be present to its eyes. The advancements that the human mind has been able to make in astronomy, offers us a feeble idea of what such a powerful intelligence would be like. The discoveries that the human mind has made in mechanics and geometry, and the laws of universal gravity, have enabled the human mind to achieve a description of the past and future states of the celestial system of the world [i.e., the past and future motions of comets and planets]. Applying the same method to other objects of its knowledge, the human mind has succeeded in finding the general laws that govern observed events and in predicting the events which current circumstances will produce in the future. All these efforts in the search for truth have tended to lead the human mind toward the kind of vast intelligence which we have just mentioned, but from which the human mind will always remain infinitely removed.

> **QUICK REVIEW**
> Encouraged by Newton's laws of motion, Laplace argued that human actions are determined.

The regularity which astronomy shows us in the movements of the comets doubtless exists also in all phenomena. The curve described by a simple molecule of air or vapor is regulated in a manner just as certain as the planetary orbits.[45]

---

[45] Pierre Simon de Laplace, *A Philosophical Essay on Probabilities* (1812), trans. Frederick Truscott and Frederick Emory (New York: John Wiley & Sons, 1902), excerpts from ch. 2, 3–6.

Laplace is suggesting two arguments for his view that human actions are not free. First, he points out, everything must work according to the "laws of nature." By the laws of nature he means the physical, chemical, biological, and psychological laws that determine how things operate. Second, he claims, "every event must have a cause that produces it." Since human actions are events, they, too must have a cause. The causes of human actions, he suggests, are people's motives. So people's motives work according to the laws of nature. That means that a person's action is the result of the motives he had and the laws of nature that caused those motives to produce that action. When a person acts, therefore, he is not free to choose other alternatives. His choice can only be what his motives and the laws of nature cause him to choose. Laplace does not mean, of course, that when we act we feel some kind of force within us that makes us do things even if we do not want to do them. Laplace is suggesting the opposite. He is suggesting that what we do depends on what we want and on the laws of nature that lead us to satisfy our wants. When we act, therefore, we are doing what we want to do. But we could not have done anything else. The laws of nature ensure that we will act exactly as our wants cause us to act.

But Laplace suggests a second argument for determinism. Laplace notes the "advancements that the human mind has been able to make in astronomy." He is talking here about Newton's discovery of the universal laws of motion and gravity. These laws of motion and gravity have let us predict the future positions of planets and comets. We predict these by first getting information about the position, mass, and velocity of a planet or comet. Then we use Newton's laws to figure out the position to which it will move in the future. Now just as we are able to predict the future positions of planets and comets, a powerful intelligence should be able to predict the future of every molecule in the world. For every molecule, Laplace says, must obey the same universal laws that govern the planets and comets. So by knowing the current position, mass, and velocity of every molecule in the world, a powerful mind could use Newton's universal laws to figure out all their future positions. Humans, of course, are made up of molecules. So such a powerful mind would be able to predict the future actions of every human being. But this means that every person's future actions are completely determined by the current position of his molecules and Newton's laws. When a person acts, then, he does not have the freedom to choose any other alternative and so he is not free.

It may seem to us that we are free because we do what we are motivated to do. But this appearance of freedom is not the reality. It is just a result of our ignorance of the laws that govern us through our motives. Eventually, Laplace thought, we will discover more detailed laws that govern human actions. Then we will see clearly that human freedom is nothing but an illusion.

In our own time, determinism has been encouraged by psychological theories, such as those of Sigmund Freud. Freud himself did not explicitly espouse a determinist position. But many of his followers used his theories to argue that unconscious psychological desires are the real causes of the actions people think they chose freely. Psychological mechanisms place human actions squarely within the causal chain of nature. For example, the contemporary philosopher John Hospers holds that "the unconscious is the master of every fate and the captain of every soul":

A man is faced by a choice: shall he kill another person or not? Moralists would say, here is a "free" choice—the result of deliberation, an action consciously entered into. And yet, though the agent himself does not know it, and has no awareness of the forces that are at work within him, his choice is already determined for him: his conscious will is only an instrument, a slave, in the hands of a deep unconscious motivation which determines his action. If he has a great deal of what the analyst calls "free-floating guilt," he will not; but if the guilt is such as to demand immediate absorption in the form of self-damaging behavior, this accumulated guilt will have to be discharged in some criminal action. The man himself does not know what the inner clockwork is; he is like the hands on the clock, thinking they move freely over the face of the clock.[46]

We noted earlier that determinism seems to rule out human freedom and responsibility. Philosophers who accept determinism agree it rules these out. If people cannot help but make the choices they make, then they do not have the ability to choose other alternatives. In this sense, they lack freedom. They also lack responsibility because people are morally responsible only for what they do freely. Determinism therefore rejects the idea that we are each morally responsible for our actions. The determinist view of reality, then, can be summarized in the following argument:

1. All actions are causally determined by previous conditions and the laws of nature.

2. If all actions are causally determined by previous conditions and the laws of nature, then people do not act freely and are not morally responsible for their actions.

3. So, people do not act freely and are not morally responsible for their actions.

We should mention that the first premise of this argument is the basic claim of determinism. All determinists accept that first premise. Most determinists also accept the second premise. But some determinists reject the second premise. Determinists who reject the second premise are usually called "compatibilists." Compatibilists try to argue that the basic claim of determinism, the first premise, is compatible with freedom. We will discuss their views of the compatibilists below.

The "previous conditions" that determinists say determine our actions differ from one philosopher to another. As we saw, Laplace thought the previous conditions were the motives a person happened to have. Hospers, however, says the previous conditions that determine our choices are unconscious mental forces such as "unconscious guilt." Others have suggested that the previous conditions consist of a person's character, temperament, desires, perceptions, beliefs, needs, interests, unconscious desires, habits, addictions, and so on. Many have also suggested that events in our environment should also be included among the previous conditions that determine our actions. A person will respond one way to events in one environment, and respond in a different way to events in a different environment. For example, the way I act when I am interacting with strangers in a store is different from the way I act when I am interacting with my family at

ANALYZING THE READING

Determinists have suggested that many different factors are causes of our actions including motives, unconscious mental forces, character, needs, interests, desires, and so on. These factors, determinists say, cause our actions by operating in accordance with the laws of nature. However, some critics of determinism raise this objection: If our minds know such a psychological factor is operating in us, we can choose not to act on that factor. For example, if I realize my reason for doing something is unconscious guilt, I can decide not to do it. If I realize I am doing something for a bad motive or an evil desire, I can decide not to do it. But this is not the way that causes following the laws of nature operate. For example, a falling rock cannot decide to stop falling. A log being carried by a river current cannot decide to stop moving. So our ability to choose not to act on any psychological factor we know about shows our actions are not caused by those factors operating in accordance with the laws of nature. Do you think this objection to determinism is right? Why?

---

[46] John Hospers, "What Means This Freedom?" in *Determinism and Freedom in the Age of Modern Science*, ed. Sidney Hook (New York: New York University Press, 1958).

home. So some determinists argue that events in our environment are also among the previous conditions that cause us to act as we do.

The implications of determinism are disturbing. If determinism is true, then punishment, at least in the traditional sense, makes little sense. More broadly, if determinism is true, then it makes no sense to hold individuals responsible for their actions, whether for good or evil. The saint should no more be praised than the criminal should be punished. For neither is ultimately responsible for what he or she did. Regret would also make no sense because one cannot regret doing what one could not help but do.

But is determinism correct? Perhaps events in the natural world are determined, but should human actions be assimilated to natural events? When we act, don't we directly experience our freedom? Aren't we sometimes directly aware that we have control over our actions and so are morally responsible at that moment for the actions we choose? Some philosophers have argued that unlike objects in nature, which are determined, human beings are free.

Libertarianism

But showing that determinism is wrong is not easy. For how can we human beings be outside the causal chain of nature? No philosopher has argued so vigorously in favor of freedom as Jean-Paul Sartre. Sartre utterly rejects determinism. Instead, Sartre argues for a form of what is sometimes called **libertarianism**. A libertarian holds that people have control over what they do and are free to make choices other than the ones they actually make.

We saw in Chapter 2 that Sartre's existentialism claims that we are free to choose the actions that make us who we are. So he also claims we are fully responsible for what we have become and what we will be. Sartre claims, then, that we are radically and absolutely free. But how does Sartre answer the determinist? How does he argue for our freedom in the face of a universe of causes that operate according to the laws of nature?

Jean-Paul Sartre: "Thus human reality does not exist first in order to act later; but for human reality, to be is to act, and to cease to act is to cease to be."

Lipnitzki/Roger Viollet/Getty Images

Sartre's argument for freedom depends on a fascinating analysis of how humans choose. Sartre points out that when a person does anything, he intends to achieve something by his action. And this means that when a person acts he has in mind a future situation that does not yet exist. That is, to do anything, a person has to think about moving from his situation as it exists right now, to a future situation that does not yet exist. Suppose, for example, that I decide to change jobs. Then I must have thought about moving from my present job situation, to a future job situation that does not yet exist. So to act, I have to think about a future job situation that does not yet exist and that is different from my present job situation. We are able to do this, Sartre claims, because we are conscious beings. Our human consciousness has the ability to mentally distance itself from its present concerns and think of a future that is different from the present. In other words, we can mentally stand back from our present situation and think of a different future that does not yet exist. Once

QUICK REVIEW
Sartre argues that human consciousness can withdraw itself from any existing situation to seek a future that does not exist, so humans are not determined by any existing situation but are free and responsible.

we think that a different future is possible, we begin to see our present situation in a new way. For example, when I realize I could have a different job, I start to see what my present job lacks and the possibilities a different future job offers. Moreover, my consciousness can turn the possibilities of the future situation and what my present lacks, into motives that will move me to act. I do this by forming the intention to change my situation. By making this choice in my consciousness I decide to make the possibilities of the future and the lacks of the present my motivation to change. This ability of our consciousness to stand back from its present situation, to conceive of a different situation that does not yet exist, and to turn what the present lacks and the possibilities of the future into a motive that moves me, is the basis of our freedom. We are free because our consciousness has these abilities. Here is Sartre's argument in his own words:

It is strange that philosophers have been able to argue endlessly about determinism and free-will . . . without ever attempting first to make explicit the structures contained in the very idea of action. . . . We should first observe that an action is on principle intentional. . . . But if this is the case, we establish that an action necessarily implies as its condition the recognition of a "desideratum", that is, of an objective lack or negativity. . . . This means that . . . [to act] consciousness must withdraw itself from the world of which it is conscious and leave the level of being [i.e., what exists] to approach that of non-being [i.e., what does not yet exist].

Insofar as man is immersed in the historical situation, he will not even succeed in conceiving of the failures and lacks in [, for example,] a political organization or economy. This is . . . because he apprehends it in the fullness of its being, and because he cannot even conceive that he can exist in it otherwise. It is necessary for man to change such an opinion [of his situation] and, in terms of what it is not [i.e., of what it lacks], to acknowledge its harshness and the sufferings it imposes. Both of these can be motives for conceiving of another state of affairs in which things would be better. It is on the day that he can conceive of a different state of affairs that a new light falls on his troubles and suffering and that he *decides* these are unbearable.

[For example,] a [suffering] worker in 1830 was incapable of revolting . . . for he . . . did not represent his sufferings to himself as unbearable. He adapted himself to them . . . because he lacked the education and reflection necessary for him to conceive of a social state in which these sufferings would not exist. Consequently, *he does not act*. It is only after he has formed the project of changing the situation that it will appear intolerable to him. This means he must first stand away from it. He must then conceive an ideal state of affairs as presently something that is still nothing [i.e., does not yet exist]. And he must conceive his actual situation as something that would be nothing [i.e., would no longer exist] if the ideal state of affairs was present. He will have to conceive of his happiness as accompanying that ideal situation and so as presently nothing [i.e., as presently not existing]. And then he must return to his present situation to illuminate it in light of the fact his happiness is nothing right now [i.e., does not exist right now]. Only then can he declare: "I am not happy!" [And then he will act.]

Two important consequences result. (1) No factual state whatever it may be (the political and economic structure of society, a psychological "state," etc.) is capable by itself of motivating any act whatsoever. For an act is a projection of [human consciousness] . . . toward what is not, and what is can in no way determine by itself what is not. (2) No factual state can determine consciousness to apprehend it as a negativity or as a lack. . . .

This means that it is by a pure wrenching away from himself and the world that the worker can conceive his suffering as unbearable and consequently can make it the motive for his revolutionary action. This implies for consciousness the permanent possibility of effecting a rupture with its own past, of wrenching itself away from its past so as to be able to consider it in the light of non-being and so as to be able to confer on it the meaning which it has in terms of the meaning of a project which it has not yet adopted. Under no circumstances can the past in any way by itself produce an act. That is, the past cannot by itself produce the thought of an end which turns back upon itself so as to illuminate the past.[47]

My consciousness, then, has the ability to stand back from the present, conceive a different future, and make the lacks of the present and possibilities of the future my motivation to change. My present situation, Sartre argues, cannot determine the future situation I choose because I imagine the future as what is different from the present. Moreover neither the lacks of the present nor possibilities of the future can by themselves motivate me to act. I must decide in my consciousness to make them my motive to act.

Sartre points out that the determinist says people's temperament, character, or passions, etc., cause their actions. The determinist is right, Sartre admits. A person's temperament, character, passions, or other present circumstances can determine what he does. But these can determine what a person does only if the person decides to make them his motives. That is, my temperament, passions, etc., determine what I do only if I choose in my consciousness to make them my motives to act. As he says: "No factual state, whatever it may be (the political and economic structure of society, a psychological "state," etc.) is capable by itself of motivating any act whatsoever." Our consciousness always has the ability to conceive and choose a future that is different from our present circumstances. Our present environment, passions, character, etc., cannot cause us to act until we decide in our mind to make them our motives. And what we decide within our conscious minds, Sartre holds, is in our full control. Sartre is adamant about the freedom of consciousness:

ANALYZING THE READING

Sartre claims that in our consciousness or mind we can freely decide which factors in our present situation are going to be the causes of our actions. He concludes that this answers the determinist who says that the factors in our present situation cause us to do what we do. Do you think Sartre's claim really answers the determinist? Why or why not? How do you think the determinist would respond to Sartre's claim?

> Man is condemned to be free: condemned, because he did not create himself, yet nonetheless free, because once cast into the world, he is responsible for everything he does. Existentialists do not believe in the power of passion. They will never regard a great passion as a devastating torrent that inevitably compels man to commit certain acts. . . . They think that man is responsible for his own passion. Neither do existentialists believe that man can find refuge in some given sign that will guide him on earth; they think that man interprets the sign as he pleases. . . .
>
> To give you an example that will help you to better understand . . ., I will mention the case of one of my students, . . .his father had broken off with his mother. . . . His older brother had been killed in the German offensive of 1940, and this young man, with primitive but noble feelings, wanted to avenge him. His mother, living alone with him and deeply hurt by the partial betrayal of his father and the death of her oldest son, found her only comfort in him. At the time, the young man had the choice of going to England to join the Free French Forces, which would mean abandoning his mother—or remaining by her side to help her go on with her life. He realized that his mother lived only for him and that his absence—perhaps his death—would plunge her into utter despair. He also realized that, ultimately, any action he might take on her behalf would provide the concrete benefit of helping her to live, while any action he might take to leave and fight would be of uncertain outcome and could disappear

---

[47] Jean-Paul Sartre, *L'Etre et le Neant*, trans. H. E. Barnes (London: Methuen, 1957; original work published 1943), 433–437.

THINKING LIKE A PHILOSOPHER

1. Sartre argues that our consciousness or mind has the ability to freely decide which "passion," desire, character trait, or other factor we will allow to determine or cause our actions. Think about some recent important decisions you have made when you felt different factors attracting you toward different actions or decisions. Would you say that each time you felt free to decide which factor you would act on? That is, did you feel your mind was free to decide which factor or factors you would turn into your motive for acting? Do you think that you were able to choose freely or do you think that in the end you just did what the strongest desire was pulling you toward doing? Describe with as much detail as you can remember what went on in your mind at the time. Describe the moment or moments at which you felt most free.

2. Think about a situation in which you felt intense desire. Did you feel you were free to choose whether or not to give in to your desire?

3. What do you think Sartre would say about a person who said she felt a desire that was so strong and intense that she was powerless to resist it?

pointlessly like water in sand. . . . He was therefore confronted by two totally different modes of action. . . . What could help him make that choice? The Christian doctrine? No. The Christian doctrine tells us we must be charitable, love our neighbor . . . choose the "narrow way," et cetera. But what is the narrow way? Whom should he love like a neighbor, the soldier or the mother?

When I last saw him, he was saying: "All things considered, it is feelings that matter; . . . If I feel that I love my mother enough to sacrifice everything else for her . . . then I should stay by her side. If, on the contrary, I feel that my love for my mother is not strong enough, I should go." But how can we measure the strength of a feeling? What gave any value to the young man's feelings for his mother? Precisely the fact that he chose to stay with her.

In other words, feelings are developed through the actions we choose; therefore I cannot use them as guidelines for action. . . . Catholics will reply: "But there are signs!" Be that as it may, it is I who chooses what those signs mean.[48]

In Sartre's view, then, we are radically free. Nothing external can motivate us to act until our own consciousness chooses to make it our motive. However, once we are aware of our freedom and the responsibility it puts on us, Sartre held, we will feel "anguish." We can escape this anguish by pretending we are not free. For example, we may pretend that our genes or our upbringing or our environment have caused us to make the choices we have made. Or we may pretend that forces beyond our control or unconscious mental states have shaped our decisions. When we so pretend, said Sartre, we act in "bad faith." That is, we deceive ourselves. Self-deception, or bad faith, is the attempt to avoid anguish by pretending we are not free. But pretending we are unfree does not make us unfree. We always remain free and the denial of our freedom through bad faith does not change that fact.

Of course Sartre does not think that we can just do anything that comes into our minds. He does not think that I can fly if I choose, nor that I can engage in time travel by just choosing to do so. Sartre identifies what he calls the "human condition." This consists of the factual conditions that we cannot change and within which we are forced to act. As he puts it:

> There is, nevertheless, a universal human condition. [This includes] all the limitations which beforehand define man's fundamental situation in the universe. His historical situations are variable: man may be born a slave in a pagan society or may be a feudal baron, or a proletarian. But what never vary are the necessities of being in the world, of having to labor and to die there.[49]

---

[48] Jean-Paul Sartre, *Existentialism Is a Humanism*, trans. Carol Macomber (New Haven, CT: Yale University Press, 2007), excerpts from 29–31.

[49] Jean-Paul Sartre, *Existentialism is a Humanism*, trans. Philip Mairet, in Walter Kaufman, ed., *Existentialism from Dostoyevsky to Sartre* (New York: Meridian Books, 1956), 303.

These factual conditions we did not choose and do not control. The freedom we have, then, is a freedom we exercise within this factual world. I freely choose what I do within the limits imposed by the factual world.

But within the limits of our factual world, Sartre insists, our consciousness is free to choose. In consciousness we have the ability to stand back from the many factors in our present situation that pull us in different directions. In our consciousness we can think of a future that is different from our present. And in light of that future and of what our present lacks, our consciousness is free to decide which factors we will act on. In making such choices within our consciousness, we make ourselves what we are.

We choose freely, then, regardless of the character our heredity has given us or the passions and desires we feel. We freely decide which of these factors will become the causes that determine our actions. So, Sartre holds, we are fully responsible for our actions.

We should note that many of Sartre's ideas were developed in partnership with Simone de Beauvoir (1908–1986). De Beauvoir was the greatest female existentialist and from the age of 21, she and Sartre were lovers and collaborators. She agreed that humans are not determined and must accept ultimate responsibility for what they are. But she focused on the implications for women in particular. Women, de Beauvoir argued, are subject to social influences that attempt to rob them of an awareness of their own freedom. They must overcome these constraints through courageous self-assertion. In *The Second Sex,* de Beauvoir argues that in our male-dominated society, men define women wholly in terms of men's own nature. A woman is simply "the other," the nonmale person who relates to the male. Moreover, women accept this role and thereby forgo their freedom to define and make themselves. They choose thereby to become mere things for men. Women must reject the male myths that they allow to define what they are. They must instead collectively create woman as a free and independent being. This will require, she says, overcoming the social and economic institutions through which men get women to accept a kind of enslavement. Social and economic liberation is key if women are to accept their freedom.

The future, then, is not fixed according to the existentialist. There is not just one possible path leading from the past into the future, as the determinist says. Instead, the existentialist is a libertarian. He or she holds that the future branches off into many possible paths. Of course, we will choose only one of those futures. But we could have chosen a different future. We are free because we could have chosen other than the way we did.

The libertarian, then, rejects the determinist's claim that previous conditions and the laws of nature alone cause all human actions. But the libertarian agrees with the determinist on one important point. The libertarian agrees that if determinism were true, then people could not act freely and could not be morally responsible for their actions. We can summarize the views of the libertarian, then, in the following argument:

1. People act freely and they are morally responsible for their actions.

2. If all actions were casually determined by previous conditions and the laws of nature, then people would not act freely and they would not be morally responsible for their actions.

3. So, not all actions are causally determined by previous conditions and the laws of nature.

ANALYZING THE READING

Explain what you think Sartre would say about a person with an addiction, such as an addiction to heroin or to smoking cigarettes. Do addictions prove that Sartre is wrong when he claims that people can freely decide which factors will determine their actions? Explain why. Would Sartre be able to say that addictions were part of the factual conditions that can make up a particular person's "human condition"? Would Sartre be able to say that although an addicted person is not free to resist feeding his addiction, he is free to choose to get treatment for his addiction so that he will later be able to resist feeding his addiction?

QUICK REVIEW

Libertarians hold that (1) humans are free and responsible, (2) determinism rules out such freedom and responsibility, and (3) human acts are not causally determined.

PHILOSOPHY AND LIFE

Does Our Brain Make Our Decisions Before We Consciously Make Them?

Four scientists found that your brain appears to determine what you will do about seven seconds before you "freely" decide to do it. In their study, the four scientists found that brain activity indicating which hand participants would use to press a button near each hand was present in the brain seven seconds before the participants consciously decided which hand to use. They wrote:

> The impression that we are able to freely choose between different possible courses of action is fundamental to our mental life. However, it has been suggested that this subjective experience of freedom is no more than an illusion and that our actions are initiated by unconscious mental processes long before we become aware of our intention to act.... We directly investigated which regions of the brain predetermine conscious intentions and the time at which they start shaping a motor decision. [Our] subjects carried out a freely paced motor-decision task while their brain activity was measured using functional magnetic resonance imaging [fMRI] machines. [fMRI machines produce images of the brain that show what parts of the brain are active when the image is made.] Subjects were asked ... to freely decide between [pressing] one of two buttons [and to indicate] when their motor decision was consciously made.... We found ... brain regions encoded [indicated] with high accuracy whether the subject was about to choose the left or right response prior to the conscious decision.... [One] region was in [the] frontopolar cortex.... The predictive information in the fMRI signals from this brain region

was already present 7 seconds before the subject's [conscious] motor decision....
[T]his prior activity is not an unspecific preparation of a response. Instead, it specifically encodes how the subject is going to decide.... [T]he lead times are too long to be explained by any timing inaccuracies in reporting the onset of awareness.

Some scientists have concluded from experiments like these that if our unconscious brain determines our decisions before we have even consciously made a decision, then our feeling that we consciously and freely make our decisions is an illusion: Our unconscious brain, not our conscious mind, makes our decisions.

QUESTIONS

1. Explain why the experiment is supposed to indicate that free will is "an illusion."

2. Do you see any way of arguing that even if the experiment is correct, free will is not an illusion?

3. Some people have suggested that choosing which hand to use to press a button is not the kind of complex decision in which we humans express our freedom, such as a decision to marry or to choose a certain career. These complex human decisions indicate that we have free choice, so the experiment does not really show that we are not free. Do you agree with this suggestion?

Source: Chun Siong Soon, Marcel Brass, Hans-Jochen Heinze, and John-Dylan Haynes, "Unconscious Determinants of Free Decisions in the Human Brain," *Nature Neuroscience*, April 13, 2008.

Yet do we have the kind of freedom that Sartre attributes to us? Is the criminal wholly to blame for his crimes? Do environment and heredity play a larger role in what we do than Sartre admits? Are you wholly responsible for who and what you are today? Yet if you deny that you are free and responsible, are you really using this denial as an excuse to escape your responsibility? Is the denial of freedom just a form of bad faith?

Not all libertarians take their stand on Sartre's analysis of consciousness. Some libertarians have argued that the scientific theory of quantum physics also implies that previous conditions do not determine our future. As we saw earlier, quantum theory holds that at the subatomic level, a particle does not simultaneously possess both a definite position and a definite velocity. So we cannot predict both its exact position and its exact velocity at a future moment. At the subatomic level, therefore, the future is not determined by the past.

But not everyone accepts the arguments of libertarians. Determinists have claimed that Sartre makes human choices mysterious and unexplainable. Others argue that Sartre's views fly in the face of what we know about human psychology and the extent to which we are shaped by our past and our present environment. Moreover, determinists have argued that the appeals to quantum theory are beside the point. What is at stake is human behavior at the level of ordinary objects, they say, not the behavior of subatomic particles.

Compatibilism

But libertarianism is not the only way of saving freedom and responsibility. Some philosophers espouse compatibilism. And compatibilism accepts determinism yet also accepts freedom and moral responsibility. **Compatibilism** rejects the view that determinism rules out freedom and responsibility. Instead, compatibilists argue, causal determinism is compatible with freedom. How is this possible?

Compatibilism saves freedom by redefining it. According to the compatibilist, to say that a person is free is to say that the person is not impeded by *external* restraints or confinements. A person wearing handcuffs or in prison, for example, is not free. But a person who can do what her own desires or character prompt her to do is free. Still, because a person's desires and character are molded by her heredity and upbringing, they are causally determined by external factors. Ultimately, then, a person's actions are determined by the previous causes that formed her desires and character. But so long as the person is not prevented or forced to act by external forces, we can say the person acts freely.

One of the first philosophers to propose a compatibilist view was the British materialist Thomas Hobbes:

> LIBERTY, or freedom, signifies properly the absence of opposition; by [this], I mean [the absence of] external impediments to motion.... [When] living creatures ... are imprisoned, or restrained with walls or chains ... we ... say they are not at liberty.... [When] man ... finds no[thing to] stop [him from] doing what he has the will, desire, or inclination to do [he is at liberty].... Liberty and necessity are consistent.... [Like] the water that has not only liberty, but a necessity of descending by the channel; so, likewise ... the actions which men voluntarily do ... because they proceed [from] their will, proceed from liberty, and yet because every act of man's will and every desire and inclination proceeds from some cause, and that from another cause, in a continual chain ... [all actions also] proceed from necessity. So that to him that could see the connexion of those causes, the necessity of all men's voluntary actions would appear manifest.[50]

QUICK REVIEW
Hobbes argued that freedom is the absence of physical restraints, so when restraints are absent, our acts are free and responsible even though they are causally determined.

Notice how Hobbes begins his treatment by providing a definition of freedom. But the definition does not define free actions in terms of having no causes. Instead, Hobbes declares that freedom is "the absence of external impediments to motion." Hobbes provides no argument for his definition. But he does give some examples of "external impediments to motion." Impediments to motion include being imprisoned and being "restrained by walls or chains." Hobbes makes it perfectly clear, that although we are "free" when we do what our desires or character prompt us to do, our actions are still determined. They are determined because our desires and character were themselves caused by previous events or conditions. So Hobbes believes that freedom is compatible with determinism.

---

[50] Thomas Hobbes, *Leviathan, in Hobbes Selections*, ed. Fredrick J. E. Woodbridge (New York: Scribner's, 1930), ch. 21, 369–371.

The kind of compatibilist theory that Hobbes offered has since been proposed numerous times by other philosophers. Some provide more argument to support their claims than Hobbes did. In the following passage, for example, the American philosopher Walter Stace (1886–1967) argues for his version of compatibilism. Stace identifies several examples of actions that people would say are "free," and other examples they would say are "unfree." He divides these examples into two separate lists. He then analyzes his lists in order to figure out what distinguishes the acts in one list from those in the other:

Free Acts	Unfree Acts
Gandhi fasting because he wanted to free India.	A man fasting in the desert because there is no food.
Stealing bread because one is hungry.	Stealing because one's employer threatened to beat one.
Signing a confession because one wanted to tell the truth.	Signing because the the police beat one.
Leaving the office because because one wanted lunch.	Leaving because forcibly removed.

[A] definition is correct if it accords with a common usage of the word defined. . . . [So] to find the correct definition of free acts we must discover what characteristic is common to all the acts in the left-hand column, and absent from the acts in the right-hand column. . . . Is being uncaused . . . the characteristic of which we are in search? It cannot be, because although . . . all the acts in the right hand column have causes, . . . so also do the acts in the left-hand column. Mr. Gandhi's fasting was caused by his desire to free India, the man leaving his office by his hunger, and so on. Moreover, there is no reason to doubt that these causes of the free acts were in turn caused by prior conditions, and that these were again the results of causes, . . . back indefinitely into the past. Any physiologist can tell us the causes of hunger. What caused Mr. Gandhi's . . . desire to free India . . . is more difficult to discover. But it must have had causes. Some of them may have lain in peculiarities of his glands or brain, others in his past experiences, others in his heredity, others in his education. . . . The only reasonable view is that all human actions, both those which are freely done and those which are not, are . . . determined by causes . . .

What, then, is the . . . characteristic which is present to all the acts in the left-hand column and absent from all those in the right-hand column? Is it not obvious that, although both sets of actions have causes, the causes of those in the left-hand column are of a different kind from the causes of those in the right-hand column? The free acts are all caused by desires, or motives, or by some sort of internal psychological states of the agent's mind. The unfree acts, on the other hand, are all caused by physical forces or physical conditions, outside the agent. Police arrest means physical force exerted from the outside; the absence of food in the desert is a physical condition of the outside world.

ANALYZING THE READING

1. According to Stace free actions are those whose cause is inside of us, while unfree actions are those whose cause is outside of us. Do you agree with Stace's definition of "free" and "unfree" actions? Can you think of any actions that are unfree yet are caused by something inside of you?

2. Stace says that since free actions are defined as those that are caused by something inside of us, they still have causes exactly like the determinist says all events do. So free actions are compatible with determinism. Does this way of showing that "free actions" are compatible with determinism seem legitimate to you? Why or why not?

3. Suppose the "real problem of freedom" is this: How can people have the freedom to do something other than what they actually did? Determinism answers by saying people never have such freedom. Libertarianism answers by saying people's consciousness gives them that freedom. But compatibilism fails to answer the real problem of freedom. Explain why this criticism of compatibilism is right or why it is wrong.

> We may therefore frame the following rough definitions. Acts freely done are those whose immediate causes are psychological states in the agent. Acts not freely done are those whose immediate causes are states of affairs external to the agent. It . . . is obvious that all those actions of men which we should ordinarily attribute to the exercise of their free will, . . . are in fact . . . caused by their own desires, wishes, thoughts, emotions, impulses, or other psychological states. [51]

Notice that Hobbes and Stace differ in a major respect. Hobbes gives no argument, while Stace does. Stace claims that "common usage" should determine what "free" and "unfree" mean. He then argues that "free" actions are not actions that have no cause. What distinguishes "free" actions, he says, is that their immediate causes are "internal psychological states of the agent's mind." But the immediate causes of "unfree" actions are "external to the agent."

So Stace's conclusions are similar to those of Hobbes. Both agree that actions are unfree when they are the result of an "external" impediment such as being imprisoned or held by chains. Both agree that actions are free when they "proceed" from a person's internal will, desires, or inclinations. And both agree that even "free" actions are determined by previous events or conditions. "Free" actions are determined because our wills, desires, and inclinations are caused by previous events or conditions. So all actions are ultimately caused by previous events and conditions operating according to the laws of nature.

In the passages quoted above Hobbes and Stace do not discuss how moral responsibility fits in with their compatibilist views. But it should be clear that compatibilists can recognize moral responsibility. To say that a person is morally responsible for an action is to say the action originated in that person. Thus, when a person's actions are caused by her inner desires and her character, they originate in her. So she is morally responsible for them.

Another issue that is not discussed in the passages we quoted from Hobbes and Stace is the possibility of internal forces that can render a person's action unfree. How a compatibilist would deal with this issue, however, is not so clear. The passage by Stace says actions are free when they are caused by a person's "internal" psychological states, and unfree only when they are caused by "external" states of affairs. But take the example of a person addicted to smoking, alcohol, or heroin. Most of us would say such a person's action is unfree when his addiction drove him to do it. Yet an addiction is an "internal" state of the person and not an "external" state. So in terms of Stace's definition of free, an action caused by an addiction should be free. We can say the same about actions caused by mental illnesses, compulsions, obsessions, tics, depression, neuroses, unconscious drives and desires, and so on. Actions caused by these internal factors, most would say, are unfree. Yet Stace's view of "free" and "unfree" would classify them as free.

The compatibilist, then, agrees with the libertarian that people are free and morally responsible for their actions. But the compatibilist also agrees with the determinist that our actions are determined by previous conditions and the laws of

THINKING LIKE A PHILOSOPHER

1. Think of a situation in which you felt an intense desire to do something. Did you feel at the time that you were free to choose whether or not to give in to your desire? Think of several choices you have made. When you made those choices do you think you had a feeling of freedom? Or did you feel that you absolutely had to choose what you chose?

2. Stace says that free actions have their causes inside of us, while unfree actions have their causes external to us. Think of several examples from your own life that Stace would say were free actions, and several that Stace would say were unfree actions.

[51] W. T. Stace, "Is Determinism Inconsistent with Free Will?" in W. T. Stace, *Religion and the Modern Mind* (Harper Collins Publishers, 1952), excerpts from 256–258.

QUICK REVIEW
Compatibilists hold that
(1) people act freely and
are morally responsible
for their actions, but
(2) freedom and moral
responsibility require
that people's actions be
causally determined by
their desires and character,
so (3) people act freely and
are morally responsible, but
their actions are causally
determined by their desires
and character.

nature. In fact, compatibilists argue, freedom and moral responsibility *require* determinism. For compatibilists define a free action as an action that results from the person's desires and character. So a person's action is free in the compatibilist sense only if it is *caused by* the person's desires and character as determinism says it is. If human actions had no cause like libertarians claim, then they would not be caused by the person's interior desires and character. Then a person's actions would not be free in the compatibilist's sense of free.

We can summarize the views of the compatibilist in the following argument:

1. People act freely and are morally responsible for their actions.

2. If people act freely and are morally responsible for their actions then all their actions are causally determined by previous conditions and the laws of nature.

3. So, people act freely and are morally responsible for their actions, and all their actions are causally determined by previous conditions and the laws of nature.

Although compatibilism appears to marry freedom with determinism, doesn't it leave the key question unanswered? If we are not free to act against our desires, then isn't there still a clear sense in which we are not free? Maybe we are "free" in the sense that we are not chained down nor physically restrained from acting. But aren't we still unfree in the more important sense that we do not ultimately control what we do? If a person is not free to choose her desires, and these desires determine her actions, then isn't she ultimately unfree? How can we hold a person responsible for the actions that flow from her desires if she does not control her desires?

QUICK REVIEW
Critics say compatibilism
ignores the real issue: Are
we unfree in the sense
that our acts are causally
determined?

Another issue that creates problems for the compatibilist is the possibility of internal forces that make a person's action unfree. Stace says actions are free when they are caused by a person's "internal" psychological states, and unfree when they are caused by "external" states of affairs. But as we saw earlier Stace's view does not seem to adequately account for the way addictions and several other internal forces operate. Addictions clearly drive the addict to engage in actions that will satisfy his or her addiction, and most of us would not want to say that those actions were freely chosen. An addiction is clearly a causal force that compels the addict's actions and those actions are undeniably unfree. Yet an addiction is not an external state of affairs. It is, instead, an internal state of the person. So according to Stace's definitions of free and unfree, those actions should be free actions. Stace's definitions, then, seem to be mistaken.

Actions caused by addictions, mental illnesses, compulsions, neuroses, and so on, create a serious problem for the compatibilist. The problem is that there is no clear way to draw a line between internal causes that make our actions "free," and internal causes that make our actions "unfree." We can't say, for example, that internal causes make our actions free when they make us do what we want. For addicts definitely want to feed their addiction yet their actions are not free. We can't say that internal causes make our actions free when they don't "force" us to act. For unconscious desires don't "force" us to act yet the actions they cause are not free. So there is no clear way for the compatibilist to define free actions in a way that distinguishes them from unfree actions. But the compatibilist has to come up with a correct definition of "free" or his whole theory collapses. For the whole point of compatibilism is to give us a definition of "free" that shows free actions are compatible with the idea that all our actions are determined. Yet it turns out that the compatibilist can't give us any clear definition of "free" at all.

Still, many philosophers today are compatibilists. Several have taken on the challenge of writing a new definition of "free action" that shows free actions are compatible with determinism. Some have said free actions are the result of desires or factors that can respond to reasons. Others have said free actions are those that come from desires or factors we want to have. But looking at these new approaches to compatibilism would require much more space than we have here.

It is not clear, then, whether or not compatibilism can really reconcile freedom with determinism. Yet the other views on freedom and responsibility that we have examined seem to be equally problematic. Because it denies freedom and moral responsibility, determinism does not accord with how we generally experience our own actions. Libertarianism seemingly preserves freedom and responsibility but at the expense of scientific respectability. Compatibilism tries to reconcile freedom and responsibility with determinism. But it seems to leave the important question unresolved in some ultimate sense. Which view of the reality or unreality of freedom makes the most sense?

The Two Worlds View. Some philosophers have suggested that perhaps we are both free and determined, as the compatibilists claim. But these philosophers do not argue that we need to redefine *freedom*. Perhaps, these philsophers say, we are simply stuck with two different ways of looking at human reality. Perhaps we have to see ourselves as both free and determined. This is the view of the great German philosopher Immanuel Kant (1724–1804):

> Is it possible that we take one point of view when we think of ourselves as free causes, and another point of view when we see ourselves as determined effects?
> ... Insofar as he knows himself through his senses, man must see himself as part of the world of sense. But insofar as he assumes he has a conscious active self, he must regard himself as part of the world of understanding. ...
> So a rational being has two points of view from which he can regard himself. ... First, to the extent that he belongs to the world of sense, he sees himself as subject to the laws of nature. Second, to the extent that he belongs to the world of understanding, he sees himself as subject only to moral rules that are based on reason. ... And as a rational being that belongs to the world of understanding, man must think of his will as free ... [52]

Here Kant is suggesting that we have two ways of understanding ourselves and the world we live in. First, we can think of ourselves as part of the world that we observe when we use our senses. This is the world that science tries to explain through scientific laws. When we think of ourselves in this way, we are looking at ourselves as one of the world's objects or things. And we feel that objects in this world have to be causally determined. We are forced to assume that everything that happens in the world we perceive must have a cause. So as part of this world, we have to see our own actions as determined by some cause or other. But Kant also suggests that we can think of ourselves as conscious beings who act in the world. When we think of ourselves in this way, we have to think of ourselves as free. We have to think of ourselves as free because if we thought other forces were determining our acts, we would not believe that we ourselves were really acting. We would think of our actions as the actions of those forces and so not our own actions. If I am to see myself as really acting, I must assume that what I am doing comes out of my own choices and is not caused by forces external to me.

Kant does not see any way of escaping these two different ways of looking at ourselves. We sometimes have to look at ourselves as physical objects, particularly when we try to explain our actions in terms of the laws of a science like psychology. But we

QUICK REVIEW
Kant says when we act, we have to assume we are free, and when we try to explain our acts scientifically, we have to assume we are determined. Both viewpoints are necessary.

---

[52] Immanuel Kant, *Foundations of the Metaphysics of Morals*, sec. 3. Translated by Manuel Velasquez.

sometimes also have to look at ourselves as free conscious beings, particularly when we try to understand ourselves as beings who act in the world. Determinism, then, is not a feature of the world itself. It is a feature of one *way of looking at ourselves* and our world. Libertarianism is also not a feature of the world itself. Rather, it is a feature of a second way of looking at ourselves and our actions. But both ways are inescapable.

Many people today agree with Kant. The philosopher/psychologist Steven Pinker, for example, writes the following:

> Science and morality are separate spheres of reasoning. Only by recognizing them as separate can we have them both. . . . A human being is simultaneously a machine and a sentient free agent, depending on the purposes of the discussion. . . . The mechanistic stance allows us to understand what makes us tick and how we fit into the physical universe. When those discussions wind down for the day, we go back to talking about each other as free and dignified human beings.[53]

Here Pinker is agreeing with Kant. When we are "playing the morality game," he says, we have to think of ourselves as free. When we are "playing the science game," we have to think of ourselves as deterministic machines. Unfortunately, he argues, we need to play both of these "games." So we have to see ourselves as free agents when we are discussing morality, and as deterministic machines when discussing science.

So, are we free or determined? Are we responsible agents or passive victims? Was Darrow right? Or was Sartre right? Or were both right, as Kant and Pinker suggest? As we mentioned at the very beginning of this discussion of freedom, these questions are incredibly important for us. But in the end you have to decide for yourself how these critically important questions should be answered.

PHILOSOPHY AT THE MOVIES

Watch *Gattaca* (1997) in which Vincent Freeman, living in a future when government uses a person's genes to determine his role in society, wants to become an astronaut, but because his DNA limits him to menial jobs, he must pay a disabled athlete with good genes for the blood, tissue, and urine samples that let him pass the gene tests for astronaut training in which he does well until he is discovered. Is the world of Gattaca free or determined? Is it both? Explain.

3.7 Is Time Real?

There is something that the discussions of determinism and freedom have assumed we understand. Both the determinist and the indeterminist assume we know what it is for one event or action to cause another. But causality involves time: the movement from an earlier cause toward its later effect. So they assume that we understand what time is. But do we? Let us see.

Time and Human Life

Time seems to be the most familiar of all realities. To every action, appointment, event, experience, happening, phenomenon, circumstance, situation, sensation,

> **QUICK REVIEW**
> Time is an intimate aspect of who we are and the lives we live, yet difficult to understand.

---

[53] Steven Pinker, *How the Mind Works* (New York: Norton, 1997), 56.

incident, adventure, occasion, quest, affair, occurrence, and climax we assign a time. We continuously talk about what happened "yesterday," what we are doing "today," and what we plan to do "tomorrow." We use the notion of time as easily as our lungs take in air. We have no trouble understanding the meaning of "past," "present," "future," "then," "now," "before,"

Sometimes time seems like an unstoppable river continuously flowing past a bank on which we stand.

"after," "when," "whenever," "later," "earlier," "always," "never," "soon." Yet what is time? When we ask the question, the reality that seemed so familiar slips away. As Saint Augustine wrote, "If no one asks me, I know what time is; if someone asks and I want to explain it, I do not know."[54]

Yet time is an intimate aspect of who we are and how we feel. Time, in fact, makes us who we are. To find out who I am, I need to look into my memory of my past and see what I've done and where I've been, how I've acted and responded to the needs and demands of others and to the events of my life. The same is true of other people. My understanding of who they are is based on how I have experienced them in the past: what I have seen them do and how I have seen them act. For example, have I seen them act with integrity and courage, or with expedience and cowardliness? Many of our feelings, too, depend on time. Take regret, for example. I feel regret about what is in the past that I wish I had not done. I feel regret because I cannot change the past.

Time seems especially mysterious because it seems to flow or move ever onward past us or with us. Sometimes it seems like an unstoppable river continuously flowing past a bank on which we stand. An event we look forward to in the future comes nearer to us carried in the river of time. It approaches, it is finally here, and then it passes us and flows away from us into the past. Sometimes it seems as if we ourselves are in the river, carried along by the river of time whether we want to be or not. It moves us inexorably forward no matter what we do, sweeping us past events lying along its banks. We grow, mature, and age. Our bodies move on from the immaturity of childhood, through the bloom of youth, into the maturity of adulthood, and on into the gradual decay of age. We go places, do things, and have fun. Then these actions, pleasures, and enjoyments become vivid memories. Eventually they grow dim, and finally are forgotten. All the while death, that final end of time for us, approaches ever closer. The flow of time seems to carry us inexorably toward death. We are like swimmers caught in a current, being swept onward toward a waterfall.

Augustine: Only the Present Moment Is Real

What is this time, whose flow seems so familiar, so ordinary, so threatening? To many philosophers, it has seemed that the flow of time we experience is so strange that in some sense it must be unreal. For example, Saint Augustine after puzzling long

---

[54] Augustine, *Confessions*, bk. 11, ch. 14. Translated by Manuel Velasquez.

and hard over the nature of time, came to the conclusion that time in a sense does not exist:

> A day contains 24 hours; during the first of these hours the rest do not yet exist; during the last of these hours the first no longer exist. . . . A single hour contains minutes that vanish as they pass. Whatever minutes have passed no longer exist, and whatever still remain do not yet exist. If we can conceive of an instant of time that cannot be divided into yet shorter moments, that is the only point of time that can exist at present. And that point flies at such lightning speed from being future to being past, that it can have no duration at all. . . . Time passes from that which does not yet exist, through that which does not endure, into that which no longer exists.[55]

So, the present instant is the only part of time that is real according to Augustine. The rest—everything in our lives that is past and everything that is future—does not exist. The past and the future have only a shadowy mental existence in our mind. Memory preserves past instants, and by anticipation we can think about the future. But outside the mind, in reality, there exists only the changing point-like instant of time that makes up the present.

However, Augustine suggested an important distinction between time from the point of view of God and time as we experience it. Think of it like this: God is outside time. From God's point of view, time is like a line of events that lies stretched out before Him. Every event and every moment of our lives lies on the line, earlier ones to the left and later ones to the right. This time line of events does not flow. In fact, nothing on the line ever changes. Everything on it is fixed. This is time from God's point of view. Notice that although nothing on the line of time changes from being future to being past, events still lie "before" or "after" each other. Time from God's point of view has "before" and "after" but no "future," "present," or "past." On the other hand, time from our point of view is very different. We are in time. We experience time as a movement along the time line of events.

THINKING LIKE A PHILOSOPHER

1. Augustine said that if no one asks me, I know what time is, but if someone asks I do not know. Try to do what Augustine says is hard: Explain what time seems to be to you. Describe as carefully as you can how you experience the sensation of the flow of time. What are its qualities? Do you feel that time flows faster during some periods and more slowly during others? When does it seem to you to flow fast and when does it seem to you to flow slowly?

2. Augustine says only the present thinnest instant of time is real. All the rest either no longer exists or does not yet exist. Do you agree that is how you experience time? Suppose that you were convinced that only objective time is real. Would this reduce your anxieties about aging, dying, or losing those you love? Why or why not?

For us, time is experienced as flowing by, one instant at a time. Time that was future becomes present and moves on to become the past. Moreover, we experience the past as frozen while the future is not yet fixed.

We have, then, two very different ways to think about the time in which we live. The first is time as a fixed series of events, or points on a line. The series or line contains all events, each located before, after, or at the same time as other events on the line. And the whole series or line is being viewed as if from someplace outside time. The second way to think about time is time as we experience it from within time. Within time we experience time as a flow from the future, through the present, and into the past. Let us call time as a fixed line of events—time as God views it, according to Augustine—the *objective* view of time. Let us call time as we experience it the *subjective* view of time. Philosophers today generally refer to subjective time as the "A

---

[55] Ibid., bk. 11, chs. 15, 18, 20, 21.

series" and objective time as the "B series." (The philosopher McTaggart, whom we discuss later, invented the terms "A series" and "B series.")

Why should these two views of time matter? Some people have felt that peace of mind can be found only in taking the objective view of time. The subjective view of time is the source of all our pain and sorrow. It is in subjective time that we endure separations from loved ones and from everything else that we treasure. As time flows onward, those we love will all age, their youth will dissipate, middle age will end, and eventually they will die. Our bodies weaken and waste away in subjective time. Childhood is present momentarily, then departs and is gone; adolescence is briefly there then vanishes. Things we buy or make always decay, wear out, fall apart, and are lost to us. Saint Augustine put it like this:

> My life is a distraction and dispersal [in time]. . . . I am wasted and scattered on things which are to come and which pass away. . . . Time is spent in grieving. . . . I am spilled and scattered among times whose order I do not know. My thoughts, the innermost bowels of my soul, are torn apart with the crowding tumults of change, and so it will be until I die.[56]

On the other hand, if we can adopt the view of time as objective, then perhaps we will not feel the pain and sorrow of separation and loss as intensely. We can see that from outside time nothing changes. Everything that happens, everyone we loved, is still there, fixed in objective time, never lost. We can, perhaps, see that from God's point of view, nothing is lost but always remains and endures. Loss and separation exist only from our point of view in subjective time, not in objective time.

We can, perhaps, understand why many philosophers have argued that subjective time is not real and that only objective time exists. For example, the existentialist philosopher Merleau-Ponty argued that the flow of time as we experience it cannot be real. The only real time is objective time, the fixed series of events. We experience time as changing and moving from the past toward the future because of the way our mind relates to real objective time. Our mind makes it seem as if we are moving along the fixed series of events that makes up objective time. However, real time (objective time) does not change. The flow of time we feel is an illusion produced because we can only experience objective time one moment at a time.

McTaggart: Subjective Time Is Not Real

But the philosopher who argued most vigorously that the flow of time as we experience it is unreal is the idealist British philosopher J. M. E. McTaggart (1886–1925). McTaggart pointed out that we can think of time as a fixed series of moments, each one "before" or "after" the others. This is objective time, or what he called the "B series." We can also think of time as a sequence of flowing moments, each of which changes from being "future" to "present" to "past." This is subjective time, or what he referred to as the "A series." McTaggart argued that if time did flow as it seemed to flow in the A series, then the same moment would first be "future," then it would be "present," and then it would be "past." But "past," "present," and "future" are incompatible with one another. The past excludes both future and present. The present excludes both past and future. The future excludes both past and present. Because "past," "present," and "future" are necessarily incompatible with one another, it is impossible for the same thing—the same moment—to be

---

[56] Ibid., bk. 11, ch. 29.

future, present, and past. Yet if time did flow, then every moment would have to be future, and then be present, and then be past. The A series, our subjective idea of time, then, is inherently contradictory and so cannot be real:

> Past, present and future are incompatible determinations. Every event must be one or the other, but no event can be more than one. If I say that any event is past, that implies that it is neither present nor future, and so with the others. And this exclusiveness is essential to change, and therefore to time. For the only change we can get [if time changes as in the A series] is from future to present, and from present to past.
>
> The characteristics [past, present, and future], therefore, are incompatible. But every event has them all [in the A series]. If *M* is past, it has been present and future. If it is future, it will be present and past. If it is present, it has been future and will be past. Thus all the three characteristics belong to each event. How is this consistent with their being incompatible? . . .
>
> I believe that nothing that exists can be temporal, and that therefore time [as the A series] is unreal.[57]

ANALYZING THE READING

McTaggart argues that the features of being past, present, and future are "incompatible" with each other in the sense that the same thing cannot have all three features. Yet if subjective time was real, then each moment would be future, then present, then past. But since the same thing cannot be all three in this way, the same moment cannot be future, then present, then past. So moments cannot flow from being future, to present, to past. This means time cannot flow; so subjective or flowing time must not be real. Do you see any problems with McTaggart's argument?

> **QUICK REVIEW**
> McTaggart argues that only subjective time is really time because the very idea of subjective time with moments that are future, present, and past is contradictory, so time is not real.

Moreover, McTaggart claimed, only the A series is really time. For time requires change, and the events or moments in objective time—the B series—do not change. Time, in the B series, is an unchanging, fixed series of events frozen onto the line that makes up the series. This is not really time. Only the A series could really count as time. And because the A series is impossible, time cannot be real.

Many philosophers have agreed with McTaggart's view that subjective time—the A series—is unreal. But they have rejected McTaggart's claim that the B series—objective time—is not really time at all. The B series, or objective time, they argue, is really a kind of time; in fact, it is the only kind of time that is real. For these philosophers, then, objective time is real, and subjective time is not.

The Australian philosopher J. J. C. Smart agrees with McTaggart's view that our experience of time as passing is an illusion. If we wanted to, he argued, we could get rid of words like *past, future,* and *now,* and talk only about where things happen in objective time. For example, we would not say the Industrial Revolution was in "the past." Instead we would say the Industrial Revolution lies in objective time at a point, *t,* that is before the year 1900. Once we give up talking about past, present, and future, we will see that events don't move from being future to being past. They are all fixed in objective time and don't change at all. So, the flow of time we think we experience is really an illusion. It is not real. Objective time, however, is real.

In some ways, the denial of subjective time is comforting. Perhaps nothing ends, nothing dies, nothing changes. Everything is there, fixed in the frozen vastness of objective time. Yet are the arguments of these philosophers correct? Suppose that Smart is right, and we can stop using words that refer to past, present, and future. Will this get rid of our experience of time as flowing past us and as carrying us on through youth, old age, and death? Just because we do not talk about something, does this mean that it is no longer there?

---

[57]   J. M. E. McTaggart, *The Nature of Existence* (Cambridge: Cambridge University Press, 1927), vol. 2, bk. 5, ch. 33, p. 20.

Or let us look at McTaggart's argument. McTaggart argues that past, present, and future are inconsistent notions. And since reality must remain consistent, reality can't have a past, present, and future. But can't McTaggart's argument be turned on its head? Can't we say that because reality is consistent, and because reality has a past, present, and future, these notions must be consistent notions?

Kant: Time Is a Mental Construct

Is it really possible for us to dismiss the flow of time? Aren't we like an ostrich with its head in the ground when we try to tell ourselves that subjective time is not real? Can we really believe that the subjective time of anticipation and loss, of birth, growth, and decay is not real? Yet some philosophers have gone even further. Some philosophers have argued that all time is unreal.

Immanuel Kant, for example, claimed that time is simply a construct of the human mind. It is a mental construct whether we are talking about subjective or objective time. He argued for this view by asking us to consider our sense experiences. The sensations that flow into us through our senses, he argued, come into us as a parade of colors, shapes, sounds, tastes, feels, and smells. By themselves, these ever-changing sensations would be a mere jumble of meaningless sense impressions. But the mind immediately imposes order and meaning on them.

To get a sense for what Kant means, imagine that you had been born blind and had lived your whole life with absolutely no idea of what seeing even was. Then, suppose an operation was found that cured your blindness so that one day, as you sat on your hospital bed, the bandages were removed from your eyes and you suddenly started seeing flashing lights, flowing colors, and changing shapes. Your first visual experiences would be an incomprehensible and meaningless jumble of ever-changing sensations. Dr. Pawan Sinha, who supervised more than two hundred surgeries that restored sight to children who were born blind, reported: "these first moments for the newly sighted are blurry, incoherent, and saturated by brightness—like walking into daylight with dilated pupils—and swirls of colors that do not make sense as shapes or faces or any kind of object."[58] Thus, during your first few moments of sight you would see lights, swirling colors, and changing shapes that made no sense to you. Such visual sensations are an example of what Kant means when he says that the sensations that flow into us from our senses are in themselves a mere meaningless jumble. Undoubtedly, as you lay there on your hospital bed, your mind would begin trying to put these sensations into some sort of order. It would try to organize them into stable patterns and regularities. Your mind would have to do this to make sense of what you were seeing. Kant claimed that we could not understand or comprehend the many sensations that flood into us unless our minds first impose some kind of order and regularity onto them.

According to Kant, space and time are the two basic systems that the mind uses to organize this flow of changing sensations. What happens is that the mind organizes its sensations by putting each sensation at a specific point in space and in time. Your mind does this by assigning the sensation to some object located at a specific place in time and space. Thus, space and time are mental maps that the mind uses to organize its sensations by locating them in this spatial and temporal "grid." When a sensation enters the mind, the mind assigns it to some object that it locates in the spatial and temporal maps we carry around inside our heads. Or the mind simply assigns it to a specific point in time and space. We might say, for example, "That red is the surface color of that apple right there." Or "That heat I feel is coming from

---

[58] Pawan Sinha, quoted in Patrick House, "What People Cured of Blindness See," *The New Yorker*, August 28, 2014.

this boiling pot." Or "That sound is coming from over here." Or "That crashing noise yesterday came from over there near that rock." Every sensation is thus assigned a location in our mental map of space and time. The most basic mental map we use is our time map because we assign every single sensation to a specific point in time. But some sensations (such as sounds) might not be given a specific location in space. In this passage Kant calls our mental time map a "representation":

> Time is a necessary representation, lying at the foundation of all our perceptions. With regard to phenomena in general, we cannot think away time from them, and represent them to ourselves as out of and unconnected with time. But we can quite easily represent to ourselves time empty of any phenomena. Time is therefore given *a priori*. In it alone is all reality of phenomena possible.[59]

 THINKING LIKE A PHILOSOPHER

According to Kant, time is a kind of mental map that each of us carries around in our minds and that lets us organize our perceptions by assigning each a position in the map of time. Yet some scientific theories, such as Einstein's theory of relativity, say that time can be stretched, slowed, or sped up. And theories about "black holes" indicate that time slows down for anything that approaches them. Do you see any conflict between such scientific theories and the idea that time is a kind of mental map in our own minds?

Here Kant is pointing out that we necessarily have to think of each of our sensations as occurring at a particular time. Sensations require time because we cannot even have a sensation unless it occurs at a specific time. On the other hand, we can easily imagine time continuing in our minds even without any sensations occurring in that time. Time, then, does not depend on the sensations we experience, and we can have the time map in our heads without any sensations in it. Time is something that is already in our mind before we experience any sensations. So, the mind must construct time before it has any sensations. It must do this so it has a means of ordering its sensations as they enter through the senses. The mind does this by locating each sensation at some point on the time map. Kant argues that the mind also groups these sensations together into objects located in its mental map of space. (We might think, for example, "This crunchy hardness, sweetness, and reddish color all belong to this apple right here.") Kant argues, in fact, that the mind puts together everything in the world we see around us by grouping its sensations into objects. But the key point is that time is nothing more than a construct of the mind. Even objective time is not a feature of things as they really exist in themselves, apart from our minds. Time, then, in a very true sense, is not real but is a mere mental construct. (You can find a much fuller explanation of Kant's philosophy in the Historical Showcase at the end of Chapter 6.)

Many scientists, however, have disagreed with Kant. They have claimed that time really exists "out there" in objects. Still, for science, they claim, the time that is really "out there" is objective time, not subjective time. Subjective time, as we experience it, flows from the future into the past. Moreover, the past, as we experience it, cannot change, whereas the future is indeterminate and can still change. So, in time as we experience it, the fixed past is radically different from the indeterminate future. For science, however, there is no difference between past time and future time. In a scientific formula, scientists claim, we can calculate the future exactly as we can the past. In most theories and mathematical formulas of the physical sciences, then, subjective time is not real. Einstein himself said, "You have to accept the idea that subjective time with its emphasis on the 'now' has no objective meaning . . . the

---

[59]   Immanuel Kant, *Critique of Pure Reason, Transcendental Aesthetic,* quoted in *Great Treasury of Western Thought,* ed. Mortimer J. Adler and Charles Van Doren (New York: R. R. Bowker, 1977), 1247.

distinction between past, present and future is only an illusion, however persistent."[60] Only objective time, Einstein felt, can be real.

Bergson: Only Subjective Time Is Real

But don't all the attempts to convince us that the flow of time is unreal seem wrong? Isn't the flow of time something we directly and undeniably experience? For example, we often wish that a future event were here, such as the end of school, or a celebration, or a vacation. At such moments don't we feel ourselves stuck in the present and powerless to make time move faster? And sometimes we are sorry that an event ended that we wish had continued, such as a pleasurable event, or time spent with a friend, or even a person's life. At such moments don't we feel the inexorable movement of time carrying us away from the past into the future? Doesn't the mind gradually fill with memories of the past, and only of the past? Don't we experience the flow of time that carries us past birth, through childhood, into adulthood, and on to the slow decline of age? Surely, all of this must be real.

The French philosopher Henri Bergson (1859–1941) agrees. Bergson argues that the scientist's objective time is just a conceptual abstraction. It is a construct of the mind. The image of time as a line is just that: an image. The concept of objective time is just that: a concept. Neither images nor concepts, he argues, can get at the reality. Only what we directly experience—what we "intuit"—is real. What we directly experience or "intuit" within ourselves is the flow of time. We directly experience ourselves as changing and as flowing through time. Bergson calls this experience the "intuition of duration":

> If I search in the depth of my being . . . I find . . . a continuous flux which is not comparable to any flux I have ever seen. There is a succession of states, each of which announces that which follows and contains that which precedes it. They can, properly speaking, only be said to form multiple states when I have already passed them and turn back to observe their track. In reality no one of them begins or ends, but all extend into each other . . .
>
> The unrolling of our duration resembles in some of its aspects the unity of an advancing movement and in others the multiplicity of expanding states; and, clearly, no metaphor can express one of these two aspects without sacrificing the other. If I use the comparison of the spectrum with its thousand shades, I have before me a thing already made, while duration is continually in the making. If I think of an elastic which is being stretched, or of a spring which is extended or relaxed, I forget the richness of color, characteristic of duration that is lived, and see only the simple movement by which consciousness passes from one shade to another. The inner life is all this at once: variety of qualities, continuity of progress, and unity of direction. It cannot be represented by images.
>
> But it is even less possible to represent it by concepts, that is, by abstract, general or simple ideas. . . . If a man does not himself have the intuition of the constitutive duration of his own being, nothing will ever give it to him, concepts no more than images.
>
> We easily persuade ourselves that by setting concept beside concept we can reconstruct the whole of the object with its parts, thus obtaining, so to speak, its intellectual equivalent. In this way we believe that we can form a faithful representation of

QUICK REVIEW
Bergson argued that objective time is a mental construct, whereas the duration of subjective time that we experience is real.

ANALYZING THE READING

Bergson argues that time as we experience it has duration. In fact, something could not be real time if it did not have duration. The idea of objective time, however, is the idea of time without duration. So objective time could not be real time. It is a mere abstract set of concepts, and no matter how many concepts are added to concepts, they cannot add up to the reality of duration. Is Bergson right that time must have duration so only subjective time is real?

---

60   Quoted in Paul Davies, "Time," in *The Experience of Philosophy,* ed. Daniel Kolak and Raymond Martin (Belmont, CA: Wadsworth, 1993), 88.

MindTap To read more from Bergson's *An Introduction to Metaphysics*, click the link in the MindTap Reader or go to the Questia Readings folder in MindTap.

> duration by setting in line the concepts of unity, multiplicity, continuity, finite or infinite divisibility, etc. There precisely is the illusion.... For ... these concepts, laid side by side, never actually give us more than an artificial reconstruction of the object, and they can only symbolize certain general aspects. It is therefore useless to believe that with them we can seize a reality of which they present to us the shadow alone ...
>
> However much I manipulate the concepts ... I never obtain anything which resembles the simple intuition that I have of duration.[61]

Real time, then, for Bergson, is subjective time. The flowing time that I experience as moving from future, through present, and into the past is real. I directly intuit this time. On the other hand, objective time is an intellectual reconstruction and thus is an illusion.

Yet is Bergson correct? Do we really have this so-called **intuition** of flowing time? Many people have claimed that they do not have such an intuition. Others have claimed that even if they have this intuition, it is nothing more than an illusion. Real time has to be objective time.

Who is right? Is subjective time real, or is only objective time real? Do things end? Do we and our loved ones die and vanish into nothing? Or is every life and event fixed eternally in objective time? Perhaps it depends on your point of view. Perhaps we cannot get by with only one of these two ways of approaching time. Both may be necessary, and maybe we should reject neither as unreal. When we do science and perhaps when we think about God, we may have no choice but to use the idea of objective time. When we think of ourselves and our human lives, we may have no choice but to use the idea of subjective time. Perhaps both are real.

PHILOSOPHY AT THE MOVIES

Watch *Terminator II: Judgment Day* (1991) or *Terminator III: Rise of the Machines* (2003), both of which feature computers in the future fighting a losing war against the few humans who have survived their initial attack. The computers send a "cyborg" robot into the past to kill John Connor, the person destined to become the leader of the humans, while the humans send back a robot to protect John Connor. Several time loops and paradoxes occur in these films. Which concept or concepts of time does the action of these films presuppose? Explain.

Chapter Summary

We opened this chapter by noting that what we ultimately consider real reflects and influences not only how we see ourselves, but also what is most important to us. Our answers to questions about what is real, which fall in the realm of metaphysics, tell us what we think ultimately matters. We discussed a number of metaphysical views, including the materialism-idealism controversy, and the responses of pragmatism and analytic philosophy. We then turned to discuss the contemporary revival of a kind of idealism in the postmodern views that antirealism has proposed. We saw how antirealists have raised the possibility that we may live in different worlds. In particular we discussed how men and women may live in different worlds. We then

---

[61] Henri Bergson, *An Introduction to Metaphysics*, trans. T. E. Hulme (London: Macmillan, 1913), selections from 9, 10, 13, 15, 16, and 20.

looked at the issue of whether and how freedom can fit into our view of reality. We discussed the two main options—determinism and libertarianism—and how compatibilism tries to reconcile them. We ended by discussing how our ideas of time affect our views of reality. The main points made in the chapter are as follows:

3.1 What Is Real?

- Metaphysics is the branch of philosophy that asks what reality and being are, and thereby asks what ultimately matters to us.

3.2 Reality: Material or Nonmaterial?

- Materialism is the position that reality is ultimately matter. Hobbes, an early materialist, argued that only physical objects are real.

- Idealism is the position that reality is immaterial: idea, mind, or spirit, for example. Bishop Berkeley, an absolute idealist, argued that because all that our minds perceive are our own ideas, only our minds and our ideas can be real.

- thinking critically Conditional arguments using the "if-then" connective are valid when their logical form is that of a valid argument; otherwise they are invalid.

3.3 Reality in Pragmatism

- Pragmatism, as developed in the United States by Peirce, James, and Dewey, rejects all views that have no practical consequences for our lives. In the writings of James, pragmatism admits the idea of multiple realities or worlds, and refuses to consider any claims but those focused on "fruits, consequences, facts."

3.4 Reality and Logical Positivism

- Logical positivists, who base their views on how language works, have argued that metaphysics is based on linguistic confusions. Logical positivists such as Alfred J. Ayer and Rudolph Carnap argue that metaphysical statements about reality are meaningless expressions of emotion and not statements of fact.

- thinking critically A categorical syllogism is valid when (1) the middle term refers to a whole category in a premise; (2) a term in the conclusion that refers to a whole category also refers to the whole category in a premise; (3) both premises are not negative; and (4) the conclusion is negative if a premise is negative.

3.5 Antirealism: The Heir of Pragmatism and Idealism

- Postmodern antirealists say no reality exists independent of our language and the systems we use to describe our world. Different languages and different systems of classification create different realities. Some feminists argue that by shaping our languages men have created a reality that favors them and oppresses women.

3.6 Is Freedom Real?

- Determinism has significant implications for our views on freedom, moral responsibility, and punishment. It has played a significant role in our judicial system.

● Determinists like Laplace hold that all human actions are caused by previous events and the laws of nature, and most conclude that freedom and responsibility are not real; libertarians hold that human actions are free so determinism is false, and existentialists like Sartre argue that human consciousness is what makes our freedom possible; compatibilists like Hobbes and Stace try to reconcile determinism and human freedom by redefining the concept of freedom.

● Kant claimed that determinism and freedom arise from two different but inescapable ways of thinking about ourselves and our actions.

3.7   Is Time Real?

● Time may be thought of as objective time, which does not flow from the future into the past, or as subjective time, which we experience as flowing from the future into the past.

● Many philosophers and scientists have agreed that real time is objective time, whereas subjective time is an illusion that does not exist. Henri Bergson has argued that subjective time is real, whereas objective time is a conceptual abstraction and not real.

3.8 Readings

The two readings that follow are based on one of the issues discussed in this chapter, the question of freedom and determinism. Does freedom exist in our universe or are all things determined by forces we do not control?

The first reading, *Oedipus the King*, has been called the greatest play ever written. Written almost 2,500 years ago it has been performed thousands of times and hundreds of books and thousands of articles have been written about it. The play was even the basis for one of Freud's most important concepts, the so-called "Oedipus complex." The play is about a king who does everything he can to avoid a terrible fate that he is warned awaits him. Yet by his own actions and his character he makes his fate inevitable. The play raises issues of freedom and determinism, of fate and of character, of seeking the truth yet being unwilling to see the truth. Above all it raises the question whether we are free and in control of our own destiny.

The second reading is by the late American philosopher Robert Solomon. Solomon devoted his life as a philosopher to investigating the hard questions that life throws at us. In the reading he discusses what the notions of fate and fatalism can offer us today and he refers to Oedipus to illustrate his ideas. Solomon points out that we still speak of significant turning points in our lives as "fated." He argues that fate is not determinism. Instead, fate refers to events whose occurrence makes sense in light of the story of our lives and our own character. "Fated events" are not events whose occurrence was determined because they were caused by previous conditions and the laws of nature, as determinism holds. Instead they are events whose occurrence makes sense in light of our character and the way we have allowed our lives to unfold. Fated events are events that were bound to happen to a person given the character that person has and the way that person's life was unfolding. That idea of fate has much to offer to us because it lets us understand how the character we develop and the way we choose to have the story of our lives unfold, ensure that some things are bound to happen to us.

SOPHOCLES

Oedipus the King

[Scene: Thebes, a Greek city during ancient times. Oedipus is king of Thebes. The former ruler, King Laius, was murdered several years earlier while on a journey. Shortly after the king's death Oedipus arrived in Thebes and found it under attack by the Sphinx, a winged monster that devoured anyone who could not answer her riddle: "What walks on four legs in the morning, two legs at noon, and three in the evening?" But Oedipus cleverly answered, "Man." Enraged because his answer was right, the Sphinx killed herself, and the city was freed. In gratitude the city made Oedipus their king and he married the former king's widow, Jocasta. Jocasta's brother, Creon, befriended Oedipus and helped him rule the city. Several years later misfortune has struck the city in the form of diseases that kill the people and their animals and destroy their harvests. The desperate citizens of Thebes have come to Oedipus for help, since he once before had saved their city. The play opens with a crowd of citizens, the "Chorus," praying in front of the doors to Oedipus' palace. Oedipus emerges from the palace to talk with the citizens.]

OEDIPUS: My children! Why are you kneeling here, crying, and praying so loudly to the gods? The incense from your rituals can be smelled throughout the city. You, old Priest! Tell me why you have come here.

PRIEST: Oedipus, my lord and king. Your own eyes can see our city being destroyed. It's like a ship sinking into a sea of blood. Disease has rotted our harvests, and disease is killing our sheep and cattle. Our women, too are sick. And their babies are born dead. And a plague has swooped down on us. The plague has taken so many into Death's kingdom, the city is almost empty. Great king, we have come to you, old and young alike, to beg your help. You freed our city from the monster Sphinx who once enslaved us. Perhaps the gods or your own wisdom might now inspire you to find a way to save us once again. You are our king, and so we ask you now to keep our city from sinking.

OEDIPUS: My poor children. How well I know the terrible plight that brings you here. I have felt the pain of each of you. I, too, have wept, and pondered how we might find a way out of our misfortune. I sent my wife's brother, Creon, to ask the oracle of the god Apollo whether there is anything I can do to save our city. It is strange he has delayed so long, for he should have returned by now. But when he comes, I will do everything the god's oracle tells me to do.

PRIEST: Your words are well-timed, Lord Oedipus, for there he is.

OEDIPUS: He looks happy! Perhaps he brings good news that will save our city.

[Creon Enters]

OEDIPUS: My royal brother! What did Apollo's oracle say?

CREON: Should I speak here in front of everyone, my Lord?

OEDIPUS: Speak here where everyone can hear. I feel more sorry for them than for myself.

CREON: Very well. The Oracle of Apollo said that to save our city we must rid ourselves of a putrid impurity that wounds us and that we have allowed to grow and fester here.

OEDIPUS: An impurity? What does that mean, and how do we get rid of it?

CREON: The oracle is talking about a murderer who must be banished or, whose blood must be shed to avenge the blood he shed. It is this murderer's guilt that is destroying our city.

OEDIPUS: But who is this murderer and who was his victim?

CREON: Before you came here, my Lord, we had a king named Laius.

OEDIPUS: I never met him, but I know about him.

CREON: He was murdered, and Apollo now demands his murderers be punished.

OEDIPUS: That was so long ago, where could they be now?

CREON: According to Apollo's oracle, they live here within our city.

OEDIPUS: Was Laius murdered here or somewhere else?

CREON: The king was on a journey to visit Apollo's oracle, and never returned.

OEDIPUS: Did his attendants say what happened?

CREON: All were killed but one. And all he would say was that the king was murdered by a group of bandits, not by a killer acting alone. We would have pursued that clue, but that was when our troubles with the monster Sphinx overwhelmed us, and surviving its attacks was more urgent than trying to solve a killing.

OEDIPUS: Well I will start a new search and bring the truth about his murder into the light. This wound that afflicts our city hurts me as well and I have to heal it. Whoever killed King Laius might strike again and try to kill me also. Rise up now, my children, and gather up your things. Know that I will do everything in my power to heal this murderous wound.

PRIEST: We are done here, then, fellow citizens. We have what we came for. Apollo has spoken through his oracle and now he will save us and heal the sickness that is killing our city.

[Oedipus, Creon, and the Priest exit. The chorus of citizens remains.]

CHORUS: Sweet voice from Apollo's oracle, what does your message mean? It makes us fearful and mystifies us. We dread your message, Apollo, god of healing. What past sin are we now paying for? What debt has the past laid on us? Our sufferings have multiplied beyond number. The plague is killing us and we cannot stop it. Our crops are dying and our women now are barren. Our children die and are left unburied and naked on the ground.

[Enter Oedipus]

OEDIPUS: Citizens of Thebes! Citizens of this great city! Hear my proclamation. If anyone knows who murdered king Laius, I order you to reveal it. Even if it was you, speak up and no harm will come to you other than exile. You will be able to leave our land safe and untouched. And if you know who the murderer is but fear to say his name, then I forbid you to take him into your home, or talk with him or pray with him. Send him away from your house because Apollo's own oracle has told us that he is the wound that is destroying our city. I curse this evildoer. May he live in misery for the rest of his wretched life. He murdered a great man, a man who was your king before me. Now that I am king, the successor to his throne, to his bed, to his wife, and father of the children my wife would have given him, I will avenge him as if he was my father. Citizens, find the murderer of your glorious king. Search everywhere for him.

CHORUS: Sire, we did not kill him, and do not know who did. But since the gods gave us this problem, the gods should give us the solution and tell us who the murderer was.

OEDIPUS: Well said, but no one can force the gods to speak.

CHORUS: True, but our prophet Tieresias, though he is blind, can see what the gods can see. Ask him who the murderer was.

OEDIPUS: I have sent for him already. For Creon earlier made the same suggestion and insisted that I question Tieresias. He should be here any moment.

CHORUS: Look, Sire! Someone brings him to you now.

[Enter Tieresias, the blind prophet led by a boy, accompanied by two guards]

OEDIPUS: Tieresias! Holy seer, you can see all things, what is hidden and what lies uncovered, whether in heaven or here on earth. Although your eyes are blind, great Prophet, you have surely sensed how sick the city is. Apollo's oracle revealed that our city will be healed only if we find the murderers of king Laius. We have to either kill them or exile them forever from our city. Help us now and tell us if in your prophetic mind you can see anything that might save our city.

TIERESIAS: Oh God! I had forgotten about this, or I would not have come. Let me return to my home, I beg you, Lord Oedipus. For your sake and mine abandon this search for Laius' murderer.

OEDIPUS: For shame, Tieresias! If you know something and do not tell us, you are betraying us and destroying your own city.

TIERESIAS: Me? I am not the one that will destroy this city. But I know where your foolish quest will take you, and I do not want to help you get there.

OEDIPUS: So you will not tell us what you know? Oh you are an angry spiteful old man.

TIERESIAS: Don't accuse me of being angry, Oedipus, when you are blind to the anger in your own heart, the anger that has made you what you are.

OEDIPUS: And who would not be angry when he sees how you insult our city.

TIERESIAS: I will say no more. Rage all you want. Vent your pent-up anger against me as you wish.

OEDIPUS: Now I am angry, Tieresias, angry enough to tell you what I think. I think that you were one of the men who plotted the king's assassination. Maybe if you weren't blind, you would have killed him with your own hands.

TIERESIAS: What? You are accusing me? Listen, then, to my words, and remember to do what you said you would do to the murderer. The wound that has sickened this city is you.

OEDIPUS: Oh, you are shameless! Do you think you can make these slanderous taunts and get away with it? Who made you say that?

TIERESIAS: You! You goaded me into saying it against my will.

OEDIPUS: I did not hear it clearly, Tieresias. Say it again so I can be sure of what you said.

TIERESIAS: I said: you are the murderer of the man whose murderer you seek.

OEDIPUS: Tieresias, you will regret those words. You will not get away with insulting me twice.

TIERESIAS: Shall I say something that will make you even angrier? Listen, then. In your ignorance, you commit the vilest of sins with those you love the most; shameful acts whose evil you cannot see.

OEDIPUS: Do you think you will get away with saying that? If so your mind is as blind as your eyes. Who put you up to this, Tieresias? Wait! Was this all Creon's idea?

TIERESIAS: You are to blame, Oedipus, not Creon.

OEDIPUS: Of course! I see it now! Creon, once my trusted friend, envies me and is plotting to take my throne. He is next in line for my royal wealth and power. So he schemed with this charlatan beggar-priest who thinks he'll rule by Creon's side when I am gone. Stupid priest: with all your magic you could not solve the deadly riddles of the Sphinx that held the city captive. But when I arrived, using nothing but my wits I solved the puzzle and shut the monster's mouth for good. Tieresias, you are nothing but a greedy fraud, and you will pay for this. And so will Creon.

CHORUS: Lord Oedipus! You and the Prophet have both spoken out in anger. Do not spend this time in quarrels, but work together to find the answer to Apollo's oracle.

TIERESIAS: Lord Oedipus, though you are king, I have the right to speak in my defense. I serve no one but Apollo and certainly not Creon. Hear me: You say that I am blind, but you are the one who cannot see. You do not see the foul sinfulness in which you live, nor do you know whom you have married. You are blind to who your parents were and cannot see how you have sinned against your own family, both those who live and those who are now dead. Your mother and your father's curse will one day drive you like a double-edged sword out of this land, and the eyes that now see the light will then see only endless darkness.

OEDIPUS: I do not have to listen to your insults. Leave my house at once and never return. You are a fool.

TIERESIAS: Perhaps I am a fool, though your parents thought me wise. I will leave now. But before I go, hear this, you and everyone. The one you're looking for, the one you cursed, the man you condemned for Laius' murder, that man is here. Although you think that he's a foreigner, he is a native, born here in Thebes. Soon he will trade his sight for blindness and his purple robes for beggar's rags. Then he'll grope his way out of our city with a blind man's stick. He will be revealed to be father and brother to his own children, son and husband of the mother who gave him birth. She took him and his father into her own bed, and he took his father's life. Ponder these things, my lord Oedipus. If I am wrong, say then that I am a fool.

[Exit Tieresias led by a boy; Oedipus exits into his palace.]

CHORUS: Who is this unnamed person, who has shed blood and steeped himself in horrors that no tongue can talk about? He should flee this place as quickly as he can. But it's useless to try to flee the Fates who surely will pursue and find

him anyway. The Prophet's words make us fearful and they fill us full of doubts. Are his words true? We do not know. Only the god Zeus and his son Apollo can know everything men have done. What we know for sure is that Oedipus saved us when the winged Sphinx ensnared us in her riddles. We will not condemn him until everything is proven beyond a doubt.

[Enter Creon]

CREON: Citizens, I've come because I'm told the king has accused me of a serious crime against the city. I'm here to clear my name. I could never be a traitor to my city and my friends.

CHORUS: He spoke in anger, Creon, and surely didn't mean it. Look, he's coming now.

[Enter Oedipus]

OEDIPUS: How dare you come here after scheming to take my thrown, Creon. Why did you hatch this plot against me? Do you think I'm some kind of fool? Did you think I wouldn't punish you because you're my own wife's brother?

CREON: Listen to me, Oedipus, and hear my defense before you pass judgment on me. What crime do you accuse me of?

OEDIPUS: Weren't you the one who told me to talk to that stupid prophet!

CREON: Yes, I suggested that.

OEDIPUS: How many years has it been since Laius was murdered?

CREON: Many years. It was a long time ago.

OEDIPUS: Then why, during all those years, didn't that prophet ever say a word about me?

CREON: Why? I don't know why.

OEDIPUS: Creon, since you are my brother in law, I've let you share in ruling our great city. Yet now you've betrayed me, and tried to take my throne. I should kill or exile you.

CREON: Listen, to me, Oedipus. Why would I want to be king and live in constant fear when I already have all the power and anything else that I could want. I have all the comforts I desire and can sleep peacefully without the terrible responsibilities of a king. You give me whatever I want. I have wealth, respect, people honor me. And I have it all without having to live in constant fear and worry. Why would I give all that up? What more would I have that I don't already have? I would never plot against you. If you want proof, go to the oracle and ask if I am telling you the truth. If you learn that I have plotted against you, then sentence me to death. I won't fight against it. But don't throw away a true friend. I know that in time you'll find out what happened. And then you'll know I am not a villain.

CHORUS: He speaks wisely, Lord Oedipus. Those who act in anger risk everything. But wait, my lords. Here comes Jocasta. She comes at a good time. She can help you settle this.

[Enter Jocasta, queen and Wife of Oedipus]

JOCASTA: You two should be ashamed fighting with each other when the whole city is sick and dying.

CREON: Sister, your husband here does me great wrong. He wants to kill or exile me for something I did not do.

JOCASTA: Oedipus, my husband. I'm sure that Creon speaks the truth. For God's sake, and for my sake, don't do what you're thinking of doing.

OEDIPUS: You're asking me to accept that I should be the one that's killed or banished. But you are more to me than anything. I'll let him go, then. Yet I will still detest him. I will always detest him.

[Creon Exits]

JOCASTA: My Lord! What was it that made you so angry?

OEDIPUS: Creon was planning to take my throne. He says that I murdered Laius.

JOCASTA: Why would he say that?

OEDIPUS: He didn't say it directly. He got that evil prophet to accuse me.

JOCASTA: The prophet? Oh, Oedipus, then you have nothing to worry about. Listen, no human being can really prophesy. I know what I'm saying. An oracle came to Laius once. The oracle told Laius that he would have a son with me, and that he was fated to be killed by that son. But see, the king was killed by a gang of thieves at a crossroads, or so I was told. And as for the son, we did have a son. But three days after he was born Laius pierced his ankles, fastened them together, and had him taken to be left on a hillside to die. So what the oracle prophesied never happened. The oracle was wrong when it prophesied our son would kill his father. Poor Laius was so frightened by that false prophesy. But the oracle was completely wrong. So pay no attention to what any prophet says.

OEDIPUS: Oh, Jocasta. What I think I heard you say has terrified me. Did you say that king Laius was killed at a crossroads?

JOCASTA: That is what I was told.

OEDIPUS: Where was this crossroads?

JOCASTA: It was where the road from Delphi crosses the road from Daulis.

OEDIPUS: When was this?

JOCASTA: It was right before you arrived here at our city.

OEDIPUS: Jocasta, describe Laius to me.

JOCASTA: Why he was tall, and his hair was almost white. He looked a lot like you. He was traveling in a carriage with five servants and a coachman.

OEDIPUS: My God, I may have cursed my own self! Who told you all this?

JOCASTA: You're frightening me, Oedipus. One servant escaped and got back here safely with that story.

OEDIPUS: Where is he now?

JOCASTA: He returned here after Laius was killed and saw you were king. He begged me privately to send him into the hills to be one of my shepherds. I agreed and sent him away, so he's there.

OEDIPUS: Jocasta, send a message to him immediately. Tell him to come here as quickly as he can.

JOCASTA: I will, my Lord. But why do you need to see him? Oedipus, tell me what worries you?

OEDIPUS: Jocasta, I'm afraid I may already have said too much about punishing Laius' killers. But I'll tell you. My father was the king of Corinth. Polybos was his name. I had a good life growing up in Corinth and had everyone's respect. But one night, at a dinner, one of our guests got drunk. He stood up and accused me of being a bastard. I was furious, but said nothing. The next day I told my parents and they were as angry as I was. I went then to the oracle. And the Oracle told me awful things. That it was my fate to sleep with my mother and murder my own father. When I heard that, I left Corinth and my parents so the awful prophesies could never come true. As I was traveling, I came to that very crossroads where you say Laius was murdered. I was on foot, and as I approached the crossroads a carriage like you describe came toward me. An old man was in the carriage. One of his servants came up to me and tried to force me off the road. I got angry and beat him. Then the coachman tried to push me away and I struck him hard. The old man in the carriage was leaning out and trying to jab my head with a pointed staff. I gave him a blow and he fell out of the carriage, onto the road, and lay still. When the other servants came at me I somehow managed to kill them. One ran away. The others, including the old man, were all dead. Jocasta, could that have been king Laius? Oh, God, don't let that be. If it was, then when I cursed his murderer I cursed myself. And I would be sleeping in the very bed of the man I murdered. These bloody hands would be the ones that killed the king and then made love to you, his own wife. I am filthy, filled with evil! I pray to all the gods that none of this is true.

CHORUS: Lord Oedipus, we too pray to God that it was not the king you met. But do not accuse yourself until you meet this shepherd and learn the truth from him.

JOCASTA: But why must you talk with the shepherd, Oedipus?

OEDIPUS: You said it was a "gang of thieves" that killed king Laius. If several men killed him, then I was not his murderer since I was traveling alone.

JOCASTA: I will send for him now. But whatever he says, it won't prove the prophesy about Laius and his son was right. Because Laius' poor son died on a hillside when he was a baby.

[Exit Jocasta with Oedipus]

CHORUS: Let us always keep the eternal laws of heaven. They were not made by men. And if a man, with contempt for them, breaks those laws, a terrible death should punish him. If crimes against the eternal law go unpunished, if those who break that law live happily, then the gods no longer deserve our worship.

[Enter Jocasta with a servant carrying flowers]

JOCASTA: Good citizens, I am going to the temple to offer flowers and incense to the God. I'm fearful that Oedipus is alarming himself with baseless worries. So I will go and pray to God to let him escape the curse he himself put on the murderer.

[Messenger enters]

MESSENGER: May God bless you, my lady! Can you show me to the palace of the king. I bring a message for him.

JOCASTA: May God bless you too, good sir. I am the wife of the king. What message do you bring us?

MESSENGER: I come from Corinth, and I bring good news. Although it may also pain you a little. King Polybos is dead. And the people of Corinth want Oedipus to be their new king.

JOCASTA: [to the servant] Run quickly and tell the king. Oh, thank you, God! The oracle was wrong! Oedipus fled Corinth so he would not kill this king who is now dead. And Oedipus had nothing to do with his death.

[Oedipus enters]

OEDIPUS: My dear Jocasta, why did you send for me?

JOCASTA: This messenger comes from Corinth. He says that your father, Polybos, has died.

OEDIPUS: What did you say? How did he die?

MESSENGER: He died of old age.

OEDIPUS: Jocasta, you were right! Why on earth do we believe in prophesies? They prophesied that I would kill my father. But now he's dead, and I never raised a hand against him. The prophesies of oracles are worthless!

JOCASTA: I told you, Oedipus. Life is ruled by chance and the future is unknowable. We have to take what life brings us as it comes.

OEDIPUS: Messenger, what about my mother? An oracle told me once that I was fated to sleep with my own mother and kill my father. So I've stayed away from Corinth all these years. And oh how I have missed them.

MESSENGER: Is that why you left Corinth?

OEDIPUS: YES, I feared the oracle.

MESSENGER: Well you had nothing to fear. Polybos was not your father. No more than I am. I gave you to him as a gift with my own hands.

OEDIPUS: What are you saying? Are you telling me that I am your son? Or that you bought me from someone else?

MESSENGER: No, neither of those. You were found on a hillside. In those days I was a shepherd and I saved your life. I can prove it. Your ankles must still bear the scars.

OEDIPUS: Why do you bring up those old pains?

MESSENGER: When you were found your feet were pierced through at your ankles and tied together. I myself pulled out the cords. But the man who gave you to me would know more about all this than I do.

OEDIPUS: You were not the one who found me? Someone else did?

MESSENGE: Yes. It was another shepherd. He was one of king Laius' shepherds.

OEDIPUS: Jocasta, do you know who he's talking about? Is he talking about the shepherd we sent for?

JOCASTA: What does it matter? Don't pay any more attention to anything he says, Oedipus. For God's sake, look no farther into this.

OEDIPUS: How can I do that when I am so close to finding who I am?

JOCASTA: Listen to me, Oedipus, for your own sake, I'm begging you to stop. What I am already suffering is more than anyone should bear.

OEDIPUS: Even if I learn my mother was a slave, Jocasta, I have to know the truth.

JOCASTA: My poor Oedipus. May God help you. I pray that He does not let you learn the truth about who you are.

OEDIPUS: I have to know! [He speaks to a servant.] You, there! Go and bring the shepherd to me quickly.

JOCASTA: Oh Oedipus, my poor, poor child. That's all I can call you now. That's the last name I will ever call you by.

[Exit Jocasta]

OEDIPUS: Whatever happens will happen. I will learn the secret of my birth. Even if it means learning that my mother was just a slave.

[Oedipus' servants bring in an old man]

OEDIPUS: At last. I think this is the shepherd we've been waiting for.

MESSENGER: Yes, that's him.

OEDIPUS: Old man, come here and answer my questions. Were you once a personal servant of king Laios?

MESSENGER: Yes, I was. But for most of my life I've worked as a shepherd.

OEDIPUS: Look at this man here. Do you recognize him?

SHEPHERD: No, no I can't. I don't remember ever seeing him.

MESSENGER: What? Don't you remember giving me a baby to raise as my own?

SHEPHERD: Why are you asking me that?

MESSENGER: Do you see this man here? This man was that baby!

HERDSMAN: Shut up, you fool! God damn you!

OEDIPUS: Don't get angry at him, old man. Just answer my questions. If you don't, a bit of pain will make you talk.

SHEPHERD: Please, my lord. I am an old man. Please don't hurt me.

OEDIPUS: [To his servants] Twist his arms back, that will make him talk.

SHEPHERD: Oh God! What do you want to know.

OEDIPUS: Did you once give him a baby?

SHEPHERD: I did. And now I wish I had died before that day.

OEDIPUS: If you don't tell me the truth, you will die now. Where did the baby come from? Was it your own child or did the baby come from someone else?

SHEPHERD: It was not mine. I beg you, my Lord. Please don't ask me any more questions.

OEDIPUS: Tell me where the baby came from or I'll kill you with my own hands!

SHEPHERD: It came from the king's house.

OEDIPUS: Was it a slave's? Was it the baby of an unmarried woman?

SHEPHERD: Oh, God, I'm so close to saying the awful truth.

OEDIPUS: Awful or not, I have to hear it, old man!

SHEPHERD: It was his. But your wife should be the one to tell you what happened.

OEDIPUS: My wife gave you the baby?

SHEPHERD: Yes, my lord.

OEDIPUS: How could the baby's mother have been so heartless?

SHEPHERD: Because she feared the oracle. The oracle said the baby would kill his parents.

OEDIPUS: Why did you give the baby away to this man here?

SHEPHERD: I felt sorry for the baby. I thought he would take the baby somewhere far from here. He saved the baby, but for the worst fate of all. If you are the man he says you are, then you were born to live in misery.

OEDIPUS: Everything! Everything! Everything has come true! Light of the sun let me never see you again. Look now at what I am. I should never have been born. I am cursed in how I've lived and cursed in how I've killed.

[Oedipus runs into the palace, and the others follow him, except the Chorus]

CHORUS: We live and we die and our lives are pointless. Whose happiness ever lasts? Whose happiness is nothing more than an illusion? Oedipus excelled before all others and won power, honors, happiness. He killed the Sphinx, saved the city and won the throne. But now who envies him?

[A servant enters]

SERVANT: Oh, Citizens, our great queen Jocasta is dead!

CHORUS: Poor miserable woman! How did she die?

SERVANT: She killed herself. She came into the house in a rage, ran straight to her bedroom, tearing out her hair and screaming king Laius' name. She slammed the door shut. But we could hear her calling out to Laius and screaming about the child who killed him and with whom she bred more evil children. She cried about the husband who was father to her husband and the child with whom she had more children. Then she was quiet. But moments later Oedipus burst in shouting for a sword. He ran into the bedroom and saw his wife hanging from a rafter, the rope twisted tight around her neck. He cried and wailed while he cut her loose and then laid her on the floor. As she lay there he. . . .What he did was terrible to watch. He tore the brooches with their long needles from her clothes. He lifted them up high and plunged them down into his own eyeballs. He cried out: "These eyes will never see the monstrous crimes I committed. They will never look on the faces of my forbidden children. They will never know the little ones I love so much." He kept jabbing the needles into his eyes, again and again. Blood spurted out from his eyes and streamed down his face.

CHORUS: How is he now? Has his grief been soothed at all?

SERVANT: He has been shouting for someone to take him before the citizens of Thebes so they can see the man who was the murderer of his father and his own mother's. . . . But I cannot say that awful word.

[Oedipus enters, blood streaming from his eyes]

CHORUS: Oh this is, indeed an ugly sight! Our poor wretched king.

OEDIPUS: Oh the pain! The agonizing pain! Where am I going? Everything is dark. A horrible darkness is all around me. I will go mad. I feel this stabbing pain and desperate guilt for all my crimes.

CHORUS: Oedipus, what demon has made you blind your own eyes?

OEDIPUS: The gods have made my punishment complete. But it was my own hands that pierced my eyes. Why should I have eyes when what I see disgusts me? I curse that man who saved my life when I should have been left to die on the hillside.

CHORUS: Death would be better now, Oedipus, than living on with blinded eyes.

OEDIPUS: Give me no more advice. What I did was best. My suffering is all my own.

CHORUS: Here comes Creon.

[Creon enters]

CREON: Oedipus, I haven't come to mock you nor blame you for what you've done. Come inside. You should not be a public spectacle like this.

OEDIPUS: Oh noble Creon. I have badly wronged you and you owe me nothing. But I ask that you quickly take me far away from here. Let me go up into the hillsides so I can live where I should have died long ago. I do not know why I was saved for this wretched fate. And I ask you to give an honorable burial to your sister who lies inside. As for my children, Creon, my two sons are grown men and can take care of themselves. But look after my poor daughters. Would you let me touch them and cry with them?

[Enter Antigone and Ismene, Oedipus' daughters, crying]

OEDIPUS: Are those my daughters I hear crying? My little darlings. Come, let me take you in my arms, the arms of your brother and your father. I am so sorry for you. How bitter have I made your lives.

CREON: Come, then Oedipus. I will have you taken outside the city. But your children will stay here.

OEDIPUS: Do not take them away from me!

CREON: You are not the one who gives the orders now, Oedipus.

[Creon and Oedipus exit. The daughters help lead him.]

CHORUS: Look on at Oedipus now. He solved the great riddle of the sphinx and became a mighty king. But now see him thrown down by despair. Count no man happy until he reaches the end of his life without disaster.

Source: Sophocles, *Oedipus the King* 429 BC, translated and abridged by Manuel Velasquez. Copyright © 2015 by Manuel Velasquez.

ROBERT C. SOLOMON

Fate and Fatalism

Fatalism is the idea that what happens (or has happened) in some sense has to (or had to) happen. Such beliefs seem to involve a peculiar sense of necessity. It is not logical necessity. . . . It is not scientific or causal necessity (it precedes modern science by millennia) and should not be confused or conflated with what is often called "determinism." . . . What is necessary seems to be only the outcome, regardless of causes, regardless of agency. Thus, Oedipus was fated to kill his father and marry his mother no matter what he or anyone else might do to prevent it and quite apart from the circuitous causal route that it took for him to get there. And in Sophocles' version, at least, there is little mention of the gods.

Particularly subject to fate are those definitive moments in life: birth, marriage, children, going broke, finding oneself at war, or being caught up in a natural calamity (legally, an "act of God"), and, of course, death. Especially fascinating are those seemingly insignificant encounters, coincidences, slips, and misunderstandings that, in retrospect, have momentous consequences. It is fate and fatalism, ultimately, that explain why heroes like Hector and Achilles have to die, why the Hebrew temple was destroyed, why hurricane Andrew hit just as the newlyweds were putting the finishing touches on the new house, why some people are rich and so many are poor, why a young girl should die "before her time." It is fate and fatalism that answer such plaintive questions as "Why me?" and "Why should this burden fall on us, of all people, especially now?" But what kind of "answer," what kind of explanation, would this be?. . . .

To put the matter bluntly, the necessity that is invoked by fate and fatalism is not scientific necessity but rather what we might call "narrative" necessity. The analog is the "logic" of a novel or movie plot. . . . The Nietzschean admonition "live your life like a work of art" should be taken with a grain of salt and demands a certain caution, but it does not follow that we do not conceive of our lives as an ongoing story with a developing plot, albeit with unexpected twists and turns, all the time. Indeed, it takes a considerable effort, whether by way of an existentialist "gratuitous act" or by way of a desperate authorial disclaimer ("the life you are witnessing has no plot or purpose"), to deny this. (But then, of course, such acts or disclaimers become yet another chapter heading in the ongoing drama of one's life.) . . .

To appeal to fate and fatalism is nothing other than to insist that in terms of the overall plot (whatever that may turn out to be) an act or event has considerable significance. It is therefore not to say that "it could not have turned out otherwise." One might say (following Aristotle and later Hegel) that fate and fatalism have teleological significance, that is, that it can be argued to be "necessary" (perhaps looking back in retrospect) insofar as it is part of the path to some ultimate purpose. It forms an intrinsic part of the narrative as it unfolds. If the story had unfolded in some other way, then that development instead of this one would have been deemed "necessary."

There is at least one interpretation of fate and fatalism that remains well within the bounds of common sense and scientific thinking and leaves room for freedom (if not free will) as well. It is also compatible with determinism (and therefore supports a modest "compatibilism" in the problem of free will) and removes the mystery and superstition that usually surround discussions of fate and fatalism. This interpretation is often associated with Heraclitus, who said, simply, that fate is character.

Aristotle famously based his theory of tragedy on the notion of a "tragic flaw" or hamartia in the tragic hero's character. Thus, Oedipus' tragedy is often "explained" by appeal to his tyrannical arrogance, his obstinacy, and his refusal to listen to either Teiresias or his wife/mother. Whether or not this is conducive to an adequate understanding of tragedy (or faithful to Aristotle), it shows quite dramatically the insistence that tragic fate can be "explained" in a way that both satisfies determinism and leaves ample room for all sorts of choices by the protagonist while preserving our sense of fatalism.

If fate is character, then it is easy to see how what we do and what happens to us is to a large extent determined, but we can also be held responsible and consider ourselves the authors of our actions. David Hume and John Stuart Mill, in modern times, were willing to accept determinism (even if conjoined with skeptical doubts) and nevertheless managed to fit agency and responsibility into its domain. They suggested that an act is free (and an agent responsible) if it "flows from the person's character." This saved the notions of agency and responsibility, it was very much in line with our ordinary intuitions about people's behavior, and it did not try to challenge the scientific paradigm. . . . Heraclitus' fragment makes it quite clear that fate is not in the hands of the gods or in any hands other than our own, although it is important not to read too much of the modern notions of "free will" and "autonomy" into this claim. The idea that someone will very likely "turn out" in such-and-such a way is a perfectly common-sense notion. . . .

Consider the idea that someone will very likely "turn out" in such-and-such a way: a naughty boy becomes a punk kid, then becomes a juvenile delinquent, then turns into a petty thief, and then later becomes a "hardened" criminal. The neighbors and some of his family members wag their fingers as they say (with each new chapter) "I told you so." The childhood whiz kid on the other hand becomes an honors student and scholarship winner, and then she becomes a famous scientist. No surprises there, even though she surmounted many obstacles and prejudices on her way to success. Her friends and neighbors say, "I always knew." It would be daft to deny that character provides some sense of narrative necessity (as well as a partial causal account), but it would be equally daft to insist that such "necessity" carries with it the strict determination of the outcome. Could things have turned out otherwise? Of course. But when people speak of fate they are not talking in terms of some peculiar sense of causal necessity. . . . The juvenile delinquent can be rightly held responsible for his increasingly criminal acts, and the successful scientist may be properly praised for her realization of the talents she first displayed as a child. To be sure, no narrative of the unfolding of character can leave out the details of environmental factors, seemingly chance occurrences and intrusions, and (especially) the influence of other people. But neither environmental factors nor the influence of other people undermines this commonsensical notion of fate as the apparently necessary and even "inevitable" unfolding of character. Environment, chance, and other people may act as co-determining factors, but Heraclitus' focus on the "internal necessity" of personal character (virtues, talents, traits, flaws, vices, and liabilities) is what we mean by "fate.

With regard to explanations of outcomes on the basis of character, do determinism and fatalism differ? . . . The difference, in general, is of the kind mentioned above. Fatalism is the narrative thesis that some action or event was bound to happen because it "fits" so well with the agent's character.

Psychological determinism, by contrast, is the science-minded thesis that whatever action or event takes place can be explained in terms of specific psychological causes. Fatalism, traditionally conceived, insists only on the necessity of the outcome, no matter what the causes may be. Thus, the standard example of fatalism is poor Oedipus, who was cursed and doomed to kill his father and marry his mother no matter what he (or his parents) might do to prevent it. There are many philosophical morals and conundrums to squeeze out of this old tale, but the only point to be repeated here is that the what of fate need make no specific commitments to any how. This does not mean that determinism is false, of course, since one might and indeed must insist that there is some chain of events and causes leading up to Oedipus' tragic deeds. But although this may well interest the scientist it is not the main concern of the fatalist.

The naughty boy who ends up doing hard prison time no doubt has a nasty biography filled with intermediate causes, but for those who "told you so" the important point is that this is how he would end up, quite apart from the causal details. So, too, the intervening successes and influences of the scientist-scholar are, so far as the fatalist is concerned, only secondary. The outcome is necessarily quite independent of the causal necessity of the outcome. Again, the difference between them is not so much the presence or absence of a causal explanation. The difference between them is the attribution of special significance to the outcome in terms of the overall story. . . .

"Fate is character" is a good way into a sensible notion of fate that even the most obstinate scientist can accept. It shows quite clearly in what ways fatalism and determinism are compatible and even mutually supporting. It also weakens the modal notion of necessity considerably, since it now becomes obvious that what is necessary from the standpoint of fate and fatalism is neither logically nor causally necessary and may well have turned out otherwise. The necessity is so only retrospectively (or by way of anticipation), given the plot of the narrative. If the naughty boy had turned out to be a successful entrepreneur or the young scientist a frustrated housewife one might still speak of fate but tell a very different story.

"Fate is character" also shows the inescapable human-interest aspect of fatalism, for what would "character" refer to if not those personal charms and annoyances, successes and failures, those virtues and vices that render our relationships so complicated and explain our enduring interest in people, whether through gossip or professional psychology? Science, including the still struggling science of character formation, may explain character, and character may in turn account for what we do, but our sense of fate and fatalism has a different kind of story to tell. It is the story of who we are and of what happens to us and how what happens fits into the larger scheme of things. It is the dramatic story, not the scientific one, even if many or most of the details are the same. Thus, fate and fatalism focus "locally" on what is most significant about us, our births, our sweetest romances, our best successes, our worst failures, our calamities, our deaths.

But, to conclude this, determinism and fatalism make two quite different claims and tell two very different stories. The first insists that whatever happens can (in principle) be explained in terms of prior causes (events, states of affairs, and inherent structures, plus the laws of nature) and so tells a causal story of the form "here is how this came about." The second insists that whatever happens must happen, but there need not be an effort to specify the causal etiology behind the modal "must." To be sure, it would also be a mistake to interpret fatalism as excluding any such effort, and Oedipus' behavior and its terrible outcome can be explained, step by step, as one event causing another. But that would surely miss the point of the fate/fatalism narrative, which is that the outcome has a dramatic significance whatever the path to that outcome. To confuse causal and narrative necessity or to add some mysterious agency and insist that fatalism depends on the whims of the gods or frivolous fates or any other mysterious force is to weaken or force us to dismiss what was and still can be a quite sensible and appealing philosophical thesis. Thus, it is important that we neither reduce fatalism to determinism nor oppose the two in such a way that determinism becomes the respectable scientific thesis while fatalism is relegated to ancient mythology and poetry.

Source: Robert C. Solomon, "On Fate and Fatalism," *Philosophy East and West*, Vol. 53, No. 4 (2003), 435–454. Excerpts from pp. 435, 436, 438, 445, 446, 447, 448, 449. Reprinted by permission of the editors of Philosophy East and West.

3.9 HISTORICAL SHOWCASE

Hobbes and Berkeley

We have suggested throughout this chapter that people's metaphysical views influence their views of human nature. Two seventeenth-century philosophers—Thomas Hobbes and George Berkeley—illustrate the profound impact a metaphysical view can have on one's view of human nature.

Hobbes, as was briefly mentioned earlier, proposed the metaphysical view that everything in the universe is material. The view led him to propose a materialistic view of human nature. Hobbes believed that humans are, in effect, complicated machines. Berkeley, on the other hand, advanced the metaphysical claim that everything in the universe is spiritual or nonmaterial. This claim then led him to hold a thoroughly spiritualistic view of human nature: To be human is to be a kind spirit.

Examining the views of Hobbes and Berkeley in some detail will help us see how metaphysics is related to the positions we take on other philosophical issues, in particular on the issue of human nature. It will become clear, also, how metaphysics can influence our views of God and society.

HOBBES

Thomas Hobbes was a thoroughgoing materialist: He held that only material objects exist. In this respect he differed considerably from his contemporary, René Descartes (whom we showcase in the next chapter). Descartes carried over from medieval philosophers like Aquinas the view that reality consists of both material and immaterial (or "spiritual") entities. Hobbes rejected this dualistic view. The recent astronomical discoveries of Copernicus, Kepler, and Galileo had all been based on the observation of moving bodies. Influenced by their approach to reality, Hobbes reasoned that perhaps all reality could be explained in terms of the motions of bodies in space.

Born prematurely in 1588 when his mother, overcome with fear at the approach of the invading Spanish navy, went into early labor, Hobbes throughout his youth had a melancholy personality that earned him the nickname of the Crow. The son of a clergyman, Hobbes was sent at the age of 14 to study at Oxford, where he tells us he learned to hate philosophy. However, he apparently learned

Thomas Hobbes: "The Universe is corporeal, that is to say body, . . . and that which is not body is no part of the Universe. And because the Universe is all, that which is no part of it is nothing, and, consequently, nowhere."

enough so that when he graduated in 1608 he was hired by the wealthy and aristocratic Cavendish family as a tutor for their sons. He later remarked that the job left him more than enough time to read and study while his young charges were "making visits" in town. Traveling with the Cavendish family gave Hobbes the opportunity to see much of Europe and to become acquainted with the great thinkers of the period, especially the Italian astronomer Galileo, who at this time was busily tracing the motions of the heavenly bodies with the aid of geometry. At about the age of 40, probably under Galileo's influence, Hobbes came to the conclusion that everything in the universe could be explained in terms of the motions of material bodies and that geometry could provide the basic laws of their motions. He attempted to work out the details of this philosophy in a remarkable series of writings that included his masterpiece *Leviathan* and a trilogy bearing the titles *De Corpore (On Material Bodies)*, *De Homine (On Man)*, and *De Cive (On the Citizen)*. Hobbes' final years were relatively happy. He died in 1679, famous for his materialistic philosophy and the political theories that grew out of it.

Hobbes was unequivocal in claiming that matter is all there is in the universe:

> The Universe, that is the whole mass of things that are, is corporeal, that is to say body; and has the dimensions of magnitude, namely, length, breadth, and depth. Also every part of body is likewise body, and has the like dimensions. And, consequently, every part of the Universe is body, and that which is not body is no part of the Universe. And because the Universe is all, that which is no part of it is nothing, and, consequently, nowhere.[1]

(Hobbes' archaic spelling has been modernized in this and following quotations.)

In Hobbes' view, the characteristics and activities of all objects, including human beings, can be explained in purely mechanical terms:

> For seeing life is but a motion of limbs, the beginning whereof is in some principal part within; why may we not say, that all *automata* (engines that move themselves by springs and wheels as does a watch) have an artificial life? For what is the *heart*, but a *spring*; and the *nerves*, but so many *strings*; and the *joints*, but so many *wheels*, giving motion to the whole body, such as was intended by the artificer?[2]

Hobbes attempted to apply this **mechanism** to explain the mental activities of human beings. Many philosophers, Descartes in particular, believed that the mental activities of perceiving, thinking, and willing were evidence that human minds are spiritual or nonmaterial. Mental activities (thinking) and mental contents (thoughts) seem to have no physical characteristics (that is, they have no color, size, or position and seem to be nonbodily). Hobbes was particularly concerned with showing that even mental activities could be entirely explained in terms of the motions of material bodies. He begins this task by first arguing that all of our thoughts originate in our sensations (or, as he writes, in "sense"). And sensations, he claims, are nothing more than motions in us that are caused by external objects. These motions in us travel through our nerves to our brains:

---

[1]   Thomas Hobbes, *Hobbes Leviathan* (Oxford: Clarendon, 1909; original work published 1651), 524.

[2]   Ibid., 8.

Concerning the thoughts of man, I will consider them first singly, and afterwards in train or dependence upon one another. . . .

The origin of them all, is that which we call SENSE [sensation], for there is no conception in a man's mind, which has not at first, totally, or by parts, been begotten upon the organs of sense. . . .

The cause of sense is the external body, or object, which presses the organ proper to each sense . . ., which pressure, by the mediation of the nerves, and other strings and membranes of the body, continues inwards to the brain and heart, causes there a resistance, or counter-pressure, or endeavor [movement] of the heart . . ., which endeavor [movement], because [it is] *outward,* seems [to us] to be some matter without. And this *seeming* or *fancy,* is that which men call *sense.* [Sense] consists, as to the eye in *light,* or *color* . . .; to the ear, in a *sound;* to the nostril, in an *odor;* to the tongue . . ., in a *savor;* and to the rest of the body, in *heat, cold, hardness, softness,* and such other qualities as we discern by *feeling.*

All [these] qualities . . . are, in the object that causes them, but so many . . . motions of the matter, by which it presses our organs. Neither in us, that are pressed, are they anything else, but . . . motions; for motion produces nothing but motion. . . . [Just] as pressing, rubbing, or striking the eye makes us fancy a light, and pressing the ear produces a din, so do the bodies we see, or hear, produce the same [sensations] by their . . . action.[3]

Once the motion created in our senses has traveled to the brain, the brain retains this motion, much like water continues moving after the wind stops. This "decaying" motion in our brain is the residual image that we retain in our memory. Thus, our memory of an object is nothing more than the residual motion the object leaves impressed on our brain:

When a body is once in motion, it moves, unless something else hinders it, eternally; and whatever hinders it, cannot in an instant, but [only] in time, and by degrees, quite extinguish it. And as we see in the water, though the wind cease, the waves [continue] . . . rolling for a long time after, so also it happens in that motion which is made in the internal parts of man. . . .

This decaying sense, when we would express the thing itself, . . . we call *imagination.* . . . But when we would express the decay, and signify that the

sense is fading, old, and past, it is called *memory.* So that imagination and memory are but one thing.[4]

But what does all of this have to do with thinking? Hobbes held that when we are thinking, we are merely linking together the decaying images (or motions) that we have retained in our memory. Our thinking activities are thus nothing more than a sequence of motions linked together, usually as they are linked together when we first experienced them as sensations. Sometimes our thinking is "un-guided," as when we daydream, and sometimes it is "regulated," as when we are trying to solve some problems:

By consequence or TRAIN of thoughts, I understand that succession of one thought to another, which is called, to distinguish it from discourse in words, *mental discourse.*

When a man thinks on anything whatsoever, his next thought after is not altogether . . . casual. . . . The reason . . . is this. All fancies [images] are motions within us, relics of those made in the sense. And those motions that immediately succeeded one another in the sense, continue also together after sense. . . .

This train of thoughts, or mental discourse, is of two sorts. The first is *unguided, without design,* and inconstant, wherein there is not passionate thought, to govern and direct those that follow to itself, [such] as the end and scope of some desire, or other passion, in which case the thoughts are said to wander and seem impertinent one to another, as in a dream. . . .

The second is more constant, as being *regulated* by some desire and design. . . . From desire arises the thought of some means we have seen produce the like of that which we aim at; and from the thought of that, the thought of means to that mean; and so continually, till we come to some beginning within our own power. . . . The train of regulated thoughts is of two kinds: one, when an effect imagined we seek the causes, or means that produce it. . . . The other is, when imagining anything whatsoever, we seek all the possible effects that can by it be produced.[5]

But "trains of thoughts" are not the only things produced by the motions that begin in our senses and end in the imaginations of our brains. The motions of our imaginations also produce motions in our organs of appetite (which Hobbes thought

---

[3]   Ibid., 12.

[4]   Ibid., 13–14.
[5]   Ibid., 18–20.

were located mainly in the heart); these are called *desires*. The motions called desires, in turn, are what lead us to engage in "voluntary actions":

> There be in animals, two sorts of *motions* peculiar to them. One [is] called *vital* . . . such as the *course of the blood,* the *pulse,* the *breathing,* the *concoction, nutrition, excretion, etc.* . . . The other is . . . *voluntary motion,* as to *go,* to *speak,* to *move* any of our limbs, in such manner as is first fancied in our minds. . . . And because *going, speaking,* and the like voluntary motions, depend always upon a precedent thought . . . it is evident that the imagination is the first internal beginning of all voluntary motion. . . . These small beginnings of motion, within the body of man, before they appear in walking, speaking, striking, and other visible actions, are commonly called ENDEAVOR.
> This endeavor, when it is toward something which causes it, is called APPETITE, or DESIRE. . . . And when the endeavor is from something, it is generally called AVERSION. . . . That which men desire, they are also said to LOVE, and to HATE those things for which they have aversion. . . . But whatsoever is the object of any man's appetite or desire, that . . . he . . . calls *good,* and the object of his hate and aversion, *evil.* . . .
> As, in sense, that which is really within us is, as I have said before, only motion, caused by the action of external objects. . . . So, when the action of the same object is continued from the eyes, ears, and other organs to the heart, the real effect there is nothing but motion or endeavor, which consists in appetite or aversion, to or from the object moving [us].
> When in the mind of man, appetites, and aversions, hopes, and fears, concerning one and the same thing, arise alternately; and divers good and evil consequences of the doing, or omitting the thing propounded come successively into our thoughts; so that sometimes we have an appetite to it; sometimes an aversion from it; sometimes hope to be able to do it; sometimes despair, or fear to attempt it; the whole sum of desires, aversions, hopes and fears continued till the thing be either done, or thought impossible, is that we call DELIBERATION. . . .
> In *deliberation,* the last appetite, or aversion, immediately adhering to the action, or to the omission thereof, is what we call the WILL. . . . *Will,* therefore, is *the last appetite in deliberating.*[6]

Thus, Hobbes concluded, not only can a materialist philosophy fully account for all our obviously physical characteristics, but it can also account for all of those inner mental activities that other philosophers take as evidence of a spiritual or nonmaterial mind: sensing, remembering, thinking, desiring, loving, hating, and willing. These mental activities do not require us to say that some kind of nonmaterial reality exists in addition to the material objects in the world. There is no such thing as a nonmaterial reality: Everything consists of matter and its motions.

Hobbes felt that his materialistic philosophy also provided the foundations for a social philosophy. By examining the basic material characteristics of human individuals, he felt he could explain why our societies are structured as they are. Hobbes began by maintaining that the central desires that affect the relations between individuals inevitably lead them to quarrel with one another:

> So that in the nature of man, we find three principal causes of quarrel. First, competition; secondly, diffidence; thirdly, glory.
> The first makes men invade for gain; the second, for safety; and the third, for reputation. The first use violence, to make themselves masters of other men's persons, wives, children, and cattle; the second, to defend them; the third, for trifles, as a word, a smile, a different opinion, and any other sign of undervalue, either direct in their persons, or by reflection in their kindred, their friends, their nation, their profession, or their name.[7]

Because of these antagonistic drives, individuals would inevitably strive "to destroy or subdue one another" if it were not for the restraints that the "common power" of government is able to impose on them. If people were in a "state of nature"—that is, if they were in the situation they were in before any government restrained them from harming one another—they would be constantly at war, and life would be miserable:

> Hereby it is manifest, that during the time men live without a common power to keep them all in awe, they are in that condition which is called war, and such a war as is of every man against every man. . . . In such condition, there is no place for industry, because the fruit thereof is uncertain: and consequently no culture of the earth; no navigation, nor use of the commodities that may be imported by sea; no commodious building; no instruments of

6 Ibid., 39, 41, 46, 47.

7 Ibid., 234–296.

moving, and removing, such things as require much force; no knowledge of the face of the earth; no account of time; no arts; no letters; no society; and which is worst of all, continual fear, and danger of violent death; and the life of man, solitary, poor, nasty, brutish, and short.[8]

To escape the brutal state of nature into which their passions continually push them, people at last decide to form a government (or, as Hobbes calls it, a Leviathan). This government is meant to set up a "common power" possessing enough force to establish law and order and thereby put an end to fighting. We set up a government by entering into a "social contract" with one another. That is, we make an agreement (or "covenant") with one another to hand over all power to a person or a group. That person or group then becomes the "sovereign" ruler and has the authority to use the power or force of the citizens themselves to enforce the law (which the sovereign makes) and to establish peace and order. We thus emerge from the dreadful state of nature by becoming "subjects" and taking on the constraints of life in a civil society:

> The final cause, end, or design of men, who naturally love liberty and dominion over others, in the introduction of that restraint upon themselves, in which we see them live in common wealths, is the foresight of their own preservation, and of a more contented life thereby; that is to say, of getting themselves out from that miserable condition of war, which is necessarily consequent, as has been shown, to the natural passions of men, when there is no visible power to keep them in awe, and tie them by fear of punishment to the performance of their covenants . . . .
>
> The only way to erect such a common power, as may be able to defend them from the invasion of foreigners, and the injuries of one another, and thereby to secure them in such sort, as that by their own industry, and by the fruits of the earth, they may nourish themselves and live contentedly; is, to confer all their power and strength upon one man, or upon one assembly of men, that may reduce all their wills, by plurality of voices, unto one will: which is as much to say, to appoint one man, or assembly of men, to bear their person; and every one to own, and acknowledge himself to be the author of whatsoever he that so bears their person, shall act, or cause to be acted, in those things which concern the common peace and safety; and

therein to submit their wills, every one to his will, and their judgments, to his judgment. This is more than consent or concord; it is real unity of them all, in one and the same person, made by covenant of every man with every man, in such manner, as if every man should say to every man, *I authorize and give up my right of governing myself, to this man, or to this assembly of men, on this condition, that you give up your right to him, and authorize all his actions in like manner. . . .* [T]his is the generation of the great LEVIATHAN. . . . And he that carries this person, is called SOVEREIGN, and said to have *sovereign power;* and everyone besides, his SUBJECT.[9]

Thus, the materialist philosophy that Hobbes created also gave him the basic concepts he needed to explain the formation of governments. Governments are simply the outcome of the motions we call "desires." Desires lead people to fight with one another (for their material possessions), and this results in a continual "war of all against all." A further desire or motion, the desire for peace, then leads people to form governments.

BERKELEY

George Berkeley is perhaps the most famous of all those idealist philosophers who hold that reality is primarily spiritual and not material. To some extent, Berkeley was reacting to the philosophy of materialists such as Hobbes, whose views were becoming popular in the wake of the growing influence of the new sciences. Such materialist philosophies, Berkeley felt, left no room for God and thus were inimical to religion. What better way to combat atheism than to prove that materialism was false and that all reality is spiritual!

Berkeley was born in 1685 in Kilkenney, Ireland. As a teenager, he was sent to Trinity College in Dublin, where he graduated with a master's degree in 1707. Berkeley stayed on at Trinity College as a teacher for six years. There, at the age of 24 , he finished writing what was to become the classic exposition of an idealist philosophy, *A Treatise Concerning the Principles of Human Knowledge.* In 1713, Berkeley left Trinity College. He was by now an ordained Protestant minister, and in 1729 he and his recent bride traveled as missionaries to Newport, Rhode Island, where he planned to organize a college that would eventually be established in Bermuda. But funding

---

[8] Ibid.

[9] Ibid., 128, 131–132.

George Berkeley: "All of the choir of heaven and furniture of the earth, in a word all those bodies which compose the mighty frame of the world, have no substance without a mind. Their being is to be perceived. Consequently, so long as they are not actually perceived by me or other created spirits, they must either have no existence at all or else exist in the mind of some eternal spirit."

for the college never materialized, and in 1731 he returned to England. In 1734, Berkeley became a bishop in the Church of England and was assigned to the diocese of Cloyne in Ireland. Sixteen years later, at the age of 65, he retired to Oxford with his wife and family. There he died in 1753.

Berkeley held the view that all we know or perceive of the world around us are the sensations we have: the colors, sights, sounds, and tastes we experience. We commonly attribute these sensations to material objects outside us. When our eyes see a small round patch of red, for example, we might infer that outside us there exists a material object that we call an apple and that light coming from this material object causes our eyes to have the sensation of red color. However, Berkeley questioned this inference. He pointed out that we really have no reason to say that in addition to the sensations we experience within our minds, there *also* exists outside us (or, in his words, "without us") some kind

of material objects. We do not even have any idea what these so-called material objects would be like, for all we perceive are our sensations, and these sensations are clearly not material objects because our sensations exist entirely in our minds (or, in Berkeley's words, "our spirits"). All that exists besides our minds, or "spirits," Berkeley concluded, are the sensations we perceive in our minds and the mental images we voluntarily form in them. Berkeley used the term *ideas* to refer to the contents of our minds, including both the sensations we have and the mental images we form. Thus, for Berkeley, the world consists entirely of minds ("spirits") and ideas.

Berkeley summarized his view in the Latin slogan *esse est percipi,* which means "to exist is to be perceived": The only things that exist, besides minds, are the ideas perceived within minds. As he flamboyantly asserted, "All the Choir of Heaven and the furniture of earth, in a word all those bodies which compose the mighty frame of the world, have no substance without a mind."[10] Thus, Berkeley was a complete idealist: He held the view that reality consists of nothing more than the ideas in our minds.

Berkeley's views are most clearly expounded in the short work he titled *A Treatise Concerning the Principles of Human Knowledge.* He opens the treatise with a remark expressing what many newcomers to philosophy feel: that philosophy seems to create more "doubts and difficulties" than it resolves:

> Philosophy being nothing else but the study of wisdom and truth, it may with reason be expected that those who have spent most time and pains in it should enjoy a greater calm and serenity of mind, a greater clearness and evidence of knowledge, and be less disturbed with doubts and difficulties than other men. Yet so it is, we see the illiterate bulk of mankind that walk the high road of plain common sense, and are governed by the dictates of nature, for the most part easy and undisturbed. To them nothing that is familiar appears unaccountable or difficult to comprehend. They complain not of any want of evidence in their sense, and are out of all danger of becoming skeptics. But no sooner do we depart from sense and instinct to follow the light of a superior principle, to reason, meditate, and reflect on the nature of things, but a thousand scruples spring up in our minds

10   George Berkeley, *A Treatise Concerning the Principles of Human Knowledge,* in *The Works of George Berkeley,* vol. 1, ed. George Sampson (London: George Bell & Sons, 1897), 181–182.

concerning those things which before we seemed fully to comprehend. Prejudices and errors of sense do from all parts discover themselves to our view; and, endeavoring to correct these by reason, we are insensibly drawn into uncouth paradoxes, difficulties, and inconsistencies, which multiply and grow upon us as we advance in speculation, till at length, having wandered through many intricate mazes, we find ourselves just where we were, or, which is worse, sit down in a forlorn skepticism.[11]

To resolve the "uncouth paradoxes, difficulties, and inconsistencies" that give philosophy a bad name, Berkeley undertakes to examine "the first principles of human knowledge"—that is, the primary sources from which we draw all our knowledge.

He begins by pointing out that if we look into our minds, we will see that everything we know consists either of sensations ("ideas imprinted on the senses or perceived by attending to the passions") or mental images ("ideas formed by help of memory and imagination"). Consequently, each object we know in the world around us (such as an "apple, a stone, a tree, a book and the like") is really nothing more than a collection of ideas (sensations of color, touch, smell, taste, or hearing). In addition to ideas, he notes, there are also "active beings" or "minds." In fact, ideas can exist only in minds. Because all objects consist of ideas and because ideas can exist only in the mind, it follows that the objects in the world exist only in the mind! Berkeley argues for this startling conclusion in the following passages:

> It is evident to anyone who takes a survey of the *objects* of human knowledge that they are either ideas actually imprinted on the senses, or else such as are perceived by attending to the passions and operations of the mind, or lastly, ideas formed by help of memory and imagination—either compounding, dividing, or barely representing those originally perceived in the aforesaid ways. By sight I have the ideas of light and colors, with their several degrees and variations. By touch I perceive, for example, hard and soft, heat and cold, motion and resistance, and of all these more and less either as to quantity or degree. Smelling furnishes me with odors, the palate with tastes, and hearing conveys sounds to the mind in all their variety of tone and composition. As several of these are observed to accompany each other, they come to be marked by one name, and so to be reputed as one thing.

Thus, for example, a certain color, taste, smell, figure, and consistency having been observed to go together are accounted one distinct thing signified by the name "apple"; other collections of ideas constitute a stone, a tree, a book, and the like sensible things—which as they are pleasing or disagreeable excite the passions of love, hatred, joy, grief, and so forth.

But, besides all that endless variety of ideas or objects of knowledge, there is likewise something which knows or perceives them and exercises diverse operations, as willing, imagining, remembering, about them. This perceiving, active being is what I call "mind," "spirit," "soul," or "myself." By which words I do not denote any one of my ideas, but a thing entirely distinct from them, wherein they exist or, which is the same thing, whereby they are perceived—for the existence of an idea consists in being perceived.

That neither our thoughts, nor passions, nor ideas formed by the imagination exist without the mind is what everybody will allow. And it seems no less evident that the various sensations or ideas imprinted on the sense, however blended or combined together (that is, whatever objects they compose), cannot exist otherwise than in a mind perceiving them—I think an intuitive knowledge may be obtained of this by anyone that shall attend to what is meant by the term "exist" when applied to sensible things. The table I write on I say exists, that is, I see and feel it; and if I were out of my study I should say it existed—meaning thereby that if I was in my study I might perceive it, or that some other spirit actually does perceive it. There was an odor, that is, it was smelled; there was a sound, that is to say, it was heard; a color or figure, and it was perceived by sight or touch. This is all that I can understand by these and the like expressions. For as to what is said of the absolute existence of unthinking things without any relation to their being perceived, that seems perfectly unintelligible. Their *esse* is *percipi*, nor is it possible they should have any existence out of the minds or thinking things which perceive them.

It is indeed an opinion strangely prevailing amongst men that houses, mountains, rivers, and, in a word, all sensible objects have an existence, natural or real, distinct from their being perceived by the understanding. But with how great an assurance and acquiescence soever this principle may be entertained in the world, yet whoever shall find in his heart to call it in question may, if I mistake not, perceive it to involve a manifest contradiction. For what are the fore-mentioned objects but the things we perceive by sense? And what do we perceive besides our own ideas or

---

11   Ibid., 161.

sensations? And is it not plainly repugnant that any one of these, or any combination of them, should exist unperceived? . . .

But, say you, though the ideas themselves do not exist without the mind, yet there may be things like them, whereof they are copies or resemblances, which things exist without the mind in an unthinking [material] substance. I answer, an idea can be like nothing but an idea; a color or figure can be like nothing but another color or figure. If we look ever so little into our thoughts, we shall find it impossible for us to conceive a likeness except only between our ideas. Again, I ask whether those supposed originals or external things, of which our ideas are the pictures or representations, be themselves perceivable or not? If they are, then they are ideas and we have gained our point; but if you say they are not, I appeal to anyone whether it be sense to assert a color is like something which is invisible; hard or soft, like something which is intangible; and so of the rest. . . .

But, [suppose] it were possible that solid, figured, movable substances may exist without the mind, corresponding to the ideas we have of bodies, yet how is it possible for us to know this? Either we must know it by sense or by reason. As for our senses, by them we have the knowledge only of our sensations, ideas, or those things that are immediately perceived by sense, call them what you will; but they do not inform us that things exist without the mind, or unperceived, like to those which are perceived. This the materialists themselves acknowledge. It remains, therefore, that if we have any knowledge at all of external things, it must be by reason, inferring their existence from what is immediately perceived by sense. But what reason can induce us to believe the existence of bodies without the mind, from what we perceive, since the very patrons of matter themselves do not pretend there is any necessary connection betwixt them and our ideas? I say it is granted on all hands (and what happens in dreams, frenzies, and the like, puts it beyond dispute) that it is possible we might be affected with all the ideas we have now, though no bodies existed without resembling them. Hence it is evident the supposition of external bodies is not necessary for the producing of our ideas; since it is granted they are produced sometimes, and might possibly be produced always in the same order we see them in at present, without their concurrence . . .

But, say you, surely there is nothing easier than to imagine trees, for instance, in a park, or books existing in a closet, and nobody by to perceive them. I answer you may so, there is no difficulty in it; but what is all this, I beseech you, more than framing in your mind certain ideas which you call books and trees, and at the same time omitting to frame the idea of anyone that may perceive them? But do you yourself perceive or think of them all the while? This therefore is nothing to the purpose; it only shows you have the power of imagining or forming ideas in your mind; but it does not show that you can conceive it possible the objects of your thought may exist without the mind. To make out this, it is necessary that you conceive them existing un-conceived or unthought of, which is a manifest repugnancy. When we do our utmost to conceive the existence of external bodies, we are all the while only contemplating our own ideas. But the mind, taking no notice of itself, is deluded to think it can and does conceive bodies existing unthought of or without the mind, though at the same time they are apprehended by or exist in itself. A little attention will discover to anyone the truth and evidence of what is here said, and make it unnecessary to insist on any other proofs against the existence *of material substance.*[12]

Berkeley's views were naturally accused of leading to skepticism, the view that we cannot know anything about reality. For Berkeley's views are but a short step away from the view that because the ideas in our minds might be false and because all we know are the ideas in our minds, we can never know anything for sure about the real world. However, Berkeley did not intend his idealist philosophy to encourage skepticism. On the contrary, he felt that "the grounds of Skepticism, Atheism and Irreligion" lay in materialism. Those who hold that only matter exists, he felt, were inevitably led to the view that God does not exist because God is a nonmaterial spirit. The best way to combat atheism, then, is to prove that matter does not exist and that, on the contrary, only spirits and their ideas exist. If spirits and ideas are the only reality, in knowing these we know all the reality there is. Thus, skepticism, like atheism, is false.

Berkeley, in fact, took great pains in his attempt to show that God exists. God is a crucial part of his universe and plays an essential role as the source of the world we see displayed before our senses. If we examine the ideas in our minds, he argues, we will see that some of them require the existence of another "spirit" to produce them, and this is God.

---

12 Ibid., 179, 180–182, 186–187, 189.

God produces in us the sensations that we perceive as reality and ensures that we perceive an orderly reality in which we can plan our lives and look easily toward the future. Berkeley concludes that the "surprising magnificence, beauty, and perfection" of the orderly display that God creates in our minds and that we call the world should fill us with admiration:

> I find I can excite [some] ideas in my mind at pleasure, and vary and shift the scene as oft as I think fit. It is no more than willing, and straightway this or that idea arises in my fancy [imagination]; and by the same power it is obliterated and makes way for another....
>
> But whatever power I may have over my own thoughts, I find the ideas actually perceived by sense have not a like dependence on my will. When in broad daylight I open my eyes, it is not in my power to choose whether I shall see or no, or to determine what particular objects shall present themselves to my view; and so likewise as to the hearing and other senses; the ideas imprinted on them are not creatures of my will. There is therefore some *other* will or spirit that produces them.
>
> The ideas of sense are more strong, lively, and distinct than those of the imagination; they have likewise a steadiness, order, and coherence, and are not excited at random, as those which are the effects of human wills often are, but in a regular train or series, the admirable connection whereof sufficiently testifies to the wisdom and benevolence of its Author. Now the set rules or established methods wherein the mind we depend on excites in us the ideas of sense are called "the laws of nature"; and these we learn by experience which teaches us that such and such ideas are attended with such and such other ideas in the ordinary course of things.
>
> This gives us a sort of foresight which enables us to regulate our actions for the benefit of life. And without this we should be eternally at a loss; we could not know how to act on anything that might procure us the least pleasure or remove the least pain of sense. That food nourishes, sleep refreshes, and fire warms us; that to sow in the seedtime is the way to reap in the harvest; and in general to obtain such or such ends, such or such means are conducive—all this we know, not by discovering any necessary connection between our ideas, but only by the observation of the settled laws of nature, without which we should all be in uncertainty and confusion, and a grown man no more knows how to manage himself in the affairs of life than an infant just born....
>
> But if we attentively consider the constant regularity, order, and concatenation of natural things, the surprising magnificence, beauty, and perfection of the larger, and the exquisite contrivance of the smaller parts of the creation, together with the exact harmony and correspondence of the whole, but above all the never-enough-admired laws of pain and pleasure, and the instincts or natural inclinations, appetites, and passions of animals; I say if we consider all these things, and at the same time attend to the meaning and import of the attributes: one, eternal, infinitely wise, good, and perfect, we shall clearly perceive that they belong to the aforesaid spirit, "who works all in all," and "by whom all things consist." ...
>
> It is therefore plain that nothing can be more evident to anyone that is capable of the least reflection than the existence of God, or a spirit who is intimately present to our minds, producing in them all that variety of ideas or sensations which continually affect us, on whom we have an absolute and entire dependence, in short "in whom we live, and move, and have our being." That the discovery of this great truth, which lies so near and obvious to the mind, should be attained to by the reason of so very few, is a sad instance of the stupidity and inattention of men who, though they are surrounded with such clear manifestations of the Deity, are yet so little affected by them that they seem, as it were, blinded with excess of light.[13]

Berkeley's idealist philosophy, then, provided him with what he thought was an irrefutable proof of the existence of spiritual reality, including God, and of the nonexistence of the material world on which Hobbes and other materialists insisted.

QUESTIONS

1. Carl Sagan said that "each human being is a superbly constructed astonishingly compact, self-ambulatory computer." In what respects is this similar to Hobbes' view? In what respects does it differ?

2. As the contemporary philosopher J. J. C. Smart writes, "By 'materialism' I mean the theory that there is nothing in the world over and above those entities which are postulated by physics. Thus I do not hold materialism to be wedded to the billiard-ball physics of the nineteenth century. The less visualizable particles of modern physics count

---

13   Ibid., 191–192, 247–248.

as matter [for me]." In what respects is Smart's materialism similar to Hobbes'? In what respects does it differ? Does Smart's materialism have any philosophical implications that are radically different from Hobbes'?

3. Hobbes claims that you are nothing more than your physical body (or your brain). If this is true, then *you* are exactly the same as *your body* (or your brain), so whatever is true of *you* must be true of *your body*. But consider the following objection to Hobbes: "Although *you* can be morally blameworthy or praiseworthy, can we say that *your body* or *your brain* is morally blameworthy or praiseworthy? Although *you* can have wishes (for example, to do math) or thoughts (for example, about philosophy), does it make sense to say that *your body* or *your brain* has these wishes or thoughts? Although *you* can love God, isn't it absurd to say *your body* or *your brain* loves God? Although it makes sense to say that *you* have a body, does it make sense to say that *your body* has a body?" Evaluate these criticisms.

4. Do you think Hobbes' description of the quarrelsomeness of human nature is an accurate description of your own self? Of others? Is Hobbes correct in claiming that without the restraints of government, you would involve yourself in a continual "war against every man" and that your life would be "solitary, poor, nasty, brutish, and short"?

5. Must a materialist philosophy like Hobbes' take a pessimistic view of human beings?

6. Do you agree with Berkeley's criticism that philosophy inevitably draws us "into uncouth paradoxes, difficulties, and inconsistencies, which multiply and grow as we advance, till, at length, . . . we find ourselves just as we were, or, which is worse, sit down in a forlorn skepticism"? What assumptions about the purpose and nature of philosophy does Berkeley make? How does this compare to Plato's conception of philosophy?

7. Do you think this is an adequate summary of Berkeley's main argument: "All the objects we perceive are only ideas; ideas exist only in minds; therefore, all the objects we perceive exist only in minds"? Do you think that any parts of this argument are false? Explain.

8. The English writer Dr. Samuel Johnson once said something like the following as he kicked a rock: "There! I thus refute Berkeley!" Would this show that Berkeley's idealism is false? Why?

9. Berkeley's idealism is very different from the way we usually think of the world, but does it make any *practical* difference? Would anything be different for you if Berkeley is correct? Should you do anything differently?

4 Philosophy, Religion, and God

The highest that man can attain in these matters is wonder.

GOETHE

4.1 The Significance of Religion

LEARNING OBJECTIVES: When finished, you'll be able to:

- Explain the importance of the choice between belief and unbelief.
- Define religion and distinguish it from religious belief, religious experience, and theology.

4.2 Does God Exist?

LEARNING OBJECTIVES: When finished, you'll be able to:

- Explain and critically evaluate the ontological, cosmological, and design arguments for the existence of God.
- thinking critically Identify and evaluate an argument from analogy.

4.3 Atheism, Agnosticism, and the Problem of Evil

LEARNING OBJECTIVES: When finished, you'll be able to:

- Explain the difference between atheism and agnosticism.
- Define the Problem of Evil and critically evaluate the claim that evil shows that God does not exist.
- thinking critically Understand how formal and informal fallacies can affect discussions of religion and God.

4.4 Traditional Religious Belief and Experience

LEARNING OBJECTIVES: When finished, you'll be able to:

- State and critically evaluate James' view that our passional nature should determine what to believe when an option is living, forced, and momentous.
- Define what a numinous religious experience is and evaluate the claim that such an experience provides reasonable grounds for belief in God.

4.5 Nontraditional Religious Experience

LEARNING OBJECTIVES: When finished, you'll be able to:

- Explain and evaluate Kierkegaard's view that only subjective thinking can know the truth about God, and Tillich's view that God cannot be proved but only experienced as one's ultimate concern.
- Explicate and evaluate the feminist claim that traditional religious concepts of God are sexist.
- Describe some of the central claims of Hinduism and Buddhism and how these differ from traditional Western approaches to religion.

Chapter Summary

4.6 Readings: Fyodor Dostoevsky, excerpt from *The Brothers Karamazov*

William P. Alston, "The Inductive Argument from Evil and the Human Cognitive Condition"

4.7 Historical Showcase: Aquinas, Descartes, and Conway

© Naturalhit/Shutterstock.com

251

4.1 The Significance of Religion

Perhaps no other area of life is as important yet contains such excruciating uncertainties as religion. Consider "The Road," a very brief "parable" told by John Hick:

> Two men are traveling together along a road. One of them believes that it leads to the Celestial City, the other that it leads nowhere. But since this is the only road there is, both must travel it. Neither has been this way before, therefore neither is able to say what they will find around each corner. During their journey they meet with moments of refreshment and delight, and with moments of hardship and danger. All the time one of them thinks of his journey as a pilgrimage to the Celestial City. He interprets the pleasant parts as encouragements and the obstacles as trials of his purpose and lessons in endurance, prepared by the king of that city and designed to make him a worthy citizen of the place when at last he arrives. The other, however, believes none of this, and sees their journey as an unavoidable and aimless ramble. Since he has no choice in the matter, he enjoys the good and endures the bad. For him there is no Celestial City to be reached, no all-encompassing purpose ordaining their journey; there is only the road itself and the luck of the road in good weather and in bad.
>
> They do not entertain different expectations about the coming details of the road but only about its ultimate destination. Yet, when they turn the last corner, it will be apparent that one of them has been right all the time and the other wrong. ... [T]he choice between theism [belief in God] and atheism [belief in no god] is a real and not merely an empty or verbal choice.[1]

ANALYZING THE READING

The "parable" of "The Road" has numerous details. Explain what each detail symbolizes. For example, the road itself symbolizes life. The celestial city is a symbol for heaven or the afterlife. Explain each of the other symbols. Are there any symbols or details that do not make sense to you?

So much depends on the choice between belief and unbelief! There is no greater influence on one's view of oneself and one's destiny than the choice between belief and unbelief. For example, Judaism and Christianity believe that humans stand midway between nature and spirit. We are on the one hand finite, bound to earth, and capable of sin. On the other hand, we can transcend nature because we are "made in the image of God." As such we possess the divine (Godlike) qualities of consciousness and the ability to love. We possess reason and an intellect capable of apprehending the universe. Both Judaism and Christianity proclaim that being made in the image of God humans can achieve infinite possibilities. Shakespeare expressed this view: "What a piece of work is a man! How noble in reason! How infinite in faculty! In form, in moving, how express and admirable! In action how like an angel! In apprehension how like a god!"[2]

Those who reject all religious belief do not see themselves as transcending nature. In fact, in their eyes nature is all there is. For those who reject religion, humans are certainly not immortal. Nor do they have any kind of spiritual nature. Those who reject religion do not see human life as having a supernatural destiny. One can find, of course, a temporal meaning to life that can make life before death fulfilling. But everything ends at death and we have no destiny at all beyond death. Shakespeare also expressed this sentiment when he wrote these lines, late in his life: "Life's but a walking shadow, a poor player that struts and frets his hour upon the stage, and then is heard no more; it is a tale told by an idiot, full of sound and fury, signifying nothing."[3]

QUICK REVIEW
The choice between belief and unbelief influences one's view of oneself and much more.

---

[1]   J. H. Hick, *Philosophy of Religion* (Englewood Cliffs, NJ: Prentice Hall, 1973), 91.
[2]   William Shakespeare, *Hamlet Prince of Denmark*, act II, scene II, lines 300–303.
[3]   William Shakespeare, *Macbeth*, act V, scene v, lines 24–28.

Obviously, the choice to accept or to reject religion can deeply influence our view of ourselves and of our destiny. As the example of Shakespeare suggests, our religious choices can change as we travel on our journey through life. And such changes can transform profoundly how we look at ourselves and our final destiny. Yet, as Hick's parable of the "The Road" implies, the choice to accept or reject religious belief will not be validated or refuted until the end of our journey—if then. Which, then, should we choose? Which choice—to accept or reject religious belief—is more reasonable during the journey? That is the basic question we address in this chapter: How reasonable is religion?

Defining Religion

Before we turn to address this question directly, however, we should briefly look at a more basic issue. What exactly is religion? Although religion is extremely difficult to define, we should attempt to get a clearer idea of what it is before we continue.

When you hear the word *religion,* what do you think of? A church? A synagogue? A mosque? Belief in God? For many people, the word *religion* refers to an institutionalized belief in God and the teachings of some group such as Catholics, Jews, or muslims. Yet some religions do not have a belief in God. Buddhism, for example, although usually considered a religion, has no belief in a personal God. Other "noncreedal" religions have few or no official beliefs. The Unitarian Universalist Church, for example, has no official belief or creed and "no requirement to believe in a god of any sort."[4] Some religions, such as the Episcopal Church, have highly institutionalized rituals. Others, like the Quaker Church, have little ritual. Many religions stress personal commitment and a relationship with the sacred, often a Supreme Being. Other religions, like animistic religions, place little importance on personal commitment or on relating to a Supreme Being. It is better, perhaps, to identify features that most religions have, than to try to give a definition that covers all possible religions. That is the approach we will take. Yet, as we will see, even then qualifications will be necessary.

Professor Ninian Smart suggests that religion has six dimensions.[5] Not all six are found in all religions. But every religion shares most of these to some degree. The six are (1) doctrine, or a set of beliefs about the universe and its relation to the supernatural, such as the belief that there is a single God who created the universe or the belief that the universe is controlled by the law of karma; (2) experience of, or an emphasis on, events in which the believer feels immediately and strikingly the presence of God or of a supernatural dimension; (3) myth, or a set of stories that convey sacred or special meaning, such as the story of Adam and Eve or the story of the illumination of the Buddha; (4) ritual, or acts of worship, prayer, sacraments, and readings of sacred scriptures; (5) morality, or a set of rules and precepts that

THINKING LIKE A PHILOSOPHER

1. What kinds of beliefs or behavior would someone have to adopt before you would be willing to say that the person is "religious"? What does the term mean to you?
2. According to Smart, religions have all or most of six dimensions, including doctrines, rituals, etc. Explain the six dimensions of the religion you know best. For example, in Catholicism the doctrines are the creed, pronouncements of the Pope, and Biblical teachings, while its rituals are the Mass and the other sacraments. If you don't know all the dimensions of the religion you know best, use the Internet to find out.
3. Think of a religion other than your own that you have wanted to know more about, such as Islam or Buddhism. Using the Internet, find and explain the six dimensions of that religion.

---

4   See the Unitarian Universalist Church Association of Congregations website at http://uua.org/index.shtml.
5   Ninian Smart, *Worldviews* (New York: Charles Scribner's Sons, 1983).

believers are enjoined to follow; and (6) organization, or an organized social group that preserves and perpetuates the religion.

People often express their religion in institutionalized ritual and orthodox beliefs. Yet religion is not just an institution. Nor is it a collection of doctrines, nor a set of stylized rituals. Morality, feeling, and emotion are also important features of religion. In fact, many people today feel that the emphasis on ritual and organizational structure has blurred religion's real import. It has obscured the importance of a deep and personal experience with the object of one's religious belief. Many religious leaders have spoken in terms of personal commitment, experience, and need. In so doing, they have recognized one of the roots from which religion springs. That root is our unending search for meaning and fulfillment.

In our investigation of religion, however, we will set aside many of Professor Smart's dimensions of religion. We will, instead, concentrate on two: religious doctrine and religious experience. Our aim is to look closely at the issue that is critical for the person considering the fundamental choice between belief and unbelief. The choice that raises the question Hick's parable points to: Is religion reasonable? So, we will look at how reasonable it is to believe what religion asks us to believe, and to trust the experiences religion asks us to trust.

Religious Belief, Religious Experience, and Theology

In this chapter, we will often speak of **religious belief**. We use this term in its most general sense to refer to a religion's doctrines about the universe and people's relation to the supernatural. We will also use the term *religious experience*. By religious experience we mean an experience of this supernatural dimension. Having experienced this dimension, a person may feel an intense personal relationship with the rest of creation, perhaps with a Creator. In a sense we all seek religious experience. That is, we search for an experience of that which can transcend us—can go beyond our finite lives and concerns—and can give an ultimate meaning to our lives. Religious belief and experience continue to be of intense philosophical interest. And, as we have argued, religious belief and experience are intimately joined to the issue of self.

Where do we find religious experience today? Some find it in the existence of a personal God. Therefore, we begin by examining the reasonableness of the most basic religious belief. That is, we will look at whether it is reasonable to believe that God exists. We then look more closely at what religious belief itself is and whether religious belief is reasonable. However, many people relate to the divine without relating to a Supreme Being. They believe that religious experience is an intimately personal encounter with the source of all reality. So we turn next to discussing religious experience to develop a clearer understanding of what it is and whether it makes sense. Finally, there are many Westerners who turn to Eastern thought in their search for a belief that is reasonable. They may turn to Hinduism or Buddhism, for example. We therefore look briefly at some major themes in Eastern religious traditions.

It is important not to confuse the philosophy of religion with theology. Literally speaking, **theology** means simply the rational study of God. In practice, however, the term is usually reserved for the rational study of religious beliefs by scholars committed to those beliefs. Theologians study the religious beliefs of a community with the assumption that those religious beliefs are true. By contrast, philosophers approach religious beliefs without these assumptions: For the philosopher, these assumptions must themselves be proved.

QUICK REVIEW
Religious belief refers to doctrines held about a supernatural dimension; *religious experience* refers to experience of this supernatural dimension.

QUICK REVIEW
Theology, the study of religious beliefs, assumes that God exists and the beliefs are true; the philosophy of religion studies religious beliefs but does not assume that they are true or that God exists.

PHILOSOPHY AT THE MOVIES

Watch *Water* (2005) which takes place in India and in which Chuyia, a little girl married to an old man who has died, must, according to Hindu Scriptures, live out her life with other widows in an "ashram" (Hindu monastery). There she is befriended by Kalyani, a beautiful young widow who must work as a prostitute to support the ashram and who falls in love with a man whom Hindu Scriptures forbid her to marry. How does religion in this film affect who and what each character thinks he or she is, that is, affect their self-understanding? In what sense are the beliefs that force the widows to live in the ashram and that prevent Kalyani from marrying, "religious" beliefs? In what sense are they not "religious" beliefs?

4.2 Does God Exist?

The most common way for people of a Judeo-Christian culture to find their place in the scheme of things is through a relationship with a personal God. **Theism** is belief in a personal God who is creator of the world, and **theists** are those who believe in such a God. **Monotheism** is the belief that there is only one God. Most of us have been raised to believe that the God of monotheism is an individual loving Being. Having created the universe, He cares for each individual, actively participates in the life of each person, and listens to and answers the prayers of individuals.

This theistic concept has perhaps never been under greater attack than it is today. We live in a period that has often pitted traditional religious concepts against the growing weight of scientific discovery. Can we, *should* we, believe in the God of theism, or must we modify this belief, perhaps even abandon it in light of what science has found? Even theologians are asking whether the believer can any longer believe in a traditional God. They are questioning an idea that has centuries of tradition behind it and that is a cornerstone of the lives of many people today. For many the traditional God is the basis not only of our religious beliefs and experiences but also of our conception of ourselves and our place in the universe.

Consider, for example, a scientific discovery that still amazes, yet has been accepted fact since 1995 when the Hubble telescope was used to count the galaxies. The visible universe around us contains about 125 billion galaxies with billions of stars in each. Each star is a sun like our own, and many—perhaps most—have planets like those that revolve around our own sun. And beyond the visible universe there are undoubtedly hundreds of billions—perhaps an infinity—more galaxies. Can we even comprehend an individual divine person who could rule over such an immense multitude of worlds? And how are we to believe that such a God is personally concerned with each person's daily life and immortal destiny on our own tiny planet? All our traditional ideas of God shrink in the great vastness of the universe that science has uncovered.

> **QUICK REVIEW**
> Scientific discoveries and theories today challenge religious belief, although for some, science strengthens belief.

THINKING LIKE A PHILOSOPHER

Do you believe in God? If you do, then, as best you can, explain your own reasons for thinking God exists. Are any of your reasons for believing in God similar to any of the arguments for God in the chapter? Are your reasons based on a personal experience like those discussed in the chapter? Do you think you believe not because you have your own reasons for believing but because you were just raised to believe? If so, explain the problems with that position. If you do not believe in God, explain your own reasons for thinking God does not exist or for remaining agnostic. Are your reasons for not believing in God similar to the arguments for atheism discussed in the chapter? Do you think you have no real reasons for disbelieving but were just raised that way? If so, explain the problems with that position.

Science has brought many of us to ask today not only if we accept the traditional concept of God, but also if there is any God at all. Yet despite the rise of science and the decay of many traditional religious forms, religion thrives in this country. Although science might shake the beliefs of many people, just as many continue to hold fast to their belief in a personal caring God. And this belief continues to be their way of locating themselves in the scheme of things. Others, as we will see, even find in science a new basis for religious belief. In fact, the relationship between science and religion has never been one of complete opposition nor complete harmony. Science has often called the claims of religion into question, but at other times the claims of science have been used to support religious claims.

We begin our overview of philosophy and religion with some of the arguments for the existence of God. It is vital to recognize the purpose of these arguments: to advance the personal quest to know God. Knowledge of God was and continues to be one of the most significant topics occupying thinkers. The arguments advanced for God's existence are one element in this centuries-long attempt to attain a rational knowledge of God.

We present the arguments for the existence of God as illustrations of a traditional way by which people have fortified their religious convictions, strengthened their relationship with a personal God, and discovered something about that God. In reading these arguments, notice their reliance on reason and sense experience. And keep in mind the contrasting approach, which we will also examine, of believing on a nonrational basis. We will discuss this latter approach and how it serves as the basis for religious belief for many people. In reading this chapter, then, you will begin to mine two rich veins in the development of religious thought, the rational and the nonrational.

The Ancient of Days.

© Whitworth Art Gallery, The University of Manchester, UK/The Bridgeman Art Library

The Ontological Argument

Earlier theologians had suggested arguments that God's existence is self-evident. But Saint Anselm (1033–1109) was the first to assert this kind of argument in a formal, self-conscious manner. Anselm was a Benedictine monk, a philosopher, and the archbishop of Canterbury. He argued that if we merely think about what God is, we will see that God has to exist. Anselm's argument, now known as the ontological argument, relied on reason alone. Later arguments for God's existence (like the "cosmological arguments" we discuss next) would be based on what we discover about the world when we look around us. But Anselm held that the mind, by merely reasoning about its own ideas, could arrive at the realization that God exists.

The **ontological argument** is an argument that deduces the existence of God from the mere idea we have of God. God, Anselm reasoned, is "that than which nothing greater can be conceived." Since we understand this idea of God (i.e., we understand the meaning of these words), this idea of God exists in our minds. Now, what if we believed that God was just an idea in our minds and that God did not exist in the real world? If so, we could easily conceive of something greater: a real God who exists in the real world. For the real thing is greater than the mere idea of that thing. So Anselm concluded, if God is "that than which nothing greater can be conceived," then God must exist outside our minds, not just within.

This is about as distilled a version of Anselm's ontological argument as one is likely to get. To appreciate Anselm's argument fully, however, you must follow it in his most important philosophical work, the *Proslogion*. While reading the following passages, keep in mind the impulse behind it. In the words of Anselm the point of it is: "*Credo ut intelligam*"—"I believe in order that I may understand." Thus, without belief, one can have no understanding of God:

> Truly there is a God, although the fool has said in his heart, there is no God.
>
> And so, Lord, You, who gives understanding to faith, allow me ... to understand that You exist and that You are what we believe You are. And, indeed, we believe that You are a being than which nothing greater can be conceived. But perhaps such a being does not exist, for hasn't the fool said in his heart, there is no God (Psalms xiv.1)? But, at any rate, this very fool, when he hears of this being of which I speak—a being than which nothing greater can be conceived—understands what he hears. And what he understands is in his understanding even if he does not believe it exists.
>
> For, it is one thing for an object to be in one's understanding, and another to understand that the object exists. When a painter first conceives of a painting he will later create, he has the painting in his understanding. But he does not yet believe it exists, since he has not yet painted it. But after he has produced the painting, he will both have it in his understanding, and he will also believe that it exists, because he has made it.
>
> Hence, even the fool [who denies that God exists] must agree that he has in his understanding, at least, the idea of that than which nothing greater can be conceived. For, when he hears this idea, he understands it. And whatever he understands, exists in his understanding. But assuredly that than which nothing greater can be conceived, cannot merely exist in his understanding. For, suppose he believed it existed only in his understanding. Then he could conceive of this being also existing in reality, which would be greater.
>
> Therefore, if that, than which nothing greater can be conceived, existed only in the understanding, it would not be that than which something greater could be conceived. But obviously this is impossible. Hence, there is no doubt that there is a being, than which nothing greater can be conceived, and this being exists both in the understanding and in reality. ... There is then, so truly a being than which nothing greater can be conceived to exist, that it cannot even be conceived not to exist. And this being is You, O Lord, our God.[6]

ANALYZING THE READING

1. How would you explain the meaning of the phrase, "a being than which nothing greater can be conceived"? Explain the meaning of that phrase in a way that a 10-year-old child could understand.

2. According to Anselm, when I understand the meaning of a phrase that refers to some object, the object "exists in the understanding." Do you agree? Why? Is Anselm confusing the *idea* we have of an object with the *object* itself? That is, he seems to say that understanding a phrase that refers to an object means the *object* exists in the understanding. Should he only conclude that the *idea* of the object exists in the understanding? If you carefully distinguish the *idea* of an object from the *object* itself, how would that affect Anselm's argument?

3. Anselm claims that existing in reality is greater than merely existing in the mind. What do you think this claim means? Explain what you think it means in a way that a 10-year-old child could understand.

A key term in this argument is the word "greater." What does Anselm mean by "greater" when he says that God is that than which nothing "greater" can be conceived? And what does the word mean when he says something that exists in reality is "greater" than something that merely exists in the mind? In Section 3.1 of Chapter 3, we saw that the philosopher Robert Nozick argued that to say

---

6   Saint Anselm, *Saint Anselm: Basic Writings,* trans. S. N. Deane (La Salle, IL: Open Court Publishing, 1962).

Saint Anselm, Archbishop of Canterbury. "There is a being, than which nothing greater can be conceived, and this being exists both in the understanding and in reality."

something is real is to say that it has "value, meaning, importance, and weight." He later adds "power" to this list. Anselm's word "greater" can be understood in terms of Nozick's notion of reality. Within Anselm's argument, we can understand "greater" to mean something like "of greater value" or "more important" or "more powerful."[7] Anselm assumes that if a thing exists in reality it has more value, importance, and power than if it just exists in the mind. Anselm, therefore, seems to be arguing as follows: God is "that than which nothing greater can be conceived." Since we understand this idea of God, the idea of God exists in our minds. But we can conceive of something greater than a God that exists only in our minds, namely a God who exists in reality. A God that exists in reality is greater than a God that exists only in our minds, because a God that exists in reality has more power, value, and importance than a God that exists only in our minds. So if God is that than which nothing greater can be conceived, we must conceive of Him as existing in reality and not just in our minds. Therefore, we must agree that God exists in reality.

Objections to Anselm. Anselm has had his supporters over the years. But many more philosophers seem to have attacked the ontological argument than have supported it. Many philosophers believe the German philosopher Immanuel Kant put his finger on the basic problem with the ontological argument. Kant wrote:

THINKING LIKE A PHILOSOPHER

1. What is your concept of God? Describe as well as you can what you think God is.
2. Would you agree that God is greater than anything you can conceive? (That is, does your idea of God match this description of God, or do you think most people's ideas of God match this description?) Have you ever thought of God in this way? Do you think of God in any way that contradicts the idea that God is greater than anything you can conceive?
3. Some philosophers have suggested that Anselm's argument is really trying to draw out the full meaning of the ideas we have about God. Suppose that is true. What else do you think you would be able to say about God if God is greater than anything you can conceive? Do you agree with Anselm that one of the things you would have to say is that He exists?

> Existence is not a real predicate, that is, it is not a kind of concept that can be added to the concept of a thing. Existence is merely the positing of a thing [in the real world]. . . . Now, if I take the subject (God) with all its predicates (omnipotence, etc.), and say: God exists, or, There is a God, I add no new predicate to the concept of God, I merely affirm

---

[7] See Stephen T. Davis, *God, Reason and Theistic Proofs* (Grand Rapids, MI: WM. B. Eerdmans Publishing Company, 1997), 19; Davis says we should "read greatness as *power, ability, freedom of action,*" in Chapter V of his *Proslogium.* Anselm equates "that than which nothing greater can be conceived" as including that "which exists through itself and creates all other things from nothing" (i.e., as what is omnipotent so "more powerful" than anything else), and as also including being "just, truthful, blessed, and whatever it is better to be than not to be." From this one can also infer that for Anselm, one thing is "greater" than another when it is, to a greater degree, "whatever it is better to be than not to be."

the existence of God with all His predicates ... However many predicates—even all the predicates that completely determine what it is—I may think belong to a thing, I do not in the least add anything at all to its concept when I add the statement: This thing exists. ... Even if I think of a being as the highest reality, without defect or imperfection, the question will still remain, Does this being exist or not?[8]

MindTap To read more from Kant's *Critique of Pure Reason*, click the link in the MindTap Reader or go to the Questia Readings folder in MindTap.

A "predicate" for Kant is just a quality or feature of a thing. And existence, he says, is not a predicate, that is, not a quality. Kant is saying that there is a fundamental difference between the *qualities* of a thing and its *existence*. Existence is not a quality. But, he claims, Anselm's argument wrongly assumes existence is a quality. So Anselm's argument fails. To understand Kant's point consider this: Most qualities are qualities a thing can have to a greater or lesser degree. That is, most qualities can be possessed to a greater or lesser degree. But a thing cannot have existence to a greater or lesser degree. A thing either exists or it does not. A thing cannot exist a little bit and then exist a little bit more. Existence is all or nothing; it does not come in degrees. Most qualities are different. Most qualities are the type that can be present to a greater or lesser degree. For example, red is a quality and so one thing can be redder than another. Now Anselm claims that existing in reality is "greater" than just existing in the mind. But that claim says that existence comes in degrees. It says one thing can have a "greater" degree of existence than another. But existence doesn't come in degrees like that. It does not come in degrees because it is not a quality that can be present to a greater or lesser degree. So Anselm's argument assumes that existence is a quality that can be present to a greater or lesser degree. But that is a false assumption. Existence is not a quality at all or, as Kant puts it, existence is not a predicate.

Although many have agreed with Kant's objection to Anselm's argument, others have questioned whether Kant is right. The key issue is Kant's claim that "existence is not a predicate." Kant does not give a full argument for this claim, which has led some philosophers to ask: "Why should we accept Kant's claim that existence is not a predicate?"[9] If we instead accept the idea that existence is a predicate, then Anselm's argument seems to be valid and sound. So although most philosophers agree with Kant's criticism of the ontological argument, some believe that Kant is wrong. They believe that existence is a kind of quality and so it can be part of the concept of God like Anselm says.

Another objection to Anselm's argument, however, is that it seems to allow us to magically prove that many bizarre things exist. One of Anselm's own fellow monks named Gaunilo made this objection. If Anselm was right, Gaunilo argued, then someone could prove that a perfect island that is "the island greater than which none can be conceived" would have to exist. For if such an island existed only in the mind, it would not be "the island greater than which none can be conceived." In this way, we could prove that the island—or any other "perfect" kind of thing we want such as the perfect flea or the perfect cow—has to exist in reality. But if he accepted that proof for the existence of an island, Gaunilo said, then he was "a greater fool" than the person who made up the proof. Gaunilo begins his

☑ QUICK REVIEW
Kant claimed that Anselm wrongly assumed existence is a real property (or "predicate") that can be part of the concept of a thing—of the concept "that than which nothing greater can be conceived." But some philosophers argue that it is Kant that was wrong because existence can be a property.

---

8 Immanuel Kant, *Critique of Pure Reason,* trans. Norman Kemp Smith (New York: St. Martin's, 1929; original work published 1781), 504–505.

9 For example, B. Miller, "In Defense of the Predicate 'Exists,'" *Mind,* vol. 84 (1975), 338–354; J. Hintikka, "Kant, Existence, Predication and the Ontological Argument," in S. Knuttila and J. Hintikka, eds., *The Logic of Being* (Dordrecht: Reidel, 1986), 249–268; J. Shaffer, "Existence, Predication, and the Ontological Argument," *Mind,* vol. 71 (1962), 307–325.

objection by asking the reader to consider a "Lost Island" that is "superior" to any other land:

> [This island] is blessed with all kinds of priceless riches and an abundance of delights ... and ... is superior in its abundance to any other lands that men inhabit. Now, if anyone described this island to me in this way, I will easily understand what he said. There is nothing difficult about that. But suppose he should then go on to say the following, as if it logically follows: "You can no more doubt that this island ... truly exists somewhere in reality than you can doubt that it is in your mind. For it is superior to exist not only in the mind alone but also in reality. Therefore it must exist. For if it did not exist, then any other land that exists in reality would be superior to it. And then this island, that you conceive as superior to all others, will not be superior to all others." If, as I say, someone wanted to persuade me in this way that this island really exists, I would think that he was joking. Otherwise I would find it hard to decide which of us is the bigger fool, myself for agreeing with him, or him for thinking that he had proved the existence of this island.[10]

Anselm agreed that only a "fool" would try to use his argument to prove that there exists an island "greater than which none can be conceived." (This was a not-too-subtle dig at Gaunilo.) The reason his argument works when it is applied to God, but not when it is applied to a finite thing like an island, he said, is because God and only God, is infinitely perfect. Unlike any finite thing, God has all perfections—such as omnipotence—to an infinite degree and so is indeed greater than anything else we can conceive, and so has to exist in reality. But a finite thing like an Island cannot have all perfections to an infinite degree otherwise it would be God. So a finite thing cannot be a thing "greater than which none can be conceived" and so it does not have to exist in reality. In other words, Anselm was arguing that each finite thing has to lack some perfection. Consequently, some other thing that did not lack that particular perfection would be greater in that particular respect. So no finite thing could be conceived to be greater in all respects than any other thing.

Since Saint Anselm of Canterbury proposed his ontological argument many others have offered their own versions of the argument. These include, in the seventeenth century, René Descartes, Gottfried Leibniz, and Baruch Spinoza, and, in the twentieth century, Charles Hartshorne, Norman Malcolm, Alvin Plantinga, and Kurt Gödel. In spite of their ingenious efforts, however, most philosophers still question whether the ontological argument is correct. Most accept Kant's criticism that existence is not a predicate as Anselm assumes it is.

The Cosmological Argument

Aquinas and the Chain of Motion. The next important attempt to justify God's existence was that of the Christian philosopher Saint Thomas Aquinas (1225–1274). Aquinas is generally considered the greatest of all the rational theologians. His arguments are systematically organized and borrow many ideas from Aristotle. In his monumental works *Summa Theologica* and *Summa Contra Gentiles,* Aquinas offers a total of five proofs. The two proofs on which we focus here each begin with an observation about the physical universe. They are called

---

[10]   Gaunilo, *Pro Insipiente (On Behalf of the Fool)*, 1078. Translated by Manuel Velasquez.

cosmological arguments because they are based on a study of the cosmos. (For Aquinas' other proofs and a fuller discussion of his philosophy, see the Historical Showcase at the end of this chapter.)

Aquinas borrowed key parts of his cosmological argument from Aristotle. The argument begins with the observation that things in the universe "are moving":

> It is evident that some things in the world around us are moving. Now if something is moving, it must have been moved by something else. But if that which moves the things we see around us is itself moving, then it too must have been moved by something else, and that by something else again. But this cannot go on to infinity because then there would be no first mover. So there must be a first mover that is not itself moved, and this is God.[11]

Aquinas' point is that if any object in our universe is moving, it must have been moved by something else that was also moving. And this second moving object must have been moved by something else that was also moving. And this third moving object must have been moved by a fourth moving object, and so on. But a chain of moving objects in which the motion of each depends on the motion of an earlier moving object has to derive its original motion from somewhere. Aquinas argues that this chain of motion cannot be just an infinite chain that never had an originating mover. For if there were nothing that first started things moving, then they would never have begun to move. So, he concludes, there must be a "First Mover"—that is, a being in whom all the motions of our universe originate. This being, of course, would have to be very different from the beings we see around us. For unlike the beings in our own experience, this being must be able to initiate motion without itself being moved. For if it moved as other things in our universe move, then it, too, would have to be moved by something else and would not be the "First Mover."

It is important to understand what Aquinas is getting at here. He is saying that in our universe, any moving thing has to derive its motion from some other moving thing. All motion in our universe is derivative or dependent. This is the nature of motion as we experience it in our universe. The existence of derivative motion in our universe then leads us inexorably back to the existence of a being who initiates the motion in the universe but does not itself move. This being has to be utterly unlike anything we know in our own universe. And this, Aquinas notes, is what we mean by God. Is Aquinas' argument correct? Before we discuss that question, let's look at a second, more sophisticated kind of cosmological argument that Aquinas also presents.

Aquinas' second cosmological argument starts by noting that things in this universe are caused. That is, their existence is caused by other things. In fact, the existence of anything in this universe must be caused by something else because nothing in this universe can cause itself to exist. Aquinas then reasons that these observed effects are the last in a chain of such effects. But this chain cannot go back endlessly in time because then there would be no beginning to the existence of the things in our universe, so nothing would now exist. The chain of dependent existents, like the chain of dependent motions, must start somewhere. Specifically, the chain of causes must start with a being whose own existence is uncaused. This being, Aquinas notes, is what we mean by God. Later, Aquinas explains that this being, whose existence is uncaused, has to be very different

---

[11] Thomas Aquinas, *Summa Contra Gentiles*, bk. 1, ch. 13, translated by Manuel Velasquez.

QUICK REVIEW
Aquinas' second cosmological proof says: (1) Some things are caused to exist by other things. (2) What is caused to exist must be caused by another thing, for nothing can cause itself to exist. (3) The series of causes cannot extend back infinitely, for then there would be no beginning to the existence of the series of causes, so no causes would exist at all. (4) So, there is a first cause of existence, and this is God.

from the beings we know in our universe. For the existence of a being in our universe is always caused by some other being. The fact that all existence in our universe always depends on some other existent, then, inexorably leads us to a being that whose existence does not depend on anything. Such a being would be utterly unlike anything in our universe. It would be the uncaused, nondependent origin of all other existents.

Aquinas' second cosmological argument is explained in the following passage from his *Summa Theologica*:

> [Another] way [of proving God's existence] is based on the nature of efficient causes. In the world we see around us, there are ordered lines of efficient causes [in which each member of the line produces the next member]. But nothing can be its own efficient cause, since then it would have to exist prior to itself and this is impossible. Now it is not possible for a line of efficient causes to extend to infinity. For in any line of efficient causes, the first is the cause of the intermediate ones, and the intermediate ones cause the last one. Now if we remove any of the causes, we remove all the remaining effects. So if there were no first cause then there would be no last cause nor any intermediate ones. But if a line of efficient causes extended back to infinity, then we would find no first cause. Consequently, if the line of causes extended back to infinity, there would be no intermediate causes nor any last causes in existence in the universe. But we know this is false. So it is necessary to admit that there is a first efficient cause. And this we call God.[12]

QUICK REVIEW
Some critics say that Aquinas' views on motion were disproved by the scientific laws of motion Newton discovered, but supporters of Aquinas argue that his views can be reconciled with Newtonian science.

Objections to Aquinas. Scientists and philosophers have raised several objections to Aquinas' cosmological arguments. A first objection to Aquinas' cosmological arguments arose out of the scientific discoveries of the seventeenth century. The most important of these was Sir Isaac Newton's discovery of the three laws of motion and universal gravitation. These laws are still regarded today as the foundations of our scientific understanding of the ordinary motions of everyday objects. Newton's first law of motion showed that a moving object continues moving forever on its own so long as an external force does not interfere. So, critics conclude, God is not needed to explain why the objects we see all around us are moving as they are. But defenders of Aquinas have responded to this objection. They have claimed that his argument should be interpreted as applying to the initiation of motions or, more simply, to acceleration. For an object to accelerate or begin moving, even according to Newton's laws, it must be acted on by an outside force. Something, therefore, is needed to explain how all of the motion we see in the universe ultimately began, and this "something" is God.

ANALYZING THE READING

1. How is Aquinas' first cosmological argument similar to the second one? How are they different?

2. State Aquinas' two arguments in writing, using the "If-then" connective. That is, state each argument with two premises and a conclusion. The first premise should state the fact or observation to which the argument appeals or on which it is based. The second premise should say that IF that fact is true, THEN God exists. The conclusion, of course, is that God exists. When you're done, continue on to the next question.

3. The textbook raises several objections to Aquinas' two arguments. Using the two arguments you just wrote down, explain which premise each objection is trying to criticize. Some of the objections, for example, object to the way Aquinas interprets or understands the "fact" or "observation" to which he appeals. Others object to what Aquinas believes that fact or observation implies. When done, go on to the next question.

4. Do you agree with any of the objections to Aquinas' argument? Why?

---

[12]   Saint Thomas Aquinas, *Summa Theologica*, I, q.2, a.3. This edited translation is by Manuel Velasquez.

A more perplexing objection to Aquinas concerns his claim that there can be no **infinite regress** in the causal series or chains he describes. But why not? Isn't it possible that the universe has existed forever and that things in it have been moving and causing each other forever? Isn't it possible that the universe has always been around and that motion and causality have always operated within it?

Aquinas agreed that the universe may have existed forever and so the chain of motions and causes might stretch back in time infinitely. So he argued that even if the universe existed forever and the chain of motions and causes stretches back in an infinite regress, a First Cause is still necessary. Aquinas reasoned that an infinite regress of causes would allow each individual link in the causal chain to be accounted for by a previous link. But the existence of the entire chain itself would still need to be explained. Similarly, in an infinite regress of motions, the motion of each moving thing can be accounted for by the motion of a prior moving thing. But the question still arises: What is the origin of the motion of the entire chain? To explain how the entire chain of causes, or motions, came into existence, Aquinas claimed, we must posit a God who ultimately creates it all. He does not create it at the beginning of time and then lets it keep running by itself. Instead, he brings it into existence and continuously keeps it in existence through every moment of time. So even if the universe has existed for an infinite length of time, God is needed to keep it in existence throughout that entire time.

The eighteenth-century philosopher David Hume, however, objected to Aquinas' claims about an infinite regress of motions and causes. Hume argued that if there was an infinite regress of motions and causes, an explanation of the whole chain was not required. Hume wrote:

> [If] I show you the particular causes of each individual in a collection of twenty particles of matter, I should think it very unreasonable, should you afterwards ask me, what was the cause of the whole twenty. For this is sufficiently explained in explaining the cause of the parts.[13]

Hume is arguing that if each of the individual links in the causal chain can be explained, no additional explanation of the whole is needed. The explanation of every part is a sufficient explanation of the whole. The same kind of logic can be applied either to motions or to efficient causes. In other words, if Hume's argument has merit, there is no need or any logical justification for positing a first mover or a first cause of existence.

Yet is it clear that Hume is right? Notice that Hume's objection relies on the assumption that the whole is not greater than the sum of its parts. Critics of Hume say that this assumption is false. If so, then an explanation is required for both the parts and the whole. And so Aquinas would be right after all.

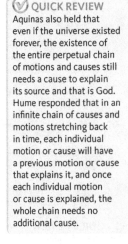

QUICK REVIEW
Aquinas also held that even if the universe existed forever, the existence of the entire perpetual chain of motions and causes still needs a cause to explain its source and that is God. Hume responded that in an infinite chain of causes and motions stretching back in time, each individual motion or cause will have a previous motion or cause that explains it, and once each individual motion or cause is explained, the whole chain needs no additional cause.

THINKING LIKE A PHILOSOPHER

1. Ask several people you know who believe there's a God, what reasons they have to think that God exists. Do any of their reasons take the form of a cosmological argument for God?

2. Many people express their reason for believing in God with expressions like: "Something must have made this universe, it couldn't have just come from nowhere." Or "The goodness, beauty, and wisdom I see in the universe had to come from somewhere." Or "Everything has to have an explanation, so there must be something that explains the universe." Have you ever heard these or similar expressions? These are all informal versions of a cosmological argument. Take one of these expressions and expand it into a full cosmological argument. How do you think the objections to Aquinas' cosmological argument would apply to these informal versions of the cosmological argument?

---

13   David Hume, *Dialogues Concerning Natural Religion*, pt. IX, in *The Philosophical Works of David Hume* (Edinburgh: Adam Black and William Tait, 1826), Vol. 2, 500.

Moreover, contemporary supporters of the cosmological argument have claimed that we now know the universe did not exist forever anyway. They base this claim on the discovery by astronomers during the twentieth century that the universe began with a "Big Bang" about 13.75 billion years ago. The discovery of the Big Bang is an important example of a scientific discovery that had a major impact on religion, this time in an apparently positive way. As we mentioned earlier, the universe we see around us consists of billions of galaxies. Each galaxy is a cluster of billions of stars. And each star is a sun like our own sun, perhaps also with planets revolving around it. During the early decades of the twentieth century, American astronomer Edwin Hubble discovered that the universe around us is expanding. All the galaxies in the universe are moving outward and away from each another. They are moving away as if propelled apart by a terrific explosion that suddenly expanded the universe a very long time ago. But if the universe is expanding, then sometime in the past it would have been smaller than now. And before that smaller yet. Astronomers concluded that about 13.75 billion years ago, the universe began as a hot, incredibly tiny, and very dense, point. That tiny point exploded suddenly into a huge inflating expanse of matter and space. And it has continued inflating outward to form the gigantic and still expanding universe we see around us. This theory received substantial support in 1963. That year two scientists, Arno Penzias and Robert Wilson, discovered that the whole universe is suffused with a microwave radiation. That radiation could only be explained as the leftover heat from the Big Bang. That explosive expansion—the Big Bang—marked the beginning of the universe and set everything in the universe moving and changing as it is still doing today. Until the Big Bang occurred, the universe as we know it did not exist. There was no time, no space, and no objects other than an incredibly tiny point into which the whole universe was densely packed. With the Big Bang, ordinary matter, space, and time all came into existence.

Many philosophers have asserted that the Big Bang is exactly the kind of starting point of the universe that the cosmological argument points toward. If the Big Bang theory is correct, then the universe has not existed forever. There could then be no infinite chain of motions and causes stretching backward in time forever. Instead, we must conclude that the universe has existed for only a few billion years and that it had a beginning. Supporters of the cosmological arguments claim that only an infinitely powerful being can account for the beginning of the universe. And that infinitely powerful being is God.

Yet even if the Big Bang theory is correct, does it really prove there is a God that created the universe? Could something other than God have caused our universe to come into existence? Some cosmologists have speculated, for example, that the universe we know was caused by events in some other unknown universe. And events in that universe may have been caused by some other unknown universe, and so on to infinity. In short, even if the universe as we know it had a beginning, can we be sure that ours is not one of an infinite series of universes that goes back forever? Critics, however, have pointed out that there is little scientific evidence supporting these speculations. In the absence of any evidence for such infinite regresses, they say, we should accept that our universe had a beginning and that God initiated that beginning.

A third important set of objections to the cosmological argument argue that its conclusion contradicts its premise. Critics point out that Aquinas insists everything must have a cause. But if this is so, then shouldn't we ask what caused God? The notion of an uncaused cause seems to contradict the premise that everything has a cause. The nineteenth-century German philosopher Arthur Schopenhauer (1788–1860) expressed this objection succinctly. He wrote: The law of universal causation "is not so

PHILOSOPHY AND LIFE

Religion and Science

The highly respected scientific journal *Nature* regularly publishes articles on the relationship between religion and science. An article published in 2004, for example, asserts that science and faith have collided with "explosive force" over the issues of "nanotechnology, artificial intelligence, cloning, creationism and genetic modification." According to the authors of the article, stem cell research, in particular, has strained the relationship between faith and science because it involves a clash between the "religion-based belief in the sanctity of human life even … of an embryo," and the "desire to alleviate suffering and cure disease" which are the aims of stem cell research. Dr. Francis Collins, a Christian scientist who heads up the National Human Genome Research Institute, is quoted as saying he is "intensely conflicted" about stem cell research. This conflict between the "religion-based" value of embryonic life, and stem cell research which destroys human embryos, the article claims, lay behind the decision of President George W. Bush—who is himself an evangelical Christian—to forbid the use of federal funds to pay for any stem cell research that destroyed more embryos. (This Bush policy ended with President Barack Obama.) Not all scientists feel that religion and science are opposed. The National Academy of Sciences, the most distinguished group of scientists in the United States, declares on its website that "Scientists and theologians have written eloquently about their awe and wonder at the history of the universe and of life on this planet, explaining that they see no conflict between their faith in God and the evidence for evolution." On the website of the BioLogos Foundation, Francis Collins (the Christian scientist quoted earlier) defends "the compatibility of Christian faith with what science has discovered about the origins of life and the universe." Collins argues that many scientific findings, such as the Big Bang and the universal effectiveness of our mathematics, "point" to a God, and that scientific theories such as evolution can be reconciled with faith.

QUESTIONS

1. Are there any aspects of science that make you more inclined to religious belief? Less inclined?

2. Should the sincere religious beliefs of those in public office (such as the president) influence policies regarding scientific research that they put in place?

3. Are the National Academy of Sciences and Dr. Francis Collins right, or do some scientific theories contradict faith?

Sources: Tony Reichhardt, David Cyranoski, and Quirin Schiermeier, "Religion and Science," *Nature*, December 9, 2004; 432:666; National Academy of Sciences website at http://www.nationalacademies.org/evolution/Compatibility.html; Francis Collins on BioLogos Foundation website at http://biologos.org/about.

accommodating as to let itself be used like a cab for hire, which we dismiss when we have reached our destination."[14]

Yet Aquinas has a response to those who object that he contradicts himself because he says everything has a cause yet God has no cause. Aquinas claims only that everything *in our universe*—the world of finite objects we experience—has a cause. He claims this because every thing in our universe is a limited, dependent being. Such dependent beings require the existence of a being that is utterly different from them. Their existence requires an infinite being that is not dependent on anything. Such a being is not another object in our universe of finite dependent things. As creator such a being could not exist in this universe of things that must have a cause. Why would we think that it could be otherwise? Why would we think that God could just be like any other object in the world around us? How could our universe of dependent things be explained by some other dependent thing within our universe? The whole point of his arguments, Aquinas might say, is to show that the finite, dependent, and contingent nature of our world requires a being who is not finite, not dependent, and not contingent. It requires an "unmoved" mover of everything and an "uncaused" cause of everything that exists.

---

[14] Quoted in C. J. Ducasse, *A Philosophical Scrutiny of Religion* (New York: Ronald Press, 1953), 335.

Several contemporary theologians who are sympathetic to Aquinas have interpreted his first-cause argument in a new way. In a way, in fact, that brings out some of its important implications. These theologians claim that the endless series that the argument tries to dismiss should not be understood as a mere regress of events in time. Instead it should be interpreted as a regress of explanations for the universe. John Hick (1922–2012), who taught at Cambridge University, is among those who make this claim. He suggests that the argument is saying that some facts in the universe are "rendered intelligible" by other facts. And these facts are made intelligible by yet other facts, which in turn are rendered intelligible by other facts. At the end of such a series of explanations, he says, there must be a reality which is "self-explanatory." This reality is one "whose existence constitutes the ultimate explanation of the whole." If there is no such ultimate reality, he claims, then the universe is "a mere unintelligible brute fact."[15]

Hick's point is that Aquinas' cosmological argument can be seen as setting a choice before us. We can choose to see the universe around us as an ultimately intelligible home that makes sense and can be explained in a rational way. That choice is the choice to accept the basic rightness of the cosmological argument. Or we can see the universe as something that is just an unexplainable, unintelligible, ultimately "absurd" place into which we have been cast for no reason at all. To make that choice is to reject the cosmological argument.

Yet Hick appears to leave us with a dilemma: Either a first cause exists, or the universe makes no sense. But can't the universe make sense as something that is simply there? Or is Hick right in his claim that without an ultimate explanation, the universe is literally senseless? But how can we be sure that the universe is not "a mere unintelligible brute fact"? Is it possible that in the last analysis the universe just doesn't make sense? Yet to take the route that the universe does not make sense seems to contradict the foundations of science itself. For science is based on the idea that the universe is intelligible. Are we willing to abandon so much?

A final objection to the cosmological argument that we should consider is that it does not seem to prove that a loving personal God exists. It shows only that there is some powerful force that is the source of all the motions and causes we see operating in the cosmos. Aquinas would probably acknowledge this problem. But he would point out that this does not mean his arguments are wrong, only that what they tell us about God is very limited. The cosmological arguments by themselves are intended only to show that there is a creator. Much more analysis of the implications of this and other arguments for God's existence is needed. Only such analysis could show that the being that created the universe is a loving, all-knowing, and all-powerful person.

One of the arguments that Aquinas thought could provide insight into what God is like, is what we now call the "design argument." The design argument, in his words, says that although they lack intelligence, "natural creatures act for an end" and could not do so "unless they are directed toward that end by some being that has knowledge and intelligence, much like an archer directs an arrow toward its target." But the most well-known version of the argument from design is the version that was crafted not by Aquinas, but by William Paley.

The Design Argument

The design argument is the most popular of the arguments for God's existence. Simply put, the **design argument** states that the order and purpose we see in nature indicate that an intelligent being designed it. As we will see, the design argument has turned out to be the battleground where much of the fighting between religion

QUICK REVIEW
Some of his defenders say Aquinas may be interpreted as believing that an endless series of explanations in which one thing is explained by some other thing ends up being no explanation at all.

QUICK REVIEW
Critics object that the cosmological argument does not prove a loving and personal God exists. Aquinas might respond that this objection does not show his argument is wrong, only that it has a limited purpose.

---

[15] Hick, *Philosophy of Religion*, 21.

and science is now being waged. Discussing the design argument, therefore, will reveal much about the relation between religion and science. It will show us both how science can be used to support religion and how it can be used to discredit it.

The "Divine Watchmaker." The argument from design is still accepted today by many scientists. These include biologist Edmund W. Sinnot, physicist and cosmologist Paul Davies, as well as by many theologians and philosophers, such as Robert E. D. Clark, Richard Swinburne, Alvin Plantinga, and Michael A. Corey. In 1802, theologian William Paley presented what is now the classic expression of the design argument. Paley compared natural organisms to the mechanism of a watch. He argued that the design evident in a watch implies that an intelligent watchmaker must have made it. Similarly, the design we see in natural organisms implies that an intelligent "Divine Agency" created them:

> In crossing a heath, suppose I pitched my foot against a *stone*, and were asked how the stone came to be there. I might possibly answer, that for anything I knew to the contrary, it had lain there for ever: nor would it perhaps be very easy to show the absurdity of this answer. But suppose I had found a *watch* upon the ground, and it should be inquired how the watch happened to be in that place; I should hardly think of the answer which I had before given, that for anything I knew the watch might have always been there. Yet why should not this answer serve for the watch as well as for the stone? Why is it not as admissible in the second case as in the first? For this reason, and for no other, viz. that when we come to inspect the watch, we perceive (what we could not discover in the stone) that its several parts are framed and put together for a purpose, e.g., that they are so formed and adjusted as to produce motion, and that motion so regulated as to point out the hour of the day; that if the different parts had been differently shaped from what they are, of a different size from what they are, or placed after any other manner, or in any other order, than that in which they are placed, either no motion at all would have been carried on in the machine, or none which would have answered the use that is now served by it. ... This mechanism being observed ... the inference, we think, is inevitable, that the watch must have had a maker; that there must have existed, at some time, and at some place or other, an artificer or artificers, who formed it for the purpose which we find it actually to answer; who comprehended its construction and designed its use. ...
>
> [E]very indication of contrivance, every manifestation of design, which existed in the watch, exists in the works of nature; with the difference, on the side of nature, of being greater and more, and that in a degree which exceeds all computation. I mean, that the contrivances of nature surpass the contrivances of art, in the complexity, subtlety, and curiosity, of the mechanism; and still more, if possible, do they go beyond them in number and variety; yet, in a multitude of cases, are not less evidently mechanical, not less evidently contrivances, not less evidently accommodated to their end, or suited to their office, than are the most perfect productions of human ingenuity. ...
>
> Every observation which was made [above] concerning the watch, may be repeated with strict propriety concerning the eye, concerning animals, concerning plants, concerning, indeed, all the organized parts of the works of nature. ...

QUICK REVIEW
Paley's argument from design says: (1) If we find an artifact, like a watch, that is designed to achieve a purpose, we can conclude it was made by an intelligent being. (2) But things we find in nature, especially living things and their parts, are designed to achieve a purpose. (3) So, by **analogy**, we can conclude they were made by an intelligent being, and this is God.

ANALYZING THE READING

1. Your textbook suggests that Paley's argument is an "argument by analogy." Assume it is an argument by analogy. Does his argument meet the four requirements of a good argument by analogy as explained in the Thinking Critically box?

2. Some philosophers have said that Paley's argument is not an argument by analogy but is, rather, an "inference to the best explanation" (a kind of argument that your textbook explained in Chapter 2 in its discussion of Darwin's argument). Explain how Paley's argument can be explained as an "inference to the best explanation."

3. Darwin objects to Paley's argument, particularly Paley's claim that the human eye has the marks of being designed by an intelligent being. Does Darwin's objection interpret Paley's argument as an argument by analogy or as an inference to the best explanation? In other words, is Darwin objecting to Paley's *analogy*, or is he objecting to Paley's *explanation*. Explain.

> Were there no example in the world of contrivance, except that of the eye, it would be alone sufficient to support the conclusion which we draw from it, as to the necessity of an intelligent Creator. ... If there were but one watch in the world, it would not be less certain that it had a maker. ... So it is with the evidences of a Divine agency.[16]

As was the custom of religious thinkers of his day, Paley called on a long list of examples from the sciences (especially biology) to make his argument. He pointed to the migration of birds, the instincts of animals, and the adaptability of species to their environments. All of these, he said, suggested a plan and a planner. But for Paley, the most impressive example of a natural creation that was obviously made by an intelligent designer was the eye. He wrote: "there is precisely the same proof that the eye was made for vision, as there is that the telescope was made for assisting it." To drive his point home, Paley presented a detailed description of the eye and its parts. Those details, he felt, showed that the eye had to be produced by an intelligent creator. Intelligence was needed to carefully design it, then select and assemble its complex parts so that together they would serve the purpose of sight. He pointed out that the eye was precisely shaped so that its lens focused light on its sensitive interior exactly where the laws of optics required. The skull was hollowed out into a socket exactly sized to enclose and protect the eye. The exterior skin was shaped into an eyelid that carefully protected the eye, wiped it, and closed it in sleep. A gland was provided to produce tears that continuously washed the eye. A tube from the eye to the nose was placed precisely so that it would drain the tears that washed the eyes. "Are there in any work of art whatever," Paley asked, "purposes more evident than those which this organ fulfills?"

 thinking critically • **Arguments by Analogy**

Paley's argument is usually described as an "argument by analogy." An "analogy" is a comparison between two similar things. An **argument by analogy** claims that since two things are alike in certain respects, they are probably alike in another related respect. A scientist, for example, might argue that since rats and humans are biologically similar, a drug that cures a disease in rats will probably cure the same disease in humans. In other words, since rats and humans have certain biological similarities, they will probably share a characteristic that is related to those similarities.

An argument by analogy like Paley's is not a deductive argument. Since its conclusion is only probable, it is an inductive argument. The conclusion of an argument by analogy is only probable because although two things may share many similarities, they may also differ in other relevant ways. For example, they may differ in ways that prevent one from having the characteristic that the other has. So an argument by analogy will not hold up if we know there are significant relevant differences between the two things that are being compared.

An argument by analogy, then, requires that two things, say x and y, have the same characteristics, say F; it requires that one of those things, say x, has another characteristic, K, that is related to F; and it requires that we know of no relevant differences between x and y. All this may be clearer if we express it in terms of the basic form that any argument by analogy should have:

1. x and y both have characteristics F.
2. x also has characteristic K, which is related to F.

16   William Paley, "Natural Theology," in *The Works of William Paley* (Philadelphia: Crissy & Markley, 1857), 387–485.

3. There are no known relevant differences between x and y.
4. So y probably has characteristic K.

For example, in 2009 Novavax, a drug company, developed a vaccine against the HINI flu virus which was spreading over the entire world at that time. To test whether the vaccine worked, they gave it to ferrets which can also be infected by the HINI flu virus and which have many biological similarities to humans. Novavax found that the ferrets became immune to the HINI virus when they received the vaccine. So Novavax concluded that the vaccine would also make humans immune to the virus. They (correctly) reasoned:

1. Ferrets and humans can both be infected by the HINI virus and they have many of the same biological characteristics.
2. Ferrets become immune to HINI when given the new vaccine and such immunity is related to an animal's biological characteristics.
3. Humans are not different from ferrets in any known relevant way.
4. So humans probably will become immune to HINI when given the new vaccine.

Since Paley's argument is an argument by design, it too will have the form mentioned earlier. If we put Paley's argument into the form of an argument from analogy, we have:

1. Watches and living organisms both have parts precisely adjusted to achieve a purpose.
2. A watch is designed by an intelligent agent, and its design is related to the precise adjustment of its parts to achieve its purpose.
3. Watches and living organisms do not differ in any known relevant way.
4. So living organisms are probably made by an intelligent agent.

Is Paley's argument by analogy a good argument? From our brief discussion it should already be clear that whether an argument by analogy is a strong argument—and how strong of an argument it is—depends on four things:

1. The premises must all be true.
2. The greater the number of characteristics shared by the two things being compared, the better the argument is.
3. The characteristics the two things share should be related to the additional characteristic, K, that one thing has and that the conclusion claims the other one has. (Here, one characteristic is "related" to a second characteristic, K, when having the one characteristic increases the probability of having the second characteristic, K. Sometimes we can't explain why two characteristics are related; we just know from past experience that they are.)
4. There should be no relevant differences between x and y. A "relevant" difference is one that decreases (perhaps to zero) the probability that y will also have the characteristic K that x has.

If we evaluate Paley's argument using the four requirements of a strong argument by analogy, does his turn out to be a strong or a weak argument? This is an evaluation you should be able to make on your own, by asking whether his argument meets the four requirements just mentioned.

> **QUICK REVIEW**
> An argument by analogy is a good or strong argument if its premises are true, the two things being compared share many of the same characteristics, the shared characteristics are related to the additional characteristic that one thing has and the other is claimed to have, and there are no relevant differences between the two things.

But what did other philosophers say about Paley's argument by design?

Objections to the Design Argument. Even before Paley published his design argument, the British philosopher David Hume had objected to earlier versions of the design argument. Hume pointed out a fundamental problem with any argument from design. We have the experience of people making and designing watches, he pointed out. So we know that the orderly design we see in the mechanism of the watch was put there by an intelligent agent. But we have never experienced how an animal, or an eye, or a universe is made. So for all we know, the order we see in an animal, or an eye, or the entire universe may not have been produced in the same way that the order we see in a watch was produced. For all we know, the order we see in the world was produced by the world itself:

> Order, arrangement, or the adjustment of final causes, is not of itself any proof of design; but only so far as it has been experienced to proceed from that principle. For all we can know *a priori*, matter may contain the source or spring of order originally within itself as well as mind does; and there is no more difficulty in conceiving, that the several elements, from an internal unknown cause, may fall into the most exquisite arrangement, than to conceive that their ideas, in the great universal mind, from a like internal unknown cause, fall into that arrangement.[17]

Hume was questioning a key assumption in the argument from design (you might ask yourself which of Paley's premises Hume was questioning). The argument from design assumes that an intelligent agent must produce the complex order found in any object. But we have no basis for this assumption, Hume argues. Perhaps the order found in some things is produced by a mechanism that is not intelligent. For all we know, Hume argued, the order in the universe might have been produced by random processes over a long period of development. We know from past experience that the order of a watch was produced by an intelligent watchmaker. But we have no experience of how a universe comes to be, so we cannot assume to know that its order originated in the design of a god.

But the most powerful objection to Paley was the theory of evolution that Charles Darwin proposed. Darwin provided exactly what Hume could only suggest. He provided a mechanism that could produce order and the appearance of design from random processes. This mechanism was natural selection. Over millions of years natural selection could produce organisms perfectly adapted to their environments.

As we saw in Chapter 2, Darwin claimed that life developed through random "variations" that were selected by the "struggle for survival." Through these processes of natural selection, those organisms whose variations allow them to adapt would survive. The rest would die, until all surviving organisms ended up being perfectly adapted to their environment. Each organism and each of its parts seemed to have been carefully designed for a purpose. The whole organism seemed designed to survive in its environment. And each of its organs seemed to have been designed to carry out the functions that enable the whole organism to survive. But the appearance of design and purpose is an illusion. Both the organism and its parts were the result of the blind processes of natural selection. Taking direct aim at Paley's favorite example, Darwin argued that even the apparent "design" of the eye resulted from the nonintelligent processes of evolution:

> To suppose that the eye, with all its inimitable contrivances for adjusting the focus to different distances, for admitting different amounts of light, and for the correction of spherical and chromatic aberration, could have been formed by natural selection, seems, I freely confess, absurd in the highest possible degree. Yet reason tells me, that if numerous gradations from a perfect and complex eye to one very imperfect and simple, each grade being useful to its predecessor, can be shown to exist ...

QUICK REVIEW

Hume objected that although we know how artifacts like watches are made, we have no knowledge of how nature and living things are made, so for all we know nature and living things are produced by a nonintelligent mechanism.

QUICK REVIEW

Darwin argued that the nonintelligent mechanism of evolution through natural selection, working over millions of years, can produce living things whose parts seem designed to achieve some purpose.

MindTap To read more from Hume's *Dialogues Concerning Natural Religion*, click the link in the MindTap Reader or go to the Questia Readings folder in MindTap.

---

17 David Hume, *Dialogues Concerning Natural Religion*, pt. II, in *The Philosophical Works of David Hume* (Edinburgh: Adam Black and William Tait, 1826), Vol. 2, 444.

then the difficulty of believing that a perfect and complex eye could be formed by natural selection, though insuperable by our imagination, can hardly be considered real. ... In living bodies, variation will cause the slight alterations, generation will multiply them almost infinitely, and natural selection will pick out with unerring skill each improvement. Let this process go on for millions on millions of years; and enduring each year on millions of individuals of many kinds; and may we not believe that a living optical instrument might thus be formed as superior to one of glass, as the works of the Creator are to those of man?[18]

Despite the challenges of Darwin's theory of evolution, many still feel that a Designer's hand is revealed in the intricate complexities of nature. Some concede that organisms evolve through natural selection. But, they argue, natural selection is the instrument God uses to design and produce life. In Chapter 2, we saw the philosopher George Mavrodes make that argument. He suggests that "there was a divine **teleology** in this process, a divine direction at each crucial stage in accordance with divine plan or intention." If the complex order we see in nature was put there by God through natural selection, that order is evidence of God's intelligent design. This approach, in other words, accepts the theory of evolution, but adds to it the idea that evolution is directed.

But critics reply that natural selection could not be directed by God. Natural selection is based on random variations and mechanical processes. These processes are often cruel (natural selection requires that the weak be killed by the strong, for example). And they produce many creatures with useless or painful characteristics. Such cruelty and the random and mechanical nature of evolution suggest it is not "intelligently directed." Evolutionary processes should not be seen as the work of an intelligent loving Creator. They are random, blind, unconscious forces.

Paley's New Defenders: Intelligent Design. Contemporary proponents of "intelligent design" have countered that these critics of Paley are wrong. William A. Dembski, for example, made that argument in *Intelligent Design: The Bridge between Science and Theology*. There he claims that the complexity of living organisms cannot be explained by random processes. They require the admission of "intelligent design" or purpose:

> Intelligent design is the field of study that investigates *signs of intelligence*. It identifies those features of objects that reliably signal the action of an intelligent cause. ... Designed objects like Mount Rushmore exhibit ... features or patterns [that] constitute signs of intelligence. Proponents of intelligent design, known as *design theorists*, purport to study such signs formally, rigorously, and scientifically. In particular, they claim that a type of information, known as *specified complexity*, is a key sign of intelligence. ... What is specified complexity? Recall the novel *Contact* by Carl Sagan (1985). In that novel, radio astronomers discover a long sequence of prime numbers from outer space. Because the sequence is long, it is *complex*. Moreover, because the sequence is mathematically significant, it can be characterized independently of the physical processes that bring it about. As a consequence, it is also *specified*. Thus, when the radio astronomers in *Contact* observe specified complexity in this sequence of numbers, they have convincing evidence of extraterrestrial intelligence. ... [M]any special sciences already employ specified complexity as a sign of intelligence—notably forensic science, cryptography, random number generation, archeology, and the search for extraterrestrial intelligence. Design theorists take these methods and apply them to naturally occurring systems.[19]

QUICK REVIEW
Defenders of the argument from design argue that even if evolution is a fact, the believer can still hold that evolution is the means by which God produces living things and their parts.

QUICK REVIEW
Dembski, a proponent of intelligent design, argues that the "specified complexity" (their improbability and their susceptibility to being independently defined) of the arrangement of molecules in genes implies they were produced by an intelligence and not by chance or by natural laws.

[18] Charles Darwin, *On the Origin of Species by Natural Selection* (London: John Murray, 1859), 186–189.
[19] William Dembski, "In Defense of Intelligent Design," in *Oxford Handbook of Religion and Science,* ed. Philip Clayton (New York: Oxford University Press, 2006).

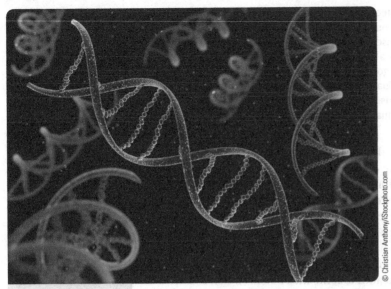

DNA double helix chromosome conceptual three-dimensional rendering with blue, green, and brown luminescent highlights.

Dembski claims that the genes that direct how living organisms form, develop, and behave provide evidence of intelligent design. The evidence is the fact that genes have "specified complexity." Genes consist of complex sequences of hundreds of protein molecules. So their arrangement exhibits "complexity." The arrangement of these molecules is not just any random arrangement, but the one that will achieve a certain goal. That is, genes are arranged to produce a living organism and direct its life functions so that it flourishes. Such an arrangement has "specificity." This means, first, that the arrangement can be specified (defined) as that arrangement that will achieve a certain specific goal. And, second, such a specification can be made independently of the arrangement itself. That is, it is unlike a random arrangement which could only be defined by listing each molecule in the arrangement).

Dembski argues that the "specified complexity" of genes cannot be produced by chance, nor by the laws of nature. Instead, he claims, the specified complexity of genes requires intelligence. He argues, first, that hundreds of protein molecules cannot come together by chance in exactly the complex arrangement required to produce a living organism and make it flourish. The probability that something of such complexity would occur by chance is so tiny that it would take longer to occur than the universe has existed. Second, he claims, the specific protein sequences of genes could not have been produced by natural laws. The protein molecules in the gene have to be brought together in the specific sequence needed to achieve a specific goal. That is, they must be arranged to produce a living organism and then direct its life functions so that the organism will flourish. There are no physical laws, he claims, that can bring proteins together according to whether they will produce a living organism and direct its life functions. Third, Dembski argues, the specified complexity of genes is evidence that genes are the product of intelligent design. It requires intelligence, he claims, to produce the specified complexity of genes. Genes are so complex that it is improbable that their specific arrangement could arise without the intervention of an intelligent agent.

Notice that Dembski is no longer using an argument by analogy as Paley did. He has turned to using an inference to the best explanation. He is claiming that the best explanation for what he calls "specified complexity" is that an intelligent being produced it. Not surprisingly, critics have attacked this fundamental premise of his argument. Critics claim that there are mechanical nonintelligent forces that can produce specified complexity. In fact, they argue, that is precisely what the nonintelligent processes of natural selection do. Other critics have attacked the concept of "specified complexity" itself as untenable.

Paley's New Defenders: The "Fine Tuning" Argument. Recently, some philosophers have proposed a version of the design argument to the arguments of intelligent design proponents. But this new design argument appeals to what is called the "fine tuning" of the universe. (This argument, as we will see, is also an inference to the best explanation.) Paley, and supporters like Dembski, appealed to biological organisms as evidence of design. But such appeals are subject to the objection that evolution can explain such "design." The new "fine tuning" argument appeals to the physical laws and physical constants of the physical universe. No one can use evolution against such an argument because evolution has nothing to do with the physical laws and constants of the universe. Physicist Paul Davies explains the argument in his book *The Mind of God.* In his book he points out that the physical laws of the universe seem designed specifically to ensure that human life can develop and flourish. If the force of gravity had been stronger by a tiny degree or weaker by a tiny amount, then galaxies, stars, and planets could not have formed. If the density of matter in the early universe had been higher by a minuscule amount, everything would have collapsed into black holes. If it had been just minutely lower, galaxies and stars could never have formed. If the universe was expanding a tiny bit faster, then galaxies would not have formed. If it was expanding a tiny fraction more slowly, then galaxies would have collapsed into black holes. Atomic particles have exactly the numerical properties needed to form into the elements needed for life, such as carbon and oxygen. If any of the numerical properties of atomic particles had been a tiny fraction higher or lower, life could never have developed in our universe.

Davies points out that all of these laws, forces, expansion rates, and atomic properties could have had any of an infinite range of different values. The probability that out of this almost infinite range of values our universe would have the specific ones needed to support life is infinitesimal. The probability, he writes, is one chance out of "a one followed by a thousand billion billion zeroes, at least."[20] So it seems extremely improbable that our universe could have turned out like it did unless these laws, forces, and numerical properties were deliberately selected. That is, unless they were picked so as to allow humans to exist in this universe. The physical laws and numerical constants that govern the universe, then, are "finely tuned" to produce those conditions that enable us to live and flourish. And the best explanation of this improbable "fine tuning" is that those laws and constants were deliberately selected by an intelligent creator of the universe.

Several scientists accept this new "fine tuning" version of the argument from design. They include George Ellis (author of *Before the Beginning*), J. C. Polkinghorne (author of *One World: The Interaction of Science and Theology*), and Holmes Rolston (author of *Science and Religion*). But many others believe this new argument from design has the same weakness that Paley's had. The argument assumes that the order we see in the universe had to be produced by an intelligent being. But we saw Hume object that for all we know some nonintelligent mechanism produced the patterns we see in the universe. Many critics of the fine-tuning version of the argument from design have repeated Hume's objection. In fact, some propose a specific mechanism that could explain the improbable fine

ANALYZING THE READING

1. Dembski argues that "specified complexity" can only be produced by an intelligent being. Would Hume's objection to the design argument apply to Dembski's argument? Why? Would Darwin's? Why?

2. The idea that an infinity of universes exists is supposed to explain the improbability of the "finely tuned" universe in which we live, but without requiring an intelligent Creator. Explain how the existence of an infinity of universes would explain the fact that the fine tuning of the universe is highly improbable.

3. Ellis says that the "case for the multiverse is inconclusive" because on principle science does not have, and can never have, any way of observing anything outside our universe. Suppose Ellis is right. Do you think that since the multiverse theory can never be proved or disproved by science, it is "unscientific"? Suppose Ellis is right and those who propose the multiverse theory can never prove it. Does that mean the theory is not a valid objection to the claim that the improbability of the universe requires an intelligent creator? Why?

[20] Paul Davies, *Other Worlds* (London: Dent, 1980), 56.

tuning of the universe. They suggest that perhaps there exist an infinite number of other universes each with different laws and numerical properties. If there are an infinite number of other universes, then it was not improbable that at least one of them would turn out to have the conditions necessary to support life. In fact, if there exist an infinity of universes, it would be almost certain that some of them would have the conditions life needs. We just happen to live in one of those.

But how could an infinity of universes exist? Several scientists have proposed theories that might explain how there could be an infinite number of other universes with laws and numerical properties different from ours.[21] The "oscillating universe" theory says that perhaps the universe has exploded in a Big Bang and then contracted an infinite number of times. And perhaps each time it explodes into existence, the "new" universe has different laws and numerical properties. So there would be an infinite number of universes each with different laws and properties.

The "many worlds" theory of quantum physics says that each time a subatomic event occurs that could turn out in two or more ways, the universe splits into two or more universes. In each universe one of those ways actually turns out to be the way the event occurred. Since trillions upon trillions of subatomic events occur throughout the universe, trillions upon trillions of universes continuously come into existence. And each of those universes would keep producing trillions upon trillions more universes. So there would not be an infinity of universes, but certainly a very large number.

The "eternal inflation" theory says our universe has inflated to an infinite size. So it could contain an infinite number of distinct regions of space, each as big as our own visible universe. And each region of space could have different laws and numerical properties. Each such region of space would in effect be a separate "universe." And there would be an infinite number of them.

But supporters of the fine-tuning argument respond that these "multiverse" scenarios are bizarre speculations. None are supported by any real scientific evidence. George F. R. Ellis is one of the world's leading scientists and cosmologists (and not a proponent of the fine-tuning argument). He argues that "the case for the multiverse is inconclusive." The case is inconclusive because other universes beyond our own necessarily "remain beyond our capacity to see, now or ever." So "we have no information about these regions and never will." He concludes that multiverse theories lack the "empirical testing [that] is the core of science."[22] Supporters of the fine-tuning argument claim that their critics have no real alternative explanation for our finely tuned universe. Supporters say their critics resort to unprovable theories as if they were real scientific explanations. In the absence of any other legitimate explanation, supporters say, we must accept the conclusion that God produced the fine tuning of the universe to make life possible for us.

THINKING LIKE A PHILOSOPHER

1. The argument from design is often said to be the most popular of all the arguments for God's existence. Do you personally find this argument appealing at this point in your life? Have you ever found that argument appealing? If the argument appeals to you, what phenomena do you think are most convincing evidence for God? If the argument does not appeal to you, what is it about the argument that makes you reject it?

2. Suppose the multiverse theory is right, and our universe is just one among trillions of trillions of trillions of others. Would that make you feel more awe at the power of God, or more certain that we are so insignificant that God could not be any more concerned about what happens to us than we are about what happens to bacteria?

21 George F. R. Ellis, "Does the Multiverse Really Exist?" *Scientific American,* vol. 305 (2011), issue 2 (August), 38–43.
22 See Max Tegmark, "Parallel Universes," *Scientific American,* vol. 288 (2003), issue 5 (May), 40–51.

Debate about the argument from design, then, lives on in this latest confrontation between science and religion. After Darwin, many philosophers and theologians thought science had fatally wounded the design argument and most abandoned it for dead. But the surprising new evidence of fine tuning that science itself discovered has resurrected it from the dead. Now it is the most vigorous and dynamic of all the arguments. But at its heart lies a key assumption: unusual or improbable design demands a conscious designer. You must decide for yourself whether this assumption makes sense of the world as you know and experience it. If you accept the argument from design it can lead you to feel awe and reverence for the universe because you see it as the handiwork of an intelligent Creator. Or, if you reject it, it can leave you feeling that in the end the universe must be accepted as a beautiful, intricate, and amazing product of the blind workings of physical processes.

PHILOSOPHY AT THE MOVIES

Watch *The Exorcism of Emily Rose* (2005), based on a true story, in which a young woman, Emily Rose, believing she is possessed by the devil, asks a priest to perform an exorcism during which she dies, leading to the priest's arrest for negligent homicide and a trial at which the jurors must decide whether Emily died of natural or supernatural causes. Should belief or disbelief in the existence of God affect a juror's decision? Why? Do the proofs for God's existence affect what you think might have been going on in Emily's death?

The Exorcism of Emily Rose.

4.3 Atheism, Agnosticism, and the Problem of Evil

As we've just seen, various philosophers have pointed out what they consider to be obvious flaws in each of the traditional proofs for God's existence. These and other objections to the arguments for the existence of God have led many people to the conclusion that the existence of God is uncertain. Although agnostics have concluded that they just don't know whether or not God exists, atheists go a step further and decide that they know that God does not exist. Let's look first at atheism.

Atheism

Atheism denies the major claims of all varieties of theism. In the words of Ernest Nagel (1901–1985), an atheist himself, "Atheism denies the existence ... of a self-consistent, omnipotent, omniscient, righteous and benevolent being who is distinct from and independent of what has been created."[23]

---

[23]   Quoted in *Encounter: An Introduction to Philosophy*, ed. Ramona Cormier, Ewing Chinn, and Richard Lineback (Glenview, IL: Scott Foresman, 1970), 224.

Religious people sometimes portray atheists as evil curmudgeons. But, as Nagel points out, philosophical atheists tend to share a number of respectable characteristics. First, many agree with the idea that sense observation and public verification are instrumental to truth and that scientific method is the best approach to gain reliable knowledge of the material world around us. This idea is, in fact, a fundamental belief of many atheists. As Nagel states, "It is indeed this commitment to the use of an empirical method which is the final basis of the atheistic critique of theism."

Second, and as a consequence of believing that sense observation and public verification provide the only reliable basis of knowledge, atheists also tend to be materialists. As Nagel bluntly puts it: "An atheistic view of things is a form of materialism."

Third, as a result of the view that nothing more exists beyond our material world, many thoughtful atheists have focused their moral and social concerns on the world here and now. They have taken firm stands against authoritarianism, oppression, and war while stressing the importance and value of the individual. For example, the philosopher Bertrand Russell was an anti-war activist, who opposed British imperialism, and condemned totalitarian governments. Because atheists cannot fortify their moral positions with promises of haven or threats of hell, they must rely on what Nagel calls "a vigorous call to intelligent activity—activity for the sake of realizing human potentialities and for eliminating whatever stands in the way of such realization."

But the fourth and defining characteristic of atheists is the belief that there are good reasons to believe that God does not exist. What can such reasons look like? We have seen several objections to the arguments for the existence of God. But even if these objections were correct, all they would show is that we don't have a good proof that God exists. But God might exist even though we can't prove He exists. So is it possible, instead, to prove that God does not exist? Here we consider perhaps the major argument against the existence of God, the problem of evil. More than any other consideration, the problem of evil has led many to atheism.

> **QUICK REVIEW**
> Atheists believe there are good reasons to think there is no God. Many atheists base their atheism on the ability of science and the scientific method to explain the material world, and so focus their concerns on the world here and now.

The Problem of Evil.   Clearly, humans and other living things continue to be beset by all kinds of evils: sickness, pain, suffering, and death. Here are but a few examples taken from news reports:[24]

> PHILADELPHIA—Police said that a 3-year old boy died after being tortured by the adults responsible for his care. . . . Police say that he was kicked, punched and had his hands, feet and rear end burned with a blowtorch. . . . 22-year old Nadera Batson was arrested and charged with murder. . . . [H]er boyfriend, Marcus King, has also been implicated in the boy's death.
>
> PAYNESVILLE, MIN.—Fire burned through a barn at one of Minnesota's largest rabbit farms early Wednesday morning, killing hundreds of the animals. . . . The rabbits were literally burned alive in their cages. . . "There were roughly 100 moms in there," said Scott, "and they all had eight to nine babies with them at the time."
>
> KATHMADU—Rescue teams began arriving in Nepal's devastated capital Monday to help terrified and homeless survivors of a 7.8 magnitude quake that killed more

---

24   The four stories are, respectively, from: "3-Year Old Boy Dies After Being Tortured, Burned by Baby Sitters," *Salem-News*, July 16, 2011, accessed March 10, 2012, from http://www.salem-news.com /articles/july162011/child-burned-dies.php; Mark Saxenmeyer, "Hundreds of Rabbits Die in Stearns County Barn Fire," KSAX.*com*, February 22, 2012, accessed March 10, 2012, from http://ksax.com /article/stories/S2508647.shtml?cat510230; New Vision, "Nepal Quake Death Toll Surges to 3,200," NewVision.Com, April 27, 2015, accessed April 28, 2015, at www.newvision.co.ug/news/667494 -nepal-quake-death-toll-surges-to-3-200.html; Associated Press, "Storms Demolish Small Towns in Ind., Kr.; 37 Dead," *The Augusta Chronicle*, March 2, 2012, accessed March 10, 2012, from http:// chronicle.augusta.com/latest-news/2012-03-02/storms-kill-15-3-states.

than 3,200 people in the impoverished nation. The earthquake also triggered an avalanche on Mount Everest which killed at least 18 climbers. Powerful aftershocks and heavy rains hampered rescue efforts. Said shopkeeper Rabi Shrestha: "I don't know why the gods want us to suffer like this."

HENRYVLLE, IND.—A string of violent storms demolished small towns in Indiana and cut off rural communities in Kentucky as an early season tornado outbreak killed more than 30 people, and the death toll rose as daylight broke on Saturday's search for survivors.

Are these kinds of events compatible with the claim that there exists an all-good, all-knowing, all-powerful Creator? A Creator, in other words, who is benevolent, omniscient, and omnipotent? Is not this belief in a benevolent God at least paradoxical in the face of such events? If God is benevolent, He would surely not want people and other living things to suffer. If God is omniscient, He surely knows when people and other living things are suffering. If God is omnipotent, surely God could prevent any suffering He wants to prevent. Yet the evil of suffering obviously exists. Is God perhaps not all-powerful or not all-knowing? Or is it that God does not want to prevent suffering? But if God does not want to prevent suffering, then God seems to have evil intentions, which certainly isn't consistent with the nature of a benevolent God.

In his *Dialogues Concerning Natural Religion,* a discussion of the arguments for God's existence, Hume considers the question of evil. His conclusion, in the words of one of his characters, Philo, is that our experience of the world argues against the existence of an all-good, all-powerful being:

My sentiments, replied Philo, are not worth being made a mystery of; and, therefore, without any ceremony, I shall deliver what occurs to me with regard to the present subject. It must, I think, be allowed that, if a very limited intelligence whom we shall suppose utterly unacquainted with the universe were assured that it was the production of a very good, wise, and powerful being, however finite, he would, from his conjectures, form *beforehand* a different notion of it from what we find it to be by experience. Nor would he ever imagine, merely from these attributes of the cause of which he is informed, that the effect could be so full of vice and misery and disorder, as it appears in this life. Supposing now that this person were brought into the world, still assured that it was the workmanship of such a sublime and benevolent being, he might, perhaps, be surprised at the disappointment, but would never retract his former belief if founded on any very solid argument, since such a limited intelligence must be sensible of his own blindness and ignorance, and must allow that there may be many solutions of those phenomena which will forever escape his comprehension. But supposing, which is the real case with regard to man, that this creature is not antecedently convinced of a supreme intelligence, benevolent, and powerful, but is left to gather such a belief from the appearances of things—this entirely alters the case, nor will he ever find any reason for such a conclusion. He may be fully convinced of the narrow limits of his understanding, but this will not help him in forming an inference concerning the goodness of superior powers, since he must form that inference from what he knows, not from what he is ignorant of. The more you exaggerate his weakness and ignorance, the more diffident you render him, and give him the greater suspicion that such subjects are beyond the reach of his faculties. You are obliged, therefore, to reason with him merely from the known phenomena, and to drop every arbitrary supposition or conjecture.[25]

---

[25]   David Hume, *Dialogues Concerning Natural Religion,* pt. XI, in *The Philosophical Works of David Hume* (Edinburgh: Adam Black and William Tait, 1826), Vol. 2, 516–517.

Hume is arguing that ahead of time one might assume that the Creator of the universe is "a very good, wise, and powerful being." The natural conclusion should be that the universe He created would have no "vice and misery and disorder." But the universe we experience has a great deal of "vice and misery and disorder." So if we want to remain committed to the belief that the Creator is "good, wise, and powerful" we will have to rationalize away this evil. We might say, perhaps, that evil is just beyond our ability to comprehend. But suppose we were not already committed to the belief that the Creator is "good, wise, and powerful." Suppose that, instead, we are willing to accept whatever conclusion the evidence around us suggests. Then our experience of the world could not support the claim that it was created by "a very good, wise, and powerful being." Instead the evidence would argue against the existence of such a being.

There are two ways of understanding Hume. First, Hume may be suggesting a *deductive* argument that proves that a benevolent, omniscient, and omnipotent God *necessarily* does not exist. He would be suggesting what we now call the "logical problem of evil," which is this kind of argument:

1. If a benevolent, omniscient, and omnipotent God exists, then there could be no evil in our world.

2. But there is evil in our world.

3. Therefore, a benevolent, omniscient, and omniscient, and omnipotent God does not exist.

In this "logical problem of evil," premise (1) is supposed to express the idea that it is a logical contradiction to say both that (A) "A benevolent, omniscient, and omnipotent God exists" and that (B) "There is evil in our world." In other words, it is impossible for both (A) and (B) to be true together. Or, to express this in terms we used when we explained logical validity: Premise (1) says it is impossible to imagine a situation in which both (A) and (B) are true.

On the other hand, Hume may be suggesting an *inductive or probable* argument that claims only that the evidence supports the conclusion that God *probably* does not exist. In this case, he would be suggesting what we now call the "evidential problem of evil," which is an argument like this:

1. There is evil in our world.

2. The best explanation of the evil in our world is that there is no benevolent, omniscient, and omnipotent God.

3. Therefore, there probably is no benevolent, omniscient, and omnipotent God.

This argument or "evidential problem of evil" is an inference to the best explanation. The reason why the conclusion is only probable is because in an inference to the best explanation, it is always possible that there is a better explanation but we just haven't found it yet.

For many philosophers, the problem of evil is the "logical problem of evil." J. L. Mackie, for example, writes:

In its simplest form the problem is this: God is omnipotent; God is wholly good; and yet evil exists. There seems to be some contradiction between these three propositions, so that if any two of them were true the third would be false. But at the same time all three are essential parts of most theological positions: the theologian, it seems, at once must and cannot consistently adhere to all three.[26]

Mackie believes it is a "contradiction" to say "(A) God is omnipotent and (B) God is wholly good and (C) Evil exists." These cannot all be true, he says, because "good is opposed to evil, in such a way that a good thing always eliminates evil as far as it can, and there are no limits to what an omnipotent thing can do."[27] But is Mackie right? As we have seen, to say that (A), (B), and (C) are contradictory, is to say that it is impossible to imagine a situation in which (A), (B), and (C) are all true. So the challenge to the believer is to come up with a situation—even an imaginary situation would do the job—in which (A), (B), and (C) are all true. Do you think it is possible to meet this challenge? If you could then you would have proven that (A), (B), and (C) are not mutually contradictory.

For some philosophers, however, the problem of evil is the "evidential problem of evil." Take, for example, the philosopher William L. Rowe. He grants that a theist could explain evil and continue to believe a benevolent, omniscient, omnipotent God exists. A theist could do this by saying that God has to allow evil in order to achieve a greater good or prevent a greater evil. For example, believers might say God permits suffering because that is the only way that humans can become morally virtuous, and this greater good outweighs the evil of suffering. Or believers might say God permits suffering because that is the only way to prevent the greater evil of people sinking into vice. But surely, Rowe claims, not all evil is like this. He gives the example of a fawn caught in a fire:

ANALYZING THE READING

1. The "logical problem of evil" says that statement (A) "A benevolent, omniscient, and omnipotent God exists" contradicts statement (B) "There is evil in our world." Explain why statement (A) contradicts statement (B). That is, explain why (A) rules out (B) and (B) rules out (A)? In other words, if (A) contradicts (B), then there is no situation in which (A) and (B) are *both* true; so explain why there is no situation in which (A) and (B) are both true.

2. When you explained why (A) contradicts (B) you had to bring in additional information than what (A) and (B) contain. For example, you might have had to add the idea that "A good god would not allow evil if he could prevent it." Or perhaps you added "An omniscient god would know about every evil as it happens." Make a list of all the additional claims you had to add to explain why (A) contradicts (B). Do you think any of these additional claims might be false? Why? If one of your additional claims is false, will (A) still contradict (B)? Why?

3. Mackie's version of the "logical problem of evil" says the three statements "God is omnipotent," "God is wholly good," and "Evil exists" seem to involve a contradiction yet all are "essential parts of most theological positions." Why does he claim the three are "essential parts of most theological positions"? Do you agree with his claim? Could a Christian, for example, give up one of the three statements?

Taking human and animal suffering as a clear instance of evil which occurs with great frequency in our world, the argument for atheism based on evil can be stated as follows:

1. There exist instances of intense suffering which an omnipotent, omniscient being could have prevented without thereby losing some greater good or permitting some evil equally bad or worse.

---

26 J. L. Mackie, "Evil and Omnipotence," in Marilyn McCord Adams and Robert Merrihew Adams (eds.), *The Problem of Evil* (New York: Oxford, 1990), 25.
27 Ibid., 26.

2. An omniscient, wholly good being would prevent the occurrence of any intense suffering it could, unless it could not do so without thereby losing some greater good or permitting some evil equally bad or worse.

3. There does not exist an omnipotent, omniscient, wholly good being. [Premise] (2) seems to express a belief that accords with our basic moral principles, principles shared by both theists and non-theists. If we are to fault the argument for atheism, therefore, it seems we must find some fault with its first premise.

[Premise (1)] Suppose in some distant forest lightning strikes a dead tree, resulting in a forest fire. In the fire a fawn is trapped, horribly burned, and lies in terrible agony for several days before death relieves its suffering. So far as we can see, the fawn's intense suffering is pointless. For there does not appear to be any greater good such that the prevention of the fawn's suffering would require either the loss of that good or the occurrence of an evil equally bad or worse. Nor does there seem to be any equally bad or worse evil so connected to the fawn's suffering that it would have had to occur had the fawn's suffering been prevented. Could an omnipotent, omniscient being have prevented the fawn's apparently pointless suffering? The answer is obvious, as even the theist will insist. An omnipotent, omniscient being could have easily prevented the fawn from being horribly burned, or, given the burning, could have spared the fawn the intense suffering by quickly ending its life, rather than allowing the fawn to lie in terrible agony for several days. Since the fawn's intense suffering was preventable and, so far as we can see, pointless, doesn't it appear that premise (I) of the argument is true, that there do exist instances of intense suffering which an omnipotent, omniscient being could have prevented without thereby losing some greater good or permitting some evil equally bad or worse?[28]

ANALYZING THE READING

1. Rowe suggests his "evidential" argument can only show God "probably" exists because "for all we know there is some good outweighing the fawn's suffering to which that suffering is connected in a way we do not see." What does he mean? Give an example of how there might be a good that *requires* the fawn's suffering and *outweighs* the fawn's suffering? In other words, suggest some greater good that God could achieve only by allowing the fawn's suffering.

2. Consider this statement: "The existence of evil can show only that God is either not all-knowing or not omnipotent; it cannot show that God does not exist." Is this statement correct?

3. A playwright once wrote, "If God is good, He is not God; if God is God, He is not good." Explain what he meant.

The suffering of an animal, then, seems pointless. Such examples of intense suffering do not seem to achieve a greater good nor prevent a greater evil. So Rowe concludes they apparently cannot be explained by the theory that God allows evil to achieve a greater good or avoid a greater evil. Yet note that Rowe's last sentence in the quotation above is a question. He does not simply assert premise (1) is true. In fact he later says: "the truth is that we are not in a position to prove that (1) is true." The reason we cannot prove (1) is that "for all we know, there is some... good outweighing the fawn's suffering to which that suffering is connected in a way we do not see." So in the end, Rowe points out, he can only conclude that an omnipotent, omniscient, wholly good being *probably* does not exist.

A few years later the philosopher Paul Draper made a key addition to the argument of the "evidential problem of evil".[29] Rowe's example of "gratuitous" (i.e., pointless) evil, Draper suggested, is much better explained by the hypothesis that if

---

[28] William L. Rowe, "The Problem of Evil and Some Varieties of Atheism," *American Philosophical Quarterly*, vol. 16 (1979), 335–341.

[29] Paul Draper, "Pain and Pleasure: An Evidential Problem for Theists," *Nous*, vol. 23, no. 3, 331–350.

there are supernatural beings, they just don't care about the gratuitous suffering we experience in this world. In short, an omniscient, omnipotent God may exist, but He is probably not benevolent.

Are the "evidential" arguments of Rowe and Draper right? Is it true that at least some terrible evils are pointless, and that the best explanation of such evils is that either there is no God or God does not care?

Theistic Responses to the Problem of Evil. Several theists have responded to the kind of evidential problem of evil argument that Rowe and Draper advance. They have argued that God could not have created the world without evil, or that by allowing evil God achieves a greater good. One approach argues that although God created the world, he had to create a finite world and this finiteness is the source of evil. Yet God does not create that evil.

The early Christian theologian Saint Augustine (354–430), for example, argued that evil is a privation. That is, evil is the loss of what is good from an entity that is in itself still good. Sickness, for example, is the lack of health in a person, and the existence of a person is in itself good. Only God, he claims, can be perfectly and completely good. So, anything that is not God must necessarily lack some good. God's creation, in other words, cannot be God. So it must be finite and limited, and so must contain incomplete goodness and the possibility of the loss of goodness. Such a privation of goodness is what we mean by evil. Yet God had good reason to create this finite and limited universe with its limited goodness. For by creating a finite universe He created something good. He created a finite and limited good, of course, but it is still a true good.

> What, after all, is anything we call evil except the privation of good? In animal bodies, for instance, sickness and wounds are nothing but the privation of health ... For evil is not a substance; the wound or the disease is a defect of the bodily substance which, as a substance, is good. Such evil, then, is a privation of that good which is called health.
>
> The creator of all nature is supremely good. But nature is not supremely and immutably good as is its Creator. Thus the good in created things can be diminished or increased. When their good is diminished, that is evil. Still, even if it is diminished, something must remain of the thing's original nature as long as it exists at all. For no matter what kind or however insignificant a thing may be, the good which is its nature cannot be destroyed unless the thing itself is destroyed. ... When, however, a thing is corrupted [i.e., when it loses some of the good it had], its corruption is an evil because it is, to that degree, a privation [a loss] of the good. Where there is no privation of the good, there is no evil. Where there is evil, there is a corresponding diminishment of the good.[30]

MindTap Go to MindTap to watch a video covering Saint Augustine's beliefs on the relationship of science and religion.

QUICK REVIEW
Augustine argued that God produces what is good and only what is good. Because evil is the absence of good, God does not produce evil. Moreover, what God creates must be finite and lack some good. So, if God is to create a finite world, and thereby bring at least some goodness into existence, it has to contain some evil.

Augustine concludes that it is wrong to argue that the existence of evil shows an all-good and all-powerful God does not exist. Instead, evil exists because a finite world has to contain some evil or privation of good if it is to be distinct from the all-good God. God *could not* prevent evil in our universe unless He were to have created another God like himself. So even an omnipotent God cannot create a finite world that has no evil.

But many critics of Augustine claim that his argument seems to dodge the issue. Call sickness lack of health, if you wish, the fact remains that people experience pain

---

30 Augustine of Hippo, Enchiridion, trans. Albert C. Outler, ch. IV, para. 12, accessed April 27, 2015, at www.ccel.org/ccel/augustine/enchiridion.chapter4.html.

and suffering, which they regard as evil. Why does an all-powerful God allow such tremendous and painful "absences of good"? Surely a benevolent omnipotent God could have created a world with less pain and less evil than ours contains. Surely he could have created a world with less of the seemingly gratuitous suffering we see all around us.

But the most common way believers have dealt with the problem of evil is to claim that God had to allow evil to achieve a greater good. Some have done this by arguing that human freedom is the cause of evil. Proponents of this view argue that God made us free. Because we are free, we are free to do evil as well as good. Even an omnipotent God could not make us free yet not free to do evil. Here is how Richard Swinburne states this argument:

> The free-will defense claims that it is a great good that humans have a certain sort of free will, which I will call free and responsible choice, but that, if they do, then necessarily there will be the natural possibility of moral evil. (By the "natural possibility" I mean that it will not be determined in advance whether or not the evil will occur.) A God who gives humans such free will necessarily brings about the possibility, and puts outside his own control, whether or not that evil occurs. It is not logically possible—that is, it would be self-contradictory to suppose—that God could give us such free will and yet ensure that we always use it in the right way. ... Free and responsible choice is ... the free will ... to make significant choices between good and evil, which make a big difference to the agent, to others, and to the world. ... It is good that the free choices of humans should include genuine responsibility for other humans, and that involves the opportunity to benefit or harm them.[31]

THINKING LIKE A PHILOSOPHER

1. Philosophers distinguish between "moral evils" and "natural evils." Give some examples of natural evils that have inflicted serious pain and suffering on you or those you love. What are some "moral evils" others have inflicted on you or those you love that caused you serious pain and suffering? Describe what you felt (i.e., your *feelings, emotions,* and *desires*) about the evils at the time. For example, did you feel anger, frustration, sadness, a thirst for revenge, a sense of betrayal? Were your feelings about the natural evils different from those you felt about the moral evils? If so, then explain why you think your feelings were different. If not, explain why they *should have been* different, and why you think they weren't.

2. According to Swinburne, "A God who gives humans free will necessarily brings about the possibility, and puts outside his own control, whether or not that evil occurs." From what you know about how your own free will works, do you agree with Swinburne? That is, when you choose to do something good, do you always feel the possibility of doing evil? Could you imagine yourself ever *feeling free* to choose what is good *without also feeling* you could choose evil?

However, critics of the "free will defense" claim there are several problems with the argument. First, and most importantly, the argument does not explain all kinds of evil. Philosophers usually distinguish "moral evils" from "natural evils." A moral evil is one that is intentionally produced by a human being or that a human being could have prevented but intentionally did not. Examples of moral evils would include the pain and suffering people cause by murders, beatings, stabbings, torturing, and so on. A natural evil, on the other hand, is one that is produced by natural processes and whose production does not require the intentional actions or omissions of humans. Examples include the pain and suffering caused by earthquakes, lightning strikes, hurricanes, tornadoes, and floods. It also includes the pain and suffering that animals and other nonhumans cause. The problem with the free will defense is that although it may give a satisfactory account of moral evils, it ignores natural evils. Humans do not produce

---

31   Richard Swinburne, *Is There a God?* (New York: Oxford University Press, 1996), 98–99.

natural evils. So, the argument that human freedom produces evil can only explain the source of moral evils. It cannot explain why natural evil exists. And so it leaves open the possibility that either God causes natural evils or God does not exist.

A house in the Lower Ninth Ward in New Orleans, Louisiana. This house was approximately one-quarter mile from the break in the levy. A river of water hit it. Stoops lay empty with no houses behind them. This photo was taken about nine months after Hurricane Katrina. Natural evils like this pose a problem for the "free will defense."

The second problem with the free will defense is that it is not clear that it even gives a good account of moral evils. Perhaps God does leave people free to do evil. But why would an all-powerful God let us inflict such horrendous evils on each other? After all, if God is all-powerful, God could have made us capable of inflicting only a limited amount of suffering on each other. We are vulnerable, easily injured creatures to begin with. Why not make us incapable of inflicting a tremendous amount of suffering on each other?

John Hick, whom we saw earlier in this chapter, provides a different explanation of why God might allow evil. In his book *Philosophy of Religion,* Hick suggests that a world without suffering would be unsatisfactory. Building on the views of the early Christians, Hick points to the idea that humans are made in the image of God. But, he suggests, they have not yet achieved the kind of likeness to God that Christ embodied. The world, then, "with all its rough edges," must be the stage on which this remaining part of the creative process takes place. And the world could not serve that purpose if God did not allow evil.

To support his claim, Hick asks us to imagine what the world would be like if God did not allow any evils in it. Imagine the world was a "paradise from which all ... pain and suffering" were excluded.[32] In such a world, people could not injure each other. A murderer's knife might turn to paper, or his bullets might melt into thin air. When thieves robbed a bank, the money they took would miraculously return to the bank. All "fraud, deceit, conspiracy and treason" would no longer have any harmful effects on society. People would no longer be injured in accidents. A child, for example, who fell from a tall building, would somehow float safely down to the ground. Reckless driving would never result in death or injury. People would not have to work because they would not suffer any harm if they refused to work. Most importantly, we would not have to be concerned about each other because none of us would ever face any "real needs or dangers."

 THINKING LIKE A PHILOSOPHER

Hick claims that a world without "pain, failure, sadness, frustration, and defeat" would not enable people to develop "the moral qualities of human personality." Good moral qualities are personal qualities like kindness, selflessness, generosity, maturity, etc. If you look back on your life, does your own experience tend to support or disprove Hick's claim? For example, in your own life do you think you acquired good "moral qualities" only when you had to suffer "pain, failure, sadness, frustration, and defeat"? Or do you think that suffering "pain, failure, etc." made it harder for you to develop good moral qualities? Can you think of ways in which you could, or actually have, acquired good moral qualities without having to go through "pain, failure, sadness, frustration, and defeat"? Do you think you have any specific good moral qualities that you could only have acquired by going through "pain, failure, sadness, frustration, and defeat"?

---

[32] Hick, *Philosophy of Religion,* 45–46.

PHILOSOPHY AND LIFE

God's Omniscience and Free Will

According to the traditional Western concept of God, God is **omniscient**—that is, God is all-knowing. But does God's knowledge leave any room for **free will?** Many people believe it does not. If God is all-knowing, they claim, then humans cannot be free. Here is how they argue:

1. Suppose God is all-knowing.

2. If God is all-knowing, then God knows what I will do in the future.

3. God cannot be wrong, so if God knows what I will do in the future, then it has to happen.

4. So what I will do in the future has to happen.

5. But if what I will do in the future has to happen, then I am not free to do anything else.

6. So I am not free—I am not able to do anything other than what God now knows I will do.

But this conclusion is distressing to believers. For if our actions are not free, then we cannot be held responsible for them. That is, I cannot be blamed for doing something if I was not able to do anything else. But if we can't be blamed for anything we do, then what of traditional doctrines of heaven and hell? How can we be punished for something if we couldn't do anything else? How can

we "repent" if we never had the ability to avoid any sinful action? How can I be blamed for what I had no power to change?

To avoid these conclusions, believers have rejected one or more of the premises of the preceding argument. Some reject point 1 and say God is not all-knowing—his knowledge is limited. Others reject point 2 and say God does not know now what I will do in the future because I have not yet decided what I will do and God leaves me free to decide what I will do. Others reject point 3 and say that God can be wrong because God is a fallible God. But, obviously, none of these options is very attractive to the believer.

QUESTIONS

1. If you are a believer, do you agree with the preceding argument? If you don't agree with it, which premise do you think you should reject?

2. Suppose that instead of "God," the preceding argument was about a supercomputer that knew everything that would happen in the future and was infallible. Assuming such a supercomputer is possible, would the argument still work?

How would this kind of world work? Hick suggests that nature would no longer operate through general laws we must learn and respect if we want to avoid pain and death. Instead, nature would work through "special providences." Gravity, for example, would usually operate, but would be suspended when allowing it to operate would end in someone being injured. Objects would sometimes be hard and solid, but would become soft when necessary to avoid an injury. Science would become useless since the world would no longer operate by fixed unchanging laws. Our lives would become like a kind of aimless dream in which "we would float and drift at ease."

In such a "hedonistic paradise," Hick claims, our ethical concepts "would have no meaning." If doing wrong, for example, involves harming someone, then there could be no wrongdoing in such a world. Nor could any actions be right as distinct from wrong. A moral virtue like courage would have no point in a world in which there are no dangers. Generosity and kindness would likewise be pointless since no one would have unmet needs or require the help of others. Prudence also would not be possible in a world without a stable environment.

A world without evil, then, might promote pleasure. But it would not enable people to develop "the moral qualities of human personality." In that respect, such a world, Hicks claims, would be the worst of all possible worlds. If our world is to be one in which we can become morally good people, then, it must be a world very much like the world in which we actually live. That is, it must operate by regular laws. It must, Hick concludes, be a world with real dangers, one in which people have problems and must overcome obstacles. It must be a world in which pain, failure, sadness, frustration, and defeat are all real possibilities. In short, it must be a world with some evils. And if it did not contain the evils our world contains, then it would have to contain others instead.

Yet regardless of the "theodicies" that people like Hicks and others have attempted, evil remains a large obstacle to belief in God. Persons of faith may be indifferent to evil as a problem because they are willing to say they can't begin to fathom God's mystery.

Not so, however, for the atheist. For the atheist, the problem of evil is a plain and unanswerable reason for concluding that God does not exist. Yet many people charge atheism with ignoring the persistent belief in a force superior to humankind. Belief in that force gives many hope, confidence, faith, and love in the face of troubles that may seem too heavy to carry. To strip them of belief may leave them ill equipped to cope with life and, possibly, morally bankrupt. But such sentiments hardly provide evidence that the atheist is wrong.

Finally, consider this observation about atheism, which is more of an insight than a criticism. Ernest Nagel, the self-proclaimed atheist we met earlier, said atheism involves a "commitment." It involves a commitment in much the same way that theism or monotheism does. In other words, empirically minded atheists erect their position as much on a commitment of faith as those who hold religious positions. All the characteristics of atheism that Nagel cites are founded as much on a categorical commitment as are the characteristics of the religionist. The commitments obviously differ. The religionist's commitment is to remaining open to the possibility of a nonempirical access to a spiritual reality. The atheist's commitment is to empiricism as a method of knowing a material world. But by what criterion could we judge that the empiricist-atheistic commitment is more sound than the theistic commitment?

Agnosticism

Having studied the arguments for and against the existence of God, many thinkers claim that neither side is convincing. As a result, they say they just don't know whether God exists—a position known as **agnosticism**.

The nineteenth-century English scientist Thomas Huxley was a well-known agnostic. For Huxley, agnosticism is based on the principle that "it is wrong for a man to say that he is certain of the objective truth of any proposition unless he can produce evidence which logically justifies that certainty."[33] Huxley believed the arguments for and against God's existence were both inconclusive. So he suspended **judgment**, about the existence of God, just as he did about ultimates such as matter and mind. As Huxley put it:

> We have not the slightest objection to believe anything you like, if you will give us good grounds for belief; but, if you cannot, we must respectfully refuse, even if that refusal

[33] Quoted in *Encounter: An Introduction to Philosophy*, ed. Ramona Cormier, Ewing Chinn, and Richard Lineback, 227.

should wreck morality and insure our damnation several times over. We are quite content to leave the decision to the future. The course of the past has impressed us with the firm conviction that no good ever comes of falsehood, and we feel warranted in refusing even to experiment in that direction.[34]

Why We Believe: Freud's View. But if it is unclear whether God exists, how can the agnostic explain why so many of us continue to believe? In his short work *The Future of an Illusion,* Sigmund Freud suggested an influential answer to that question. Freud, who was the founder of modern psychoanalysis, was hostile to religious belief. He suggested that our belief in God is an "illusion" that has its origins in "infantile" needs. People have no good reason to believe in God, he claimed. Yet people continue to believe because they have an "infantile" need to feel someone is protecting and watching over them. This need leads them to believe that there is a being that watches out for them. And they imagine that this being is like the father who looked after them when they were children. In a later work, *New Introductory Lectures in Psychoanalysis,* Freud summarized his view in the following words:

THINKING LIKE A PHILOSOPHER

Freud claims that the memory of one's father and one's ongoing need for protection are the reason why a person believes in God, and he seems to think this is "infantile" and not a good thing. Do you believe in God? If you do, then think about how you think and feel about God; do you see and turn to God primarily as a source of protection and comfort? Would that be infantile? Would it be a bad thing? Why? If you do not believe in God, then based on the people you've known who believe in God, would you say that they seemed to see God mainly as a source of protection and comfort? Do you see that as bad? Why?

✓ QUICK REVIEW
Freud claimed that people believe because they have an "infantile" need to believe someone like a "father" is still watching over them.

The God-Creator is openly called Father. Psychoanalysis has concluded that he really is the father, clothed in the grandeur in which he first appeared to the small child. The religious man's picture of the creation of the universe is the same as his picture of his own creation.... He therefore looks back on the memory-image of the overrated father of his childhood, exalts it into a Deity, and brings it into the present and into reality. The emotional strength of this memory-image and the lasting nature of his need for protection are the two supports of his belief in God.[35]

ANALYZING THE READING

Freud suggests that your memory of how your father protected you when you were a child, and your ongoing need for protection, lead people to imagine a God exists who still takes care of you. Freud gives no evidence or argument for this suggestion, except that in Christianity God is called "Father." What kind of evidence could prove or establish that Freud is right? What kind could prove that he is wrong?

Freud's suggestion is intriguing. And many people today accept it. But is it true? Is there any way of proving that it is true? Perhaps not. Freud offers even less in the way of proof than traditional believers and atheists have offered for their beliefs about God. Moreover, even if Freud is correct, and our belief in God originates in "infantile" needs, does this show that belief in God is an "illusion"?

---

[34]   Thomas H. Huxley, "Agnosticism and Christianity" (1889), 309-365, in *Collected Essays,* vol. 5, *Science and Christian Tradition* (New York: D. Appleton and Company, 1902), 318.

[35]   From Sigmund Freud, *New Introductory Lectures in Psychoanalysis* (New York: W. W. Norton & Company, 1965).

thinking critically • Formal and Informal Fallacies

No other subject matter raises the intense kinds of arguments that discussions of religion and God do. Unfortunately, these discussions are often rife with fallacies, that is, with bad arguments, and Freud's argument may perhaps be an example. It will be useful to look at what formal and informal fallacies are, and see how they can affect discussions of religion and God.

A fallacy is a defective argument, a case of bad or faulty reasoning. Fallacies present inadequate evidence, or, more often, no evidence at all, for the conclusion they are supposed to support. They are, in short, bad arguments, sometimes so bad that they hardly deserve to be called arguments at all. Nevertheless, we are often taken in by fallacies, and to avoid this it will help if you know what they are. There are two broad groups of fallacies: formal fallacies and informal fallacies.

Formal fallacies are arguments that are offered as sound logical arguments when in fact they have an invalid form. We have already seen some formal fallacies and here it is enough to remind ourselves of the two most common formal fallacies, the fallacy of *denying the antecedent* and the fallacy of *affirming the consequent*:

If p, then q	If p, then q
Not-p	q
So Not-q	So p

Arguments with either of these forms are always bad arguments. Nevertheless, we frequently make such fallacious arguments, and just as frequently they fool us. Here is an example of the fallacy of denying the antecedent: "If you could prove God exists, then religion would be justified, but you can't prove God exists, so religion is not justified." And here is an example of affirming the consequent: "If God is good, then he would create a world in which we could enjoy ourselves; but God has created a world in which we can enjoy ourselves, so God must be good." Both of these are invalid, and so bad arguments, although to some people—maybe even to you—they look like good ones. Don't be fooled!

While formal fallacies are bad arguments because they have an invalid form, *informal fallacies* are bad arguments because of their content, that is, because the content of the claims they make do not provide real support for their conclusions. There are many kinds of informal fallacies, but here are some of the most important ones:

Appeal to emotion. This common fallacy is the attempt to establish a claim not by providing good reasons for the claim but by appealing to the passions or prejudices of the audience. Here's an example: "If you don't accept that God exists, you're going to Hell!" Emotional appeals may persuade people to accept a claim, but they do not provide any evidence that the claim is true.

Inappropriate appeal to authority. Another common fallacy is the attempt to establish a conclusion by appealing to an "authority" who is not an expert on the subject of the claim, or who has a motive to mislead, or who is known to be unreliable, or whose claim is highly improbable on its face. A few years ago, for example, a journalist working for the tabloid *Weekly World News* wrote that "scientists have determined" that heaven is "a mind-boggling 3-billion light years from earth" because the Hubble telescope sighted "a shining white city" suspended in space "roughly 3 billion light-years away." Relying on the tabloid's journalist to prove a claim about heaven's location would be an inappropriate appeal to authority.

Ad hominem argument. This is an argument that attacks the person making an argument instead of addressing the argument itself. I use an *ad hominem* argument, for example, when someone argues that God does not exist and I reject his argument because "He's an evil person." The moral character of the person who makes a claim is irrelevant to whether the claim is true or false.

Argument from ignorance. This kind of argument claims that because there is no evidence that something is false, it must be true. For example, I am arguing from ignorance if

QUICK REVIEW
Fallacies are defective arguments that present inadequate evidence or no evidence at all for their conclusions. Formal fallacies are arguments with an invalid form; informal fallacies are arguments that are bad because of their content. The most common formal fallacies are *denying the consequent* and *affirming the antecedent*. Common informal fallacies include *appeal to emotion, inappropriate appeal to authority, ad hominem, argument from ignorance, begging the question, hasty generalization, biased statistics, genetic fallacy, forgetful induction,* and *post hoc ergo propter hoc*.

I say that because you cannot prove that God does not exist, God must exist. But the lack of evidence against a claim is not in itself evidence in favor of a claim.

Begging the question. This fallacy is also called a circular argument. It is an argument in which the premises or reasons used to prove a conclusion already assume that the conclusion is true. For example, I am begging the question if I argue, "What the bible says must be true because the bible says it is the word of God."

Hasty generalization. This type of fallacy occurs when an inductive generalization is not based on a sufficiently large sample. For example: "All of my friends who are religious are really happy people, so all religious people must be really happy persons." The few religious people who happen to be my friends do not form a sufficiently large sample to base on it a conclusion about millions of others.

Biased statistics. An inductive generalization makes this fallacy when it relies on a sample that's not representative. When surveys dealing with religious issues poll people from only one social class or from only one region of the United States and draw conclusions about everyone in the United States, they generally make the fallacy of biased statistics.

Genetic fallacy. This fallacy occurs when a person argues that the causal origin of a belief or claim is evidence that it is false or that it is true. For example, the geneticist Dean Hammer claimed in his book, *The God Gene: How Faith Is Hardwired into Our Genes,* that a human gene called $VMAT_2$ causes spiritual feelings including feelings of the presence of God. Some people then argued that genes must cause us to believe in God, so the belief that God exists must be false. But this argument is fallacious since even if our genes cause our belief in God, the belief might still be true, since whether a belief is true does not depend on where the belief came from. The *cause* of a belief is not *evidence* for or against the truth of the belief.

Forgetful induction. This is the fallacy of failing to take into account all the evidence that might affect one's conclusion and, in particular, ignoring evidence that would disprove one's conclusion or shed doubt on one's conclusion. A person, for example, might argue that astrology is a true theory on the basis of astrology predictions that turned out to be correct, while ignoring astrology's many predictions of things that didn't happen.

Post hoc ergo propter hoc. This Latin phrase, which means "after it, therefore caused by it," refers to the fallacy of arguing that since a first event occurred *before* a second one, the first must have *caused* the second. This is also sometimes called the fallacy of *false cause.* An example of a *post hoc ergo propter hoc* fallacious argument is when a person claims that since she prayed before she recovered from an illness, her prayer must have caused her recovery.

There are many kinds of fallacies, then, and you should be able to recognize and point them out when people try to use them to get you to accept their claims. Any of them has the power to ensnare a person who is not careful. In fact, as we mentioned earlier, Freud's argument that belief in God is an "illusion" might be a fallacy. But we leave it to you to determine whether his argument or other arguments in this chapter are fallacies.

Why We Believe: Kant's View. The philosopher Immanuel Kant proposed an explanation of why we believe in God even though we cannot prove that God exists. Unlike Freud, Kant did not conclude that belief in God is "an illusion." Kant proceeded by noting that the world is often unjust. Morally good people often suffer unhappiness, while evil people often prosper. But the fact that the good sometimes suffer while the evil sometimes prosper should not lead us to reject God. On the contrary, Kant argued, the fact that this world is unjust should lead us to believe in God. For the fact that the world is unjust obligates us to pursue a world that is just. And this obligation in turn requires we believe in a God who alone can bring about a perfectly just world:

QUICK REVIEW
Kant argued that our morality forces us to believe in the possibility of a just world where evil is punished and good is rewarded, and this is possible only if there is a God and an afterlife. So, we have to believe in a God and an afterlife.

We ought to strive to bring about the supreme good [perfect justice]. Because we ought to bring about this supreme good, it must be possible for it to exist. ... But the supreme good is possible in the world only if there exists a Supreme Being who can bring about a world in which happiness is correlated with moral goodness. Now a being that is capable of bringing about a just world as the moral law requires, is an intelligence (a rational being). And a being that acts according to the requirements of the moral law, has a will. Therefore, the supreme creator of the world, whose existence must be supposed if the *sumum bonum* is possible, is a Being who causes the world by His intelligence and will ... that is, God.[36]

Kant is arguing that we feel an obligation to work for a world in which justice prevails. This would be a world in which moral goodness is rewarded with happiness and evil with punishment. But, claims Kant, if we have an obligation to do something, then it must be possible for us to do it. For we cannot have a moral obligation to do something that is impossible. So, because we have an obligation to work for a world in which justice prevails, we must believe it is possible for such a world to exist. In other words, we must believe that it is possible for a world to exist in which good people are happy and evil people are not. Such a world is possible only if there is a God who will punish the evil and reward the good, perhaps in some afterlife. So, since our obligation to pursue a just world forces us to believe a just world is possible, we must believe that there exists a God who can make such a world possible.

Kant's suggestion, like Freud's, is an intriguing response to our inability to either prove or disprove that God exists. It is an alternative to agnosticism. But, again, we must ask this: Is it reasonable? Unlike Freud, as we noted, Kant does not claim that belief in God is an illusion. Kant claims only that even if God's existence cannot be

THINKING LIKE A PHILOSOPHER

1. According to Kant, the realization that the world is unjust should make us feel an obligation to make it more just. Do you think that Kant's claim applies to you? For example, think about the times that you have seen that a person or group was being treated unjustly. Perhaps something was being taken from them unjustly, or perhaps they were being unjustly oppressed, or maybe someone was violating their rights. Has seeing or learning that such injustices were being inflicted on others made you feel you should do something about it? For example, does seeing an injustice make you angry or upset at those who are injuring others unjustly, so that if you could, you would do something to them or do something to help their victims?

2. Kant also claims that your desire for justice extends to an afterlife. That is, Kant claims that when you see injustice, your desire for justice makes you think that unjust people *certainly must* get what they deserve in an afterlife. Do you think Kant is right, at least as far as your own feelings go?

proved, and even if evil in the world casts doubt on God's existence, we are still forced to believe that God exists. We are forced to believe in God—that is, if we feel that we have an obligation to make this a better, more just world. However, Kant's argument leaves open the question of whether really God exists. Although we must *believe* that God exists, we cannot *know* that God exists.

Perhaps, then, neither the existence or nonexistence of a theistic God can be proved. But lack of certain evidence does not make the question any less important. Even if we feel we lack sufficient evidence, we still must live our lives as if we believe or disbelieve. If we disbelieve, we will not join a church, pray, or worship. We will not feel the presence of God as we walk through a hushed forest of tall trees. If we believe, however, we will not only do these things, but we will also see ourselves as having a spiritual dimension, perhaps one that survives after death. In short, if we lack belief, then we will live our lives in one way, and if we believe, we will live in another way. The question is this: Is it possible to be an agnostic in practice? In the end, mustn't the agnostic choose to live either as a believer or as a nonbeliever?

---

[36] Immanuel Kant, *Critique of Practical Reason*, trans. T. K. Abbot (London: Longmans Green, 1927), pt. 1, bk. 2, ch. 2, para. 5, pp. 220–222.

PHILOSOPHY AT THE MOVIES

Watch *Shadowlands* (1993), the true story of C. S. Lewis, a teacher at Oxford who meets, befriends, and eventually marries Joy Gresham, an American woman who then discovers she has terminal cancer and whom Lewis comes to love deeply before she dies. Early in the film, how does C. S. Lewis view the problem of evil? What are his views on the problem of evil toward the end of the film? Is Lewis at any point in the film an agnostic? Does he at any point consider atheism?

4.4 Traditional Religious Belief and Experience

Religious Belief

Many believers agree that the arguments for and against the existence of God are inconclusive. Yet this hardly matters to them because their belief does not depend on rational proofs. Instead, they believe because belief seems to cohere—to fit—with their life experience and who they are. In short, they do not have conclusive proof of their beliefs, but they choose to believe "for reasons of the heart."

"The Will to Believe"

Is it legitimate to base belief on a personal decision made with the heart instead of the head? Are we justified in choosing to believe without irrefutable reasons for believing? In a classic address titled "The Will to Believe," the American pragmatist William James confronted these issues. (After he gave the speech he said he should have titled it "The Right to Believe.") The thrust of James' views is captured in the following excerpt from "The Will to Believe":

MindTap To read more from James' *The Will to Believe, and Other Essays in Popular Philosophy*, click the link in the MindTap Reader or go to the Questia Readings folder in MindTap.

Let us give the name of hypothesis to anything that may be proposed to our belief. … Next, let us call the decision between two hypotheses an option. Options may be of several kinds. They may be: (1) living or dead; (2) forced or avoidable; (3) momentous or trivial; and for our purpose we may call an option a genuine option when it is of the forced, living, and momentous kind:

1. A living option is one in which both hypotheses are live ones. If I say to you: "Be a theosophist or be a Mohammedan," it is probably a dead option, because for you neither hypothesis is likely to be alive. But if I say: "Be an agnostic or be Christian," it is otherwise: trained as you are, each hypothesis makes some appeal, however small, to your belief.

2. Next, if I say to you: "Choose between going out with your umbrella or without it," I do not offer you a genuine option, for it is not forced. You can easily avoid it by not going out at all. … But if I say, "Either accept this truth or go without it," I put on you a forced option, for there is no standing place outside of the alternatives. Every dilemma based on a complete logical disjunction, with no possibility of not choosing, is an option of this forced kind.

3. Finally, if I were [the arctic explorer] Dr. Nansen and proposed to you to join my North Pole expedition, your option would be momentous; for this would probably be your only similar opportunity, and your choice now would either exclude you from the North Pole sort of immortality altogether or put at least the chance of it into your hands. … [On the other hand,] an option is trivial when the opportunity is not unique, when the stake is insignificant, or when the decision is reversible if it later proves unwise. …

QUICK REVIEW
James held that when an option is a "genuine"—a "living, momentous, and forced"—option that "by its nature cannot be decided on intellectual grounds," it is legitimate (not wrong) to choose on the basis of our "passional nature," even without sufficient evidence in support of the option we choose.

The thesis I defend is, briefly stated, this: Our passional nature not only lawfully may, but must, decide an option between propositions, whenever it is a genuine option that cannot by its nature be decided on intellectual grounds; for to say, under such circumstances, "Do not decide, but leave the question open," is itself a passional decision,—just like deciding yes or no,—and is attended with the same risk of losing the truth.

Wherever the option between losing truth and gaining it is not momentous, we can throw the chance of gaining truth away, and at any rate save ourselves from any chance of believing falsehood, by not making up our minds at all till objective evidence has come. In scientific questions, this is almost always the case; and even in human affairs in general, the need of acting is seldom so urgent that a false belief to act on is better than no belief at all. . . .

[But] moral questions immediately present themselves as questions whose solution cannot wait for sensible proof. A moral question is a question not of what sensibly exists, but of what is good, or would be good if it did exist. . . .

Turn now from these wide [moral] questions of good, to a certain class of questions of fact, questions concerning personal relations, states of mind between one man and another. Do you like me or not?—for example. Whether you do or not depends, in countless instances, on whether I meet you half-way, am willing to assume that you must like me, and show you trust and expectation. The previous faith on my part in your liking's existence is in such cases what makes your liking come. But if I stand aloof, and refuse to budge an inch until I have objective evidence, until you shall have done something apt, . . . ten to one your liking never comes. . . .

But now, it will be said, these are all childish human cases, and have nothing to do with great cosmic matters, like the question of religious faith. Let us then pass on to that.

We see, first that religion offers itself as a momentous option. We are supposed to gain, even now, by our belief, and to lose by our nonbelief, a certain vital good. Secondly, religion is a forced option, so far as that good goes. We cannot escape the issue by remaining skeptical and waiting for more light, because, although we do avoid error in that way if religion be untrue, we lose the good, if it be true, just as certainly as if we positively chose to disbelieve. . . .

If religion be true and the evidence for it be still insufficient, I do not wish, by putting your extinguisher upon my nature (which feels to me as if it had after all some business in this matter), to forfeit my sole chance in life of getting upon the winning side,—that chance depending, of course, on my willingness to run the risk of acting as if my passional need of taking the world religiously might be prophetic and right. All this is on the supposition that it [i.e., being religious], really may be prophetic and right, and that, even to us who are discussing the matter, religion is a live hypothesis which may be true.

In concreto, the freedom to believe can only cover living options which the intellect of the individual cannot by itself resolve; and living options never seem absurdities to him who has them to consider. When I look at the religious question as it really puts itself to concrete men, and when I think of all the possibilities which both practically and theoretically it involves, then this command [that we must wait until that we shall put a stopper on our heart, instincts, and courage, and wait—acting of course meanwhile more or less as if religion were not true till doomsday, or till such time as our intellect and senses working together may have raked in evidence enough—this command, I say, seems to me the queerest idol ever manufactured in the philosophic cave.[37]

 THINKING LIKE A PHILOSOPHER

James does not believe that only religious decisions have the four features of being living, forced, momentous, and incapable of being decided on intellectual grounds. He claims that moral decisions and decisions about whether to trust in a personal relationship also have these four features. Describe some incidents from your own life when you faced decisions that were living, forced, momentous, and incapable of being decided on intellectual grounds. Did you use your "passional nature" to make these decisions? Describe how you went about making the decisions you actually made.

37   William James, *The Will to Believe, and Other Essays in Popular Philosophy* (New York: Longmans, Green and Co., 1898), 2–4, 11.

James is claiming that it is sometimes rationally and morally justified to believe something without adequate intellectual evidence for the belief. It is justified when we face a "momentous, living, and forced option" where to "not decide ... is itself a decision" and the option "cannot by its nature be decided on intellectual grounds." It is legitimate to rely on "our passional nature" to decide such options even without sufficient intellectual evidence for either option. Without understanding his terms as James understands them, we can easily misconstrue what he is saying.

First, consider James' statement that "we may call an option a genuine option when it is of the forced, living, and momentous kind." What does this mean? By the word *option* James means a choice among beliefs or "hypotheses" that may be proposed to us, such as whether or not to believe in God. Some options are what James calls "genuine" options—that is, they are choices we have to make and they will affect our lives in a significant way. James explains that "genuine" options are "living, forced, and momentous." An option is *living* when it proposes a belief that we can take seriously. For example, choosing whether to believe in the ancient Greek gods Zeus, Hera, or Apollo is not a living option for us, although it was for the ancient Greeks. Second, an option is *forced* when it's a choice you cannot escape by deciding not to choose. For example, if someone proposes, "Either vote for me or vote for my opponent," you can avoid making a decision by not voting at all. On the other hand, if someone says, "Either come follow me or don't," you are forced to make a choice. Even choosing not to choose would be making a choice: the choice not to follow. Finally, an option is *momentous* when the opportunity is unique, the stakes are important, and the decision is irreversible. If a depressed man, for example, is choosing whether or not to leap over a cliff to his death, his option is momentous.

Next, consider James' view that we are sometimes faced with an option "that cannot by its nature be decided on intellectual grounds." By this, he means that the intellectual evidence for both alternatives is and must be inadequate, or the intellectual reasons for both alternatives are balanced. That is, the reasons in favor of one option are as good or as bad as the reasons favoring the other option. For example, the question whether you will still be alive ten years from now is one that "cannot by its nature be decided on intellectual grounds."

According to James, we may rationally and morally rely on our "passional nature" to decide an option that is living, forced, momentous, and cannot be decided on intellectual grounds. What is our "passional nature"? For James, our "passional nature" consists of our nonintellectual interests, emotions, desires, hopes, fears, commitments, and so forth. They are the nonintellectual part of who we are. So, James is saying that when a "genuine" option can't be decided on intellectual grounds, it is legitimate to decide it by relying on our emotions, desires, hopes, and so on.

James does not mean that one should simply rely on our emotions to believe in anything for which there is no good evidence. When options are not living, forced, and momentous, James claims we should not make up our minds until all the evidence is in. Otherwise we risk falling into needless error. Most scientific questions and human issues we are likely to face, he points out, are not genuine options and we should not rely on our passional nature to decide them. In other words, in most real choices the need to act is not forced on us nor is the choice momentous. So if the evidence is lacking, we should wait for more evidence before making up our minds. We should rely on our "passional nature" only when facing "living, forced, and momentous" choices that "cannot be decided on intellectual grounds." In such cases, "as men who may be interested at least

ANALYZING THE READING

According to James, it is not wrong to rely on our passional nature to make decisions when the options are living, forced, momentous, and cannot by their nature be decided on intellectual grounds. Why does James claim it is legitimate to base decisions on our passional nature when they have these four features, but it is not legitimate when decisions lack one of these four features? Do you think James is right?

as much in positively gaining truth as in merely escaping dupery," we cannot sit back and wait to make our decision. We have to decide because waiting to decide is itself a decision. Only when choices of that kind arise are we intellectually and morally justified to rely on our interests, emotions, desires, and so forth. James believes that there are several areas of our lives where such choices inevitably arise. These include when we must make important moral decisions, or decide whether to trust in a personal relationship such as a love relationship or a friendship. And, of course, such choices are also inevitable when deciding questions of religious belief.

Granted, for some people religious belief is not a living option. But for most it is. To these people, James says that religious belief is also a momentous option. People stand to gain much by their belief and to lose much by their unbelief. The option of belief or unbelief is also a forced option. If people choose to wait to avoid error, they risk losing the chance of attaining the good that religious belief promises. If the ice cream stand closes while you are debating your choice, the result will be the same as if you had chosen to have no ice cream. And for many, religious belief is also an option "that cannot by its nature be decided on intellectual grounds." James himself argues that the intellectual evidence in favor of belief balances the evidence against it. So there is no intellectual evidence that is absolutely persuasive on either side. Yet the decision whether to believe in God is living, momentous, and forced. So we not only can but *should* allow our "passional nature" to decide it.

Critics of James' View. James' view obviously rejects the claim that we should not believe unless we have sufficient and strong evidence in favor of belief. One critic of James' view, and, in fact, the person against whom he was arguing, is W. K. Clifford. In an earlier essay "The Ethics of Belief" Clifford asserted "it is wrong always, everywhere and for anyone, to believe anything upon insufficient evidence." Clifford argued that our beliefs affect other people. If we allow ourselves to believe things without sufficient evidence, he argued, we may harm others directly. But we will also harm society at large by making it "credulous."

A ship owner was about to send to sea an emigrant-ship. He knew she was old, and not over well built at the first; that she had seen many seas … and often had needed repairs. Doubts had been suggested to him that possibly she was not seaworthy. These doubts preyed upon his mind; … He thought that perhaps he ought to have her thoroughly overhauled and refitted, even though this should put him at great expense. Before the ship sailed, however, he succeeded in overcoming these melancholy reflections. He said to himself that she had gone safely through so many voyages and weathered so many storms that it was idle to suppose she would not come safely home from this trip also. He would put his trust in Providence, which could hardly fail to protect all these unhappy families that were leaving their fatherland to seek for better times elsewhere. … In such ways he acquired a sincere and comfortable conviction that his vessel was thoroughly safe and seaworthy; he watched her departure with a light heart, and benevolent wishes for the success of the exiles in their strange new home that was to be; and he got his insurance money when she went down in mid-ocean and told no tales.

What shall we say of him? Surely this, that he was guilty of the death of those men. It is admitted that he did sincerely believe in the soundness of his ship; but the sincerity of his conviction can in no wise help him, because he had no right to believe on such evidence as was before him. … The reason of this judgment is not far to seek: it is that … the belief held by one man

ANALYZING THE READING

1. Clifford suggests the example of a ship owner who without sufficient evidence decides that his ship is seaworthy when it is not. Is this example relevant to the question whether we should decide a religious question without sufficient evidence? Why or why not?

2. Clifford believes that credulity is something that spreads. That is, he claims that if I am credulous about one thing, then I will become credulous about other things. And he claims that if one person in society is credulous, then others in society will become credulous. Is Clifford right about both of these claims?

was of great importance to other men. But … no belief held by one man, however seemingly trivial the belief, and however obscure the believer, is ever actually insignificant or without its effect on the fate of mankind, we have no choice but to extend our judgment to all cases of belief whatever.

Belief, … is ours not for ourselves but for humanity. … If I let myself believe anything on insufficient evidence, there may be no great harm done by the mere belief; it may be true after all, or I may never have occasion to exhibit it in outward acts. But I cannot help doing this great wrong towards Man, that I make myself credulous. [In addition] the danger to society is not merely that it should believe wrong things, though that is great enough; but that it should become credulous, and lose the habit of testing things and inquiring into them …

The harm which is done by credulity in a man is not confined to the fostering of a credulous character in others, and consequent support of false beliefs. Habitual want of care about what I believe leads to habitual want of care in others about the truth. … By such a course I shall surround myself with a thick atmosphere of falsehood and fraud, and in that I must live. To sum up: it is wrong always, everywhere, and for anyone, to believe anything upon insufficient evidence.[38]

QUICK REVIEW

Clifford and other critics of James claim that it is always wrong to believe without sufficient evidence and to rely on our passional nature when something cannot be decided on intellectual grounds. James responds that their claim itself has no sufficient evidence, so critics like Clifford must rely on their passional nature to accept their claim. So Clifford and his critics implicitly accept James' view that it is sometimes legitimate to believe without sufficient evidence.

Clifford's conclusion was unequivocal. It is always wrong to believe without sufficient evidence. And he meant this in a moral sense: it is morally wrong for a person to believe without sufficient evidence. For by believing without evidence I may not only harm others, I will also wrong myself by making myself credulous, and wrong society by making those around me both credulous and careless with the truth.

James responded to Clifford by arguing that questions of belief give us two options. We can choose to protect ourselves from believing something false by withholding our belief if the evidence is insufficient. Or we can choose to protect ourselves from missing out on the truth by sometimes choosing to believe even if the evidence is insufficient. Which is the better option? James wrote:

We may regard the chase for truth as paramount, and the avoidance of error as secondary; or we may, on the other hand, treat the avoidance of error as more imperative, and let truth take its chance. Clifford, in the instructive passage which I have quoted, exhorts us to the latter course. Believe nothing, he tells us, keep your mind in suspense forever, rather than by closing it on insufficient evidence incur the awful risk of believing lies. You, on the other hand, may think that the risk of being in error is a very small matter when compared with the blessings of real knowledge, and be ready to be duped many times in your investigation rather than postpone indefinitely the chance of guessing true. I myself find it impossible to go with Clifford. We must remember that these feelings of our duty about either truth or error are in any case only expressions of our passional life. Biologically considered, our minds are as ready to grind out falsehood as veracity, and he who says, "Better go without belief forever than believe a lie!" merely shows his own preponderant private horror of becoming a dupe. He may be critical of many of his desires and fears, but this fear he slavishly obeys. He can not imagine any one questioning its binding force. For my own part, I have also a horror of being duped; but I can believe that worse things than being duped may happen to a man in this world: so Clifford's exhortation has to my ears a thoroughly fantastic sound. It is like a general informing his soldiers that it is better to keep out of battle forever than to risk a single wound. Not so are victories either over enemies or over nature gained.[39]

ANALYZING THE READING

Read over the selections by Clifford and James' response to Clifford. Do you think James really answered Clifford? That is, do you think James' reply showed that Clifford was wrong to conclude "it is wrong always, everywhere, and for anyone, to believe anything upon insufficient evidence"? Or was Clifford's real argument left standing? Who is right, James or Clifford?

[38]   William K. Clifford, "The Ethics of Belief," *Contemporary Review*, vol. 29 (December 1876–May 1877), 289–309; excerpts from 289, 290, 292, 294, 295.
[39]   James, *The Will to Believe*, 18–19.

James' point here is that when faced with a momentous, living, and forced option to believe, there is a cost to be paid if we choose never to believe without sufficient evidence. The cost is that by never believing without sufficient evidence, we may miss out on the truth. On the other hand, there is also a cost to be paid if we choose to believe sometimes without sufficient evidence when faced with such momentous, living, and forced options. The cost is that the policy to believe sometimes without sufficient evidence may lead us to believe a falsehood. Which policy should we adopt? In the end, James subtly implies, the choice between these policies is itself a "genuine option" that cannot be decided on intellectual grounds. So we have to choose between these two policies on the basis of our passional nature! James points out that even Clifford had to choose on the basis of his own passional nature. He chose to withhold belief because of his "horror" of falling into error, a "fear he slavishly obeys." So he, too, chose on the basis of emotion. We are in the same boat insofar as we, too, must choose between these two policies on the basis of our passional nature.

James' argument is relevant not only for those who believe in a personal God. It is also relevant for those whose experience suggests the world has a spiritual dimension, but not necessarily a Supreme Being. James' view of the role of feeling and emotion in religious belief also provides a basis for belief in a sacred dimension based on personal experience. Just what constitutes a personal experience of the sacred is a complex question, of course. But individuals often appeal to personal experience as their justification for religious belief. We turn now to discuss personal experience as the ground of belief.

Personal Experience of the Divine

Many believers, maybe most, do not need any rational proof for their religious belief. Many people say they believe in God because they have experienced God or a religious dimension of reality. They may describe an experience, in fact, that was deeper and more real than their sensory experiences.

For many people, such religious experiences are simply quiet moments in which they have "felt" a divine presence. Consider this report of a 17-year-old boy:

> Sometimes as I go to church, I sit down, join in the service, and before I go out I feel as if God was with me, right side of me, singing and reading the Psalms with me. . . . And then again I feel as if I could sit beside him, and put my arms around him, kiss him, etc. When I am taking Holy Communion at the altar, I try to get with him and generally feel his presence.[40]

Other people claim to have had a more vivid direct experience of God or of a divinity. Here is how St. Teresa described one of her religious experiences:

> One day when I was at prayer . . . I saw Christ at my side—or, to put it better, I was conscious of Him, for I saw nothing with the eyes of the body or the eyes of the soul. He seemed quite close to me and I saw that it was He. As I thought, He was speaking to me. Being completely ignorant that such visions were possible, I was very much afraid at first, and could do nothing but weep, though as soon as He spoke His first word of assurance to me, I regained my usual calm and became cheerful and free from fear. All the time Jesus Christ seemed to be at my side.[41]

> **QUICK REVIEW**
> Many believe in God not on the basis of rational proofs but because of a direct personal experience of the divine.

---

[40] William James, *The Variety of Religious Experience* (New York: The Modern Library, 1936), 71.

[41] St. Teresa of Avila, *The Life of St. Teresa of Avila by Herself*, quoted in Davis, op. cit., 124.

And here is how the Old Testament prophet Isaiah described his encounter with God:

> In the year that King Ussiah died, I saw the Lord sitting on a throne, high and lofty … Seraphs were in attendance above him; each had six wings; with two they covered their faces, and with two they covered their feet, and with two they flew. And one called to another and said: "Holy, Holy, Holy is the Lord of hosts; the whole earth is full of his glory" … And I said: "Woe is me! I am lost, for I am a man of unclean lips, and I live among a people of unclean lips; yet my eyes have seen the King, the Lord of Hosts.[42]

What is the nature of such experiences? In his *Varieties of Religious Experience,* James suggests that such experiences seem to usually have two characteristics. One is *ineffability*—that is, the experience cannot be adequately described in words. The other is a noetic quality—that is, to the individual the experience is a source of knowledge, often illuminations full of meaning, truth, and importance.

Rudolf Otto is a German theologian who wrote *The Idea of the Holy,* a classic study of religious experience. He used the term "numinous experience" to describe an experience in which the power or presence of a divinity or supernatural reality was felt or perceived. Based on his study of many such experiences, Otto claimed that a numinous experience had several characteristic qualities. First, the experience is accompanied by a kind of amazement, fear, even terror, at the power and awesome nature of what is being experienced. Second, what is experienced attracts, fascinates, and draws one in with an almost irresistible force. Third, what is experienced is wholly unlike anything that one has encountered before. Fourth, the person having the numinous experience feels unworthy and insignificant in the presence of a sacred reality. Fifth, the experience is suffused with a sense of mystery. And sixth, the experience is accompanied by bliss, a feeling of fulfillment, of contentment and satisfaction. Of course, not all of these qualities are present in all religious experiences of the divine, and in some cases they may be extremely attenuated. The characteristics Otto identifies, however, are widely thought to communicate well what a numinous experience is like.

The point, however, is that many people approach religion through such numinous experiences. Such experiences of God or of a supernatural dimension of reality convince them that God or a supernatural dimension of reality exists. But should such experiences be trusted? Is it rational to believe that God or a supernatural dimension of reality exists on the basis of such experiences? The philosopher Stephen T. Davis offers the following argument to support his claim that religious experiences can be a legitimate basis for belief in God:

THINKING LIKE A PHILOSOPHER

1. Have you, or someone you know well, ever had a "numinous" experience, perhaps one in which the five qualities Rudolf Otto mentions were extremely attenuated? If so, how would you describe the experience? Sometimes when people walk through a forest, watch a spectacular sunset, or climb to the top of a high mountain, they can be struck with awe at the beauty and majesty of what they see. Have you ever had such experiences? Would you call them numinous experiences? Read over the "report" of the 17-year-old boy quoted in the textbook. Have you ever had a similar experience? Would you call it a numinous experience?

2. Do you think it is possible to have a numinous experience yet not believe in God? Read over the vision of the Buddha described at the end of Chapter 1. The Buddha did not believe in God, although he did believe in an "ultimate reality." Did he have a numinous experience?

3. How would you distinguish a real from a false religious experience?

---

[42] Isaiah, 6: 1–4.

1. Throughout human history, and in very many human societies and cultures, people claim to have experiences of God or of some Godlike being.

2. The claim that those experiences are veridical is more probable than the claim that they are delusive.

3. Therefore, probably God or some Godlike being exists.[43]

The Ecstasy of Saint Teresa (close-up). Gian Lorenzo Bernini (1598–1680). Location: S. Maria della Vittoria, Rome, Italy.

© Scala/Art Resource, NY

Davis' first premise is clearly true and uncontroversial. The term *veridical* in the second premise of Davis' argument means "real" or "genuine." The second premise means, therefore, that when a person claims to have experienced God through a numinous experience, that person's claim is probably true. And if it is true that a person really experienced God, of course, it follows that God really exists.

But what can be said in favor of premise (2), that is, in support of the claim that numinous experiences are probably real experiences of God (or of a supernatural reality)? Davis claims that one reason for accepting (2) is the "principle of credulity" proposed by philosopher Richard Swinburne. Swinburne explains the principle of credulity in this way:

> I suggest that it is a principle of rationality that (in the absence of special considerations), if it seems (epistemically) to a subject that x is present, then probably x is present; what one seems to perceive is probably so. How things seem to be is good grounds for a belief about how things are. ... [Therefore] in the absence of special considerations, all religious experiences ought to be taken by their subjects as genuine, and hence as substantial grounds for belief in the existence of their apparent object—God, or Mary, or Ultimate Reality, or [the Greek god] Poseidon.[44]

By "seems (epistemically) to a subject that x is present" Swinburne means that the person's perception of x is the reason the person believes that x is present. So the principle of credulity basically says that we are justified to rely on our perceptions, unless we have a special reason not to trust a particular perception. Such "special considerations" might include things like the following. I was dreaming when I had the perception. I was diagnosed with schizophrenia at the time of the perception. I had just taken LSD when I had the perception. Or: I have well-supported knowledge that the perception is unreal because it was the perception of a man carrying his head under his arm.

QUICK REVIEW

Davis argues that many people claim to have experiences of God, that such experiences are probably veridical, so probably God exists. Swinburne supports the claim that numinous experiences are probably real experiences of God with his principle of credulity, which states that in the absence of special considerations, "if it seems (epistemically) to a subject that x is present, then probably x is present."

QUICK REVIEW

Critics argue that Swinburne's principle of credulity should not be applied to numinous experiences because the unusual nature of such experiences should count as a "special consideration" against accepting those experiences as veridical. Swinburne replies that numinous experiences are not unusual and the only reason for claiming that no numinous experiences should be taken as veridical is if one assumes God does not exist, but that is what has to be proven.

---

[43] Davis, op. cit., 128.
[44] Richard Swinburne, *The Existence of God* (Oxford: Oxford University Press, 1979), 254.

But why should we accept the principle of credulity? According to Swinburne, we already accept the principle and have no choice but to continue doing so. For we must rely on our perceptions virtually every moment we are awake. If we were not justified in relying on our perceptions of the world, then everything we think or believe about the world would be unjustified. We must rely on our perceptions even to get information from others since we have to perceive what they say or what they write. Moreover, precisely because the principle of credulity is so fundamental, there is no way to prove it (or disprove it). For in order to prove it I would have to rely on at least some perceptions. So any proof would depend on the principle and thus would be circular.

Nevertheless, critics have objected to Swinburne's principle of credulity. Even if we accept the principle of credulity for ordinary perceptions, they argue, it is not acceptable to use it for perceptions during a "numinous experience." A numinous experience is extremely unusual. Its unusual nature should count as a "special consideration" against relying on one's perceptions during such an experience. But Swinburne replies to this objection, first, that numinous experiences are not unusual. They are extremely common. He cites surveys which show that millions and millions of people today have such experiences. Second, Swinburne claims, even if some numinous experiences are false, this does not mean that all of them are. The only reason we can have for thinking that all numinous experiences are false is because we think God does not exist. But such a "reason" assumes to know the very thing that has to be proven: whether God exists.

If we accept Swinburne's principle of credulity, then we have a reason to accept the second premise of Davis' argument. Assuming his first premise is true, it shows religious experiences provide reliable evidence that "probably God exists." But why is Davis only willing to say God "probably" exists? Undoubtedly because Davis believes that although some religious experiences are "veridical," it is at least possible that none of them are. We may someday discover, for example, that all religious experiences are the product of a brain misfunction. Davis apparently believes that is unlikely. Nevertheless, it remains a possibility. And since that possibility remains, his argument can only be a probabilistic one.

Yet the claim that people have direct experiences of the divine can still be questioned. How can a finite human being experience an infinite God? If we experience something, then mustn't we experience it through the senses that we have? And if so, then won't it have to have sensory qualities such as colors, sounds, feelings, and shapes? But certainly God does not have these sensory qualities. So how can what we experience be God?

Despite these issues, we see in many people a continuing and intense search for a direct experience of a divine dimension. Many people feel a need to locate themselves in the cosmic scheme of things. Often, they reject traditional religious prescriptions and instead follow their own sense of what religion means to them. This pursuit takes many forms. Among them are the New Age movement, self-healing, consciousness expansion, and the human potential movement. But all reject some or all of traditional religion.

In the following section, we discuss three religious movements that also reject traditional religion. These are radical theology, feminist theology, and the study of Eastern religious traditions. Although quite different in content and methodology, they are similar in their search for religious experience outside of its traditional forms.

PHILOSOPHY AT THE MOVIES

Watch *The Apostle* (1997) in which Eulis "Sonny" Dewey, a foot-stomping, shouting, charismatic Texas preacher, becomes so enraged when he finds his wife Jessie (also a minister) is sleeping with the youth minister that he hits the younger man in the head with a baseball bat, which sends the man into a coma and forces Sonny to flee to Louisiana where he starts preaching in a renovated country church using the alias "Apostle E. F." Do you think Sonny believes on intellectual grounds? How would William James and W. K. Clifford view Sonny's grounds of belief? Who is right? Which, if any, of the religious experiences many people in this film seem to have are "numinous experiences."

4.5 Nontraditional Religious Experience

Radical Theology

For many of us traditional religion and traditional religious belief are no longer meaningful. Some philosopher-theologians have responded by developing a school of theology that deviates in radical ways from traditional theism. The radical theologians, as these thinkers are often termed, feel that our relationship with God is more experiential than rational. The roots of this view can be traced to thinkers like the Danish philosopher Søren Kierkegaard (1813–1855).

Kierkegaard. The northern European society into which Kierkegaard was born was thoroughly Christian. But it had adopted a stylized formal kind of religious life that, Kierkegaard believed, lacked the passion that should be at the heart of religion. Where the Christians around him should have felt fear, they were complacent. Where they should have shown intensity, they were smugly self-satisfied. To put it bluntly, Kierkegaard was revolted by these self-professed pillars of Christianity. In works such as *Philosophical Fragments* and *Concluding Unscientific Postscript,* Kierkegaard railed against them. And he also worked out an uncompromising view of Christianity that was both new and yet very old.

Central to Kierkegaard's religious thought is his distinction between the objective and subjective thinker. This is essentially a distinction between one who relies on reason and one who relies on faith. The objective thinker strikes an intellectual, dispassionate, scientific posture toward things, including his life and religion. In effect, the objective thinker adopts the view of an observer. In contrast, the subjective thinker is passionately and intensely involved with his life and religion. Truth for the subjective thinker is not just a matter of accumulating evidence to establish

Søren Aabye Kierkegaard. "The thing is to find a truth which is true for me, to find the idea for which I can live or die."

© Hulton Archive/Getty Images

a viewpoint. Truth is a profound personal concern. Kierkegaard contrasts the importance of subjective truth as opposed to objective truth in this selection from his personal journal:

> What I really lack is to be clear in my mind what I am to do, not what I am to know, except insofar as a certain understanding must precede every action. The thing is to understand myself, to see what God really wishes me to do; the thing is to find a truth which is true *for me*, to find *the idea for which I can live and die*. What would be the use of discovering so-called objective truth, of working through all the systems of philosophy and of being able if required, to review them all and show up the inconsistencies within each system;—what good would it do me to be able to develop a theory of the state and combine all the details into a single whole, and so construct a world in which I did not live, but only held up to the view of others;—what good would it do me to be able to explain the meaning of Christianity if it had no deeper significance *for me* and *for my life*;—what good would it do me if truth stood before me, cold and naked, not caring whether I recognized her or not, and producing in me a shudder of fear rather than a trusting devotion? I certainly do not deny that I still recognize an *imperative of understanding* and that through it one can work upon men, *but it must be taken up into my life*, and that is what I now recognize as the most important thing.[45]

ANALYZING THE READING

What is the difference between "objective truth" and "subjective truth"? Notice that for Kierkegaard, subjective truth is, first, a belief that is "true for me" and, second, a belief that expresses an "idea for which I can live and die" or expresses an idea that has "significance for me and for my life." So based on these two features of subjective truth, what would "objective truth" be?

Several themes are worth noting in this entry. First, Kierkegaard is desperately seeking clarity. Specifically, he wants clarity about action, about what he is to do, not an intellectual form of certainty. Second, notice the emphasis he gives to subjective truth, to what is "true *for me*" and has "significance *for me* and *for my life*." This is a recurring theme in Kierkegaard's thought. Reality must be understood from the subjective perspective of the self who chooses and acts. Third, notice Kierkegaard's intense focus on personal decision and what "I can live and die" for, and can "take up into my life." For Kierkegaard, the self is an outcome of our choices and commitments. Through our decisions we create who we are, we create the reality of the self. Finally, observe Kierkegaard's religiosity. Kierkegaard was deeply religious, and the central issue of his life and thought was what it means to be a Christian.

 THINKING LIKE A PHILOSOPHER

1. Describe some of the beliefs you hold that you would say are subjective truths, and some that you would say are objective truths.
2. Kierkegaard says that subjective truths are more important than objective truths. Do you feel the same way? Why?

Although Kierkegaard emphasizes subjective thinking, he never denies that objective thinking has its place. He simply asserts that life's most central concerns cannot be addressed by objective analysis. Indeed, from Kierkegaard's view, life's most important questions defy objective analysis. Religious commitment, in particular, says Kierkegaard, is not open to objective thinking. It is not open to objective thinking because it is a relationship with God who always remains a mystery. Religion and religious belief, then, are a confrontation with the unknown person

---

45 Søren Kierkegaard, *The Journals of Kierkegaard*, trans. A. Dru (London: Collins, 1958), 44. Reprinted by permission of Alexander Dru.

of God, not with something knowable. In the following passage from *Philosophical Fragments*, Kierkegaard demonstrates what he means:

> But what is this unknown something with which Reason collides when inspired by its paradoxical passion, with the result that it unsettles even man's knowledge of himself? It is the Unknown. It is not a human being, in so far as we know what man is; nor is it any other known thing. So let us call this unknown something: *the God*. It is nothing more than a name we assign to it. The idea of demonstrating that this unknown something (the God) exists, could scarcely suggest itself to Reason. For if the God does not exist it would of course be impossible to prove it; and if he does exist it would be folly to attempt it. For at the very outset, in beginning my proof, I would have presupposed it, not as doubtful but as certain (a presupposition is never doubtful, for the very reason that it is a presupposition), since otherwise I would not begin, readily understanding that the whole would be impossible if he did not exist. But if when I speak of proving the God's existence I mean that I propose to prove that the Unknown, which exists, is the God, then I express myself unfortunately. For in that case I do not prove anything, least of all an existence, but merely develop the content of a conception. . . .
>
> The works from which I would deduce God's existence are not directly and immediately given. The wisdom in nature, the goodness, the wisdom in the governance of the world—are any of these manifest, perhaps, upon the very face of things? Are we not here confronted with the most terrible temptations to doubt, and is it not impossible finally to dispose of all these doubts? But from such an order of things I will surely not attempt to prove God's existence; and even if I began I would never finish, and would in addition have to live constantly in suspense, lest something so terrible should suddenly happen that my bit of proof would be demolished. From what works then do I propose to derive the proof? From the works as apprehended through an ideal interpretation, i.e., such as they do not immediately reveal themselves. But in that case it is not from the works that I make the proof; I merely develop the idea I have presupposed, and because of my confidence in *this* I make so bold as to defy all objections, even those that have not yet been made. In beginning my proof I presuppose the ideal interpretation, and also that I will be successful in carrying it through; but what else is this but to presuppose that the God exists, so that I really begin by virtue of confidence in him?[46]

In this passage Kierkegaard explains the failure of rational theorizing—of objective thinking—in religious matters. He argues that the attempt to "prove" God's existence by using our reason is pointless. When we use our reason to think about God, he claims, our reason encounters a major obstacle. The obstacle is that God is absolutely unknowable. God is the great unknown something. A person may respond to this unknown by trying to use reason to prove that it exists. But that exercise is pointless. If God does not exist, then, of course, there would be no way to prove that He exists. For you cannot "prove" something that is false. On the other hand, if God does exist and a person tries to prove that He exists the person's "proof" must begin by assuming that He exists. That is, a rational "proof" of God must assume the very thing it is trying to prove. For example, suppose you try to argue that God must exist because something had to create the universe. Then in that very idea of a "something" that creates the universe you have assumed the existence of the god you wanted to prove. In any proof of God, the conclusion is always implicit in the premises. All the "proof"

> **QUICK REVIEW**
> Kierkegaard distinguishes objective thinking (dispassionate, scientific) from subjective thinking (passionate, involved). Religious belief is not open to objective thinking, and it is useless to try to prove God's existence. This causes "anguish."

46 Søren Kierkegaard, *Philosophical Fragments*, trans. David Swenson (Princeton, NJ: Princeton University Press, 1936). Copyright © 1936, 1962 by Princeton University Press.

ANALYZING THE READING

1. For Kierkegaard "objective thinking" is thinking that relies on reason and tries to be intellectual, dispassionate, and objective about what it decides to believe or do; "subjective thinking" is thinking that relies on faith and on feeling and passion when deciding what to believe or do. Kierkegaard says that the decision to believe in God cannot be based on objective thinking (i.e., reasoning) about the proofs of God's existence. What argument does he give for saying this? Do you think he's right? Why?

2. According to Kierkegaard, if I really think I can prove that God exists, all I am doing is to "presuppose that the God exists, so that I really begin by virtue of confidence in him." Explain what he means.

 ## THINKING LIKE A PHILOSOPHER

1. How would you describe what Kierkegaard calls a "leap of faith"? Explain how a personal but *nonreligious* decision can be a leap of faith.

2. Do you agree with Kierkegaard that basic religious beliefs and decisions should be a leap of faith? Or do you believe religious beliefs and decisions should be based on reason and objective truth? What are some of the religious decisions you have made? For example, did you ever decide you would continue to believe in God or decide you would not start or would not continue to believe in God? Would you say those decisions were a leap of faith? Would you say they were based more on subjective thinking or on objective thinking?

3. Would you describe any of the nonreligious decisions you have made during your own life as a leap of faith? If so, what were they? Are you happy now with the decisions you made?

does is draw out the content of the concepts in the premises. Or suppose you try to prove that God must exist because of the wisdom and goodness you see in nature. Then your proof will be based on the fact that you interpret nature as exhibiting wisdom and goodness. In that decision to interpret nature as a sign of God's wisdom and goodness, you have assumed that God exists. Reason or "objective thinking," then, is not a pathway to God. God is not subject to rational, objective analysis. But if the point of religion and religious faith is not to know God through rational objective analysis, just what is their point? To *feel, act, and commit oneself*, rather than to know.

Rational thinking, which is what objective thinkers try to use to understand matters of religion, may give us an intellectual idea of God. But that is not religion. Religion is not a relationship with our ideas about God. It is, rather, a relationship with another person, that is, with God. Objective thinking not only provides little on which to base a relationship with God, it can undermine that relationship. "I contemplate the order of nature," says Kierkegaard, "in the hope of finding God, and I see omnipotence and wisdom; but I also see much else that disturbs my mind and excites anxiety. The sum of all this is objective uncertainty."

Faced with objective uncertainty and the failure of objective analysis and rational "proofs," we are anguished. This anguish is compounded by the anticipation of our own death and feelings of insignificance in the face of the eternal order of things. The debates go on; our lives ebb away. Only a decision, Kierkegaard argues, can end the rational reflections and debates that objective thinking keeps spinning.

Kierkegaard calls this decision the "leap of faith." It is a commitment to a relationship with God that defies objective analysis. It is a leap that is made alone and in "fear and trembling." Of course, we may choose not to make the leap of faith. We may, instead, try to minimize our suffering by continuing our rational reflections and objective analysis. But for this alternative, Kierkegaard has only sarcasm. "*The two ways*," he says: "one is to suffer; the other is to become a professor of the fact that another suffered."

> When someone is to leap he must certainly do it alone and also be alone in properly understanding that it is an impossibility ... the leap is the decision. ... I am charging the individual in question with not being willing to stop the infinity of reflection. Am I requiring something of him, then? ... And what do I require of him? I require a *resolution*. And in that I am right, for only in that way can reflection be stopped. ... The

beginning can occur only when reflection is stopped, and reflection can be stopped only by something else, and this something else is something altogether different from the logical, since it is a resolution.[47]

Kierkegaard believed that *what* we choose in those crucial moments is not as important as *how* we choose. When making a significant choice we must choose passionately, with energy and an awareness of the significant consequences of our choices. We must do this, for example, when choosing whether to marry, or whether to do what is morally right or morally wrong, or whether to become a serious Christian.

> If you will understand me aright. I should like to say that in making a choice it is not so much a question of choosing the right, as of the energy, the earnestness, the pathos with which one chooses. Thereby the personality announces its inner infinity, and thereby, in turn, the personality is consolidated. Therefore, even if a man were to choose the wrong, he will nevertheless discover, precisely by reason of the energy with which he chose, that he had chosen the wrong. For the choice being made with the whole inwardness of his personality, his nature is purified and he himself brought into immediate relation with the eternal Power whose omnipresence interpenetrates the whole of existence.[48]

We make a free "leap of faith" when we make significant choices in the absence of a clear knowledge that we are choosing correctly. In such moments, we are both attracted and repelled by a future that is unknown, and we feel anxiety at making a "leap" into the "nothingness" of an unknown future. For example, when we look over the edge of a cliff, we feel anxiety. We may feel repelled by the thought of falling over, and at the same time almost have an urge to jump into the "nothingness." Our anxiety arises from our realization that we are free to do it. For Kierkegaard, this was particularly true of the "leap of faith" in which we choose to trust in God without any intellectual proof that God exists. We must often, perhaps always, make our important life choices without full intellectual knowledge of what our choices will bring. And so we feel both repelled and attracted by the leap into an unknown future.

Note that in the passage above, Kierkegaard says that in choosing "the personality is consolidated." That is, through our choices we become ourselves. We come to exist; we become real; we become a self. Kierkegaard does not say there are no right and wrong choices. But he believed that if people choose earnestly and passionately, they will know when they have made a wrong choice and will be able to get back on the right track.

Even this brief sketch of Kierkegaard's thought shows the extent to which he recast traditional religion. Traditional theism emphasized objective thinking

ANALYZING THE READING

1. Kierkegaard claims that it is more important to make choices passionately, with "energy, earnestness, and pathos," than it is to make the right choices. What does he mean by this? Do you think his claim is generally true? Why? What do you think are the types of choices for which Kierkegaard's claim is certainly correct?

2. What are some of the choices you have made that you would now say were made with "energy, earnestness, and pathos"? Looking back on those choices, would you say they were good choices or not?

QUICK REVIEW
Religion and God must be approached through a "leap of faith," a commitment that defies objective analysis.

---

[47] Søren Kierkegaard, *Concluding Scientific Postscript*, trans. Howard V. Hong and Edna H. Hong (Princeton, NJ: Princeton University Press, 1992), 102, 113.

[48] Søren Kierkegaard, *Either/Or—A Fragment of Life*, trans. David F. Swenson and Lillian Marvin Swenson (Princeton, NJ: Princeton University Press, 1949), vol. 2, p. 141.

© Alfred Eisenstaedt/Pix Inc./Time and Life Pictures/Getty Images

Paul Tillich "If you start with the question whether God does or does not exist, you can never reach Him."

and a rational approach to God. Kierkegaard replaced these with subjective thinking and a leap of faith that looks not toward knowledge, but toward a relationship with "the God." The authentic Christian is not the thinker, but the passionate doer and actor. "It is impossible to exist without passion," he wrote, "unless we understand the word 'exist' in the loose sense of a so-called 'existence.'" Kierkegaard urges us to make those anxiety-filled leaps of faith that make us who we are. But most of all, Kierkegaard urges us to take our religion seriously and embrace it passionately.

Tillich. The chief exponent of radical theology in modern time has been Protestant theologian Paul Tillich (1886–1965). Tillich, an existentialist, contends that traditional theism has viewed God as *a* being and not as *being itself*. This view, he claims, is a profound error and the source of many more errors. For that view sees God as one being among others. But God is not an individual being as we are. God is, rather, existence itself, the origin of the existence of all individuals, yet not another individual among them. We must look at why Tillich says this, and what he means.

Like Kierkegaard, Tillich believes that traditional theism's attempts to "prove" God exists are mistakes. They have ended by turning God into an object:

> If you start with the question whether God does or does not exist, you can never reach Him; and if you assert that He does exist, you can reach Him even less than if you assert that He does not exist. A God about whose existence or non-existence you can argue is a thing beside others within the universe of existing things. And the question is quite justified whether such a thing does exist, and the answer is equally justified that it does not exist.[49]

God cannot be proved, as if God were an object for which one was searching. Doing that makes him just one more object along with all the others in the universe. Such "objectification" limits the deity and raises the very kinds of doubts that lead to a loss of faith.

Tillich argues that the proofs for God's existence have not just fostered an erroneous view of God. They have led to disbelief in God. The proofs have led us to bring God into our subject–object view of reality. "He" is an object for us as subjects, becoming the target for our prayers, worship, and supplications. From

---

[49]   This and the following Tillich quotations are from Paul Tillich, *The Courage to Be* (New Haven, CT: Yale University Press, 1952). Excerpts from 4–5.

this perspective "He" becomes almost a *thing* to which we direct ourselves. At other times we make ourselves an object for God and turn God into an all-knowing, all-powerful subject. Since we are neither, the relationship must be one of superior (God) to inferior (us), controller to controlled, subject to object, master to servant. An antagonistic tension results. As Tillich says:

> He deprives me of my subjectivity because he is all-powerful and all-knowing. I revolt and try to make him into an object, but the revolt fails and becomes desperate. God appears as an invincible tyrant, the being in contrast with whom all other things are without freedom and subjectivity.[50]

This image of God as "invincible tyrant," he feels, is itself a refutation of the rational approach of traditional theism. It is a more telling refutation than all the objections to the traditional proofs for God's existence. Tillich believes that this view of God as tyrant is "the deepest root of the Existentialist despair and the widespread anxiety of meaninglessness in our period."

If Tillich and other radical theologians reject the theistic concept of God, what do they offer as a substitute? What kind of God do they believe in? For Tillich, as we said, God is not one entity among other entities. Instead, God is "the ground of being." That is, God is the foundation and source of all existence. This ground of being transcends the individual God of traditional theism and can dissipate the anxiety of our doubt and meaninglessness. This ground of being is not provable because it cannot be. It is neither an object nor a subject. It is present, although hidden, in every divine-human encounter.

That God is the "ground of being" is only one of Tillich's many difficult concepts. "Depth" is another difficult concept that is central to his thought. "Depth is what the word God means," he writes, realizing that for many the word may have no meaning. "If the word has not much meaning for you, translate it," advises Tillich, "and speak of the depths of your life, of the source of your being, of your ultimate concern, of what you take seriously without reservation." Tillich writes:

> What does the metaphor *depth* mean? It means that the religious aspect points to that which is ultimate, infinite, unconditional in man's spiritual life. Religion, in the largest and most basic sense of the word, is ultimate concern. And ultimate concern is manifest in all creative functions of the human spirit. It is manifest in the moral sphere as the unconditional seriousness of the moral demand. Therefore, if someone rejects religion in the name of the moral function of the human spirit, he rejects religion in the name of religion.
>
> Ultimate concern is manifest in the realm of knowledge as the passionate longing for ultimate reality. Therefore, if anyone rejects religion in the name of the cognitive function of the human spirit, he rejects religion in the name of religion.

ANALYZING THE READING

1. Tillich says that the traditional proofs for the existence of God encourage us to see God as "an invincible tyrant." Explain why he probably believes that the proofs would lead people to see God in this way. Do you agree?

2. Tillich claims that the view of God as tyrant is "the deepest root of the Existentialist despair and the widespread anxiety of meaninglessness in our period." What do you think he means by this? Do you agree? Why?

---

[50] Ibid.

Ultimate concern is manifest in the aesthetic function of the human spirit as the infinite desire to express ultimate meaning. Therefore, if anyone rejects religion in the name of the aesthetic function of the human spirit, he rejects religion in the name of religion. You cannot reject religion with ultimate seriousness, because ultimate seriousness, or the state of being ultimately concerned, is itself religion. Religion is the substance, the ground, and the depth of man's spiritual life. This is the religious aspect of the human spirit.[51]

THINKING LIKE A PHILOSOPHER

1. Explain what Tillich thinks a person's "ultimate concern" is. Describe what your own "ultimate concern" (or concerns) is at this point in your life.
2. Tillich says that anyone who has an ultimate concern believes in God. Would you say that your ultimate concern is a kind of belief in God? That is, do you see your ultimate concern as somehow sacred, or as a concern for something that is greater than your finite self?
3. The ultimate concern of some people is money, and the ultimate concern of others is power. Do you think it would be right to describe such people as having turned money or power into their God? Would this be part of what Tillich means when he says that a person who has an ultimate concern believes in God? Why?

QUICK REVIEW
For Tillich, God is "the source of your ultimate concern" and "of what you take seriously without reservation." So, anyone who has an ultimate concern believes in God.

QUICK REVIEW
But it is unclear what Tillich means by "God," and statements he makes about what "God" is seem to be mere tautologies.

Thus, to be religious is to have an ultimate concern. If there is something about which you deeply and truly care, then you are religious; you have a religion. And the object of your ultimate concern is the way that God is manifested to you.

An atheist might say, "I do not believe in God." But Tillich would say that this is virtually impossible. For a genuine atheist would have to be someone who does not believe that there is anything that is worth caring about deeply. Anyone who has an "ultimate concern" believes in God. The only people who can rightly call themselves atheists are those who can say, "Life has no depth. Life is shallow. Being itself is surface only." Tillich writes: "If you could say this in complete seriousness, you would be an atheist; but otherwise you are not. He who knows the depth knows about God."

Tillich is no escapist, no dodger of doubt. On the contrary, he accepts the concrete world of finite values and meanings. We must use this finite world with all its imperfections, skepticism, and meaninglessness to confront what is ultimately real: being. And the ground of all being is God. Through our experience of the being we confront in our finite world and our willingness to care deeply and seriously about the ultimate meaning and value of that being, we experience God. Everyone, therefore, "who knows the depth," experiences God.

Besides the questions raised by his many elusive concepts, Tillich's theology provokes other objections. By saying that God is the object of a person's ultimate concern, he seems to be doing away with what we have traditionally recognized as God. Even the atheist who is ultimately concerned about something, Tillich claims, can be said to believe in God. But what could this possibly mean? The atheist is someone who does not believe in that which we call God. How can such a person believe in God if, say, he or she is deeply committed to atheism itself as the ultimate concern? What does "God" mean here? Related to this is the objection that Tillich's statements about God are nothing but tautologies. In logic a **tautology** is a statement whose predicate repeats its subject. When Tillich says, "He who knows the depth knows about God," is he actually saying, "He who knows about God knows about God"? When he argues, "If one is ultimately concerned or has the courage to be, then one knows God," isn't he saying, "If one knows God or knows God, then one knows God"?

Tillich claimed to have had an experience of divine presence. He experienced a merging with some fundamental reality, and this experience became the foundation

---

[51] Paul Tillich, *Theology of Culture*, ed. Robert C. Kimball (London: Oxford University Press, 1964), 6–7.

of many of his views. Of course, no one may question Tillich's personal experience; it is as personal as one's thoughts and feelings. But his interpretation of his experience can be questioned. We can and should ask for his reasons for interpreting that experience as resulting from contact with the ground of all being. Tillich must verify that this "ground of all being" is real and was the cause of his transcendent experiences.

Tillich would probably reply that knowledge about the God he describes—the ground of all being—is a unique kind of knowledge. Such knowledge is different from the intellectual kind of knowledge we have about ordinary things. He would argue that his knowledge transcends empirical data and defies scientific verification. It is knowledge whose source is much closer to mystical intuition than to sense experience or reason. This knowledge, he might say, is rooted in what Rudolf Otto called a "numinous experience." As we saw, in such an experience a person feels or perceives a divine presence as an awesome almost irresistible force. And as William James noted, such experiences can be the source of illuminations full of meaning. But even if Tillich's experience was a numinous experience, does that put it beyond all questioning?

Feminist Theology

Many feminists have also challenged the traditional Western concept of God and religion. Their most important objections are that God is portrayed as male and is associated with religious beliefs and practices that are oppressive to women.

For example, God has traditionally been said to have no sex, and many philosophers have been careful to emphasize this point. Yet these same philosophers, as well as the majority of people, continue to use male pronouns—*He and Him*—to refer to God. Both Christianity and Judaism have traditionally characterized "Him" in male roles, particularly as a male parent, a "Father." The result is that in Western people's real, practical, and lived religious experience, God is thought of as a male despite the denials of philosophers and theologians. In her groundbreaking book *Beyond God the Father,* the feminist philosopher and theologian Mary Daly has argued that this male conception of God has had a profoundly oppressive impact on women:

> If God in "his" heaven is a father ruling his people then it is in the "nature" of things and according to divine plan and the order of the universe that society be male dominated. Within this context, a *mystification of roles* takes place: The husband dominating his wife represents God "himself." The images and values of a given society have been projected into the realm of dogmas and "Articles of Faith" and these in turn justify the social structures which have given rise to them and which sustain their plausibility.[52]

Moreover, in a surprising reversal of biological fact, Christianity and Judaism have suggested that the woman is born from the man's body and not the man from the woman's. The Old Testament story that Eve, the first female, was made out of Adam's rib implies that males are prior to females and are their source. The Judeo-Christian Bible also implies that sin and evil originated with a woman—Eve—who tempted the man—Adam—into the "Fall." Subsequently, Christianity went on to hold that salvation has to come from a male person—Jesus Christ, who is the "Son

---

[52] Mary Daly, *Beyond God the Father* (Boston: Beacon, 1974), 206.

of God" and whom God sent forth to be crucified as a sacrifice to save us all from sin and evil. Christianity has also given mostly to males—priests and pastors—the authority to lead Christians in their daily lives, and many of the major Christian religions—such as Roman Catholicism—still refuse to ordain women as priests or allow them to become bishops. The most orthodox segments of Judaism have also similarly allowed only males—rabbis—to play leadership roles.

Daly, perhaps the most articulate feminist critic of traditional religious beliefs, summarizes her criticisms of religion in general, and Christianity in particular, in these propositions:

> There exists a planetary sexual caste system [patriarchy], essentially the same in Saudi Arabia and in New York, differing only in degree.
> This system is masked by sex role segregation, by the dual identity of women, by ideologies and myths. ...
> All of the major world religions function to legitimate patriarchy. This is true also of the popular cults such as the Krishna movement and the Jesus Freaks.
> The myths and symbols of Christianity are essentially sexist. Since "God" is male, the male is God. ...
> The myth of feminine evil, expressed in the story of the Fall, is reinforced by the myth of salvation/redemption by a single human being of the male sex [Jesus Christ]. The idea of a unique divine incarnation in a male, the God-man of the "hypostatic union," is inherently sexist and oppressive. Christolatry is idolatry.[53]

QUICK REVIEW
Feminist theologian Daly holds that the traditional concept of God is male, sexist, oppressive to women, and legitimates patriarchy— the rule of men over women. We must reject it, especially in its Christian form, and replace it with "the Goddess."

Daly argues that by making God male, males have been able to use God to justify and maintain their power and authority over women: It is right for males to rule because the highest "Lord"—God—and the "savior"—Jesus Christ—are male. Moreover, because women are the source of evil and had their origins in man (Adam's rib), it is appropriate that they be ruled by men. Thus, the traditional male concept of God has played and continues to play a major role in keeping women oppressed and dominated by men.

Daly and other feminist thinkers have suggested that the male concept of God cannot be reformed because it has too many masculine connotations that make it oppressive to women. Maleness is an essential part of the traditional Western concept of God and cannot be separated from it. Instead, the concept must be abandoned, allowed to wither and die, and replaced with new religious symbols and concepts associated with "the Goddess":

ANALYZING THE READING

1. Do you agree that the Western concept of God is sexist? If not, how do you respond to Daly's criticisms?

2. Do you think Mary Daly is right to claim that the traditional Western concepts of God and religion are so sexist they should be discarded, or do you think Pamela Young is right that traditional religious concepts and practices can be reformed?

> For some feminists concerned with the spiritual depth of the movement, the word "God" is becoming increasingly problematic, however. This by no means indicates a movement in the direction of "atheism" or "agnosticism." ... Some reluctantly still use the word "God" while earnestly trying to divest the term of its patriarchal associations, attempting to think perhaps of the "God of the philosophers" rather than the overtly masculist and oppressive "God of the theologians." But the problem becomes increasingly troublesome, the more the "God" of the various Western philosophers

---

[53] Mary Daly, "The Qualitative Leap Beyond Patriarchal Religion," *Quest* 1, no. 4 (Spring 1975), 20.

is subjected to feminist analysis. "He"—"Jahweh"—still often hovers behind the abstractions, stunting our own thought, giving us a sense of contrived doublethink. The word "God" just may be inherently oppressive. . . .

For an increasing minority of women—and even for some men—"Goddess" is becoming more functional, meaningful, and loaded with healing associations. . . . The use of the expression, "The Goddess," is a way ... of exorcising the male "God," and of affirming a different myth/reality.[54]

A significant and growing number of women, Daly holds, are breaking away from the Judeo-Christian concept of God. That concept "legitimates patriarchy—the prevailing power structure and prevailing world view." Efforts to reform these traditional structures and views, she claims, are useless. Such efforts will "eventually come to be recognized as comparable to a Black person's trying to reform the Ku Klux Klan." Instead, feminists who seek a religious dimension in their lives should find meaning in "the Goddess." Many women are already creating a revolutionary and powerful new community, a new "sisterhood." These new female communities reject the prevailing male view that power must be understood as power *over* people. Within this new sisterhood, power is experienced as the "power of presence to ourselves and to each other." This new feminist movement is not hierarchical. That is, unlike male organizations, it is not based on leaders who have "power" over their followers. Thus, the notion of "the Goddess" will not lead to an oppressive female-dominated society like the male-dominated society that the male God produced.[55]

Daly is perhaps the harshest and most extreme critic of traditional religious concepts. Many men feel put off by her strong language and unrelenting attacks on everything that is male. Yet many of her criticisms of religion are incisive and telling blows against the often oppressive maleness of the traditional Western concept of God. That sexism undeniably affects much of traditional Western religious thought and practice. Nor can it be denied that these sexist traditions have been used to justify the so-called right of men to rule over women. Thus, although one might argue with this or that element of the feminist perspective represented by Daly, much of what she says rings true.

Yet many feminists, while agreeing with much of Daly's critique, have objected to some of her claims. Some feminist theologians have questioned whether the male concepts of God and religion are as irredeemable as Daly claims. For example, the feminist theologian Pamela Young writes, "Although for Christians it is in Jesus that they see God's presence, God's love and care exemplified, that this decisive revelation has taken place in a man is, in a very real sense, accidental."[56] Young argues that the male qualities attached to the concept of God and to Christianity are not necessary to either. Male qualities are "accidental" or nonessential elements of traditional religious concepts and practices. Male qualities got attached to God and to Christianity because they originated in human societies that were already sexist and dominated by males. Young argues that it is the task of the feminist to identify the sexist, oppressive, and male elements that have infected religious thinking and reform them.

It is unclear whether feminists such as Young can succeed in purging the Western concepts of God and religion of their sexist leanings. Daly may be correct when she writes that "dressing up old symbols just will not work for women who are conscious

---

[54] Ibid., 33.
[55] Ibid., 28.
[56] Pamela Dickey Young, *Feminist Theology/Christian Theology* (Minneapolis: Fortress Press, 1990), 97, 98, 99, 101.

of sexist religiosity." Both Daly and Young are inviting us to come with them on different journeys toward an understanding of God and religion that is neither sexist nor oppressive. But where either of those journeys will lead—or even whether they will succeed in going anywhere—is still unclear. Yet those journeys matter to all of us. For each one of us has to make his or her own journey toward an acceptance—or rejection—of God and religion. And for many of us, rejection or acceptance of God and religion will depend on how flawed we believe them to be.

Eastern Religious Traditions

Eastern religious traditions are many and varied. It is neither our intention nor within our capabilities to mention all of them, let alone discuss them fully. We can only outline some of the central beliefs of two related Eastern religions, Hinduism and Buddhism. Many Westerners have turned to these for meaningful religious experience.

Dharmachakra, Wheel of Transmigratory Existence (paper).

Boltin Picture Library / The Bridgeman Art Library

Hinduism. One of the oldest Eastern traditions is Hinduism. Hinduism has been practiced by hundreds of millions of people in India and elsewhere for about five thousand years. Hinduism has many divisions and subdivisions. In fact, Hinduism is so diversified that it is very difficult to describe as a whole or to generalize about it. Any attempt at description is bound to be an oversimplification. A further complication is that our language has no precise equivalents for certain Indian terms and concepts.

With awareness of these limitations, let us begin with the literary sources of Hindu teaching. Although many texts form the body of Hindu scripture, one has influenced Hindu thought more than any other: the *Bhagavad Gita* or the *Song of the Lord*. The *Bhagavad Gita* is part of the great epic *Mahabharata*. The *Bhagavad Gita* descries a long conversation between the god Krishna, and a warrior prince, Arjuna, on the eve of a great battle. Reading the *Bhagavad Gita* will introduce you to the principal concepts of Hinduism, as well as to beautiful poetry.

One concept found in the *Bhagavad Gita* is the idea that one fundamental reality underlies the multiplicity of things we see around us. This underlying reality is the ultimate source of the whole universe. This ultimate reality is the absolute, or *Brahman*, that sustains all things, is all things, yet is also beyond all things. In the following selections from the *Bhagavad Gita*, Lord Krishna, speaks as the *avatar* or visible manifestation of Brahman:

> I have no beginning and am Lord of all that exists. ... The entire universe is pervaded by Me, yet my form is not seen. All living things have their being in Me, yet I am not limited by them. ... Though I, the Supreme Self, am the cause and beholder of all, yet I remain outside them all. ... I am the oblation, the sacrifice and the worship. I am the fuel and the chant. I am the butter offered to the fire, I am the fire itself, and I am the act of offering. I am the Father of the universe and its Mother. I am its Nourisher and its Grandfather. I am the Knowable and the Pure. I am Om, and the Sacred Scriptures. I am the Goal, the Sustainer, the Lord, the Witness, the Home, the Shelter, the Lover and the Origin. I am Life and Death. I am the Fountain and the imperishable Seed. I am the Heat of the Sun. I release and hold back the Rains.

I am Death and Immortality. I am Being and Non-Being. ... I am the Self, seated in the hearts of all beings. I am the beginning and the life, and I am the end of them all. ... I am the knowledge of spirituality. I am the discussion between disputants. ... I am all-devouring Death. I am the origin of all that shall happen. I am fame, fortune, speech, memory, intellect, constancy and forgiveness. I am the gambling of the cheat and the splendor of the splendid. I am victory. I am effort. I am the purity of the pure. ... The aspects of my divinity are endless.[57]

Brahman is present behind everything and causes whatever there is. It is unlimited, incomprehensible, all-pervasive, omnipresent, and unchangeable. The many objects we see around us are illusions. They are the illusory manifestations of Brahman.

A correlative Hindu idea is the concept of *Atman.* Atman is a deep *consciousness* that lies within each of us. Atman is beneath all our living, sensing, and conscious thinking activities and beneath all our dreaming and waking experiences. Atman is not the ordinary individual self we commonly call "I" or "me." The individual self that we are aware of and refer to as "me" is also an illusion. Beneath the illusionary individual self that I am aware of, however, lies my real self, Atman, or my deep consciousness. Atman is the *profound inner consciousness* of which I am not ordinarily aware. It is a *consciousness* within myself that, though not sensed, directs everything I do. The Atman within each of us has lived forever and will continue to live forever. This is the basis of the Hindu doctrine of reincarnation. Each person's body eventually dies, but his deep consciousness, his Atman, continues to live in a different body. Here is how the *Bhagavad Gita* expresses these ideas. At this point in the *Bhagavad Gita* prince Arjuna has said that he grieves for the many people that will die in the battle that awaits him. To this Lord Krishna answers:

Wise people grieve neither for the dead nor for the living. For there was never a time when I did not exist, nor when you, nor when any king did not exist. Nor will there ever be a time when we shall cease to be. Just as the soul, Atman, acquires a child's body, then a youth's body, and then an aged body during this life, similarly, the soul, Atman, acquires another body after death. ... The visible physical body is perishable and transitory. But the invisible soul, Atman, is eternal. Atman is indestructible. No one can destroy the imperishable Atman. This is the way you and all others are Atman. A soul, Atman, pervades all that we see. Nothing can destroy Atman. But the material bodies which this eternal, indestructible, immeasurable soul inhabits are all finite. ... Just as a man discards his threadbare robes and puts on new ones, so the soul, Atman, throws off its worn-out bodies and takes fresh ones. [58]

 THINKING LIKE A PHILOSOPHER

The central concepts of Hinduism, like Brahman, Atman, karma, and the wheel of existence, are very different from the basic concepts of Western religions. Do you think that the possibility of choosing to believe Hinduism could ever be what James calls a "live" option for you? Do you think it could ever be a true "live" option for most Americans? Why?

Yet, I can become aware of the Atman within through meditation that achieves an enlightened inner self-consciousness. Such an enlightened self-consciousness is one that sees beyond the many differentiated illusionary things we perceive and beyond the illusionary self. It is a direct awareness of one's deep consciousness, Atman.

---

[57] Shri Purahit Swami, translator, *The Bhagavad Gita,* excerpts from chs. 4, 9, 10.

[58] Ibid., excerpts from ch. 2.

When, through mediation, I am able to contact the Atman-consciousness within. I will see that my inner deep consciousness is identical with Brahman. That is, I will truly and profoundly realize my unity with Brahman. I will see that the ultimate reality that underlies everything in the universe is identical with the deep consciousness within myself. Our deepest inner consciousness, then, is the ultimate reality that is the source of the illusory universe we see around us.

In Hindu thought, the highest spiritual value is enlightenment, by which one is illuminated. More importantly, enlightenment liberates us from the wheel of existence. Repeated existence is the destiny of those who do not achieve enlightenment.

To understand enlightenment, you must understand the law of karma, the law of sowing and reaping. Each of us, through what we do or do not do, determine his or her destiny. If we are particularly evil, we may find ourselves reborn as something less than human. If we are noble, we may be reborn as especially favored humans. In that way we are continually born, we continually die, and we are reborn again. We will keep turning on this wheel of existence until we achieve enlightenment. That alone can release us from the series of rebirths and from the endless striving to cling to material things.

Buddhism. Another major Eastern tradition is Buddhism, contained in the teachings of its founder, Siddhartha Gautama, or the Buddha. Because Gautama found no evidence for belief in a personal God, his teachings are a diagnosis of and a prescription for the "disease" of living.

The Buddha preached the Four Noble Truths. As we saw in Chapter 2, he held that nothing in the universe endures. To try to cling to what is impermanent inevitably ends in loss and suffering. Buddhism recognizes the wheel of life. Everything that lives must die, and is then forced to rise, repeat life again, and then fall again into death in a ceaseless round of loss and suffering. Our cravings keep us returning to this passing world through successive "rebirths." Release from this suffering, the Buddha preached, can be gained only by putting an end to our craving for pleasure, for continued life, and for power. And the key to ending this craving is following the Noble Eightfold Path:

> And this is the Noble Truth of Sorrow. Birth is sorrow, age is sorrow, disease is sorrow, death is sorrow; contact with the unpleasant is sorrow, separation from the pleasant is sorrow, every wish unfulfilled is sorrow—in short, all the five components of individuality are sorrow.
>
> And this is the Noble Truth of the Arising of Sorrow. It arises from craving, which leads to rebirth, which brings delight and passion, and seeks pleasure now here, now there—the craving for sensual pleasure, the craving for continued life, the craving for power.
>
> And this is the Noble Truth of the Stopping of Sorrow. It is the complete stopping of that craving, so that no passion remains, leaving it, being emancipated from it, being released from it, giving no place to it.
>
> And this is the Noble Truth of the Way which leads to the Stopping of Sorrow. It is the Noble Eightfold Path—[having] Right Views, Right Resolve, Right Speech, Right Conduct, Right Livelihood, Right Effort, Right Mindfulness, and Right Concentration.[59]

ANALYZING THE READING

1. Read the the First Noble Truth of the Buddha. Explain in your own words what you think it means. Use the Internet if you need more clarification. Do you think there is any truth to what it says? Explain why.

2. Explain in your own words what you think the second noble truth means. Again, use the Internet if you need more clarification. Do you believe there is any truth to what the second noble truth says? Explain why.

3. What would you say are the main reasons many Westerners are attracted to Eastern thought?

---

[59] William Theodore de Bary, *Sources of Indian Tradition,* vol. 1, from Samyutta Nikaya (New York: Columbia University Press, 1958), 99.

The First Noble Truth is concerned with the suffering that we experience in living within an impermanent universe. All the main events of life, the First Noble Truth says, are filled with sorrow because they are all related to what we must eventually lose. Since nothing lasts, we are doomed to repeatedly suffer the pain of losing what we love or desire. The Second Noble Truth identifies the cause of this suffering. We suffer because we grasp and try to cling to what never lasts. This clinging is due to **avidya**—ignorance and unawareness of the illusory nature of the things around us. The person who lacks awareness is committed to the world of things and illusion, **maya**. Such a person is unaware of the deeper fundamental reality behind the world of illusion. The unaware person tries to control herself and her environment. These attempts are futile. The result is frustration and the viciously circular pattern of life called **samsara**, the cycle of births and deaths. The Third Noble Truth concerns the ending of samsara, called **nirvana**—release or liberation. We achieve nirvana when we stop grasping and clinging and become aware of the profound reality that underlies all things. Release from the cycle of births and deaths comes when we at last enter a state in which all difference between oneself and fundamental reality is obliterated. That state defies definition or description. The Fourth Noble Truth describes the Eightfold Path of the Buddha's **dharma**. Dharma is the Buddha's moral doctrine about what we must do to end the grasping and clinging that leads to frustration and is an obstacle to finding nirvana. We will examine this concept more carefully in Chapter 7.

Differences between East and West. Obviously, there is much more to Hinduism and Buddhism than we have outlined. Still, these sketches already suggest some of the major differences between Eastern and Western religious thought.

First, the East rejects the West's "objectified" God. There is no claim of a personal, all-knowing, all-good, all-powerful, and all-loving divine individual as there is in the Western tradition. So Eastern thinkers have generally not been as preoccupied with debating God's existence as Western thinkers have been. As a corollary, Buddhism does not share the Western view that there is a moral law commanded by God. There is no moral law whose transgression leads to eternal damnation. In short, our tradition presents a God who expects us to behave in a certain way. In contrast:

> The Buddha's precepts of conduct—abstinence from taking life, taking what is not given, exploitation of the passions, lying, and intoxication—are voluntarily assumed rules of expedience, the intent of which is to remove the hindrances to clarity of awareness. Failure to observe the precepts produces bad "*karma*" not because *karma* is a law or moral retribution, but because all motivated and purposeful actions, whether conventionally good or bad, are *karma* insofar as they are directed to the grasping of life. Generally speaking, the conventionally "bad" actions are rather more grasping than the "good."[60]

Moreover, whereas the traditional thrust of Western religion has been to align us with a loving Creator, Eastern thought aims to ground us in an ultimate reality. To do so, Eastern thought generally prescribes discipline, self-control, moderation, and detachment. Although these values are accepted in Western religious practice, they are often practiced as a means to an end: salvation and reward. They are ways of attaining wisdom and truth, but they are also ways of avoiding damnation.

---

[60] Alan Watts, *The Way of Zen* (New York: Pantheon, 1957), 61.

Perhaps these differences explain why there has been a growing interest in the United States in Eastern thinking and religions. Many have turned from traditional faiths in favor of Buddhism, yoga, Transcendental Meditation, Vedanta, and so on. Of course, converts to Eastern religions have not stopped asking about their place in the scheme of things. On the contrary, they are asking perhaps more intensely than ever before. Many of those who have turned to Eastern religions have found little meaning in traditional Western religious concepts and practices. Traditional notions of self, Judeo-Christian doctrines and the emphasis on a personal relationship with God, are no longer meaningful. Many features of Eastern thought attract people to explore in new directions. Such features include, of course, the Eastern emphasis on consciousness and inner growth and the importance of discipline, practice, and method. They also include a distrust of doctrines and dogmas; and hope for integrating body and intellect, feelings and reason. But a central feature seems to be the reevaluation and redefinition of one's concept of the divine and one's relationship to it.

The many differences between Eastern thought and Western outlook should not be ignored. In the end, those differences raise the fundamental questions that the Westerner must ask about Eastern religion. Is it too alien to be truly understood by us? Is it too alien to meet our standards of what is reasonable? Is it too alien to be ultimately meaningful for us?

PHILOSOPHY AT THE MOVIES

Watch *Spring, Summer, Winter, Fall and Spring* (2003) which tells the story of a Buddhist monk and his very young apprentice as they move through the cycles of life, desire, attachment, loss, search, redemption, and death. The story takes place on a small floating monastery that is drifting on a lake in a mountainous forest where the monk teaches the boy prayer and meditation and respect for life, until the boy enters adolescence and falls in love with a girl whom he follows away from the monastery, only to return many years later after the monk has died and after he has changed considerably. What aspects of Buddhist thought do you see in this movie? Are Tillich's claims about people's "ultimate concern" supported in this film? Do Mary Daly's criticisms apply to the Buddhism you see in this movie?

Chapter Summary

Clearly, the philosophy of religion has had a long and illustrious history that continues to unfold. The concept of religious experience is inextricably linked with who we are. For one way in which we define ourselves is by our place in the cosmos, our place in the overall scheme of things. But that relationship between ourselves and the cosmos is the space within which religion lives.

The potential for what we have been calling religious experience is staggering. In the future, areas of conscious awareness that we hardly dream of today may open up. This awareness will no doubt be accompanied by a deep and reverent sensitivity to the profound mystery of life and our wondrous part in it.

All religions, then, speak of our need to find our place in the cosmic scheme of things. In the West, these have been sought through a relationship to a personal God, and many arguments have been assembled to prove that God's existence. Seeing weaknesses in the theistic position, however, many people have adopted atheism or agnosticism.

Whether or not the arguments for God are sound, the question of religious belief persists and affects our lives. For many people, belief arises from their personal religious experience. In this connection, we examined whether it was reasonable to believe on the basis of religious experience. We then looked at movements that reject the traditional Western approach to religion. These included radical theology, feminist theology, and Eastern religious thought. The main points of this chapter are:

4.1 The Significance of Religion

- Religions differ profoundly: Some do not believe in God, some have no official beliefs, and some are not institutionalized.

- Six dimensions characterize most religions: (1) doctrine, (2) experience, (3) myth, (4) ritual, (5) morality, and (6) organization.

4.2 Does God Exist?

- Anselm's ontological argument claims that God, as "that than which nothing greater can be conceived," must exist.

- The cosmological argument of Aquinas argues that the motions and effects we see in the world demand an origin in an unmoved mover and an uncaused cause.

- William Paley's design argument claims the order we see in nature implies that it was produced by an intelligent deity; a contemporary version says the improbability of the fine tuning in the universe requires a God, and critics reply that if we live in a "multiverse" such fine tuning is not improbable.

- thinking critically An argument by analogy claims that since two things are alike in certain respects, they are probably alike in another related respect.

4.3 Atheism, Agnosticism, and the Problem of Evil

- Atheism and agnosticism are responses to the difficulties in the traditional arguments for a theistic God.

- Atheism claims that we know that God does not exist, arguing particularly that the existence of evil implies there is no God. Theists argue that evil is necessary for good, in particular the good of human free will.

- Agnostics claim that we do not know whether or not God exists.

- Freud and Kant argued that people cannot help but believe in a God.

- thinking critically Fallacies, which often intrude into discussions of religion and God, are defective forms of reasoning, and include both formal and informal fallacies.

4.4 Traditional Religious Belief and Experience

- William James held that a "living, momentous, and forced" option that "cannot be decided on intellectual grounds" must be decided on the basis of our "passional nature," even without sufficient evidence in support of the option we choose; such was the case with religious belief.

- Many people believe in God not because of rational proofs but because of a direct personal experience of the divine. Davis and Swinburne argue such experiences are veridical.

4.5 Nontraditional Religious Experience

- Radical theology, as presented by Søren Kierkegaard and Paul Tillich, rejects traditional rational proofs of God. Kierkegaard sees religion as a "leap of faith"; Tillich sees religion in terms of one's "ultimate concern."

- Feminist theology has argued that much in the Western concept of God and religion is sexist and that these sexist notions have been used to oppress women.

- Eastern religious views, such as Hinduism and Buddhism, reject the Western traditional view of God, and both advocate the search for enlightenment.

4.6 Readings

The following two readings are both concerned with the Problem of Evil. The first is drawn from the classic Russian novel, *The Brothers Karamazov*, by Fyodor Dostoevsky. In the reading, one of the brothers, Ivan, is speaking to his younger brother, Alyosha, who has entered a monastery and is now a novice monk preparing to take the vows by which he will forever renounce marriage and possessions and devote himself to prayer and service to God. Alyosha is a gentle young man with a simple faith, a genuine love for all humanity, and a wisdom beyond his years. Ivan, a university student, is a brilliant and logical thinker who searches for a rational explanation for everything and who is tortured by religious doubts due to his inability to reconcile a loving God with the existence of suffering. The conversation described in the reading, which is central to Dostoevsky's novel, shows Ivan explaining the reasons for his doubts to Alyosha. In the second reading, the American philosopher William P. Alston argues against a key premise that is assumed to be true by probable (or "inductive") arguments that say evil is evidence that God probably does not exist (including the argument Ivan makes in the first reading). All arguments that say evil is evidence that a good God probably does not exist assume that a good God could and would have prevented at least some of the evils in our world. (Alston uses Rowe's version of that assumption as an example.) Alston argues that we humans just do not have the mental abilities to know whether that assumption is true or not. Notice that Alston is, in effect, trying to answer the argument that Ivan explains to Alyosha, in Dostoevsky's *The Brothers Karamazov*. Who is right, Alston or Ivan?

FYODOR DOSTOEVSKY

Excerpt from *The Brothers Karamazov*

"I must make one confession," Ivan began. "I could never understand how one can love one's neighbours. It's just one's neighbours, to my mind, that one can't love, though one might love those at a distance ... For anyone to love a man, he must be hidden, for as soon as he shows his face, love is gone."

"Father Zossima has talked of that more than once," observed Alyosha. "He, too, said that the face of a man often hinders many people not practised in love, from loving him. But yet there's a great deal of love in mankind, and almost Christ-like love. I know that myself, Ivan."

"Well, I know nothing of it so far, and can't understand it, and the innumerable mass of mankind are with me there. ... But enough of that. I simply wanted to show you my point of view. I meant to speak of the suffering of mankind generally, but we had better confine ourselves to the sufferings of the children. ... Children can be loved even at close quarters, even when they are dirty. ... Are you fond of children, Alyosha? I know you are, and you will understand why I prefer to speak of them. If they, too, suffer horribly on earth, they must suffer for their fathers' sins, ... but that reasoning is of the other world and is incomprehensible for the heart of man here on earth. The innocent must not suffer for another's sins, and especially such innocents! ... You don't know why I am telling you all this, Alyosha? My head aches and I am sad."

"You speak with a strange air," observed Alyosha uneasily, "as though you were not quite yourself."

"By the way, a Bulgarian I met lately in Moscow," Ivan went on, seeming not to hear his brother's words, "told me about the crimes committed by Turks and Circassians in all parts of Bulgaria .... They burn villages, murder, outrage women and children. ... These Turks took a pleasure in torturing children, too; cutting the unborn child from the mother's womb, and tossing babies up in the air and catching them on the points of their bayonets before their mothers' eyes. Doing it before the mothers' eyes was what gave zest to the amusement."...

"Brother, what are you driving at?" asked Alyosha. ...

"You see, I am fond of collecting certain facts, and, would you believe, I even copy anecdotes of a certain sort from newspapers and books, and I've already got a fine collection.... I've collected a great, great deal about Russian children, Alyosha. There was a little girl of five who was hated by her father and mother, 'most worthy and respectable people, of good education and breeding.' ... This poor child of five was subjected to every possible torture by those cultivated parents. They beat her, thrashed her, kicked her for no reason till her body was one bruise. Then, they went to greater refinements of cruelty—shut her up all night in the cold and frost in a privy, and because she didn't ask to be taken up at night (as though a child of five sleeping its angelic, sound sleep could be trained to wake and ask), they smeared her face and filled her mouth with excrement, and it was her mother, her mother did this. And that mother could sleep, hearing the poor child's groans! Can you understand why a little creature, who can't even understand what's done to her, should beat her little aching heart with her tiny fist in the dark and the cold, and weep her meek unresentful tears to dear, kind God to protect her? Do you understand that, friend and brother, you—pious and humble novice? Do you understand why this infamy must be and is permitted? Without it, I am told, man could not have existed on earth, for

he could not have known good and evil. Why should he know that diabolical good and evil when it costs so much? Why, the whole world of knowledge is not worth that child's prayer to dear, kind God! ... I am making you suffer, Alyosha. I'll leave off if you like."

"Never mind. I want to suffer, too," muttered Alyosha.

"One picture, only one more, because it's so curious, so characteristic. ... It was in the darkest days of serfdom at the beginning of the century. ... There was in those days a general of aristocratic connections, the owner of great estates. ... One day a serf-boy, a little child of eight, threw a stone in play and hurt the paw of the general's favourite hound. 'Why is my favourite dog lame?' He is told that the boy threw a stone that hurt the dog's paw. 'So you did it.' The general looked the child up and down. 'Take him.' He was taken—taken from his mother and kept shut up all night. Early that morning the general comes out on horseback, with the hounds, his dependents, dog-boys, and huntsmen, all mounted around him in full hunting parade. The servants are summoned for their edification, and in front of them all stands the mother of the child. The child is brought from the lock-up. It's a gloomy, cold, foggy, autumn day, a capital day for hunting. The general orders the child to be undressed; the child is stripped naked. He shivers, numb with terror, not daring to cry ... 'Make him run,' commands the general. 'Run! run!' shout the dog-boys. The boy runs ...'At him!' yells the general, and he sets the whole pack of hounds on the child. The hounds catch him, and tear him to pieces before his mother's eyes! ... Well—what did he deserve? To be shot? To be shot for the satisfaction of our moral feelings? Speak, Alyosha!"

"To be shot," murmured Alyosha, lifting his eyes to Ivan with a pale, twisted smile.

"Bravo!" cried Ivan delighted. "You're a pretty monk! So there is a little devil sitting in your heart, Alyosha Karamazov!" ...

Ivan for a minute was silent, his face became all at once very sad. ...

"I must have justice, or I will destroy myself. ... I want to see it, and if I am dead by then, let me rise again, for if it all happens without me, it will be too unfair. ... I want to see with my own eyes [that harmony when] the hind lies down with the lion and the victim rises up and embraces his murderer. I want to be there when everyone suddenly understands what it has all been for. ... But then there are the children, and what am I to do about them? That's a question I can't answer. ... Listen! If all must suffer to pay for the eternal harmony, what have children to do with it, tell me, please? It's beyond all comprehension why they should suffer, and why they should pay for the harmony. ... Some jester will say, perhaps, that the child would have grown up and have sinned, but you see he didn't grow up, he was torn to pieces by the dogs, at eight years old. Oh, Alyosha, I am not blaspheming! I understand, of course, what an upheaval of the universe it will be when everything in heaven and earth blends in one hymn of praise and everything that lives and has lived cries aloud: 'Thou art just, O Lord, for Thy ways are revealed.' When the mother embraces the fiend who threw her child to the dogs, and all three cry aloud with tears, 'Thou art just, O Lord!' then, of course, the crown of knowledge will be reached and all will be made clear. But what pulls me up here is that I can't accept that harmony. ... It's not worth the tears of that one tortured child who beat itself on the breast with its little fist and prayed in its stinking outhouse, with its unexpiated tears to 'dear, kind God'! It's not worth it, because those tears are unatoned for. They must be atoned for, or there can be no harmony. But how? How are you going to atone for them? Is it possible? By their being avenged? But what do I care for avenging them? What do I care for a hell for oppressors? What good can hell do, since those children have already been tortured? ... And if the sufferings of children go to swell the sum of sufferings that was necessary to pay for truth, then I protest that the truth is not worth such a price. I don't want the mother to embrace the oppressor who threw her son to the dogs! ... I don't want harmony. ... Besides, too high a price is asked for harmony. ... And so I hasten to give back my entrance ticket, and if I am an honest man I am bound to give it back as soon as possible. And that I am doing. It's not God that I don't accept, Alyosha, only I most respectfully return him the ticket."

"That's rebellion," murmured Alyosha, looking down.

"Rebellion? I am sorry you call it that," said Ivan earnestly. ... "Tell me yourself, I challenge your answer. Imagine that you are creating a fabric of human destiny with the object of making men happy in the end, giving them peace and rest at last, but that it was essential and inevitable to torture to death only one tiny creature—that baby beating its breast with its fist, for instance—and to found that edifice on its unavenged tears, would you consent to be the architect on those conditions? Tell me, and tell the truth."

"No, I wouldn't consent," said Alyosha softly.

Source: From Fyodor Dostoyevsky, *The Brothers Karamazov,* Constance Garnett, translator (New York: The Lowell Press, 1912).

WILLIAM P. ALSTON

The Inductive Argument from Evil and the Human Cognitive Condition

William Rowe [a critic who argues that evil is evidence that God probably does not exist, claims (as all such critics claim)]:

(1) There exist instances of intense suffering which an omnipotent, omniscient being could have prevented without thereby losing some greater good or permitting some evil equally bad or worse.

... [I will argue we do not have the ability to know whether (1) is true or not. First, can the critic claim that there are particular cases of suffering that God has no good reason to allow and that God could miraculously prevent by intervening in the natural order? To claim this] ... we would have to be justified in supposing that God would have a sufficient reason to make, in this case, an exception to the general [laws of Nature]. And how could we be justified in supposing that? We would need an adequate grasp of the full range of cases from which God would have to choose whatever exceptions He is going to make, if any, to the general policy of letting nature take its course. Without that we would not be in a position to judge that ... a [particular] evil is among the n% of the cases most worthy of being miraculously prevented. And it is abundantly clear that we have and can have no such grasp of this territory as a whole. We are quite unable, by our natural powers, of determining just what cases, or even what kinds of cases, of suffering there would be throughout the history of the universe if nature took its course. We just don't know enough about the constituents of the universe even at present, much less throughout the past and future, to make any such catalogue. And we could not make good that deficiency without an enormous enlargement of our cognitive capacities. Hence we are in no position to judge that God does not have sufficient reason for refraining from interfering in [a particular] case.

[Second, can the critic claim] that God could have instituted a quite different natural order, one that would not involve human and animal suffering, or at least much less of it? Why couldn't there be a natural order in which there are no viruses and bacteria the natural operation of which results in human and animal disease, a natural order in which rainfall is evenly distributed, in which earthquakes do not occur, in which forests are not subject to massive fires? To be sure, even God could not bring into being just the creatures we presently have while subjecting their behavior to different laws. For the fact that a tiger's natural operations and tendencies are what they are is an essential part of what makes it the kind of thing it is. But why couldn't God have created a world with different constituents so as to avoid subjecting any sentient creatures to disease and natural disasters? Let's agree that this is possible for God. But then the critic must also show that at least one of the ways in which God could have done this would have produced a world that is better on the whole than the actual world. For even if God could have instituted a natural order without disease and natural disasters, that by itself doesn't show that He would have done so if He existed. For if that world had other undesirable features and/or lacked desirable features in such a way as to be worse, or at least no better than, the actual world, it still doesn't follow that God would have chosen the former over the latter. It all depends on the overall comparative worth of the two systems.... I merely want to show that the critic is not justified in supposing that some alternative natural order open to God that does not involve suffering (to the extent that we have it) is better on the whole.

There are two points I want to make about this.... First, it is by no means clear what possibilities are open to God. Here it is important to remember that we are concerned with metaphysical possibilities (necessities ...), not merely with conceptual or logical possibilities in a narrow sense of 'logical'. The critic typically points out that we can consistently and intelligibly conceive a world in which there are no diseases, no earthquakes, floods, or tornadoes, no predators in the animal kingdom, while all or most of the goods we actually enjoy are still present. He takes this to show that it is possible for God to bring about such a world. But, as many thinkers have recently argued, consistent conceivability (conceptual possibility) is by no means sufficient for metaphysical possibility,

for what is possible given the metaphysical structure of reality. To use a well worn example, it may be metaphysically necessary that the chemical composition of water is H_2O since that is what water essentially is, even though, given the ordinary concept of water, we can without contradiction or unintelligibility, think of water as made up of carbon and chlorine. Roughly speaking, what is conceptually or logically (in a narrow sense of "logical") possible depends on the composition of the concepts, or the meanings of the terms, we use to cognize reality, while metaphysical possibility depends on what things are like in themselves, their essential natures, regardless of how they are represented in our thought and language.

It is much more difficult to determine what is metaphysically possible or necessary than to determine what is conceptually possible or necessary. The latter requires only careful reflection on our concepts. The former requires—well, it's not clear what will do the trick, but it's not something we can bring off just by reflecting on what we mean by what we say, or on what we are committing ourselves to by applying a certain concept. To know what is metaphysically possible in the way of alternative systems of natural order, we would have to have as firm a grasp of this subject matter as we have of the chemical constitution of familiar substances like water and salt. It is clear that we have no such grasp. We don't have a clue as to what essential natures are within God's creative repertoire, and still less do we have a clue as to which combinations of these into total lawful systems are doable. We know that you can't have water without hydrogen and oxygen and that you can't have salt without sodium and chlorine. But can there be life without hydrocarbons? Who knows? Can there be conscious, intelligent organisms with free will that are not susceptible to pain? That is, just what is metaphysically required for a creature to have the essential nature of a conscious, intelligent, free agent? Who can say? Since we don't have even the beginnings of a canvass of the possibilities here, we are in no position to make a sufficiently informed judgment as to what God could or could not create by way of a natural order that contains the goods of this order (or equal goods of other sorts) without its disadvantages.

One particular aspect of this disability is our inability to determine what consequences would ensue, with metaphysical necessity, on a certain alteration in the natural order. Suppose that predators were turned into vegetarians. Or rather, if predatory tendencies are part of the essential natures of lions, tigers, and the like, suppose that they were replaced with vegetarians as much like them as possible. How much like them is that? What other features are linked to predatory tendencies by metaphysical necessity? We may know something of what is linked to predation by natural necessity, e.g., by the structure and dispositional properties of genes. But to what extent does metaphysical possibility go beyond natural possibility here? To what extent could God institute a different system of heredity such that what is inseparable from predation in the actual genetic code is separable from it instead? Who can say? To take another example, suppose we think of the constitution of the earth altered so that the subterranean tensions and collisions involved in earthquakes are ruled out. What would also have to be ruled out, by metaphysical necessity? (Again, we know something of what goes along with this by natural necessity, but that's not the question.) Could the earth still contain soil suitable for edible crops? Would there still be mountains? A system of flowing streams? We are, if anything, still more at a loss when we think of eradicating all the major sources of suffering from the natural order. What metaphysical possibilities are there for what we could be left with? It boggles the (human) mind to contemplate the question.

The second main point is this. Even if we could, at least in outline, determine what alternative systems of natural order are open to God, we would still be faced with the staggering job of comparative evaluation. How can we hold together in our minds the salient features of two such total systems sufficiently to make a considered judgment of their relative merits? *Perhaps* we are capable of making a considered evaluation of each feature of the systems (or many of them), and even capable of judicious comparisons of features two-by-two. For example, we might be justified in holding that the reduction in the possibilities of disease is worth more than the greater variety of forms of life that goes along with susceptibility to disease. But it is another matter altogether to get the kind of overall grasp of each system to the extent required to provide a comprehensive ranking of those systems. We find it difficult enough, if not impossible, to arrive at a definitive comparative evaluation of cultures, social systems, or educational policies. It is far from clear that even if I devoted my life to the study of two primitive cultures, I would thereby be in a position to make an authoritative pronouncement as to which is better on the whole. How much less are we capable of making a comparative evaluation of two alternative natural orders, with all the indefinitely complex ramification of the differences between the two ...

I have drawn on various limits to our cognitive powers, opportunities, and achievements in arguing that we are not in a position to deny that God could have [a sufficient] reason for various cases of suffering. In conclusion it may be useful to list the cognitive limits that have formed the backbone of my argument.

1. *Lack of data.* This includes, inter alia, the secrets of the human heart, the detailed constitution and structure of the universe, and the remote past and future, including the afterlife if any.

2. *Complexity greater than we can handle.* Most notably there is the difficulty of holding enormous complexes of fact—different possible worlds or different systems of natural law—together in the mind sufficiently for comparative evaluation.

3. *Difficulty of determining what is metaphysically possible or necessary.* Once we move beyond conceptual or semantic modalities (and even that is no piece of cake) it is notoriously difficult to find any sufficient basis for claims as to what is metaphysically possible, given the essential natures of things, the exact character of which is often obscure to us and virtually always controversial. This difficulty is many times multiplied when we are dealing with total possible worlds or total systems of natural order.

4. *Ignorance of the full range of possibilities.* This is always crippling when we are trying to establish negative conclusions. If we don't know whether or not there are possibilities beyond the ones we have thought of, we are in a very bad position to show that there can be no divine reasons for permitting evil.

5. *Ignorance of the full range of values.* When it's a question of whether some good is related to [an evil] in such a way as to justify God in permitting [that evil], we are, for the reason mentioned in question 4., in a very poor position to answer the question if we don't know the extent to which there are modes of value beyond those of which we are aware. For in that case, so far as we can know, [the evil] may be justified by virtue of its relation to one of those unknown goods.

6. *Limits to our capacity to make well considered value judgments.* The chief example of this we have noted is the difficulty in making comparative evaluations of large complex wholes.

... The point is that the critic is engaged in attempting to support a particularly difficult claim, a claim that there isn't something in a certain territory, while having a very sketchy idea of what is in that territory, and having no sufficient basis for an estimate of how much of the territory falls outside his knowledge. This is very different from our more usual situation in which we are forming judgments and drawing conclusions about matters concerning which we antecedently know quite a lot, and the boundaries and parameters of which we have pretty well settled.

Source: From William P. Alston, "The Inductive Argument from Evil and the Human Cognitive Condition," *Philosophical Perspectives,* vol. 5 (1991), pp. 29, 54, 55, 59, 60

4.7 HISTORICAL SHOWCASE

Aquinas, Descartes, and Conway

In this chapter, we have examined a broad range of philosophical issues raised by belief in God. But we have tended to treat these issues in isolation from other philosophical questions. By contrast, most major philosophers have felt that questions about God are deeply related to other important philosophical issues. For this reason, philosophers' views on God have profoundly influenced their positions on other philosophical questions.

Here we showcase three philosophers whose views about God determine their views on other important philosophical issues: Thomas Aquinas, René Descartes, and Anne Conway. By examining their work, we get an idea of how these three philosophers incorporate God into a large philosophical system. Moreover, in becoming acquainted with them, we will see how a person's position on one philosophical issue can dramatically affect and interact with that person's views on other issues in philosophy.

Saint Thomas Aquinas (oil on silvered copper).

National Trust Photographic Library/The Bridgeman Art Library

AQUINAS

No period of history has been more preoccupied with religion than the medieval era, and the greatest of the medieval thinkers was Thomas Aquinas. Although Aquinas was influenced by the writings of Aristotle, he was also deeply affected by the events of the fifteen centuries (322 BCE to 1225 CE) that separated him from Aristotle, Plato, and the other Greek philosophers. Those centuries saw the Roman Empire (circa 300 BCE to circa 500 CE) rise and spread over Europe and also witnessed the birth of Christianity at the very height of the empire's power. They also saw the collapse of civilization, as barbarian tribes repeatedly invaded the empire until, after centuries of battering, it was destroyed and Europe descended into the Dark Ages. During the Dark Ages, Christianity spread gradually, but most philosophy ceased while men and women concentrated on surviving in the barbaric world that Europe had become.

It was not until Aquinas' times that conditions in Europe once again became conducive to philosophical activities and that new centers of learning—the first universities—were established. But the Europe that emerged from the Dark Ages had become completely Christianized; consequently, philosophy tended to focus on religious concerns.

It was only natural that Thomas Aquinas' thinking should focus on the philosophical problems raised by the religion that now dominated Europe.

Born in 1225 to a wealthy family of the Italian nobility, Saint Thomas Aquinas was raised to hold high office in the Roman Catholic Church, a position that his family hoped would prove advantageous to their political fortunes. In preparation for this career, the family sent him at the age of 5 to study in a Benedictine monastery, where he remained until he entered the University of Naples at the age of 14. At Naples, Thomas came into contact with the Dominicans, an inspiring order of monks dedicated to poverty and to service through teaching. Despite vigorous opposition from his family, Thomas entered the Dominican Order in 1241, dashing his family's hopes for his ecclesiastical career. Four years later, the order sent him to the new University of Paris to study under Albert the Great, a scholar of towering intellect already famous for his knowledge of Aristotle's doctrines. Under Albert's influence, Thomas began to draw heavily on Aristotle's teachings, gradually producing a brilliant synthesis of Christian theology and Aristotelian philosophy. Aquinas remained a dedicated Christian scholar and teacher throughout his life, churning out a prodigious number of writings until his death in 1274. In his two greatest works, the *Summa Contra Gentiles* and the *Summa Theologica*, Thomas addresses virtually every philosophical issue raised by Christianity and resolves them in a way that many feel is philosophically sound yet true to the Christian faith. Aquinas' philosophy, in fact, has often been called the Christian philosophy and is still held by a large number of Christians.

Aquinas did not confuse religious faith with philosophy. With great care he distinguished among truths that are known by faith, truths that are known by reason, and truths that are known by both faith and reason. Philosophy, he held, consists of truths that our unaided reason can discover by reflecting on our natural experience in the world. Theology, on the other hand, begins with truths that have been revealed by God through Scripture and accepted by faith, and from these revealed truths draws further religious truths. There is some overlap between philosophy and theology, however, because some truths that can be discovered by our unaided reason have also been revealed by God:

Some truths about God exceed the capacity of our human reason. An example of this is the truth that God is three persons in one. But there are some truths that reason by its very nature is also able to discover. Examples of these are the truths that God exists, that there is only one God, and similar truths. In fact, these truths about God have been proved by several philosophers who have relied completely on the light of their natural reason.[1]

Aquinas' Five Proofs. Central to Aquinas' philosophy are his famous five proofs for the existence of God (one of which is the cosmological proof), some of which were influenced by Aristotle's views on causes. Each of the proofs begins by pointing to some aspect of the world we experience: its motion, its causality, its contingency, its imperfection, or its unthinking order. Each proof then argues that this aspect of the world cannot account for itself: Each aspect depends for its existence on something—a Divine Being—that is utterly different from the objects we experience. The motion of objects demands the existence of an unmoved mover, the causality we see at work demands the existence of something that is uncaused, the contingency of objects demands the existence of something that is noncontingent, the existence of imperfect objects demands the existence of something that is perfect, and the existence of order among objects that do not think demands the existence of something that thinks and that produces that order:

That God exists can be proved in five ways.

The first and clearest way is the argument from motion. It is certain and evident to our senses that some things in the world are in motion. Now if something is moved, it must be moved by something else. ... For nothing can change from being potentially in motion to being in a state of actual movement unless something else that is in actual movement acts on it. ... So whatever is moving must be moved by something else. Now if that by which it is moved is itself moving, then it, too, must be moved by something else, and that by something else again. But this cannot go on to infinity because then there would be no first mover. And if there were no first mover, then nothing would move since each subsequent mover will move only to the extent that it is moved by the

---

[1]   Saint Thomas Aquinas, *Summa Contra Gentiles*, I, q.3, a.2. This edited translation is by Manuel Velasquez.

motion imparted by the first mover. The [other] parts of a staff, for example, will move only to the extent that the [top of the] staff is moved by the hand. Therefore, there must be a first mover that is not moved. And this first unmoved mover is what we mean by God.

The second way is based on the nature of efficient causes. In the world we see around us, there are ordered lines of efficient causes [in which each member of the line produces the next member]. But nothing can be its own efficient cause, since then it would have to exist prior to itself and this is impossible. Now it is not possible for a line of efficient causes to extend to infinity. For in any line of efficient causes, the first is the cause of the intermediate ones, and the intermediate ones cause the last one. Now if we remove any of the causes, we remove all the remaining effects. So if there were no first cause then there would be no last cause nor any intermediate ones. But if a line of efficient causes extended back to infinity, then we would find no first cause. Consequently, if the line of causes extended back to infinity, there would be no intermediate causes nor any last causes in existence in the universe. But we know this is false. So it is necessary to admit that there is a first efficient cause. And this we call God.

The third way is based on contingency and necessity. It proceeds as follows. We find in nature things that are contingent. These are things that are generated and that can corrupt, and which therefore can exist or can cease to exist. Now it is impossible for such contingent things to exist forever. For if it is possible for something to cease existing, then eventually a moment will come when it will cease to exist. Therefore, if everything were contingent, then eventually everything would have ceased existing. If this happened, then even now nothing would exist, because something can start to exist only through the action of something that already exists. It follows that not everything is contingent, that is, some things must exist necessarily, that is, forever. Now every necessary thing is caused to exist forever either by something else or not by anything else. But as we proved above, it is impossible for a line of causes to be infinite. So there must exist something which derives its necessary existence from itself and not from something else, and which causes the existence of all other necessary beings. This is what we all mean by God.

The fourth way is based on the degrees of perfection that we find in things. Among the objects in our world some are more and some less good, true, noble, and the like. But to say that a thing has more or less of a certain perfection is to say that it resembles to a greater or lesser degree something which perfectly exemplifies that perfection. ... So there must be something which is most perfectly true, most perfectly good, most perfectly noble, and, consequently, which most perfectly exists (since, as Aristotle shows, those things that are perfectly true also exist perfectly). Now that which most perfectly exemplifies some quality, also causes other things to have that quality to a greater or lesser degree. Fire, for example, which most perfectly exemplifies the quality of heat, is the cause of the heat in hot things. Therefore, there must be something which is the cause of the being, goodness, and every other perfection in things. And this we call God.

The fifth way of proving God's existence is based on the order in the universe. We see that things which lack knowledge, such as natural objects, act for an end. That is, their activity is always or nearly always aimed at achieving the best result. It is clear, therefore, that their activity is not produced by chance but by design. Now things which lack knowledge cannot move unerringly toward an end unless they are directed toward that end by some being that has knowledge and intelligence much like an arrow is directed toward its target by an archer. Therefore there must exist an intelligent Being Who directs all natural things toward their respective ends. This Being we call God.[2]

Aquinas says that each of the five proofs for the existence of God tells us something about God. The first proof implies that unlike anything in the universe, God imparts motion to everything without moving and therefore without being in time or being material. The second implies that unlike anything we know, God is the uncreated creator that causes everything to exist. The third tells us that—again unlike anything in our experience—God cannot cease existing because God's existence does not depend on anything else. The fourth tells us that unlike anything in the universe, God is perfect goodness, perfect truth, perfect nobility, and perfect existence. And the fifth tells us that God is the supremely wise intelligence in whom all the order in the universe originates.

---

2   Saint Thomas Aquinas, *Summa Theologica*, I, q.2, a.3. This translation copyright © 1978 by Manuel Velasquez.

Nevertheless, Aquinas cautions, there is such a vast gulf between ourselves and God that the knowledge of God that we can glean from the five proofs is very imperfect. Each proof merely tells us that some aspect of the universe we experience requires the existence of something else that is *unlike* anything in that universe and therefore *unlike* anything in our experience. Aquinas expresses this idea by asserting that although the proofs show us *that* God is, they do not tell us *what* God is. The proofs give us what Aquinas calls a "negative way" of knowing God. They do not give us a positive conception of God but lead us to *remove* certain ideas from our conception of God: God is *not* in motion, God is *not* created, God is *not* dependent, God is *not* imperfectly good, God is *not* a blind unintelligent force.

Analogical Knowledge of God. But does this *via negativa*—this negative approach—provide us with the only knowledge we have of God? Are we doomed to know only what God is *not* and never to have any positive knowledge of God? At first sight, it would seem that we could never have any positive knowledge of God because all our positive knowledge is based on our experience of the universe, and God is unlike anything in our experience. However, Aquinas identifies an imperfect kind of positive knowledge of God that is open to us. He calls this "knowledge by analogy" or "analogical knowledge" of God.

Aquinas explains analogical knowledge as follows: He points out that there are certain words—such as *good, wise,* and *loving*—that we apply both to God, whom we do not experience, and to human creatures, whom we do experience. We say, for example, that God is good, wise, and loving, and we say that this or that person of our experience is good, wise, or loving. We could conceivably be applying such words to both God and humans in any of three ways.

First, the words could have a *univocal* meaning—that is, they could have exactly the same meaning when applied to God, whom we do not experience, as when applied to the humans we do experience. But this is impossible because God and humans are so unlike that the goodness, wisdom, and love of God must be different from the goodness, wisdom, and love we experience in humans:

> It is impossible for a word to be applied univocally to both God and the creatures he produces. For when an effect is not equal to the power of the cause that produced it, the effect receives only an imperfect likeness of the cause: that is, the effect will be like the cause only to an imperfect degree. . . . Thus, when the word "wise" is applied to human beings, the word in a way comprehends and includes in its meaning the thing to which it refers [i.e., imperfect wisdom as we experience it and as God produced it]. But this is not so when the word is applied to God. For when the word "wise" is applied to God it refers to something [perfect wisdom] that exceeds the meaning of the word and which is not comprehended.[3]

Second, then, words applied to both God and creatures could have an *equivocal* meaning: They could mean something totally different when applied to each. But this, too, is inadequate, Aquinas insists. If the words we use changed their meaning when we applied them to God, then we could not say anything at all about God. For we would never know what our words meant when we applied them to God because their meaning derives entirely from our experience of creatures:

> Neither can we say that words that are applied to God and creatures have a purely equivocal sense, although some thinkers have held this view. If words that applied to both God and creatures were purely equivocal, then our experience of creatures would not allow us to know anything about God nor to prove anything about God. For the words we used in our reasoning would always be exposed to the fallacy of equivocation. [They would have one meaning in part of our reasoning and another meaning in another part.] Now this is contrary to the procedure of some philosophers, such as Aristotle, who managed to prove many things about God. It also contradicts scripture which says "The invisible things of God are clearly seen, being understood from the things that He created."[4]

Humans, then, must reflect God's nature to some degree because they are God's creation: The goodness, wisdom, and love of humans that we experience must reflect imperfectly the perfect goodness, wisdom, and love of God, in whom they originate. So, Aquinas concludes, the third and correct way in which we apply to God certain words whose meaning is based on our experience of humans is *by analogy.* Words such as *wise, good,* and *loving* are applied both to God and humans with an *analogical* meaning. The

---

3   Ibid., I, q.13, a.5.
4   Ibid.

words do not have a completely different meaning when applied to each, but their meaning is also not exactly the same:

> We have to conclude that these words are applied to both God and creatures in an *analogous* sense, that is, with a meaning that is based on a relationship. ... For example, the word "healthy" can be applied to a medicine as well as to an animal because of the relationship the medicine has to the health of the animal: the medicine is the cause of the animal's health. In a similar way, words can be applied to both creatures and to God in an analogous and not in a purely univocal nor in a purely equivocal sense. Consider that we can apply to God only words whose meanings we draw from our experience of creatures. Consequently, when we apply a word to both God and creatures, its meaning has to be based on the relationship that creatures have to God: they are related to God as to their origin and their cause in whom all their perfections pre-exist in a way that excels their existence in creatures. Now this kind of common possession of perfections is the basis of a kind of meaning that is midway between pure univocation and pure equivocation. When a word is applied analogically in this way to two different beings its meaning does not remain completely identical as with univocal uses, nor does it have completely different meanings as in equivocal uses.[5]

Our experience of humans, then, gives us an imperfect but positive knowledge of attributes that exist in God in a perfect way. We can never fully comprehend God's own unique and perfect goodness, wisdom, and love, which are quite different from our imperfect and partial goodness, wisdom, and love. So *good, wise,* and *loving* do not have exactly the same meaning when applied to God and humans. Nevertheless, we do experience the partial goodness, wisdom, and love of humans and know that it reflects the perfect goodness, wisdom, and love of God from whom they derive. This knowledge allows us to say that there is some similarity of meaning among *good, wise,* and *loving* when used to describe both God and humans.

The Law of God. The universe that God created, Aquinas holds, is governed by laws that are imposed by God. Aquinas calls these laws the *eternal law,* and

he likens God to a ruler or a craftsman who fashions the laws of the universe:

> Before any craftsman makes something, he must have in his mind an idea of what he will make. Similarly, before a ruler governs his subjects, he must have in his mind some idea of what his subjects are to do. The craftsman's idea of what he will make constitutes a plan of the object to be made (it is also part of what we call his skill). And the ruler's idea of what his subjects are to do constitutes a kind of law. ... Now since God is the wise creator of the universe, He is like a craftsman who makes something. And He is also like the ruler since He governs every act and motion of every single creature. Consequently, the idea in God's wise mind, according to which everything was created, can be called a plan (or an ideal model, or even a part of God's skill); and since everything is also governed according to this same idea, it can also be called a law. So the eternal law is nothing more than a plan in God's mind, in accordance with which every act and motion of the universe is directed.[6]

The laws that order the universe govern creatures through the natural forces and inclinations that were made part of their natures when they were created. As part of that universe, human beings are also subject to the eternal law of God through the natural inclinations within us that move us toward our own ends and activities. Unlike other creatures, however, human beings use their reason to direct themselves toward their ends:

> It is clear from the preceding article that the eternal law is the guide and standard for everything that is subject to God's provident direction. Clearly, therefore, the activities of all creatures are equally determined by the eternal law. Their activities are determined by the natural forces and inclinations that were made part of their natures when they were created [by God]. These natural forces and inclinations cause creatures to engage in their appropriate activities and attain their appropriate ends.
> Now rational creatures [such as humans] are also subject to God's provident direction, but in a way that makes them more like God than all other creatures. For God directs rational creatures by instilling in them certain natural inclinations and [reasoning] abilities that enable them to direct themselves as well as other creatures. Thus human beings also are subject to the eternal law and they too derive from that law certain natural

---

5   Ibid.

6   Ibid., I–IIae, q.93, a.1.

inclinations to seek their proper ends and proper activities. These inclinations of our nature constitute what we call the "natural law" and they are the effects of the eternal law imprinted in our nature.

Thus, even scripture suggests that our natural ability to reason (by which we distinguish right from wrong) in which the natural law resides, is nothing more than the image of God's own reason imprinted on us. For Psalm Four asks, "Who will show us what is right?" and it answers, "The light of Thy Mind, O Lord, which has been imprinted upon us."[7]

Aquinas argued that morality is based on these "natural inclinations" or this "natural law" that God instilled within us. Our reason perceives as good those things toward which we are naturally inclined and perceives as evil whatever is destructive of those goods. It is morally right to pursue the goods toward which we are naturally inclined and morally wrong to pursue what is destructive of those goods. Thus, natural law is the basis of morality:

A thing is good if it is an end that we have a natural inclination to desire; it is evil if it is destructive of what our nature is inclined to desire. Consequently, those kinds of things that our nature is inclined to desire are perceived by our reason as good for our human nature. And our reason will conclude that those kinds of things ought to be pursued in our actions. But if our reason sees a certain type of thing as destructive of what human nature is inclined to desire, it will conclude that that type of thing ought to be avoided.

We can therefore list the basic [moral] precepts of the natural law by listing the kinds of things that we naturally desire. First, like every other nature, human nature is inclined to desire its own survival. Consequently it is a natural [moral] law that we ought to preserve human life and avoid whatever is destructive of life. Secondly, like other animals, human nature is inclined to desire those things that nature teaches all animals to desire by instinct. For example, all animals have an instinctive desire to come together in a union of male and female, and an instinctive desire to care for their young. [So it is morally right to pursue these things.] Thirdly, human nature is inclined to desire those goods that satisfy our intellects. This aspect of our nature is proper to human beings. Thus, human nature is inclined to desire knowledge

(for example, to know the truth about God) and to desire an orderly social life. Consequently, it is a natural [moral] law that we ought to dispel ignorance and avoid harming those among whom we live.[8]

Thus, for Aquinas, the God whose existence is implied by an imperfect universe is also the God who creates the moral laws that we come to know by reflecting on our basic human inclinations. God is not only the foundation of the existence of the universe but also the foundation of morality.

DESCARTES

The role that God plays in the philosophy of Descartes is different from the role that God plays in other philosophies, such as that of Aquinas. For Aquinas as well as for other philosophers, God's existence is a conclusion we reach by coming to know the world around us. For Descartes, however, God is the One who guarantees that we can come to know the world around us. For Descartes, God is not a Being whom we come to know *after* we know the world around us; instead, God is a Being whom we must know about *before* we can know anything for certain about the world around us. God does not come at the end of knowledge but at the beginning.

There are many other differences between Descartes and Aquinas. Some of these differences undoubtedly reflect the changes that had taken place in Europe during the 350 years between them. Europe was no longer dominated by a single religion: Protestantism had appeared to compete with Catholicism. The physical sciences were emerging under the impetus of the new discoveries and theories of Galileo and Copernicus. Many of the new modern nations of Europe had already established themselves with their own particular languages, governments, and cultures. The New World of the Americas was being explored. And everywhere fresh minds were bubbling with new ideas and disputing the old medieval views—including those of Aquinas—that had so long dominated European intellectual life.

René Descartes was born in 1596 in Touraine, the son of a councillor of the Parliament of Brittany. A brilliant young man, he was sent in 1604 to study

---

[7] Ibid., I–IIae, q.91, a.2.

[8] Ibid., I–IIae, q.94, a.2.

Portrait of René Descartes (1596–1650)
c. 1649 (oil on canvas) (detail of 32939).
This painting is after the lost original that
was painted in 1649. Artist: Frans Hals
(1582/83–1666).

Louvre, Paris, France/Lauros/Giraudon/The Bridgeman Art Library

in the Jesuit college of La Fleche, where, although he was impressed by the precision of mathematics, he was deeply distressed by the disputes and doubts that surrounded all other realms of knowledge, especially philosophy. The end of school, in 1612, left him feeling unsettled and dissatisfied. As he later wrote in his *Discourse on Method,* a short philosophical work in which he described how he came to formulate his own philosophy:

> As soon as I had completed the entire course of study at the close of which one is usually received into the ranks of the learned, ... I found myself embarrassed with so many doubts and errors that it seemed to me that the effort to instruct myself had no effect other than the increasing discovery of my own ignorance. And yet I was studying at one of the most celebrated Schools in Europe.... I was delighted with Mathematics because of the certainty of its demonstrations and the evidence of its reasoning. ... On the other hand, ... I shall not say anything about Philosophy, but that, [although] it has been cultivated for many centuries by the best minds that have ever lived, ... nevertheless no single thing is to be found in it which is not subject to dispute, and in consequence which is not dubious. ... [A]s to the other sciences, inasmuch as they derive

their principles from Philosophy, I judged that one could have built nothing solid on foundations so far from firm.[9]

Disillusioned, Descartes joined the army at the age of 17 and began to travel, hoping that by studying "the great book of the world" he would find more truth than he had found in school:

> This is why, as soon as age permitted me to emerge from the control of my tutors, I entirely quitted the study of letters. And resolving to seek no other knowledge than that which could be found in myself, or at least in the great book of the world, I employed the rest of my youth in travel, in seeing courts and armies, in speaking with men of diverse temperaments and conditions, in collecting varied experiences, in proving myself in the various predicaments in which I was placed by fortune, and under all circumstances bringing my mind to bear on the things which came before it, so that I might derive some profit from my experience.[10]

But the young Descartes found himself as dissatisfied by the many conflicting opinions he encountered on his travels with the army as he had been by his formal studies in school. This led him one fateful winter day to resolve to see whether he could reach the truth by studying his own inner being:

> [During the time] I only considered the manners of other men I found in them nothing to give me settled convictions; and I remarked in them almost as much diversity as I had formerly seen in the opinions of philosophers. ... But after I had employed several years in thus studying the book of the world and trying to acquire some experience, I one day formed the resolution of also making myself an object of study and of employing all the strength of my mind in choosing the road I should follow. ... I was then in Germany, ... returning from the coronation of the Emperor to rejoin the army, [when] the setting in of winter detained me in a quarter where, since I found no society to divert me, while fortunately I had also no cares or passions to trouble me, I remained the whole day shut up alone in a stove-heated room where I had complete leisure to occupy myself with my own thoughts.[11]

---

9   René Descartes, *Discourse on Method,* in *The Philosophical Works of Descartes,* vol. 1, trans. and ed. Elizabeth S. Haldane and G. R. T. Ross (Cambridge: Cambridge University Press, 1911), 83, 85, 87.
10   Ibid., 86.
11   Ibid., 87.

There in his quiet little "stove-heated room," Descartes thought back to the careful method of reasoning that he had admired in mathematics. This method, Descartes felt, begins with "simple" truths that are so "clearly and distinctly perceived" that they cannot be doubted and proceed to the more complex truths that rest on the simple truths. Perhaps this method of reasoning could be used in other fields to establish all truth with certitude:

> Those long chains of reasoning, simple and easy as they are, of which geometricians make use in order to arrive at the most difficult demonstrations, had caused me to imagine that all those things which fall under the cognizance of man might very likely be mutually related in the same fashion; and that, provided only that we abstain from receiving anything as true which is not so, and always retain the order which is necessary in order to deduce the one conclusion from the other, there can be nothing so remote that we cannot reach to it, nor so recondite that we cannot discover it. ... Considering also that of all those who have hitherto sought for the truth in the Sciences, it has been the mathematicians alone who have been able to succeed in ... producing reasons which are evident and certain, I did not doubt that it had been by means of a similar method that they carried on their investigations.[12]

Convinced that in mathematics he had found an instance of the only reliable method for discovering truth, Descartes summarized his new method in four rules:

> The first of these was to accept nothing as true which I did not clearly recognize to be so: that is to say, carefully to avoid precipitation and prejudice in judgments, and to accept in them nothing more than what was presented to my mind so clearly and distinctly that I could have no occasion to doubt it.
> The second was to divide up each of the difficulties which I examined into as many parts as possible, and as seemed requisite in order that it might be resolved in the best manner possible.
> The third was to carry on my reflections in due order, commencing with objects that were the most simple and easy to understand, in order to

rise little by little, or by degrees, to knowledge of the most complex. ...
> The last was in all cases to make enumerations so complete and reviews so general that I should be certain of having omitted nothing.[13]

Believing that he now had a method for pursuing the truth, Descartes left his little room and again took up his travels. Nine years passed before he felt ready to apply his method to philosophical issues:

> Inasmuch as I hoped to be able to reach my end more successfully in converse with man than in living longer shut up in the warm room where these reflections had come to me, I hardly awaited the end of winter before I once more set myself to travel. And in all the nine following years I did nothing but roam hither and thither.... Nine years thus passed away before I had taken any definite part in regard to the difficulties as to which the learned are in the habit of disputing, or had commenced to seek the foundation of any philosophy. ... [Then I] resolved to remove myself from all places where any acquaintances were possible, and to retire to this country [Holland, where] ... I can live as solitary and retired as in deserts the most remote.[14]

Here, in solitude, Descartes began writing a long series of "meditations." Slowly, he built a philosophy that, he was convinced, was as solid and certain as mathematics because it relied on the same method. He began by putting his first rule into practice by "rooting out of my mind" all opinions that were the least bit doubtful. Through this "method of doubt," Descartes came upon the basic truth that was to serve as the "simple" principle from which he would "rise to the most complex":

> I do not know that I ought to tell you of the first meditations there made by me, for they are so metaphysical and so unusual that they may perhaps not be acceptable to everyone. ... Because I wished to give myself entirely to the search after Truth, I thought that it was necessary for me to take an apparently opposite course, and to reject as absolutely false everything as to which I could imagine the least ground of doubt, in order to see if afterwards there remained anything in my belief

12 Ibid., 91–92.

13 Ibid., 92.
14 Ibid., 98–100.

that was entirely certain. Thus, because our senses sometimes deceive us, I wished to suppose that nothing is just as they cause us to imagine it to be; and because there are men who deceive themselves in their reasoning and fall into fallacies, even concerning the simplest matters of geometry, and judging that I was as subject to error as was any other, I rejected as false all the reasons formerly accepted by me as demonstrations. And since all the same thoughts and conceptions which we have while awake may also come to us in sleep without any of them being at that time true, I resolved to assume that everything that ever entered into my mind was no more true than the illusions of my dreams.

But immediately afterwards I noticed that while I thus wished to think all things false, it was absolutely essential that the "I" who thought this should be something, and remarking that this truth, "I think, therefore I am" was so certain and so assured that all the most extravagant suppositions brought forward by the skeptics were incapable of shaking it, I came to the conclusion that I could receive it without scruple as the first principle of the Philosophy which I was seeking.

And then, examining attentively that which I was, I saw that I could conceive that I had no body, and that there was no world nor place where I might be; but yet that I could not for all that conceive that I was not. On the contrary, I saw from the very fact that I thought of doubting the truth of other things, it very evidently and certainly followed that I was. On the other hand, if I had only ceased from thinking, even if all the rest of what I had ever imagined had really existed, I should have no reason for thinking that I had existed. From that I knew that I was a substance the whole essence or nature of which is to think, and that for its existence there is no need of any place, nor does it depend on any material thing; so that this "me," that is to say, the soul by which I am what I am, is entirely distinct from body, and is even more easy to know than is the latter; and even if body were not, the soul would not cease to be what it is.

After this I considered generally what in a proposition is requisite in order to be true and certain; for since I had just discovered one which I knew to be such, I thought that I ought also to know in what this certainty consisted. And having remarked that there was nothing at all in the statement, "I think, therefore I am" which assures me of having thereby made a true assertion, excepting that I see very clearly that to think it is necessary to be, I came to the conclusion that I might

assume, as a general rule, that the things which we conceive very clearly and distinctly are all true—remembering, however, that there is some difficulty in ascertaining which are those that we distinctly conceive.

Following upon this, and reflecting on the fact that I doubted, and that consequently my existence was not quite perfect (for I saw clearly that it was a greater perfection to know than to doubt), I resolved to inquire whence I had learnt to think of Something more perfect than I myself was. And I recognized very clearly that this conception must proceed from some Nature which was really more perfect. As to the thoughts which I had of many other things outside of me, like the heavens, the earth, light, heat, and a thousand others, I had not so much difficulty in knowing whence they came, because, remarking nothing in them which seemed to render them superior to me, I could believe that, if they were true, they were dependencies upon my nature, in so far as it possessed some perfection; and if they were not true, that I held them from nothing, that is to say, that they were in me because I had something lacking in my nature. But this could not apply to the idea of a Being more perfect than my own, for to hold it came from nought would be manifestly impossible; and because it is no less contradictory to say of the more perfect that it is what results from and depends on the less perfect, than to say that there is something which proceeds from nothing, it was equally impossible that I should hold it from myself. In this way it could not but follow that it had been placed in me by a Nature which was really more perfect than mine could be, and which even had within itself all the perfections of which I could form any idea—that is to say, to put it in a word, which was God. To which I added that since I knew some perfections which I did not possess, I was not the only being in existence; but there was necessarily some other more perfect Being on which I depended, or from which I acquired all that I had.[15]

Thus, Descartes was led by his method to realize that he existed, that he had a soul, and, most important, that God existed, for, as Descartes reasoned, God is the foundation of all truth. God is not a deceiver, and God ensures that whatever we "clearly and distinctly" understand is true. Error arises only when

---

15 Ibid., 100–102.

we pass judgment on matters that are not clearly and distinctly understood:

> For, first of all, I recognize it to be impossible that He should ever deceive me; for in all fraud and deception some imperfection is to be found, and although it may appear that the power of deception is a mark of subtlety or power, yet the desire to deceive without doubt testifies to malice or feebleness, and accordingly cannot be found in God. ...
>
> Whence, then, come my errors? They come from the sole fact that since the will is much wider in its range and compass than the understanding, I do not restrain it within the same bounds, but extend it also to things which I do not understand ....
>
> But if I abstain from giving my judgment on anything when I do not perceive it with sufficient clearness and distinctness, it is plain that I will act rightly and will not be deceived. But if I decide to deny or affirm [what is not clear and distinct], then I no longer make use as I should of my free will. ...
>
> So long as I restrain my will within the limits of my knowledge so that it forms no judgment except on matters which are clearly and distinctly represented to it by the understanding, I can never be deceived. For every clear and distinct perception is without doubt something and hence cannot derive its origin from what is nothing, but must of necessity have God as its author—God, I say, who, being supremely perfect, cannot be the cause of any error; and consequently we must conclude that such a perception is true.[16]

Having found the source of truth and knowledge, Descartes turned to the final major philosophical question that confronted him: Did the material world around him really exist, or was it merely a figment of his imagination?

> Now that I have noted what must be done to arrive at a knowledge of the truth, my principal task is to endeavor to emerge from the state of doubt into which I have these last days fallen, and to see whether nothing certain can be known regarding material things. ... Nothing further remains, then, but to inquire whether material things exist. ... I find that ... there is in me a certain passive faculty

of perception, that is, of receiving and recognizing the ideas of material things. ... But, since God is no deceiver, it is very manifest that He does not communicate to me these ideas directly and by Himself, nor yet by the intervention of some creature [different from the material objects I think I perceive]. For since He has given me no faculty to recognize that this is the case, but, on the other hand, a very great inclination to believe that they are conveyed to me by material objects, I do not see how He could be defended from the accusation of deceit if these ideas were produced by causes other than material objects. Hence we must allow that material things exist.[17]

Thus, the existence of a perfect God is our only guarantee that our knowledge about the world is accurate. If it were not for God, we could never be sure that any of our so-called knowledge of external reality is true. For earlier philosophers, God is primarily the foundation of reality, what accounts for the existence of the objects in the universe. But for Descartes, God is primarily the foundation of our knowledge, what accounts for the fact that we can know the objects in our universe.

Descartes' philosophy made him famous, and within a short time at least two of the crowned heads of Europe were asking his advice. In 1649, Descartes received an invitation from Queen Christina of Sweden, who requested him to instruct her in the mysteries of philosophy. Being eager to please her, Descartes traveled north to Sweden and there began tutoring the busy queen at the only hour she had free: five o'clock in the morning. The bitter cold and the early hour combined to weaken Descartes' health, and within a few months he caught pneumonia. On February 11, 1650, Descartes died.

ANNE CONWAY

Although both Aquinas and Descartes give God a very prominent position in their philosophies, Anne Conway more thoroughly developed a philosophy based wholly on the nature of God. She was truly obsessed by the idea of a God who is perfect in every way, and her fascinating and visionary philosophy is an attempt to describe the consequences of this idea. Unfortunately, because Conway was a woman in a male-dominated society, her work was

---

[16] René Descartes, *Meditations on First Philosophy*, in *Philosophical Works of Descartes*, vol. 1, trans. and ed. Elizabeth S. Haldane and G. R. T. Ross (Cambridge: Cambridge University Press, 1911), 172, 175–176, 178.

[17] Ibid., 179, 185, 191.

largely ignored, and when male philosophers took over her ideas, they failed to attribute them to her.

Conway was born on December 14, 1631, into a wealthy, energetic, and intellectually talented English family headed by Elizabeth and Heneage Finch, a lawyer. Tragically, her father died just a week before her birth. Virtually nothing is known of Anne's childhood other than that she received a remarkably full education. In 1651, she married Edward Conway, a wealthy landowner with some connections to the court of Charles II. Several philosophers, including Henry More and Ralph Cudworth, were frequent guests at their house; through them, especially More, Anne came in contact with some of the major philosophical currents of the age.

Throughout her life, Conway was plagued by migraine headaches. These may have been partially responsible for her death in 1679 at the age of 48. Conway died while her husband was away in Ireland, and his friends, wanting to let him see her before she was buried, had her body pickled in wine and stored in a vat in his library until he returned to bury her.

Toward the end of her life, Conway wrote a short work called *The Principles of the Most Ancient and Modern Philosophy,* which was published after her death. In that work she traced the fundamentals of her philosophical views.

Conway begins her philosophy focused on God, the most perfect of all beings. From this simple beginning, she deduces in a rationalist manner the main characteristics of the universe as she sees it. Although she does not attempt to prove that God exists, she goes to great lengths to explain what God has to be like. Because God is perfect, he must possess all perfections, including unlimited ("infinite") wisdom, goodness, justice, omniscience, and omnipotence. God is also a "spirit"—that is, a being capable of thinking and awareness. Although God has no physical body (and so no shape), he is the creator of the life, the bodies, and all other goods that creatures have:

> God is a Spirit, Light, and Life, infinitely Wise, Good, Just, Mighty, Omniscient, Omnipresent, Omnipotent, Creator and Maker of all things visible and invisible. ... He hath no manner of darkness or corpority [physical body] in him, and so consequently no kind of Form of Figure whatsoever. ... He is in a true and proper sense a creator

of all things, who doth not only give them their Form and figure, but also being, life, body, and whatsoever else of good they have.[18]

God, Conway holds, cannot change because he is already perfect. If he were to change, he would then have to become either more perfect or less perfect. But he cannot become more perfect, for he is already fully perfect, and neither can he become less perfect, for then he would not be God.

Moreover, Conway argues, because God is unchanging, he is outside of time. To see what she means, it may help consider that, when we say that time is passing, we mean that certain changes have occurred: The hands of a clock have moved across its face, or the sun above us has moved across the sky. But imagine that everything in our universe came to a complete stop so that nothing changed in any way: Absolutely nothing moved, and everything remained completely fixed in a frozen state. In such a completely frozen universe, nothing would distinguish one moment from another. Time would then be meaningless. Time requires change; without change, there is no time. Thus, Conway claimed, time itself is nothing but change. Because God is unchanging, God is not in time: He exists outside of the universe of time and change in a timeless state called "eternity," where the whole history of the universe appears before him as if in a single present, unchanging moment. By contrast, all creatures change and so are subject to time:

> In God there is neither time nor Change, nor Composition, nor Division of parts: He is wholly and universally one in himself and of himself, without any manner of variety or mixture. ... For ... Times ... are nothing else but successive Motions and operations of created beings. ... The eternity of God himself hath no times in it; nothing therein can be said to be past, or to come, but the whole is always present. ... And the reason hereof is manifest; because time is nothing else but the successive motion or operation of creatures; which motion or operation, if it should cease, time would also cease, and the creatures themselves would cease with time. Wherefore such is the nature of every creature, that it is in motion, or hath a

---

18   Anne Conway, *The Principles of the Most Ancient and Modern Philosophy,* ed. Peter Loptson (Boston: Martinus Nijhoff, 1982; original work published 1692), 149.

certain motion, by means of which it advances forward, and grows to a farther perfection. And seeing in God there is no successive motion or operation to a farther perfection; because he is most absolutely perfect. Hence there are not times in God or his eternity.[19]

Conway argues that although God is completely free to create whatever he chooses to create, he had to create us. God is free, yet he has to do what he does. How is this possible? How can God be both free and unfree? Conway explains that there is nothing greater than God that can force him to do anything: There is no external force that can make him do one thing rather than another. So, God is completely free from any *external* forces. But God is perfectly good, so he cannot be "indifferent" (unconcerned) about doing good; that is, his own inner goodness forces him to do what is good. So, whatever God does, he does it because it is a good thing to do. Therefore, although God is free from external forces, he is also unfree because his own inner goodness forces him to do whatever is good. Because it is good to create good things, God is forced to create good creatures:

> Although the Will of God be most free, so that whatsoever he doth in the behalf of his creatures, he doth freely without any external violence, compulsion, or any cause coming from them—whatsoever he doth, he doth of his own accord—Yet that indifference of acting, or not acting, can by no means be said to be in God. … Seeing his infinite wisdom, goodness, and justice is a law unto him, which he cannot transgress. … Hence therefore it evidently follows that it was not indifferent to God, whether he would give being to his creatures or no; but he made them out of a certain internal impulse of his divine wisdom and goodness, and so he created the world or creatures as soon as he could.[20]

In fact, Conway argues, because God has to create anything that is good, and because there are infinite numbers of good things that an all-powerful God can create, God must create infinite numbers of creatures inhabiting infinite numbers of worlds:

> These attributes duly considered, it follows that creatures were created in infinite numbers, or that there is an infinity of worlds or creatures made of God: for seeing God is infinitely powerful, there can be no number of creatures so great, that he cannot always make more: and because, as is already proved, he doth whatsoever he can do [that is good]; certainly his will, goodness, and bounty is as large and extensive as his power; whence it manifestly follows that creatures are infinite, and created in infinite manners, so that they cannot be limited or bounded with any number or measure.[21]

Not only are there infinite numbers of worlds in the universe around us, but there are also infinite numbers of worlds within each of us, and within each of these worlds in us is another infinity of worlds, and within each of these worlds another infinity of worlds, and so on. For God can create ever-smaller good things or "monads" within each good thing he creates, and, after all, God must create whatever is good:

> Also by the like reason is proved, that not only the whole body or system of creatures considered together is infinite, or contains in itself a kind of infinity; but also that every creature even the least that we can discern with our eyes, or conceive in our minds, hath therein such an infinity of parts, or rather entire creatures, that they cannot be numbered; even as it cannot be denied that God can place one creature within another, so he can place two as well as one, and four as well as two, so also eight as well as four, so that he could multiply them without end, always placing the less within the greater.… This being sufficient to demonstrate that in every creature, whether the same be a spirit or a body, there is an infinity of creatures, each whereof contains an infinity and again each of these, and so *ad infinitum*.[22]

Thus, for Conway, creativity is one of God's essential attributes: For God to be God, he must create. And, Conway holds, this creativity is from all eternity, so for an infinite length of time an infinity of creatures have existed. The universe is infinite in time as it is infinite in creatures.

According to Conway, the essential difference between God and the infinite creatures he creates is changeability. God, as we have seen, does not change and is outside of time. However, the creatures he creates all change in time. Although God

---

[19] Ibid., 149, 154, 155.
[20] Ibid., 157, 158.

[21] Ibid., 158–159.
[22] Ibid., 159–160.

is perfect and cannot become better or worse, creatures are imperfect and so can change for the better or for the worse. But their changes into better or worse creatures are governed by God's justice.

At this point, Conway reaches a breathtaking conclusion. She argues that God's justice demands that over time each creature change into a higher or lower kind of creature. Consider, Conway suggests, that all creatures have a soul or a spirit. Now what is to become of this spirit at death?

> Now I demand, unto what higher perfection and degree of goodness, the being or essence of a horse doth or may attain after he hath done good service for his master, and so performed his duty, and what is proper for such a creature? Is a horse then a mere fabrick or dead matter? Or hath he a spirit in him, having knowledge, sense, and love, and divers other faculties and properties of a spirit? If he hath, which cannot be denied, what becomes of this spirit when the horse dies?[23]

Conway's answer is simple. If a creature has done good deeds in its life, she proposes, then justice demands that at death it be changed into a better creature. On the other hand, if a creature has done evil in its life, then at death justice demands it change into a lower creature. Thus, Conway argues, because God is just, his justice requires a kind of transmigration of spirits. Men and any other creatures who do evil are changed at death by God's justice into worse creatures, whereas creatures who do good are changed by God's justice into better ones:

> Now we see how gloriously the justice of God appears in this transmutation of things out of one species into another; and that there is a certain justice which operates not only in men and angels, but in all creatures, is most certain; and he that doth not observe the same may be said to be utterly blind: for this justice appears as well in the ascension of creatures as in their descension; that is, when they are changed into the better and when into the worse; when into the better, this justice distributes to them the reward and fruit of their good deeds; when into the worse, the same punishes them with due punishments, according to the nature and degree of the transgression. ...

> For example: is it not just and equitable, if a man on earth liveth a pure and holy life, like unto the heavenly angels, that he should be exalted to an angelical dignity after death, and be like unto them ...? But if a man here on earth lives so wickedly and perversely that he is more like a devil raised from hell than any other creature, if he dies in such a state without repentance ... shall not such deservedly become like devils ...? But if a man hath neither lived an angelical or diabolical, but a brutish, or at leastwise an animal or sensual life on earth; so that his spirit is more like the spirit of a beast than any other thing: shall the same justice most justly cause that as he is become a brut, as to his spirit ... that he also (at least as to his external form in bodily figure) should be changed into that species of beasts, to whom he was inwardly most like ...?[24]

But Conway's greatest contribution to philosophy lies in her method of bringing the body and the spirit together. The philosopher Descartes, before her, had claimed that humans have both a body and a spirit. But the body, Descartes claimed, is utterly different from and distinct from the spirit: They are two different and separate things. So different are they that it seems that the body and the spirit cannot possibly affect each other. That set the basic problem for philosophy after Descartes: How is the body related to the spirit when they are two different and separate things?

Conway avoids Descartes' problem by proposing that body and spirit are not two different things, but rather that they are merely aspects or qualities of the same thing. Every creature, Conway claims, exhibits both bodily qualities and spiritual qualities. Even the "lowest" physical creatures such as rocks and plants have some rudimentary spiritual consciousness, some minimal levels of awareness, life, and thinking. On the other hand, even the "highest" spiritual creatures, such as angels, have some residual bodily qualities, some minimal degree of physical qualities. Everything in the universe, then, is both bodily and spiritual. So, body and spirit are not to be thought of as *things*. Instead, they are merely two different kinds of qualities that all creatures possess to a greater or lesser degree.

Conway provides several arguments in support of her view that every creature—even something like a rock—has both physical and spiritual qualities.

---

[23] Ibid., 180–181.

[24] Ibid., 184, 185.

For example, she argues that whatever God creates has to have some of his qualities: God communicates something of himself to each thing he creates. Because God is a spirit, everything he creates has to have some spiritual qualities. Moreover, God creates creatures so that they can share eternal life with him. But how can they do this unless they have spiritual qualities?

> For seeing God is infinitely good and communicates his goodness in finite ways to his creatures; so that there is no creature which doth not receive something of his goodness, and that very largely: and seeing the goodness of God is a living goodness, which hath life, power, love, and knowledge in it, which he communicates to his creatures, how can it be that any dead thing should proceed from him or be created by him? ... Has not God created all his creatures of this end, that in him they might be blessed and enjoy his divine goodness, in their several states and conditions? But how can this be without life or sense?[25]

Thus, the universe as conceived by Conway is much richer and more dynamic and orderly than other philosophers had ever suggested. Not only are there an infinity of worlds within worlds in her vision of the universe, but these infinite numbers of creatures are all living, thinking, and feeling creatures as well. Everything in the universe is alive and has some degree of awareness, from the simplest grain of dust to the highest angel. Moreover, although there is a constant churn of change as creatures continuously mutate into higher or lower creatures, this change is all regulated by God's justice, which ensures that each creature at death will be reborn into the kind of creature it deserves to be.

Perhaps because Conway was a woman, and so condemned to be ignored by a world thoroughly dominated by males, her thought had very little direct impact on philosophy. However, after her death, the German philosopher Gottfried Leibniz (1646–1716) studied her work and based his own famous views on those of Conway. Leibniz took from Conway the idea that God creates infinitely many "monads" (without, of course, giving her credit for the idea). Leibniz also took from her the idea that God's goodness compels him to create good things,

as well as the idea that because God is perfectly good, the universe of creatures he creates also has to be perfectly good. Thus, through Leibniz and other male philosophers, many of the major ideas of Conway entered the mainstream of philosophy, although the men who took over her ideas relegated her name to obscurity.

Conway's philosophy is notable not only for its unwavering focus on God, but also because of the view that it provides of human beings. Conway's views on God's justice and the transmigration of creatures, in fact, are very similar to the Hindu religious view of karma and rebirth. Hindu religious thought has traditionally held that at death all living creatures are reborn as new living creatures. The kind of creature one becomes after death depends on one's karma—that is, the totality of good or evil deeds one has performed during one's past. If one's deeds were good, then one is reborn into a higher creature; if one's deeds were evil, then one is reborn into a lower animal. Conway's philosophy comes to exactly the same conclusions, but on the basis of a conception of God that is much more familiar to Westerners.

QUESTIONS

1. Evaluate each of Aquinas' proofs for the existence of God. Why do you think a believer like Aquinas would be concerned with proving God's existence? Does it make sense to believe without proof? Why or why not?

2. Does Aquinas' theory of analogy really explain how it is possible for religious believers to speak about God? Contemporary theories of language hold that words mean whatever we, the speakers of the language, intend them to mean. How can we intend words to have a meaning that we do not understand when applied to God? Does Aquinas' theory imply that God must be like the world that God creates?

3. Compare the interests and approaches of Descartes and Aquinas. What accounts for these differences? Which seem to be more "modern"? Why?

4. How useful are Descartes' four rules for discovering the truth? Could you use them, for example, as the basis for discovering the truth about God for yourself? Explain.

5. Descartes criticized all philosophy prior to his because "no single thing is to be found in it which is

---

[25] Ibid., 196.

not subject to dispute, and in consequence which is not dubious." Explain whether this criticism applies to Descartes' own philosophy and to his own views about God. Why would Descartes have felt that his philosophy was immune from his criticism?

6. Is Descartes correct in claiming that "if I abstain from giving my judgment on anything when I do not perceive it with sufficient clearness and distinctness, it is plain that I will act rightly and will not be deceived"? Do you decide of your own free will to believe what you believe?

7. Explain why Conway holds that God is "outside of time." Do you agree with Conway's view that time is change? Explain your answer.

8. Explain Conway's view that God is both free and unfree.

9. Explain why Conway believes that God's justice requires transmigration.

10. How, exactly, did Conway try to avoid Descartes' body/mind problem? Do you think she succeeded in doing so? Explain your answer.

5 The Sources of Knowledge

A man is but what he knows.

FRANCIS BACON

All I know is what I read in the papers.

WILL ROGERS

OUTLINE AND LEARNING OBJECTIVES

5.1 Why Is Knowledge a Problem?

LEARNING OBJECTIVES: When finished, you'll be able to:

- Explain how the controversy over recovered memories shows the importance of understanding what knowledge is.
- Discuss why it is important, for society and for ourselves, to understand the sources of reliable knowledge.
- Explain why memory is not an original source of knowledge.

5.2 Is Reason the Source of Our Knowledge?

LEARNING OBJECTIVES: When finished, you'll be able to:

- Describe and criticize Descartes' views on knowledge and Plato's argument for innate ideas.
- Explain and critically evaluate the rationalist claims that reason is a source of knowledge and that some knowledge is innate.

5.3 Can the Senses Account for All Our Knowledge?

LEARNING OBJECTIVES: When finished, you'll be able to:

- Describe and criticize Locke's and Berkeley's empiricist views on the source of our knowledge and our knowledge of the "external" world.
- Explain Hume's view that sense experience is the only source of knowledge and evaluate his argument that it is unjustified to claim that there is an external world or that real causality exists.
- **thinking critically** Identify and evaluate inductive generalizations.
- Explain the problem of induction, how it is related to Hume, and why it is difficult to solve.

5.4 Kant: Does the Knowing Mind Shape the World?

LEARNING OBJECTIVES: When finished, you'll be able to:

- Explain how Kant's theory of knowledge combines rationalism and empiricism.
- Explain how Kant showed that we can know the synthetic *a priori* statements of mathematics and natural science.
- Critically evaluate Kant's claim that Hume's skepticism is mistaken because the mind organizes its sensations into the world as we know it.
- Describe how Kant's views were later modified by romantic philosophers, anthropologists, and constructivist psychologists and sociologists.

5.5 Does Science Give Us Knowledge?

LEARNING OBJECTIVES: When finished, you'll be able to:

- Explain and critically evaluate inductionism, the hypothetical method, falsifiability, and Kuhn's theory of scientific knowledge.
- Explain how each is related to empiricism, rationalism, and Kant.
- **thinking critically** Distinguish science from pseudoscience.

© John Navajo/Shutterstock.com

Chapter Summary

5.6 Readings

Ambrose Bierce, "An Occurrence at Owl Creek Bridge"

Peter Unger, "A Defense of Skepticism"

Thomas Nagel, "How Do We Know Anything?"

5.7 Historical Showcase: Hume

One of the fundamental branches of philosophy is epistemology, the study of knowledge. Specifically, epistemology deals with the nature, sources, limitations, and validity of knowledge. Epistemological questions are basic to all other philosophical inquiries. Everything we claim to know, whether in science, history, or everyday life, amounts to little if we cannot justify our claims. Thus, neither a concept of human nature and self, nor a theory of the universe, nor even an assertion about an ordinary event ("This lemon tastes sour" or "It is raining") escapes the need for justification. Epistemology presents us with the task of explaining how we know what we claim to know, how we can find out what we wish to know, and how we can judge someone else's claim to know. Epistemology addresses a variety of problems: the sources, reliability, and extent of our knowledge; the nature of truth; linguistic meaning; scientific knowledge; and how we interpret each other's actions and words. This and the next chapter deal with these major epistemological topics. This chapter focuses on the question of *how* true knowledge is acquired—its sources or bases—and the next examines the *nature* of true knowledge.

5.1 Why Is Knowledge a Problem?

Your ideas about who you are depend on what you think you know. In fact, nothing is more important to understanding yourself than your knowledge of your past. Your past has made you what you are. Your memories of that past—of parents, of the home you grew up in, of the friends and experiences you have had—constitute your understanding of who you now are. Yet how do you know whether your memories are true? Consider the following account written by a young college student:

> Jana never calls. I live a long way away and she is my only sibling, but she never calls . . . .
>
> Suddenly, out of the blue, she was calling me, talking to me, sharing her life with me . . . . [But] the circumstances that finally broke down the barriers between us were catastrophic, unspeakable. Our parents, my dear sister told me, had repeatedly abused her when she had been very young.
>
> I was stunned. "This abuse was . . . sexual?"
>
> "Yes, sexual."
>
> "And they both were involved?"
>
> "Yes, they and others."
>
> "Are you sure?"
>
> "YES, OF COURSE I AM!"
>
> I was furious with my parents. I had left home a few years back under the cloud of ongoing arguments with them and, since then, I had been slowly trying to patch

things up. This revelation shattered the reconciliations, shattered even the desire to make the effort. With each of the many collect phone calls I accepted from Jana, my parents became more and more strangers, less the people I remembered knowing as a child. When I commented on this fact, Jana taught me about repressed memories. I was frightened beyond description. My entire life was nothing more than my memories of it. If suddenly those are taken away, if suddenly they are found to be fiction, then what am I? I too am fiction. I am the man with amnesia who knows not even his name. I am a 24-year-old adult with no memories of what really happened to him as a child. It was in the midst of that horror of no longer knowing who the hell I was that I began to search desperately for answers. . . . Jana called every other day or so to tell me new stories of abuse that had gurgled up from the black well-spring of repressed memories in her unconscious mind. Abuse by groups. Abuse with guns. Abuse with various crude medical instruments. Abuse by physical and psychological torture.

It was in this atmosphere of dread and disgust that I discovered I too had been sexually abused as a kid. . . . I discovered my own personal experiences with the help of a psychiatric social worker. . . . The therapist suggested that it would be odd if I had been left alone while my sister had been so harmed. . . . No wonder I couldn't remember anything about my childhood! It was too horrible to remember! Over the next couple sessions she walked me through what she called "relaxation therapy." Whatever I should see, assuming it wasn't too happy, I was to consider truth. . . .

The clarity of the new memories was striking, photographic. So much better than my old memories, those fake cover-up daydreams I'd used to help me suppress the truth; they had all been cloudy. I was beginning to feel like a survivor, like I was on to the truth and it was just a matter of time until I could feel whole again. The trouble was, the closer I came to being "whole," the worse I felt. I was flunking my college classes. I was calling in to work sick. I was smoking a lot. I didn't shave. I didn't eat well. And I didn't care. . . .

Dr. Michael Fane, a psychiatrist ...was my lucky break. He ran the clinic where my therapist worked, and part of the deal was that I had to have one diagnostic session with him before treatment proceeded. I explained to him my situation, my recent discovery of abuse, and the things I believed had been done to me. . . . [But during the diagnostic session Dr. Fane explained how such memories can be fabricated by one's own mind and how "recovered memories" may not be true at all.] By the next morning I would wake up to find my faith in my new memories shattered. . . . I had never heard of False Memory Syndrome at this point in my life, but I knew that I had it.[1]

Working with Dr. Fane over many sessions, the college student who wrote this account decided his "recovered" memories of sexual abuse were false memories. But his sister, Jana, remains convinced that her memories are true. She has broken off all contact with her parents, whom she now sees as monsters who turned her into a dysfunctional person. She believes that her brother, who refuses to accept her knowledge that their parents sexually abused them, is "in denial" of the truth.

Jana and her brother are not the only people who fear that the most fundamental things they thought they knew about themselves might be completely false. Today, tens of thousands of men and women believe they have recalled formerly repressed memories of being sexually abused. The abuse, they feel, was inflicted by parents, siblings, relatives, and family friends when they were children. Before entering therapy, they claimed, they had no knowledge of the acts but suffered

---

[1] Eleanor Goldstein and Kevin Farmer, *True Stories of False Memories* (Boca Raton, FL: Social Issues Resources Series, 1993), 117, 118, 199, 120, 125. Used by permission of the publisher.

from a variety of "symptoms." These symptoms included depression, anxiety, eating disorders, sexual problems, and difficulty with intimacy. Sometimes the recovered memories include terrifying details. Some have recalled torture, participation in satanic rituals, animal sacrifices, and even murder.

The theory of "recovered memories" has stirred fierce controversy. Supporters of the theory cite studies based on clinical practice. For example, Judie Alpert, a professor of applied psychology at New York University, asserts the following:

> There is absolutely no question that some people have repressed some memories of early abuse that are just too painful to remember. In their 20s and 30s some event triggers early memories, and slowly they return. The event has been so overwhelming that the little girl who is being abused can't tolerate to be there in the moment, so she leaves her body, dissociates, as if she is up on a bookshelf looking down on the little girl who is being abused. Over time, she pushes it deep down because she can't integrate the experience.[2]

MindTap To read more about repression from Elizabeth Loftus, click the link in the MindTap Reader or go to the Questia Readings folder in MindTap.

Other psychologists flatly deny that these theories are scientifically valid. Professor Elizabeth Loftus is professor of psychology at the University of Washington. She asserts that the theory that people can repress memories of repeated traumatic experiences in childhood and recall them decades later is false:

> If repression is the avoidance in your conscious awareness of unpleasant experiences that come back to you, yes, I believe in repression. But if it is a blocking out of an endless stream of traumas that occur over and over that leave a person with absolutely no awareness that these things happened, that make them behave in destructive ways and re-emerge decades later in some reliable form, I don't see any evidence for it. It flies in the face of everything we know about memory.[3]

The controversy over repressed and recovered memories is a dramatic illustration of some profound issues raised by our views about knowledge. These include our views of what knowledge is, how we acquire it, how we establish its truth, and whether science gives us the truth. It shows how important it is to be clear about these issues. As Jana's brother says, if one accepts recovered memories as true knowledge, then one's identity can become a mere "fiction." And the parents one may have thought he knew may turn out to be "strangers." If we believe recovered memories provide true knowledge of past crimes, then we must believe that many people who are living comfortable lives should be cast into the deepest prisons. If we accept that the studies supporting the theory of recovered memory are valid science, then we will agree that recovered memories provide true knowledge of past crimes.

QUICK REVIEW
The controversy on recovered memories, and court cases based on them, raise urgent questions about how we acquire knowledge, how we know the truth, and whether science gives us truth.

Yet are recovered memories a source of true knowledge, and is the theory of recovered memories valid science? Many critics of recovered memories remind us of the seventeenth-century Salem witch trials. During these trials, many women were condemned to death because men "knew" they were witches. They "knew" this because of the women's supposedly witchlike behavior and accepted theories of witchcraft. Indeed, how often have entire societies found themselves deluded about the valid sources of knowledge and truth? For several hundred years, European society and science believed that the earth was flat and that it lay at the center

---

[2] Quoted in Leon Jaroff, "Lies of the Mind," *Time*, November 29, 1993, 52; for a more recent review of the literature on the controversy over recovered memories, see Elizabeth F. Loftus and Deborah Davis, "Recovered Memories," *Annual Review of Clinical Psychology*, vol. 2 (2006), 469–98.

[3] Ibid.

of the universe. Everyone believed that the sun, planets, and stars revolved around the earth. When Copernicus, Galileo, and others suggested that this was a mistake, they were condemned and persecuted by church authorities. Church authorities believed that Scripture is the only source of true knowledge. According to Scripture, they claimed, the earth lies at the center of the universe. During the Nazi era, German society claimed that it was a "scientific fact" that the Germanic races were superior to all others. So they rounded up Jews and Gypsies, imprisoned them, tortured them, and eventually murdered millions. Here in the United States researchers claimed their scientific studies showed that white races are genetically superior to blacks. They concluded that race-based public policies are justified. And in the recent past, reputable scientists claimed that women were inferior to men and that society should treat them as such.

All these events show the importance—both to us personally and to our society—of looking carefully at the issues of truth and knowledge. What is knowledge? What is truth? What is the difference between true scientific knowledge and bogus theories of pseudoscience? What are the valid sources of knowledge and truth?

In this chapter, we examine the question of how reliable knowledge is acquired. We ask what distinguishes the way in which reliable knowledge is acquired from the way in which unreliable beliefs are acquired. In the next chapter, we examine what true knowledge *is* instead of looking at how it is *acquired*.

Acquiring Reliable Knowledge: Reason and the Senses

How do we acquire reliable knowledge? What is the source or basis of our knowledge? Philosophers have given considerable attention to questions about the sources of knowledge. One way of approaching the subject, though by no means the only way, is to examine two views about the sources of our knowledge: rationalism and empiricism. **Rationalism** is the view that knowledge of the world can be obtained by relying on reason without the aid of the senses. In this view, reason is the key source of the knowledge we have about the universe. So what distinguishes real knowledge from mere opinion, in the rationalist view? Real knowledge is based on the logic, the laws, and the methods of reason. The best example of real knowledge, many rationalists hold, is mathematics. Mathematics is a kind of knowledge that is obtained entirely by reason and that we use to understand the universe.

Empiricism, on the other hand, is the view that knowledge about the world can be attained only through sense experience. According to the empiricist, real knowledge is based on what sight, hearing, smell, and other senses tell us about reality, not what people discover in their heads.

In this chapter, we look more closely at these two seminal theories of the sources of our knowledge. We will then consider an influential alternative, *transcendental idealism.* Transcendental idealism attempts to integrate the insights of empiricism

© Photothèque R. Magritte-ADAGP/Art Resource, NY/ARS, NY

The False Mirror, René Magritte. Are there different kinds of knowledge? If there are, how can each be obtained? What are their sources? What are their limits? Rationalists endorse reason, arguing that only rational knowledge is certain. Empiricists contend that reason can only relate the facts that are presented by the senses.

and rationalism. We will end by looking at how these theories relate to the knowledge generated by science. We will also discuss whether scientific knowledge can be distinguished from pseudoscience.

The Place of Memory

Before we turn to these tasks, however, you might be asking a question: So where does memory fit into all this? After all, when we discussed recovered memories, the key question was whether people's "recovered" memories yield real knowledge of distant events. So shouldn't we discuss memory as a source of knowledge in addition to sense experience and reason?

To answer this question, let us look more closely at what memory is. Memory is, basically, the ability to bring facts or past experiences into our present consciousness or activities. However, there are different kinds of memory. Some philosophers have argued that we have at least three kinds of memory: habit memory, personal memory, and factual memory. *Habit memory* is our ability to remember how to do something that we learned in the past, such as how to ride a bicycle or how to ski. Habit memory is our ability to bring into our present activities the skills we learned by past experience. *Personal memory* is our ability to bring into our present consciousness a representation of events that we personally and directly experienced in the past. I use personal memory, for example, when I remember personally talking with you yesterday or personally playing with my cousin many years ago. Finally, *factual memory* is our memory of all the facts that make up our knowledge of the world. For example, I remember that George Washington was the first president of the United States. Of course I personally acquired the facts that make up my factual memories. But I did not personally experience those facts. For example, I didn't personally experience Washington's presidency.

Memory is obviously a critically important aspect of knowledge, as shown by the cases of recovered memories. Without memory of my past, I wouldn't have any knowledge of who I am. Nor could I retain any knowledge of the world around me, nor have the knowledge I need to relate to the people I love and to the things that matter to me. In fact, without memory, I would retain no knowledge whatsoever.

But is memory a *source* of the fundamental knowledge we have? Apparently not. Any knowledge that I now remember I must have acquired earlier, through some other more fundamental source. For example, my personal memories consist of things that I experienced through my senses—what I directly saw, heard, touched, tasted, or felt. My habit memories are skills I also acquired by working with my senses and learning through the experience of practicing. And my factual memories I acquired through reading or hearing, or through using my reason to think things out for myself. In each case memory does not bring any new knowledge to me but merely preserves knowledge that I acquired through some other source. If we are to study the source of the knowledge we have, then, we should not study memory itself, but the sources from which our memories were acquired. And the two basic sources of all of our knowledge and memories, most philosophers agree, are sense perception and reason. For these reasons, then, we will only discuss sense perception and reason as sources of knowledge. We will not directly discuss memory as a source of knowledge.

THINKING LIKE A PHILOSOPHER

The text suggests there are three kinds of memory: habit memory, personal memory, and factual memory. What are some examples from your own life of each of these three kinds of memory?

PHILOSOPHY AT THE MOVIES

Watch *The Crucible* (1996), which is based on the play by Arthur Miller and portrays the Salem, Massachusetts, witch trials of 1692 where several men and women accused of witchcraft were jailed, tortured, and executed when a group of teenage girls testified against them. Analyze each of the main characters—John Proctor, his wife Elizabeth, the Reverend Parris, the Reverend Hale, and Judge Danforth—and explain what each assumes are valid and reliable sources of knowledge. In what ways does this movie show the importance of having a correct understanding of what real knowledge is, what the valid sources of knowledge are, and how "knowledge" should be tested and evaluated to ensure it really is knowledge?

5.2 Is Reason the Source of Our Knowledge?

Rationalism is the view that reason, without the aid of sensory perception, is capable of arriving at some truths about the world. **Perception** refers to seeing, hearing, smelling, touching, and tasting, as well as sensing our inner states. Perception, then, includes the processes by which we sense or perceive the qualities of ordinary physical things like their colors, shapes, sounds, smells, textures, tastes, etc., as well as our inner states like emotions or feelings of pain. When rationalists say at least some of our knowledge is based on reason rather than perception, they mean that we do not rely on these sensory processes for all of our knowledge about the world around us.

In effect, rationalists contend that the source of some of our knowledge is not our perceptual experience but our mental processes. They hold that we acquire some knowledge about the world around us through reasoning and not by observing it with our senses. That is, we acquire some truths about the world by just thinking and reasoning inside our minds.

At first sight, this view may strike you as an astonishingly stupid view: How can we know anything about the world around us without first observing it? But before you brush aside this view of knowledge, think a little about how mathematicians work and how their work differs from that of other scientists. Scientists such as chemists and physicists work in laboratories, where they conduct experiments and observe the results. Astronomers use giant telescopes to observe the stars. Biologists use microscopes to determine what living organisms are like. In short, these scientists need to observe the external world to check whether their theories are true. Not so the mathematician. The mathematician typically works huddled over her desk, perhaps with the shades drawn. Yet she can discover mathematical theorems in her windowless office by using nothing more than pencil, paper, and reason. The mathematician does not need to observe the external world to check whether her theories are true. Yet the mathematical theories she discovers by reasoning in her mind can accurately describe the vast universe outside her office.

Because such knowledge does not depend on sense experience, rationalists call it a priori knowledge. *A priori* knowledge is knowledge that we know has to be true, without having to rely on sense observations. That is, by using just our reason without relying on our senses, we know *a priori* claims are true and that they necessarily have to be true. Moreover, the rationalist holds, some of the knowledge that we discover by just using reason underlies our understanding of the universe. When astronomers investigate black holes and stars in galaxies billions of miles away, they use the theories of the mathematician. When physicists explore the intricacies of subatomic

> **QUICK REVIEW**
> Rationalists claim that not all knowledge of the world around us is acquired through sense observation. For example, mathematical knowledge is acquired by reasoning alone without observation of the world, yet it tells us how the world works.

particles they must rely on the mathematician's theories. When biologists examine the chemistry of DNA, they too must use the theories the mathematician reasoned out. The great scientist Albert Einstein wondered how the mathematician's theories could describe the world so precisely. He asked: "How is it possible that mathematics, a product of human thought that is independent of experience, fits so excellently the objects of physical reality?" In fact, mathematics can reveal facts about the world that scientific observation has not yet discovered. In 1867, for example, James Maxwell expressed all that was known about electromagnetic fields in four mathematical equations. The mathematics of the equations showed that radio waves—unknown at the time—had to exist. But it took twenty years before scientists detected them.

Similar points may be made about the laws of logic. The laws of logic include propositions like: "At least one of any two contradictory propositions must be false." Or: "No proposition can both be and not be true at the same time." These laws of logic are also not established by observation. Yet they underlie all our reasoning about the world around us. So, reason, without relying on sense experience, can give us knowledge of truths about the world. And these truths are so basic that much of our other knowledge depends on our prior knowledge of these truths.

ANALYZING THE READING

A priori knowledge is knowledge we know is true independently of perception. The textbook gives the examples of mathematical truths, truths of logic, and several others. Can you give examples not in your textbook, of some mathematical truths that you know for sure you did not get from experience because you could never have experienced what the truths say? Can you think of other things that you can know are true without ever having to check it out with your senses?

Rationalists do not necessarily believe that all knowledge is acquired through reason alone. Many of them agree that we get some of our knowledge by observing things with our senses—for example, whether the sun is shining, whether giraffes have spots, whether dinosaurs existed. But the rationalist holds that *some* of our knowledge about reality is acquired without sense experience, and that this includes some of the most basic knowledge we have.

Rationalists also insist that some of the knowledge we acquire by using reason alone is knowledge about the world around us. We obviously have knowledge that is not based on sensory experience but that is also not about the world, For example, we know that all bachelors are unmarried. But such knowledge is true by definition. So it does not give us any information about the world. However, the rationalist claims that some of our knowledge about the world is acquired by the use of reason alone, without sense experience. For example, some rationalists have held that the laws of logic and of mathematics tell us what the world has to be like and that these laws are established solely by reason. But the laws of logic and mathematics are not the only examples of knowledge we did not discover by using our senses. Other examples include these propositions: (1) Every event has a cause. (2) The shortest distance between two points on a plane surface is a straight line. (3) The universe follows the same laws in all of its parts. (4) The processes of the universe are regular and can be explained by consistent laws. The rationalist points to these as other examples of fundamental knowledge about the world we did not get by using our senses.

Western philosophers are not the only thinkers who have believed that some of our knowledge is not based on sense experience. Eastern philosophy has given birth to several rationalist views of knowledge. Almost all schools of Indian philosophy agree that sense perception is a source of some knowledge. But several Indian philosophers also claim that sense perception is ultimately erroneous. Therefore, we must rely on other sources of knowledge to investigate reality. A good example of a rationalist non-Western thinker is the great Indian philosopher Shankara (788–822).

Shankara was a charismatic mystic, saint, and poet who founded the Advaita Vedanta school of philosophy before he died at the young age of 32. Shankara's philosophy can be summed up in this statement: "Brahman [Ultimate Reality] is real, the world is false, and the self is not different from Brahman." A basic idea that Shankara developed is the idea of "sublation." Sublation is the process of correcting an error about reality when it is contradicted by a different but more correct understanding of reality. For example, a thirsty man in a desert might run to a mirage of water he sees in the distance. But when he gets there and finds nothing but sand, he realizes and corrects his error.

According to Shankara, hallucinations, dreams, mirages, and other illusions give rise to errors. But we "sublate" these errors when we see that they are contradicted by other things our senses show us in the world around us. But more important, Shankara said, is that everything in the world around us that we perceive with our senses can also be sublated. It is sublated when through study of the Hindu Scriptures, through reasoning, and through meditation we come to know the ultimate reality. That ultimate reality he called Brahman. When we come to know Brahman, the ultimate reality that underlies everything, we realize that the world we perceive is an illusion compared to the reality of Brahman. For example, a dream has its own reality yet is an illusion in comparison to the world our senses reveal. In the same way the world our senses reveal has its own reality yet is an erroneous illusion in comparison to Brahman. Moreover, argues Shankara, by meditating we can come to experience our own deepest self. This deepest self is pure inner consciousness. As we know and understand this deepest self, we will realize there is no difference between our self and other selves nor between our self and all other things. Then we will also recognize that this pure self is Brahman. At that point we will realize who and what we really are and attain bliss as ignorance disappears.

QUICK REVIEW
The Indian philosopher Shankara was a rationalist who held that our knowledge of ultimate reality is not acquired through our senses but through reasoning and meditation.

What is important to notice about Shankara's philosophy is his key idea that the senses are not a source of knowledge of ultimate reality. Instead, thinking, study, reasoning, and meditating are the key to knowing the ultimate reality—the Self that is identical with Brahman. And thinking reveals the illusory nature of the world that our senses perceive.

The history of Western philosophy also records the thinking of many other outstanding rationalists, including Plato (circa 428–348 BCE), Saint Augustine (354–430), Benedict Spinoza (1632–1677), Anne Conway (1631–1679), Gottfried Wilhelm Leibniz (1646–1716), and Georg Hegel (1770–1831). Three important rationalists living today include Noam Chomsky, Laurence Bonjour, and Peter Carruthers. The most noteworthy rationalist, however, is René Descartes. We already met Descartes when we discussed his dualist view of human nature in Chapter 2. An interesting fact we have not yet mentioned is that Descartes was an accomplished mathematician and that he invented analytic geometry. His mathematical thinking undoubtedly influenced his rationalist view of knowledge. We will begin our discussion of rationalism with Descartes because his ideas have been so influential in Western thought.

Descartes: Doubt and Reason

It's not hard to identify with Descartes' point of departure—an attitude of doubt or **skepticism** toward what we think we know. Today, we might call his frame of mind distrust. Descartes suffered a kind of epistemological "credibility gap." He was unsure about the truth of much that he had been taught to believe. Descartes was driven to this point by the many intellectual, scientific, and religious upheavals that his world was undergoing.

MindTap Descartes is an important figure in the study of knowledge. Go to MindTap to watch a video exploring his historical context and explaining the reasoning behind one of his important insights.

Only a few decades before Descartes was born, Martin Luther had launched the great Protestant revolution. The Protestant revolution engulfed all of Europe and gave birth to the religious wars that rocked the continent for decades. Church doctrines that everyone had accepted as eternal dogmas were suddenly cast into doubt. Moreover, scientists such as Copernicus and Galileo were challenging views that had been accepted for more than two thousand years. Copernicus rejected the view that the earth was at the center of the universe and that the sun revolved around it. In place of this old theory, Copernicus argued that the earth revolves around the sun. Galileo questioned established theories about the nature of the moon and the planets and theories about motion that were just as established.

We live in an age much like that of Descartes. Ours is an era of rapid change and new discoveries, of constant sensory input, and of an information explosion. Smartphones, computers, the Internet, blogs, Facebook, and Twitter move information around the globe instantly. Stock prices fall in Japan, and seconds later they drag down stock markets in the United States. Television programs aired in Los Angeles instantaneously create a stir in Europe. The flow of new discoveries in science, medicine, and technology is so fast and so massive that no one can keep up. Settled ideas about our universe are regularly overthrown. The universe we once thought was stable is actually expanding rapidly. An enigmatic energy called "dark energy" is pushing everything apart. We discovered that at the center of every galaxy are strange "black holes," massive objects whose gravity not even light can escape. The visible stars and galaxies we thought were the whole universe have turned out to be only about 15 percent of all the matter there is. A mysterious invisible "dark matter" accounts for about 85 percent of all the rest of the matter in the universe. Advances in medicine have extended life in ways that created troubling new questions about when life ends. Genetic engineering has found ways to "clone" replicas of any organism and raised new questions about the wisdom of manipulating life and even creating it. This rapid, continuous flow of information and new discoveries can leave us unsteadily wobbling between the old and the new.

Just as new discoveries leave us uncertain and disoriented, the people of the seventeenth century were afflicted with uncertainty. How should they reconcile the new ideas of Copernicus and Galileo with their old religious, philosophical, and scientific beliefs? Indeed, the age of Descartes was marked by a profound questioning of established religious doctrines and time-honored scientific theories. Amid this destabilizing questioning, Descartes searched for something firm to believe in. He looked for some fixed foundation on which he could stand amid the dizzying changes he was experiencing. Impressed by the clarity and reliability of mathematics Descartes came to believe its methods might provide a path to the certitude he sought. Mathematical reasoning, he felt, could be a model of reasoning that could yield the certain knowledge his skeptical age needed:

> The long chains of simple and easy reasoning by means of which geometers are accustomed to reach the conclusions of their most difficult demonstrations, had led me to imagine that all things, to the knowledge of which man is competent, are mutually connected in the same way, and that there is nothing so far removed from us as to be beyond our reach, or so hidden that we cannot discover it, provided only we abstain from accepting the false for the true, and always preserve in our thoughts the order necessary for the deduction of one truth from another.[4]

---

[4] René Descartes, *Discourse on the Method of Rightly Conducting the Reason, and Seeking Truth in the Sciences*, in *The Philosophical Works of Descartes*, vol. 1, trans. and ed. Elizabeth S. Haldane and G. R. T. Ross (Cambridge, England: Cambridge University Press, 1911).

Filled with the kind of doubt, uncertainty, and anxiety that many of us experience today, then, Descartes turned to the methods of mathematics. Perhaps mathematics' method of relying on absolutely certain truths, and inferring new truths from those, might help him find the unshakable knowledge he wanted. Hoping to discover such unshakable truth, Descartes examined each of his beliefs, asking himself whether it could be accepted as undeniably true:

All that up to the present time I have accepted as most true and certain I have learned either from the senses or through the senses; but it is sometimes proved to me that these senses are deceptive, and it is wiser not to trust entirely to any thing by which we have once been deceived. . . .

At the same time I must remember that I am a man, and that consequently I am in the habit of sleeping, and in my dreams representing to myself the same things or sometimes even less probable things, than do those who are insane in their waking moments. How often has it happened to me that in the night I dreamt that I found myself in this particular place, that I was dressed and seated near the fire, whilst in reality I was lying undressed in bed! At this moment it does indeed seem to me that it is with eyes awake that I am looking at this paper; that this head which I move is not asleep, that it is deliberately and of set purpose that I extend my hand and perceive it; what happens in sleep does not appear so clear nor so distinct as does all this. But in thinking over this I remind myself that on many occasions I have in sleep been deceived by similar illusions, and in dwelling carefully on this reflection I see so manifestly that there are no certain indications by which we may clearly distinguish wakefulness from sleep that I am lost in astonishment. And my astonishment is such that it is almost capable of persuading me that I now dream. . . .

I have long had fixed in my mind the belief that an all-powerful God exists by whom I have been created such as I am. But how do I know that He has not brought it to pass that there is no earth, no heaven, no extended body, no magnitude, no place, and that nevertheless I possess the perceptions of all these things and that they seem to me to exist just exactly as I now see them? And, besides, as I sometimes imagine that others deceive themselves in the things which they think they know best, how do I know that I am not deceived every time that I add two and three, or count the sides of a square, or judge of things yet simpler, if anything simpler can be imagined? But possibly God has not desired that I should be thus deceived, for He is said to be supremely good. If, however, it is contrary to His goodness to have made me such that I constantly deceive myself, it would also appear to be contrary to His goodness to permit me to be sometimes deceived, and nevertheless I cannot doubt that He does permit this.

I shall then suppose, not that God who is supremely good and the fountain of truth, but some evil genius not less powerful than deceitful, has employed his whole energies in deceiving me; I shall consider that the heavens, the earth, colors, figures, sound, and

ANALYZING THE READING

Descartes suggests that we can know anything there is to know by using the "chains of simple and easy reasoning" with which "geometers are accustomed to reach [their] conclusions." Think back to the geometry classes you've taken. What are the "chains of simple and easy reasoning" Descartes is talking about here? (Although maybe you didn't think they were so "simple and easy"!) What do you think Descartes might have in mind when he says we could use the reasoning methods of geometry to discover whatever we want to know about "all things"?

ANALYZING THE READING

1. According to Descartes God or an "evil genius" could do something to him that would make him see, hear, feel, taste, and smell everything around him exactly as he is doing right now, while, in reality, nothing existed around him. If God or an "evil genius" is deceiving him in this way, is there any way Descartes could know that they were doing this to him?

2. Descartes says that for all he knows, God or an evil genius might be deceiving him right now. So, he says, he will suspend his judgment about whether anything around him is what it appears to be. Do you think it's possible for anyone to do this? That is, is it possible for you to make yourself believe something just by deciding to do that? And is it possible for you to make yourself stop believing something you've always believed? Is belief like a light switch that you can turn on or off as you wish? Or is belief something that is forced on you by the events around you?

QUICK REVIEW

To find indubitable foundational truths, Descartes tried to doubt all his beliefs by realizing that everything might be a dream or an illusion of a powerful god; any beliefs that could not be doubted would be basic indubitable truths. One was "I think, therefore I am."

all other external things are nothing but the illusions and dreams of which this genius has availed himself in order to lay traps for my credulity. I shall consider myself as having no hands, no eyes, no flesh, no blood, nor any senses, yet falsely believing myself to possess all these things; I shall remain obstinately attached to this idea, and if by this means it is not in my power to arrive at the knowledge of any truth, I may at least do what is in my power [i.e., suspend my judgment], and with firm purpose avoid believing any false thing, or being imposed upon by this arch deceiver, however powerful and deceptive he may be.[5]

 THINKING LIKE A PHILOSOPHER

Descartes says that for all he knows he might be dreaming and that "there are no certain indications by which we may clearly distinguish wakefulness from sleep." Have you ever had such a clear dream that even afterwards you thought it might not have been a dream? Have you ever had a dream in which you wondered whether you were dreaming? Do you think Descartes is right that there are no "certain indications" by which you can tell whether you are dreaming or not? Notice he suggests that in dreams things do not seem as "clear and so distinct" as they do when we are awake. Do you think this "clarity and distinctness" indicate a clear difference between your own dreaming and being awake? Do you think you can tell whether you are in a dream by checking to see how "clear and distinct" things seem to be? Is it possible that you could be dreaming right now?

Thus, Descartes took doubt to its outer limits. Our sense perceptions, he held, may be illusions or the products of our own dreams or hallucinations. Our ideas may be nothing more than the products of an evil, all-powerful devil that puts these ideas in our minds. In this way, Descartes came to doubt everything of which he could not be certain. He then asked this question: Is there anything that survives this attempt to cast doubt on absolutely everything? Is there any truth that is so certain that it cannot be doubted even if an evil genius deceives me? Ultimately, he discovered what he felt was an indubitable truth: "I think, therefore I am."

> Without doubt I exist even if he deceives me, and let him deceive me as much as he will, he can never cause me to be nothing so long as I think that I am something. So that after having reflected well and carefully examined all things, we must come to the definite conclusion that this proposition: I am, I exist, is necessarily true each time that I pronounce it, or that I mentally conceive it.[6]

ANALYZING THE READING

1. Descartes comes to the conclusion that even if he is being deceived about everything else, he can be absolutely certain that he exists. But is this conclusion really so certain as he thinks it is? Is it possible for an all-powerful God or evil genius to deceive him even about his own existence? Why?

2. Why does Descartes come to the conclusion that any idea that is "clear and distinct" must be true? What does it mean to say that an idea is "clear and distinct"?

Descartes reasoned that even if he was being deceived about everything else, he could not be deceived about the fact that he was thinking he was being deceived. That is, even if everything he thought about was an illusion, he could not doubt that he was thinking about that illusion. And if he was thinking, then he must exist. Thus, the doubting self is a self whose existence cannot be doubted. And it is a self that not only doubts but also affirms, wills, and imagines—in short, we can be certain the thinking self exists.

Descartes, then, was absolutely certain of the truth of the proposition "I think, therefore I am." But then he asked himself: What was it about this proposition that made him so certain of its truth?

5   René Descartes, "Meditation One," in *Meditations on First Philosophy*, vol. 1, *The Philosophical Works of Descartes*, trans. and ed. Elizabeth S. Haldane and G. R. T. Ross (Cambridge, England: Cambridge University Press, 1911), 145, 147, 148.

6   René Descartes, "Meditation Two," op. cit., 150.

After this I considered generally what in a proposition is requisite in order to be true and certain; for since I had just discovered one which I knew to be such, I thought that I ought also to know in what this certainty consisted. And having remarked that there was nothing at all in the statement, "I think, therefore I am" which assures me of having thereby made a true assertion, excepting that I see very clearly that to think it is necessary to be, I came to the conclusion that I might assume, as a general rule, that the things which we conceive very clearly and distinctly are all true.[7]

So Descartes concludes that what makes him certain about the idea that "I think, therefore I am" is the clarity and distinctness with which he apprehends this idea. From this conclusion he draws a crucial lesson: Clarity and distinctness are the marks of truth. What exactly does Descartes mean by clarity and distinctness? Descartes apparently believes that we have a clear idea of something when we know exactly what it is—that is, when we know its essential properties or essential nature. And we have a distinct idea of something when we can distinguish it from other things.

But what is the source of our clear and distinct ideas? Where do those clear and distinct ideas come from? This is an important question, for in answering it, Descartes lays a rationalistic basis for knowledge. He answers that question in one of the most epistemologically important of all his writings, his *Second Meditation*. There Descartes attempts to explain how thinking and reasoning without the aid of the senses can be the source of real knowledge about the world. In the selection that follows, note how he abstracts from the sense qualities of a piece of wax to demonstrate why the mind—not the senses—is the ultimate criterion of knowledge. In this way, he establishes a rationalistic foundation for knowledge:

ANALYZING THE READING

Usually we say an *idea or belief in our mind* is true if it corresponds with what the *real world outside* our mind is like. In other words, whether an idea is true depends on what the *real world* outside us is like, not on what the *idea in our mind* is like. For example, suppose I want to know whether my idea that it's raining is true. I can't find out if that idea is true by just thinking about that idea in my head. No matter how much I examine that idea and think about its qualities *in my head*, I will not be able to figure out whether it's true or not. To find out if it's true, I have to check the real world and see if the rain is actually coming down in *the real world outside my head*. But Descartes is claiming that just by examining an idea in my head to see if it has the qualities of being "clear" and "distinct" I will be able to tell if it is true. He is claiming that if we see in our head that an idea is "clear" and "distinct" then we can know it is true without checking the real world. Do you think Descartes could be right? Why?

Let us begin by considering the commonest matters, those which we believe to be the most distinctly comprehended, to wit, the bodies [i.e., physical objects] which we touch and see. Not indeed, bodies in general, for our general ideas about bodies are usually somewhat confused. But let us consider a single specific body. Let us take, for example, this piece of wax: it has been taken quite freshly from the hive, and it has not yet lost the sweetness of the honey which it contains; it still retains some of the odor of the flowers from which it was collected; its color, its figure, its size are apparent; it is hard, cold, easily handled, and if you strike it with the finger, it will emit a sound. Finally all the things that are requisite to cause us distinctly to recognize a body, are met with in it. But notice that while I speak and bring it near the fire, what remained of the taste leaves it, the smell evaporates, the color changes, the shape is destroyed, its size increases, it becomes a liquid, it gets hot, so hot one can hardly handle it, and when one strikes it now, no sound is emitted. Does the same wax remain after these changes? We must confess that it remains; no one would judge otherwise. What then did I know so distinctly in this piece of wax? It could certainly be nothing that any of my senses informed me about, since all

> **QUICK REVIEW**
> Using the example of a piece of wax that the mind knows is the same physical body when it melts but that to the senses looks completely different, Descartes concludes that reason, without the aid of the senses, is what knows the body of the wax.

---

[7]   René Descartes, *Discourse*, op. cit., 101.

those things that we got from taste, smell, sight, touch, and hearing, we now see have changed, and yet we know the same wax remains.

… We must then grant that … it is my mind alone which perceives … [what] this piece of wax [is]…. But what is this piece of wax which cannot be understood except by the mind? It is certainly the same thing that I see, touch, imagine, and it has remained the same thing that I thought it was from the beginning. But what must particularly be observed is this: it itself is perceived neither by an act of vision, nor of touch, nor of imagination … but only by an intuition of the mind.[8]

ANALYZING THE READING

Descartes argues that when the hardened wax melted it lost all the qualities that our senses could detect. So to our senses, the hardened wax vanished and a new thing appeared, the melted puddle. But our minds know that the hardened wax and the melted wax are the same physical thing. So he concludes that our mind, not our senses, is the source of that knowledge that the hardened and melted wax are the same thing. Is Descartes' argument right? Do you think there is any way that he might actually have relied on our senses to know that the hard wax and the melted wax are the same thing? Explain.

Descartes points out here that our minds know that as it melts, the wax remains the same body of wax although to our senses all of its qualities have changed. Thus, our knowledge of what the wax itself is—an enduring physical body—does not derive from the senses or the imagination. If that knowledge were derived from the senses, we would have to say that when the wax melts, it is no longer what it was because to our senses nothing remains of what it used to be. Consequently, our knowledge that the melted wax is the same thing as the unmelted wax is something that we know with the mind and not with the senses. Thus, Descartes concludes, our knowledge of what a thing essentially is is grasped by an "intuition" of the mind. That is, the mind understands the essential nature of a thing by a direct insight into its essential nature. In the case of the wax, we know the solid wax and the melted wax are the same because our mind grasps its essential nature as a physical body. Because we know its essential nature, we know that it remains essentially the same physical body even when all its perceivable qualities change. Once again Descartes reveals his rationalist leanings.

Descartes' view that reason is the ultimate source of our most basic knowledge, even of what we perceive with our senses, is an example of extreme rationalism. Not all rationalists are as thoroughgoing as Descartes. Some rationalists hold that although some of our basic knowledge derives completely from reason, some of it also depends on the senses. The extreme rationalist, like Descartes, holds that all our basic or "foundational" knowledge derives solely from reason. And it is derived without the aid of the senses. Descartes does believe, of course, that we acquire some ideas through our senses. He notes, for example: "But if I hear a noise, if I see the sun, or if I

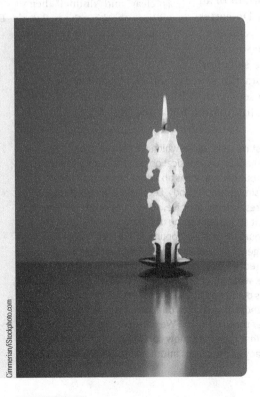

Our minds know that the solid wax and the melted wax are the same body, although to our senses all of its qualities have changed.

Cimmerian/iStockphoto.com

---

8   Descartes, "Meditation Two," op. cit., 154–155.

feel its heat, I have all along judged that these sensations proceeded from certain objects existing out of myself."[9] Our knowledge of sounds, of what the sun looks like and what its heat feels like, are examples of a kind of simple knowledge of the world "outside" us. Such knowledge, Descartes suggests, is acquired through the senses. But our knowledge of the essential nature of the body that gives off sounds or that glows like the sun or that emits heat, is acquired by the mind alone.

The extreme nature of Descartes' rationalism is especially evident in the way he approaches our knowledge of God and the world. Descartes argues that an imperfect creature like himself could not make up the idea of a perfect God. He concludes that the source of such an idea must be something perfect—God. So he concludes that this perfect being, God, must exist.

> It is clear by the natural light of reason that there must at least be as much reality in the efficient and total cause of a thing, as in the thing that is its effect. For, from where could the effect derive its reality, if not from its cause? And in what way can this cause communicate this reality to something else, unless it possessed that reality in itself? And from this it follows, not only that something cannot proceed from nothing, but likewise that what is more perfect—that is to say, something which has more reality within itself—cannot proceed from the less perfect....
>
> Now by the name God I understand a substance that is infinite, eternal, immutable, independent, all-knowing, all-powerful, and by which I myself and everything else... have been created. But all these characteristics are such that the more diligently I attend to them, the less do they appear capable of proceeding from me alone. Therefore, from what has been already said, we must conclude that God necessarily exists. For... I could not have the idea of an infinite substance—since I am finite—if it had not proceeded from some substance which was truly infinite.[10]

Notice that in these kinds of reasonings, Descartes never appeals to the testimony of his senses. His claims appeal only to the "clear and distinct" ideas in his mind. This is because he is a rationalist and so he believes that reason is the source of his basic knowledge about the world. He also reveals his rationalist approach to knowledge when he argues that the world and other people exist. He argues for this conclusion by reasoning entirely with the clear and distinct ideas within his mind. Could a perfect God, he asks, deceive me into perceiving my own body, the outer world, and other individuals, as I obviously do? Could He deceive me into thinking they exist when in fact they do not?

> There is . . . in me a certain passive faculty of perception, that is, of receiving and recognizing the ideas of sensible things,. . . Since God has given me . . . a very great inclination to believe that they are conveyed to me by corporeal objects, I do not see how He could be defended from the accusation of deceit if these ideas were produced by causes other than corporeal objects. Hence we must allow that corporeal things exist.[11]

ANALYZING THE READING

1. Descartes claims that "by the light of natural reason" he knows that there has to be as much reality in a cause as there is in its effect. Is Descartes' claim appropriate in light of his earlier assumption that God or an evil genius are deceiving him? Why?

2. Descartes argues that he has in himself the idea of a perfect infinite being. But he is finite and far from perfect. So he could not have produced his idea of a perfect infinite being, so God must have produced it. Write out Descartes' argument in full, using the "If...then..." logical form. What does Descartes' argument assume? Do you think that assumption (or assumptions) is true? Why?

---

9   Descartes, "Meditation Six," op. cit., 191.
10 Descartes, "Meditation Three" in *Meditations on First Philosophy*, 162, 165, 166.
11 Descartes, "Meditation Six," op. cit., 191.

ANALYZING THE READING

Descartes argues that since God does not deceive, and since God gave him an inclination to believe that his perceptions are caused by objects outside himself, those objects must exist. Do you see anything wrong with this argument? Explain.

QUICK REVIEW

Descartes argues that he could not have produced the idea of a perfect being, God, and neither could he have acquired it through the senses; only God could have put it into his mind, so God must exist. Because God is good, He does not deceive, so we can rely on the powers of knowing He has given us.

Keep in mind that at this point Descartes knew only that God and he, a thinking thing, existed. True, he did perceive his own body and the outer world. But consistent with his method of doubt, he had reasoned that these might be illusions. But he has now proved that a perfect being exists. Is such trickery and deception inherent in the idea he has of a perfect being? He concludes that the essential nature of a perfect being rules out deception. Therefore, he reasons, the world and what we perceive within it do indeed exist, since otherwise God would be deceiving us. But notice that he does not say he knows they exist because *his senses* tell him they exist. His senses only provide "ideas of sensible things" and ideas can be illusions that correspond to nothing real. The only way he knows that his ideas are connected to existing objects is because his *reason* came to that conclusion using its clear and distinct ideas. Descartes is here sticking to his rationalist view that reason is the source of our basic knowledge about the world.

Innate Ideas

But another question remains: How do these clear and distinct ideas get into our minds? Where do they come from if not the senses? Descartes and other rationalists used the notion of innate ideas to answer this question. **Innate ideas** are ideas that are present in the mind from birth: We are born with them. The rationalist, Plato, for example, believed that we are born with certain ideas fully formed in our minds—for example, the concepts of geometry. But, at birth, these ideas are hidden away in the depths of the mind or memory, so the young infant is not consciously aware of them. As the person grows up, these ideas can slowly emerge into the person's awareness.

THINKING LIKE A PHILOSOPHER

Many rationalist philosophers believe that we know some truths that no one ever taught us and that we could not have discovered by observing the world around us. The text gives several examples of such truths. Do you feel that you know some truths and that no one ever taught you and you did not discover by observing the world around you? What are some examples truths that you yourself know but would have a hard time explaining how you came to know they were true?

What kind of ideas might be innate? Some rationalists have believed that at least the basic principles of logic and math are innate. These include the basic axioms of geometry, such as the proposition that the shortest distance between two points is a straight line. They also include the basic laws of arithmetic, such as the proposition that if equal numbers are added to equal numbers, the results are equal. Moreover, some rationalists believe that the basic rules of science are also innate. This includes, for example, the rule that every event has to have a cause. Some rationalists have believed that not only are *propositions* like these innate but that some individual *concepts* are also innate. These concepts include the concepts of "point," "line," "straight," "equality," "event," and "cause."

Why would anyone think that such propositions and concepts are innate? This question is at the heart of a problem that we still struggle with today: Where else could our knowledge of these propositions and concepts have come from? Many philosophers agree with Descartes that we cannot come to know these propositions and concepts by observing the world around us. In other words, we cannot know these by looking at things outside the mind. The things we see around us never quite live up to these propositions and concepts. For example, in geometry, mathematicians think of a line as having no thickness and a point as having no size.

But the lines we see in the world around us are always more or less thick. And points are always of one size or another. In arithmetic, as we conceptualize it in our minds, *equal* means perfectly identical. Yet in the world around us, two objects are never perfectly identical to each other. Or consider the proposition that *every event has a cause.* In the world around us and over a lifetime, we may observe perhaps a few hundred thousand or even a few million events. Yet we certainly do not observe *every event.* How then is it that our minds know, without observing all events, that *every* event must have a cause?

Apparently, there are certain propositions and concepts that are in our mind, yet it seems we do not come to know these by observing things in the world around us. Where, then, does our knowledge of these come from? According to some rationalist philosophers, we are born with this knowledge. The rationalist philosopher Plato, in particular, often discussed this issue in his dialogues. His demonstration of how we become aware of the innate ideas we have is clearer than the explanations of Descartes or other rationalists, so we will focus on his arguments. In his dialogue, *Meno,* Plato provides what is probably the best example of innate ideas. The dialogue describes a slave boy as he becomes aware of some innate ideas he had in his mind but did not know he had.

Plato's *Meno.* In *Meno,* Plato tells us how Socrates once made a slave boy "remember" his knowledge of geometry by showing him some imperfect figures drawn on the ground. Socrates shows the slave boy a square that is supposed to be two feet by two feet, or four square feet in size (see Figure 5.1a). Socrates asks the boy how he would draw a second square that is exactly twice the size of the first square. At first, the boy says that if you double the length of each side of the first square, you will get a second square that is exactly twice the size of the first square. But when Socrates draws a second square that is approximately four feet by four feet (Figure 5.1b), the boy quickly realizes that his first answer is wrong. If you double the length of each side of a square, you get a new square that is exactly four times as big as the first square. Yet the boy knows this without making exact measurements of the squares that Socrates draws on the ground. And even if the boy had measured the squares, they would probably not have turned out to be exactly the right sizes. So, where did the boy's knowledge come from?

Socrates then repeats his original question: How do you draw a second square that is exactly twice the size of the first square? The boy hesitates. Socrates draws a diagonal line from one corner to the other in the first square (Figure 5.1c). Then, he draws a second, larger square, using this diagonal line as the side of the larger square. Socrates asks the boy how big this second square is. The boy is unsure. So Socrates draws some diagonals in the larger square, dividing it into four small triangles (Figure 5.1d). Then, Socrates invites the boy to count the triangles in the first square and the triangles in the second square. Immediately, it flashes on the boy:

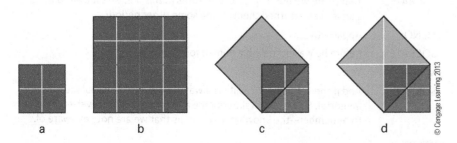

a   b   c   d

© Cengage Learning 2013

Figure 5.1 Socrates used similar diagrams to prove his theory of innate ideas.

The second square drawn on the diagonal has to be exactly twice the size of the first square! The boy "knows" this, even though, again, he does not measure Socrates' very imperfect figures. Plus, if he had measured the squares that Socrates drew on the ground, it would certainly have turned out that the second square was not exactly twice the size of the first square. So, again, where did the boy's knowledge come from? It could not have come from just looking at how big the second square was compared to the first. For, again, the squares Socrates draws on the ground are rough, crooked, and inexact. So the big square is not exactly twice as big as the small one. In a discussion with Meno, the master of the slave, Socrates answers the question about where the boy's knowledge came from:

SOCRATES: What do you say of your slave, Meno? Weren't all of his answers given out of his own head?

MENO: Yes, his answers were all his own.

SOCRATES: And yet, you just told us that you never taught him geometry?

MENO: That's true.

SOCRATES: But he had these opinions somewhere inside him, didn't he?

MENO: Yes.

SOCRATES: So the person who does not know something may still have true opinions about the subject buried within himself without actually being aware of them?

MENO: He may.

SOCRATES: And just now these opinions were stirred up in the boy, as if in a dream. But if we asked him many more of these same kinds of questions, in many different forms, wouldn't he eventually come to know the subject as well as anyone else?

MENO: I think so.

SOCRATES: Without anyone telling him the answers, he can recover his knowledge from within himself, if he is only asked questions?

MENO: Yes.

SOCRATES: And this spontaneous recovery of the knowledge that is in him is a form of remembering what is already in him?

MENO: True.

SOCRATES: And this knowledge which he now remembers, he must have acquired at some earlier time?

MENO: Yes. . . .

SOCRATES: Has anyone ever taught him these things? You should know, Meno, since he was raised in your house?

MENO: No, no one ever taught him this.

SOCRATES: Then, if he did not acquire these truths in this life, isn't it clear that he acquired and learned them during some other period?

MENO: Apparently.

SOCRATES: Before he was born with a human form?

MENO: Yes. . . .

SOCRATES: And if the truth about reality is always in our soul, the soul must be immortal. So we must take courage and try hard to discover—that is, to remember—the knowledge within us that we are not yet aware of.[12]

---

[12]   Plato, *Meno*, 85c–86a. This translation © 1998 by Manuel Velasquez.

In this fascinating dialogue, Plato tries to show that there is only one way we could have come to have our knowledge of geometry. We could not have acquired our knowledge of geometry by observing things after we were born or by being told these things. We must have had this knowledge in some form in our minds at birth. But how did it get into our minds? Plato answers: We must have acquired this knowledge before we were born! Before we were born, Plato believes, our souls must have lived in a different and perfect world. In that world we actually observed perfectly shaped lines, squares, and triangles, along with other perfect ideas. When we are born into this imperfect world, we carry those perfect ideas within us, buried in the depths of memory.

Most rationalist philosophers reject Plato's claim that before we were born we existed in another perfect universe. But many rationalists, including Descartes, accept Plato's more basic insight. This is the insight that we do not acquire the basic truths of math and science by observing the world around us but are born with them or they develop naturally in us. In the following passage, Descartes indicates his agreement with Plato's fundamental insight:

> [W]e come to know them [innate ideas] by the power of our own native intelligence, without any sensory experience. All geometrical truths are of this sort—not just the most obvious ones, but all the others, however abstruse they may appear. Hence, according to Plato, Socrates asks a slave boy about the elements of geometry and thereby makes the boy able to dig out certain truths from his own mind which he had not previously recognized were there, thus attempting to establish the doctrine of reminiscence. Our knowledge of God is of this sort.[13]

Descartes thought that some of the foundational ideas on which all our knowledge is based are contained fully formed in our reason from the time we are born. But we do not become aware of them until later. As he put it: [W]hen we say that an idea is innate in us, we do not mean that it is always there before us. This would mean that no idea was innate. We simply mean that we have within ourselves the faculty of summoning up the idea." When we summon up an innate idea, we become aware of it as if we were recalling a memory. In Descartes' words: "on first discovering [innate ideas] it seems that I am not so much learning something new as remembering what I knew before; or it seems like noticing for the first time things which were long present within me although I had never turned my mental gaze on them before." Descartes believed, for example, that human beings are born with innate ideas of the three fundamental kinds of things in the universe. These are God, minds, and material bodies. It takes time for us to become consciously aware of these ideas, Descartes thought, but we know how to use these ideas even before we think directly about what their nature is. His example of the wax shows this. Everyone—even a child—knows that a physical body is a thing that continues to exist even as all its qualities change. This is why, he notes, everyone knows that the solid wax and the melted wax are the same physical body. We each know from childhood what a body is, at least well enough to know that when wax melts it is still the same body of wax. The idea of a body, then, is innate and fully formed and operating in our mind even before we have consciously thought about what a body is. But not everyone agreed with this view of innate ideas.

Leibniz: Innate Ideas Are "Tendencies." Among those who disagreed with Descartes was another rationalist, Gottfried Wilhelm von Leibniz (1646–1716). Leibniz specifically disagreed with Descartes' view that the mind has fully formed

---

[13] René Descartes, letter of 1643, in John Cottingham, Robert Stoothoff, and Dugald Murdoch (eds.), *The Philosophical Writings of Descartes*, vol. 3 (Cambridge: Cambridge University Press, 1984), 222–223.

PHILOSOPHY AND LIFE

Innate Ideas?

Two recent scientific studies suggest that people have innate ideas that are not learned through sense experience but are present from birth. One study by Perin, Berger, and Markram examined how neurons are organized in the brains of newborns. Neurons are brain cells that process, transmit, and preserve thoughts and information. Scientists believe that neurons represent or "encode" information or thoughts by forming circuits that connect them with each other. According to the authors, "*neuronal circuitry is often considered a clean slate that can be... arbitrarily molded by experience.*" In other words, scientists believed that at birth the brain contained no encoded information, and that whatever information brain neurons encoded after birth came from sense experiences. However, the study discovered that many neurons are already connected in small networks from birth. The study concluded that "*experience cannot freely mold* all the neurons of the brain, because from birth the brain contains "*neuronal groups that ...emerged during embryonic development independent of experience.*" In short, these small networks of neurons seem to represent innate concepts that are present in the brain from birth and independent of sense experience.

The second study, by Hespos and vanMarle, reviewed earlier research on the concepts babies seem to have. The study states:

> We review how object and substance knowledge interfaces with number knowledge systems [in infants]. The evidence supports the view that certain core principles about these domains are present as early as we can test for them and the nature of the underlying representation is best characterized as primitive initial concepts that are elaborated and refined through learning and experience. ... Infants have detailed knowledge about how objects behave and interact from the first weeks of life.

The authors go on to say that experiments with babies as young as two months suggest they possess such "initial concepts." How do scientists know what babies are thinking? Scientists rely on the expressions on babies' faces and on other responses babies make when they see physical objects

being manipulated by the scientists. For example, when babies are shown a ball rolling behind a small screen and coming out on the other side, they show very little reaction and very soon look away from the scene. Apparently such a scene conforms with their knowledge of how physical objects behave. But when they are shown a ball rolling behind a small screen and not coming out the other side, babies seem surprised, they stare at the screen for a long time, and then perhaps look behind the screen for the missing ball. Such experiments have shown that babies know that physical objects continue to exist even when they are not seen, and know that physical objects don't just blink out of existence. Other similar experiments have shown that babies know what a physical object is, know that physical objects continue to exist even when one is not looking at them, know that two physical objects cannot occupy the same space at the same time, and know that physical objects cannot pass through each other. Babies also know that liquid substances do not behave like physical objects, that liquids can separate, and that objects (like a straw) can pass through them. Finally, babies seem to have some knowledge of small numbers—for example, they know the difference between one cookie, two cookies, and three cookies (they prefer the larger quantity!).

QUESTIONS

1. Do these studies show that babies have the kind of innate ideas that Descartes, Plato, and other rationalists had in mind?

2. Do you see any similarities between the claims Descartes makes about his wax example and the findings of these studies?

Sources: Rodrigo Perin, Thomas K. Berger, and Henry Markram, "A Synaptic Organizing Principle for Cortical Neuronal Groups," *Proceedings of the National Academy of the Sciences*, March 2011; Susan J. Hespos and Kristy vanMarle, "Physics for Infants: Characterizing the Origins of Knowledge about Objects, Substances, and Number," *Wiley Interdisciplinary Previews: Cognitive Science*, vol. 3 (January/February 2012), no. 1, pp. 19–27.

innate ideas within itself. Leibniz agreed that we do not acquire our knowledge of the most basic truths about the world by observing the world around us. He also agreed that those truths must somehow be innate in us, that is, in some sense we are born with them. But Leibniz was not willing to say that we are born with fully formed truths or concepts in our minds. Innate ideas, Leibniz claimed, are in us only as "tendencies" or "dispositions":

> If there were veins in a block of marble which marked out the shape of Hercules rather than other shapes, then that block would be more determined to that shape and Hercules would be innate in it, in a way, even though labor would be required to expose the veins and to polish them into clarity, removing everything that prevents them from being seen. This is how ideas and truths are innate in us—as inclinations, dispositions, tendencies, or natural potentials, and not as actualities.[14]

At birth, the mind does not come equipped with fully formed innate ideas. Rather, at birth people's minds have only an inborn capacity or tendency to form those ideas. As people mature, their experiences gradually shape these tendencies and turn them into fully formed ideas.

Rationalists generally have agreed with Plato, Descartes, and Leibniz that we have innate ideas. Still, the theory of innate ideas is difficult for other philosophers to accept. How can we have knowledge inside our minds, they ask, if we are not aware of it? To say that we "know" something is to say that we at least believe it. But how can we believe something without being aware of it? To many philosophers, it seems pointless to say that we have knowledge if we are not aware of it. But if we do not accept the theory of innate ideas, how do we answer the question the theory is meant to solve? That is, how do we acquire our knowledge of so many basic truths that seem to lie beyond what our observations of the world around us can provide?

ANALYZING THE READING

Suppose the rationalists are right when they claim that we know some truths that no one ever taught us and that we could not have discovered by observing the world around us. Some rationalists explain those truths by saying they are innate; that is, we either are born with them in our minds or they develop naturally in our minds as we grow up. What are some ways that you think the presence of such truths in our minds could be explained, without relying on the rationalist theory of innate ideas?

Jainism. Western philosophers are not the only ones who have argued in support of a rationalist theory of innate ideas. Some of the philosophers of India have made similar claims. Take Jainism, for example, an important philosophy of India. Jainism originated several centuries before Christ and today is still embraced by some six million people. (The great twentieth-century philosopher Mohandas K. Gandhi was a Jain philosopher.) Jain philosophers hold that even before our senses perceive an object, we already have the knowledge of that object in our minds.[15] When we see an object, our perception of the object merely serves to uncover the innate knowledge of that object that we already had within us. The philosophers of Jainism hold that every human being carries within his or her mind a complete knowledge of everything in the universe. What explains our unconscious but complete knowledge

---

14 Gottfried W. Leibniz, "New Essays on the Human Understanding," in *Leibniz Selections*, ed. Philip P. Wiener (New York: Charles Scribner's Sons, 1951), 373.
15 Bibhu Padhi and Minakshi Padhi, *Indian Philosophy and Religion: A Reader's Guide* (Jefferson, NC: McFarland, 1990), 67.

of the universe? According to the philosophers of Jainism, the mind is not limited by time or space but is present everywhere. Because our mind is everywhere, it must know everything. But throughout most of our lives we are unaware of the unlimited knowledge within us. Our past unethical actions and decisions (perhaps in former lives!) create a veil of impurity that covers over the potentially unlimited knowledge within us, hiding it from us. Nevertheless, we can get rid of the baggage of our past wrongdoing and can also free ourselves from our bondage to material things. When we achieve this we will be liberated and will become fully conscious of our Godlike knowledge. Key to our future liberation is the practice of *ahimsa*, the avoidance of all aggression, injury, or harm to other living things. Until then, we must be satisfied with recovering the innate knowledge that is within us piece by piece through the use of our intellect and our senses.

We will end this discussion of rationalism by considering what Descartes' views suggest about "recovered memories." Some people with recovered memories have made the point that "the clarity of the new memories is striking, photographic." Descartes probably would strongly object to applying his theories to memories of sense experiences like these. But he did hold that clarity and distinctness of ideas were indicators of true knowledge. The clarity, the detailed sharpness, and the distinctness of many recovered memories suggest they are "clear and distinct." So perhaps those qualities imply they can be accepted as true knowledge. That is, the inherent qualities of recollected memories validate them as sources of knowledge about the past. Indeed, that is exactly what many lawyers have argued: The clarity and distinctness of recovered memories prove that they must be true. For example, one attorney is quoted as saying this during a trial: "I find it highly unlikely that someone who can remember what pattern was on the wallpaper and that a duck was quacking outside the bedroom window where she was molested by her father when she was four years old is making it up. Why in the hell would your mind do this?"

Some juries hearing cases of childhood sexual abuse based on sharply detailed recovered memories have also agreed. They, too, have thought that the clarity and distinctness of recovered memories make them self-evidently true. A follower of Descartes might even argue that because God is not a deceiver, He would not put such clear and distinct memories in our minds unless they were true. But we should ask ourselves this important question: Are we justified in claiming that memories need no external validation and that they are self-evidently true when they are clear and distinct? Does the clarity and distinctness of a memory—or of any other idea—really guarantee its truth, as Descartes claimed? But if the inherent clarity and distinctness of recovered memories do not show they are self-evident sources of knowledge of the past, then how are they to be validated?

> **QUICK REVIEW**
> If Descartes' criteria of "clearness and distinctness" as indicators of valid knowledge are applied to recovered memories (something Descartes would probably not allow), they would suggest that such memories are valid.

PHILOSOPHY AT THE MOVIES

Watch *Proof* (2005) which tells the story of Catherine and her father, Robert, who died a couple of days earlier. Robert was a brilliant mathematician until he became mentally ill, forcing Catherine to cut short her own studies in mathematics, and return home to take care of him. Catherine gives her boyfriend a notebook in which someone has written the proof of a revolutionary mathematical theory. Although Catherine claims she wrote the proof herself, her boyfriend and her sister suspect her father wrote the proof. Explain what rationalism would say is the source of our knowledge of a mathematical proof like the one in the notebook.

5.3 Can the Senses Account for All Our Knowledge?

Both in the East and in the West, a view of the sources of knowledge emerged that contrasted sharply with rationalism. This opposing view of knowledge is now called "empiricism." Empiricism is the view that all knowledge about the world comes from or is based on the senses. Empiricists were explicitly reacting to the claims of the rationalists. Empiricists claimed that the human mind contains nothing except what sense experience has put there. Thus, all ideas originate in sense experience. Consequently, empiricism teaches that true knowledge is *a posteriori*. That is, it depends on experience. Real knowledge is empirically verifiable or falsifiable by our sense experience.

Empiricism obviously makes a lot of sense where our ordinary knowledge of the world is concerned. It is by using our senses that we learn that the sky is blue, that trees are green, that lemons taste sour, and that the seasons change in a regular cycle. Sense observations also underlie almost all the knowledge of the natural sciences. Sense observations are the source of the astronomer's knowledge that Halley's comet returns to earth every seventy-five years. They are the source of the chemist's knowledge that when oxygen and hydrogen burn, they produce water. They are the basis of the physicist's knowledge that at the surface of the earth objects fall at the accelerating rate of 32 feet per second. And they are the source of the biologist's knowledge that monkeys form social hierarchies. In all these cases, our knowledge comes from, and is based on, sense experience.

It is not surprising, then, that many Eastern as well as Western philosophers have embraced empiricism. For example, the Charvaka philosophers of India, whom we mentioned in Chapter 3, were empiricists. They held that the only valid source of knowledge is sense perception. Other Indian philosophers, such as the philosophers of the Nyaya (which means "Logic") school, can also be classified as empiricists. The Nyaya philosophers agreed that there are other valid sources of knowledge besides sense perception. But they claimed that all other sources of knowledge ultimately depend on sense perception. For example, in reasoning or "inference," we must ultimately reason from knowledge that we acquired from perception. Likewise, knowledge acquired from the testimony of others ultimately depends on someone's sense perception.[16]

In the West, empiricism has also had a long history. Elements of empiricism can be found in the writings of Aristotle (384–322 BCE), Saint Thomas Aquinas (1225–1274), Sir Francis Bacon (1561–1626), and Thomas Hobbes (1588–1679). The most noteworthy empiricists, however, were the three philosophers John Locke (1632–1704), George Berkeley (1685–1753), and David Hume (1711–1776).

Locke and Empiricism

John Locke was the first to launch a systematic attack on the views of the rationalists. Locke argued that the rationalists went astray when they claimed that "there are in the

MindTap Can we truly trust our senses, as empiricism puts forth? Go to MindTap to watch a video exploring our perception of color.

QUICK REVIEW
Western empiricists such as Locke, Berkeley, and Hume, and Indian Charvaka and Nyaya philosophers hold that all our knowledge comes through sense observations.

John Locke: "For since the mind, in all its thoughts and reasonings, hath no other immediate objects but its own ideas, it is evident that our knowledge is only conversant about them."

© Lebrecht Music and Arts Photo Library/Alamy

---

[16] Stephen H. Phillips, "Epistemology, Indian Schools of," in *Encyclopedia of Philosophy* (New York: Macmillan, 1967), vol. 3, 390.

understanding certain innate principles ... which the soul receives in its very first being, and brings into the world with it." According to Locke, the only real argument the rationalists produced for their belief in innate ideas was the argument from "universal consent." That is, because people everywhere have certain ideas in their minds, such ideas must be innate. The fundamental problem with this argument, Locke claimed, is that there are no ideas that all human beings are aware of:

> But ... this argument of universal consent, which is made use of to prove innate principles, seems to me a demonstration that there are none such: because there are none to which all mankind give a universal assent.... For, first, it is evident that all children and idiots have not the least apprehension or thought of them. And the want of that is enough to destroy that universal assent which must needs be the necessary concomitant of all innate truths.[17]

Locke claimed the mind is a blank slate—in Latin, a *tabula rasa*—on which experience makes its mark. Blank slates, of course, contain no ideas of any kind, neither innate nor acquired. In *An Essay Concerning Human Understanding*, he states the nature of his proposed doctrine clearly:

> Let us then suppose the mind to be, as we say, white paper, void of all characters, without any ideas:—How comes it to be furnished? Whence comes it by that vast store which the busy and boundless fancy of man has painted on it with almost endless variety? Whence has it all the *materials* of reason and knowledge? To this I answer, in one word, from *experience*. In that all our knowledge is founded.... Our observation employed either about external sensible objects or about the internal operations of our minds ... is that which supplies our understandings with all the *materials* of thinking. These two are the fountains of knowledge, from whence all the ideas we have, or can naturally have, do spring.... First, our senses, conversant about particular sensible objects, do convey into the mind several distinct perceptions of things, according to those various ways wherein those objects do affect them. And thus we come by those [simple] *ideas* we have of yellow, white, heat, cold, soft, hard, bitter, sweet, and all those which we call sensible qualities ... Secondly, the other fountain from which experience furnishes the understanding with ideas is the perception of the operations of our own mind within us.... And such are [the simple ideas of] perception, thinking, doubting, believing, reasoning, knowing, willing, and all the different actings of our own minds.[18]

ANALYZING THE READING

Do you agree with Locke's claim that we had to acquire all the ideas in our minds through our sense experiences, that is, through our perceptions either of the world around us or of our own interior states? Can you think of any concepts or truths that you think you could not have acquired through your sense perceptions?

✅ QUICK REVIEW
Locke argued that there were no ideas that all humans share, so no "innate" ideas that all people have when they come into the world. Instead, at birth the mind is a tabula rasa, or blank slate, that only experience can fill.

There is an obvious objection to Locke's claim that all our ideas come either from our sense perceptions or from perceptions of our mental operations. The objection is that we obviously have ideas that we do not get through sense perception nor from perceptions of our mental operations. For example, the idea of gratitude is not something we see walking around outside of us, nor is it one of the "actings of our own minds." What is the source of such ideas? Locke claimed that we

---

17   John Locke, *An Essay Concerning Human Understanding*, ed. A. C. Fraser (Oxford: Clarendon, 1894), I, ii, 4–5. Note that in the excerpts from Locke I have changed the word "doth" to "does," "hath" to "has," and "without" to "outside." The changes involving "doth" and "hath" substitute modern English for seventeenth-century English, which makes the text easier for a modern reader to understand. The change of "without" to "outside" substitutes a word that today means what the word "without" meant in seventeenth-century English. This avoids misunderstanding this key word whose more common meaning today is *with no*, or *with the lack of*.
18   Ibid., II, i, 2–5.

ourselves construct such ideas. We put them together from the building blocks of "simple" ideas we get from our senses or from our awareness of our mental activities:

> The mind has a power to consider several [simple ideas] united together as one idea . . . as itself has joined them together. Ideas thus made up of several simple ones put together, I call *complex*;—such as are beauty, gratitude, a man, an army, the universe. . . . In this faculty of repeating and joining together its ideas, the mind has great power in varying and multiplying the objects of its thoughts, infinitely beyond what sensation or reflection furnished it with: but all this still confined to those simple ideas which it received from those two sources, and which are the ultimate materials of all its compositions.[19]

It's tempting to be lulled by the apparent simplicity and common sense of Locke's assertions about knowledge. But automatic acceptance misses important philosophical issues. Consider the fact that we humans make all sorts of claims. Some are apparently ordinary ones such as "It's raining," "It's the hottest day of the year," and "The lemon is sour." Others are more complex such as "$E = mc^2$." Most people would say, and for at least the simplest of these statements even a rationalist like Descartes would agree, that these claims are based on sense perception. If you ask people, for example, how they know it's raining, they might tell you to go outside and *see* for yourself. If you ask them how they know that today is the hottest day of the year, they might tell you they *looked* out the window and then *listened* to the weather report. If asked how they know that a lemon is sour and sugar is sweet, they might tell you to *taste* them yourself. The question of knowledge, it seems, is bound up with what we perceive. Through perception we feel confident that we *know* how things are.

But should we be so confident? Can't there be a difference between things as they "really" are and our perception of them? Are things always necessarily what they appear to be to our senses? Suppose you're in a hospital recovering from an operation and still somewhat groggy from the anesthesia. Just then you see your long-dead grandfather walk into your room. You pinch yourself, blink, shake your head, turn away, and look back, but he's still standing there. Eventually he leaves. But you're left wondering: Was he really there, as your senses insisted he was?

Obviously, things in reality can be different from what our senses seem to perceive. And this difference can undermine our claim to know things on the basis of our senses. This is a fundamental epistemological problem that arises with all sense-based knowledge claims. Two responses can be made to this problem: Either (1) we claim that no distinction exists between what I seem to experience and what things are like in reality. For example, we can say there is no difference between my experience of my grandfather in my room and what is really in my room. Or (2) we agree that what we experience must be distinguished from the reality itself. For example, my experience of my grandfather must be distinguished from what is really in my room. In the first instance, (1), we face serious and perhaps insurmountable difficulties. For we are

ANALYZING THE READING

Locke claims that *"complex" ideas* like "beauty, gratitude, etc." are ideas that we create by putting together several simpler ideas. And some of those simpler ideas might themselves be made out of even simpler ideas. Ultimately, we should be able to break any idea down into the *completely simple ideas* we got through our senses, like "yellow, white, heat, cold, soft, hard, bitter, sweet," and other or the *completely simple ideas* we get from "the operations of our own mind within us," like "thinking, doubting, believing, reasoning, knowing, willing, etc." Try the following experiment to see if Locke is right. Choose any "idea" that seems to be a *complex idea* and is not a *completely simple idea*. Now see if you can break that complex idea down into the completely simple ideas that Locke says we get through our senses and from inside our minds. Are you able to do that with any complex idea? Next, try to construct at least one complex idea by putting together some of Locke's completely simple ideas. Are you able to create any complex idea this way? What do these experiments tell you?

---

[19] Ibid., II, xii, 1–2.

claiming that reality is indistinguishable from our experience. In other words there's no difference between your experience of your grandfather and what is actually in your room. More generally there is no difference between your experience and reality. This claim will guarantee we know reality on the basis of our sense experience. But it will mean that the universe consists of nothing more than perceptions and ideas. As we saw earlier, the idealist philosopher George Berkeley took this position.

If we take the second option, (2), we face equally serious difficulties. For once we agree that our perceptions are distinct from reality, how can we know whether our perceptions square with reality? In fact, if we distinguish our perceptions of things from the way things actually are, we raise the possibility that our perceptions may never match reality.

When he developed his theory of knowledge, Locke took option (2). He asserted not only that knowledge originates in sense experience. But he also asserted that physical objects exist outside us that cause our perceptions and that are independent of our perceptions of them. In effect, he distinguished between our *perceptions* of objects, and the *objects* that cause us to have those perceptions. He wrote: "I can no more doubt, whilst I write this, that I see white and black, and that something really exists that causes that sensation in me, than that I write or move my hand."[20] But although Locke distinguished between external objects and the ideas they cause in us, he held that we directly perceive only our ideas and not the external objects. Notice in the following passage how he states these claims:

> It is therefore the actual receiving of ideas from outside [us] that gives us notice of the existence of other things, and makes us know, that something does exist at that time outside us, which causes that idea in us; . . . e.g. while I write this, I have, by the paper affecting my eyes, that idea produced in my mind, which, whatever object causes [it], I call white; by which I know that that quality or accident . . . does really exist, and has a being outside me. And of this, the greatest assurance I can possibly have, and to which my faculties can attain, is the testimony of my eyes, which are the proper and sole judges of this thing; . . .
>
> The notice we have by our senses of the existence of things outside us, though it be not altogether so certain as our intuitive knowledge, or the deductions of our reason employed about the clear abstract ideas of our own minds; yet it is an assurance that deserves the name of knowledge. If we persuade ourselves that our faculties act and inform us right concerning the existence of those objects that affect them, it cannot pass for an ill-grounded confidence: for I think nobody can, in earnest, be so skeptical as to be uncertain of the existence of those things which he sees and feels. At least, he that can doubt so far, . . . will never have any controversy with me; since he can never be sure I say anything contrary to his own opinion. As to myself, I think God has given me assurance enough of the existence of things outside me. . . . This is certain: the confidence that our faculties do not herein deceive us, is the greatest assurance we are capable of, concerning the existence of material beings. . . .
>
> But yet if, after all this, any one will be so skeptical as to distrust his senses, and to affirm that all we see and hear, feel and taste, think and do, during our whole being, is but the series and deluding appearances of a long dream, whereof there is no reality; and therefore will question the existence of all things, or our knowledge of anything: I must desire him to consider, that, if all be a dream, then he doth but dream that he makes the question, and so it does not much matter that a waking man should answer him.[21]

---

20   Ibid., IV, xi, 2.
21   Ibid., IV, xi, 2, 3, 8.

Thus, for Locke our knowledge of things is more accurately termed our knowledge of our *ideas* of things. And so the key problem arises: How can we be sure that the ideas we have are accurate representations of external objects? And even more disconcerting: How can we be sure that there even are any external objects? Locke was obviously aware of this problem. An indication of this is the slight tone of desperation in the passage above. Locke seems determined to assure us that things really do exist outside us and our perceptions really do show us what they are like. Yet he realizes in the end that the existence of the external world is only a belief that he attributes to God. "God," he writes, "has given me assurance enough of the existence of things outside me."

Primary and Secondary Qualities. Locke argued that we can be sure that at least some of our ideas are accurate representations of things in the external world. According to Locke, every physical object has certain qualities that are in the object itself whether or not anyone perceives them. These he called **primary qualities**. Generally, primary qualities can be measured—for example, size, shape, and motion. These measurable qualities, he wrote, "give us an idea of the thing as it is in itself."[22] Locke also held that there are qualities that the object itself does not have, but that seem to us to be qualities of the object. For example, when we perceive a ripe apple, we perceive its color, smell, texture, and maybe even its taste. Before it ripens we perceive the apple to have a green color; when ripe it looks red, and after it rots it may have another color. And it may have one color in the midday sun and another at sunset. When fresh the apple may smell sweet; when rotting it may smell putrid. What exactly are these types of qualities—these colors, smells, textures, tastes? What we term color and smell, and so on, Locke claimed, are merely powers in the apple that cause these sensations in us. The color and smell are not qualities in the apple itself, but merely ideas it causes in us:

> Qualities thus considered in bodies are, First, such as are utterly inseparable from the body, in what state soever it be; and such as in all the alterations and changes it suffers, all the force can be used upon it, it constantly keeps; and such as sense constantly finds in every particle of matter which has bulk enough to be perceived; and the mind finds inseparable from every particle of matter.... Take a grain of wheat, divide it into two parts; each part has still solidity, extension, figure, and mobility: divide it again, and it retains still the same qualities; and so divide it on, till the parts become insensible; they must retain still each of them all those qualities.... These I call original or primary qualities of body, which ... produce simple ideas in us, viz. solidity, extension, figure, motion or rest, and number....
>
> Secondly ...[there are] qualities which in truth are nothing in the objects themselves but power to produce various sensations in us ...as colors, sounds, tastes, etc. These I call secondary qualities. The ideas of primary qualities of bodies are resemblances of them, and their patterns do really exist in the bodies themselves, but the ideas produced in us by these secondary qualities have no resemblance of them at all. There is nothing like our ideas [of secondary qualities] existing in the bodies themselves.... The particular bulk, number, figure, and motion of the parts of fire or snow are really in them,- whether any one's senses perceive

ANALYZING THE READING

Locke gives a list of the characteristics of primary qualities when he discusses the "Qualities thus considered in bodies." For example, he says that primary qualities are those that "sense constantly finds in every particle of matter." Some of the characteristics of primary qualities lead him to say that primary qualities really exist in objects outside of us. Secondary qualities, however, do not really exist "in the objects themselves." What do you think are the characteristics of primary qualities that lead Locke to say that objects outside of us have to possess the primary qualities we perceive?

---

[22] Ibid., II, viii, 2, 3.

them or no: and therefore they may be called real qualities because they really exist in those bodies. But light, heat, whiteness, or coldness, are no more really in them than sickness or pain is in manna. Take away the sensation of them; let not the eyes see light or colors, nor the ears hear sounds; let the palate not taste, nor the nose smell, and all colors, tastes, odors, and sounds...vanish and cease.[23]

PHILOSOPHY AND LIFE
Science and the Attempt to Observe Reality

Can we ever observe the world as it is, independently of ourselves? Or do our very attempts to observe the world always *change* the world? Psychologists and sociologists often face this problem, because the very fact that people are being observed leads them to behave differently from how they would behave if they were not being observed. The more accurately you try to determine how angry you feel, for example, the less you experience the anger you are trying to observe.

Or consider the results of a famous series of experiments called the Hawthorne studies, which tried to discover what kinds of job conditions would improve the productivity of workers. Workers were observed under various different working conditions (including noise, darkness, bright light, music, silence). The Hawthorne researchers discovered, much to their surprise, that the productivity of the workers they studied always improved no matter what the conditions. It was only much later that the researchers realized that it was the fact that the workers were being *observed* and were being rewarded with so much *attention* that led them to be more productive. Making objective observations—that is, observations that are not contaminated by the observer's activities and choices—is very difficult when observing the psychological or social world.

But surely the *physical* world can be observed objectively—that is, without it being changed by our observations. Or can it? Consider the problem of trying to measure precisely the temperature of a volume of warm water: If we insert a thermometer into the water, the temperature of the thermometer will change the original temperature of the water.

But it is when we reach the basic constituents of all matter—subatomic particles—that our attempts to observe the physical world most radically alter that world. For to observe that world, we must shoot some kind of radiation (light rays or gamma rays) at it and observe the reflected radiation. But the energy of the radiation always disturbs the subatomic particles, leaving us uncertain about what was there before the observation. In fact, modern physics explicitly holds that on principle it is impossible to observe subatomic particles without disturbing them so much that we cannot be sure where they are or how fast they are moving. Here is how a physics textbook explains the impossibility of observing the subatomic world in a way that would eliminate our uncertainty about that world:

> In Newtonian mechanics, still applicable to the macroscopic world of matter, both the position and velocity of a body are easily calculable; e.g., both the position and the velocity of the earth in its orbit can be known precisely at any instant. Inside the atom this is not possible. We have already learned that electrons orbiting within atoms can absorb light energy in units proportional to the frequency of the light and that in doing so they shift energy levels. Now suppose that we could "see" an electron. You need light to see it, but when you turn on the light to see it, the electron absorbs some of the light energy and instantly moves to another energy level with a different velocity. This is implied in Heisenberg's uncertainty principle: *It is impossible to obtain accurate values for the position and momentum of an electron simultaneously.* In other words, observation causes a reaction on the thing observed... . This principle of uncertainty ... sets fundamental limits upon our ability to describe nature.

QUESTIONS

1. What implications do the Hawthorne experiments and the uncertainty principle have for epistemology?

2. Do the Hawthorne experiments and the uncertainty principle demonstrate that we can never hope to know the world as it really is?

Sources: Augustine Brannigan and William Zwerman, "The Real 'Hawthorne Effect,'" *Society* 38.2 (Jan./Feb. 2001): 55–60; Verne H. Booth, *Elements of Physical Science: The Nature of Matter and Energy* (London: Macmillan, 1970), 327–328.

---

[23] Ibid., II, viii, 9, 15, 17.

Locke claims that the tree has in itself no green color; it has only the power to produce in our senses a "sensation" that we call green. This claim, he thinks, is proved by the fact that a sensation will "vanish and cease" as soon as our senses stop observing. Primary qualities, however, are in bodies whether we are observing them or not; for when we perceive a body it always has primary qualities, and our minds cannot think of a body without primary qualities. Primary qualities, Locke concludes, "really exist in the bodies themselves" and so their ideas in us are "resemblances of them."

So according to Locke we know how things are because our ideas of primary qualities actually resemble the primary qualities of objects in the external world. For example, if we experience the tree as being a certain height, we can trust that idea to represent how the tree really is; if we experience it to have a certain shape, we can trust that idea to represent how the tree really is. Thus, Locke believed, we can come to have true knowledge of the things around us by having sense experiences of their primary qualities, since these sense experiences represent the qualities external entities actually have.

Problems with Locke. But the nagging questions we noted earlier still remain. First, how do we know that our perceptions truly or accurately represent the external world? Locke claims that we know our ideas of primary qualities accurately represent the qualities of external objects. But the fact is that according to Locke we have no direct knowledge of any external objects so we have no direct knowledge of their actual primary qualities. All the information we have about external objects is what our perceptions provide. Apart from these perceptions we know nothing about external objects. So there is no way that we can check whether our perceptions are giving us accurate information about external objects. We cannot check whether external objects have either the primary or secondary qualities our senses say they have.

But there is a more troubling issue. How do we even know that there are external objects? Locke tried to answer this question with the assertion that *something* outside us had to cause our perceptions so we know at least that something is out there. The production of ideas in us, whether of primary or secondary qualities, claimed Locke, is evidence that there are things outside us that are producing these ideas in us:

> When our senses do actually convey into our understandings any idea, we cannot but be satisfied that there does something *at that time* really exist outside us, which does affect our senses, and by them give notice of itself to our apprehensive faculties, and actually produce that idea which we then perceive; and we cannot so far distrust their testimony, as to doubt that such *collections* of simple ideas as we have observed by our senses to be united together, do really exist together.[24]

But how can Locke be sure of any of this? If all we know are the ideas in us, how can Locke, or anyone else, know that there are things outside us that are causing these ideas? How can we know that, as he says, "there does something *at that time* really exist outside us, which does affect our senses"?

In Locke's own time other empiricists objected that he could not account for the accuracy and origin of our ideas. The foremost challenge was presented by the Irish bishop George Berkeley, whom we met in Chapter 3. There we were

MindTap To read more from Locke's *An Essay Concerning Human Understanding*, click the link in the MindTap Reader or go to the Questia Readings folder in MindTap.

QUICK REVIEW
Critics of Locke say we have no way of knowing whether our experiences are accurate copies of objects outside us, or even whether objects exist outside us.

---

[24] Ibid., IV, xi, 9

interested in Berkeley's idealism—that is, his metaphysical view of what reality is. Here, we will be interested in his views on knowledge, that is, what we can *know* about reality. The two are, as we will see, related. But it is important to keep in mind that, though related, they are not the same. This point is especially important when discussing Berkeley. For, as we will see, Berkeley often moves from claims about what we can know, to claims about what reality is like. But you should always question that kind of move. If, for example, you do not *know* whether anybody is in the room next door, does that entitle you to conclude that *in reality* there is nobody next door?

Berkeley and Subjectivism

George Berkeley agreed with Locke that all our ideas originate in sensory experience. He also accepted Locke's argument that secondary qualities are ideas in us, not in external objects. But Berkeley insisted that Locke's primary qualities are also ideas in us, not in external objects. Primary qualities, like secondary qualities, he claimed, are mind-dependent and exist only in the mind. Both primary qualities and secondary qualities, then, are **subjective**. That is, they do not exist independent of a mind. In *A Treatise Concerning the Principles of Human Knowledge*, Berkeley argued for these claims:

> They who assert that figure, motion, and the rest of the primary or original qualities do exist without mind in unthinking [material] substances, do at the same time acknowledge that colors, sounds, heat, cold and such like secondary qualities, do not; which they tell us are sensations, existing in the mind alone.... Now if it be certain that those original [primary] qualities are inseparably united with [the] other sensible [secondary] qualities, and not, even in thought, capable of being abstracted [separated] from them, it plainly follows they exist only in the mind [since they are inseparable from secondary qualities that exist only in the mind]. But I desire anyone to reflect, and try whether he can, by any abstraction of thought conceive the extension and motion of a body without all other sensible [secondary] qualities. For my own part, I see evidently that it is not in my power to frame an idea of a body extended and moving but I must ...give it some color or sensible [secondary] quality, which is acknowledged to exist only in the mind. In short, extension, figure and motion, abstracted from [separated from] all other [secondary] qualities, are inconceivable. Where therefore the other sensible [secondary] qualities are, there must these [primary qualities] be also, to wit, in the mind and nowhere else.... I shall farther add, that, after the same manner as modern philosophers prove certain sensible qualities to have no existence in Matter, or without the mind, the same thing may be likewise proved of all other sensible qualities whatsoever. Thus, for instance, it is said that heat and cold are affections only of the mind, and not at all patterns of real beings, existing in the corporeal substances which excite them, for that the same body which appears cold to one hand seems warm to another. Now, why may we not as well argue that figure and extension are not patterns or resemblances of qualities existing in Matter, because to the same eye at different stations, or eyes of a different texture at the same station, they appear various, and cannot therefore be the images of anything settled and determinate without the mind? ...In short, let any one consider those arguments

ANALYZING THE READING

Locke argued that primary qualities like size, weight, motion, etc., really existed in the material objects we perceive outside of us because our minds "find [primary qualities] inseparable from every particle of matter." In other words, we cannot imagine a material object without these primary qualities. However, Locke said, secondary qualities do not really exist in objects outside of us. Berkeley replies that Locke is wrong because we also cannot imagine a material object without any secondary qualities. So if secondary qualities do not exist in objects outside of ourselves, primary qualities also do not exist outside our minds. Who is right, Locke or Berkeley? Why?

✅ **QUICK REVIEW**
Berkeley argued that Locke's primary qualities are as mind-dependent as Locke had claimed secondary qualities are.

which are thought manifestly to prove that colors and taste exist only in the mind, and he shall find they may with equal force be brought to prove the same thing of extension, figure, and motion.[25]

If heat or cold is a secondary quality and exists only in the mind, then primary qualities like figure and extension also exist only in the mind. For figure and extension, as Locke claimed, are inseparable from the secondary qualities. Berkeley also points out that bodies do not retain their primary qualities unchanged any more than they retain their secondary qualities. For example, the shape of a coin appears round from one angle and flat from another. Why? Because, says Berkeley, all qualities, including primary qualities, are dependent on us. So as we change our perspective, so do the primary qualities of the object. Primary qualities are as mind-dependent as secondary qualities.

But Berkeley attacked more than Locke's claim that primary qualities exist in external objects. Berkeley also attacked Locke's claim that our ideas of primary qualities correspond to the qualities of external objects. That is, he attacked Locke's claim that primary qualities accurately represent the qualities of external objects. Berkeley argued that on principle, our ideas cannot represent any external reality:

> [But] what do we perceive besides our own ideas or sensations? And is it not plainly repugnant that any one of these, or any combination of them, should exist unperceived? . . . The sensible qualities are color, figure, motion, smell, taste, etc., i.e. the ideas perceived by sense. Now, for an idea to exist in an unperceiving [material] thing is a manifest contradiction, for to have an idea is . . . [the same] as to perceive; that therefore wherein color, figure, and the like qualities exist must perceive them [i.e., such qualities must exist in a mind] . . . But, say you, though the ideas themselves do not exist without the mind, yet there may be things like them, whereof they are copies or resemblances, which things exist without the mind in an unthinking [material] substance. I answer, an idea can be like nothing but an idea; a color or figure can be like nothing but another color or figure. If we look but ever so little into our thoughts, we shall find it impossible for us to conceive a likeness except only between our ideas. Again, I ask whether those supposed originals or external things, of which our ideas are the pictures or representations, be themselves perceivable or no? If they are, then they are ideas and we have gained our point [for what is perceived has to be an idea]; but if you say they are not, I appeal to any one whether it be sense to assert a color is like something which is invisible; [or whether] hard or soft, [can be] like something which is intangible; and so of the rest.[26]

QUICK REVIEW

Berkeley argued that Locke was wrong to claim that the ideas of primary qualities are accurate copies of the qualities of external material bodies. Since an idea can only be like another idea, our ideas of primary qualities must be copies of other ideas (i.e., primary qualities must be ideas). Since ideas can exist only in the mind, primary qualities can exist only in the mind and so are not qualities of external material bodies.

ANALYZING THE READING

1. Berkeley states that we do not perceive anything "besides our own ideas or sensations." In other words, we only perceive "our own ideas or sensations." Do you think Berkeley's statement is true? Have you ever perceived one of your sensations? If you did, what did it look like? Would it be more accurate to say you perceive things *by means of* your sensations but do not perceive the *sensations themselves*? Suppose that it is true that we perceive by means of our sensations but do not actually perceive the sensations themselves. If this is true, then how would it affect Berkeley's argument for the claim that the world we see consists of nothing more than ideas and sensations in our minds? If we don't really perceive our own sensations, would Berkeley's argument be refuted?

2. Berkeley says a critic might agree that ideas only exist in the mind, but the critic might say they are "copies or resemblances" of objects that exist outside the mind. Berkeley "answers" this objection by saying "an idea can be like nothing but [another] idea." In other words ideas can only be "copies or resemblances" of other ideas. Do you think Berkeley has really "answered" his critic? Think about this: Would you say that a painting can only be a "copy or resemblance" of another painting? Or could a photograph only be a "copy or resemblance" of another photograph? What do you think is the mistake that Berkeley is making in his "answer"?

---

25 George Berkeley, *A Treatise Concerning the Principles of Human Knowledge*, in *The Works of George Berkeley*, (London: Thomas Tegg and Son, 1837), paras. x, xiv, xv, pp. 9–10.

26 Ibid., paras. iv, vii, viii, p. 9.

THINKING LIKE A PHILOSOPHER

Can you make yourself think what Berkeley wanted you to think? That is, can you convince yourself that everything you see around you is actually nothing more than a perception or idea inside your mind? What does it feel like, or what do you think it would feel like, to really believe that everything you see around you is really inside your head?

QUICK REVIEW

Berkeley argued Locke was wrong to claim that we know there are external objects because they must cause our sensations. We have no access to such objects, Berkeley argued, and just as dreams are not caused by external objects, our perceptions need not be caused by external objects.

QUICK REVIEW

Both primary and secondary qualities, Berkeley argued, are sensations in us and so are mind-dependent. Besides minds and their sensations and ideas, nothing exists.

ANALYZING THE READING

Samuel Johnson is a famous British writer and is the second most quoted person in the English language after Shakespeare. A friend of his once described a conversation he had with Johnson in these words: "After we came out of the church, we stood talking of Bishop Berkeley's ingenious [attempt] to prove the nonexistence of matter and that every thing in the universe is merely idea. I observed that though his doctrine is not true, it is impossible to refute it. I never shall forget the alacrity [quickness] with which Johnson answered, striking his foot with mighty force against a large stone, till he rebounded from it: 'I refute it *thus!*'" Why did Johnson think he was refuting Berkeley by kicking the stone so hard his boot bounced back? How would Berkeley answer Johnson's "refutation." Which do you think is right: Johnson's refutation or Berkeley's answer? Why?

Berkeley is making two points here. First, ideas obviously can only exist in a mind. But any qualities we perceive—colors, shapes, smells, solidity—are ideas. So all qualities, including primary qualities, can only exist in a mind. Secondly, an idea can only be similar to another idea. Ideas, that is, can be accurate copies only of other ideas. So if our ideas of primary qualities are accurate copies of primary qualities, those primary qualities must be ideas. And since ideas can only exist in a mind, primary qualities must exist in the mind.

Our ideas, then, do not represent the primary qualities of material objects outside the mind. The only thing our ideas can accurately represent are other ideas—and such ideas, like all ideas, must exist in the mind.

In a final blow to Locke's philosophy, Berkeley struck at the key weakness in Locke's view. This was Locke's assertion that we know there are external objects because something must be causing our sensations:

> But, though it were possible that solid, figured, movable substances may exist without the mind, corresponding to the ideas we have of bodies, yet how is it possible for us to know this? Either we must know it by sense or by reason. As for our senses, by them we have the knowledge only of our sensations [and] ideas, . . . but they do not inform us that things exist without the mind . . . like to those which are perceived. . . . [So] if we have any knowledge at all of external things, it must be by reason, inferring their existence from what is immediately perceived by sense. But . . . it is granted on all hands (and what happens in dreams . . . puts it beyond dispute) that it is possible we might be affected with all the ideas we have now, though there were no bodies existing without resembling them.[27]

Locke's assumption that our sensations had to be caused by external objects was unjustified, Berkeley claimed. Just as our dreams do not need to be caused by external objects, so too the sensations we have need not be caused by anything at all. We perceive only the sensations in our minds and know nothing beyond our sensations. So we cannot check whether there are external objects that cause our sensations. As we noted in the last chapter, Berkeley drew from these considerations about what we can know, the metaphysical conclusion that the reality we see consists of ideas in our minds.

Earlier we said that reality could be different from what our senses say it is. You may think you see your dead grandfather, but he might not really be there. There are, we said, two possible responses to this problem. One is the response Locke opted to take. He agreed that what we experience is not the same as the reality itself. But that left him with an unanswerable question: How can we ever know that what we perceive is what reality is really like? Berkeley clearly decided to take the other option. He says that what we perceive is the same as reality. That is, reality is nothing more than what we

---

[27] Ibid., para. xviii, p. 11.

perceive: The two are one and the same. By taking this option, Berkeley avoided the problem of trying to figure out how we can know our perceptions match reality. But he has ended up with a strange world in which nothing exists but ideas and minds.

Berkeley's thinking could have become solipsism. This is the view that only I exist. Everything and everyone else is just an idea in my mind. So that what is real is whatever seems real to me in my own mind. To avoid such excesses, Berkeley argued that God keeps the world of ideas in existence even when I do not perceive it. God always has the world—a world composed of ideas, of course—"in mind," and what is real is the world in God's mind, not just what seems real to me. Thus God ensures the objectivity of our knowledge by guaranteeing a stable world of ideas that exists independent of myself. The ideas in God's mind are the ultimate criteria of objective reality and of whether our ideas are true or mistaken.

But given Berkeley's claims, the existence of God creates a major problem for him: How can he know that God exists? If we cannot know that any external material objects exist, how can he know that an external nonmaterial being like God exists? In a dialogue he wrote, Berkeley anticipates just such an objection. In the dialogue Hylas represents Locke, and Philonus represents Berkeley.

HYLAS:	Answer me, Philonus. Are all our ideas perfectly inert beings? Or have they any agency included in them?
PHILONUS:	They are altogether passive and inert.
HYLAS:	And is not God an agent, a being purely active?
PHILONUS:	I acknowledge it.
HYLAS:	No idea therefore can be like unto, or represent, the nature of God.
PHILONUS:	It cannot.
HYLAS:	Since therefore you have no idea of the mind of God, how can you conceive it possible that things should exist in His mind? . . . You admit . . . that there is a spiritual Substance, although you have no idea of it; while you deny there can be such a thing as material Substance, because you have no idea of it. Is this fair dealing? To act consistently, you must either admit Matter or reject Spirit.[28]

"Admit Matter or reject Spirit" was a choice Berkeley was unwilling to make. Berkeley was a Christian, an Anglican bishop, in fact. So his attack on the idea of an external material reality was motivated by his desire to rid the world of materialism. Materialism, he thought, was the ultimate source of atheism and the greatest obstacle to religion. So he hoped to convince the world that there is no material reality—that everything is spiritual, either idea or mind. If he succeeded, then perhaps the world would no longer be misled by materialism and would instead turn to God. That desire prompted the ingenious efforts that resulted in what he called his philosophy of "immaterialism." But that philosophy relied on the theory that all we know are ideas in our mind, and we have no knowledge of external material objects. Consequently, we cannot claim external material objects exist. But as Hylas suggests in the passage above, if he was logical, he would have to admit that his view of knowledge left him no reason to think God exists either. Berkeley was unwilling to admit that, and so he claimed that the orderliness of some of his ideas gave him knowledge of a God who produces that order. But the view that we know only what is in our minds had logically led him to conclude that we cannot know that "external

---

[28] George Berkeley, *Three Dialogues Between Hylas and Philonus*, vol. 1, *The Works of George Berkeley*, ed. George Sampson (London: George Bell & Sons, 1897), 364–365.

material objects" exist. That same logic should have led him to conclude that we cannot know that an external independent "God" exists.

But Berkeley made another questionable move. Berkeley's basic claim was that since we can know only the ideas in our mind, we cannot know what lies outside our minds. Fair enough. But Berkeley then went on to claim that since we have no knowledge of objects outside the mind, they do not exist. In other words, he assumed that if we don't know about something, it must not exist. That assumption is clearly false. It moves from a claim about the extent of our knowledge to a claim about things that lie beyond our knowledge.

Like Locke, Berkeley had adopted empiricism—the view that our only source of knowledge are the sense experiences we have. He used this empiricist claim to argue that all we know are the sense perceptions in our mind. Locke had earlier reached the same conclusion. But Berkeley then took the next logical step. He reasoned that the things we see around us must be nothing more than perceptions in our mind and we cannot claim that external objects exist. Locke had been unwilling to take this second step. He said the perceptions in our minds are distinct from the real external world. Then he simply asserted he was "assured" that the external world exists and we too should be assured. Thus Berkeley was more willing than Locke to follow the logic of his empiricism. But Berkeley was not willing to follow empiricism further than the claim that the world we see is just an idea in our minds and we do not know what lies beyond. He was not willing to say that we therefore do not know whether there is a God out there. In short, Berkeley recoiled from empiricism when it threatened his deepest religious convictions. So he asserted that God must exist because some of his ideas are more orderly than others. He was therefore unwilling to take empiricism to its logical conclusion. But Berkeley remains a critically significant figure. For he represents an important step in the logical development of empiricism. As we will see, the Scottish philosopher David Hume, unlike Locke and Berkeley, was willing to extend empiricism to its logical limits. Many believe he took it too far.

Hume and Skepticism

It's fair to say that David Hume pushed Locke's and Berkeley's empiricism to a complete skepticism. That is, empiricism led him to a denial of the possibility that we can have certain knowledge about much of what we all take for granted. How Hume came to his skeptical conclusions is a long and complex affair, which we can only sketch here. (For a fuller discussion of Hume, see the Historical Showcase at the end of this chapter.)

As an empiricist, Hume followed Locke and Berkeley in claiming that all our knowledge of the world is based on our perceptions. Hume asserts that perceptions take two forms, what he terms *impressions* and *ideas*. The distinction between them and how they relate to knowing are vital to understanding Hume's thought. In *An Enquiry Concerning Human Understanding*, Hume explains his ideas and impressions:

> Here, therefore, we may divide all the perceptions of the mind into two classes or species, which are distinguished by their different degrees of force and vivacity. The less forcible and lively are commonly denominated *Thoughts* or *Ideas*. The other species want a name in our language, and in most others; I suppose, because it was not requisite for any, but philosophical purposes, to rank them under a general term or appellation. Let us therefore use a little freedom, and call them *Impressions*; employing that word in a sense somewhat different from the usual. By the term *impression*, then, I mean all our more lively perceptions, when we hear, or see, or feel, or love, or hate,

or desire, or will. And impressions are distinguished from ideas, which are the less lively perceptions of which we are conscious, when we reflect on any of those sensations or movements above mentioned.[29]

Thus, those impressions we get directly from the senses are quite vivid—for example, those of a color we see or an emotion we feel. However, when we later recall the color or emotion, our memories of them are less vivid than the original impressions were. Similarly, when we think or imagine colors or emotions, our thoughts and images are less vivid than the original impressions. The pain you feel when you hammer your thumb is an impression; the memory of what you felt is an idea. You'll probably agree the pain is a bit more "vivid" than your memory of the pain. Every idea we have in our heads, Hume claimed, has to come from some earlier sense impression. What about ideas we have of things we've never perceived with our senses, such as a golden mountain or a pink elephant? Hume answers that in such cases our imagination combines impressions that were earlier acquired from our senses. He writes: "When we think of a golden mountain, we only join two consistent ideas, *gold* and *mountain*, with which we were formerly acquainted." In short, the senses are the source of all our knowledge:

> It seems a proposition, which will not admit of much dispute, that all our ideas are nothing but copies of our impressions, or, in other words, that it is impossible for us to think of anything, which we have not antecedently felt, either by our external or internal senses.

From this insight, Hume drew a portentous conclusion. He concluded that there can be no genuine knowledge without corresponding sense impressions. This is a crucial point for Hume. He claims that all real knowledge must be derived from impressions. And impressions come from our outer senses (sight, hearing, touch, taste, smell) or from our inner senses (our inner feelings, such as anger, sorrow, fear). Consequently, we cannot have genuine knowledge of a thing unless we can point to the impression from which the idea of that thing is derived. As he puts the point:

> When we entertain ... any suspicion that a philosophical term is employed without any meaning or idea (as is but too frequent), we need but enquire, from what impression is that supposed idea derived? And if it be impossible to assign any, this will serve to confirm our suspicion [that the term has no meaning].[30]

Causality as Habit. Hume repeatedly used the principle that we can have real knowledge only if we can point to a sense impression from which it is derived. Using that principle he was able to prove that many of our common "ideas" are meaningless.

> **QUICK REVIEW**
> Hume accepted Berkeley's view that all we experience are our own sensations and ideas, which he called "impressions." Because all our knowledge is derived from sense impressions, he argued that if an idea is not derived from a sense impression, it is meaningless or nonexistent.

ANALYZING THE READING

Hume claims that all our thoughts, ideas, memories, images, and anything else in our minds either (1) is derived from our perceptions of what is outside us or inside us, or (2) is created by "joining" together ideas that were derived from perceptions of what is outside us or inside us. So everything in our minds ultimately must be capable of being traced back to some perceptions of something outside us or inside us. Do you think Hume is right? Hume argues for his claim by saying that no matter what idea you choose, if you examine it long enough you will see that it is derived from perceptions or created from perceptions. Can you think of any concept you have in your mind that you did not derive from perceptions or create from perceptions? What would the rationalists say to Hume?

> **QUICK REVIEW**
> Because the idea of causal connection is not derived from any sense impression, it does not exist in the real world; causality is nothing more than the habitual expectation that events in the future will be followed by the same kind of events that followed them in the past. This habitual expectation is formed by repeatedly seeing the same sequence of events.

---

[29] David Hume, *An Enquiry Concerning Human Understanding*, ed. L. A. Selby-Bigge (Oxford: Clarendon, 1894), sec. 2, para. 18.

[30] Ibid., sec. 2, para. 17.

ANALYZING THE READING

1. Hume claims that there are some "philosophical" ideas for which it is "impossible to assign" any "impression [from which] that supposed idea derived." Does this contradict anything he said earlier about all the ideas in our minds? How do you think Hume would answer you if you objected that his claim about philosophical ideas contradicts what he said earlier about all ideas?

2. According to Hume, the philosopher's "idea of [causal] power or necessary [causal] connection" cannot be perceived when we look at one thing causing another (like one moving billiard ball causing another one to move). Since "we can have no idea of anything which never appeared to our outward sense or inward sentiment," he concludes that "we have no idea of [causal] connection or [causal] power at all." Try to put Hume's argument into its logical form. Does Hume contradict himself in this argument? Hume says his conclusion is really that "these *words* are absolutely without any meaning." Can this fix the contradiction he might have made in his argument?

A key idea that he argues is mistaken is our idea of **causality**. Philosophers and others commonly think that when one event causes another the first event exerts some kind of "power" or force that compels the second to necessarily happen. That is, we believe that the cause forces the effect to happen so that the effect necessarily has to happen when the cause acts. According to the common view, then, there is some kind of real connection between a cause and its effect, and when the cause acts, the effect has to follow. But Hume asks us to look carefully at any case of one object causing another object to do something. Take, for example, a rapidly moving billiard ball that strikes a second billiard ball so that the second ball moves rapidly away. No matter how hard we look, he says, all we will see is one ball moving quickly, then touching the second ball, and then the second ball moving quickly. We see nothing more. Specifically, we see no necessary connection between the objects, no power or influence going from one to the other. We just see one event followed by another event but see nothing anywhere between them:

> To be fully acquainted, therefore, with the idea of [causal] power or necessary [causal] connection, let us examine its impression; and in order to find the impression with greater certainty, let us search for it in all the sources, from which it may possibly be derived.... When we look about us towards external objects, and consider the operation of causes, we are never able, in a single instance, to discover any power or necessary connection; any quality, which binds the effect to the cause, and renders the one an infallible consequence of the other. We only find, that the one does actually, in fact, follow the other. The impulse of one billiard-ball is attended with motion in the second. This is the whole that appears to the outward senses.... Consequently, there is not, in any single, particular instance of cause and effect, anything which can suggest the idea of power or necessary connection.... And as we can have no idea of any thing which never appeared to our outward sense or inward sentiment, the necessary conclusion seems to be that we have no idea of [causal] connection or [causal] power at all, and that these words are absolutely without any meaning when employed either in philosophical reasoning or common life.[31]

We can perceive no connection between a cause and its effect. So, Hume concludes, a cause does not pass some kind of mysterious influence to the effect that forces the effect to occur. Events simply succeed each other. What, then, is the source of our feeling that when one billiard ball strikes another, the second ball has to—necessarily must—move? The source of that feeling, Hume asserts, is habit. Hume argues that when we repeatedly see an event of one kind followed by an event of a second kind, the mind forms the habit of expecting to see the second when it sees the first. From then on when we see the first kind of event, the expectation of seeing the second kind is aroused in our mind. For example, suppose that over and over we see that when one moving billiard ball strikes a second, the second ball starts moving. Then our mind

---

[31]   Ibid., sec. 7, pt. 1, para. 50.

will form the habit of expecting to see the second ball move when we see the first ball strike it. From then on, seeing one moving billiard ball strike another will arouse in us a feeling of expectation that next we will see the second ball move. The feeling that the cause somehow forces or compels the effect to necessarily happen is all in our minds. We project this feeling of expectation on to the events, so that we think the necessity is in the events. But it is nothing more than a feeling in our minds:

> The idea of necessity arises from some impression. There is no impression conveyed by our senses, which can give rise to that idea. It must, therefore, be derived from some internal impression, or impression of reflection. There is no internal impression, which has any relation to the present business, but that propensity, which custom produces, to pass from an object to the idea of its usual attendant. This therefore is the essence of necessity. Upon the whole, necessity is something that exists in the mind, not in objects; nor is it possible for us ever to form the most distant idea of it, considered as a quality in bodies. Either we have no idea of necessity, or necessity is nothing but that determination of the thought to pass from causes to effects and from effects to causes, according to their experienced union. . . .
>
> I am sensible, that of all the paradoxes, which I have had, or shall hereafter have occasion to advance in the course of this treatise, the present one is the most violent. . . . Before we are reconciled to this doctrine, how often must we repeat to ourselves, *that* the simple view of any two objects or actions, however related, can never give us any idea of power, or of a connection between them; *that* this idea arises from the repetition of their union; *that* the repetition neither discovers nor causes any thing in the objects, but has an influence only on the mind, by that customary transition it produces; *that* this customary transition is, therefore, the same with the power and necessity, which are consequently qualities of perceptions, not of objects, and are internally felt by the soul, and not perceived externally in bodies? There is commonly an astonishment attending every thing extraordinary; and this astonishment changes immediately into the highest degree of esteem or contempt, according as we approve or disapprove of the subject. I am much afraid, that although the foregoing reasoning appears to me the shortest and most decisive imaginable, yet with the generality of readers the bias of the mind will prevail, and give them a prejudice against the present doctrine. . . .[32]

THINKING LIKE A PHILOSOPHER

Hume says his "doctrine" of causality is "the most violent" of all his claims. He seems to mean that his claims about causality will require "violent" changes in people's beliefs. Do you feel this way about Hume's claims about causality? Which of his claims about causality do you think would require the biggest changes in your own views if you believed them? Do you believe Hume's claims about causality? Suppose Hume's claims about causality are true; then which of your views would you have to change?

Notice that Hume in this passage thinks his "doctrine" of causality is new and requires a "violent" change in our beliefs. His doctrine, he thinks, will be so hard for people to accept, that he actually repeats his whole argument again in the second paragraph! But even after reviewing his argument again, he says, most readers will still hold a "bias" and "prejudice" against his view. Why does Hume think his view of causality requires "violent" change and is sure to arouse "bias" and "prejudice"? One reason is related to Christianity. Before Hume everyone assumed that causes themselves forced effects to happen. Causal forces, they thought, were real and exist in objects themselves, not in our minds. So when Christians said that God caused the world to exist, they were saying that God possessed real causal powers or forces. But if causal forces are all in our mind, then it makes no sense to say God himself has causal powers. So Hume's doctrine destroys the reality of the causal connection that Christians said exists between God and the world.

---

[32] David Hume, *A Treatise of Human Nature*, bk. I, pt. III, sec. xiv.

Yet Hume was not done. Not only is causality nothing more than a feeling of expectation in our minds, even this expectation is unjustified. Hume argues that we have no good reason to expect that future causes will produce the same effects that they have produced in the past. It is true, for example, that in the past when one rolling billiard ball hit another, the second started to move. But what justification do we have to believe this will always happen in the future? What reason do we have to think that future causes and effects will follow each other like they have in the past? Hume argues that we have no justification for thinking that in the future causes will have the same kind of effects that we've observed in the past:

All reasoning may be divided into two kinds, namely, demonstrative reasoning or that concerning relations of ideas, and . . . [probable] reasoning or that concerning matter of fact and existence. That there are no demonstrative arguments in the case seems evident; since it implies no contradiction that the course of nature may change, and that an object, seemingly like those which we have experienced, may be attended with different or contrary effects. May I not clearly and distinctly conceive that a body, falling from the clouds, and which, in all other respects, resembles snow, has yet the taste of salt or feeling of fire? Is there any more intelligible proposition than to affirm, that all the trees will flourish in December and January, and decay in May and June? Now whatever is intelligible, and can be distinctly conceived, implies no contradiction, and can never be proved false by any demonstrative argument or abstract reasoning *a priori*.

If we be, therefore, engaged by arguments to put trust in past experience, and make it the standard of our future judgment, these arguments must be probable only, or such as regard matter of fact and real existence, according to the division above mentioned. But that there is no argument of this kind, must appear, if our explication of that species of reasoning be admitted as solid and satisfactory. We have said that all arguments concerning existence are founded on the relation of cause and effect; that our knowledge of that relation is derived entirely from experience; and that all our experimental conclusions proceed upon the supposition that the future will be conformable to the past. To endeavor, therefore, the proof of this last supposition by probable arguments, or arguments regarding existence, must be evidently going in a circle, and taking that for granted, that which is the very point in question. . . .

THINKING LIKE A PHILOSOPHER

When Hume discusses the possibility that things in the future might not happen like they have in the past, he says: "This happens sometimes, and with regard to some objects. Why may it not happen always, and with regard to all objects?" Can you think of any events that you think are a real possibility for your own future and that would change almost "all objects" in your life? For example, are there any specific catastrophes that you think are real possibilities in the future and that would probably change everything in your personal life? What are those? Suppose there are some such specific catastrophes that are real possibilities. Does the real possibility that the future might not be like the past mean that you should change anything in your present life? Explain.

For all inferences from experience suppose, as their foundation, that the future will resemble the past, and that similar powers will be conjoined with similar sensible qualities. If there be any suspicion that the course of nature may change, and that the past may be no rule for the future, all experience becomes useless, and can give rise to no inference or conclusion. It is impossible, therefore, that any arguments from [past] experience can prove this resemblance of the past to the future, since all these arguments are founded on the supposition of that resemblance. Let the course of things be allowed hitherto ever so regular, that alone, without some new argument or inference, proves not that, for the future, it will continue so. In vain do you pretend to have learned the nature of bodies from your past experience. Their secret nature, and consequently all their effects and influence, may change, without any change in their sensible qualities. This happens sometimes, and with regard to some objects. Why may it not happen always, and with regard to all objects? What logic, what process of argument secures you against this supposition?[33]

Notice that Hume begins by pointing out that there are only two ways to establish that the future will be like the past. One way is to use deductive reasoning or what Hume calls "demonstrative reasoning." As we've seen, this is the kind of argument in which, if the premises are true, the conclusion is necessarily true. But, Hume points out, the claim that the future will be like the past is not necessarily true, since things could change in the future. So the claim cannot be the conclusion of a deductive argument. The claim, then, must be based on inductive reasoning or what Hume calls "probable reasoning." This is the kind of reasoning that moves from premises about what has been true in some cases, to a conclusion about what probably will be true in all similar cases. For example, from observing that several bodies of different weight all fell at the same speed, Galileo concluded that all bodies probably fall to earth at the same speed. But Hume points out that using inductive reasoning to prove that the future will be like the past is circular reasoning. Inductive reasoning says that what was true in the past will probably be true in the future. So inductive reasoning itself relies on the assumption that the future will be like the past. Hume goes on to point out that it is useless to rely on our past experience to show that our past experience is reliable. Hume has in mind the person who might say that the reason we know the future will be like the past is because in the past, future events have always turned out to be like past events. True enough, Hume grants. But that could change in the future. "This happens sometimes, and with regard to some objects," he says, "why may it not happen always, and with regard to all objects?" In short, if we are questioning whether our past experience is reliable, we cannot use our past experience to prove our past experience is reliable, since the future may not be like the past. So, without circular reasoning we have no way to justify our expectation that in the future events will follow each other like they have in the past. Not only is causality nothing more than an expectation in our mind, but this expectation itself is unjustified.

 THINKING LIKE A PHILOSOPHER

Hume claims that you are not justified in thinking that events in your future will follow each other like they have in your past. Do you agree with him that you personally do not have any legitimate reason to think that events in your future will follow each other just like they have in your past? If you think he's wrong, then what is your personal reason for thinking that events in your future will follow each other like they have in your past? Is your personal reason just a case of circular reasoning? That is, are you using your past experience to show that your past experience is a reliable guide for your future? If you agree with Hume that you personally do not have any real reason to think that events in your future will follow each other as in your past, what do you think this means for the plans you have made for your future?

Hume's question whether we are justified in thinking that future events will be like those we experienced in the past is now called the "problem of induction." But Hume's question is only one of a larger group of questions we classify as part of the problem of induction. Hume pointed out that when we make claims about future causes and effects on the basis of our past experience, we go beyond our experience. But we go beyond our experience in other important ways that are not related to causes and their effects. And Hume casts serious doubts on our justification for going beyond our experience in those other ways too. To understand how large and serious the problem of induction is, it helps to know what "inductive generalizations" are. Inductive generalizations are explained in the Thinking Critically box that follows. Read through that and then you should be able to get a better understanding of how serious Hume's problem of induction is for all of us.

---

[33] David Hume, *An Enquiry Concerning Human Understanding,* op. cit., sec. 4, pt. 2.

⚙ thinking critically • Inductive Generalizations

The problem regarding causal reasoning that Hume pointed to is actually a special instance of a more general problem called the "problem of induction." To understand the general problem, it helps to have a good understanding first of what an "inductive generalization" is.

An inductive generalization is a probable argument whose premises are claims about what is true in *some* cases, and whose conclusion is a claim about what *probably* will be true in *all* similar cases. The limited group of cases described in the premises is called the "sample," and the entire group of cases described in the conclusion is called the "population." Here's a simple one-premise example of an inductive generalization:

1. The 1,500 Toyotas that readers of *Consumer Reports* have owned were very reliable.
2. So probably all Toyotas will be very reliable.

Here the *sample* consists of the 1,500 Toyotas owned by readers of *Consumer Reports*, and the *population* consists of all Toyotas.

The premises of an inductive generalization may contain explicit statistics about the sample. The argument will then apply the statistics about the sample in the premises, to the whole population in the conclusion. For example:

1. 90 percent of the 1,500 Toyotas that readers of *Consumer Reports* have owned were very reliable.
2. So probably 90 percent of all Toyotas will be very reliable.

Notice that although the first example above contains no explicit statistics, it *assumes* that we are talking about 100 percent of the sample and 100 percent of the population:

1. [100 percent of] The 1,500 Toyotas that readers of *Consumer Reports* have owned were very reliable.
2. So probably [100 percent of] all Toyotas will be reliable.

Like all probable arguments, an inductive generalization is a *strong* argument if its premises make the conclusion very probable, and *weak* if they do not. So how do you figure out the strength of an inductive generalization? The strength of an inductive generalization depends on two factors: *how large* the sample is, and *how representative* the sample is:

a. All other things being equal, the larger the sample is, the stronger the argument will be. But note that if the members of the population are extremely similar to each other—like the virtually identical bolts made by a factory machine—a very small sample can provide a strong argument.

b. The more representative the sample is, the stronger the argument. A sample is representative to the extent that its characteristics match the relevant characteristics of the whole population. (e.g., if one third of the population has relevant characteristic X, then one third of the sample should have characteristic X.) A relevant characteristic is one that could affect the feature that is being generalized; below we explain what "feature that is being generalized" means.

An inductive generalization always assumes (or explicitly indicates) that its sample is appropriately large and representative. We can summarize all this by saying that if all the premises and assumptions of an inductive generalization are made explicit, it will have the following form:

1. N percent of the A's in a group are F.
2. That group of A's is a large and representative sample of A's.
3. So probably N percent of all A's are F.

Here N is a numerical percent (which is often omitted), A's are the members of the population and the sample, and F is the feature or features being generalized.

We obviously make inductive generalizations all the time. In fact, when we reason about what will probably happen now or in the future, we are making an inductive generalization. But our everyday generalizations usually don't mention percentages and don't provide much information about how large or representative our sample is. And very often they don't even mention that the conclusion is only probable. We might say, for example, "The three Toyota Corollas I've owned turned out to be pretty reliable, so I think all Toyota Corollas are going to be reliable," or "All five of my Chinese friends are smart and study a lot, so I think all Chinese must be like that." If we assume that one Toyota Corolla is pretty much identical to another in all the relevant characteristics, then our generalization about Toyotas might be a strong one, although a sample of three is very small. But Chinese, like any other group of people, differ from each other in numerous ways that are relevant to how smart and studious a person is. So generalizing from a sample of five relies on a sample that is neither large enough nor representative. When we argue from a sample that's too small, we make a "hasty generalization." Hasty generalization is one of the fallacies we identified in the Thinking Critically box in Chapter 4 entitled "Formal and Informal Fallacies." And if our sample is not representative, we say it is "biased." The fallacy of "biased statistics" is another fallacy we identified in Chapter 4. The generalization involving my Chinese friends commits the fallacy of being a hasty generalization, and it uses a sample that is not representative so it is also biased.

QUICK REVIEW

Hume's criticism of causal reasoning applies to all inductive generalizations and is now called the "problem of induction" which asks: What justification do we have for inferring that what was true of a sample in the past will be true of a whole population in the future? Arguing that since inductive generalization has been successful in the past it will be successful in the future is itself an inductive generalization and so assumes that inductive generalization is justified, which is what must be proved.

If you have read through the Thinking Critically box, you should understand how inductive generalizations work. So let's return to Hume's "problem of induction." The problem of induction is this: Are we justified in thinking that what was true of a *sample* of items in the past will be true of *all* such items in the future? What justifies this move from *some past* observations to *all future* observations? Notice that the problem of induction has two parts: (1) what justifies an inference from *some* items we have observed to *all* those items we have not observed, and (2) what justifies an inference from *past* observations to *future* observations? Both parts of the problem of induction ask whether inductive generalizations are justified in moving beyond the evidence provided by their premises. But Hume only noticed the second part, (2), of the problem of induction. So the problem of induction to which Hume drew our attention is actually not just a problem that involves future causes and their effects. It is a problem that afflicts all inductive generalizations. And it is a large problem for us because, as mentioned in the Thinking Critically box, we use inductive generalizations every time we reason about what will happen now or in the future. And, obviously, we do that hundreds of times a day.

The problem of induction can't be solved by providing standards for good inductive generalizations. As the Thinking Critically box on inductive generalization showed, we have such standards. For example, in an inductive generalization, the sample must be large and representative. But the problem of induction generalization remains: How do we know that what was true of a large and representative sample of things in the past will be true of all such things in the future?

You might think that one way to argue that we can rely on inductive generalization is by pointing to how successful it is: It's justified because

ANALYZING THE READING

1. Hume argues that we have no legitimate justification for assuming that in the future events will follow each other just like they have in the past. Is he right? Can you think of any argument, evidence, or reason that would show that our past experience is a reliable guide to what will happen in the future?

2. How is the problem of induction related to Hume's claim that we have no reason to think the future will be like the past? How does the problem of induction go beyond Hume's claim?

it works! Inductive generalization successfully shows us what we have to do to boil water, to bake a cake, to relieve a headache, to go to the moon, and to send a rocket to Mars. Since it's been so successful, it must be reliable. But there's a problem here. As Hume points out, that argument is circular. It assumes what it is supposed to prove. The argument is saying that because inductive generalization has been so successful in the past, we know it will be successful in the future. But this assumes that what has been true in the past will be true in the future. Yet this assumption is what has to be justified!

Or you might want to argue that we can rely on inductive generalization because we know that nature is uniform and that the world follows regular patterns. So we know that a pattern we observed in nature yesterday is the one we will see in nature in the future. But as Hume also pointed out, this argument, too, assumes what it is supposed to prove. It says that since nature has been uniform in the past, it will be uniform in the future. So it assumes that what has been true in the past will be true in the future. But that, again, is the very assumption that has to be justified.

You might even be tempted to say that we should just stop making inductive generalizations if we don't know whether they can be justified. But we can't stop. You can prove this to yourself by trying to go through a single day—even a single hour—without doing something that is based on an inductive generalization. You won't succeed. All your experience lies in the past, and you have to rely on that past experience as you plan and move into your future. So you are forced to continuously generalize from what you've experienced in the past to what you will experience in your future. Inductive generalization is inescapable. It is also too useful to give up. Inductive generalization amplifies and expands our knowledge in remarkably useful ways. It takes the relatively few things you've experienced in your past and says that what you experienced then will apply always and everywhere you go. For example, you've seen that fire can hurt you, that being nice to people makes them be nice to you, that if you eat a lot you'll put on weight, and so on. And so all these and other things you learned at home will continue to be true when you leave home and travel through the world. In fact, inductive generalization lets astronomers take what scientists discover here on our little planet and apply it to the entire universe. In view of all we would have to give up, how can we possibly stop using inductive generalizations?

Is there an answer, then, to Hume's problem of induction? Is our reliance on inductive generalizations justified? To this day, no one has come up with an answer that has persuaded everyone. Nevertheless, when we discuss Immanuel Kant in the next section, we will see an answer that has persuaded at least some philosophers.

Can We Know an External World Exists? Hume's views suggested another disturbing possibility: Perhaps the external world does not exist at all. True, we assume there is an external, regular, and predictable world outside us. But how can we know for sure that there is a world beyond our sense impressions when all we know are our own impressions? We have no way of peering beyond these impressions, no way of going beyond these impressions to see whether they are connected to an external world. Because we know only what our sense impressions convey to us, and our sense impressions say nothing about the external world, we cannot say an external world exists:

> Almost before the use of reason, we always suppose an external universe, which depends not on our perception, but would exist, though we and every sensible creature were absent or annihilated. . . . [But] by what argument can it be proved,

that the perceptions of the mind must be caused by external objects, entirely different from them, though resembling them (if that be possible)...? It is a question of fact, whether the perceptions of the senses be produced by external objects, resembling them: how shall this question be determined? By experience surely; as all other questions of a like nature. But here experience is, and must be entirely silent. The mind has never anything present to it but the perceptions, and cannot possibly reach any experience of their connection with objects. The supposition of such a connection is, therefore, without any foundation in reasoning.... The mind has never anything present to it but [its] perceptions, and cannot possibly reach [beyond them to] any experience of their connection with [external] objects. The supposition of such a connection is, therefore, without any foundation in reasoning.[34]

ANALYZING THE READING

1. Hume argues that we have no reason to think that a real world exists beyond our perceptions. Yet, unlike Berkeley, he does not claim that there is no real world beyond our perceptions, that is, that no real world exists beyond our perceptions. Why not?

2. Also unlike Berkeley, Hume does not claim that the world we perceive *is* the real world. That is, he does not go on to claim that the real world is nothing but an idea in our minds. Why not? Are these differences between Berkeley and Hume important? Why?

Hume concedes that we always act *as if a* real external world of things exists. The apparent constancy in things leads us to believe that they have an independent existence external to us. But we have no reason to think that our impressions are connected with independent external things. There is no way for us to reach beyond our impressions to an external world.

This discussion may resemble Berkeley's doctrine that to be is to be perceived. But recall that Berkeley said there's a God who keeps things in existence when no person is perceiving them. Hume, who is more consistent, does not rely on any such theological prop. Indeed, how could he? After all, we prove that God exists by showing that the things around us had to be caused by God. But Hume has shown that causality is just a habit that repeated events create in our minds. There are no causal powers or forces connecting causes to their events. So, we cannot say that the things around us are caused by real causal powers that exist in God. Yet Hume is unwilling to say outright that God's existence cannot be proved. Notice how his argument stops short of a definite conclusion in the following passage in which he is discussing the existence of God:

THINKING LIKE A PHILOSOPHER

Hume argues that we cannot know whether anything exists beyond our perceptions. That is, that we cannot know whether there is a real world outside of our minds. Do you think Hume is right and that you yourself don't know whether there is a real world outside your own mind? How do you think your life would have to change if you really believed there was no real world outside your mind?

It is only when two *species* of objects are found to be constantly conjoined, that we can infer the one from the other; and were an effect presented, which was entirely singular, and could not be comprehended under any known *species*, I do not see, that we could form any conjecture or inference at all concerning its cause. If experience and observation and analogy be, indeed, the only guides which we can reasonably follow in inferences of this nature; both the effect and cause must bear a similarity and resemblance to other effects and causes, which we know, and which we have found, in many instances, to be conjoined with each other. I leave it to your own reflection to pursue the consequences of this principle. I shall just observe, that,... the antagonists of Epicurus always suppose the universe, an effect quite singular and unparalleled, to be the proof of a Deity, a cause no less singular and unparalleled...[35]

---

34 Ibid., sec. 12, pt. 1, paras. 118 and 119.
35 Ibid., sec. 11, para. 115.

Notice that Hume states all the premises for an argument, but omits the conclusion. He says only "I leave it to your own reflection to pursue the consequences of this principle." What are the consequences? The "principle" is that we can say one thing is the cause of another only if we have observed things of the first kind causing things of the second kind. But he notes that "the antagonists of Epicurus" pointed out that the universe is one of a kind, and God is one of a kind. This means that we can never observe the kind of thing that God is, causing the kind of thing the universe is. The obvious conclusion is that we can never know that God is the cause of the universe. Yet Hume does not state this "obvious" conclusion. Why not? Perhaps because Hume was writing during a period of harsh religious persecution. Nonbelievers of any kind, particularly atheists, could find themselves in prison or worse. Under those circumstances, it was best for him to be cautious and never state in writing that he is an atheist.

Hume's empiricism ends in virtually complete skepticism about everything. Hume begins with the basic claim of empiricism that the source of all our knowledge is sense perception. He concludes that we can never know whether or not any of our ideas about the external world are accurate, or even whether there is an external world. Since the only knowledge we have is what our ideas and perceptions provide, we can have no knowledge of anything beyond them. We also cannot know whether anything really causes anything else to happen. Nor are we justified in thinking that our past experience is a reliable guide to our future. And although he never explicitly said as much, we also cannot know whether there is a God.

Perhaps all this was inevitable. Locke, the earliest of our three empiricists, also began with the basic empiricist claim that sense perception is the source of all our knowledge. Like Hume he assumed that our perceptions were distinct from the world outside the mind. This raised the possibility that the perceptions within us might not correspond to the real world outside or that there might be no world outside. But Locke said God gave him "assurance" that an external world exists and that our perceptions accurately reflect at least its primary qualities. Our next empiricist, Berkeley, however, was not so assured. He too accepted the basic claim that sense perception is the source of all our knowledge. He concluded that the entire universe must consist of perceptions in our minds, and there is no external material world. Yet God sustains that world of perceptions when no one else is around to perceive it. So Berkeley backed away from empiricism where God was concerned. Though logic would suggest he could not know whether God existed, Berkeley affirmed God's existence anyway. The third and latest of our three empiricists is Hume. And Hume was willing to go all the way with the empiricist claim that sense perception is our only source of knowledge about the world. Hume faced up to the possibility that the ideas in our minds may not correspond to a reality outside the mind. And unlike Locke and Berkeley, Hume did not rely on God to save him from skepticism. With cold logic, Hume argued that we cannot know whether our ideas and sense perceptions correspond to reality. Indeed, Hume claimed, we are acquainted only with the impressions and ideas in our minds and have no access to any other reality.

Many contemporary philosophers are inclined to agree with Hume. For example, Barry Stroud argues that we must accept Descartes' claim that we might be dreaming. In other words, our perceptions might not correspond to any reality outside the mind. Like Locke and Hume, Stroud takes the option of assuming that what we perceive is distinct from what is real. But once we accept the possibility that our perceptions might not represent a real world outside our minds, Hume's skepticism, he argues, is inevitable. We have no way of checking to see what the real world behind our perceptions might be like. For we must rely on the perceptions within us, and those perceptions do not tell us whether anything exists beyond themselves. So real knowledge of the world is forever lost to us:

> If we are in the predicament Descartes finds himself in at the end of his *First Meditation* we cannot tell by means of the senses whether we are dreaming or not; all the sensory experiences we are having are compatible with our merely dreaming of a world around us while that world is in fact very different from the way we take it to be. Our knowledge is in that way confined to our sensory experiences. There seems to be no way of going beyond them to know that the world around us really is this way rather than that. . . .
>
> What *can* we know in such a predicament? We can perhaps know what sensory experiences we are having, or how things seem to us to be. At least that much of our knowledge will not be threatened by the kind of attack Descartes makes on our knowledge of the world beyond our experiences. What we can know turns out to be a great deal less than we thought we knew before engaging in that assessment of our knowledge. Our position is much more restricted, much poorer, than we had originally supposed. We are confined at best to what Descartes calls "ideas" of things around us, representations of things or states of affairs which, for all we can know, might or might not have something corresponding to them in reality. We are in a sense imprisoned within those representations, at least with respect to our knowledge. Any attempt to go beyond them to try and tell whether the world really is as they represent it to be can yield only more representations, more deliverances of sense experience which themselves are compatible with reality's being very different from the way we take it to be on the basis of our sensory experiences. . . .
>
> We would be in the position of someone waking up to find himself locked in a room full of television sets and trying to find out what is going on in the world outside. For all he can know, whatever is producing the patterns he can see on the screens in front of him might be something other than well-functioning cameras directed on to the passing show outside the room. The victim might switch on more of the sets in the room to try to get more information, and he might find that some of the sets show events exactly similar or coherently related to those already visible on the screens he can see. But all those pictures will be no help to him without some independent information, some knowledge that does not come to him from the pictures themselves, about how the pictures he does see before him are connected with what is going on outside the room. The problem of the external world is the problem of finding out, or knowing how we could find out, about the world around us if we were in that sort of predicament. It is perhaps enough simply to put the problem this way to convince us that it can never be given a satisfactory solution.[36]

QUICK REVIEW
Contemporary philosophers such as Barry Stroud agree with Hume's view that we have no way of knowing whether there is any external world beyond our sensory experiences.

MindTap To read more from Barry Stroud's *The Significance of Philosophical Skepticism*, click the link in the MindTap Reader or go to the Questia Readings folder in MindTap.

If Stroud is right then given Hume's assumptions we cannot avoid his skeptical conclusions. Once we have decided that our only source of knowledge is our perceptions and that our perceptions are distinct from the real world, skepticism seems inevitable.

But although Hume arrived at skeptical conclusions on every front, those conclusions seem to have had little effect on his ordinary daily life. Hume tells us that he found too much enjoyment in being "merry with my friends" to stay with the "darkness" of his skepticism:

> The *intense* view of these manifold contradictions and imperfections in human reason has so wrought upon me, and heated my brain, that I am ready to reject all belief and reasoning, and can look upon no opinion even as more probable or likely than another. Where am I, or what? From what causes do I derive my existence, and to what condition

---

[36] Barry Stroud, *The Significance of Philosophical Skepticism* (Oxford: Clarendon, 1984), 31–33.

shall I return?. . . What beings surround me? and on whom have I any influence, or who have any influence on me? I am confounded with all these questions, and begin to fancy myself in the most deplorable condition imaginable, environed [surrounded] with the deepest darkness, and utterly deprived of the use of every member and faculty.

THINKING LIKE A PHILOSOPHER

1. Hume claims that thinking about skepticism was so "intense" that it "heated [his] brain," made him feel he was in a "deplorable... darkness," and put him into a "delirium." If you yourself fully believed everything Hume claimed, do you think you would feel the same? Why?

2. Hume says that he could not long continue thinking about his skeptical views, and his natural desire for "amusement" would pull him away from those "speculations" and make him instead enjoy dining, playing games, and conversing with his friends. Would you say that this describes your own reactions when you spend time thinking about Hume's skeptical arguments? Is there anything hypocritical in Hume's decision to continue on with his own life as if nothing had happened, after telling his readers that their most basic convictions were completely unjustified?

Most fortunately it happens, that since reason is incapable of dispelling these clouds, nature herself suffices to that purpose, and cures me of this philosophical melancholy and delirium, either by relaxing this bent of mind, or by some avocation, and lively impression of my senses, which obliterate all these chimeras. I dine, I play a game of back-gammon, I converse, and am merry with my friends; and when after three or four hours' amusement, I would return to these speculations, they appear so cold, and strained, and ridiculous, that I cannot find in my heart to enter into them any farther.[37]

Hume's point is that we are unable to remain permanently in a skeptical frame of mind. My own human nature takes over and forces me to leave the skeptical thinking and reasoning that have "heated my brain" and "utterly deprived [me] of the use of every member and faculty." So human nature takes me away from the "delirium" of skepticism and ensures that, instead, "I dine, I play a game of back-gammon, I converse, and am merry with my friends."[38]

We began this chapter with a discussion of the controversy over the theory of recovered memories. Does empiricism shed any light on that controversy? Clearly, the empiricist would deny the rationalist view that when recovered memories are clear and distinct, they must be true. An empiricist such as Locke would instead say that ideas provide true knowledge only when they are based on sense experience. Hume would agree, holding that ideas should never be accepted as true unless they can be shown to have been "derived" from some "sense impression." Recovered memories, then, should not be accepted unless they can be corroborated with some kind of independent sense experience. A skeptic in the spirit of Hume might want to go further. A skeptic might want to say that, just as we must remain skeptical about our ordinary perceptions, we also must remain skeptical about recovered memories. "The mind," Hume suggested, "is a kind of theater, where several perceptions successively make their appearance, pass, re-pass, glide away, and mingle in an infinite variety of postures

The Dream, Henri Rousseau. "All the sensory experiences we are having are compatible with our merely dreaming of a world around us while that world is in fact very different from the way we take it to be."

The Museum of Modern Art, Licensed by SCALA/Art Resource, NY

---

37   David Hume, *A Treatise of Human Nature*, bk. I, pt. IV, sec. vii.
38   Ibid.

and situations." When memories are "recovered" in therapy, the Humean skeptic might suggest, they simply become one more element in this jumble of ideas in the mind. It is no more possible to know whether one of them is true than it is to establish that any of our other ideas correspond to an independent reality.

But not all philosophers have accepted Hume's skepticism. In fact, Hume's skepticism led Immanuel Kant in the eighteenth century to analyze what we could really know. His investigations resulted in a unique blend of empiricism and rationalism called *transcendental idealism*. This new approach to knowledge, Kant claimed, is the only way to resolve the problems that rationalists and empiricists have left us with.

PHILOSOPHY AT THE MOVIES

Watch *Contact* (1997) in which Dr. Ellie Arroway, a scientist who conducts research for SETI (Search for Extra Terrestrial Intelligence) by scanning outer space with a radio telescope, one day discovers a radio signal from distant intelligent beings that provides plans for a machine to journey to their part of the universe, a journey Ellie wants to undertake. Is Ellie an empiricist at the beginning of this movie? At the end? How do Ellie's views on knowledge affect the beliefs she is willing to accept? Does the movie suggest any reasons why Ellie's views on knowledge may be wrong?

5.4 Kant: Does the Knowing Mind Shape the World?

The question that concerned the German philosopher Immanuel Kant (1724–1804) was how to deal with Hume's wholesale skepticism. He sensed that philosophy had reached a pivotal point. The rationalists had claimed that the mind, by itself, is a source of knowledge. The empiricists replied that the senses are the only valid sources of knowledge, and Hume went on to argue that the senses provide no evidence for the causal laws of science. Kant agreed that all our knowledge of the world begins with our senses as the empiricists claimed. But he argued that the mind by itself (as rationalists insisted) can provide us with knowledge of the laws of science. In arguing this, Kant fashioned a new view of knowledge that claims that both reason and the senses contribute to our knowledge of the world.

Kant's new view is now called **transcendental idealism**. It holds that the world that appears to be around us is a world that our mind constructs. Our mind arranges the sensations that come from its senses into orderly structures or patterns. But these orderly structures and patterns are provided by the mind itself. In other words, the senses are the source of the sensations that the mind arranges into the world we experience. But the way those sensations are arranged—their orderly structure—comes from the mind. Because the mind arranges everything we perceive according to its own rational rules or laws, the mind can know these laws that govern everything we perceive. Although these ideas of Kant are difficult to comprehend, their originality and depth well repay the effort it takes to understand them.

QUICK REVIEW
Kant tried to show that, as empiricists claimed, our knowledge begins with the senses, but as rationalists claimed, the mind is a source of knowledge of universal laws.

Hume's Challenge

In *The Critique of Pure Reason*, his most important work, Kant accepted Hume's view that our knowledge about the world is based on sense perception. Nevertheless, he added, reason or the mind also contributes something to our knowledge and is part of the source of our knowledge:

> There is no doubt that all of our knowledge begins with experience. For how could our faculty of knowledge awake into action if objects did not stimulate our senses? Whatever stimulates our senses in part serves to produce a sense impression and in part serves to bring the activity of our understanding into action. Our understanding compares these impressions, joins them together or separates them, and in that way it turns the raw material provided by sense impressions into the awareness of objects that we call experience. In the order of time, therefore, we have no knowledge before experience, and with experience all our knowledge begins.
>
> But although all our knowledge begins with experience, it does not follow that all of it is produced by experience. For it may well be that even our experiential knowledge consists partly of what we receive through our sense impressions, and partly of something that our own faculty of knowledge contributes from itself. And we may not be able to distinguish easily the part that our own faculty of knowledge contributes, from the part provided by the raw material our senses provide. It may take a great deal of practice and attention to become skilled in distinguishing one from the other.
>
> So this raises a question that requires closer examination and that cannot just be given an off-hand answer. The question is this: Is there any part of our knowledge that is independent of our experience, and is even independent of the impressions that our senses provide? If we have such knowledge it would be *a priori* knowledge [i.e., knowledge prior to experience], and would be different from the empirical knowledge that has its source *a posteriori* from experience [i.e., knowledge posterior to experience].[39]

Notice that in this passage Kant has given a brief summary of his fundamental view. Our senses provide the basic sensations of color, shape, odors, sounds, etc. Then our mind or "understanding" takes these basic sensations and somehow joins them together to form the objects that we experience.

So Kant agreed with Hume that our senses provide sense impressions like tastes, smells, sounds, and colors. But our senses don't show us any of the relationships among the objects we perceive. For example, as Hume said, we don't see causal relationships, we just see events repeatedly following each other. Kant concluded that the mind has to be the source of our knowledge of the relationships among the objects we perceive. That is, the mind itself must provide whatever relationships we know exist between objects. To understand what Kant meant, it is important to see exactly where Kant agreed with Hume and where he disagreed.

The Basic Issue

Kant believed that Hume's arguments had almost destroyed science. Hume had argued that the universal laws of science, particularly cause-and-effect laws, go beyond the evidence of our senses. Scientists observe a few times that certain causes are followed by certain effects. They see several times, for example, that when one moving object hits another similar object, the two bounce away from each other with equal velocities. Scientists infer a universal law from these observations. For example, Newton inferred his third law of motion, "*Every* action will *always* cause an equal and opposite reaction." But how do scientists know that the sequence of events they see a few times will repeat itself *every* time in the future? Hume asserted that scientists cannot know this. So he claimed they have no justification for jumping from

---

39   Immanuel Kant, *Critique of Pure Reason*, 2nd ed., trans. Norman Kemp Smith (London: Macmillan, 1929; original work published 1781), 1–2.

what they observe *sometimes* in the *past* to conclusions about what will happen *every time* in the *future*. The universal laws of science, then, go beyond the evidence provided by our sense observations and so are ultimately unjustified. This, of course, was the problem of induction that Hume had pointed to.

When Kant read Hume's arguments, he woke up to the fact that our unthinking acceptance of the laws of science may have no firm foundation:

> I openly confess that my recollection of David Hume was the very thing which many years ago first awoke me from my dogmatic slumber and gave my investigations in the field of speculative philosophy a quite new direction. But I was far from following him in the conclusions at which he arrived.[40]

Kant agreed with Hume that in some fields of knowledge we reach conclusions that go beyond the evidence our senses provide. The most important for us here are two fields of knowledge:

1. *Mathematics,* such as geometry which contains universal laws like "The shortest distance between any two points is always a straight line"; and arithmetic, which gives us universal statements such as "The sum of 3 and 7 always equals 10."

2. *Natural science,* where we find universal statements such as "Every event must have a cause," and "Every action causes an equal and opposite reaction."

Kant used special terminology to describe these statements or laws that go beyond the evidence our senses can give us. These statements, Kant said, are *synthetic a priori* statements. Synthetic statements are statements that describe or give us information about the world around us. For example, the statement that "Every event must have a cause" tells us how things will always happen in the universe around us. Kant contrasted synthetic statements with *analytic* statements. *Analytic* statements, he said, do not give us information about the world because they are true or false by definition. For example, "All triangles have three sides" is analytic because, by definition, a triangle is a three-sided figure. *A priori* statements, on the other hand, are universal and necessary statements that tell us what *must* be true of *every* member of some group. For example, geometry tells us that the shortest distance between *any* two points *must* be a straight line. As Kant (and Hume) pointed out, *a priori* statements go beyond what we can observe with our senses. They go beyond what we observe because usually (1) we can't observe *all* the members of a group and (2) our senses can't tell us what *must* be, but only what is. We establish that *a priori* statements are true by using the reasoning processes of the mind, such as the mental reasoning processes we use in mathematics. Kant contrasted *a priori* statements with what he calls *a posteriori* statements such as "Some swans are black," which we can establish only by observation.

Synthetic *a priori* statements, then, are statements that really describe the world, yet they go beyond what we can observe with our senses. Hume said that such statements are unjustified

✓ QUICK REVIEW
Hume argued that when scientists observe that *sometimes* in the *past* one event caused another and conclude that this will happen *every* time in the *future*, they cannot really know this conclusion is true.

✓ QUICK REVIEW
Kant wanted to show that, despite Hume, we have real knowledge of statements that are synthetic (give us information about the world) and *a priori* (universal statements that go beyond what our senses can perceive) in mathematics and natural science.

ANALYZING THE READING

1. Give some examples that are not in the textbook of synthetic statements and analytic statements, and of *a priori* statements and *a posteriori* statements. The textbook gives several examples of synthetic *a priori* statements. Can you think of any examples of synthetic *a priori* statements that are not in the textbook? Can you give some examples of synthetic *a posteriori* statements and of analytic *a priori* statements?

2. Kant agreed that synthetic *a priori* statements go beyond the evidence our senses can provide. Pick some synthetic *a priori* statement. Using that statement as an example, explain why our senses cannot provide the evidence needed to prove that the synthetic a priori statement you picked is true.

---

[40] Immanuel Kant, *Prolegomena to Any Future Metaphysics,* trans. Lewis White Beck (New York: Bobbs-Merrill, 1950), 8.

precisely because they go beyond what we can observe. But Kant wanted to prove that such statements are justified, at least in mathematics and in the natural sciences. Kant also claimed that although synthetic *a priori* statements describe the world, we know they are true by mental reasoning that does not rely on the senses. This, of course, Hume had absolutely denied. According to Hume, any statements that describe the world must rely on the senses.

Space, Time, and Mathematics

Kant set out to show, then, that synthetic *a priori* statements in mathematics and natural science are justified. And he wanted to show that we know synthetic *a priori* statements are true by pure mental reasoning that does not rely on sense observations. Hume adamantly denied both of these claims.

To prove his claims, Kant began by accepting Hume's view of the senses. All our knowledge of the world begins with the sensations that stream into us through our senses: colors, shapes, sounds, tastes, feels, smells. Hume said as much when he wrote, "The mind is a kind of theater where several perceptions successively make their appearance, pass, re-pass, glide away, and mingle in an infinite variety of postures and situations."[41] Kant agreed. But Kant noticed something both empiricists and rationalists had missed. It is true that sensations stream into us through our senses. Yet we do not experience a mere display of sensations streaming through us. When you look around the room you do not merely see numerous patches of color streaming past your vision. Instead, you see *objects*, such as your desk, some books, a computer, and the walls of the room. The world we experience is not a mere jumble of numerous sensations but an organized world of stable objects.

The same is true of your other senses. Each sense presents a stream of changing sensations. But you experience these sensations as belonging to solid objects outside you. If you listen and observe right now, for example, you do not just sense ringing, booming, rustling sound sensations in your ears. Instead, you hear noises that seem to come from particular places in the room around you. The rustling noises are from the papers on your desk. The booming sound you attribute to a truck outside driving past your house. The ringing you attribute to the cell phone lying on your desk. Each sensation of sound, sight, touch, and smell seems to be the sound, sight, touch, or smell of an object located somewhere in the space around you.

How can this be? How is it that the stream of ever-changing sensations we receive through our senses is transformed into the objects that we perceive? Sensations cannot arrange themselves on their own, Kant claimed. So it must be the mind that organizes them into the objects we perceive around us. This remarkable insight of Kant—that the mind organizes its sensations into the objects we see in the world around us—is the key to his theory of knowledge. Kant saw that the orderly world of objects we experience is a world the mind must construct from its sensations.

In particular, Kant argued, the mind organizes its sensations into objects by making them appear to be located in the space "outside" of us. The mind makes space appear to us as something that is outside of us and surrounds us. But space, he argued, is just a structure in the mind that the mind uses to organize its sensations. It is like a mental map or mental setting that the mind uses to organize its sensations as they flow in through the senses. As our senses perceive colors, sounds, shapes, and odors, the mind puts those sensations together into objects. And the mind organizes those objects by placing each one into this mental map we call space. For example, suppose

---

[41] David Hume, *A Treatise of Human Nature*, ed. L. A. Selby-Bigge (Oxford: Clarendon, 1894), 252–253.

PHILOSOPHY AND LIFE
Knowledge and Gestalt Psychology

Some patterns of visual stimulation are more meaningful to us than others. Consider the following pattern. How would you describe it?

—————————————   —————————————

—————————————   —————————————

—————————————

—————————————   —————————————

—————————————

Probably you'd say that you see three sets of two horizontal lines each, rather than six separate lines. This is because you perceive items close to each other as a whole. Now consider this pattern:

```
O   X   O
O   X   O
O   X   O
```

Because we perceive items that resemble each other as units, you'd probably describe what you see as two vertical rows of circles and one of X's rather than three horizontal rows of circles and X's.

Why is one pattern of visual stimulation meaningful while another is not? One answer lies in past experience: Patterns that outline shapes are meaningful if they match shapes that you have experienced and remembered. But meaningfulness also seems to be imposed by the organization of the visual system.

Some years ago, a group of German psychologists, Kurt Koffka and Wolfgang Köhler among them, studied the basic principles of organization in perception. They insisted that a perception of form is an innate property of the visual system. This group of psychologists became known as Gestaltists, from the German word *gestalt*, meaning "form."

Gestaltists focus on subjective experience and the exploration of consciousness. They see the most significant aspect of experience as its wholeness or interrelatedness. Thus, Gestaltists believe that any attempt to analyze behavior by studying its parts is futile because such an approach loses the basic characteristic of experiences: their organization, pattern, and wholeness. For Gestaltists, no stimulus has constant significance or meaning. It all depends on the patterns surrounding events. For example, a 5'10" basketball player looks small when seen as part of a professional basketball team, but normal size as part of a random group of individuals.

As part of their focus on subjective experience and the exploration of consciousness, Gestalt psychologists formulated a number of descriptive principles of perceptual organization. Two are illustrated previously in the two simple patterns: the principles of similarity and proximity.

QUESTIONS

1. What do you think Gestaltists owe to the theories of knowledge that preceded their investigations?

2. What connections do you see between Gestalt psychology and the views of Kant?

---

your eyes perceive a rectangular whiteness spread over a larger rectangular brownish area. Meanwhile your ears hear a rustling sound and your fingers feel a smooth thin surface between them. Your mind will join this color, sound, and feel together into the object you recognize as a sheet of paper. The larger brownish area it will put together into the object you recognize as your desk. And it positions the paper object in space about twenty inches in front of your eyes, and the desk it positions below that. But your mind makes it appear as if this mental space within you is actually spread out all around outside you. So you perceive the paper-object and desk-object as things located in a space outside you. Yet that space you seem to see outside you, exists only in your mind. It is like a mental map in which your mind positions the objects it constructs from the sensations that flow in through your senses. To you your mental map with the objects positioned in it appears to be the space that you perceive all around you. But that is a kind of illusion the mind creates.

The space that you have in your mind, then, has to be in your mind before you can even perceive any objects. For without some kind of mental map your mind could not organize its sensations into objects. Then all you would be conscious of is a flow of ever-changing sensations. Your mind with its jumble of sensations would appear exactly as Hume described it: "a kind of theater where several perceptions successively make their appearance, pass, repass, glide away, and mingle in an infinite variety of postures and situations." Fortunately, that is not what we experience. We experience an orderly stable world of objects that seem to be solidly positioned in a space outside us.

But how does Kant know that space is a structure within our minds? How does he show that it is a mental structure that we must have before we perceive the objects we perceive? Couldn't space be something that really exists outside of us and that we learn about after we see objects arranged in space outside of us?

Kant gave several arguments to show that space had to exist inside of us before we could even perceive objects as being located outside of us. First, Kant points out that we could not even think of objects as "outside" of us unless we already knew what space was because *outside* refers to space. So, space must first be in our mind, before we can even start to think of objects as being "outside" of us in space. So space is not something we can get to know from things outside of us. We must be aware of what space is before we can even think of things as being "outside" of us. Second, Kant argues, we can imagine space without any objects in it. But it is impossible to imagine a world of objects that is not in a space. So space is something that we need to perceive objects, but we can be aware of space even before we perceive objects. So space cannot be an idea that we learn about after we start perceiving objects. We must be aware of it even before we perceive objects. Third, he argues, space is not some kind of concept or idea that we form from our experience of seeing objects in space. For space is not a concept at all. Concepts are general ideas that apply to many individual things. Take, for example, the concept of a *horse*. There are many horses, of course, and the concept horse applies to each individual horse. But space is not a general idea that applies to many individual things. Instead, there is only one single space. We can talk about several different "spaces" of course. But such spaces are just parts of the one single space in which all things exist. So space is not a concept we derive from seeing objects in space. Here are Kant's arguments in a passage from his major work, *Critique of Pure Reason*:

> Through our mind's outer senses, we make objects appear to us as if they were outside of us and in space. In space they are given a specific shape, size, and location relative to each other. . . . But what is space. . . ?

ANALYZING THE READING

1. Kant gives three arguments by which he tries to prove that space is not a concept we get by observing objects outside of us, but is, instead, a single unified system that we must have in our minds even before we observe any objects outside of us. Can you summarize those three arguments in your own words? Do you think those arguments are right? Why?

2. According to Kant, every single object we perceive now or in the future has to be in space and time. What reason does he provide for this claim?

3. Kant says that the truths of geometry have to apply to every object we experience now or any time in the future. What reason does he provide for this claim?

First, space is not a . . . concept [we] derived from our outer experiences. If I refer some of my sensations to an object outside myself (that is, to something in another region of space from that in which I find myself), or if I perceive objects as separated by being located in different places, I already have to possess an awareness of space as the framework or setting in which those spatial relationships exist. . . . So I cannot derive an awareness of space by experiencing things as "outside" myself or as spatially separated from each other. On the contrary, my prior possession of an awareness of space is what makes it possible for me to experience things as "outside" myself or as spatially separated from each other.

Second, space is something of which we have a necessary *a priori* awareness that enables us to experience outer perceptions. For we cannot imagine a state of affairs in which there is no space, yet we can easily imagine space with no objects in it. So we have to regard space as something that makes it possible for objects to appear to us, not as a concept that we construct from objects that appear to us. Space is something of which we have an *a priori* awareness that necessarily makes it possible for outer objects to appear to us...

[Third,] Space is not a general concept. It is, instead, a single thing of which we have a direct awareness. For we can only be aware of a single space. Any talk of "many spaces" is always understood to refer to *parts* of the one unique space around us. And space is not something that is assembled from such "spaces" like parts from which the whole of space was put together. On the contrary, we think of any parts of space as existing within one all-encompassing space. Space is essentially *single*. It is only by marking out boundaries within it that we can talk about parts of space or "many spaces." Thus our idea of space is of a single thing of which we have an a priori direct awareness.

Space is not a property of things in themselves nor of their relationships to each other. That is, space is not something that attaches to objects themselves and that would remain even if we completely removed ourselves and our own capacity to perceive things.... Space is nothing other than the form in which all appearances of outer sense must appear. That is, space is a part of our perceptual ability within which all our outer perceptions must appear.[42]

Space, then, is not something that exists independently outside of us. Space is something in the mind that the mind uses to organize its sensations into the stable objects we perceive. And that space appears to us to be outside of us.

Moreover, Kant claimed, time, like space, is also a structure in the mind. The mind makes it seem to us as if we and the objects around us exist in time. But time is just another mental structure that the mind uses to organize the many sensations it receives. Just as the mind organizes its sensations into objects that it positions in space, it also positions these objects at specific points in time. To prove this, Kant used arguments that were almost identical to those he used to show that space is a mental structure with which the mind organizes its sensations. He argued, for example, that "Time is not a ... concept ... derived from any experience" because before we can experience things happening "before" or "after" or "simultaneous with" other things, "the awareness of time [must be] presupposed."[43] Time must be present in our minds before we can perceive objects as existing in time.

In effect, then, Kant argued that space and time don't exist independently and apart from us. Time and space exist only as mental structures within our minds. They are part of the human mind's ability to experience sensations as objects in space and time.

Kant claimed, then, that space and time are structures in the mind. This claim gave him a way to prove that the universal laws of mathematics really do apply to every object in the universe we perceive.

☑ QUICK REVIEW
Space and time, Kant claimed, are structures in the mind that we use to organize our many sensations. Geometry consists of the laws of space and arithmetic consists of the laws of time. So, by reasoning about the structures of space and time within us, we can have real knowledge of the synthetic *a priori* laws of mathematics—that is, of the universal laws of geometry and arithmetic.

THINKING LIKE A PHILOSOPHER

Kant says that the space you see around yourself is really all in your mind, and that your mind creates the illusion that space is outside yourself. Does this make sense to you? Do you think it could be true? To get a sense of what Kant means, imagine a video game in which you wear goggles that put tiny video screens in front of each of your eyes. The screens produce a three-dimensional image so that to you it looks as if you are standing on an alien planet with galaxies swirling overhead. (Several versions of this technology are already available, of course.) Do you think it might be possible for your mind to do what goggles like this can do? How would the experience of wearing such goggles be different from the experience of having your mind create the illusion that space is outside you?

---

42 Immanuel Kant, *Critique of Pure Reason*, B38. Page numbers here refer to the *Akademie* editions of the *Critique*; "A" refers to the first edition, and "B" to the second. While I am responsible for the translations, I have leaned heavily both on Jonathan Bennett's highly interpretive but also highly readable translation published as part of his online "Early Modern Texts" (earlymoderntexts.com), and on the translation by Paul Guyer and Allen Wood published in 1998 by Cambridge University Press.

43 Ibid., B46.

We get the laws of mathematics, Kant asserts, by reasoning about the structures of space and time that we carry around within our own minds. Geometry, for example, gives us truths about space, such as the law that the shortest distance between any two points *in space* is a straight line. And arithmetic gives us the laws of numbers that, Kant says, are the result of adding units successively *in time*. That is, arithmetic gives us truths about time. So we can discover the truths of geometry and arithmetic by thinking about the structures of space and time that are in our minds. Since the structures of space and time are in our minds, we can discover the truths of geometry and arithmetic without making any sense observations. This is why the mathematician can discover mathematical truths by just reasoning in her mind. She can do this because mathematical truths are just truths about the structures of space and time she has in her mind.

Kant also called attention to the fact that our minds put every object we perceive into these structures of space and time. In fact, he argued, we cannot perceive anything that is not positioned in space and time. So, every object we perceive, or can ever perceive, has to obey the laws of space and time, which are the laws of geometry and arithmetic. We can be certain, then, that the synthetic *a priori* laws of mathematics must apply to every object in the universe we perceive. In other words, although the truths of mathematics go beyond the evidence of our senses, we know that they are true and must apply to all the objects in the universe we see around us. Moreover, we know that these truths will continue to be true of any objects we perceive in the future. We know this because any objects we perceive in the future will have to be in space and time. Otherwise we could not even perceive them. Without space and time we would experience a jumble of sensations instead of stable orderly objects. So we know that the truths of mathematics will have to be true of any objects we perceive in the future.

Kant's theory of space and time, then, allowed him to solve part of Hume's problem of induction. Hume had argued that for all we know, the future might not be like the past. So we are not justified in thinking that our past experience is a reliable guide to what will happen in the future. Kant replied that we actually have very good reason to think that the future will be like the past, at least where space and time are concerned. Whatever objects we perceive in the future will have to be located in space and time. So any truths about space and time must continue to be true of any objects we perceive in the future.

Causality and the Unity of the Mind

But if Kant really was to answer Hume's skepticism, he had to prove that we also are justified in believing that the causal laws of science will continue to be true in the future. Kant proves this in a way that is similar to the way he proves that we are justified in believing the synthetic *a priori* statements of mathematics apply to all objects. Kant points out that the objects we perceive around us change through time. So when the mind organizes its sensations into objects, it constructs objects that can change. Kant argues that the mind puts these changes—that is, these events—into causal relationships with each other. So, we can be certain that every event (change in an object) that we perceive is caused by some prior event (a prior change in an object).

To understand Kant's argument for these claims, notice what you see when you look at the world around yourself. You perceive objects that change over time but that remain the same object. We receive a stream of sensations, and these are organized into objects that change yet are still the same object. For example, suppose I pick up an egg to fry for breakfast. A white oval patch of color appears in my vision. I feel a cool hard shell and then hear a cracking sound. Then I see a transparent flowing stuff with a yellow blob fall into a round thing that radiates heat. There it lies for a few moments and then it gradually changes into a bubbly patch of white color with a smaller circle of yellow color at its center. I start to smell a distinct odor and hear a sizzling noise. Finally I see the whole thing slide onto a circular patch of blue color, which is, of course, my plate. Now during this whole process I am not just aware of colors, shapes, sounds, smells, and other sensations. Instead, I perceive an object that changes over time. I see an egg being broken, and then the contents of the same egg being fried, And finally I see the same egg, now cooked, being slid onto my blue plate. I perceive an object, the egg, that undergoes changes as time passes, yet remains the same object.

Kant argued that to transform our sensations into objects that change as time passes, the mind has to do three things to its sensations. First, it has to "run through" or receive the many different sensations as they stream into the mind from the senses. Second, it has to remember each sensation when it vanishes and is replaced by a new sensation. Third, the mind has to be conscious that the earlier sensations and the later ones are all sensations of the same object. As I cooked breakfast, for example, my mind apprehended the many different sensations of colors that my senses brought into my mind as the egg was cracked and its contents were fried. The mind has to remember each of these different color sensations as each appears, then vanishes and is replaced by a different one. And thirdly, the mind must recognize that all these different sensations belong to the same object. That is, I must recognize that it is the same egg when I break it, when I fry it, and when I slide it onto my plate. Here is how Kant describes this process:

QUICK REVIEW

Kant said we perceive objects that change over time. To perceive such an object, the mind must collect and remember sensations, and be aware these belong to the same object. But to collect, remember, and be aware of sensations in this way means that the mind is a unified awareness that endures through time. And because the mind is a unified awareness, it can know the many sensations it receives only if it connects them all into a unified world of interrelated objects.

> First, in order to change many different [sensations] into a unified perception, it is necessary for the mind to run through and collect its many different [sensations]. I call this mental action the "synthesis of apprehension." This action is aimed directly at the multiple sensations which can not on their own combine themselves into a single unified perception. . . .
>
> [Second,] it is clear that I will have to grasp each of these many different sensations one after the other. But if I kept dropping the earlier sensations from my thoughts and did not keep reproducing them [in my memory] as I go on to grasp the next one, then a complete perception [of an enduring object] could never form. I could have no thoughts about it, not even the most basic thoughts about space and time. The synthesis of apprehension [mentioned earlier] must therefore be combined with [what I call] the "synthesis of reproduction."...
>
> [Third,] if we did not recognize that what we are sensing now is the very same thing we were sensing earlier, then all those activities of reproducing [and keeping in mind] the earlier series of sensations would be in vain. For the present sensation would be a new one unrelated to the collection of sensations that had been gradually put together earlier. The many different sensations would then never be able to constitute a whole thing, since they would lack the kind of unity that only consciousness can provide.[44]

The mind, then, has this amazing power to gather its sensations together, to keep each one in its memory, and then to join them together into a single object by its ability to recognize that the many different sensations it has gathered together are sensations of the same object. Truly amazing!

Now the mind can do all this, Kant points out, only if the mind itself also endures through time. For my mind to collect, remember, and recognize the sensations that

---

[44] Ibid., A99–A103.

come to me at different times, my mind has to be present through each of these times. So the process of constructing my perception of an object that remains the same object as it changes over time requires that my mind remains the same mind during that process. This means, according to Kant, that the mind must be a single unified awareness that remains the same unified awareness as time passes. As you will see next, this idea that the mind is a single unified awareness is the key step in Kant's argument. In fact, Kant made up a special term for this unified awareness. He called it the "transcendental principle of unity."

Kant argues that because the mind is a unified awareness it requires unity in what it perceives. That is, if the mind is to bring its many sensations together into a world of objects, the mind *must* see that world as a unified whole. In fact, he pointed out, because the mind is a single awareness, it can know many different sensations only if they are all brought together into its single unified awareness. And to be contained in one unified awareness, sensations *must* be joined together into one connected unified whole:

> Sensations would be nothing to us, and would not concern us in the least, if they could not be taken up into our [unified] consciousness. Knowledge is impossible in any other way. We are *a priori* conscious that we remain completely the same while we experience all those perceptions that we are capable of knowing. For perceptions cannot be perceptions of anything for me unless they are brought together with my other perceptions into [my] single unified consciousness. This principle stands firm *a priori*, and may be called the "transcendental principle of unity" for all our many different perceptions and sensations.[45]

ANALYZING THE READING

According to Kant, our minds have to create a single interconnected world of objects out of the many different sensations streaming from our senses. Explain why Kant says our minds have to do this. Does his argument seem right to you? Why?

QUICK REVIEW
One of twelve relationships that the mind uses when it connects its many sensations into a single unified world of interrelated objects is the relationship of cause and effect. The mind must connect its sensations with causal relationships so it can see changes in these objects as independent of itself. So, the unified independent world of changing objects we see around us must be governed by cause-and-effect relationships.

Kant's point is that the mind connects and unifies its sensations into a unified world of interrelated objects because *it must*. My mind *must* connect my various sensations together because they must all be brought into my unified awareness.

It may help to summarize Kant's argument up to this point. Kant says (1) we perceive objects that change in time yet remain the same objct. (2) To perceive such an object the mind must collect and remember the sensations it receives at different times. And it must recognize that the sensations all belong to the same object. (3) To collect, remember, and recognize sensations that enter us at different times, the mind has to remain the same unified awareness during those times. (4) Since the mind is a unified awareness, it can be aware of many different sensations only if they are joined together into a single unified whole. (5) So, if the mind is to be aware of many different sensations, it must connect them together into a single unified whole—that is, a single unified world of interconnected objects.

What connections does the mind make among the changing objects it puts together from its sensations? Kant says that the objects the mind connects into the unified world we perceive around us are connected to each other by twelve kinds of relationships or "categories." The most important of these for our purposes is the relationship of cause and effect, which Hume had tried to undermine. How does Kant show that the changing objects that must be connected into a unified world must be connected by cause and effect?

---

[45] Ibid., A116.

Kant notes that the objects we perceive as being outside ourselves change independently of us. In other words, the events I see in the world are not events I produce, but events that occur independently of myself. So, Kant argues, the mind has to impose cause-and-effect relationships on the events that we perceive. Otherwise those events would seem to be happening inside us, and would not appear to be happening in the objects we perceive outside ourselves. If the events I see were not *caused* by other events in the world, he argues, I would not be able to tell the difference between events happening in the world outside and events happening in me. Kant gives two examples. One is the example of looking at a house. Suppose I first look at the right side of the house, then move my head and now see the left side of the house; or I can just as easily move my head the other way from left to right. Here, Kant says, the changes I perceive are really changes in me. The house itself did not change. And I know this because I could make the change go in either direction: from left to right or from right to left. Kant's other example is watching a ship on a river being carried by the current from upstream to downstream. This time, he points out, the change of the ship's position is being caused by the river current. And I know it is being caused by something in the world outside myself because the change is not reversible. I cannot make the ship move from downstream to upstream by turning my head, in the way that I could move from the right side of the house to the left or the left to the right by turning my head. So I know that the change in the boat is happening to the boat itself; it is not a change in myself. So I also know that an object in the world outside me is itself changing only if I see the change as a change that is caused by something outside me. So my mind has to impose causal relationships on events in the world if I am going to see those events as happening outside of myself. But, in fact, I do see a world of objects that change outside of me. So, my mind must impose cause-and-effect relationships on all the events we see happening in the objects outside of ourselves. Here is how Kant himself makes these points:

Suppose I see a ship being driven downstream [by a river's current]. My perception of its position downstream comes after my perception of its position upstream. Moreover, it is impossible ... for me to perceive the ship first downstream and then later upstream. The order in the sequence of my perceptions of the ship, then... is determined, and my apprehension of those perceptions is tied to that fixed order. However, [consider] the example of a house [I am looking at]. My perceptions of the house can begin at the rooftop and end at the ground. Or I could begin my perceptions at the bottom of the house, and end them at the top. Similarly, I could have my perceptions of the house... move from right to left, or move from left to right. In my various perceptions of the house, then, there is no fixed order that makes it necessary for me to begin my perceptions in one way ... rather than another. But when I am perceiving an event that is happening [in the world itself, like the ship], a causal law must be present that makes the order of my perceptions follow each other in a necessary order.

For suppose that nothing happens before a certain event that makes that event follow according to a causal law. Then [like in the house example], the order of my perceptions would be determined completely by the way I myself was apprehending them, that is, the order would be subjective [in me]. The order of my perceptions would not be objectively determined [i.e., determined by the objects I perceive] in a way that

ANALYZING THE READING

1. Kant says that any events that we experience as events that are happening outside of us have to be causally connected to other events outside of us. Explain the argument Kant gives for this claim. How do Kant's example of a ship and of a house help him in his argument?

2. Kant says that the causal laws of science have to apply to any object we perceive outside of ourselves, now and in the future. Explain why he says this.

determined which perception would occur first and which would occur later. In such a case we would have only a play of sense impressions that would not be related to the object itself.... And in such a case I would not be able to say that events are actually happening in that [object itself] that appears before me. All I could say is that one perception followed another, which could be merely subjective [in me] and would not be a determination of the object. So I would not be able to say that I had knowledge about [what is happening in] the object itself.

So if we experience that an event is actually happening [in the objects we perceive], then we have to presuppose that something happened before that event, and the event followed whatever it was that happened, according to a causal law. For without presupposing that, I could not say that the event was occurring in the object itself, since the mere fact that my perceptions follow each other in a certain order but are not determined by a causal law does not justify my claim that the order of events was happening in the object I was perceiving. I can make the relationship of events objective only if I presuppose there is a causal law in accordance with which the sequence of my perceptions is determined by previous events. Only if I make that presupposition can I experience something happening [in the objects I perceive.][46]

To understand what Kant is saying, consider the following example. Suppose you are standing at the end of an ocean pier gazing out at the ocean watching a distant sail boat that seems to be standing still. As you watch it, the sail boat seems to move forward a little bit and then stop again. Now, did the boat itself move, or did the boat seem to move because you moved your eyes? That is, was the movement of the boat a change in *your perceptions* of the boat or a change in *the boat itself*? Kant says the only way to answer this question is by whether or not the change was the result of a cause acting on the boat. Suppose, for example, that the change in the position of the boat was caused by something outside yourself. For example, suppose the change was caused by a wind that came up and caused the boat to move and then stop. Then you know that the boat itself moved, and it was not just you moving your eyes. On the other hand, if nothing outside you caused the boat to move, then the movement was just a change in you, not in the boat itself. So you see events as happening in the objects outside yourself only if those events are caused by other events outside yourself. That is, events will appear to be happening in the objects outside of you only if those events are caused by other events outside of you. Now Kant has already shown that the world you perceive outside yourself is constructed by your mind. But that means that the events in the world your mind constructs have to be caused by other events in that world. Otherwise, you would not see that world as being outside you. If the events you perceive were not being caused by other outside independent events, everything would seem to be happening inside you. So your mind has to connect events causally if you are to see them as happening in objects outside yourself. And that means that all those events you see as events happening in objects outside yourself must be caused by other events outside yourself. In short, any events we see happening in the world outside of us have to be causally connected to other events in the world outside of us. In other words, we cannot even experience events happening in the world outside us, unless those events are causally connected to other events in the world outside us.

Let's pause to summarize once again. Kant argued (1) that the mind is a unified awareness. (2) So, if it is to be aware of its many sensations, it must connect these sensations together into the unified world of connected objects you perceive outside yourself. (3) One of the ways the mind connects its sensations into a single unified world you see *outside* yourself is by connecting all its events causally. That is,

---

[46]   Ibid., A192–A195

every event you perceive as happening in objects outside yourself must be caused by some other event. (4) These causal relationships are connections the mind *must* make so that the world of objects appears to be unified and *outside of us*. That is, any events that I believe are happening in the world outside myself must be caused by other events in the world outside myself. (5) The world of objects we perceive outside of us, then, has to be a unified world in which all events have a cause.

Kant concludes that this proves that Hume was wrong about the causal laws of science. Hume had pointed out that we do not actually see causal relationships, so he concluded that we cannot know there are real causal relationships in the world. Kant partly agreed. True, we do not see causality because it is a relationship between objects and is not a visible object. But we still know that causality is operating in the world. We know it's there because the mind puts it there. The mind puts it there so that we will perceive a unified world and that world will appear to be outside of us. All events that we will ever perceive as part of this external independent world, then, must be caused by other events in that same world!

The implications of Kant's views are huge! First, if Kant is right, the world we see around us is a world that our own mind constructs. Sensations stream into us, and the mind organizes these into the interrelated changing objects that make up the world we perceive. Second, if Kant is right, then cause and effect are, and always will be, part of the world as we perceive it. Hume, then, was wrong when he claimed that we have no reason to think that events are really connected together by the universal and necessary causal laws of science. On the contrary, events in the world *we* perceive will always have to be connected by cause and effect. Moreover, Hume was wrong when we said we are unjustified in believing that what we experience in the past is a reliable guide to the future. That is, we have no reason to think that the future will be like the past. But if Kant is right, then the causal laws we discovered operating in the world outside of us must continue to operate in the future world we perceive outside of ourselves. For otherwise, we would not be able to perceive it as a world outside of us! So Hume's problem of induction is solved. We are justified in believing that the future will be like the past.

QUICK REVIEW
Contrary to what Hume said, scientists can know that every event they perceive must have a cause. They can know this because the mind must put causality into the world it perceives so it can bring this unified independent world of objects into its unified mind.

ANALYZING THE READING

Kant claims that he answered several of the challenges Hume proposed. Kant said he showed Hume was wrong when he said we have no justification for assuming the future will be like the past. He showed Hume was wrong when he said that causes and effects are all in our minds, not in the world we perceive outside ourselves. And he showed that Hume was wrong when he said we cannot know whether our ideas are accurate representations of the world that we see outside ourselves. Explain how Kant showed that Hume was wrong on each of these points.

However, there is a consequence to Kant's view that is troubling. If Kant is right, then the things we see around us might not be the way things are in themselves. What we see outside of us is a world our minds have put together out of its sensations. But perhaps the world as it really is in itself is not like the world that appears to us and that our mind has put together for us to experience. For all we know, the world that appears to us is utterly unlike the world as it is in itself. Expressing a view called **phenomenalism**, Kant called the world that our minds construct, and that appears to us to be outside of us, the "phenomenal" world. The world as it might be in itself, apart from our mind, he called the "noumenal" world. Clearly, we can never know what the noumenal world is really like. All we can ever know is the phenomenal world that we perceive after the mind has put it together out of our sensations. We see the world that appears to us after our mind has put it together using its internal structures of space, time, and causality. But a creature—an alien for example—with a different mind might not see a world that appears to be in space and time and connected by causality. The mind of an alien might put together a world that appeared utterly different from the world that appears to us. But the alien, too, would not know what the world was like in itself. The alien and other members of his alien race would see their

QUICK REVIEW
We perceive only the world as it has been constructed by the mind out of its sensations (the phenomena), and we do not perceive the world as it is in itself (the noumena).

phenomenal world, but, like us, they could never know what the noumenal world was like in itself.

Kant, then, agreed with the empiricists' claim that the senses provide the sensations we need to know anything about the world around us. But the rationalists are also right when they claim that our minds can know the universal laws that order the world. For example, we can know that in the world that we see, every event will have a cause. We can come to know some of these laws by simply reasoning inside our minds because these laws are inside our minds to begin with. Yet they are also in the world as *we* perceive it because the mind puts them there when it constructs the unified world of changing objects outside ourselves.

Notice that Kant also resolved a key problem of skepticism with which both the rationalists and the empiricists had struggled. How can we know that our ideas accurately represent the world outside of us? Descartes raised doubts about whether our ideas about the world were accurate. For all we know, what we perceive "in" our minds might not really be what is "out there" in the world. Hume concluded that we can never know whether our ideas accurately represent the world "outside" or even whether there is such a world. But Kant responded to Hume's skepticism with an answer that was simple but revolutionary. We know our ideas can represent the world accurately because the mind itself constructs the world. Thus, Kant claimed, skepticism is banished.

Kant wrote that his revolutionary claim that the world must conform to the mind was a kind of "Copernican" revolution in knowledge.[47] Copernicus revolutionized astronomy by rejecting the view that the sun revolves around the earth and replacing it with the view that the earth revolves around the sun. In a similar way, Kant replaced the view that the mind must conform to the world (i.e., our mind must make its knowledge match what the world is like) with the view that the world must conform to the mind (i.e., what the world is like depends on what our mind makes it be). Only this revolutionary view, Kant held, has the power to free us from skepticism.

Constructivist Theories and Recovered Memories

Theories like Kant's are sometimes called *constructivist* theories because they hold that reality as we know it is constructed by us. We put together the world as we know it, and for each of us there is no reality apart from the reality we build.

A number of psychologists have developed constructivist theories of the human individual, including George Kelly, Ernst von Glaserfeld, and Humberto R. Maturana. Constructivist psychologists claim people construct their reality using meanings and expectations from their past experiences. The so-called radical constructivists hold that the only world we know is the world we construct, and we cannot affirm any reality beyond that world. In his book, *Radical Constructivism: A Way of Knowing and Learning*, psychologist von Glaserfeld writes: "Constructivism, thus, does not say there is no world and no other people, it merely holds that insofar as we know them, both the world and others are models that we ourselves construct."[48]

Several sociologists have also developed constructivist theories. They include Kenneth Gergen, Peter Berger, and Thomas Luckmann. Berger and Luckmann, for example, in their classic book *The Social Construction of Reality*, argue that the members

---

[47]   Ibid., Bxvi.
[48]   Ernst von Glaserfeld, *Radical Constructivism: A Way of Knowing and Learning* (London: The Falmer Press, 1995), 137.

of a society together construct their common reality. That reality consists of the categories, meanings, and institutions they reinforce in their interactions with each other.

The idea that we construct what we know as the "real world" clearly has profound implications but is easily misunderstood. For example, consider the phenomenon of recovered memories of childhood sexual abuse discussed earlier. What might a Kantian approach to such recovered memories say? Are such memories valid sources of knowledge? Think about this before we leave Kant and his followers.

The person in therapy who recovers her repressed memories gradually constructs a detailed picture of a past reality. That new reality is often very different from the reality that she had previously remembered. In the spirit of Kant, we might want to say that the past world that is constructed from these memories must be as fully real as the world that we currently see around us. After all, the world that we see around us is also constructed by the mind. So it is no more "privileged" and no more "real" than the world that our mind might gradually piece together out of its recovered memories. So, for the person who comes to believe in a past world in which she was sexually abused, that awful world is every bit as real. Consequently, it must be taken as seriously as the present world that her mind similarly constructed. In the spirit of Kant someone might say that recollected memories should be accepted since they are part of the reality constructed from the memories themselves. Perhaps some of Kant's "romantic" followers might accept this conclusion, especially those who think that each of us constructs his or her own world.

However, Kant would object that this conclusion overlooks an important part of his theory. In his theory, we can know only one real world: the world in which objects are causally related to each other. In the world we see around us, for example, bullets can cause death, and fire can cause painful burns. So, bullets and fires are part of the real world. Other "worlds" that our minds might construct—like the worlds of our dreams—are not real because they are not causally related to the world around us. For example, a bullet that I shoot in a dream cannot cause someone's death in the real world, and a fire that I dream cannot cause someone in the real world a painful burn. If recollected memories provide true knowledge of reality, then, the events they depict must be more than mental constructs. Real events must be causally related to the actual world around us.

QUICK REVIEW
Kant would agree that recovered memories are valid sources of knowledge only if they are causally connected to the world we perceive around us.

This aspect of Kant's theory can shed light on whether recovered memories are valid sources of knowledge. His theory implies that recollected memories can be taken as a true basis of knowledge only if the events they depict have some causal connection to the world around us. People who suspect they may be survivors of childhood sexual abuse need to determine whether the world they remember is more than a mental construct. Kant would say that they need to find independent causal effects of the abuse in the real world. That is, causal effects that indicate the abuse was actually part of the real world, such as recordings or bodily injuries.

Still, not everyone has agreed with Kant's theory. Many insist that our sense experience must conform to an independent world of things if it is to give us real knowledge. We want to know if the world that we construct from our sense experience is an accurate picture of the world that is really there, independent of our sense experience. Kant would say that we can never know what reality is like apart from our mental construct of it. Thus, Kant's theory that we construct the world we see around us seems to drive us to a deep skepticism about our ability to know the world as it really is apart from how it appears to us.

One problem with Kant's position is that in his view, the senses are our basic link to reality. So the question arises again whether there is a difference between reality and what we experience. If experience is the only true basis of knowledge, then it is reasonable to question the reliability of the senses as sources of that knowledge.

After all, the mind can't organize our sensory experiences until it receives them. Of course, Kant claims that what we perceive may not correspond to how things are in themselves—what we perceive is already informed by the categories. Thus, we never perceive things as they are in themselves. If things in themselves are unknowable, then we appear to be faced with a skepticism that is very close to Hume's. We could also wonder about Kant's categories. Are they the same for everyone or, as some constructivists claim, different for different people?

Despite these problems, Kant's views, and the views of his followers, are a serious attempt to analyze the sources of our knowledge. Kant not only shows the limitations that the sources of our knowledge impose on us, but also validates knowledge within the world as it appears to us. More specifically, Kant is noteworthy for his portrayal of the active nature of the mind. This conception of our mind's role as a creator of the world we perceive provides a revolutionary way of considering the nature of the self and the world we know.

> **✅ QUICK REVIEW**
> Kant's theory leaves us with a kind of skepticism about whether we can know reality as it really exists independently of the workings of our mind.

PHILOSOPHY AT THE MOVIES

Watch *Criminal* (2004) in which Richard, a seasoned con man, teams up with Rodrigo, a young man just beginning to con people, and the two decide to try to sell a counterfeit antique bank note to a rich collector named Hannigan who is staying in the hotel run by Richard's sister, Valerie. How do the cons of Richard and Rodrigo early in the film depend on the way their victims construct their world? How do your expectations lead you to construct what you see in the film in a way that lets the filmmaker lead you to the conclusions he wants? Does the fact that the expectations of the film's victims and your own expectations about the film lead you and the victims to construct the world in a certain way support or undermine the theories of Kant and/or his followers?

Movies with similar themes: *Matchstick Men* (2003), *Ocean's Eleven* (2001), *Ocean's Twelve* (2004), and *Ocean's Thirteen* (2007).

5.5 Does Science Give Us Knowledge?

We have examined three approaches to knowledge. We began by discussing the rationalist view, that some of our knowledge of reality derives from reason and does not rely on the senses. We then looked at the empiricist view that our knowledge of reality all derives from our sense experience. And lastly, we looked at Kant's view, that reason can know the fundamental structures of reality but our knowledge of the world depends on our sense experience.

How do these approaches to knowledge help us understand the knowledge we think we possess? As we will see now, these approaches to knowledge can help us separate real knowledge from its counterfeits. We are surrounded by claims about astrology, ESP, psychic predictions, the prophecies of Nostradamus, the healing powers of crystals and pyramids, UFOs, paranormal phenomena, parapsychology, clairvoyance, psychokinesis, reincarnation, and so on and so on. How can we tell which, if any, of these claims we should take seriously? In one way or another, they all claim to be "scientific." But are they? The approaches to knowledge we've studied can help us answer that question. They can help us separate real scientific knowledge from views that claim to be scientific but are not. We will turn now to look at the nature of scientific knowledge in order to see how the approaches to knowledge are related to science. Our aim is to determine how true scientific knowledge differs from pseudoscience (i.e., from bogus science). The three approaches to knowledge have made important contributions to our understanding of science. And these contributions can help us see how science differs from pseudoscience.

For many people today, science is the most reliable source of knowledge. Many of us hold that scientific claims about the world are as close to the truth as we can get. People use the term *scientific* to suggest reliability, validity, and certainty. Thus, when we want to say that a certain belief is unreliable or dubious, we say it is "unscientific." On the other hand, we describe a claim as "scientific" when we want to distinguish it from claims that are fraudulent or based on superstition or prejudice. The methods of the sciences, many of us hold, are the best methods we have for getting genuine knowledge of reality. But what are these methods, and what justifies our reliance on them?

Perhaps the most obvious characteristic of science is its reliance on sense observation. In fact, for many people a theory is scientific to the extent that it is based on sense observations. Empiricists, in particular, claim that science is justified because it is based on sense observations. But what, exactly, does this mean? Clearly, when we just observe, say, a falling rock we don't immediately "see" that it is falling at an accelerating rate of 32 feet per second per second. Much less do we "see" this law of falling bodies. How, then, are scientific laws and theories supposed to be related to our sense observations?

Inductive Reasoning and Simplicity

One of the earliest views of the relationship between scientific theories and sensory observations is *inductionism*. This view holds that science is based on inductive reasoning. That is, it is based on reasoning that moves from many particular observations to claims about the general laws that govern what we observe. Inductive reasoning was first suggested as the core of the scientific method by the philosopher Francis Bacon (1561–1626). In fact, Bacon has been called the father of empiricism. Unlike most of his contemporaries, Bacon refused to unquestioningly accept the views of the ancient Greek philosophers. Bacon insisted that instead scientists should investigate nature by careful sense observation and experimentation. They should collect as many facts as possible about the subject they are studying, perhaps using experiments to generate additional facts. Once all the facts are collected, they should carefully sift through the facts, looking for common patterns. By doing this they will be able to derive general laws about those facts. As he put it, scientists will be able to move "from … sense and particulars up to the most general propositions."

> **QUICK REVIEW**
> Inductionism holds that scientific knowledge is based on sense observation: making particular observations, generalizing to general laws, and confirming the laws through additional observations.

Two centuries after Bacon, another philosopher, the empiricist John Stuart Mill (1806–1873), tried to improve on Bacon. He proposed what he called *canons*, or methods of **induction**. These were rules for determining which generalizations the facts and observations of the scientist supported. In the spirit of Bacon, Mill claimed that scientific method is characterized by three features:

1. *The accumulation of particular observations.* Scientific method begins with the collection of as many observed facts as possible about the subject we are investigating.

2. *Generalization from the particular observations.* Scientific method then proceeds by inferring general laws from the accumulated particular facts.

3. *Repeated confirmation.* Scientific method continues to accumulate more particular facts to see whether the generalization continues to hold true. The more particular instances of a "law" we find, the more confirmation the law has and the higher its probability.

For the inductionist, real science differs from unscientific superstitions by its reliance on observations, generalization, and repeated confirmation. The pseudosciences, on the inductionist view, are not based on these.

Several scientists have relied on this empiricist idea of science. They have proceeded by compiling observations, generalizing from these, and repeatedly confirming the generalizations. For example, during the seventeenth century, Galileo Galilei (1564–1642) studied falling objects. Most scientists of his time were content to accept the commonsense opinion of Aristotle, who had declared that objects fall faster the heavier they are. But Galileo decided to find out for himself. He devised a number of experiments in which he repeatedly measured how fast metal balls of different weights fell when dropped about a hundred feet. Much to his surprise, he found that every ball fell at the same rate, no matter how heavy it was. Moreover, Galileo also found that as each ball fell, it moved faster and faster. Pressing his study, Galileo built long, smooth inclined planes and rolled balls down them. For years he worked, carefully releasing the balls and timing them. After many observations, he formulated an important generalization. It was that all objects fall to the earth at the same constantly accelerating rate of 32 feet per second per second. Aristotle was wrong. Countless scientists after Galileo have confirmed his law of falling bodies, making it a highly probable law.

In a similar way, Gregor Mendel (1822–1884) formulated the basic laws of heredity. He grew and repeatedly cross-bred peas and observed the numbers of offspring with certain colors and shapes in each generation. From these observations, he generalized his laws, which say, for example, that in the second generation the ratio of a dominant genetic trait to a recessive trait is 3:1. Mendel's laws have been repeatedly confirmed by biologists and are now accepted as some of the fundamental laws of biology.

But inductionism carries several problems. One major problem we already saw when we were discussing Hume and the problem of induction. The problem is that every generalization has to go *beyond* the observations on which it is based. For example, Galileo observed relatively few balls falling short distances before formulating his generalization. Since a generalization goes beyond its evidence, the evidence cannot really prove the generalization. Another problem is that a large number of different generalizations will fit any set of observations. All those different generalizations are equally "confirmed" by the observations of the scientist. For example, Galileo observed several falling metal balls as they dropped a hundred feet and found that each time they were moving at an accelerating rate. From these observations, he could have concluded (1) that objects fall at an accelerating rate until they drop one hundred feet and then they fall at a uniform rate, or (2) that objects fall at an accelerating rate until they reach a certain speed and then they begin to slow down, or (3) that objects fall at an accelerating rate at those locations where Galileo measured their fall, but sometimes they fall at a uniform rate in other places. Clearly, there are an infinite number of other generalizations that would also fit Galileo's observations. If so many other generalizations fit the observations, why should we accept one generalization rather than another?

Some inductionists have pointed to the criterion of *simplicity* as a way of deciding among competing generalizations. The scientist generally chooses the simplest generalization that will fit her sensory observations. None of the generalizations suggested in the last paragraph, for example, is as simple as Galileo's.

✔ QUICK REVIEW
But generalizations always go beyond finite observations, and many generalizations can fit any finite set of observations. So, sense observations by themselves cannot select the correct general laws. Also, great scientific theories are not mere generalizations. Reason must play a role in science.

ANALYZING THE READING

The text says that one problem with the theory of inductionism is that any set of observations will support an infinite number of generalizations. Another is that inductionism can explain how observations support simple low-level laws, but it cannot explain how observations support the fundamental theories of science. Explain these problems. How do you think the inductionist would respond to these two criticisms?

PHILOSOPHY AND LIFE
Society and Truth

In *The Art of Awareness*, J. Samuel Bois reports the following experiment:

> A psychologist employed seven assistants and one genuine subject in an experiment where they were asked to judge how long was a straight line that they were shown on a screen. The seven assistants, who were the first to speak and report what they saw, had been instructed to report unanimously an evidently incorrect length. The eighth member of the group, the only naive subject in the lot, did not know that his companions had received such an instruction, and he was under the impression that what they reported was really what they saw. In one-third of the experiments, he reported the same incorrect length as they did. The pressure of the environment had influenced his own semantic reaction and had distorted his vision. When one of the assistants, under the secret direction of the experimenter, started reporting the correct length, it relieved that pressure of the environment, and the perception of the uninformed subject improved accordingly.

QUESTION

1. To what extent does our sense knowledge depend on what we think we *should* be seeing?

_____

Source: J. Samuel Bois, *The Art of Awareness* (Dubuque, IA: William C. Brown, 1973).

But simplicity seems to be a rationalist criterion, not an empiricist criterion. Simplicity is based on the idea that the world must follow simpler rather than more complex laws. And this criterion does not seem to be established by sense observation but by reason. Thus, the inductionist method of empiricism seems forced to incorporate an element of rationalism into its procedures.

But even if the inductionist can deal with this problem, a more serious problem awaits. Inductionism is not an adequate explanation of the relationship between scientific knowledge and sense observations. The problem is that almost none of the great scientific theories are mere generalizations from a few facts. For example, as we saw in Chapter 2, Darwin's theory of evolution claims that species evolve as a result of inherited variations and natural selection. Darwin did not establish his theory by observing a few species evolve in this way and then generalizing to the conclusion that all species evolve like this. In fact, Darwin never observed the evolution of any species because the evolution of a single species would take many lifetimes. So contrary to the view that science is based on induction, Darwin's scientific theory was not a generalization based on a few sense observations.

Simple low-level scientific laws are sometimes established by induction, of course. But the greatest and most fundamental *theories* of science were not established by induction alone. Galileo's law of falling bodies is an example of a relatively simple and low-level law that, we can argue, was established by induction. But this law describes the behavior of a very limited range of objects: those that fall to the surface of the earth. On the other hand, Isaac Newton (1642–1727) developed a comprehensive theory with three laws of motion and a law of universal gravitation. Newton's theory explains the motions of the moon, of planets, and of distant stars and galaxies, as well as of objects that fall to the surface of the earth. Yet Newton did not establish his theory by merely generalizing from some sensory observations. Instead, he seems to have familiarized himself with the previous findings of numerous scientists. Then he creatively fashioned a comprehensive theory that drew all of their findings together. More than that, his theory went beyond them in a way that no one had suspected was possible. Clearly, scientific method consists of more than mere inductive generalizations. But what is this "more"?

The Hypothetical Method and Falsifiability

Since induction cannot account for broad scientific theories, many thinkers have turned in a different direction. What distinguishes scientific knowledge, they have claimed, is the use of the *hypothetical method*. William Whewell (1794–1866) was a critic of Mill. He pointed out that advances in scientific knowledge do not depend only on generalizations based on several observations. Whewell contended the greatest scientific advances occur when a scientist makes a creative guess or **hypothesis** to explain a phenomenon. After that the scientist will turn to sense observations and experimentation to *test* this hypothesis. But the key step is the creative guess or hypothesis:

> The conceptions by which facts are bound together are suggested by the sagacity of discoverers. This sagacity cannot be taught. It commonly succeeds by guessing; and this success seems to consist in framing several tentative hypotheses and selecting the right one. But a supply of appropriate hypotheses cannot be constructed by rule, nor without inventive talent.[49]

Darwin's theory of evolution seems to be a good example of what Whewell had in mind. Darwin's theory began as a hypothesis intended to explain a large number of facts. These included the discovery that fossils buried in ancient layers of rock were different from but related to surviving species. They included the observation that living species occurred in groups that seemed related as if they had common ancestors. They included also the discovery that some butterfly species had gradually changed color over time in ways that made them more likely to escape being eaten by birds. And they included the discovery that certain species had become extinct apparently as a result of competition with other species. And so on. All of these facts could be explained, he held, by his hypothesis on the evolution of species. Namely, that species change over time by a process of natural selection, in which species that are best adapted to their environment survive and reproduce. So Darwin's theory of evolution was not a mere generalization from observations. It was, instead, a creative idea advanced to explain a large number of facts. Darwin showed that all the varieties of animals and plants, both fossilized and living, could be put into a sequence that showed evolution over immense periods of time. More significant, his theory explained how this evolution had taken place. After Darwin, countless biologists used his theory to guide their investigations and experiments. They used it also to decide which observations were worth making.

At the very heart of the scientific method, then, is an element, a contribution, made by reason. Reason—the ability to synthesize, to relate, and to creatively formulate new conceptual structures—seems to be the source of the hypotheses that scientists develop and use to guide their research. This is an important point because it implies that reason makes an essential contribution to science. Moreover, it is a point that the transcendental idealist Kant made. In his *Critique* he wrote that reason is the source of the basic "questions" or hypotheses that the scientist uses to explore

---

49   William Whewell, *History and Philosophy of the Inductive Sciences* (1840), quoted in Stewart Richards, *Philosophy and Sociology of Science* (New York: Schocken, 1984), 529.

the world of nature. As he points out, even Galileo was guided by a hypothesis when he decided to test his law of falling bodies by rolling metal balls down long, smooth inclined planes:

> When Galileo caused balls, the weights of which he had himself previously determined, to roll down an inclined plane; when Torricelli made the air carry a weight which he had calculated beforehand to be equal to that of a definite volume of water; or in more recent times when Stahl changed metals into oxides, and oxides back into metal, by withdrawing something and then restoring it, a light broke upon all students of nature. They learned that reason has insight only into that which it produces after a plan of its own, and that it must not allow itself to be kept, as it were, in nature's leading-strings, but must itself show the way with principles of judgment based upon fixed laws, constraining nature to give answers to questions of reason's own determining. Accidental observations, made in obedience to no previously thought-out plan, can never be made to yield a necessary law, which alone reason is concerned to discover. Reason, holding in one hand its principles, according to which alone concordant appearances can be admitted as equivalent to laws, and in the other hand the experiment which it has devised in conformity with these principles, must approach nature in order to be taught by it. It must not, however, do so in the character of a pupil who listens to everything that the teacher chooses to say, but of an appointed judge who compels the witnesses to answer questions which he has himself formulated.[50]

In formulating a hypothesis, the scientist turns away from the senses. She relies on reason to help her create new relationships, new structures, and new connections. And she uses reason to organize these into a theory that orders, systematizes, and explains whatever facts other scientists have found. In formulating hypotheses, Kant might have said, the scientist also relies on other "laws of reason," such as the criterion of simplicity. Then, the scientist returns to sensory observations. She asks whether the theory accurately predicts new observations, or suggests fresh research and new experiments. Or whether it points the way toward other corroborating observations. Thus, sense observations are essential to scientific method. Yet the creative use of reason is equally essential to the hypothetical methods used by science.

The most influential proponent of the hypothetical method in the twentieth century was Karl Popper (1902–1994). Popper was an empiricist philosopher. He agreed that scientific theories are not mere generalizations from experience. And he also agreed that science progresses by formulating hypotheses that can explain many different phenomena and guide later research. But, he claimed, those are not the factors that really distinguish the claims of science from unscientific claims. What distinguishes scientific claims or hypotheses is that they can be *falsified* by empirical observations.

Many unscientific theories are said by their supporters to be confirmed by observation and experience. For example, astrologers point to observed events that are consistent with some of their predictions and say that these verify their theories. Similarly, people who believe extrasensory perception selectively point to facts that tend to confirm their theories. But any theory, Popper pointed out, can be shown to be consistent with some observed facts. Science does not proceed by trying to find facts that confirm a theory. Instead, the mark of science is that it tries to *disprove* or *falsify* proposed theories. A real scientific theory is not just

QUICK REVIEW
Whewell's "hypothetical method" view of science says reason formulates generalizations and broad theories that are tested by sense observations and experiments. Popper added that they must be capable of being falsified by observable events.

---

[50] Kant, *Critique of Pure Reason*, Pxiii.

ANALYZING THE READING

1. What is the hypothetical method? Is the hypothetical method nothing more than a version of an argument to the best explanation that was explained in Chapter 2? Is the hypothetical method more than an argument to the best explanation? If so, what is the additional factor or factors that the hypothetical method proposes that are not proposed by an argument to the best explanation?

2. In what way is the view that science depends on the hypothetical method an improvement on the inductionist theory?

3. In what way was Popper's theory of falsification an improvement on the view that science depends on the hypothetical method?

one that is confirmed by some observations that suggest it is true, but one that survives repeated attempts to prove it is false. Popper wrote, "there is no more rational procedure than the method of trial and error—of conjecture and refutation; of boldly proposing theories; of trying our best to show that these are erroneous; and of accepting them tentatively if our critical efforts are unsuccessful."[51]

Popper claimed, then, that a scientific theory must be *capable of being falsified by observable events.* This does not mean that scientific statements are those that are actually shown to be false. Rather, a statement is scientific when some observable events or discoveries exist that *could* show the statement is false. Science advances when the scientist formulates a hypothesis that implies that some observable event will occur. Then he and others try to falsify the hypothesis by experiments and observations that see whether the predicted event occurs as the hypothesis said. If a theory stands up to many attempts to falsify it, then we are justified in believing it. The more times we try to prove it false, and fail, the more reliable the theory is. For example, astronomers had noticed that the orbit of the planet Uranus was irregular; Newton's theory of motion predicted that the disturbance was caused by the gravitational attraction of an unknown planet in a certain orbit near Uranus. When astronomers searched that part of the sky, they eventually discovered the planet Neptune. Thus, Newton's theory made the kind of prediction that could prove it was false. Instead, the prediction turned out to be true, thereby confirming the theory. Newton's theory also predicts the trajectories of cannon balls and the motions of everything from trains to molecules. All these predictions could have disproved his theory if they turned out to be wrong. Instead, the predictions turned out true, thereby providing even more confirmation for his theory.

Similarly, Darwin's theory of evolution predicted that fossilized organisms in older Cambrian rock formations would be simpler than those in more recent Cambrian rock. The theory of evolution hypothesizes that organisms develop gradually from simple to increasingly complex forms. If evolution is true, then older pre-Cambrian formations should contain simpler fossil forms than those in the Cambrian layers of rocks. That is exactly what biologists found in 1947 in pre-Cambrian rocks in Australia. So the prediction of the theory of evolution was not wrong, and the theory was not falsified; it was instead confirmed.

The hypothetical method and Popper's falsifiability criterion imply that scientific theories are only probable. They are always open to revision based on new evidence or a new interpretation of existing evidence. A scientific hypothesis may predict certain events, and these events may occur as the hypothesis suggests. But it is always possible that other predictions of the hypothesis, not yet tested, may turn out to be wrong. A scientific hypothesis, like a generalization, always goes beyond the limited facts or observations that it was formulated to explain. For this reason, it is always open to refutation; it is always merely probable, never certain.

---

[51] Karl Popper, *Conjectures and Refutations* (1963), quoted in Richards, *Philosophy and Sociology of Science*, 52.

Paradigms and Revolutions in Science

Popper's view, however, ignores the extent to which scientists are human beings who work and socialize together in communities. They are trained in universities to accept certain theories and research methods. And they are deeply convinced that the basic theories of their subject are correct. As a result, scientists tend to continue to accept a basic theory even if they run into observations that falsify the theory. In fact, despite Popper's claim that scientists are continuously trying to disprove their theories, the opposite seems to happen more often. Scientists may stubbornly cling to a theory for decades after the appearance of experimental results that are inconsistent with the theory.

The American philosopher and historian of science Thomas Kuhn (1922–1996) studied science as a social phenomenon. He argued that we should think of scientific knowledge as the product of communities of scientists who accept and work with that knowledge. An example of such a community is the community of biologists who accept and use Darwin's theory. Another example is the community of astronomers who accept and use Newton's and Einstein's theories. And a third example is the community of chemists who accept and use molecular theory. A person who decides to become a scientist gets a long "indoctrination" into the accepted theories and research methods of his scientific community. Kuhn calls the theories accepted by a scientific community, together with their research methods, a "paradigm" of what science is for that community. The student-scientist is taught the paradigm of the community of scientists he wants to join. That is, he is taught the basic theories of the field and the correct methods for applying and extending those theories. Examples of paradigms are the theory of the atom in chemistry, the Copernican theory that the earth and planets revolve around the sun in astronomy, and the theory of evolution in biology. In each case, the community of scientists working in the field accepted the basic theory, and used it to guide their research. According to Kuhn:

> These remarks should begin to clarify what I take a paradigm to be. It is, in the first place, a fundamental scientific achievement and one which includes both a theory and some exemplary applications to the results of experiment and observation. More important, it is an open-ended achievement, one which leaves all sorts of research still to be done. And, finally, it is an accepted achievement in the sense that it is received by a group whose members no longer try to rival it or to create alternates for it. Instead, they attempt to extend and exploit it in a variety of ways.[52]

Moreover, Kuhn argued, science does not always grow gradually, as the inductionists and the falsificationists say it does. Instead, science leaps forward through major *revolutions*. Most of the time, scientists hold onto their theories even if a few observations show up that do not fit the theory. Such observations are called "anomalies." So long as there are relatively few anomalies scientists hold on to their theories. But when too many observations accumulate that do not square with a theory, a "crisis" results. Some scientists, particularly younger ones, start to rethink the theory. They develop new theories that take the anomalies into account. Then a revolution may occur in the scientific community. Some scientists (usually the older established ones) continue to hold on to the old theory while other (usually young) scientists turn to the new theory. New research programs and methods are

---

[52] Thomas Kuhn, "The Function of Dogma in Scientific Research," in *Scientific Knowledge: Basic Issues in the Philosophy of Science*, ed. Janet A. Kourany (Belmont, CA: Wadsworth, 1987), 259.

developed for this new theory, and when young people enter the field, they start to get indoctrinated into the new theory. Eventually the new theory becomes the new paradigm for that field of science:

> Scientific revolutions are here taken to be those noncumulative developmental episodes in which an older paradigm is replaced in whole or in part by an incompatible new one. . . . Why should a change of paradigm be called a revolution? ... Political revolutions are inaugurated by a growing sense, often restricted to a segment of the political community, that existing institutions have ceased adequately to meet the problems posed by an environment that they have in part created. In much the same way, scientific revolutions are inaugurated by a growing sense, again often restricted to a narrow subdivision of the scientific community, that an existing paradigm has ceased to function adequately in the exploration of an aspect of nature to which that paradigm itself had previously led the way. In both political and scientific development, the sense of malfunction that can lead to crisis is prerequisite to revolution.[53]

 QUICK REVIEW
During scientific revolutions, older scientists try to hold on to the old theories and resist the new paradigm. Kuhn suggests that the new paradigm is not necessarily truer than the old.

The history of science is filled with examples of such scientific revolutions, Kuhn said. One example is the change from the medieval theory that the sun revolves around the earth to the revolutionary theory of Copernicus that the earth revolves around the sun. Another is the change from Newton's theory that time and space are absolute and unchanging to the revolutionary new theory of Einstein that time and space are relative. And another is the change from the theory that animal and plant species do not change to Darwin's revolutionary new theory of evolution. The new paradigms, Kuhn insisted, gave us new ways of seeing the world, new ways of thinking, and new goals and methods for investigating nature.

Kuhn's insights into the way that science progresses are extremely valuable. But they leave an important question unanswered: What is the difference between real science and claims that are unscientific? Kuhn's view seems to provide us with no way of answering this question other than to say that a theory is scientific if a community of scientists accepts it. As he wrote in one of his early works, "What better criterion could there be [of scientific knowledge] than the decision of the scientific group?"[54] Kuhn's view suggests that true scientific knowledge must be consistent with the knowledge prevailing among a community of scientists. Yet any group of people might claim to be a "community of scientists." Take, for example, the International Flat Earth Research Society (http://theflatearthsociety.org). It claims to be a group of scientists who aim "to establish as a fact that this earth is flat and plane and that it does not spin and whirl 1000 miles an hour and to expose modern astronomical science as a fraud, myth, a false religion." How can we distinguish real science from bogus science when we don't know how to distinguish a community of real scientists from a community of bogus scientists?

THINKING LIKE A PHILOSOPHER

1. Kuhn explains science as a social activity that a community of scientists engage in, and he argues that scientists do not really try to falsify their theories like Popper says they do. He also claims that scientists are not willing to change their theories, and that new theories emerge only after the scientists who believed in the old theories die off and are replaced by a younger generation of scientists who prefer the new theories. Are any of Kuhn's views about what science is similar to the views of science that you have been taught in your science classes?
2. If you think about the science classes that you have taken, which of the views of science described in this chapter seem to match the view of science that you received in your science classes?

---

[53]   Thomas Kuhn, "The Nature and Necessity of Scientific Revolutions," *in Scientific Knowledge*, 311.
[54]   Thomas Kuhn, *The Structure of Scientific Revolutions* (London: Oxford University Press, 1973).

In his later writings, Thomas Kuhn responded to this important question:

> What, I ask to begin with, are the characteristics of a good scientific theory? ...First, a theory should be accurate: Within its domain, that is, consequences deducible from a theory should be in demonstrated agreement with the results of existing experiments and observations. Second, a theory should be consistent, not only internally or with itself, but also with other currently accepted theories applicable to related aspects of nature. Third, it should have broad scope: In particular, a theory's consequences should extend far beyond the particular observations, laws, or subtheories it was initially designed to explain. Fourth, and closely related, it should be simple, bringing order to phenomena that in its absence would be individually isolated and, as a set, confused. Fifth—a somewhat less standard item, but one of special importance to actual scientific decisions—a theory should be fruitful of new research findings: it should, that is, disclose new phenomena or previously unnoted relationships among those already known.[55]

QUICK REVIEW
Kuhn suggested a good scientific theory was accurate, consistent with other accepted theories, broad, simple, and fruitful.

Many of the criteria that Kuhn suggests here are closely related to the rationalist tradition. For example, the criterion of consistency is not established by sense observation. It is based on reason, on the idea that rationality demands consistency. The same can be said about his criterion that a good scientific theory must bring "order" into our sensory observations. This, we have suggested, is a function of reason.

The views of science we've looked at suggest that it incorporates elements from empiricism, rationalism, and Kant. Inductionism says science relies on sense observations, a source of knowledge that empiricists emphasize. The hypothetical method, especially in its appeal to simplicity and consistency, incorporates rationalist criteria. And the creative use of reason to formulate hypotheses that guide research and bring order to our sense observations is supported by Kant.

But as we noted at the beginning of this discussion one of the things we hope to draw from this discussion of the sources of knowledge is an understanding of how science differs from pseudoscience. We turn now to that issue. In the Thinking Critically box that follows, we will summarize the conclusions we can now draw about what scientific knowledge is. We will line them up in a form that should allow us to use those conclusions to evaluate whether claims should count as science or pseudoscience.

thinking critically • Distinguishing Science from Pseudoscience

Let's try now to summarize what we've seen and reach some conclusions about what distinguishes science from pseudoscience.

First, our discussion of inductionism suggests that particularly in the establishment of low-level laws, science relies on the inductive method of observation, generalization, and repeated confirmation by new observations. When rival generalizations are in all other respects equal, scientists tend to accept the simplest one, the one that accounts for the facts most economically. But more important than simplicity is the number and variety of new observations that confirm a generalization. Pseudosciences, on the other hand, do not rely on the inductive method to establish any of their claims.

Second, the discussion of the hypothetical method suggests that especially in the establishment of general theories—and also in the establishment of some low-level

---

55 Thomas Kuhn, *The Essential Tension: Selected Studies in Scientific Tradition and Change* (Chicago: University of Chicago Press, 1977), 321.

Are theories about the existence of UFOs scientific? Are they falsifiable?

QUICK REVIEW

The scientific method seems to be distinguished from pseudoscience by the following: (1) it is based on sense observation and rationality; (2) it relies on the inductive method for its low-level laws; (3) it proceeds by formulating hypotheses that can guide research, (4) that are falsifiable, (5) and that are widely accepted in the community of scientists; and (6) its theories are accurate, consistent with other accepted theories, broad, simple, and fruitful.

laws—scientific knowledge requires the creative formulation of hypotheses that can guide research and be tested by observation. Not all creative guesses or hypotheses are on an equal level. A scientific hypothesis must not only be testable by observation. It must also make predictions that can be observed, and it must be capable of guiding new research and suggesting new experiments that can test the hypothesis. Pseudoscientific theories, like astrology, do not provide the basis for this kind of research and experiments.

Third, as Popper suggested, a critical element of a scientific theory is that it must be *falsifiable:* The theory must make predictions that can be shown to be false by observation. This means that science does not use a selective approach to evidence. Scientists do not pick out only the evidence and observations that agree with their theories. Instead, they continually look for *disconfirming* evidence as well as confirming evidence. This approach contrasts with, say, the methods of "psychics," who point out the events that match their predictions, but conveniently ignore the predictions that never came true. Because science is always on the lookout for disconfirming evidence, scientific theories are never certain but only probable, always open to refutation by future observations.

Fourth, a scientific theory is one that is widely accepted in the community of scientists; they use the theory to guide their research but may abandon it in a scientific revolution when confronted with too many anomalies for which the theory can no longer account. This means that the evidence on which scientific theories are based must be made available to other people. Experiments or observations that confirm a theory must be capable of being replicated or repeated by others in the community of scientists. This approach contrasts with the methods of, say, UFO researchers, who rely on "sightings" by individuals that cannot be duplicated or repeated by others. Moreover, when confronted with sufficient "anomalies" that cannot be explained by their theory, scientists will eventually abandon a theory, whereas pseudoscientific groups will not. For example, astrologers have tenaciously clung to their theories for centuries, no matter how much evidence has accumulated against them.

Fifth, as Kuhn suggests, a scientific theory must meet five criteria: (1) It must be in accurate agreement with observations; (2) it must be consistent with other prevailing scientific theories; (3) it must have broad consequences that extend beyond the phenomena it was originally designed to explain and that organize and relate phenomena that were previously thought to be disconnected; (4) it must be as simple as possible and simpler than the phenomenon to be explained; and (5) it must be fruitful by suggesting fresh research and new experiments. Pseudoscientific theories generally do not meet these five criteria.

These features of science generally are not shared by the many pseudoscientific claims that we read in newspapers and magazines and find on the Internet. They distinguish genuine science from, say, biorhythm theory, theories of extrasensory perception, parapsychology, astrology, pyramid power, and UFOs. These nonscientific theories are not in agreement with what many other people have observed, they are not consistent with science, they are used as ad hoc explanations of past events but cannot explain or predict future events, they do not look for evidence that can disprove or falsify the theories, they do not help us organize and understand phenomena that were previously felt to be disconnected, and they certainly do not lead to new research programs or fresh scientific experiments. Instead, they are simply grab-bag theories: Their supporters grab at any new findings that seem to agree with their theory, and they stuff these findings into their bag of "evidence."

Is the Theory of Recovered Memories Science or Pseudoscience?

We discussed earlier the controversy over the theory of repressed memory and of recovered memory therapy. Proponents of this theory, as we saw, claim that the theory is scientifically valid. But how does the theory fare when measured against the features that distinguish a real scientific theory from pseudoscience? On several counts, the theory of repressed memory and of recovered memory therapy measures up quite favorably. For example, the theory is widely accepted in the community of scientists composed of psychologists. It is accepted particularly by those belonging to the psychoanalytic school.

THINKING LIKE A PHILOSOPHER

What are some examples of pseudosciences that you're familiar with and that are not mentioned in the textbook? Which of the features that characterize a real science does your example of a pseudoscience lack?

Furthermore, the theory is in accurate agreement with observations made in clinical practice. It is consistent with several other psychological theories. It seems to have implications that extend beyond the phenomenon of recovered memories. It has been very successful at organizing and relating psychological phenomena that were previously thought to be disconnected. And it is fruitful in suggesting fresh research and experiments. Yet in other respects the theory seems to fail as a genuine scientific theory. In particular, one of the disturbing aspects of recovered memory theory is that it may not be falsifiable. In fact, efforts of critics to disprove the theory have typically been met with the response that the critics are "in denial." And patients in therapy are sometimes encouraged to believe that "the existence of profound disbelief is an indication that memories are real." The theory's apparent lack of susceptibility to falsification appears to be its weak point. But this is crucial. For if a theory cannot be falsified then, as Popper pointed out, it can hardly be counted as a scientific theory.

The scientific validity of the theory of repressed memory and of recovered memory therapy is a complex and troubling issue. It is an issue that demonstrates the importance of having clear views on the valid sources of knowledge and of scientific truth. And it is an issue that readers might profitably continue to pursue on their own, using the concepts and understandings they have developed in the course of this chapter.

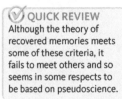

QUICK REVIEW
Although the theory of recovered memories meets some of these criteria, it fails to meet others and so seems in some respects to be based on pseudoscience.

PHILOSOPHY AT THE MOVIES

Watch *Kinsey* (2004), which portrays the life of famous sex researcher Alfred Kinsey, who revolutionized the study of human sexual behavior as well as society's approach to sexuality. Which of the various theories of science and scientific knowledge are confirmed or discontinued by Kinsey's approach to research and by the discoveries he made?

Movie with a related theme: *A Beautiful Mind* (2001).

Chapter Summary

The issues of who we are and how we are to live are tied to the question of knowledge. Historically, philosophers have asked this question: If there are different kinds of knowledge of reality, how can they be obtained? The most common view is that there are two main sources of such knowledge: reason—favored by the rationalists—and sense observation—favored by empiricists. Among the outstanding rationalists is René Descartes, who attempted to demonstrate the validity of *a priori* knowledge—that is, knowledge independent of sensory perception.

In vigorous reaction to Descartes and the rationalists are the British empiricists: Locke, Berkeley, and Hume. They insist that all knowledge of reality is *a posteriori*—that is, it follows from experience. One crucial problem that empiricists face arises from their distinction between an objective world and our perception of that world. If these are differentiated, how do we know that our experiences correspond with how things are? Locke's answer is that our experiences represent the outside world. Berkeley says that all we ever know are our own ideas; only conscious minds and their perceptions exist. For Hume, reality is not truly knowable.

Immanuel Kant proposed his theory of transcendental idealism to demonstrate that knowledge of reality is possible. Although Kant argues that true knowledge of reality has its basis in sensory experience, he also claims that the mind has innate capacities to order that sensory experience and thus arrive at knowledge.

We have seen that modern science incorporates elements of all these traditions. Scientific "knowledge" is based on induction and simplicity, on the hypothetical method and creativity, on falsifiability and predictive power, on wide acceptance by the community of scientists, as well as on accuracy, consistency, explanatory power, the ability to relate what was previously disconnected, and fruitfulness. Pseudoscientific theories such as astrology do not possess these features.

The main points of this chapter, then, are the following:

5.1   Why Is Knowledge A Problem?

- To understand and resolve controversies like the controversy over recovered memories, it is necessary to have an understanding of what knowledge is.

- There are two common views regarding the sources of knowledge: rationalism and empiricism.

- Memory does not provide us with new knowledge, but preserves knowledge that we acquire from other sources.

5.2   Is Reason the Source of Our Knowledge?

- René Descartes was a rationalist concerned with discovering something that he could hold as true beyond any doubt. He concluded that reason provides our knowledge of the essential nature of reality, that the existence of God guarantees that we are not deceived, and that some of our knowledge is innate. All of this, he claimed, could be established by reason alone.

- With the example of a slave boy who reveals his knowledge of geometry, Plato argued that we have an innate knowledge of geometry that we acquired in a previous existence.

5.3   Can the Senses Account for All Our Knowledge?

- Empiricism states that all knowledge comes from or is based on sensory perception and is *a posteriori*.

- John Locke held that we have knowledge of the primary qualities of things, such as their size, shape, and weight, and that such primary qualities really exist in external objects. Secondary qualities such as colors, smells, and sounds are sensations in us caused by the powers of external objects; these qualities do not really exist in external objects. We know the external world through the primary qualities we perceive by our senses, and we know there are external objects because they must cause our sensations.

- According to George Berkeley's subjectivist theory of knowledge, we know only our own ideas. He argues that Locke's primary qualities are as mind-dependent as secondary qualities, and that we have no knowledge of external material objects.

● David Hume pushed Locke's and Berkeley's empiricism to its logical conclusion, arguing that all knowledge depends on our sense impressions and that we cannot claim something exists unless we perceive it through some sense impression. Since we have no sense impressions of the self, an external world, or of causal relations, we cannot say these are real. Moreover, we have no justification for claiming that our past experiences of causes provide us knowledge of future causes.

● The problem of induction is the problem of showing that we are justified in claiming that since some things were observed to have certain features in the past, all of those types of things will have those same features in the future.

● thinking critically Inductive generalizations are probable arguments whose premises indicate that something is true of a limited sample, and whose conclusion claims that the same is true of the whole population. Their strength depends on how large and how representative the sample is.

5.4   Kant: Does the Knowing Mind Shape the World?

● Immanuel Kant's transcendental idealism, an alternative to empiricism and rationalism, distinguishes between things as we experience them (phenomena) and things as they are in themselves (noumena); we know phenomena but have no knowledge of noumena. The mind, claimed Kant, organizes our sensations and posits relationships among them by arranging these sensations into the world we perceive. Through an awareness of these relationships, we acquire knowledge that is synthetic and *a priori*, such as our knowledge of causal relationships. The mind organizes its many sensations into a unified world because it is a unified awareness and so must unify its many sensations to bring them into its unified awareness. The mind unifies its many sensations by connecting them with causal relationships and other kinds of relationships.

5.5   Does Science Give Us Knowledge?

● Inductionism is the view that all science is based on the process of sensory observation, generalization, and repeated confirmation. This process is often used to establish scientific laws, and simplicity is one criterion for choosing among competing generalizations.

● The hypothetical method view says that science is also based on the creative formulation of hypotheses whose predictions are then tested and used to guide research. Karl Popper argued that falsifiability is a criterion of scientific theories.

● Thomas Kuhn argued that scientific theories are those that are widely accepted by a community of scientists. They are the basis of paradigms that guide research but that are abandoned in a scientific revolution, when too many anomalies appear that cannot be accounted for by the paradigm.

● Scientific theories must be accurate, consistent with other widely accepted theories, capable of explaining phenomena other than those they were developed to explain, capable of organizing phenomena that were previously thought to be unrelated, and fruitful insofar as they generate new research and new discoveries.

5.6 Readings

The first reading that follows is the intriguing story "An Occurrence at Owl Creek Bridge" by Ambrose Bierce. As a Southern planter is being hanged by Union soldiers during the Civil War, he falls free and, escaping, travels the many miles to his wife and the home he desperately wants to see again, only to lose them in the final moment of an illusion. Bierce's story forces us to ask whether we can know that we are not deceiving ourselves about the world we see around us.

In the next article, contemporary philosopher Peter Unger argues that in fact we can never know for sure whether our beliefs about the world are true or whether they are deceptions introduced into our mind by some "exotic" means or by our ordinary impulses. Unger begins by considering what he calls the "exotic and bizarre case of a deceiving scientist" who artificially implants false beliefs in our minds, and then he goes on to consider more "ordinary" cases of being deceived by our natural impulses. He concludes that we can never really know anything about the external world. Unger suggests that if we are to be rational and undogmatic, we should stop using the words "I know."

In the last article, Thomas Nagel, also a contemporary philosopher, raises the possibility that all of our knowledge about the world around us might be a giant illusion. He then examines an argument by which people have sometimes tried to prove that such skepticism is meaningless. However, Nagel concludes that this argument against skepticism fails. Yet, he suggests, we have no choice but to live as if our ordinary beliefs about the world around us are true.

AMBROSE BIERCE

An Occurrence at Owl Creek Bridge

I

A man stood upon a railroad bridge in northern Alabama, looking down into the swift water twenty feet below. The man's hands were behind his back, the wrists bound with a cord. A rope closely encircled his neck. It was attached to a stout cross-timber above his head and the slack fell to the level of his knees. Some loose boards laid upon the sleepers supporting the metals of the railway supplied a footing for him and his executioners—two private soldiers of the Federal army, directed by a sergeant who in civil life may have been a deputy sheriff. At a short remove upon the same temporary platform was an officer in the uniform of his rank, armed. He was a captain. A sentinel at each end of the bridge stood with his rifle in the position known as "support," that is to say, vertical in front of the left shoulder, the hammer resting on the forearm thrown straight across the chest—a formal and unnatural position, enforcing an erect carriage of the body. It did not appear to be the duty of these two men to know what was occurring at the center of the bridge; they merely blockaded the two ends of the foot planking that traversed it.

Beyond one of the sentinels nobody was in sight; the railroad ran straight away into a forest for a hundred yards, then, curving, was lost to view. Doubtless there was an outpost farther along. The other bank of the stream was open ground—a gentle acclivity topped with a stockade of vertical tree trunks, loopholed for rifles, with a single embrasure through which protruded the muzzle of a brass cannon commanding the bridge. Midway of the slope between the bridge and fort were the spectators—a single company of infantry in line, at "parade rest," the butts of the rifles on the ground, the barrels inclining slightly backward against the right shoulder, the hands crossed upon the stock. A lieutenant stood at the right of the line, the point of his sword upon the ground, his left hand resting upon his right. Excepting the group of four at the center of the bridge, not a man moved. The company faced the bridge, staring stonily, motionless. The sentinels, facing the banks of the stream, might have been statues to adorn the bridge. The captain stood with folded arms, silent, observing the work of his subordinates, but making no sign. Death is a dignitary who when he comes announced is to be received with formal manifestations of respect, even by those most familiar with him. In the code of military etiquette silence and fixity are forms of deference.

The man who was engaged in being hanged was apparently about thirty-five years of age. He was a civilian, if one might judge from his habit,* which was that of a planter. His features were good—a straight nose, firm mouth, broad forehead, from which his long, dark hair was combed straight back, falling behind his ears to the collar of his well-fitting frock coat. He wore a mustache and pointed beard, but no whiskers; his eyes were large and dark gray, and had a kindly expression which one would hardly have expected in one whose neck was in the hemp. Evidently this was no vulgar assassin. The liberal military code makes provision for hanging many kinds of persons, and gentlemen are not excluded.

The preparations being complete, the two private soldiers stepped aside and each drew away the plank upon which he had been standing. The sergeant turned to the captain, saluted and placed himself immediately behind that officer, who in turn moved apart one pace. These movements left the condemned man and the sergeant standing on the two ends of the same plank, which spanned three of the crossties of the bridge. The end upon which the civilian stood almost, but not quite, reached a fourth. This plank had been held in place by the weight of the captain; it was now held by that of the sergeant. At a signal from the former the latter would step aside, the plank would tilt and the condemned man go down between two ties. The arrangement commended itself to his judgment as simple and effective. His face had not been covered nor his eyes bandaged. He looked a moment at his "unsteadfast footing," then let his gaze wander to the swirling water of the stream racing madly beneath his feet. A piece of dancing driftwood caught his attention and his eyes followed it down the current. How slowly it appeared to move! What a sluggish stream!

He closed his eyes in order to fix his last thoughts upon his wife and children. The water, touched to gold by the early sun, the brooding mists under the banks at some distance down the stream, the fort, the soldiers, the piece of drift—all had distracted him. And now he became conscious of a new disturbance. Striking through the thought of his dear ones was a sound which he could neither ignore nor understand, a sharp, distinct, metallic percussion

---

*Clothing.—Ed.

like the stroke of a blacksmith's hammer upon the anvil; it had the same ringing quality. He wondered what it was, and whether immeasurably distant or near by—it seemed both. Its recurrence was regular, but as slow as the tolling of a death knell. He awaited each stroke with impatience and—he knew not why—apprehension. The intervals of silence grew progressively longer, the delays became maddening. With their greater infrequency the sounds increased in strength and sharpness. They hurt his ear like the thrust of a knife; he feared he would shriek. What he heard was the ticking of his watch.

He unclosed his eyes and saw again the water below him. "If I could free my hands," he thought, "I might throw off the noose and spring into the stream. By diving I could evade the bullets and, swimming vigorously, reach the bank, take to the woods and get away home. My home, thank God, is as yet outside their lines; my wife and little ones are still beyond the invader's farthest advance." As these thoughts, which have here been set down in words, were flashed into the doomed man's brain rather than evolved from it the captain nodded to the sergeant. The sergeant stepped aside.

II

Peyton Farquhar was a well-to-do planter, of an old and highly respected Alabama family. Being a slave owner and like other slave owners a politician he was naturally an original secessionist and ardently devoted to the Southern cause. Circumstances of an imperious nature, which it is unnecessary to relate here, had prevented him from taking service with the gallant army that had fought the disastrous campaigns ending with the fall of Corinth, and he chafed under the inglorious restraint, longing for the release of his energies, the larger life of the soldier, the opportunity for distinction. That opportunity, he felt, would come, as it comes to all in war time. Meanwhile he did what he could. No service was too humble for him to perform in aid of the South, no adventure too perilous for him to undertake if consistent with the character of a civilian who was at heart a soldier, and who in good faith and without too much qualification assented to at least a part of the frankly villainous dictum that all is fair in love and war.

One evening while Farquhar and his wife were sitting on a rustic bench near the entrance to his grounds, a gray-clad soldier rode up to the gate and asked for a drink of water. Mrs. Farquhar was only too happy to serve him with her own white hands. While she was fetching the water her husband approached the dusty horseman and inquired eagerly for news from the front.

"The Yanks are repairing the railroads," said the man, "and are getting ready for another advance. They have reached the Owl Creek bridge, put it in order and built a stockade on the north bank. The commandant has issued an order, which is posted everywhere, declaring that any civilian caught interfering with the railroad, its bridges, tunnels or trains will be summarily hanged. I saw the order."

"How far is it to the Owl Creek bridge?" Farquhar asked.

"About thirty miles."

"Is there no force on this side of the creek?"

"Only a picket post half a mile out, on the railroad, and a single sentinel at this end of the bridge."

"Suppose a man—a civilian and student of hanging—should elude the picket post and perhaps get the better of the sentinel," said Farquhar, smiling, "what could he accomplish?"

The soldier reflected. "I was there a month ago," he replied. "I observed that the flood of last winter had lodged a great quantity of driftwood against the wooden pier at this end of the bridge. It is now dry and would burn like tow."

The lady had now brought the water, which the soldier drank. He thanked her ceremoniously, bowed to her husband and rode away. An hour later, after nightfall, he repassed the plantation, going northward in the direction from which he had come. He was a Federal scout.

III

As Peyton Farquhar fell straight downward through the bridge he lost consciousness and was as one already dead. From this state he was awakened—ages later, it seemed to him—by the pain of a sharp pressure upon his throat, followed by a sense of suffocation. Keen, poignant agonies seemed to shoot from his neck downward through every fiber of his body and limbs. These pains appeared to flash along well-defined lines of ramification and to beat with an inconceivably rapid periodicity. They seemed like streams of pulsating fire heating him to an intolerable temperature. As to his head, he was conscious of nothing but a feeling of fullness—of congestion. These sensations were unaccompanied by thought. The intellectual part of his nature was already effaced; he had power only to feel, and feeling was torment. He was conscious of motion. Encompassed in a luminous cloud, of which he was now merely the fiery heart, without material substance, he swung through unthinkable arcs of oscillation, like a vast pendulum. Then all at once, with terrible suddenness, the light about him shot upward with the noise of a loud splash; a frightful roaring was in his ears, and all was cold and dark. The power of thought was restored; he knew that the rope had broken and he had fallen into the stream. There was no additional strangulation; the noose about his neck was already suffocating him and kept the water from his lungs. To die of hanging at the bottom of a river!—the idea seemed to him ludicrous. He opened his eyes in the darkness and saw above him a gleam of light, but how distant, how inaccessible! He was still sinking, for the light became fainter and fainter until it was a mere glimmer. Then it began to grow and brighten, and he knew that he was rising toward the surface—knew it with reluctance, for he was now very comfortable. "To be hanged and drowned," he thought, "that is not so bad; but I do not wish to be shot. No; I will not be shot; that is not fair."

He was not conscious of an effort, but a sharp pain in his wrist apprised him that he was trying to free his hands. He gave the struggle his attention, as an idler might observe the feat of a juggler, without interest in the outcome. What splendid effort!—what magnificent, what superhuman strength! Ah, that was a fine endeavor! Bravo! The cord fell away; his arms parted and floated upward, the hands dimly seen on each side in the growing light. He watched them with a new interest as first one and then the other pounced upon the noose at his neck. They tore it away and thrust it fiercely aside, its undulations resembling those of a water snake. "Put it back, put it back!" He thought he shouted these words to his hands, for the undoing of the noose had been succeeded by the direst pang that he had yet experienced. His neck ached horribly; his brain was on fire; his heart, which had been fluttering faintly, gave a great leap, trying to force itself out at his mouth. His whole body was racked and wrenched with an insupportable anguish! But his disobedient hands gave no heed to the command. They beat the water vigorously with quick, downward strokes, forcing him to the surface. He felt his head emerge; his eyes were blinded by the sunlight; his chest expanded convulsively, and with a supreme and crowning agony his lungs engulfed a great draught of air, which instantly he expelled in a shriek!

He was now in full possession of his physical senses. They were, indeed, preternaturally keen and alert. Something in the awful disturbance of his organic system had so exalted and refined them that they made record of things never before perceived. He felt the ripples upon his face and heard their separate sounds as they struck. He looked at the forest on the bank of the stream, saw the individual trees, the leaves and the veining of each leaf—saw the very insects upon them: the locusts, the brilliant-bodied flies, the grey spiders stretching their webs from twig to twig. He noted the prismatic colors in all the dewdrops upon a million blades of grass. The humming of the gnats that danced above the eddies of the stream, the beating of the dragon flies' wings, the strokes of the waterspiders' legs, like oars which had lifted their boat—all these made audible music. A fish slid along beneath his eyes and he heard the rush of its body parting the water.

He had come to the surface facing down the stream; in a moment the visible world seemed to wheel slowly round, himself the pivotal point, and he saw the bridge, the fort, the soldiers upon the bridge, the captain, the sergeant, the two privates, his executioners. They were in silhouette against the blue sky. They shouted and gesticulated, pointing at him. The captain had drawn his pistol, but did not fire; the others were unarmed. Their movements were grotesque and horrible, their forms gigantic.

Suddenly he heard a sharp report and something struck the water smartly within a few inches of his head, spattering his face with spray. He heard a second report, and saw one of the sentinels with his rifle at his shoulder, a light cloud of blue smoke rising from the muzzle. The man in the water saw the eye of the man on the bridge gazing into his own through the sights of the rifle. He observed that it was a gray eye and remembered having read that gray eyes were keenest, and that all famous marksmen had them. Nevertheless, this one had missed.

A counter-swirl had caught Farquhar and turned him half round; he was again looking into the forest on the bank opposite the fort. The sound of a clear, high voice in a monotonous singsong now rang out behind him and came across the water with a distinctness that pierced and subdued all other sounds, even the beating of the ripples in his ears. Although no soldier, he had frequented camps enough to know the dread significance of that deliberate, drawling, aspirated chant; the lieutenant on shore was taking a part in the morning's work. How coldly and pitilessly—with what an even, calm intonation, presaging, and enforcing tranquillity in the men—with what accurately measured intervals fell those cruel words:

"Attention, company! ...Shoulder arms! ...Ready! ...Aim! ...Fire!"

Farquhar dived—dived as deeply as he could. The water roared in his ears like the voice of Niagara,

yet he heard the dulled thunder of the volley and, rising again toward the surface, met shining bits of metal, singularly flattened, oscillating slowly downward. Some of them touched him on the face and hands, then fell away, continuing their descent. One lodged between his collar and neck; it was uncomfortably warm and he snatched it out.

As he rose to the surface, gasping for breath, he saw that he had been a long time under water; he was perceptibly farther down stream—nearer to safety. The soldiers had almost finished reloading; the metal ramrods flashed all at once in the sunshine as they were drawn from the barrels, turned in the air, and thrust into their sockets. The two sentinels fired again, independently and ineffectually.

The hunted man saw all this over his shoulder; he was now swimming vigorously with the current. His brain was as energetic as his arms and legs; he thought with the rapidity of lightning.

"The officer," he reasoned, "will not make that martinet's error a second time. It is as easy to dodge a volley as a single shot. He has probably already given the command to fire at will. God help me, I cannot dodge them all!"

An appalling splash within two yards of him was followed by a loud, rushing sound, *diminuendo*, which seemed to travel back through the air to the fort and died in an explosion which stirred the very river to its deeps! A rising sheet of water curved over him, fell down upon him, blinded him, strangled him! The cannon had taken a hand in the game. As he shook his head free from the commotion of the smitten water he heard the deflected shot humming through the air ahead, and in an instant it was cracking and smashing the branches in the forest beyond.

"They will not do that again," he thought; "the next time they will use a charge of grape. I must keep my eye upon the gun; the smoke will apprise me—the report arrives too late; it lags behind the missile. That is a good gun."

Suddenly he felt himself whirled round and round—spinning like a top. The water, the banks, the forests, the now distant bridge, fort and men— all were commingled and blurred. Objects were represented by their colors only; circular horizontal streaks of color—that was all he saw. He had been caught in a vortex and was being whirled on with a velocity of advance and gyration that made him giddy and sick. In a few moments he was flung upon the gravel at the foot of the left bank of the stream— the southern bank—and behind a projecting point which concealed him from his enemies. The sudden arrest of his motion, the abrasion of one of his hands on the gravel, restored him, and he wept with delight. He dug his fingers into the sand, threw it over himself in handfuls and audibly blessed it. It looked like diamonds, rubies, emeralds; he could think of nothing beautiful which it did not resemble. The trees upon the bank were giant garden plants; he noted a definite order in their arrangement, inhaled the fragrance of their blooms. A strange, roseate light shone through the spaces among their trunks and the wind made in their branches the music of Æolian harps. He had no wish to perfect his escape—was content to remain in that enchanting spot until retaken.

A whiz and rattle of grapeshot among the branches high above his head roused him from his dream. The baffled cannoneer had fired him a random farewell. He sprang to his feet, rushed up the sloping bank, and plunged into the forest.

All that day he traveled, laying his course by the rounding sun. The forest seemed interminable; nowhere did he discover a break in it, not even a woodman's road. He had not known that he lived in so wild a region. There was something uncanny in the revelation.

By nightfall he was fatigued, footsore, famishing. The thought of his wife and children urged him on. At last he found a road which led him in what he knew to be the right direction. It was as wide and straight as a city street, yet it seemed untraveled. No fields bordered it, no dwelling anywhere. Not so much as the barking of a dog suggested human habitation. The black bodies of the trees formed a straight wall on both sides, terminating on the horizon in a point, like a diagram in a lesson in perspective. Overhead, as he looked up through this rift in the wood, shone great golden stars looking unfamiliar and grouped in strange constellations. He was

sure they were arranged in some order which had a secret and malign significance. The wood on either side was full of singular noises, among which—once, twice, and again—he distinctly heard whispers in an unknown tongue.

His neck was in pain and lifting his hand to it found it horribly swollen. He knew that it had a circle of black where the rope had bruised it. His eyes felt congested; he could no longer close them. His tongue was swollen with thirst; he relieved its fever by thrusting it forward from between his teeth into the cold air. How softly the turf had carpeted the untraveled avenue—he could no longer feel the roadway beneath his feet!

Doubtless, despite his suffering, he had fallen asleep while walking, for now he sees another scene—perhaps he has merely recovered from a delirium. He stands at the gate of his own home. All is as he left it, and all bright and beautiful in the morning sunshine. He must have traveled the entire night. As he pushes open the gate and passes up the wide white walk, he sees a flutter of female garments; his wife, looking fresh and cool and sweet, steps down from the veranda to meet him. At the bottom of the steps she stands waiting, with a smile of ineffable joy, an attitude of matchless grace and dignity. Ah, how beautiful she is! He springs forward with extended arms. As he is about to clasp her he feels a stunning blow upon the back of the neck; a blinding white light blazes all about him with a sound like the shock of a cannon—then all is darkness and silence!

Peyton Farquhar was dead; his body, with a broken neck, swung gently from side to side beneath the timbers of the Owl Creek Bridge.

Source: Ambrose Bierce, "An Occurrence at Owl Creek Bridge," *Current Literature, A Magazine of Record and Review*, vol. 21 [1897], no. 3, pp. 237–239.

PETER UNGER

A Defense of Skepticism

A CLASSICAL FORM OF SKEPTICAL ARGUMENT

There are certain arguments for skepticism which conform to a familiar … pattern or form. These arguments rely, at least for their psychological power, on vivid descriptions of exotic *contrast cases*. The following is one such rough argument, this one in support of skepticism regarding any

alleged *knowledge of an external world*. The exotic contrast case here concerns an evil scientist, and is described to be in line with the most up to date developments of science, or science fiction. We begin by arbitrarily choosing something concerning an external world which might conceivably, we suppose, be *known*, in one way or another, e.g., that there are rocks or, as we will understand it, that there is at least one rock.

Now, first, *if* someone, anyone *knows* that there are rocks, then the person *can know* the following quite exotic thing: There is *no* evil scientist deceiving him into *falsely* believing that there are rocks. This scientist uses electrodes to induce experiences and thus carries out his deceptions, concerning the existence of rocks or anything else. He first drills holes painlessly in the variously colored skulls, or shells, of his subjects and then implants his electrodes into the appropriate parts of their brains, or protoplasm, or systems. He sends patterns of electrical impulses into them through the electrodes, which are themselves connected by wires to a laboratory console on which he plays, punching various keys and buttons in accordance with his ideas of how the whole thing works and with his deceptive designs. The scientist's delight is intense, and it is caused not so much by his exercising his scientific and intellectual gifts as by the thought that he is deceiving various subjects about all sorts of things. Part of that delight is caused, on this supposition, by his thought that he is deceiving a certain person, perhaps yourself, into falsely believing that there are rocks. He is, then, an evil scientist, and he lives in a world which is entirely bereft of rocks.

Now, as we have agreed, (1) *if you know* that there are rocks, then you *can know* that there is no such scientist doing this to you [i.e., deceiving you to falsely believe that there are rocks]. But (2) no one *can* ever *know* that this exotic situation does *not obtain;* no one *can* ever *know* that there is *no* evil scientist who is, by means of electrodes, deceiving him into falsely believing there to be rocks. That is our second premise, and it is also very difficult to deny. So, thirdly, as a consequence of these two premises, we have our skeptical conclusion: (3) You never *know* that there are rocks. But of course we have chosen our person, and the matter of there being rocks, quite arbitrarily, and this argument, it surely seems, may be generalized to cover any external matter at all. From this, we may conclude, finally, that (4) nobody ever *knows* anything about the external world.

[A philosopher's] attempt to reverse our argument will proceed like this: (1) According to your argument, nobody ever *knows* that there are rocks. (2) But I *do* know that there are rocks. This is something concerning the external world, and I do know it. Hence, (3) somebody *does know* something about the external world. . . . And so, while I might not have known *before* that there is no such scientist, at least (4) I *now* do know that there is no evil scientist who is deceiving me into falsely believing that there are rocks. So far has the skeptical argument failed to challenge my knowledge successfully that it seems actually to have occasioned an increase in what I know about things.

While the robust character of this reply has a definite appeal, it also seems quite daring. Indeed, the more one thinks on it, the more it seems to be somewhat foolhardy and even dogmatic. One cannot help but think that for all this philosopher really can *know*, he might have all his experience artificially induced by electrodes, these being operated by a terribly evil scientist who, having an idea of what his "protege" is saying to himself, chuckles accordingly. . . .

[Suppose you were this philosopher.] Now, we may suppose that electrodes are removed, that your experiences are now brought about through your perception of actual surroundings, and you are, so to speak, forced to encounter your deceptive tormentor. Wouldn't you be made to feel quite *foolish*, even *embarrassed*, by your claims to *know*'? Indeed, you would seem to be exposed quite clearly as having been, not only wrong, but rather irrational and even dogmatic. . . .

It seems much better, perhaps perfectly all right, if you are instead only *confident* that there is no such scientist. It seems perfectly all right for you to *believe* there to be no evil scientist doing this. If you say, not only that you believe it, but that you have some *reason* to believe this thing, what you say *may* seem somewhat suspect, at least on reasoned reflection, but it doesn't have any obvious tint of dogmatism or irrationality to it. . . .

ORDINARY CASES

Largely because it is so exotic and bizarre, the case of a deceiving scientist lets one feel acutely the apparent irrationality in thinking oneself to know. But the exotic cases have no monopoly on generating feelings of irrationality.

[For example,] you may think you *know* that a certain city is the capital of a certain state, and you may feel quite content in this thought while watching another looking the matter up in the library. You will feel quite foolish, however, if the person announces the result to be *another* city, and if subsequent experience seems to show that announcement to be right. This will occur, I suggest, even if you are just an anonymous, disinterested bystander who happens to hear the question posed and the answer later announced. This is true even if the reference was a newspaper, *The Times*, and the capital was changed only yesterday. But these feelings will be very much less apparent, or will not occur at all, if you only feel very confident, at the outset, that the city is thus-and-such, which later is not announced. You might of course feel that you shouldn't be quite so confident of such things, or that you should watch out in the future. But you probably *wouldn't* feel, I suggest, that you were *irrational* to be confident of that thing at that time. Much less would you feel that you were *dogmatic* in so being. . . .

It is hard for us to think that there is any important similarity between such common cases as these and the case of someone thinking himself to *know* that *there are rocks*. Exotic contrast cases, like the case of the evil scientist, help one to appreciate that these cases are really essentially the same. By means of contrast cases, we encourage thinking of all sorts of new sequences of experience, sequences which people would never begin to imagine in the normal course of affairs. How would you react to such developments as *these*, no matter *how* exotic or unlikely? It appears that the proper reaction is to feel as irrational about claiming knowledge of rocks as you felt before, where, e.g., one was apparently caught in thought by the library reference to the state's capital. Who would have thought so, before thinking of contrast cases? Those cases help you see, I suggest, that in *either* case, no matter whether you are in fact right in the matter or whether wrong, thinking that you *know* manifests an attitude of dogmatism. Bizarre experiential sequences help show that there is no essential difference between any two external matters; the apparently most certain ones, like that of rocks, and the ones where thinking about *knowing* appears, even without the most exotic skeptical aids, *not* the way to think.

Source: Reprinted from *Ignorance* by Peter Unger. Copyright © Oxford University Press, 1975.

THOMAS NAGEL

How Do We Know Anything?

Ordinarily you have no doubts about the existence of the floor under your feet, or the tree outside the window, or your own teeth. In fact most of the time you don't even think about the mental states that make you aware of those things: you seem to be aware of them directly. But how do you know they really exist? Would things seem any different to you if in fact all these things existed *only* in your mind—if everything you took to be the real world outside was just a giant dream or hallucination, from which you will never wake up? …

How can you know that isn't what's going on? If all your experience were a dream with *nothing* outside, then any evidence you tried to use to prove to yourself that there was an outside world would just be part of the dream. If you knocked on the table or pinched yourself, you would hear the knock and feel the pinch, but that would be just one more thing going on inside your mind like everything else. It's no use: If you want to find out whether what's inside your mind is any guide to what's outside your mind, you can't depend on how things *seem*—from inside your mind—to give you the answer.

But what else is there to depend on? All your evidence about anything has to come through your mind—whether in the form of perception, the testimony of books and other people, or memory—and it is entirely consistent with everything you're aware of that *nothing at all* exists except the inside of your mind. . . .

Some would argue that radical skepticism of the kind I have been talking about is meaningless, because the idea of an external reality that *no one* could ever discover is meaningless. The argument is that a dream, for instance, has to be something from which you *can* wake up to discover that you have been asleep; a hallucination has to be something which others (or you later) *can* see is not really there. Impressions and appearances that do not correspond to reality must be contrasted with others that *do* correspond to reality, or else the contrast between appearance and reality is meaningless.

According to this view, the idea of a dream from which you can never wake up is not the idea of a dream at all: it is the idea of *reality*—the real world in which you live. Our idea of the things that exist is just our idea of what we can observe. (This view is sometimes called verificationism.) Sometimes our observations are mistaken, but that means they can be corrected by other observations—as when you wake up from a dream or discover that what you thought was a snake was just a shadow on the grass. But without some possibility of a correct view of how things are (either yours or someone else's), the thought that your impressions of the world are not true is meaningless.

If this is right, then the skeptic is kidding himself if he thinks he can imagine that the only thing that exists is his own mind. He is kidding himself, because it couldn't be true that the physical world doesn't really exist, unless somebody could *observe* that it doesn't exist. And what the skeptic is trying to imagine is precisely that there is no one to observe that or anything else—except of course the skeptic himself, and all he can observe is the inside of his own mind. So solipsism is meaningless. It tries to subtract the external world from the totality of my impressions; but it fails, because if the external world is subtracted, they stop being mere impressions, and become instead perceptions of reality.

Is this argument against solipsism and skepticism any good? Not unless reality can be defined as what we can observe. But are we really unable to understand the idea of a real world, or a fact about reality, that can't be observed by anyone, human or otherwise?

The skeptic will claim that if there is an external world, the things in it are observable because they exist, and not the other way around: that existence isn't the same thing as observability. And although we get the idea of dreams and hallucinations from cases where we think we *can* observe the contrast between our experiences and reality, it certainly seems as if the same idea can be extended to cases where the reality is not observable.

If that is right, it seems to follow that it is not meaningless to think that the world might consist of nothing but the inside of your mind, though neither you nor anyone else could find out that this was true. And if this is not meaningless, but is a possibility you must consider, there seems no way to prove that it is false, without arguing in a circle. So there may be no way out of the cage of your own mind. This is sometimes called the egocentric predicament.

And yet, after all this has been said, I have to admit it is practically impossible to believe seriously that all the things in the world around you might not really exist. Our acceptance of the external world is instinctive and powerful: we cannot just get rid of it by philosophical arguments. Not only do we go on acting *as if* other people and things exist: we *believe* that they do, even after we've gone through the arguments which appear to show we have no grounds for this belief. (We may have grounds, within the overall system of our beliefs about the world, for more particular beliefs about the existence of particular things: like a mouse in the breadbox, for example. But that is different. It assumes the existence of the external world.)

If a belief in the world outside our minds comes so naturally to us, perhaps we don't need grounds for it. We can just let it be and hope that we're right. And that in fact is what most people do after giving up the attempt to prove it: even if they can't give reasons against skepticism, they can't live with it either. But this means that we hold on to most of our ordinary beliefs about the world in face of the fact that (a) they might be completely false, and (b) we have no basis for ruling out that possibility.

We are left then with three questions:

1. Is it a meaningful possibility that the inside of your mind is the only thing that exists—or that even if there is a world outside your mind, it is totally unlike what you believe it to be?
2. If these things are possible, do you have any way of proving to yourself that they are not actually true?
3. If you can't prove that anything exists outside your own mind, is it all right to go on believing in the external world anyway?

Source: From *What Does It All Mean? A Very Short Introduction to Philosophy* by Thomas Nagel. © 1987 by Thomas Nagel. Reprinted by permission of Oxford University Press, Inc.

5.7 HISTORICAL SHOWCASE

Hume

This showcase features a British philosopher who profoundly influenced our views on human knowledge: David Hume. Hume raised profound questions about what we can know, what humans are, and whether God exists.

The man who most deeply influenced our modern perspectives on knowledge is the eighteenth-century philosopher David Hume. To a large extent, the philosophers who followed Hume either enthusiastically embraced his empiricist views or desperately sought to refute his claims. In either case, they were reacting to the radical empiricism he formulated. Everyone who comes after Hume must take his arguments into account.

This chapter showcases Hume because of his pervasive influence on our views of knowledge. In addition, by considering Hume's work, you can appreciate how our views of knowledge can affect our views of human nature, God, and the sciences. Hume's empiricist views on knowledge led him to raise crucial questions in all of these areas.

David Hume, the "ultimate skeptic," was born in 1711 into a comfortable family who lived on a small country estate called Ninewells in Edinburgh, Scotland. Hume's father died when David was 2. His mother, who took over the task of rearing him, said of the boy: "Davey is a well-meanin' critter, but uncommon weakminded." Nevertheless, a few weeks before his twelfth birthday, Hume entered Edinburgh University, where his family hoped he would be able to earn a degree in law. But university life was unpleasant for Hume, and two years later he dropped out without finishing his degree, having convinced his family that he could as easily study law at home. As Hume later wrote, "My studious disposition, my sobriety, and my industry gave my family a notion that the law was a proper profession for me. But I found an insurmountable aversion to everything but the pursuits of philosophy and general learning, and while they fancied I was poring over [the legal texts of] Voet and Vinnius, Cicero and Vergil were the authors which I was secretly devouring."[1] As a teenager, Hume sat around the house reading, all the while complaining he was being forced to struggle with various physical and mental ailments.

Then, in his late teens, Hume convinced himself that he had found a truly new philosophy. As he put it, "There seemed to be opened up to me a new Scene of Thought, which transported me beyond measure and made me, with an ardour natural to young men, throw up every other pleasure or business to apply entirely to it." David then spent much of his day trying to think out and express to others the "new" thoughts he believed that he had discovered.

Although living at home, Hume apparently managed to get around. At the age of 22 he was accused by a young woman named Anne Gal-braith of fathering her child, who had been conceived out of wedlock. Hume was sent away to work in the office of a Bristol merchant, but before the year was out he had quit the job he so detested and was sent to live in France on a tiny allowance. There, he spent the next three years living in "rigid frugality" while writing a book, *A Treatise of Human Nature*, in which he tried to express his new philosophy. The book was published in 1737, and by 1739 David was once again living at home in Ninewells, confident that he would soon be famous. To his bitter disappointment, when the book appeared, no one cared: "It fell dead-born from the press, without reaching such distinction as even to excite a murmur from the zealots."[2]

In 1745, Hume tried to get a position teaching ethics at Edinburgh University but was turned down. Instead, he took the job of tutor to a young marquise, who unfortunately turned out to be insane. The next several years Hume spent alternately working as a secretary for a general and living at home. He wrote continuously during this period, producing, among other things, a much shorter and simplified version of his *Treatise* titled *An Enquiry Concerning Human Understanding* and numerous essays on politics, literature, history, and economics. In 1752, Hume secured a position as librarian at Edinburgh University but was fired when the curators objected that his selection of books, such as *The History of Love-Making Among the French*, was obscene.

But by 1763 Hume's writings had made him famous, and that year, when he traveled to France as secretary for the British ambassador, he found himself at the center of the intellectual life of Parisian high society. There, he met

David Hume: "Here, therefore, is a proposition which might banish all metaphysical reasonings: When we entertain any suspicion that a philosophical term is employed without any meaning, we inquire, from what impression is that supposed idea derived? And if it be impossible to assign any, this will confirm our suspicion."

© Scottish National Portrait Gallery, Edinburgh, Scotland/The Bridgeman Art Library

---

1   David Hume, *The Essays Moral, Political and Literary* (Oxford: Oxford University Press, 1963), 608.

2   Ibid.

and had an intense love affair with the Countess de Boufflers. Three years later, having grown homesick, Hume left the countess and returned to England. After working for three years as undersecretary of state, Hume retired in 1769 to Edinburgh, where he lived "very opulent" and, finally, very famous, until his death in 1776.

Like Berkeley before him, Hume based his philosophy on the observation that all of our genuine knowledge (or "thoughts") about the world around us derives from the sensations provided by our senses. To explain this, Hume divided the contents of our minds into two groups, our sensations (which he called *impressions*) and our thoughts. All our thoughts, he held, are "copies" of our sensations and are derived from them. Even complex thoughts about things that do not exist, such as the thought of a golden mountain, are formed by putting together memories of simple sensations we once experienced: the sensation of gold and the sensation of mountain. Hume concluded that because genuine knowledge depends on prior sensory experience, assertions that are not based on sensory experience cannot be genuine knowledge:

> Everyone will readily allow that there is a considerable difference between the perceptions of the mind when a man feels the pain of excessive heat or the pleasure of moderate warmth, and when he afterwards recalls to his memory this sensation or anticipates it by his imagination. . . .
>
> Here, therefore, we may divide all the perceptions of the mind into two classes or species, which are distinguished by their different degrees of force and vivacity. The less forcible and lively are commonly denominated *Thoughts* or *Ideas*. . . . Let us . . . use a little freedom and call [the other class] *Impressions*. . . . By the term *impression*, then, I mean all our more lively perceptions, when we hear, or see, or feel, or love, or hate, or desire, or will. . . .
>
> Nothing, at first view, may seem more unbounded than the thought of man. . . . What never was seen or heard of, may yet be conceived. . . .
>
> But though our thought seems to possess this unbounded liberty, . . . all this creative power of the mind amounts to no more than the faculty of compounding, transposing, augmenting, or diminishing the materials afforded us by the senses and experience. When we think of a golden mountain, we only join two consistent ideas, *gold* and *mountain*, with which we were formerly acquainted. . . . In short, all the materials of thinking are derived either from our outward or our inward sentiments. . . . Or, to express myself in philosophical

language, all our ideas or more feeble perceptions are copies of our impressions or more lively ones.

> To prove this, the two following arguments will, I hope, be sufficient. First: When we analyze our thoughts or ideas, however compounded or sublime, we always find that they resolve themselves into such simple ideas as were copied from a precedent feeling or sentiment. Even ... the idea of GOD as meaning an infinitely intelligent, wise, and good Being, arises from reflecting on the operations of our own mind, and augmenting, without limit, those qualities. . . .
>
> Second: If it happens, from a defect of the organ, that a man is not susceptible of [some] sensation, we always find that he is as little susceptible of the correspondent ideas. A blind man can form no notion of colors, [nor] a deaf man of sounds.
>
> Here, therefore, is a proposition which . . . might . . . banish all that jargon which had so long taken possession of metaphysical reasonings. . . . When we entertain any suspicion that a philosophical term is employed without any meaning or idea (as is but too frequent), we need but inquire, *from what impression is that supposed idea derived?* And if it be impossible to assign any, this will serve to confirm our suspicion.[3]

Hume's "proposition"—that meaningful concepts must be "derived" from "impressions"—was a crucial step in his attempt to undermine our claims to knowledge. If a concept is not based on the sensations or "impressions" of our sense experience, he held, then it must be meaningless. Hume applied this idea ruthlessly. He argued that claims about the existence of an external world are meaningless. All we are acquainted with are the sensations we have. We have no grounds, then, for saying that an external world also exists that somehow causes us to have those sensations:

> By what argument can it be proved, that the perceptions of the mind must be caused by external objects, . . . and could not arise either from the energy of the mind itself, . . . or from some other cause still more unknown to us?
>
> It is a question of fact, whether the perceptions of the senses be produced by external objects resembling them: how shall this question be determined? By experience surely, as all other questions of a like nature. But here experience is, and must be entirely silent. The mind has never anything present to it but the perceptions, and cannot possibly reach any experience of their connection with

³   David Hume, *An Enquiry Concerning Human Understanding*, ed. L. A. Selby-Bigge (Oxford: Clarendon, 1894), 17–20.

objects. The supposition of such a connection is, therefore, without any foundation in reasoning.[4]

Not only are we unable to know whether there is an outer world; we are also unable to claim that there is any *inner self*. The very idea of a personal *me*, of the inner person called "I," has no foundation, Hume claims:

> There are some philosophers who imagine we are every moment intimately conscious of what we call our SELF; that we feel its existence and its continuance in existence; and are certain, beyond the evidence of a demonstration, both of its perfect identity and simplicity....
>
> Unluckily all these positive assertions are contrary to that very experience which is pleaded for them, nor have we any idea of *self*.... For from what impression could this idea be derived?... If any impression gives rise to the idea of self, that impression must continue invariably the same, through the whole course of our lives; since self is supposed to exist after that manner. But there is no impression constant and invariable. Pain and pleasure, grief and joy, passions and sensations succeed each other, and never all exist at the same time. It cannot, therefore, be from any of these impressions, or from any other, that the idea of self is derived; and consequently there is no such idea....
>
> For my part, when I enter most intimately into what I call *myself* I always stumble on some particular perception or other, of heat or cold, light or shade, love or hatred, pain or pleasure. I never can catch *myself* at any time without a perception, and never can observe anything but the perception....
>
> [S]etting aside some metaphysicians..., I may venture to affirm of the rest of mankind, that they are nothing but a bundle or collection of different perceptions, which succeed each other with an inconceivable rapidity, and are in a perpetual flux and movement.... The mind is a kind of theater, where several perceptions successively make their appearance, pass, re-pass, glide away, and mingle in an infinite variety of postures and situations.[5]

We cannot know whether there is any outer world beyond our sensations because all we are acquainted with are our sensations. Neither can we know whether there is an inner self because, again, all we experience is a constant flow of sensations, and we never perceive,

among these sensations, an object called an inner self. All we can say, Hume claims, is that we are "a bundle or collection of different perceptions." Beyond the existence of *these* perceptions, we can know nothing.

What, then, is left for us to know? Perhaps a great deal. For we are at least acquainted with the perceptions our senses display before us. And from these perceptions we can reason to others. For example, if I perceive a flame, then I know that there will be heat; if I hear a voice, then I know that a person must be present. This kind of knowledge is based on our knowledge of cause and effect. I have learned that flames *cause* heat, so I reason from the flame to the heat; I have found that voices are the *effects* of people, so I reason from the voice to the person. In fact, all the natural sciences consist of laws based on our knowledge of cause and effect. On the basis of a few experiments, for example, the science of physics asserts that if an object is dropped, gravity will cause it to fall at 32 feet per second per second. Clearly, then, from the present things we perceive, our knowledge of causes enables us to know what the future will be like. And all the natural sciences—physics, chemistry, biology—are based on this kind of causal knowledge.

But Hume, in a devastating attack on knowledge, argues that none of our knowledge of cause and effect has a rational basis. And if our causal knowledge is not rationally justified, then all the natural sciences are similarly unjustified. Hume begins by pointing out that all our knowledge of causal laws rests on our experience of the world:

> All reasoning concerning matter of fact seems to be founded on the relation of *Cause and Effect*.... A man, finding a watch or any other machine in a desert island, would conclude that there had once been men in that island. All our reasonings concerning fact are of the same nature.... The hearing of an articulate voice and rational discourse in the dark assures us of the presence of some person. Why? Because these are the effects of the human [being]....
>
> If we would satisfy ourselves, therefore, concerning the nature of that evidence which assures us of matters of fact, we must inquire how we arrive at the knowledge of cause and effect.
>
> I shall venture to affirm, as a general proposition which admits of no exception, that the knowledge of this relation ...arises entirely from experience, when we find that any particular objects are constantly conjoined with each other.[6]

---

4   Ibid., 152–153.
5   David Hume, *A Treatise of Human Nature*, ed. L. A. Selby-Bigge (Oxford: Clarendon, 1896), 251–253.

6   Hume, *An Enquiry Concerning Human Understanding*, 26–27.

All causal knowledge, Hume is saying, is based on our experience that in the past, events of one kind have been "constantly conjoined" with events of another kind. In the past, for example, I may have seen that when one billiard ball hits another, the second ball always rolls away. Thus, the event of one billiard ball striking another has been "constantly conjoined" in my past experience with the event of the second ball rolling away. All the causal laws of the natural sciences and all the causal knowledge of our everyday lives, then, are based on our past experience of such "constant conjunctions." But this scientific and everyday reliance on past experience, Hume points out, raises a problem. How do we know that past experience is a reliable guide to the future?

> We always presume when we see like sensible qualities, ... that effects similar to those which we have experienced will follow from them. . . . The bread which I formerly ate nourished me. . . . But does it follow that other bread must also nourish me at another time? The consequence seems nowise necessary. . . . These two propositions are far from being the same: *I have found that such an object has always been attended with such an effect*, and *I foresee, that other objects which are, in appearance similar, will be attended with similar effects*. The connection between these two propositions is not intuitive.[7]

In this passage, Hume suggests that all causal reasoning is based on the *assumption* that the future will be like the past. When I see a flame and reason that it will be hot, it is because *in the past* when I perceived flame I also perceived heat. But, Hume asks, how do we know that the future will be like the past? Clearly, there is no way of *proving* that the future will be like the past:

> That there are no demonstrative arguments in the case seems evident, since it implies no contradiction that the course of nature may change, and that an object, seemingly like those which we have experienced, may be attended with different or contrary effects. May I not clearly and distinctly conceive that a body falling from the clouds, and which in all other respects resembles snow, has yet the taste of salt or feeling of fire? Is there any more intelligible proposition than to affirm that all the trees will flourish in December and January and decay in May and June? Now whatever is intelligible and can be distinctly conceived, implies no

contradiction and can never be proved false by any demonstrative argument.[8]

So, we cannot *prove* with "demonstrative arguments" that the future will be like the past. Perhaps, then, we know that the future will be like the past because of *past experience?* No, Hume replies, we cannot use past experience to show that the future will be like the past. For if we don't know that the future will be like the past, then we don't know that *past* experience is a reliable guide. To argue that past experience proves we can rely on past experience is to argue in a circle:

> For all inferences from experience suppose, as their foundation, that the future will resemble the past, and that similar powers will be conjoined with similar sensible qualities. If there be any suspicion that the course of nature may change, and that the past may be no rule for the future, all experience becomes useless, and can give rise to no inference or conclusion. It is impossible, therefore, that any arguments from experience can prove this resemblance of the past to the future, since all these arguments are founded on the supposition of that resemblance. Let the course of things be allowed hitherto ever so regular, that alone, without some new argument or inference proves not that for the future it will continue so. Their secret nature and consequently all their effects and influence, may change, without any change in their sensible qualities. This happens sometimes, and with regard to some objects: why may it not happen always, and with regard to all objects? What logic, what process of argument, secures you against this supposition?[9]

Hume's conclusion is devastating: We have no way of *knowing* that causal claims are justified. All the causal laws of the sciences and our everyday causal reasonings are based on an assumption that we cannot prove or rationally justify: the assumption that the future will be like the past. But if we cannot rationally show that the future will be like the past, then why do we continually move past our experience to conclusions about the future? Because, Hume claims, we are creatures of nonrational habit:

> Suppose [a person] has lived so long in the world as to have observed similar objects or events to be

7 Ibid., 33–34.

8 Ibid., 35.
9 Ibid., 37–38.

constantly conjoined together. What is the consequence of this experience? He immediately infers the existence of one object from the appearance of the other. . . . There is some . . . principle which determines him to form such a conclusion.

This principle is CUSTOM or HABIT. For wherever the repetition of any particular act or operation produces a propensity to renew the same act or operation, without being impelled by any reasoning or process of the understanding, we always say that this propensity is the effect of *custom*. . . .

Custom, then, is the great guide of human life. It is that principle alone which renders our experience useful to us, and makes us expect, for the future, a similar train of events with those which have appeared in the past.[10]

All claims about causal connections, then, are based on our experience that, in the past, events of a certain kind have been "constantly conjoined" with events of another kind. And habit moves us from this past experience to the conclusion that, in the future, all similar events will be similarly conjoined. In other words, from our past experience of the constant conjunction of events, we conclude by habit that one kind of event "causes" a second kind. But we cannot provide any rational justification for this habit of moving from the past to the future. All the causal laws of the sciences and all the causal "knowledge" of everyday life are based on nonrational "habit."

We cannot know whether an external world exists; we cannot say that the self exists; we cannot rationally justify the causal laws of any of the natural sciences or the causal reasonings of our everyday life. Can skepticism extend further? Yes. Hume went on to attack the foundations of religious belief: the claim that God exists.

Hume believed that the best arguments for God's existence were causal arguments: those that hold that God must exist because the design of the universe requires an all-powerful intelligent Creator. But all causal reasonings depend on past experience, Hume points out, and we have no past experience of other gods creating universes. Although our past experience of human beings and their products leads us to say that things such as watches require intelligent human creators, we have no past experience of other universes and gods that could lead

us to say that universes require intelligent gods to create them:

In works of *human* art and contrivance, it is allowable to advance from the effect to the cause, and returning back from the cause, to form new inferences concerning the effect. . . . But what is the foundation of this method of reasoning? Plainly this: that man is a being whom we know by experience. . . . When, therefore, we find that any work has proceeded from the skill and industry of man, as we are otherwise acquainted with the nature of the animal, we can draw a hundred inferences concerning what may be expected from him; and these inferences will all be founded in experience and observation.

The case is not the same with our reasonings from the works of nature. The Deity is known to us only by his productions, and is a single being in the universe, not comprehended under any species or genus, from whose experienced attributes or qualities we can, by analogy, infer any attribute or quality in him. . . .

I much doubt whether it be possible for a cause to be known only by its effect ... [when it has] no parallel and no similarity with any other cause or object that has ever fallen under our observation. It is only when two species of objects are found to be constantly conjoined, that we can infer the one from the other; and were an effect presented, which was entirely singular, and could not be comprehended under any known *species*, I do not see that we could form any conjecture or inference at all concerning its cause. If experience and observation and analogy be, indeed, the only guides which we can reasonably follow in inferences of this nature, both the effect and cause must bear a similarity and resemblance to other effects and causes which we know, and which we have found in many instances to be conjoined with each other. I leave to your own reflection to pursue the consequences of this principle.[11]

The consequence of this principle, of course, is that we cannot argue from the existence of an orderly universe to the existence of an intelligent God. Hume's skepticism, then, leaves our edifice of knowledge in shambles. The external world, the self, the causal laws of the natural sciences, our everyday causal reasoning, and our religious claims are all called into question. Can knowledge be saved? Many people think that Hume's arguments definitively

---

10   Ibid., 42–44.

11   Ibid., 143–144, 148.

destroyed all hope that it might be. But in Germany, a very ordinary man, Immanuel Kant, was spurred by Hume's skepticism into constructing what many people look on as the most breathtakingly creative response that could be made to Hume. Whether that response succeeded, you must decide after reading the showcase on Kant in the next chapter.

QUESTIONS

1. How would you explain Hume's distinction between "impressions" and "ideas"? How can Hume say that all ideas are "copies" of impressions? Does Hume bring up any ideas that he himself says are *not* copies of impressions?

2. Hume says that philosophical terms must be tested by asking "from what impression is that supposed idea derived?" Do you think this is a good test? Are there any terms or "supposed ideas" that you would have to reject if you applied this test to your own ideas? If you applied this test to Hume's own philosophical terms, do you think they would all pass his test? Why?

3. How are Hume's ideas about the self similar to the Buddhist view of the self examined in Chapter 2? Do you think Hume's view of the self is a correct analysis of *your* self? Why?

4. How would you summarize Hume's criticism of the assumption that the future will resemble the past? Can you detect any weaknesses in his criticism? Explain in your own words what Hume means when he writes, "It is impossible, therefore, that any arguments from experience can prove this resemblance of the past to the future, since all these arguments are founded on the supposition of that resemblance."

5. Hume asserts that all ideas are copies of impressions. Is this a generalization from his own experience? If so, then how do you think Hume would respond to this criticism: "Because Hume has shown that past experience cannot provide real knowledge of the future, he cannot claim to know that all ideas must be, now and in the future, copies of impressions"?

6. Do you see any way of showing that Hume must be mistaken in his claim that the causal laws of the sciences rest on nothing more than "habit"?

6 Truth

No one is so wrong as the man who knows all the answers.

THOMAS MERTON

OUTLINE AND LEARNING OBJECTIVES

6.1 Knowledge and Truth

LEARNING OBJECTIVE: When finished, you'll be able to:

- Explain why knowledge has been defined as a justified true belief, and why this definition has been questioned.

6.2 What Is Truth?

LEARNING OBJECTIVES: When finished, you'll be able to:

- Explain and evaluate the correspondence, coherence, and pragmatic views of truth.
- Explain why these views matter.

6.3 Does Science Give Us Truth?

LEARNING OBJECTIVES: When finished, you'll be able to:

- Describe some of the main strengths and weaknesses of the instrumental, realist, and conceptual relativist views of science.
- Explain how these views of science are related to the pragmatic, correspondence, and coherence theories of truth.

6.4 Can Interpretations Be True?

LEARNING OBJECTIVES: When finished, you'll be able to:

- Explain why truth matters when interpreting texts.
- Relate the correspondence, pragmatic, and coherence views of truth to Aquinas', Wittgenstein's, and Gadamer's views of true interpretations.

Chapter Summary

6.5 Readings

Ryunosuke Akutagawa, "In a Grove"

Hugh Tomlinson, "After Truth: Post-Modernism and the Rhetoric of Science"

John Searle, "Reality and Truth"

6.6 Historical Showcase: Kant

6.1 Knowledge and Truth

Suppose you have a girlfriend. You're a young man and have been dating her for a long time. Although you love her passionately, you're unsure that she still loves you. You're not sure about her love because she doesn't seem as interested in your company as she used to be. Sometimes she seems bored with you and more interested in others. Yet when you ask her, she says, 'Yes, I still love you very much." Is she telling you the truth? The very thought that she might not be telling the truth makes you miserable. You ask her outright whether she's telling you the truth. She's offended that you should doubt her. "Of course I'm telling you the truth!" she says. "Of course I still love you!" Perhaps for several days you decide that you'll take her words as true. After all, when you suspect her words are false, you feel awful. Since it makes you feel better and because you're *pragmatic,* you decide to accept that her words are true. At least this way you feel the way you want to feel.

Even though we distinguish between truth and falsity hundreds of times a day, we may have difficulty expressing that distinction. What is truth? *La condition humaine* (the human condition), 1933. Artist: René Magritte, (1898–1967), Belgian. Location: private collection.

Gianni Dagli Orti/Private Collection/The Art Archive/Picture Desk/© 2010 C. Herscovici, London/Artist Rights Society (ARS), New York

But then you start to feel bad again and think that this kind of truth isn't what you need. Getting at the truth about your lover, you think, is more than just accepting whatever succeeds in making you feel good. So, you start thinking about a different kind of truth. You think that maybe the truth about her love lies in what her actions indicate. Her protestations of love just don't fit with what you believe her actions show; in other words, her statements don't *cohere* with your beliefs about what her actions mean. You tell her that you don't think she's telling you the truth when she says she loves you because her actions show that her love has gone. She replies that you're mistaken. You're putting meanings on her actions that aren't there. Her actions don't mean she is bored with you, she says. It's just that she feels relaxed around you now and feels she can be herself without always needing to put up a happy front with you. Now you're extremely perplexed. You were ready to think that her words were true only if they fit with your beliefs about what her actions meant. Yet you aren't sure now whether these beliefs of yours about what her actions mean are themselves true.

THINKING LIKE A PHILOSOPHER

The textbook describes how difficult it was for a certain young man to know the truth about how his girlfriend felt about him. Describe a similar situation in which you were involved. That is, describe a situation in which you had a strong desire to know the truth about how another person felt about you, yet could not seem to find out. How would you describe the kind of truth you were trying to get? Did you eventually get the truth? How did you know it was the truth?

Then you become convinced that the truth you most want is the truth about what really lies in her heart. You want the facts. What matters isn't what makes you feel good inside yourself or what fits with the other beliefs inside your head. What you want is the truth about what's out there in the real world; you want the truth about what's really going on there inside her heart. What you want to know is whether what she says *corresponds* with what in fact her real feelings are. So, though you dread the answer, you ask her, "What do you really feel in your heart toward me?" Her response leaves you even more perplexed: "I'm not sure I know.

I think the feelings I have for you are feelings of love. But I don't think I understand myself, or love, well enough to be sure. I think I have a lot of feelings toward you in my heart, but I'm often confused about my feelings and don't quite know what they are or what they mean. That's all I can tell you."

Now you're completely at a loss. You thought you could get at the truth if you could just get outside yourself and find out what was really there inside her heart. Yet what is in her heart is as amorphous as a cloud. You wonder now what truth itself is or even if there's such a thing as truth. Is truth just what makes us have the good feelings we want to have? Is it what fits with our system of beliefs and meanings? Is truth about what corresponds with the facts in the real world outside of us? What do we mean, then, when we say that a belief or statement is true?

The history of philosophy records several ways of looking at truth that are similar to the three kinds of truth you've just been considering. The pragmatic theory says, roughly, that our beliefs are true when they work (i.e., when they get us what we want). The coherence theory says that a belief is true when it fits with our other beliefs and meanings. The correspondence theory says that a belief is true when it corresponds with what is "out there" in the real world. Each of these makes a unique contribution to understanding the nature of truth. As our short discussion already suggests, it's important to be clear about what truth means. And it's particularly important when we're searching for the truth about ourselves and our relationships with others. Shortly, we'll look at the three theories starting with the correspondence theory, and then the coherence view, and ending with the pragmatic theory. Later, when we look at truth in science and in interpretation, we will see that these three theories again play an important role in understanding truth in both of these areas.

Before we look at truth, however, we need to say something about the concept of knowledge. In the last chapter we were able to discuss the sources of knowledge without anything more than our ordinary everyday understanding of what we mean by knowledge. But when discussing the concept of truth, the lack of a clear understanding of knowledge can get us into trouble. So we'll look briefly, now, at what knowledge means. We'll also say a few brief words about what philosophers call "truth-bearers."

QUICK REVIEW
In different situations in real life we seem to believe *truth* means different things and is established in different ways: Truth may be (1) what gets us what we want, (2) what fits with our other beliefs and meanings, and (3) what corresponds with what is "out there" in the real world.

Knowledge as Justified True Belief

What do you mean when you say you *know* something? For instance, "I know my girlfriend loves me." Just what do you mean when you say that? Stating the question more formally, if we let *p* represent any proposition, what are you asserting when you claim: "I know that *p*"?

For one thing, you must *believe* that *p* is the case. If you *know* that your girlfriend loves you, then you have to at least *believe* she does. Imagine what your friends would think if you said, "I know that my girlfriend loves me, but I don't believe she does." They'd think you were talking a bit weirdly, and rightly so. After all, if you're claiming to know something, how can you not believe it? Of course, we sometimes seem to dissociate belief from knowledge, as in "I know the president has been assassinated, but I just don't believe it!" However, this is a rhetorical utterance. We *do* believe it; otherwise, we wouldn't be shocked. Intellectually we believe it, but emotionally we're incredulous. To assert that you know *p*, then, is to assert at least that you believe *p*. Thus, "I know *p*" implies "I believe *p*."

 THINKING LIKE A PHILOSOPHER

The textbook argues that you know something only if it is something that you believe, that you are justified in believing, and that is true. Otherwise you don't have real knowledge but, at most, just a belief. What are some of the beliefs you have that you feel count as real knowledge. Explain for each of those beliefs why you are justified in having that belief. Explain for each of those beliefs how you know that the belief is true.

Knowledge also implies having evidence or justification for what you believe. When you say, "I know that my girlfriend loves me," you imply not only that you believe it but also that you have some evidence or reasons to believe it. So, "I know *p*" implies "I have evidence or justification for *p*." Suppose that someone claimed to know that the stock market will plunge next week. You'd likely ask, "How do you know that?" If the person responds, "I just believe it for no reason," you wouldn't think that he really knows the market will fall. Belief indicates merely an attitude toward something; it may, however, not be justified, and then could not count as knowledge. A belief is justified when you have adequate evidence or reasons for the belief. If someone claims to know that the stock market will plunge next week, she is implying that she believes it and that her belief is justified, that is, she has adequate evidence or sufficient reasons for his belief.

So, can we say that knowledge is a justified belief? Not quite. Suppose you believe your girlfriend loves you, and your justification for that belief is that she has told you she loves you several times. But a week later you discover she has been having an affair with your best friend and although she stopped loving you several months ago, she has not wanted to hurt you and so has been lying about her feelings toward you. Can you continue to say that last week you knew she loved you? No. If your belief that she loved you was false, then you cannot say that you *knew* she loved you. You would have to say that you *thought* she loved you, but you didn't really *know* how she felt. Knowledge is more than having a justified belief. Real knowledge requires that what you say you know has to be true. Knowledge is a justified belief that's *true*. You may believe your girlfriend loves you, and your belief may be justified. Still, to *know* she loves you, you need more than justified belief: Your belief must also be true.

QUICK REVIEW
The traditional view of knowledge says that it is justified true belief.

We have now reached a useful and traditional characterization of knowledge. Knowledge is (1) a belief that is (2) justified and (3) true. But how adequate is this traditional characterization of knowledge? Is knowledge nothing more than a justified true belief? Is having a justified true belief sufficient for having knowledge, or does knowledge involve something more?

ANALYZING THE READING

Edmund Gettier showed that knowledge is more than justified true belief by giving examples of people whose belief was true and justified, yet was not knowledge. The belief was not knowledge because it turned out to be true by accident. Can you come up with your own example of someone whose belief is true and justified yet is not knowledge?

Unfortunately, it turns out that the notion of justified true belief does not fully capture what knowledge is. Knowledge is more than a justified true belief. But figuring out what more it involves is very difficult. To understand this difficulty, consider the following example of a person who has a justified true belief but does not have knowledge. Incidentally, this kind of example is called a *Gettier example,* after the philosopher Edmund Gettier, who first drew our attention to these examples and to the difficulties that they raise for our concept of knowledge.

Suppose that John is a very careful person who before today has never made a mistake. Today he plans to buy some low-fat milk at the store. By mistake, however, he incorrectly tells his friend Sam that he intends to buy whole milk. Later, when John goes to the store (still planning to buy low-fat milk), he accidentally picks up a container of whole milk. Not realizing his second mistake, he pays for the milk and leaves the store with it. Now suppose that someone asks Sam whether he knows what kind of milk John bought at the store. Sam, of course, replies that he knows that John bought whole milk. Notice that Sam is indeed justified in thinking that John bought whole milk because he knows that John tells the truth and has never before made a mistake. Sam also believes that John bought whole milk. And, by accident, it is true that John bought whole milk. So, Sam has a justified true belief. Nevertheless, we would all agree that Sam doesn't really know that John bought whole milk. Because Sam's belief was based on a falsehood (the statement that John made when he told Sam that he intended to buy whole milk) that turned out to be true entirely by accident, we are reluctant to say that his belief is genuine knowledge. Yet it is a justified true belief.

This example shows that knowledge is more than a justified true belief. But what more is needed to have genuine knowledge? Unfortunately, we cannot say. Many philosophers have spent a lot of time and effort trying to uncover what this "more" is. Yet no one has come up with a solution that has persuaded everyone. Nevertheless, we do know that knowledge requires at least a justified true belief.[1] And for our purposes, that characterization of knowledge should be enough to avoid any major confusions in our discussions of truth.

There is one more clarification we need to make related to what can be true. Discussions of truth often raise this question: What kinds of things can be true? It turns out that lots of things can be true. We can say a friend, for example, is a true friend. A painting can be a true representation of someone. An archer's aim can be true. We can say of someone that she is a true perfectionist, or a true musician, or a true artist. A story can be a true story. Someone can show her true feelings.

ANALYZING THE READING

The textbook suggests that many things can be true including a true friend, a true story, a true perfectionist, a true artist, and a person's true feelings. What do you think "true" means in each of these cases. For example, what does it mean to say that someone is a *true* friend?

Yet none of these uses of true have yet identified the kind of truth we discussed above and will discuss in the rest of this chapter. In our discussion of the problem of knowing what a lover thinks of us, we were talking about truth as it applies to a person's beliefs and statements. That is the kind of truth we will discuss here. What kinds of things can be true in this sense of true? Obviously beliefs and statements can be true in this sense, but also propositions, sentences, thoughts, utterances, declarations, and judgments. These are all called "truth-bearers" because they are the kinds of things that can bear the quality of being true.

Philosophers have often debated whether all the truth-bearers we just listed should be allowed to count as genuine truth-bearers. Some philosophers have argued that some of the truth-bearers on our list do not qualify as genuine truth-bearers. Others have argued that some of these truth-bearers are true only in a degenerative and derivative sense, and others have held that some of these truth-bearers don't even exist! Those debates force us to say here, at the beginning of our discussion, what we will count as genuine truth-bearers. We are going to be generous and allow all of the things we listed to be truth-bearers. For the most part, however, we will be talking about truth as it applies to beliefs, propositions, and statements. And, to keep things simple, we will use these three terms interchangeably. For example, we will sometimes talk about a certain statement as true, and then almost immediately talk about the equivalent belief or proposition as true. The point that needs to be made here is that you should not think that we are implying something important when we change from using one of these terms to using a different one. Throughout this chapter these three—beliefs, propositions, and statements—will be used as equivalent, or at least similar, kinds of truth-bearers.

---

[1]   Gettier's essay and several attempts to deal with this issue can be found in Paul K Moser and Arnold vander Nat, eds., *Human Knowledge: Classical and Contemporary Approaches,* 3rd ed. (New York: Oxford University Press, 2002).

PHILOSOPHY AT THE MOVIES

Watch *The Truman Show* (1998), in which Truman Burbank, not realizing that all his life he has lived in a television studio staged to look like a small town with "friends" who are really actors, and also not realizing that all his activities have been continuously televised to people around the world, finally tries to escape when it dawns on him that nothing around him is what it seems to be. Is Christof right when he says to Truman: "There's no more truth out there than there is in the world I created for you"? What does truth mean for Christof? Is Truman justified in believing that the town around him is real? Should having beliefs that are justified matter to Truman so long as he's happy? Why? Is it better to be happy and deceived or to struggle but know the truth? Why?

6.2 What Is Truth?

In June 2004, a Belgian jury found Marc Dutroux guilty of murder. He had kidnapped, imprisoned, and repeatedly raped six girls—all children—and murdered four of them. Two of the girls he murdered were 8-year-olds who starved to death in a dungeon in his basement and two others he buried alive. Dutroux made several videos of himself raping the children. The Dutroux case dragged on for almost ten years amid numerous charges that government officials were protecting Dutroux. Dutroux claimed he was part of a ring of pedophiles that included government officials in Belgium and around Europe for whom he procured children. A young woman, Regina Louf, came forward and said that she had been a victim of that ring. As a child, she said, she had been sexually abused and tortured by the pedophile group Detroux described and to which he belonged. She identified several members of the ring, and many of them were highly respected people. They included police officers, bankers, doctors, businessmen, judges, politicians, and members of the nobility. Then, several other women came forward with similar stories. Faced with an outraged public, the government appointed the Dutroux Inquiry Commission to get to the truth about the Dutroux case.[2]

The meetings of the Commission were televised and often heated. During a Commission meeting, two witnesses, a policeman named Lesage and a judge named Doutrewe, were questioned about an important file on Dutroux. Under oath, the policeman testified that he had sent the file to the judge who had to have received it. The judge, also under oath, asserted vehemently that the file was not sent to him and so he never received it. The next day Professor Yves Winkin, a well-known professor of anthropology, was interviewed by *Le Soir*, a Belgian newspaper:

> *Le Soir:* The confrontation [between Officer Lesage and Judge Doutrewe] was stimulated by an almost ultimate search for truth. Does truth exist?

---

[2]   The information in this paragraph is based on the following sources: BBC News, "Belgian Sex Ring 'Ignored,'" January 22, 2002, http://news.bbc.co.uk/27hi/europe/1774436.stm (accessed June 10, 2009); BBC News, "Regina Louf's Testimony," May 2, 2002, http://news.bbc.co.uk/1/hi/programmes/correspondent_europe/1962244.stm (accessed June 10, 2009); BBC News, "Belgium's X-Files—An Olenka Frenkiel Investigation," May 2, 2002, http://news.bbc.co.uk/2/hi/programmes/correspondent/1944428.stm (accessed June 10, 2009); Rachael Bell, "Marc Dutroux," Tru TV Tru Crime Library,http://www.trutv.com/library/crime/serial_killers/predators/dutroux/evil_1.html (accessed June 10, 2009); Institute for the Study of Globalization and Covert Politics, "Beyond the Dutroux Affair," http://www.isgp.eu/dutroux/Belgian_X_dossiers_of_the_Dutroux_affair.htm#girl (accessed June 10, 2009).

Winkin: I think that all the work of the Commission is based on a sort of presupposition that there exists, not *a* truth, but *the* truth—which if one presses hard enough, will finally come out. However, anthropologically, there are only partial truths, shared by a larger or smaller number of people: a group, a family, a firm. There is no transcendent truth. Therefore, I don't think that judge Doutrewe or officer Lesage are hiding anything: both are telling their truth. Truth is always linked to an organization, depending upon the elements that are perceived as important. It is not surprising that these two people, representing two very different professional universes, should each set forth a different truth.[3]

Winkin's statement about the Dutroux Commission has significant implications about the nature of truth. First, it implies that what is true in relation to one person need not be true in relation to another person. Truth is relative. Whether a statement is true depends on who makes the statement. Second, it claims that there is no such thing as *the* truth about whether government officials who are pedophiles were protecting Dutroux. That is, in Winkin's view there's no such thing as the real "objective" truth. There is no objective truth about whether there's a ring of powerful people in Europe who kidnap, abuse, and torture children. And there is no objective truth about whether those powerful people were protecting Dutroux

David Martin/AFP/Getty Images

Accused pedophile Marc Dutroux pretends to have a heart attack in front of the courthouse upon his arrival to appear before the Council Chamber in 2002.

from prosecution. If your group "shares" the belief that there is ring of pedophiles operating throughout Europe, then it's true that there is. But if your group doesn't share these beliefs, then it isn't true that such a ring exists. Third, in Winkin's view we can't even say that it's either true or false that Lesage sent the file to Judge Doutrewe. If you're Lesage, then because you just *believe* you sent the file, it's really *true* that you sent it. And if you're Doutrewe, then you don't *believe* Lesage sent the file, so it's really *true* that he didn't. Both beliefs are really true even though they contradict each other.

Winkin's view of truth is one that many philosophers also hold. Some theories of truth would at least partially support Winkin's views. These include, as you will see, some versions of the pragmatic and the coherence theories of truth. But there is at least one theory that firmly rejects Winkin's views, and that is the correspondence theory of truth.

Correspondence Theory

Undoubtedly the most popular theory of truth is the **correspondence theory**. The correspondence theory says that truth is an agreement or correspondence between a proposition and some fact in the real world. Take the proposition that "Water boils at 212 degrees Fahrenheit at sea level." The correspondence theory says this is a true proposition because it corresponds with the fact that in the real world, water boils at 212 degrees Fahrenheit at sea level. The correspondence theory assumes, then, that there is a real world whose existence does not depend on our beliefs, thoughts, or perceptions. That is, it assumes that a real world exists whether or not we believe it, think about it, or perceive it. This independent world or reality contains facts. And a belief, statement, or proposition is true when what it states corresponds with a fact in this real independent world.

> **QUICK REVIEW**
> The correspondence theory says that a proposition is true when it agrees with or corresponds to a fact.

---

[3]   Quoted in Alan Sokal and Jean Bricmont, *Fashionable Nonsense* (New York: Picador USA, 1998).

Truth and Paradox

The concept of truth was intensively studied by logicians during the twentieth century. In fact, the vigorous attempts that logicians and mathematicians made to clarify the notion of truth led to some of the greatest and most far-reaching mathematical discoveries of the century. Much of this work was inspired by the realization that the very notion of truth seems to give rise to troublesome paradoxes and contradictions.

One of the earliest examples of the troublesome contradictions that the notion of truth can create is attributed to the ancient Greek philosopher Eubulides, who wrote, "A man says that he is not telling the truth. Is what he says true or false?" If what the man says is true, then the man is not telling the truth, so what he says must be false! But if what the man says is false, then it is false that he is not telling the truth, so what he says must be true! Thus, assuming what the man says is true leads us to a contradiction, and assuming what the man says is not true also leads us to a contradiction. In either case, the very notion of truth seems to generate a contradiction.

The same kinds of contradictions are generated by much simpler statements, such as "This statement is not true" or

> The sentence in the box on this page is false.

But why should it matter that the very concept of truth generates contradictions? Because, unfortunately, once a single contradiction is allowed, it is easy to prove with rigorous logic that any *statement whatsoever* is true. That is, anything can be proved once you accept a contradiction. This is fairly easy to show.

Let the letter Q stand for any statement you want, such as "Unicorns exist." Now suppose that you accept as true the statement "God is good." Call this statement

P. And suppose you also accept as true the contradictory statement "God is not good." Call this statement *not-P*. Now consider the following statement:

1. *Either P is true or Q is true.*

You must accept that statement 1 is true because you previously accepted that *P* is true. However, because you also accepted *not-P*, this means that *P* is not true. That is, you must also accept statement 2:

2. *P is not true.*

Now you have accepted statements 1 and 2. But from statements 1 and 2, of course, it logically follows that

3. *Q is true.*

And so you must accept that *Q* is true—that is, that unicorns exist! By accepting the contradiction that *P* is true and that *not-P* is also true, we can logically prove that unicorns exist. In fact, anything at all can be proved with rigorous logic once a contradiction is accepted.

The terrible consequences that would follow should the concept of truth involve contradictions were what led twentieth-century logicians and mathematicians to invest considerable energy in trying to come up with ways to avoid contradictions. Unfortunately, this work has not yet come to any firm conclusions. The possibility that our notion of truth may be contradictory still lurks.

1. Can you conceive of some ways of avoiding the contradictions that truth seems to involve?

2. Can you conceive of some ways of avoiding the argument that once a contradiction is accepted, anything can be proved?

The correspondence theory has had a long history. Aristotle stated a simplified form of the theory when he said in his *Metaphysics* that "to say of what is that it is, and of what is not that it is not, is true." Presumably, he meant that if what a statement says corresponds with the facts of reality, then it is true. Aquinas provided a somewhat fuller but still succinct version of the theory. He wrote the following in his treatise *On Truth:* "A judgment is said to be true when it conforms to the external reality." Several more recent philosophers have proposed versions of the correspondence theory. These have included Descartes, Locke, Hume, and Kant.

Russell's Correspondence Theory. Bertrand Russell, a twentieth-century British philosopher, is a classic example of a correspondence theorist. Russell maintains that there is a realm of facts whose existence does not depend on us. A belief is true when it corresponds with a fact—that is, when it corresponds to some fact in the real world. Thus, the belief that Paris is in France is true because that belief corresponds to the fact that Paris is in France. In *The Problems of Philosophy*, Russell expresses his position:

> [I]t is to be observed that the truth or falsehood of a belief always depends upon something which lies outside the belief itself. If I believe that Charles I died on the scaffold, I believe truly, not because of any intrinsic quality of my belief, which can be discovered by merely examining the belief, but because of an historical event which happened two and a half centuries ago. If I believe that Charles I died in his bed, I believe falsely: no degree of vividness in my belief, or of care in arriving at it, prevents it from being false, again because of what happened long ago, and not because of any intrinsic property of my belief. Hence, although truth and falsehood are properties of beliefs, they are properties dependent upon the relations of the beliefs to other things, not upon any internal quality of the beliefs.
>
> . . . the above requisite leads us to adopt the view—which has on the whole been commonest among philosophers—that truth consists in some form of correspondence between belief and fact.[4]

In the preceding passage, Russell claims that the truth or falsity of a belief does not depend on the nature of the belief itself, but on something "outside the belief." In particular, truth is a relationship between a belief and things in the world outside the belief. In other words, truth is a "correspondence between belief and fact."

Russell goes on to try to explain what he means by "correspondence"—that is, what it means to say that a belief "corresponds" to a fact. Russell calls the constituents or parts of a belief its "objects" or "object-terms." For example, in the belief that Booth shot Lincoln, the objects are *Booth, shot,* and *Lincoln.* Russell claims that when we believe something, we relate things—that is, we arrange them in a certain order or relationship. In a statement of the belief, this order is indicated by word arrangement. For example, the belief that Booth shot Lincoln is different from the belief that Lincoln shot Booth. Although their object-terms are the same, their order or relationship is different. What makes one true and the other false? The arrangement of the object terms in the true belief corresponds to the way things are arranged in a fact. If the relationship among the terms in the *belief* or *statement* is the same as the relationship of the corresponding objects in a *fact*, then the belief or statement is true:

> Thus a belief is *true* when it corresponds with a certain associated complex [fact], and *false* when it does not. Assuming, for the sake of definiteness, that the objects of the belief are two terms and a relation, the terms being put in a certain order by the "sense" of the believing, then if the two terms in that order are united by the relation into a

THINKING LIKE A PHILOSOPHER

The correspondence theory of truth says that a belief is true if it corresponds with a fact. What are some of the beliefs you have that you know are true? What is the fact or facts with which each of those beliefs corresponds? How can you be sure that each of those beliefs corresponds to the fact or facts it is supposed to correspond to?

QUICK REVIEW
Russell explains correspondence by saying that a sentence corresponds to a fact when the relations among the words or constituents of the sentence mirror the relations among the terms or parts of a fact.

ANALYZING THE READING

Russell argues for the correspondence theory of truth by identifying a "requisite" of a theory of truth, and then saying that the requisite leads to the view that the correspondence theory of truth is the correct theory of truth. What does this requisite seem to be, and how does the correspondence theory of truth meet this requisite? Do you agree that a theory of truth must meet this requisite?

---

4   Bertrand Russell, *The Problems of Philosophy* (London: Oxford University Press, 1912), 283–284.

complex [fact], the belief is true; if not, it is false. This constitutes the definition of truth and falsehood that we were in search of. Judging or believing is a certain complex unity of which a mind is a constituent; if the remaining constituents, taken in the order which they have in the belief, form a complex unity [i.e., a fact], then the belief is true; if not, it is false. . . . We may restate our theory as follows: If we take such a belief as 'Othello believes that Desdemona loves Cassio', we will call Desdemona and Cassio the *object-terms*, and loving the *object-relation*. If there is a complex unity 'desdemona's love for Cassio', consisting of the object-terms related by the object-relation in the same order as they have in the belief, then this complex unity is called the *fact corresponding to the belief*. Thus a belief is true when there is a corresponding fact, and is false when there is no corresponding fact.[5]

ANALYZING THE READING

1. Russell tries to explain what "corresponds" means by arguing that a belief "corresponds" to a fact when the "terms" in the *belief* are related to each other in the same way that the respective "objects" in the *fact* are related to each other. The textbook claims that it does not seem that objects (such as people) in a fact can be related to each other in the same way that the terms in a belief are related. How do you think Russell would answer the textbook's claim? Can you think of a way to defend Russell by suggesting what it might mean to say that the terms of a belief are related to each other in the way that the objects of a fact are related?

2. The textbook suggests that Russell assumed that a belief was a kind of "picture" of a fact, yet a belief is not a picture at all. But could Russell respond that actually beliefs are like pictures in some important ways? Explain how Russell could respond to the criticism that he wrongly assumed that a belief was a kind of picture of a fact.

For Russell, then, a belief is true when and only when it relates its object-terms in the same way that the corresponding objects are related in a real fact. Take, for example, my belief that Joe loves Mary. This belief is true if the way that my belief relates Joe, love, and Mary is the same way that Joe, love, and Mary are related in the real world. That is, the belief is true if in the real world it is a fact that Joe loves Mary.

But notice how puzzling this is. For example, what are the "objects" in a belief? Beliefs aren't physical things made up of "objects," so it is not clear exactly what the "objects" of a belief are. Moreover, when Russell gives examples of the "objects" of a belief, his examples are the words that make up a sentence, like "Desdemona" and "loves" and "Cassio." So let's assume that the "objects" of a belief are more or less equivalent to the words of the sentence that expresses the belief. Then Russell seems to be saying that a belief or a sentence that expresses the belief is true when the words of the sentence are related to each other in the same way that the parts of a fact are related to each other. But this is even more puzzling: How can the *people*, Desdemona and Cassio, be related to each other in the same way that *words* are related to each other? Words are related by their physical positions on paper, but people are not. So how can the relationship between words or object-terms be the same as the relationship between the real objects that make up a fact? Russell seems to assume that beliefs or sentences are like pictures. A picture is an accurate representation of a scene when the parts of the picture are related to each other in the same way that the parts of the scene are related to each other. So Russell seems to think a belief is true when its parts are related to each other in the same way that the parts of the fact are related to each other. But the whole trouble with this approach is that beliefs and sentences are not pictures of things. In fact, they are not even remotely like pictures.[6]

---

5 Ibid., 285.
6 On the relationship between Russell and the Picture Theory of language, see Edna Daitz, "The Picture Theory of Meaning," *Mind*, New Series, vol. 62, no. 246 (April 1953), 184–201, and V. Hope, "The Picture Theory of Meaning in the Tractatus as a Development of Moore's and Russell's Theories of Judgment," *Philosophy*, vol. 44, no. 168 (April 1969), 140–148.

But a correspondence theory of truth doesn't need all of Russell's complicated machinery of facts, objects, relationships, and so on. All that a correspondence theory of truth requires is the simple idea that whether beliefs are true depends on the way things are in the real world. So not surprisingly there are other correspondence theories of truth that are simpler than Russell's. For example, the American philosopher Roderick Chisholm gives us this short formula as a summary of his theory of truth:

> T is a sentence token that is true in $L =_{def} T$ is a sentence token and there is a state of affairs h such that (1) T expresses h in L and (2) h obtains.[7]

In this formula, a "sentence token" is just a particular sentence; L means a language; h refers to some state of affairs; and $=_{def}$ is equivalent to "by definition means that." So in ordinary words, Chisholm's summary says: To say that a sentence of some language is true, by definition means that (1) the sentence expresses a state of affairs and (2) that state of affairs obtains. Or, in short, a sentence is true if and only if it expresses a state of affairs that obtains in reality.

There are, then, different versions of the correspondence theory of truth. Some focus on beliefs, others on statements, others on propositions. Some say that "facts" make beliefs true. Others say that "states of affairs" make them true, and still others say that "conditions" in the real world make them true. Some say that beliefs must "mirror" or "picture" the real world. Others say that they must correctly "describe" the real world. And yet others say that they must "express" what obtains in the real world. But what they all have in common is the basic claim that truth depends on what the real world is actually like.

Because it seems so natural and reasonable, most philosophers have accepted some version of the correspondence theory of truth. In the West, some of its more prominent early adherents, as indicated earlier, have included Aristotle and Aquinas. In the East, almost all the great schools of India have implicitly or explicitly assumed the correspondence theory. Take, for example, the members of the great Nyaya-Vaisesika or "Logic" school of Indian philosophy. These Indian philosophers claimed that a belief or an "awareness" is true when it reflects or corresponds to a fact that is independent of our consciousness. Our knowledge of facts, they go on to argue, can come from perception, reasoning, analogy, or the testimony of others. Today, a number of contemporary Western philosophers have defended the correspondence theory of truth. Among them are David M. Armstrong, Donald Davidson, John Searle, and many others.

Challenges to the Correspondence Theory. Although the correspondence theory seems reasonable, many philosophers have raised significant objections to it. One key problem is that the correspondence theory assumes we can determine whether our beliefs correspond to or match a reality that is external to ourselves. As we saw in the last chapter, many philosophers have questioned this assumption. We know only what our senses perceive, they argue, and we don't know anything about the world beyond our senses. Since we know only what our senses tell us, how can we ever get beyond them to check whether what they tell us "corresponds" to what the real world is like? How can we compare our beliefs, which are based on what we perceive, to a world we cannot perceive? So if the correspondence theory says truth depends on a reality we can't know, then doesn't it put truth forever out of our reach?

QUICK REVIEW
Critics say that the correspondence theory wrongly assumes we can determine whether our beliefs correspond to an external reality; but our only access to an external world is through our senses and we cannot know whether our senses give us an accurate picture of an external reality because we cannot get beyond our senses to check this out.

---

[7] Roderick M. Chisholm, *Theory of Knowledge*, 2nd ed. (Englewood Cliffs, NJ: Prentice Hall, 1977), 138.

✓ QUICK REVIEW
Other critics say we cannot define the fact to which a true statement is supposed to correspond without using the true statement itself. Searle replies that this is because the word *fact* is supposed to indicate the conditions in reality that make a specific proposition true. This is a significant use of *fact*, but it means that a fact can be defined only in relation to the proposition it makes true.

Then there's the question of just what a *fact* is. Critics claim that *fact* as used by correspondence theorists means nothing more than "true proposition," as in "It's a fact that I'm six feet tall." To show this, critics ask this question: To which fact is a true proposition supposed to "correspond"? For example, to which fact does the proposition "The cat is on the mat" correspond? The obvious answer is that "the cat is on the mat" corresponds to the fact that the cat is on the mat. But then identifying the fact to which a true proposition corresponds requires using the true proposition itself. So the correspondence theory merely says that a true proposition is one that corresponds to what the proposition says. This seems circular. We are saying a proposition is true if it corresponds to what the proposition says. But that doesn't really tell us anything! What is gained by this? The correspondence theory seems pointless.

American philosopher John Searle, who agrees with the correspondence theory, has tried to answer the objection that its reliance on facts makes it pointless.[8] He agrees that true propositions are those that correspond to facts. And he admits that if you want to identify the fact to which a true proposition corresponds, you have to use the proposition itself. There is no getting around that. But this does not make the correspondence theory pointless. Searle argues that the word *fact* was developed precisely so that we could refer to what it is in the real world that makes a proposition true. That is, we use the word *fact* to refer to the conditions in the real world that make a specific proposition true. In his words, a specific fact is just a proposition's "truth conditions." What are "truth conditions"? The "truth conditions" of a proposition are what has to be present in the real world in order for the proposition to be true. Take, for example, the proposition "The cat is on the mat." For this proposition to be true, the real world has to contain the existence of the cat, the mat, and the cat's being on the mat. So the truth conditions of "The cat is on the mat" are the existence in the real world of the cat, the mat, and the cat's being on the mat. But there's an easier way to say" "the existence in the real world of the cat, the mat, and the cat's being on the mat." We can just say "the fact that the cat is on the mat." That is, the purpose of the word *fact* is to let us refer to, and talk about, the truth conditions of a proposition. So the fact and the proposition have to go together. But this doesn't mean that the word *fact* doesn't tell us something important. It's important because it tells us that what makes a proposition true is a specific set of conditions in the real world. In other words, the importance of the word *fact* is that it lets us say that it is something about the real world that makes a proposition true. Connecting truth to facts means propositions are not made true by our own beliefs nor the beliefs of our society. Searle believes, in fact, that the reason the correspondence theory of truth is important is precisely because it connects truth to facts. That is, it is critically important that facts determine the truth. If it is a fact that the cat is on the mat, then no matter what I believe or society believes, it is true that the cat is on the mat.

But why is it important to relate facts to truth? To understand why this is important, let's go back to the case of Marc Dutroux. Dutroux is the man who tortured, raped, and murdered four little girls. Recall what the anthropology Professor Yves Winkin said about the Dutroux case. He said "there is no transcendent truth," and

ANALYZING THE READING

Searle argues that the word *fact* was developed so we could talk about those things in the real world that make a belief or proposition true. And the idea that truth is related to facts is, Searle thinks, a very important idea. Explain why it is important for a theory of truth to connect beliefs with facts.

---

8   John R. Searle, *The Construction of Social Reality* (New York: Free Press, 1995).

"there are only partial truths, shared by a larger or smaller number of people." "Truth," he said, "is always linked to an organization, depending upon the elements that are perceived as important." Winkin's point is that truth does not depend on what the facts in the real world are. Instead, what is true depends on the beliefs or interests of groups. What does Winkin's view of truth imply about Marc Dutroux? Winkin's view of truth seems to imply that whether Dutroux is guilty does not depend on what the facts are. The truth about Dutroux depends on the beliefs and interests of the group you are talking about. Searle's view of the importance of facts is diametrically opposed to this kind of view of truth. Searle's view claims that truth depends on facts or conditions in our real world, not on what people happen to believe or are interested in. Searle's views on the role of facts implies that the truth about Dutroux depends on conditions in the real world, not on the beliefs people have in their minds.

Yet it is not clear that Searle's defense of facts works, and some critics say it clearly doesn't. Moreover, even if Searle is right, critics claim that there are other problems with the correspondence theory. The correspondence theory uses the word *corresponds*, yet *corresponds* is a word that is even more unclear and confusing than the word *fact*. Just what does it mean to say that a true belief "corresponds" to a fact or a state of affairs? It doesn't correspond in the way that a color sample on a color chart corresponds with a color of paint on a wall. With color samples, there's a resemblance between the sample and the wall paint. Yet there's no resemblance between a belief and a fact or state of affairs, or between a sentence and a fact or state of affairs. And a belief does not seem to correspond to a fact in the way that a picture mirrors the scene it portrays, which is what Russell's theory proposes. Does a statement correspond to a fact in the way that titles of books on library cards correspond to the books themselves? Is there a similar sort of one-to-one correspondence between statements and facts? Just as for each book there's a card, and for each card a book, so also for each statement there's a fact and for each fact a statement? If so, what have we gained? It seems at least as clear to say that a true proposition describes an actual state of affairs and thus dispose of the inherently misleading term *correspondence*.

Finally, there is the problem of negative statements. To what fact or state of affairs does the negative statement "No unicorns exist" correspond? Does it correspond to some sort of negative fact? But what is a negative fact or negative state of affairs? And what about hypothetical statements like "If it rains, then the ground gets wet"? Are there supposed to be "hypothetical facts" to which hypothetical statements correspond? But what on earth would a hypothetical fact look like?

> **QUICK REVIEW**
> Critics also say we cannot explain what *correspondence* means and cannot explain to what "facts" true negative statements and true hypothetical statements correspond.

Coherence Theory

According to the **coherence theory** of truth, a belief is true if it "coheres" with a group of accepted beliefs that also "cohere" with each other. Truth is not correspondence between a belief and a fact in the real world. Instead, truth consists of coherence between a belief and other beliefs. But these terms need to be explained. Most importantly, what does "coherence" mean? And what is "a group of accepted beliefs"? And just who is supposed to "accept" these beliefs?

We'll start by clarifying what "coherence" means. The word *coherence* usually refers to the relationship between things when they "stick together" well. Yet the coherence theory of truth is supposed to be about beliefs. But how can beliefs "stick together"? Is there some kind of special glue for beliefs? No, of course not. In the coherence theory of truth, coherence refers to the relationship among beliefs when they are *consistent* with each other and *support* each other. Beliefs are consistent with each other when they can both be true at the same time. And they support each other when one makes the other more probable. For example, the belief that it's raining and the belief that the sky is cloudy are consistent beliefs. But the belief that it's raining and the belief that it's not raining are inconsistent since both cannot be true at the same time. Moreover, the belief that it's raining supports the belief that the sky is cloudy. For if it's raining then probably the sky is cloudy.

Geometry is a good example of a limited system of beliefs that are consistent and support each other. Geometry constructs an entire system of "truths," or theorems, by deducing the theorems from a few basic statements, or "axioms." All the theorems of geometry are consistent with each other. And each theorem is supported by the other theorems and axioms from which it is deduced.

Let's turn next to what the coherence theory of truth means by "accepted." A belief is "accepted" when someone thinks that belief is true. If someone thinks it's raining, for example, then she "accepts" the belief that it's raining. But just who is this "someone" supposed to be? That is, who is supposed to "accept" the group of beliefs that the coherence theory is talking about? That question is not so easy to answer because different coherence theories explain this "someone" in different ways. Some coherence theories say the "accepted" beliefs they are talking about are those accepted by an "omniscient" being who knows everything. According to this kind of coherence theory, then, a belief is true when it coheres with that group of coherent beliefs that an omniscient being would accept. But most coherence theories say that the "someone" they are talking about are ordinary people. Some say that the "someone" is a group of people that together would know everything human beings could ever know. Then a belief would be true if it coheres with the coherent beliefs accepted by people who together know everything we can know. Other coherence theories say the "someone" consists of the people alive today that together would know everything we know today. So a true belief would be one that coheres with the coherent beliefs accepted by those people who together know everything we know today.

The main ideas that most coherence theories use should now be clearer. So we can turn to look now at the coherence theory of truth that a particular philosopher proposed.

Brand Blanshard (1892–1987) was an articulate twentieth-century proponent of the coherence theory of truth. Blanshard, a rationalist, was also a staunch defender of idealism. Like Berkeley, Blanshard argued that what we directly perceive exists only in the mind. As he wrote in his autobiography: "I have never been able to accept the realist view that the objects of direct experience are independent of consciousness. Indeed, everything we sense or feel seems to me to exist only in consciousness."[9] Unlike Berkeley, however, Blanshard did not claim that what we perceive is all there is. He acknowledged that a material world, perhaps made up of atoms, could exist beyond what we directly perceive.

Brand Blanshard:
"A judgment of fact can be verified only by the sort of apprehension that can present us with a fact, and this must be a further judgment. And an agreement between judgments is best described not as a correspondence, but as coherence."

Yale University Library

---

9   Brand Blanshard, "Autobiography," in Paul Arthur Schilpp, ed., *The Philosophy of Brand Blanshard* (Chicago: Open Court Publishing Company, 1980), excerpts from 142.

But Blanshard's most important contributions were his views on reason, particularly the idea that reason strives to develop a complete and coherent body of truths about the universe. Blanshard argued that the aim of all our thinking is to develop a system of truths about the universe that would contain everything there is to know about that universe. Although we already know many things, our present system of knowledge is far from complete. We try to increase our system of beliefs by bringing new beliefs into it, and by using it to expand our knowledge into what is still unknown. Blanshard explains these ideas in the following passage from his major work, *The Nature of Thought*:

> To think is to seek understanding. And to seek understanding is an activity of mind that is marked off from all other activities by a highly distinctive aim. This aim . . . is to achieve systematic vision: so to apprehend what is now unknown to us as to relate it, and relate it necessarily, to what we know already. We think to solve problems; and our method of solving problems is to build a bridge of intelligible relation from the continent of our knowledge to the island we wish to include in it. . . . Thought in its very nature is the attempt to bring something unknown or imperfectly known into a sub-system of knowledge, and thus also into that larger system that forms the world of accepted beliefs. That is what explanation is.[10]

This attempt to understand things by relating them to the "larger system that forms the world of accepted beliefs" is at the heart of Blanshard's coherence view of truth. Blanshard believed that our minds possess a desire to know everything. This desire leads us to try to expand our "system of accepted beliefs" to include whatever can be known. We have, in short, a natural desire to know and we satisfy it by continuously adding new true beliefs to those we already accept.

Blanshard argued that we determine whether a new belief is true by seeing whether it fits our "system of accepted beliefs." If the new belief is consistent with our accepted beliefs, and is supported by them, then we accept the belief as true and add it to our previously accepted beliefs. If it is inconsistent with our accepted beliefs or is not supported by them, then we will reject it as false. Blanshard is convinced that we do not determine whether a belief is true by checking whether it "corresponds" with the facts. Correspondence with facts is not the criterion of truth that we actually use. The "test" we always use to determine whether a belief is true, Blanshard argued, is whether it coheres with the beliefs we already accept. He argues for these claims in the following passage:

> Now I think it can be shown that coherence is our test, the final and invariable test [of truth], when our beliefs are under pressure. . . . Take first the judgments of fact: "Burr killed Hamilton in a duel." [and] "That is a cardinal on the branch yonder."

THINKING LIKE A PHILOSOPHER

Blanshard claims that we all have a desire to know everything there is to know about the world. Do you think this is true of you? If so, how strong would you say that desire is in you? Would you say that although there are some things you want to know everything about, there are others that you don't care to know anything about? If so, what are the things you have a desire to know about, and what are the things you don't care to know about? Do you think it is possible that some day humanity might know everything there is to know?

THINKING LIKE A PHILOSOPHER

Blanshard gives two examples of the process by which we test the truth of a new belief, to see if we should add it our other beliefs. One example is "Burr killed Hamilton in a duel," and another is "That is a cardinal on the branch yonder." Find a different example of a fact taken from today's news. Now explain step by step how you would use Blanshard's coherence test of truth to figure out whether you should bring that new "fact" into your system of accepted beliefs.

---

[10] Brand Blanshard, *The Nature of Thought*, vol. II (London: George Allen & Unwin Ltd., 1939), excerpts from 261.

As regards the first of them ... the slightest consideration will show that the use of correspondence as a test [of its truth] is here out of the question; one of the terms that are to correspond is irrecoverably gone. ... Our test in such cases must clearly be found elsewhere. And the more we reflect, the plainer it becomes that this test is the way our judgment is implicated with a host of further judgments that we are compelled to make when we investigate. If this belief about Hamilton is true, then a thousand references in newspapers, magazines, and books, and almost endless facts about the fortunes of Hamilton's family, about the later life of Burr, and about American constitutional history, fall into place in a consistent picture. If it is false, then the most credible journalists, historians and statesmen, generation after generation, may be so deluded about events that happen before the eyes of a nation that no single historical fact is any longer above suspicion. If evidence of this weight is to be rejected, then in consistency we must go on to reject almost every hint that takes us beyond immediate perception. And intellectually speaking, that would pull our house about our heads. What really tests the judgment is the extent of our accepted world that is implicated with it. ... And that is the test of coherence [not correspondence] ...

[Next,] take the judgment, "That bird is a cardinal". ... This is supposed to be fact, unadulterated brute fact, given directly to our senses and providing a solid reality to which our thought is to correspond. But no bird is a mere sense datum, or even a collection of sense data. ... To recognize a cardinal is a considerable intellectual achievement, for to do it one must grasp, implicitly but none the less really, the *concept* of cardinal, and this can only be done by a leap far out of the given into ideal classification. The most ignorant person among us who achieves such recognition could unpack from it a surprising wealth of contents. The idea of living organisms, the thought of the bird kingdom and its outstanding characteristics, the notions of flight and a peculiar song and a determinate color—these and many other notions are so bound up with the identification that our thought would lose its character with the removal of any one of them. ... And these essential elements, at least at the time and for the most part, are not given in sense at all. They are elements in a theory, and a theory of no little complexity, which is based on sense data if you will, but could not possibly consist of them.[11]

ANALYZING THE READING

1. According to Blanshard every "fact" is really just a bunch of beliefs you already have about that kind of fact, and there is no such thing as a "pure" fact that consists of just the fact with no related beliefs. Do you think this claim is true? If not, can you think of any fact that does not in the end come down to being a bundle of beliefs?

2. Blanshard argues that every so-called "fact" consists of beliefs you already have. So if you try to check whether a new belief "corresponds" to a fact, you will be checking whether the new belief corresponds to beliefs you already have. And checking whether a new belief corresponds to beliefs you already have is the same as checking whether the new belief "coheres" with the beliefs you already have. So in the end, if you try to check whether a new belief is true, you will be checking whether it coheres with beliefs one already has. Is this argument of Blanshard valid? Is it sound? Explain why or why not.

QUICK REVIEW
We cannot test if a belief about the past is true by comparing it to the facts since the facts are gone; so we must test it by its coherence with other beliefs about the past. And if we try to test if a belief about the present is true by comparing it to the facts, we end up testing it by its coherence with other beliefs. So coherence is the only test for truth.

Blanshard is making two points here. First, he argues that we can figure out whether a belief about the past is true, only by seeing if it coheres with the beliefs we already have. We cannot test a belief about the past by seeing if it corresponds to the facts, since the facts are no longer present. We therefore have to rely on the beliefs we already have. Second, Blanshard argues that we also do not determine whether a belief about the present is true by checking whether it corresponds with the facts. Blanshard points out that every so-called "fact" is really just a bunch of beliefs we already have about that the so-called "fact." Even what looks like a pure fact about a bird is really a bundle of beliefs we have about birds. So if we try to see whether a new belief "corresponds" with the facts, we always end up checking whether it corresponds with other beliefs. And checking a new belief against our other beliefs amounts to asking if the belief "coheres" with our other beliefs.

---

[11] Ibid., excerpts from 226–228.

In short, we always test whether our beliefs are true by seeing whether they cohere with the "system" of beliefs we already have. But Blanshard points out that although we use coherence with our beliefs to *test* whether new beliefs are true, this does not prove that truth itself *means* coherence with our beliefs. Using a certain test to see if an object has a certain quality does not prove that the quality means the same as the test. For example, we use a thermometer to "test" what the temperature is, but that does not show that "temperature" means "the use of a thermometer." So Blanshard must next argue that truth means coherence with our beliefs. He argues, basically, that since we use coherence to *test* whether our beliefs are true, truth would have to *mean* coherence with accepted beliefs.

> [First,] if one holds that truth is correspondence, one cannot intelligibly hold . . . that it is tested by coherence. . . . Suppose that we construe experience into the most coherent picture possible, remembering that among the elements included will be such secondary qualities as colors, odors, and sounds. Would the mere fact that such elements as these are coherently arranged prove that anything precisely corresponding to them exists 'out there'? I cannot see that it would, even if we knew that the two arrangements had closely corresponding patterns. . . . If you place the nature of truth in one sort of character and its test in something quite different, you are pretty certain, sooner or later, to find the two falling apart. In the end, the only test of truth that is not misleading is the special nature or character that is itself constitutive of truth.
> [Second,] in order to know that experience corresponds to fact, we must be able to get at that fact, unadulterated with idea, and compare the two sides with each other. And we have seen . . . that such a [pure] fact is not accessible.[12]

ANALYZING THE READING

Blanshard claims that "if you place the nature of truth in one sort of character and its test in something quite different, you are pretty certain, sooner or later, to find the two falling apart." What does he mean by this? Why is this claim important to his attempt to show that the "nature of truth" is correspondence with our accepted beliefs?

Blanshard's argument here is simpler than it looks. First, he is arguing, we would not be able to use coherence to figure out whether new beliefs are true, if "true" meant "correspondence with facts." For showing that a belief coheres with other beliefs would not show that it corresponds with facts. But we have already seen that we always use coherence to determine whether new beliefs are true. So truth cannot mean correspondence with facts. So, he concludes, truth must mean coherence with accepted beliefs. Second, he argues, if truth was correspondence with facts, then we would need to have access to pure facts. But he has shown that we never reach a pure fact. All facts come to us in the form of beliefs we already have about that "fact." Since all so-called "facts" are really just a bunch of our accepted beliefs, truth cannot mean correspondence with facts. Truth, then, must mean coherence with our accepted beliefs.

Blanshard's view, then, is that truth itself is nothing more nor less than coherence with the "system that forms the world of accepted beliefs." But it is important to understand what Blanshard means by the "system that forms the world of accepted beliefs." Through most of his discussion Blanshard writes as if he is talking only about the accepted beliefs of each individual person. So he seems to be saying that a belief is true if it coheres with an individual person's own accepted beliefs. Yet notice that this would mean that truth can change because people's accepted beliefs change. Blanshard avoids saying that truth can change by distinguishing two different "systems" of beliefs. There is, first, what he calls the ideal "completed system of knowledge." This completed system includes every truth that can be known about the universe

---

[12] Ibid., excerpt from 268.

organized so that each truth makes the others necessary. In this completed system, Blanshard writes, "everything real and possible is coherently included." Second, there are the incomplete systems of beliefs that we each carry around in our minds. These include some scientific knowledge, and many unorganized bits of cloudy memories and ideas. *Ultimately*, a belief is true if it coheres with the "completed system of knowledge." But we do not yet have that completed system of knowledge. So *in practice* we have to rely on our incomplete system of beliefs to determine what is true.

> While the truth of a judgment does consist in the last resort in its relations to a completed system, no sensible person would claim to know these in detail. . . . The system we actually work with is always less than the whole; at the best it is the mass of scientific knowledge bearing on the point in question; on the average it is a cloudy congeries of memories, suggestions and inferences, ill-organized in the extreme, and yet capable of subconscious mobilization and use. . . . For all the ordinary purposes of life, coherence does not mean coherence with some inaccessible absolute, but with the system of present knowledge. . . . [So] what the standard [of truth] means *in practice* is [coherence with] the system of present knowledge as apprehended by a particular mind. That system changes; hence what coheres with it at one time may not cohere with it at another; thus in practice we shall be justified in accepting at one time what later we must reject. . . .[But] we have neither said nor implied that truth itself changes. What we have said is that while truth as measured by the ultimate standard is unchanging, our knowledge of that truth does change—which is a very different thing.[13]

ANALYZING THE READING

According to Blanshard there are two "systems" of beliefs: the one "apprehended by a particular mind" and the "completed system" of knowledge. How do these differ? Why does he distinguish the two systems? Blanshard does not say whose mind would hold the "completed system" of beliefs. In light of what the "completed system" would have to contain, could a single person hold it all in her mind? Could a large group of persons hold it all in their minds? Could God?

 THINKING LIKE A PHILOSOPHER

According to Blanshard, in a complete system of knowledge, "every proposition would be entailed by the others." Do you think that to some degree your own beliefs are like this? That is, do you think that you drew some of your beliefs from other beliefs you had? For example, if you believe there is an afterlife, then you probably drew that belief from other religious beliefs you had. And your belief that 222 + 333 = 555 you probably just now drew from other beliefs you have about the numbers "2," "3," and "5," and what "+" and "=" mean. What are some examples of beliefs you have that you deduced from other beliefs?

QUICK REVIEW
Blanshard argues that, in practice, we accept something is true when it coheres with our present knowledge, but the ultimate standard for truth is coherence with a complete system of knowledge about the universe.

As these passages show, Blanshard was an extremely careful and thoughtful rationalist. As we noted earlier, he believed that our reason is driven to seek a "complete system of knowledge" about the universe. In this ideal system of true beliefs, all beliefs would be consistent with all other beliefs, and each would support the others. He writes that in "a completely satisfactory system . . . every proposition would be entailed by the others jointly and even singly, no proposition would stand outside the system." Beliefs support each other in the sense that one could be deduced from the others. The whole set of beliefs would be highly ordered, like the "system" theorems that can be deduced from the axioms of geometry.

Blanshard conceded that we have not yet achieved such an ideal system and was not sure that we ever would. Nevertheless, he insisted that the truth of our beliefs is ultimately measured by their coherence with this ideal and complete system of knowledge. In practice, however, we must each rely on our own partial approximation to that ideal. But he was convinced that we each seek that ideal complete system and that the ongoing expansion of our knowledge is moving toward it.

---

[13] Ibid., excerpts from 270–272.

PHILOSOPHY AND LIFE

Historical Facts

Julius Caesar crossing the Rubicon to begin a civil war against Pompey, 49 BCE.

What is a historical fact? Take, for example, what passes for a simple historical fact: "In the year 49 BCE, Caesar crossed the Rubicon." This is a familiar fact, and one of some importance. Yet, as the most distinguished American historian Carl L. Becker pointed out more than a half century ago, this simple fact has strings tied to it. It depends on numerous other facts so that it has no meaning apart from the web of circumstances that produced it. This web of circumstances, of course, was the chain of events arising out of the relation of Caesar to

Pompey, the Roman Senate, and the Roman Republic. As Becker states,

> Caesar had been ordered by the Roman Senate to resign his command of the army in Gaul. He decided to disobey the Roman Senate. Instead of resigning his command, he marched on Rome, gained the mastery of the Republic, and, at last, we are told, bestrode the narrow world like a colossus. Well, the Rubicon happened to be the boundary between Gaul and Italy, so that by the act of crossing the Rubicon with his army Caesar's treason became an accomplished fact and the subsequent great events followed in due course. Apart from these great events and complicated relations, the crossing of the Rubicon means nothing, is not an historical fact properly speaking at all. . . . [It is] a symbol standing for a long series of events which have to do with the most intangible and immaterial realities, viz.: the relation between Caesar and the millions of people of the Roman world.

Clearly, for Becker "the simple historical fact" is only a symbol, an affirmation about an event. And because it's hardly worthwhile to term a symbol cold or hard, indeed dangerous to call it true or false, one might best speak of historical facts as being more or less appropriate.

QUESTIONS

1. Could Becker's analysis be applied to this statement: "The Japanese bombed Pearl Harbor on December 7, 1941?"

2. Would it be accurate to say that historians deal not with an event but with statements that affirm the fact that the event occurred? If so, what's the difference?

Source: Carl L. Becker, "What Are Historical Facts?" Quoted in *Coming Age of Philosophy*, ed. Roger Eastman (San Francisco: Canfield, 1973), 451–452.

Blanshard, of course, is not the only philosopher to have accepted the coherence theory of truth. In the West, the great rationalist philosophers Spinoza and Hegel accepted the coherence theory. So did several modern empiricists, such as Otto Neurath and C. G. Hempel. And, of course, the coherence theory was embraced by idealist philosophers, including H. H. Joachim and F. H. Bradley. Some contemporary coherentists include Dummett, Putnam, and Rescher.

Several Eastern philosophers also embraced the coherence view of truth. In the previous chapter, we met the great seventh-century Indian philosopher Shankara. Shankara held that a judgment about reality should be "sublated" when it does not fit in with other, fuller judgments about reality. This is a form of the coherence theory. Several members of the Yogacara school of Buddhist philosophy also accepted a form of coherentism. For example, the Indian philosopher Dharmakirti (circa 600–660) accepted the coherence theory. Dharmakirti said that any belief or "awareness" based on sense perception should be rejected if it does not cohere or agree with the fuller system of beliefs we have. In his view, coherence with other beliefs or "awarenesses" is both the nature of truth and the way we determine whether a belief or an awareness is true.

Still, is the systemic coherence of beliefs with one another by itself a guarantee of truth? Recall that until the sixteenth century, almost everyone believed that the earth was the center of the solar system. Why did everyone believe this? Because it made sense and accorded with commonsensical observation. It fit in with the widespread experience of things and with religious belief. Moreover, in the second century CE the astronomer Ptolemy developed this earth-centered view into a complicated but consistent theory. His theory, which said that the sun revolves around the earth, could even be used to predict astronomical events successfully. In fact, the major difference between Ptolemy's theory and the theory of Copernicus which replaced it was that Copernicus' was simpler. (With the refinements that Kepler, Galileo, and Newton later proposed, its predictions were also more accurate.) Yet both theories were consistent. The point is that coherence does not seem to distinguish between consistent truth and consistent error. A judgment may be true if it is consistent with other judgments, but what if the other judgments are false? If first judgments are not true, they can produce a system of consistent error.

Another issue is one that Blanshard himself recognized. If beliefs are true when they cohere with an individual's personal set of beliefs, then what is true today may not be true tomorrow. This will lead to problems. For example, if people in the Middle Ages accepted the belief that the earth is flat, then at that time it was true that the earth is flat. But since we know today that the earth is not flat, today it is not true that the earth is flat. But truth cannot change in this way. If the earth is not flat then it is as true that it was not flat in the Middle Ages as it is today, even if people in the Middle Ages "accepted" the belief that it was. So there is a problem when we try to define truth in terms of the accepted beliefs of real individuals or groups. Blanshard tries to get around this problem by claiming that there is an ideal "complete" system of beliefs that includes everything that can be known. Ultimately, he says, beliefs are true only if they cohere with that ideal system that contains all true beliefs. In relation to that complete system of beliefs, then, truth does not change. But the problem is that this seems to tell us nothing. For what is this "complete system" of beliefs? Clearly, it is not the system of beliefs of any one person today, nor of any one person in the future. And probably, as Blanshard admits, such a complete group of beliefs will probably never exist. Basically, then, Blanshard's "complete system" seems to be nothing more than an imaginary set of beliefs that is imagined to contain all true beliefs. So Blanshard is saying that a belief is "ultimately" true when it "coheres" with that group of beliefs that contains all true beliefs. Which seems to just mean that a belief is true if it is one of the true beliefs. That, however, seems to tell us nothing. The problem that Blanshard is faced with seems to be a problem for any theory that says that truth is coherence with accepted beliefs. If the accepted beliefs are those of a real individual or a real group, then truth would have to change, which seems wrong. But if the accepted beliefs are some ideal set of all true beliefs, then the theory seems to just be saying that a belief is true when it is one of the true beliefs. And that seems to take us nowhere.

But the correspondence and coherence theories do not exhaust all the options. There is a third major theory of truth called the pragmatic theory of truth.

✓ QUICK REVIEW
Critics point out that in the past, societies accepted beliefs that we now know were false, such as "The sun revolves around the earth." So testing a belief by seeing if it coheres with our other beliefs will often mean testing it against false beliefs.

✓ QUICK REVIEW
Critics say that if truth is coherence with the beliefs of a specific individual or group, then truth will change, which seems wrong. But saying truth is coherence with an ideal system of all true beliefs seems to mean a belief is true if it is one of the true beliefs, and this is not helpful.

Pragmatic Theory

The evident weaknesses in the correspondence and coherence theories led philosophers to suggest another theory of truth. This was the pragmatic theory of truth. The pragmatic theory of truth says that a belief is true if it is "expedient," that is, useful. For example, in science a belief may be useful for making accurate predictions.

In the West, the pragmatic theory of truth was a cornerstone of pragmatism, the essentially American philosophy mentioned in Chapter 3. We saw that pragmatism developed in the writings of Charles S. Peirce (1839–1914), William James (1842–1910), and John Dewey (1859–1952). The American pragmatists rejected both the correspondence and the coherence theories of truth. Both, pragmatists claimed, wrongly saw truth as "inert" and neither recognized how people's interests affect what they take as truth. The pragmatists proposed usefulness as the measure of truth and insisted that truth should take into account the consequences of accepting a belief. In a nutshell, the pragmatic view of truth holds that a belief is true if it is useful to believe. A belief in ordinary life could be accepted as true, if accepting the belief meets people's needs and interests over a long period of time. In science a belief might be accepted if after a prolonged period it passed the scientist's tests and helped the scientist explain and predict events. At a biological level, a belief might be accepted if it aids us individually or collectively in the struggle for survival.

Many Eastern philosophers have accepted versions of the pragmatic view of truth. One was the Indian philosopher Vatsyayana (circa 350 BCE) who wrote the oldest commentary on the *Nyayasutra*. Vatsyayana stated in the opening passage of his commentary that the truth of a belief is known by its fruits. A false belief is one that leads us to engage in the wrong actions and prevents us from getting what we want. A true belief is one that has successful results. There are several other Eastern philosophers who adopted the pragmatic view of truth. But here we will focus on the pragmatic theory of truth as it was articulated by the American pragmatists.

American Pragmatism and Truth. The American pragmatists rejected older European philosophies that saw truth primarily in rationalistic terms. Especially objectionable to the pragmatists was the traditional idea of truth as something fixed. Pragmatists saw truth as dynamic and changing, subjective and relative. Like the correspondence and coherence theories, the pragmatic theory of truth has many versions. But the classic version was put forth by William James in *Pragmatism: A New Name for Some Old Ways of Thinking*. In it, he clearly distinguishes the pragmatic theory from other theories of truth:

> Truth, as any dictionary will tell you, is a property of certain of our ideas. It means their "agreement," as falsity means their disagreement, with "reality." Pragmatists and intellectualists both accept this definition as a matter of course. They begin to quarrel only after the question is raised as to what may precisely be meant by the term "agreement," and what by the term "reality," when reality is taken as something for our ideas to agree with.
>
> In answering these questions the pragmatists are more analytic and painstaking, the intellectualists more offhand and unreflective. The popular notion is that a true idea must copy its reality. Like other popular views, this one follows the analogy of the most usual experience. Our true ideas of sensible things do indeed copy them. Shut your eyes and think of yonder clock on the wall, and you get just such a true picture or copy of its dial. But your idea of its "works" (unless you are a clock-maker) is much less of a copy, yet it passes muster, for it in no way clashes with the reality. Even though it should shrink to the mere word "works," that word still serves you truly; and when you speak of the "time-keeping function" of the clock, or of its spring's "elasticity," it is hard to see exactly what your ideas can copy.

You perceive that there is a problem here. Where our ideas cannot copy definitely their object, what does agreement with that object mean? Some idealists seem to say that they are true whenever they are what God means that we ought to think about that object. Others hold the copy-view all through, and speak as if our ideas possessed truth just in proportion as they approach to being copies of the Absolute's eternal way of thinking.

These views, you see, invite pragmatistic discussion. But the great assumption of the intellectualists is that truth means essentially an inert static relation. When you've got your true idea of anything, there's an end of the matter. You're in possession; you *know*; you have fulfilled your thinking destiny. You are where you ought to be mentally; you have obeyed your categorical imperative; and nothing more need follow on that climax of your rational destiny. Epistemologically you are in stable equilibrium.

Pragmatism, on the other hand, asks its usual question. "Grant an idea or belief to be true," it says, "what concrete difference will its being true make in any one's actual life? How will the truth be realized? What experiences will be different from those which would obtain if the belief were false? What, in short, is the truth's cash-value in experiential terms?"

The moment pragmatism asks this question, it sees the answer: *True ideas are those that we can assimilate, validate, corroborate and verify. False ideas are those that we cannot.* That is the practical difference it makes to us to have true ideas; that, therefore, is the meaning of truth, for it is all that truth is known as.

This thesis is what I have to defend. The truth of an idea is not a stagnant property inherent in it. Truth *happens* to an idea. It *becomes* true, is *made* true by events. Its verity *is* in fact an event, a process: the process namely of its verifying itself, its *verification*. Its validity is the process of its validation.

But what do the words *verification* and *validation* themselves pragmatically mean? They again signify certain practical consequences of the verified and validated idea. It is hard to find any one phrase that characterizes these consequences better than the ordinary agreement-formula—just such consequences being what we have in mind whenever we say that our ideas "agree" with reality. They lead us, namely, through the acts and other ideas which they instigate, into or up to, or towards, other parts of experience with which we feel all the while—such feeling being among our potentialities—that the original ideas remain in agreement. The connections and transitions come to us from point to point as being progressive, harmonious, satisfactory. This function of agreeable leading is what we mean by an idea's verification. . . .

The importance to human life of having true beliefs about matters of fact is a thing too notorious. We live in a world of realities that can be infinitely useful or infinitely harmful. Ideas that tell us which of them to expect count as the true ideas in all this primary sphere of verification, and the pursuit of such ideas is a primary human duty. The possession of truth, so far from being here an end in itself, is only a preliminary means towards other vital satisfactions.

"The true," to put it very briefly, is only the expedient in the way of our thinking, just as "the right" is only the expedient in the way of our behaving. Expedient in almost any fashion; and expedient in the long run and on the whole of course; for what meets expediently all the experience in sight won't necessarily meet all farther experiences equally satisfactorily. Experience, as we know, has ways of *boiling over*, and making us correct our present formulas.

Let me now say only this, that truth is *one species of good*, and not, as is usually supposed, a category distinct from good, and co-ordinate with it. *The true is the name of whatever proves itself to be good in the way of*

ANALYZING THE READING

James claims that true ideas are those that we can "validate" and "verify." James also states that a "verified and validated idea" is one that has "certain practical consequences," namely the consequence of gradually leading us to what is "progressive, harmonious, satisfactory." Explain what James seems to mean by "validate" and "verify." That is, explain how an individual or a society would "validate" and "verify" an idea according to James.

ANALYZING THE READING

The word *expedient* means useful. So what does James mean by the claim: *"'The true,' to put it very briefly, is only the expedient in the way of our thinking, just as 'the right' is only the expedient in the way of our behavior."* What does James mean by "useful" or "expedient"? Note that he adds the words: "and expedient in the long run and on the whole, of course." What do these words add to his claim?

belief and good, too, for definite, assignable reasons. Surely you must admit this, that if there were no good for life in true ideas, or if the knowledge of them were positively disadvantageous and false ideas the only useful ones, then the current notion that truth is divine and precious, and its pursuit a duty, could never have grown up or become a dogma. In a world like that, our duty would be to shun truth, rather. But in this world, just as certain foods are not only agreeable to our taste, but good for our teeth, our stomach and our tissues; so certain ideas are not only agreeable to think about, or agreeable as supporting other ideas that we are fond of, but they are also helpful in life's practical struggles. If there be any life that it is really better we should lead, and if there be any idea which, if believed in, would help us to lead that life, then it would be really *better for us* to believe in that idea, *unless, indeed, belief in it incidentally clashed with other greater vital benefits.*

Ought we ever not to believe what it is *better for us* to believe? And can we then keep the notion of what is better for us, and what is true for us, permanently apart? Pragmatism says no, and I fully agree with her.[14]

 MindTap To read more from William James' *Pragmatism: A New Name for Some Old Ways of Thinking,* click the link in the MindTap Reader or go to the Questia Readings folder in MindTap.

According to James, we do not base truth on a comparison of a statement with some objective external reality. Neither are true beliefs based on their coherence with other beliefs. In James' view, the essential problem with those outlooks is that their adherents have failed to ask the right questions. They shouldn't ask how judgments correspond or relate to reality, but *what difference they make.* For James, the truth of an idea or judgment depends on what he calls "the practical difference it makes" in our lives. We should accept a belief if it has progressive, harmonious, and satisfactory consequences. But beliefs have to be tested, investigated, and used by a community for a long period of time. If they continue to lead to useful consequences we should accept them as true. For example, believing in our scientific theories has enabled us to make great technological progress. Believing in the ideas of democracy has made our lives with one another and our society more harmonious. And believing in the many bits of practical knowledge that we use to make our way through our world has made our daily lives more satisfactory. So, we accept all these beliefs. And accepting them for these reasons makes them count as true.

THINKING LIKE A PHILOSOPHER

1. Give some examples of rules about life that you think you have accepted as true on the basis of what the pragmatist James calls "the practical difference it makes" in your life? For example, a rule you might have accepted as true is the Golden Rule: "You should do unto others as you would have them do unto you." And you might have accepted it because you found that when you accepted that rule you had more harmonious and satisfactory relationships with people.
2. What were the "harmonious and satisfactory" consequences that followed from accepting as true those rules that you just gave as examples to question 1 above?

Modern Pragmatism. Pragmatism continues to be one of the most vigorous living philosophies. In fact, many contemporary philosophers believe that pragmatism is the most vital and promising of all approaches to truth. Nevertheless, contemporary pragmatists approach truth differently from William James. Whereas James gave a definition of *truth,* modern pragmatists tend to argue that we should forget about trying to define this elusive idea. Instead, we should get on with the more important activity of living in open-minded, democratic communities. Richard Rorty, one of the foremost living philosophers and a staunch advocate of pragmatism, writes the following:

We pragmatists . . . are making the purely *negative* point that we would be better off without the traditional distinctions between knowledge and opinion, construed as the distinction between truth as correspondence to reality and truth as a commendatory

14 William James, *Pragmatism: A New Name for Some Old Ways of Thinking* (New York: Longmans, Green, 1907), 198–199.

term for well-justified belief. Our opponents call this negative claim "relativistic" because they cannot imagine that anybody would seriously deny that truth has an intrinsic nature. So when we say that there is nothing to be said about truth save that each of us will commend as true those beliefs which he or she finds good to believe, the realist is inclined to interpret this as one more positive theory about the nature of truth: a theory according to which truth is simply the contemporary opinion of a chosen individual or group. Such a theory would, of course, be self-refuting. But we pragmatists do not have a theory of truth, much less a relativistic one.[15]

Nevertheless, Rorty holds that what can be said about the notion of truth is that truth is whatever has passed society's "procedures of justification." He proposes "the ethnocentric view that there is nothing to be said about either truth or rationality apart from descriptions of the familiar procedures of justification which a given society, ours, uses in one or another area of inquiries."[16] Thus, the modern pragmatist, much like William James, wants to get rid of the traditional idea that truth is correspondence with an external reality. Instead, the modern pragmatist wants us to recognize that when people say something is true, they are merely trying to "commend" it as good to believe. We commend a statement as true when it passes the tests that our community uses to distinguish what is true from what is false. Different communities, of course, may have different procedures or criteria for separating true from false. Scientists use one set of procedures for deciding what they will accept as true, whereas poets, lawyers, literary critics, and movie producers use others. But no group's procedures lead to more truth about reality than any other group's. One group's truth about an independent reality cannot be "privileged" as more true than the truths of other groups. There are many truths that emerge from the many different procedures that different communities use. And they each use these different procedures because they have found that these procedures produce worthwhile or useful results.

QUICK REVIEW
The contemporary pragmatist Rorty claims we do not need theories of truth; the most we can say is that we "commend" as true whatever passes our community's "procedures of justification." Because there are many communities, there are many different but equally valid truths.

Criticisms of Pragmatism. Pragmatism has been the subject of intense criticism. The main criticism has been that it seems to base truth on the fallible judgments of human communities. What's true may be justified for a certain community to believe, but what's justified for them to believe isn't necessarily true. Pragmatism seems to reduce epistemology to psychology.

To understand this basic criticism of pragmatism, consider a simple fact: What we were justified in believing yesterday may turn out to be false today. For example, five hundred years ago people were justified in believing the sun revolved around the earth since they had good evidence for that belief and no evidence to the contrary. Today, we know the sun does not revolve around the earth. Pragmatism does not seem to be able to account for this simple fact. Pragmatism says that truth is whatever a community is justified in believing after it has used its "procedures of justification." So the pragmatist would have to say that five hundred years ago it was true that the sun revolved around the earth because people were justified in believing it did then. Since we are justified in believing it does not, it is false today that the sun revolves around the earth! This seems clearly absurd.

QUICK REVIEW
This kind of pragmatic theory seems to imply that when our community all thought that the earth was flat, it really was true that it was flat. But this seems wrong.

Some pragmatists have tried to deal with this objection. Instead of saying that truth is what any community would be justified in believing, they say it is only what an "ideal community" would be justified in believing. An ideal community is one

15   Richard Rorty, "Science as Solidarity," in *Dismantling Truth*, ed. Hilary Lawson and Lisa Appignanesi (New York: St. Martin's, 1989), 11.
16   Ibid., 11.

that continues investigating indefinitely, examines all the evidence, makes no mistakes, and is open to all points of view. Truth, then, must be judged by what this ideal community would be justified in believing. So it is correct that five hundred years ago people were justified in believing that the sun revolved around the earth. But the pragmatist does not have to conclude that five hundred years ago it was true that the sun revolved around the earth. For an ideal community would not believe that the sun ever revolved around the earth. So the pragmatist can say that it was not true that the sun revolved around the earth five hundred years ago even if people then thought it did. The "ideal community" idea lets pragmatists say people can be justified in believing something false, without having to say that what they believe is true. A belief that a group is justified in believing but that is untrue is simply a belief that an ideal community would not be justified in believing.

However, this response seems to replace one kind of "metaphysical garbage" with another kind. Pragmatists have said that the idea that truth requires an external reality to which true beliefs must "correspond" is so much "metaphysical garbage." But to say that we must believe in an "ideal community" to know the difference between true and false seems also to be metaphysical garbage.

Moreover, what view should pragmatists have about their own views about truth? Shouldn't they say that their theory is true if it is more useful than other theories? But in what sense is the pragmatic theory more useful than the more traditional correspondence theory of truth or coherence theory of truth? Any judgment about usefulness seems to involve a large dose of subjectivity. Couldn't traditional philosophers claim that their views of truth are better in terms of their own preferences? It seems that they can.

Does Truth Matter?

These debates over the nature of truth may at first seem dry and irrelevant. What does it matter whether the correct view of truth is the correspondence theory, the coherence theory, or the pragmatic theory? After all, whatever truth is, it seems that we will continue to believe the same truths and live the same lives. But, in fact, the parties to these debates are fighting over matters that directly affect each of us. It affects, for example, our views on the case with which we began our discussion of truth. This was the case of Marc Dutroux, accused of killing four children and of being part of a ring of pedophiles that included powerful men throughout Europe who protected him. As we saw, Professor Winkin claimed there is no objective truth about these matters and that the truth depends on the beliefs and interests a group happens to "share." Where do the three theories of truth stand on these issues?

Consider, first, that both the coherence and the pragmatic views are opposed to the correspondence view of truth. This is only natural because the correspondence view holds that truth is objective. That is, it holds that truth depends on what the real world is like, not on what a particular person or group accepts. Both the coherence and pragmatic views, on the other hand, reject the idea that truth is objective in this way. Instead, they hold that the truth of a claim depends on what the group that makes the claim accepts. The coherence theory says that a claim is true if it coheres with the other beliefs that a group accepts. The pragmatic theory says that a claim is true if it is useful for a group to believe it or it passes the procedures of justification the group uses. Both theories agree that if a group accepts a claim (because it coheres with their other beliefs or because it passes their procedures of justification or because it is useful to believe), then the claim is true for that group. Moreover, any conflicting claims accepted by other groups are equally true (if they meet the same criteria). One group's accepted claims are as true as the accepted claims of any other group. So to reject the correspondence view of truth is to reject objectivity and to choose a relativist view that sees each group's accepted claims as equally valid.

We must be careful, though, in how we use the words *relativist* and *relativism*. Rorty and other pragmatists say that, in a sense, they are not relativists about truth. They are not relativists, Rorty claims, if by *relativism* we mean that every belief is as good as any other and truth is whatever a group believes. Such relativism, Rorty has said, is just a "bogeyman" intended to "frighten children." However, he concedes, pragmatists agree that they are relativists about truth if by *relativism* we mean that truth is whatever a group *accepts because it passes that group's procedures of justification*. Pragmatists are relativists, then, in this more restricted sense.

But why does it matter that pragmatism and coherence are relativist views of truth? Consider some consequences of rejecting the correspondence theory and opting for the pragmatic or coherence theories of truth. Suppose we accept the pragmatic or coherence theories of truth. Then we must agree that one group's accepted claims are as true as any other group's accepted claims if the reason their claims are accepted is because they pass their procedures of justification or because they are useful to believe or because they cohere with their system of accepted beliefs. We must agree that if, for such reasons, members of a racist group accept the claim that they are superior to other races, their claim is as true as our claim that no race is superior to another. We must agree that if, for those reasons, males as a group accept the claim that they are superior to women, then their claim is as true as women's claim that males are not superior to females. And if, for those reasons, a group accepts that the Holocaust never happened, then that claim is as true as historians' claim that Nazi Germans slaughtered six million Jews during World War II. If the ring of pedophiles Marc Dutroux identified accepts that sex with children is good, for those reasons, then their claim is as valid as another group's claim that having sex with children is evil.

In short, if truth means what the coherent or pragmatic theories say it means, then whatever one group accepts can be as true as what an opposing group accepts. One group's biases, prejudices, or superstitions can be as legitimate as the objections that other groups may raise to these biases, prejudices, or superstitions. If truth is not objective, then the consequence, it seems, is that any claim accepted by a group can be a legitimate truth.

For many who hold a relativist theory of truth, these consequences are not necessarily bad. For example, some pragmatists hold that toleration is a critically important value that only relativism can preserve. Toleration is the virtue of acknowledging that we do not have a monopoly on truth and that the claims of others may be as valid as the claims we accept. Toleration is the virtue that relativism prizes. Defenders of relativism say it is inclusive and democratic, and that objective views of truth are exclusive and undemocratic. Objective views of truth are exclusive and undemocratic because they imply that the views of some groups are wrong and so they exclude such views.

So, you see that the choice among the theories of truth is not an abstract irrelevant exercise. A lot hangs on which theory you ultimately accept. If you opt for objectivity, you will move toward the correspondence view that truth depends on facts about the world independent of what any group happens to accept. Accepting objectivity may lead you to say that some views (like the views of a racist or a pedophile) are wrong no matter how many people accept them. On the other hand, if you opt for relativism, you will move toward the coherence or pragmatic view that truth depends on what this or that group accepts. Accepting relativism may lead you toward a more tolerant, inclusive, and democratic recognition that the views of others are equally valid. Both paths are attractive; both paths have dangerous pitfalls.

✓ QUICK REVIEW

The correspondence theory of truth says truth depends on an objective reality, but the coherence and pragmatic theories say truth depends on what a group accepts. Such relativist theories imply that beliefs accepted by any group are true and as valid as any other beliefs, no matter how racist, superstitious, nonhistorical, or biased.

✓ QUICK REVIEW

Defenders of relativist theories argue that their views on truth are more tolerant, democratic, and inclusive than an objective theory such as correspondence. Although the theories to some extent can be seen as complementary theories about truth in different realms, our lives can force us to choose one or the other.

Reconciling the Theories of Truth

Is there any way to reconcile the three theories? Can we say, for example, that each of the theories tells us only part of what truth is and that you need all the theories to get a full picture of truth? To a certain extent, this is possible, and some philosophers have proposed as much.[17] One simple way to do this is to view each theory as appropriate for some domains of knowledge, but not necessarily for others. Unquestionably, for example, the correspondence theory fits our beliefs about the empirical physical realm. This domain includes the beliefs we have about the ordinary objects around us and the claims that science makes about the nature of the physical and biological world. Suppose I say it's true that New York is three thousand miles from Los Angeles, it's true that a fire needs oxygen, or it's true that it's raining. Then I am probably taking *truth* to mean "correspondence." If the statements correspond to the facts, then I accept them as true.

On the other hand, the coherence theory provides some insight into truth in the domains of mathematics, of logic, of the legal decisions courts make, and of works of fiction. For example, the theorems of geometry are deduced from geometry's axioms and other theorems. And judges in courts of law try to keep their decisions consistent with the body of previous legal decisions. When we say the theorems of geometry or the decisions of a judge are true, the coherence theory seems to provide a useful understanding of what that kind of truth is.

Finally, the pragmatic test seems to reveal the meaning of truth as applied to the domain of value judgments. Thus, "Lying is wrong," "Pleasure is an intrinsic good," and other such statements form an important part of our lives. So do value judgments in the arts, politics, education, and other walks of life. Frequently, the best—and sometimes the only—way to verify such judgments is by asking what the consequences of believing such judgments are. Do these beliefs lead to satisfying lives? The pragmatic theory thus helps us understand what truth can mean in the realm of values.

ANALYZING THE READING

A pluralist theory of truth holds that each of the three theories of truth may be used to understand what truth means in different "domains of discourse." The textbook mentions several domains of discourse and suggests the theory of truth that might apply to each. What are some domains of discourse (or kinds of knowledge) that are not mentioned in the textbook? Explain which of the three theories of truth you think would be the right theory to use to explain what truth means in those domains.

So we can see the theories of truth as complementing, rather than opposing, each other. This approach to truth is sometimes called a "pluralist" view of truth because it accepts all three views of truth and sees each as applying to specific "domains of discourse." It is a view that sees truth as being more than a single quality or property or that accepts that there are different ways of being true. Mathematical beliefs may have the kind of truth that the coherence theory proposes, while descriptive beliefs about ordinary objects can have the kind of truth the correspondence theory proposes. Rather than forcing ourselves to choose among three incompatible theories, we can use the resources of all of them to understand truth in the various domains of discourse in which we seek knowledge.

Still, this strategy of approaching the theories of truth as complementary can take us only a certain distance. For the question still remains: How are we to evaluate a claim that others accept when we disagree with that claim and when it has an impact on the way we live? Since the disagreement is about a single claim, different domains of discourse are not involved. The truth of the claim has to be understood in the light

---

[17]   This view is now called "Alethic Pluralism"; see C. Wright, *Truth and Objectivity* (Cambridge, MA: Harvard University Press, 1992), and M. P. Lynch, *Truth as One and Many* (Oxford: Clarendon Press, 2009).

of a single theory of truth. Shall we be tolerant pragmatists and say, for example, that racist or sexist groups are entitled to their views? What if their racism or sexism is directed against us? Or what shall we say about a ring of adults who believes sex with children is good? Shall we be tolerant relativists and say that their belief is as valid as ours? Or shall we opt for an objective view of truth and say that their belief is false and that we should track them down and not allow them to act on it?

Our lives together, then, can still force us to choose between the objectivity and exclusivity of the correspondence theory and the relativism and tolerance of the coherence or pragmatic theories. It seems that where our lives intersect, at least, we must opt for one or the other of these theories. Such choices have momentous consequences for who you are. For in a very real sense, the kind of person you are depends on how you respond to such choices. Will you become the tolerant relativist who accepts that racists, sexists, and pedophiles have their views and you have yours? Or will your convictions about the objectivity of truth lead you to take firm stands for what you see as the truth?

PHILOSOPHY AT THE MOVIES

Watch *The Usual Suspects* (1995) in which Verbal, an eyewitness to a waterfront explosion, explains to the police how he and four other men got together in jail after they were arrested on suspicion of stealing a truck, and how they ended up at the scene of the explosion. What is true and what is false in this movie? On what view of truth do you base your answer? Does the film depend on one theory of truth more than another? Explain.

© Photos 12/Alamy

6.3 Does Science Give Us Truth?

🔵 **MindTap** What can science tell us about how we obtain knowledge? Go to MindTap to watch a video about how scientists understand the relationship between the brain, memory, and knowledge.

In the previous chapter, we discussed the scientific method as a source of knowledge. We noted that it incorporates elements of empiricism, rationalism, and transcendental idealism. But we did not answer this question: Does science give us the truth? Now that we have looked closely at the question "What is truth?" let's return to the issue of whether there is truth in science. Does our discussion of the three theories of truth help us understand scientific truth?

Many people hold that science clearly gives us the truth about the world. After all, science has enabled us to do amazing things. It has shown us how to cure hundreds of deadly diseases. It has let us put people into space and on the moon. Science has shown us how to send our voices and moving pictures over thousands of miles and how to build computers that make a million calculations in a fraction of a second. It has enabled the invention of radios, rockets, telescopes, the hydrogen bomb, computers, vaccines, antibiotics, heart transplants, cars, airplanes, submarines, and satellites. All this and much more testifies to the power of our scientific knowledge. These successes, many believe, are clear proof that science gives us the truth. Yet does it?

To focus our inquiry, we're going to need examples of what a scientific theory is. So we will take a very quick look at two theories: the standard theory of matter and Copernicus' theory of the solar system. We will see that it's not so easy to know in what sense, if any, they are true.

Since the beginning of the twentieth century, scientists have accepted the atomic theory of matter. This theory says that the objects around us are made of atoms. Each atom consists of a small central nucleus made up of protons and neutrons and a surrounding cloud of electrons. For many years, scientists held the theory that protons, neutrons, and electrons were the building blocks from which all things are made. But experiments eventually led scientists to a new theory: The protons and neutrons are themselves made of even smaller, more basic particles. The experiments that led scientists to change their theories were done in gigantic tubes called *particle accelerators* or *colliders*, some over a mile long. From one end of one of these tubes, a device shoots particles (electrons and atoms) toward the other end. At the other end, these particles smash into other particles at terrific speeds. These collisions can be detected in "cloud chambers" or "bubble chambers." Inside these chambers the speeding particles and collisions make tiny tracks or lines that can actually be seen and photographed (see Figure 6.1). Some collisions can also

© Omikron/Photo Researchers, Inc.

Figure 6.1   Photograph of the tracks made in a bubble chamber when a tiny subatomic particle—a proton—collided with another particle in the area at the center right and broke up into at least nine particles. The tracks left by these nine particles branch away from the point of collision and streak toward the bottom of the image. The various spirals scattered around the bubble chamber are other tracks left by electrons whose trajectories were curved by strong magnets.

be detected using Geiger counters and other sensitive instruments that record the collisions. In these collisions, electrons sometimes bounce off of the particles at the other end, like tiny billiard balls hitting each another. In other collisions, protons and neutrons seem to break apart into smaller particles when struck by the speeding electrons.

As a result of these experiments with colliders, scientists now accept what they call the standard theory of matter. This theory says that all the ordinary physical objects in the universe—from toads and trees to stars and galaxies—are made up of four kinds of tiny basic particles. These consist of two kinds of "quarks," which make up the protons and neutrons in the nuclei of atoms. A third type of basic particles are electrons, which surround the nuclei of atoms. And the fourth type consists of neutrinos, which move very fast, have virtually no mass, and seem to shoot out of nuclear reactions. These four kinds of particles are held together and acted upon by four forces. One is a strong nuclear force, which holds quarks together in the atomic nucleus. The second is a weak nuclear force, which sets off certain kinds of radioactive decay. The third is electromagnetism, which builds atoms into molecules and molecules into the physical objects we see. And the fourth is gravity, which holds together the planets, stars, and whole galaxies. Each of these four forces is associated with or "carried" by a particle. Photons carry the electromagnetic force. Gluons carry the strong nuclear force. Bosons carry the weak force. And gravitons carry gravity. This standard theory of matter is today accepted as a true theory of the fundamental structure of all the matter in our universe. Our question is: What does it mean to say that this theory of matter is "true"?

The Instrumentalist View

If you asked them, most scientists would say that the standard theory of matter is true. Yet what does that mean? Well, ask yourself this: What does it mean to say that quarks, neutrinos, and electrons exist? No one has ever seen or heard or touched one of these particles, and no one ever will. They are unobservable "theoretical entities." That is, they are entities mentioned in the standard theory and other theories, but we cannot directly observe them. So in what sense is it true that these theoretical entities exist?

Perhaps you might want to say that it is "true" that unobservable theoretical entities like electrons exist in the following sense. The standard theory of matter says that electrons and the other theoretical entities exist. This theory predicts that when bits of matter collide at very high speeds, they will break apart into the basic particles it describes. Those collisions will make the dials on Geiger detectors move and will leave little tracks in cloud chambers. Now, in fact, when scientists shoot bits of matter together at extremely high speeds in particle accelerators the dials on Geiger detectors move and the tracks appear exactly as the theory predicts. The accuracy of these predictions shows that the theory is true. So, it is "true" that electrons exist insofar as accepting the theories in which electrons play a role allows us to make successful predictions.

Still, do successful predictions indicate that a theory is true and that its theoretical entities exist? Couldn't the theory just be a formula that works but that isn't literally true? Granted, the theory lets scientists predict what they will see when they shoot bits of matter together. But this successful prediction does not necessarily mean that the theory is literally true. Nor does successful prediction mean that it is literally true that these theoretical entities exist.

In fact, many scientists and philosophers interpret the standard theory as saying something like this: "If we *assume* that matter is partly made of little electrons, we can predict that the dials on detectors will move when matter collides. But this does not mean it is literally true that little electrons exist. It only means that with this assumption we can make accurate predictions." In short, photons, gluons, gravitons, and bosons are only imaginary things mentioned in theories that let us predict what will happen in certain experiments. Scientific theories that describe such unobservable theoretical entities are not true in the same literal sense that, say, it is true that the moon exists. Instead, such theories are *assumed* to be true even though we cannot say they are *really* true. And they are assumed to be true because that assumption allows us to use the theories to predict what will happen.

This view of scientific theories and of theoretical entities is called the instrumentalist view of scientific theories. You have probably noticed that this view has some similarities to the pragmatic theory of truth. In fact, the instrumentalist view incorporates some fundamental aspects of the pragmatic theory of truth. The **instrumentalist view**, like the pragmatic theory, emphasizes that truth in science is related to whether a theory "works." That is, whether a theory works determines whether the theory is acceptable. However, unlike the pragmatic view of truth, the instrumentalist view does not claim that scientific theories are literally true when they work. By saying that a theory "works," the instrumentalist means that it lets us accurately predict what will happen when we do certain things. But the instrumentalist does not believe that the unobservable theoretical entities of the scientific theory really exist. They are invented or fictitious entities that serve as useful but imaginary constructs. They are useful because if we act *as if* they exist, we can make accurate scientific predictions.

The instrumentalist view has a long history. For example, in the sixteenth century, the astronomer Copernicus proposed that the earth and the planets revolve around the sun. As noted earlier in this chapter, everyone then believed that the earth stood still and the sun and planets revolved

ANALYZING THE READING

The instrumentalist view of science claims that scientific theories are true only in the sense that they allow scientists to predict events. Explain what this claim means. Do you think this claim is right? What reasons do you think led or could lead some philosophers to embrace the instrumentalist view?

around it. This was the theory of the astronomer Ptolemy. People believed that God, who created the universe, put humans and the earth at the center of the universe. Theologians claimed that the Bible itself declares that the sun revolves around the earth and the earth stands still. And church authorities were willing to persecute anyone who opposed these views. So, in the preface to Copernicus' book, a friend of his wrote that Copernicus was not trying to describe the real universe. Instead, Copernicus' proposal was just an imaginary model meant to "save the appearances." That is, it gave scientists a way of accurately calculating and predicting where the sun and the planets would appear in the sky. Readers, he wrote, should not take Copernicus' proposal as a description of the real structure of the universe. In reality, the sun revolves around the earth. Copernicus' proposal that the earth and planets revolve around the sun was just a useful but fictitious device for calculating the positions of the planets. In short, Copernicus' theory that the earth revolves around the sun should be interpreted instrumentally.

Most scientists at the time agreed. In reality, they said, the earth stood still at the center of the universe while the sun and planets spun around it as Ptolemy said. Copernicus' assumption that the sun stood still while the earth and planets spun around it was false. But this false assumption, they felt, gave them a better way of calculating where the planets would be on any given day in the future. Here is how a book on astronomy written in 1594 put it: "Copernicus affirms that the earth turns about and that the sun stands still in the midst of the heavens, by help of which false supposition he has made truer demonstrations of the motions and revolutions of the celestial spheres, than ever were made before."[18]

But as time passed scientists found additional problems with the old view of Ptolemy that the sun revolves around the earth. A growing number of scientists then began to think that Copernicus' proposal was a description of the way the universe really worked. This belief got some of those scientists into trouble with the church. The most famous was Galileo Galilei. In 1632, he published *A Dialogue Concerning the Two Great World Systems.* In that work he argued that Copernicus' view was an accurate description of the way the universe really was. For his efforts, Galileo was put on trial by the church's Inquisition. The Inquisition condemned Galileo for "vehement suspicion of heresy" and sentenced him to house arrest for life. Eventually, Galileo had to retract his views. Nevertheless, the future would vindicate his rejection of the instrumentalist interpretation of Copernicus' theory. How then did Galileo interpret Copernicus? He interpreted his theory according to the "realist" view of science.

The Realist View of Science

The **realist view** of scientific truth is an alternative to the instrumentalist view. The realist view is, in fact, a version of the correspondence theory of truth. According to the realist view, scientific theories are literally true or false. The standard theory, we saw, describes quarks, neutrinos, gluons, bosons, gravitons, and other unobservable entities. The realist view of science says that if the standard theory of matter is true, these entities

THINKING LIKE A PHILOSOPHER

Suppose the realist view of science is correct. How would that affect the way you see the world around you: the planets, the milky way, the stars, the plants, and the animals you see. Suppose the instrumentalist view of science is correct. How would that affect the way you see the world around you?

---

[18] Quoted in Michael R. Gardner, "Realism and Instrumentalism in Pre-Newtonian Astronomy," *in Scientific Knowledge,* ed. Janet A. Kourany (Belmont, CA: Wadsworth, 1987), 370.

really exist. More generally, any true scientific theory, such as Copernicus' heliocentric theory, describes the way the universe really is.

According to the realist, the world around us contains entities whose existence is independent of us. These entities have properties and relationships that are also independent of us. That is, the world is made up of entities whose relationships and qualities do not depend on our beliefs or theories. According to the realist, science tries to explain this world by discovering the properties and relationships its entities have. A scientific theory is true if the entities and properties it talks about exist as the theory says they do and if they have the relationships the theory says they have. That is, the realist says a scientific theory is true when the entities and properties it refers to and the relationships it describes *correspond* to real entities that exist in the world and their real relationships and properties. For example, if the standard theory of matter is true, then electrons, gluons, and quarks are real and they really have the properties and relationships the theory says they have. If Copernicus' theory of the universe is true, then the planets, earth, and sun move and are really related to one another as his theory says they are.

Realists and instrumentalists have very different views about the aim of science. According to the instrumentalist, the aim of science is to make accurate predictions, ultimately so that we can satisfy our human needs. For the realist, the aim of science is to provide true explanations of the world by telling us exactly what properties and relationships its entities have. Notice also that the realist and the instrumentalist differ on how science proceeds. According to the instrumentalist, the scientist *invents* or makes up useful scientific truth. But according to the realist, the scientist *discovers* scientific truth. The realist believes that the facts a true theory describes were already there before the scientist discovered or described them. So the truths of the theory already existed even before the theory was formulated. The instrumentalist believes that truth does not exist until the scientist invents it and shows that it gives us the right predictions.

Realists argue that scientific theories give us accurate predictions simply because they correspond to the way the world is. Theories are not true because they make accurate predictions, as the instrumentalist holds. Rather, they make accurate predictions because they correspond to reality. Moreover, says the realist, most scientists will not say that they are trying to make up imaginary entities that can help them predict the future. Instead, they will say that they are trying to discover what reality is really like. That is, they are trying to figure out what entities really exist, what properties they really have, and how they are really related.

QUICK REVIEW

The realist view of science is based on the correspondence theory of truth and says a theory is true if the entities, properties, and relationships that it describes *correspond* to real entities, properties, and relationships in the world. Theories are discovered, not invented. The aim of science is to provide accurate descriptions of the universe. Theories allow accurate predictions because they are true; they are not true because they allow accurate predictions.

ANALYZING THE READING

According to the textbook, instrumentalists hold that the scientist invents or makes up useful scientific truths, while realists hold that the scientist discovers scientific truth. Explain what this means. Why can't the instrumentalist say that the scientist discovers scientific truths? Why can't the realist say that the scientist invents or makes up useful scientific truths?

The Conceptual Relativist View

A third view of scientific truth, the **conceptual relativist view**, shares many characteristics of the coherence theory of truth. Conceptual relativism owes much to the philosophy of Thomas Kuhn, whom we discussed in the preceding chapter. Many people whom Kuhn has influenced have come to the conclusion that a true scientific theory is nothing more than a theory that a community of scientists accepts. A community of working scientists, they claim, has its own unique way of seeing the world. The scientists who are members of the community have their own way of conducting research and their own research programs. They have their own way of interpreting what happens in their experiments and their own theories and beliefs about nature. And they have their own values about what counts in scientific

QUICK REVIEW

The conceptual relativist view of scientific theories is based on Kuhn and the coherence theory of truth. It says that communities of scientists accept research methods, programs, theories, and values that form a "conceptual framework" that is true by definition. New findings or beliefs are true if they fit in with the community's conceptual framework.

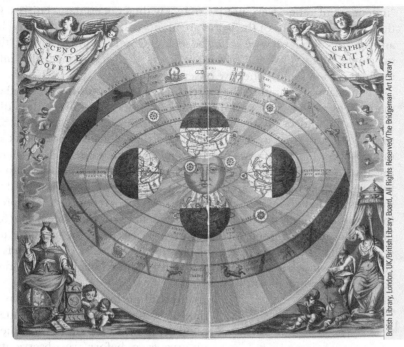

A seventeenth-century rendering of Copernicus' model for the earth and planets revolving around the sun. Scenographia: Systematis Copernicani Astrological Chart, c.1543, devised by Nicolaus Copernicus (1473–1543) from *The Celestial Atlas, or the Harmony of the Universe (Atlas coelestis seu harmonia macrocosmica),* c.1660. Andreas Cellarius (seventeenth century).

research. These research methods, theories, and values are the "conceptual framework" that a community of scientists has and that defines their community.

For example, astronomers before Copernicus believed in an older theory that could be found in the writings of Aristotle and Ptolemy. This theory said that the sun and planets revolve around the earth. Astronomers combined this theory with religious beliefs and values that said God put the earth at the center of the universe. And they looked at the sky with the naked eye to confirm these theories. These theories, methods, values, and beliefs were the conceptual framework of astronomers before Copernicus. After Copernicus, scientists began to believe that they should not place so much value on ancient books and texts. Neither should they rely on the church to decide scientific matters. They began to believe that, instead, they should rely on their own observations. They began to look at the sky by using the newly discovered telescope. They came to believe in Copernicus' theory that the earth and planets revolve around the sun. These new beliefs, methods, theories, and values made up a new conceptual framework.

According to the conceptual relativist, the beliefs that make up the conceptual framework of a community of scientists are true by definition. New scientific findings or new scientific theories are true if they fit in with the accepted conceptual framework of that community. For the conceptual relativist, then, what is true in science is what coheres with the theories, values, and research methods that define a community of scientists. A particular research finding is true or false only in relation to a particular conceptual framework. The standard theory of matter is true, for example, if it fits in with the beliefs, the methods, the values, and the other theories of contemporary physicists. Copernicus' theory is true if it fits in with the beliefs, methods, and other theories of contemporary astronomers.

Conceptual relativists argue that both the realist and instrumentalist views are radically flawed. Both the realist and the instrumentalist mistakenly believe that they can somehow know or observe the real world independently of their theories. Instrumentalists believe that they can independently check the world to see whether a theory's predictions are accurate. Realists believe that they can independently check the world to see whether a theory corresponds with reality. Yet these "independent" checks are not possible, say the conceptual relativists. Our observations and perceptions of the world are always colored and influenced by our beliefs and theories about what we *should* be seeing. Observations are always "theory laden," say conceptual relativists. Consequently, our theories about reality influence what we think we are seeing when we observe reality.

For example, suppose that a scientist who believes in the standard theory of matter sees a little white trail in a cloud chamber. She will see the little trail as the track left behind by an electron as it moved through the chamber. She will see it this way because that is what the standard theory leads her to think she is seeing. On the other hand, suppose you or I looked at the same vapor trail without knowing anything about the standard theory of matter. Then, all we would see would be little wispy lines that appeared and then vanished inside a glass bottle. In fact, our theories and beliefs influence even our ordinary perceptions. As you read this page, for example, you do not just see black scratches on white paper, which is all that an illiterate person might see. Instead, you see words that have meaning and sense. You see meaningful words instead of black scratches because of the beliefs and theories you have about what books and writing are. These beliefs and theories affect what you see when you look at this page.

QUICK REVIEW

Conceptual relativists say all observations are "theory laden." In other words, they are influenced by our values, beliefs, and theories—our conceptual frameworks—about what we should be seeing. So, theories cannot be verified by somehow observing the real world independently of our theories as instrumentalists and realists assume; we can see only if our theories fit in with the beliefs and theories we already accept.

THINKING LIKE A PHILOSOPHER

The conceptual relativist claims that it is not possible to know or observe the real world independently of our theories. That is, what we observe is always influenced and colored by what our beliefs and theories tell us we should be observing. Explain what this claim means by using an example of some object that you can observe inside your room right now. Explain how your prior beliefs and assumptions about what you are looking at influences what you see when you observe that object. Compare what you see when you observe that object to what an alien from another planet might see if he were to observe the same object. Do you agree with the claim of the conceptual relativist?

According to the conceptual relativist, then, theories can never be checked against some independent reality. Our theories influence what we observe even before we observe it. So we can only check our theories by seeing how they fit in with our other accepted theories and beliefs together with any new theory-laden observations we make. We can never escape this web of previously accepted beliefs and theories. Since theories can be checked only against other theories, we say a scientific theory is true when it fits in with our other accepted theories and beliefs.

These claims of the conceptual relativist theory of science, of course, are similar to the claims of the coherence theory of truth. The coherence theory of truth says that beliefs can never be checked against some pure fact. Every so-called fact, the coherence theory claims, is laden with beliefs that make it impossible to get at the pure fact. Consequently, the coherence theory claims, we can only check our beliefs against the system of beliefs that we already accept.

The conceptual relativist view that theories cannot be checked to see how well they describe an independent reality has an important implication. It implies that we cannot say that one theory explains or describes reality more accurately than another. Nevertheless, Kuhn argues, science periodically undergoes "conceptual revolutions." For example, when Copernicus' new theory replaced the old theory that the sun revolves around the earth, this was a "conceptual revolution." Kuhn suggests that when a new theory replaces an old one in such a revolution, there may be no rational reason for saying that the new theory is better than the old one. Many conceptual relativists who have followed Kuhn have agreed with this important suggestion. They have concluded that there often are no grounds for saying that one conceptual framework is better than another. That is, sometimes at least, we cannot say that one conceptual framework corresponds to reality better than another or even that one necessarily gives us better predictions. Truth in science is ultimately nothing more than coherence with an accepted conceptual framework.

When scientists abandon one framework and replace it with another, we often must attribute the change to nonrational causes and events. Scientists do not necessarily change their frameworks because they believe the new one describes or predicts events better than the old one did.

Conceptual relativists, then, reject the realist view that true scientific theories explain or describe what the universe is really like. Scientific theories do not "correspond" to a real world that is independent of our theories. Conceptual relativists also reject the instrumentalist view that scientific theories are true if they can be used to predict the future. For conceptual relativists a scientific theory is true if it coheres or fits in with the conceptual framework of a community of working scientists. Thus, conceptual relativism is similar to the coherence theory of truth.

We saw earlier that we can interpret truth in at least three ways: as correspondence, as coherence, and as pragmatic. We have seen now that we can also interpret truth in science in three ways: according to the realist view, the instrumentalist view, and the relativist view. These three ways of understanding truth in science are similar to the three views of truth we examined earlier in this chapter. Which of these is correct? No one can answer that question for you. Scientists and philosophers themselves are divided on this question. In fact, the question itself is a paradox. For in asking which of these three views of truth is correct, aren't you asking which of them is true? Yet doesn't each interpret the meaning of truth in a different way? Truth in science, it has turned out, is much more complicated than it first appeared to be.

QUICK REVIEW
Periodically, communities of scientists exchange one conceptual framework for another in a "conceptual revolution." But the new framework is not more true than the old; it does not more accurately describe an independent real world or necessarily make more accurate predictions. It just better achieves whatever values are prized in the community's conceptual framework.

PHILOSOPHY AT THE MOVIES

Watch *Living Proof* (2008; originally a TV movie), which tells the true story of Dr. Denny Slamon, a UCLA physician and researcher conducting research on the drug Herceptin because he believes it will stop the growth of certain breast cancer tumors by binding to a protein molecule that regulates the replication of tumor cells, a process that is not directly observable. What view of scientific truth does this movie seem to accept? What view of scientific truth do the various characters in this movie seem to hold?

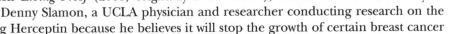

6.4 Can Interpretations Be True?

Science is not the only area of our lives where truth is important but difficult to pin down. Truth is also crucial to us when we try to interpret books, poems, movies, scripture, and people's words and actions. When someone speaks to you, you need to interpret that person's *words*: What did she mean by that? When you see someone doing something, you interpret her *actions*: Why did she do that, and what is the meaning of what she did? When you read a poem or watch a movie, you need to interpret it: What is the poem or movie trying to say? When you go to church or read the Bible, you try to interpret the words of passages in scripture. When a lawyer or a judge looks at a statute or even the Constitution, she must interpret it to determine its meaning.

But when is an interpretation true and what is a "true" interpretation? Suppose you chance upon this passage in the Bible: "You shall not lie with a male as with a woman; it is an abomination" (Leviticus 18:22). What does it mean? Obviously, you say, it is pointing out that homosexual activities are immoral. Yet many biblical scholars say that this "obvious" interpretation is mistaken. Homosexual relations between males, they say, were part of the ritual practices of some of the religions that opposed Judaism when this text was written. What the text is really saying, then, is to avoid the ritual practices of foreign religions. So which interpretation is true? The "obvious" one that first occurred to you or the one that some biblical scholars have proposed? And what do you mean when you say one is true and the other is false?

Or instead take a poem, such as William Blake's famous "The Tyger":

Tyger! Tyger!

Cybermartu/iStockphoto.com

Tyger! Tyger! Burning bright
In the forests of the night,
What immortal hand or eye
Could frame thy fearful symmetry?

In what distant deeps or skies
Burnt the fire of thine eyes?
On what wings dare he aspire?
What the hand dare seize the fire?

And what shoulder, and what art,
Could twist the sinews of thy heart?
And when thy heart began to beat,
What dread hand? And what dread feet?

What the hammer? What the chain?
In what furnace was thy brain?
What the anvil? What dread grasp
Dare its deadly terrors clasp?

When the stars threw down their spears,
And watered heaven with their tears,
Did he smile his work to see?
Did he who made the Lamb make thee?

Tyger! Tyger! Burning bright
In the forests of the night,
What immortal hand or eye
Could frame thy fearful symmetry?[19]

What does this poem mean? Some literary experts have argued that the Tyger is here a symbol of the evil self who "sustains its own life at the expense of its fellow-creatures."[20] The "forests of the night," they claim, symbolize for Blake the "fallen world"—that is, the material world where evil reigns. The Lamb is a symbol for Jesus Christ. The answer to the question Blake asks at the end is: No, the God who made the Lamb did not make the evil in the heart of the evil predator. Yet other critics argue for an opposite interpretation: "There can be no doubt that *The Tyger* is a poem that celebrates the holiness of tiger-ness."[21] They claim that the word "*forests* suggests tall straight forms, a world that for all its terror has the orderliness of the tiger's stripes." Blake, they say, transforms the ferocity of the tiger into the symbol of goodness. Still a third group of critics have claimed that the tiger in Blake's poem is *both* good and evil. A fourth group of critics say it is "beyond good and evil." Yet others conclude that the poem "is a maze of questions in which the reader is forced to wander confusedly."[22] What, then, is the true interpretation of the poem? And what would it mean to say a certain interpretation is the "true" interpretation?

19 William Blake, "The Tiger," in Edwin Ellis, ed., *The Poetical Works of William Blake*, vol. I (London: Chatto & Windus: 1906), 85.
20 Kathleen Raine, "Who Made the Tyger," *Encounter*, June 1954, 50.
21 E. D. Hirsch, *Innocence and Experience* (New Haven, CT: Yale University Press, 1964), 247–248.
22 L. J. Swingle, "Answers to Blake's 'Tyger': A Matter of Reason or of Choice," *Concerning Poetry* 2 (1970), 67.

Or take a legal text. In 1868, Congress ratified the Fourteenth Amendment to the United States Constitution. The amendment states: "No State shall make or enforce any law which shall . . . deny to any person . . . the equal protection of the law." What is the true interpretation of this text? Some legal scholars say it clearly means that a state cannot support a preferential treatment program. A preferential treatment program gives preference to women or minorities over white males when applying for jobs or colleges. Such programs, they argue, do not treat white males as equal to women or minorities. So such programs "clearly" violate the meaning of the Constitution's Fourteenth Amendment. Other legal scholars have argued that women and minorities have been disadvantaged in the past. Preferential programs are needed now to make them more equal to white males. So, these scholars say, the true meaning of the Fourteenth Amendment clearly allows preferential treatment programs.[23] Who is right? What is the true interpretation of the Constitution? Some might want to reply that the Supreme Court decides its true interpretation. But this only pushes the problem back a step. How should the judges of the Supreme Court decide which is the true interpretation? And what would it mean to say that their interpretation is the "true" interpretation?

Hermeneutics is the study of the interpretation of words and actions. The word comes from the name of the ancient Greek god Hermes, who carried messages from the gods up in heaven to mortals down on earth. The messages were transmitted through "oracles," humans with the ability to hear and report these messages. But often the messages of the gods were unclear, ambiguous, or had multiple meanings. So recipients of the messages relied on professional interpreters to explain them. Hermeneutics developed from these attempts to interpret the words of the gods. But it was not the Greek gods that gave interpreters their hardest problems. Hermeneutics became an even larger concern for those who believed in the Judaic and Christian God.

Symbolic Interpretation and Intention

For both Christianity and Judaism, the Bible contains the words of God because God inspired the writers to write these words. But like the words of the Greek oracles, the words of the Bible can be unclear, ambiguous, or can be interpreted in many different ways. How can a believer know what he or she must do if the Bible can be interpreted in many ways? Which interpretation should he or she live by?

During the Middle Ages, philosophers and theologians developed new interpretations of several biblical passages. Many believed that besides its literal meaning, a biblical passage could have deeper symbolic meanings. Take, for example, the thirteenth-century philosopher-theologian Thomas Aquinas (1225–1274). Aquinas held that a biblical text could have many "spiritual" interpretations. And, he claimed, they could all be true:

> The first and basic meaning of a [biblical] text is the historical or literal meaning conveyed by the words themselves. But the things and events described by the literal meaning can also have a meaning. This is the spiritual meaning of the [biblical] text . . . . Now

> **THINKING LIKE A PHILOSOPHER**
>
> Pick a movie that you have recently seen and that you feel had a deeper meaning or message than a movie that provides pure entertainment. What is the meaning or message that you think the movie was trying to communicate? Discuss the movie with a friend who saw the same movie and ask your friend what meaning or message he or she felt the movie was trying to communicate. Are you both in complete agreement about your interpretations of the movie, or do you differ on some (maybe all) points? If you disagree on some points, do you think there is any way the two of you could come to an agreement on how the movie should be interpreted?

> **QUICK REVIEW**
> When we interpret books, poems, legal texts, scriptures, and people's words and actions, we must make sure that our interpretations are true. But what is a true interpretation? *Hermeneutics* is the study of interpretations.

---

[23] See Howard N. Meyer, *The Amendment That Refused to Die: Equality and Justice Deferred: The History of the Fourteenth Amendment* (Aurora, ON, Canada: Madison Books, 2000).

there are three kinds of spiritual meaning. First, things and events in the Old Testament can symbolize things and events in the New Testament. This is called the allegorical sense [of a biblical text]. Second, the actions of Jesus Christ described or symbolized [in the text] express how we ought to live. This is the moral meaning [of the biblical text]. Third, the things described in the Bible can symbolize what eternal glory [after death] will be like. This is the anagogical sense. So a word in the Bible can have several meanings.[24]

In some ways, Aquinas' willingness to accept many true interpretations made the problem of interpretation worse. How can a believer know which interpretation of the Bible is true if there can be many interpretations? Aquinas' solution was simple: The Church decides which interpretations of the Bible are true and which are false. In particular, the Church decides which symbolic interpretations are true.

But doesn't this solution create even more problems? First, how is the Church itself supposed to decide which interpretations are true? How is it to choose among the many literal and symbolic interpretations that human creativity can devise? Setting the Church up as an authority just pushes the problem back one step. These difficulties suggest a deeper problem with symbolic interpretations. Aren't symbolic interpretations really examples of seeing what you want to see? Aren't symbolic interpretations arbitrary? Symbolic interpretations seem to allow the reader to read into a text whatever meaning the reader would like to see.

Two hundred years after Aquinas, the Protestant reformer Martin Luther weighed in on the issue. He solved it by rejecting the whole idea of symbolic interpretations. There was, he said, only one true meaning of scripture, and that is the literal meaning. The nineteenth-century philosopher Friedrich Schleiermacher (1768–1834) agreed with Luther's view. But he provided an argument for this view. A text is a product of the history and culture of the person who wrote it, he said. So to interpret the text, we have to know the historical situation of the author. We have to figure out, in short, what the author was thinking and intending when he wrote whatever he wrote. As he put it: "The language and the history of the time the writer was living in is the context within which individual texts have to be interpreted."

Schleiermacher is not the only one who argued that there is one true and literal interpretation of a text. The philosopher Wilhelm Dilthey (1833–1911) also argued that the true interpretation of a text is the meaning the original human author intended. To find this original meaning, he claimed, we need to put ourselves in the place and time of the historical author and try to understand what he intended by the words he wrote. To understand the actions or words of any person, we must "relive" the life of the other person. This applies, he said, not only to interpreting words but also to interpreting anything that humans produce. It applies to our attempts to interpret art, poetry, speeches, laws, and even human history itself.

Schleiermacher and Dilthey, like Aquinas, obviously embraced the correspondence theory of truth. A true interpretation is one that corresponds to what

---

[24] Thomas Aquinas, *Summa Theologica*, I, Q. 1, a. 10, trans. and abridged by Manuel Velasquez.

the original author of a poem, law, scripture passage, or work of art intended. But Aquinas took the true interpretation to be the one that God intended because he felt God was in a sense the ultimate author of scripture. And God, he believed, could intend a scriptural passage to have more than one meaning. But Schleiermacher and Dilthey insisted we must look for what the historical human authors of a text intended. To try to understand God's intentions seems beyond our limited powers.

Many scholars accept the ideas of Schleiermacher and Dilthey. Literary critics have carefully studied what life was like at the time a poet such as Blake wrote to figure out what he intended the words of his poem to mean. Legal scholars have argued that to interpret a law like the Fourteenth Amendment, we need to get back to what those who originally passed the law intended it to mean. And theologians have studied life in ancient Palestine to try to determine what the human authors of the Bible meant by the words they used.

But there's another way to think about interpretation. Ask yourself this: Why is interpretation even needed? Why are there many possible ways of interpreting texts? Isn't the real problem the ambiguity of language? If the language and words that we use to express our meaning were perfectly clear and unambiguous, then would there even be a problem of interpretation? What if we could develop a language that was completely clear and unambiguous? Wouldn't this eliminate the possibility of different interpretations? Wouldn't an unambiguous language eliminate the need for hermeneutics?

Wittgenstein and the Ideal Clear Language

The idea of an unambiguous language was first suggested by the seventeenth-century rationalist philosopher Gottfried Leibniz (1646–1716). Leibniz argued that a perfect language in which we could express our ideas with complete clarity would be of immense value. In this perfect language, he said, "there will be no equivocations or amphibolies, and everything which will be said intelligibly in that language will be said with propriety."[25] Disagreements over interpretations, he said, could be settled "by calculating" the true meaning in this perfect language.

Leibniz never completed his ideal language. But in the early part of the twentieth century, the Austrian philosopher Ludwig Wittgenstein (1889–1951) took up that task. Wittgenstein published a seventy-five-page book titled *Tractatus-Logico-Philosophicus* in 1921. His book changed the course of philosophy. Wittgenstein claimed to provide the basics of the kind of ideal language that Leibniz had only dreamed about. In his book he described an ideal language that, he claimed, could express all legitimate meanings unambiguously.

Reality, he argued, consists of facts, both complex facts and simple facts. The simplest facts are "atomic facts," and complex facts are built out of these atomic facts. The propositions of an ideal language, he said, will provide "pictures" of these facts. A proposition will correctly picture a fact—and so will be true—when it has the same kind of "structure" the fact has. That is, a true proposition must have words that correspond to the parts of the fact it expresses, and the structure of the words must correspond to the structure of the parts of the fact. (Wittgenstein's views on truth are very similar to those of Russell who was his teacher, friend, and

QUICK REVIEW
Dilthey agreed that the only true interpretation of a text is the meaning that its human author intended, and finding this requires putting ourselves in the place and time of the historical author to "relive" his life.

QUICK REVIEW
Aquinas, Luther, Schleiermacher, and Dilthey all accepted the correspondence theory of truth: A true interpretation is one that corresponds to what the author (God for Aquinas, the human author for the others) intended.

QUICK REVIEW
Wittgenstein argued that a problem with interpreting language is that it is unclear; what is needed is an ideal language that is unambiguous. He set about describing such a language.

QUICK REVIEW
Wittgenstein said the world consists of complex facts made up of atomic facts and that an ideal language consists of complex propositions made up of elementary propositions. Elementary propositions represent atomic facts. A proposition is true when the structure of its elementary parts corresponds to the structure of the atomic facts that make up the complex fact it represents.

---

[25] Gottfried Leibniz, "Preface to the General Science," in *Leibniz Selections*, ed. Philip P. Wiener (New York: Scribner's, 1951), 16.

collaborator.) Wittgenstein, who wrote in an oracular fashion himself, expressed these points in his *Tractatus-Logico-Philosophicus*:

MindTap To read more from Ludwig Wittgenstein's *Tractatus-Logico-Philosophicus*, click the link in the MindTap Reader or go to the Questia Readings folder in MindTap.

> The world is the totality of facts, not of things....
> The object is the fixed, the existent....
> In the atomic fact the objects are combined in a definite way.
> The way in which objects hang together in the atomic fact is the structure of the
>   atomic fact....
> We make to ourselves pictures of facts....
> The elements of the picture stand, in the picture, for the objects.
> The picture consists in the fact that its elements are combined with one another in a
>   definite way.
> That the elements of the picture are combined with one another in a definite way,
>   represents that the things are so combined with one another.
> This connection of the elements of the picture is called its structure.[26]

✓ QUICK REVIEW
In this ideal language, all facts can be expressed unambiguously. If something cannot be expressed in this ideal language, it is illegitimate to try to say it at all.

In an ideal language, Wittgenstein argues, the simplest atomic facts will be expressed by simple elementary propositions. Just as complex facts are made up of atomic facts, in an ideal language complex propositions will be made up of elementary propositions. With this ideal language, Wittgenstein claimed, all facts can be expressed in a clear and unambiguous way. In fact, wrote Wittgenstein, "Everything that can be thought of at all can be thought of clearly; everything that can be said can be said clearly."[27]

✓ QUICK REVIEW
Wittgenstein's theory was based on the correspondence theory of truth and said that a proposition is true when its structure accurately "pictures" the structure of the fact it represents.

Wittgenstein's theory of language was, in effect, a hermeneutic. Wittgenstein held that the only legitimate meanings were those that could be expressed in his ideal language of facts. If a meaning could not be expressed or "spoken" in his ideal language, it was not legitimate. As he put it, "Whereof one cannot speak, thereof one must be silent."[28] This meant that only factual propositions could be legitimate since only factual propositions could be expressed in his language. Moreover, since all propositions could have only one meaning, they all could have only one interpretation. The true interpretation of any proposition, then, was its meaning. And its meaning was the fact that it expressed.

ANALYZING THE READING

Both Leibniz and Wittgenstein thought that it is possible to create an artificial language in which anything could be stated so clearly that there would be no disagreement about how the statement should be interpreted. Do you think it is possible to create such a language? Why? Would such a language have any value? Why?

Clearly, Wittgenstein had embraced a correspondence theory of truth. Propositions are true when they correspond to the facts. Meanings are legitimate only when they can be expressed in propositions that correspond to facts.

But as Wittgenstein got older, he abandoned his search for an ideal language of facts. He also left behind his allegiance to the correspondence theory of truth. And he again changed the course of philosophy.

The older Wittgenstein came to believe that his whole earlier approach to language had been wrong. It was a mistake, Wittgenstein argued in his later life, to think that language can serve a single purpose and express a single meaning. His idea that a language can provide an unambiguous picture of reality was based on this mistake. We must instead acknowledge that we use language for many different purposes and in many different human activities or "games." The meaning

---

[26]   Ludwig Wittgenstein, *Tractatus-Logico-Philosophicus*, 1.1 and 2.026–2.1512, quoted in *The Great Treasury of Western Thought*, ed. Mortimer J. Adler and Charles Van Doren (New York: R. R. Bowker, 1977), 403, 1267.

[27]   Ibid., 4.116.

[28]   Ibid., 6.57.

of language or a text cannot be isolated from our human activities. The meaning of a language or a text does not depend on the "facts" it pictures. Instead, the meanings of language depend on how people use language in the many different activities of life:

> But how many kinds of sentences are there? You say assertion, question, and command?—There are *countless* kinds, countless different kinds of use of what we call "symbols," "words," "sentences." And this multiplicity is not something fixed, given once for all; but new types of language, new language-games, as we may say, come into existence, and others become obsolete and get forgotten. . . . Here the term "language game" is meant to bring into prominence the fact that the *speaking* of language is part of any activity, or of a form of life.[29]

QUICK REVIEW
The older Wittgenstein argued that the meaning of a text does not depend on the "facts" it pictures, but on the meaning people give it as they use it in the many activities or "games" of life. Language can have many meanings if it is used in many different games.

These later views of Wittgenstein became vitally important for hermeneutics. Wittgenstein himself did not directly discuss the topic of hermeneutics. Nevertheless, his views have clear implications for that topic. First, if he is right, then the dream of a clear language is just that: a dream. Second, and more important, the meaning of words is not a fixed thing. So, the true interpretation of a text is also not fixed. The meaning of a text arises from the meaning that people give it as they use it in their life activities. Meaning is use. The true interpretation of a text, then, is the interpretation that people give it as they use it.

Clearly, in these later views Wittgenstein no longer holds the correspondence theory of truth. His view of truth is now much closer to the pragmatic theory of truth. For example, an interpretation of a scripture is true for a group of people if it is an interpretation that has a use in their forms of life. The same can be said for poetry and art. A true interpretation of a poem may be one that can enrich and give significance to the life of the reader. And the true interpretation of a law, such as the Fourteenth Amendment, depends on the needs and concerns of those who must use the law to order their society.

QUICK REVIEW
The true interpretation of a text is the interpretation that people give it in the game of life in which it is used. This view is based on a pragmatic theory of truth because it says that an interpretation of a text is true if it is an interpretation that people find useful in one of their life activities.

While Wittgenstein was developing his new views on meaning in England, European philosophers were also developing new views on meaning. Wittgenstein had developed his new views by rejecting his own older view that language can have only one meaning. European philosophers developed their new views by rejecting the view that there is one true interpretation of a text. Dilthey and Schleiermacher had said that the one true interpretation of a text is the meaning that the original author intended. But many European philosophers now objected that we can't ever really know the intentions of the original author. This is especially the case if the author lived centuries ago in a different culture. The most important of these new European philosophers is the German philosopher Hans-Georg Gadamer (1900–2002).

Gadamer and Prejudice

Gadamer pointed out that when a person tries to interpret someone's words, she must rely on the resources provided by her own personal experience and culture. Our culture consists of the values and beliefs of our time and our society. The culture that we absorb as we grow up is a "prejudice" that influences how we interpret someone else's words. For example, suppose that because of the way I was raised

---

[29] Ludwig Wittgenstein, *Philosophical Investigations*, 3rd ed., trans. G. E. M. Anscombe (New York: Macmillan, 1953), 11e.

in my culture, I believe in angels and devils. Then, when I read a Bible story about how Jesus cast devils out of a man, I may interpret the story as literally true. But suppose I grew up in a culture that does not believe in devils. Then, when I read this story, I may interpret it as a story that just symbolizes the ability of Jesus to overcome evil. My prior cultural beliefs prejudice how I interpret the story. There is no way to rid ourselves completely of these prejudices, says Gadamer. We have to interpret the words and actions of people in terms of our own historical culture. We can try to understand and correct our prejudices. But we can never completely escape them.

Texts, then, must be interpreted from the perspective of one's own personal experience and culture. That means that people from different cultures or historical periods must interpret texts differently. But none of these interpretations is more true than the others. As Gadamer puts it, "A text is understood only if it is understood in a different way every time."[30] A text, then, does not have a single true interpretation. Instead, the true meaning of a text depends on who is reading it and when and where they are reading it. A text can have as many true interpretations as there are people who read it:

> An inevitable difference between the interpreter and the author [is] created by the historical distance between them. Every age has to understand a transmitted text in its own way, for the text is part of the whole of the tradition in which the age takes an objective interest and in which it seeks to understand itself. The real meaning of a text, as it speaks to the interpreter, does not depend on the contingencies of the author and whom he originally wrote for. It certainly is not identical with them for it is always partly determined also by the historical situation of the interpreter and hence by the totality of the objective course of history.[31]

However, Gadamer did not think that we can just dream up any interpretations we want and pin them on texts. Instead, says Gadamer, interpreting a text is like talking to a person. We speak, and then the other person speaks; then, with a better understanding of the person, we speak again. Then, the other person also speaks again, and the process continues. In the same way, Gadamer insists, we have to carry on a dialogue with the text. First, we interpret the text in terms of the prejudices and concerns of our culture. Then, we try to understand what new things the text itself is trying to express and what it might have meant in its culture. When we do this, our own cultural prejudices change and get closer to the meaning of the text. Then, we use our newly informed cultural prejudices to come up with a better interpretation of the text. We try again to understand the text itself and its meaning in its own culture. Again our cultural prejudices change, coming closer to the meaning of the text. As we continue this dialogue, we keep developing better and more true interpretations of the text. Still, we never completely get rid of our prejudices.

ANALYZING THE READING

Schleiermacher and Dilthey argued that the true interpretation of a biblical text is the meaning intended by the person who wrote the text, so to know that true interpretation one must study the writer and his historical context. But Gadamer argued that it is not possible to know what the person who wrote a blibical text really meant because we will always be prejudiced by our own cultural views. Explain who you think is right and why.

---

[30] Hans-Georg Gadamer, *Truth and Method*, trans. and ed. Garrett Barden and John Cumming (New York: Seabury, 1975), 275.

[31] Ibid., 274–275.

Our interpretations are always a combination of our own cultural prejudices and what the text was trying to say in its own culture.

Gadamer, then, seems to hold a coherence view of truth. The true interpretation is the one that best coheres with both the prejudices of our own culture and what we believe the text meant in its own culture. Truth emerges from the union of these two cultural "horizons." Still, there are many true interpretations. For an interpretation that fits the prejudices of people living in one culture and time may not fit the prejudices of those from other cultures and times.

If Gadamer is correct, then a poem like Blake's "The Tyger" has no single true interpretation. Moreover, whatever its true meaning, it is *not* necessarily the meaning that Blake intended. Instead, it means whatever you, the reader, interpret it to mean in light of your own cultural values and beliefs and what you believe the poem seems to be trying to say. Similarly, a law, such as the Constitution's Fourteenth Amendment, has no single true interpretation. It means whatever we, today, interpret it to mean in light of both of the current cultural values of U.S. society and what we believe the amendment seems to have meant in the past. And a scripture text has no single true meaning. It means whatever the believers of each age interpret it to mean in light of their own cultural concerns and what they believe the scripture was intended to mean in the culture within which it was written.

Is Gadamer right? Is there no single true interpretation of our words and actions? Many people believe so. But not everyone. Some thinkers, such as E. D. Hirsch, argue that Gadamer and his followers have confused the "meaning" of a text with its "significance."[32] The meaning of a text is what the author intended to convey literally with the words that he used. The significance of a text is the implications the text has for our actions and lives. Although the significance of a text can change from one person or culture to another, Hirsch claims, its meaning remains the same. To find this fixed true meaning of a text, he argues, we have to do what Dilthey suggested: We have to discover what the author intended. A true interpretation is the one that corresponds with the author's intention.

We are left with a choice that in the end comes down to deciding among the theories of truth. Aquinas, Schleiermacher, and Dilthey tell us that the true interpretation is the one that corresponds with the intentions of the author, whether that author is a person or God. Wittgenstein suggests that any interpretation is true if it is one that gives pragmatic significance to our forms of life. And Gadamer tells us that a true interpretation is one that coheres with the prejudices of our culture and what we believe a text meant in its own culture.

PHILOSOPHY AT THE MOVIES

Watch *The People vs. Larry Flynt* (1996), which tells the story of Larry Flynt, publisher of the pornographic magazine *Hustler*, and his attempts to defend himself against being charged with illegally making and selling pornography. In this film, what views are apparent on what the true interpretation of the Constitution is?

---

[32] E. D. Hirsch, *Validity in Interpretation* (New Haven, CT: Yale University Press, 1967).

Chapter Summary

We opened this chapter by noting that knowledge is at least warranted true belief. We discussed the various modes of warrantability as they apply to various kinds of statements. We then discussed three theories of truth: the correspondence, coherence, and pragmatic theories. And we explored three related views of truth in science. The main points of this chapter are:

6.1 Knowledge and Truth

- Knowledge is at least justified true belief, but Gettier examples show that something more is required for genuine knowledge.

6.2 What Is Truth?

- The three traditional theories of truth are the correspondence, coherence, and pragmatic theories.

- The correspondence theory of truth claims that the truth of a statement depends on its relation to facts. A statement is true if and only if it corresponds to some fact. Objection: If we know only our sensory experiences, how can we ever get outside them to verify what reality actually is? What does correspondence mean? Precisely what is a fact?

- The coherence theory of truth claims that the truth of a statement depends on its relation to other statements. A statement is true if and only if it coheres or fits in with the system of beliefs that we already accept. Objection: Coherence is no guarantee of truth. A system of mutually supporting and consistent, but false beliefs can produce a coherent system of consistent error.

- The pragmatic theory claims that truth depends on what works. A statement is true if and only if it effectively solves a practical problem and thereby experientially satisfies us. The pragmatist sees the human as needing to use the practical consequences of beliefs to determine their truth and validity. Objection: There's no necessary connection between truth and workability. Truth is rendered a psychological, not an epistemological, concern, and it can become relative.

- It is important to understand which theory of truth is most acceptable to us since some theories imply that truth is relative while others imply that truth is objective. This difference affects how we respond to people or groups whose beliefs are different from our own.

6.3 Does Science Give Us Truth?

- There are three views of truth in science: the instrumentalist, realist, and conceptual relativist views. The instrumentalist view has similarities to the pragmatic theory, the realist view to the correspondence theory, and the conceptual relativist view to the coherence theory.

6.4 Can Interpretations Be True?

- Truth is important for hermeneutics, which is the attempt to interpret people's words and actions.

- For Aquinas, scripture has many true symbolic interpretations, but the true interpretation is the one that corresponds to what the author intended and the ultimate author of scripture is God. For Schleiermacher and Dilthey, the only true interpretation is the one that corresponds to what the historical author intended.

- Wittgenstein abandoned his early ideal of a clear language of facts in which all texts would have a clear meaning, and proposed, pragmatically, that the meaning of words depends on how they are successfully used in a "form of life," so texts can have as many true interpretations as there are forms of life in which it is used.

- For Gadamer, an interpretation emerges from uniting our cultural "prejudices" with what the text was trying to say in its own culture, so there are as many true interpretations of a text as there are cultural contexts with which an interpretation can cohere.

In the final analysis, no single theory—correspondence, coherence, or pragmatic—may provide a complete solution to the problem of truth. Each has shortcomings and strengths. Equally important, each theory can play a part in the way we understand truth in the search for and discovery of self.

6.5 Readings

The world-famous and classic short story about truth, "In a Grove," is our first reading. This story is considered the masterpiece of Ryunosuke Akutagawa, a Japanese writer whom many believe is Japan's greatest short story writer and after whom Japan's most prestigious literary award, the Akutagawa Prize, is named. Akutagawa wrote the story when he was 30 years old and shortly afterward began suffering hallucinations. Five years later he committed suicide. His story is about a murder witnessed by several people. But each person's account of the event is different. Is there any more to the event than these different accounts? Is the truth about the event whatever each person accepts as true, so that there are many truths? That seems to be one way to interpret Akutagawa's story. But is that the true interpretation of the text? Akutagawa seems to indicate that there is a single underlying reality that all the accounts agree on, such as that the murder occurred, that a woman, her husband, and a bandit were involved, and so on. So did Akutagawa mean for us to understand that there is a true account of the real factual event, but each person's own view of the event is colored by his or her interests? Or, like the story itself initially suggests, is the true interpretation of his story whatever each reader accepts as true?

In the second reading philosopher Hugh Tomlinson argues against the traditional view of truth, which holds that there is one reality and a true account must correspond to that reality. This traditional view, he claims, must give way to the new postmodern view that our concepts and language shape reality itself so that there is no single underlying reality to which true accounts must correspond. He concludes that "there are . . . many truths."

In the third reading, however, John Searle argues that the view that there is one "way that things really are" is a presupposition of all language, debates, opinions, and theories. Accounts are true if they correspond to that one "way that things really are," so not all accounts of an event are equally true. If Akutagawa's story is interpreted as saying that there is a true account of the real factual event and that conflicting accounts merely reflect a person's interests, then Searle supports him. But if his story is interpreted as saying that there are many truths, then Tomlinson supports him. Yet is there a single true interpretation of the story itself? And what is a true interpretation? (Akutagawa's story has been made into a movie seven times, the last in 2012.)

RYUNOSUKE AKUTAGAWA

In a Grove

THE TESTIMONY OF A WOODCUTTER QUESTIONED BY A HIGH POLICE COMMISSIONER

Yes, sir. Certainly, it was I who found the body. This morning, as usual, I went to cut my daily quota of cedars, when I found the body in a grove in a hollow in the mountains. The exact location? About 150 meters off the Yamashina stage road. It's an out-of-the-way grove of bamboo and cedars.

The body was lying flat on its back dressed in a bluish silk kimono and a wrinkled head-dress of the Kyoto style. A single sword-stroke had pierced the breast. The fallen bamboo-blades around it were stained with bloody blossoms. No, the blood was no longer running. The wound had dried up, I believe. And also, a gadfly was stuck fast there, hardly noticing my footsteps.

You ask me if I saw a sword or any such thing?

No, nothing, sir. I found only a rope at the root of a cedar near by. And . . . well, in addition to a rope, I found a comb. That was all. Apparently he must have made a battle of it before he was murdered, because the grass and fallen bamboo-blades had been trampled down all around.

"Was a horse nearby?"

No, sir. It's hard enough for a man to enter, let alone a horse.

THE TESTIMONY OF A TRAVELING BUDDHIST PRIEST QUESTIONED BY A HIGH POLICE COMMISSIONER

The time? Certainly, it was about noon yesterday, sir. The unfortunate man was on the road from Sekiyama to Yamashina. He was walking toward Sekiyama with a woman accompanying him on horseback, who I have since learned was his wife. A scarf hanging from her head hid her face from view. All I saw was the color of her clothes, a lilac colored suit. Her horse was a sorrel with a fine mane. The lady's height? Oh, about four feet five inches. Since I am a Buddhist priest, I took little notice about her details. Well, the man was armed with a sword as well as a bow and arrows. And I remember that he carried some twenty odd arrows in his quiver.

Little did I expect that he would meet such a fate. Truly human life is as evanescent as the morning dew or a flash of lightning. My words are inadequate to express my sympathy for him.

THE TESTIMONY OF A POLICEMAN QUESTIONED BY A HIGH POLICE COMMISSIONER

The man that I arrested? He is a notorious brigand called Tajomaru. When I arrested him, he had fallen off his horse. He was groaning on the bridge at Awataguchi. The time? It was in the early hours of last night. For the record, I might say that the other day I tried to arrest him, but unfortunately he escaped. He was wearing a dark blue silk kimono and a large plain sword. And, as you see, he got a bow and arrows somewhere. You say that this bow and these arrows look like the ones owned by the dead man? Then Tajomaru must be the murderer . . .

THE TESTIMONY OF AN OLD WOMAN QUESTIONED BY A HIGH POLICE COMMISSIONER

Yes, sir, the corpse is the man who married my daughter. He does not come from Kyoto. He was a samurai in the town of Kokufu in the province of Wakasa. His name was Kanazawa no Takehiko, and his age was twenty-six. He was of a gentle disposition, so I am sure he did nothing to provoke the anger of others.

My daughter? Her name is Masago, and her age is nineteen. She is a spirited, fun-loving girl, but I am sure she has never known any man except Takehiko. She has a small, oval, dark-complected face with a mole at the corner of her left eye.

Yesterday Takehiko left for Wakasa with my daughter. What bad luck it is that things should have come to such a sad end! What has become of my daughter? I am resigned to giving up my son-in-law as lost, but the fate of my daughter worries me sick. For heaven's sake leave no stone unturned to find her. I hate that robber Tajomaru, or whatever his name is. Not only my son-in-law, but my daughter . . . (Her later words were drowned in tears.)

TAJOMARU'S CONFESSION

I killed him, but not her. Where's she gone? I can't tell. Oh, wait a minute. No torture can make me confess what I don't know. Now things have come to such a head, I won't keep anything from you.

Yesterday a little past noon I met that couple. Just then a puff of wind blew, and raised her hanging scarf, so that I caught a glimpse of her face. Instantly it was again covered from my view. That may have been one reason; she looked like a Bodhisattva.

At that moment I made up my mind to capture her even if I had to kill her man.

Why? To me killing isn't a matter of such great consequence as you might think. When a woman is captured, her man has to be killed anyway. In killing, I use the sword I wear at my side. Am I the only one who kills people? You, you don't use your swords. You kill people with your power, with your money. Sometimes you kill them on the pretext of working for their good. It's true they don't bleed. They are in the best of health, but all the same you've killed them. It's hard to say who is a greater sinner, you or me. (An ironical smile.)

But it would be good if I could capture a woman without killing her man. So, I made up my mind to capture her, and do my best not to kill him. But it's out of the question on the Yamashina stage road. So I managed to lure the couple into the mountains.

It was quite easy. I became their traveling companion, and I told them there was an old mound in the mountain over there, and that I had dug it open and found many mirrors and swords. I went on to tell them I'd buried the things in a grove behind the mountain, and that I'd like to sell them at a low price to anyone who would care to have them. Then . . . you see, isn't greed terrible? He was beginning to be moved by my talk before he knew it. In less than half an hour they were driving their horse toward the mountain with me.

When he came in front of the grove, I told them that the treasures were buried in it, and I asked them to come and see. The man had no objection— he was blinded by greed. The woman said she would wait on horseback. It was natural for her to say so, at the sight of a thick grove. To tell you the truth, my plan worked just as I wished, so I went into the grove with him, leaving her behind alone.

The grove is only bamboo for some distance. About fifty yards ahead there's a rather open clump of cedars. It was a convenient spot for my purpose. Pushing my way through the grove, I told him a plausible lie that the treasures were buried under the cedars. When I told him this, he pushed his laborious way toward the slender cedar visible through the grove. After a while the bamboo thinned out, and we came to where a number of cedars grew in a row. As soon as we got there, I seized him from behind. Because he was a trained, sword-bearing warrior, he was quite strong, but he was taken by surprise, so there was no help for him. I soon tied him up to the root of a cedar. Where did I get a rope? Thank heaven, being a robber, I had a rope with me, since I might have to scale a wall at any moment. Of course

it was easy to stop him from calling out by gagging his mouth with fallen bamboo leaves.

When I disposed of him, I went to his woman and asked her to come and see him, because he seemed to have been suddenly taken sick. It's needless to say that this plan also worked well. The woman, her sedge hat off, came into the depths of the grove, where I led her by the hand. The instant she caught sight of her husband, she drew a small sword. I've never seen a woman of such violent temper. If I'd been off guard, I'd have got a thrust in my side. I dodged, but she kept on slashing at me. She might have wounded me deeply or killed me. But I'm Tajomaru. I managed to strike down her small sword without drawing my own. The most spirited woman is defenseless without a weapon. At least I could satisfy my desire for her without taking her husband's life.

Yes, . . . without taking his life. I had no wish to kill him. I was about to run away from the grove, leaving the woman behind in tears, when she frantically clung to my arm. In broken fragments of words, she asked that either her husband or I die. She said it was more trying than death to have her shame known to two men. She gasped out that she wanted to be the wife of whichever survived. Then a furious desire to kill him seized me. (Gloomy excitement.)

Telling you in this way, no doubt I seem a crueler man than you. But that's because you didn't see her face. Especially her burning eyes at that moment. As I saw her eye to eye, I wanted to make her my wife even if I were to be struck by lightning. I wanted to make her my wife . . . this single desire filled my mind. This was not only lust, as you might think. At that time if I'd had no other desire than lust, I'd surely not have minded knocking her down and running away. Then I wouldn't have stained my sword with his blood. But the moment I gazed at her face in the dark grove, I decided not to leave there without killing him.

But I didn't like to resort to unfair means to kill him. I untied him and told him to cross swords with me. (The rope that was found at the root of the cedar is the rope I dropped at the time.) Furious with anger, he drew his thick sword. And quick as thought, he sprang at me ferociously, without speaking a word. I needn't tell you how our fight turned out. The twenty-third stroke . . . please remember this. I'm impressed with this fact still. Nobody under the sun has ever clashed swords with me twenty strokes. (A cheerful smile.)

When he fell, I turned toward her, lowering my blood-stained sword. But to my great astonishment she was gone. I wondered to where she had run away. I looked for her in the clump of cedars. I listened, but heard only a groaning sound from the throat of the dying man.

As soon as we started to cross swords, she may have run away through the grove to call for help. When I thought of that, I decided it was a matter of life and death to me. So, robbing him of his sword, and bow and arrows, I ran out to the mountain road. There I found her horse still grazing quietly. It would be a mere waste of words to tell you the latter details, but before I entered town I had already parted with the sword. That's all my confession. I know that my head will be hung in chains anyway, so put me down for the maximum penalty. (A defiant attitude.)

THE CONFESSION OF A WOMAN WHO HAS COME TO THE SHIMIZU TEMPLE

That man in the blue silk kimono, after forcing me to yield to him, laughed mockingly as he looked at my bound husband. How horrified my husband must have been! But no matter how hard he struggled in agony, the rope cut into him all the more tightly. In spite of myself I ran stumblingly toward his side. Or rather I tried to run toward him, but the man instantly knocked me down. Just at the moment I saw an indescribable light in my husband's eyes. Something beyond expression . . . his eyes make me shudder even now. That instantaneous look of my husband, who couldn't speak a word, told me all his heart. The flash in his eyes was neither anger nor sorrow . . . only a cold light, a look of loathing. More struck by the look in his eyes than by the blow of the thief, I called out in spite of myself and fell unconscious.

In the course of time I came to, and found that the man in blue silk was gone. I saw only my husband still bound to the root of the cedar. I raised myself from the bamboo-blades with difficulty, and looked into his face; but the expression in his eyes was just the same as before.

Beneath the cold contempt in his eyes, there was hatred. Shame, grief, and anger. . . . I don't know how to express my heart at that time. Reeling to my feet, I went up to my husband.

"Takejiro," I said to him, "since things have come to this pass, I cannot live with you. I'm determined to die, . . . but you must die, too. You saw my shame. I can't leave you alive as you are." This was all I could say. Still he went on gazing at me with loathing and contempt. My heart breaking,

I looked for his sword. It must have been taken by the robber. Neither his sword nor his bow and arrows were to be seen in the grove. But fortunately my small sword was lying at my feet. Raising it over head, once more I said, "Now give me your life, I'll follow you right away." When he heard these words, he moved his lips with difficulty. Since his mouth was stuffed with leaves, of course his voice could not be heard at all.

But at a glance I understood his words. Despising me, his look said only, "Kill me." Neither conscious nor unconscious, I stabbed the small sword through the lilac-colored kimono into his breast.

Again at this time I must have fainted. By the time I managed to look up, he had already breathed his last—still in bonds. A streak of sinking sunlight streamed through the clump of cedars and bamboos, and shone on his pale face. Gulping down my sobs, I untied the rope from his dead body. And . . . and what has become of me since I have no more strength to tell you. Anyway I hadn't the strength to die. I stabbed my own throat with the small sword, I threw myself into a pond at the foot of the mountain, and I tried to kill myself in many ways. Unable to end my life, I am still living in dishonor. (A lonely smile.) Worthless as I am, I must have been forsaken even by the most merciful Kwannon. I killed my own husband. I was violated by the robber. Whatever can I do? Whatever can I . . . I . . . (Gradually, violent sobbing.)

THE STORY OF THE MURDERED MAN, AS TOLD THROUGH A MEDIUM

After violating my wife, the robber, sitting there, began to speak comforting words to her. Of course I couldn't speak. My whole body was tied fast to the root of a cedar. But meanwhile I winked at her many times, as much as to say "Don't believe the robber." I wanted to convey some such meaning to her. But my wife, sitting dejectedly on the bamboo leaves, was looking hard at her lap. To all appearances, she was listening to his words. I was agonized by jealousy. In the meantime the robber went on with his clever talk, from one subject to another. The robber finally made his bold, brazen proposal. "Once your virtue is stained, you won't get along well with your husband, so won't you be my wife instead? It's my love for you that made me be violent toward you."

While the criminal talked, my wife raised her face as if in a trance. She had never looked so beautiful as at that moment. What did my beautiful wife say in answer to him while I was sitting bound there? I am lost in space, but I have never thought of her answer without burning with anger and jealousy. Truly she said, . . . "Then take me away with you wherever you go." This is not the whole of her sin. If that were all, I would not be tormented so much in the dark.

When she was going out of the grove as if in a dream, her hand in the robber's, she suddenly turned pale, and pointed at me tied to the root of the cedar, and said "Kill him! I cannot marry you as long as he lives." "Kill him!" she cried many times, as if she had gone crazy. Even now these words threaten to blow me headlong into the bottomless abyss of darkness. Has such a hateful thing come out of a human mouth ever before? Have such cursed words ever struck a human ear, even once? Even once such a . . . (A sudden cry of scorn.) At these words the robber himself turned pale. "Kill him," she cried, clinging to his arms. Looking hard at her, he answered neither yes nor no . . . but hardly had I thought about his answer before she had been knocked down into the bamboo leaves. (Again a cry of scorn.) Quietly folding his arms, he looked at me and said, "What will you do with her? Kill her or save her? You have only to nod. Kill her?" For these words alone I would like to pardon his crime.

While I hesitated, she shrieked and ran into the depths of the grove. The robber instantly snatched at her, but he failed even to grasp her sleeve.

After she ran away, he took up my sword, and my bow and arrows. With a single stroke he cut one of my bonds. I remember his mumbling, "My fate is next." Then he disappeared from the grove. All was silent after that. No, I heard someone crying. Untying the rest of my bonds, I listened carefully, and I noticed that it was my own crying. (Long silence.)

I raised my exhausted body from the root of the cedar. In front of me there was shining the small sword which my wife had dropped. I took it up and stabbed it into my breast. A bloody lump rose to my mouth, but I didn't feel any pain. When my breast grew cold, everything was as silent as the dead in their graves. What profound silence! Not a single bird-note was heard in the sky over this grave in the hollow of the mountains. Only a lonely light lingered on the cedars and mountains. By and by the light gradually grew fainter, till the cedars and bamboo were lost to view. Lying there, I was enveloped in deep silence.

Then someone crept up to me. I tried to see who it was. But darkness had already been gathering round me. Someone . . . that someone drew the small sword softly out of my breast in its invisible hand. At the same time once more blood flowed into my mouth. And once and for all I sank down into the darkness of space.

Source: "In a Grove", from *Rashomon and Other Stories* by Ryunosuke Akutagawa, translated by Takashi Kojima. Copyright 1952 by Liveright Publishing Corporation. Used by permission of Liveright Publishing Corporation.

HUGH TOMLINSON

After Truth: Post-Modernism and the Rhetoric of Science

COMMON-SENSE REALISM

The modern notion of truth draws much of its plausibility from a set of metaphysical views which form an "externalist" perspective on the world, what Putnam has called a "God's Eye point of view".[1] This perspective is now deeply embedded in our "common-sense" attitude to the world. The "common-sense realist" sees the world as being objectively ordered independently of all human activity.

. . . According to the [common sense] realist:

the world consists of some fixed totality of mind-independent objects. There is exactly one true and complete description of "the way the world is". Truth involves some sort of correspondence between words or thought-signs and external things and sets of things.[2]

This correspondence view of truth provides . . . a picture which fits with the way [in] which we use simple sentences about ordinary material objects. We look to the world, to the "thing referred to", in order to decide whether such sentences are appropriate or not: To decide whether "there is food in the fridge", I can look in the fridge. . . .

According to the realist picture, "truth" is given by a particular relationship between words and world: a sentence is true when it corresponds to the world. This involves two aspects: the items to be related and the relationship itself. From his own perspective, the realist must be in a position to give a coherent account of both.

The items to be related seem obvious and straight-forward: words and objects. The commonsense realist thinks of the world as consisting, paradigmatically, of unproblematically identifiable physical objects with simple properties. From a "God's Eye point of view" the world "really is" divided up into objects, independently of human description and ordering.

This view of objects runs counter to the whole thrust of modern philosophy since Kant.... It was Kant's fundamental insight that "we are giving the orders", that both concepts and experience are necessary components of knowledge. We can only have experience of a world which is already structured by our concepts; it is "our world". What counts as a particular object depends on the classificatory concepts which we use. We cannot "leap outside" these concepts and directly compare them with "un-conceptualized objects"....

It seems that all that words can ever be related to are objects which depend on the words used. Truth is, then, not "objective" and unique, but "subjective" in the sense that it depends on the particular language used. There are as many truths as there are languages.

RELATIVISM AND POST-MODERNISM

The post-modernist story is a simple one: realism, in any of its forms, cannot be made coherent in its own terms. We have, as Putnam says, reached "the demise of a theory that lasted for over two thousand years. That it persisted so long and in so many forms in spite of the internal contradictions and obscurities which were present from the beginning testifies to the naturalness and strength of the desire for a God's Eye View."[3]

REFERENCES

1. See Hilary Putnam, *Reason, Truth and History* (Cambridge: Cambridge University Press, 1981), 50ff.
2. Ibid., 49.
3. Putnam, *Reason, Truth and History*, 74.

Source: Reprinted from Hugh Tomlinson, "After Truth: Post-Modernism and the Rhetoric of Science" in *Dismantling Truth: Reality in the Post-Modern World*, ed. Hilary Lawson and Lisa Appignanesi (New York: St. Martin's, 1989). Copyright © Hilary Lawson and Lisa Appignanesi.

JOHN SEARLE

Reality and Truth

Among the ... positions that form our cognitive Background, perhaps the most fundamental is a certain set of presuppositions about reality and truth. Typically when we act, think, or talk, we take for granted a certain way that our actions, thoughts, and talk relate to things outside us.... [W]e take the following for granted: there exists a real world that is totally independent of human beings and of what they think or say about it, and statements about objects and states of affairs in that world are true or false depending on whether things in the world really are the way we say they are. These two Background presuppositions have long histories and various famous names. The first, that there is a real world existing independently of us, I like to call "external realism.".... The second view, that a statement is true if things in the world are the way the statement says they are, and false otherwise, is called "the correspondence theory of truth." This theory comes in a lot of different versions, but the basic idea is that statements are true if they correspond to, or describe, or fit, how things really are in the world, and false if they do not....

[E]xternal realism underlies ... the correspondence theory of truth. Thinkers who wish to deny the correspondence theory of truth ... typically find it embarrassing to have to concede external realism ...

I do not believe it makes any sense to ask for a justification of the view that there is a way that things are in the world independently of our representations, because any attempt at justification presupposes what it attempts to justify. Any attempt to find out about the real world at all presupposes that there is a way that things are. That is why it is wrong to represent external realism [the claim that there exists a real world that is totally independent of all our representations, thoughts, language, and so on] as the view that there are material objects in space and time, or that mountains and molecules, and so on, exist. Suppose there were no mountains and molecules, and no material objects in space and time. Then those would be facts about how the world is, and thus would presuppose external realism. That is, the negation of this or that claim about the real world presupposes that there is a way that things are, independently of our claims . . . [E]xternal realism is not a theory. It is not an opinion I hold that there is a world out there. It is, rather, the framework that is necessary for it to be even possible to hold opinions or theories about such things as planetary movements. When you debate the merits of a theory such as the heliocentric theory of the solar system, you have to take it for granted that there is a way that things really are. Otherwise, the debate can't get started. Its very terms are unintelligible. But that assumption, that there is a way that things are independent of our representations of how they are, is external realism. External realism is not a claim about the existence of this or that object, but rather a presupposition of the way we understand such claims. . . . This does not mean that realism is an unprovable theory; rather, it means that realism is not a theory at all, but the framework within which it is possible to have theories.

Source: From John Searle, *Mind, Language and Society* (New York: Basic Books, 1998), excerpts from pp., 12, 13, 31, 32. Copyright © 1999 John R. Searle. Reprinted by permission of Basic Books, a member of the Perseus Books Group.

6.6 HISTORICAL SHOWCASE

Kant

In the previous chapter, we saw how Hume's empiricism led philosophy into the dead end of skepticism. If Hume's radical empiricism is accepted, then we can never hope to learn the truth about ourselves, God, or the universe.

In this chapter, we showcase a philosopher who claimed to have found a way around Hume's skepticism and who, in doing so, revolutionized our views about knowledge and truth. This is the eighteenth-century philosopher Immanuel Kant.

Immanuel Kant (1724–1804) is regarded by many as the greatest of all philosophers, especially in the field of epistemology. His unique contribution was to argue that the world we experience is a world that our own mind constructs. Our mind can know the truth about the world we experience, he argued, because that world is constructed by the mind itself.

We showcase Kant in this chapter because of the radical and profound contributions he made to our conceptions of knowledge

© Private Collection/The Bridgeman Art Library International

Immanuel Kant: "There can be no doubt that all our knowledge begins with experience. But though all our knowledge begins with experience, it does not follow that it all arises out of experience. For it may well be that even our empirical knowledge is made up of what we receive through impressions and of what our own faculty of knowledge supplies from itself."

and truth. But reading Kant also allows us to see how his revolutionary views about knowledge influenced his views on morality and God. Kant is a good example of how our epistemological views affect our positions on other philosophical issues.

Although he revolutionized philosophy, Kant lived a very ordinary life. He spent all of his 80 years in the small town in which he was born: Königsberg (now Kaliningrad, Russia). There he grew up, and there he went to college, supporting himself in part by his winnings from playing pool with other students. Kant remained in Königsberg after graduating, eventually becoming a teacher at the local university. As a teacher, Kant came to schedule his activities so precisely that neighbors used to set their clocks when he passed their houses on his daily afternoon walk. Although Kant remained a bachelor all of his life, he had a number of close women friends and had a reputation for being a funny, witty, and entertaining host at the dinner parties he frequently had.

The Problem of Synthetic *a Priori* Knowledge

MindTap Kant described his own work as a "revolution," which may not have been overstating things! Go to MindTap to watch a video discussing Kant's work on the theory of knowledge.

Although Kant never left his birthplace, books put him in touch with all the intellectual currents of the eighteenth century. He was well acquainted with the tremendous new discoveries in the natural sciences and was especially impressed with Newton's discoveries in physics. But when Kant came across the writings of Hume, these discoveries seemed threatened. For Hume argued that our so-called scientific knowledge is not rationally justified. In particular, he pointed out that the cause-and-effect laws of science go beyond the evidence scientists have for them. Scientists observe a *few times* that certain events have been conjoined *in the past,* and they conclude that those kinds of events *must always* cause each other *in the future.* But how do scientists know that events must always be causally connected in the future as in the past?

Kant realized that Hume's objection was devastating. If Hume was correct, then all our scientific knowledge was unjustified. Moreover, Kant soon discovered that other areas of knowledge also contained judgments that went beyond the evidence of our senses:

> I openly confess that my recollection of David Hume was the very thing which many years ago first interrupted my dogmatic slumber and gave my investigations in the field of speculative philosophy a quite new direction. I was far from following him in the conclusions at which he arrived. . . .
>
> I therefore first tried to see whether Hume's objection could not be put into a general form. I soon found that the concept of the connection of cause and effect was by no means the only concept by which the understanding thinks the connection of things *a priori* [that is, independently of experience].[1]

Kant found three areas of knowledge in which our statements about the world go beyond the evidence provided by our sensory experience:

1. In the sciences of geometry and arithmetic. For example:
   "The shortest distance between two points must always be a straight line."

   "The square of the hypotenuse of a right-angle triangle must always equal the sum of the squares of the other two sides."
   "The sum of 798 and 857 must always equal 1655."
2. In the natural sciences. For example: "All events must always have a cause."
3. In philosophical metaphysics. For example: "There must exist a God that causes the universe."

Kant termed these *synthetic* statements to indicate that each gives us genuine information about the world around us. For example, geometry tells us that the world will always obey the law that the square of the hypotenuse of right triangles equals the sum of the squares of the other two sides, and the natural sciences tell us that all events must have a cause. By contrast, Kant used the term *analytic* to refer to statements that merely give us information about the meanings of words, such as "Bachelors are unmarried males."

Kant also called the statements in the list *a priori,* pointing out two features of such statements: First, as Hume said, these statements go beyond what we can establish through our sensory experience. For example, we could never check *all* right triangles, yet geometry says the square of their hypotenuses *always* equals the sum of the squares of the other two sides. Second, we establish that these statements *must* be true by relying on our thought processes. The laws of geometry, for example, are established in the mind. *A priori* statements, then, are necessary and universal: They state something that we know by mental processes *must* be true and that *always* holds. By contrast, Kant used the term *a posteriori* to refer to statements that can be established by sensory observations, such as "This room is empty" and "The sky above is blue." *A posteriori* statements are neither necessary nor universal.

But how can we know *a priori* propositions about the world without going outside of our minds? For example, how do we know that the outer world must always obey the laws of geometry when we can establish these laws completely within the mind? How do we know that every event must always have a cause when we have not examined every event? Is Hume correct in saying that such synthetic *a priori* statements are unjustified?

> Now the proper problem of pure reason is contained in the question: How are *a priori* synthetic judgments possible? . . .

---

[1] Immanuel Kant, *Prolegomena to Any Future Metaphysics,* trans. Lewis White Beck (New York: Bobbs-Merrill, 1950), 8.

Among philosophers, David Hume came nearest to envisaging this problem, but still he was very far from conceiving it with sufficient definiteness and universality. He occupied himself exclusively with the synthetic proposition regarding the connection of an effect with its cause, and he believed himself to have shown that such an *a priori* proposition is entirely impossible.... If he had envisaged our problem in all its universality, ... he would then have recognized that, according to his own argument, pure mathematics, which certainly contains *a priori* synthetic propositions, would also not be possible....

In the solution of our above problem, then, we are at the same time deciding as to the possibility of the employment of pure reason in establishing and developing all those sciences which contain *a priori* knowledge of objects, and have therefore to answer the questions: How is pure mathematics possible? How is pure science of nature possible? ... How is metaphysics ... possible?[2]

To save our knowledge from Hume's skepticism, Kant had to show that we are justified in making statements that give us real information about the world but are established completely within the mind. To solve that problem, Kant embarked on what he called "a critique of pure reason"—an investigation of what our minds can know apart from the senses.

Space, Time, and Mathematics

Kant began his investigation by granting Hume's view of our senses. Hume pointed out that all our knowledge of the world begins with sensations within us: colors, shapes, sounds, tastes, feels, smells. The senses, Hume said, provide us with a continual stream of endlessly changing:

> perceptions which succeed each other with an inconceivable rapidity and are in a perpetual flux and movement....The mind is a kind of theater, where several perceptions successively make their appearance, pass, re-pass, glide away, and mingle in an infinite variety of postures and situations.[3]

But Kant noticed something Hume had missed. It is true that all we receive from the senses are the sensations within us. Yet we do not *experience* a mere display of sensations within us. When I open my eyes, I do not experience changing sensations of light and colors playing in my vision. Instead, I see *objects* that appear to be *outside* of me. For example, when I look down, I see not a squarish blob of whiteness but the white page of a book a few inches away. Somehow, the sensations (colors and shapes) that continually play in my vision appear to me as objects outside of me.

The same is true of my other senses. They, too, provide only a stream of sensations within me. But I experience them as belonging to particular objects outside of me. For example, I do not merely sense ringing, booming, rustling sound sensations in my hearing. Instead, I hear noises that seem to come from some particular place in the room: perhaps a rustling noise from the pages of my book or a voice from a particular person in front of me. Each sensation of sound, feel, and smell appears to be the sound, feel, and smell of objects outside me.

Kant argued that somehow our mind takes these many separate sensations and *organizes* them into objects that appear to be outside ourselves, in space. It is as if my mind carries within it a three-dimensional representation of space, and every sensation is given a position in this mental image of space.

In fact, Kant argues, we could not experience objects as being outside of us without this three-dimensional representation of space in our minds. Even to perceive objects as outside of ourselves, we *already* have to know what outside is—that is, we have to know what space is. Moreover, although we can imagine an empty space without objects, we cannot imagine an object that is not in space. This also proves, according to Kant, that our mental representation of space has to be in our minds prior to our experience of objects:

> Space is not an empirical concept which has been derived from outer experiences. For in order that certain sensations be referred to something outside me (that is, to something in another region of space from that in which I find myself), and, similarly, in order that I may be able to represent them as outside and alongside one another, and ... as in different places, the representation of space also must be presupposed. The representation of space cannot, therefore, be ... obtained from the relations of outer ... [experience]. On the contrary, this outer experience is itself possible at all only through that representation.
>
> Space is a necessary *a priori* representation which underlies all outer perceptions. We can never represent to ourselves the absence of space, though we can quite well think of it as empty of

2   Immanuel Kant, *Critique of Pure Reason*, trans. Norman Kemp Smith (New York: St. Martin's, 1929; original work published 1781), B19, B22.
3   David Hume, *A Treatise of Human Nature*, ed. L. A. Selby-Bigge (Oxford: Clarendon, 1896), 252–253.

objects. It must therefore be regarded as the condition of the possibility of ... [sensory experiences], and not as ... [something] dependent on them.[4]

Space, then, is merely a mental representation that helps us organize our sensations so that they appear to us to be objects outside of us. There is nothing more to space than this mental image. Space does not exist independently of us outside our mind:

> Space does not represent any property of things in themselves, nor does it represent them in their relation to one another. That is to say, space does not represent any determination that attaches to objects themselves and which remains even when abstraction has been made of all the subjective conditions of perception.
>
> It is therefore solely from the human standpoint that we can speak of space, of extended objects, etc. ... This predicate can be ascribed to things only insofar as they appear to us, that is, only to objects of sensibility [of the senses].[5]

Kant's view—that space does not exist outside the mind—may seem strange. But his view provides the key to one of his major questions: How do we know that the laws of geometry must hold true for all objects in the world even though these laws are established within the mind? Kant's solution is simple and brilliant.

First, he argues, the laws of geometry are nothing more than the laws of the mental image of space that is in our minds. That is why we can establish the laws of geometry by simply examining our inner image of space without having to examine the outer world.

Second, Kant points out, the mind puts every object we experience into this mental representation of space. All our sensations are organized by the mind into objects within its representation of space so that they appear to us as if they exist in space outside. Every object we experience will have to appear within this mental image and therefore must obey its laws. Because the laws of geometry are the laws of our mental representation, every object we experience will have to obey the laws of geometry.

Thus, Kant provides a solution to the problem that had puzzled philosophers for centuries: How do we know without going outside our minds that all objects obey the laws of geometry? The only solution, Kant held, is that we establish the laws of geometry completely *a priori* by simply looking within our own minds' three-dimensional image of space. We know all the objects we perceive will obey these laws because the mind places all objects within this mental image so that for us they are in space.

Using similar arguments, Kant showed that all our experience must obey the laws of arithmetic. The laws of arithmetic, he said, are the laws of time: They are laws about how units follow one after another, just like numbers follow one after another.

But where do we get our image of time? Just as we organize sensations by inserting them in space, we also organize them by inserting them in time. So, time is also one of the structures of the mind. Time is like a long filing system we use to organize our sensations by placing each one at a certain point in the system. Because the image of time is within us, we can know its laws just by examining it. And because the mind makes everything we experience appear to be in time, everything must obey the laws of time. And these laws are the laws of arithmetic.

So the synthetic *a priori* statements of geometry and arithmetic are justified. Although these statements give us information about the structure of the world, we do not have to examine every object in the world to know these statements hold true of everything we will ever perceive. The synthetic *a priori* statements of geometry and arithmetic can be established by simply examining our inner images of time and space. Space and time are merely structures within the mind in which we position the objects our mind makes out of the sensations it receives so that to our minds these objects exist in space and time.

Our Unified Mind Must Organize Sensations into Changing Objects

But Kant also had to show that the synthetic *a priori* statements of the natural sciences were justified. In particular, he had to show that the causal laws of science were justified. How did he do this? Kant's solution to this problem is remarkably similar to his solution to the problem of geometry and mathematics. Kant points out that the mind organizes its sensations so that they appear to us as objects that change through time. How does the mind do this? The mind organizes its sensations into such independent objects

---

[4]   Kant, *Critique*, B38, B39. (Note that the word *intuition* has been replaced here and elsewhere in the translations that follow with the more familiar term *perception*. Of course, while a perception for Kant is an intuition, it is only one kind of intuition and so "intuition" has a broader meaning than perception. But in the contexts where I substitute the word "perception" for the word "intuition" Kant is primarily referring to sensory intuitions and so the term "perception" will serve.)

[5]   Ibid., B42–B43.

by using twelve rules or "categories." The most important of these rules or categories turns out to be the basic law underlying the natural sciences: that all perceived events must have a cause. So, just as we know that every object we experience will be organized in space and time, we can also be sure that every event we experience will be causally related to other events. How exactly did Kant prove this? Kant's argument is difficult, but with a bit of work it can be understood.

Kant first points out that our sensations appear to us to be of independent objects that last through time and that change. For example, during the time I look at a book, I believe that I continue seeing the same book. My sensations appear to me to be of an object that lasts through time. And as I turn its pages, the same book appears to me to be changing.

To make my sensations appear to be changing objects, Kant says, the mind has to bring its sensations together in three ways. First, the mind has to receive or "apprehend" the many separate sensations provided by the senses. For example, each separate moment I look at the changing white book, my senses produce new and different sensations of white color. To keep perceiving the book, then, I have to keep receiving all of these separate sensations. Second, the mind has to remember the past sensations. For example, in perceiving the book, I have to keep in mind the past sensations of white as I receive new sensations. If I continually forgot the past sensations, it would be as though a new book were continually appearing before me each moment. Third, the mind has to connect or relate the later sensations to the earlier ones. That is, the mind has to recognize that the earlier sensations and the later ones are sensations of the same object. For example, I must recognize that my later, slightly different sensations of the book are sensations of the same book I saw earlier. Otherwise, the earlier and later sensations would appear to me as many separate images of different books floating in my memory. This recognition or connection of earlier and later sensations is what finally makes me believe that I am seeing the same book but that it is changing through time:

> Each perception [of an object] is made up of a multiplicity [of sensations] . . . . In order to change this multiplicity [of separate sensations] into a single thing [an object], it is necessary first to run through and collect the multiplicity [of sensations]. This act I call the "synthesis of apprehension." . . .

> But if I were always to drop out of thought the earlier sensation . . . and did not reproduce them [in my memory] while advancing to the next ones, then a complete perception [of an object] would never form. . . . The synthesis of apprehension is therefore inseparably connected with [what I will call] the "synthesis of reproduction."

> [Moreover,] if we were not conscious that what we are thinking of now is the same as what we thought a moment before, all reproduction in the series of perceptions would be in vain. Each perception would . . . be a new one. . . . The multiplicity could never form a whole, because it would not have that unity that [my] consciousness alone can give it [by recognizing that what I perceive now is the same as what I perceived earlier].[6]

But the mind's ability to collect sensations into unified objects that change through time would not be possible unless the mind itself also lasted through time. For example, suppose that I am looking at a book and receiving new sensations of white color each passing moment. If the later sensations are to be connected to the earlier ones, the *same* mind has to receive the earlier and the later ones. This means my mind has to last through time: It has to last through the earlier and later sensations. Thus, the process of receiving, remembering, and connecting sensations into objects that last through time requires a mind that also lasts through time. The unification of sensations into objects requires a "unified" mind that connects sensations:

> [But] there can be in us no kind of knowledge, no connection or unifying of one bit of knowledge with another, unless there is a unified consciousness which precedes all the data of perception. . . . This pure original unchanging consciousness I call "transcendental apperception."[7]

The mind, then, is a single consciousness that remains the same through time, contrary to Hume's claim that the mind is only a bundle of disconnected sensations. In fact, Kant argues, the mind *must* connect its sensations because it must bring all these separate sensations into itself:

> If we want to discover the internal foundation of this unifying of perception . . ., we must begin with

---

6   Immanuel Kant, *Kritik der Reinen Vernunft* [*Critique of Pure Reason*] (Leipzig, Germany: Johann Friedrich Hartknoch, 1981), A99–A103. This translation is by Manuel Velasquez.

7   Ibid., A107.

pure [transcendental] apperception. Sensations would be nothing to us, and would not concern us in the least, if they were not received into our [unified] consciousness. . . . Knowledge is impossible in any other way. We are conscious *a priori* of our own enduring identity with regard to all perceptions we know. Our enduring identity is a necessary condition for us to have these perceptions. For perceptions could not be perceptions of anything for me unless they . . . could at least be connected together into [my] one consciousness. This principle stands firm *a priori*, and may be called the "transcendental principle of the unity" of all the multiplicity of our perceptions (and therefore also of sensation).[8]

What Kant is saying here is that our mind connects and unifies its sensations because it *has to*. It has to connect them together because the many sensations my senses produce must all enter one mind: my own single mind. But to enter into my one mind, they have to be brought together into one.

As Kant says, this point—that the mind *has to* unify its sensations—is crucial. If the mind has to unify its sensations into objects, then we know that the connections the mind imposes on objects are necessary.

What kinds of connections does the mind make between objects? Kant argues that there are twelve kinds of connections or "categories" that the mind must impose on its sensations. Only the most important of these, the relation of cause and effect, concerns us here.

Causality Is in the World As We Experience It

Kant tries to show that the mind *must* impose causal relationships on its sensations if they are to appear as objects that change independently of us. Kant begins his argument by pointing out that changes we perceive can follow one another in an order that I can determine or in an order that is fixed. But changes whose order I determine are not changes in independent objects outside of me; they are merely changes in me. For example, if I look first at the roof of a house and then at the windows, the order of my perceptions is determined by my own will. I can change the order by simply looking first at the windows and then at the roof. So, these changes in my perceptions are merely changes in *me*. They are not independent changes in the *objects* outside of me. On the other hand, changes whose order is

fixed or "necessary" are changes that I see as changes in independent objects outside of me. For example, if I see a boat being carried down a river by the current, I will first perceive the boat upriver, and then I will perceive the boat downstream. The order of these perceptions cannot be determined by my own will: I cannot change the order. So, I know that the changes in my perceptions of the boat are changes in the *objects* outside of me, not merely changes in *me*. And I know this only because the order of these changes is fixed by necessary causal laws and not by me. If our sensations are to appear as objects that change independently of ourselves, they must be related by causal laws:

The Principle of the succession of time, according to the Law of Causality: All changes take place according to the law of connection between cause and effect.

Proof: The apprehension of the multiplicity of phenomena is always successive. The perceptions of the parts [of objects] follow one upon another. . . . Thus, for instance, the apprehension of the multiplicity in the phenomenal appearance of a house that stands before me is successive. . . . Every apprehension of an event is [similarly] . . . a perception following on another perception. But as this applies to all synthesis of apprehension, as in the phenomenal appearance of a house, that apprehension would not be different from any other.

But I observe that if in a phenomenon which contains an event I call the antecedent state of perception A, and the subsequent B, B can only follow A in my apprehension, while the perception A can never follow B, but can only precede it. I see, for instance, a ship gliding down a stream. My perception of its place below follows my perception of its place higher up in the course of the stream, and it is impossible in the apprehension of this phenomenon that the ship should be perceived first below and then higher up. We see, therefore, that the order in the succession of perceptions in our apprehension is here determined, and our apprehension regulated by that order. In the former example of a house my perceptions could begin with the apprehension of the roof and end in the basement, or begin below and end above; they could apprehend the manifold of the empirical perception from right to left or from left to right. There was therefore no determined order in the succession of these perceptions. . . . [But] in the apprehension of an event there is always a rule which makes the order of successive perceptions necessary. . . . Thus only can I be justified in saying, not only of my apprehension, but of the phenomenon itself, that there exists in it a succession, which

_____
8   Ibid., A116.

is the same as to say that I cannot arrange the apprehension otherwise than in that very order. . . .

If therefore experience teaches us that something happens, we must always presuppose that something precedes on which it follows by rule. Otherwise I could not say of the object that it followed, because its following in my apprehension only, without being determined by rule in reference to what precedes, would not justify us in admitting an objective following. It is therefore always with reference to a rule by which phenomena as they follow, that is as they happen, are determined by an antecedent state, that I can give an objective character to my subjective synthesis (of apprehension); nay, it is under this supposition only that an experience of anything that happens becomes possible.[9]

Thus, Kant proved that all events in the world we experience have to be causally connected. Let us review the steps of his argument. First, Kant showed that the mind connects ("synthesizes") its sensations into objects that last through time. It does this through apprehension, reproduction, and recognition. Second, this connecting of sensations into objects shows that our mind is unified. Third, because the mind is unified, it *must* connect its sensations together. Fourth, one of the connections the mind must impose on its sensations is the connection of cause and effect, for our sensations would not seem to us to be sensations of independently changing objects unless they were causally connected to one another.

Hume, then, was wrong. Hume said that the laws of the sciences are not well founded, in particular the laws of causality: We have no evidence that events must always be causally connected to one another. However, Kant proved that all events we experience in the world outside of us *must* be connected by causal laws. For that world is a world that the mind puts together out of its sensations by bringing these sensations together into a single mind. To bring sensations together so that they seem to be sensations of independently changing objects, the mind must connect them by causal relations. The mind, that is, *must* use the category of cause and effect to connect our sensations so that they appear to us as the independently changing world of trees, oceans, mountains, and stars that we see around us. Only by recognizing that we construct the world in our mind in this way, Kant says, can we escape Hume's skepticism about the causal laws of science.

Kant called the world as it appears in our minds the phenomenal world and distinguished it from the noumenal world. The noumenal world is the collection of things as they exist in themselves apart from our perception of them in our mind. Clearly, we can never know what the noumenal world is like: All we can know is the phenomenal world of things as they appear to us after they have been organized by the mind.

What about Hume's skepticism about God? Reluctantly, Kant agreed that we cannot *prove* that there is a God. The cosmological proofs for God, Kant pointed out, say that God must exist because God had to "cause" the universe. But the only causality in the universe is the causality our own minds put there; the concept of a cause is merely a category of the mind, nothing more. So, we cannot appeal to causality to prove that God exists. Other metaphysical arguments for the existence of God, Kant held, make similar illegitimate use of concepts that are merely categories of the mind. None of these metaphysical arguments are valid proofs of the existence of God.

But Kant's views on God do not end here. Kant attempted to show that the existence of God should be accepted on the basis of our moral commitments. To understand this aspect of Kant, we must examine his views on morality.

Two Versions of the Categorical Imperative of Morality

Kant argued that a person is moral to the extent that he or she follows a principle he called the **categorical imperative**: "I ought never to act unless I can will my maxim to serve as a universal law." For Kant, a "maxim" is the reason a person has for doing something. And a maxim "serves as a universal law" if every person consistently acts on that reason. So, the categorical imperative is the moral principle that whenever I do something, my reasons for doing it must be reasons that I would (and could) be willing to have everyone act on. For example, suppose that I wonder whether I should help the needy, and my reason for being reluctant to help them is simply that I do not want to take the trouble. According to Kant, I must ask myself this: Would I be willing to have everyone refrain from helping others when they did not want to take the trouble? Clearly, I would *not be* willing to have everyone do this because I myself might need the help of others in some situations. Therefore, it would be wrong for me to refrain from helping those in need. Kant claims that sometimes it is absolutely *impossible* for everyone to act on

9   Immanuel Kant, *Critique of Pure Reason*, trans. Friedrich Max Müller (New York: Macmillan, 1896), 774, 155–160.

the immoral reasons we are tempted to act on. In such cases, it is absolutely immoral to act on those reasons:

> The ordinary reason of humanity in its practical judgments agrees perfectly with this, and always has in view the principle here suggested. For example, suppose that I ask myself: Would it be morally permissible for me to make a promise I do not intend to keep when I am in trouble?... The shortest and most unerring way for me to discover whether a lying promise is consistent with duty is to ask myself: Could I will to have my maxim (that is, the principle, "I will get out of my difficulties with false promises") serve as a universal law, for myself as well as for others; and would I be able to say to myself, "Everyone may make a false promise when he finds himself in a difficulty that he cannot escape in any other way"? As soon as I ask myself these questions, I become aware that although I might desire to lie, I could not will to have lying become a universal law. For if lying promises became the rule, there would soon be no promises at all. There would be no promises because people would stop believing each other when they said that they intended to keep their promises; and if one person over hastily accepted the lying promise of another, that person would soon learn to do the same thing to others. So as soon as my maxim became a universal law, it would destroy itself.
>
> I do not, therefore, need any great genius to see what I have to do so that my will can be morally good. Even if I have very little experience of the world, even if I cannot prepare for all contingencies ahead of time, all I have to ask myself is this: Could you will to have your maxim serve as a universal law? If not, then you should not act on that maxim.[10]

How does Kant argue for the categorical imperative? For Kant, moral right and wrong depend on the interior motives on which the person acts. Kant argues that to the degree that a person is interiorly motivated merely by self-interest or by the pleasure he gets from an action, the action "has no moral worth." A person's behavior has moral worth only to the extent that the person is motivated by "duty"—that is, by the belief that all human beings ought to act this way. Consequently, an action has moral worth only to the extent that the person is motivated by reasons that he or she feels everyone else can and ought to act on.

Kant claimed that the categorical imperative could be expressed in a second way: "Act in such a way that you always treat humanity, whether in your own person or in the person of any other, never simply as a means, but always at the same time as an end." Never treat people *only* as means but always also as ends. By this, Kant means that we should never treat people only as tools to be manipulated or forced into serving our interests. Instead, we should always treat people as ends—that is, as free rational persons who must be given the opportunity to decide for themselves whether they will go along with our plans:

> A man who is thinking of making a lying promise will realize that he would be using others merely as means because he would not be letting them participate in the goal of the actions in which he involves them. For the people I would thus be using for my own purposes would not have consented to be treated in this way and to that extent they would not have participated in the goals to be attained by the action. Such violations of the principle that our humanity must be respected as an end in itself are even clearer if we take examples of attacks on the freedom and property of others. It is obvious that the person who violates such rights is using people merely as means without considering that as rational beings they should be esteemed also as ends; that is, as beings who must be able to participate in the goals of the actions in which they are involved with him.[11]

According to Kant, this second way of expressing the categorical imperative is really equivalent to the first. The first version says that what is morally right for me must be morally right for others, or that everyone must be treated the same. The second version says that just as I give myself the opportunity to decide what I will do, I must also give others the same opportunity or, again, that everyone must be treated the same. However, unlike the first version, the second version emphasizes that morality requires us to respect the freedom of all rational persons.

The Moral Argument for God's Existence

Kant points out that if the categorical imperative defines morality, then morality and happiness do not necessarily coincide. For the morally good person is the one who follows the categorical imperative even when this is not in her self-interest and even when she takes no pleasure in doing so. Consequently, morally good people often suffer and fail to get what is in their self-interest. On the other hand, evil people who consistently pursue their self-interest and pleasure, even by taking advantage of others, often prosper. In this world, good people who

[10] Immanuel Kant, *Grundlegungzur Metaphysik derSitten [Groundwork of the Metaphysics of Morals]*, in *Immanuel Kant Werkausgabe*, vol. 7, ed. Wilhelm Weischedel (Frankfurt, Germany: Insel Verlag Wiesbaden, 1956), 28–30. This translation copyright © 1987 by Manuel Velasquez.

[11] Ibid., 62.

deserve happiness often do not receive it, whereas evil people who do not deserve it do receive it.

This mismatch between morality and happiness is wrong, Kant holds, and all of us believe that it ought not to be this way. In fact, we feel an obligation to seek a world where the good prosper and the evil do not, and our sense of obligation requires us to believe that such a world is possible. Kant calls such a perfect world a *summum bonum*, the supremely good state of affairs. But, he says, only a good God could bring such a perfect world into existence (perhaps in another life). So, if we believe such a world is possible (and we have an obligation to believe it is), we must assume that God exists. Thus, although we cannot prove that God exists, morality forces us to assume so:

> We ought to endeavor to promote the *summum bonum*, which, therefore must be possible. Accordingly, the existence of a cause of all nature, distinct from nature itself, and containing the principle of this connection, namely the exact harmony of happiness with morality, is also *postulated*. . . . The *summum bonum* is possible in the world only on the supposition of a Supreme Being having a causality corresponding to moral character. Now a being that is capable of acting on the conception of laws is an *intelligence* (a rational being), and the causality of such a being according to this conception of laws is his will; therefore the supreme cause of nature, which must be presupposed as a condition of the *summum bonum*, is a being which is the cause of nature by *intelligence* and *will*, consequently its author, that is God. . . . Now it was seen to be a duty for us to promote the *summum bonum*. Consequently it is not merely allowable, but it is a necessity connected with duty as a requisite, that we should presuppose the possibility of this *summum bonum*. And as this is possible only on condition of the existence of God, it inseparably connects the supposition of this with duty; that is, it is morally necessary to assume the existence of God.[12]

Thus, Kant shifted the argument for God's existence away from metaphysics, where every other philosopher had placed it. Other philosophers had assumed that God's existence had to be proved by relying on metaphysical concepts such as the concept of causality, and such arguments had been ruthlessly demolished by the skepticism of Hume. Kant tried to show that these arguments had to fail because metaphysical concepts are merely categories in our minds; they can tell us nothing about things as they are in themselves. Instead, Kant claimed, we must believe in God on the basis of our moral commitments: Morality forces us to hold that God exists. For morality tells us that good people must be rewarded and evil ones punished, and only a God could bring about such a *summum bonum*. By thus placing belief in God in the realm of morality, Kant hoped, belief would be secure from the attacks of Humean skepticism.

Despite his very ordinary life, then, Kant's philosophy was truly revolutionary. Kant taught us to believe that the world conforms to the categories of the mind, whereas we had always assumed that the mind must conform its categories to the world. He taught us that morality requires us to respect the freedom of others whether or not this pleases us and, consequently, that being moral and being happy may not coincide in this life. And he taught us to believe in God on the basis of morality instead of on the basis of metaphysical arguments. These were truly new ways of looking at the universe, new ways of thinking about ourselves and the world in which we live. It is hard to imagine a more revolutionary view of our situation.

QUESTIONS

1. In your own words, explain Kant's problem: "How are *a priori* synthetic judgments possible?"

2. Summarize in your own words how Kant tries to show that *a priori* synthetic judgments in geometry and arithmetic are possible.

3. In your own words, why does Kant say that our mind *must* connect its sensations together into objects? Why does Kant say that the mind must connect its sensations into objects that are causally connected? In your view, does Kant really answer Hume?

4. Some people have said that Kant cannot be called a rationalist or an empiricist. Why do you think they say this? Do you see any rationalist elements in Kant? Do you see any empiricist elements?

5. Is Kant's first version of the categorical imperative the same as the **Golden Rule**? (Do unto others as you would have them do unto you.)

6. In your view, what would Kant's categorical imperative imply about the morality of suicide? About the morality of the death penalty? Explain.

7. Do you believe that Kant's argument for accepting the existence of God is correct? Why?

---

[12] Immanuel Kant, *Critique of Practical Reason*, trans. T. K. Abbott (London: Longmans Green, 1927), 220–222.

7 Ethics

Ethics is not a doctrine about how to make ourselves happy but about how we are to be worthy of happiness.

IMMANUEL KANT

7.1 What Is Ethics?

LEARNING OBJECTIVE: When finished, you'll be able to:

- Explain what it means to say that ethics is the study of morality.

7.2 Is Ethics Relative?

LEARNING OBJECTIVE: When finished, you'll be able to:

- Describe and critically evaluate the theory of ethical relativism.

7.3 Do Consequences Make an Action Right?

LEARNING OBJECTIVE: When finished, you'll be able to:

- Explain, evaluate, and use the theories of ethical egoism, act utilitarianism, and rule utilitarianism.

7.4 Do Rules Define Morality?

LEARNING OBJECTIVE: When finished, you'll be able to:

- Explain, evaluate, and apply scriptural divine command theories, natural law theory, Kantian ethics, and Buddhist ethics.

7.5 Is Ethics Based on Character?

LEARNING OBJECTIVES: When finished, you'll be able to:

- Explain, evaluate, and use virtue ethics.
- Explain and critically evaluate the ethic of caring as a feminist ethic.

7.6 Can Ethics Resolve Moral Quandaries?

LEARNING OBJECTIVES: When finished, you'll be able to:

- Apply ethical theories to the moral issues of abortion and euthanasia.
- thinking critically Engage in moral reasoning that uses ethical theory and avoids fallacious moral thinking.

Chapter Summary

7.7 Readings

Fyodor Dostoyevsky, "The Heavenly Christmas Tree"

Peter Singer, "Famine, Affluence, and Morality"

7.8 Historical Showcase: Nietzsche and Wollstonecraft

Miłosz_G/Shutterstock.com

7.1 What Is Ethics?

Our moral decisions are an inescapable part of who we are. Listen to the voices of these young men and women:

> All the other times when I did care about [birth control], when I was so afraid, I didn't get any satisfaction out of it at all, even during the whole intercourse. It seemed so one-way. Here I'm so wrapped up in being scared and he's getting the good end of it. He's not really worrying about what's going to happen to you. He's only worrying about himself. This time I think what I really thought was if you don't think about it, maybe you'll get something out of it. So I guessed it wouldn't be a hassle, I wouldn't worry about it. And I did get a lot more out of it, not worrying about it. I had thought about getting birth control pills with my boyfriend before, but that worked to where it was a one-way street for his benefit, not for mine. It would be mine because I wouldn't get pregnant, but safe for him, too, because I wouldn't put him on the spot. So I get sick of being used. I'm tired of this same old crap; forget it. I'm not getting pills for his benefit. So I never got them and I never thought I would have to 'cause I wasn't looking for anyone since I was tired of being used. Sex was a one-way street. He gets all the feelings, girls have all the hassles. She gets more emotional and falls head over heels while he could give a damn. I'm sick of it, so I thought, Hang it all [and got pregnant].[1]

THINKING LIKE A PHILOSOPHER

Has a friend of yours ever considered having an abortion? If so, did you tell her how you felt about abortion? If none of your friends has had to consider this, then imagine one of your friends was considering having an abortion. What would you tell her if she asked for your advice?

> I was 26 and she was 22. . . . For her it was the second [abortion]. . . . She was 16 the previous time, and the guy had blamed her and was cruel about it. Having to go through it again traumatized her. I didn't know what to do. It numbed me out. My feelings for her and about her were pretty twisted. . . . She broke up eventually with me in a cut-and-dried, cold fashion, which I think was the result of the abortion. . . . To this day, I feel loss. I have a lack of understanding as to why it's so hard for me to accept how I feel, the pain or hurt or whatever it is. I want to derail it, but I think about it when I'm alone or when somebody brings it up. I don't really allow the feeling, even now, as I talk about it. I'm knotting in the stomach, uptight. . . . I feel guilty. Morally, in this day and age, it's not the end of the world. I don't see it as taking life away. I feel guilty in the sense that it's an unpleasant situation. You did start something, but I don't feel it's killing. If I did, I'd go nuts, I suppose.[2]

> [After this abortion,] I'd like to get married and have a baby, but I doubt I ever will. I look too much for love and adoration, and I get them mixed up with sex. I guess I do it to get people to validate me. . . . [After the abortions,] I never think about the babies at all. . . . I remember a conversation I had with a friend who'd just had an abortion. It's just an embryo, I told her, preferring to use the clinical definition. It's not a being, just a bunch of splitting cells. My friend said, "It's murder. How can you deny it's a life? It's murder, but it's justifiable homicide." . . . I agree with her, of course, but I just won't admit it. . . . Truth is hard to take, and I just don't know if I'm ready for it.[3]

These remarks remind us of the personal and moral questions we all must face. Should I think about the morality of my sexual relationships? Is it wrong to use people? Must I take responsibility for the consequences of my actions? Is abortion moral? They also remind us of the public decisions we must make as a society. Should we support

1   Quoted in Kristin Luker, *Taking Chances: Abortion and the Decision Not to Contracept* (Berkeley: University of California Press, 1975), 127–128.
2   Quoted in Arthur B. Shostak and Gary McLouth, *Men and Abortion* (New York: Praeger, 1984), 86.
3   Quoted in Linda Bird Franke, *The Ambivalence of Abortion* (New York: Random House, 1978), 63.

the legality of abortions? Should we force unwed fathers to support their children? Should we provide sexual education in grade schools? Should we provide welfare to unwed mothers? We can answer these kinds of questions only on the basis of our moral values. Much of what we are and do, in fact, is determined by our moral values because our values shape our thoughts, feelings, actions, and perceptions.

Our values are, to a large extent, absorbed from the society around us. We absorb them from family and friends; from television, radio, and the Internet; from books and magazines, from Church and school. As children we adopt the values of our culture without thinking, much like how we learn to speak our native language, or learn the rules of good manners. Yet given the large and pervasive influence our values have on who we are, what we believe, and what we do, this unreflective embrace of values is not necessarily a good thing. To unthinkingly adopt the values proposed by those around you is to live your life according to the values they have chosen for you, not those you have chosen for yourself. The fundamental question is this: Will you live the life that other people want you to live and do what they want you to do? Or will you move through your life on a road you have mapped out for yourself? Will you live someone else's life, or will you live by values you have chosen for yourself?

To examine your values, to shape and rethink them in the light of your own experience and your own reasoning, is the philosophical task of ethics, the subject of this chapter.

Ethics is the study of morality. It is a branch of philosophy that tries to determine what things in life are morally good and which actions are morally right. So ethics deals with morality, but it is not the same as morality. **Morality** consists of the standards that an individual or a group has about what is right and wrong or good and evil. Your moral standards include, for example, your beliefs about whether it's wrong to lie to your friends or wrong to tell one friend what another told you in confidence. Your moral standards include your beliefs about whether it's wrong to cheat on your girlfriend or your boyfriend. They include your views about the morality of forcing sex on an unwilling partner. And they include your views on racism, sexism, suicide, abortion, and euthanasia. Moral standards, then, are rules or statements that indicate the kinds of actions that are morally wrong or morally right, and the kinds of values that are morally good. The Ten Commandments, for example, is a list of ten moral standards. Generally speaking, moral standards deal with matters to which we attach great importance. Typically they involve serious harm or injury to others or to oneself. Consider the moral standards we have against lying, theft, rape, murder, child abuse, assault, slander, fraud, suicide, greed, and using addictive drugs. All of these plainly deal with matters that we feel are important because they involve the infliction of serious harm to others or to oneself.

As we suggested earlier, ethics "studies" these kinds of moral standards. People engage in ethics when they examine their moral standards or those of society and ask whether they are reasonable or unreasonable. In other words, when we ask whether our moral standards are supported by good reasons or poor ones or no reasons at all.

 MindTap How do our values bear out given only a split second to react? Go to MindTap to watch a video presenting an experiment that tests this question.

✓ QUICK REVIEW
We daily face moral questions that should be answered by values we have chosen for ourselves.

💬 THINKING LIKE A PHILOSOPHER

1. The textbook explains what moral standards are. Can you make a list of what you feel your main moral standards are? Next, analyze your list. What generalizations would you make about the items on your list? For example: Do they all or mostly involve your actions toward other people? Are they all or mostly related to your religious beliefs?

2. This book suggests that people "engage in ethics when they examine their moral standards and ask whether they are reasonable or unreasonable." What are some moral standards you absorbed as a child that you now think are unreasonable? As you look over your past life, what moral standards have you changed *because* you came to believe they were unreasonable? Explain.

A person starts to do ethics when she takes the moral standards absorbed from family, church, and society—and critically evaluates them. Do the standards really make sense? What are the reasons for or against these standards? Why should I continue to believe in them? What can be said in their favor, and what can be said against them? Are they reasonable or stupid? You may have once asked yourself, for example, whether you should tell your friend the truth about her boyfriend or lie to her. Telling the truth would just hurt her feelings and make her upset with you. So is it sometimes permissible to lie? Are some things—such as people's feelings—more important than telling the truth? Why is honesty between friends important, anyway? What makes lying wrong? Is lying wrong because lying injures people? Then, is lying right when telling the truth will hurt people more? What makes something right and wrong, and why are these so important?

When a person asks these kinds of questions about her moral standards or about the moral standards of her society, she has started to do ethics. Ethics, then, is a study of moral standards that aims at developing standards that are reasonable, and that we have decided for ourselves are justified. It is, in short, the attempt to ensure that the standards we live by are truly our own standards, chosen because we ourselves believe they are reasonable. It is choosing our moral standards because we ourselves have decided they are reasonable and not because others decided for us.

We begin our study of ethics by looking at an important challenge to ethics. This is the theory philosophers call ethical relativism. Ethical relativism holds that moral right and wrong depend on the society or culture to which you belong. As you will see, this theory implies that we cannot say that one group's moral beliefs are any better or worse than another's. But as you will also see, the theory of ethical relativism carries with it a number of serious problems.

ANALYZING THE READING

The textbook suggests that the purpose of ethics is to develop moral standards that are reasonable. What does "reasonable" mean? What are some characteristics of a moral standard that would make it an unreasonable one? Describe some of the moral standards of your friends or other people you know that you think are unreasonable? What is it about those beliefs that leads you to say they are unreasonable?

QUICK REVIEW

Ethics is the study of morality; it involves reflecting on one's moral standards or the moral standards of a group or a society, and asking whether they are reasonable.

PHILOSOPHY AT THE MOVIES

Watch *The Woodsman* (2004), which recounts the story of Walter, a convicted sex offender just released from prison, who, trying to start a new life with Vickie who's aware of his history, finds he can escape neither himself nor his past. What values do you think should guide Vickie as she tries to decide how to relate to Walter? Should Walter be allowed to start a new life as he wants to do? Why or why not?

7.2 Is Ethics Relative?

Ethics is not the only way to study morality. Sociology, anthropology, psychology, and other social sciences also study morality. But the social sciences study morality through a descriptive or factual investigation of moral behavior and beliefs. These social sciences are concerned with how people *in fact* behave or what people *in fact* believe about moral right and wrong. Ethics, on the other hand, asks how people *ought* to behave or what people *ought* to believe about moral right and wrong. For example, anthropologists tell us that the Inuit (Eskimos) used to abandon their elderly on the ice and allow them to die of starvation and exposure. They also inform us that in certain tribes in Nigeria, when twins were born one of the infants was killed.[4] Such twin infanticide seems to have been morally acceptable to those Nigerian tribes at the time. But anthropology, as such, does not try to determine whether it was right or wrong for the Inuit to abandon their elderly or for Nigerian tribes to kill a twin at birth. Ethics, on the other hand, tries to answer the question of whether it is *morally right* for the Inuit, in their circumstances, to abandon their elderly. And it asks whether killing twins is *right* for African tribes, in their circumstances. The social sciences ask what people actually do or actually believe about moral right and wrong. But ethics asks what people ought to do or ought to believe about moral right and wrong.

Although ethics and the social sciences study morality in very different ways, both have addressed one important issue: moral diversity. Many anthropologists have emphasized how different the moralities of different societies are. For example, many societies think that slavery is unjust, whereas others have felt slavery is permissible. Some societies believe that infanticide is wrong, but other societies practice it frequently. Some see female circumcision as a moral obligation while others condemn the practice, calling it "female genital mutilation." In fact, societies differ about the morality of a long list of practices. They differ on abortion, polygamy, patricide, slavery, suicide, discrimination, genocide, homosexuality, euthanasia, pedophilia, and torturing animals.

QUICK REVIEW
Descriptive relativism affirms that societies differ in their moral standards.

This diversity of moral standards has led virtually all anthropologists—and almost everyone else—to embrace a view called *descriptive relativism*. Descriptive relativism holds that different societies or cultures have different moralities. That is, what the people of one society or culture *believe* is morally wrong, people of other cultures often *believe* is morally right. This kind of relativism is called "descriptive" because it tries only to describe the moral beliefs and standards of each culture. It does not take a position on whether the actions of people in one culture really are morally wrong or really are morally right. Nor does descriptive relativism hold that anyone ought to live by any of those standards. That is, it does not take a position on whether anyone's moral standards tell us anything about what anyone ought to do. Although certain questions still surround the issue, descriptive relativism is accepted by virtually everyone. But some philosophers and anthropologists have gone beyond descriptive relativism and embraced *ethical relativism*.

QUICK REVIEW
Ethical relativism is the view that what is morally right or wrong depends on one's culture or society and that there is no single correct set of moral standards that everyone should follow everywhere and always.

Ethical relativism (also referred to as "moral relativism") is the view that not only do a person's beliefs about moral right and wrong depend on her culture, but that moral right and wrong themselves depend on a person's culture. Ethical relativism is the view that claims about moral right and wrong are really claims about what is morally right or wrong according to a specific culture or society. The ethical relativist holds that each society has a culture and moral standards are part of that culture. When a person is raised within the culture of a society, she "internalizes" that culture along with its moral standards. That is, she comes to perceive and value what her culture tells her she should perceive and value. A form of behavior is then morally right for that person if and only if the moral standards of her culture say it is morally right.

 THINKING LIKE A PHILOSOPHER

Do you now or have you ever held the view that whether an action is morally wrong depends on what a person believes about morality? If so, would you describe your view as descriptive relativism or as ethical relativism? That is, was it your view that what a person *thinks* is wrong depends on what they believe about morality (which is a kind of descriptive relativism)? Or was it your view that a person's action really is wrong if she believes it's wrong, and is really not wrong if she believes it's not wrong (which is a form of ethical relativism)?

4   Helen L. Ball and Catherine M. Hill, "Twin Infanticide," *Current Anthropology*, vol. 37, no. 5 (December 1996), 856–863.

Ethical relativism differs significantly from descriptive relativism. As we noted, descriptive relativism holds that what people *believe* is morally right and wrong differs from one society to another. Ethical relativism, however, holds that what *actually is* morally right and wrong differs from one society to another. According to the ethical relativist, the moral standards of a person's culture tell us what that person *really ought* to do, not just what she *believes* she ought to do. And no other moral standards exist except the moral standards of each society's culture. So the only moral standards a person can use to judge moral right and wrong are those of her own society's culture. The standards of a person's culture determine what that person ought to do, and those are the only standards she can use to determine what she ought to do.

Although ethical relativism is different from descriptive relativism, the two are related. The main argument in support of ethical relativism relies on descriptive relativism. That argument goes something like this. Descriptive relativism, which we know is true, tells us that right and wrong differ from one society to another. Now if there was a single set of "correct" moral standards that everyone should follow, then right and wrong would not differ from one society to another. Surely if there was a single set of correct moral standards, then everyone would know those standards and everyone would accept them. Since people everywhere do not accept the same moral standards, there is no single set of correct moral standards that everyone should follow. The only moral standards there are, then, are those we find embedded in each society's culture. And those moral standards are the ones that tell each of us what is morally right or morally wrong.

The anthropologist Melville J. Herskovits (1895–1963) was a well-known supporter of ethical relativism, although he called it "cultural relativism." He summarized the view of the ethical relativist in a talk he presented several years ago. He first explained that there were significant differences between the moral standards of European cultures and those of African cultures. He then went on to say:

> Differences of this sort, and the many others that have been revealed by the cross-cultural approach, have led us to a concept technically called "cultural relativism." This concept holds that there is no absolutely valid moral system, any more than there is an absolutely valid mode of perceiving the natural world. The traditions of a people dictate what for them is right and wrong, how they are to interpret what they see and feel and hear, and they live according to these imperatives. . . . How does the individual come to know the values of his society? These are learned through a process that I have been forced, for want of a better word, to call enculturation. In its essence, this is . . .socialized learning, to which all human beings are exposed. Most of the enculturative process is effortless; we learn our cultural lessons so well that our knowledge is internalized and comes to have a strong emotional as well as cognitive content.[5]

Notice three points that Herskovits makes. First, he claims that no moral system can be said to be "absolutely valid." In other words, there are no moral standards that all people ought to live by. There are only the moral standards of each person's own cultural traditions. Second, he claims that what is morally right or wrong for a person is "dictated" by what that person's culture or "traditions" say is right or wrong. And third, he claims that the moral standards a person accepts are acquired through a process of "enculturation." This third point means that moral standards have no rational basis. That is, people and societies do not think, reason, and debate

---

[5]   Melville J. Herskovits, *Cultural Relativism: Perspectives in Cultural Pluralism*, ed. Frances Herskovits (New York: Random House, 1972).

about their moral standards. All moral standards are merely the traditions that a society's ancestors happen to have handed down to the present generation. And the present generation unthinkingly and uncritically accepts them.

The theory of ethical relativism brings with it a shipload of problems. First, the theory claims that the only moral standards we can use to evaluate right and wrong are those of our own culture. Apart from these cultural standards, there exist no other correct or "objective" moral standards. Every moral standard, then, is just the moral standard of this or that cultural group. But if the only standards we can use to evaluate right and wrong are those our own culture gives us, then we have no way to evaluate or criticize our own moral standards. We cannot evaluate our own moral standards because we would have to use those same moral standards to evaluate them.

Suppose, for example, that our moral standards said slavery is morally right. Then if ethical relativism is correct, we could not say that our standards are mistaken and that slavery is wrong. We could not say that, because we can only use the moral standards of our own culture to evaluate the morality of slavery. And those moral standards tell us slavery is not wrong. Since there is no correct or objective standard we can appeal to, we are stuck with accepting what our own moral standards say about slavery. Or so the ethical relativist implies.

We also could not evaluate the moral standards of another culture. For suppose that another culture's standards were different from ours. Suppose their culture said slavery is morally right, but our culture said slavery is morally wrong. Then ethical relativism would give us no way of determining that their moral standard about slavery is mistaken and ours is correct, or that theirs is correct and ours is mistaken. There are no other standards we can use to evaluate both of our standards, except our own standards or their own standards. For the relativist tells us there is no correct or objective standard apart from the standards of each person's culture. So to determine which standard is right—ours or theirs—we have to use either our standards or their standards. But if we use our standards to judge whether slavery is morally wrong, this will just tell us that our standard is correct and theirs is wrong. And if we use their standards, this will just tell us that theirs is right and ours is wrong. So the only conclusion we can draw is that our standards agree with our standards, and their standards agree with their standards! We are still left wondering whose standards about slavery are right. In the end we would not be able to determine whether theirs are mistaken or ours are. We could only say that ours are different from theirs, not that ours are mistaken and theirs are right, or the other way around.

Ethical relativism implies, then, that we cannot say our own moral standards are mistaken. Nor can we say the moral standards of another culture are mistaken, only that they are different. Yet ethical relativism seems to be telling us that we can't do what we do all the time. We are able to criticize our own moral standards, for example, and conclude that our standards are mistaken. Before our Civil War, the moral standards of American society said that slavery is morally justified. But a large number of Americans eventually reasoned that slavery is built on the idea that some people are not equal to others and that idea is false and unreasonable. Economic self-interest kept the South from publicly admitting that, and the result was the Civil War. But the point is that many Americans were able to mentally step outside their culture and rationally evaluate their own moral standards and decide they were wrong. Culture is not a prison that keeps us locked within its walls. Moreover, people are also able to rationally evaluate the moral standards of other cultures. We can rationally say that if a culture thinks it is morally right to destroy another racial, ethnic, or religious group, that culture is mistaken. We can rationally say, for example, that the murders of six million Jews during the Holocaust was wrong, that the mass murders of two million Cambodians by the Khmer Rouge in the 1970s was

QUICK REVIEW

Ethical relativism claims that the only moral standards we can use to determine right and wrong are those of our own society; but this would mean that we cannot evaluate whether our own standards or those of another society are mistaken. Yet we can criticize our own standards and those of other cultures.

wrong, that the mass murder of the Tutsi in Rwanda in 1994 was wrong, that the murder of Bosnian Muslims by the Serbs in 1995 was wrong, and that the killings of the non-Arab people of Darfur between 2003 and 2006 was wrong. Even though the moral standards of the cultures of the murderers might have approved of their killings, we can confidently say that they were mistaken.

Another problem with ethical relativism lies in the relationship it sees between a culture's moral standards and people's moral views. The theory of ethical relativism says that something is morally right for a person if the moral standards of that person's culture say it is morally right. This claim of the ethical relativist seems wrong. Suppose that all the members of my culture hold that abortion is morally right. In other words the moral standards of my culture say that abortion is morally right. If the ethical relativist is correct, then abortion has to be morally right for me. And I have to accept that, regardless of what my own reasoning might tell me about abortion. Or suppose that everyone else in my culture believes that slavery is right. Then my culture's moral standards would tell me that slavery is right, and I have to accept that. It would be wrong for me to think that slavery is unjust even if my own reasoning led me to that conclusion. Since, according to ethical relativism, the moral norms of my society define what is right or wrong for me, I have to conform to those norms. For the ethical relativist, morality must be, as Herskovits says at one point, "conformity to the code of the group." In other words, ethical relativism implies that morality is conforming to the moral beliefs of the group to which you belong. And that, also, seems mistaken.

Another problem with ethical relativism that critics often raise is a problem with the argument that is supposed to prove it. The ethical relativist argues that the many cultural disagreements about moral matters show that no moral standards are valid for all societies. But philosopher James Rachels points out a problem with this argument:

> The fact that different societies have different moral codes proves nothing. There is also disagreement from society to society about scientific matters: in some cultures people believe that the earth is flat, and that evil spirits cause disease. We do not on that account conclude that there is no truth in geography or in medicine. Instead, we conclude that in some cultures people are better informed than in others. Similarly, disagreement in ethics might signal nothing more than that some people are less enlightened than others. At the very least, the fact of disagreement does not, by itself, entail that truth does not exist. Why should we assume that, if ethical truth exists, everyone must know it?[6]

Yet another problem with ethical relativism is that if ethical relativism is true, then moral disagreements should be impossible. This is a strange conclusion because the relativist says that ethical relativism is true *because people and societies disagree* about moral issues. But consider this: The relativist says that claims about moral right and wrong are really claims about what is morally right or wrong according to one's culture. So suppose you and I are arguing about abortion because you say abortion is wrong, and I say abortion is not wrong. Then, according to the relativist, you are saying abortion is wrong by *your* culture's standards, and I am saying it is not wrong by *my* culture's

---

6   James Rachels, "Can Ethics Provide Answers?" *Hastings Center Report* 10, no. 3 (June 1980): 34.

standards. But then we don't disagree! You are talking about your culture's standards, and I am talking about my culture's standards. So there is no real disagreement because we are talking about two different things.

Just as individuals cannot disagree about morality, societies also cannot disagree. At least not if ethical relativism is correct. For when the members of one society say something is right, they are, according to the relativist, just talking about what their culture accepts. And any society that seems to disagree will really be talking about what their culture accepts. So although the two societies seem to disagree, they are really just talking about two different things. But this seems false. Both societies and individuals can disagree about a moral issue, and when they disagree they are often talking about, and disagreeing about, the same thing. Moreover, if societies could not disagree about some moral issues, then the ethical relativist's own argument would have to be mistaken. For the ethical relativist argues for his theory by pointing out that societies disagree about morality. Yet his own theory of ethical relativism implies that societies cannot disagree about morality.

There are other problems with ethical relativism. Is it really true that there are no moral standards that all societies recognize? Think about it. If a society is going to survive, don't its members have to accept some moral standards about how they should behave toward one another? Won't a society collapse if its members don't recognize the moral standard to refrain from arbitrarily murdering their neighbors? Won't the language of a society collapse if its members don't recognize the moral standard of telling the truth? Won't a society's ability to make contracts and agreements collapse if its members don't recognize the obligation to keep one's promises? Although societies may differ in some of their moral beliefs, aren't there certain basic moral standards that all societies have to accept just to survive?

ANALYZING THE READING

The textbook argues that if ethical relativism is correct, then people from different cultures could not disagree about the morality of any kind of behavior. Give an example of a kind of behavior that you know two different cultures disagree on. Explain why ethical relativism could not say that people from those cultures disagree about the morality of that kind of behavior.

Moreover, even when two societies seem to have different moral standards, at a deeper level the two societies may share the same moral values. Take "twin infanticide," the practice of killing one of the two babies when twins are born. As we noted earlier, twin infanticide used to be common in certain Nigerian tribes but condemned by most Western societies. Western societies condemn infanticide of any kind because they value human life. Does this mean that societies that practice twin infanticide do not value human life? Not necessarily. Anthropologists found that societies that permit twin infanticide exist in harsh and demanding environments. In those environments food is scarce and malnourishment is widespread. In such circumstances, "The feeling is that the mother cannot successfully nurse both twins and that if she tried both would die. Through infanticide, at least one twin has a chance."[7] It is not just the twin's lives that are at risk: "In attempting to nurse and carry two infants, the mother's health might also suffer, with consequences for other children in the family."[8] So societies that permit twin infanticide apparently do so because they, too, value human life. But to secure the value of human life in their harsh environments, such societies must resort to the extreme measure of twin infanticide. Nigerian tribes, then, may share the same fundamental moral values we have. But their different circumstances may lead them to accept as moral those practices that would be immoral in our more affluent circumstances.

---

[7]   Ball and Hill, "Twin Infanticide," op. cit., 858.
[8]   Ibid.

In spite of the many objections to ethical relativism, however, we should not reject the theory altogether. A fundamental point the theory is trying to make is that we should be tolerant of the moral beliefs of others. In particular, we should not assume that our own moral beliefs are the correct ones or even the best ones. The moral beliefs embedded in a culture have developed over many centuries in response to the particular circumstances of that culture. Societies that face extreme hardships must adapt to those hardships with moralities that may look very different from ours. Yet their moralities may be trying to achieve the same basic moral values for which we all strive. In fact, some societies may have hit upon moral outlooks that are much better responses to the world than our own. We should, then, be tolerant and respectful of those different moral outlooks.

Yet having respect and tolerance does not mean that we cannot rationally criticize and evaluate the moral standards of other cultures and of our own culture. A relativist like Herskovits says we "internalize" our moral standards by just absorbing them from our culture, apparently without thinking. To some extent—maybe to a large extent—this is true. Yet it is always possible for us to think about the standards we have "internalized" and to rationally evaluate and criticize them. For example, we can ask whether our own moral standards or those of our own groups—family, friends, society—are reasonable. We can ask whether they are consistent and whether they look toward the well-being of our whole society. We can ask whether they conform to the facts of human nature and whether they respect the dignity of persons. And we can ask whether they help produce admirable moral characters. We can ask these questions not just about our own moral standards but about those of other cultures. Questions like these may convince us that our own moral standards are unreasonable and that the moral standards of other societies are more reasonable than ours. That would not necessarily be a bad thing to learn! But by reasoning in this way, we are trying to figure out what is "really" or "absolutely" right or wrong. Ethical relativism, however, insists that your culture must determine your moral beliefs regardless of your own reasoning. So the theory of ethical relativism would not allow you to reach your own conclusions about right and wrong. For the ethical relativist, as Herskovits says, to be moral is to "conform" to the "dictates" of the morality of your society. Morality, for the relativist, is a form of social conformity.

We can't explore ethical relativism any further. Whether or not we agree with ethical relativism, each of us must still decide for ourselves what we ought to do and how we ought to live. Such decisions require that we have some reasonable moral standard on which to base our decisions. So, whether or not you accept ethical relativism, the question remains: What are reasonable beliefs to hold about how I ought to live?

PHILOSOPHY AT THE MOVIES

Watch *Nowhere in Africa (Nirgendwo in Afrika)* (2001) in which Walter, a Jew living in Germany during the Nazi era, travels to Africa as World War II is about to break out. When he has his family join him there, he discovers that, while his daughter Regina quickly adjusts to their new home, his wife, Jettel, dislikes Africa and their life there. List the many ethical issues this movie raises. Was it wrong for Jettel to agree to the British soldier's request? Was it wrong for Walter to insist the family return to Germany? Does this film depict descriptive relativism? Ethical relativism? Does the film imply or reject the idea that people of different cultures ultimately have the same values?

Movie with a related theme: *Enemy Mine* (1985).

7.3 Do Consequences Make an Action Right?

Consider this true story:

> Matthew Donnelly was a physicist who had worked with X-rays for thirty years. Perhaps as a result of too much exposure, he contracted cancer and lost part of his jaw, his upper lip, his nose, and his left hand, as well as two fingers from his right hand. He was also left blind. Mr. Donnelly's physicians told him that he had about a year left to live, but he decided that he did not want to go on living in such a state. He was in constant pain—one reporter said that "at its worst, he could be seen lying in bed with teeth clenched and beads of perspiration standing out on his forehead." Knowing that he was going to die anyway, and wanting to escape his misery, Mr. Donnelly begged his three brothers to kill him. Two refused, but one did not. The youngest brother, 36-year-old Harold Donnelly, carried a .30-caliber pistol into the hospital and shot Matthew to death.[9]

When questioned, Harold Donnelly said that he did not feel that killing his brother was immoral. It was much better for his brother to die than to suffer the terrible consequences of continuing to live. The *consequences* justified the killing.

Traditionally, many ethicists have said that we should decide moral right and wrong by looking at the consequences of our actions. If the consequences are good, the act is right. If the consequences are bad, the act is wrong. Thus, a **consequentialist theory** judges the morality of an action by how good or bad its consequences are. In particular, consequentialists consider the amount of nonmoral good and the amount of nonmoral bad that an action produces. The morally right action is the one that produces more good (or less bad) nonmoral consequences compared to any other action that could be performed in its place. Note that consequentialists say we should evaluate the morality of an action by considering only its *nonmoral* consequences. Consequentialists look only at nonmoral consequences because it would be circular to define an immoral action as one that has immoral consequences. To avoid circularity, consequentialists insist we must look only at the nonmoral consequences of our actions. Suppose a consequentialist is evaluating whether it is moral for Harold to kill his brother Matthew. A consequentialist would look at the *pain* that Matthew would avoid if Harold killed him. He would consider the *sorrow* that Harold will probably feel when Matthew is dead. He would also consider the *suffering* Harold would undergo if he has to go to prison for killing his brother. He would take into account the *distress* Harold might feel knowing he killed his own brother. And he would also consider the *satisfactions* Harold and his family would feel knowing that Matthew was no longer suffering, and so on. But the consequentialist would not consider whether Harold's action was unjust or violated Matthew's moral rights. Nor would he consider whether Harold was selfish, or whether killing his brother would lead him to commit other immoral actions.

A consequentialist theory, then, determines what is right on the basis of what is good. But we need to distinguish two kinds of goods: instrumental goods and intrinsic goods. Instrumental goods are good because they get us other good things. Intrinsic goods are good in themselves; they are desirable for themselves and not because of what else they might get us. For example, having a wisdom tooth removed is not a pleasant experience. But it is instrumentally good because it is a means to the good of having healthy teeth. On the other hand, the pleasures of skiing are intrinsically good. They are desirable for themselves and not for some further good they can get us. Similarly, an intrinsically evil or bad thing is undesirable in itself.

---

[9] James Rachels, *The Elements of Moral Philosophy* (New York: Random House, 1986), 82.

And an instrumentally evil or bad thing is undesirable because it will produce some other evil. Some things, of course, can be both instrumentally good and intrinsically good, or both instrumentally evil and intrinsically evil.

According to consequentialists, the rightness or wrongness of our actions depend on how much *intrinsic* good they produce, and how much *intrinsic* evil they diminish. So what things are intrinsically good? Consequentialists have not agreed on an answer to that question. Nevertheless, a good number have adopted **hedonism.** This is the view that only pleasure or happiness is intrinsically good and that only pain or unhappiness is intrinsically evil. In other words, only pleasure is desired for itself and not for what it can get us, and only pain is disliked for itself and not for other losses it may inflict on us. Even if pleasure brought us no other benefits we would still desire it; and even if pain inflicted no other losses on us we would still dislike it. All other things, hedonists claim, are good to the extent that they bring us pleasure or happiness and to the extent they diminish pain or unhappiness. For example, the ancient Greek philosopher Epicurus (341–270 BCE) argued that pleasure is the chief goal of life. But we must weigh our pleasures carefully to ensure that they do not later cause us greater pain:

The purpose of all our actions is to be free from pain and fear, and, when we have attained this, the tempest of the soul will be laid to rest, since a living creature does not need to search for something that is lacking, nor to look for anything else by which the good of the soul and of the body will be fulfilled. . . . We speak of pleasure as the starting point and the goal of a happy life because it is our primary kindred good and because every act of choice and aversion originates with it, and because we come back to it when we judge every good by using the feeling of pleasure as our criterion. . . . And since pleasure is our first and kindred good, we should not choose every pleasure whatsoever, but pass over pleasures when they will later produce greater pains. And we should consider a pain superior to other pleasures when submission to the pain brings us as a consequence a greater pleasure. Although all pleasure is good because it is a kindred good, not all pleasure should be chosen, just as all pain is evil and yet not all pain is to be shunned. It is by measuring one against another, and by looking at their conveniences and inconveniences, that all these matters must be judged. . . . When we say, then, that pleasure is the purpose of life, we do not mean the pleasures of the prodigal or the pleasures of sensuality. . . . I mean, instead, the pleasure that consists in freedom from bodily pain and mental agitation. The pleasant life is not the product of one drinking party after another or of having sex with men or women, or of eating the delicacies of a luxurious meal. On the contrary, it is the result of sober thinking—namely, investigation of the reasons for every act of choice and aversion, and elimination of those false ideas about the gods and death which are the chief source of mental disturbances.[10]

ANALYZING THE READING

Epicurus claims that there is a difference between the pleasures that we should choose and the pleasures that should not be chosen. What is the difference? How would you describe the kind of pleasure that we should choose? How would you describe the kind of pleasure that should not be chosen? Why does he say that we should not choose "the pleasures that should not be chosen"?

Some consequentialists claim that other things besides pleasure are intrinsically good. Different consequentialists at various times have claimed that knowledge, justice, consciousness, friendship, adventure, being esteemed, health, beauty, and so on, are intrinsic goods. Some associated the good with self-realization, the full development of people's capacities and abilities. Some Christian consequentialists have identified the good with love. They have argued that actions are right to the extent

10 Epicurus, "Letter to Menoeceus," in *The Philosophy of Epicurus*, ed. George K. Strodach (Evanston, IL: Northwestern University Press, 1963), 175.

that they increase the amount of love in the world. Other philosophers have been "pluralists," holding that there are many kinds of intrinsic goods. So consequentialists are not necessarily hedonists.

An obvious question arises here. Whose good and whose evil should a consequentialist consider? When examining the consequences of an action, are we supposed to consider the consequences the action has only for the person performing the action? Or are we supposed to consider the consequences the action will have on everyone? For example, think again about Harold and his brother Matthew in the hospital again. Clearly the consequences just for Harold are different from the consequences for Harold, Matthew, his family, etc. When deciding what to do, then, should we consider the consequences only for the agent, or should we consider the effects on everyone who is affected by the agent's action? The answers to these questions form the basis for the two main kinds of consequentialist theories: egoism and utilitarianism.

> **QUICK REVIEW**
> Some consequentialists hold that intrinsic goods include not just pleasure but also knowledge, power, beauty, self-realization, or love.

Ethical Egoism

Some ethicists claim that when deciding the morality of an action, only the good and bad consequences for the agent matter. That is, the only consequences of her actions a person should consider are the consequences of her actions on herself. These ethicists are called *egoists*. **Ethical egoism** contends that we act morally when we act in a way that best promotes our own long-term interests. So, ethical egoism is the view that an action is morally right if it produces more good and fewer bad consequences for me than any other action I could perform in its place. Here is how American libertarian author Harry Browne argued for ethical egoism:

> The Unselfishness Trap is the belief that you must put the happiness of others ahead of your own. Unselfishness is a very popular ideal, one that's been honored throughout recorded history. . . . So perhaps we should look more closely at the subject to see if the ideal is sound. . . .
>
> Each person always acts in ways he believes will make him feel good or will remove discomfort from his life. . . . One man devotes his life to helping the poor. Another one lies and steals. . . . One woman devotes herself to her husband and children. Another one seeks a career as a singer.
>
> In every case, the ultimate motivation has been the same. Each person is doing what he believes will assure his happiness. . . . For the thief and the humanitarian each have the same motive—to do what he believes will make him feel good. In fact, we can't avoid a very significant conclusion: Everyone is selfish. Selfishness isn't really an issue, because everyone selfishly seeks his own happiness.[11]

> **QUICK REVIEW**
> Ethical egoism claims that a morally right action is one that produces more good and fewer bad consequences for oneself than any other action.

Browne is saying that the belief that you should put the happiness of others ahead of your own happiness is false. He is suggesting, in other words, that you should put your own happiness ahead of the happiness of others. Why should you always put your own happiness ahead of the happiness of others? Because, Browne argues, everyone else always puts their own happiness ahead of the happiness of others.

ANALYZING THE READING

Browne argues that since every person does "what he believes will assure his happiness," then "everyone is selfish." Put his argument into its logical form using the "if . . . then . . ." form of premises. Make sure you supply any assumed premises that Browne does not state but that are needed to make the argument valid. What is the assumed premise? Do you agree with this assumed premise? Why? What would Rachels say about it?

---

[11] Harry Browne, *How I Found Freedom in an Unfree World* (Macmillan Publishing Co., 1973); copyright owned by Pamela Wolfe Browne at http://www.trendsaction.com, email PLWBrowne@HarryBrowne.org.

Browne's argument seems to rely on a view about people that is called "psychological egoism." Psychological egoism—a view we discussed in Chapter 2—holds that people always act out of self-interest. Notice that *ethical* egoism holds that people *ought* to act out of self-interest, but *psychological* egoism holds that people *always* act out of self-interest, whether they ought to or not. In the passage above, Browne is arguing, then, that since everyone always acts out of self-interest, you and everyone else ought to always act out of self-interest. Browne does not tell us why he thinks psychological egoism implies ethical egoism; the two, after all, are different. Browne may think that since everyone else always acts out of self-interest, in fairness you too should act out of self-interest. Or he might think that morality requires you to do only what you are able to do. Since you are only able to act out of self-interest, morality must require you to act out of self-interest. But notice that it is odd to say that everyone *ought* to be selfish if everyone *already is* selfish. If everyone is going to act selfishly anyway, why would you have to tell them that they ought to do so?

Problems of Ethical Egoism. Many philosophers believe that arguments like Browne's are mistaken because psychological egoism is mistaken. One argument for claiming that people always act out of self-interest is that when people do something, it is always the case that they wanted to do it. Otherwise why would they have done it? Since people always do what they want to do, the psychological egoist argues, their actions are always motivated by selfishness. American philosopher James Rachels criticizes this argument in the following passage:

> It is the object of a want that determines whether it is selfish or not. The mere fact that I am acting on my wants does not mean that I am acting selfishly; that depends on what it is that I want. If I want only my own good, and care nothing for others, then I am selfish; but if I also want other people to be well-off and happy, and if I act on that want, then my action is not selfish.[12]

QUICK REVIEW
Problems with ethical egoism include: It is unclear what is morally right when people's interests conflict; ethical egoism is not impartial because it favors one's own interests, so it is not consistent with a moral point of view.

Critics also claim that ethical egoism runs into problems when people's interests conflict. Suppose we are competing against each other, say in a race, so that it is in your interests to win the race, and it is in my interests to win the race. The philosopher Kurt Baier (1917–2010) argued that in situations like these ethical egoism leads to contradictions and so has to be false. If we are competing in a race, then it is in my interests to win, so (according to ethical egoism) I ought to win. Yet, claims Baier, it is wrong to prevent someone from doing what he ought to do, so it is wrong for you to prevent me from winning. Yet it is also in your interests to win the race, so it is also wrong for you to not prevent me from winning. But then ethical egoism has led us into a contradiction: that it is wrong for you to prevent me from winning and also wrong for you to not prevent me from winning.

QUICK REVIEW
Utilitarianism claims that a morally right action is one that produces more good and fewer bad consequences for everyone than any other action. For traditional utilitarians good consequences consist of pleasure or happiness, and bad consequences consist of pain or unhappiness.

Some ethicists think that the most serious weakness of ethical egoism is that it is inconsistent with "the moral point of view." Any theory of ethics, these critics argue, must evaluate people's actions from the moral point of view. By the "moral point of view," they mean the point of view of someone who is impartial, that is, who is not biased in favor of one individual or group over another. Kurt Baier, for example, described the moral point of view as the point of view "of an independent, unbiased, impartial, objective, dispassionate, disinterested observer."[13] Ethical egoism, Baier and others have argued, is clearly not consistent with the moral point of view because it claims that you should be partial to your own interests.

---

[12] Rachels, op. cit., 58.
[13] Kurt Baier, *The Moral Point of View* (Ithaca, NY: Cornell University Press, 1958), 201.

Utilitarianism

In contrast to ethical egoism, utilitarianism asserts that the standard of morality is the promotion of good for everyone and not just for oneself. In brief, utilitarianism claims that a morally right action is one that produces more good or fewer bad consequences for everyone than any other action that could be performed in its place. Again, as with all consequentialist positions, good and evil mean nonmoral good and evil.

Jeremy Bentham (1748–1832) and John Stuart Mill (1806–1873) are the classic proponents of utilitarianism. Both claimed that only pleasure or happiness has intrinsic value, while pain or unhappiness are intrinsically evil. Their utilitarianism was, in short, based on a hedonistic philosophy. In the words of John Stuart Mill, author of the short but influential work, *Utilitarianism:*

MindTap To read more from John Stuart Mill's *Utilitarianism*, click the link in the MindTap Reader or go to the Questia Readings folder in MindTap.

> The creed which accepts as the foundation of morals, Utility, or the Greatest Happiness Principle, holds that actions are right in proportion as they tend to promote happiness, wrong as they tend to produce the reverse of happiness. By happiness is intended pleasure, and the absence of pain; by unhappiness, pain, and the privation of pleasure. . . . [T]he happiness which forms the utilitarian standard of what is right in conduct, is not the agent's own happiness, but that of all concerned.[14]

Jeremy Bentham: "Nature has placed mankind under the governance of two sovereign masters, *pain* and *pleasure*. They govern us in all we do, in all we say, in all we think. The principle of utility recognizes this subjection."

© UCL Art Collections, University College London, UK/The Bridgeman Art Library

As we noted earlier, some consequentialists claim that other things besides happiness or pleasure are intrinsically good. Such consequentialists would say that those other goods should be considered when determining moral right and wrong. But traditional utilitarians like Mill and Bentham claim that pleasure and the absence of pain are the only intrinsic goods on which morality depends. Since we will here focus primarily on traditional utilitarianism, we will assume that *good* refers to pleasure or happiness.

Like Mill's *Utilitarianism,* Bentham's *Introduction to the Principles of Morals and Legislation* is a classic of utilitarianism. Bentham's book asserts that the quantities of pleasure and pain our actions produce are the fundamental criteria of moral right and wrong. He explains this in the following passage, where he describes what is sometimes called Bentham's "utilitarian calculus." Notice that in the passage Bentham begins by appealing to psychological egoism. Yet he ends by claiming we should act in the interests of others.

THINKING LIKE A PHILOSOPHER

Pick a day during which you will be doing the kind of things you ordinarily spend most of your time doing. During the entire day try to base all your actions on Mill's principle of utilitarianism, by doing only what you think will produce the greatest amount of happiness for the largest number of people. At the end of the day, write an account of how your day went. What did you learn about utilitarianism?

---

[14] John Stuart Mill, *Utilitarianism* (1871), excerpts from ch. 2.

Nature has placed mankind under the governance of two sovereign masters, *pain* and *pleasure*. It is for them alone to point out what we ought to do, as well as to determine what we shall do. On the one hand the standard of right and wrong, on the other the chain of causes and effects, are fastened to their throne. They govern us in all we do, in all we say, in all we think: every effort we can make to throw off our subjection, will serve but to demonstrate and confirm it. In words a man may pretend to abjure their empire: but in reality he will remain subject to it all the while. The *principle of utility* recognizes this subjection. . . .

By the principle of utility is meant that principle which approves or disapproves of every action whatsoever, according to the tendency which it appears to have to augment or diminish the happiness of the party whose interest is in question: or, what is the same thing in other words, to promote or to oppose that happiness. . . .

By utility is meant that property in any object, whereby it tends to produce benefit, advantage, pleasure, good, or happiness (all this in the present comes to the same thing), or (what comes again to the same thing) to prevent the happening of mischief, pain, evil, or unhappiness to the party whose interest is considered; if that party be the community in general, then the happiness of the community. . . .

An action then may be said to be conformable to the principle of utility or, for shortness sake, to utility (meaning with respect to the community at large), when the tendency it has to augment the happiness of the community is greater than any it has to diminish it. . . . Of an action that is conformable to the principle of utility one may always say . . . that it . . . ought to be done, or . . . that it is right it should be done. . . . [or] that it is a right action.

These [following criteria] are the circumstances which are to be considered in estimating a pleasure or a pain. . . . [When] the value of a pleasure or a pain is considered, it will be greater or less, according to seven circumstances: to wit. . . .

1. Its *intensity*.
2. Its *duration*.
3. Its *certainty* or *uncertainty*.
4. Its *propinquity* or *remoteness*.
5. Its *fecundity* [the chance it has of being followed by sensations of the *same* kind: that is, pleasures, if it be a pleasure; pains, if it be a pain].
6. Its *purity* [the chance it has of not being followed by sensations of the *opposite* kind: that is, pains, if it be a pleasure; pleasures, if it be a pain].
   And one other; to wit:
7. Its *extent*; that is, the number of persons to whom it *extends*; or (in other words) who are affected by it.

To take an exact account then of the general tendency of any act by which the interests of a community are affected, proceed as follows. Begin with any one person of those whose interests seem most immediately to be affected by it: and take an account: Of the value of each . . . *pleasure* which appears to be produced by it . . . [and] the value of each *pain* which appears to be produced by it. . . .

ANALYZING THE READING

Bentham claims that "Nature has placed mankind under the governance of two sovereign masters, pain and pleasure." What does he mean by this? How does Bentham's claim that pain and pleasure are our "sovereign masters" compare to psychological egoism?

THINKING LIKE A PHILOSOPHER

Bentham provides a list of criteria or "seven circumstances" to measure the amount of pleasure and pain an action produces. Take any two actions you have recently done. List the one or two main pleasures and pains you believe each action produced. Now use Bentham's seven circumstances or criteria to estimate how large each pleasure was, and how large each pain was. Now, for each action, subtract the amount of pain it produced from the amount of pleasure it produced. Now determine which action produced the greatest amount of pleasure after you subtracted its pain. What does this exercise show you?

QUICK REVIEW

Bentham claims pain and pleasure govern us in all we do; his principle of utility says that morally right actions are those that increase the happiness or pleasures of the community, and that the pleasures and pains our actions produce for everyone should be measured so that we can choose the one that produces the greatest quantity of pleasure or the least quantity of pain for everyone affected by the action.

Sum up all the values of all the *pleasures* on the one side, and those of all the *pains* on the other. The balance, if it be on the side of pleasure, will give the *good* tendency of the act . . . with respect to the interests of *that individual* person; if on the side of pain, the *bad* tendency of [the act].

[Then] take an account of the *number* of persons whose interests appear to be concerned; and repeat the above process with respect to each [person]. *Sum up* the numbers expressive of the degrees of *good* tendency which the act has with respect to each individual . . . to whom the tendency of it is *good* upon the whole . . . do this again with respect to each individual . . . to whom the tendency of it is *bad* upon the whole. Take the *balance* which if on the side of *pleasure*, will give the general *good tendency* of the act, with respect to the total number or community of individuals concerned; if [the balance is] on the side of pain, [it will indicate] the general *evil tendency* [of the act] with respect to the same community.[15]

ANALYZING THE READING

According to Bentham, an action "ought to be done" if it "has the tendency to augment the happiness of the community." So we ought to seek the pleasure of others, not just our own. Is there any conflict between his view that we ought to seek the pleasure of others, and his earlier statement that pain and pleasure are our "sovereign masters" and "govern us in all we do,. . . say,. . . [and] think"? Explain.

MindTap To read more from Jeremy Bentham's *Introduction to the Principles of Morals and Legislation*, click the link in the MindTap Reader or go to the Questia Readings folder in MindTap.

Notice how clearly Bentham tells us that utilitarianism requires *measuring* the *quantity* of pleasures and pains an action causes for *everyone*. The morally right action is the one that will produce the highest *quantity* of pleasure for everyone or the lowest *quantity* of pain for everyone. Bentham argues that we can measure the quantity or size of the pleasures and pains our actions produce. We can measure them by how intense they are, how long they last, how certain they are to occur, and so on. But Bentham is not so clear about a key assumption he makes. He assumes that when we are trying to decide what we ought to do, we already know what our alternatives are. That is, he assumes we have identified all the actions we could perform at that moment. Once we know what choices we have, we can then use utilitarianism to figure out which action is the morally right one to choose. To figure out which action is right we must first *add* up all the pleasures each action produces. Then we must *add* up all the pains each will produce. Finally, we must *subtract* each action's *total quantity* of pains from that action's *total quantity* of pleasures. We must do this, of course, for each and every action that we could perform at that moment. We then choose the one action that will produce the greatest quantity of pleasure compared to all the other actions we could perform. But when all the actions we could perform will produce more pain than pleasure, we should choose the one that will produce the lowest quantity of pain. The action with the highest amount of pleasure or lowest amount of pain is the morally right action, according to Bentham's utilitarianism.

The view that pleasures and pains can be measured and then added and subtracted from each other has been criticized often. What yardstick can we use to measure the "intensity" or "propinquity" or "purity" of pleasures and pains? Moreover, suppose one kind of pleasure is as intense, as long, as certain, etc., as a second kind of pleasure. Must we conclude they are equally valuable? Suppose the pleasure of drinking a beer is as intense, as long, etc., as the pleasure of helping a friend with her

QUICK REVIEW

In Bentham's utilitarianism, good consequences consist of happiness or pleasure, and bad consequences consist of unhappiness or pain; the quantity of pleasure produced by an action is measured by its intensity, duration, certainty, likelihood to produce more pleasure, and so on.

ANALYZING THE READING

Epicurus, Bentham, and Mill were all hedonists. They all claimed pleasure is the only good that we desire for itself and not for what it can get us. They also thought pleasure and happiness were the same thing. Are there other fundamental values in human life besides pleasure that we desire just for themselves and not for what they can get us? If so, what are they?

15 Jeremy Bentham, *Introduction to the Principles of Morals and Legislation* (1823), excerpts from chs. 1 and 4.

problems. Does it follow they are equally valuable? And how can we compare the pleasures and pains you feel to those I feel? What if I insist that my pleasures and pains are much more intense than yours, while you insist yours are more intense? How can we possibly know who is right?

Perhaps not surprisingly, Mill thought Bentham was too focused on the quantitative aspects of pleasure and pain. So Mill suggested that the *quality* of pains and pleasures is as important or perhaps even more important than their *quantity*. In particular, Mill argued that the uniquely human "pleasures of the intellect, of the feelings and imagination, and of the moral sentiments" have "a much higher value . . . than those [pleasures] of mere sensation" which other animals can experience:

It is quite compatible with the principle of utility to recognize the fact, that some kinds of pleasure are more desirable and more valuable than others. It would be absurd that . . . the estimation of pleasures should be supposed to depend on quantity alone. If I am asked, what I mean by difference of quality in pleasures, or what makes one pleasure more valuable than another . . . there is but one possible answer. Of two pleasures, if there be one to which all or almost all who have experience of both give a decided preference, irrespective of any feeling of moral obligation to prefer it, that is the more desirable pleasure. If one of the two is, by those who are competently acquainted with both, placed so far above the other that they prefer it, even though knowing it to be attended with a greater amount of discontent, and would not resign it for any quantity of the other pleasure which their nature is capable of, we are justified in ascribing to the preferred enjoyment a superiority in quality, so far outweighing quantity as to render it, in comparison, of small account.

Now it is an unquestionable fact that those who are equally acquainted with, and equally capable of appreciating and enjoying both [higher and lower pleasures], do give a most marked preference to the manner of existence which employs their higher faculties. Few human creatures would consent to be changed into any of the lower animals, for a promise of the fullest allowance of a beast's pleasures; no intelligent human being would consent to be a fool, no instructed person would be an ignoramus, no person of feeling and conscience would be selfish and base, even though they should be persuaded that the fool, the dunce, or the rascal is better satisfied with his lot than they are with theirs. They would not resign what they possess more than he for the most complete satisfaction of all the desires which they have in common with him. . . . It is better to be a human being dissatisfied than a pig satisfied; better to be Socrates dissatisfied than a fool satisfied. And if the fool, or the pig, are of a different opinion, it is because they only know their own side of the question. The other party to the comparison knows both sides.[16]

In this famous passage, Mill claims one kind of pleasure is more valuable than a second kind if most people prefer the first over the second after experiencing both. This point is important. For it suggests that the value we give to a particular kind of pleasure should be determined by the value most experienced people would give it. Moreover, he claims, most people would prefer the higher pleasures to the lower pleasures. So the higher pleasures are more valuable than the lower ones. You may object that Mill is clearly wrong here. You may feel most people prefer the "lower" pleasures of sex, food, and drink, over the "higher" pleasures of, say, listening to a Beethoven symphony. But to prove his point, Mill proposes a "thought experiment." Imagine that somehow you were forced to choose between two

---

[16]   Mill, *Utilitarianism*, excerpts from ch. 2.

options: (1) becoming an animal whose "lower" pleasures were all fully satisfied but who could experience none of the "higher" pleasures, or (2) remaining a human being who could experience the "higher" pleasures but who was otherwise "dissatisfied." Would you choose (1) or (2)? Mill thinks that virtually everyone would prefer (2). So he concludes that everyone prefers the higher pleasures over the lower ones.

If we accept Mill's view, then when we assess the pleasures and pains of an action, we must first decide which are "higher" and which are "lower." Then we should give the "higher" pleasures greater values than the "lower" ones. We can then go on to add up the values of all the pleasures produced by the action and subtract the values of its pains. We should go through this process for each and every action we could perform when we make our choice. Finally, we should choose the action that will produce the greatest amount of pleasure or happiness (or the least amount of pain or unhappiness if all the actions we could perform will produce more pain than pleasure).

Notice that utilitarianism will not necessarily tell me that the morally right action is the one that seems to be morally right. For example, if in a certain situation lying or cheating or stealing produces more happiness than the alternatives, then that is the morally right thing to do. For the

THINKING LIKE A PHILOSOPHER

Do Bentham and Mill convince you? That is, do they convince you that utilitarianism is correct in its basic claim that an action is morally right if and only if it produces more pleasure or less pain for everyone, than any other action? Do you agree that any type of action whatsoever can be morally justified if it produces a sufficiently large amount of pleasure?

utilitarian the conventional morality most of us usually follow is deeply flawed. Conventional morality rigidly insists that certain kinds of actions are morally right no matter what their consequences are. This is unreasonable, utilitarians claim. We should not thoughtlessly follow the conventional morality we received from family, church, or friends. We need to be critical with our conventional morality and if it seems to make unreasonable demands on us, then we should set it aside and do what is reasonable. And the utilitarian will insist that in every situation what is reasonable is what will produce the best consequences for everyone.

Bentham's utilitarian views differed from Mill's in a significant way. Bentham seems to have had in mind a particular kind of utilitarian theory called **act utilitarianism**. But in some passages of his work on utilitarianism, Mill seems to have advocated a different kind called **rule utilitarianism**.

Act Utilitarianism. Act utilitarianism says that the morally right action is the one that will produce the greatest amount of pleasure or the least amount of pain for everyone, compared to all the other alternatives. In other words, before you act, ask yourself this: What will be the consequences of my actions not only for myself but for everyone? And, just as important: How do the consequences of each action I could perform compare to the consequences of each of my other alternatives? If an action produces more happiness or pleasure than any other action I could perform in its place, then the action is morally right. If the action produces more unhappiness or pain than some of the other actions I could take, then the action is morally wrong. In effect, for act utilitarians, the end justifies the means. This can create problems.

Take the following case: You are a judge living in a small town in South Africa many years ago. The police bring a black man before you and charge him with raping a white woman the night before. The woman, who is the only witness, has positively identified him although the rape took place in the dark of night. The rape has incensed the townspeople, and a mob of vigilantes has formed. The mob declares that if you do not agree to sentence the black man to death, they will raid the black settlement outside the town and kill several dozen black women in revenge.

QUICK REVIEW
Act utilitarianism claims
that the morally right
action is the particular act
that itself produces more
pleasure and less pain for
everyone. Act utilitarianism
seems to sometimes
require injustices and rights
violations.

You know that they will carry out this threat and that you have no way of stopping them. A few hours ago, by sheer improbable coincidence you happened to be alone at the bedside of a dying friend who—just before dying—confessed that he had committed the rape. It would be useless to bring this utterly improbable story to the mob. They would simply accuse you of trying to get the black man off the hook by making up an unlikely story. What should you do?

The implications of act utilitarianism are clear. You should sentence the black man to death although you know that he is innocent. By sentencing him to death, you will sacrifice one innocent life to save the lives of several dozen other innocent black women. If you declare him innocent, you would save one life but condemn several others to death. Utilitarianism here seems to require us to condemn an innocent man to death. But condemning an innocent man to death seems highly unjust and a violation of the innocent man's moral rights.

Rule Utilitarianism. Some utilitarians have argued that we get into such dilemmas when we use the utilitarian principle to judge *particular acts*. Instead, they argue, we should only use the utilitarian principle to determine which *moral rules* we should follow. The rules we should follow, of course, are those that will have the best consequences. Those rules should serve as our moral rules. Once we know which moral rules we should follow, we can then use those rules to determine which particular acts we should perform. Some of Mill's writings indicate that this was the approach he took. He wrote: "the standard of morality" consists of "the rules and precepts for human conduct, by the observance of which an existence [exempt as far as possible from pain, and as rich as possible in enjoyments] might be. . . . secured to all mankind."[17] This approach, called rule utilitarianism, holds that the *moral rules* that should govern what we do are those that will produce the greatest happiness for everyone. The particular actions we should perform are those that such moral rules require. When our particular actions follow those moral rules, our actions are morally right.

Imagine, for example, that I borrow a friend's new car. And suppose that while driving, I accidently drive too close to a road sign and dent the side of her car. So I have to decide whether I should tell her that I dented her new car. Or should I lie and tell her that someone dented the car when I left it in a parking lot? Let's suppose that if I lie no one will ever know, and no one, including myself, will ever feel the least bit of pain as a result of my lie. My friend's auto insurance will pay for the damage to her car. To the insurance company the money they pay is an insignificant sum that they have already taken into account as the cost of doing business. On the other hand, if I tell the truth my friend will feel extremely upset and angry with me. I will have to pay for the dent and that will impose a large and painful burden on me. So what should I do? Act utilitarianism would tell me that of the two options I have, the morally right one is to lie. Lying will produce the greatest amount of happiness and least amount of pain for everyone. Rule utilitarianism, however, would tell me that I have to first ask myself: What moral rule about lying will produce the most happiness for everyone? It is clear, let us suppose, that lying generally ends up producing more unhappiness than telling the truth. If so, then the moral rule about lying that we should follow is: Always tell the truth. So in the situation I'm in, I should follow that rule and tell my friend the truth.

Rule utilitarians claim that their approach will avoid problems like those of the judge in the South African town. They would say the judge must ask himself: What moral rule about punishment would generally produce the most happiness for everyone?

---

[17] Ibid.

The judge should see, then, that judges should operate with the rule "Judges should never punish people for something they didn't do." Clearly, if everyone followed this rule, it would have the best consequences for everyone. People would know that the legal system would never arbitrarily punish them. So they would not suffer the fear and anxiety of never knowing how the courts would deal with them. That would not be true of the opposite alternative—the rule that judges can sometimes punish people for things they didn't do. This second alternative would produce much worse consequences over the long term. For this second rule would surely create fear, anxiety, and uncertainty among people. Consequently, say rule utilitarians, the moral rule judges should follow is "Never punish people for something they did not do." So in the South African judge's particular situation, the right thing to do is to set the innocent black man free. That is the morally right thing to do even if condemning this innocent man in this particular case would produce more happiness for everyone. In short, we should try to find and follow those rules that will have the best consequences for everyone over the long term. We should do that instead of trying to do what will have the best consequences at one particular time.

But is it that simple? Consider, first, the problem of trying to figure out the consequences of promoting one rule over another. What research can establish with any certainty that one rule will have better social consequences than another? Given our general ignorance of how societies function, it seems impossible to give definitive answers to this question. The rules of our conventional morality have been developed over many thousands of years. Following those rules will probably leave us all better off than trying to come up with new rules we can only hope will leave everyone better off.

Second, rules that allow for exceptions seem to promise more happiness than rules that don't. But such rules are problematic. We have suggested, for example, that judges should follow the rule "Judges should never punish people for something they didn't do." But wouldn't society be better off if judges followed this second rule: "Judges should never punish people for something they didn't do, *except in those instances where punishing them will leave everyone better off?*" This second rule will ensure that we do not *generally* punish innocent people. But it will allow exceptions when punishing the innocent will increase happiness. In such cases following the first rule will not produce the most happiness for everyone. But the second rule will produce the most happiness even in those cases in which the first rule would not. So this second rule has better consequences than the first rule. So the South African judge should follow this second rule.

But notice that following the second rule will again lead the judge to execute the innocent black man. Thus, rules that allow for exceptions would likely produce the most happiness. But such rules allow the same injustices and rights violations that act utilitarianism does. It is not clear, then, that rule utilitarianism is really an improvement over act utilitarianism.

ANALYZING THE READING

You and five friends are exploring a cave when a cave-in traps you all in a large chamber. The only way out is a small hole. Tom, who is fat, is the first to try to crawl through the hole and gets stuck. For two days you all try to pull or push him out but only wedge him in tighter. The air is becoming hard to breathe because oxygen is running out. But Tom can breathe fresh air on the other side of the hole. One of you has a small dynamite charge that can blow his body out of the hole. This will kill him. You have only a few hours of oxygen left. Should you use the dynamite to save the five of you? What would act utilitarianism say? What would rule utilitarianism say? What would you say? Why?

Some Implications of Utilitarianism

Despite these difficulties, many people believe that utilitarianism provides a powerful analysis of ethics. To get a better understanding of utilitarianism and its strengths and weaknesses, let us consider a specific issue. We'll look at what utilitarianism implies for a moral issue raised at the beginning of this chapter: our sexual behavior.

Sex is central to human life and raises a bewildering variety of moral questions. Are some forms of sexual activity—for example, incest, pedophilia, and adultery—always morally deficient? Or are there no limits on what is morally permissible in sex? For act utilitarianism, the answer is straightforward: Any action is morally right if it produces more happiness for everyone than any other action. This means any sexual activity can be morally permissible—incest, pedophilia, or adultery—in some circumstances. Sexual activities are almost always intensely pleasurable. At least sometimes they will produce a greater balance of pleasure over pain than any other alternative. Many act utilitarians have reached exactly that conclusion. Richard Taylor, for example, is a utilitarian. In his book *Having Love Affairs* he offers an act utilitarian justification of adultery. He argues that extramarital affairs based on love often produce more good than harm for a married person. And the good often outweighs the harms to a greater degree than all other alternatives. In such circumstances, he concludes, adultery is morally justified:

> The joys of illicit and passionate love, which include but go far beyond the mere joys of sex, are incomparably good. And it is undeniable that those who never experience love affairs, and who perhaps even boast of their faultless monogamy year in and year out, have really missed something.[18]

Taylor goes on to argue that if revealing an affair to one's spouse will injure the spouse and the marriage relationship, then one should conceal the affair. Lying is justified, on act utilitarian grounds, if the net benefits of lying to one's spouse about an affair are greater than those of telling the truth. Other philosophers have used similar arguments to justify gay and lesbian sexual acts. Some have argued that if the partners are consenting adults who take suitable contraceptive precautions, incest can be moral. This approach to sex would seem to rule out only those sexual acts that clearly involve harmful violence or great risks of harm. For example, this approach rules out violent rape or casual sex that risks contracting AIDS or some other venereal disease.

But is this approach to sex too permissive? Are some sexual acts, such as incest or pedophilia, intrinsically wrong? Isn't it immoral for the adulterer to break his marriage promises and then lie about it to his spouse? Perhaps even utilitarians would find Taylor's analysis too facile. Utilitarianism urges us to look beyond the immediate pleasure an action produces for oneself. It says we should also consider the beneficial and harmful consequences that our actions will produce for all others now and in the future. When seen in this light, act utilitarianism might condemn many sexual activities because of their harmful effects on the individual or society.

In fact, a rule utilitarian approach to the ethics of sexuality focuses on such broader social effects explicitly. It asks whether the long-term social consequences of moral rules that permit a certain type of sexual activity will benefit or harm society. The Ramsey Colloquium developed such an argument against various forms

---

[18]   Richard Taylor, *Having Love Affairs* (Buffalo, NY: Prometheus, 1982), 12.

of sex. The Ramsey Colloquium is a group of Christian and Jewish scholars. They argue that moral doctrines that permit adultery, divorce, and homosexuality will prove harmful to society:

> It is important to recognize the linkages among the component parts of the sexual revolution. [W]idespread adultery, easy divorce, . . . and the gay and lesbian movement have not by accident appeared at the same historical moment. They have in common a declared desire for liberation from constraint—especially constraint associated with an allegedly oppressive culture and religious tradition. They also have in common the pre-supposition that the body is little more than an instrument for the fulfillment of desire, and that the fulfillment of desire is the essence of the self. Finally, they all rest on a doctrine of the autonomous self. We believe it is a false doctrine that leads neither to individual flourishing nor to social well-being.
>
> Marriage and the family—husband, wife and children, joined by public recognition and legal bond—are the most effective institutions for the rearing of children, for the directing of sexual passion and for human flourishing in community. . . . Gay and lesbian "domestic partnerships" should not be socially recognized as the moral equivalent of marriage. Marriage and the family are institutions necessary for our continued social well-being. In an individualistic society that tends to liberation from all constraint, they are fragile institutions in need of careful and continuous support.[19]

ANALYZING THE READING

Do you agree with the Ramsey Colloquim claim that "widespread adultery, easy divorce, and the gay and lesbian movement" have lead "neither to individual flourishing nor to social well-being"? Why?

✓ QUICK REVIEW

Rule utilitarians such as the Ramsey Colloquium argue that moral rules that prohibit adultery, divorce, and homosexuality will produce more pleasure and less pain than other rules, so it is wrong to engage in adultery, divorce, and homosexuality. Critics argue that it is not clear that such rules will have the consequences the Ramsey Colloquium claims they will.

The Ramsey Colloquium argues that moral rules tolerant of homosexuality, adultery, and divorce have harmful consequences on families and on society. They imply that it is wrong to accept and follow such permissive moral rules. But is this rule utilitarian view about the morality of sexual activities correct? Is it clear to you that the acceptance of the moral permissibility of adultery, divorce, and homosexuality has the harmful effects that critics allege? Some have argued that the reasons for the decline of the family are many and complex, and that it is simplistic to blame this decline on permissive sexual attitudes. The problem with rule utilitarian arguments like these is that they place such heavy burdens of information gathering on us. And act utilitarian arguments do the same. How are we to know exactly what the significant future consequences of our moral rules or our individual actions will be?

Despite the questions it raises, utilitarianism identifies an important aspect of morality. It is true that future consequences are difficult to predict. Yet no one can deny that morally upright behavior, including sexual behavior, should attend to the consequences of what we do. We cannot deny that we should try to minimize the future harms that our sexual behaviors might inflict on

 THINKING LIKE A PHILOSOPHER

The Ramsey Colloquium says that adultery, divorce, and the gay and lesbian movement have harmed both individuals and society. Do you think your own life or the life of any of your friends has been affected by any of these factors? Explain. Do you have any gay friends? If so, do you agree they assume "the body is little more than an instrument for the fulfillment of desire"? Do you think any of your heterosexual friends assume this?

ourselves and others. The problem is that consequences are not all that matter in ethics. Therefore, we must turn to different approaches to ethics that can help us discern the other important elements of the moral life.

---

[19] The Ramsey Colloquium, "Morality and Homosexuality," in *Today's Moral Issues,* ed. Daniel Bonevac (Mountain View, CA: Mayfield, 1996), 272–274.

PHILOSOPHY AT THE MOVIES

Watch *Extreme Measures* (1996) in which Guy Luthan, a young doctor working in a hospital, comes upon an agitated patient wandering the streets who suffers convulsions and then dies. When Luthan tries to find out where the patient came from, he is accused of a crime and fired by the hospital. This makes him more determined to uncover the patient's background, until he stumbles upon a secret medical project that promises great benefits for humanity.

Movie with related theme: *Abandon Ship!* (sometimes titled *Seven Waves Away;* 1957).

7.4 Do Rules Define Morality?

A **nonconsequentialist theory** maintains that the morality of an action depends on factors other than consequences. The two main types of nonconsequentialist theories are those that propose a single rule to govern human conduct and those that propose multiple rules. Two single-rule nonconsequentialist theories are the divine command theory and Immanuel Kant's ethical theory. Buddhist ethics represents a kind of multiple-rule theory.

Divine Command Theory

The **divine command theory** is a nonconsequentialist normative theory that says we should always do the will of God. Whatever the situation be, if we do what God commands, then we do the right thing; if we disobey God's commands, then, no matter what the consequences, we do wrong. There are two main types of divine command theories. One type holds that God's commands are found in sacred scriptures and the other says that God's commands are found in human nature.

Scriptural Divine Command Theories. A divine command theory does not state that we should obey God's laws because in so doing we will promote our own or the general good. Perhaps obeying God will accomplish these ends. But the sole justification for obeying God's law is that God wills it. Divine command theory also does not defend the morality of an action by promising some supernatural reward. True, perhaps God will reward the faithful, and perhaps behaving righteously is in one's best long-term interests. But divine command theorists wouldn't justify moral actions on such egoistic grounds.

For divine command theorists, morality is independent of what any individual thinks or likes and what any society happens to sanction. God establishes moral laws. Those laws are eternally true and are universally binding on all people, regardless of whether everyone obeys them. Such divinely established laws are interpreted in a religious tradition. And usually they are expressed in that religion's sacred scriptures. The Ten Commandments found in the Old Testament of the Jewish scriptures are a good example:

> And God spoke all these words, saying, I am the Lord your God . . . you shall have no other gods before me. . . . Remember the Sabbath day, to keep it holy. . . . Honor your father and your mother. . . . You shall not kill. You shall not commit adultery. You shall not steal. You shall not bear false witness against your neighbor. You shall not covet your neighbor's house. You shall not covet your neighbor's wife, or his manservant, or his maidservant, or his ox, or his mule, or anything that is your neighbor's.[20]

---

[20] Exodus 20:2–17.

Christians accept this Judaic view of God's commands. But for Christians the more significant expression of God's will in the New Testament of the Christian scriptures are the words of Jesus:

> And Jesus lifted up his eyes on his disciples, and said:. . . . I say to you that hear, Love your enemies, do good to those who hate you, bless those who curse you, pray for those who abuse you. To him who strikes you on the cheek, offer the other also; and from him who takes away your cloak do not withhold your coat as well. Give to everyone who begs from you; and of him who takes away your goods, do not ask them back again. And as you wish that men should do to you, do so to them.[21]

Finally, contrast these expressions of God's commands with what adherents of Islam accept as the expression of God's will in the Koran, the scriptures of Islam:

> Thy Lord has decreed you shall not serve any but Him, and to be good to your parents. . . . And give the kinsman his right, and the needy, and the traveller; and never squander. . . . And keep not thy hand chained to thy neck, nor outspread it widespread altogether. . . . And slay not your children for fear of poverty. . . . And approach not fornication. . . . And do not approach the property of the orphan save in the fairest manner. . . . And fulfill the covenant. And fill up the measure when you measure, and weigh with the straight balance. . . . And pursue not what thou has not knowledge of. . . . And walk not in the earth exultantly. All of that—the wickedness of it is hateful in the sight of thy Lord.[22]

These laws, claim their adherents, apply to everybody everywhere. And their value does not depend on what produces human satisfaction, either individually or for society. The justification of such moral laws is divine authority expressed through humans and their institutions and scriptures.

However, even a cursory look at scriptural divine command theory reveals some inherent weaknesses. First, and as the preceding samples make excruciatingly clear, different sacred scriptures exist. Which one expresses what God commands? It is true that there is some overlap in what each says. For example, both Judaism and Islam say that God commands us to respect our parents. But they differ in many respects about the specifics of what God commands. How are we to know which of these scriptures is right? Which one should we follow? Beyond that, how do we know that any of these writings represent the inspired word of God? Some assert that the scriptures say so. But isn't it circular reasoning to say that because a book says it's true, it must be true? And what of the fact that all these scriptures assert that they are the true, inspired word of God? Beyond that, can we be sure that God even exists? What help are these scriptural commands to the unbeliever, the agnostic, and the atheist? If morality is following what some religions say are God's commands, does it follow that the unbeliever can have no morality? And if God does exist, can we be sure that God expressed His law in one source and not in another?

There is also a deeper, more fundamental problem, one that we saw when we discussed Plato's *Euthyphro* in Chapter 1. The problem, in fact, is sometimes called the "Euthyphro problem." The problem is this: Are actions right because God commands them, or does God command them because they are right? If God commands certain actions *because* they are right, then morality does not depend on God but on a power superior to God that determines what actions are right. This consequence is not acceptable to most believers. On the other hand, if actions are

> **QUICK REVIEW**
> Divine command theory is a nonconsequentialist theory that says the morally right action is the one that God commands, for example, in scripture. Critics argue that there are too many conflicting scriptures and that we cannot know which one reports the true commands of God; also, if something is right because God commands it, then even cruelty could be morally right.

---

[21] Luke 6:27–31.
[22] Sura 17:22–39.

Do you now believe or have you ever believed that moral right and wrong are based on what God commands? If so, do you think that if God said an action that had always been wrong was actually morally right, then that action would be morally right from that time on? For example, could God, by commanding it, make incest, adultery, torturing innocent children, and pedophilia morally right? How do your answers relate to the "Euthyphro problem"?

right *because* God commands them, then anything that God commands must be right. Should God command cruelty and torture, then cruelty and torture would be morally right—a consequence that is also difficult to accept. So whether God commands actions because they are right, or they are right because God commands them, we reach a consequence that is unacceptable.

There is another kind of ethics that also appeals to God's command but that, paradoxically, does not require belief in God. This is natural law ethics.

Natural Law Ethics. Natural law ethics holds that humans should live according to nature. The Stoics, followers of the school of thought originally founded by Zeno around 300 BCE, held a natural law ethic. They believed that there is a universal natural order in the world put there by God. And the human mind can discover that natural order. To the extent that humans live according to this universal order, particularly as it is exhibited in their own human nature, they will flourish and be happy.

The ancient Stoic philosopher Epictetus (circa 50–130), for example, wrote the following:

> The business of the wise and good man is to live conforming to nature: and as it is the nature of every soul to assent to the truth, to dissent from the false, and to remain in suspense as to that which is uncertain; so it is its nature to be moved toward the desire of the good, and to aversion from the evil; and with respect to that which is neither good nor bad it feels indifferent. . . . When the good appears, it immediately attracts to itself; the evil repels from itself.[23]

Here, Epictetus is saying that if we look at human nature, we will see that it has certain natural tendencies. We have a natural tendency to believe what we discover is true, to reject what is false, and to suspend belief about matters we are unsure of. In the same way, we have a natural tendency to desire what we judge is good for us and a natural tendency to feel repelled by what we judge is bad for us. We also have a natural tendency to feel indifferent about what is neither beneficial nor harmful to us. The morally good person, he suggests, is the person who lives according to these basic natural tendencies. The morally evil person is the one who violates these basic tendencies, perhaps by gratifying his cravings for things that his judgment says are bad for him. Moral rightness, then, is conduct that conforms to these natural tendencies.

What does this have to do with God and God's commands? The key idea is that God made human nature. So, if one lives according to what human nature requires, one is living according to what God intended when He made humans. If you live according to your nature, Epictetus says, then you can be "conscious that you are obeying God." In short, the requirements of human nature are the commands of God. Humans can discover those commands by looking at their own nature, and in following these commands they are morally good.

Natural law ethics (including the key idea that to follow human nature is to obey God's will), then, began with the ancient Greeks. But the Christian philosopher and theologian Thomas Aquinas is regarded as the classical proponent of natural law

---

[23] Epictetus, *Discourses,* III, 3.

PHILOSOPHY AND LIFE

Embryonic Stem Cell Research

Human embryonic stem cells are cells taken from several-days-old embryos and are capable of turning into virtually any type of human cell, from blood cells to muscle, skin, brain, stomach, heart, pancreatic, or liver cells. Stem cells are perfect for replacing the diseased or injured tissues of patients with spinal cord injuries, heart disease, diabetes, osteoarthritis, and rheumatoid arthritis, and those of burn and stroke victims. Scientists believe that if stem cells from aborted embryos are implanted into the brains of patients suffering from Alzheimer's disease (which causes memory loss) or Parkinson's disease (which causes tremors, rigidity, and eventually complete paralysis), the embryo's cells could take over the functions the patient's own brain cells can no longer perform, and the patient could recover fully or partially. Researchers believe that stem cells from aborted embryos can be transplanted into the pancreatic tissues of diabetics, into the brain tissues of patients with Huntington's disease, into the spines of patients with multiple sclerosis, into the livers of patients with Hurler's syndrome, or into the tissues of patients suffering from more than 155 genetic disorders and could produce full or partial cures of these crippling illnesses. Some researchers have suggested that injecting stem cells into muscle or skin can enhance these tissues, raising the possibility that athletes could take embryonic stem cell injections to improve their performance or that embryonic cells could be used for cosmetic purposes.

Opponents of abortion have argued that to use, or conduct research on, stem cells is morally wrong because acquiring embryonic stem cells involves aborting or destroying the embryo, which they believe is a human being. In 1995, Congress imposed a ban prohibiting spending federal funds on "research in which a human embryo or embryos are destroyed, discarded, or knowingly subjected to risk of injury or death." After his election, President George W. Bush was lobbied by patient groups, scientific organizations, and the biotechnology industry to lift this ban. Antiabortion groups urged him not to do so. On August 9, 2001, Bush announced that he would allow federal funding for such research but only on stem cells already in existence, not on any stem cells acquired through future destruction of embryos. Bush's decision left both supporters and opponents of stem cell research unhappy. But on March 9, 2009, newly elected President Barack Obama reversed the Bush policy. Declaring that the previous administration had "forced what I believe is a false choice between sound science and moral values," Obama lifted the ban on using federal funds for stem cell research regardless of the source of the stem cells. Although many scientists celebrated the new policy, antiabortion groups saw it as a defeat for morality on a basic question of human life. The antiabortion groups sued to reverse the policy but in July 2011 a federal judge ruled that the Obama administration had legal authority to enact the policy.

QUESTIONS

1. In your view, is it moral to transplant or conduct research on the cells of aborted embryos? Would it be moral to abort an embryo intentionally to provide researchers with stem cells? Would it be moral to use stem cells to improve athletic performance or for cosmetic purposes?

2. In your judgment, is a ban on the use of federal funds for embryonic stem cell research immoral? Was Bush's 2001 decision immoral? Was Obama's 2009 decision immoral?

Source: American Association for the Advancement of Science, "AAAS Policy Brief: Stem Cell Research," http://www.aaas.org/spp/cstc/briefs/stemcells (accessed March 3, 2004); Claudia Kalb, "A New Stem Cell Era," *Newsweek*, online edition, March 9, 2009, http://www.newsweek.com/id/188454 (accessed May 28, 2009).

ethics. Aquinas held that because God created the universe, the laws that govern it are laws that God imposed on it. In particular, God imposed on human beings certain "natural laws" through the natural inclinations that He built into human nature when He created humans. The most important of these inclinations are our reasoning abilities:

> Now rational creatures [such as humans] are also subject to God's provident direction, but in a way that makes them more like God than all other creatures. For God directs rational creatures by instilling in them certain natural inclinations and [reasoning] abilities that enable them to direct themselves as well as other creatures. Thus human

beings also are subject to God's eternal law and they too derive from that law certain natural inclinations to seek their proper ends and proper activities. These inclinations of our nature constitute what we call the "natural law" and they are the effects of God's eternal law imprinted in our nature.[24]

According to Aquinas, morality arises when our reason becomes aware of the "natural inclinations" that God built into human nature. Our reason tells us, Aquinas claims, that what we are naturally inclined to desire is good. And it also tells us that we ought to pursue those kinds of goods toward which we are naturally inclined. Each of the kinds of goods we naturally desire is the basis of a moral rule that says we ought to pursue that kind of good and avoid whatever might destroy it:

A thing is good if it is an end that we have a natural inclination to desire; it is evil if it is destructive of what our nature is inclined to desire. Consequently, those kinds of things that our nature is inclined to desire are perceived by our reason as good for our human nature. And our reason will conclude that those kinds of things ought to be pursued in our actions. But if our reason sees a certain type of thing as destructive of what human nature is inclined to desire, it will conclude that that type of thing ought to be avoided.

We can therefore list the basic [moral] precepts of the natural law by listing the kinds of things that we naturally desire. First, like every other nature, human nature is inclined to desire its own survival. Consequently it is a natural [moral] law that we ought to preserve human life and avoid whatever is destructive of life. Secondly, like other animals, human nature is inclined to desire those things that nature teaches all animals to desire by instinct. For example, all animals have an instinctive desire to come together in a union of male and female, and an instinctive desire to care for their young. [So it is morally right to pursue these things.] Thirdly, human nature is inclined to desire those goods that satisfy our intellect. This aspect of our nature is proper to human beings. Thus, human nature is inclined to desire knowledge (for example, to know the truth about God) and an orderly society. Consequently, it is a natural [moral] law that we ought to dispel ignorance and avoid harming those among whom we live.[25]

Thus, by reflecting on our natural human inclinations, we can discover the specific types of goods that God commands humans to pursue. These are human life, family, knowledge, and an orderly society. Actions are morally right when they aim at securing these types of goods, and they are morally wrong when they aim at destroying these types of goods.

Some examples might clarify what Aquinas means and might also clarify some important features of natural law ethics. Consider the issue of suicide. Aquinas held that suicide was immoral. But he did not condemn suicide merely because the Christian scriptures say that it is wrong to take one's life. Instead, Aquinas argued that human nature has a built-in inclination to desire life. That is, each of us instinctively wants to stay alive and instinctively avoids threats to our life. Since we are naturally inclined to desire life, Aquinas held, our reason knows immediately that life is a

ANALYZING THE READING

1. According to Aquinas, all human beings have a natural desire for life, for union with a spouse and family, for knowledge, and for an orderly society. Do you agree with this? That is, do you feel that these are all fundamentally good things and worth seeking? Why or why not? Do you think there are other values that should be on this list? That is, are there other values that you believe every human desires simply because that is how all humans are made?

2. Aquinas claims that actions are wrong when they are destructive of these goods and right when they tend to promote these goods. Do you agree? Why?

---

24 Saint Thomas Aquinas, *Summa Theologica*, I–II, Q. 91, a. 2. This translation copyright © 1978 by Manuel Velasquez.
25 Ibid., I–II, Q. 94, a. 2.

fundamental human good that we should promote and not destroy. And because God is the source of this inclination, the requirement that we should not destroy life is His command. Suicide, then, is wrong because it destroys what our reason knows is a fundamental human good and by destroying this good, suicide violates the command of God. Or consider the issue of social injustice, which Aquinas also considered immoral. We are naturally inclined to desire an orderly society, he claimed. That is, our human nature has a built in inclination to socialize with others in communities that are peaceful, law-abiding, and orderly. But social injustices, he argued, undermine or destroy the fundamental good of social order. Consequently, it is wrong to engage in activities that lead to social injustice. It would be wrong, for example, to support laws or policies that discriminate against minorities or that allow some to starve while others live in luxury. Other kinds of activities, like theft, fraud, assault, and deception, also undermine or destroy the basic good of social order and so are also immoral.

But what are we to do when there are conflicts among the basic goods toward which we are inclined? That is, what are we to do when we can secure one basic good only by destroying another? What should I do, for example, when I can defend my own life only by destroying the life of one who wants to kill me? Killing in self-defense destroys the basic good of the aggressor's life, yet it promotes the basic good of the life of his victim. To deal with such conflicts, Aquinas proposed what is now called the "principle of double effect." Aquinas suggested that actions sometimes produce two or more effects. Killing in self-defense is that kind of action since it saves one life by destroying another. Aquinas argued that when actions have such double effects, one good and one evil, what matters is one's intention and that the good effect be proportionate to the bad effect.

> There is nothing to prevent an act from having two effects, only one of which is intended, while the other effect is not part of the agent's intention. Now the moral nature of an act depends on the intention with which it is done and not on what the agent did not intend. The act of self-defense is the kind of act that can have two effects. One is the saving of one's life and the other is the death of the aggressor. Now in an act of self-defense one's intention is to save one's own life, and saving one's life is not morally wrong since it is natural to try to keep oneself in existence as far as possible. Nevertheless, even if an act is carried out with a good intention, it will be morally wrong if its destructiveness is out of proportion to the end [that one seeks]. For example, if a man, acting in self-defense uses more violence than is needed the act is morally wrong. But if he repels an attack with a moderate amount of violence his act of self-defense is not morally wrong.[26]

The idea Aquinas spells out in this short paragraph has far-reaching implications. In fact, some natural law proponents have argued that Aquinas' principle of double effect can by itself serve as an entire ethical theory. But what exactly is Aquinas' principle of double effect? In the paragraph above Aquinas explicitly mentions two factors: a good intention and that the bad effect must be proportionate to the good. Natural law philosophers have argued that a third factor is implicit in Aquinas' discussion but is not mentioned. The third factor is that the good effect cannot be achieved without the bad. When one kills in self-defense, for example, there is usually no way to save one's life without killing the attacker. The principle of double effect, then, says that when one's action has a good effect and a bad effect, the action is *not morally wrong*: If (1) one's intention aims at the good and not the evil,

---

[26] Ibid., II–II, Q. 64, a. 7.

(2) the good can't be achieved without the evil, and (3) the good is proportional to the evil. "Proportional" here means that the good that is achieved is of equal or greater value than the evil that is inflicted. An example may clarify what Aquinas means. Suppose that during a battle a soldier is attacked. Suppose (1) the soldier is intent only on saving his life and even regrets the injuries he inflicts on his attacker. Suppose (2) the only way to save his life is by killing his attacker. And (3) the good of saving his life is proportional to the evil of taking the life of another since one life is of equal value to another. Then it was not morally wrong for the soldier to kill his attacker. But it would be morally wrong for the soldier to intentionally kill someone who is not threatening anyone's life. It would be morally wrong for the soldier to kill his attacker if there is some other way of saving his own life. And it would be morally wrong to take someone's life for something of less value than human life, such as money.

Today, there are many philosophers who have adapted Aquinas' natural law theory. For example, the Australian philosopher John Finnis (1940–) presented a sophisticated natural law theory in his book *Natural Law and Natural Rights*. But Finnis argues that we need to revise Aquinas' four fundamental goods and expand them to include seven basic forms of good:

> ### ANALYZING THE READING
>
> The principle of double effect says that if an action has a bad and a good effect, it is not wrong to do it if we intend only the good effect, the good cannot be attained without the bad, and the good effect is proportional to the bad. Describe an action that has the bad effect of destroying one of the basic goods and the good effect of preserving one of the basic goods. Would the principle of double effect say that your action is not morally wrong? Explain why.

> Now besides life, knowledge, play, aesthetic experience, friendship, practical reasonableness, and religion, there are countless objectives and forms of good. But I suggest that these other objectives and forms of good will be found, on analysis, to be ways or combinations of ways, of pursuing (not always sensibly) and realizing (not always successfully) one of these seven basic forms of good, or some combination of them.[27]

Natural law theory does not raise all of the problems that scriptural divine command theories raise. For example, natural law theory does not have to deal with the problem that many different scriptures exist, each claiming to tell us what God commands. In fact, one of the most important advantages of natural law theory is that one does not even have to believe in God to accept the theory. For the theory claims that morality is based on living according to our human nature, and this claim does not require belief in God. All people, whether they believe in God or not, can discover what morality requires by reflecting on their own human nature. Those who believe in God, of course, will take the additional step of concluding that because God made human nature, it embodies what God intends for humans. But the unbeliever can reject this additional step and still agree that our human nature is the best guide to moral right and wrong.

Neither does natural law theory have to deal with the problem that God might command something that is bad for us. For in natural law theory, whatever is good for our nature is what God commands. And what God commands when He makes our nature will be what is good for us.

Nevertheless, natural law theory has many critics. For example, critics have asked why we should be morally obligated to pursue the goods that our natural inclinations seek. Why are our *inclinations* the measure of what is morally good for us? Isn't it at least logically possible that we might be naturally inclined to things that are not necessarily good for us? Children often have desires for things that are bad

---

[27] John Finnis, *Natural Law and Natural Rights* (Oxford: Oxford University Press, 2011), 90.

for them. Isn't it possible for adults to similarly have inclinations toward what is evil? In addition, doesn't natural law have some damaging ambiguities? For example, natural law doesn't seem sure exactly what the fundamental goods are supposed to be. Aquinas argued that there were four, whereas modern natural law philosopher Finnis has opted for a rather different group of seven. How are we to decide not just how many there are, but exactly what they are supposed to be?

Finally, consider the problem of conflicts between fundamental goods. These are situations in which pursuing one good requires destroying another. Clearly, such conflicts are common in human life. Aquinas uses the principle of double effect to deal with such conflicts. He claims that we must only intend to preserve the one good and not intend to destroy the other good. But, in such cases, can we really limit our intention to the pursuit of the good? When I am forced to kill a person in self-defense, for example, don't I really intend to destroy the life of that person? When I foresee that one of my actions will have many effects, don't I necessarily intend those effects to happen? But if the principle of double effect doesn't work, then won't the problem of conflicts between fundamental goods end up destroying natural law theory?

> **QUICK REVIEW**
> Critics of natural law ethics say that it is not clear why we are morally obligated to follow our natural inclinations, it is not clear exactly what goods we are naturally inclined toward, and it is not clear that one can keep from intending a foreseen evil as the principle of double effect says one must.

Implications of Divine Command Ethics

Although divine command ethics has several limitations, many philosophers think it can shed some light on ethical questions. One of the topics that divine command theorists have addressed is the topic we earlier discussed in relation to utilitarian theory: sexual activity. What light can natural law theory shed on the morality of sex?

Natural law theory claims that we must take seriously the basic goods toward which sexual activity is naturally oriented. Some natural law ethicists have argued that it is clear that sex is naturally oriented toward the good of procreation which is part of the basic good of family. Consequently, it is immoral to engage in any sexual activity that does not remain open to this good. John Finnis argues as follows:

> [T]he choice to exclude the possibility of procreation while engaging in intercourse is always, and in an obvious and unambiguous way . . . a choice directly and immediately against a basic value. . . . And if a question is raised about solitary sexual acts or sexual intercourse outside the vagina (whether homo- or heterosexual), the [natural law] response . . . turns on the fact that all sexual activity . . . [must retain] . . . a sufficient openness and respect towards [this basic procreative value]. . . . [S]ome sexual acts are (as types of choice) always wrong because [they are] an inadequate response, or direct closure, to [this] basic procreative value.[28]

In this natural law approach, a sexual activity is immoral and "unnatural" if it cannot result in pregnancy or if we take steps to block the possibility of a pregnancy. This would condemn as "unnatural" a wide range of sexual activities. It would condemn homosexual sex, oral sex, anal sex, masturbation, bestiality, sex with dead bodies, sex with inanimate objects, and sadomasochistic sex.

For many people, the moral condemnation of such forms of sex is exactly right. They believe natural law theory (as Finnis interprets it) has identified the basic purpose of sex—reproduction.

ANALYZING THE READING

Finnis' natural law theory seems to say that "procreation" is the "basic value" at which an act of sexual intercourse naturally aims. This seems to mean that the natural purpose of sexual intercourse is procreation. So anything that prevents an act of sexual intercourse from achieving its natural purpose of procreation is morally wrong. What are the differences between this natural law theory of John Finnis and Aquinas' natural law theory? What are the similarities? Is either theory correct? Why?

---

[28] John Finnis, "Natural Law and Unnatural Acts," *Heythrop Journal* 11, no. 4 (October 1970): 380.

And they believe it correctly evaluates sexual activities as unnatural when they do not further this basic purpose. Moreover, many people reject the utilitarian view that any action can be justified if it provides enough good consequences. Some actions, they feel, are intrinsically wrong regardless of their consequences. So they agree with Finnis' natural law claim that certain kinds of sexual activities are intrinsically immoral whatever their consequences. In fact, many people (rightly or wrongly) describe as "unnatural" those sexual activities that natural law condemns. They agree, for example, that it is unnatural to have sex with animals, sex with the dead, sadomasochistic sex, and so on.

Yet can't sex serve many purposes other than procreation, such as pleasure, intimacy, play, and communication? Why should reproduction be singled out as the only morally relevant purpose of sex? Suppose that in some sense, say a biological or functional sense, the purpose of our sexual organs is reproduction. Still, why should this biological fact make it immoral to use them for other purposes? In an evolutionary or biological sense, the purpose of teeth is to chew food and the purpose of eyes is to see. But is there anything immoral about using one's teeth to pry the top off a beer bottle or to use one's eyes to flirt? Granted evolution has adapted our sexual organs for the function of procreation. Still, these organs also have other functions, including that of providing pleasure. What is wrong with using them solely for the latter purpose?

However, there are other, more liberal natural law approaches to sex. For example, Donald Levy provides a different approach to sexual matters. He rejects the view that sexual activities are necessarily wrong when they cannot issue in reproduction. Instead, he argues, sexual activities are unnatural and immoral when they deny a basic good without necessity and do so for the sake of sexual pleasure. This understanding of natural law, Levy suggests, does not imply that, say, homosexuality is unnatural:

> [W]hat I count as the basic human goods can be rather completely listed: life, health, control of one's bodily and psychic functions, the capacity for knowledge and love. . . . I suggest that an unnatural act is one that denies a person (oneself or another) one or more of these basic human goods without necessity, that is, without having to do so in order to prevent losing some other basic human good. . . . Denying oneself or another a basic human good without some other basic human good being expected or intended to be made possible thereby is always wrong. . . .
>
> The perverted is a subclass of the unnatural. When a person denies himself or another one of the basic human goods (or the capacity for it) and no other basic human good is seen as resulting thereby, and when pleasure is the motive of the denial, the act is perverted. When the pleasure is sexual, the perversion is sexual.
>
> The child molester is a case of sexual perversion. . . . [T]he young girl sexually initiated by an older person can easily be traumatized; that there is no way of undoing the harmful effects with the ease and certainty with which they were induced establishes the correctness of classifying the case as one of sexual perversion. . . .
>
> That perversion degrades is a necessary truth . . . as I have defined perversion. . . . Although the definition of [perversion] does not, by itself, produce criteria strong enough to allow us to be decisive in the important case of homosexuality, the definition [does] seem to require rape to be included among the sexual perversions . . . [because] rape does degrade.[29]

ANALYZING THE READING

Compared to Finnis, is Levy's interpretation of natural law theory more similar or less similar to Aquinas' view?

✅ QUICK REVIEW

Finnis, a natural law ethicist, claims that sexual acts that "exclude the possibility of procreation" are "unnatural" and so are morally wrong. Other natural law ethicists, such as Levy, argue that sexual acts are not necessarily wrong when they exclude procreation, but only when they destroy a basic human good.

---

[29]   Donald Levy, "Perversion and the Unnatural as Moral Categories," *Ethics* 90, no. 2 (January 1980): 191–202. Reprinted by permission of The University of Chicago Press.

Levy is suggesting here that we do not have to interpret natural law as saying that the morality of a sexual act depends on whether the act can result in procreation. Instead, he suggests, natural law should be seen as saying that a sexual act is morally wrong only if it *destroys* a concrete instance of a basic human good. For example, child molestation is wrong because it destroys the psychic functioning of the child (which is part of the child's human life). Rape is wrong because it destroys the psychic functioning of the adult victim. It is difficult to say, on the other hand, that homosexuality is destructive of a basic human good, and so that it is unnatural or morally wrong. Levy's natural law approach leads to a more tolerant view of homosexuality and, perhaps, of other forms of sex. In this respect it seems more aligned with contemporary views of sexual morality than Finnis' approach.

Yet perhaps we should not so quickly dismiss the more conservative natural law views of philosophers like Finnis. It is true that the natural law view of Finnis has significant problems. Still, his view alerts us to an aspect of sex that is morally important, namely, the relationship of sexual intercourse to reproduction. For the fact that sexual intercourse can result in pregnancy raises important moral issues for anyone considering sex.

Philosophers have not been indifferent to the objections brought against natural law theory and other divine command theories. In the eighteenth century, Immanuel Kant presented a nonconsequentialist theory based not on divine authority but on human reason alone.

PHILOSOPHY AT THE MOVIES

Watch *Breaking the Waves* (1996) in which Bess, a sweet, simple girl who speaks to God, marries Jan, a big man who works on an oil rig and who, when paralyzed from the neck down in a work accident, asks Bess to sleep with another man, a request that Bess sees as a sacrifice God wants and that she believes will save Jan. Does this film hold that actions are right because God commands them or that God commands certain actions because they are right? Do the bells at the end indicate that God was truly speaking to Bess? Is it morally right for Bess to do what she believes God commands her to do? Does this movie suggest any problems with divine command ethics, or does it support divine command ethics?

© Photos 12/Alamy Stock Photo

Kant's Categorical Imperative

Of all philosophers, the German philosopher Immanuel Kant has had the greatest influence on contemporary ethics. Kant was a deeply religious man. Yet he rejected divine command theories of ethics as well as utilitarian theories. Kant held that a person has the ability to decide for herself what she will do and her reasons for doing it. Kant called this ability to choose for oneself "autonomy of the will." He argued that a legitimate theory of ethics must recognize our autonomy. He contrasted autonomy with heteronomy. *Heteronomy* is allowing someone else or something else to determine what we should do. The trouble with divine command theories is that they say that the Church or the Bible or human nature should determine what we should do. Utilitarian theories are worse. Utilitarian theories say that our desires for pleasure should determine the actions we should perform. So both divine command theories and utilitarian theories are heteronomous and both fail to recognize human autonomy. A theory of ethics, Kant held, should respect our freedom to choose subject only to the idea that what is morally permissible for us should also be permissible for everyone. Kant argues for these views by analyzing the notions of "a good will," moral "duty," and what he calls "maxims," which are the reasons we have for doing what we do.

The "Good Will."   The "will," for Kant, is our ability to choose what we will do and the reasons on which we will act. As such, the will is at the core of who a person is and why the person behaves as he or she does. So if we want to determine what a morally good person is and what the morally good person does, we must begin by asking what a morally good will is. That is precisely where Kant begins one of his greatest works, the *Foundations of the Metaphysics of Morals*. In the following passage from the first pages of this work, Kant argues that only a good will—that is, only the will of a good person—is "good without qualification." So we ought to strive to have a good will (i.e., to be a good-willed person).

> It is impossible to think of anything in the universe—or even beyond it—that is good without qualification, except a good will. Intellectual talents such as intelligence, cleverness, and good judgment are undoubtedly good and desirable in many respects; so also are character traits such as courage, determination, and perseverance. But these gifts of nature can become quite evil and harmful when they are at the service of a will that is not good. It is the same with gifts of fortune such as power, wealth, honor, and even health and that general well-being and contentment we call happiness. These will produce pride and conceit unless the person has a good will, which can correct the influence these have on the mind and ensure that it is adapted to its proper end. Moreover, an impartial rational spectator would not feel any pleasure at seeing a person without a good will enjoying continuous happiness. Thus it seems that having a good will is a necessary condition for even deserving happiness.[30]

QUICK REVIEW
The will is a person's ability to make decisions on the basis of reasons. Kant argues that nothing is good without qualification except a good will, and a good will is one that chooses what is morally right because it is right and not because it is enjoyable or in one's self-interest.

Kant believed, then, that since a good will is good without qualification, we should strive to have a good will. But what is a "good will"? That is, when is a person's will good? Kant claims that a good will (the will of a good person) is not the will of someone who does what is morally right only out of self-interest. Nor is a person's will good when she does what is right only because she wants the pleasure or enjoyment she gets from doing what is right. Instead, a person's will is good when the person does what is morally right simply because she believes it is morally right. Kant argues for this claim by asking us to consider three examples of people who do what is morally right. But the first example of people does what is right only because it is in their own interests to do so. The second example of people does what is right only for the sake of the pleasure it gives them. The third example of people also does what is right only for the pleasure they get from doing what is right. Kant contrasts these kinds of people with a person who does what is right only because she believes it is right. Only such a person, Kant claims, has a good will.

QUICK REVIEW
Kant argued the following: (1) A person with a good will does what is right because she believes it is morally right to do it. (2) To believe it is morally right to do something is to believe it is what all human beings ought to do. (3) Therefore, a person with a good will—a good person—is one who does what is right because she believes it is what all human beings ought to do.

> We must next develop the idea of a will that is esteemed as good in itself. . . . To do this, we will look at the notion of doing one's moral duty, which is related to the notion of a good will. . . .
>
>   We begin by considering how we sometimes do what we have a moral duty to do, but we do it not *because* we believe it is our duty, but for some other reason. . . . Take as our first example, a shop-keeper who has a moral duty not to overcharge his immature customers. And when he has a lot of competition the smart shop-keeper will not overcharge anyone but will keep to a fixed price for each customer. Because he charges everyone the same, even a child will be willing to buy from him. So the shop-keeper treats his customers honestly but we would not say he does so for the sake of moral duty or fairness. He acts out of self-interest. . . . Nor would we say he treats all his customers

---

30   Immanuel Kant, *Grundlegung zur Metaphysik der Sitten [Groundwork of the Metaphysics of Morals]*, in *Immanuel Kant Werkausgabe*, vol. 7, ed. Wilhelm Weischedel (Frankfurt, Germany: Insel Verlag Wiesbaden, 1956), 18. This translation copyright © 1987 by Manuel Velasquez.

the same *because* it gives him pleasure to treat his customers well. He does what is right but does it out of self-interest [and we can see his action has no moral value].

Secondly, consider that we each have a duty to continue living, and almost everyone also enjoys living. But for that reason, the anxious care most people take to continue living, [we can see,] has no intrinsic [moral] value. . . . People continue living, which is their moral duty, but they don't do so *because* they are motivated by their moral duty. On the other hand, imagine a person who has suffered so much adversity and . . . sorrow that he no longer enjoys living and wishes he were dead. Yet suppose he continues living . . . because he believes that is his moral duty. [It is clear that] such a person's reason for living does have moral value.

Thirdly, think about how we each have a moral duty to help others when we can. Now some people have such sympathetic natures that. . . . they enjoy. . . . making others happy. . . . I claim that when one helps others *only* for the sake of the enjoyment one gets, . . . one's action has no true moral value. Such actions have no more moral value than anything else one might do for the enjoyment one will get from doing it, such as seeking to be honored. . . . On the other hand, imagine someone whose mind is clouded by a sorrow that has extinguished all feelings toward others, yet who has the power to help those in distress. . . . Suppose he tears himself out of his dead insensibility and helps them not because it is enjoyable for him, but because he believes he has a moral duty to help them. [Clearly] at that point his action will have genuine moral value. . . .

So we are left . . . with this proposition: our actions have true moral value precisely when . . . [they are done] not because we enjoy doing them, [nor because they are in our self-interest], but because we believe it is our moral duty to do them.[31]

> ### ANALYZING THE READING
>
> Kant claims that when a person helps others *only* for the sake of the pleasure or enjoyment helping others gives him (the "only" is important here), his action does not have any moral value. That is, although his action is not morally evil, it is also not morally good; it is morally neutral. Do you agree with Kant? Explain.

Duty and the First Version of the Categorical Imperative. The person with a morally good will, then, is the person who does what is right because he believes it is his moral duty to do it. But what does it mean to say that something is one's moral duty? Kant answers this question by pointing out that we feel respect for what we believe everyone is morally required to do. That is, if I believe a certain kind of conduct is a moral duty, I "respect" or look up to that kind of conduct as something required by a moral law that everyone ought to follow. In Kant's words: "Duty is the necessity of acting from respect for a law" and "a law is an objective principle valid for every rational being and a principle on which everyone ought to act."[32] So a person has a morally good will when the person does what is right because he believes it is something required by a moral law that everyone ought to follow. Kant concludes that a person is morally good when the person does only what he believes that everyone is required to do.

Kant summarizes this conclusion in what he calls the principle "of the categorical imperative": "*I ought never to act except in such a way that I can will that my maxim should become a universal law.* "[33] A maxim is the reason a person in a certain situation has for doing what he does, and that maxim would "become a universal law" if every person in a similar situation chose to do the same thing for the same reason. So Kant's categorical imperative says that it is morally right for a person to do something for a certain reason if and only if the person would be willing to have everyone

MindTap Do you think you could live by Kant's principle? Does it make sense to? Go to MindTap to watch a video about Kant's views on ethics and discussion of how they can bear out in the real world.

---

[31] Ibid., 24–25.
[32] Ibid., 28 and 50.
[33] Ibid., 29.

in a similar situation do the same thing for the same reason. Kant claims that this principle is the fundamental principle of morality.

In the following passage, Kant gives four examples to illustrate what the categorical imperative requires in practice. Notice that in the first two examples Kant asks whether the maxim on which a person wants to act *could be* a law that everyone in the world had to follow, while in the second two examples he asks whether the person *would be willing* to live in a world in which that maxim was a law everyone had to follow.

QUICK REVIEW
Kant concludes that it is morally right for me to do something for a certain reason only if I could be willing to have everyone in a similar situation do the same thing for that same reason. In other words, it is morally wrong for me to do something unless it is something that everyone could do and that I am willing to have everyone do.

We will now enumerate a few duties [that follow from the categorical imperative]. We will adopt the usual practice of classifying duties into perfect and imperfect duties and subclassifying each of these into duties to ourselves and duties to others.

1. *Perfect duty to oneself.* Imagine a man who has been reduced to despair by a series of misfortunes. Suppose he feels tired of living, but is still able to ask himself whether it would be contrary to duty to take his own life. So he asks whether the maxim of his action could become a universal law of nature. His maxim is this: "Out of self-love I will adopt the principle that I will end my life once it contains more evils than satisfactions." Our man can then ask himself whether this principle, which is based on the feeling of self-love, can become a universal law of nature that everyone follows. He will see at once that a system of nature that contained a law that destroyed life by means of the very feeling whose function it is to sustain life would contradict itself. Therefore, such a law could not be part of a system of nature. Consequently, his maxim cannot become a universal law of nature so it violates the basic principle of morality.

2. *Perfect duty to others.* Imagine another person who finds himself forced to borrow some money. He knows that he will not be able to repay it, but he also knows that nobody will lend him anything unless he [falsely] promises to repay it. So he is tempted to make such a [false] promise. But he asks himself: Would such a promise be consistent with moral duty? If he were to make such a promise the maxim of his action would be this: "When I need money, I will borrow it and promise to repay it even if I know that I will never do so." Now I personally might be able to live according to this principle of self-interest. But the question is: Is it right? So I ask myself: What if my maxim were to become a universal law that everyone followed? Then I see at once that it could never even become a universal law of nature since it would contradict itself. For suppose it became a general rule that everyone is to make promises even when they never intend to keep them. Then promising itself could not continue, nor could we gain those benefits we hoped to gain by promising. For people would no longer believe anyone's promises, but would mock all "promises" as empty deceptions. [Since my maxim cannot become a universal law, it is morally wrong for me to act on it.]

3. *Imperfect duty to oneself.* Imagine a third man who has a useful natural ability that he could develop through practice and exercise. However, he is comfortably situated and would rather indulge in pleasure than make the effort needed to develop and improve himself. But he asks himself whether his maxim of neglecting his natural gifts as he is tempted to do is consistent with his duty. He sees then that a system of nature could conceivably exist with such a universal law, even if everyone (like the South Sea islanders) were to let his talents rust and devoted his life to idleness, amusement, and sex—in a word, to pleasure. But although his maxim *could* be conceived as a universal law of nature, he would not be willing to have it be a universal law of nature; that is, he would not be willing to have such a law implanted in us like a natural instinct. For our natural abilities enable us to achieve whatever goals we might have, so every rational person who has any goals whatever necessarily wants to have his abilities develop.

4. *Imperfect duty to others.* Imagine a fourth man who is prosperous, while he sees that others have to put up with great wretchedness. Suppose he could help them but he asks himself: What concern is it of mine? Let everyone have whatever happiness God

QUICK REVIEW
Kant argues that committing suicide, making false promises, failing to develop one's talents, and failing to help those in need are all morally wrong because they are all actions that not everyone could do, or actions that I would not be willing to have everyone do even toward me.

or his own efforts can give him. For my part I will not steal from people or envy their fortune. But I do not want to add to their well-being or help them when they are in need! Undoubtedly, if such a way of thinking became universal, the human race could continue to exist; it might even be better off than if everyone were to talk about sympathy and good will and occasionally practiced it, but generally continued to cheat whenever they could and betrayed and violated the rights of others. However, although that maxim *could* be a universal law of nature, one would not be willing to have it be a universal law of nature for then one's will would be inconsistent with itself. For we know that many situations will arise in which one will need the love and help of others. So if one's maxim were a law of nature, one would find oneself in a world deprived of the help he knows he will need.[34]

ANALYZING THE READING

Which of the following actions would be wrong according to Kant's first version of the categorical imperative: living with your parents and never working; giving all your money to the poor; counterfeiting money; committing adultery; cheating at poker; deciding to never help the poor; breaking off all communication with your family; cheating on your girlfriend or boyfriend; cheating on your spouse; cheating on your income taxes; refusing treatment for a painless but terminal disease. Explain how the actions that are wrong violate Kant's first version of the categorical imperative.

So Kant's **categorical imperative** says it is morally right for me to do something for a certain reason only if I could be willing to have everyone in a similar situation do what I do for that same reason. Kant's examples show that the categorical imperative really has two aspects. It says I should not do something for a certain reason unless (1) everyone *could* do the same thing for the same reason, and unless (2) I would be *willing* to have everyone do the same thing for the same reason. Notice that these two moral requirements correspond roughly to two common ways in which we identify wrongful actions. First, when someone is considering doing something wrong, we sometimes ask them: "What if everyone did that?" When we ask "What if everyone did that?" we are asking people to consider part (1) of Kant's categorical imperative. Second, when someone is considering doing something wrong, we also sometimes ask them, "How would you like it if everyone did that to you?" When we ask this, we are asking people to consider part (2) of Kant's categorical imperative.

In the preceding passage, Kant provided four examples of how the categorical imperative should be applied. Some additional examples may make his views clearer. Take the first aspect of Kant's categorical imperative: I should never do something for a certain reason *unless everyone can do the same thing for that same reason.* Consider this example: Is it wrong for you to cheat on an exam because you want to? Kant would say this: Ask yourself whether everyone could cheat on an exam when they wanted to. Could cheating for such a reason be universal? Clearly, if everyone always cheated on exams when they wanted to, the very practice of giving exams would break down. For what teacher would give an exam knowing that everyone who wants to is going to cheat on it? Because it is not possible for everyone to cheat on exams whenever they want, it is wrong for you to cheat on this exam merely because you want to. Or consider a game, such as poker or football or checkers. Is it wrong for you to secretly cheat during a game because you want to win? Ask yourself whether it is possible for everyone to always cheat at games because they want to win. Obviously, if everyone always cheated at games when they wanted to win, all game activities would soon break down and cease. Since it is not possible for everyone to cheat at games whenever they want, it is wrong for you to cheat at a game whenever you want. Or consider lying. Is it wrong for you to lie because you want to hide what you are really thinking? If everyone lied whenever they wanted to

---

[34] Ibid., 28, 51–55.

hide their thoughts, then no one's utterances could be trusted. So language would soon break down and no one would be able to make even lying statements. Because everyone cannot lie to hide their thoughts, it is wrong for you to do so. In short, the first aspect of Kant's categorical imperative says that it is wrong to make an exception of yourself: If everyone cannot do something for the reason you are doing it, then it is wrong for you to do it.

Kant's categorical imperative has a second aspect. The second aspect says some actions are wrong, not because everyone could not do them, but because we are *not willing* to have everyone do them. For example, consider racism. Is it wrong to discriminate against some people because you do not like their race? Ask yourself whether you would be willing to have everyone discriminate against others when they didn't like those people's race. Now, it is possible for a world to exist in which everyone discriminates like this. But would you be willing to live in such a world? Probably not. For if everyone discriminates against people whose race they don't like, then you are likely to sometimes be discriminated against. And you probably are not willing to have people do that to you. So, discriminating against others because you do not like their race is wrong for you.

A Second Version of the Categorical Imperative: Treating People as Ends. Although Kant claimed that there is only one categorical imperative, he also felt that we could express it in more than one way. The first version of the categorical imperative says, in effect, that what is morally right (or wrong) for one person must be morally right (or wrong) for everyone. This implies that everyone is of equal value. In Kant's words, everyone has the same "absolute value," an idea he also expressed by saying that everyone is an "end in himself." Because everyone is of equal value, no one should be used to serve the interests of another without their consent. Every person should always be respected as having an "absolute value." Kant summarized these ideas by restating his categorical imperative in these words: *Act so that you always treat people as ends in themselves, and never merely use them as means.* In the following passage, he explains this second version of the categorical imperative and illustrates it with four examples:

> Now I say that man and generally any rational being exists as an end in himself. In all his actions, whether they concern himself or other rational beings, we must always regard a man as an end and not merely as a means to be arbitrarily used by this or that will. . . . Accordingly [a second version of] the categorical imperative can be formulated as follows: *So act as to treat humanity, whether in your own person or in that of any other, always as an end and never merely as a means.* We will now inquire whether this version can be applied in practice. We will again consider our previous four examples:
>
> 1. *Strict duty to oneself.* A person who is thinking of committing suicide should ask himself whether his action is consistent with the idea that humanity is an end in itself. If he kills himself to escape his suffering, he is using a person (himself) merely as a means to maintain a tolerable existence. But a person is not a thing. That is to say, a person [including oneself] cannot be used merely as a means, but must always be respected as an end in himself. I cannot, therefore, dispose of my own person by mutilating, despoiling, or killing myself. . . .
> 2. *Strict duty to others.* A man who is thinking of making a lying promise will realize that he would be using others merely as means because he would not be letting them participate in the goal of the actions in which he involves them. For the people I would thus be using for my own purposes would not have consented to be treated in this way and to that extent they would not have participated in the goals to be attained by my action. . . .

3. *Meritorious duty to oneself.* We should not only refrain from violating our own humanity as an end in itself, but we should also try to make our actions harmonize with the fact that our humanity is such an end. Now humanity has certain abilities that we can perfect to a greater or lesser extent. . . . When we neglect to develop these abilities we are not doing something that is destructive of humanity as an end in itself. But such neglect clearly does not advance humanity as an end in itself.

4. *Meritorious duty to others.* All men by nature want to be happy. Now humanity probably could survive even if people never helped each other achieve their happiness, but merely refrained from deliberately harming one another. But this would only be a negative way of making our actions harmonize with the idea that humanity is an end in itself. The positive way of harmonizing with this idea would be for everyone to help others achieve their goals so far as he can. The goals of every person who is an end in himself should also be my goals if my actions are really to be in full harmony with the idea that the person's humanity is an end in itself.[35]

Kant's second version of the categorical imperative implies that we should not use people as objects, as things we merely use to achieve our goals. Instead, he claims, we should always at the same time allow them to choose whether or not they will join us in our actions. As he puts it in the second example above, a person must let others "participate in the goal of the actions in which he involves them."

Again, some additional examples may clarify what Kant has in mind in this second version of the categorical imperative. For Kant, to respect a person as an *end* is to respect her capacity to freely and knowingly choose for herself what she will do. To treat a person as a means is to use the person to achieve my personal goals. In effect, this second version of the categorical imperative says that we should treat people only as they freely and knowingly consent to be treated. So we should not merely use them as a means to our own goals without informing them of what we are doing. Kant would say that it is wrong to force or manipulate a person into doing something. When I manipulate or force a person to do something, I am failing to treat the person as she has freely and knowingly consented to be treated.

Think next about whether it is wrong to lie or steal from a person. Lying or stealing involves doing something to a person without her free and knowing consent and so these are both wrong. What about helping those in great need? Kant would say that when people are in great need (such as the very poor), their ability to choose for themselves is compromised. But we have a duty to promote people's capacity to choose for themselves. So we should help those whose poverty prevents them from exercising their capacity to choose for themselves.

Notice that Kant is not saying that it is wrong to use people for our own ends. He is saying only that it is wrong to use people for our own ends *when we have not given them a choice in the matter.* For example, suppose you order a taxi driver to take you to the airport. Clearly, you are "using" the driver as a "means" to get to the airport. Does this

 THINKING LIKE A PHILOSOPHER

Think of something that you or a friend did that you believe was morally wrong. Explain why it was wrong by using Kant's first version of the categorical imperative to show that it was wrong. Next, explain why it was wrong by using Kant's second version of the categorical imperative to show that it was wrong.

ANALYZING THE READING

Which of the following actions would be wrong according to Kant's second version of the categorical imperative: pickpocketing; crossing the street against a red light; smoking; using heroin; having sex with someone who is too drunk to object; refusing to go to a doctor for a serious illness; speeding on a highway; refusing to fight in a war your government has declared. Explain how the actions that are wrong violate Kant's second version of the categorical imperative.

---

[35] Ibid., 68.

make it immoral? Kant would doubtless say that it is not wrong. For when the taxi driver accepted the job of driving a taxi, he was consenting to take people to the destination they ordered him to. So, when you now order him to take you to the airport, you treat him as a means, but at the same time you are treating him as he *previously* consented to be treated. So you do not merely treat him as a means, but also as an end in himself.

Notice also that Kant is not saying that it is wrong to do things to people that at the moment they do not want you to do. Take, for example, a teacher who flunks a student or a judge who puts a lawbreaker in jail. Clearly, neither the student nor the lawbreaker wants to be treated this way. So, is it immoral to do this to them? Kant would probably again say that in reality each is being treated as he *previously* consented to be treated. The student consented to be graded by the teacher when he signed up for the course knowing what it required. The lawbreaker consented to be treated according to the laws of this country when he chose to live or remain in it knowing what its laws required.

Finally, notice that this second version of the categorical imperative also corresponds to some common ways we have of indicating that an action was wrong. Consider, for example, how often you have heard friends say something like: "He just used me!" or "She was just using me!" or "He just treated me like an object!" Such expressions are direct descendants of Kant's second version of the categorical imperative: do not use people merely as means. Or consider how people often say that there is nothing wrong with sex between "consenting adults." Or how often we say that before treating a patient or experimenting on a person, one should get the person's "informed consent." Such expressions are directly related to Kant's claim that people must be treated as ends, that is, as they have consented to be treated.

⊘ QUICK REVIEW
Critics say Kant's theory cannot deal with conflicts among duties. Critics also claim that his theory implies that certain acts (such as lying) are always wrong no matter what the circumstances might be, and this implication seems mistaken.

Conflicts. Nevertheless, Kant's theory has a few problems. First, duties frequently conflict, and Kant's theory does not seem to give us an obvious way of resolving such conflicts. If, as Kant argues, it is always wrong to tell a lie and always wrong to break a promise, then which do I choose when these duties conflict? Second, the acts that the categorical imperative says are *always* wrong do not always seem wrong. For example, Kant says that it is wrong to lie, no matter what good might come of telling the lie. Yet is it wrong to lie to save your life? To save someone from serious pain or injury? There seems to be no compelling reason why such actions should be prohibited without exception.

Some Implications of Kantian Ethics. Many people today believe that Kantian ethics provides rich insights into the moral life. To see more clearly the kind of understanding of morality that Kant's ethics provides, let us consider the topic we discussed earlier: sexual behavior. Philosopher Thomas Mappes says the idea it is wrong to "use another person" or treat her like "an object" derives from Kant's principle that we should not use a person "merely as a means." But what, exactly, do these Kantian ideas imply about ethics in sex? Mappes explains what it is to use a person sexually:

> The morally significant sense of "using another person" is best understood by reference to the notion of voluntary informed consent. . . . Using another person (in the morally significant sense) can arise in at least two important ways: via coercion, which is antithetical to voluntary consent, and via deception, which undermines the informed character of voluntary consent. . . . It seems clear, then, that A may sexually use B in at least two distinctive ways, (1) via coercion and (2) via deception.

There are a host of clear cases in which a [fully competent adult] person "uses" another precisely because the former employs deception. . . . Consider this example. One person, A, has decided, as a matter of personal prudence based on past experience, not to become sexually involved outside the confines of a loving relationship. Another person B, strongly desires a sexual relationship with A but does not love A. B, aware of A's unwillingness to engage in sex without love, professes love for A, thereby hoping to win A's consent to a sexual relationship. B's ploy is successful; A consents. When the smoke clears and A becomes aware of B's deception it would be both appropriate and natural for A to complain, "I've been used."

Forcible rape is the most conspicuous, and most brutal way of sexually using another person via coercion. . . . A man who rapes a woman by the employment of sheer physical force, by simply overpowering her, employs occurrent coercion. . . . When the victim of rape is treated as if she were a physical object, there we have one of the most vivid examples of the immoral using of another person.

Frequently, forcible rape involves not occurrent coercion but dispositional coercion. In dispositional coercion, the relevant factor is not physical force but the threat of harm. . . . For example, a man threatens to kill or beat a woman if she resists his sexual demands. She "consents," that is, she submits to his demands. . . . [But] it is coerced.

Although the threat of immediate and serious bodily harm stands out as the most brutal way of coercing consent to sexual interaction, we must not neglect the employment of other kinds of threats to this same end. . . . Consider . . . the following case: Mr. Supervisor makes a series of increasingly less subtle sexual overtures to Ms. Employee. These advances are consistently and firmly rejected by Ms. Employee. Eventually, Mr. Supervisor makes it clear that the granting of "sexual favors" is a condition of her continued employment. . . . [This] case [also] . . . involve[s an] attempt to sexually use another person.[36]

> **QUICK REVIEW**
> Using Kant's theory, Mappes argues that it is wrong to sexually use a person through coercion or deception, which is why rape and sexual harassment of employees are wrong.

Kant's theory is clearly useful for helping us see what our moral obligations are. In fact, in some respects, it sheds more light on common dilemmas in sexual matters than do other approaches to the morality of sex. For Kant's theory identifies the central importance of showing respect for the dignity of our sexual partners. And it calls our attention to the key significance of consent in morally legitimate sexual interactions.

However, some people have criticized this Kantian approach to sex, saying that, like utilitarianism, it is too permissive. Utilitarianism approves of any sexual activity if its pleasures sufficiently outweigh its pains. Yet the Kantian approach seems to approve of virtually any consensual sexual activity. This seems to allow all sexual activity between informed and voluntarily consenting adults. It would allow incest and adultery if the parties involved give their consent. For many people, this is a morally objectionable result.

> **QUICK REVIEW**
> Critics say that Kant's theory implies that any kind of sexual activity between informed and consenting persons is morally right, and this seems too permissive. Other critics argue that free, rational consent may not be possible where sex is concerned.

Moreover, many have questioned whether the Kantian approach to sex makes idealistic assumptions about how real our consent can be. In the throes of sexual desire, in the sexual heat of the moment, are people really able to give their voluntary informed consent? Isn't the sometimes overwhelming power of sex incompatible with free, rational consent? Feminists have suggested that sexual roles are designed to ensure male dominance over women and to mask from women their own real sexual desires and needs. In the context of such false consciousness, isn't the Kantian faith in informed consent unreal? For example, does the prostitute genuinely consent to her situation? Some feminists have even questioned whether any woman truly consents to sex.

---

[36] Thomas A. Mappes, "Sexual Morality and the Concept of Using Another Person," in *Social Ethics: Morality and Social Policy,* ed. Thomas A. Mappes and Jane S. Zembaty (New York: McGraw-Hill, 1992).

PHILOSOPHY AT THE MOVIES

Watch *Liar, Liar* (1997) in which Fletcher Reed, a successful lawyer and habitual liar who regularly breaks his promises to spend time with his son, Max, misses Max's birthday party. When Max makes a birthday wish that for a full day his father be unable to lie, Fletcher finds that no matter how much he struggles, he cannot lie—which makes it particularly difficult to defend his client in court. Kant claims that the categorical imperative implies that it is always wrong to lie; utilitarianism claims that it is permissible to lie if lying has better consequences than any other alternative. What is the view of this movie?

Buddhist Ethics

Buddhist ethics cannot be considered a divine command theory because Buddhism does not believe in a God that issues commands. Yet Buddhism provides important insight into the moral life, and for centuries it has influenced the moral behavior of millions. Because many people in the West today are turning to it for enlightenment, here we briefly consider its implications for ethics.

We can begin with two generalizations about Buddhism's approach to ethical behavior. First, intentional actions are supremely important because, as our karma, they determine our destiny. The basic meaning of the word *karma* is "action." But karma also refers to the consequences of one's action, primarily on oneself. For the Buddhist, a person's intentional actions are not isolated events. Instead, what we intentionally do now determines what we become and so the influence of our intentional actions moves forward into our future. Classical Buddhism understood this in terms of the doctrine of successive rebirths—what you are in this life is determined by what you did in your past lives. But some contemporary Buddhists interpret karma in terms of a single human life—what you are today is determined by the choices you made earlier in your present life. In either case, our intentional actions are all important in determining who and what we now are as well as who and what we will become.

A second generalization we can make about Buddhism is that its ethics is a form of wisdom and not a set of obligations. The following passage, which is attributed to the Buddha, makes that point. It is taken from the *Digha Nikaya*, or *The Long Discourses of the Buddha*, one of the oldest records of the teachings of the Buddha:

> Morality is washed all round with wisdom, and wisdom is washed all round with morality. Wherever there is morality, there is wisdom and wherever there is wisdom there is morality. From the observing of the moralities comes wisdom and from observing of wisdom comes morality. Morality and wisdom together reveal the height of the world. It is just as if one should wash one hand with the other or one foot with the other; exactly so is morality washed round with wisdom and wisdom with morality.[37]

The point is important. Unlike Western ethics, Buddhist ethics does not conceive of ethics as a set of obligations, rights, or duties. Nor is Buddhist ethics a set of imperatives, nor a set of standards for evaluating our actions or assigning blame. Ethics is, instead, the accumulated wisdom we have about how to deal with what Buddhism considers the fundamental problem of human life: suffering. We will return to this point after we look at the way Buddhism deals with suffering.

---

[37] *Dighanikaya*, vol. 1, ed. T. W. Rhys Davies and J. E. Carpenter (Melksham, Wilts, UK: Pali Text Society, 1947), 124.

To understand the central role of suffering in Buddhist ethics, we must return to the Four Noble Truths. We very briefly mentioned these in Chapter 4, but we must now examine them more closely by looking at their implications for ethics:

Buddha: **"Morality is** washed all round with wisdom, and wisdom is washed all round with morality. . . . It is just as if one should wash one hand with the other or one foot with the other; exactly so is morality washed round with wisdom and wisdom with morality."

And this is the Noble Truth of Suffering. Birth is suffering, aging is suffering, disease is suffering and death is suffering; contact with the unpleasant is suffering; separation from the pleasant is suffering; every wish unfulfilled is suffering—in short, all the five components of individuality related to clinging are suffering.

And this is the Noble Truth of the Origin of Suffering. It arises from craving, which leads to rebirth accompanied by pleasure and lust, which leads to seeking pleasure now here, now there; that is, it leads to the craving for sensual pleasure, the craving for continued life, the craving for power.

And this is the Noble Truth of the Stopping of Suffering. It is the complete stopping of that craving so that nothing of it remains, giving it up, relinquishing it, being freed from it, not relying on it.

And this is the Noble Truth of the Way which leads to the Stopping of Suffering. It is the Noble Eightfold Path—[having] Right Understanding, Right Intention, Right Speech, Right Conduct, Right Livelihood, Right Effort, Right Mindfulness, and Right Concentration.[38]

MindTap To read more from *Sources of Indian Tradition*, by William Theodore de Bary, click the link in the MindTap Reader or go to the Questia Readings folder in MindTap.

Buddhism sees itself as the solution to a human problem, and the First Noble Truth explains that problem: suffering. Suffering pervades our world and our existence: It is a universal human experience. We feel pain, both the bodily pains of diseases and injuries, and the mental anguish of losing those we loved and losing what we desired. We continuously experience the frustration of living in a world where nothing remains the same and nothing lasts. Our bodies age, our strength and skills decline, we suffer diseases and death. All our pleasures are temporary. The intensity of the love and passion we felt for a lover subsides and ends. The excitement and enthusiasm we experience when we first get something we wanted settles into indifference or even disappointment. The five "components of individuality" are all subject to suffering. This includes suffering in our bodies, our feelings, our perceptions, our mental activities, and our consciousness.

But we cannot alleviate suffering unless we know what its causes are. The Second Noble Truth is an explanation of the fundamental causes of our suffering. The fundamental cause of suffering, the Buddha claimed, is our craving for things. Our cravings are continually frustrated because nothing is permanent. We crave pleasure but all pleasures are short-lived; we crave continued life yet we must die; and we

QUICK REVIEW
The Four Noble Truths of Buddhism are as follows: (1) Whatever is tied to our individuality, such as birth, age, disease, death, and pain, brings suffering. (2) We suffer because we crave things: pleasure, life, power. (3) Only putting an end to craving will end our suffering. (4) Craving can be ended only by following the Noble Eightfold Path of right understanding, right thought, right speech, right conduct, right livelihood, right effort, right mindfulness, and right concentration.

---

[38] William Theodore de Bary, *Sources of Indian Tradition*, vol. 1, from *Samyutta Nikaya* (New York: Columbia University Press, 1958), 99.

crave power, yet all power is fleeting. Craving manifests itself in three vices: attachment to some things, aversion to other things, and confusions about the true nature of the things we crave. These are vices because they are at the root of suffering.

The Third Noble Truth makes the point that since craving is the fundamental cause of suffering, we can eliminate suffering by eliminating craving. Specifically, we must eliminate our attachments, our aversions, and our confusions. Three confusions are crucial. The first is the confused belief that things in the world are permanent. The second is the confused belief that we are individual selves. And the third is the confused belief that human existence is not all suffering.

The Fourth Noble Truth explains the way that craving can be eliminated. Craving, the root of suffering, can be eliminated by following the Eightfold Path, namely by cultivating (1) correct understanding, (2) correct resolve, (3) correct speech, (4) correct conduct, (5) correct livelihood, (6) correct effort, (7) correct mindfulness, and (8) correct concentration.

To have *correct understanding* one must not only understand, accept, and live according to the Four Noble Truths. But correct understanding also requires becoming genuinely convinced of three basic ideas. These three critical convictions are that nothing is permanent, that there is no self, and that all life is suffering. Failure to accept that nothing is permanent leads us to continually seek permanence in what is impermanent. Failure to accept that we have no self leads us to assume we have a self that we must care for when in fact we have none. Thinking we have a self leads us to seek happiness for the self through activities that increase the sufferings of others or oneself. And thinking some aspects of life are not suffering leads us to see what is actually undesirable as attractive. Of these three failures of understanding, however, the most fundamental is the belief that one is an enduring individual self. From that false belief flows all our selfishness and our clinging to things. *Correct resolve* refers to having both the determination and the detachment needed to follow and remain on the Eightfold Path. To have *correct speech* is to refrain from saying what is false or useless, and to use speech only to benefit others and not to add to their suffering. The precept on correct speech prohibits lying, slandering, gossiping, cursing, and creating dissension. And it enjoins honesty, friendliness, sincerity, and clarity. *Correct conduct* is behavior that does not harm oneself or others, that is, behavior that does not cause suffering. Specifically, it means not injuring others and not destroying or stealing their property. It means avoiding fornication and killing. And it means refraining from personal habits that abuse one's body, that allow one's body to deteriorate, or that pollute the body and its organs in any way. Having a *correct livelihood* means making one's living in occupations that do not increase the sufferings of others—humans or animals. This is usually seen as ruling out occupations like weapons manufacturing, butchering or hunting animals, or making and selling alcoholic drinks. It also rules out occupations that create attachments or cravings, such as marketing that arouses consumer desires for things. *Correct effort* refers to keeping one's mind focused on what matters and not allowing oneself to get sidetracked by distracting thoughts and desires. What matters most and what one must stay focused on is the Eightfold Path. The word *effort* implies an act of the will and indicates the importance of using one's will to stay on the Eightfold Path. *Correct mindfulness* is being completely aware of what is happening in one's mind and body. This includes an awareness of one's physical body, one's sensations, one's mind, and one's thoughts. Exercises such as concentrating on one's breathing or paying full attention to what one is doing at the moment can help one achieve correct mindfulness and move toward insight and enlightenment. Finally, *correct concentration* is achieving a meditative state of pure consciousness in which there is "neither perception nor non-perception." This is enlightenment, a state of consciousness in which there are no thoughts, nor ideas, nor any other contents in one's mind. The Buddhist progresses toward this state in four stages. First, he rids himself of all negative desires and thoughts and allows only positive feelings. Second, he eliminates all intellectualization. Third, he eliminates all feelings including positive ones. And, finally, he eliminates all sensations so that only pure undistracted awareness remains.[39]

It's important not to view the precepts of the Eightfold Path as a set of absolute rules. Buddhism, as we saw, stresses the elimination of suffering, not the fulfillment of obligations. In other words, blind obedience to the precepts is not encouraged because they are merely means to an end: the elimination of suffering. Unlike Western morality, Buddhist ethics does not see violations of the precepts of the Eightfold Path as sinful or as evil wrongdoing that deserves blame. Nor are they seen as God's commands since Buddhism does not include a belief in God. Instead, violations of the Eightfold Path are simply obstacles that prevent us from being released from suffering. So violations of these precepts should not be seen as morally blameworthy. Instead, they should be seen as behaviors and thoughts that increase our attachments and cravings and thereby immerse us more deeply in the causes of suffering. Violations of the Eightfold Path then, are not morally blameworthy but they inflict profound damage on us. Violations tighten the bonds that keep us tied to the cause of our suffering and make release from that suffering more difficult. Keeping that in mind, let us ask what Buddhism can tell us about the issue of sexual ethics which we discussed in relation to the other ethical approaches.

Buddhism distinguishes between the conduct expected of a Buddhist monk, and that expected of a Buddhist layperson. The Buddhist monk must conduct himself in a manner that is conducive to achieving "correct concentration" or enlightenment. Since indulging in sex will increase a person's cravings and attachments, it is clearly not conducive to achieving enlightenment. For that reason sex in any form is absolutely forbidden to the monk. The monk voluntarily accepts this rule of complete abstinence from sexual activity. If he should violate this basic rule he must leave the order of monks.

Buddhist laypeople are not expected to live according to the strict rules of the monk. But in both of the major traditions of Buddhism laypeople are expected to follow the so-called "Five Precepts." These Five Precepts can be understood as making the Eightfold Path, particularly "Correct Conduct," more specific. The Five Precepts are described as "gifts" by the Buddha:

> Now, there are these five gifts, five great gifts—original, long-standing, traditional, ancient, unadulterated, unadulterated from the beginning—that are not open to suspicion, will never be open to suspicion, and are not faulted by knowledgeable contemplatives and Brahmans. Which five?
>
> First for a disciple of the noble ones, [is] abandoning the taking of life, abstaining from taking life. . . .
>
> Next is abandoning taking what is not given (stealing), the disciple of the noble ones abstains from taking what is not given. . . .
>
> Next is abandoning illicit sex, the disciple of the noble ones abstains from illicit sex. . . .
>
> Next is abandoning lying, the disciple of the noble ones abstains from lying. . . .
>
> Next is abandoning the use of intoxicants, the disciple of the noble ones abstains from taking intoxicants.[40]

 THINKING LIKE A PHILOSOPHER

Consider each of the Five Precepts of Buddhism in relation to your life. Would you say that your life has pretty much followed the Five Precepts? Are there some precepts that you have found more difficult than others? Which are these and why do you think they have been more difficult?

---

[39] Michael C. Brannigan, *Striking a Balance: A Primer in Traditional Asian Values* (Plymouth, United Kingdom: Lexington Books, 2010), 51–61.

[40] *Abhisanda Sutta*, translated by Thanissaro Bhikkhu, 1997, accessed May 10, 2015, at: http://www.accesstoinsight.org/tipitaka/an/an08/an08.039.than.html.

The Five Precepts do not seem to be too difficult to understand. Yet they encompass more than is apparent at first sight. The first precept, against taking life, for example, rules out intentionally killing any living creature whatsoever, or causing someone to kill a living creature. The precept also rules out injuring one's own body or that of any other person, as well as injuring other living things. The second precept prohibits theft. But the prohibition of theft is seen as also including the prohibition of fraud, cheating, forgery, counterfeiting, refusing to repay a debt, cheating a customer, and extortion. The third precept we will comment on below. The fourth precept prohibits lying, but is interpreted as also prohibiting deception, deceit, and exaggeration, as well as divisive speech, slander, abusive or angry speech, and gossip. The fifth precept prohibits drinking alcohol but is also interpreted as prohibiting the selling of alcohol.

But the precept that most concerns us is the third one, "abandoning illicit sex." What is "illicit sex"? The commentary on the Five Precepts in the *Visuddhimagga* by the Buddhist monk Buddhaghosa (circa 400) provides some clarification. Buddhaghosa is regarded as the most important interpreter of the writings of early Buddhism. According to Buddhaghosa by "illicit sex" the Buddha meant "intercourse with men and then also with . . . women who have been betrothed, women bought with money, kept women. . . . " So the third of the Five Precepts rules out homosexual acts, adultery, prostitution, and having a mistress, as well as having sex with an engaged woman or any girl under the protection of a relative. But keep in mind that these forms of sex are not ruled out because they are evil, sinful, or blameworthy. They are ruled out because they produce pleasure, and pleasure intensifies craving and attachment. Yet note that some sexual activities are not ruled out even though they also are pleasurable. The precepts do not rule out sex between married partners, for example. Why does Buddhaghosa specifically rule out homosexual acts, adultery, prostitution, and having a mistress? The reason is because he saw these as activities that also affect others. Specifically, he believed that these activities produced suffering in others. Adultery, for example, affects the adulterer's spouse, causing suffering. The relation to suffering is also the reason why, according to other Buddhist commentators, the third precept also prohibits rape and incest. And the most fundamental aim of Buddhism, of course, is to reduce and eliminate suffering.

The focus of Buddhism, then, is not on the wrongness of these or any other moral activities but on the elimination of suffering. Because the pursuit of sexual pleasure leads us away from this key goal, it is to be set aside. And if one is unwilling to follow the monk by abstaining from sex altogether, one should at least ensure that one's sexual activities do not increase the suffering of others.

ANALYZING THE READING

The text emphasizes that unlike Western ethics, Buddhist ethics does not consist of obligations, rights, or duties, and does not see violations of the Eightfold Path or of the Five Precepts as sinful or deserving of blame. Does this mean that "Buddhist ethics" is not really ethics but more like some advice about life?

PHILOSOPHY AT THE MOVIES

Watch *Little Buddha* (1993) in which a group of Tibetan Buddhist monks determines that a boy living in Seattle named Jesse Conrad is the reincarnation of a great deceased Buddhist teacher named Lama Dorje. They travel to Seattle to find him and then ask his parents if they can take the boy back to Tibet for testing to determine whether he is in fact the reincarnation of Lama Dorje. What roles do the Noble Eightfold Path and the Five Precepts play in this movie? What role does the idea of karma play in this movie? What other key Buddhist beliefs does this movie demonstrate?

© KPA Honorar & Belege/United Archives Gmb/Alamy

7.5 Is Ethics Based on Character?

The ethical theories we've discussed so far provide principles or rules focused on actions. That is, those theories give us rules or principles that define the *actions* we are morally obligated or have a moral duty to perform or avoid. Utilitarianism is based on the principle that "*actions* are right in proportion as they tend to promote happiness, wrong as they tend to produce the reverse of happiness." Kant based his ethics on the principle that one should "*act* so as to treat humanity . . . always as an end and never merely as a means." Modern ethics has been concerned mostly with studying rules or principles like these, which tell us which *actions* are morally right or how people ought to *act.*

Many philosophers now feel dissatisfied with this approach to ethics. One major problem, they say, is that this approach results in disagreements that cannot be resolved. Utilitarians disagree with Kantians, and both disagree with followers of natural law ethics. Contemporary philosopher Alasdair MacIntyre writes:

> The most striking feature of contemporary moral utterance is that so much of it is used to express disagreements; and the most striking feature of the debates in which these disagreements are expressed is their interminable character. I do not mean by this just that such debates go on and on—although they do—but also that they apparently can find no terminus. There seems to be no rational way of securing moral agreement in our culture.[41]

MacIntyre and others argue that modern ethics has become too preoccupied with such conflicting rules and principles. As a result it has forgotten a part of morality that earlier ages recognized: moral virtue or character. The moral life, MacIntyre and others suggest, is not just a matter of actions and rules. The moral life is about becoming a good person. It is about cultivating morally desirable character traits like honesty, courage, compassion, and generosity. We should stop focusing on action-based rules about which we will inevitably disagree. Instead of looking at how we should act, ethics should concern itself with the kind of person we can become. Ethics should study the character traits or "virtues" of the morally good person and explain how we can develop and acquire these traits. Ethics should not emphasize *doing* but *being*; it should look not at what we ought to do but at what we ought to *be.*

Virtue ethics is a kind of ethics that takes the approach that MacIntyre and others have called for. Virtue ethics looks at those character traits that we call virtues, like courage, generosity, kindness, good humor, self-control, and so on. It asks questions such as these: What are the character traits or virtues of a morally good person? What exactly is a virtue? How are virtues related to our nature as human beings? How are virtues developed?

This approach to ethics is not new. It is, in fact, an approach that the ancient Greek philosophers such as Aristotle made the cornerstone of their moral philosophy. But as MacIntyre pointed out, philosophers have neglected this approach to ethics until recently. Many who have turned to explore virtue ethics have looked to Aristotle as one of the clearest and best explanations of what the human virtues are. There is no better way of understanding virtue ethics than by examining his views. As part of our discussion of his virtue theory, we will also look at his views on friendship and love. We then turn to examine a controversial issue: whether the virtues of women should differ from those of men.

---

[41] Alasdair MacIntyre, *After Virtue* (Notre Dame, IN: University of Notre Dame Press, 1984), 3.

Aristotle's Theory of Virtue

In his great work *Nicomachean Ethics*, Aristotle proposed an answer to this question: What are the virtues appropriate for human beings? Aristotle saw a virtue as a kind of ability to habitually respond to circumstances in the right way. Courage, for example, is a virtue. So the person with courage is the person who has the ability to habitually respond to fearful situations in the right way, that is, courageously. But what, exactly does that mean? What is a courageous response to a situation? And what of the other virtues? What is generosity, for example, and what kind of response to situations does generosity involve?

Aristotle began his discussion of virtue with an analysis of happiness. His assumption was that human virtues should be related to happiness. Happiness, he wrote, is the ultimate aim of everything we do. The virtues of a good person should be related to this ultimate aim of ours. That is, there should be a close connection between having the virtues of a morally good person and being happy. After all, if human virtues are not related to happiness, then why should we pursue them?

But how is happiness achieved? Aristotle argued that human beings can be happy only if they fulfill their basic human purpose or "function." That is, humans can be happy only if they act as humans are specifically meant to act. Since only humans can reason, Aristotle concluded that humans are meant to act with reason. So we humans can achieve happiness only if we have the ability to act with reason. That is, we will be happy only if we have the ability to act as our reason tells us to act. In short, happiness requires being able to use our reason in the choices we make. Aristotle then suggested that having a virtue is having the ability to do something and to do it well. For example, we say a musician has the virtues of a musician if in addition to being able to play music, she has the ability to do it well. So the virtues that are specific to humans should be related to the ability to act with reason and to do it well. Such virtues should not only enable us to act as humans are specifically meant to act. They should also be the key to human happiness since happiness is achieved by doing what we are specifically meant to do. Aristotle makes these points in the following passages from *Nicomachean Ethics*:

> Every action and pursuit is thought to aim at some good.... If, then, in all our activities there is some end we seek for its own sake so that everything else is a means to that end, obviously it will be our highest and best end. Clearly there must be some such end since everything cannot be a means to something else. For then there would be nothing for which we ultimately do anything and everything would be pointless....
>
> Now happiness seems more than anything else to answer to this description. For happiness is something we always choose for its own sake and never as a means to something else. But things like fame, pleasure, reason, virtue, and so on, are chosen partly for themselves but they are also chosen as a means to happiness, since we believe that they will bring us happiness. But we never seek happiness for the sake of these things or as a means to any other thing....

ANALYZING THE READING

1. Aristotle says that each action we do is a means to some end. And usually that end is a means to some further end. And that further end is usually a means to some yet further end; and that is a means to... etc. For example, I study to pass an exam; I want to pass the exam to pass the course; I want to pass the course to get my college degree; I want a college degree to get a good job; I want a good job to make money; I want money to... etc. Is Aristotle right that *your* actions are links in chains of means to further ends, which are means to further ends, which are means to further ends, etc.? Explain why.

2. Aristotle then claims these chains of means to further ends must terminate in "some end we seek for its own sake" and not as a means to a further end, because otherwise "there would be nothing for which we ultimately do anything and everything would be pointless." Is Aristotle's claim true? That is, do you agree that if there was nothing we were ultimately seeking for itself, "everything would be pointless"? Explain why.

So it appears that happiness is the ultimate end and that by itself it would make life worthwhile and lacking in nothing. We also feel that it is the most desirable of all things, and not just one good thing among others. . . . Happiness is something final and by itself it would be sufficient for us. It is the end we seek in all that we do.

The reader may think that in saying that happiness is our ultimate end we are merely stating a platitude. So we must be more precise about what happiness involves.

Perhaps the best approach is to ask what the specific purpose or function of a human being is. For the good and the excellence of all things that have a [11] purpose—such as musicians, sculptors, or craftsmen—depend on their purpose. So if human beings have a purpose, their good will be related to their purpose. But how could humans not have a purpose if even carpenters and tanners have a purpose? Are humans born for no purpose? Since a human being's eye, hand, foot, and in general each of his parts has a purpose, can we take it as given that a human being also has a purpose apart from that of each of his parts? But what could the purpose or function of a human being be?

Our biological activities we share in common even with plants, so these activities cannot be the purpose or function of humans since we are looking for what is specific to human beings. The activities of our senses we also plainly share with other things: horses, cattle, and other animals. So there remain only the activities that belong to the rational part of a human being. . . . So the specific purpose or function of a human being involves the activities of that part of his soul that is related to reason, or that at least is obedient to reason. For one part of us consists of reason, the part that thinks, while another part of us does not think but can obey reason. . . .

Now the function of a thing is the basis [of its goodness], but its good is something added to this function. For example, the function of a musician is to play music, and the good musician is one who not only plays music but who in addition does it well. So, the good for a human being would have to be something added to this function of carrying on the activities of reason. It would be carrying on the activities of reason but doing so well. But a thing carries out its proper functions well when it has the proper virtues. So the [ultimate] good for a human being is carrying out those activities of his soul [which involve reason] and doing so with the proper virtue or excellence.[42]

ANALYZING THE READING

Aristotle argues that since every part of a human being has a purpose, a human being as a whole must have a purpose. Put his argument into its logical form. What is the assumption he makes but does not explicitly state? Is his assumption true? Why?

QUICK REVIEW

Aristotle's ethic of virtue says humans will achieve happiness—their ultimate end—only by fulfilling their specific purpose, which is to exercise their reason, and to do so in an excellent or virtuous way.

Notice that Aristotle's conclusion is that we will achieve our ultimate good—happiness—if we are able to use our reason and use it well. And the ability to use our reason and use it well is the ability to act with virtue. In short, the virtue that is characteristic of a human being is the ability to use our reason and use it well.

Aristotle points out that it is not enough to just have a theoretical knowledge of virtue. We are looking at virtue in order to learn how to act with virtue, not just to learn how to define it. That means that we need to ask how the virtue of using our reason well relates to the actions we choose. So the question is: How do we use our reason well in the choices we make?

THINKING LIKE A PHILOSOPHER

1. According to Aristotle, each of your actions is done for some end; and usually that end is a means to some further end; and that further end is a means to some yet further end; and that further end is a means to some even further end, etc. Give some examples from your own life of some actions you do for some end, and how this is a means to some further end, and how that further end is a means to some yet further end, and how that is a means to. . . etc.

2. Aristotle claims that happiness is the ultimate end you seek as the last end in each of these chains of means to an end, which is a means to an end, which is a means to an end, etc. Looking at your own life, would you say that his claim about happiness is true? Explain why his claim seems to be true in your life or why you would say it has not been true in your life.

---

42 Aristotle, *Nicomachean Ethics*, bk. 1, chs. 2, 7. This translation copyright © 1992 by Manuel Velasquez.

Our choices are decisions we make about our desires, emotions, and actions. Aristotle points out that we can allow our desires, emotions, and actions to go too far or not go far enough. Take, for example, the emotion of fear. A person can feel excessive fear, and then he will tend to respond with cowardliness. Or a person may not feel enough fear, and then he will tend to respond with recklessness. The same is true of our desires. We can allow ourselves to desire pleasure too much and then we become lustful, or we can have an insufficient desire for pleasure and then become austere. Both extremes are bad, Aristotle points out. Our desires, emotions, and actions, then, can be excessive or they can be deficient. Since both extremes are bad, they are vices. The good, or the virtuous choice, then, has to lie somewhere between those extremes. That point of moderation between an excessive and deficient response to situations, then, is the point that the person of virtue would choose. A person with the virtue of courage, for example, will keep his fear from becoming too excessive, or from being too deficient. Such a person will neither be cowardly nor reckless, but courageous. Aristotle calls the point of moderation between excess and deficiency the "mean" between the extremes. So the person of virtue is the person who is able to choose the mean.

But how is all this related to using our reason in the choices we make? There is an important relationship, Aristotle believed, between the point of moderation that the person of virtue would choose, and our reason. The relationship is that only our reason can tell us where that point of moderation lies. To know, for example, whether we are letting our fear go too far, we need to be able to judge what kind of response is appropriate for the situation we face. As Aristotle says, we must know how to respond "at the right time, on the right occasion, toward the right persons, with the right object, and in the right fashion." If I see a large growling dog, for example, and feel fear, I have to figure out what kind of response is appropriate. Suppose the dog is threatening a child. Then responding by allowing my fear to get the best of me would be cowardly. Controlling my fear so I can rescue the child is the appropriate response and would be courageous. But suppose that instead of a child, the growling dog is standing over a book I dropped. Then rushing in and grabbing the book would be reckless, not courageous. It would be reckless because the value of the book is not worth the risk of getting bitten. But to know that, I had to use my reason. Only by using my reason can I figure out what kind of response to my fear is appropriate for a situation. So only reason can tell me where the point of moderation lies between excess and deficiency in our desires, emotions, and actions.

So we must use our reason in the choices we make in order to know the point of moderation a virtuous person would choose. But just having reason tell us where the virtuous point lies is not enough. I may know intellectually, for example, what my appropriate response should be when I see a dog threatening a child. But if I don't have the ability to control my fear, I won't be able to respond in the courageous way I know I should respond. So to respond to a situation in a virtuous manner, I must have the ability to get my desires, emotions, and actions to respond as my reason says they should respond. And that ability is what a virtue is. A virtue is the ability to habitually get my desires, emotions, and actions to respond as my reason says they should. Aristotle makes these points in the following passage:

> Our inquiry does not aim at theoretical knowledge like other inquiries do. For we are inquiring not so that we can learn what virtue is, but so that we can become virtuous. Otherwise our inquiry will be useless. So we must examine the nature of our actions and ask how we ought to act. . . .

To begin with, consider that the expert in any field is the one who avoids doing what is excessive as well as what is deficient. Instead he seeks to hit the mean and chooses it. . . . Acting well in any field is achieved by looking to the mean and bringing one's actions into line with this standard of moderation. For example, people say of a good work of art that nothing could be taken from it or added to it, implying that excellence is destroyed through excess or deficiency but achieved by observing the mean. The good artist, in fact, keeps his eyes fixed on the mean in everything he does. . . .

Virtue, therefore, must also aim at the mean. For human virtue deals with our feelings and actions, and in these we can go to excess or fall short or we can hit the mean. For example, it is possible to feel fear, confidence, desire, anger, pity, pleasure, . . . and so on, either too much or too little—both of which extremes are bad. But to feel these at the right times, and on the right occasions, and toward the right persons, and with the right object, and in the right fashion, is the mean between the extremes and is the best state, and is the mark of virtue. In the same way, our actions can also be excessive or can fall short or can hit the mean.

Virtue, then, deals with those feelings and actions in which it is wrong to go too far and wrong to fall short but in which hitting the mean is praiseworthy and good. . . . It is a habit or acquired ability to choose . . . what is moderate or what hits the mean as determined by reason.

ANALYZING THE READING

According to Aristotle, a virtue is the ability to choose the mean between extremes in our emotions, desires, and actions. Do you think he's right when he claims that the mean between extremes is always the virtuous choice? Explain why or why not.

But it is not enough to speak in generalities. We must also apply this to particular virtues and vices. Consider, then, the following examples.

Take the feelings of fear and confidence. To be able to hit the mean [by having just enough fear and just enough confidence] is to have the virtue of courage. . . . But he who exceeds in confidence has the vice of recklessness, while he who has too much fear and not enough confidence has the vice of cowardliness.

The mean where pleasure . . . is concerned is achieved by the virtue of temperance. But to go to excess is to have the vice of self-indulgence or lust, while to fall short is to have the vice of being austere or unfeeling. . . .

Or take the action of giving or receiving money. Here the mean is the virtue of generosity. . . . But the man who gives to excess and is deficient in receiving has the vice of being prodigal, while the man who is deficient in giving and excessive in taking has the vice of being stingy. . . .

With regard to how one spends money the mean is tastefulness, while the vice of being deficient in this respect is cheapness, and the vice of excess is vulgarity or ostentatiousness.

Or take the desire for the attention of others. The mean is self-confidence, while being excessive in this is the vice of vanity and being deficient is the vice of self-abasement.

There is also the desire to be honored and esteemed by others. Here the mean is the virtue of proper self-respect, while the excess is the vice of being overly-ambitious and the deficiency is the vice of lacking ambition. . . .

The feeling of anger can also be excessive, deficient, or moderate. The man who occupies the middle state is said to have the virtue of being even-tempered, while the one who exceeds in anger has the vice of being bad-tempered, and the one who is deficient in anger has the vice of being apathetic.

In telling the truth about oneself, the mean is the virtue of honesty, while exaggerating the truth is the vice of boastfulness, and understating the truth is the vice of false humility.

✓ QUICK REVIEW
Excellence in any field is achieved by hitting the mean and not by excess or deficiency. So being virtuous in our actions and feelings is achieved by hitting the mean as determined by reason and avoiding excess or deficiency in our actions and feelings.

 THINKING LIKE A PHILOSOPHER

Aristotle gives a list of several virtues and vices. Which of these virtues would you say you have at this point in your life? How would you describe each of those virtues? Which of Aristotle's virtues would you say you don't really have but would like to have? What would it mean to you if you had them? Which of his vices would you say you have at this point in your life? Have any of these prevented you from getting or being something you wanted? Which of your vices that do you most wish you didn't have?

As for being generally pleasant toward people, the mean is friendliness, while the vice of excess is being obsequious and the vice of being deficient is surliness. . . .

With respect to being entertaining to others, the mean is being witty, while going to excess is being a buffoon and being deficient is being boorish. . . .

In relation to the feeling of shame the mean is having self-esteem, while the vice of excess is being self-conscious and the vice of deficiency is being shameless.[43]

For Aristotle, then, a virtue is the ability to be reasonable in our actions, desires, and emotions, and to be reasonable is to act with moderation. We said earlier that human happiness required being able to act as reason tells us to act. We see now that this means that we must have virtue. For virtue is the ability to habitually act as our reason tells us to act. Developing virtue, then, is the key to achieving happiness.

We are not born with such virtues, Aristotle points out, but acquire them by training in our communities. In particular, we acquire them in youth by being trained repeatedly to respond to situations in a reasonable manner. As Aristotle puts it, we become virtuous by being trained to act virtuously in the appropriate situations until it becomes a habit. At first, acting virtuously is difficult, but when we have acquired the virtue, it becomes easy and satisfying:

As is the case with any skill, we acquire the virtues by first doing virtuous acts. We acquire a skill by practicing the activities involved in the skill. For example, we become builders by building, and we learn to play the harp by playing the harp. In the same way, we become just by doing just acts, temperate by doing temperate acts, and courageous by doing acts of courage. . . .

Both the moral virtues and the corresponding vices are developed or destroyed by similar kinds of actions, as is the case with all skills. It is by playing the harp that both good and bad harp players are produced [good players by repeatedly playing well, poor players by repeatedly playing poorly]. And the same is true of builders and all the rest: by building well they develop into good builders, and by building badly into bad builders. In fact, if this were not so they would not need a teacher and everyone would be born either good or bad at their trade. The same holds for the virtues. By what we do in our interactions with others we will develop into just persons or into unjust ones; and by the way we respond to danger, training ourselves to respond with fear or with confidence, we will become either cowardly or courageous. The same can be said of our appetites and feelings of anger: By responding in one way or another to these we will become either temperate and even-tempered or self-indulgent and ill-tempered. In short, acts of one kind produce character traits of the same kind. This is why we should make sure that our actions are of the proper kind: for our character will correspond to how we act. It makes no small difference, then, whether a person is trained in one way or another from his youth; it makes a very great difference, in fact, all the difference.

Not only are character traits developed and destroyed in the same way, they also manifest themselves in similar ways. This is something we can actually see with strength. Strength is produced by taking plenty of nourishment and doing plenty of exercise, and it is the man with strength, in turn, that is best able to do these things. It is the same with the virtues. By abstaining from pleasures we develop temperance, and it is the man with temperance that is best able to abstain from them. The same holds for courage: by habituating

THINKING LIKE A PHILOSOPHER

Identify a virtue or virtues that you learned at home. Aristotle claims that a virtue is learned when one is trained to repeatedly do the act of the virtue. For example, the virtue of courage is learned when one is forced to repeatedly do acts of courage until it becomes a habit. As far as you can remember, is this the way that you acquired the virtue or virtues that you were taught at home? Describe what you can remember of how you learned the virtue or virtues.

✓ QUICK REVIEW

Virtue is acquired by repeatedly being made to act virtuously until it becomes a habit; vices are acquired by repeatedly acting viciously until it becomes a habit. When a virtue is acquired, one is able to do virtuous acts and to feel pleasure in virtuous acts.

---

[43] Ibid., bk. 2, chs. 6, 7.

ourselves to disregard danger and to face it, we become courageous, and it is when we have become courageous that we are best able to face danger.

A test of the presence of a certain character trait is the pleasure or pain that accompanies our actions. The person who abstains from bodily pleasures and feels pleased at this, is temperate, while the person who feels pain at having to abstain is self-indulgent. And the person who stands his ground against fearful things and takes pleasure in this or at least is not pained, is courageous, while the man for whom this is painful is a coward.[44]

But can virtue theory help us deal with the specific moral issues we face? Let's consider the issue that we discussed earlier when examining other approaches to morality: sexual behavior. As Aristotle notes, our moral character is shaped through the actions we choose, and our character in turn influences the actions we choose. Through our actions, we shape the kind of person we gradually become, and the kind of person we are is, in turn, expressed through our actions. So to assess the morality of a behavior, we must look at the kind of character that the behavior produces, and the kind of character that such behavior expresses. If the behavior tends to produce a virtuous character and is the expression of a virtuous character, then it is morally right. If it produces a vicious character or is the expression of a vicious character, then it is morally wrong. Now consider how philosopher Janet Smith uses this approach to evaluate the moral quality of adultery:

The very importance of the attempt to live an ethical life lies in the fact that in acting the individual forms herself or himself either for the better or for the worse. One of the foremost questions to be asked by the moral agent in the decision to do an action is: What kind of person will I become if I do this act?

Let us now consider how the choice to commit adultery might reveal and affect one's moral character. . . .

If it is true . . . that adulterers can be said to have undesirable moral characteristics and/or that they are forming undesirable moral characters through their choice to commit adultery, this would be taken as an indication. . . . that adultery is a morally bad action. . . .

For an analysis in accord with an ethics of virtue, answers to the following questions would be useful: What sort of people generally commit adultery? Are they, for instance, honest, temperate, kind, etc.?. . . . Why do adulterers choose to have sex with people other than their spouses? Are their reasons selfish or unselfish ones? Do they seem to speak of their reasons for their choice honestly or do they seem to be rationalizing? What sort of lives have they been leading prior to the action that they choose; are they the sorts of lives that exhibit the characteristics we admire?

Most may agree that some true generalizations could be made about adulterers that would lead us to think that in general adultery is not compatible with the moral virtues that we admire. The reaction of the American public to the extramarital affairs of [clergyman] Jim Bakker and [politician] Gary Hart reveal well the widespread view that lying predictably accompanies the act of adultery and that adulterers are not to be trusted. Certainly, if someone told us that he or she wanted to be an honest, trustworthy, stable and kind individual with good family relationships, and wanted to know if an adulterous affair would conflict with this goal, we would have little hesitation in advising against adultery.[45]

 THINKING LIKE A PHILOSOPHER

Janet Smith suggests that people who are unfaithful in a committed relationship (adulterers) lack the virtues of being honest, temperate, kind, etc., and instead have the vices of dishonesty, untrustworthiness, and selfishness. You may not know many adulterers. But you may know friends or acquaintances who have "cheated" on their boyfriends or girlfriends. Based on your own experience of adulterers or of friends or acquaintances who have been unfaithful in a relationship, would you agree or disagree with Smith?

QUICK REVIEW
According to the virtue theory of Smith, one can evaluate the moral quality of sexual behaviors by asking whether those behaviors develop virtues or vices.

---

44 Ibid., bk. 2, chs. 1, 2, 3.
45 Janet Smith, "Moral Character and Abortion," in *Doing and Being*, ed. Janet Graf Haber (New York: Macmillan, 1993), 442–456.

At least in the hands of Janet Smith, virtue ethics implies a conservative view of adultery. According to Smith, adultery seems to be connected with several vices. She suggests that adultery seems to be something done by people who are dishonest, intemperate, disloyal, and selfish. Adultery, then, is an act in which these vices are expressed. Moreover, she suggests, adultery seems to encourage the development of these same vices. Adultery puts people into positions where they have strong incentives to lie to their spouses, to be self-indulgent, and to be disloyal to their spouses. Thus, adultery seems to further the development of these vices. Since adultery is an expression of vice and because it tends to develop these vices further, an ethic of virtue would condemn adultery.

However, it is important to keep in mind that Smith's argument merely shows that adultery is usually associated with vices. It is possible that in some cases adultery might not be associated with lying, for example. A virtue approach such as Smith's cannot show that any action is always wrong. It can show only that certain actions, such as adultery, are usually or generally wrong.

Love and Friendship

We have so far ignored a part of our moral lives that many people associate with virtue. It is a part that many philosophers, particularly Aristotle, believe is an essential component of living morally: the ability to love and befriend others. Aristotle, for example, argued that friendship, which he believed was based on love, is a kind of virtue that is essential to human life. Since love and friendship are central to a virtuous life, and they are topics that Aristotle felt were crucial parts of his theory of virtue, we briefly examine them here.

Aristotle argued that there is a kind of "friendship" that is based on the pleasure or utility one person provides for another. But such friendships are not friendships in a full sense. Friendship in the "full sense," he argued, is based on two people's mutual recognition of the goodness of the other. Such friends, he claims, are "other selves." Aristotle's discussion of friendship is as important and insightful for us today as when it was written:

> After discussing virtue, it is only natural to turn to a discussion of friendship, since friendship is a virtue or implies virtue, and is one of life's necessities. For without friends no one would choose to live, even if he had all other goods. . . .
>
> We can identify the main kinds of friendship in terms of what someone can be loved for. . . . People can be loved for any of three reasons: because they are good, because they give us pleasure, or because they are useful to us. . . . There are, then, these three reasons for friendship. We say of a friend that we ought to wish him to have what is good. But . . . there is friendship only when this wish is reciprocated. And we should also add "when it is recognized." For . . . how could we say two people are friends if they do not know their mutual feelings? To be friends, then, they must mutually recognize that each wishes good for the other, and each must wish good to the other for one of three reasons [because the other is good, or is pleasurable, or is useful]. . . .
>
> Now those who love each other for their usefulness do not love each other for themselves but because of what one gets from the other. The same is true of those who love for the sake of the pleasure they get from each other. . . . In either case, it is not the other person himself who is loved; instead what is

💬 THINKING LIKE A PHILOSOPHER

Aristotle distinguishes three kinds of friendships: those who love each other because each is useful to the other; those who love each other because each gives pleasure to the other; and those who love each other because each sees the good in the other. Describe friendships of each of these three kinds that you have had. During the friendship did you know the kind of friendship it was? What happened?

loved is the pleasure or utility that one gets from the other. So these friendships are not real friendships [in the full sense]. . . .

For the most part the friendships of young people seem to be based on pleasure; for young people often . . . seek mainly what gives them pleasure. . . . This is why they quickly become friends and quickly cease to be so; their friendships change when the one in whom they took pleasure changes, and pleasures change quickly. . . . This is why they fall in love and then out of love so quickly. . . . Still, people who love because of the pleasure they give each other want to spend their days and lives together; for this is how they can attain what they seek in their friendship.

Friendship in the full sense is the friendship of people who are good, and who are similar in virtue; for these want what is good for each other because of the good they see in each other, and they are each good themselves. Now those who wish good to their friend for their friend's own sake are real friends; for they are friends because of who they are, and not because of what one provides the other. Their friendship, therefore, lasts as long as they are good, and the goodness of a person is an enduring thing. Such friends . . . are generally also useful to each other and find pleasure in each other. . . . [However,] such friendships are rare because good people are rare . . . and they require time and familiarity. . . . Nor can they . . . be real friends until they have come to appreciate the good that is lovable in each, and each has come to trust the other. . . . These, then, are friends without qualification; the others are counted as friends only in a qualified sense due to their resemblance to these true friends.

Friendship seems to originate in a man's relationship to himself. For the defining characteristics of friendship seem to be present in a man's relationship to himself. For (1) a friend is one who wishes good to his friend and who does what is good or seems good for his friend; (2) a friend wishes his friend to exist and live for his friend's own sake . . .; (3) Some say a friend is one with whom one spends time; (4) others say a friend is one who has the same tastes; (5) and that he is someone who grieves and rejoices with his friend. . . . Now each of these is found in the good man's relation to himself . . . For (1) he wishes for himself what is good or seems good and he does what is good . . . for himself . . .; and (2) he wishes that he himself will continue to exist and live. . . . And (3) he . . . enjoys spending time with himself since the memories of his past and his hopes for the future are good, and therefore pleasant. . . . (5) He grieves and rejoices . . . with himself; and (4) whatever he finds painful or pleasant to himself at one time, is painful or pleasant to himself at other times. . . . So since each of these characteristics are found in the good man's relationship to himself, he is related to his friend as to himself, and treats his friend as another self . . . so friendship is like one's love for oneself.[46]

THINKING LIKE A PHILOSOPHER

Aristotle describes "friendship in the full sense" as one in which each friend "is related to his friend as to himself," so he sees and treats his friend as if his friend is "another self." Have you ever had such a friendship? How would you describe it?

For Aristotle, love is central to friendship. In fact, he distinguishes the three types of friendship according to the three kinds of ways we can love a person. Yet Aristotle says very little about love itself. Just what is love? That notion obviously demands attention.

Modern philosophers who have studied love generally distinguish three types of love: *philia, eros,* and *agape. Philia* (a Greek word that gave us the name "Philadelphia," City of Brotherly Love) is the kind of brotherly love that is involved in friendship as Aristotle discussed it. It is the kind of deep mutual liking that friends or family members can have for one another. *Eros,* on the other hand, is the kind of intensely passionate attraction that one may feel toward a person or

---

46 Aristotle, *Nichomachean Ethics,* excerpts from bk. 9, chs. 1, 2, 3, and 4, and bk. 10, ch. 4. This translation © 2006 by Manuel Velasquez.

even toward a thing. One may have *eros* toward music or beauty or something else toward which one feels intensely passionate and attracted. Finally, *agape* refers to the kind of love that, in Christianity at least, God has toward people. It is also the kind of love that a person can have toward God and, by extension, that a Christian should have toward all human beings. Unlike *eros*, *agape* is not a passionate and intense attraction. And unlike *philia*, *agape* is not a response to something good, pleasurable, or useful in the beloved. Instead, *agape* is gratuitous: It is freely given. The Christian God loves (and the Christian should love) each person even when there seems to be nothing in the person that is good, pleasurable, or useful. In fact, God is not said to love people because they are good; instead, God's love *makes* people good: *Agape* is creative insofar as it creates goodness in the one who is loved.

But what is love itself? We can, of course, love many things: power, money, travel, animals, foods, art, people, and so on. Here we focus on love of one person for another person. When we have this kind of love—and maybe all kinds of love are like this—we have a strong, positive attitude toward the person's goodness or value. We see the person herself as good or valuable and respond with positive regard. But we have many kinds of strong, positive responses toward the good in people, including liking, respecting, and admiring. What more is love besides a strong, positive attitude toward a person's goodness?

One of the oldest answers to this question is based on Aristotle's suggestion that "a friend is one who wishes good to his friend and who does what is good or seems good for his friend . . . and wishes to spend time with his friend." That is, when I love you, I want you to flourish and to do well for your own sake (not for my sake), and I try to do what is good for you for your own sake (again, not for my sake). I want to be with you; I grieve when you grieve and rejoice when you rejoice. The philosopher Gabrielle Taylor tries to summarize these ideas:

> If x loves y, then x wants to benefit and be with y, etc., and he has these wants because he believes y has some determinate characteristics in virtue of which he thinks it worthwhile to benefit and be with y.[47]

To love a person, in this view, is to respond positively to something good or worthwhile in that person. But it also implies the desire to promote that person's well-being, to be with that person, and empathize with that person. On this view, then, love is a kind of relationship in which a person sees good in another and responds by doing good to that person, trying to be with that person, and so on.

However, critics of this "relationship view" of love say that it leaves out an essential aspect of love: Love is first and primarily an emotion, not a relationship. That is, love is an emotion that arises in you as a response to seeing your loved one as attractive and valuable in herself. The emotion of love is, in part, the pleasure that you feel at the thought of this unique person's existence and well-being. It is also, in part, the pain you would experience at the thought of her nonexistence or failure to do or be well. The emotion of love also includes feeling a heightened awareness and perception of the person, an attraction toward and cherishing of the person, and a desire to be with the person. From this complex emotion, this view holds, arises the sort of response that the relationship view emphasizes: doing good to the other, trying to be with the other, and so on. However, these responses are consequences of the emotion of love, not its essence.

---

47   Gabrielle Taylor, "Love," *Proceedings of the Aristotelian Society* 76 (1976): 157.

Yet another group of philosophers argues that this "emotion view" of love still leaves out a central feature of love: to love is to form a bond, a close union with another person. What kind of union is involved in love? Aristotle said that a friend is "another self." So, one way of understanding the union of lovers is as a kind of identification with the other's interests and concerns. The interests and concerns of the person I love become my interests and concerns. But another way of understanding the union of lovers is to see it as the creation of a totally new entity, a new "we." The "we" that lovers form, philosopher Robert Solomon says, is a kind of new shared identity, a "fusion of two souls" in which each lover defines who he or she is in terms of the shared relationship. "A theory of love," he writes, "is primarily a theory of the . . . shared self, a self mutually defined and possessed by two people."[48] However, opponents say that this view of the union of love goes too far because although lovers do become close, they do not fuse together into some new entity. Moreover, when love becomes this tight of a union, the lovers can lose their own identity and freedom. Love then becomes a loss of self and a kind of slavery instead of being liberating and an enhancement of who one is.

QUICK REVIEW
The union view of love says it is a kind of union between two persons; one version sees this union as identifying with the other's interests and concerns; another version says it is a "fusion of two souls" that forms a new shared identity that is a new entity, a "we."

A fourth theory of love criticizes the view that love is a response to the goodness of the loved one. This "creative" theory of love says that all love is like *agape:* It *creates* goodness in the one who is loved; it makes the loved one better. Does this refer to the fact that "love is blind," that lovers sometimes see in loved ones those qualities they want to see and fail to see their unpleasant qualities? This can't be the right understanding of the creative power of love, for this is really the creation of an irrational delusion. Instead, the true creative power of love shows itself in the way that a lover sees the potential good in another and brings it out of her. If I love you, for example, I expect and believe that you will be a good person, and seeing this, you live up to my expectation. I may also believe, and encourage you to believe, that you will succeed in what you do, and seeing this, you actually do succeed.

THINKING LIKE A PHILOSOPHER

The textbook describes four views of what love is. Based on the love relationships that you have had, which of the four views seems closest to the truth about what love is, at least as you have experienced it? Explain how your relationships or relationship exhibited the qualities that view says are the qualities that love has.

QUICK REVIEW
The creative view of love says love is not a response to the goodness already present in another person but that it creates goodness in the other person so that the loved one becomes better; love sees the potential good in another and brings it out of her.

Obviously, there are many different views on the nature of love. But perhaps they are not all wrong. It is possible, in fact, to see each of the many different views as shedding light on one of love's many different aspects. From this perspective, love is a complex reality that consists of many different aspects, each of which is emphasized by one or more of the theories. Love, then, can be seen as a relationship in which one responds to the goodness seen in another by wanting and doing what is good for her for her own sake. It will include an emotion that feels pleasure in the beloved and that feels a heightened awareness and attraction for the beloved. It can become a kind of union—a "we"—that is formed together with the beloved. And it can be creative of goodness in the beloved. Can love be all of these things? Can it be more? You must decide the answer to these questions by looking closely at your own experience of love and of the friendships that love has created in your own life.

Male and Female Ethics?

Although Aristotle (and most of his followers today) believed that love is an important part of a life of virtue, he did not put love at the center of morality. Neither did he claim that friendship and love are the most important of the virtues. But recently,

---

[48] Robert Solomon, *About Love: Reinventing Romance for Our Times* (New York: Simon & Schuster, 1988), 24.

some philosophers have argued that something akin to love should lie at the center of an adequate theory of ethics. This view of ethics developed in the context of studying whether men and women view morality in a different way. We end this exploration of virtue ethics by looking at a feminist approach to virtue ethics that makes caring and concern for others part of the very foundations of ethics.

Philosophers (usually male ones) have in the past claimed that men and women have different ethics. Often they accompany their claim with the suggestion that the ethics of women is somehow inferior to that of men. Understandably and justifiably, these claims and suggestions have angered women.

Recently, however, several female philosophers have also begun to suggest that men and women have different moralities. But they see the moralities of women are equal to or superior to those of men. In particular, they argued, men tend to focus on what an ethics of principles emphasizes, whereas women tend to focus on what an ethics of virtue emphasizes.

© Frazer Harrison / Getty Images

Carol Gilligan. The psychologist Carol Gilligan was one of the first women to suggest that men and women approach ethics differently. She is also one of the first to suggest that the ethics of women is not inferior to that of men. Gilligan is the author of the important book *In a Different Voice: Women's Conception of Self and Morality.* There she argued against the views of Lawrence Kohlberg, a psychologist whose work seems to imply that women, on average, are less morally developed than men are.

Kohlberg argued that people's moral abilities develop through stages just as their physical abilities do. For example, a child must crawl before he or she walks, and must walk before he or she runs. He called the major stages of moral development the preconventional, conventional, and postconventional levels. Parents and authority figures tell children at the first or preconventional level what is right and what is wrong. Children obey to avoid punishment. So at the preconventional level of moral development, morality focuses on the self. It is a matter of following authority and avoiding punishment. As the child matures into adolescence, he or she develops attachments and loyalties to groups: family, friends, church, and nation. These become the basis of the next level, the conventional level of morality. At the conventional level, morality is based on being accepted by those in one's groups and on following their conventional moral standards and rules. If the adolescent continues to mature morally, he or she will begin to examine and question the conventional moral standards absorbed earlier in life. The adolescent may ask whether these standards serve everyone's welfare, whether they are just, and whether they respect people's human rights. This signals the entry into the postconventional level of morality. At the postconventional level morality is based on universal moral principles of human welfare, justice, and rights.

However, not everyone develops through all the levels. Some people remain at the preconventional level all their lives. Others make it to the conventional level

Carol Gilligan:
"Moral development for a woman is marked by progress toward more adequate ways of caring for herself and others."

✓ QUICK REVIEW
Kohlberg argued that moral development moves through three levels: a preconventional level, focused on the self; a conventional level, focused on being accepted by a group and accepting the group's conventional morality; and a postconventional level, focused on moral principles. The postconventional level of moral principles is the most advanced form of morality. Most women seemed to Kohlberg to remain at the less advanced conventional level.

and then go no further. And only a minority of people seem to make it all the way to the most advanced, postconventional level. Significantly, more men than women seem to make it to Kohlberg's postconventional level. Women seem to remain often at the conventional level, where attachments and loyalties to family, friends, and others are important. This implies, according to Kohlberg's theory, that by and large women are less morally developed than men are.

Enter Carol Gilligan. Gilligan pointed out a significant flaw in Kohlberg's work: He had developed his stages of moral development by studying mostly men. So Gilligan argued that his theory really describes how men's morality develops and not how women's morality develops. Women may not advance to Kohlberg's third level of male development. But this is because they advance to a third level of female development that Kohlberg's theory ignores. Based on her own studies of women, Gilligan argued that women's morality is different from men's. Women's morality centers on caring and being responsible for others with whom they are involved in personal and loving relationships. Women end up in Kohlberg's conventional level because that is the only level that takes relationships and personal attachments into account. But women develop by showing increasing maturity in how they balance the needs of the self with their responsibilities to others. Her research, Gilligan claimed:

> reveals the existence of a distinct moral language whose evolution informs the sequence of women's development. This is the language of selfishness and responsibility, which defines the moral problem as one of obligation to exercise care and avoid hurt. The infliction of hurt is considered selfish and immoral in its reflection of unconcern, while the expression of care is seen as the fulfillment of moral responsibility. The reiterative use of the language of selfishness and responsibility and the underlying moral orientation it reflects sets the women apart from the men whom Kohlberg studied and may be seen as the critical reason for their failure to develop within the constraints of his system. [49]

Gilligan argued that moral development for a woman is marked by progress toward more adequate ways of caring for herself and for others. Women move through three levels of development. These are (1) a level at which they are overly devoted to caring for themselves, (2) a level at which they are overly devoted to caring for others, and (3) a level at which they achieve a balance between caring for self and caring for others.

Gilligan claimed that at the earliest or preconventional level of moral development, the female child sees morality as a matter of taking care of herself. As the girl moves to a second or conventional level of moral development, she comes to accept the conventional standards and norms of her friends and family. These typically emphasize that, as a woman, she should devote herself to loving and caring for others even if this means neglecting her own needs. The woman at the conventional level sees morality in terms of her responsibility to maintain the relationships in which she is enmeshed and on which others depend. If she continues to develop, she will enter a third, postconventional level of moral development. At this third level, she will begin to question the conventional standards she had earlier accepted. She will

49 Carol Gilligan, "In a Different Voice: Women's Conceptions of Self and of Morality," in *The Future of Difference*, ed. Hester Eisenstein and Alice Jardine (New Brunswick, NJ: Rutgers University Press, 1985).

QUICK REVIEW

Gilligan argued that Kohlberg's levels are those through which men's morality develops, but women's morality develops through a different sequence of levels based on caring for oneself and for others. Because women are always focused on caring relationships, they seem to always be stuck in Kohlberg's second level, but in reality they are developing through different levels of caring.

QUICK REVIEW

Gilligan claims that moral development in women moves through (1) a level in which they are overly devoted to caring for themselves, (2) a level in which they are overly devoted to caring for others, and (3) a level in which they balance caring for others and for themselves.

THINKING LIKE A PHILOSOPHER

Both Kohlberg and Noddings argue that people pass through three levels as they mature and as their moral thinking develops: the preconventional, the conventional, and the postconventional levels. What level do you think you are at? Explain why you think you are at that level. Think of people or friends that you think are at the other two levels. Explain why you think they are at the other two levels.

become critical of those standards that require her to sacrifice her own needs to take care of others. She will come to see herself as a self-in-relation-to-others and will see that caring for others is deeply related to and depends upon her caring for herself. She now sees morality in terms of maintaining relationships through caring for herself-in-relation-to-others.

According to Gilligan, this female perspective on morality is very different from the way men typically look at morality. When faced with moral decisions, women focus on the *relationships* of the people involved. They see morality as a matter of taking care of the people in these loving relationships. When men face moral decisions, they focus on the *individuals* involved. They see morality as a matter of following the moral rules or principles that apply to these individuals. Women focus on personal relationships; men focus on impartial rules and principles. In short, women exhibit the personal virtues of caring and being in relationships. But men exhibit a more impersonal focus on moral rules, principles, and obligations.

But though women tend to approach ethics differently from men, Gilligan has argued, a woman's approach to ethics is not inferior. Caring and responsibility for sustaining relationships are virtues that society greatly needs. Society, she suggests, tends to disconnect people and to promote competition, **individualism,** separation, and independence. A male emphasis on impersonal rules and principles further encourages these tendencies. Moreover, these tendencies have broken down our communities and our networks of relationships. We need the virtues of caring and responsibility for others. Or we risk becoming a society of isolated individuals who guard their individual rights but are lonely, unattached, unloving, and uncaring.

Nel Noddings. Philosopher Nel Noddings has gone further than Gilligan in developing a female ethic based on the virtue of caring. In her book *Caring: A Feminine Approach to Ethics and Moral Education,* she develops an ethic of care. Noddings holds that the "feminine" virtue of caring is more fundamental than the "masculine" focus on principles:

> One might say that ethics has been discussed largely in the language of the father: in principles and propositions, in terms such as justification, fairness, justice. The mother's voice has been silent. Human caring and the memory of caring and being cared for, which I shall argue form the foundation of ethical response, have not received attention except as outcomes of ethical behavior.[50]

Noddings argues that ethics is about specific individuals in actual encounters with other specific individuals. Ethics is not about abstract principles of justice and rights. The ethical person is the person who cares for another specific individual during an actual encounter with that unique person. The ethical person manifests her concern for that specific individual in concrete, loving deeds. In such relationships, the caring person does not consult abstract principles or universal rules that somehow fit all humanity. Nor does she reason about morality as if it were a geometry problem. Instead, she consults her immediate "feelings, needs, impressions, and . . . sense of personal ideal" and responds to the unique individual with whom she is dealing.

Noddings claims that as we grow we acquire a "growing store of memories of both caring and being cared for," and develop the capacity to care for others as well as for oneself. Gradually, the growing person forms a picture of her ideal self as a caring person. She finds the freedom to choose whether to live up to this ideal picture of herself.

---

[50] Nel Noddings, *Caring: A Feminine Approach to Ethics and Moral Education* (Berkeley: University of California Press, 1984), 1.

QUICK REVIEW
Gilligan concludes that for women, morality is focused on caring for others and maintaining personal relationships, whereas for men, morality consists of following impersonal rules and principles.

MindTap To read more from Nel Noddings, read from *Starting at Home: Caring and Social Policy* by clicking the link in the MindTap Reader or going to the Questia Readings folder in MindTap.

QUICK REVIEW
Noddings argues that a feminine ethic based on the virtue of caring for specific individuals in personal relationships is superior to a male ethic based on abstract principles of justice and rights.

QUICK REVIEW
According to Noddings, ethical behavior consists of feeling caring toward others and choosing to act on this feeling, motivated by the desire to live up to the ideal of being a caring person.

Ethical behavior arises when one feels caring for another person and freely chooses to act on this feeling motivated by the desire to live up to the ideal of being a caring person. She writes: "The source of ethical behavior is, then, in twin sentiments—one that feels directly for the other and one that feels for and with the best self, who may accept and sustain the initial feeling rather than reject it."[51]

Carol Gilligan and Nel Noddings have recently tempered their views. Both now agree that men as well as women are capable of approaching morality from the perspective of caring. Both also agree that women as well as men may approach morality in terms of universal moral principles. However, women see things in terms of the virtue of caring more instinctively than do men, who in turn are more likely to appeal to moral rules and principles.[52]

Criticisms. But a crucial question is this: Is it good that women focus on the moral virtue of caring whereas men focus on impersonal moral rules and principles? Some philosophers have argued that it is not. Our culture has traditionally said that women are "by nature" good at caring for others. Consequently it has relegated that job to women as mothers, wives, lovers, nurses, and schoolteachers. Thus, Gilligan and Noddings are indirectly encouraging this traditional view of women. And they give men more justification for avoiding the caring tasks that could enrich their lives and personalities. For example, the lives of fathers could be enriched by their spending more time nurturing and caring for their children. But Gilligan and Noddings imply that this is not a task for men, but for women.

Other philosophers have criticized the very idea of an ethics based on caring for specific individuals with whom we have personal relationships. Such an ethics seems too narrow to encompass all our moral concerns. Clearly, we are personally related to only a few people. Through modern technology, however, our actions affect many more people than those with whom we can have personal relationships. For example, the environmental pollution that we produce with our machines and products can harm people far distant from us in time and space. Yet we will never know most of these people and never have a personal relationship with them. If ethics is only a matter of caring for those with whom we have concrete personal relationships, then ethics will not reach very far. It will have nothing to say, for example, about the wrongness of harming unknown others through environmental pollution.

The jury is still out in the case of the feminist ethic of care. This approach to ethics is still relatively young and requires more exploration and discussion. We have discussed it here to see what a feminist theory of virtue might look like, a theory that places personal relationships, love, and caring at the heart of ethics.

Conclusions

Clearly, the virtue approach to ethics differs greatly from the principles approach that Mill, Kant, and others employ. The virtue approach, in fact, reminds us of several things that the rules approach neglects. First, as we have already noted, the virtue

---

ANALYZING THE READING

Gilligan and Noddings have argued that men tend to approach moral issues and moral decisions in a way that is different from the approach of women. Describe both the male and the female way of approaching and dealing with moral issues and decisions. Based on your experience, would you agree or disagree with Gilligan and Noddings? Explain why.

QUICK REVIEW
Gilligan and Noddings now agree that both men and women can approach morality either from a caring perspective or from universal moral principles, but women tend to deal with moral issues in terms of the caring relationships involved, whereas men tend to deal with them from a principle-based perspective.

QUICK REVIEW
Critics claim that an ethic of care merely reinforces sexist stereotypes of women that drive women into the "caring" professions and forces women to care for others whatever the costs because that is what they are good at. Other critics say that an ethic of care cannot deal with moral issues that involve people with whom we have no personal relationship.

---

[51] Ibid., 80.
[52] See Carol Gilligan, "Moral Orientation and Moral Development," in *Women and Moral Theory*, ed. Eva Feder Kittay and Diana T. Meyers (Totowa, NJ: Rowman & Littlefield, 1987), 19–33; see also the articles in *Mapping the Moral Domain*, ed. Carol Gilligan, Victoria Ward, and Jill McLean (Cambridge, MA: Center for the Study of Gender, Education, and Human Development, 1988).

approach emphasizes the character of the morally good person and the development of that character. The principles approach neglects character and focuses instead on one's duties and obligations. Yet character is undoubtedly a fundamental moral concern. Isn't each of us vitally concerned about the sort of person we are becoming? Doesn't each of us care about the sort of character we display? Isn't our character at the core of who we are, as well as at the center of how we relate to others?

Second, the virtue approach reminds us of the importance of community and early training, which the principles approach ignores. As Aristotle says, a person's character is developed by "training" and learning within communities. Such communities include family, church and school, and associations like gangs, corporations, and prisons. These all shape our character by the values they prize and the traits they encourage or discourage. Thus, the idea of community is critically important to virtue ethics, but it is largely ignored by the principles approach.

Third, this approach to ethics reminds us of the importance of our ideals about what people should be like and the virtues that the ideal person displays. These are exemplified by the examples of heroes and idols our society holds up and praises. The lives of morally exemplary people can illustrate virtue more clearly than anything else and can also inspire us to imitate them. Among such people are Jesus, Saint Theresa of Avila, Socrates, Joan of Arc, the Buddha, Mother Teresa, Mahatma Gandhi, Florence Nightingale, Martin Luther King, Jr., Rosa Parks, Malcolm X, Harriet Truman, and César Chávez. The lives of these and many others have inspired millions to cultivate the virtues they exhibited in their lives.

Fourth, the virtue approach encourages us to look closely at aspects of our moral lives that are almost ignored by a principles approach, such as friendship and love. Focusing on rights, obligations, moral rules, and moral principles tends to blind us to the roles that love, friendship, and other virtues play in our lives. Moreover, the virtue approach explores how character develops and evolves through a person's life. This helps us understand how virtues like caring and concern can be developmentally related to a person's progress through the various stages of life. And this helps us see how they can form the basis for an important approach to the ethical life, an approach that may be particularly attractive to women.

Because virtue theory provides such powerful insights into our moral lives, many philosophers today have embraced it. Many see it as better than an ethic of rules and principles, such as utilitarianism and Kantian ethics. For example, Alasdair MacIntyre has urged the adoption of virtue theory as the best way to understand the "narrative" of our moral lives:

> If human life is understood as a progress through harms and dangers, moral and physical, which someone may encounter and overcome in better and worse ways and with a greater or lesser measure of success, the virtues will find their place as those qualities the possession and exercise of which generally tend to success in this enterprise and the vices likewise as qualities which likewise tend to failure. Each human life will then embody a story whose shape and form will depend upon what is counted as a harm and danger and upon how success and failure, progress and its opposite, are understood and evaluated.[53]

But the virtue approach is not without its difficulties. The main problem that critics have raised about virtue ethics is that it does not help answer the kinds of moral questions that people most frequently ask. People seem to turn to ethics when they face situations in which they must decide what to do and the morality of

◯ QUICK REVIEW
The virtue approach to ethics emphasizes people's character, stresses that our communities shape our character, reminds us of the importance of moral exemplars, and calls our attention to important aspects of the moral life, such as love, friendship, caring, and concern.

---

[53] Alasdair MacIntyre, *After Virtue*, 135.

the alternatives is unclear. For example, an unmarried woman finds herself pregnant and asks herself, "Should I have an abortion?" Or a woman whose injured husband has been diagnosed as "brain dead" is asked in the hospital whether she wants to have his life-support system disconnected. In such situations, people ask themselves, "What should I do?" instead of "What should I be?" But virtue ethics does not directly address the question of what one should *do*. The woman considering an abortion and the one considering disconnecting her husband's life support are not helped by virtue theory. How will they be helped, for example, by the advice that the good person has the virtues of honesty, courage, compassion, and generosity? They don't want to know what kind of character they should develop but what they should do right now. There is a question about the morality of actions, not the morality of character. In situations such as these, an ethics of principle seems much more helpful than an ethics of virtue. An ethics of principle provides rules that can help us see which actions are moral and which are not.

QUICK REVIEW
Critics of virtue theory argue that it offers no guidance when people want to know what they should do, not what kind of person they should be.

PHILOSOPHY AT THE MOVIES

Watch *Iris* (2001), the true story of British writer and philosopher Iris Murdoch and her relationship with her husband, John Bayley. The movie traces her life from the time when she and John first meet and fall in love as young teachers to the period forty years later when Alzheimer's disease gradually robs her of her memory and leaves her completely dependent on John's care. Make a list of Iris Murdoch's and John Bayley's virtues and vices as portrayed in the movie. On which of these virtues does the movie place the highest value? Which do you think are most valuable? Are there any traits of Iris Murdoch that the movie portrays as virtues but that most people would portray as vices, or traits portrayed as vices that most would consider virtues?

7.6 Can Ethics Resolve Moral Quandaries?

Now that we have completed our overview of major ethical theories, we should ask this question: How should we use these theories in our own moral lives? Unfortunately, the answer to this question is not simple. As we have seen, all the theories have shortcomings. Yet each theory identifies factors that we should take into account when we make moral decisions. Utilitarianism tells us to consider the pleasures and pains our actions will cause. Natural law theory says to keep in mind the basic goods our nature prompts us to pursue. Kant reminds us of the obligations we believe all humans should live up to. He also points to the importance of treating people as ends and not as mere means. And Aristotle, Gilligan, and Noddings tell us of the importance of the virtues and vices our actions both express and develop. Thus, each theory focuses our attention on morally important aspects of the moral life that the other theories tend to ignore. If we want to make sure we take all the morally relevant features of our situation into account, we should assess our actions in the light of all the theories and not just of one of them.

 This, of course, complicates things because the theories may conflict with one another. Our lives sometimes place us in situations in which utilitarian theory may tell us to do one thing, while Kantian theory or virtue tells us to do something else. Such conflicts are unavoidable in a world like ours, where all situations are multi-faceted. In the real world, the situations we confront do not have a single or a few simple features. They present us with many complex characteristics and qualities, multiple relationships, and complicated histories. One theory will pick out a subset of these features and use them to decide what to do, while another will focus on

QUICK REVIEW
No single ethical theory can elucidate all aspects of all moral decisions, yet each identifies some of the ethical considerations involved in moral decisions. By using all the theories, we come to see all or most of the considerations we need to take into account when making moral decisions.

different features, and so may lead us to a different conclusion. This is a point that the American pragmatist philosopher John Dewey makes:

> In view of the part played by the actual conflict of . . . [moral theories] in moral situations and the genuine uncertainty which results as to what should be done, I am inclined to think that one cause for the inefficacy of moral philosophies has been that in their zeal for a unitary view they have oversimplified the moral life. The outcome is a gap between the tangled realities of practice and the abstract forms of theory. A moral philosophy which should frankly recognize the impossibility of reducing all the elements in moral situations to a single commensurable principle, which should recognize that each human being has to make the best adjustment he can among . . . [theories] which are genuinely disparate, would throw light upon the actual predicaments of conduct and help individuals in making a juster estimate of the force of each competing [theory].[54]

As Dewey suggests, we have to recognize that in real life our moral decisions can involve uncertainty because our moral principles can conflict with each other. But he suggests this does not mean that the different approaches to ethics are useless. When we face a moral issue, we can consider each of the theories in turn, and ask what each of them would say about throws on the issue. That will give us a full and informed understanding of all the factors that we should take into consideration when making moral decisions. But in the end, as Dewey notes, "each human being has to make the best adjustment he can" among these various theories. This means that we have to weigh and think about the various different factors identified by the theories. We need to decide which features of the situation seem most important or seem to carry the most weight. And then we must make our decision. The fundamental value of studying and understanding ethical thought is not to find a theory that will automatically make our decisions for us. Instead, the aim is to find conceptual tools and theoretical frameworks that are reasonable and that help us see what is morally important in human life. Ethics is the search for reasonable ethical values and moral principles that will help us make our own informed decisions in complex moral situations. Thus, while the study of ethical theories makes us aware of the many moral options available to us, each of us must make his or her own ultimate decisions.

We will look at two issues now to illustrate how the ethical theories can help identify the morally significant aspects of a moral issue. The two issues we will look at are important life and death moral issues that many of us are destined to face (or perhaps have already faced). These are the issues of euthanasia and abortion.

Abortion

Abortion is a moral issue that raises many questions about life and death. It raises questions about what a person is and when one becomes a person. It raises questions about the meaning of life that is just beginning. And it raises questions about the moral rights of women and the moral duties of men.

Abortion is the deliberate ending of a pregnancy before live birth. In 1973, the U.S. Supreme Court ruled in the case of *Roe v. Wade* that the Constitution guarantees each citizen a fundamental "right to privacy." And, it held, "the right of personal privacy includes the abortion decision, but this right is qualified and must be considered against important state interests in regulation." The Supreme Court ruling said government may not make laws restricting abortions performed during the first

---

54 John Dewey, "Three Independent Factors in Morals" [1930] in John Dewey, *The Later Works, 1925–1953*, vol. 5, ed. Jo Ann Boydston (Carbondale: Southern Illinois University Press, 1981–1989).

six months of pregnancy. But during the last three months of pregnancy, government "in promoting its interest in the potentiality of human life, may, if it chooses, regulate, and even proscribe, abortion except where it is necessary, in appropriate medical judgment, for the preservation of the life or health of the mother."

Although the Supreme Court settled the *legal* issue, the *moral* issue still remains. When, if ever, is it moral for a person to choose to have an abortion? The issue of abortion frequently raises conflicting feelings in the person faced with the situation. Consider the real case of this mother of three (anonymously named "Jane Doe") and the contradictory emotions and moral judgments that tear at her:

> We were sitting in a bar on Lexington Avenue when I told my husband I was pregnant. . . . [T]he news was greeted with shocked silence. . . . My husband talked about his plans for a career change in the next year, to stem the staleness that fourteen years with the same investment banking firm had brought him. A new baby would preclude that option. The timing wasn't right for me either. I had just taken on a full-time job. A new baby would put me right back in the nursery. . . . It was time for us, we tried to rationalize. There just wasn't room in our lives now for another baby. We both agreed. And agreed. And agreed.
>
> How could it be that I, who am so neurotic about life that I step over bugs rather than on them . . . could so arbitrarily decide that this life shouldn't be? "It's not a life," my husband had argued, more to convince himself than me. "It's a bunch of cells smaller than my fingernail." But any woman who has had children knows that certain feeling in her taut, swollen breasts, and the slight but constant ache in her uterus that signals the arrival of a life.
>
> When my name was called [at the abortion clinic], my body felt so heavy the nurse had to help me into the examining room. I waited for my husband to burst through the door and yell "stop," but of course he didn't.
>
> "You're going to feel a burning sensation now," [the doctor] said, injecting Novocaine into the neck of the womb. The pain was swift and severe, and I twisted to get away from him. He was hurting my baby, I reasoned. . . . "Stop," I cried. "Please stop." He shook his head, busy with his equipment. "It's too late to stop now," he said. "It'll just take a few more seconds."
>
> What good sports we women are. And how obedient. Physically the pain passed even before the hum of the machine signaled that the vacuuming of my uterus was completed, my baby sucked up like ashes after a cocktail party.[55]

QUICK REVIEW
Although the Supreme Court in 1973 ruled that state laws had to allow abortions in the first six months of pregnancy, the morality of abortion remains undecided. Many, including those who have had abortions, often have contradictory feelings about the ethics of having an abortion.

QUICK REVIEW
Some argue that the fetus is not a person with a right to life because it lacks certain mental traits, but critics respond that infants, retarded adults, and future generations also lack these traits yet have a right to life.

Clearly, Jane Doe's decision to have an abortion was an agonizing one. It was one filled with contradictory feelings and distressing uncertainties. We must certainly sympathize with her anguish and the anxious doubts she had about what she was doing even as she did it. But let us also ask the question that lay behind her anguish: Was this abortion morally justified?

Many people who say abortion is not wrong argue that the fetus is not a "person." Because only persons have a moral right to life, they conclude, the fetus does not have a moral right to life. For example, philosopher Mary Anne Warren asks us to imagine that an alien encountered new creatures on some planet. How would the alien know whether such creatures were mere animals that could be killed and eaten or were, instead,

ANALYZING THE READING

1. Warren claims that a being is a "person" with a moral right to life if and only if the being has the five "traits" that she lists (or has most of them). Put each of her five traits into your own words.

2. Imagine yourself in the position she suggests: You are an alien who has landed on a planet and want to know whether the creatures you see are persons with a moral right to life, or whether it is morally right to kill and eat them. Would the traits she lists enable you to make this decision? Why or why not?

---

55 From "Jane Doe, 'There Just Wasn't Room in Our Lives for Another Baby,'" *The New York Times*, May 14, 1976. Copyright © 1976 by the New York Times Co. Reprinted by permission of the author.

persons with a moral right to life? She argues that a creature is a person only if it exhibits five traits:

> I suggest that the traits which are most central to the concept of personhood, or humanity in the moral sense, are, very roughly, the following:
>
> 1. Consciousness (of objects and events external and/or internal to the being), and in particular the capacity to feel pain;
> 2. Reasoning (the *developed* capacity to solve new and relatively complex problems);
> 3. Self-motivated activity (activity which is relatively independent of either genetic or direct external control);
> 4. The capacity to communicate, by whatever means, messages of an indefinite variety of types, that is, not just with an indefinite number of possible contents, but on indefinitely many possible topics;
> 5. The presence of self-concepts, and self-awareness, either individual or racial, or both.
>
> We needn't suppose that an entity must have *all* of these attributes to be properly considered a person.... All we need to claim, to demonstrate that a fetus is not a person, is that any being which satisfies *none* of (1)–(5) is certainly not a person.[56]

Fetuses do not have any of the five traits Warren lists. So she concludes, "a fetus is a human being which is not yet a person, and which therefore cannot coherently be said to have full moral rights." This view is similar to the suggestion of Jane Doe's husband that the fetus is "just a bunch of cells." But critics have objected to this type of argument by pointing out that many of those we see as full persons do not have Warren's five traits. These include infants, retarded adults, the mentally ill, and future generations. Some lack one or two of Warren's required traits, and some have none of them. Yet infants, retarded adults, and future generations, critics claim, clearly have a moral right to life. So the criteria she suggests must be mistaken. Yet neither is it clear that we can prove that fetuses *are* persons. Like Jane Doe, we are left with the troubling uncertainties that the fetus may be a human "life" and "a baby," yet perhaps it might not be. Many philosophers have concluded that the issue of abortion can't be decided by arguments about whether a fetus is or is not a person.

A Kantian Approach. Although the arguments over the "personhood" of the fetus have been inconclusive, there are other ways of approaching the morality of abortion. British philosopher Richard Hare argues that a Kantian approach to ethics, summarized by the Golden Rule, shows abortion is generally immoral:

> [T]he Christian "Golden Rule" [and] the Kantian Categorical Imperative [provide the same type of argument].... [But] I shall use that form of the argument which rests on the Golden Rule that we should do to others as we wish them to do to us.
>
> It is a logical extension of this form of argument to say that we should do to others what *we are glad was* done to us. Two (surely readily admissible) changes are involved here. The first is a mere difference in the two tenses which cannot be morally relevant. Instead of saying that we should do to others as we wish

ANALYZING THE READING

Hare uses a version of the Golden Rule to show that abortion is usually morally wrong. What version of the Golden Rule does he use? Explain how that version of the Golden Rule shows that it is wrong "to terminate any pregnancy which will result in the birth of a person having a life like ours." Explain why this conclusion does not show that all abortions are morally wrong. Do you agree with Hare's conclusion? Why?

---

[56] Mary Anne Warren, "On the Moral and Legal Status of Abortion," *The Monist*, vol. 57 (1973), no. 4: 100.

them (in the future) to do to us, we say that we should do to others as we wish that they had done to us (in the past). The second is a change from the hypothetical to the actual; instead of saying that we should do to others as we wish that they had done to us, we say that we should do to others as we are glad that they did to us. I cannot see that this could make any difference to the spirit of the injunction. . . .

The application of this injunction to the problem of abortion is obvious. If we are glad that nobody terminated the pregnancy that resulted in our birth, then we are enjoined not, *ceteris paribus*, to terminate any pregnancy which will result in the birth of a person having a life like ours.[57]

QUICK REVIEW
Hare claims that because we should do to others what we are glad was done to us, we should not abort a fetus that would have a life like ours if we are glad we were not aborted.

This kind of Kantian approach reaches what we can call a "conservative" position on abortion. It allows aborting a mentally defective fetus that would not have a life like ours. But it would condemn having an abortion for the sake of one's career, for example.

A Utilitarian Approach. However, many utilitarians propose a different approach to abortion. Some have argued that abortion is not morally wrong. They have appealed to the principle that any action that, on balance, has better consequences than the alternatives is morally permissible. Since abortion sometimes has better consequences than any other alterative, they argue, it is sometimes morally justified. Among the consequences that might justify an abortion they have suggested are avoiding financial burdens, avoiding disgrace, or avoiding the birth of a defective infant. But utilitarians are quick to point out that we should take into account all the consequences of our actions, including the effects on our future behavior. For example, philosopher Jane English argues that once the fetus comes to look like a person, killing it will lessen the respect we have for persons in general. At that point, then, it would be wrong to abort the fetus:

QUICK REVIEW
Utilitarians argue that abortion is justified when it has better consequences than the alternatives.

> Even if a fetus is not a person, abortion is not always permissible, because of the resemblance of a fetus to a person [and the bad consequences that killing such person-like creatures would have on our behaviors toward persons]. . . . [So] it would be wrong for a woman who is seven months pregnant to have an abortion just to avoid having to postpone a trip to Europe. In the early months of pregnancy when the fetus hardly resembles a baby at all, then, abortion is permissible whenever it is in the interests of the pregnant woman or her family. The reasons would only need to outweigh the pain and inconvenience of the abortion itself. In the middle months when the fetus comes to resemble a person, abortion would be justifiable only when the continuation of the pregnancy of the birth of the child would cause harm—physical, psychological, economic or social—to the woman. In the later months of pregnancy, even on our current assumption that a fetus is not a person, abortion seems to be wrong except to save a woman from significant injury or death.[58]

MindTap To read more from Jane English and other authors in *The Ethics of Abortion*, click the link in the MindTap Reader or go to the Questia Readings folder in MindTap.

QUICK REVIEW
English, a utilitarian, claims that it is wrong to abort a fetus in the late months of pregnancy—when it looks like a person—because doing so lessens the respect we have for persons in general.

The utilitarian argument of Jane English comes to the conclusion that the Supreme Court was right to prohibit abortions only in the last three months of pregnancy. Moreover, her utilitarian argument would perhaps imply that the abortion decision of Jane Doe was justified. Yet can we be certain that the consequences of an abortion are better than the consequences of having allowed the fetus to be born? Can we know that the future life of a fetus will produce less happiness than the happiness produced by aborting it?

---

[57] R. M. Hare, "Abortion and the Golden Rule," *Philosophy & Public Affairs* 4, no. 3 (Spring 1975): 207.
[58] Jane English, "Abortion and the Concept of a Person," in *The Ethics of Abortion*, ed. R. M. Baird and S. E. Rosenbaum (Buffalo, NY: Prometheus, 1989), 83–92.

The Value of a Future Life Approach. Another approach to abortion has some similarities with natural law theory. This is the approach proposed by philosopher Don Marquis. Marquis begins by pointing out that killing an adult human being is morally wrong. He then asks: Why do we see killing an adult as wrong? He answers that it is wrong because it deprives one of a fundamental good: one's own future life with all its experiences, activities, projects, and enjoyments. He then argues that since it is wrong to deprive an adult of this good, it must be equally wrong to deprive a fetus of that same good:

> [W]e can start from the following unproblematic assumption concerning our own case: it is wrong to kill us. Why is it wrong?. . . . The loss of one's life deprives one of all the experiences, activities, projects, and enjoyments that would otherwise have constituted one's future. . . . Therefore, when I die, I am deprived of all of the value of my future. Inflicting this loss on me is ultimately what makes killing me wrong. . . . The claim that the primary wrong-making feature of a killing is the loss to the victim of the value of its future has obvious consequences for the [15] ethics of abortion. The future of a standard fetus includes a set of experiences, projects, activities, and such which are identical with the futures of adult human beings and are identical with the futures of young children. Since the reason that is sufficient to explain why it is wrong to kill human beings after the time of birth is a reason that also applies to fetuses, it follows that abortion is prima facie seriously morally wrong.[59]

ANALYZING THE READING

Marquis argues that abortion is wrong for the same reason that we feel killing an adult is wrong, that is, it deprives the victim of the value that their future life would have. Critics say his argument "by analogy" is mistaken. Put Marquis' argument into the logical form of an argument by analogy (Chapter 4, Section 4.2). Do you agree that Marquis' argument by analogy is flawed?

Marquis' argument is an argument by analogy. Critics have argued that his analogy is mistaken. Adult humans can be said to have a future that is "theirs" because they have planned that future themselves and have some control over that future. Fetuses, obviously, cannot think and so there is no future that they have planned for themselves or that they can control. So, critics claim, fetuses do not have a future that is "theirs" as adults do, so killing them takes nothing from them that was "theirs." Marquis' argument has been widely debated. But you will have to judge for yourself whether it is acceptable.

Virtue Theory's Approach. One last perspective on abortion that we can examine is an approach based on virtue theory. As we have seen, virtue theory can evaluate the morality of behavior by examining the kind of moral character that such behavior produces. If behavior produces virtue, then it is morally desirable; if it produces vices, then it is morally wanting. Notice how Janet Smith takes precisely this approach:

> The one characteristic that is nearly universal among women deciding to have abortions is that they are engaged in relationships that are not conducive to raising a child. . . .
> The relationships of women who have abortions seem characterized by instability, poor communication, and lack of true mutuality. Those involved in such relationships seem to be characterized by irresponsibility and confusion about what they really want—which results in them being dishonest both with themselves and with their partners. . . . Studies

---

59   Don Marquis, "Why Abortion Is Immoral," *The Journal of Philosophy,* vol. 86, no. 4 (April 1989), 183–202. Excerpts (176 words) from 189, 190, and 192.

show that the women having abortions . . . display carelessness and indifference in their use of contraception. . . . These women seem not to have much self-knowledge, nor do they seem to be self-determining—they seem to be "letting things happen" that, were they reflective and responsible individuals, they might not accept as actions for themselves. . . . They . . . characterize abortion and indeed their own decision as taking a human life. If, then, it is a virtue to act in accord with one's principles, many of the women having abortions seem not to have this virtue and are acting in a way that will not advance their possession of it.

An ethics of virtue assesses actions by the type of character that produces and chooses these actions. Abortion, in the eyes of this interpreter, does not fare well as a moral action, according to this analysis.[60]

QUICK REVIEW
Using virtue theory, Smith argues that abortion is wrong because it produces and is produced by a moral character characterized by the vices of irresponsibility, dishonesty, carelessness, indifference, and lack of principles.

From the perspective of an ethics of virtue as Smith understands virtue ethics, abortion does not appear to be a morally upright option. Abortion is wrong, she claims, because it produces a moral character characterized by vices. The vices it seems to produce include carelessness, irresponsibility, dishonesty, and lack of principles. Were any of these traits evident in the characters of Jane Doe and her husband? If not, then this would tend to undermine Smith's argument. But it is important to keep in mind, as Smith herself admits, that her argument shows only that certain vices are *usually* associated with abortion. It is always an open possibility that for some people, the traits generally associated with abortion will not accompany their decision to have an abortion.

Comparing Approaches. The various theories of ethics we have examined provide us with insight into different aspects of the morality of abortion. None of the theories by itself is adequate, for each is limited to a particular perspective on the ethics of abortion. Utilitarianism alerts us to the importance of reflecting on the good and bad consequences of choosing to have or to reject an abortion, both for ourselves and for society. Kant reminds us that it is important to ask what the significance of a fetus's future life is and whether we ourselves would value having such a life. The natural law focus on the value of a future life reminds us of the loss that abortion may involve. Virtue ethics reminds us of the importance of personal responsibility and integrity in choosing for or against abortion. These theories, then, reveal several significant considerations that we should consider when assessing abortion.

Yet these theories cannot decide the issue for you. They tell you only what you should consider when making up your own mind about the morality of abortion. In the end, it is you who must reflect on and weigh the importance of each of the considerations to which the moral theories point. And it is you who must decide which of these considerations seems the most reasonable and seems to carry the most weight.

Euthanasia

Literally, *euthanasia* means "good death." But the term today refers to knowingly taking the life of a person suffering from a painful and incurable disease, as long as the action is intended to be merciful. Often, we distinguish between active and passive euthanasia. The distinction (which some philosophers question) is based on the difference between killing someone and allowing someone

QUICK REVIEW
In passive euthanasia, a person is allowed to die from a disease without treatment that could prolong her life; in active euthanasia, something is done or given to the person that causes her death.

---

[60] Janet Smith, "Moral Character and Abortion," in *Doing and Being,* ed. Joram G. Haber (New York: Macmillan, 1993), 442–454.

© S. P. Rayner/iStockphoto.com

to die. In passive euthanasia, death is caused by the patient's disease, which is allowed to run its course without any treatment that might prolong the patient's life. In active euthanasia, the immediate cause of death is not the patient's disease but something that is done or given to the patient to cause his or her death, such as a lethal drug. To focus our discussion, consider this case:

On Sunday, June 21, 1992, Jennifer Cowart, age thirty-two, and her brother George Kowalski, age twenty-eight, traveled to Pensacola Beach, Florida, for a day of relaxation. At the end of the day, Jennifer and George were heading back to their vehicle when Jennifer noticed a go-kart track. The two entered the track, bought tickets, and began riding. Within one minute, Jennifer's go-kart bumped into one of the side guardrails, flipped on its side, and burst into flames. Jennifer was seat-belted in the go-kart and could not get out. George tried to run into the fire to save his sister, but the flames were too intense. Bystanders attempted to use a fire extinguisher, but it did little to lessen the inferno. Jennifer was trapped in the burning go-kart for two minutes when her seat belt finally burned through and she fell to the ground. George grabbed his sister and pulled her away from the fire. Jennifer was alive. She was lying on the asphalt alert, oriented, and coherent. She had suffered 3rd and 4th degree burns covering ninety-five percent of her body. She was suffering the worst pain imaginable. At the scene, Jennifer begged the rescue personnel to "let me die." Instead, Jennifer was flown to a burn center in Mobile, Alabama, where she remained for one year until she . . . died. Medical personnel described Jennifer as suffering from the most agonizing physical pain they had ever witnessed. They said there was no way to effectively alleviate Jennifer's pain without permanently sedating her, which would have resulted in death. Thus, this was not done. Jennifer was so badly burned that her two children (age nine and five) were not permitted to see her for the entire one-year period she was hospitalized. Jennifer was aware that she had lost her ears, nose, fingers, toes, and that she had very limited use of her legs and arms. She knew she would forever have problems with her kidneys, liver, lungs, and all other body organs. She knew that she was so badly disfigured that if she ever got out of the hospital and went to any public place that people would be frightened of her. . . . I could not stop asking the question: "Who gave the medical profession the authority to keep Jennifer alive under these conditions?" She had been begging to die, and her chance of survival was less than ten percent. Yet, the medical providers made the decision to perform heroic efforts to save her.[61]

Clearly, the author of this true account is not asking whether the doctors had the legal authority to keep Jennifer alive. The author is asking, instead, whether the doctors had a moral right to keep her alive. He is suggesting that perhaps the doctors should have allowed her to die without any treatment aimed at prolonging her life. Or perhaps he is suggesting that they should have attempted "permanently sedating her, which would have resulted in death." If her doctors allowed her to die without any life-prolonging treatment, that would be "passive euthanasia." But administering sedative drugs with the intention of causing her death would have been a form of "active euthanasia."

---

61 Martin Levin, "Physician-Assisted Suicide: Legality and Morality," accessed August 31, 2012, at http://www.levinlaw.com/news/2002/5/8/physician-assisted-suicide-legality-and-morality. Reprinted with the permission of the author.

Natural Law: Pro and Con. Whatever the legality of euthanasia might be, the moral question still remains: Is active euthanasia morally permissible? The conservative position on this question has been set out by many natural law ethicists, such as J. Gay-Williams:

> Every human being has a natural inclination to continue living. Our reflexes and responses fit us to fight attackers, flee wild animals, and dodge out of the way of trucks. In our daily lives we exercise the caution and care necessary to protect ourselves. Our bodies are similarly structured for survival. . . . Euthanasia does violence to this natural goal of survival. It is literally acting against nature because all the processes of nature are bent towards the end of bodily survival. . . .
>
> By reason alone, then, we can recognize that euthanasia sets us against our own nature. Furthermore, in doing so, euthanasia does violence to our dignity. Our dignity comes from seeking our ends. When one of our goals is survival, and actions are taken that eliminate that goal, then our natural dignity suffers. Unlike animals, we are conscious through reason of our nature and our ends. Euthanasia involves acting as if this dual nature—inclination towards survival and awareness of this as an end—did not exist. Thus, euthanasia denies our basic human character and requires that we regard ourselves or others as something less than fully human.[62]

QUICK REVIEW
Gay-Williams uses natural law ethics to argue that because we have a natural inclination toward life and because our dignity comes from seeking that toward which we have a natural inclination, it is wrong to destroy life through euthanasia.

The natural law position, then, argues that life is a fundamental human good whose inviolable value we can discover by reflecting on our natural inclinations. Because active euthanasia destroys this fundamental human good, it is immoral. Therefore, it would have been wrong for Jennifer's doctors to give her a large dose of sedation with the intention of causing her death.

Yet recall that natural law theory recognizes that a person's actions can sometimes have a "double effect." These are cases where the person's action has the effect of securing a basic human good, but also has the effect of destroying a basic human good. So one effect is good, the other is bad. We summarized Aquinas' analysis of the ethics of double effect in the following words:

> If an action has two effects, one good and one bad, the action is *not morally wrong* if: (1) one's intention aims at the good and not the bad effect, (2) the good effect can't be achieved without the bad effect, and (3) the good effect is proportional to the bad effect. "Proportional" here means that the good effect is of equal or greater value than the bad effect.

Natural law philosophers have used Aquinas' principle of double effect to justify passive euthanasia in cases like Jennifer Cowart's. In her case, relief from her intense suffering is a good, while the loss of her life is bad. Natural law philosophers have therefore argued as follows. So long as (1) Jennifer's doctors are not doing anything to her with the intention of causing her death, and (2) Jennifer's release from pain cannot be brought about without her death, and (3) the good of relief from such intense pain is proportional to the bad effect of her death, then allowing her to die without any life-prolonging treatment would not be wrong. In Jennifer's case, then, even Gay-Williams' conservative interpretation of natural law would allow Jennifer to die by passive euthanasia. Some natural law philosophers would even make a case for doing what the author of Jennifer's story suggests: "permanently sedating her, which would have resulted in death." They would argue that her doctors

---

[62] J. Gay-Williams, "The Wrongfulness of Euthanasia," in *Intervention and Reflection: Basic Issues in Medical Ethics,* ed. Ronald Munson (Belmont, CA: Wadsworth, 1979).

would have been justified in trying to relieve her pain even with such a large dose of sedation that it risked killing her. So long as her doctors intend only to relieve her pain and are not intending or trying to kill her, then it would not be wrong to give her a dose of sedation that carried an extremely high risk of killing her. Their argument would be: (1) In administering the large dose of sedation, Jennifer's doctors intend only to relieve her pain and are not giving her the sedation with the intention of killing her. (2) Jennifer's release from pain cannot be brought about without a dose of sedation that is also likely to have the effect of killing her. (3) The good of relieving her intense pain is proportional to the evil of risking her death.

But we have seen that natural law reasoning has some shortcomings. In particular, natural law does not make clear why we have a moral obligation to follow our natural inclinations. Perhaps a natural law ethicist could respond that we are obligated to follow our natural inclinations because these embody God's commands. Yet what light can such a divine command approach to euthanasia provide for the nonbeliever?

Utilitarianism: Pro and Con. Utilitarianism provides a different approach to euthanasia. Philosopher James Rachels expresses the utilitarian argument in favor of active euthanasia as follows:

> Terminal patients sometimes suffer pain so horrible that it can hardly be comprehended by those who have not actually experienced it. . . . The argument from mercy says: euthanasia is justified because it provides an end to that. . . .
>
> I want now to present a . . . version of the argument from mercy, which is inspired by utilitarianism. I believe that the following argument is sound and proves that active euthanasia can be justified:
>
> 1. If an action promotes the best interests of everyone concerned, and violates no one's rights, then that action is morally acceptable.
> 2. In at least some cases, active euthanasia promotes the best interests of everyone concerned and violates no one's rights.
> 3. Therefore, in at least some cases active euthanasia is morally acceptable.
>
> How can it be wrong to do an action that is merciful, that benefits everyone concerned, and that violates no one's rights?[63]

It is important to notice that Rachels qualifies his argument with the proviso that "no one's rights" should be violated by an act of euthanasia. Rachels wants to rule out the possibility of involuntary euthanasia. Involuntary euthanasia is euthanasia in which the patient does not consent to being put to death. Rachels believes that Kant's theory implies that a patient has the right

---

ANALYZING THE READING

The textbook suggests that the principle of double effect would allow Jennifer's doctors to use passive euthanasia to allow her to die, or even to give her so much sedation that it would have a very high risk of killing her. Suppose you agree with the principle of double effect. But suppose you think it is being used wrongly in Jennifer's situation by the textbook. Which of the three requirements of the principle of double effect could you argue was not being correctly used? Explain why.

✓ QUICK REVIEW

Rachels uses utilitarianism to argue that when euthanasia benefits everyone concerned by putting an end to a person's pain and suffering and violates no one's rights, it is morally justified.

ANALYZING THE READING

Rachels argues that utilitarianism would hold that active euthanasia is morally right so long as the patient consented to it. Suppose you were a rule utilitarian and you disagreed with Rachel's conclusion. How could a rule utilitarian argue that active euthanasia even with the patient's consent is morally wrong?

---

[63]   James Rachels, "More Impertinent Distinctions and a Defense of Active Euthanasia," in *Biomedical Ethics*, ed. Thomas A. Mappes and Jane S. Zembaty (New York: McGraw-Hill, 1981), 355–359.

to refuse to be put to death. So active euthanasia is not justified when it violates this right to refuse consent.

Obviously, Rachels disagrees with the natural law position on euthanasia. In Rachels' view, it would have been morally legitimate for a doctor to have put Jennifer to death. Yet, does the utilitarian argument ignore the broader consequences of euthanasia? In most cases, won't the death of a person inflict great grief, emotional pain, distress, and even economic deprivation on those who are left behind? Moreover, once we allow physicians to put to death those who request it, will physicians gradually lose their commitment to saving life? Will society move down a slippery slope toward allowing doctors to put to death anyone whose life society deems no longer valuable?

A Kantian Approach. Rachels holds that his conclusion is supported not only by utilitarianism but also by a Kantian approach to euthanasia. One problem with utilitarianism is that it assumes that only consequences matter when evaluating an action. Yet consequences can be extremely difficult to predict. A Kantian approach has the advantage that it does not rely on trying to predict the consequences:

> Kant argued that we should act only on rules that we are willing to have applied universally; that is, we should behave as we would be willing to have everyone behave. . . . If we would not be willing for the rule to be followed universally, then we should not follow it ourselves. Thus, if we are not willing for others to apply the rule to us, we ought not apply it to them.
>
> The application of all this to the question of euthanasia is fairly obvious. Each of us is going to die someday, although most of us do not know when or how. But suppose you were told that you would die in one of two ways, and you were asked to choose between them. First, you could die quietly, and without pain, from a fatal injection. Or second, you could choose to die of an affliction so painful that for several days before death you would be reduced to howling like a dog, with your family standing by helplessly, trying to comfort you, but going through its own psychological hell. It is hard to believe that any sane person, when confronted by these possibilities would choose to have a rule applied that would force upon him or her the second option. And if we would not want such a rule, which excludes euthanasia, applied to us, then we should not apply such a rule to others.[64]

ANALYZING THE READING

Rachels offers a Kantian argument to show that active euthanasia is morally right. Would Kant accept the argument Rachels offers or would he say that Rachels is not using his categorical imperative correctly? Explain.

QUICK REVIEW

Rachels also uses Kantian ethics to argue that because we would not be willing to live by a rule that forced us to suffer pain when we had a terminal illness instead of being put painlessly to death, it is wrong to apply such a rule to others.

This Kantian approach also implies that it would have been morally permissible to put Jennifer Cowart to death by means of active euthanasia. Yet we have seen that Rachels believes Kant's theory implies that active euthanasia requires informed consent. Yet does that proviso assume an ideal situation that is often absent in a hospital situation? A person hospitalized for a painful terminal illness may be drugged, depressed, and even subject to the subtle manipulations of his exhausted family. How realistic is it to expect that such a person would be able to make choices that are free and rational?

Comparing Views. The moral theories of natural law, utilitarianism, and Kantian ethics, then, do not agree on the subject of euthanasia. But this does not mean that the three approaches are useless. On the contrary, each approach again calls our attention to one or more of the factors that we must take into account to evaluate

---

[64] Ibid.

the morality of active euthanasia. Natural law reminds us that human life is a basic good with intrinsic value. It informs us that we should not take life without serious cause and without due consideration. The utilitarian argument of Rachels suggests that in some cases the evil of pain may override the value of the basic good of life. And Rachels' proviso reminds us of the key importance of securing a person's consent before administering euthanasia. Finally, the Kantian argument reminds us of our fundamental interdependence. What we may want others to do for us when we are in need, we should consider doing for those presently in need.

⚙️ thinking critically • Moral Reasoning

We said earlier that ethical theories do not automatically tell us what we should do in a specific situation or about a specific issue such as abortion. For one thing, the theories can provide conflicting advice. Moreover, each theory considers only one or a few of the morally important aspects of a situation, so each theory by itself provides an incomplete assessment of the situation. For these reasons, using the theories to help us make our moral decisions requires considering what each theory says, and trying to use the insights of all the theories.

But how do we go about doing this? What kind of reasoning or thinking is involved in making a conscientious moral decision? We can, of course, be sloppy in the way we make our moral decisions, for example, by making our decisions solely on the basis of our emotions. But how would we make a moral decision if we were conscientiously trying to do our best by making the best use of our reasoning and thinking abilities? We can summarize the process of reasoning that can lead up to a conscientious moral decision in five steps:

1. Recognizing that a situation raises an ethical issue.
2. Getting the relevant facts about the situation.
3. Identifying the options for responding to the situation.
4. Evaluating the ethics of each of the options.
5. Making a decision.

To understand these five steps, let us discuss them one by one.

1. *Recognizing that a situation raises an ethical issue.* Before we can even start to think about the ethical issues a situation raises, we need to recognize that such issues are present. We noted earlier that moral standards are those that deal with matters that involve harming or injuring others or oneself. Situations that raise ethical issues, then, will be those that involve serious harm or injury to others or to oneself. Such situations would include, for example, lying that has serious consequences for others or using street drugs to which we ourselves can become addicted. But not all injuries raise ethical issues (a painful medical operation, for example, might not raise any ethical issues). In addition a situation that raises an ethical issue is one in which the harm that is inflicted is the kind that potentially could violate our moral standards. This does not mean that we *know* the harm or injury violates our moral standards. It only means that we *suspect it could* violate our moral standards. The suspicion or feeling that harm that is being inflicted, or could be inflicted, may violate our moral standards signals that we face a situation that raises ethical issues and so requires closer ethical scrutiny.

2. *Getting the relevant facts about the situation.* In order to clarify whether an ethical issue is actually present in a situation we face, and to determine what the issue is, we must inform ourselves about the situation. We need to answer questions like these: What exactly is the harm that is involved and how certain are we that it will occur? Who is harmed and how many are harmed? Is there something special about those who are harmed (for example, have they committed a crime)? Who is inflicting the harm, is their action intentional, and what is their relationship to those whom

they are harming (for example, are there any promises, commitments, obligations, or family relationships between them)? How significant is the harm and how imminent is it? Are any benefits produced by the harm and if so, what are those benefits, how large are they, and who receives them? Are there any other morally relevant features of the situation; that is, are there any other facts that can influence or make a difference to the moral assessments we make about the situation?

3. *Identifying the options for responding to the situation.* When we are clear about the nature of the situation, we can turn to asking what others or we *could* do about the situation. This does not mean trying to figure out what others or we *should do* about the situation. Instead, it means identifying the many different things we *could do* to respond to, or deal with, the situation. What are the various courses of action that we could take to deal with the situation? What does each of these courses of action involve; that is, what are the probable consequences of each course of action?

4. *Evaluating the ethics of each of the options.* This is the point at which the ethical theories we have studied can and should enter into our moral reasoning. We ask how each of the courses of action available to us measures up to the moral principles advanced by the theories of ethics we have studied, in light of all the relevant facts. In particular, and given the facts we have, we ask:

    a. The utilitarian question: Which course of action will produce the most benefits and do the least harm?

    b. The Kantian questions: Which course of action treats everyone involved as ends and not merely as means, and which course of action would I be willing to have everyone adopt in any similar situation?

    c. The natural law question: Which course of action best respects the basic human goods of life, family, knowledge, and an orderly society?

    d. The virtue questions: Which course of action expresses a morally virtuous character or will tend to develop a morally virtuous character? Which course of action expresses a morally vicious character or will tend to develop such a character?

5. *Making a decision.* After considering what each of these theories says about each of the options available to us, we must choose that course of action that we believe is best supported by the theories. Sometimes, of course, the theories will conflict. In such cases, we must do our best to figure out which theory seems most relevant or germane to the kind of ethical issue that is involved, or which theory we believe should be given the greatest weight in the particular situation.

We should note that one of the most common mistakes people make in their moral reasoning is being inconsistent: failing to reach the same conclusions about cases that are the same in all relevant respects. When we are dealing with nonmoral matters, we generally recognize that if two things are the same in all relevant respects, then a judgment we make about one should also apply to the other. For example, if two apples are exactly alike in ripeness, sweetness, texture, size, shape, color, and everything else related to evaluating their commercial grade, then if one is judged to be "Grade A," the other should also be judged to be "Grade A." More generally: Consistency requires that two things should be treated the same when they are the same in all the relevant respects, that is, in all the respects that are relevant to the treatment in question.

Unfortunately, when we are reasoning about moral matters, we often fail to live up to the consistency requirement. We may reason, for example, to the conclusion that other people are behaving immorally when they lie about their experience on their job resumes. Yet when we (or a friend or family member) "exaggerate" our experience on our own job resume, we may tell ourselves that it is morally permissible for us to engage in that kind of "white lie." When we do this, we violate the consistency requirement unless there are relevant differences between our situation and the situation of those we condemned for falsifying their job resume. All reasoning should be consistent, and consistency in moral reasoning means at least that we must be willing to accept the consequences of making the same moral judgments about ourselves that we make about others who are in circumstances that are the same as ours in all the relevant respects. (Two sets of circumstances are the same in all the relevant respects when all those factors that have a bearing on the judgment that an action is right or wrong in one set of circumstances are also present in the other.)

We tend to violate the consistency requirement in our moral reasoning because we do not want to admit, even to ourselves, that we are guilty of the same wrongs that we attribute to others. In fact, we engage in a number of fallacious mental tricks to avoid reasoning to the conclusion that what we are doing or intend to do is immoral. We *use euphemisms* to convince ourselves that our situation does not raise ethical issues. Businessmen, for example, refer to firing people as "downsizing"; government officials refer to torture as "enhanced interrogation techniques"; politicians refer to lies as "misstatements" or "less than precise words." We *rationalize* the harms we inflict by telling ourselves that we do it in pursuit of a worthy cause. The president of a company, for example, may fraudulently deceive his stockholders by telling himself that he is doing it for the sake of his employees. We *diminish the magnitude of the harm* we do by comparing it to other larger evils. I may think, for example, that the office supplies I steal at work are inconsequential compared to what I have seen others do or compared to the wrongs I think the company has inflicted on me. We *dehumanize those we harm* so we can avoid seeing that we are injuring human beings like ourselves. For example, we may think of the employees we fire as "human resources"; during the U.S. war in Vietnam soldiers referred to enemy soldiers as "gooks"; Hitler referred to the Jewish population as "the Jewish problem," and referred to murdering them as "the final solution." And we *attribute to others the responsibility* for harmful actions we have carried out. We may injure someone and think, "He (the victim) forced me to do it," or "He (the victim) had it coming to him," or "My boss made me do it," or "I was just following orders."

These are but a few of the fallacious mental tricks that we use to inconsistently avoid accepting the judgment of a piece of moral reasoning that concludes that we are guilty of the same wrongs that we attribute to others. We should strive to avoid them, just like we try to avoid other fallacious ways of thinking.

PHILOSOPHY AT THE MOVIES

Watch *The Sea Inside (Mar Adentro)* (2004), the true story of Ramon Sampedro, a Spanish quadriplegic who for decades fights government officials to allow him to end his life, while friends like the woman Rosa try to convince him that his life is worth living. Do you believe that Ramon Sampedro is justified in asking for euthanasia? Why or why not? Were officials justified in preventing him from practicing euthanasia on himself? Explain your answers in terms of the moral theories described in this chapter.

Chapter Summary

Whether or not we choose to acknowledge them as such, the moral values we hold and the obligations we feel constitute expressions of who we are, how we see things, and how we wish to be seen by others. In choosing a moral lifestyle, we're really defining who we are. Nevertheless, if our morality is to be an expression of the self we have truly chosen to be, we must carefully reflect on our values and decide for ourselves whether or not they are reasonable. We must weigh their merits and liabilities in the light of our own lives, circumstances, and understanding of human nature. Such reflection places heavy emphasis on self-growth, especially on increasing our knowledge and awareness of self and the world.

The main points of the chapter are:

7.1 What Is Ethics?

- Ethics is the study of those values that relate to our moral conduct, including questions of good and evil, right and wrong, and moral responsibility.

7.2 Is Ethics Relative?

- The descriptive study of ethics, which raises the issue of ethical relativism, studies ethics from a factual point of view. Ethics is the search for principles of moral behavior that are reasonable.

7.3 Do Consequences Make an Action Right?

- Consequentialist theories claim that the morality of an action depends only on its consequences.

- Egoism is the consequentialist position that states the following: Always act in such a way that your actions promote your best long-term interests.

- Act utilitarianism is the consequentialist position that states this: Always act so that your actions produce the greatest happiness for everyone.

- Rule utilitarianism is the consequentialist position that states the following: Always follow those rules that tend to produce the greatest happiness for everyone.

7.4 Do Rules Define Morality?

- Nonconsequentialist theories claim that the morality of an action depends on factors other than consequences.

- Divine command theory is a nonconsequentialist theory that enjoins us to follow the law of God. There are scriptural and natural law versions of divine command theory.

- Kant's categorical imperative is a nonconsequentialist position that states this: Always act in such a way that your reasons for acting are reasons you could will to have everyone act on in similar circumstances, and always treat persons as ends and not merely as means.

- Buddhism emphasizes intentional action and ties morality to wisdom. Its moral code is expressed in the precepts of the Eightfold Path cultivate correct understanding, correct intention, correct speech, correct conduct, correct livelihood, correct effort, correct mindfulness, and correct concentration.

7.5 Is Ethics Based on Character?

- Virtue ethics identifies the character traits of the morally good person; it emphasizes the kind of person we should become instead of principles of action. Some virtue theories argue that male and female virtues differ.

7.6 Can Ethics Resolve Moral Quandaries?

- Application of the normative theories to issues such as abortion and euthanasia suggests that each theory provides important and distinctive insights into factors that should be taken into account when making moral decisions.

● thinking critically Conscientious moral reasoning involves: (1) recognizing that a situation raises ethical issues, (2) getting the relevant facts, (3) identifying your options, (4) evaluating the ethics of each option, and (5) making a decision. It also fulfills the consistency requirement and avoids fallacious mental tricks by which we seek to escape the consistency requirement.

7.7 Readings

The following readings focus on a pressing moral issue that we did not have the space to discuss in this chapter: What moral obligations, if any, does each of us have toward the poor? The first selection, "The Heavenly Christmas Tree," is a classic short story by Fyodor Dostoyevsky that raises this moral question. In his story, Dostoyevsky asks us to consider a situation that, he suggests, "must have happened somewhere at some time." His story describes the plight of an impoverished boy wandering the streets of a large city on Christmas Eve. In the second reading, Australian philosopher Peter Singer, an avowed utilitarian, argues that we have an obligation to help the starving people of the world even if this means doing without luxuries. Singer claims that if we can prevent something bad from happening without sacrificing anything that is of comparable value, then we are obligated to prevent it. Because starvation is bad, we are obligated to prevent it, and because luxuries—such as more clothes or a better music system—are not of comparable value to preventing starvation, we are obligated to spend our money on preventing starvation rather than on such luxuries.

FYODOR DOSTOYEVSKY

The Heavenly Christmas Tree

I am a novelist, and I suppose I have made up this story. I write "I suppose," though I know for a fact that I have made it up, but yet I keep fancying that it must have happened somewhere at some time, that it must have happened on Christmas Eve in some great town in a time of terrible frost.

I have a vision of a boy, a little boy, six years old or even younger. This boy woke up that morning in a cold damp cellar. He was dressed in a sort of little dressing gown and was shivering with cold. There was a cloud of white steam from his breath, and sitting on a box in the corner, he blew the steam out of his mouth and amused himself in his dullness watching it float away. But he was terribly hungry. Several times that morning he went up to the plank bed where his sick mother was lying on a mattress as thin as a pancake, with some sort of bundle under her head for a pillow. How had she come here? She must have come with her boy from some other town and suddenly fallen ill. The landlady who let the "corners" had been taken two days before to the police station, the lodgers were out and about as the holiday was so near, and the only one left had been lying for the last twenty-four hours dead drunk, not having waited for Christmas. In another corner of the room a wretched old woman of eighty, who had once been a children's nurse but was now left to die friendless, was moaning and groaning with rheumatism, scolding and grumbling at the boy so that he was afraid to go near her corner. He had got a drink of water in the outer room, but could not find a crust anywhere, and had been on the point of waking his mother a dozen times.

He felt frightened at last in the darkness: it had long been dusk, but no light was kindled. Touching his mother's face, he was surprised that she did not move at all, and that she was as cold as the wall. "It is very cold here," he thought. He stood a little, unconsciously letting his hands rest on the dead woman's shoulders, then he breathed on his fingers to warm them, and then quietly fumbling for his cap on the bed, he went out of the cellar. He would have gone earlier, but was afraid of the big dog, which had been howling all day at the neighbor's door at the top of the stairs. But the dog was not there now, and he went out into the street.

Mercy on us, what a town! He had never seen anything like it before. In the town from which he had come, it was always such black darkness at night. There was one lamp for the whole street, the little, low-pitched, wooden houses were closed up with shutters, there was no one to be seen in the street after dusk, all the people shut themselves up in their houses, and there was nothing but the howling of packs of dogs, hundreds and thousands of them barking and howling all night. But there it was so warm and he was given food, while here—oh, dear, if he only had something to eat! And what a noise and rattle here, what light and what people, horses and carriages, and what a frost! The frozen steam hung in clouds over the horses, over their warmly breathing mouths; their hoofs clanged against the stones through the powdery snow, and every one pushed so, and—oh, dear, how he longed for some morsel to eat, and how wretched he suddenly felt. A policeman walked by and turned away to avoid seeing the boy.

Here was another street—oh, what a wide one, here he would be run over for certain; how everyone was shouting, racing and driving along, and the light, the light! And what was this? A huge glass window, and through the window a tree reaching up to the ceiling; it was a fir tree, and on it were ever so many lights, gold papers and apples and little dolls and horses; and there were children clean and dressed in their best running about the room, laughing and playing and eating and drinking something. And then a little girl began dancing with one of the boys, what a pretty little girl! And he could hear the music through the window. The boy looked and wondered and laughed, though his toes were aching with the cold and his fingers were red and stiff so that it hurt him to move them. And all at once the boy remembered how his toes and fingers hurt him, and began crying, and ran on; and again through another window-pane he saw another Christmas tree, and on a table cakes of all sorts—almond cakes, red cakes and yellow cakes, and three grand young ladies were sitting there, and they gave the cakes to any one who went up to them, and the door kept opening, lots of gentlemen and ladies went in from the street. The boy crept up, suddenly opened the door and went in. Oh, how they shouted at him and waved him back! One lady went up to him hurriedly and slipped a coin into his hand, and with her own hands opened the door into the street for him! How frightened he was. And the coin rolled away and clinked upon the steps; he could not bend his red fingers to hold it tight.

The boy ran away and went on, where he did not know. He was ready to cry again but he was afraid, and

ran on and on and blew his fingers. And he was miserable because he felt suddenly so lonely and terrified, and all at once, mercy on us! What was this again? People were standing in a crowd admiring. Behind a glass window there were three little dolls, dressed in red and green dresses, and exactly, exactly as though they were alive. One was a little old man sitting and playing a big violin, the two others were standing close by and playing little violins and nodding in time, and looking at one another, and their lips moved, they were speaking, actually speaking, only one couldn't hear through the glass. And at first the boy thought they were alive, and when he grasped that they were dolls he laughed. He had never seen such dolls before, and had no idea there were such dolls! And he wanted to cry, but he felt amused, amused by the dolls. All at once he fancied that some one caught at his smock behind: a wicked big boy was standing beside him and suddenly hit him on the head, snatched off his cap and tripped him up. The boy fell down on the ground, at once there was a shout, he was numb with fright, he jumped up and ran away. He ran, and not knowing where he was going, ran in at the gate of some one's courtyard, and sat down behind a stack of wood: "They won't find me here, besides it's dark!"

He sat huddled up and was breathless from fright, and all at once, quite suddenly, he felt so happy: his hands and feet suddenly left off aching and grew so warm, as warm as though he were on a stove; then he shivered all over, then he gave a start, why, he must have been asleep. How nice to have a sleep here! "I'll sit here a little and go and look at the dolls again," said the boy, and smiled thinking of them. "Just as though they were alive! . . . ." And suddenly he heard his mother singing over him. "Mommy, I am asleep; how nice it is to sleep here!"

"Come to my Christmas tree, little one," a soft voice suddenly whispered over his head.

He thought that this was still his mother, but no, it was not she. Who it was calling him, he could not see, but some one bent over and embraced him in the darkness; and he stretched out his hands to him, and . . . and all at once—oh, what a bright light! Oh, what a Christmas tree! And yet it was not a fir tree, he had never seen a tree like that! Where was he now? Everything was bright and shining, and all round him were dolls; but no, they were not dolls, they were little boys and girls, only so bright and shining. They all came flying round him, they all kissed him, took him and carried him along with them, and he was flying himself, and he saw that his mother was looking at him and laughing joyfully. "Mommy, Mommy; oh, how nice it is here, Mommy!" And again he kissed the children and wanted to tell them at once of those dolls in the shop window. "Who are you, boys? Who are you, girls?" he asked, laughing and admiring them.

"This is Christ's Christmas tree," they answered. "'Christ always has a Christmas tree on this day, for the little children who have no tree of their own. . . . '" And he found out that all these little boys and girls were children just like himself; that some had been frozen in the baskets in which they had as babies been laid on the doorsteps of well-to-do Petersburg people, others had been boarded out with Finnish women by the Foundling and had been suffocated, others had died at their starved mother's breasts in the Samara famine, others had died in the third-class railway carriages from the foul air; and yet they were all here, they were all like angels about Christ, and He was in the midst of them and held out His hands to them and blessed them and their sinful mothers. . . . And the mothers of these children stood on one side weeping; each one knew her boy or girl, and the children flew up to them and kissed them and wiped away their tears with their little hands, and begged them not to weep because they were so happy.

And down below in the morning the porter found the little dead body of the frozen child on the wood stack; they sought out his mother too. . . . She had died before him. They met before the Lord God in heaven.

Why have I made up such a story, so out of keeping with an ordinary diary, and a writer's above all? And I promised two stories dealing with real events! But that is just it, I keep fancying that all this may have happened really—that is, what took place in the cellar and on the wood stack; but as for Christ's Christmas tree, I cannot tell you whether that could have happened or not.

Source: Fyodor Dostoyevsky, *Short Stories* (New York: Books, Inc., 1900).

PETER SINGER

Famine, Affluence, and Morality

Note: When Singer wrote this article the Indian state of Bengal was suffering from a severe famine and its fleeing citizens became refugees in neighboring countries, producing the Bengal emergency to which Singer wants to apply his argument.—Ed.

. . . I begin with the assumption that suffering and death from lack of food, shelter, and medical care is bad. I think most people will agree about this, although one may reach the same view by different routes. I shall not argue for this view. People can hold all sorts of eccentric positions, and perhaps from some of them it would not follow that death by starvation is in itself bad. It is difficult, perhaps impossible, to refute such positions, and so for brevity I will henceforth take this assumption as accepted. Those who disagree need read no further.

My next point is this: if it is in our power to prevent something bad from happening, without thereby sacrificing anything of comparable moral importance, we ought, morally, to do it. By "without sacrificing anything of comparable moral importance" I mean without causing anything else comparably bad to happen, or doing something that is wrong in itself, or failing to promote some moral good, comparable in significance to the bad thing we can prevent. This principle seems almost as uncontroversial as the last one. It requires us only to prevent what is bad, and not to promote what is good, and it requires this of us only when we can do it without sacrificing anything that is, from the moral point of view, comparably important. I could even, as far as the application of my argument to the Bengal emergency is concerned, qualify the point so as to make it: if it is in our power to prevent something very bad from happening, without thereby sacrificing anything morally significant, we ought, morally, to do it. An application of this principle would be as follows: if I am walking past a shallow pond and see a child drowning in it, I ought to wade in and pull the child out. This will mean getting my clothes muddy, but this is insignificant, while the death of the child would presumably be a very bad thing.

The uncontroversial appearance of the principle just stated is deceptive. If it were acted upon, even in its qualified form, our lives, our society, and our world would be fundamentally changed. For the principle takes, firstly, no account of proximity or distance. It makes no moral difference whether the person I can help is a neighbor's child ten yards from me or a Bengali whose name I shall never know, ten thousand miles away. Secondly, the principle makes no distinction between cases in which I am the only person who could possibly do anything and cases in which I am just one among millions in the same position.

I do not think I need to say much in defense of the refusal to take proximity and distance into account. The fact that a person is physically near to us, so that we have personal contact with him, may make it more likely that we *shall* assist him, but this does not show that we *ought* to help him rather than another who happens to be further away. If we accept any principle of impartiality, universalizability, equality, or whatever, we cannot discriminate against someone merely because he is far away from us (or we are far away from him). Admittedly, it is possible that we are in a better position to judge what needs to be done to help a person near to us than one far away, and perhaps also to provide the assistance we judge to be necessary. If this were the case, it would be a reason for helping those near to us first. This may once have been a justification for being more concerned with the poor in one's own town than with famine victims in India. Unfortunately for those who like to keep their moral responsibilities limited, instant communication and swift transportation have changed the situation. From the moral point of view, the development of the world into a "global village" has made an important, though still unrecognized, difference to our moral situation. Expert observers and supervisors, sent out by famine relief organizations or permanently stationed in famine-prone areas, can direct our aid to a refugee in Bengal almost as effectively as we could get it to someone in our own block. There would seem, therefore, to be no possible justification for discriminating on geographical grounds.

There may be a greater need to defend the second implication of my principle—that the fact that there are millions of other people in the same position, in respect to the Bengali refugees, as I am, does not make the situation significantly different from a situation in which I am the only person who can prevent something very bad from occurring. Again, of course, I admit that there is a psychological difference between the cases; one feels less guilty about doing nothing if one can point to others, similarly placed, who have also done nothing. Yet this can make no real difference to our moral obligations. Should I consider that I am less obliged to pull the drowning child out of the pond if on looking around I see other people, no further away than I am, who have also noticed the child but are doing nothing? One has only to ask this question to see the absurdity of the view that numbers lessen obligation. It is a

view that is an ideal excuse for inactivity: unfortunately most of the major evils—poverty, overpopulation, pollution—are problems in which everyone is almost equally involved.

If my argument so far has been sound, neither our distance from a preventable evil nor the number of other people who, in respect to that evil, are in the same situation as we are, lessens our obligation to mitigate or prevent that evil. I shall therefore take as established the principle I asserted earlier. As I have already said, I need to assert it only in its qualified form: if it is in our power to prevent something very bad from happening, without thereby sacrificing anything else morally significant, we ought, morally, to do it.

The outcome of this argument is that our traditional moral categories are upset. The traditional distinction between duty and charity cannot be drawn, or at least, not in the place we normally draw it. Giving money to the Bengal Relief Fund is regarded as an act of charity in our society. The bodies which collect money are known as "charities." These organizations see themselves in this way—if you send them a check, you will be thanked for your "generosity." Because giving money is regarded as an act of charity, it is not thought that there is anything wrong with not giving. The charitable man may be praised, but the man who is not charitable is not condemned. People do not feel in any way ashamed or guilty about spending money on new clothes or a new car instead of giving it to famine relief. (Indeed, the alternative does not occur to them.) This way of looking at the matter cannot be justified. When we buy new clothes not to keep ourselves warm but to look "well-dressed" we are not providing for any important need. We would not be sacrificing anything significant if we were to continue to wear our old clothes, and give the money to famine relief. By doing so, we would be preventing another person from starving. It follows from what I have said earlier that we ought to give money away, rather than spend it on clothes which we do not need to keep us warm. To do so is not charitable, or generous. Nor is it the kind of act which philosophers and theologians have called "supererogatory"—an act which it would be good to do, but not wrong not to do. On the contrary, we ought to give the money away, and it is wrong not to do so. . . .

Source: From *Philosophy and Public Affairs,* vol. 1, no. 3 (Spring 1972): 231–235, 238–240, 242–243. Copyright © 1972 by Princeton University Press. Excerpts reprinted by permission of Princeton University Press.

7.8 HISTORICAL SHOWCASE

Nietzsche and Wollstonecraft

Many people are skeptical about the claims of morality, holding that morality is a sham of some kind. In this showcase, therefore, we discuss the views of a nineteenth-century philosopher who was completely skeptical about morality: Friedrich Nietzsche.

We then discuss the views of Mary Wollstonecraft. Wollstonecraft accepted a view of morality very much like Kant's view that morality is based on reason. Her confidence in ethics and reason is the basis of her view that women are, and should be treated as, the equals of men. Far from being skeptical of morality, she saw it as the foundation of sexual equality and built on it the first clearly articulated feminist philosophy.

By considering and contrasting the views of these philosophers, you may find it easier to make up your own mind about the future and reality of moral principles.

Nietzsche

The most powerful attack ever launched against morality was made by Friedrich Nietzsche. Nietzsche was born in 1844 in Roeken, Germany. His father having died when Nietzsche was 4, he was raised in a household consisting of his mother, sister, grandmother, and two aunts. In 1864, Nietzsche went off to college, studying first at the University of Bonn and then transferring to the University of Leipzig. There, perhaps experiencing the first effects of his freedom, Nietzsche soon contracted syphilis, which at that time was incurable. The disease had little immediate effect on his scholarly skills, however, and he soon managed to impress his professors, particularly the widely respected Friedrich Ritschel. When Nietzsche graduated from Leipzig, Ritschel gave him an enthusiastic recommendation, and in 1869 Nietzsche quickly secured a position as a professor at the University of Basel. Unfortunately, his health soon began to deteriorate because of his disease, and in 1878 poor health forced Nietzsche to resign his position. Most of the rest of his life was spent in terrible loneliness. Several times he proposed marriage to different women but was firmly rejected by each. In 1889, Nietzsche abruptly went mad. He spent much of the next eleven years in a madhouse or under the care of his doting sister. He died on August 25, 1900.

Friedrich Nietzsche: "God is dead! God remains dead! And we have killed him! How shall we console ourselves, the most murderous of all murderers? Shall we not ourselves have to become Gods?" Friedrich Nietzsche, portrait. German philosopher.

"GOD IS DEAD"

In the major writings he produced before he went mad, Nietzsche proposed the insightful view that the traditional values and ethical systems of the West were collapsing even as he wrote. The major source of their collapse, he felt, was the loss of belief in God. "God is dead," he declared, having been killed by our own modern philosophies and beliefs. Because we no longer believe in God, it is difficult for us to believe in the traditional values and ethical views that Christians and others have defended by appealing to God. The death of God has left us floating directionless in a cold, empty space. Nietzsche announced the death of God by using the highly poetic image of a madman:

> *The Madman.*—Have you ever heard of the madman who on a bright morning lighted a lantern

and ran to the market-place calling out unceasingly: "I seek God! I seek God!"—As there were many people standing about who did not believe in God, he caused a great deal of amusement. Why! is he lost? said one. Has he strayed away like a child? said another. Or does he keep himself hidden? Is he afraid of us? Has he taken a seavoyage? Has he emigrated?—the people cried out laughingly, all in a hubbub. The insane man jumped into their midst and transfixed them with his glances. "Where has God gone?" he called out, "I mean to tell you! *We have killed him,—you and I! We are all his murderers!* But how have we done it? How were we able to drink up the sea? Who gave us the sponge to wipe away the whole horizon? What did we do when we loosened this earth from its sun? Whither does it now move? Whither do we move? Away from all suns? Do we not dash on unceasingly? Backwards, sideways, forwards, in all directions? Is there still an above and below? Do we not stray, as through infinite nothingness? Does not empty space breathe upon us? Has it not become colder? Does not night come on continually, darker and darker? Shall we not have to light lanterns in the morning? Do we not hear the noise of the gravediggers who are burying God? Do we not smell the divine putrefaction?—for even Gods putrefy! Who will wipe the blood from us? With what water could we cleanse ourselves? What lustrums, what sacred games shall we have to devise? Is not the magnitude of this deed too great for us? Shall we not ourselves have to become Gods, merely to seem worthy of it? There never was a greater event,—and on account of it, all who are born after us belong to a higher history than any history hitherto!"—Here the madman was silent and looked again at his hearers; they also were silent and looked at him in surprise. At last he threw his lantern on the ground, so that it broke in pieces and was extinguished. "I come too early," he then said, "I am not yet at the right time. This prodigious event is still on its way, and is travelling,—it has not yet reached men's ears. Lightning and thunder need time, the light of the stars needs time, deeds need time, even after they are done, to be seen and heard. This deed is as yet further from them than the furthest star,—*and yet they have done it!*"—It is further stated that the madman made his way into different churches on the same day, and there intoned his *Requiem aeternam deo*.[1]

But the death of God, for Nietzsche, was not necessarily a bad thing. For belief in God had encouraged the illusion that there are universal and absolute truths that everyone must accept. In fact, Nietzsche maintained, there is no absolute truth. Instead, all our beliefs are nothing more than so many interpretations or "perspectives," ways we have of looking at the world. There is an indefinite number of possible interpretations of the world, all of them equally true and equally false. But some of these are more useful than others because some have the advantage of enabling us to live and gain power over the world. Such "useful" beliefs, although as false as any others, are the ones we count as part of the "truth." As Nietzsche put it, "*Truth is that sort of error* without which a particular type of living being could not live. The value for *life* is ultimately decisive."[2]

WILL TO POWER

Although Nietzsche did not believe that there is one "true" interpretation of the universe, he did think that some interpretations or ways of understanding the universe are better than others. Every event in the universe, Nietzsche maintained, can be interpreted as being produced by a force he called the "will to power." It was a useful hypothesis, he felt, to interpret events in the universe in terms of something with which we are familiar—the activity of our own wills:

> We must risk the hypothesis that everywhere we recognize "effects" there is an effect of will upon will; that all mechanical happenings, insofar as they are activated by some energy, are willpower, will-effects.—Assuming, finally, that we succeeded in explaining our entire instinctual life as the development and ramification of one basic form of will (of the will to power, as I hold); assuming that one could trace back all the organic functions to this will to power, including the solution of the problems of generation and nutrition (they are one problem)—if this were done, we should be justified in defining *all* effective energy unequivocally as *will to power*.[3]

If everything in the universe is interpreted as a result of a will to power, then all human actions must also be seen as outcomes of the will to power. The primary drives of human beings are not the pursuit of pleasure and the avoidance of pain (as Mill had argued). Instead, human beings are primarily

1   Friedrich Nietzsche, *The Joyful Wisdom*, trans. Thomas Common, in *The Complete Works of Friedrich Nietzsche*, vol. 10, ed. Oscar Levy (New York: Macmillan, 1944), 167–169.

2   Quoted in Frederick Copleston, *A History of Philosophy*, vol. 7 (Garden City, NY: Doubleday, 1963), 183.

3   Friedrich Nietzsche, *Beyond Good and Evil*, trans. M. Cowan (Chicago: Henry Regnery, 1955), 43.

motivated by the desire to increase their power over things and over people. As Nietzsche put it, "Life itself is essential assimilation, injury, violation of the foreign and the weaker, suppression, hardness, the forcing of one's own forms upon something else, ingestion and—at least in its mildest form—exploitation."[4] In fact, Nietzsche felt, our theories and beliefs about the world should also be seen as instruments of the will to power. Interpretations of the world are instruments we use to extend our power over the world and over one another.

Just as there are no absolute truths about the world, so also there are no absolute truths about morality. Any morality, Nietzsche claimed, is also merely an interpretation of the world: "There are no moral phenomena, only moralistic interpretations of phenomena," and "There are no moral facts." Like any other kind of interpretation, a morality cannot be said to be absolutely true or false; it can only be a more-or-less useful instrument for the will to power. Moralities, then, are interpretations used as instruments to exert power over others or over the natural world. For example, Nietzsche argues that Kant, like every other moralist, proposed his moral theory to impose his own values:

> Apart from the value of such assertions as "there is a categorical imperative in us," one can always ask: What does such an assertion indicate about him who makes it? There are systems of morals which are meant to justify their author in the eyes of other people; other systems of morals are meant to tranquilize him, and make him self-satisfied; with other systems he wants to crucify and humble himself; with others he wishes to take revenge; with others to conceal himself; with others to glorify himself and gain superiority and distinction;—this system of morals helps its author to forget, that system makes him, or something of him, forgotten; many a moralist would like to exercise power and creative arbitrariness over mankind; many another, perhaps, Kant especially, gives us to understand by his morals that "what is estimable in me, is that I know how to obey—and with you it *shall* not be otherwise than with me!"[5]

Mill's argument for utilitarianism, Nietzsche argues, was also an attempt to impose on others his personal preferences. In Mill's case, these were preferences he shared with his fellow British citizens. Utilitarian arguments are merely an attempt to impose on the world the values of the English:

> Observe, for example, the indefatigable, inevitable English utilitarians. . . . In the end, they all want *English* morality to be recognized as authoritative, inasmuch as mankind, or the "general utility," or "the happiness of the greatest number,"—no! the happiness of *England* will be best served thereby. They would like, by all means, to convince themselves that the striving after *English* happiness, I mean after *comfort* and *fashion* (and in the highest instance, a seat in Parliament), is at the same time the true path of virtue; in fact, that insofar as there has been virtue in the world hitherto, it has just consisted in such striving.[6]

The ethical systems proposed by the major moral philosophers, then, are nothing more than manifestations of the will to power. The same is true of the popular moralities the masses follow. In his survey of the history of moralities, Nietzsche wrote, he had discovered two basic kinds of popular moralities. One kind was the "slave moralities" that weak people—especially the Christians—had devised as instruments to acquire power over the strong. The other kind was the "master moralities" that had been devised by the strong to assert their power over the weak.

A master morality will normally develop in those individuals who are the strongest, those who are born with the power to dominate others. This type of morality values strength, intelligence, courage, revenge, and power seeking. In this morality a person is good to the extent that he or she has the strength to overpower others. This type of morality extols the individual.

On the other hand, a slave morality is fashioned by weak groups of people. A slave morality values whatever is useful or beneficial to the weak, such as sympathy, kindness, pity, patience, humility, and helping those in need. In a slave morality, the good person is the one who helps the weak, whereas the dominating individual is seen as evil. Slave moralities are the moralities of the herd because they extol the group and not the individual:

> In a tour through the many finer and coarser moralities which have hitherto prevailed or still prevail on the earth, I found certain traits recurring regularly together and connected with one another, until finally two primary types revealed

---

4   Ibid., 201.
5   Friedrich Nietzsche, *Beyond Good and Evil*, trans. Helen Zimmern, in *The Complete Works of Friedrich Nietzsche*, vol. 2, Oscar Levy, ed. (New York: Macmillan, 1944), 106.

---

6   Ibid., 174.

themselves to me, and a radical distinction was brought to light. There is master-morality and slave-morality;—I would at once add, however, that in all higher and mixed civilizations, there are also attempts at the reconciliation of the two moralities; but one finds still oftener the confusion and mutual misunderstanding of them, indeed, sometimes their close juxtaposition—even in the same man, within one soul. The distinctions of moral values have either originated in a ruling caste, pleasantly conscious of being different from the ruled—or among the ruled class, the slaves and dependents of all sorts. In the first case, when it is the rulers who determine the conception "good," it is the exalted, proud disposition which is regarded as the distinguishing feature, and that which determines the order of rank. The noble type of man separates from himself the beings in whom the opposite of this exalted, proud disposition displays itself: he despises them. Let it at once be noted that in this first kind of morality the antithesis "good" and "bad" means practically the same as "noble" and "despicable";—the antithesis "good" and "evil" is of a different origin. The cowardly, the timid, the insignificant, and those thinking merely of narrow utility are despised; moreover, also, the distrustful, with their constrained glances, the self-abasing, the dog-like kind of men who let themselves be abused, the mendicant flatterers, and above all the liars;—it is a fundamental belief of all aristocrats that the common people are untruthful. "We truthful ones"—the nobility in ancient Greece called themselves. It is obvious that everywhere the designations of moral value were at first applied to *men,* and were only derivatively and at a later period applied to *actions;* it is a gross mistake, therefore, when historians of morals start with questions like, "Why have sympathetic actions been praised?" The noble type of man regards himself as a determiner of values; he does not require to be approved of; he passes the judgment: "What is injurious to me is injurious in itself "; he knows that it is he himself only who confers honor on things; he is a creator of values. He honors whatever he recognizes in himself; such morality is self-glorification. In the foreground there is the feeling of plenitude, of power, which seeks to overflow, the happiness of high tension, the consciousness of a wealth which would fain give and bestow:—the noble man also helps the unfortunate, but not—or scarcely—out of pity, but rather from an impulse generated by the superabundance of power. The noble man honors in himself the powerful one, him also who has power over himself, who knows how to speak and how to keep silence, who takes pleasure in subjecting himself to severity and hardness, and has reverence for all that is severe and hard. "Wotan placed a hard heart in my breast," says an old Scandinavian Saga: it is thus rightly expressed from the soul of a proud Viking. Such a type of man is even proud of *not* being made for sympathy; the hero of the Saga therefore adds warningly: "He who has not a hard heart when young, will never have one." The noble and brave who think thus are the furthest removed from the morality which sees precisely in sympathy, or in acting for the good of others, or in *désintéressement,* the characteristic of the moral; faith in oneself, pride in oneself, a radical enmity and irony towards "selflessness," belong as definitely to the noble morality, as do a careless scorn and precaution in presence of sympathy and the "warm heart."—It is the powerful who *know* how to honor, it is their art, their domain for invention. The profound reverence for age and for tradition—all law rests on this double reverence,—the belief and prejudice in favor of ancestors and unfavorable to newcomers, is typical in the morality of the powerful; and if, reversely, men of "modern ideas" believe almost instinctively in "progress" and the "future," and are more and more lacking in respect for old age, the ignoble origin of these "ideas" has complacently betrayed itself thereby. A morality of the ruling class, however, is more especially foreign and irritating to present-day taste in the sternness of its principle that one has duties only to one's equals; that one may act towards beings of a lower rank, toward all that is foreign, just as seems good to one, or "as the heart desires," and in any case "beyond good and evil": it is here that sympathy and similar sentiments can have a place. The ability and obligation to exercise prolonged gratitude and prolonged revenge—both only within the circle of equals,—artfulness in retaliation, *raffnement* of the idea in friendship, a certain necessity to have enemies (as outlets for the emotions of envy, quarrelsomeness, arrogance—in fact, in order to be a good *friend):* all these are typical characteristics of the noble morality, which, as has been pointed out, is not the morality of "modern ideas," and is therefore at present difficult to realize, and also to unearth and disclose.—It is otherwise with the second type of morality, *slave-morality.* Supposing that the abused, the oppressed, the suffering, the unemancipated, the weary, and those uncertain of themselves, should moralize, what will be the common element in their moral estimates? Probably a pessimistic suspicion with regard to the entire situation of man will find expression, perhaps a condemnation of man, together with his situation.

The slave has an unfavorable eye for the virtues of the powerful; he has a skepticism and distrust, a *refinement* of distrust of everything "good" that is there honored—he would fain persuade himself that the very happiness there is not genuine. On the other hand, *those* qualities which serve to alleviate the existence of sufferers are brought into prominence and flooded with light; it is here that sympathy, the kind, helping hand, the warm heart, patience, diligence, humility, and friendliness attain to honor; for here these are the most useful qualities, and almost the only means of supporting the burden of existence. Slave-morality is essentially the morality of utility. Here is the seat of the origin of the famous antithesis "good" and "evil":—power and dangerousness are assumed to reside in the evil, a certain dreadfulness, subtlety, and strength, which do not admit of being despised. According to slave-morality, therefore, the "evil" man arouses fear: according to master-morality, it is precisely the "good" man who arouses fear and seeks to arouse it, while the bad man is regarded as the despicable being. The contrast attains its maximum when, in accordance with the logical consequences of slave-morality, a shade of depreciation—it may be slight and well-intentioned—at last attaches itself even to the "good" man of this morality; because, according to the servile mode of thought, the good man must in any case be the *safe* man: he is good-natured, easily deceived, perhaps a little stupid, *un bonhomme.* Everywhere that slave-morality gains the ascendancy, language shows a tendency to approximate the significations of the words "good" and "stupid."—A last fundamental difference: the desire *for freedom,* the instinct for happiness and the refinements of the feeling of liberty belong as necessarily to slave-morals and morality, as artifice and enthusiasm in reverence and devotion are the regular symptoms of an aristocratic mode of thinking and estimating.—Hence we can understand without further detail why love as a *passion*—it is our European specialty—must absolutely be of noble origin; as is well known, its invention is due to the Provençal poet-cavaliers, those brilliant ingenious men of the "gai saber" [happy science], to whom Europe owes so much, and almost owes itself.[7]

Although Nietzsche clearly favored the "master moralities" and argued that we should rid ourselves of our "slave moralities," he did not feel that one morality was more "true" than another. Because there is no longer any God, there are no longer any objective moralities. Moralities are our own inventions:

> What then, alone, can our teaching be?—That no one gives man his qualities, either God, society, his parents, his ancestors, nor himself (this nonsensical idea, which is at last refuted here, was taught as "intelligible freedom" by Kant, and perhaps even as early as Plato himself). No one is responsible for the fact that he exists at all, that he is constituted as he is, and that he happens to be in certain circumstances and in a particular environment. The fatality of his being cannot be divorced from the fatality of all that which has been and will be. This is not the result of an individual attention, of a will, of an aim, there is no attempt at attaining to any "ideal man," or "ideal happiness" or "ideal morality" with him—it is absurd to wish him to be careering towards some sort of purpose. *We* invented the concept "purpose"; in reality purpose is altogether lacking. One is necessary, one is a piece of fate, one belongs to the whole, one is in the whole—there is nothing that could judge, measure, compare, and condemn our existence, for that would mean judging, measuring, comparing and condemning the whole. *But there is nothing outside the whole!* The fact that no one shall any longer be made responsible, that the nature of existence may not be traced to a *causa prima,* that the world is an entity neither as a sensorium nor as a spirit—*this alone is the great deliverance*—thus alone is the innocence of becoming restored.... The concept "God" has been the greatest objection to existence hitherto.... We deny God, we deny responsibility in God: thus alone do we save the world.[8]

The significance of Nietzsche's attack on morality cannot be overstated. If Nietzsche is correct, then moral principles are nothing more than subtle or not-so-subtle tools that the weak use to secure their power over the strong. Morality is a sham. The moral principles proposed by Christians, utilitarians, or Kantians are nothing more than their attempt to impose their will on others. When I say, for example, that everyone should be charitable or that everyone should seek to maximize the happiness of everyone else, I am really trying to get you to be charitable to me or to maximize my happiness. Moral principles are thus nothing more than an expression of the will to power.

---

7   Ibid., 227–232.

8   Friedrich Nietzsche, *The Twilight of the Idols,* trans. A. M. Lucovici, in Oscar Levy, ed., *The Complete Works of Friedrich Nietzsche* (New York: The Macmillan Company, 1911), vol. 16, 43.

Thus, just as Hume's views had threatened epistemology, so Nietzsche's views threatened to destroy morality.

Wollstonecraft

Mary Wollstonecraft is recognized today as the first major feminist philosopher. A hard-working, independent, and enterprising woman, Wollstonecraft went against the conventions of the day. In an age when women were supposed to stay at home, Wollstonecraft left home to support herself at the age of 19 and managed to achieve what was then unthinkable: She became an internationally known philosopher.

The second of seven children, Mary Wollstonecraft was born on April 27, 1759. Her father, a gentleman farmer who managed to dissipate the small fortune he inherited from his own father, was subject to uncontrollable fits of rage, frustration, and drunkenness. As a nine-year-old, Wollstonecraft felt she had to watch "whole nights at their chamber door" to protect her mother from her father's violence.

At the age of 19, seeking independence in defiance of her parents' wishes, Wollstonecraft left home to work for two years as a live-in companion

Mary Wollstonecraft: "I see not the shadow of a reason to conclude that [the] virtues [of men and women] should differ in respect to their nature. In fact, how can they, if virtue has only one eternal standard?" John Opie (1761–1807); Mary Wollstonecraft (Mrs. William Godwin), c. 1790–1791.

to a wealthy and tyrannical widow who continually reminded her of her lower status.

Wollstonecraft was forced to return home in 1781 to care for her sick mother. Subjected once again to a violent family life, Wollstonecraft became embittered and depressed. The death of her mother in 1782 let Wollstonecraft leave home again, and she moved in with the family of her close friend Fanny Blood. Although Fanny's family was impoverished, Wollstonecraft there found peace and tranquility.

In 1784, Wollstonecraft, her two sisters, and Fanny opened a school in Newington Green, a town near London. Although the school prospered at first, it eventually ran up a huge debt and had to be closed. Needing money, Wollstonecraft turned to writing and in 1786 published *Thoughts on the Education of Daughters.* The book attracted little attention. Later that year, Wollstonecraft took the job of governess to the three daughters of Lord and Lady Kingsborough. Wollstonecraft hated her aristocratic employers, who constantly reminded her that she was of a lower social class. In a letter to her sister, she described Lady Kingsborough as a "haughty and disagreeable" woman whose "proud condescension added to my embarrassment."[9] After only ten months, Lady Kingsborough fired her.

Wollstonecraft moved to London in 1787, where she took a job as an editor and writer for a journal. Here at last she prospered. Working at the journal was intellectually exciting, and the work allowed her to devote herself to her own writing, which now succeeded beyond her dreams. During the next few years she published numerous works, including two controversial works that made her internationally famous: *A Vindication of the Rights of Men* and *A Vindication of the Rights of Women.*

Wollstonecraft fashioned a philosophy based on a fundamental moral principle that she first set out in *A Vindication of the Rights of Men,* a work devoted to refuting the elitist philosophy of Edmund Burke. Burke held that people are fundamentally unequal and that the privileges of the upper class should be preserved. Mindful of her own unhappy experiences with upper-class women, Wollstonecraft rejected Burke's view as foolish. She argued that all human beings possess reason and that reason is the source of the equal moral rights that all human beings have. As Wollstonecraft put the matter in

9   *The Collected Letters of Mary Wollstonecraft,* ed. Ralph M. Wardle (Ithaca, NY: Cornell University Press, 1979), 164.

A Vindication of the Rights of Men, where she imagines herself talking to Burke:

> The birthright of man, to give you, sir, a short defi-
> nition of this disputed right, is such a degree of
> liberty, civil and religious, as is compatible with the
> liberty of every other individual with whom he is
> united in a social compact, and the continued exis-
> tence of that compact. . . .
>
> It is necessary emphatically to repeat, that
> there are rights which men inherit at their birth,
> as rational creatures, who were raised above the
> brute creation by their improvable faculties; and
> that, in receiving these, not from their forefathers,
> but, from God, prescription can never undermine
> natural rights.[10]

According to Wollstonecraft, reason is the source of morality because it is reason that allows us to restrain our animal passions. This ability to rise above our animal nature is what sets us off from the animal world and is the source of the respect to which all humans who acquire virtue have an equal right:

> In what respect are we superior to the brute cre-
> ation, if intellect is not allowed to be the guide of
> passion? Brutes hope and fear, love and hate; but
> without a capacity to improve, a power of turning
> these passions to good or evil, they neither acquire
> virtue nor wisdom—Why? Because the Creator has
> not given them reason.
>
> Children are born ignorant, consequently
> innocent; the passions are neither good nor evil
> dispositions, till they receive a direction. . . . If
> virtue is to be acquired by experience, or taught by
> example, reason, perfected by reflection, must be
> the director of the whole host of passions. . . .
> —She must hold the rudder, or let the wind blow
> which way it list, the vessel will never advance
> smoothly to its destined port. . . . Who will venture
> to assert that virtue would not be promoted by the
> more extensive cultivation of reason?[11]

Expressing a view that she would never aban-don, Wollstonecraft claimed that to the extent that women fail to develop their reason and fail there-fore to rise above animal feeling and passion, they will not merit the respect that is due to a developed human being. When women fail to acquire the same "manly" virtues that males cultivate—fortitude,

humanity, justice, wisdom, and truth—they give up their equality with men. Burke, she points out, claimed that women should not attempt to acquire the virtues of males but should attempt instead to make themselves pleasing to men by cultivating the virtues of littleness, weakness, and beauty. But in convincing women to pursue this path, Wollstone-craft argues, Burke has robbed them of the very thing—a developed reason—that would give them a right to moral respect:

> You may have convinced them that littleness and
> weakness are the very essence of beauty; and that
> the Supreme Being, in giving women beauty in the
> most supereminent degree, seemed to command
> them, by the powerful voice of nature, not to culti-
> vate the moral virtues that might chance to excite
> respect, and interfere with the pleasing sensations
> they were created to inspire. Thus confining truth,
> fortitude, and humanity within the rigid pale of
> manly morals, they might justly argue that to be
> loved—woman's high end and great distinction—
> they should learn to list, to totter in their walk, and
> nickname God's creatures. Never, they might repeat
> after you, was any man, much less a woman, ren-
> dered amiable by the force of these exalted quali-
> ties, fortitude, justice, wisdom, and truth; and thus
> forewarned of the sacrifice they must make to these
> austere, unnatural virtues, they would be authorized
> to turn all their attention to their persons, system-
> atically neglecting morals to secure beauty.[12]

This idea, that women are rendered inferior to men by society's insistence that they not develop their rea-son and by their own acquiescence in that insistence, forms the basis of Wollstonecraft's greatest work, *A Vindication of the Rights of Women*. Here, Wollstonecraft argues that society in general and men in particular keep women in an undeveloped and morally inferior state. Tragically, women themselves acquiesce in the inferior role assigned to them by men:

> The conduct and manners of women, in fact, evi-
> dently prove that their minds are not in a healthy
> state; for, like the flowers which are planted in too
> rich a soil, strength and usefulness are sacrificed
> to beauty; and the flaunting leaves, after having
> pleased a fastidious eye, fade, disregarded on the
> stalk, long before the season when they ought to
> have arrived at maturity.—One cause of this barren
> blooming I attribute to a false system of education,
> gathered from the books written on this subject by

---

[10] From Mary Wollstonecraft, *A Vindication of the Rights of Men* (1790), in *A Wollstonecraft Anthology,* ed. Janet M. Todd (Bloomington: Indiana University Press, 1977), 65, 67.

[11] Ibid., 73–74.

[12] Ibid., 76–77.

men who, considering females rather as women than human creatures, have been more anxious to make them alluring mistresses than affectionate wives and rational mothers; and the understanding of the sex has been so bubbled by this specious homage, that the civilized women of the present century, with a few exceptions, are only anxious to inspire love, when they ought to cherish a nobler ambition, and by their abilities and virtues exact respect.[13]

It is particularly through an inferior education that women are kept in a state of immaturity and dependency, she argues. They are trained to think that they must devote themselves to pleasing men and to becoming dependent on them. Women must resist these enticements:

The education of women has, of late, been more attended to than formerly; yet they are still reckoned a frivolous sex, and ridiculed or pitied by the writers who endeavour by satire or instruction to improve them. It is acknowledged that they spend many of the first years of their lives in acquiring a smattering of accomplishments; meanwhile strength of body and mind are sacrificed to libertine notions of beauty, to the desire of establishing themselves,—the only way women can rise in the world,—by marriage. And this desire making mere animals of them, when they marry they act as such children may be expected to act:—they dress, they paint, and nickname God's creatures. . . .

In the present state of society, a little learning is required to support the character of a gentleman; and boys are obliged to submit to a few years of discipline. But in the education of women, the cultivation of the understanding is always subordinate to the acquirement of some corporeal accomplishment; even while enervated by confinement and false notions of modesty, the body is prevented from attaining that grace and beauty which relaxed half-formed limbs never exhibit. Besides, in youth their faculties are not brought forward by emulation; and having no serious scientific study, if they have natural sagacity it is turned too soon on life and manners. They dwell on effects and modifications, without tracing them back to causes; and complicated rules to adjust behavior are a weak substitute for simple principles.[14]

The popular view that women must be educated differently from men is based on the theory that the moral virtues of women are very different from those of men. Wollstonecraft argues strenuously against this popular view. Morality, she claims, is not based on gender: It is a mistake to believe that there is one morality for men and a different one for women. Women and men must be educated as equals, she argues, because both are equally endowed with reason and because a single standard of morality applies equally to men and to women. The claim that male morality is different from female morality, she argues, is what allows men to maintain a "tyranny" over women:

To account for and excuse the tyranny of man, many ingenious arguments have been brought forward to prove that the two sexes, in the acquirement of virtue, ought to aim at attaining a very different character: or, to speak explicitly, women are not allowed to have sufficient strength of mind to acquire what really deserves the name of virtue. Yet it should seem, allowing them to have souls, that there is but one way appointed by Providence to lead mankind to either virtue or happiness. . . .

I see not the shadow of a reason to conclude that their virtues should differ in respect to their nature. In fact, how can they, if virtue has only one eternal standard? I must therefore, if I reason consequentially, as strenuously maintain that they have the same simple direction, as that there is a God. . . .

Women, I allow, may have different duties to fulfill; but they are human duties, and the principles that should regulate the discharge of them, I sturdily maintain, must be the same.[15]

Wollstonecraft did not deceive herself about the difficulties of overcoming the inequalities between men and women. From childhood, an unrelenting social conditioning teaches women that their place in society is to remain dependent on men and to not develop their reason as equals to men. But Wollstonecraft is confident that women will flourish as the equals of men when they are freed from the deadening influence of this conditioning:

Novels, music, poetry, and gallantry, all tend to make women the creatures of sensation. . . . This overstretched sensibility naturally relaxes the other powers of the mind, and prevents intellect from attaining that sovereignty which it ought to attain to render a rational creature useful to others, and content with its own station: for the exercise of the understanding, as life advances, is

---

[13] Ibid., 85.
[14] Ibid., 86, 89.

[15] Ibid., 87, 90, 95.

the only method pointed out by nature to calm the passions. . . . Yet to their senses are women made slaves, because it is by their sensibility that they obtain present power. . . .

Asserting the rights which women in common with men ought to contend for, I have not attempted to extenuate their faults, but to prove them to be the natural consequence of their education and station in society. If so it is reasonable to suppose that they will change their character, and correct their vices and follies, when they are allowed to be free in a physical, moral, and civil sense.[16]

Now free of debt and a famous intellectual, Wollstonecraft traveled to France, which was then in the throes of a revolution. There, while the exhilarating madness of the French Revolution unfolded around her, Wollstonecraft met Gilbert Imlay, a dashing and liberal-thinking young American adventurer and war speculator. She fell passionately in love with him and in 1793 found herself pregnant with his child. On May 14, 1794, she gave birth to a girl, whom she named Fanny, after her friend. Imlay now withdrew his affection, and after several separations, he left her for good and went to England. In early 1795, Wollstonecraft followed him, only to learn on arriving in England that he had taken up with another woman; distraught, she tried to kill herself. After her recovery, Imlay got rid of her by talking her into taking their baby and going to Scandinavia as his business representative. Wollstonecraft returned from Scandinavia in late 1795, still hoping to be reconciled with Imlay, but found he had moved in with a young actress. Again she tried to commit suicide.

---

[16] Ibid., 98, 114.

Wollstonecraft now began to see a friend of many years, William Godwin. Gradually, she experienced their "friendship melting into love," as he came to seem like the perfect intellectual and emotional companion. By December of 1796, she was pregnant with his child. Three months later the two were married, and Mary rejoiced that she had at last found the fulfilling and tranquil relationship for which she had always longed. Tragically, only a few months later, on August 30, 1797, Mary Wollstonecraft died of complications related to childbirth.

QUESTIONS

1. Can you explain in your own words what Nietzsche means when he says that "all mechanical happenings . . . are will-power, will-effects"?

2. Explain the differences between "slave moralities" and "master moralities." Explain how slave moralities are supposed to be expressions of the "will to power." Explain how *all* moralities are supposed to be expressions of the will to power. Do you agree? Why?

3. Explain how reason makes us "superior to the brute creation," according to Wollstonecraft, and how reason is related to virtue. Can you explain why her views cannot be classified as utilitarian? Do you see any similarities between her views and those of Kant?

4. Why, according to Wollstonecraft, are the virtues of women the same as those of men? Do you agree?

5. Explain how education affects women's reason, according to Wollstonecraft, and the effect that this has on their virtue and on the respect that is due them. What does Wollstonecraft mean when she says women become "creatures of sensation and pleasure?"

6. To what extent is Wollstonecraft's criticism of the position of women still an accurate criticism of the position of all or some women today? Explain your answer.

8 Social and Political Philosophy

Freedom and bread enough for all are inconceivable together.

FYODOR DOSTOYEVSKI

OUTLINE AND LEARNING OBJECTIVES

© StudioSmart/Shutterstock.com

✓ QUICK REVIEW

Questions of social and political philosophy include: What is the legitimate role of government? What should government do for the poor? How is the individual related to society? Is the authority of the state justified? What is justice?.

8.1 What Is Social and Political Philosophy?

The U.S. government does many of the things governments have been doing for hundreds of years, such as maintaining law and order at home and conducting war against foreign enemies. But our government, like most governments today, does much more. It provides support for those who are poor, disabled, or unemployed. It pays for medical services for senior citizens. It subsidizes the businesses of farmers, fishermen, and miners. It has provided loans to banks, insurance companies, and car companies and has sometimes purchased large portions of their stock. The government pays for the education of all children. It provides college students with scholarships, subsidies, and loans. It pays for low-rent public housing, for urban mass transit systems, and for highway systems. The government is the nation's largest employer. It runs a major publishing business and underwrites the postal service. It provides or subsidizes loans to exporters, farmers, first-time homeowners, and small businesses. And thousands of government regulations now touch vast areas of U.S. life. These include antitrust regulations, labor regulations, equal opportunity regulations, employee safety regulations, medical regulations, drug regulations, and even toy regulations.

Are all these activities legitimate functions of government? Many conservative thinkers think not. Ronald Reagan, one of the most popular conservative presidents of the twentieth century, once said: "the taxing powers of government must be used to provide revenues for legitimate government purposes. It must not be used to regulate the economy or bring about social change."[1] In his view it is not legitimate for government to tax some citizens in order to provide benefits for others. Many thinkers have agreed with him. For example, economist William E. Simon holds that "the overriding principle to be revived in American political life is that which sets individual liberty as the highest political value—that value to which all other values are subordinate and which is to be given the highest priority in policy discussions. By the same token, there must be a conscious philosophical prejudice against any intervention by the state into our lives, for by definition such intervention abridges liberty."[2]

ANALYZING THE READING

1. The conservative president Ronald Reagan said tax revenues must be spent only on "legitimate government purposes." Also, "regulating the economy" or "bringing about social change" are not legitimate. What government purposes do you think he believed are "legitimate"? Do you agree with him? What programs or laws would he include as examples of "regulating the economy" and "bringing about social change"? Do you agree it is not legitimate for government to support those programs or laws? Why?

2. Economist William E. Simon claimed: "any intervention by the state into our lives... by definition... abridges liberty." Can you give some examples of the kinds of "intervention by the state into our lives" he probably had in mind? Look up the definition of "intervention." Is "abridges liberty" part of its definition? What do you think Simon's claim is supposed to mean? Simon offers one argument for his claim. What is that argument? Do you agree with the premises of that argument? Why?

Yet many Americans disagree with these conservative views. Recent Gallup polls indicate that a majority of 67 percent of Americans believes government spends too little on the issue of poverty. Other surveys indicate that 63 percent of Americans feel government should take care of people when they can't take care of themselves. Sixty-two percent feel that government ought to ensure that every citizen has enough to eat and a place to sleep. Eighty-three percent believe government should

---

[1]   Quoted in Daniel Patrick Moynihan, "Constitutional Dimensions of State and Local Tax Deductibility," *Publius: The Journal of Federalism,* Summer 1986; 16: 71–78.

[2]   Quoted in *What Is the Role of American Government?* (pamphlet) (St. Paul, MN: Greenhaven, 1988), 81.

do more to protect the environment. And 86 percent support government programs that make health care affordable and accessible.[3] In fact, many critics argue that government hasn't gone far enough in many areas. They believe taxes should be used more aggressively to correct social problems and injustices.

These claims and counterclaims raise several issues that have profound implications for how we run our society: What, exactly, should the role of government be? What is the source of the authority government wields over us? Is it just that government should play such a large role in regulating our lives? What is justice and what does justice demand of our government?

Asking how active a role government should take in the lives of its individual citizens leads to a broader question: What is the proper relation between the individual and society? Aristotle observed that a human being is a social animal. We work with, cooperate with, depend on, and otherwise relate to each other for our survival and prosperity. The totality of such *social relationships* among a group of people is *society*. A specific society is a specific group of people with shared interests, institutions, geographical location, and culture that distinguish them from other groups. Any society shapes our attitudes, values, loyalties, and outlooks. So we will also examine the relationship between the individual and society. Doing this will also shed light on the unifying theme of this text: your self-identity.

Throughout much of the discussion, we frequently refer to "the state" and its "power" or "authority." When we talk about "the state," we are not using the word in the sense in which California and New York are "states." Instead, we will use the word to refer to what we today often refer to as a "nation." A nation is a politically organized body of people who occupy a definite territory and whose government has supreme or "sovereign" authority over the people in that territory. In this sense, the United States *as a whole* is a state, but California and New York are not states. Because the state exercises its sovereign authority through its government, we sometimes use the two terms (*state* and *government*) interchangeably. Properly speaking, of course, the national government is the means through which the state exercises its authority. Because the authority of the state and the authority of the national government are really one and the same, we will often use the two terms interchangeably. Two other terms we will use interchangeably are "power" and "authority." Strictly speaking, power refers to the *ability* to control people's actions, while authority refers to the *right* to control people's actions. But authority also can be used to refer to power that an agent has the right to use to control people's actions, while power can be used to refer to authority that gives the agent the ability to control people's actions. In this second usage the terms are often used interchangeably and we will follow this second usage.

In approaching the topic of social and political philosophy, we focus on three related issues. First, we consider how the power and authority of the state may be justified. This requires a close look at social contract theory, which forms the theoretical foundations for the legitimacy of our government and its authority. Second, determining the proper role of government inevitably raises questions of fairness and justice. So we next look at some influential theories of justice that can be used to determine whether government and its actions are fair and just. But even if government is just, there is a third question: Are there any moral limits to the government's use of its power? So, third and finally, we consider whether the authority of

---

3   Gallup, "Americans Dissatisfied with Government's Efforts on Poverty," October 25, 2005, http://www.gallup.com/poll/19396/Americans-Dissatisfied-Governments-Efforts-Poverty.aspx (accessed May 30, 2009); Pew Research Center, "Independents Take Center Stage in Obama Era," May 21, 2009, http://people-press.org/reports/pdf/517.pdf (accessed May 30, 2009).

THINKING LIKE A PHILOSOPHER

1. Do you agree with the way our government runs the country? What do you think our government does well, and what do you think it does poorly?

2. How would you answer the following three questions: Is the government spending too much on welfare programs for poor people? Is the government doing enough to protect the environment? Should the government send our troops to fight wars in other countries that are not attacking our country? Do you think any of these three government activities go beyond what government has a right to do? Explain.

3. What would you say is the purpose of a government? Has the government done anything during the last five years that you think goes beyond its purpose?

government must always be obeyed, the rights that can limit the power of the state, and limits on the state's use of its power in war and terrorism.

The concepts and issues we discuss have one thing in common: They arise out of the social milieu. Although they have ethical and political implications, they do not directly involve either ethics or politics. They are not ethics because they are not primarily concerned with establishing a norm of good conduct. They are not politics because they are not concerned with the art or science of governing a state and its people. Rather, these concerns fall into the category of **social philosophy**, which is the philosophical study of society and its problems and the application of moral principles and concepts to these problems. Such concepts include the concepts of human rights, justice, and freedom. **Political philosophy** is usually considered a subdivision of social philosophy.

Political philosophy is that part of social philosophy that looks at the proper role of the state or government in society. Political philosophy addresses questions such as: What justifies the power and authority of the state? What are the moral limits on the power of the state? What is law and do we have a moral obligation to obey the laws of the state? As we noted, political philosophy is a subdivision of social philosophy, so the issues of political philosophy are also issues of social philosophy. Using the term *political philosophy*, however, reminds us that many social issues concern that political entity, the state.

PHILOSOPHY AT THE MOVIES

Watch *Snowpiercer* (2014) which takes place in a future when all life on earth has been destroyed except for a few hundred who have managed to board the Snowpiercer, a train that has been traveling around the earth for 17 years carrying humanity's last survivors. A class system has developed and a security force maintains order but those who have been forced to live in squalid conditions at the rear of the train attempt a revolt. (Note that *Snowpiercer* is a surrealistic film and so has dozens of plot points that don't make logical sense. Don't watch this film expecting realism and tight logic!) What philosophical questions about politics, society, government, and justice does this film raise for you?

Other movies with similar themes: *Elysium* (2013); *2012* (2009).

8.2 What Justifies the State and Its Power?

The state is the highest authority in a society, and has the power to define the public interest and enforce its definition. One clear example of the state doing this is the income tax system. The state sets its priorities—that is, it defines the programs and actions that it decides are in the public interest. Then, it taxes citizens to implement these programs and actions. In theory, Americans pay taxes proportional to their incomes. That is, the more they make, the greater the proportion of their income they pay in taxes. Many feel that this is fair. But the demands for government programs and services have increased. And the costs of those programs and services have also increased. As a result, the government's demand for taxes has grown. A sizable number of people think that this tax burden is now unfair, especially people who disagree with the programs for which taxes are spent.

Take, for example, a childless couple who live in an apartment and who both work, she as a doctor and he as a stockbroker. Since they rent and have no dependents, they can claim few deductions on their state and federal income taxes. But because they both earn high incomes, they pay hefty taxes every year. Yet much of their tax money goes to pay for things from which they will never benefit. This year, some of their local tax money went to pay for new school buildings, although they have no children. Some of their money went to maintain national parks, although they never plan to visit them. Besides paying for things that do not benefit them, some of their money pays for things they positively disagree with. For example, some of their state taxes fund abortion clinics, although they may feel that abortion is a form of murder. Some of their federal taxes pay for military weapons. Yet both may be pacifists and believe that it is immoral to support the military. Some of their money subsidizes the tobacco industry. Yet neither of them may smoke because both feel that smoking causes cancer. So they may feel it is a violation of their conscience to support a product that kills people.

Is it fair for government to force this couple to pay for programs that they cannot in good conscience support? Are they wrong to feel government has no right to make them do things they would not choose to do on their own? Are they wrong to feel that the government is misusing its power and authority?

But this case raises a broader question not directly related to specific government programs or measures. What justifies the authority of the state in the first place? What gives the state the right to tax, conscript, fight wars, educate, or do any of the myriad things it does? Clearly, we cannot say government has misused its authority until we know what its rightful purpose and limits are. And determining the rightful purpose and limits of government authority requires an inquiry into the source of that authority.

Political thinkers have advanced several theories to explain the legitimacy of the state and justify its authority. Some have justified the power of the state by appealing to God. Thus, some rulers have claimed their power is based on a divine right to rule. That is, God made them the rulers and so citizens have a duty to accept their authority. Others have justified the state's authority by appealing to the public interest. They have claimed that so long as the state furthers the public interest, its authority is justified. But the theory that most of us today accept is that the state is justified because citizens consent to be ruled by the state.

The most influential modern versions of this view are captured in the term *social contract*. Social contract theory is a theory of state legitimacy that has extraordinary importance for us today. **Social contract theory** says individuals agree to form governments to protect their lives, liberty, and pursuit of happiness. Their agreement or "contract" creates a government. As part of the agreement they consent to give the government the authority it needs to protect what they value. Contract theory is thus both an explanation of the origin and purpose of the state and a defense of its authority. We see versions of contract theory as far back as Plato. In *The Republic* one of Socrates' friends says:

> They say it is natural to benefit from doing wrong to another, and natural to suffer harm when one is wronged by another. But the harm of being wronged generally outweighs the benefits of wrongdoing. Consequently, when men have wronged

others and have been wronged themselves, and so have tasted both, those who are too weak to wrong others or to stop others from wronging them, make an agreement with each other to put an end to both. And that is the origin, they say of orderly society, of laws, and of agreements between men.[4]

But the most important proponents of social contract theory were Thomas Hobbes and John Locke. More recently, the philosopher John Rawls proposed a new and intriguing version of social contract theory.

Hobbes and the War of All against All

More than any other person, Thomas Hobbes was the founder of modern political philosophy. There were political theorists before him including Plato, Aristotle, Saint Augustine, and Thomas Aquinas. They claimed that the state develops naturally from smaller groups such as the family, the tribe, and the village. The state is not created by people but is an organic development that arises from our social nature. By participating in the political and social life of the state we become better and more complete human beings. In contrast, Hobbes based his political philosophy on the idea that people are not social. And the state is not a natural outgrowth from smaller societies. It is, instead, an artificial creation of human beings designed to protect us from each other.

In his classic work, *Leviathan,* Hobbes portrayed humans as selfish, unsocial creatures. They are driven by three main "passions": the desire for personal gain, for security, and for respect from others. Without government people would constantly be battling each other for personal gain, security, and respect. Human life without the "common power" of government, therefore, is constant struggle, strife, and war. So "miserable" is such an existence that it drives men to agree to give a ruler the power to force them to live in peace. That agreement is the birth of government. Here, in a version with modernized English, is what Hobbes says in his *Leviathan:*

> Nature has made men so equal, in the faculties of body and mind, that . . . the difference between man and man is not so considerable that one man can claim to himself any benefit to which another may not pretend as well as he. For as to the strength of body, the weakest has strength enough to kill the strongest, either by secret machination or by confederacy with others. . . . And as to the faculties of the mind I find yet a greater equality among men than that of strength. For prudence is but experience which equal time equally bestows on all men. . . .
>
> From this equality of ability, arises equality of hope in the attaining of our ends. And therefore if any two men desire the same thing, which nevertheless they cannot both enjoy, they become enemies, and . . . endeavor to destroy, or subdue one another. . . . If one plant, sow, build, or possess a convenient seat, others may probably be expected to come prepared with forces united, to dispossess, and deprive him, not only of the fruit of his labor, but also of his life, or liberty. . . .
>
> So in the nature of man, we find three principal causes of quarrel. First, competition; secondly, distrust; thirdly, glory. The first makes men invade for gain; the second, for safety; and the third, for reputation. The first use violence, to make themselves masters of other men's persons, wives, children, and cattle; the second, to defend them; the third, for trifles, as a word, a smile, a different opinion, and any other sign of [being] undervalued.

---

[4]   Plato, *The Republic,* bk. II, translated by Manuel Velasquez.

Hereby it is manifest, that during the time men live without a common power to keep them all in awe, they are in that condition which is called war; and such a war, as is of every man, against every man. . . .

In such condition, there is no place for industry; because the fruit thereof is uncertain: and consequently no culture of the earth; no navigation, nor use of the commodities that may be imported by sea; no commodious building; no instruments of moving and removing such things as require much force; no knowledge of the face of the earth; no account of time; no arts; no letters; no society; and, which is worst of all, continual fear and danger of violent death; and the life of man [is] solitary, poor, nasty, brutish, and short.

It may seem strange to some man that has not well weighed these things that Nature should thus dissociate and render men apt to invade and destroy one another, and he may therefore, not trusting to this inference made from the passions, desire perhaps to have the same confirmed by experience. Let him therefore consider with himself: when taking a journey he arms himself and seeks to go well accompanied; when going to sleep he locks his doors; when even in his house he locks his chests; and this when he knows there be laws and public officers, armed to revenge all injuries that shall be done him; what opinion does he have of his fellow subjects when he rides armed; of his fellow citizens when he locks his doors; and of his children and servants when he locks his chests? Does he not there as much accuse mankind by his actions as I do by my words?

To this war of every man against every man, this also is consequent: that nothing can be unjust. The notions of right and wrong, justice and injustice, have there no place. [For] where there is no common power, there is no law; where no law, no injustice. Force and fraud are in war the two cardinal virtues.

The . . . end, or design of men (who naturally love liberty, and dominion over others) in the introduction of that restraint upon themselves in which we see them live in Commonwealths, is the foresight of their own preservation, and of a more contented life thereby; that is to say, of getting themselves out from that miserable condition of war which is necessarily consequent, as has been shown, to the natural passions of men when there is no visible [common] power to keep them in awe . . .

The only way to erect such a common power, as may be able to defend them from the invasion of foreigners, and the injuries of one another, and thereby to secure them in such sort as that by their own industry and by the fruits of the earth they may nourish themselves and live contentedly, is to confer all their power and strength upon one man, or upon one assembly of men . . . and to submit their wills, everyone, to his will, and their judgments to his judgment. This is more than consent, or concord; it is a real unity of them all in one and the same person, made by covenant of every man with every man, in such manner as if every man should say to every man: "I authorize and give up my right of governing myself to this man, or to this assembly of men, on this condition; that you give up, your right to him, and authorize all his actions in like manner." This done, the multitude so united in one person is called a COMMONWEALTH; in Latin, CIVITAS. This is the generation of that great LEVIATHAN, or rather, to speak more reverently, of that mortal god to which we owe, under the immortal God, our peace and defense. For by this authority, given him by every particular man in the Commonwealth, he has the use of so much power and strength conferred

ANALYZING THE READING

1. Hobbes gives two arguments to show that without government people would be at war with each other. He says one argument is an "inference made from the passions," and the other is an argument that "confirms by experience." What are these two arguments? Do you think his arguments are valid? Are they sound? Why?

2. Hobbes suggests that before government exists, people are at war with each other and so could not cooperate or trust each other. Yet he says that people can cooperate in an agreement to form a government. Do you see a problem here? Do you think Hobbes has an answer for this problem?

3. According to Hobbes the ruler must have unlimited power over citizens if he is "by terror" to be "enabled to form the wills of them all, to peace at home, and mutual aid against their enemies abroad." Is Hobbes right?

4. Suppose Hobbes is right in everything he says. Would this show that the authority of the U.S. government today is justified?

Frontispiece to *Leviathan* by Thomas Hobbes: "Hereby it is manifest that during the time men live without a common power to keep them all in awe, they are in that condition which is called war; and such a war, as is of every man, against every man, and the life of man is solitary, nasty, brutish, and short."

Private Collection/The Bridgeman Art Library

on him that, by terror thereof, he is enabled to form the wills of them all, to peace at home, and mutual aid against their enemies abroad. And he that carries this person is called sovereign, and said to have sovereign power; and every one besides, his subject. . . .

Because the right of bearing the person of them all is given to him they make sovereign, by covenant only of one to another, and not of him to any of them, there can happen no breach of covenant on the part of the sovereign; and consequently none of his subjects . . . can be freed from his subjection. . . . Annexed to the sovereignty [is] the whole power of prescribing the rules whereby every man may know what goods he may enjoy, and what actions he may do. . . . These rules of property (or *mine* and *yours*) and of good, evil, lawful, and unlawful in the actions of subjects are the civil laws.

[The sovereign's] power cannot, without his consent, be transferred to another: he cannot forfeit it: he cannot be accused by any of his subjects of injury: he cannot be punished by them: he is judge of what is necessary for peace, and judge of doctrines: he is sole legislator, and supreme judge of controversies, and of the times and occasions of war and peace: to him it belongs to choose magistrates, counselors, commanders, and all other officers and ministers; and to determine of rewards and punishments, honor and order. . . . The sovereign power . . . is as great as possibly men can be imagined to make it. And though of so unlimited a power, men may fancy many evil consequences, yet the consequences of the want of it, which is perpetual war of every man against his neighbor, are much worse.[5]

Hobbes' social contract theory is extraordinary. First, his theory explains how governments come into existence. Governments are created when people unite and agree to give a person or persons the authority to rule over them. Second, Hobbes' theory explains why the authority of government is justified. It is justified for a simple reason: citizens agree to give the state the authority to rule them. Since citizens have given their consent the state is justified in using its authority to force them to obey. Third, Hobbes' social contract theory provides citizens with a clear explanation of the purpose of government: "to defend them from the invasion of foreigners, and the injuries of one another." And fourth, his theory explains what limits there are to the power of government. The power of government, according to Hobbes' theory, is virtually unlimited.

Why does Hobbes say the power of government must be unlimited? Consider that humans create a government out of a concern for their safety and survival. Because their lives would otherwise be "solitary, poor, nasty, brutish, and short," humans must create a government so powerful it can force them all to live in peace. That means

---

[5]   Thomas Hobbes, *Leviathan* (London: J. Bohn, 1839), excerpts from Part One, chs. 13, 17, 18, and 20.

the person or body that wields political power must have unlimited and absolute authority over all citizens. Without such absolute power, Hobbes felt, government would be unable to force people to live in peace. In the end, then, the government that individuals agree to create must become superior to the individuals who created it.

Notice also that Hobbes claims that before government exists there can be no morality. As he puts it: "The notions of right and wrong, justice and injustice, have there no place." Consequently, people can have no moral rights until government exists. Government creates all moral rights including the right to life, the right to liberty, and the right to own property. Government creates rights by choosing and enforcing the laws that grant people those rights. Hobbes felt that if a moral law could not be enforced then it amounted to nothing. Since moral laws cannot be enforced until government exists, there can be no real morality until then.

THINKING LIKE A PHILOSOPHER

1. Do you think Hobbes' description of how people would act if there was no government is at all accurate? Do you think there are neighborhoods in your city or places around the world to which Hobbes' description would apply today? If so, where are they?

2. Hobbes says that if there was no authority (like government) that kept us from harming each other, we would steal, lie, cheat, or do anything to get what we want. Do you think this is true of you? If you knew absolutely for sure you would never be caught by any authority or anyone else, would you still refrain from stealing, lying, cheating, or doing other wrongs to get what you want? What do you think people in general would do?

3. Hobbes says that a state of nature would be a war "of every man against every man." What would you do to survive in that kind of situation? Would you try to form a group that could work together to protect each other?

Hobbes lived and wrote during the civil wars that shook England during the seventeenth century. The civil wars were fought between those who wanted to be ruled by a monarch, and those who wanted to be ruled by a Parliament that represented the people. Given his defense of an absolute sovereign, it is not surprising that Hobbes sided with those who remained loyal to the monarchy. But the forces of Parliament had their own philosopher to support them. His name was John Locke.

Locke and Natural Moral Laws

We saw that Hobbes believed that, without government to restrain them, people would commit any crime to get what they want. In contrast, John Locke saw humans as essentially moral beings who would feel an obligation to obey the moral law even in the absence of government. Where Hobbes saw a lawless war as humanity's natural state, Locke saw our natural state as regulated by the moral law he called "the law of nature."

If there were no government, Locke held, people would find themselves in "a state of nature" where they would be free and equal. In the state of nature people, by using their reason, would see that they should respect the life, health, and property of others. Government, he claims, does not decree respect for the moral rights of others—our own reason does. The state of nature, then, is not a war of "every man against every man." It is, instead, populated by people who are free, rational, social and, to some extent, moral.

But if people in the state of nature are free and equal, why do they give up their freedom and equality and subject themselves to a government? People establish governments, Locke claimed, because three things are missing in the state of nature: (1) a clear interpretation of the unwritten moral law; (2) unbiased judges to resolve disputes about the moral law; and (3) a power capable of enforcing justice when someone violates the moral law. So individuals agree to create a government that can provide what the state of nature lacks, and thereby protect the natural moral rights reason "teaches" people they have. Locke explains the origin and purpose of government in these passages from his brilliant and influential work, *Essay Concerning the True and Original Extent and End of Civil Government*:

Sec. 4. To understand political power right, and derive it from its original, we must consider, what state all men are naturally in, and that is, a state of perfect freedom to order their actions, and dispose of their possessions and persons, as they think fit, within the bounds of the law of nature. . . . A state also of equality, wherein all the power and jurisdiction is reciprocal, no one having more than another. . . .

Sec. 6. But though this be a state of liberty, yet it is not a state of license. . . . The state of nature has a law of nature to govern it, which obliges every one: and reason, which is that law, teaches all mankind, who will but consult it, that being all equal and independent, no one ought to harm another in his life, health, liberty, or possessions: . . .

Sec. 27. . . .[Reason also teaches] that every man has a property in his own person: this no body has any right to but himself. The labor of his body, and the work of his hands, we may say, are properly his. Whatsoever then he removes out of the state that nature has provided, and left it in, he has mixed his labor with, and joined to it something that is his own, and thereby makes it his property. It being by him removed from the common state nature has placed it in, it has by this labor something annexed to it, that excludes the common right of other men: for this labor being the unquestionable property of the laborer, no man but he can have a right to what that is joined to, at least where there is enough, and as good, left in common for others.

Sec. 95. Men being, as has been said, by nature, all free, equal, and independent, no one can be put out of this estate, and subjected to the political power of another, without his own consent. The only way whereby any one divests himself of his natural liberty, and puts on the bonds of civil society, is by agreeing with other men to join and unite into a community for their comfortable, safe, and peaceable living one amongst another, in a secure enjoyment of their properties. . . .

Sec. 97. And thus every man, by consenting with others to make one body politic under one government, puts himself under an obligation to every one of that society, to submit to the determination of the majority, and to be concluded [bound] by it; or else this original compact, whereby he with others incorporates into one society, would signify nothing, and be no compact, if he be left free, and under no other ties than he was in before in the state of nature. . . .

ANALYZING THE READING

1. Locke says that even without government we have a moral right to own property because we each own our person, our labor, and anything that was not previously owned and into which we "mix" our labor. Examples of things not previously owned into which I mix my labor are poems I write and statues I carve out of driftwood I find on a seashore. Can you give other examples?

2. Do you agree that things become yours if they are not previously owned and you "mix" your labor into them by improving them or turning them into something useful?

3. Do you agree that we own ourselves? Our labor? Would Locke say that a slave owns himself or his labor? Why?

Sec. 119. [But what is] a sufficient declaration of a man's consent? There is a common distinction of an express and a tacit consent, which will concern our present case. Nobody doubts but an express consent, of any man entering into any society, makes him a perfect member of that society, a subject of that government. . . . The difficulty is, what ought to be looked upon as a tacit consent? And to this I say, that every man that has any possessions, or enjoyment of any part of the dominions of any government, does thereby give his tacit consent, and is as far forth obliged to obedience to the laws of that government, during such enjoyment, as any one under it; whether his possession be of land . . . or a lodging only for a week; or barely travelling freely on the highway. . . .

Sec. 123. If man in the state of Nature be so free as has been said, . . . why will he part with his freedom, and subject himself to the dominion and control of any other power? To which is it obvious to answer, that though in the state of Nature he has a right, yet the enjoyment of it is very uncertain and constantly exposed to the invasion of others; for all being kings as much as he, every man his equal, and the greater part no strict observers of equity and justice, the enjoyment of the property he has in this state is very unsafe, very insecure. This makes him willing to quit this condition which, however free, is full of fears and continual dangers; and it is not without reason that he seeks out and is willing to join in society with others . . . for the mutual preservation of their lives, liberties and estates, which I call by the general name—property.

Sec.124. The great and chief end, therefore, of men uniting into commonwealths, and putting themselves under government, is the preservation of their property; to which in the state of Nature there are many things wanting.

First, there wants an established, settled, known law, received and allowed by common consent to be the standard of right and wrong. . . .

Sec.125. Secondly, in the state of Nature there wants a known and indifferent judge, with authority to determine all differences according to the established law. . . .

Sec.126. Thirdly, in the state of Nature there often wants power to back and support the sentence when right, and to give it due execution. . . .

Sec.127. Thus mankind, notwithstanding all the privileges of the state of Nature, being but in an ill condition while they remain in it, are quickly driven into society. . . .The inconveniences that they are therein exposed to by the irregular and uncertain exercise of the power every man has of punishing the transgressions of others, make them take sanctuary under the established laws of government, and therein seek the preservation of their property. . . . And in this we have the original right and rise of both the legislative and executive power as well as of governments. . . .

Sec. 222. The reason why men enter into society is the preservation of their property. And the end why they choose and authorize a legislative is that there may be laws made and rules set, as guards and fences to the properties of all the members of the society. . . . Since it can never be supposed to be the will of the society that the legislative should have a power to destroy that which everyone designs to secure by entering into society, and for which the people submitted themselves to legislators of their own making, whenever the legislators endeavor to take away and destroy the property of the people, or to reduce them to slavery under arbitrary power, they put themselves into a state of war with the people, who are thereupon absolved from any farther obedience. . . . Whensoever, therefore, the [government] . . . shall transgress this fundamental rule of society, and either by ambition, fear, folly, or corruption, endeavor to grasp . . . an absolute power over the lives, liberties and estates of the people, by this breach of trust they forfeit the power the people had put into their hands for quite contrary ends. And it devolves to the people, who have a right to resume their original liberty and by the establishment of a new [government], . . . provide for their own safety and security, which is the end for which they are in society. [6]

ANALYZING THE READING

1. Hobbes says that without government people would not follow any moral rules and everyone would use "force and fraud" to harm others and take what they have. But Locke suggests that without government people would know that the moral law says we should not harm others, and that some or most people would generally follow the moral law. Which of these two views do you think provides the most accurate view of how people would behave if there was no government to maintain law and order? Why?

2. According to Locke, people would have moral rights even before government existed and they create government to protect those rights. But Hobbes says people can have no moral rights until government exists because moral laws are nothing until there is someone that can enforce those moral laws. Who is right?

 ## THINKING LIKE A PHILOSOPHER

1. Social contract theory says you should obey government's laws because you agreed to. Did you ever intentionally or unintentionally make such an agreement? By choosing to continue to live in this country did you "implicitly" agree to obey its laws? Is such an implicit agreement valid if you cannot leave the country? Even if you have not made an agreement to obey our laws, do you have an obligation to obey anyway? Why?

2. Locke says that if government tries to "grasp absolute power over the lives, liberties and estates of the people," it will "forfeit the power" citizens gave it, and citizens would then "have a right to resume their original liberty" and establish a new government. Locke means citizens would then have a right to overthrow government and establish a new one. Do you agree that if our government tried to do what Locke describes, it would loose the right to govern you? How far would our government have to go before you personally would be willing to fight to overthrow it?

[6] John Locke, *Essay Concerning the True and Original Extent and End of Civil Government,* vol. 4 (1690) (Oxford: Clarendon, 1894), excerpts from secs. 4, 6, 26, 27, 123, 124, 125, 126, 127, and 222.

In short, individuals make an agreement or contract to create a government that will protect their moral rights to "life, liberty, and estate"—which together Locke calls their "property." This social contract is based on the consent of the people, and all agree to abide by the decisions of the majority.

Note that in the final section (222) Locke argues that the government's authority is limited. Unlike Hobbes, Locke did not believe the power of government is unlimited. Since people form a government to protect their rights to life, liberty, and estates, government has no authority to do anything that goes beyond this basic purpose. More importantly, if government begins to take away citizens' lives, liberties, or estates citizens can take back the authority they had given it. For Locke, therefore, the authority of government is not absolute but specific and limited.

Locke also differs from Hobbes with respect to the source of morality and moral rights. We saw that Hobbes argues that government creates and gives people whatever moral rights they have. Before government, Hobbes concludes, there is no morality and so no moral rights. But Locke argues that in the state of nature, people would discover the laws of morality by using their reason. The moral law that all people can discover by using their reason, Locke argues, "teaches" that everyone has a right to life and liberty. That same moral law teaches that each person owns his own body, the labor that issues from his body, and the products into which he "mixes" his labor. So people also have a moral right to property, because each owns his body and its labor and what he makes with his labor. Locke's point is that government does not create and give people the moral rights they have. Instead, people's rights to life, liberty, and property exist independent of, and prior to, government. And the reason people have these rights before government exists is because morality is not created by government but is discovered by people independently of government.

THINKING LIKE A PHILOSOPHER

1. Locke says that "reason" can "teach us" that we should not "harm another in his life, health, liberty, or possessions." Have you ever, by using your own reason, figured out that you had a moral obligation to do something or refrain from doing it?

2. Do you think that today all your ideas about right and wrong are just those your parents or teachers taught you, or are many of them ideas that you figured out for yourself using your reason? What are some examples of both kinds of ideas?

3. If your parents or teachers had not taught you what was right and what was wrong, do you think you could have figured it out on your own using your reason? Why?

4. Have you ever felt your conscience prompting you to do something right or to refrain from something wrong? Do you think your conscience is anything like Locke's voice of "reason"?

This point is important because it explains what Locke believes the purpose of government is and why its authority is limited. For Hobbes the purpose of government is to protect people from the violence of others. People are so violent that a government with unlimited power is needed to control them. But Locke does not believe everyone is as violent as Hobbes felt they were. So Locke argues, instead, that the purpose of government is to protect people's moral rights. It is true that protecting people's moral rights will often require protecting them from the violence of others. But there are other ways that people's moral rights can be threatened. In particular, government itself may try to infringe on people's rights. Locke's theory implies that government has no authority to infringe on people's moral rights because its purpose is to protect, not violate, those rights. The authority of government, therefore, is limited by the moral rights of citizens. For Hobbes, on the other hand, government can do whatever it wants to citizens because its authority is unlimited. And since a citizen's moral rights are given by government they can be taken away by government. So Hobbes' government may legitimately take a citizen's liberty, property and, even his life. Not so in Locke. When government infringes on people's moral rights—what Locke calls their "property"—it has transgressed its authority.

Signing the Declaration of Independence, John Trumbull. Both the Declaration and Locke's contract agree that when a government infringes on the individual rights of life, liberty, and the pursuit of happiness (or "estates," for Locke), the people have a right to dismiss it.

An important consequence of the fact that it is wrong for government to violate people's rights is that people have the right to resist and rebel against government authority. Recall that Hobbes believed that resistance to the authority of the sovereign is never justified. Locke, on the contrary, regards such resistance as a fundamental moral right. And so when government itself violates citizen's moral rights, citizens have a moral right to object, resist, and even overthrow that government.

Although the contrast between Hobbes and Locke is significant, they both agree that rationality enables humans to perceive the necessity of entering a social contract to create the state. They also agree on the source of the state's authority: the consent of the governed. Locke, like Hobbes, felt that the power the state exerts is justified because it is a power that we have consented to accept. Our ancestors, Locke believed, consented to the original establishment of government. And each of us today tacitly consents again to that same government when we voluntarily choose to continue to live under that government.

Yet Locke, much more than Hobbes, also emphasized the right to liberty. It was Locke's firm belief that government must respect people's moral right to liberty. In fact, it is the duty and purpose of government to protect the individual's right to be left free to pursue happiness as he sees fit.

It is difficult to exaggerate the tremendous influence that Locke's views had on political events both during his life and long afterwards. Locke's views were adopted by several nations during what is sometimes called the "century of revolutions." In 1776, for example, the American colonies sounded a Lockean chord in these lines from the Declaration of Independence:

> We hold these truths to be self-evident. That all men are created equal. That they are endowed by their Creator with certain unalienable rights. That among these are life, liberty and the pursuit of happiness. That to secure these rights, governments are instituted among men, deriving their just powers from the consent of the governed. That whenever any Form of Government becomes destructive of these ends, it is the Right of the People to alter or to abolish it, and to institute a new Government, laying its foundation on such principles and organizing its powers in such form, as to them shall seem most likely to effect their safety and Happiness.[7]

The similarities to Locke's position are not accidental. The Declaration of Independence was written by Thomas Jefferson, an avid reader and disciple of Locke.

---

[7]   U.S. Declaration of Independence, Paragraph 2 (1776).

Contemporary Social Contract: Rawls

The social contract theories of Hobbes and Locke were severely criticized in the eighteenth century by that most skeptical of all skeptics, David Hume. Hume struck a simple but devastating blow to social contract theory. He pointed out that there never was a social contract. Governments, he argued, are established by conquest or are handed on by the right of succession. If we go back in history, he pointed out, we will find no signs of people coming together to choose their governments. Social contract is, in short, a complete fiction:

> [Some] philosophers . . . assert . . . that government in its earliest infancy arose from consent, or rather the voluntary acquiescence of the people. . . . They affirm that all men are born equal and owe allegiance to no prince or government, unless bound by the obligation and sanction of a promise. . . .
>
> But would these reasoners look abroad into the world, they would meet with nothing that, in the least, corresponds to their ideas. . . . On the contrary, we find everywhere princes who claim their subjects as their property and assert their independent right of sovereignty, from conquest or succession. We find also, everywhere, subjects, who acknowledge this right in their prince. . . . Were you to preach, in most parts of the world, that political connections are founded altogether on voluntary consent or a mutual promise, the magistrate would soon imprison you, as seditious, for loosening the ties of obedience; if your friends did not before shut you up as delirious, for advancing such absurdities. . . . Almost all the governments which exist at present, or of which there remains any record in history, have been founded originally either on usurpation or conquest or both, without any pretense of a fair consent or voluntary subjection of the people.[8]

ANALYZING THE READING

1. According to Hume history shows all governments have been founded by "conquest" or "succession" or "usurpation," and not by "voluntary consent or a mutual promise." Do you think this is true? What about the U.S. government?

2. Suppose Hume is right and no government ever began by people meeting and agreeing to a social contract. Would that show that social contract theory is completely wrong? Why?

3. Could Locke use his theory of "tacit consent" to show that Hume is wrong because everyone today makes an agreement to recognize the authority of government? Do you agree with Locke's views about tacit consent? Why?

So devastating was Hume's attack that most philosophers gave up on social contract theory. For more than a century, the theory fell out of favor, and philosophers almost completely ignored it.

Toward the end of the twentieth century, however, social contract theory once more resurfaced. Harvard philosopher John Rawls (1921–2002) reshaped social contract theory into a powerful new way of thinking about the nature of government and society.

Rawls agreed with Hume that the social contract is a historical fiction. People have not necessarily come together and decided to start their governments. However, Rawls argued, this does not matter. The significance of social contract theory is that it gives us a way of thinking about what our governments should be like. Social contract theory says that to figure out what kind of government we should have, we should imagine that we are starting our society and our government from scratch. What kind of government would we choose for ourselves if we were in this starting or "original" position and wanted to create a government that was just?

---

8   David Hume, "Of the Original Contract," in *Essays, Literary, Moral, and Political* (New York: Ward, Lock & Tyler, n.d., c. 1870), 272–273.

Rawls proposed that if we are to determine what justice and a just government are, we must set aside everything that leads us to favor ourselves over others. A just government is one that is equally fair to everyone and shows favoritism to none. But how will we set aside the things that unjustly lead us to favor ourselves over others? Rawls made an ingenious proposal. Imagine, he proposed, that we were about to start a new society and a new government. Suppose that by some miracle none of us knows anything about what he or she will be like in that new society. For example, we don't know whether we will be male or female, black or white, rich or poor, young or old, smart or dumb, talented or untalented, needy or self-sufficient, religious or atheist. Then, we would be forced to choose a government that is fair to everyone no matter what they happen to be like. If I do not know, for example, whether I will be black or white in this new society, then I will insist on a government that favors neither blacks nor whites. I will want a government that does not discriminate. Or suppose that I do not know whether in our new society I will be rich or poor, atheist or religious, talented or untalented. Then, I will insist on a government that favors neither the rich nor the poor, neither the atheist nor the religious person, and neither the talented nor the untalented. Rawls called his view "justice as fairness."

QUICK REVIEW
Rawls agrees with Hume that the social contract is a historical fiction but said that it helps us see what a just government is. Rawls argues that a just government is one we would choose to live under if we chose without knowing whether we would be rich or poor, black or white, and so forth. For under such a "veil of ignorance," we would choose a form of government that was fair to everyone by providing everyone with equal political rights and economic opportunities.

Thus we are to imagine that those who engage in social cooperation choose together, in one joint act, the principles which are to assign basic rights and duties and to determine the division of social benefits. . . . Men are to decide in advance how they are to regulate their claims against one another and what is to be the foundation charter of their society. . . .

In justice as fairness the original position of equality corresponds to the state of nature in the traditional theory of the social contract. This original position is not, of course, thought of as an actual historical state of affairs, much less as a primitive condition of culture. It is understood as a purely hypothetical situation characterized so as to lead to a certain conception of justice. Among the essential features of this situation is that no one knows his place in society, his class position or social status, nor does anyone know his fortune in the distribution of natural assets and abilities, his intelligence, strength and the like. . . . Since all are similarly situated and no one is able to design principles to favor his particular condition, the principles of justice [they choose] are the result of a fair agreement or bargain.[9]

ANALYZING THE READING

Rawls concludes that people in his "original position" will choose principles for their future society that are fair and just to everyone. They would choose fair and just principles, he says, because no one would know the kind of person they will be in their future society. Since no one knows what kind of person they will be, no one will choose principles that are unfair to any person. For example, since no one knows if they will be rich or poor, they will choose principles that are fair to both the rich and the poor. Since no one knows if they will be black or white, they will choose principles that are fair to both blacks and whites. Since no one knows if they will be male or female, they will choose principles that are fair to both males and females. Rawls concludes that in the original position people's choices must be fair: the principles they choose will necessarily be just to everyone. Do you agree with this conclusion? If you disagree, what step in his argument is wrong?

Notice what social contract has become for Rawls. It is no longer a description of how we formed the governments that we *actually* have. Instead, it is now an imaginary device that is supposed to help us determine what justice requires. If our government is to be just, then, it must live up to the principles of justice that people in the original position would choose.

---

[9]   John Rawls, *A Theory of Justice* (Cambridge, MA: Harvard University Press, 1972), excerpts from 11, 12, and 13.

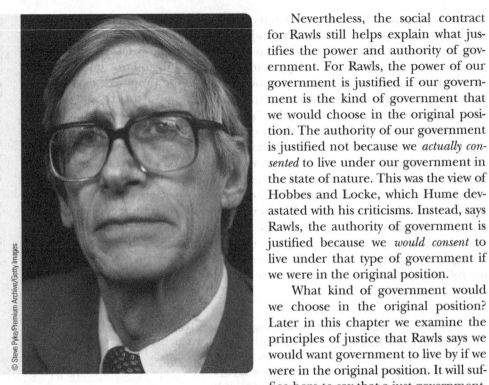

John Rawls: "...the principles of justice are the result of a fair agreement or bargain."

Nevertheless, the social contract for Rawls still helps explain what justifies the power and authority of government. For Rawls, the power of our government is justified if our government is the kind of government that we would choose in the original position. The authority of our government is justified not because we *actually consented* to live under our government in the state of nature. This was the view of Hobbes and Locke, which Hume devastated with his criticisms. Instead, says Rawls, the authority of government is justified because we *would consent* to live under that type of government if we were in the original position.

What kind of government would we choose in the original position? Later in this chapter we examine the principles of justice that Rawls says we would want government to live by if we were in the original position. It will suffice here to say that a just government, according to Rawls, is one that does not favor one way of life over another. It does not favor one religion over another. It does not favor one ethnic or racial group over another. It does not favor one culture over another. Instead, it leaves every person free to pursue the form of life that she believes suits her best. The just government is one that provides equal political rights and equal economic opportunities for everyone without showing favoritism to any.

With Rawls, we have come to the most recent major version of social contract theory. Rawls' theory has had as great an impact on thinkers today as the theories of Hobbes and Locke had in their day. Yet the theory, particularly in the version of Rawls, has been subjected to intense criticisms. We turn now to look at two major critiques of social contract theory: the communitarian critique and the feminist critique.

The Communitarian Critique

Communitarianism is the view that the actual community in which we live should be at the center of our analysis of society and government. Communitarians emphasize the social nature of human beings. They argue that our very identity—who we are—depends on our relationships to others in our communities. We are embedded in our community and its cultural practices. So, we cannot hope to understand ourselves or our government apart from our community and its

 THINKING LIKE A PHILOSOPHER

What do you think a just government should be like? Try to answer that question the way Rawls suggests. That is, imagine you came together with the other members of your society to choose the principles that the government of your society must follow in the future. And imagine you and the others do not know any of your particular qualities such as your economic class, abilities, intelligence, strength, gender, religion, race, etc. What principles would you want the government to follow if you did not know what kind of person you would turn out to be in your future society? For example: What rights should government guarantee? What should it do for the poor? Should it require equal opportunity? Should it pay for education, and how much education? What tax system should it use? Should it limit what corporate executives get paid? Remember that the principles you choose have to be acceptable to the other members of your society who also do not know their particular qualities.

cultural traditions. Although not all would identify themselves as such, several contemporary philosophers are usually identified as communitarians, including Charles Taylor, Alasdair MacIntyre, and Michael J. Sandel. Among the classical philosophers who are sometimes identified as early communitarian thinkers are Aristotle and Hegel.

The key problem with social contract theory, argue communitarians, is that it neglects people's social nature by focusing on the individual. In making this general criticism, communitarians bring a number of more specific complaints against social contract theory.

First, some communitarians have argued, the social contract theory assumes that government or the state is an artificial construct. But the state, communitarian philosophers have argued, is natural. For example, Aristotle argued long ago that government or the state is a natural outgrowth of our natural tendency to associate with other human beings. Just as the family and the tribe are outgrowths of our natural tendencies to socialize with one another, so is the state:

We get the clearest view of a thing, whether it be the state or anything else, when we see how it originates and develops. At the origins [of the state], then, we have the union of male and female, who cannot live without each other. Men and women come together so that the race may continue. Such union is not something they decide on their own to pursue. They come together in a family because, in common with other animals and plants, humans have a natural desire to reproduce themselves.... From this relationship between men and women ... comes the first association, which is the family.... When several families develop together, and their association aims at more than the supply of their daily needs, we have the first society, which is the village.... When several villages have joined together in a single complete community, large enough to be self-sufficing, the state has come into existence. Thus, the state originates in the bare needs of life. But it continues in existence for the sake of providing its members the good life. Since the earlier forms of society are natural, so is the state. For the state is their purpose and completion, and the nature of a thing is revealed in its completion. The nature of anything, in fact, is revealed when it is fully developed, whether we are speaking of a man, a horse, or a family....

In addition, we should note that the state is by nature prior to the family and to the individual, since the whole is prior to the part. For example, the whole body is prior to the foot and the hand, for if the whole body were to be destroyed, the foot and hand would die.... We know that the state is a creation of nature and that it is prior to the individual by the fact that the individual apart from the state is not

THINKING LIKE A PHILOSOPHER

1. At one point Aristotle says that the desire to pursue a family is "natural" and not something men and women "decide on their own." Do you see in yourself any kind of a desire to pursue a family? If so, is your desire a natural inborn desire or is it a learned "artificial" desire, like the desire for money or the desire to be a lawyer? Do you agree "men and women cannot live without each other"?

2. According to Aristotle, "a social instinct is implanted in all people by their nature." Do you feel a social instinct is implanted in you? Do you know anyone who does not want any kind of social relationship, not even with family members? Describe them. Do you know anyone who has a very powerful "social instinct"? Describe them.

3. Do you agree that the desire to join in groups is *natural*? People like to gather in groups to cheer for their team, or come together for a party, or dance with others at a club. What are some other examples of our desire to join groups?

ANALYZING THE READING

1. Aristotle says "the state is a creation of nature." What do you think he means by this? Is he right?

2. How does Aristotle's view of the state differ from the views of Hobbes and Locke?

3. Aristotle claims that just as a foot or a hand cannot live apart from the whole living body, the individual "is not self-sufficient" apart from society. What does he mean? Do you agree? How is this claim related to his claim that we have natural desires that can only be satisfied in social groups?

4. According to Aristotle, "the state ... is prior to the individual." What do you think he means by this? Do you agree? What is the argument Aristotle uses to show this? Is his argument a valid argument? Is it sound?

self-sufficient. The individual is like a part that is dependent on the whole. If there were a being who could not live in society or who did not need to live in society because he was self-sufficient, then he would have to either be an animal or a god. He could not be a real part of the state. A social instinct is implanted in all people by their nature.[10]

Notice that Aristotle says that the state is "prior to the individual." By this he means, first, that individuals cannot become full human beings unless they live in the state. In particular, Aristotle argued, our political abilities and social virtues emerge and develop only in the state. The state is nature's way of bringing these capacities out in us. Second, Aristotle also wants to say that the state is more important than an individual citizen. Just as the whole human body is more important than one of its parts, so the whole association of humans that we call the state is more important than one of its members.

The idea that the state is a natural outgrowth of our human nature was echoed in the nineteenth century by the German philosopher Georg Wilhelm Friedrich Hegel (1770–1831). Like Aristotle, Hegel believed that the state is the completion of all earlier human associations and more important than the individual. He also agreed with Aristotle's claim that humans can develop fully only within the state. In particular, argued Hegel, humans can develop their freedom only within the state. Moreover, the individual will develop fully only if he embraces the cultural practices of the state of which he is a member:

The State . . . is that form of reality in which the individual has and enjoys his freedom. But he can do so only if he recognizes, believes in, and wills that which is common to the whole. And this must not be understood . . . [to mean that the state] is a means provided for his benefit. Nor [is the state a means by which] each individual . . . limits his own freedom so that [every individual] can secure a small space of liberty for himself. Rather, we affirm, that Law, Morality, Government, and they alone, are the positive reality and completion of Freedom. . . .

It must further be understood that all the worth which the human being possesses— all spiritual reality, he possesses only through the State. . . . Thus only is he fully conscious; thus only is he a partaker of morality—of a just and moral social and political life. . . .

Summing up what has been said of the State, we find that . . . its vital principle, what actuates the individuals who compose it—is Morality. The State, its laws, its social arrangements, constitute the rights of its members; its natural features, its mountains, air, and waters, are their country, their fatherland, their outward material property; the history of this State is the history of their deeds; what their ancestors have produced, belongs to them and lives on in their memory. All is their possession, just as they are possessed by it; for it constitutes their existence, their being.

. . . It is this matured totality which thus constitutes one Being, the spirit of one people. To it the individual members belong; each one is the Son of his Nation, and at the same time . . . the Son of his Age. None remains behind it, still less [does anyone] advance beyond it. This spiritual Being, the Spirit of his time, is his; he is a representative of it; it is that in which he originated, and in which he lives.[11]

For Hegel, freedom is more than just not interfering with the lives of others. People are free to the extent that they can do more: The more abilities they have, the freer they are. Because the state is the arena in which people can most fully

---

[10] Aristotle, *Politics*, bk. I, ch. ii, translated by Manuel Velasquez.
[11] Georg Wilhelm Friedrich Hegel, *The Philosophy of History*, trans. J. Sibree (New York: Dover, 1956), 38, 39, 52.

Arnoldo Borja (right), a community organizer of Virginia Justice Center, organizes Latino day laborers so they can claim their political and civil rights as Americans. Hegel wrote: "all the worth which the human being possesses, he possesses only through the State. Thus only is he fully conscious and a partaker of a just social and political life." When marginalized groups claim their political and civil rights, they participate in the life of the state and experience the worth, consciousness, and justice that only participation in the state can provide.

© Alex Wong/Getty Images

develop their abilities, only in the state can the range of activities open to people be expanded and widened to their fullest extent. Therefore, only in the state can people be truly free.

Already it should be clear that the communitarian views of Aristotle and Hegel directly contradict several of the assumptions of social contract theory. First, they contradict the assumption that the state is an artificial construct. Social contract theory assumes that there is no state until people come together and deliberately think it up and create it; the state does not just naturally grow and develop. However, Aristotle and Hegel reject this assumption. The state, they argue, is a natural outgrowth of our human tendencies to live together. Social contract theory is thus mistaken in its fundamental assumption that the state is an artificial construct that humans must deliberately put together.

Second, Aristotle and Hegel contradict the assumption that before the state exists, there are fully formed people who can come together to create a state. Hobbes, Locke, and to an extent even Rawls assume this. But Aristotle and Hegel point out that it is not possible for people to develop fully before the state exists. If there were no state, humans could not know what one is, nor would they know how to go about organizing themselves into a state. And only in the state does the individual develop the freedom required to enter an agreement. In short, before there is a state, there can be no fully formed human individuals capable of coming together to form a state through some sort of agreement.

Third, and perhaps most important, communitarians agree with Hegel that the state and its cultural practices are the source of the identity of all individuals. That is, in the state we acquire the cultures and traditions that we use to define ourselves. Think, for example, of how a person growing up in the United States comes to think

ANALYZING THE READING

1. Suppose that freedom is the ability to do things, so that the more you are able to do, the freer you are. What, then, would Hegel mean when he says: "the state is that form of reality in which the individual has and enjoys his freedom"? Would he be right?

2. According to Hegel, what are all the things that make up "the state"? Keeping in mind what he means by "the state," what do you think he means when he says "all the worth which the human being possesses. . . he possesses only through the state"? Do you agree?

3. Hegel suggests that a person will develop into a fully free person "only if he recognizes, believes in, and wills that which is common to the whole." Suppose that "the whole" consists of a state's culture, its legal and political ideals, the rights its people have, its history, its land, etc. What then does Hegel mean? Is he right?

4. How does Hegel's view of the state differ from the views of Hobbes and Locke?

of himself or herself as an "American." An American thinks of himself or herself as being part of a long history that begins with the pilgrims and the thirteen colonies. An American thinks of himself or herself as part of a history that includes George Washington, Abraham Lincoln, Teddy Roosevelt, John Kennedy, and Barack Obama. An American thinks of himself or herself as part of a nation that includes its mountains and national parks, its rebellions and wars, its music and literature. In short, our very sense of who we are depends on the cultural traditions of the state to which we belong.

Yet, as we saw, the social contract view, particularly as developed by Rawls, believes that the state must support no particular culture but leave people free to choose their own cultural preferences. Michael J. Sandel, one of the foremost contemporary communitarian thinkers, has written the following about social contract theory, particularly Rawls' version:

> Its central idea is that government should be neutral toward the moral and religious views its citizens espouse. Since people disagree about the best way to live, government should not affirm in law any particular vision of the good life. Instead, it should provide a framework of rights that respects persons as free and independent selves, capable of choosing their own values and ends.[12]

QUICK REVIEW
Communitarian views, contrary to social contract theory, imply that (1) the state is not an artificial construct (2) because without the state, humans could not develop, for there would be no one to enter a social contract in "the state of nature," and (3) because our culture and traditions make us who we are, the state should support the cultural traditions of its people, including their religion, morality, and cultural values.

Sandel argues that it is a mistake to think that government should be neutral toward the different moral, religious, and cultural views found in a community. As Hegel argued, if an individual is to develop fully, she must live in a state that supports and nourishes a strong set of cultural traditions. Different states will support different cultural traditions, of course. For example, the state and government of Mexico support a culture and a tradition that are very different from those that the state and U.S. government support. But each state and its government must favor and support some set of cultural traditions. The government of each state must educate its people so that they learn about these cultural traditions and come to accept their values. For us in the United States, says Sandel, the government must support a cultural tradition that has always valued participation in the political process:

> Participating in politics . . . means deliberating with fellow citizens about the common good and helping to shape the destiny of the political community. But to deliberate well about the common good requires more than the capacity to choose one's ends and to respect others' rights to do the same. It requires a knowledge of public affairs and also a sense of belonging, a concern for the whole, a moral bond with the community whose fate is at stake. To share in self-rule requires that citizens possess, or come to acquire, [these] qualities of character, or civic virtues. But this means that [we] cannot be neutral toward the values and ends . . . citizens espouse. [We require] . . . a formative politics, a politics that cultivates in citizens the qualities of character self-government requires.[13]

Communitarians argue, then, that government must not stay away from morality and cultural values. Instead, it must strive to teach citizens the morality and cultural values that are part of their traditions.

---

[12] Michael J. Sandel, *Democracy's Discontent* (Cambridge, MA: Belknap Press of Harvard University Press, 1996), excerpt from 4.
[13] Ibid., excerpts from 5–6.

But are the communitarians right? Consider, first, the idea that the state is natural and not an artificial construct. Is this really true? Doesn't it take a great deal of human ingenuity and effort to maintain a state? Doesn't this suggest that the state is something that human beings construct? Or take the criticism that because people need a state to develop fully, they cannot form a government in the state of nature. It is true that there are some abilities that can develop only within the political institutions of the state. But are these abilities really needed for a stateless group of people to come together and agree to form a rudimentary government?

Consider, finally, what is perhaps the most important objection of communitarians. This is the objection that government should support the cultural traditions of its people. Ask yourself this: Should all cultural traditions be supported and transmitted? Before the Civil War, many whites living in the South argued that they had developed a distinct culture and way of life on their large plantations. Slavery was a part of this Southern culture. So, slavery as a cultural tradition should not be destroyed, they argued. In a similar way, many people have argued that the view that women should stay home, take care of children, and be subservient to their husbands is part of a distinct culture and way of life that should not be destroyed. Are all these cultural traditions equally valuable? If they are not, then are communitarians wrong to claim that government should support whatever traditional cultural values a nation has?

It is not clear, then, that communitarianism has made its case against the social contract tradition. However, there is a second important position that has also attacked the idea of the social contract.

Social Contract and Women

A significant and glaring set of problems can be raised with regard to the tradition of contract theory that Hobbes and Locke represent. At the heart of contract theory is the idea that authority over adults depends on their consent. Rulers have no authority to rule unless their subjects agree or consent to that rule. For Hobbes and Locke, consent alone can justify or legitimize the authority of the state. This fundamental idea is underlined in our own Declaration of Independence when it states that governments derive their just powers "from the consent of the governed." A social contract is necessary to establish the state because the contract is the means through which citizens consent to be ruled by a government.

The Traditional View. But this fundamental idea raises an important question that many women have asked: What justifies the authority that males have traditionally exercised over females, particularly in the family? For example, Hobbes writes that a family consists of "a man and his children; or of a man and his servants; or of a man, and his children, and servants together: wherein the Father or Master is the Sovereign."[14] Locke similarly tells us that in the family, "the Rule . . . naturally falls to the Man's share, as abler and stronger [than the Woman]."[15]

ANALYZING THE READING

1. Sandel claims that a person's character and virtues can develop fully only if the person participates in the decisions and activities of "the political community." Do you agree?

2. How is Sandel's view similar to Hegel's? How is it similar to Aristotle's?

3. Sandel argues that government must support and nurture those values and ends that citizens "espouse." How is this different from what Rawls claims? Who is right?

---

[14] Hobbes, *Leviathan*, ed. A. D. Lindsay (New York: J. M. Dent, 1950), 172.
[15] Locke, *Two Treatises of Government*, ed. Peter Laslett (London: Cambridge University Press, 1963), 210.

Hobbes and Locke are merely describing an old traditional view of the family, in which the man rules and the woman is ruled. But they write as if this rule of the male over the female were perfectly justified. How is this possible in view of their fundamental point that authority over adults is justified only if they consent? Do adult women, half of the human race, somehow "consent" to let men, the other half, rule over them in families? Clearly, this is not the case: Women do not enter a social contract giving men the right to rule over them. Then, doesn't it follow that it is unjustified for men to exercise authority over adult women as they have done in the traditional family?

The fact that Hobbes and Locke do not apply to women the idea that ruling requires consent should alert us to another glaring problem that their theories raise. The "free" and "equal" people who enter into the social contract and who subsequently become citizens of the state are all and only men. Women are left out. Hobbes explicitly states that "commonwealths have been erected by the Fathers, not by the Mothers of families."[16] And Locke, as we have seen, assumes that men are the "natural" heads of families, and it is these male heads of families who enter the social contract.

Thus, social contract theory, at least as developed by Hobbes and Locke, explicitly asserts that the state is created by an agreement that *males* make with one another. Because people acquire political rights only by entering such an agreement, it would seem logical to conclude that only males have political rights in the state. Hobbes and Locke were males interested in writing about how males come to be governed by a state, and they simply ignored the situation of the female half of the human race. Consequently, these philosophers failed to apply their principle that adults must be ruled by consent to the situation of women in families.

Public and Private Spheres. Why did they fail to apply their fundamental principles to the family? These failures are perhaps related to a basic assumption we all unconsciously make: that "private" or "personal" matters, such as family matters, have nothing to do with the "public" matters of politics—what happens to women within the family is a private matter unrelated to the politics that rules our public lives. Recently, however, a number of female philosophers have pointed out that this unconscious separation of the "public" from the "private" is the source of many of the political and economic inequalities to which women are subjected. For example, political philosopher Carole Pateman writes that "the dichotomy between the public and the private . . . is, ultimately, what the feminist movement is about."[17] We must examine this claim since it has important implications for how we think about the state. Understanding her claim may also help us see why Hobbes and Locke so easily ignored half of the human race and accepted the unequal position of women in the family.

Private life, for us, includes life within the family and the domestic and personal activities that take place within a home. Examples include sex; raising children; expressing intimacy, love, and affection; and doing domestic chores. Public life,

---
[16] Hobbes, *Leviathan*, 168.
[17] Carole Pateman, "Feminist Critiques of the Public/Private Dichotomy," in *Private and Public in Social Life*, ed. Stanley Benn and Gerald Gaus (London: Croom Helm, 1983), 82.

ANALYZING THE READING

1. Why does it matter that both Locke and Hobbes assume that the parties to the social contract are males?

2. Okin suggests there is a connection between "women's domestic roles" and "their inequality and segregation in the workplace." What does she mean? Do you agree?

3. What does Okin mean by the statement: "the personal is political"? What does she mean by "the political is personal"? Do you agree with either statement?

QUICK REVIEW
Feminists argue that social contract theory wrongly assumes that family structures are justified because often in families males rule over females without their consent, and social contract theory wrongly assumes that the "public" sphere of the state should not interfere with the "private" sphere of the family.

on the other hand, includes the economic and political activities that take place outside the family and the home. These include paid work, buying and selling goods, voting, running for political office, and participating in legal processes. It is taken almost for granted today that the public should not interfere with the private. "A man's home is his castle," we say, implying that the world should not interfere with what goes on in the home.

But this separation of the private and the public, several female philosophers have pointed out, places women in an unequal position. Traditionally, women have taken on the major burden of domestic work: cooking for everyone in the family, cleaning the house, doing the laundry, and caring for the children. This gives men the time and freedom to leave the home and enter public life. Thus, the labor performed by women within the private sphere gives men the freedom to participate in the public sphere, while keeping women occupied and confined in the private.

Having women occupy the private sphere and men the public is not necessarily unjust. However, in our society, real economic and political power is available only in the public world. Men are paid for the work they perform in the public world whereas women are not paid for the work they perform in the private home. So men acquire the economic power that wealth brings and many women are left economically powerless. Women may try to work for pay outside the home, of course. But they are always disadvantaged, feminists claim, because they are still expected to do most of the housework and child care. Moreover, because working women become occupied with these domestic tasks, men are free to engage in those political and legal processes that are the source of political power. Women remain occupied with domestic tasks that carry no political power. Some women may become active in public affairs, but this is always difficult. It is difficult because domestic tasks continue to encroach on their time and because their private lives have not prepared them for engaging in the public world of politics.

In short we separate the public from the private and relegate women to labor in the private sphere, thereby freeing men to take over the public world. But because the public world is the source of economic and political power, men come to hold most of the power in our society. Women either remain wholly powerless or are disadvantaged by the burdens that the private sphere puts on them even when they work outside the home. Thus, the separation of the private world from the public world is the fundamental means by which women are forced into political and economic powerlessness.

How is all this related to political theories such as social contract theory? Because private domestic matters are assumed to have nothing to do with politics, political philosophers have ignored the

Courtesy of The Advertising Archives

Traditionally, women have shouldered the major part of the unpaid work in the "private" life of the family: cooking for everyone, cleaning up the house, doing the laundry, and caring for the children. Some feminists argue this frees men to engage in the more powerful "public" life of economic and political activities, while women are relegated to a relatively powerless and unequal role.

✔ QUICK REVIEW

Feminists also argue that social contract theory divides the "public" life of politics and economics, in which men predominate, from the "private" life of the family, where women are confined to labor so that men can participate in public life. This unjustly relegates women to powerless roles, gives men political and economic power, and insulates family relations from public criticism.

 THINKING LIKE A PHILOSOPHER

1. How were household tasks divided up in your family? Did most household tasks fall on the shoulders of your mother? If so, do you think your mother resented this?

2. How do you hope that household tasks will be divided up in any family you start?

3. Do you think that it would be possible to "extend the political ideals of consent, equality, and freedom" into your family? That is, would it be possible to do only what each consents to do? To treat each as equal to the others? To allow each to be equally free? Do you think it would be right to do so? Explain.

Linda A. Cicero/Stanford News Service

private sphere of the family. Yet the work women do in the family is the basis of men's political and economic power. The contemporary political philosopher Susan Okin elaborates on these points in her book *Justice, Gender, and the Family:*

Thus feminists have turned their attention to the politics of what had previously been regarded—and . . . still is seen by most political theorists—as paradigmatically nonpolitical. That the personal sphere of sexuality, of housework, of child care and family life is political became the underpinning of most feminist thought. Feminists of different political leanings and in a variety of academic disciplines have revealed and analyzed the multiple interconnections between women's domestic roles and their inequality and segregation in the workplace, and between their socialization in gendered families and the psychological aspects of their oppression. We have strongly and persistently challenged the long-standing underlying assumption of almost all political theories: that the sphere of family and personal life is so separate and distinct from the rest of social life that such theories can justifiably assume but ignore it.

The interconnections between the domestic and the nondomestic aspects of our lives are deep and pervasive. Given the power structures of both, women's lives are far more detrimentally affected by these interconnections than are men's. Consider two recent front-page stories that appeared on subsequent days in the *New York Times*. The first was about a tiny elite among women: those who work as lawyers for the country's top law firms. If these women have children with whom they want to spend any time, they find themselves off the partnership track and instead, with no prospects of advancement, on the "mommy track." "Nine-to-five" is considered part-time work in the ethos of such firms, and one mother reports that, in spite of her twelve-hour workdays and frequent work on weekends, she has "no chance" of making partner. The article fails to mention that these women's children have fathers, or that most of the men who work for the same prestigious law firms also have children, except to report that male lawyers who take parental leave are seen as "wimp-like." The sexual division of labor in the family, even in these cases where the women are extremely well qualified, successful, and potentially influential, is simply assumed.

The next day's *Times* reported on a case of major significance for abortion rights. . . . The all-male panel of judges ruled 7 to 3 that the state may require a woman under eighteen years who wishes to obtain an abortion to notify both her parents—even in cases of divorce, separation, or desertion—or to get special approval from a state judge. The significance of this article is amplified when it is juxtaposed with the previous one. For it shows us how it is that those who rise to the top in the highly politically influential profession of law are among those who have had the least experience of all in raising children. There is a high incidence of recruitment of judges from those who have risen to partnership in the most prestigious law firms. . . . Here we find a systematically built-in absence of mothers (and presumably of "wimp-like" participating fathers, too) from high-level political decisions concerning some of the most vulnerable persons in society—women, disproportionately poor and black, who become pregnant in their teens, and their future children. It is not hard to see here the ties between the supposedly distinct public and domestic spheres.

This is but one example of what feminists mean by saying that "the personal is political," sometimes adding the corollary "the political is personal." Contemporary feminism poses a significant challenge to the long-standing and still-surviving assumption of political theories that the sphere of family and personal life is sharply distinct from the rest of social and political life, that the state can and should restrain itself from intrusion in the domestic sphere, and that political theories can therefore legitimately ignore it.[18]

✓ **QUICK REVIEW**
Okin argues that the public or nondomestic world where economic and political power is centered, and the private domestic world of the family where women are unequal and psychologically oppressed, have deep and pervasive interconnections that affect women detrimentally.

🌐 **MindTap** To read more from Susan Okin's *Justice, Gender, and the Family,* click the link in the MindTap Reader or go to the Questia Readings folder in MindTap.

---

18   Susan Okin, *Justice, Gender, and the Family* (New York: Basic Books, 1989), 125–127.

The problems that feminist thinkers have identified in political theory seem to call the whole social contract tradition into question. This tradition, and much of Western political theory, seems to be built on the assumption that our private lives and our public affairs are and should be separate. But by ignoring the private domain, the assumption ignores the most fundamental source of political and economic inequalities: the family.

Perhaps, however, it is better to see this discussion as a call to reform our ways of thinking about the family and its relationship to politics. Instead of rejecting social contract theory, perhaps we should extend its political ideals of consent, equality, and freedom into the world of the family. These political ideals, fashioned and bequeathed to us by Hobbes and Locke, need not be seen as corrupt. In fact, we may say that the reason traditional social contract theory falls short is not because of the political ideals on which it is based but because it does not extend the political ideals of consent, equality, and freedom far enough. Our task, then, is to see how the ideals of equality, freedom, and consent can be applied to family life. Is this possible? That is a question each of us, as we have moved out of the families in which we were raised and into new families of our own, must answer for ourselves.

PHILOSOPHY AT THE MOVIES

Watch *The Lord of the Flies* (1990), in which a group of schoolboys marooned on an island organize themselves into a rudimentary society, but then divide into two competing camps that descend into violence. With whose view of the state of nature and the origin of government does this film most agree: the view of Hobbes or Locke? How are the men who rescue the boys similar to the boys?

8.3 What Is Justice?

Whether we believe that government rests on individual consent or on community values, we want government to be just. But what is justice? It's common to think of justice in retributive terms—that is, in terms of crime and the punishments that government inflicts on criminals. But we can think of justice in other terms. In fact, in a larger sense, justice deals with distribution, not merely retribution. Questions arise daily, for example, about the way that wealth and income are distributed among us. On any given day about 40 to 45 million Americans live in poverty, and about 30 to 35 million of those do not know where their next meal will come from. On the other hand, the average CEO of one of the Fortune 500 companies makes about $12 million per year, or about 343 times what an average American worker makes. Are such large inequalities just? Is it just that some should be spending their money on yachts while others are starving? Figures like these raise numerous questions: Should we try to make people's incomes more equal? Should we try to channel more of our resources to those in need? If individuals belong to groups that have been unfairly discriminated against, should these persons receive special consideration and treatment? Who should have access to medical care? Only those who can afford it? Everyone who needs it? Those who are likely to benefit most?

Issues of distribution needn't be confined to wealth and goods, however. Equally important is the distribution of privilege and power. Education raises such issues. Who should have access to government-supported public education? Everyone? Everyone but immigrants? Only those who can afford to pay? Only those who show promise of benefiting society? Other questions of privilege and power can

> **QUICK REVIEW**
> Justice includes both retributive justice, which looks at how fair punishments are, and distributive justice, which looks at how fairly society distributes benefits and burdens.

also be asked. Who shall be permitted to vote? To drive? To drink? Should everyone be treated the same under the law, or should certain individuals—for example, juveniles—receive special consideration?

All these issues raise questions of distributive justice. *Distributive justice* is concerned with the fair and proper distribution of public benefits and burdens among the members of a community. Burdens include work and the costs that must be paid to develop society's productive capacities. The benefits include, of course, all the goods that people want and that society produces. Although distributive justice operates in all organizations, it applies chiefly to how government distributes benefits and burdens among its members.

Clearly, the subject of distributive justice touches many areas, from jobs to income, from taxes to medical services. Embedded in any answer to the question of how jobs should be assigned, economic goods should be distributed, income and taxes determined, and medical resources allocated will be a principle of distributive justice—that is, some assumption about the proper way of distributing what is available when there isn't enough for all. For example, it's commonly argued that jobs should be distributed on the basis of talent and ability. Again, it is sometimes said that large corporations should be given tax breaks so they can reinvest their savings, thus increasing jobs and productivity, which in turn will benefit the whole of society. President Barack Obama has claimed that medical services should be provided on the basis of need. And during the 2009 recession, the government gave away about $1 trillion taxpayer dollars to several banks, an insurance company, and some auto manufacturers, saying that these companies "needed" these funds to continue operating and that if they were to fail, the whole of society could fall into a disastrous economic depression. Each of these assertions implies some standard that should be considered in the distribution of certain resources: merit, social benefit, and need. Whether these or other principles should be taken into account is a basic concern of distributive justice.

One way of approaching questions of distributive justice is to start with what is sometimes called "formal justice." Aristotle and other philosophers argued that formal justice is the root meaning of *justice*. Formal justice is the requirement that we should treat similar people similarly. For example, if Jack and Jill carry the same amount of water for us, then we should pay them the same. We should not pay Jack more merely because he is a man. Neither should we pay Jill more merely because her skin is white and Jack's is not. Formal justice, then, is a kind of consistency. Formal justice says that we should treat two cases the same when they are the same. But this raises a key question: When should we consider people to be "the same"? In many respects, Jack and Jill are not the same. We just indicated that Jack is not white but Jill is. And Jack is a man whereas Jill is a woman. But these differences are not relevant when deciding how much each should be paid for the work each does. On the other hand, if Jill carries a bucket of water for us that is twice as big as Jack's, then this is relevant to how much each should get. The amount of work that people do is a relevant difference when deciding what they should be paid for their work. So we can state the principle of formal justice as follows:

QUICK REVIEW
The principle of formal justice says people should be treated the same when they are similar in relevant respects and differently when they differ in relevant respects. Material principles of justice indicate what kinds of differences are "relevant."

> Formal justice obtains when individuals who are similar in all respects relevant to the kind of treatment in question, are given similar benefits and burdens, and individuals who are dissimilar in a relevant respect are treated dissimilarly.

This formal principle of justice tells us something about what justice and injustice are. For example, if we agree that sex and race are not relevant differences when considering people for jobs, then the principle tells us that racial and sexual

PHILOSOPHY AND LIFE

Society and the Bomb

The decision to drop the atomic bomb that killed tens of thousands of the civilian inhabitants of the city of Hiroshima on August 6, 1945, was made while the United States was at war with Japan. Henry L. Stimson, the American Secretary of War at the time, later explained that he advised President Truman to drop the bomb on the basis of utilitarian reasoning:

> I felt that to extract a genuine surrender from the [Japanese] Emperor and his military advisers, they must be administered a tremendous shock which would carry convincing proof of our power to destroy the Empire. Such an effective shock would save many times the number of lives, both American and Japanese, that it would cost. . . . Our enemy, Japan, . . . had the strength to cost us a million more [lives]. . . . Additional large losses might be expected among our allies and . . . enemy casualties would be much larger than our own. . . . My chief purpose was to end the war in victory with the least possible cost in lives. . . . The face of war is the face of death; death is an inevitable part of every order that a wartime leader gives. The decision to use the atomic bomb was a decision that brought death to over a hundred thousand Japanese. . . . But this deliberate, premeditated destruction was our least abhorrent choice.

Objecting to this kind of utilitarian justification for killing the inhabitants of cities with nuclear weapons, philosopher–theologian John C. Ford wrote the following:

> [Is] it permissible, in order to win a just war, to wipe out such an area with death or grave injury, resulting indiscriminately, to the majority of its ten million inhabitants? In my opinion the answer must be in the negative. . . . [It] is never permitted to kill directly non-combatants in wartime. Why? Because they are innocent. That is, they are innocent of the violent and destructive action of war, or of any close participation in the violent and destructive action of war.

QUESTIONS

1. Is killing the innocent always wrong, no matter what the consequences?

2. Would you side with Stimson or Ford about the morality of dropping the bomb?

3. Do you agree that in some circumstances the use of nuclear weapons is morally permissible?

Source: Henry L. Stimson, "The Decision to Use the Atomic Bomb," *Harpers* (February 1947), 101–102, 106–107; John C. Ford, "The Hydrogen Bombing of Cities," *Theology Digest* (Winter 1957).

---

discrimination in hiring is unjust. On the other hand, if we agree that experience, skill, education, and ability are relevant when choosing people for a certain job, then it is morally just to favor those who have more experience, skills, education, and ability.

Yet the formal principle of justice does not settle all the issues. In fact, it does not settle the most pressing controversies that swirl around the issue of justice. For example, is need relevant when deciding whether it is just for government to provide welfare to people? Or take affirmative action programs, which show preference to women and minorities who have been disadvantaged in the past. Are these programs based on "relevant differences"? Are they just or discriminatory? What kinds of differences among people are relevant, and what kinds are not? The formal principle of justice leaves this fundamental question unanswered.

THINKING LIKE A PHILOSOPHER

1. Have you ever been treated in a way that violated the principle of formal justice? Describe what happened to you and explain how it violated the principle of formal justice.

2. The text suggests a simple principle of "substantive justice" that we often use to determine fairness: "first come, first served." Crowding in line, for example, violates this principle and so we think such behavior is unfair. What are some other simple principles that you personally use to determine fair or unfair behavior (other than those in the text)?

Over the centuries, philosophers and nonphilosophers have suggested many kinds of "relevant differences" among people. These are called "material" or "substantive" principles of justice. For example, a simple principle that we all think is just is "first come, first served." When we are waiting to buy tickets at a movie theater or concert, for example, we stand in a line where the first to arrive is served first, and latecomers are served last. We think it is unjust when a latecomer crowds in line ahead of us. The reason, of course, is because when waiting to receive a service or good, we believe that a relevant difference among us is who took the trouble to get there first.

But there are other, broader views of what justice means when we are talking about society. Thus, the person who invokes talent and ability as the proper principle of job distribution probably views justice in terms of merit. Likewise, the person who argues for special tax advantages for large corporations is viewing justice in terms of social utility. And those who think that medical resources should be equally available to everyone see justice chiefly in terms of equality: Everyone should be treated equally in the sense that all should have access to the same medical care. In fact, merit, social utility, and equality have served as focal points for various theories of justice down through the years and continue to exert profound influence on our current views of justice and the proper relationship between the individual and society.

Justice as Merit

Plato proposed one of the first substantive theories of justice, one associated with giving individuals what is their due. In Plato's theory, justice in the state is exactly what it is in the individual: a harmony between the various parts for the good of the whole. Social justice, then, requires cooperation among the members of a society so that society will function best. As a result, the interests of the individual must be subordinated to the larger interests and good of society.

Such a notion had significant implications for the overwhelming majority of the Greek population, who were poor and powerless. The submissive role that these people played, especially the slaves, was vital to the overall success of the society. Yet their interests and rights were kept to a minimum. Indeed, they expected reward only insofar as their actions benefited their superiors. Such an attitude could be fostered only in a rigidly structured society, whose sharply drawn class divisions left no confusion about one's place, role, or expectations in life. This is precisely the kind of society that Plato has in mind in *The Republic*: a system in which every individual has his or her place, and justice means that each person acts and is treated accordingly. In Plato's view, then, justice becomes associated with merit, in the sense that individuals are treated and given a station in life according to their talents and accomplishments. People's natural talents, Plato held, make them fit for certain social roles or statuses, and what people get depends on their role or status. In the following passage from *The Republic*, Plato indicates his position quite clearly:

Plato: **"When one who** is by nature a worker attempts to enter the warrior class, or one of the soldiers tries to enter the class of guardians, this meddling brings the city to ruin. That then is injustice. But the doing of one's own job by each class is justice and makes the city just."

© Museo Capitolino, Rome, Italy/The Bridgeman Art Library

SOCRATES: Is the exclusive aim of judges in delivering judgment that no citizen should have what belongs to another or be deprived of what is his own?

GLAUCON: That is their aim.

SOCRATES: That is what we call justice?

GLAUCON: Yes.

SOCRATES: In some way then possession of one's own and the performance of one's own task could be agreed to be justice.

GLAUCON: That is so.

SOCRATES: Consider then whether you agree with me in this: if a carpenter attempts to do the work of a cobbler, or a cobbler that of a carpenter, and they exchange their tools and the esteem that goes with the job, or the same man tries to do both, and all the other exchanges are made, do you think that this does any great harm to the city?

GLAUCON: Not really.

SOCRATES: But I think that when one who is by nature a worker or some other kind of moneymaker is puffed up by wealth, or the mob, or by his own strength, or some other such thing, and attempts to enter the warrior class, or one of the soldiers tries to enter the group of counselors and guardians, though he is unworthy of it, and these exchange their tools and the public esteem, or when the same man tries to perform all these jobs together, then I think you will agree that these exchanges and this meddling bring the city to ruin.

GLAUCON: They certainly do.

SOCRATES: The meddling and exchange between the three established orders [of workers, warriors, and guardian rulers] does very great harm to the city and would most correctly be called wickedness.

GLAUCON: Very definitely.

SOCRATES: And you would call the greatest wickedness worked against one's own city injustice?

GLAUCON: Of course.

SOCRATES: That then is injustice. And let us repeat that the doing of one's own job by the moneymaking, warrior, and guardian groups, when each group is performing its own task in the city, is the opposite: it is justice and makes the city just.

GLAUCON: I agree with you that this is so.[19]

Apparent in this selection and throughout *The Republic* is Plato's insistence not only on class distinctions but also on the natural *inequality* of individuals. For Plato, however, class distinctions are not based on birth or on one's aristocratic or other family origins. Instead, Plato argued that people, whatever their family background, have different natural talents and abilities. These natural talents and abilities—not their family backgrounds—make them fit for different social roles. At the top of society are those whose talents and accomplishments make them fit to rule. Below them are those whose natural courage and aggressiveness make them fit to enter the military class. Next come those whose skills fit them to be free workers and artisans. At the bottom, almost unmentioned by Plato, are the slaves. Those with higher social status merit more than those below them, so justice requires that they get more.

---

[19]   Plato, *The Republic*, trans. G. M. A. Grube (Indianapolis: Hackett, 1974), bk. IV. Reprinted by permission.

Aristotle also shared the assumption that individuals are unequal and that justice is giving to unequal individuals their unequal due. Indeed, in his *Politics,* Aristotle defended slavery because he believed that those who were slaves were naturally suited for that role and would be wretched and ineffectual were they made free.

> That some should rule and others be ruled is not only necessary, but advantageous; for from the hour of their birth some are marked out to be ruled, others to rule. . . . It is clear that the rule of the mind over the body, and of reason over the passions, is natural and advantageous; whereas the equality of the two or the rule of the inferior is always hurtful . . . . Where, then, there is such a difference between people as that between mind and body . . . the lower sort are by nature slaves, and it is better for them as for all inferiors that they should be under the rule of a master.[20]

QUICK REVIEW
Justice as merit holds that benefits and burdens should be distributed unequally according to people's ability, effort, achievement, or social status. Plato argued that people have different talents and abilities, so society will function best if each person plays the role for which he or she is best suited. Critics claim that such inequality is unjust.

Both Aristotle and Plato believed that the abilities, social status, and achievements of different people entitled them to different treatment and different positions in society. Justice means that each should act and be treated according to his or her abilities, achievements, and social status. We can summarize this notion of justice in a more general way in this statement of the principle of merit:

> A just society is one that distributes benefits and burdens according to merit as measured by a person's talent, ability, effort, achievement, intelligence, or social status.

THINKING LIKE A PHILOSOPHER

1. Can you describe some situations in which decisions about you were based on the principle of merit? Did you feel you were treated fairly and got what you deserved?
2. Do you think the United States should use the principle of strict egalitarianism as an ideal to aim for? Should it use the principle of moderate egalitarianism this way?
3. Is it just for you to be taxed to pay for government programs that you feel are morally wrong? Can any of the principles of justice discussed in this section help you decide this question?
4. Do you think the law requiring young people to remain in school until a certain age is just? Is the one that requires parents to enroll their children in school just? Do any of the principles of justice help you decide this question?

Notice that the principle of merit tries to put some teeth into the principle of formal justice. The principle of formal justice says that people should be treated the same except when there are relevant differences between them. In effect, Plato and Aristotle hold that the main "relevant difference" among people is *merit*—what people deserve in light of their talents and achievements. Notice that this view plays an important role in many of our perceptions of justice. We feel that among athletes it is just that the highest honors should be awarded on the basis of achievement. The gold medal should go to the one who runs or swims the fastest, the one who lifts the most, or the one who throws the discus the farthest. Many college scholarships are awarded on merit: on the grades a person achieved in high school and on standardized tests. We feel it is just when jobs are awarded according to merit as indicated by a candidate's abilities and accomplishments.

On the other hand, Plato and Aristotle might question the justice of some contemporary practices. For example, it seems safe to say that both would object to heterogeneous grouping in public schools (i.e., the practice of putting students of different abilities in the same class, as opposed to homogeneous grouping, in which only students of similar ability are placed in the same class). They would certainly object to the view that "all men are created

---

[20] Aristotle, *Politics,* bk. 1, ch. 5. Translated by Manuel Velasquez.

equal" and that everyone should have equal political rights. And they would definitely object to the view that everyone has an equal right to hold political office.

Many people today find Plato's and Aristotle's theories of justice objectionable because of their assumption that individuals have or should have an unequal status. But isn't the view that we are all equal as much an assumption as the view that we are inherently unequal? So doesn't equality require a defense as much as inequality? Can the view that people are or should be "equal" be defended?

Justice as Equality

We can readily identify with the idea of equality. After all, we have been reared in a society built on the premise that "all men are created equal." *Equal* here, of course, means "the same." Accordingly, in the United States it is widely believed that everyone is entitled to a period of roughly the same kind of education, that the sexes and races should be treated the same, that individuals should be treated the same before the law, that everyone should have the same job opportunities and the same access to medical care, that everyone should have the same right to practice religion, speak freely, travel, and so on. Similarly, we reject slavery on principle because it violates our belief that everyone is equal. We even object to snobbery, presumably because we believe that one person is not necessarily better than another because of wealth, family, intelligence, or some other source of unequal status. The point is that we needn't look far to see evidence that, at least in theory, our society is erected on a commitment to egalitarianism.

Yet what, exactly, does this commitment to equality mean? One way of trying to capture the meaning of *equality* is by taking the term quite strictly. Strict equality means exactly equal shares. This view is sometimes referred to as *strict egalitarianism*. We can summarize the view that justice is, strictly, giving to each an equal share, in the following principle of strict egalitarianism:

> In a just society, every person will be given exactly equal shares of that society's benefits and burdens.

Notice that the strict egalitarian view takes a definite position on formal justice. The strict egalitarian claims that there are *no* relevant differences among people when it comes to justice. Justice demands strict equality regardless of the differences among people.

Equality has been an ideal for Americans since the nation was founded. The Declaration of Independence states, for example, that "all men are created equal." Nevertheless, promoting strict equality leads to difficult theoretical and operational problems. To get an idea of these problems, consider the practice of heterogeneous grouping in the classroom. Since we presume that everyone is equal, we try to ensure that everyone has roughly the same educational opportunities, at least in the formative years. Accordingly, thirty students of widely differing abilities and capacities may be placed in the same class at the same time with the same instructor. Faced with such diversity, teachers aim their teaching at the nonexistent "average" student. As likely as not, the instructional level will be too high for the slowest class members and too low for the swiftest. As a result, the slowest don't learn, and the swiftest get bored; both "turn off." Is this just?

Again, modern medical technology has made the wondrous dream of organ transplants an astonishing reality. Corneas, hearts, kidneys, bone marrow, and even livers and lungs can be transplanted with more or less success. But there's a rub: Demand exceeds supply. Who should get available organs when there aren't enough to go around? By a strict egalitarian calculation, everyone who needs a heart should have an equal chance of getting it. But suppose that two people are in need of the only available heart. One of them is a renowned neurosurgeon in her forties whose survival promises to benefit countless persons. The other is a sixty-five-year-old derelict who for three decades has abused his body and whose survival will benefit no one except himself. Is it just to treat these individuals as equals in determining who will receive the heart? Or is it more just that they be treated as unequals?

The problem, of course, is that people are not equal, and their inequalities seem to demand an unequal sharing in society's resources. Human beings have different needs, different abilities, different desires, and different virtues. They put forward different efforts and have different skills and different physical abilities. In fact, humans seem to be unequal in all respects. Don't we have to take these differences into account when we distribute benefits among people? Suppose that every worker were given exactly the same wage. Then, better workers would have no incentive to work hard because hard work would get them exactly the same as loafing. Suppose that every needy person is given the same basket of goods. Then some will get more than they need, and others will get less than they need. On the other hand, if people are given exactly the same burdens, then some will get more than they can bear, whereas others will not get enough. Take the burdens of work. If everyone has to do exactly the same amount of work, then people who are unskilled or handicapped will have to do as much as people who are strong and skilled. This does not seem to be the best way to arrange work burdens. People's differences, then, seem to demand that they receive different shares of society's benefits and burdens.

Some egalitarians respond to these criticisms by proposing a more moderate form of egalitarianism. They distinguish two kinds of equality: political equality and economic equality. People have political equality when they have an equal right to participate in their political processes. Moderate egalitarians suggest that people should have equal political rights. Such equal rights include an equal right to vote, an equal right to run for political offices, equal civil rights, and equal rights to due process. Strict egalitarianism should be the rule in the political arena. But what about the economic arena? Here, say moderate egalitarians, we again have to make a distinction. Economic equality can mean either equality of income and wealth, or equality of economic opportunity. The objections that critics of strict egalitarianism make, they say, are problems that result if we try to make everyone's income and wealth equal. But differences among people have to be recognized when distributing income and wealth. On the other hand, moderate egalitarians continue, there is nothing wrong with equality of economic opportunity. Everyone should have an equal opportunity to get those jobs and positions that carry higher levels of income and wealth. Society might secure equality of economic opportunity by giving everyone the same chance at an education and by eliminating all racial and sexual discrimination in jobs and other positions. So, moderate egalitarians conclude, strict equality is justified in the political arena, and it is also justified in the economic arena if we are talking about equality of opportunity. But other economic benefits

THINKING LIKE A PHILOSOPHER

1. Can you describe some situations in which decisions about you were based on the principle of merit? Did you feel you were treated fairly and got what you deserved?
2. Do you think the United States should use the principle of strict egalitarianism as an ideal to aim for? Should it use the principle of moderate egalitarianism this way?
3. Is it just for you to be taxed to pay for government programs that you feel are morally wrong? Can any of the principles of justice discussed in this section help you decide this question?
4. Do you think the law requiring young people to remain in school until a certain age is just? Is the one that requires parents to enroll their children in school just? Do any of the principles of justice help you decide this question?

and burdens should be distributed according to relevant differences among people. This moderate form of egalitarianism can be summarized in the following principle of moderate egalitarianism:

> A just society is one in which political rights and economic opportunities are distributed equally, whereas other economic benefits and burdens are distributed unequally according to the relevant differences among people.

But is even such a modified egalitarianism correct? Aren't there some differences among people that lead us to say that even political rights should not be equal? Consider the criminal. Is it wrong to say that the convicted criminal should not have the same political rights that other citizens have? Or take the person who cannot read or the person who has an IQ less than 50. Should such people have the same right to vote as all others? Consider equality of opportunity. Can we really hope to achieve equality of opportunity? Won't differences among people always sabotage our attempts to achieve equality of opportunity? Suppose that we give everyone the same education in the hope that this will give everyone an equal opportunity to get good jobs. Some students will be more motivated, smarter, and have fewer distractions than others. Such students will graduate with better qualifications than others. So, not everyone will have the same opportunities when they graduate, even if everyone gets the same education. People's inequalities, then, seem to undercut the egalitarian's attempts to achieve both political equality and equality of opportunity.

For Plato and Aristotle, the natural differences among people posed no great problem because they associated justice with unequal merit. But for modern theorists, the tension between recognizing people's differences and pursuing equality poses an urgent problem. Indeed, it is one that philosophers have debated for several centuries and one that has given rise to the theory of justice associated with social utility.

Justice as Social Utility

One view of justice that occurs to many people today is this: Justice is what promotes the general welfare—that is, the greatest happiness of the greatest number of citizens. The ultimate criterion of justice, then, is utility: A policy or action is just when it produces more utility or happiness for the greatest number of citizens, compared to any other alternative policy or action.

As we saw in the last chapter, John Stuart Mill was one of the modern founders of utilitarianism, the view that we should aim at maximizing the happiness of society's members. Mill argued that we should always try to minimize social harms and maximize social benefits. In *Utilitarianism,* Mill discusses how the concept of justice is related to society's utility. Mill concedes that many people think that justice is completely unrelated to maximizing social utility. This is a false belief, he argues.

John Stuart Mill: "Justice remains the appropriate name for certain social utilities which are vastly more important, and therefore more absolute and imperative, than any others are as a class." John Stuart Mill (1806–1873), 1973 (oil on canvas), George Frederick Watts (1817–1904).

Although the notion of justice seems to vary among different persons, says Mill, people ultimately interpret justice in terms of utility. Thus, for example, while people may claim that justice is equality, they will readily abandon the pursuit of equality when they feel that society's utility is better served through some practice that requires inequality. Then they are likely to say, for example, that a famous surgeon and a skid-row bum should not be treated as equals in determining who should get an available heart. Because preserving the life of the surgeon promises more social benefits, it is just that the surgeon should get the heart. So utility appears to be the basis of justice even for those that think justice is based on equality, just as it is the basis for all other moral rules.

Justice, however, requires actions that differ from all the other actions that utility sanctions. The kinds of actions that are said to be just or unjust are actions that are much more important to us than any of the other actions utility requires or prohibits. Justice is concerned with those actions that support or destroy our ability to live together in peace, such as harming others, interfering with their freedom, aggression, and the use of power. Those behaviors are more vital to human well-being than any others because they determine whether society will be able to function at all. Nevertheless, although justice concerns those actions that are most important to us, they too must be judged by their utility. Actions are just when they provide more social benefits and fewer harms than any other alternative. In the following passage from *Utilitarianism,* Mill makes these points:

> While I dispute the pretensions of any theory which sets up an imaginary standard of justice not grounded on utility, I account the justice which is grounded on utility to be the chief part, and incomparably the most sacred and binding part, of all morality. Justice is a name for certain classes of moral rules, which concern the essentials of human well-being more nearly [more closely], and are therefore of more absolute obligation, than any other rules for the guidance of life.... The moral rules which forbid mankind to hurt one another ... are more vital to human well-being than any maxims which only point out the best mode of managing some department of human affairs.... It is their observance which alone preserve peace among human beings: if obedience to them were not the rule and disobedience the exception, everyone would see in everyone else an enemy, against whom he must be perpetually guarding himself.... Now it is these moralities primarily which compose the obligations of justice.
>
> Justice, [therefore,] is a name for certain moral requirements which, regarded collectively, stand higher in the scale of social utility, and are therefore of more paramount obligation than any others....
>
> Justice [, therefore,] remains the appropriate name for certain social utilities which are vastly more important, and therefore more absolute and imperative, than any others are as a class; and which, therefore, ought to be, as well as naturally are, guarded by a sentiment [that is] ... distinguished from the milder feeling which attaches to the mere idea of promoting human pleasure or convenience.[21]

ANALYZING THE READING

1. Can you think of any groups or situations in which the principle of strict egalitarianism would provide the perfect way to divide things?

2. Mill says that justice consists of moral rules that require or prohibit those kinds of actions that "are more vital to human well-being" than any other kinds of actions. But can't any kind of action, in the right circumstances, become "more vital to human well-being" than others? Take sleeping, for example. If a doctor sleeps in too late and fails to operate on a patient, the patient may die. So even sleeping can become "vital to human well-being." So does Mill really give us a way to understand how justice differs from other moral requirements? How do you think Mill could answer this objection?

---

[21]   John Stuart Mill, *Utilitarianism* (New York: Bobbs-Merrill, 1957), 68–69. Reprinted by permission.

In Mill's view, then, utility or "expediency" is the fundamental criterion in determining what is just and unjust. By expediency, Mill means what is beneficial to society. Whatever the institution, policy, or program, its justice depends ultimately on its expediency—the extent to which it will produce benefits and reduce harms for society. Is affirmative action just? It is if it produces more benefits than any other alternative proposed. Is a proportional tax system just? It is if it will produce more benefits and fewer harms than any other kind of tax system. Questions about justice may differ, but their answers are always the same: What is most expedient will be just. What is not expedient will not be just. We can summarize Mill's views in this statement of the utilitarian principle of justice:

> The just society is the one that distributes benefits and burdens in whatever way will produce the greatest social benefits or (when only net harms result) the fewest social harms for everyone in society.

Because Mill's utilitarian theory of justice is a logical extension of his ethical theories, it invites some of the same objections. First, even if what we consider expedient we also consider just, should we do so? For example, some people have argued that slavery can be expedient for a society under some conditions. In fact, some have argued that in primitive societies, slavery gave some people the leisure needed to develop knowledge and technologies that in the long run made those societies better off than if everyone had spent all their time laboring. If these arguments are correct, then the utilitarian would have to agree that slavery in such situations is just. But this seems wrong. Slavery is unjust to the slaves no matter how much it benefits the slave owners.

Second, related problem with social utility arises from the inevitable clash of individual and public interests. Sometimes the general utility can be served only at the expense of an individual or small group. Take, for example, the volatile issue of nuclear waste disposal sites. Nuclear power plants can provide a sizable fraction of the electrical power that citizens use and from which many draw significant benefits. These plants can also produce large amounts of radioactive wastes, which have to be stored somewhere. But many people fear that radioactive storage sites pose risks to individuals living near them. Is it just for the government to insist that these individuals must bear the risks for the good of society?

Justice Based on Need and Ability

Socialism is one of the major political philosophies of the modern world. Many countries base their institutions on socialism, including the communist nations. There are many different versions of socialism. Still we can say that socialism generally holds that the wealth society produces belongs to everyone and so should be shared by everyone. Some socialists advocate government ownership of all productive enterprises. In some socialist nations government distributes to everyone a share of the income and wealth produced by the enterprises government owns.

There are many kinds of socialism, so it is probably not accurate to speak of *the* socialist view of justice. Still, philosophers traditionally take the dictum that Karl Marx proposed as the socialist view on distributive justice. As Marx wrote in his short work *Critique of the Gotha Program*, "From each according to his ability, to each according to his need."[22] This idea can be summarized in what we will call the socialist principle of justice:

---

[22] Karl Marx, *Critique of the Gotha Program* (London: Lawrence and Wishart, 1938), 14, 107. This slogan was earlier stated by Louis Blanc in *L'Organization du Travail* (Paris, 1850) and later by Nikolai Lenin in his short pamphlet "Marxism on the State."

QUICK REVIEW
Justice as social utility holds that benefits and burdens should be distributed so as to maximize social benefits and minimize social harms. Critics argue that social utility wrongly implies that injustices such as slavery are sometimes just, and that it is just to sacrifice the welfare of individuals or small groups for the sake of the general welfare.

MindTap You may well know the name Karl Marx already, but do you understand how he developed his thought on economic justice? Go to MindTap to watch a video introducing the basic elements of Marx's thinking.

> In a just society work burdens should be distributed according to people's abilities, and benefits should be distributed according to people's needs.

Marx's slogan is another interpretation of what *relevant difference* could mean in the principle of formal justice. For Marx, the key differences that are relevant when distributing things justly are people's abilities and needs. Justice requires that jobs and tasks should be assigned to people according to the skills and abilities they have. Those with few or no abilities should have light or easy tasks, whereas those who are highly capable and skilled should have more demanding jobs. On the other hand, the goods that society produces should be distributed according to people's needs. These goods include food, clothing, housing, and medical care. The greater a person's need for some type of good, the more he or she should receive. The less a person needs a type of good, the less he or she should receive.

We use the principle of distribution according to need and ability in many areas of our lives. In athletics, for example, the members of a team will distribute burdens according to each team member's abilities. And team members tend to stand together and help one another according to each one's need. In business, managers sometimes use this principle when they assign tasks to workers. For example, they may give the hard and complex tasks to those with commensurate abilities. And when workers seem to have special needs, many managers will try to accommodate them by giving them extra resources. In society at large, we believe that people's needs should be one of the criteria that government uses to distribute benefits. For example, this is the key idea behind government welfare programs, aid to the needy, and loans to people in disaster areas. We also believe that income taxes should be levied according to people's ability to pay. The more people earn, we think, the more income taxes they should pay.

But the group in which use of the socialist principle is most prominent is the family. Able family members willingly work to support and help the family, whereas those who are in need are willingly supported out of the family's resources. In fact some have argued for the socialist principle by claiming societies should be model on the family.

However, Karl Marx offers a different argument. Marx argues that people should realize their human potential through work that exercises their particular abilities. This means that work should be distributed according to people's abilities. Second, he argues, the benefits produced through work should be used to promote human happiness and well-being. This implies that goods should be used first to meet people's basic needs and then their other, nonbasic needs.

But many people have objected to the socialist principle. First, they have argued that under the socialist principle there would be no relation between how hard a person works and the compensation that person receives. Compensation, after all, would be based on need, not effort. So, workers would have no incentive to work hard. Second, critics have asked, how practical is it to try to model a whole society on the family? People are self-interested and competitive. Outside the family they are not motivated by the willingness to share and help that is natural in the family. Finally, critics claim, the socialist principle can't succeed unless government forces people to live by its dictates. Under the socialist principle, people can't freely choose the job they want but must take the job that fits their abilities. So, government has to step in to decide what job best fits people's abilities and to make them take that job. Second, under socialism, people can't freely choose the goods they want but instead must take the goods that fit their basic needs. This means that government, again, has to step in and decide what goods best meet a person's needs. Therefore, to match jobs with abilities and goods with needs requires coercion or the use of force by government.

Justice Based on Liberty

Like socialism, liberalism is one of the major political philosophies of the modern age. Liberalism is the view that liberty is the most important value that society and government can promote. In particular, liberals support freedom of conscience, freedom of speech, freedom of association, and freedom of occupation. Liberals also support equal political rights and civil liberties.

During the twentieth century, liberalism divided into two camps: classical liberalism and welfare liberalism. Classical liberals favor a limited government that stays out of the free market and does not try to distribute economic goods. Welfare liberals favor a government that reduces some of the harmful effects of the free market by providing economic help to the least advantaged.

We have seen that socialism has a view on justice. Liberalism also has strong views on justice. However, because liberalism is now made up of two conflicting camps, we can expect that liberalism will have two contrasting views on justice. Let's begin with the views on justice that welfare liberals support. To get a clearer idea of these views, we look at a philosopher whom we have already met: John Rawls.

Justice in Welfare Liberalism. As we have seen earlier in this chapter, Rawls argues that the principles of justice that should govern society are those that would be chosen by people who do not know whether in their society they will be rich or poor, talented or untalented, black or white, male or female, and so forth. Principles that would be chosen behind such a "veil of ignorance," he claims, would be fair to everyone because without such knowledge, one would not choose principles that advantage the rich or the poor, the talented or the untalented, black or white, male or female, and so on. A person behind this veil of ignorance will not choose principles that are unfair to some group, Rawls claims, because that person might turn out to be a member of that group. Moreover, Rawls argues, the principles on which a stable society is based must be principles that are fair to everyone. If the principles that govern a society are perceived by some group as being unfair to themselves, then society will not be stable but subject to unrest. For this reason, also, the principles that are chosen to govern society must be fair to everyone.

What principles of justice will be fair to everyone? Rawls proposes three principles: the principle of equal liberty, the principle of equal opportunity, and the difference principle.

The *principle of equal liberty* states that "each person [must have] . . . an equal right to the most extensive scheme of equal basic liberties compatible with a similar scheme of liberties for all."[23] This principle is meant to govern primarily society's political institutions (its constitution, government, courts, legislative system, and laws). Essentially, the principle of equal liberty means that each person must have as many basic political rights and freedoms as possible, as long as everyone else can have the same ("equal") political rights and freedoms. For example, everyone must have at least the same voting rights, the same legal rights, the same right to trial by jury, the same right to run for a political office, the same freedom of speech, the same freedom of thought and conscience, the same freedom of the press, and so on. In the political sphere, then, everyone must be equal, and everyone must be granted the maximum degree of freedom compatible with everyone else having the same degree of freedom. Because the principle of equal liberty requires equality, Rawls argues, it is fair to everyone. Moreover, society's political institutions will be stable as long as they are based on this fair principle.

---

[23]   John Rawls, "Social Unity and Primary Goods", in *Utilitarianism and Beyond*, ed. Amartya Sen and Bernard Williams (Cambridge: Cambridge University Press, 1982), 159–186.

PHILOSOPHY AND LIFE

Welfare

About 14 percent of our population, or 45 million Americans, lived in poverty in 2013, and 13.4 percent or 42 million Americans had no health insurance; about one out of every five children was poor. Also in 2013, unemployment was at 7.4 percent, which meant that 11.5 million adult citizens were unemployed and looking for jobs. According to the U.S. Department of Health and Human Services, at least 591,000 Americans were homeless on any given night, and over a five-year period about 3 percent of Americans (about 8 million people) become homeless for one or more nights and are forced to sleep on the streets, in cars, or anywhere else they can find a place to lie down. Numerous cities have sprouted "tent cities" on their outskirts where homeless and jobless individuals and families live in flimsy camping tents. News reports have described the plight of the homeless:

> Jim Gibson, a 50-year-old contractor had a job and an apartment. Today he [lives in a tent and] struggles to stay clean and fed. The widower and grandfather says he is "trying to survive and look for work. The only work I've found is holding an advertising sign on a street corner."
> 53-year-old Dave Cutch . . . was a welder in Colorado. "So the company I'm working for, I get laid off," Cutch says. . . . Months went by without work. Cutch lost his house, his car was stolen, his savings ran out. "Trying to get back on my feet, you know," Cutch says. "Daily I still

> go out looking for a job. But the thing I'm running into is when I put the application in they ask me, 'Where do you live at?' And I go, 'Actually, I don't have a place to live. I'm homeless.' That's it. They don't hire me."
> 9-year-old Brehanna didn't understand. Her family was being evicted. . . . Her father, Joe Ledesma, a homebuilder for 20 years, was without a job and couldn't find another. . . . Joe Ledesma [now] spends most days searching for jobs. [His wife,] Heidi Ledesma, who at 42 is disabled because of severe arthritis in her ankles, shuffles her feet and limps. . . . She cooks for her family—not in a home, but in the crowded kitchen of a . . . homeless center. "I never thought this would happen to us," she says. "Not in a million years."

QUESTION

1. Should the government tax employed citizens to provide welfare for individuals and families like those discussed here who are jobless and homeless? Why?

Sources: *Los Angeles Times*, March 20, 2009; Richard Gonzalez, "Sacramento Tent City Reflects Economy's Troubles," NPR News, March 16, 2009, http://www.npr.org/templates/story/story.php? storyId=101900138 (accessed May 25, 2009); Mary Hudetz, "Home-builder Copes with Homelessness," *The Daily Reporter*, May 8, 2009, http://dailyreporter.com/blog/2009/05/08/homebuilder-copes-with-homelessness (accessed September 8, 2009).

Rawls' second principle is called the *principle of equal opportunity*. It is mostly supposed to govern a society's economic institutions. The principle says any social and economic inequalities must be "attached to offices and positions open to all under conditions of fair equality of opportunity."[24] This means that desirable jobs and positions must be open to anyone who is qualified. And job qualifications must be related to the requirements of the job. They must not discriminate by race, sex, or any other unrelated characteristic. The principle also means society should provide everyone with enough education needed to qualify for the desirable positions. For example, government can provide free public schools and affordable colleges.

Rawls calls his third principle the *difference principle* because it deals with the differences among people. The difference principle is also mostly aimed at economic institutions. The difference principle says that any social and economic inequalities must contribute "to the greatest benefit of the least advantaged members of society."[25] This means that unlike the political arena where everyone must be equal,

---

[24] Ibid.
[25] Ibid.

the economic arena can allow people to be unequal. That is, some people can get higher incomes, or more wealth, or positions of greater authority and respect than others. Rawls holds that inequalities will get people to work harder and contribute more. Giving greater rewards to those who work harder or contribute more will motivate people to do so. The economy will then be more productive and everyone should benefit. The difference principle says that above all, the least advantaged must benefit. The least advantaged are those at the lower levels (of income, wealth, authority, or respect). They will benefit if the added productivity raises their incomes and expectations along with everyone else's. Here is an example Rawls provides:

> To illustrate, suppose that the least advantaged are represented by the typical unskilled worker. The proposed [difference] principle requires that inequalities in wealth and income—for example, the greater shares [incomes] earned by entrepreneurs and professional persons—must be justified [by their effect on] the members of this group [of unskilled workers]. Differences in wealth and income are just only if they are to the advantage of the representative man who is worse off [such as the typical unskilled worker]. Presumably, given a background of equality of opportunity, and so on, the greater expectations of entrepreneurs and professional persons have the effect in the long run of raising the life-prospects of the laboring class. [Their higher incomes offered to entrepreneurs and professionals] provide the necessary incentives so that the economy is more efficient, industrial advance proceeds more rapidly, and so on. . . . All [such] differences in wealth and income, all social and economic inequalities, should work for the good of the least favored [who in this example is the unskilled worker].[26]

But inequalities raise the possibility of unfairness. Those who are highly disadvantaged (who cannot work or have no skills or abilities) can get left behind in a society with large inequalities. Rawls proposes using the increased productivity that inequalities provide to benefit the highly disadvantaged. For example, government can tax those who are already benefiting from society's productivity. Then it can use those taxes to pay for programs that provide support for the highly disadvantaged. He suggests, however, that there is a limit to how much government can take from those who are advantaged. If carried too far such government actions may begin to harm society's productivity or create social instability. At that point the government has reached the limit to what it can take from the advantaged to support the disadvantaged.

Let us summarize all this. Rawls' principles of justice, which we can call the principles of welfare liberalism, can be summarized as follows:[27]

The distribution of benefits and burdens in a society is just if

1. each person has the most political rights and freedoms compatible with everyone else having the same rights and freedoms, and

2. social and economic inequalities (of income, wealth, authority, or respect) are allowed only if:

   a. everyone has an equal opportunity to qualify and compete for those positions that provide higher levels of income, wealth, authority, or respect , and

   b. such inequalities provide benefits to the least advantaged persons, but not beyond the point where society's overall level of benefits begins to decline.

---

[26] John Rawls, "Distributive Justice: Some Addenda," *Natural Law Forum*, 13 (1968): 51–71.

[27] See John Rawls, *A Theory of Justice* (Cambridge, MA: Harvard University Press, 1972), 52–107.

THINKING LIKE A PHILOSOPHER

1. Rawls says a society is just only if its inequalities somehow produce benefits for the least advantaged. What do you think he means by "inequalities"? Do you think your society meets this requirement? Why?
2. Do you see any evidence that to some extent we run our country according to Rawls' principles of justice? Explain.

These principles are fair, Rawls argues, because they are based on reciprocity, on "tit-for-tat." The principle of equal liberty obviously provides equal benefits for everyone. The principle of equal opportunity gives those who have talents and abilities the opportunity to compete for the more favored jobs and positions. Their efforts thus add to the productivity of society. But the disadvantaged also benefit because the added productivity provided by the advantaged is used to benefit the disadvantaged. Thus, the advantaged get to enjoy the better jobs and positions, while the disadvantaged in turn get to benefit from the productivity of the advantaged. This reciprocity makes the result fair to everyone.

Many observers have suggested that Rawls' principles are actually the principles on which most modern democratic and capitalist societies are based. They are based on the principles of welfare liberalism at least insofar as they provide ideals toward which societies seek to move, even if in practice societies do not actually achieve them. Others, however, argue that during the last several decades most democratic capitalist societies have abandoned the attempt to move toward the ideals of welfare liberalism. In particular, societies have abandoned the attempt to support the disadvantaged, while the benefits of growing economic inequalities have only benefited the wealthiest—the "top 1%." Moreover, the influence of money on politics is now so great, they argue, that for all practical purposes even our political rights and liberties are no longer equal. They are not equal because the money of the wealthiest enables them to have a bigger say in what government does than others have.

Although many people support the ideals of fairness that Rawls' principles embody, not everyone does so. In particular, classical liberals criticize Rawls.

Justice in Classical Liberalism. One of Rawls' strongest classical liberal critics was his Harvard colleague Robert Nozick (1938–2002). Nozick agreed that in the political arena, people should be equal and should have as much liberty as is possible. But in his book *Anarchy, State, and Utopia*, Nozick points out that Rawls advocates a "patterned" theory of justice. A patterned theory is one that says goods should be distributed among the members of a society according to a certain pattern or formula. If goods are not distributed according to the formula, then goods should be taken from citizens who have too much and given to those who have too little. This has to be done until everyone has what the formula says they should have. In Rawls' case the "formula" would consist of his two principles.

Nozick objects that any patterned theory will always require the unjust use of force and coercion. People's free choices, he says, will always change any pattern that society tries to establish. Then, government will unjustly have to force some individuals to give their goods to others until the required distribution is achieved again.

Nozick provides an ingenious example to illustrate his claim. He asks us to imagine a society in which all money is already distributed according to a patterned formula (like Rawls' principles). We will call this "just" distribution D1. In D1, each person holds the money that each should justly hold, no more and no less. Now suppose that a basketball star—Wilt Chamberlain—agrees to play basketball if he can get 25 cents per ticket each game. Millions of fans freely choose to give him 25 cents to watch him play each game. As a result of these many free choices, at the end of the season Wilt Chamberlain has $250,000 more than anyone else does.

So at the end of the season, goods are no longer distributed according to the "just" distribution D1. We can call this new distribution D2. We can see that in D2 money is no longer distributed according to the concept of justice with which we began, since now Wilt Chamberlain has $250,000 more than he should have. Here is how Nozick explains his point:

> Suppose a distribution favored by one of these [patterned] conceptions is realized. Let us suppose it is your favorite one and let us call this distribution D1: perhaps everyone has an equal share, perhaps shares vary in accordance with some dimension you treasure. Now suppose that Wilt Chamberlain is greatly in demand by basketball teams, being a great gate attraction. . . . He signs the following sort of contract with a team: In each home game, twenty-five cents from the price of each ticket of admission goes to him. . . . The season starts, and people cheerfully attend his team's games; they buy their tickets, each time dropping a separate twenty-five cents of their admission price into a special box with Chamberlain's name on it. They are excited about seeing him play; it is worth the total admission price to them. Let us suppose that in one season one million persons attend his home games, and Wilt Chamberlain winds up with $250,000, a larger sum than the average income. . . . Is he entitled to this income? Is this new distribution, D2, unjust? . . . If D1 was a just distribution, and people voluntarily moved from it to D2, transferring parts of their shares that they were given under D1 (what was it for if not to do something with?), isn't D2 also just?[28]

MindTap™ To read more from Robert Nozick's *Anarchy, State and Utopia*, click the link in the MindTap Reader or go to the Questia Readings folder in MindTap.

Nozick says that this new distribution of money, D2, seems perfectly just. Yet it would be unjust according to the "patterned principles" of justice with which we began. So those principles require us to take some of Chamberlain's money and give it to others until the distribution again satisfies the principles. Thus, patterned principles require us to keep taking goods from some and giving them to others to reestablish the distribution that people's free choices continually change. However, Nozick argues that if a distribution is changed by people's free choices, then there can be nothing wrong with it. The fans knew their money was going to the basketball star, so they can have no complaint. And the goods of those who did not see the game were not affected. So there was really nothing wrong with the distribution that resulted from these free choices.

What kind of justice does Nozick propose? In keeping with his ideas about the importance of free choice, Nozick argues that justice is respecting people's free choices. Any distribution of economic benefits and burdens is just, says Nozick, if it is the result of individuals freely choosing to exchange with each other the goods that each person already owns. In summary, Nozick holds the following principle, which we can call the principle of classical liberalism:

ANALYZING THE READING

1. What does Rawls mean by "inequalities"? Explain what his "difference principle" requires.

2. How is Nozick's Wilt Chamberlain example supposed to show that Rawls' principles would force us to keep taking from some to give to others?

3. Nozick suggests that if "D1 was a just distribution and people voluntarily moved from it to D2," then D2 is also a just distribution. How would Nozick's principle of classical liberalism prove that this suggestion of his is true? Why would Nozick's suggestion show that Rawls's principles are wrong?

4. Rawls claims that his principles do not apply to "particular transactions or distributions" nor to "small scale" decisions; they apply to the "principles and policies" that "regulate social and economic equalities." Do you think that Rawls' claim answers Nozick's objection? Why?

---

[28] Robert Nozick, *Anarchy, State and Utopia* (New York: Basic Books, 1974), 161–162.

QUICK REVIEW

Justice in the welfare liberalism of Rawls requires equal liberty in society's political institutions, equal opportunity for desirable jobs and positions, and the difference principle, which says economic inequalities are just only if they produce benefits for the least advantaged. Rawls says these principles are fair to everyone and so would be chosen "behind a veil of ignorance" and would promote social stability.

Benefits and burdens are distributed justly when society allows every individual the freedom to do what he chooses to do for himself or for others, the freedom to keep what he makes for himself or what others choose to give him, and the freedom to keep what he has or give it to whomever he chooses.[29]

Nozick is raising several objections to Rawls' principles. One is that Rawls is using the better-off people in society as "means" to improve the welfare of the worst-off. Nozick regards this as fundamentally unjust because it uses people as means. As a corollary, he claims Rawls is not impartial, for he gives the least advantaged a highly privileged role. They are the ones whose welfare determines the justice of the entire economy. Finally, he objects that Rawls' principles do not allow people to keep what they earn if their earnings can be used to improve the welfare of the worst-off. Yet, Nozick claims, people are entitled to keep what they earn. And, he argues, it is wrong to take away what a person is entitled to, and to give it to someone else. A person's rights of entitlement are very important rights in Nozick's view. They are so important that they should not be violated as Rawls' principles do.

But perhaps Nozick misinterprets Rawls' when he applies the difference principle to a specific transaction. After all, Rawls' principle is about the large institutions that make the policies a society follows. It is not about the specific small-scale exchanges that Nozick describes. More important, Rawls does not argue that those who are well off have to share all of their property with the disadvantaged. He says only that society must help the most disadvantaged members. This does not mean that everyone has a right to an equal share. In other words, Rawls' concept of justice does not equate fair distribution with equal distribution, as Nozick seems to assume he does. Rawls' view is that individuals have a just claim to whatever they have earned, as long as they earned it fairly.

In the following paragraph from "A Kantian Conception of Equality," Rawls makes these very points concerning his difference principle:

> In explaining this principle, several matters should be kept in mind. First of all, it applies in the first instance to the main public principles and policies that regulate social and economic equalities. It is used to adjust the system of entitlements and rewards, and the standards and precepts that this system employs. Thus the difference principle holds, for example, for income and property taxation, for fiscal and economic policy; it does not apply to particular transactions or distributions, nor, in general, to small scale and local decisions, but rather to the background against which these take place. No observable pattern is required of actual distributions, nor even any measure of the degree of equality. . . . What is enjoined is that the inequalities make a functional contribution to those least favored. Finally, the aim is not to eliminate the various contingencies, for some such contingencies seem inevitable. Thus even if an equal distribution of natural assets seemed more in keeping with the equality of free persons, the question of redistributing these assets (were this conceivable) does not arise, since it is incompatible with the integrity of the person. Nor need we make any specific assumptions about how great these variations are: we only suppose that, as realized in later life, they are influenced by all three contingencies. The question, then, is by what criterion a democratic society is to organize cooperation and arrange the system of entitlements that encourages and rewards productive efforts. We have a right to our natural abilities and a right to whatever we become entitled to by taking part in a fair social process. The problem is to characterize this process.[30]

THINKING LIKE A PHILOSOPHER

Think of situations in your personal life where you have used each of the various types of justice discussed in these sections of the text. Describe the kinds of situations that you have found are appropriate for each type of justice?

---

29   Ibid., 160.
30   John Rawls, "A Kantian Conception of Equality," *Cambridge Review* (February 1974), 97.

Rawls' welfare liberalism is most controversial because it connects justice with aiding the least advantaged. Most, if not all, of us today agree that government should secure equal political rights. But many do not believe government should provide material goods and social services to the disadvantaged. Indeed, in the last fifteen years there has been a concerted effort to roll back welfare programs. Rawls' claim that justice requires providing goods and services to the disadvantaged put considerable distance between himself and classical liberalism.

Justice poses a profound and enduring problem for all governments. We have surveyed philosophers over a span of more than two millennia. But no single theory of justice has received universal endorsement. Our own society seems ambivalent about the relative importance of merit, social utility, equality, need, ability, and freedom. The challenge continues to be what it has always been: to find the proper balance among these often competing values.

PHILOSOPHY AT THE MOVIES

Watch *Slumdog Millionaire* (2008) in which Jamal, an eighteen-year-old who grew up in the slums of Mumbai, becomes a contestant on the Indian television game show *Who Wants to Be a Millionaire* and is suspected of cheating when he is able to answer the questions, although his answers are based on his experiences as he grew up struggling to survive as an orphan on the streets. What events, situations, or conditions portrayed in this film seem to you to be unjust? On which view(s) of justice are your views based?

Unimedia europe/Pathe films/Newscom

8.4 Limits on the State

We have seen how different thinkers—such as Hobbes and Locke—tried to show the authority of the state is morally justified even when we do not like what it is doing to us. One of these thinkers—Thomas Hobbes—thought that he had shown that the authority of the state is unlimited. In Hobbes' view, the ruler can do whatever it wants, and the citizen is obligated to obey. But most political and social philosophers have rejected Hobbes' view. They have argued that there are important moral limits on what the state may do to citizens and how it may exercise its authority. We have discussed, in fact, several philosophers who argue for at least one important limit on the state. The state must be just. Although these philosophers have very distinct views on what justice is, they all agree that a state must promote justice.

But are there any other limits on the authority of the state? For example, if the laws the state enacts are unjust, do citizens still have an obligation to obey them? And are there any limits to the state's authority other than that the state and its laws must be just? For example, do people's human rights place any limits on what the state may do to its citizens or on the kinds of laws the state may enforce? And if so, exactly what rights must the state recognize? And what about the state's relations to other states? Is a state justified, for example, in using force and violence against other states, or are there limits to their use?

These are the kinds of questions that we examine in this section. We begin by considering why the theory of civil disobedience claims that citizens are not morally required to obey the authority of the state when its laws are unjust. We then examine how the right to freedom and other human rights impose further limits on the authority of the state. Last, we discuss whether there are any moral limits on the use of violence between states. In particular what can be said about the organized violence that we refer to as "war" and the kind of violence that we now term *terrorism*.

Unjust Laws and Civil Disobedience

According to the dictionary, *law* means a general rule or body of general rules that is enforced by government and that regulates the behavior of citizens. Clearly, the laws that governments enact are not always just. The laws of the United States, for example, once supported slavery. And until the twentieth century, U.S. law not only permitted, but actually enforced racial and sexual discrimination.

Many thinkers have claimed that when laws are unjust or immoral we are under no obligation to obey them. We are not obligated to obey them because unjust laws are, in fact, not genuine laws. Recently, for example, the Catholic bishops of the United States issued a statement objecting to a new federal law. The law required all employers, including Catholic employers, to provide employees health insurance that gave them access to birth control products including some that induced abortions. Believing that abortion is an immoral form of homicide, the bishops felt that the new law forced Catholics to support abortions. It therefore required them to do something immoral and so violated their conscience:

> It is a sobering thing to contemplate our government enacting an unjust law. An unjust law cannot be obeyed. . . . If we face today the prospect of unjust laws, then Catholics in America, in solidarity with our fellow citizens, must have the courage not to obey them. No American desires this. No Catholic welcomes it. But if it should fall upon us, we must discharge it as a duty of citizenship and an obligation of faith. . . . An unjust law is "no law at all."[31]

The view on which the bishops based their statement is an old one, with roots going back to the ancient Greeks. The great Greek playwright, Sophocles, for example, wrote in his play *Antigone*, "no king's law can override the unwritten and immutable laws of God." Taking a similar stance, the Christian philosopher and theologian Saint Augustine later wrote in his work, *On Free Choice of the Will*, "An unjust law is no law at all."

Several centuries later, Saint Thomas Aquinas, who was profoundly influenced by Augustine, agreed with the claim that "an unjust law is no law at all." A human law, Aquinas held, is a true law only when it does not violate the moral law or require its citizens to violate the moral law. Morality, as Aquinas conceived it and as we saw in the last chapter, is not an arbitrary set of rules for behavior. Rather the basis of moral obligation is built into our very nature in the form of various inclinations toward the basic goods in which we find our happiness. These include the inclination that leads us to value life, the inclination that leads us to value having and raising children, and the inclination that leads us to value truth. The rules of conduct corresponding to these inherent human features Aquinas called **natural law**. Accordingly, to say that a law violates the moral law is to say that it violates the natural law that directs us toward those goods in which we find our happiness.

Aquinas reasoned that since law governs human actions, and since human actions aim at achieving happiness, law must aim at achieving the happiness of those whom it governs. That is, it must aim at the happiness of the community, or, as he sometimes put it, at the common good of all. Law, moreover, must be a product of reason, since we use our reason to figure out what we must do to achieve our aims. And since the purpose of law is to direct a community toward its own happiness, law must be made by the whole community and everyone must know what it is. Aquinas concludes in a famous definition:

---

[31]   Cheryl Wetzstein, "Bishops Plea Against Obeying 'Unjust Laws,'" *Washington Times*, April 12, 2012.

> From the four preceding considerations, we arrive at a definition of law: Law is noth-
> ing other than a directive that reason formulates, that aims at the common good of
> the community, that is made by the whole community or by a ruler who is charged
> with caring for the whole community, and that is disclosed and publicized to every-
> one in the community.[32]

The key element in this definition, of course, is the idea that a true law must
aim at the common good of the whole community. The common good of the community is achieved when each person is enabled to achieve the basic goods toward
which our nature inclines us—that is, when each person is able to live according to
the natural or moral law. A true law, Aquinas concluded, must be consistent with
the natural or moral law, and if a law violates the natural or moral law, it is not a
genuine law.

Aquinas' view on the relation between morality and the law has been a point of
great controversy. He is claiming that morality is part of the essential nature—the
essence—of law: A rule issued by a government is not a real law unless it is morally just. Although many philosophers have agreed with Aquinas, many others have
strongly objected to this way of linking law and morality. The British legal philosopher John Austin (1790–1859), for example, argued that a law is nothing more than
a command issued by the ruler, backed by threats of punishment and maintained by
a habit of obedience. Consequently, once a law has been issued by a ruler who has
the power to punish and whom citizens habitually obey, it is a valid law whether or
not it is moral, and whether we like it or not:

> The existence of law is one thing; its merit or demerit is another. Whether it be or be
> not is one enquiry; whether it be or be not conformable to an assumed [moral] stan-
> dard, is a different enquiry. A law,which actually exists is a law, though we happen to
> dislike it, or though it vary from the text by which we regulate our approbation and
> disapprobation.[33]

Opponents of Aquinas' view such as Austin are generally called *positivists.*
Positivists hold that if a piece of legislation has been passed by a legitimate authority,
it is a law that we are obligated to obey regardless of its morality. A law is a law and
must be obeyed. Whether it is moral or just is a separate question.

Notice that Aquinas' theory of law provides something that a positivist theory
cannot provide, something that has been particularly relevant to many oppressed
minorities. Aquinas' theory of law implies that citizens have the right to disobey laws
that are unjust or immoral. This conclusion follows from his idea that a true law
must accord with the natural law of morality:

> As Saint Augustine says, "that which is not just seems to be no law at all." Conse-
> quently, an ordinance is a valid law only to the extent that it is just. Now we say that
> something is just when it conforms to the [moral] principles of our reason and the
> basic moral principles of our reason are the natural law. So an ordinance enacted
> by humans is a valid law only to the extent that it conforms to the natural law.
> If an ordinance contradicts the natural law then it is not a valid law but a corruption
> of law. . . .

---

[32] Saint Thomas Aquinas, *Summa Theologica,* I-IIae, q.90, a.4; translated by the author.

[33] J. Austin, *The Province of Jurisprudence Determined,* W. Rumble (ed.), (Cambridge: Cambridge University
Press, 1995) (first published, 1832), 157.

The ordinances that human beings enact may be just or unjust. If they are just then we have a moral obligation to obey them since they ultimately derive from [the natural law which in turn is based on] the eternal law of God. . . .

However, an ordinance may be unjust for one of two reasons. First, it may be contrary to the rights of humans; and second, it may be contrary to the rights of God.

A "law" can be contrary to the rights of humans in any of three ways. First, the "law" might not be aimed at achieving the common good. This would be the case, for example, if a ruler passed legislation that imposed heavy taxes that merely fed the ruler's greed and had no communal benefits. Second, the "law" might not have been enacted by a legitimate authority. This would be the case, for example, if someone tried to enforce a law without having been delegated the legal authority to do so. Third, the "law" might distribute burdens unjustly. This would be the case, for example, if a law were aimed at achieving the common good, but the burdens involved in achieving that good were distributed unjustly among the citizens. Ordinances that are contrary to the rights of humans in any of these three ways are not valid laws but acts of violence. . . . We have no moral obligation to obey such ordinances except perhaps to avoid giving bad example or to prevent social disorder. . . .

Finally, a law can also be unjust when it is contrary to the rights of God. This would be the case, for example, if a tyrant were to pass a law requiring the worship of idols or any act that is against divine law. It is utterly wrong to obey such laws.[34]

Laws are just and must be obeyed, then, only when (1) they serve the common good of the whole community, (2) they do not exceed the authority of the law-maker, (3) they do not unjustly discriminate against some and unfairly advantage others, and (4) they do not require citizens to violate their religious beliefs. If a law fails on any of these counts, it is no law at all and so citizens have no obligation to obey it. Often this point is expressed by saying that human laws must conform to the "higher law" of morality, and when they do not, we must remain "true to our conscience" by obeying the higher law.

Although positivists have criticized the natural law view of what a true law is, many political leaders have embraced the view of Aquinas. Aquinas has been embraced particularly by those who suffer under unjust or discriminatory laws. They have advocated disobeying such laws in favor of the "higher law" of conscience. In his famous "Letter from Birmingham Jail," civil rights leader Martin Luther King Jr. relied on this point to defend his civil disobedience of segregation laws:

One may well ask, "How can you advocate breaking some laws and obeying others?" The answer is found in the fact that there are two types of laws: There are just and unjust laws. I would agree with Saint Augustine that "An unjust law is no law at all." Now what is the difference between the two? How does one determine when a law is just or unjust? A just law is a man-made code that squares with the moral law or the law of God. An unjust law is a code that is out of harmony with the moral law. To put it in the terms of Saint Thomas Aquinas, an unjust law is a human law that is not rooted in eternal and natural law. Any law that uplifts human personality is just. Any law that degrades human personality is unjust. All segregation statutes are unjust because segregation distorts the soul and damages the personality. It gives the segregator a false sense of superiority, and the segregated a false sense of inferiority. . . .

THINKING LIKE A PHILOSOPHER

Do you personally believe that if you think a law is unjust then you no longer have to obey it? Would you want to live in a county where everyone believed this? Why?

---

[34] Aquinas, *Summa*, I-IIae, q.95, a.2, and q.96, a.4. Translated by the author.

I hope you can see the distinction I am trying to point out. In no sense do I advocate evading or defying the law as the rabid segregationist would do. This would lead to anarchy. One who breaks an unjust law must do it *openly, lovingly,* . . . and with a willingness to accept the penalty. I submit that an individual who breaks a law that conscience tells him is unjust, and willingly accepts the penalty by staying in jail to arouse the conscience of the community over its injustice, is in reality expressing the very highest respect for law.[35]

MindTap To read more from Martin Luther King, Jr.'s "Letter from Birmingham Jail," click the link in the MindTap Reader or go to the Questia Readings folder in MindTap.

King drew the logical consequences from Aquinas' natural law view. If rules are true laws only when they are moral and just, then people have no obligation to obey a rule that is unjust or immoral. As King suggests in the preceding passage, he advocated nonviolent disobedience as a response to unjust laws such as laws that discriminate on the basis of race. Civil disobedience of the kind advocated by King is the act of disobeying an unjust law openly, peacefully, and with a willingness to pay the penalty in order to bring about a change in the law.

Of course, the very idea that an unjust law need not be obeyed makes many people uncomfortable. Who is to decide when a law is unjust? Clearly, each individual must decide this for himself or herself. But doesn't this doctrine lead to an anarchic and chaotic situation in which each person individually decides which rules are true laws and which are not?

In spite of these problems, for many minorities who have suffered discrimination under oppressive and unjust regimes, this right to disobey unjust laws has been critical. The great statesman of India, Mohandas K. Gandhi, who had a profound influence on King, held that oppressed people have a moral right to disobey unjust laws. Gandhi preached this view in his campaign against the British which eventually forced the British to give India its independence. Gandhi did not, however, endorse the natural law theory of Aquinas. Instead, Gandhi based his views on a foundation of Hindu spirituality that emphasized the power of truth and love, which he sometimes referred to as "soul force," or passive resistance. But like King, Gandhi advocated nonviolent resistance to unjust laws. And, like King, he held that using violence as a means to overthrow unjust laws would simply result in more violence:

ANALYZING THE READING

1. Do you think the Catholic bishops were right when they wrote "An unjust law cannot be obeyed"? Why? Is their statement ambiguous? How?

2. What would you say is the difference between Aquinas' view about the relation between a law and morality, and Austin's view of their relation? Who do you think is right? Why?

3. Both Martin Luther King and Mohandas K. Gandhi very publicly disobeyed laws they thought were unjust. Do they both give the same reasons to explain why they believed their disobedience was justified? What is the reason or reasons each gives? Both of them claim that if one disobeys an unjust law one must be willing to accept the penalty. What reasons does each give for this claim? Are their reasons the same? Do you agree with either?

QUICK REVIEW
Gandhi argued that one has a right to disobey unjust laws and advocated nonviolent "passive" resistance to unjust laws because using violence to overthrow unjust laws will lead to more violence.

Passive resistance is a method of securing rights by personal suffering; it is the reverse of resistance by arms. When I refuse to do a thing that is repugnant to my conscience, I use soul-force. For instance, the government of the day has passed a law which is applicable to me. I do not like it. If by using violence I force the Government to repeal the law, I am employing what may be termed body-force. If I do not obey the law but accept the penalty for its breach, I use soul-force. It involves sacrifice of self. . . . It is a superstition and ungodly thing to believe that an act of a majority binds a minority. Many examples can be given in which acts

MindTap Gandhi was one of the most influential political figures in the twentieth century. Go to MindTap to watch a video depicting one of his protest marches.

---

[35] Martin Luther King Jr., "Letter from Birmingham Jail," in *Civil Disobedience: Theory and Practice,* ed. Hugo Adam Bedau (New York: Pegasus, 1969), 77–78.

of majorities will be found to have been wrong and those of minorities to have been right. . . . So long as the superstition that men should obey unjust laws exists, so long will their slavery exist. And a passive resister alone can remove such a superstition. To use brute-force, to use gunpowder, is contrary to passive resistance, for it means that we want our opponent to do by force that which we desire but he does not. And, if such a use of force is justifiable, surely he is entitled to do likewise by us. And so we should never come to an agreement.[36]

It is clear, then, that our views about law are extremely important and that these views will have significant implications for the position that we take on obedience to the law and obedience to the higher law of conscience. If morality is part of the essence of law, then unjust regulations are not real laws and need not be obeyed; nonviolent—or perhaps even violent—resistance to such "laws" is morally justified in the name of a higher law.

Freedom

The liberties that concern us here are political and social freedoms, including freedom of thought, freedom of association, and the important freedom of being able to live as one wants without interference from others. History records many heroic battles fought to secure these freedoms. Freedom finds what may be its classic defense in John Stuart Mill's essay *On Liberty*, in which the British social and political philosopher presents a powerful case for liberty.

Mill's central concern in this essay is the freedom of the individual. He is specifically concerned with the extent to which government and society must be prohibited from interfering with an individual's actions and choices. In essence, Mill argues that society in general, and government in particular, must leave the individual free to live his life as he chooses so long as he is harming no one. This concern for freedom grew out of Mill's fear of what he called the "tyranny of the majority," the tendency of government—and society in general—to persecute and suppress any forms of life or ways of thinking that it dislikes, and to force individuals to conform to what the majority wants:

> The will of the people . . . practically means the will of the most numerous or the most active part of the people—the majority, or those who succeed in making themselves accepted as the majority; the people, consequently, may desire to oppress a part of their number, and precautions are as much needed against this as against any other abuse of power. . . . [I]n political speculations "the tyranny of the majority" is now generally included among the evils against which society requires to be on its guard.
>
> Like other tyrannies, the tyranny of the majority was at first, and is still vulgarly, held in dread, chiefly as operating through the acts of the public authorities. But . . . when society is itself the tyrant . . . its means of tyrannizing are not restricted to the acts which it may do by the hands of its political functionaries. Society can and does execute its own mandates. . . . Protection, therefore, against the tyranny of the magistrate is not enough; there needs protection also against the tyranny of the prevailing opinion and feeling, against the tendency of society to impose, by other means than civil penalties, its own ideas and practices as rules of conduct on those who dissent from them; to fetter the development and, if possible, prevent the formation of any individuality not in harmony with its ways, and compel all characters to fashion themselves upon the model of its own.[37]

---

[36]   Mohandas K Gandhi, *Hind Swaraj or Indian Home Rule* (1909), reprinted in *Social and Political Philosophy*, ed. John Somerville and Ronald E. Santoni (Garden City, NY: Doubleday, 1963), 510.

[37]   John Stuart Mill, *On Liberty* (London: J. M. Dent, 1910), ch. 1.

Against this tendency of society to impose a "tyranny" over the individual, Mill proposed a fundamental principle that is now sometimes called the "harm principle," which imposes a significant limit on the power of government. Mill's principle is that unless an individual's actions will harm others, he must be left free to do what he wants in three ways: free to think and say what he wants, free to live as he wants, and free to associate with others as he wants.

THINKING LIKE A PHILOSOPHER

What do you think Mill means by "the tyranny of the prevailing opinion and feeling"? Have you ever been subjected to the tyranny of prevailing opinion and feeling? If so, what was it like?

The object of this essay is to assert one very simple principle, as entitled to govern absolutely the dealings of society with the individual in the way of compulsion and control, whether the means used be physical force in the form of legal penalties or the moral coercion of public opinion. That principle is that the sole end for which mankind are warranted, individually or collectively, in interfering with the liberty of action of any of their number is self-protection. That the only purpose for which power can be rightfully exercised over any member of a civilized community, against his will, is to prevent harm to others. His own good, either physical or moral, is not a sufficient warrant. He cannot rightfully be compelled to do or forbear because it will be better for him to do so, because it will make him happier, because in the opinions of others, to do so would be wise or even right. These are good reasons for remonstrating with him, or reasoning with him, or persuading him, or entreating him, but not for compelling him, or visiting him with any evil in case he do otherwise. To justify that, the conduct from which it is desired to deter him, must be calculated to produce evil in some one else. The only part of the conduct of any one, for which he is amenable to society, is that which concerns others. In the part which merely concerns himself, his independence is, of right, absolute. Over himself, over his own body and mind, the individual is sovereign.

It is perhaps hardly necessary to say that this doctrine is meant to apply only to human beings in the maturity of their faculties. We are not speaking of children or of young persons below the age which the law may fix as that of manhood or womanhood. . . .

But there is a sphere of action in which society, as distinguished from the individual, has, if any, only an indirect interest, comprehending all that portion of a person's life and conduct which affects only himself, or if it also affects others, only with their free, voluntary, and undeceived consent and participation. . . . This, then, is the appropriate region of human liberty. It comprises, first, the inward domain of consciousness demanding . . ., absolute freedom of opinion and sentiment on all subjects practical or speculative, scientific, moral, or theological [and] the liberty of expressing and publishing [those] opinions. . . . Secondly, the principle requires liberty of tastes and pursuits, of framing the plan of our life to suit our own character; of doing as we like . . . without impediment from our fellow-creatures, so long as what we do does not harm them, even though they should think our conduct foolish, perverse, or wrong. Thirdly, . . . the liberty, within the same limits, of combination among individuals; freedom to unite for any purpose not involving harm to others: the persons combining being supposed to be of full age and not forced or deceived.[38]

Mill supported his view by arguing that this principle would promote the greatest utility or happiness for everyone in society. People must be left free, but not because they have a right to be free. Instead they must be left free because leaving people free will produce more benefits and fewer harms for society than restraining people from thinking and speaking, living, and associating as they want:

---

[38] Ibid., ch. 2, paras. 13, 15, and 16.

> I forgo any advantage which could be derived to my argument from the idea of abstract right as a thing independent of utility. I regard utility as the ultimate appeal on all ethical questions; but it must be utility in the largest sense, grounded on the permanent interests of man as a progressive being. Those interests, I contend, authorize the subjection of individual spontaneity to external control only in respect to those actions of each which concern the interests of other people.[39]

To show that "utility in the largest sense" requires liberty, Mill begins by focusing on the first kind of freedom: freedom to think and say what one wants. He argues that society will benefit if all people are allowed to believe and say whatever they want about any subject whatsoever. For if the government tries to force people to believe what it wants them to believe on some subject, it may force them to believe what is false. Moreover, free and open debate is needed to establish the truth and bring our ideas to life:

> [T]he peculiar evil of silencing the expression of an opinion is, that it is robbing the human race; posterity as well as the existing generation; those who dissent from the opinion, still more than those who hold it. If the opinion is right, they are deprived of the opportunity of exchanging error for truth; if wrong, they lose, what is almost as great a benefit, the clearer perception and livelier impression of truth, produced by its collision with error.
>
> First, if any opinion is compelled to silence, that opinion may, for aught we can certainly know, be true. To deny this is to assume our own infallibility. Secondly, though the silenced opinion be an error, it may, and very commonly does, contain a portion of truth; and since the general or prevailing opinion on any subject is rarely or never the whole truth, it is only by the collision of adverse opinions that the remainder of the truth has any chance of being supplied. Thirdly, even if the received opinion be not only true, but the whole truth; unless it is suffered to be, and actually is, vigorously and earnestly contested, it will, by most of those who receive it, be held in the manner of a prejudice, with little comprehension or feeling of its rational grounds. And not only this, but, fourthly, the meaning of the doctrine itself will be in danger of being lost, or enfeebled, and deprived of its vital effect on the character and conduct: the dogma becoming a mere formal profession, inefficacious for good, but cumbering the ground, and preventing the growth of any real and heartfelt conviction, from reason or personal experience.[40]

Mill claims, then that only free debate and exchange of ideas—the "collision of adverse opinions" in a "contest" of ideas—can establish the truth and make our beliefs vital and clear. Notice that Mill's views about the value of debate and the exchange of ideas with those who hold different ideas is at the same time an argument in support of his third kind of freedom, freedom of association. Mill does not spend much time explicitly arguing for freedom of association. He does not need to. His arguments for freedom of expression and freedom to live as one wants are themselves arguments for freedom of association.

Not only will society benefit when people are free to debate with others as they want, but it will also benefit

ANALYZING THE READING

1. What does Mill mean by "the tyranny of the majority"? Is such "tyranny" a problem for us today? Why or why not?

2. Mill gives four arguments to support his view that people must be allowed the freedom to think, say, and debate whatever they choose. What are those arguments? How does each argument incorporate the utilitarian principle that everyone should do whatever will produce the greatest benefits and fewest harms for society? Are his arguments sound?

3. Mill claims that a person will develop the combination of abilities and character that are unique to him as an individual only if he has the freedom to live as he chooses. Is his claim true? Why?

---

[39] Ibid., ch. 1, para. 14.
[40] Ibid., ch. 2, para. 64.

when people are free to live as they choose. Mill argues that the good whose value is above all others, and so whose development provides the greatest benefit to society, is the fully developed individual. And the individual can develop fully only if he is free to live as he chooses to live. Consequently, the freedom to live as one chooses to live will provide society with the greatest utility possible:

> As it is useful that while mankind are imperfect there should be different opinions, so is it that there should be different experiments of living; that free scope should be given to varieties of character, short of injury to others; and that the worth of different modes of life should be proved practically, when any one thinks fit to try them. It is desirable, in short, that in things which do not primarily concern others, individuality should assert itself . . . the free development of individuality is one of the leading essentials of well-being.
>
> The human faculties of perception, judgment, discriminative feeling, mental activity, and even moral preference are exercised only in making a choice. He who does anything because it is the custom makes no choice. He gains no practice either in discerning or in desiring what is best. The mental and moral, like the muscular powers, are improved only by being used.
>
> He who lets the world, or his own portion of it, choose his plan of life for him, has no need of any other faculty than the ape-like one of imitation. He who chooses his plan for himself, employs all his faculties. He must use observation to see, reasoning and judgment to foresee, activity to gather materials for decision, discrimination to decide, and when he has decided, firmness and self-control to hold to his deliberate decision. . . . It is possible that he might be guided in some good path, and kept out of harm's way, without any of these things. But what will be his comparative worth as a human being? . . . Among the works of man, which human life is rightly employed in perfecting and beautifying, the first in importance surely is man himself. . . .
>
> It is not by wearing down into uniformity all that is individual in themselves, but by cultivating it, and calling it forth, within the limits imposed by the rights and interests of others, that human beings become a noble and beautiful object of contemplation; and . . . by the same process human life also becomes rich, diversified, and animating, furnishing more abundant aliment to high thoughts and elevating feelings, and strengthening the tie which binds every individual to the race, by making the race infinitely better worth belonging to. In proportion to the development of his individuality, each person becomes more valuable to himself, and is therefore capable of being more valuable to others. There is a greater fullness of life about his own existence, and when there is more life in the units there is more in the mass which is composed of them. . . .
>
> To give any fair play to the nature of each, it is essential that different persons should be allowed to lead different lives. In proportion as this latitude has been exercised in any age, has that age been noteworthy to posterity. . . .
>
> Neither one person nor any number of persons, is warranted in saying to another human creature of ripe years, that he shall not do with his life for his own benefit what he chooses to do with it.[41]

Mill is arguing that the freedom to choose the life one feels is best for oneself as a unique individual is necessary to develop one's human potential. And the development of each person's human potential will provide society with the greatest possible benefit: the fully developed human being. Allowing everyone the freedom to choose to live as each wants to live, then, will provide society with more utility than any other course of action.

41 Ibid., ch. 3.

Society in general and government in particular, then, must grant each individual the freedom to believe and say what she wishes, the freedom to live as she wishes, and the freedom to associate and debate with whomever she wishes, so long as she harms no one in the process. It is wrong for society or government to interfere in the life of an adult, even if it says it is doing it for the adult's own good.

Although Mill appears to have drawn an important line of demarcation between society and individual, the distinction in some ways seems fuzzy. Mill says that society is justified in interfering in the individual's life when the individual "harms" others. But what constitutes "harm to others"? Suppose hearing you defend communism or pederasty or homosexuality or atheism makes me feel mental anguish. Can society step in and make you stop because you are inflicting the harm of mental anguish on me? If not, then what, exactly, does "harm to others" mean?

Furthermore, Mill argues that because the individual and not society is the best judge of what advances self-interest, society must leave the individual free to decide what is in his own best interests. But it seems that we do not always know our best interests. Suppose that a man who enjoys heroin "shoots up" every day and says this is in his best interests. Or suppose that a motorcyclist insists it is in his best interests to ride without a helmet. Or a driver insists that it is in her best interests to ride without a seat belt. These actions might be "doing what we like ... so long as what we do does not harm [others] even though they should think our conduct foolish, perverse, or wrong." So, according to Mill, society should leave individuals free to engage in these actions. Yet most of us would agree that these people's behavior is clearly not in their best interests. Couldn't one argue that in cases like these it is all right to interfere with their behaviors by outlawing heroin, passing laws that require motorcycle helmets, and enforcing laws that require seat belts?

Part of the problem is that Mill's concept of freedom guarantees an absolute freedom from outside interference in any adult activity that does not affect others. But this ignores our responsibility for each other. Perhaps in some cases we are morally justified in keeping others from doing things that clearly are not in their best interests.

Human Rights

The extent to which a state respects the freedom of its citizens is not the only basis for judging its justice. Many people believe that the laws of a state should also be judged by the respect that it shows for human rights. All people, they believe, have certain basic human rights, and the law should show respect for such rights. In fact, some people have held that when a law fails to respect human rights, the law is evil and need not be obeyed.

Although the notion of a right is difficult to pin down, it has played a significant role in U.S. history. For example, the Declaration of Independence asserts that "all men are endowed by their Creator with certain unalienable rights ... among these are life, liberty, and the pursuit of happiness." Several years later, the U.S. Constitution was amended to include the Bill of Rights, which guaranteed citizens the right to freedom of religion, the right to freedom of speech, the right to freedom of the press, the right to freedom of assembly, the right not to be subjected to unreasonable search and seizure, and the rights to due process and to trial by jury. In 1948, the United Nations published the Universal Declaration of Human Rights. The Declaration of Human Rights states that all human beings have "the right to own property, ... the right to work, ... the right to a just and favorable remuneration, ... [and] the right to rest and leisure." And, more recently, we have witnessed an explosion of appeals to rights—gay rights, prisoners' rights, women's rights, animal rights, smokers' rights, fetal rights, and employee rights.

Just what is a right? The philosopher H. J. McCloskey has defined a **right** as a justified entitlement or claim on others.[42] For example, if I have a right to privacy, then I have a justified claim to be left alone by others. And if I have a right to an education, then I have a justified claim to be provided with an education by society.

The flip side of a right is a **duty**, which is an obligation imposed on other individuals. That is, if someone has a right to something, then others have certain duties or obligations toward that person. If you have a right to privacy, then everyone else has a duty to leave you alone; if you have a right to an education, then society has a duty to provide you with an education. Rights always impose duties on others. That is, rights are "correlated" with duties.

There are two main kinds of rights, depending on the kind of justification or basis that they are given. There are legal rights and moral rights. *Legal rights* depend on the laws of a nation or country. For example, the laws of the United States give all citizens a legal right to equal treatment under the law. However, the laws of South Africa, throughout the 1980s and into the 1990s, failed to give black people the legal right to equal treatment.

Moral rights, or, as they are sometimes called, *human rights*, are rights that all people have simply because they are human beings. These rights are justified or supported by moral principles that impose their correlated duties on all human beings. For example, the laws of South Africa once said that black people did not have the legal right to equal treatment. Most people throughout the world felt that the South African legal system was morally wrong and that black people everywhere, including those in South Africa, have a moral right to equal treatment. Everyone has this right because the moral principle of respect for human dignity requires equality of treatment.

Moral or human rights are in a sense much more significant than legal rights because we judge legal rights in terms of people's moral rights. That is, when a country's laws violate people's moral rights, we say that the law is wrong and must be changed. The American Civil War, a bloody, costly, and tragic confrontation, was fought in part because the slavery laws of the South were seen to violate the moral rights of black Americans. The civil rights movement of the sixties was a bitter struggle to change discriminatory laws that violated the moral rights of minorities and women. And we have seen bloody clashes in South Africa, Latin America, and parts of Asia over the injustice of laws that are seen to violate the moral rights of various groups. Thus, when the law violates people's moral rights, the law must be changed.

Some philosophers divide rights into two groups: negative rights and positive rights. *Negative rights* are rights that protect freedoms of various kinds. The right to privacy, the right not to be killed, the right to travel, and the right to do what one wants with one's property are all negative rights. These rights all protect some form of human freedom or liberty. Negative rights impose a negative duty on other people. They impose a duty not to prevent others from engaging in certain actions. For example, the right of free association imposes on others the duty not to prevent people from associating with whom they please. Negative rights are sometimes called "freedoms-from" because they leave people free from the interference of others. However, negative rights impose minimal duties on others because they merely require that others not act.

Positive rights are rights that guarantee people certain goods. Positive rights include the right to an education; the right to adequate medical care, food, and

> **QUICK REVIEW**
> Rights impose duties on others; negative rights impose duties on others to leave people free to engage in certain activities; positive rights impose duties on others to provide the right holder with certain goods. Moral or human rights are rights that all humans have.

---

[42] H. J. McCloskey, "Rights—Some Conceptual Issues," *Australasian Journal of Philosophy* 54 (1976): 99–115.

The Third of May,
Francisco Goya. To what extent ought the state and its primary instrument, government, exercise authority and power over the individual? Location: Museo del Prado, Madrid, Spain.

© SCALA/Art Resource, NY

housing; the right to a fair trial; the right to a job; and the right to a clean environment. Positive rights impose a positive duty on people. They impose a duty to actively help a person to have or to do something. If the poor have a right to adequate medical care, for example, then we as a society have a duty to ensure that they are provided with such care. Consequently, respecting a positive right requires more than merely not acting; positive rights impose on us the duty to act positively on behalf of others.

Without understanding the distinction between negative and positive rights, it is hard to understand many of the social controversies that confront our society. Many people today believe that government should only enforce negative rights. They believe that the purpose of government is to guarantee only freedoms-from. Such people hold that government should not be involved in welfare programs, farm subsidies, or any other redistributive programs; ideally, government should only protect citizens from one another and from foreign invasion. But, as we have seen, many other Americans believe that government should do more than enforce these negative rights: It should also guarantee people's positive rights through programs that provide the needy with a minimum level of well-being.

Both positive rights and negative rights have been defended on the basis of a variety of philosophies. But perhaps the most influential defense of human rights has been the approach advocated by the philosopher Immanuel Kant. He maintained that every human being has a worth or a dignity that everyone else must respect. The individual's worth, Kant held, gives each person a value that is "beyond all price." Because of this intrinsic value or dignity, each person is an "end in himself"—that is, a being for whose sake we should all act. Consequently, Kant claimed, we each have a duty to respect every person's freedom, as well as to help others achieve their goals. This is the meaning of words of his that we saw in the previous chapter:

> Violations of the principle that our humanity must be respected as an end in itself are even clearer if we take examples of attacks on the freedom and property of others. It is obvious that the person who violates such rights is using people merely as

means without considering that as rational beings they should be esteemed also as ends; that is, as beings who must be able to participate in the goals of the actions in which they are involved with him. . . .

Humanity probably could survive even if people never helped each other achieve their happiness, but merely refrained from deliberately harming one another. But this would only be a negative way of making our actions harmonize with the idea that humanity is an end in itself. The positive way of harmonizing with this idea would be for everyone to help others achieve their goals as far as he can.[43]

> ### ANALYZING THE READING
>
> 1. Kant claims that human beings are "ends in themselves." How is Kant's claim similar to Mill's earlier claim that "the first in importance surely is man himself"? How is it different?
>
> 2. What is Kant's argument for his claim that we have a moral duty "to help others achieve their goals" as far as we can, and that government should provide support for those "who are not able to support themselves"? What rights was Kant defending?

Because of their human dignity, then, all persons have positive as well as negative human rights. For this reason, Kant held that government may legitimately levy taxes to pay for support for the welfare, education, and development of persons "who are not able to support themselves."[44]

Some philosophers who agree that everyone has a basic dignity interpret the notion of human dignity differently from Kant. For example, Robert Nozick has argued that human dignity implies only that people should be free from having others interfere with their lives. In short, the only rights that humans have are negative rights to be left alone. This implies that government should guarantee only people's negative rights and not their positive ones.

However, many contemporary philosophers agree with Kant's conclusions, even if they do not accept all his views. We saw earlier that Rawls endorses the idea that government should provide support for the disadvantaged. He therefore agrees that government should support people's positive rights. While Rawls has said that much of his thinking was inspired by Kant, however, he has also said that he disagrees with Kant on several points.

Thomas Donaldson is another philosopher who agrees that people have both negative and positive human rights, even though he does not believe that these are necessarily based on human dignity. Instead, Donaldson holds that human rights are rights that should fulfill three conditions: They must protect something of very great importance to human beings, they must be subject to substantial and recurrent threats, and the obligations they impose on others must be fair and affordable. Donaldson has suggested the following list of basic human rights:

1. The right to freedom of physical movement.
2. The right to ownership of property.
3. The right to freedom from torture.
4. The right to a fair trial.
5. The right to nondiscriminatory treatment (freedom from discrimination on the basis of such characteristics as race or sex).
6. The right to physical security.

> **QUICK REVIEW**
> Kant argued that because every person as an "end in himself" has an intrinsic value or dignity that everyone else must respect, each person has a duty to respect other people's freedom and to help others achieve their happiness. So, everyone has negative and positive rights.

43 Immanuel Kant, *Grundlegung zur Metaphysik der Sitten* [*Groundwork of the Metaphysics of Morals*], in *Immanuel Kant Werkausgabe*, vol. 7, ed. Wilhelm Weischedel (Frankfurt, Germany: Insel Verlag Wiesbaden, 1956). This translation copyright © 1987 by Manuel Velasquez.

44 Immanuel Kant, *The Metaphysical Elements of justice*, trans. W. Hastie (New York: Bobbs-Merrill, 1965), 93.

7. The right to freedom of speech and association.

8. The right to a minimal education.

9. The right to political participation.

10. The right to subsistence.[45]

According to Donaldson, each of these human rights protects something of great importance to human life, each is subject to recurrent threats from governments and others around the world, and each imposes fair and affordable burdens on governments or others. Consequently, all governments and citizens of all nations should be required to live up to them. In addition, Donaldson argues, the governments of the wealthier nations should help those of poorer nations provide these rights for their people.

ANALYZING THE READING

Donaldson argues that people have ten basic human rights. What is the argument that he uses to support his view that people have these ten basic human rights? Do you agree with his argument? Why?

A currently divisive issue in the United States, as we have seen, is how much the government should do to guarantee positive rights. Some contend that government already does too much. They say the executive, legislative, and judicial branches of government are poking their collective noses into areas where they do not belong. In short, by supporting positive rights government is doing what it has no legitimate authority to do. This view is related to the social contract view of Locke. Locke argued that the purpose of government is to protect our rights to life, liberty, and property. If government does anything beyond this it would be doing what it has no authority to do. But Locke's rights to life, liberty, and property are all negative rights. The right to life is not the right to be given what I need to live; it is the right not to be prevented from living, that is, the right not to be killed. The right to liberty is the right not to have others prevent me from doing what I want. And the right to property is the right not to have others prevent me from using my property as I wish. So Locke's rights are all negative rights. Many people who claim that government should not support positive rights, therefore, appeal to Locke's theory.

Others claim that government has the same authority to support positive rights that it has to support negative rights. They argue that life has grown so expensive and competitive that many are unable to meet all their needs. They conclude that government not only has the authority, but the obligation to step up to the job of supporting people's positive rights. Many people who endorse this conclusion appeal to Kant's views on human dignity.

We can close by noticing that although these positions differ, they are related to the issues that have occupied us in this chapter: What is the purpose of government? How far does government's authority extend? What does justice require of government?

War and Terrorism

We have discussed some of the moral limits on what the state may do to its citizens. But are there any limits on what the state may do to other states or to the citizens of other states? For example, is it ever wrong for nations to use violence or force upon each other? Are there any moral limits on what warring nations can do to each other? Is it ever wrong for the citizens of one nation to use violence upon the

---

[45]   Thomas Donaldson, *The Ethics of International Business* (New York: Oxford University Press, 1989), 81.

citizens of another? If the members of one group feel threatened by the members of another group, can they legitimately use violence against them?

Several violent incidents during the past two decades have made these questions particularly pressing for Americans. In 1989, when General Noriega took over the government of Panama and said that the United States was no longer welcome in Panama, the U.S. military invaded Panama and replaced Noriega with Panamanian officials who were friendly to the United States. In 1990, Iraq invaded Kuwait. The Kuwaiti government appealed to the United Nations for help, and with the blessings of the United Nations, the U.S. military subsequently went to Iraq, defeated its army, and invaded deep into its territory. On September 11, 2001, a band of terrorists flew two jets into the World Trade Center's Twin Towers in New York City, destroying the buildings and killing about 3,000 Americans. In response, the United States invaded Afghanistan and overthrew its government, the Taliban regime. The Taliban were alleged to be harboring Osama Bin Laden, the accused leader of the terrorist band that destroyed the Twin Towers. The following year, the United States invaded Iraq and overthrew the government of Saddam Hussein on the grounds that his regime was harboring weapons of mass destruction and so posed a threat to the security of the United States. Also during the past two decades, numerous terrorist groups have attacked and killed civilians—in airplanes, on subways, on trains, in buildings, and on city streets—to protest what the terrorists perceive as injustices. Suicide bombers in Iraq and Afghanistan have killed hundreds of American soldiers as well as Iraqi and Afghanistan citizens.

Thoughtful presidents, generals, and citizens have pondered the question of whether such acts of violence and war are morally justified. Our political leaders are always anxious to justify their military actions as "ethical and just." But what, exactly, are the moral principles that govern the use of force between nations? Are there any moral limits on how wars between nations should be waged? And what is the moral status of terrorism and of counterterrorism? Three main positions have been developed in the West in response to these questions: political realism, pacifism, and just war theory.

Political Realism. Political realism, sometimes called "realpolitik," is the view that there are no moral limits on what one nation may do to another in pursuit of its own interests. The classic proponent of this position is Thomas Hobbes, whom we discussed earlier. We saw that Hobbes claims that before government exists, people are in a state of nature. A point we did not discuss, however, is that Hobbes also claims that nations exist in a permanent "state of nature." Nations exist in a state of nature because there is no international body (what he calls a "common power") powerful enough to force them to behave justly with each other. This state of nature, Hobbes held, is a continual state of war. Hobbes also claims that in such a state of war, there can be no morality and so no binding moral obligations to constrain nations. Instead, the only constraint on one nation's behavior is the force or power of other nations:

> It is manifest that during the time men live without a common power to keep them all in awe, they are in that condition which is called war; and such a war as is of every man against every man. For war consisteth not in battle only, or in the act of fighting, but in a tract of time, wherein the will to contend by battle is sufficiently known. . . .
>
> But though there had never been any time wherein particular men were in a condition of war one against another, yet in all times kings and persons of sovereign authority, because of their independency, are in continual jealousies, and in the state and posture of gladiators, having their weapons pointing, and their eyes fixed on one another; that is, their forts, garrisons, and guns upon the frontiers of their kingdoms, and continual spies upon their neighbors, which is a posture of war. . . .

MindTap To read more from Thomas Hobbes' *Leviathan*, click the link in the MindTap Reader or go to the Questia Readings folder in MindTap.

> To this war . . ., this also is consequent: that nothing can be unjust. The notions of right and wrong, justice and injustice, have there no place. Where there is no common power, there is no law; where no law, no injustice . . . They are qualities that relate to men in society, not in solitude. It is consequent also to the same condition that there be no property, no dominion, no mine and thine distinct; but only that to be every man's that he can get, and for so long as he can keep it.[46]

If a form of political realism like Hobbes' is correct, then morality has no place in international relations. There is nothing morally wrong with any violent act that a nation might undertake in pursuit of its own "national interests." Right and wrong, just and unjust—are terms that can apply to individual human beings living in a society where government can enforce law and order. But they cannot be applied to the relations between nations. Consequently, the use of violence between nations can never be condemned as morally wrong or unjust. They can only criticize as imprudent or not in the nation's best interests. Wars, then, can never be said to be wrong or immoral, but only stupid or against the national interest. In a similar vein, the realist might argue that even terrorism cannot be criticized as wrong or immoral when it is undertaken by the citizens of nations against the citizens of another nation. In the view of the realist, terrorism may be stupid or useless, but it cannot be moral or immoral.

Political realism has had many defenders over the years. Many contemporary politicians and statesmen and stateswomen continue to embrace the view today. But is the view acceptable? Critics of realism argue that there is no reason to accept the political realist's claim that we cannot apply morality to the relations between nations. In fact, critics say, we apply morality to the actions of nations all the time, and there seems nothing wrong with doing so. We apply morality to the relations between nations when we say, for example, that it is unjust for a powerful nation to wage war on a weak nation merely to take over its land and resources. Or when we say that it is wrong for one nation to violate the human rights of the citizens of another nation. For example, many said it was unjust for Iraq to invade Kuwait and take over its land and oil fields in 1990. And many historians have said that it was wrong for the German Nazis to invade France and export its Jewish citizens to be killed in their concentration camps during World War II. Examples like these show that the political realist is wrong in claiming that we cannot use moral terms to judge the acts of nations, including their wars. Moreover, what reason can the realist give for thinking that morality does not apply to an area of human life? Because acts of war are the actions of human beings, and because all human actions can be judged by the standards of morality, it follows that war and terrorism can be judged "moral" or "immoral." The realist is, therefore, mistaken in thinking that morality does not apply to war.

There are other objections to political realism. The political realist assumes that there is no international body that can force nations to abide by any rules. But this, critics say, seems wrong. The critics of realism point out that today several nations have come together in groups capable of forcing one another to abide

ANALYZING THE READING

1. Describe the key claims of the political realist view. Do you think those claims are justified? Why?

2. Hobbes claims that if there is no international body powerful enough to force all other nations to behave morally toward your nation, then your nation has no obligation to behave morally toward them. Do you agree with him? Why? Can you think of any arguments that you could use to support Hobbes' claim? Is your argument valid? Is it sound?

QUICK REVIEW

Political "realists" such as Hobbes argue that because nations exist in a state of nature without a "common power" to enforce justice, they are in a "state of war" in which concepts of morality or justice do not apply. So, violence between nations is neither right nor wrong but only for or against a nation's best interests. Critics argue that because acts of war are acts of human individuals, we can and do apply moral concepts to acts of war; moreover, there are international bodies that can enforce justice.

---

[46] Thomas Hobbes, *Leviathan*, pt. 1, ch. 13.

by international laws. These groups include the United Nations, the World Trade Organization (WTO), the North Atlantic Treaty Organization (NATO) states, the European Union, the Organisation for Economic Co-operation and Development (OECD), and other regional groups of nations. These groups provide the "common power" that Hobbes said is necessary if relations between nations are to be judged by the standards of morality. Thus, there seems to be nothing to prevent even Hobbes from agreeing that morality applies to wars fought between modern nations.

Some defenders of realism have responded to these criticisms by providing a different kind of defense of realism. Some have argued that a government official has a moral obligation to advance the interests of the state regardless of what morality may say. This moral obligation, a realist may claim, is an obligation that overrides any other moral obligation a government official may have. Why does a government official have this obligation? The realist may give this argument: The purpose of government is solely to advance the interests of the nation and its citizens. Rulers and statesmen act on behalf of government; they serve as "agents" of government. When they agree to accept government office, they agree to single mindedly pursue the interests of the nation and its citizens. Therefore, the highest obligation of a government official is to do whatever will best secure the interests of the nation and its citizens. Since that is their highest moral obligation, they must not let other moral considerations prevent them from undertaking those actions that best advance the interests of the nation and its citizens. Therefore, moral considerations cannot affect the decisions of nations. The decisions of nations are made by their top officials and those officials have an obligation to not allow moral considerations to affect their decisions.

Critics of realism have responded that this argument in defense of realism concedes a key point that undermines realism. It concedes that morality applies to the actions and decisions of top government officials. If government officials do what they do because they have a moral obligation to do it, then their decisions and actions are in fact subject to morality. If morality applies to the decisions of top government officials, then it applies to the decisions they make. But the decisions of top government officials are the decisions of the nation. So morality must apply to the decisions of nations. This second argument for realism, then, implies that morality *does* apply to decisions nations make about their actions toward other nations. It seems, then, that the only consistent argument for realism is the kind of argument that Hobbes gave. But that kind of realism, we have seen, is also open to serious objections.

Pacifism. Unlike the realist, the pacifist asserts that morality applies to relations between nations. In particular morality applies to violence among nations and so to war. There are two forms of pacifism: absolute pacifism and conditional pacifism. The absolute pacifist holds that war is always wrong, while the conditional pacifist holds that although war—especially modern war—is generally wrong, in rare situations it might be justified.

Pacifists are not cowards. Many pacifists have refused to fight in the face of extreme pressures and violence directed against them. Others have accepted imprisonment and even execution rather than compromise their pacifist principles. And many have proclaimed themselves "conscientious objectors" rather than join their nation's war effort. Most democratic nations, including the United States, have laws that allow pacifists and others opposed to war to register as conscientious objectors rather than have to fight in a war. Most of these laws say that conscientious objectors must substitute some nonviolent form of public service such as serving as a medic for the military, perhaps on the battlefield.

Why do absolute pacifists hold that war is always wrong? Some absolute pacifists hold this view on religious grounds. Many Christians have held, for example, that the teachings of Jesus—"Love your enemies" and "When a man strikes you on one cheek, offer him your other cheek"—directly prohibit the use of violence, even in self-defense. During Christianity's first three centuries, most Christians accepted the view of Origen, who argued that Christians could not "go forth as soldiers" because "the Lord has abolished the sword." Many Buddhists are also pacifists because of their religion. The Buddha, the founder of Buddhism, demanded that his followers completely abstain from any violence: "Avoid killing, or harming any living thing," and "In times of war give yourself to the mind of compassion, helping living beings abandon the will to fight." Buddhists have often accepted death rather than fight in a war.

However, other absolute pacifists view war as immoral not on religious grounds but on utilitarian grounds. They argue that war is always wrong because of the terrible evils that it always inflicts. War inflicts the evils of death, intense human suffering, economic losses, widespread destruction of human goods and achievements, and moral and spiritual degradation both on those who wage the war and on those who are victimized by the war. It is unjustified, such pacifists hold, to produce such large evils unless doing so will produce correspondingly large benefit. But the evils of war are so large that no benefit can outweigh those evils. Therefore, war is always morally unjustified.

Other pacifists defend the view that war is always wrong by appealing to a deontological argument. Some pacifists, for example, adopt Kant's theory of ethics. They argue that the dignity of the human person implies that every human being has a right not to be killed and a right not to be subjected to violence. Because war necessarily inflicts violence and death on people, war is absolutely immoral.

But is the pacifist right? It is true, critics agree, that as the utilitarian argument for pacifism asserts, war involves great evils. But aren't there some human goods whose value is so large that we are justified in using war to protect those goods? Consider how, during the last century, Adolf Hitler and the German Nazi party invaded several nations and systematically tortured and exterminated millions of innocent Jewish people. Even though World War II was a great evil, critics of pacifism claim, it was justified because it stopped Hitler. Or consider the American Revolution, which was fought to free the American colonies from the tyranny of Great Britain. Wasn't the good that came from American independence worth the evils that the American Revolution produced?

Other critics of absolute pacifism have pointed out that pacifism claims violence is always wrong. It is wrong to use violence even to defend oneself against an unjust attacker or to defend another innocent victim of an unjust attacker. But this implication of pacifism is mistaken, critics claim. There is clearly nothing wrong with defending oneself against an unjust attack. Nor can it be wrong to help the innocent victim of an unjust attack. Because pacifism has such obviously false implications, it must itself be false.

Critics of the absolute version of pacifism have argued that the deontological argument for pacifism is based on inconsistent views. Philosopher Jan Narveson, for example, argues that the deontological pacifist claims it is always wrong to inflict violence on people. This pacifist claim implies that people have a right not to have violence inflicted on them. But if people have a right not to have violence inflicted on them, then they must have a right to be defended when someone inflicts violence on them. But if people have a right to be defended when others inflict violence on them, then they have a right to use violence to defend their rights. So, the absolute pacifist's claim that violence is always *wrong* leads to the contradictory conclusion that it is *right* to use violence to defend oneself against violence! Narveson concludes that the absolute pacifist is mistaken: It is not always wrong to use violence

> **QUICK REVIEW**
> Absolute pacifists hold that war is always immoral either on religious grounds or because the evils of war always outweigh the good war might produce, or because the violence of war violates human dignity. Critics argue there are some goods that outweigh the evils of war, that it is not wrong to defend oneself or others against unjust attack, and that pacifism is inconsistent because if people have a right not to be subjected to violence, then they have a right to be defended from violence even with violence.

on people. Although it is usually wrong to use violence on people, it is morally justified when defending oneself and others from violence.[47]

Some pacifists have turned away from absolute pacifism and, instead, have adopted a kind of "conditional" pacifism. The conditional pacifist agrees with the critics that in some extreme but rare situations, war might be justified. However, the conditional pacifist continues, the kinds of wars that now confront us are always wrong. It is possible, of course, to imagine an ideal war between ideally decent enemies, in which the benefits of fighting the war might outweigh its horrible costs. But such an idealistic situation is unrealistic: It does not happen in the real world in which we now live. Modern wars are fought with weapons that necessarily inflict widespread injuries and suffering on numerous innocent parties: civilians, children, the aged. When used at Hiroshima and Nagasaki, nuclear weapons inflicted tens of thousands of civilian deaths in a single instant; so-called obliteration bombing raids against the Germans during World War II killed tens of thousands at a time; "conventional" bombs used in the Korean War, the Vietnam War, and the wars in Iraq and Afghanistan also indiscriminately killed and maimed soldiers and civilians alike by the thousands. Moreover, once war is declared, nations are willing to do virtually anything to avert defeat, and their governments often unleash horrific destruction on the "enemy." So terrible are the evils inflicted by modern wars that they would always outweigh any good that realistically might be achieved through war.

However, critics argue that the conditional pacifist admits a key point that undermines the pacifist position: The conditional pacifist admits that to properly evaluate the justice of a war, one needs to weigh its costs against its benefits. Once this is admitted, critics claim, then the conditional pacifist has opened the door to the view that despite the qualms of the conditional pacifist, it may be that some wars—perhaps even modern wars—are morally justified. And if war is sometimes justified, then we must ask this question: Under what conditions is war justified? Just war theory tries to answer that question.

Just War Theory.

Just war theory rejects the realist claim that morality should not be applied to war. It also rejects the pacifist claim that war is so evil that it is always immoral. Instead, just war theory holds that although war is evil because killing is wrong, it is sometimes morally justified for a state to engage in war. It can be justified because the state has an obligation to defend its citizens, protect the innocent, and enforce justice. Just war theory sets out several principles to determine when war is morally justified.

Many thinkers have contributed to the development of just war theory, including Saint Augustine, Saint Thomas Aquinas, Francisco de Vitoria (1492–1546), Hugo Grotius (1583–1645), Samuel Pufendorf (1632–1694), and Christian Wolff (1679–1754). In modern times, the Harvard philosopher Michael Walzer has argued in his book *Just and Unjust Wars* that just war theory is the most appropriate theory for determining the ethics of war. Many government officials have agreed with Walzer. When embarking on a military campaign, government officials often make at least a show of demonstrating that their campaign follows the principles of just war

---

ANALYZING THE READING

1. What is the argument that some utilitarians have used to support the view of absolute pacifism? Do you agree with that argument? Why?

2. Explain how Kant's theory of ethics has been used to argue in favor of the absolute pacifist view?

3. Explain Jan Narveson's argument against absolute pacifism. Is his argument valid? Is it sound?

QUICK REVIEW

Conditional pacifists hold that although there might be some good that could justify some low levels of violence, modern wars inflict so much violence that their violence outweighs any possible good that could be achieved. Critics point out that the view of the conditional pacifist implies that the costs of war have to be weighed against its benefits.

---

[47] Jan Narveson, "Pacifism: A Philosophical Analysis," *Ethics* 75, no. 4 (July 1965): 259–271.

theory—even if they do not always use the term "just war theory." On May 1, 2012, for example, the U.S. government revealed that its military had been killing individual al-Qaida leaders in Pakistan using remotely piloted aircraft so precisely targeted that they could kill an individual with little collateral damage and without harming innocent civilians. When John Brennan, the then White House counterterrorism advisor, made this revelation, he delivered a lengthy speech in which he hastened to argue that "these targeted strikes against al-Qaida terrorists are indeed ethical and just." They are ethical and just, he claimed, because they adhere to the ethical "principles of the law of war that govern the use of force." The "principles of the law of war" that he appealed to in his speech were the principles of "just war theory," including, he stated, "the principle of necessity," "the principle of distinction [between innocent civilians and military targets]," "the principle of proportionality," and "the principle of humanity [that limits unnecessary suffering]."

Saint Augustine was among the first to claim that although war is evil, it is "just" if it is fought under certain conditions. However, it was Saint Thomas Aquinas who first clearly and systematically stated the criteria that a just war would have to meet. Addressing the question of whether war was ever justified, Aquinas wrote the following:

> In order for a war to be just, three things are necessary. First, the decision to wage the war must be made by a ruler who has the authority to do so. For a private individual has no right to declare war, since he can seek for redress of his rights from the tribunal of his superior. Moreover a private individual lacks the authority to call together the people, which has to be done in wartime. And as the care of the common good is committed to those who are in authority, it is their business to watch over the common good of the city, kingdom or province subject to them. And just as it is lawful for them to use the sword when they punish evil-doers in defending the common good against internal disturbances, . . . so too, it is their business to have recourse to the sword of war to defend the common good against external enemies. . . . Secondly, a just cause is required, namely that those who are attacked, should be attacked because they deserve it on account of some fault. Which is why Augustine says: "A just war is wont to be described as one that avenges wrongs, when a nation or state has to be punished, for refusing to make amends for the wrongs inflicted by its subjects, or to restore what it has seized unjustly." Thirdly, it is necessary that the belligerents should have a rightful intention, so that they intend the advancement of good, or the avoidance of evil. Hence Augustine says: "True religion looks upon as peaceful those wars that are waged not for motives of aggrandizement, or cruelty, but with the object of securing peace, of punishing evil-doers, and of uplifting the good." For it may happen that a war is declared by a legitimate authority, and for a just cause, and yet it may be unlawful because of a wicked intention. Hence Augustine says: "The passion for inflicting harm, the cruel thirst for vengeance, an unpacific and relentless spirit, the fever of revolt, the lust of power, and such like things, all these are rightly condemned in war."[48]

Clearly, it is Aquinas' view that although war is not a good thing, it is morally justified under certain conditions. The three conditions he gives can be summarized as follows:

1. *Legitimate authority.* The war must be legally declared by a public authority who is legitimately authorized to commit a people to war; the war must not be declared by a private individual or group that has not been entrusted with the care of the common good or by someone without the legal authority to declare war.

---

[48] Thomas Aquinas, *Summa Theologica*, I–II, q.40, a.1.

2. *Just cause.* The war must be pursued for a morally just cause or purpose, such as self-defense or to take back what was unjustly seized; it is wrong to engage in a war against a nation that has done nothing to deserve it.

3. *Right intention.* Those who are engaged in fighting the war must have a rightful intention; that is, they must intend only to achieve the just end and must not be motivated, for example, by a desire to inflict injury out of sheer cruelty or revenge.

In the centuries that followed, many thinkers who were sympathetic to Aquinas' just war theory nevertheless pointed out several shortcomings. For example, if a country could avoid a war through diplomacy or if a country had no hope of winning a war, then it should not go to war even if the war met Aquinas' three conditions. To fix Aquinas' theory, thinkers supplemented his three conditions with several others. Here are the four most important added conditions:

4. *Last resort.* The war must be fought only as a last resort; it is wrong to engage in a war if there are other means of achieving one's ends.

5. *Real and certain danger.* War can be declared only when there is a certain and imminent danger of an attack or invasion by a foreign power; it is wrong to launch a preemptive strike on a country merely because a government is afraid that the country might become belligerent sometime in the future.

6. *Reasonable probability of success.* There must be a reasonable probability of achieving the end for which the war is fought; it is wrong to commit a nation to a war that is hopeless or futile.

7. *Proportional end.* The war must be aimed at achieving a goal whose value is proportional to the injuries that the war will probably inflict; it is wrong to enter a war that will produce more harm than good.

These seven conditions today are referred to as the *jus ad bellum* conditions of the just war theory. *Jus ad bellum* is a Latin phrase that means "justice [when] approaching war," so these are the seven conditions that must be present when a nation enters or declares war.

But proponents of just war theory have also discussed how nations must conduct themselves during a war. These additional conditions are referred to as the *jus in bello* conditions of the just war theory. *Jus in bello* is Latin for "justice [when] in war," so it refers to the kinds of methods or means that must be used in a just war. The two *jus in bello* conditions that proponents of the just war theory have developed are these:

8. *Proportional means.* It is wrong during war to use methods of warfare that inflict harms that are not proportional to the end to be achieved; it is wrong to use weapons or methods that will inflict more suffering or deaths than are truly necessary to achieve one's ends.

9. *Noncombatant immunity.* Although it is permissible during war to target or kill military combatants (soldiers and others actively engaged in fighting a war), it is wrong to intentionally target or kill innocent noncombatants (children, the aged, and any other civilians

THINKING LIKE A PHILOSOPHER

1. Would you describe yourself as more of a political realist, or an absolute pacifist, or a conditional pacifist, or a just war theorist?

2. How many wars has the United States been involved in since you were born? Which of these was the most recent one? Was that war a just war according to the principles of just war theory? Do you know anyone who fought in that war? Based on what you know or can learn about that war by doing some research about it on the Internet, do you think it was morally just? Why?

not actively engaged in fighting a war); it is also wrong to use methods or weapons that cannot discriminate between noncombatants and combatants.

The principles of just war theory are not based on any single philosophy. The thinkers who have helped develop just war theory have proposed many different kinds of arguments for the seven *jus ad bellum* and the two *jus in bello* conditions. Aquinas, for example, defends the claim that war must be declared by a legitimate authority (principle 1). He argues that only a legitimate government has the right to take life in defense of the state, to gather its citizens into an army, and to use violence to correct wrongs. Private individuals do not have such a right and so cannot wage war. He also defends the claim that that war must be fought for a just cause (principle 2). He argues that it is wrong even for the state to take life unless it is done to defend the state and its people or to correct a wrongful injury against the state or its people. And he defends the view that war must be fought with a good intention (principle 3) because in his view, an agent's intention determines the morality of the agent's action.

Other philosophers have argued for the principles that war should be fought only as a last resort (principle 4) and only when there is a certain and imminent danger of attack (principle 5). They have argued that the killing, destruction, and sufferings of war are such great evils that war is justified only as a last resort. And the evils of war are so great that they should not be unleashed until an attack is imminent. The principle that it is wrong to commit a nation to a war that is hopeless (principle 6), that a war must aim at achieving a good that is greater than the harms it will produce (principle 7), and that methods of war must not inflict more injuries than are necessary to achieve one's ends (principle 8) have all been defended on utilitarian grounds. Such defenses have appealed to the principle of utilitarianism which states that we have a moral duty to maximize good and minimize harm. The principle that it is legitimate to target combatants or soldiers but wrong to intentionally kill innocent noncombatants (principle 9) has been defended, in part, by appealing to natural law ethics. Natural law ethics argues that it is always wrong to directly destroy an innocent human life. The principle has also been defended in part on the basis of Immanuel Kant's categorical imperative. Kant's categorical imperative states that persons should be treated as ends—that is, only as they have consented to be treated. Kantians have argued that by entering the military and going to war, soldiers have consented to engage in mortal combat and so can be killed in battle. But civilians, who are not actively engaged in fighting, have not so consented and so may not be targeted.

The theory of just war is not just a view of Western thinkers. Some Eastern philosophers have expounded versions of just war theory. Sikhism, for example, has developed the concept of "Dharam Yudh," meaning "war in defense of righteousness." Like Western philosophers, Sikhs also hold that although war is evil, it is sometimes a justified evil. The theory of Dharam Yudh holds that war is justified only if: (1) it is fought as a last resort, (2) it is not undertaken for revenge, (3) its armies are disciplined and do not include paid mercenaries, (4) the nation uses only the minimum force needed to achieve success, (5) civilians are not harmed, and (6) there is no looting or theft of property or territory.

Notice that there is substantial overlap between the theory of Dharam Yudh and just war theory.

Just war theory is subject to a number of criticisms. Pacifists have argued that historically, the theory has been used only as an excuse for going to war and has not been used to avoid war. Consequently, the pacifist claims, just war theory has encouraged war instead of having served to limit war.

Other critics have argued that just war theory is too vague. It is not clear, for example, what the theory means when it states that war must be declared by the legitimate authority. Does this mean that when citizens rebel against an unjust and oppressive government, their rebellion is always unjust? It is also not clear what the theory means by a "just cause." A just cause certainly includes defending oneself against an actively invading force or helping a weak nation defend itself against an invading force. But does just cause include attacking a nation whose government is violating the human rights of its own citizens? (As Muammar Gaddafi's Libyan regime was doing when attacked by the U.S. and other U.N. forces in 2011.) Does it include attacking a nation to prevent it from launching a future attack? (Like the United States did when it claimed it invaded Iraq in 2003 to prevent it from developing "weapons of mass destruction.") And consider the principle of "last resort." Does this principle mean that a nation has to wait until it has tried every form of persuasion and diplomacy before resorting to war? If so, then doesn't this waiting give the enemy more time to kill and strengthen its forces so it inflicts greater harm on the waiting nation? Or consider the principle of "reasonable probability of success." Does this mean that small and weak nations must never defend themselves against more powerful nations that will likely win any war against them? Neither is it clear what "proportionality" means. How is one supposed to measure the value of the goods that wars are fought for (such as a democratic government) against the loss of life war inevitably inflicts? Critics argue that since the principles of just war theory are unclear, cynics can and do misuse it to justify wars that are unjustified. Moreover, even those who honestly want to use the theory to assess the justice of a conflict find themselves hampered by its lack of clarity.

Critics have also argued that modern weapons of war have made just war theory irrelevant. Modern wars use weapons and methods of warfare that make it difficult or impossible to discriminate combatants from noncombatants. These include chemical, biological, and nuclear weapons and methods such as saturation bombing. Critics conclude that today the principle of discrimination is either useless or it condemns all wars.

Despite its critics, just war theory today is the most widely accepted theory for determining when war is morally justified. Its defenders say that although the theory is sometimes unclear, it is still clear enough to be useful in judging many wars. Moreover, many of its principles have been incorporated into international laws that define and punish war crimes. For example, principle 9 on noncombatant immunity is now part of the Geneva Protocol and the Geneva Convention. International and military courts have prosecuted soldiers and deposed leaders for war crimes based on violating noncombatant immunity.

Terrorism. So far, we have been discussing the ethics and morality of war and methods of warfare. Does this discussion shed any light on terrorism or using violence to fight it? Terrorism has been defined in many different ways. Some definitions focus on the idea that acts of terrorism are acts of violence designed to create terror among the members of a society. Others focus on the idea that terrorism is violence in pursuit of a political goal such as a more just government. And still others focus on the idea that terrorism is violence that is intentionally directed against innocent noncombatants. After reviewing all of these various definitions, political philosopher C.A.J. Coady comes to the following conclusion:

> If we define terrorism as the tactic of intentionally targeting noncombatants with lethal or severe violence for political purposes, we will capture a great deal of what is being discussed with such passion and we can raise crucial moral and political

☑ QUICK REVIEW
Coady defines terrorism as intentionally targeting noncombatants with lethal or severe violence to achieve political purposes, perhaps through the creation of fear and perhaps including the targeting of property that is related to life or security.

questions about it with some clarity. We might narrow the definition in certain respects by incorporating a reference to the idea that the attacks or threats are meant to produce political results via the creation of fear, and we could widen it by including noncombatant property as a target where it is significantly related to life and security.[49]

Defined in this way, what can we say about the ethics of terrorism and of using violence to fight terrorism? As we have mentioned, political realism would not condemn terrorism as immoral. According to the realist, morality and immorality do not apply to the actions states take against their enemies. Moreover, the political realist would hold that a nation should do everything it can to protect its citizens from terrorists and to defend its interests. So the realist would hold that all the violence and power of the state may legitimately be used to crush dangerous terrorist movements. The state may use violence against its enemies wherever they may live, even if the violence seems excessive. Any method, even the use of torture, is legitimate to the realist, if it is the most effective way to protect the nation's interests. The realist holds that morality does not apply to any actions a state may take against other states or their citizens. The realist also holds, of course, that a nation must be prudent in its use of violence. It does not want to create enemies that later harm its interests. But so long as it secures its own long- and short-range interests, the state may use as much violence as it wants to protect itself from terrorism.

☑ QUICK REVIEW
Political realism would not condemn terrorism as immoral, and it would claim that it is not wrong to use any amount of violence to protect a nation's citizens from terrorists.

The pacifist, on the other hand, would condemn terrorism as immoral. The absolute pacifist opposes all violence including terrorism and torture. The pacifist would recommend using persuasion, diplomacy, and other nonviolent methods instead of violence.

Just war theory is also clear about the ethics of terrorism, although its view is more complicated than the view of the realist or the pacifist. First, the acts of terrorists are almost never authorized by a legitimate government. So they fail principle 1 of the just war theory. (However, some terrorism is "state sponsored" and so may be authorized by a legitimate government.) Second, they are sometimes undertaken for a cause that is not just and are motivated by revenge. If so they violate principles 2 and 3. Third, most acts of terrorism lack a clear and specific goal and there is little hope that the violence will achieve its goal. So such terrorist acts violate principles 6 and 7. But the issue that just war critics of terrorism single out as most significant is that the terrorist targets innocent civilians who are noncombatants. So the terrorist violates principle 9. Just war proponents conclude that terrorism is nothing more than rationalized murder inflicted by people who lack authority, in pursuit of a hopeless goal. It is therefore morally unjustified.

☑ QUICK REVIEW
Pacifism would condemn terrorism as immoral but would not approve using violence in pursuit of terrorists.

☑ QUICK REVIEW
Just war theory would condemn terrorism because it is usually violence that is not authorized by a legitimate authority; it is usually not for a just cause and is motivated by revenge; it has no clear goal, and there is little hope that the violence will achieve its goal; and, most important, it targets and kills innocent noncombatants. Just war theory would approve the use of violence against terrorists only if it adheres to the nine principles of just war.

Since just war theory condemns terrorism as unjust, does it approve using violence to fight terrorism? Specifically, does it condemn using torture to fight the injustice of terrorism? Would it condemn torturing captured terrorists to get information from them about terrorist threats?

Just war theory holds the state must adhere to the nine principles even when fighting an unjust enemy threat. This means the state must not use more violence than necessary to achieve its ends. The threat must be real and imminent. The violence used must have a reasonable chance of success. The harms inflicted must be proportional to the good to be achieved. And the innocent must not be intentionally targeted or harmed.

---

[49] C.A.J. Coady, "Terrorism," *Encyclopedia of Ethics*, ed. L. C. Becker (New York: Garland, 1992), 1241–1244.

PHILOSOPHY AND LIFE

The Purpose of Business

Business is the single most important and all-pervasive social institution of modern societies. Everything we eat, drink, wear, read, drive, or use as entertainment is manufactured, packaged, and sold by a business; the money we spend ultimately comes from business. Even politics is overwhelmed by the influence of business.

Yet we rarely ask what its purpose is. Is the purpose of business to make profits? Or does business have a social responsibility to improve our society? In 1970, the Nobel Prize–winning economist Milton Friedman set out what became a classical but controversial view of the responsibilities of a business and its executives:

> In a free-enterprise, private-property system, a corporate executive is an employee of the owners of the business. He has direct responsibility to his employers [the stockholders]. That responsibility is to conduct the business in accordance with their desires, which generally will be to make as much money as possible while conforming to the basic rules of the society, both those embodied in law and those embodied in ethical custom. . . . There is one and only one social responsibility of business—to use its resources and engage in activities designed to increase its profits so long as it stays within the rules of the game, which is to say, engages in open and free competition without deception or fraud.

Forty years later, John Mackey, founder and CEO of Whole Foods, joined the hundreds of people who have responded to Friedman:

> I strongly disagree [with Friedman]. At Whole Foods, we measure our success by how much value we can create [not just for stockholders, but] for all six of our most important stakeholders: customers, employees, investors, vendors, communities, and the environment. Many thinking people will readily accept my arguments that caring about customers and employees is good business. . . . [Moreover,] a certain amount of corporate philanthropy is [also] good business. . . . As we mature, most people grow beyond . . . egocentrism and begin to care about others—their families, friends, communities, and countries. Our capacity to love can expand even further, to loving people from different races, religions, and countries—potentially to unlimited love for all people and even for other sentient creatures. This is our potential as human beings, to take joy in the flourishing of people everywhere. Whole Foods gives money to our communities because we care about them and feel a responsibility to help them flourish as well as possible.

Milton Friedman penned a response to John Mackey, in which he defended the principles he laid out forty years earlier:

> Whole Foods Market behaves in accordance with the principles I spelled out in my 1970 article. . . . Had it devoted any significant fraction of its resources to exercising a [real] social responsibility unrelated to the bottom line, it would be out of business by now or would have been taken over. Mackey [says] . . . "successful businesses put the customer first" [and] "Corporate philanthropy is simply good business."[As] I wrote in 1970: "It may well be in the long run [business] interests of a corporation . . . to devote resources to providing amenities to the community. . . . [T]his is one way for a corporation to generate goodwill . . . [so such] expenditures . . . are entirely . . . in its own self-interest."

QUESTIONS

1. Do you agree that in a "free-enterprise, private-property" society, a business's only duty is to "increase its profits"? Do businesses have a duty to refrain from actions that are legal but that harm employees, customers, or the environment?

2. Do you agree with Mackey's view that "love for all people" should motivate a business to "care" for and contribute to the "flourishing" of customers, employees, investors, vendors, communities, and the environment?

3. What does Friedman mean when he writes that Whole Foods "behaves in accordance with the principles I spelled out in my 1970 article"? Do you agree?

Source: Milton Friedman, "The Social Responsibility of Business Is to Increase Its Profits," *The New York Times Magazine*, September 13, 1970; M. Friedman and John Mackey, "Rethinking the Social Responsibility of Business," *Reasononline*, October 2005, http://www.reason.com/news/show/32239.html (accessed May 25, 2009).

Some have argued that these precepts show that the use of torture on captured terrorists is wrong. For example, the Bush administration admitted in October 2008 that it gave the CIA permission to use "waterboarding," sleep deprivation, beatings, and other forms of "torture" on prisoners the CIA thought were terrorists. In some cases, the prisoners the CIA accused of terrorism turned out to be innocent. Moreover, critics argued, torture inflicts more harm than needed to elicit information from prisoners. More benign techniques, they argued, are as, or more, effective than torture. Besides, torture has little chance of success because victims make up false stories to get the torture to stop. So the results of torture are unreliable. And the pain inflicted was out of proportion to the value of the information the CIA gained. If the critics are correct then just war theory would condemn the CIA's use of torture.

On the other hand, defenders of the use of torture claim that just war theory does not necessarily condemn torture. They claim that in many cases only torture can force captives to divulge valuable information they may have. Moreover, although victims might make up some false stories, these can often be checked by interviewing others. And the harm inflicted on a prisoner may be small in comparison to the value of the information forced out of him.

So just war theory clearly condemns terrorism as unjust. But it is ambiguous about the use of some forms of violence. Specifically, it does not clearly condemn nor justify the use of torture in the fight against terrorism.

Also, some utilitarian thinkers have argued that terrorism is not always as wrong as just war theory claims. It is possible to imagine a country whose citizens are subjected to great injustices by a foreign government. The only way to end those injustices may be through terrorist attacks on the citizens of the oppressive government. If terrorism is the only or least costly way to end such injustices, and if ending them is of sufficient value, then, terrorism would be morally justified. Or so some utilitarians have argued.

Entrance to the detention camp Delta on U.S. Naval station Guantanamo Bay, Cuba. President George W. Bush signed an executive order stating that the U.S. military could indefinitely imprison at Guantanamo any non-citizen accused of being involved in international terrorism; there prisoners were subjected to sleep deprivation, "waterboarding," beatings, and other acts of violence later characterized as "torture."

Friedrich Stark/Alamy

Other defenders of terrorism have used a different argument in its defense. They argue that when one state oppresses another, the citizens of the oppressor are not necessarily "innocent." If the citizens of an oppressor actively support their government's actions, those citizens become responsible for its actions. The defender of terrorism might then argue that such citizens are not "innocent." They are, therefore, legitimate targets of terrorist violence. Killing such citizens, the defender of terrorism may conclude, does not violate the principle of noncombatant immunity.

Is terrorism, then, sometimes justified, or is it always wrong? This is a question that you, the reader, will have to answer for yourself. In this short discussion of a very large, terrifying, and morally cloudy issue, we have tried to review some of the key perspectives that can be brought to bear on the moral status of terrorism. We hope that this overview will help you think through the issue on your own.

PHILOSOPHY AT THE MOVIES

Watch *The Fog of War* (2003), a documentary that interviews Robert McNamara, who during World War II helped plan the bombing of German and Japanese cities that killed thousands of their inhabitants in massive firestorms, helped plan the flights that dropped two atomic bombs on Japan, and who, as secretary of defense under two presidents, was chiefly responsible for directing the failed war in Vietnam. Which view of war does this film seem to support: political realism, pacifism, or just war theory? Which view does McNamara seem to support?

Other movie with similar themes: *All Quiet on The Western Front* (2016).

Chapter Summary

This chapter opens by keying on a recurring issue in any determination of the proper relation between individual and society: the problem of justice. Since the time of the Greeks, philosophers have proposed theories associating justice with merit, social utility, and fairness (equality). A related issue is how the state justifies its claims to power and authority. Although there are a number of theories of the legitimacy of the state, contract theory is the view on which our own society's conception of power and governance is based. Even if the power of the state can be justified by contract theory, though, the question remains: What, if any, are the limits to the power of the state? Whatever their leaning, contract theorists believe that the state and government have the right and duty to exercise control through law, which has traditionally demarcated individual and society. Laws guarantee freedom from interference, but in a broader sense they also guarantee positive rights.

The main points of the chapter are:

8.1   What Is Social and Political Philosophy?

- Social philosophy is the philosophical study of society and its problems and the application of moral principles to these problems, including the problems of human rights, justice, and freedom.

- Political philosophy is the subdivision of social philosophy that focuses on the proper role of the state or government in society.

8.2   What Justifies the State and Its Power?

- Many today accept a contractual justification for the power and authority of the state—that is, the state acquires its legitimacy through the consent of the governed.

- Contract theory has its roots in the thought of Thomas Hobbes and John Locke.

- Contract theory was revived in the twentieth century by John Rawls, who argues that the social contract is an imaginary device for determining what a just society and government would be like.

- Contract theory has been criticized by communitarians, who argue that it ignores the social nature of human beings, and by feminists, who argue that it assumes a nonconsensual division between the private realm of the family, to which women are relegated, and the public realm of politics and economics, in which men participate.

8.3   What Is Justice?

- Distributive justice refers to the fairness with which a community distributes benefits and burdens among its members; the principle of formal justice says that equals should be treated equally.

- The classical Greek view of justice, as expressed by Plato and Aristotle, associates justice with merit.

- Egalitarians argue either for strict equality or for equality of political rights and economic opportunities.

- The socialist principle of justice is summarized in Karl Marx's slogan: "From each according to his ability, to each according to his need."

- Although welfare liberals such as John Rawls argue that justice requires economic aid for the disadvantaged, classical liberals such as Robert Nozick argue that people's free choices should be respected in all economic matters.

- Several British philosophers of the eighteenth and nineteenth centuries, among them John Stuart Mill, associate justice with social utility, which raises the problem of balancing individual rights and interests with the common good.

8.4   Limits on the State

- Thomas Aquinas argued that the laws of the state must be consistent with natural law and that citizens have no obligation to obey a human law when it violates natural law and so is unjust.

- The laws of the state must be consistent with the right to freedom. The right to freedom, such as is enumerated in the Bill of Rights, provides guarantees against state interference.

- Human rights are classified into negative and positive rights. Although everyone agrees that the laws of the state must be changed when they conflict with human rights, some hold that the state need only enforce people's negative rights, whereas others hold that governments must also provide for people's positive rights.

- Political realism, pacifism, and just war theory are three views on the morality of war. Political realism says that morality does not apply to war, whereas pacifism says that war is immoral. Just war theory says that war is evil but is morally justified if it meets both the *jus ad bellum* conditions (legitimate authority, just cause, right intention, last resort, real and certain danger, reasonable probability of success, proportional end) and the *jus in bello* conditions (proportional means and noncombatant immunity). Just war theory also condemns terrorism.

8.5 Readings

Is war morally justified? The first reading is taken from E. M. Remarque's famous novel on World War I, a realistic and terrifying polemic against war. In the reading, Paul Baumer, a young German soldier fighting in the trenches, gets lost as he crawls along the ground trying to find his own company during a bombardment. He takes shelter in a muddy shell hole while machine gun bullets fly just above his head. In the second reading, philosopher Bertrand Russell argues that although some wars may have been morally justified in the past, wars today cannot be morally justified. He argues that the great evils that modern wars unleash far outweigh the goods for which modern wars are fought. These readings should prompt you to ask whether our own government's use of war and violence to achieve its ends is morally justified.

ERICH MARIA REMARQUE

From *All Quiet on the Western Front*

A shell crashes. Almost immediately two others. And then it begins in earnest. A bombardment. Machine-guns rattle. Now there is nothing for it but to stay lying low. Apparently an attack is coming. Everywhere the rockets shoot up. Unceasing.

I lie huddled in a large shell-hole, my legs in the water up to the belly. . . .

[Then] I have this one shattering thought: What will you do if someone jumps into your shell-hole? Swiftly I pull out my little dagger, grasp it fast and bury it in my hand once again under the mud. If anyone jumps in here I will go for him; it hammers in my forehead; at once, stab him clean through the throat, so that he cannot call out; that's the only way; he will be just as frightened as I am, when in terror we fall upon one another, then I must be first.

The rattle of machine-guns becomes an unbroken chain. Just as I am about to turn round a little, something heavy stumbles, and with a crash a body falls over me into the shell-hole, slips down and lies across me.

I do not think at all, I make no decision—I strike madly home, and feel only how the body suddenly convulses, then becomes limp, and collapses. When I recover myself, my hand is sticky and wet.

The man gurgles. It sounds to me as though he bellows, every gasping breath is like a cry, a thunder—but it is only my heart pounding. I want to stop his mouth, stuff it with earth, stab him again, he must be quiet, he is betraying me; now at last I regain control of myself, but have suddenly become so feeble that I cannot any more lift my hand against him.

So I crawl away to the farthest corner and stay there, my eyes glued on him, my hand grasping the knife—ready, if he stirs, to spring at him again. But he won't do so any more; I can hear that in his gurgling. . . .

These hours . . . The gurgling starts again—but how slowly a man dies! For this I know—he cannot be saved. Indeed I have tried to tell myself that he will be, but at noon this pretence breaks down and melts before his groans. If only I had not lost my revolver crawling about, I would shoot him. Stab him I cannot.

By noon I am groping on the outer limits of reason. Hunger devours me, I could almost weep for something to eat, I cannot struggle against it. Again and again I fetch water for the dying man and drink some myself.

This is the first man I have killed with my hands, whom I can see close at hand, whose death is my doing. . . .

But every gasp lays my heart bare. This dying man has time with him, he has an invisible dagger with which he stabs me: Time and my thoughts.

I would give much if he would but stay alive. It is hard to lie here and to have to see and hear him.

In the afternoon, about three, he is dead.

I breathe freely again. But only for a short time. Soon the silence is more unbearable than the groans. I wish the gurgling were there again, gasping, hoarse, now whistling softly and again hoarse and loud.

It is mad, what I do. But I must do something. I prop the dead man up again so that he lies comfortably although he feels nothing any more. I close his eyes. They are brown, his hair is black and a bit curly at the sides.

The mouth is full and soft beneath his moustache; the nose is slightly arched, the skin brownish; it is now not so pale as it was before, when he was still alive. For a moment the face seems almost healthy;—then it collapses suddenly into the strange face of the dead that I have so often seen, strange faces, all alike.

No doubt his wife still thinks of him; she does not know what has happened. He looks as if he would often have written to her; —she will still be getting mail from him—Tomorrow, in a week's time—perhaps even a stray letter a month hence. She will read it, and in it he will be speaking to her.

My state is getting worse; I can no longer control my thoughts. What would his wife look like? Like the little brunette on the other side of the canal? Does she belong to me now? Perhaps by this act she becomes mine. I wish Kantorek were sitting here beside me. If my mother could see me—The dead man might have had thirty more years of life if only I had impressed the way back to our trench more sharply on my memory. If only he had run two yards farther to the left, he might now be sitting in the trench over there and writing a fresh letter to his wife.

But I will get no further that way; for that is the fate of all of us: if Kemmerich's leg had been six inches to the right; if Hay Westhus had bent his back three inches further forward—

The silence spreads. I talk and must talk. So I speak to him and say to him: Comrade, I did not want to kill you. If you jumped in here again, I would not do it, if you would be sensible too. But you were only an idea to me before, an abstraction that lived in my mind and called forth its appropriate response. It was that abstraction I stabbed. But now, for the first time, I see you are a man like me. I thought of your hand-grenades, of your bayonet, of your rifle; now I see your wife and your face and our

fellowship. Forgive me, comrade. We always see it too late. Why do they never tell us that you are just poor devils like us, that your mothers are just as anxious as ours, and that we have the same fear of death, and the same dying and the same agony—Forgive me, comrade; how could you be my enemy? If we threw away these rifles and this uniform you could be my brother just like Kat and Albert. Take twenty years of my life, comrade, and stand up—take more, for I do not know what I can even attempt to do with it now.

It is quiet; the front is still except for the crackle of rifle-fire. The bullets rain over; they are not fired haphazardly, but shrewdly aimed from all sides. I cannot get out.

"I will write to your wife," I say hastily to the dead man, I will write to her, she must hear it from me, I will tell her everything I have told you, she shall not suffer, I will help her, and your parents too, and your child—

His tunic is half open. The pocketbook is easy to find. But I hesitate to open it. In it is the book with his name. So long as I do not know his name perhaps I may still forget him, time will obliterate it, this picture. But his name, it is a nail that will be hammered into me and never come out again. It has the power to recall this forever; it will always come back and stand before me.

Irresolutely I take the wallet in my hand. It slips out of my hand and falls open. Some pictures and letters drop out. I gather them up and want to put them back again, but the strain I am under, the uncertainty, the hunger, the danger, these hours with the dead man have confused me, I want to hasten the relief, to intensify and to end the torture, as one strikes an unendurably painful hand against the trunk of a tree, regardless of everything.

There are portraits of a woman and a little girl, small amateur photographs taken against an ivy-clad wall. Along with them are letters. I take them out and try to read them. Most of it I do not understand, it is so hard to decipher and I know scarcely any French. But each word I translate pierces me like a shot in the chest;—like a stab in the chest.

My brain is taxed beyond endurance. But I realize this much, that I will never dare to write to these people as I intended. Impossible. I look at the portraits once more; they are clearly not rich people. I might send them money anonymously if I earn anything later on. I seize upon that, it is at least something to hold on to. This dead man is bound up with my life, therefore I must do everything, promise everything, in order to save myself; I swear blindly that I mean to live only for his sake and his family, with wet lips I try to placate him—and deep down in me lies the hope that I may buy myself off in this way and perhaps even yet get out of this; it is a little stratagem: if only I am allowed to escape, then I will see to it. So I open the book and read slowly:—Gerard Duval, printer.

With the dead man's pencil I write the address on an envelope, then swiftly thrust everything back into his tunic.

I have killed the printer, Gerard Duval. I must be a printer, I think confusedly, be a printer, a printer—

Source: Excerpt from Erich Maria Remarque, *All Quiet on the Western Front*, trans. A. W. Wheen (Boston: Little, Brown and Company, 1958), chap. 9, pp. 217, 219, and 223–229. [Copyright 1929, 1930 by Little Brown and Company; Renewed 1957, 1958 by Erich Maria Remarque.]

BERTRAND RUSSELL

The Ethics of War

I.

It is necessary, in regard to any war, to consider, . . . the evils inseparable from war and [that are] equally certain whichever side may ultimately prove victorious. So long as these are not fully realized, it is impossible to judge justly whether a war is or is not likely to be beneficial to the human race. Although the theme is trite, it is necessary therefore briefly to remind ourselves what the evils of war really are.

To begin with the most obvious evil: large numbers of young men, the most courageous and the most physically fit in their respective nations, are killed, bringing great sorrow to their friends, loss to the community, and gain only to themselves. Many others are maimed for life, some go mad, and others become nervous wrecks, mere useless and helpless derelicts. Of those who survive many will be brutalized and morally degraded by the fierce business of killing, which, however much it may be the soldier's duty, must shock and often destroy the more humane instincts. As every truthful record of war shows, fear and hate let loose the wild beast in a not inconsiderable proportion of combatants, leading to strange cruelties, which must be faced, but not dwelt upon if sanity is to be preserved.

Of the evils of war to the noncombatant . . . it is not necessary to enlarge. . . . Even assuming the utmost humanity compatible with the conduct of military operations, it cannot be doubted that, if the troops of the Allies penetrate into the industrial regions of Germany, the German population will have to suffer a great part of the misfortunes which Germany has inflicted upon [its opponents]. . . .

The evils which war produces outside the area of military operations are perhaps even more serious, for though less intense they are far more widespread. Passing by the anxiety and sorrow of those whose sons or husbands or brothers are at the front, the extent and consequences of the economic injury inflicted by war are much greater than is usually realized. It is common to speak of economic evils as merely material, and of desire for economic progress as grovelling and uninspired. . . . But with regard to the poorer classes of society, economic progress is the first condition of many spiritual goods and even often of life itself. An overcrowded family, living in a slum in conditions of filth and immorality, where half the children die from ignorance of hygiene and bad sanitation, and the remainder grow up stunted and ignorant–such a family can hardly make progress mentally or spiritually, except through an improvement in its economic condition. And without going to the very bottom of the social scale, economic progress is essential to the possibility of good education, of a tolerable existence for women, and of that breadth and freedom of outlook upon which any solid and national advance must be based. . . . It cannot be doubted that the desire on the part of the rich to distract men's minds from the claims of social justice has been more or less unconsciously one of the motives leading to war in modern Europe. Everywhere the well-to-do and the political parties which represent their interests have been the chief agents in stirring up international hatred and in persuading the working man that his real enemy is the foreigner. Thus war, and the fear of war, has a double effect in retarding social progress: it diminishes the resources available for improving the condition of the wage-earning classes, and it distracts men's minds from the need and possibility of general improvement by persuading them that the way to better themselves is to injure their comrades in some other country. . . .

II.

Are there any wars which achieve so much for the good of mankind as to outweigh all the evils we have been considering? I think there have been such wars in the past, . . . For the purposes of classification we may roughly distinguish four kinds of wars, though of course in any given case a war is not likely to be quite clearly of any one of the four kinds. With this proviso we may distinguish: (1) Wars of Colonization; (2) Wars of Principle; (3) Wars of Self-defence; (4) Wars of Prestige. Of these four kinds I should say that the first and second are fairly often justified; the third seldom, except against an adversary of inferior civilization, and the fourth, which is the sort to which the present war (World War I) belongs, never. Let us consider these four kinds of war in succession.

By a war of colonization I mean a war whose purpose is to drive out the whole population of some territory and replace it by an invading population of a different race. Ancient wars were very largely of this kind, of which we have a good example in the Book of Joshua. In modern times the conflicts of Europeans with American-Indians, Maories, and other aborigines in temperate regions, have been of this kind. . . . In order that such wars may be justified, it is necessary that there should be a very great and undeniable difference between the civilization of the colonizers and that of the dispossessed natives. It is necessary also that the climate should be one in which the invading race can flourish. When these conditions are satisfied the conquest becomes justified, though the actual fighting against the dispossessed inhabitants ought, of course, to be avoided as far as is compatible with colonizing. Many humane people will object in theory to the justification of this form of robbery, but I do not think that any practical or effective objection is likely to be made.

Such wars, however, belong now to the past. . . . What are nowadays called colonial wars do not aim at the complete occupation of a country by a conquering race; they aim only at securing certain governmental and trading advantages. They belong, in fact, rather with what I call wars of prestige, than with wars of colonization in the old sense . . .

III.

The second type of war which may sometimes be justified is what may be called the war of principle. To this kind belong the wars of Protestant and Catholic, and the English and American civil wars. In such cases, each side, or at least one side, is honestly convinced that the progress of mankind depends upon the adoption of certain beliefs–beliefs which, through blindness or natural depravity, mankind will not regard as reasonable, except when presented at the point of the bayonet. Such wars may be justified: for example, a nation practising religious toleration may be justified in resisting a persecuting nation holding a different creed. . . . But wars of principle are much less often justified than is believed. . . . It is very rarely that a principle of genuine value to mankind can only be propagated by military force: as a rule, it is the bad part of men's principles, not the good part, which makes it necessary to fight for their defence. And for this reason the bad part rather than the good rises to prominence during the progress of a war of principle. A nation undertaking a war in defence of religious toleration would be almost certain to persecute those of its citizens who did not believe in religious toleration. A war on behalf of democracy, if it is long and fierce, is sure to end in the exclusion from all share of power of those who do not support the war. . . . This common doom of opposite ideals is the usual, though not the invariable, penalty of supporting ideals by force. While it may therefore be conceded that such wars are not invariably to be condemned, we must nevertheless scrutinize very skeptically the claim of any particular war to be justified on the ground of the victory which it brings to some important principle. . . .

Men do right to desire strongly the victory of ideals which they believe to be important, but it is almost always a sign of yielding to undue impatience when men believe that what is valuable in their ideals can be furthered by the substitution of force for peaceful persuasion. To advocate democracy by war [for example] is only to repeat, on a vaster scale and with far more tragic results, the error of those who have sought it hitherto by the assassin's knife and the bomb of the anarchist.

IV.

The next kind of war to be considered is the war of self-defence. This kind of war is almost universally admitted to be justifiable. The justification of wars of self-defence is very convenient, since so far as I know there has never yet been a war which was not one of self-defence. Every strategist assures us that the true defence is offence; every great nation believes that its own overwhelming strength is the only possible guarantee of the world's peace and can only be secured by the defeat of other nations. . . . The claim of each side to be fighting in self-defence appears to the other side mere wanton hypocrisy, because in each case the other side believes that self-defence is only to be achieved by conquest. So long as the principle of self-defence is recognized as affording always a sufficient justification for war, this tragic conflict of irresistible claims remains unavoidable.

In certain cases, where there is a clash of differing civilizations, a war of self-defence may be justified on the same grounds as a war of principle. I think, however, that, even as a matter of practical politics, the principle of nonresistance contains an immense measure of wisdom if only men would have the courage to carry it out. The evils suffered during a hostile invasion are suffered because resistance is offered . . . What one civilized nation can achieve against another by means of conquest is very much less than is commonly supposed. It is said, both here and in Germany, that each side is fighting for its existence; but when this phrase is scrutinized, it is found to cover a great deal of confusion of thought induced by unreasoning panic. We cannot destroy Germany even by a complete military victory, nor conversely, could Germany destroy England even if our Navy were sunk and London occupied by the Prussians. English civilization, the English language, English manufactures would still exist, and as a matter of practical politics it would be totally impossible for Germany to establish a tyranny in this country. If the Germans, instead of being resisted by force of arms, had been passively permitted to establish themselves wherever they pleased, the halo of glory and courage surrounding the brutality of military success would have been absent, and public opinion in Germany itself would have rendered any oppression impossible. . . .

In a word, it is the means of repelling hostile aggression which make hostile aggression disastrous. . . . As between civilized nations, therefore, nonresistance would seem . . . the course of practical wisdom. Only pride and fear stand in the way of its adoption.

V.

The last kind of war we have to consider is what I have called the war of prestige. Prestige is seldom more than one element in the causes of a war, but it is often a very important element. . . . Men desire the sense of triumph, and fear the sense of humiliation which they would have in yielding to the demands of another nation. Rather than forego the triumph, rather than endure the humiliation, they are willing to inflict upon the world all those disasters which it is now suffering and all that exhaustion and impoverishment which it must long continue to suffer. The willingness to inflict and endure such evils is almost universally praised; it is called high-spirited, worthy of a great nation, showing fidelity to ancestral traditions. The slightest sign of reasonableness is attributed to fear, and received with shame on the one side and with derision on the other. In private life exactly the same state of opinion existed so long as duelling was practised, and exists still in those countries in which this custom still survives. It is now recognized, at any rate in the Anglo-Saxon world, that the so called honor which made duelling appear inevitable was a folly and a delusion. It is perhaps not too much to hope that the day may come when the honor of nations, like that of individuals, will be longer measured by their willingness to inflict slaughter.

Source: From Bertrand Russell, "The Ethics of War," in *Justice in Wartime* (Chicago: The Open Court Publishing Co., 1916), pp. 20–39.

8.6 HISTORICAL SHOWCASE

Marx and Rawls

Two social philosophies tend to dominate much of our contemporary debate over the appropriate nature of our society: Marxism and liberalism. These two philosophies, in fact, tend to dominate much of the thinking of modern societies. The democratic and capitalist nations mainly adhere to the tenets of liberalism, whereas the socialist and communist nations continue to see themselves (even as they undergo tremendous changes) as adherents to the tenets of Marxism.

Therefore, it is appropriate for us to showcase in this chapter on society two thinkers—Karl Marx and

John Rawls—who present and argue for the principles underlying these two dominant social philosophies. The writings of Marx are the origins of those social philosophies that call themselves Marxist, and John Rawls is considered by many to have articulated the central principles of modern liberalism.

Marx

Karl Marx, a seminal social philosopher of the modern age, is widely misunderstood. Marx was born in 1818 in Trier in the Rhineland to Jewish parents who, faced with anti-Semitism, turned Lutheran. After

Karl Marx: "What constitutes the alienation of labor? First, that the work is *external* to the worker, that it is not part of his nature; and that, consequently, he does not fulfill himself in his work but denies himself, has a feeling of misery rather than well-being, does not develop freely his mental and physical energies but is physically exhausted and mentally debased." Portrait of Karl Marx (1818–1893), c. 1970 (chromolitho). Artist: Chinese School (twentieth century).

completing his studies at the gymnasium in Trier, Marx attended the universities of Bonn and Berlin.

When Marx entered the University of Berlin in 1836, the dominant intellectual influence throughout Germany and at the university was the philosophy of Georg Hegel (1770–1831). Central to Hegel's thought was the idea that reality is not fixed and static, but changing and dynamic. Life is constantly passing from one stage of being to another; the world is a place of constant change. But Hegel did not believe the change itself is arbitrary. On the contrary, he thought it proceeds according to a well-defined pattern or method, termed a **dialectic**.

The idea of the dialectic is that reality is full of contradictions. As reality unfolds, the contradictions are resolved and something new emerges. The procedure of the dialectical method can be represented as follows:

Thesis. Assertion of position or affirmation.

Antithesis. Assertion of opposite position or negation.

Synthesis. Union of the two opposites.

The Hegelian dialectic presumably expresses the process of development that Hegel believed pervades everything. By this account, there is only one reality: Idea. The only thing that is real is the rational; the Idea is thought itself thinking itself out. The process of thought thinking itself out is the dialectic.

In thinking itself out, thought arrives at the main antithesis to itself: inert matter. At this point Idea objectifies itself in matter: It becomes Nature or, for Hegel, the creation of the world. Life is the first sign of synthesis. Thought reappears in matter, organizing plants and displaying conscious instinct in animals. Ultimately, thought arrives at self-consciousness in human beings. The dialectic continues through human history.

To understand a society or culture, therefore, it is crucial to recognize the dialectical process that is operating. Each period in the history of a culture or society has a character of its own. This character can be viewed as a stage in the development from what preceded it to what follows it. This development proceeds by mental or spiritual laws. In effect, a culture has a personality of its own. Indeed, by Hegel's reckoning, the whole world or all of reality can be identified with a single character or personality—with what Hegel variously called *the Absolute, world self,* or *God* (taken in a pantheistic sense). All of human history, then, can be viewed as the progressive realization of this Absolute Spirit that is the synthesis of the thesis, Idea thinking itself out, with the antithesis, Idea spread out into Nature.

While at the University of Berlin, Marx read Hegel's complete works. He was drawn to a revolutionary aspect of Hegel's philosophy, namely, that history moves through a dialectical process of development. Marx also joined the Berlin Club of Young Hegelians but soon became convinced that philosophy alone was inadequate to change the world. What was needed was social and political action.

After completing his doctoral dissertation in 1841, Marx turned to socialistic journalism, taking an editorial position in 1842 at the *Rheinische Zeitung* (*Rhineland Gazette*). In this position, Marx became familiar with the social problems of the day and deepened the social orientation of his thought. Soon he became editor in chief of the newspaper and took it in a radical direction, conducting a campaign against Christian religion and the Christian state. As a result, the newspaper was shut down by the state censor in March 1843.

The suppression of the *Rheinische Zeitung* marked a new period in Marx's intellectual development, during which he began to formulate his materialistic concept of history and eventually became a communist. Also during this time, which he spent in Paris, Marx turned to a critical examination of Hegelian thought and in 1843 published an article on the subject: "Introduction to the Critique of Hegel's Philosophy." The article portrayed religion as an illusion resulting from the fact that the world is alienated and estranged from its real nature. Total revolution, Marx argued, is necessary to emancipate society from this condition.

Marx's critique of Hegel was significantly influenced by the work of Ludwig Feuerbach (1804–1872). In his *Essence of Christianity* (1841), Feuerbach had tried to show that Hegel's idealism was wrongheaded in that it had succeeded in eliminating physical reality. By contrast, Feuerbach held that philosophy is the science of reality, which consists of physical nature. Part of the illusion Feuerbach saw in Hegel was Hegel's belief in Absolute Spirit or God progressively realizing itself in history. In fact, according to Feuerbach, the ideas of religion are produced by human beings as a reflection of their own needs. Because individuals are dissatisfied or "alienated" in their practical lives, they need to believe in illusions such as those fostered in Hegelian philosophy. Thus, metaphysics is no more than an "esoteric psychology"; it is the expression of feelings within ourselves rather than truths about the universe. In particular, religion is the expression of alienation. Individuals can be freed from the illusions of religion only by realizing their purely human destiny in this world.

Feuerbach's influence on Marx was so great that Marx grew convinced that dialectical philosophy would avoid idealism by starting from human reality rather than from an ideal Absolute Spirit. Also, it could avoid mechanistic materialism by taking the concrete nature of the human being as its initial principle.

Although his reading of Feuerbach altered Marx's view of Hegel, Marx did preserve Hegel's notions of historical development and of alienation. These he wove into his own materialist concept of history. Like Hegel, Marx saw historical development operating in everything, but this development was material in character, not spiritual. The key to all history lay not in the individual's idea but in the economic conditions of his or her life. Again, while adopting Hegel's notion of alienation, Marx did not see it as metaphysical or religious in nature, but social and economic.

Marx's view of alienation can be found in his "Economic and Philosophic Manuscripts" (1844). His materialistic concepts of history can be found in various works of the same period: *The Holy Family* (1845), *The German Ideology* (1846), and *The Poverty of Philosophy* (1847). Until recently, Marx was best known as the author of *Das Kapital* (1867) and the *Communist Manifesto* (1848), which he wrote with friend and collaborator Friedrich Engels. Today, largely as a result of the publication of his early writings, the philosophical aspect of Marx's work has caught scholars' attention. Indeed, it is now thought that Marx's later writings cannot be fully understood and interpreted without reference to his earlier works, especially "Economic and Philosophic Manuscripts" and *The German Ideology*.

VIEW OF HISTORY

Distinctive in Marx's understanding of the world as a whole is his interpretation of history. Marx was firmly convinced that he had discovered a scientific method for studying the history of human societies, that eventually there would be a single science that combined the science of mankind with natural science. Accordingly, he held that there are universal laws behind historical change. Just as we can predict natural events such as eclipses, we can predict the future large-scale course of history from a knowledge of these laws. Just as physicists aim to uncover the natural laws of the universe, so Marx believed that he was laying bare the economic laws of modern society, the material laws of capitalist production. These laws, presumably, are working with iron necessity toward inevitable results.

Like Hegel, Marx held that each period in each culture has its own character and personality. Therefore, the only true universal laws in history are those concerned with the process by which one stage gives rise to the next. He viewed this developmental process as roughly divided into the Asiatic, the ancient, the feudal, and the "bourgeois" (capitalist) phases. When conditions are right, said Marx, each stage must give way to the next. Ultimately, capitalism will give way to communism. Writing with Engels in the *Communist Manifesto*, Marx puts it this way:

> *The history of all hitherto existing society is the history of class struggles.*
>
> Freeman and slave, patrician and plebian, lord and serf, guild-master and journeyman, in a word, oppressor and oppressed, stood in constant opposition to one another, carried on an uninterrupted,

now hidden, now open fight, a fight that each time ended, either in a revolutionary re-constitution of society at large, or in the common ruin of the contending classes.

In the earlier epochs of history, we find almost everywhere a complicated arrangement of society into various orders, a manifold gradation of social rank. In ancient Rome we have patricians, knights, plebians, slaves; in the middle ages, feudal lords, vassals, guild-masters, journeymen, apprentices, serfs; in almost all of these classes, again, subordinate gradations.

The modern bourgeois society that has sprouted from the ruins of feudal society, has not done away with class antagonisms. It has but established new classes, new conditions of oppression, new forms of struggle in place of the old ones.

Our epoch, the epoch of the bourgeoisie, possesses, however, this distinctive feature; it has simplified the class antagonisms. Society as a whole is more and more splitting up into two great hostile camps, into two great classes directly facing each other: Bourgeoisie and Proletariat.[1]

Marx believed that the universal laws operating in history are economic in nature. Moreover, he saw a causal connection between the economic structure and everything in society such that the mode of production of material life determines the general character of the social, political, and spiritual processes of life. In a word, the economic structure is the real basis by which everything else about society is determined.

Based on this view of history, Marx predicted that capitalism will become increasingly unstable economically. The class struggle between the *bourgeoisie* (ownership class) and *proletariat* (working class) will increase, with the proletariat getting both poorer and larger in number. The upshot will be a social revolution: The workers will seize power and eventually institute the new communist phase of history.

VIEW OF HUMAN NATURE

Related to Marx's view of history is his view of human nature, which we alluded to in Chapter 2. Apart from some obvious biological factors, such as the need to eat, Marx denies the existence of any essential human nature—that is, something that is true of every individual at all times everywhere. However, he does allow that humans are social beings, that to speak of human nature is really to speak about the totality of social relations. Accordingly, whatever any of us does is a social act, which presupposes the existence of other people standing in certain relations to us. In short, everything is socially learned.

The social influence is especially apparent in every activity of production. Producing what we need to survive physically is a social activity: It always requires that we interact and cooperate with others. Given Marx's account, it follows that the kind of individuals we are and the kinds of things we do are determined by the kind of society in which we live. In other words, for Marx it isn't the consciousness of individuals that defines their beings, but their social being that determines their consciousness. In commenting incisively on this point, professor of philosophy Leslie Stevenson writes the following:

> In modern terms, we can summarize this crucial point by saying that sociology is not reducible to psychology, i.e., it is not the case that everything about men can be explained in terms of facts about individuals; the kind of society they live in must be considered too. This methodological point is one of Marx's most distinctive contributions, and one of the most widely accepted. For this reason alone, he must be recognized as one of the founding fathers of sociology. And the method can of course be accepted whether or not one agrees with the particular conclusions Marx came to about economics and politics.[2]

Professor Stevenson goes on to point out that despite Marx's denial of individual human nature, Marx is prepared to offer at least one generalization about human nature. It is that humans are active, productive beings who distinguish themselves from other animals by the central, overriding fact that they produce their own means of subsistence. Indeed, according to Marx, it is not only natural for humans to work for their livings but right as well. Thus, by Marx's account, the life of productive activity is the right one for humans.

Granted that it is proper for humans to work for their livings, what may be said about the product of that work? Like Locke before him and numerous other thinkers after him (including Rawls and

---

[1]   Karl Marx and Friedrich Engels, *Communist Manifesto*, trans. Samuel Moore (Chicago: Regnery, 1969).

[2]   Leslie Stevenson, *Seven Theories of Human Nature* (London: Oxford University Press, 1974), 54.

Nozick), Marx thought that individuals have a legitimate claim to the product of their own labor. But Marx rejects the notion that they are entitled to own property that they have not personally produced. Neither is property ownership permissible when it enriches the already affluent at the expense of other people, thereby forcing these people to work without benefit of the products of their labor. But this, according to Marx, is precisely what capitalism encourages: the exploitation of the large working class (proletariat) at the hands of the affluent few who own the means of production (bourgeoisie). Again, here are Marx and Engels writing on this subject in the *Communist Manifesto:*

> The bourgeoisie, wherever it has got the upper hand, has put an end to all feudal, patriarchal, idyllic relations. It has pitilessly torn asunder the motley feudal ties that bound man to his "natural superiors," and has left remaining no other nexus between man and man than naked self-interest, callous "cash payment." It has drowned the most heavenly ecstasies of religious fervor, of chivalrous enthusiasm, of Philistine sentimentalism, in the icy water of egotistical calculation. It has resolved personal worth into exchange value, and in place of the numberless indefeasible chartered freedoms, has set up that single, unconscionable freedom—Free Trade. In one word, for exploitation, veiled by religious and political illusions, it has substituted naked, shameless, direct, brutal exploitation.
>
> The bourgeoisie has stripped of its halo every occupation hitherto honored and looked up to with reverent awe. It has converted the physician, the lawyer, the priest, the poet, the name of science, into its paid wage-laborers.
>
> The bourgeoisie has torn away from the family its sentimental veil, and has reduced the family relation to a mere money relation.
>
> The bourgeoisie has disclosed how it came to pass that the brutal display of vigor in the Middle Ages, which Reactionists so much admire, found its fitting complement in the most slothful indolence. It has been the first to show what man's activity can bring about. It has accomplished wonders far surpassing Egyptian pyramids, Roman aqueducts, and Gothic cathedrals; it has conducted expeditions that put in the shade all former Exoduses of nations and crusades.
>
> The bourgeoisie cannot exist without constantly revolutionizing the instruments of production, and thereby the relations of production, and with them the whole relations of society. Conservation of the old modes of production in unaltered form, was, on the contrary, the first condition of existence for all earlier industrial classes. Constant revolutionizing of production, uninterrupted disturbance of all social conditions, everlasting uncertainty and agitation distinguish the bourgeois epoch from all earlier ones. All fixed, fast-frozen relations, with their train of ancient and venerable prejudices and opinions, are swept away, all new-formed ones become antiquated before they can ossify. All that is solid melts into air, all that is holy is profaned, and man is at last compelled to face, with sober senses, his real conditions of life, and his relations with his kind.
>
> The need of a constantly expanding market for its products chases the bourgeoisie over the whole surface of the globe. It must nestle everywhere, settle everywhere, establish connections everywhere.
>
> The bourgeoisie has through its exploitation of the world-market given a cosmopolitan character to production and consumption in every country. To the great chagrin of Reactionists, it has drawn from under the feet of industry the national ground on which it stood. All old-fashioned national industries have been destroyed and are daily being destroyed. They are dislodged by new industries, whose introduction becomes a life and death question for all civilized nations, by industries that no longer work up indigenous raw material, but raw material drawn from the remotest zones; industries whose products are consumed, not only at home, but in every quarter of the globe. In place of the old wants, satisfied by the productions of the country, we find new wants, requiring for their satisfaction the products of distant lands and climes. In place of the old local and national seclusion and self-sufficiency, we have intercourse in every direction, universal interdependence of nations. And as in material, so also in intellectual production. The intellectual creations of individual nations become common property. National one-sidedness and narrow-mindedness become more and more impossible, and from the numerous national and local literatures there arises a world-literature.
>
> The bourgeoisie, by the rapid improvement of all instruments of production, by the immensely facilitated means of communication, draws all, even the most barbarian, nations into civilization. The cheap prices of its commodities are the heavy artillery with which it batters down all Chinese walls, with which it forces the barbarians' intensely obstinate hatred of foreigners to capitulate. It compels all nations, on pain of extinction, to adopt the bourgeois mode of production; it compels them to introduce what it calls civilization into their midst, i.e., to become bourgeois themselves. In a word, it creates a world after its own image.

The bourgeoisie has subjected the country to the rule of the towns. It has created enormous cities, has greatly increased the urban population as compared with the rural, and has thus rescued a considerable part of the population from the idiocy of rural life. Just as it has made the country dependent on the towns, so it has made barbarian and semi-barbarian countries dependent on the civilized ones, nations of peasants on nations of bourgeois, the East on the West.

The bourgeoisie keeps more and more doing away with the scattered state of the population, of the means of production, and of property. It has agglomerated population, centralized means of production, and has concentrated property in a few hands. The necessary consequence of this was political centralization. Independent, or but loosely connected provinces, with separate interests, laws, governments and systems of taxation, became lumped together in one nation, with one government, one code of laws, one national class-interest, one frontier and one customs-tariff.

The bourgeoisie, during its rule of scarce one hundred years, has created more massive and more colossal productive forces than have all preceding generations together. Subjection of Nature's forces to man, machinery, application of chemistry to industry and agriculture, steam-navigation, railways, electric telegraphs, clearing of whole continents for cultivation, canalization of rivers, whole populations conjured out of the ground—what earlier century had even a presentiment that such productive forces slumbered in the lap of social labor?[3]

According to Marx, the result of bourgeoisie exploitation is alienation, a key concept in his political and social philosophy.

CONCEPT OF ALIENATION

Marx borrowed his notion of alienation from Hegel and also from Feuerbach. For Hegel, alienation has its roots in a distinction between a subject and supposedly alien object. For Marx, the human can be considered the subject, and nature—that is, the human-created world—can be viewed as object. Humans are alienated from nature, from the world and the social relations they create. What is the cause of this alienation? Marx is rather fuzzy about this. At one point he traces its roots to the ownership of private property. Elsewhere he says that private property is not the cause but the effect of alienation. Whether private property is a cause or effect of alienation, one thing is evident: Marx associates alienation with economics, with the ownership of private property. Specifically, alienation consists of individuals not fulfilling themselves in work. Rather, because work is imposed on them as a means of satisfying the needs of others, they feel exploited and debased. What about workers who are paid handsomely for their efforts? Nevertheless, says Marx, they remain estranged. Insofar as the fruits of their labor are enjoyed by someone else, the work ultimately proves meaningless to them.

In the following selection from his "Economic and Philosophic Manuscripts," Marx summarizes his notion of alienation as the separation of individuals from the objects they create, which in turn results in separation from other people and ultimately from oneself:

> We shall begin from a *contemporary economic* fact. The worker becomes poorer the more wealth he produces and the more his production increases in power and extent. The worker becomes an ever cheaper commodity the more goods he creates. The *devaluation* of the human world increases in direct relation with the *increase in value* of the world of things. Labor does not only create goods; it also produces itself and the worker as a *commodity*, and indeed in the same proportion as it produces goods. . . .
>
> All these consequences follow from the fact that the worker is related to the *product of his labor* as to an *alien* object. For it is clear on this presupposition that the more the worker expends himself in work the more powerful becomes the world of objects which he creates in face of himself, the poorer he becomes in his inner life, and the less he belongs to himself. It is just the same as in religion. The more of himself man attributes to God the less he has left in himself. The worker puts his life into the object, and his life then belongs no longer to himself but to the object. The greater his activity, therefore, the less he possesses. What is embodied in the product of his labor is no longer his own. The greater this product is, therefore, the more he is diminished. The *alienation* of the worker in his product means not only that his labor becomes an object, assumes an *external* existence, but that it exists independently, *outside himself*, and alien to him, and that it stands opposed to him as an autonomous power. The life which he has given to the object sets itself against him as an alien and hostile force. . . .
>
> The worker becomes a slave of the object; first, in that he receives an *object of work*, i.e.,

---

3   Marx and Engels, *Communist Manifesto*.

receives *work*, and secondly, in that he receives *means of subsistence*. Thus the object enables him to exist, first as a *worker*, and secondly, as a *physical subject*. The culmination of this enslavement is that he can only maintain himself as a *physical subject* so far as he is a *worker*, and that it is only as a *physical subject* that he is a worker. . . .

What constitutes the alienation of labor? First, that the work is *external* to the worker, that it is not part of his nature; and that, consequently, he does not fulfill himself in his work but denies himself, has a feeling of misery rather than well-being, does not develop freely his mental and physical energies but is physically exhausted and mentally debased. The worker, therefore, feels himself at home only during his leisure time, whereas at work he feels homeless. His work is not voluntary but imposed, *forced labor*. It is not the satisfaction of a need, but only a *means* for satisfying other needs. Its alien character is clearly shown by the fact that as soon as there is no physical or other compulsion it is avoided like the plague. External labor, labor in which man alienates himself, is a labor of self-sacrifice, of mortification. Finally, the external character of work for the worker is shown by the fact that it is not his own work but work for someone else, that in work he does not belong to himself but to another person. . . .

We arrive at the result that man (the worker) feels himself to be freely active only in his animal functions—eating, drinking and procreating, or at most also in his dwelling and in personal adornment—while in his human functions he is reduced to an animal. The animal becomes human and the human becomes animal.

Eating, drinking and procreating are of course also genuine human functions. But abstractly considered, apart from the environment of human activities, and turned into final and sole ends, they are animal functions.

We have now considered the act of alienation of practical human activity, labor, from two aspects: (1) the relationship of the worker to the *product of labor* as an alien object which dominates him. This relationship is at the same time the relationship to the sensuous external world, to natural objects, as an alien and hostile world; (2) the relationship of labor to the *act of production* within *labor*. This is the relationship of the worker to his own activity as something alien and not belonging to him, activity as suffering (passivity), strength as powerlessness, creation as emasculation, the *personal* physical and mental energy of the worker, his personal life (for what is life but activity?), as an activity which is directed against himself; independent of him and not belonging to him. This

is *self-alienation* as against the above-mentioned alienation of the *thing*.[4]

Marx goes on to infer yet a third aspect of estranged labor from the preceding two: the estrangement of the individual from the species itself. But this needn't concern us here.

In Marx's view, when workers are alienated, they cannot be free. They may have the political and social freedoms of speech, religion, and governance that classical liberals delineate. But freedom from government interference and persecution does not necessarily guarantee freedom from economic exploitation. And it is for this kind of freedom, freedom from alienation, that Marx and Engels feel such passion.

SENSE OF FREEDOM

How can humans be free of alienation? To begin with, they must recognize that the key to freedom and the lack of it lies in economics. Therefore, humans must return to a "natural" state in which they and their labor are one. Marx here recognizes the corrupting influence of society and calls for a conception of the state that will allow humans to be unselfish and nondestructive. But don't misunderstand. Marx is not advocating the end of work. On the contrary, he holds that work is humanizing, ennobling. Thus, he is urging people to liberate themselves from alienated work. Without this kind of freedom, which is basically a freedom from material need, other freedoms are a sham.

Basically, Marx prescribes a fairer distribution of wealth as a means for combating alienation and ensuring freedom. For Marx, justice requires that the means of production be owned by everyone. In unvarnished terms, in part this means no ownership of property except for those products a person makes directly. It also means an end to the worker/owner distinction, thereby making everyone a laborer who shares in the benefits of his or her labor. Specifically, Marx calls for nationalization of land, factories, transport, and banks as a way of attaining freedom from alienation. But insofar as Marx presumably believes that (1) the state is the basis of all social ills, and (2) nationalization evidently will exacerbate this by concentrating power in the hands of the state, it

---

[4] Karl Marx, "The Economic and Philosophic Manuscripts of 1844," in *Karl Marx: Early Writings*, trans T. B. Bottomore. Copyright © T. B. Bottomore, 1963. Used with permission of McGraw-Hill Book Co.

isn't at all clear how such institutional changes could affect freedom. This observation has led Leslie Stevenson to suggest that we understand Marx as saying,

> at least in his early phase, that alienation consists in the lack of community. In other words, since the State is not a real community, individuals cannot see their work as contributing to a group of which they are members. It would follow that freedom from alienation would be won by decentralizing, not nationalizing, the State in genuine communities or "communes." These entities would be characterized by the abolition of money, specialization, and private property.[5]

Indeed, it may be this community element of Marx's vision that explains why Marx continues to win and hold followers. After all, it is difficult to disagree with such ideas as a decentralized society in which individuals cooperate in communities for the common good, technology is harnessed and directed for the interest of all, and the relationship between society and nature is harmonized. At the same time, Marx gives no good reason for assuming that the communist society will achieve any of these ideals. In fact, if the history of Russia in the past century is any indication, quite the opposite seems the case.

Rawls

Some countries today claim to be based on the socialist views proposed by Karl Marx, including the People's Republic of China, the Republic of Cuba, the Socialist Republic of Vietnam, and the Lao People's Democratic Republic; seven others that describe themselves as "socialist" nations have been greatly influenced by the ideas of Marx. Much of the rest of the world, however, consists of countries that by and large follow a philosophy termed *liberalism*. Liberalism has its roots in the individualism of John Locke and John Stuart Mill. At the heart of early liberalism was the view that the best society is one in which individuals are left free to pursue their own interests and fulfillment as each chooses. As Mill argued, the only restraints to which adult individuals should be subject are those necessary to keep one individual from harming others.

Contemporary liberalism has retained this fundamental commitment to individual liberty but has added to it an awareness of the extent to which

economic realities can indirectly limit an individual's liberty. For example, the choices of a poor person are much restricted by that person's poverty, whereas wealth and property endow the rich with choices and power not available to the poor. Therefore, contemporary liberalism has tended to incorporate the view that citizens who are well off can be required to provide economic support for the poor through taxes that pay for welfare programs. Contemporary liberalism has also tended to accept the view that individuals should be given some protection against the economic power of businesses through laws that protect the worker. Undoubtedly, these contemporary modifications of liberalism have been influenced by Marx. To a large extent, in fact, contemporary liberalism is the response that capitalist societies have made to Marx.

Perhaps the best representative of contemporary liberalism is John Rawls, a philosopher who taught at Harvard University. In his now-classic work *A Theory of Justice*, Rawls presents a brilliant and often passionate argument in support of contemporary liberalism. Many philosophers hold, in fact, that the modern world is faced with a fundamental choice between two kinds of societies: the kind of socialist society advocated by Marx and the kind of liberal society advocated by Rawls.

Rawls was born in 1921 in Baltimore, Maryland. While he was growing up he lost two of his four brothers, one to diphtheria and the second to pneumonia. Both brothers caught the disease that killed them from Rawls who had caught each disease only a few days before they did. Their deaths weighed on Rawls for many years. When he completed high school in 1939 he enrolled in Princeton University where he played on the university's baseball team. There he began thinking seriously of entering a seminary and becoming a Roman Catholic priest. But the United States had entered World War II, so when he graduated from Princeton, Rawls enlisted as an infantryman. During the war Rawls saw fighting in the Pacific and when he witnessed the terrible randomness of death, his religious beliefs began to waver. When he learned about the cruelties of the Holocaust he lost his faith completely.

At the end of the war, Rawls returned to Princeton where, in 1950, he received his doctorate in philosophy. From 1953 to 1959 he taught at Cornell University and then moved to the Massachusetts Institute of Technology. In 1962, he moved to Harvard University where he taught for the next thirty years. The U.S. war in Vietnam was just starting

---

5   Stevenson, *Seven Theories of Human Nature*, 58.

and although Rawls was a quiet and private person, he began speaking out against the United State's involvement in Vietnam. His reflections on the justice of the war the United States was pursuing in Vietnam led him to begin thinking deeply about the moral limits of government power, and the morality of civil disobedience and conscientious objection. In 1971 these reflections became part of a book on justice that he had been working on since 1957 entitled *A Theory of Justice*. Although this book is generally acknowledged to be Rawls' greatest work, he published five more influential books before he died. Rawls was described as a quiet, witty, and modest man devoted to his students, but even more so to his wife, Margaret, and their two sons and two daughters. In 1995 Rawls suffered a stroke and was forced to retire completely from teaching. In 1999, President Clinton awarded him the National Humanities Metal. Rawls continued writing until his death on November 24, 2002.

For Rawls, the most important question to ask about a society is this one: Is it just? The laws and institutions of a society must embody justice, or they must be changed:

> Justice is the first virtue of social institutions, as truth is of systems of thought. A theory however elegant and economical must be rejected or revised if it is untrue; likewise laws and institutions no matter how efficient and well-arranged must be reformed or abolished if they are unjust....
> The only thing that permits us to acquiesce in an erroneous theory is the lack of a better one; analogously, an injustice is tolerable only when it is necessary to avoid an even greater injustice. Being first virtues of human activities, truth and justice are uncompromising.[6]

If we are to analyze the justice of society, Rawls claims, we must look not at the particular actions of individuals but at society's basic political, economic, and social *institutions*, or what he calls society's "basic structure." Like Marx, Rawls acknowledges that social institutions and social inequalities have a deep and profound effect on the individual's chances in life. A society's institutions are what primarily determine what we can do and what our lives as individuals will be like. From the very beginning of our development they favor some of us and hamper others:

> The primary subject of justice is the basic structure of society, or more exactly, the way in which the major social institutions distribute fundamental rights and duties and determine the division of advantages from social cooperation. By major institutions I understand the political constitution and the principal economic and social arrangements. Thus the legal protection of freedom of thought and liberty of conscience, competitive markets, private property in the means of production, and the monogamous family are examples of major social institutions. Taken together ... the major institutions define men's rights and duties and influence their life-prospects, what they can expect to be and how well they can hope to do. The basic structure is the primary subject of justice because its effects are so profound and present from the start. The intuitive notion here is that this structure contains various social positions and that men born into different positions have different expectations of life.... In this way the institutions of society favor certain starting places over others. These are especially deep inequalities. Not only are they pervasive, but they affect men's initial chances in life. It is these inequalities ... to which the principles of social justice must in the first instance apply.[7]

But what principles and rules should govern our social institutions? What guidelines and formulas should we follow when designing our institutions if those institutions are to be just? Rawls proposes two "principles of justice" that, he claims, embody the fundamental requirements of justice. He states them as follows:

1. Each person [must have] an equal right to the most extensive scheme of equal basic liberties compatible with a similar scheme of liberties for all.

2. Social and economic inequalities [must] meet two conditions: they must be

   a. To the greatest expected benefit of the least advantaged members of society, and

   b. Attached to offices and positions open to all under conditions of fair equality of opportunity.[8]

Rawls explains that these two principles are supposed to govern two different parts of the "basic structure" of a society:

---

6 John Rawls, *A Theory of Justice* (Cambridge, MA: The Belknap Press of Harvard University Press, 1971), excerpts from 3–4,

7 Ibid., excerpt from 7.
8 John Rawls, "Some Reasons for the Maximin Criterion," *American Economic Review*, 64 (1974): 141–146.

The formulation of the principles assumes that we can usefully divide the social structure into two more or less distinct parts, the first principle applying to one, the second to the other. We are to distinguish between [first] those aspects of the social system which define and secure the equal liberties and opportunities of citizenship and [second] those aspects which establish or permit social and economic inequalities. The fundamental freedoms, that is, the main political rights, liberty of conscience and freedom of thought, the basic civil rights, and the like—these are all required to be equal by the first principle. The second principle applies to the distribution of income and wealth and to the structure of political and economic institutions insofar as these involve differences in organizational authority. While the distribution of wealth and authority is not required to be equal, it must [benefit the least advantaged]. . . . Further offices and positions must be open to all.

The first part of the second principle [should] be rendered in the following way. Assuming the framework of institutions required by fair equality of opportunity to obtain, the higher expectations of those better situation in the basic structure are just if and only if they work as part of a scheme which improves the expectations of the least advantaged members of society. The intuitive idea here is that the social order should not establish and secure the more attractive prospects of those better off unless doing so is to the advantage of those less fortunate. . . .

To illustrate, suppose that the least advantaged are represented by the typical unskilled worker. The proposed [first part of the second] principle requires that inequalities in wealth and income—for example, the greater distributive shares earned by entrepreneurs and professional persons—must be justified to the members of this group. Differences in wealth and income are just only if they are to the advantage of the representative man who is worse off. Presumably, given a background of equality of opportunity, and so on, the greater expectations of entrepreneurs and professional persons have the effect in the long run of raising the life-prospects of the laboring class. They provide the necessary incentives so that the economy is more efficient, industrial advance proceeds more rapidly, and so on. . . . All differences in wealth and income, all social and economic inequalities, should work for the good of the least favored.[9]

In short, Rawls' two principles require equal political rights, equality of opportunity, and help for the disadvantaged. The first principle, which applies mainly to political institutions, requires equal political freedom and equal political rights. But the second principle, which applies mainly to economic institutions, does not require economic equality. However, it does require that everyone have an equal opportunity to compete for the better jobs and positions. Moreover, according to the second principle, any economic inequalities—such as jobs or positions with higher incomes—must incentivize people to be more productive with their talents. And such added productivity must be used to help the least advantaged.

But why should we accept these two principles of justice? Rawls argues that to understand why we should accept these two principles, we should engage in a kind of imaginary experiment. Imagine, he says, that before people formed a society, they could all gather together in a large meeting. And suppose that at this imaginary first meeting (or "original position"), no one knew what place each person would have in their future society. No one knew whether he or she would turn out to be rich or poor, owner or worker, ruler or ruled. In fact, suppose that no one knew even whether he or she would turn out to be male or female, intelligent or stupid, healthy or sick, strong or weak, black or white. In other words, suppose that everyone at this original meeting is "behind a veil of ignorance," where no one knows what each will be like in the future society.

Suppose, then, that the people at this original meeting had to choose the basic rules or principles that would govern their future society. Clearly, Rawls says, the parties in such an original position would have to be perfectly fair to everyone because no one would know who he or she might turn out to be. In such a situation, a person would not choose principles that favor whites over blacks because in their future society that person might turn out to be black. Neither would a person choose principles that favor the rich over the poor because the person might turn out to be poor. In short, the veil of ignorance would force everyone to choose principles that would be perfectly just to everyone:

> Imagine that those who engage in social cooperation choose together ... the principles which are to assign basic rights and duties and determine the division of social benefits.. .. [They] must decide

9   John Rawls, "Distributive Justice: Some Addenda," *Natural Law Forum*, 13 (1968): 51–71.

once and for all what is to count among them as just and unjust. The choice which rational men would make in this hypothetical situation . . . determines the principles of justice.

In justice as fairness the original position of equality corresponds to the state of nature in the traditional theory of the social contract. This original position is . . . a purely hypothetical situation. . . . Among the essential features of this situation is that no one knows his place in society, his class position or social status, or his fortune in the distribution of natural assets and abilities, his intelligence, strength, and the like... The principles of justice are chosen behind [this] "veil of ignorance." . . . Since all are similarly situated and no one is able to design principles to favor his particular condition, the principles of justice are the result of a fair agreement or bargain. . . . The name "justice as fairness" conveys the idea that the principles of justice are agreed to in an initial situation that is fair.[10]

What principles would be chosen in such an "original position"? Rawls suggests that for people living in a democracy, the two main options would be utilitarian principles and his two principles. He then argues that people in the original position would not choose to live under utilitarian principles. Utilitarian principles, Rawls claims, sometimes require some people to suffer losses for the sake of maximizing society's utility. Clearly, a person in the original position would not agree to this because that person might turn out to be one of the people forced to suffer losses.

Once justice is thought of as arising from an original agreement of this kind, it is evident that the principle of utility is problematical. For why should rational individuals who have a system of ends they wish to advance agree to a violation of their liberty for the sake of a greater balance of satisfactions enjoyed by others? It seems more plausible to suppose that, when situated in an original position of equal right, they would insist upon institutions which return compensating advantages for any sacrifices required. A rational man would not accept an institution merely because it maximized the sum of advantages irrespective of its effect on his own interests. It appears, then, that the principle of utility would be rejected as a principle of justice.[11]

Instead of choosing utilitarian principles, Rawls claims, the parties would settle on his two principles of justice. Recall that the first principle says that everyone must have equal political rights. The second says that any inequalities must be available to everyone and must benefit the least advantaged.

There is the following argument for holding that the two principles would be acknowledged [in the original position]. . . . Since there is no way for anyone to win special advantages for himself, each would consider it reasonable to acknowledge the first principle (that of equal liberty) as an initial principle. There is, however, no reason why they should regard this position as final, for if there are inequalities which satisfy the second principle, the immediate gain which equality would allow can be considered as intelligently invested, in view of its future return. If, as is quite likely, these inequalities work as incentives to better efforts, the members of this society may look on them as concessions to human nature. They, like us, may think that people should ideally want to serve one another. But, since they are mutually self-interested, their acceptance of these inequalities is merely the acceptance of the relations in which they actually stand and a recognition of the motives which lead them to engage in their common practices. ... Provided that the conditions of the [second] principle are met, there is no reason why they should not allow such inequalities.[12]

Rawls' argument is that the parties to the original position would choose the first principle, which requires equal political freedoms for everyone, because each person would want to be equal to everyone else in the political sphere. However, he claims, the parties would agree to allow social and *economic* inequalities if such "inequalities set up various incentives which succeed in eliciting more productive efforts" from people. For example, offering higher incomes to talented people can spur them on to use their talents to produce more goods, and this added productivity can benefit everyone. But the parties to the original position will each want to have an equal chance at these more lucrative positions. Consequently, they will insist that these positions be "open to all under conditions of fair equality of opportunity." Moreover, the parties to the original position will want to protect themselves in case they turn out to be among the "least advantaged."

---

[10]   *Theory of Justice,* excerpts from 11–13.
[11]   John Rawls, "Distributive Justice," in *Philosophy, Politics, and Society,* ed. Peter Laslett and W. G. Runciman (Oxford: Blackwell, 1967), 58–82.
[12]   John Rawls, "Constitutional Liberty," in *Nomos: Justice,* vol. VI (New York: Atherton Press, 1963) 98–125.

So they will agree that the benefits produced by allowing inequalities should be used to help the least advantaged.

Rawls' two principles, then, are the principles that he thought anyone—ourselves included—would choose if he or she were in the original position behind the veil of ignorance. And because the veil of ignorance in the original position requires us to be absolutely fair and just to everyone, the two principles we would choose would have to be just and so express what justice requires.

And what does justice require of us, according to Rawls? Certainly not the kind of socialist state advocated by Marx, in which individuals are not free to own the means of production; in which all land, factories, transport, and banks are controlled by the state; and in which free markets are prohibited. Neither does justice require an absolute equality. Instead, Rawls argues, justice requires freedom and *political* equality. In particular, justice requires political liberty, equality of opportunity, and aid to the poor. And although it does not *require* private ownership of the means of production, and free markets, nevertheless it allows these. Justice also allows *economic* inequalities, and it requires that the state must provide adequate welfare programs for the disadvantaged.

In short, justice requires more or less what the social, economic, and political institutions of most modern liberal democracies require. This is perhaps not surprising because Rawls' philosophy is intended to defend Western liberal ideals. It is, perhaps, the most powerful alternative to contemporary Marxism and the most powerful contemporary defense of liberalism.

QUESTIONS

1. In your own words, explain what the bourgeoisie is and how it developed. Does the bourgeoisie exist today? Explain.

2. To what extent does Marx's concept of alienation apply to modern workers? To what extent does it apply to modern college students? How would Marx analyze the contemporary trend toward careerism among today's college students (i.e., the trend to see a college education as preparation for a job or a career instead of as a humanizing and liberating activity)?

3. Explain in your own words what Rawls' "original position" is and why it is supposed to show us the meaning of justice. Do you agree that using the original position is an adequate way of determining what justice requires? Why? Do you think that Rawls' two principles of justice are adequate? Why?

4. How do Rawls' views about society differ from Marx's? What assumptions do you think Marx and Rawls make that lead each of them to such different conclusions?

5. What do you think Rawls would have said about the justice or injustice of making pornography illegal? About making drugs such as marijuana and cocaine illegal? About nationalizing businesses? About the international problem of poverty?

9 Postscript: The Meaning of Life

There is both pleasure and pain in tragedy and comedy, not only on the stage, but on the greater stage of human life.

PLATO

OUTLINE AND LEARNING OBJECTIVES

9.1 Does Life Have Meaning?

LEARNING OBJECTIVES: When finished, you'll be able to:

- Interpret the question whether life has meaning and explain why it is important.
- Explain why some argue that the question itself is meaningless.

9.2 The Theistic Response to Meaning

LEARNING OBJECTIVE: When finished, you'll be able to:

- Describe how some have found the meaning of life in a divine reality, and critically evaluate this view.

9.3 Meaning and Human Progress

LEARNING OBJECTIVE: When finished, you'll be able to:

- Describe how some have found the meaning of life in human progress, and critically evaluate this view.

9.4 The Nihilist Rejection of Meaning

LEARNING OBJECTIVE: When finished, you'll be able to:

- Describe the nihilist response to the question of whether life has meaning and explain how nihilists have argued for their response; critically evaluate the nihilist view.

9.5 Meaning as a Self-Chosen Commitment

LEARNING OBJECTIVE: When finished, you'll be able to:

- Explain the idea of subjective meaning as something created by the individual and why some have held this view; critically evaluate this view.

Chapter Summary

We have completed our overview of the central questions of philosophy: What am I? Is there a God? What is real? What can I know? What is truth? What ought I to do? What is a just society? We close now with a look at a question that is usually omitted from introductory courses in philosophy. That question is: Does life have any meaning? Introductory courses omit it in part because it is a difficult question. Yet for many people it is an urgent question and demands an answer. It may have been what brought them to philosophy in the first place.

It is fitting to conclude our philosophical journey with this question. As you will see, our discussion will draw from, and rely on, what you learned in earlier chapters. Because you have now examined the central issues of philosophy, therefore, you are better prepared to look into this question. By drawing on your earlier learning this chapter will also help bring together what you have learned. This chapter, then, draws out some of the consequences of the earlier chapters. For this reason, we call this closing chapter a "postscript."

MindTap What do you think of Albert Camus's idea that whether life is worth living is the "one truly serious philosophical problem"? Can you answer this one important question? Go to MindTap to watch a video about a group of people who have decided upon their answer.

9.1 Does Life Have Meaning?

Perhaps the most important question in philosophy is the question "Does life have meaning?" The French existentialist philosopher Albert Camus (1913–1960), in fact, argued that it is the only important question:

> There is but one truly serious philosophical problem, and that is suicide. Judging whether life is or is not worth living amounts to answering the fundamental question of philosophy. All the rest—whether or not the world has three dimensions, whether the mind has nine or twelve categories—comes afterwards. These are games; one must first answer [the fundamental question]. . . .
>
> If I ask myself how to judge that one question is more urgent than another, I reply that one judges by the actions it entails. I have never seen anyone die for the ontological argument. Galileo, who held a scientific truth of great importance, abjured it with the greatest ease as soon as it endangered his life.
>
> In a certain sense, he did right. That truth was not worth the stake. Whether the earth or the sun revolves around the other is a matter of profound indifference. To tell the truth, it is a futile question. On the other hand, I see many people die because they judge that life is not worth living. I see others paradoxically getting killed for the ideas or illusions that give them a reason for living (what is called a reason for living is also an excellent reason for dying). I therefore conclude that the meaning of life is the most urgent of questions.[1]

ANALYZING THE READING

1. Camus claims that the urgency of a question depends on the seriousness of the action or choice the question entails. What does he say is the most serious action or choice we face? Do you agree?

2. What, therefore, is the most urgent question?

3. How is this most urgent question related to the question whether life has meaning?

4. What follows about how urgent the question whether life has meaning is? Do you agree with Camus? Do you agree that all other questions are "games" or "of profound indifference" or "futile"? Why?

QUICK REVIEW
Camus claimed that the most urgent and "the one truly serious question in philosophy" is the question whether life has meaning and is thus worth living, because people are willing to die for this question.

People often ask about the meaning of life when death enters their lives. The death of someone they love or their own death may be imminent. Death brings everything we are or ever hoped to be to a complete end. What's the point of all our striving, then? At such times human life may seem brief and insignificant in the face of the

---

[1]   Albert Camus, "An Absurd Reasoning," from *The Myth of Sisyphus and Other Essays*, trans. Justin O'Brien (New York: Knopf, 1955).

great immensity and eternity of the universe. And that universe itself may seem to offer only an unconcerned and uncaring impersonal coldness. All these factors can lead people to question whether human life, and their life in particular, has any meaning.

But for many people, the question whether life has any meaning arises even when death is not near. Many people seem to reach a point in their lives when nothing seems to have any value. The things they have spent their lives chasing begin to seem pointless. They may feel like Shakespeare's Macbeth when he realized that all his killing, striving, and achievement had left him with nothing but despair:

> Life's but a walking shadow, a poor player
> That struts and frets his hour upon the stage
> And then is heard no more. It is a tale
> Told by an idiot, full of sound and fury,
> Signifying nothing.

The despair that gripped Macbeth is the despair of a person convinced that life is pointless and has no meaning. Perhaps no one has written of such despair more poignantly than the great Russian novelist Leo Tolstoy (1828 -1910):

In my writings I had advocated what to me was the only truth, that it was necessary to live in such a way as to derive the greatest comfort for oneself and one's family.

Thus I proceeded to live. But five years ago something very strange began to happen with me: I was overcome by minutes at first of perplexity and then of an arrest of life, as though I did not know how to live or what to do, and I lost myself and was dejected. But that passed, and I continued to live as before. Then those minutes of perplexity were repeated oftener and oftener, and always in one and the same form. These arrests of life found their expression in ever the same questions: "Why? Well, and then?"

At first I thought that those were simply aimless, inappropriate questions. . . . But the questions began to repeat themselves oftener and oftener, answers were demanded more and more persistently, and like dots that fall in the same spot, these questions, without any answers, thickened into one black blotch. . . .

I felt that what I was standing on had given way, that I had no foundation to stand on, that what I had lived by no longer existed, and that I had nothing to live for. . . .

It was as though I had just been living and walking along and had come to an abyss, where I saw clearly that there was nothing ahead but perdition. And it was impossible to stop and go back, and impossible to shut my eyes, in order that I might not see that there was nothing ahead but suffering and imminent death,—complete annihilation.

What happened to me was that I, a healthy, happy man, felt that I could not go on living,—an insurmountable force drew me on to find release from life. . . . The thought of suicide came to me as naturally then as the thought of improving my life had come to me before.

All this happened to me when I was surrounded on every side by what is considered to be complete happiness. I had a good, loving, and beloved wife, good children, and a large estate, which grew and increased without any labor on my part. I was respected by my neighbors and friends, more than ever before, was praised by strangers, and, without any self-deception, could consider my name famous. . . . And while in such condition I arrived at the conclusion that I could not live. . . .

This mental condition expressed itself to me in this form: my life is a stupid, mean trick played on me by somebody. . . . Involuntarily I imagined that there, somewhere, there was somebody who was

 THINKING LIKE A PHILOSOPHER

Nearly everyone at one time or another has thought about suicide. Camus considers suicide the most serious philosophical question, and Tolstoy considered suicide when he felt life was meaningless. Have you ever considered suicide? When? Do you agree that suicide is the most serious question?

THINKING LIKE A PHILOSOPHER

1. Do you think it is important for your life to have a meaning or is this a question that doesn't really matter to you? If you are having a lot of fun or are just happy and content, do you think it would be better for you to ignore the question?
2. At this point in your life, what do you think is the meaning or purpose of your life?
3. If you were to become depressed like Tolstoy did, do you think the meaning you attribute to your life would help you through such a crisis?

now having fun as he looked down upon me and saw me, who had lived for thirty or forty years, learning, developing, growing in body and mind, now that I had become strengthened in mind and had reached that summit of life from which it lay all before me, standing as a complete fool on that summit and seeing clearly that there was nothing in life and never would be. And that was fun to him. . . .

I could not ascribe any sensible meaning to a single act or to my whole life. I was only surprised that I had not understood this from the start. All this had long ago been known to everybody. Sooner or later there would come diseases and death (they had come already) to my dear ones and to me, and there would be nothing left but stench and worms. All my affairs, no matter what they might be, would sooner or later be forgotten, and I myself should not exist. So why should I worry about all these things? How could a man fail to see this and live,—that was surprising! A person could live only so long as he was drunk; but the moment he sobered up, he could not help seeing that all that was only a deception, and a stupid deception at that!. . .

"My family?" I asked myself. But my family, my wife and children, they are also human beings. They are in precisely the same condition that I am in: they must either live in the lie or see the terrible truth. Why should they live? Why should I love them, why guard, raise, and watch them? Is it for the same despair which is in me, or for dullness of perception? Since I love them, I cannot conceal the truth from them,—every step in understanding will lead them up to this truth. And the truth is death."

And in order to free myself from that terror, I wanted to kill myself. The terror of the darkness was too great, and I wanted as quickly as possible to free myself from it by means of a noose or a bullet. It was this feeling that more than anything else drew me on toward suicide.[2]

Tolstoy—then one of the world's most acclaimed writers—concluded that life had no meaning. His family and his writing had earlier sustained him. In his love for his family he had found "the only truth," and in poetry and art he had found "reflections of life" that had sustained him. But now he felt that "the truth is death." Ahead of him and everyone he loved lay death. Eventually everything anyone had been or done in life would disintegrate and be forgotten. And that, he came to believe, made life pointless. Art and family sustained him no longer and he fell into a deep suicidal depression.

We will return to Tolstoy shortly when we examine how he eventually answered the question of the meaning of life. Here we need to note only that Tolstoy's need to find meaning in life is a need that many of us have felt. Or will someday feel. Events may eventually force us to ask whether the things we have devoted our lives to achieving have any real meaning. This question, which has brought many people to philosophy, is the question that we now discuss.

What Does the Question Mean?

But what, exactly, does this question mean? There are some philosophers who have claimed that the question itself has no meaning. The question is literally

---

2   Leo Tolstoy, *My Confession*, trans. Leo Wiener (Boston: Dana Estes & Company, Publishers, 1904), 16–24.

meaningless. This is the position of the logical positivists, whose empiricist views we saw earlier. Take A. J. Ayer, for example. He argued that besides tautologies, the only meaningful questions are factual questions, that is, questions we can answer by sense observation. The question whether life has meaning, he claims, is not a factual question. So the question itself has no meaning.

> . . . there is no sense in asking what is the ultimate purpose of our existence, or what is the real meaning of life. . . . The position is not that our existence unfortunately lacks a purpose which, if the fates had been kinder, it might conceivably have had. It is rather that those who inquire, in this way, after the meaning of life are raising a question to which it is not logically possible that there should be an answer. . . . If a question is so framed as to be unanswerable, then it is not a matter for regret that it remains unanswered. It is, therefore, misleading to say that life has no meaning; for that suggests that the statement that life has a meaning is factually significant, but false; whereas the truth is that, in the sense in which it is taken in this context, it is not factually significant.[3]

But most people today believe that the logical positivists are mistaken. In particular, people reject the idea that the only meaningful statements are tautologies and factual claims our senses can verify. In fact, many of our most pressing social, religious, and moral questions seem to make perfectly good sense. Yet they cannot be resolved through the use of our senses. Moreover, many modern philosophers have shown—as we will see—that the question of the meaning of life can have a perfectly understandable meaning.

But if the question is not meaningless, what, then, does it mean? One way of understanding the question "What is the meaning of life?" is to take it as asking whether my life has a larger or more important purpose than merely living. In other words, is my individual life related to something larger and more significant that gives my finite life value?

This seems to be the way that Leo Tolstoy understood the question. Despite being respected and loved, he fell into a deep depression when he began to feel that life is meaningless. Tolstoy came out of his profound funk when he decided that to have meaning, his finite life had to be related to the infinite God.

9.2 The Theistic Response to Meaning

Perhaps the most common way that people answer the question whether life has meaning is in terms of their relationship to God. This is an ancient response to the question. For example, we saw in Chapter 2 that Thomas Aquinas argues that everything has a purpose, including human beings:

> Now here on earth, the simplest elements exist for the sake of compound minerals; these latter exist for the sake of living bodies, among which plants exist for animals, and animals for humans. . . . Now humans naturally desire, as their ultimate purpose, to know the first cause of all things. But the first cause of all things is God. So the ultimate purpose of human beings is to know God.[4]

---

[3] A. J. Ayer, "The Claims of Philosophy," from E. D. Klemke and Steven M. Cahn, eds., *The Meaning of Life* (New York: Oxford University Press, 2008), 201.

[4] Thomas Aquinas, *Summa Contra Gentiles*, bk. III, ch. 22, paras. 7, 8, ch. 25, para. 11, translated by Manuel Velasquez.

Aquinas' view can be called the theistic response to the question of meaning. The theistic response claims that human life has meaning because humans are part of a plan or providential order devised by God. Within that plan, all things in the universe have purpose and value. The purpose of finite human beings, in particular, is to know the infinite God and be united with Him. Life on earth, while brief, is valuable insofar as it is a preparation for that future union with that infinite God. Human life, then, is not a tiny, insignificant, and meaningless "hour upon the stage" that ends with nothing. Human life has a meaning because each person is related to an infinite significant whole within which each finite individual has a place.

This theistic response is the one that led Tolstoy out of his depression. As Tolstoy wrote:

> I understood that it was not right for me to look for an answer to my question in rational knowledge, and that the answer given by rational knowledge was only an indication that the answer might be answered . . . only when into the discussion of the question should be introduced the question of the relation of the finite to the infinite. I also understood that, no matter how irrational and monstrous the answers might be that faith gave, they had this advantage that they introduced into each answer the relation of the finite to the infinite, without which there could be no answer.
>
> No matter how I might put the question, "How must I live?" the answer of faith is, "According to God's law." "What result will there be from my life?"—"Eternal torment or eternal bliss." "What is the meaning which is not destroyed by death?"—"The union with infinite God, paradise."
>
> Thus, outside rational knowledge, which had to me appeared as the only one, I was inevitably led to recognize that all living humanity had a certain other non-rational knowledge, faith, which made it possible to live. . . . It alone gave to humanity answers to the questions of life, and, in consequence of them, the possibility of living.
>
> Ever since humanity had existed, faith had given the possibility of living, and the chief features of faith were everywhere one and the same. No matter what answers faith may give, its every answer gives to the finite existence of man the sense of the infinite,—a sense which is not destroyed by suffering, privation, and death. Consequently in faith alone could we find the meaning and possibility of life.
>
> Then I began to cultivate the acquaintance of the believers from among the poor, the simple and unlettered folk, of pilgrims, monks, dissenters, peasants. . . . I began to examine closely the lives and beliefs of these people, and the more I examined them, the more did I become convinced that they had the real faith, that their faith was necessary for them, and that it alone gave them a meaning and possibility of life. . . .
>
> I began to love these people. . . . Thus I lived for about two years, and within me took place a transformation. . . . What happened with me was that the life of our circle—of the rich and the learned—not only disgusted me, but even lost all its meaning. All our acts, reflections, sciences, arts—all that appeared to me in a new light. I saw that all that was mere pampering of the appetites, and that no meaning could be found in it; but the life of all the working masses, of all humanity, which created life, presented itself to me in its real significance. I saw that that was life itself and that the meaning given to this life was truth, and I accepted it.

ANALYZING THE READING

1. Tolstoy implies that if life has no meaning, then it is logical to choose suicide. Does Camus agree? Do you agree? Why or why not?

2. Tolstoy suggests that if human life ends with nothing more than "death—complete annihilation," then it has no meaning. Is he right? If human life did not end with death but went on forever, would human life then necessarily be meaningful? In other words, is eternal life by itself sufficient to make life meaningful? Is eternal life necessary to make life meaningful?

3. Tolstoy suggests that "faith" relates "the finite existence of man" to something "infinite" that is "not destroyed by suffering, privation, and death," namely, "union with infinite God." Why would "union with infinite God" give Tolstoy the meaning he wanted?

> I renounced the life of our circle, having come to recognize that that was not life, but only a likeness of life, that the conditions of superabundance in which we lived deprived us of the possibility of understanding life and that, in order that I might understand life, I had to understand not the life . . . of us, the parasites of life, but the life of the simple working classes, of those who produced life, and the meaning which they ascribed to it.
>
> This meaning, if it can be expressed, was like this: Every man has come into this world by the will of God. God has so created man that every man may either ruin his soul or save it. The problem of each man in life is to save his soul; in order to save his soul, he must live according to God's command, and to live according to God's command, he must renounce all the luxuries of life, must work, be humble, suffer, and be merciful.[5]

There is, of course, not just one theistic response. Each of the world's religions provides its own interpretation of the infinite divine reality in relation to which finite human life has meaning. So each provides a different account of the larger whole that gives life meaning. Some, like Islam, infuse life with meaning in a way that is much like the theistic response of Christianity. Other religions, like Hinduism and Buddhism, relate human life to a view of the universe that is very different. Hinduism asserts the doctrine of rebirth and karma and holds out the goal of absorption into Brahman after ascending the stages of consciousness. Buddhism asserts the doctrine of rebirth and of liberation from that great wheel of rebirth through the eightfold way whose goal is enlightenment. But despite their profound differences, all religions give meaning to life in a similar way. They relate the individual to a divine reality that is larger and more significant than the individual.

QUICK REVIEW
Each religion offers its own view of the cosmic whole in terms of which human life has meaning, but all theistic views give meaning to life by relating the individual to a divine reality that is larger and more important than the individual is.

The theist response to the search for meaning satisfies many believers, but it also raises difficult questions. First, the response obviously depends on accepting the belief that God exists or that some kind of divine reality exists. However, when we discussed the many proofs for the existence of God in Chapter 4, we saw that it is very difficult to prove that God exists. The theist response will say little to the nonbeliever.

Second, as the Austrian philosopher Kurt Baier (1917–2010) has argued, there is something "morally repugnant" about the theist response. He writes:

> It is degrading for a man to be regarded as merely serving a purpose. If, at a garden party, I ask a man in livery, "What is your purpose?" I am insulting him. I might as well have asked, "What are you *for*?" Such questions reduce him to the level of a gadget, a domestic animal, or perhaps a slave. I imply that *we* allot to *him* the tasks, the goals, the aims which he is to pursue; that *his* wishes and desires and aspirations and purposes are to count for little or nothing. We are treating him, in Kant's phrase, merely as a means to our ends, not as an end in himself.[6]

The theist view claims, according to Baier, that humans have meaning because they have a purpose that God assigns them. But to see humans in this way is to see them as objects or tools that God uses. Yet as we saw when we discussed Kant's views on ethics, humans should be treated as ends and never used merely as means.

Third, the philosopher Kai Nielsen has argued that the theist response is illogical.[7] The theistic response says: God has a purpose for my life; therefore, my life has

QUICK REVIEW
Critics argue that the theistic response is irrelevant to the nonbeliever. Baier claims that to say humans have a purpose assigned to them by God reduces humans to tools that God is using. Nielsen says from the fact that someone else (e.g., God) has a purpose for me, it does not follow that my life has meaning because values are not established by facts.

---

5 Leo Tolstoy, *My Confession*, 53–72.
6 Kurt Baier, "The Meaning of Life," in *The Meaning of Life: A Reader*, ed. E.D. Klemke and Steven M. Cahn (New York: Oxford University Press, 2008), 101.
7 Kai Nielsen, "Linguistic Philosophy and 'the Meaning of Life,'" in *The Meaning of Life*, ed. Sanders and Cheney, 129–154.

meaning. But the second part of this statement does not follow from the first. For example, suppose that when you were born, your father had a purpose for you. Suppose he wanted you to carry on the family name and take over the family business. Clearly, from the fact that your father had this purpose for you, it does not follow that your life must have meaning. Similarly, even if God or some being out in the universe somewhere has a purpose for you, it does not follow that your life must have a meaning. A life with meaning seems to be a life one values, and facts about other beings—even facts about God—cannot determine what one values.

9.3 Meaning and Human Progress

Some philosophers agree that life has meaning only if it is related to something more significant than the individual. But they have not agreed that it is a divine reality that gives life meaning. They have proposed instead that contributing to human progress gives life meaning.

The German philosopher Georg Hegel, for example, argued that history shows progress. "The History of the world," Hegel wrote, "is none other than the progress of the consciousness of freedom."[8] As history develops, Hegel claims, people come to recognize that humans are essentially free. And as this recognition grows more people are allowed to be free. In the ancient "Oriental" empires of China, India, and Egypt, Hegel claims, only one person, the emperor, was free. Everyone else was treated despotically. These empires were succeeded by the Greek and Roman empires, in which all citizens were recognized as free. But their slaves had no freedom. The Greek and Roman empires, then, recognized that only *some* are free. These empires were eventually succeeded by the nations of the modern world which Hegel calls the "German nations." Modern nations abolished slavery and all people were finally recognized as free:

> The Orientals did not attain the knowledge that Spirit—Man as such—is free. And because they did not know this, they were not free. They only understood that one person was free [the emperor]. But for this reason, the freedom of that one was arbitrary. The ferocity and brutal reckless passion of one emperor, alternated with his successors' mildness and tame desires. And the latter, too, was only an accident of Nature, as arbitrary as the former. That one person, the emperor, was therefore only a Despot. He was not really a free man.
>
> The consciousness of Freedom first arose among the Greeks. Consequently they were free. But they and the Romans likewise, knew only that some are free—not man as such. Even Plato and Aristotle did not realize this. The Greeks, had slaves. Their whole life and the maintenance of their splendid liberty, was based on the institution of slavery. This fact, moreover, allowed that liberty only an accidental, transient and limited growth. And it produced a rigorous thraldom of our common nature—of the human.
>
> The German nations, influenced by Christianity, were the first to attain the consciousness that man, as man, is free. That it is the freedom of Spirit, which constitutes its essence.[9]

ANALYZING THE READING

1. Hegel claims that human history has progressed by gradually expanding the freedom of everyone. Do you agree?

2. According to Hegel you can find meaning in your life by helping humanity move toward a better, more perfect, and freer world. Do you think he is right?

---

8   Georg Wilhelm Friedrich Hegel, *The Philosophy of History*, trans. J. Sibree (New York: Dover, 1956), 19.
9   Ibid., 18.

The progress that we see in history, Hegel holds, is not continuous. Here history moves forward, there it pauses, and there it may briefly regress. But in its overall sweep, history keeps moving toward a better and more perfect world:

> The mutations which history presents have been long characterized in general, as an advance to something better, more perfect. . . . This peculiarity in the world of mind has indicated in the case of man . . . a real capacity for change, and that for the better—an impulse of perfectibility. . . .
> Universal history—as already demonstrated—shows the development of the consciousness of Freedom on the part of Spirit, and of the consequent realization of that Freedom. This development implies a gradation—a series of increasingly adequate expressions or manifestations of Freedom.[10]

QUICK REVIEW
Hegel argues that the larger reality that gives an individual life meaning is the historical progress of the world toward an ever greater consciousness of freedom. The individual's life has meaning to the extent that he or she takes part in this progressive movement of history by participating in the spirit of the age, the way in which freedom is evolving in his time.

Hegel claims that if the individual person deliberately becomes a part of this progressive movement of history, his or her life will have meaning. In fact, as we saw in Chapter 2, Hegel argues that apart from this forward sweep of history, the individual cannot find meaning. All meaning for the individual lies in entering and participating in the "spirit" of his or her age, the particular way in which freedom is evolving during the individual's lifetime.

Other philosophers have also proposed that we can see progress in history and that by taking part in this progress the individual finds meaning in life. Karl Marx, who adopted many of Hegel's ideas about how history moves from an Asiatic, through an ancient, and on to a modern society, also felt that history was progressing toward a better and more perfect world. However, progress for Marx is economic progress: "In broad outline, the Asiatic, ancient, feudal and modern bourgeois modes of production may be designated as epochs marking progress in the economic development of society."[11] For Marx, the more perfect future world would be a world without economic classes—the classless society: "In place of the old bourgeois society, with its classes and class antagonisms, we shall have an association in which the free development of each is the condition for the free development of all."[12] Such a society would be a just society in which, as we saw in Chapter 8, benefits and burdens are distributed according to need and ability. To find meaning in life, the individual must join in the struggle to overthrow the old capitalist structures, which will give way to the new, classless society.

QUICK REVIEW
Marx also argues that the meaning of life is found by participating in the progressive movement of history, but for him history was progressing economically toward a classless society, and meaning lay in joining in the struggle to overthrow old capitalist structures and thereby help achieve the classless society.

Others have proposed different ways to contribute to human progress. Some have suggested that as scientific knowledge progresses, life acquires meaning for the scientist through the contributions that he or she makes to this progress. Others suggest that society can evolve and become better, and that by contributing to making ours a better or more just society a person's life can have meaning. Still others believe that human life can be made better in many different ways, and so for them life has meaning when they contribute to any of these ways of making human life better.

MindTap Like Marx, the Mexican artist Diego Rivera saw human progress in terms of economic systems. Go to MindTap to watch a video showing his master work, the mural "Man, Controller of the Universe," and explaining what it depicts.

But do these ideas of progress make sense today? Does history really reveal any kind of progress toward a goal? Doesn't history, on the contrary, exhibit decline, not progress? Take, for example,

THINKING LIKE A PHILOSOPHER

If you sat down to write the story of your life, do you think that your life's story would exhibit progress? Why? Would it exhibit meaning? Why?

---

10 Ibid., 54, 63.
11 Karl Marx, *Toward a Critique of Political Economy*, 13: 10, trans. A. Wood, quoted in *A Dictionary of Philosophical Quotations*, ed. A. J. Ayer and Jande O'Grady (Oxford, England: Blackwell, 1992), 291.
12 Karl Marx and Friedrich Engels, *Manifesto of the Communist Party*, 6: 505, quoted in *Dictionary of Philosophical Quotations*, 288.

the state of the environment. Isn't the environment dirtier, uglier, more polluted, more crowded, and more degraded today than ever before? Or look at the state of the world. Haven't the grim experiences of two world wars in the past century and two smaller wars in the first decade of the present century, been enough to put an end to the traditional idea of progress and to optimistic feelings about the future? The title of a widely read book by historian Oswald Spengler that was written after World War I seems to be a perfect description of our situation: *Decline of the West.* Critics argue that personal meaning and value cannot be based on this kind of history.

Moreover, if there is human progress in history, then it must have a goal, and this goal must be valuable. But why should we accept the idea that greater freedom or a "classless society" or any other goal must have value for *me*? Why should such goals matter to me? Even if we feel such goals are valuable, how can we be sure that history is moving to achieve them? If humans have free will (which we discussed earlier), then doesn't this mean that there is no way of knowing ahead of time that humans will choose to move toward some specific goal?

Yet many people today believe that humanity is in some sense still progressing. They believe that our lives can have meaning by contributing toward this progress and by "making this a better world." For example, the historian Charles Van Doren has argued that although there is little evidence for progress in economic, political, moral, or artistic matters, there is nonetheless clear progress in human knowledge.[13] Although we might not be be making ourselves better people, we are increasing our knowledge. Because of the cumulative efforts of many thinkers and scientists we know more now than we ever did in our earlier history. And that increase in knowledge has made our lives incomparably better, healthier, longer, and more comfortable than they were even a hundred years ago. To the extent that people contribute to the continual expansion of this valuable treasure of knowledge, they are making ours a better world and so their life has had a meaning.

9.4 The Nihilist Rejection of Meaning

Yet for many people the ideas of being part of God's plan or of contributing to human progress no longer make sense. Unable to find meaning in God or human progress, many philosophers have argued that life has no meaning. The German philosopher Arthur Schopenhauer argued, for example, that everything passes away and "that which in the next moment exists no more, and vanishes utterly, like a dream, can never be worth a serious effort." Schopenhauer concluded that "All good things are vanity, the world in all its ends [is] bankrupt, and life [is] a business which does not cover its expenses":

> A quick test of the assertion that enjoyment outweighs pain in this world, or that they are at any rate balanced, would be to compare the feelings of an animal engaged in eating another with those of the animal being eaten. . . .
>
> History shows us the life of nations and finds nothing to narrate but wars and tumults; the peaceful years appear only as occasional brief pauses and interludes. In just the same way the life of the individual is a constant struggle, and not merely a metaphorical one against want or boredom, but also an actual struggle against other people. He discovers adversaries everywhere, lives in continual conflict and dies with sword in hand. . . .

---

[13]   Charles Van Doren, *A History of Knowledge* (New York: Random House, 1991).

That human life must be some kind of mistake is sufficiently proved by the simple observation that man is a compound of needs which are hard to satisfy; that their satisfaction achieves nothing but a painless condition in which he is only given over to boredom; and that boredom is a direct proof that existence is in itself valueless, for boredom is nothing other than the sensation of the emptiness of existence.[14]

The contemporary American philosopher Richard Taylor also argues for the view that when viewed objectively, human life has no meaning:

A perfect image of meaninglessness . . . is found in the ancient myth of Sisyphus. Sisyphus, it will be remembered, betrayed divine secrets to mortals, and for this he was condemned by the gods to roll a stone to the top of a hill, the stone then immediately to roll back down, again to be pushed to the top by Sisyphus, to roll down once more, and so on again and again, forever. Now in this we have the picture of meaningless, pointless toil, of a meaningless existence that is absolutely never redeemed.

But if we supposed that these stones, instead of rolling back to their places, . . . were assembled at the top of the hill . . . in a beautiful and enduring temple, then the aspect of meaninglessness would disappear. His labors would then have a point. . . . Meaningfulness would at least have made an appearance.

Which of these pictures does life in fact resemble?

Look at a busy street any day, and observe the throng going hither and thither. To what? Some office or shop, where the same things will be done today as were done yesterday, and are done now so they may be repeated tomorrow . . . most such effort is directed only to the establishment and perpetuation of home and family; that is, to the begetting of others who will follow in our steps to do more of the same. . . . Our achievements, even though they are often beautiful, are mostly bubbles; and those that do last, like the sand-swept pyramids, soon become mere curiosities. . . . Nations are built upon the bones of their founders and pioneers, but only to decay and crumble before long, their rubble then becoming the foundation for others directed to exactly the same fate.[15]

ANALYZING THE READING

1. Both Schopenhauer and Taylor claim that life is meaningless. But they have different reasons for thinking life is meaningless. What are their reasons and how do they differ?

2. Taylor claims that if Sisyphus used the stones to build a beautiful temple, his life would have meaning. Would Schopenhauer agree? Why or why not?

3. Taylor claims that if Sisyphus had an "unappeasable desire" to roll stones, his life would have meaning. Would Schopenhauer agree? Why or why not?

The views of both Schopenhauer and Taylor are based on the *nihilist* view that there is no larger whole to which we can relate and that can be a source of meaning. Both God and the idea of progress no longer make sense. Moreover, human life and all that humans produce are too insignificant and fleeting to be a source of meaning. Human life is just an endless repetition of the same meaningless events that came before. What is left?

Although Taylor believes that when viewed objectively our lives are meaningless, he also argues that there is a sense in which our lives have a kind of subjective meaning. He writes:

Let us suppose that the gods, while condemning Sisyphus to the fate just described, at the same time [were] merciful by implanting in him . . . a compulsive impulse to roll stones. . . . His one desire in life is to roll stones.

---

14 Arthur Schopenhauer, *Essays and Aphorisms*, trans. R. J. Hollindale (London: Penguin Books, 1970), 41–50.
15 Richard Taylor, "The Meaning of Life," in *The Meaning of Life*, ed. Klemke, 146.

> If Sisyphus had a keen and unappeasable desire to be doing just what he found himself doing, then, although his life would in no way be changed, it would nevertheless have a meaning for him. . . . We find that our lives do indeed still resemble that of Sisyphus, but . . . the strange meaningfulness they possess is that of the inner compulsion to be doing just what we were put here to do, and to go on doing it forever. This is the nearest we may hope to get to heaven.

Taylor is saying that so long as the activities of our life satisfy desires we happen to have, our life will have meaning for us. Life will possess "meaningfulness" for a person so long as the person wants to do what he or she is doing.

To many the kind of meaningfulness that Taylor suggests life can have will seem to be no meaning at all. For example, while Tolstoy despaired that life had no meaning, he was satisfying his desires. Yet he questioned whether satisfying his desires itself had a point. If someone asks "What is the meaning of life," it will not help to answer: "to satisfy your desires." That answer will only lead to the question: "But what is the point of *that?*"

Nevertheless, Taylor's suggestion comes close to another kind of answer that can be given to the question whether life has any meaning. That is the answer proposed by some existentialists: The meaning of life is what you choose to make it.

THINKING LIKE A PHILOSOPHER

1. Do you agree with Taylor that meaninglessness is essentially the kind of pointlessness that Sisyphus' life represents? Do you agree that our lives or the lives of most people around you are like Sisyphus' life?
2. Taylor's view of what makes life meaningful is different from Tolstoy's view. Which of the two is more plausible to you?

9.5 Meaning as a Self-Chosen Commitment

Some philosophers, such as R. M. Hare, have argued that the nihilist response is mistaken.[16] The nihilist argues life does not have an "objective" meaning, a meaning that does not depend on what one chooses or believes. So the nihilist concludes life has no meaning. But, Hare claims, life can have a "subjective" meaning, a meaning that depends on one's choices and beliefs. Life will have "subjective" meaning if one (a) chooses goals that give direction to one's life and (b) believes that these goals are valuable and worth pursuing. Family, country, religion, friends—all these can become my personal goals. And if these matter to me, then by choosing to pursue them, I can give my life meaning and value.

Many philosophers have agreed that the goals we choose to pursue can give life a "subjective" meaning. One of the earliest was Kierkegaard. As we saw in Chapter 4, Kierkegaard claims the starting point in life is choosing something for which one is willing to live or die:

> What I really lack is to be clear in my mind what I am to do, not what I am to know, except insofar as a certain understanding must precede every action. The thing is to understand myself, to see what God really wishes me to do; the thing is to find a truth which is true for me, to find the idea for which I can live and die. Of what use would it be to me to discover a so-called objective truth, to work through philosophical systems so that I could, if asked, make critical judgments about them, could point out the fallacies in each system; of what use would it be to me to be able to develop

---

---

16 See R. M. Hare, "Nothing Matters," in *The Meaning of Life,* ed. Klemke, 241–247.

a theory of the state, .. [or] to be able to formulate the meaning of Christianity . . . if it had no deeper meaning for me and for my life?[17]

Kierkegaard described three lifestyles, which he called *aesthetic, ethical,* and *religious.* Which of these lifestyles was best for oneself, he felt, is never clear. Yet the key to living authentically is to make a decisive choice among them. And, by so choosing, one creates the meaning of one's life:

> Every human being . . . has a natural need to formulate a life-view, a conception of the meaning of life and of its purpose. The person who lives aesthetically also does that, and the popular expression heard in all ages . . . [to describe this stage of life is]: One must enjoy life. . . . We encounter [some aesthetic] life-views that teach that we are to enjoy life . . . [through something] outside the individual. This is the case with every life-view in which wealth, honors, noble birth, etc., are made life's task and its content. . . . [Other] life-views teach that we are to enjoy life . . . [through something] within the individual himself . . . ordinarily defined as talent. It [may be] a talent for practical affairs, a talent for business, a talent for mathematics, a talent for writing, a talent for art, a talent for philosophy. Satisfaction in life, enjoyment, is sought in the unfolding of this talent. . . .
>
> In contrast to an aesthetic life-view . . . we often hear about another life-view that places the meaning of life in living for the performance of one's moral duties. This is supposed to signify an ethical view of life. . . . [But it is] a mistake to [see duty as something that is imposed] from outside the individual. . . . The truly ethical person . . . does not have duty outside himself but within himself. . . . When a person has felt the intensity of duty with all his energy, then he is ethically mature, and then duty will break forth within him. . . .
>
> The story of Abraham [in the Bible] contains . . . a teleological suspension of the ethical. . . . [Abraham faithfully obeyed God's command to sacrifice his beloved son although human sacrifice violated his ethical duty; at the last moment, God stopped Abraham's hand.] Abraham represents faith. . . . He acts by virtue of the absurd. . . . By his act he transgressed the ethical altogether and had a higher telos outside it, in relation to which he suspended it. . . . Why then does Abraham do it? For God's sake and—the two are wholly identical—for his own sake. He does it for God's sake because God demands this proof of his faith; he does it for his own sake so that he can prove it.[18]

 THINKING LIKE A PHILOSOPHER

1. Kierkegaard says that choosing to commit yourself to a religious belief is like a "leap" into something that you cannot prove and for which you cannot give rational reasons. Do you agree? Is religion related to your beliefs about the meaning of life?
2. Are you religious? If so, have you found that belief is like a "leap"? If not, is your reason for not being religious related to the idea that religious belief is like a "leap" into something you cannot prove and that has no rational reasons?

Notice that for Kierkegaard, the meaning of life is subjective. It is by our personal or subjective choice of an aesthetic, ethical, or religious life that we determine the meaning of life for us. For example, we can choose to pursue wealth or honor, or enjoyment of our talents. Then the pleasure these provide becomes the meaning of life for us. But the individual may come to feel such a life has little value. Then, he must choose to stay at the aesthetic stage, whose attractions he knows or commit himself to the ethical stage. The commitment to the ethical stage of life involves embracing one's ethical obligations and pursuing pleasure within the bounds of

---

[17] Søren Kierkegaard, *The Journals of Kierkegaard,* trans. and ed. A. Dru (London: Collins, 1958), 44.
[18] Søren Kierkegaard, *Either/Or,* vol. II, trans. Howard V. Hong and Edna H. Hong, reprinted in Denise Peterfreund White, ed., *Great Traditions in Ethics,* 8th ed. (Belmont, CA: Wadsworth, 1996), 228–230, 232.

ethics. Moral integrity and honesty become the meaning of life. At first, one confidently assumes that one can live up to the moral law. But in time the individual realizes he cannot do all that morality requires, and he experiences guilt or sin. The individual must then choose. Will he remain at the ethical level and keep trying but failing to do what ethics demands? Or will he admit that he needs God to save him from his guilt, and so choose to move to the religious stage?

But the move to the religious stage is a "leap" that is filled with uncertainty. As Kierkegaard puts it: "All Christianity is rooted in the paradoxical, whether one accepts it as a believer, or rejects it precisely because it is paradoxical. Aye, it lies in fear and trembling, which are the desperate categories of Christianity, and of the leap."[19] The religious stage is a commitment of one's life to something that cannot be rationally proved or rationally understood. The move to the religious stage requires a "leap of faith" like Abraham's decision to trust God when God commanded him to sacrifice his son. Such a leap of faith is made alone, without any guarantee of being right. It is a leap made in "fear and trembling." But we must choose, and what we choose becomes the meaning of life for us.

Many years later, the French philosopher Jean-Paul Sartre took up several of these existential themes. Sartre was an atheist. But he agreed that the meaning of life is the result of a choice. Neither God nor human progress can provide us with purpose and meaning unless we choose to commit ourselves to these. So it is our choice itself that makes them meaningful and valuable to us.

We met Sartre earlier when we were discussing human nature in Chapter 2 and when we discussed existentialism in Chapter 3. Recall that Sartre holds that there are no fixed values to give meaning to our lives. There are no fixed values because there is no God and so there is no one to establish values for us. Until we choose, life has no set value we should pursue and so no objective meaning or purpose. But by choosing to pursue a cause, a religion, a life goal, I make these valuable and make them the meaning of my life. Here is how Sartre puts this idea:

> God does not exist and we have to face all the consequences of this. The existentialist is strongly opposed to a certain kind of secular ethics which would like to abolish God . . . [but hold] that values exist all the same, inscribed in a heaven of ideas.
>
> The existentialist, on the contrary, thinks it very distressing that God does not exist, because all possibility of finding values in a heaven of ideas disappears along with Him. There can no longer be an a priori Good, since there is no infinite and perfect consciousness to think it. Nowhere is it written that the Good exists, that we must be honest, that we must not lie; because the fact is we are on a plane where there are only men.
>
> If God does not exist, we find no values or commands to turn to which legitimize our conduct. So, in the bright realm of values, we have no excuse behind us, nor justification before us. We are alone, with no excuses. . . .
>
> [Some] may object that "your values are not serious, since you choose them yourselves." To that I can only say that I am very sorry that it should be so. But I have excluded God and, there must be somebody to

QUICK REVIEW
Sartre, an atheist, claims that only subjective meaning is possible and that we give subjective meaning to our lives by choosing to commit ourselves to something and thereby giving it value; nothing has value before it is chosen. Critics argue that one must believe something is valuable before one can choose to devote oneself to it.

ANALYZING THE READING

1. Kierkegaard says that for the individual at the ethical stage moral duty is not "outside himself, but within himself." What do you think he means by this?

2. According to Kierkegaard, the religious stage requires acting "by virtue of the absurd." What do you think he means by this?

3. Kierkegaard implies that the ethical stage of life is in some sense better than the aesthetic stage of life, and that the religious stage is in some sense better than the ethical stage. Would Sartre agree with this? Do you agree with this? Why?

4. Sartre claims that if God does not exist, then there are "no values or [moral] commands to turn to." What are his reasons for this claim? Is he right?

---

19   Soren Kierkegaard, *Kierkegaard's Concluding Unscientific Postscript*, trans. David F. Swenson (Princeton: Princeton University Press, 1941), 96.

invent values. We have to take things as they are. And moreover, to say that we invent values means nothing else but this: life has no meaning a priori. Before you come alive, life is nothing; it's up to you to give it a meaning, and its value is nothing else but the meaning that you choose.[20]

But in the end, doesn't Sartre leave us without a compass as we struggle to find meaning in our lives? If Sartre is right, then before we choose nothing has value, but when we choose a thing it acquires value for us. If so then we should be able to find meaning in our lives by choosing anything at all. For we can give value to anything by choosing it. But this is clearly not true. A person cannot think that her life has meaning if she chooses to devote it to making tiny little piles of sand on the beach. To believe life has meaning, we must choose goals or causes that we think had value even before we chose them. Otherwise, why would we choose them? Why would we choose to devote our lives to something that does not yet have any value?

Sartre and Kierkegaard, then, may be right when they claim that nothing can give my life meaning unless I choose it and make it my own. But Sartre, at least, seems wrong to claim that before I choose, nothing has value. On the contrary, what I choose to devote my life to must be something that I already believe is valuable and worth pursuing. If it has no value before I choose it, then I will not choose it. And so it will not give my life meaning.

So does life have meaning? For many people, life does have meaning because they believe that they have a part to play in a larger whole that gives life value and purpose. Such objective meaning might come from being part of a larger divine plan, or from contributing to human progress. But for many, these sources of meaning are no longer significant. Some reject God; some reject the idea of human progress; others reject both. The result is that many accept nihilism: They conclude that life has no meaning.

But Kierkegaard and Sartre reveal another possibility. They suggest the possibility of creating subjective meaning through our choices. In a way, even those who look to God or human progress for meaning must choose to commit themselves to these. But if subjective meaning can be created through choice, then the range of meaning is wider than God and human progress. Life can have meaning through a commitment to any of a variety of human concerns. For one person, meaning may come through a commitment to family or to loving relationships. For some meaning may come through a commitment to art, to political life, or to healing or helping others. For another, meaning may come through a commitment to living an ethical life of moral integrity. And for yet others it may come through a commitment to religious faith.

But the key question is the one that Sartre forces us to face: Can anything we choose—whatever it might be—make life meaningful for us? If Sartre is right, then meaning is easy. We can find meaning by committing ourselves to the pursuit of money, the pursuit of pleasure, or even to making little piles of sand on the ocean shore. But if Sartre is wrong, then meaning is not so easy to come by. If Sartre is wrong then life can have meaning only if we commit ourselves to an ideal that, ahead of time, we know is worth pursuing. As Kierkegaard suggests, finding meaning may require the difficult choice of ever more authentic stages of life. Meaning may be the result of finding at each stage that what I have committed myself to is not worthy enough and that I need more. If so, then at each stage meaning requires a commitment to what I know has value, and has value even before I choose it.

MindTap To read more from Jean-Paul Sartre's *Existentialism and Human Emotions*, click the link in the MindTap Reader or go to the Questia Readings folder in MindTap.

QUICK REVIEW
The idea of subjective meaning suggests that because meaning can be created through our choices, life can have meaning through our commitment to any of a wide variety of worthy human concerns, such as family, art, loving relationships, raising children, healing, helping, moral integrity, and religious faith.

---

[20] Jean-Paul Sartre, *Existentialism and Human Emotions* (New York: Philosophical Library, 1957), 23, 49.

PHILOSOPHY AT THE MOVIES

Watch *About Schmidt* (2002) in which Warren Schmidt, after retiring from his job as an actuary and having his wife die, feels useless and alienated, and travels in a Winnebago to visit his daughter to try to convince her not to marry a waterbed salesman. What is the meaning of life for Warren's friend Ray? Does the movie seem to agree with Ray? Does Warren believe or come to believe that his life has a meaning? Explain. What does it mean when at the end of the movie Warren cries over the picture that Ndugu drew? Is he crying because he sees that life has meaning after all or because he sees that life has no meaning?

Chapter Summary

We have now come to the end of our philosophical journey. If you must leave a philosophy course having learned only one thing, the prized possession might be to travel with a philosophical attitude. Having a philosophical attitude means having one's eyes open as one journeys through the many decisions that will give shape and meaning to our lives.

A philosophical attitude is not achieved with a single philosophy course, although it may begin with one. Rather, the philosophical attitude needs lifelong nurturing to flourish and strengthen. And it requires something else—courage— the courage to continue on the journey once begun.

The main points of this chapter are:

9.1 Does Life Have Meaning?

- For many people, the question of whether life has any meaning arises even when death is not near.

- Logical positivists claim the question is meaningless.

9.2 The Theistic Response to Meaning

- The theistic response to the question of the meaning of life holds that the meaning of life is to be explained in terms of the individual's relationship to a larger and more significant divine reality.

9.3 Meaning and Human Progress

- Hegel and Marx define the meaning of life in terms of contributing toward human progress. For Hegel, history progresses toward a fuller expansion of freedom; for Marx, history progresses toward a classless society.

9.4 The Nihilist Rejection of Meaning

- The nihilist response to the meaning of life is the claim that life has no meaning, a view that Arthur Schopenhauer embraced.

9.5 Meaning as a Self-Chosen Commitment

- The existentialists Søren Kierkegaard and Jean-Paul Sartre argue that the meaning of life is created by what one chooses; for Sartre things have no value apart from our choices, while for Kierkegaard God has value even apart from our choices.

Glossary

All terms highlighted in the text are defined in this glossary. Some of these terms carry nuances that are unmentioned here. Every attempt has been made to be concise without being misleading.

A

a posteriori pertaining to knowledge that is empirically verifiable; based on inductive reasoning from what is experienced

a priori pertaining to knowledge whose possession is logically prior to experience; reasoning based on such knowledge

act utilitarianism in normative ethics, the view that an action is morally right if it produces the greatest happiness for the greatest number of people

agnosticism a claim of ignorance particularly of religious matters; the claim that God's existence can be neither proved nor disproved

analogy a comparison of two things in an argument which is intended to demonstrate that since the two share one aspect, they must share another as well

anthropomorphism the attributing of human qualities to nonhuman entities, especially to God

antirealism the doctrine that the objects of our senses do not exist independently of our perceptions, beliefs, concepts, and language

argument a group of statements consisting of premises and conclusions of such a type that the premises are intended to prove or demonstrate the conclusion

argument from design *see* design argument

atheism denial of theism; the view that God or a god does not exist

atman the Hindu idea of the true self; the ego or soul; pure consciousness

autonomy the freedom of being able to decide for oneself by using one's own rationality

avidya in Buddhism, the cause of all suffering and frustration; ignorance or unawareness that leads to clinging

axiom a proposition regarded as self-evident or true

B

behaviorism a school of psychology that restricts the study of human nature to what can be observed rather than to states of consciousness

Brahman the Hindu concept of an impersonal Supreme Being; the source and goal of everything; the ultimate reality

C

categorical imperative Immanuel Kant's ethical formula: Act as if your maxim (general rule by which you act) could be willed to become a universal law; the principle that what is morally right for one person in one set of circumstances is also morally right for anyone else in similar circumstances

categorical syllogism the most important kind of categorical argument. The categorical syllogism contains exactly *two premises* and *a conclusion*. In addition, a categorical syllogism contains only *three terms*

causality, causation events connected together as cause and effect; the relationship between two events in which one brings about or produces the other

cause whatever is responsible for or leads to a change, motion, or condition; an event that brings about another event

coherence theory a theory contending that truth is a property of a related group of consistent statements

communitarianism view that the actual community in which we live should be at the center of our analysis of society and government

compatibilism view that rejects the idea that determinism rules out freedom and responsibility and that argues instead that causal determinism is compatible with freedom

conceptual relativist view the view that a true scientific theory is nothing more than a theory that coheres with the conceptual framework accepted by a community of scientists

consequentialist theory in ethics, the position that the morality of an action is determined by its nonmoral consequences

contract theory in social philosophy, the doctrine that individuals give up certain liberties and rights to the state, which in turn guarantees such rights as life, liberty, and the pursuit of happiness

correspondence theory a theory contending that truth is an agreement between a proposition and a fact

cosmological argument argument for the existence of God that claims that there must be an ultimate causal explanation for why the universe as a totality exists

critical thinking the kind of thinking we do when we base our beliefs and actions on unbiased and valid reasoning that uses well-founded evidence, that avoids false generalizations and unrecognized assumptions, and that considers opposing viewpoints

---

D

deduction the process of reasoning to logically certain conclusions

deductive argument an argument in which the premises are intended to show that the conclusion must necessarily be true so long as the premises are true

deductive reasoning *see* deduction

defining characteristic a characteristic in whose absence a thing would not be what it is

design argument an argument for the existence of God that claims that the order and purpose manifest in the working of things in the universe require a God

determinism the theory that every event is caused or determined by previous conditions and events together with the physical, biological, and psychological laws that govern reality; the view that human actions are completely determined by what the laws of nature cause us to do

dharma in Buddhism, one's duty as set forth by the Buddha; the principles whereby self-frustration is ended; the Eightfold Path prescribed by the Buddha

divine command theory a non-consequential normative theory that says we should always do what God commands; the view that actions are morally right if and only if God commands or permits them, and morally wrong if and only if God forbids them

dualism a theory that holds that reality is composed of two distinct kinds of substances, neither of which can be reduced to the other, such as spirit/matter or mind/body

duty in ethics, an obligation; what one is morally required to do; what a morally upright individual must do

---

E

egoism ethical theory that contends that we act morally when we act in a way that promotes our own interests

empiricism the position that knowledge has its origins in and derives all of its content from experience

essence that which makes an entity what it is; that defining characteristic in whose absence a thing would not be itself

ethical egoism in ethics, the view that we act morally when we act in a way that promotes our own interests

ethical relativism a view that denies the existence of any universally applicable moral standard; a view that claims that the truth or validity of a moral standard is not absolute but depends on the standards held or accepted by a social group

ethics the branch of philosophy tries to determine the good and right thing to do

existence actuality

existentialism a twentieth-century philosophy that denies any essential human nature and holds that each of us creates our own essence through our free actions

---

F

free will the capacity or power to act without one's actions being causally determined by events or conditions outside one's control

functionalism explanation of mental activities and states as terms that mediate or relate perceptual inputs and behavioral outputs

---

G

Golden Rule the ethical rule that holds: Do unto others as you would have them do unto you

---

H

hedonism the view that only pleasure is intrinsically worthwhile

human nature what constitutes something as a human being; what makes us different from anything else; the collection of qualities that make us human

hypothesis in general, an assumption, statement, or theory of explanation, the truth of which is under investigation

---

I

idealism in metaphysics, the position that reality is ultimately non-matter; the view that reality consists of mind and its contents

identity theory the theory that mental states are really physical brain states

indeterminism the view that some individual choices are not causally determined by preceding events over which the individual has no control

individualism the social theory that emphasizes the importance and primacy of the individual, of his or her rights, and of his or her independence of action

induction the process of reasoning to probable explanations or judgments

inductive reasoning *see* induction

inference to the best explanation an argument that assumes that the theory that best explains a large set of facts is probably true

infinite regress an infinite series of causally or logically related terms that has no first or initiating term

innate ideas ideas that, according to some philosophers such as Plato, can never be found in experience but that are inborn

instrumentalist view in epistemology, the view that scientific theories can be true only in the sense that they enable us to accurately predict what will happen and that any unobservable entities postulated by the theory do not literally exist

intuition a source of knowledge that does not rely on the senses or reason but on direct awareness of something

J

judgment asserting or denying something in the form of a proposition

K

karma the Hindu law of sowing and reaping; the law that, according to Hinduism, determines that the form and circumstances we assume in each reincarnated state depend upon our actions in prior incarnations

L

libertarianism in metaphysics, the view that determinism is false and that people are free to choose to act other than they do; in social philosophy, the view that the right to freedom from restraint takes priority over all other rights

logical positivism the philosophical school of thought, associated with Carnap and Ayer, that claims that only analytic and empirically verifiable statements are meaningful and that because metaphysical and ethical statements are neither, the latter are meaningless

M

materialism the metaphysical position that reality is ultimately composed of matter

maya in Buddhism, the world of illusion

mechanism the view that all natural processes can be explained in terms of mechanical laws that govern matter and its motions

metaphysics the branch of philosophy that studies the nature of reality

monism the view that reality is reducible to one kind of thing or one explanatory principle

monotheism the view that there is a single God

morality the standards that an individual or a group has about what is right and wrong or good and evil

N

natural law a pattern of necessary and universal regularity; a universal moral imperative derived from the nature of things; a moral standard inferred from the nature of human beings that indicates how everyone ought to behave

nihilism the view that nothing exists, that nothing has value; the social view that conditions are so bad that they should be destroyed and replaced by something better

nirvana in Buddhism, enlightenment that comes when the limited clinging self is extinguished

nonconsequentialist theory in ethics, a theory that holds that the morality of an action is determined by more than just its consequences

O

objective possessing a public nature that is independent of us and our judgments about it

objective idealism the position that ideas exist in an objective state; associated originally with Plato

omniscient all-knowing

ontological argument an argument for the existence of God based on the nature of God's being

P

perception the processes of seeing, hearing, smelling, touching, and tasting; an observation made through these processes

phenomenalism the belief, associated with Kant, that we can know only appearances (phenomena) and never what is ultimately real (noumena), that the mind has the ability to sort out sense data and provide relationships that hold among them

philosophy the love of wisdom; the activity of critically and carefully examining the reasons behind our most fundamental assumptions

political philosophy that part of social philosophy that looks at the nature and proper role of the state or government in society

positivism the view that only analytic and empirically verifiable propositions are meaningful; the view that all nonanalytic knowledge must be derived from or based on what can be empirically experienced or perceived

postmodernism late-twentieth-century movement that rejects the view that there is only one reality and that through rational inquiry we are progressing toward an ever fuller unified scientific understanding of that one reality

pragmatism the philosophical school of thought, associated with Dewey, James, and Peirce, that tries to mediate between idealism and materialism by rejecting all absolute first principles, tests truth through workability, and views the universe as pluralistic

pre-Socratics the Greek philosophers before Socrates

primary qualities according to Locke, those qualities that inhere in an object, including size, shape, weight, and so on

psychological egoism the view that human beings are so constituted that they must always act out of self-interest

R

rationalism the position that reason alone, without the aid of sensory information, is capable of arriving at the knowledge of some undeniable truths

realism the doctrine that the objects of our senses exist independently of their being experienced

realist view the view that scientific theories are literally true or false and that the unobservable entities postulated in a scientific theory really exist if the theory is true

reason the capacity for thinking logically and making inferences; the process of following relationships from thought to thought and of ultimately drawing conclusions

reductionism the view that one kind of thing is constituted by or reducible to another kind of thing; in particular the view that processes such as thought and life are nothing more than physical or chemical processes

relativism the view that the truth or falsity of a class of propositions depends upon the beliefs held by a social group; the view that all human judgments are conditioned by factors such as culture and personal experience

religious belief the doctrines of a religion about the universe and one's relation to the supernatural

right a justified entitlement or claim on others

rule utilitarianism the normative ethical position that we should act so that the rule governing our actions is the one that would produce the greatest happiness for the most people if everyone were to follow it

S

samsara in Buddhism, the cycle of birth and life

scientific method a form of investigation based on collecting, analyzing, and interpreting sense data to determine the most probable explanation

self the ego or "I" that exists in a physical body and that is conscious and rational

sense data images or sensory impressions

skepticism in epistemology, the view that no knowledge of reality is possible

social philosophy the philosophical study of society including the study of the application of moral principles to the problems of society, and the study of the nature of freedom, equality, justice, political obligation, and the state

solipsism an extreme form of subjective idealism, contending that only I exist and that everything else is a product of my subjective consciousness

soul an immaterial entity that is identified with a consciousness, mind, or personality

sound argument an argument that is both valid and has true premises

subjective that which refers to, or depends on, the knower; that which exists in the consciousness but not apart from it

subjective idealism in epistemology, the position that all we ever know are our own ideas

T

tautology a statement whose predicate repeats its subject in whole or in part or is true by definition

teleology the view that natural organisms have a purpose or are designed to achieve an end; a view that maintains that purposes inhere in nature and affirms that the universe either was consciously designed for, or is operating under some partly conscious, partly unconscious, purpose

theism the belief in a personal God who intervenes in the lives of the creation

theology the rational study of God, including religious doctrines

transcendental idealism in epistemology, the view that the *form* of our knowledge of reality derives from reason but its *content* comes from our senses

V

valid in logic, having a conclusion that follows from the premises by logical necessity

value *(as a verb)* to impose worth on something; to believe that something has worth

value *(as a noun)* an object or quality that is believed to have worth or be desirable; that which is worthy of pursuit; that which is, or ought to be, regarded highly or held dear

virtue ethics in ethics, a moral theory that holds that the moral life should be concerned with cultivating a virtuous character rather than following rules of action

Index

Time Period	Important Philosophers	Political, Cultural, and Scientific Events of Period
1500 B.C.	Vedic and Upanishad Philosophers of India (c. 1500–700 B.C.) Buddha (c. 560–480 B.C.) Thales (c. 624–545 B.C.) Confucius (c. 551–479 B.C.)	Shang Dynasty (1600–1027 B.C.) loosely unites China India's first kingdoms rise (1500–330 B.C.) by Ganges River Mycenaean civilization declines in Greece; city-states Athens and Sparta rise (1200–700 B.C.) Homer writes *Illiad* and *Odyssey* (c. 750 B.C.)
500 B.C.	Heraclitus (c. 500 B.C.) Parmenides (c. 500 B.C.) Zeno of Elea (c. 490–430 B.C.) Protagoras (c. 481–411 B.C.) Socrates (c. 470–399 B.C.) Democritus (c. 460–370 B.C.) Thrasymachus (c. 450 B.C.) Perictione (c. 450–350 B.C.) Plato (c. 427–348 B.C.) Aristotle (384–322 B.C.) Mencius (c. 372–289 B.C.) Epicurus (341–270 B.C.) Cicero (106–43 B.C.) Lucretius (c. 98–55 B.C.)	Hindu epic *Ramayana* written (c. 500 B.C.) Asoka (272–231 B.C.) rules first empire of India Greeks defeat Persians at Salamis (480 B.C.) Pericles (495–429 B.C.) leads Athens during "Golden Age"; builds Acropolis, promotes drama of Sophocles, Euripides, and Aristophanes, sees flowering of art, mathematics, philosophy In Peloponnesian War, Sparta defeats Athens (431–404 B.C.) Histories of Herodotus (484–425) and Thucydides (460–395) Alexander the Great (356–323 B.C.) unites ancient western world and spreads Greek culture as far as India Old Testament Pentateuch completed (c. 400 B.C.) Founding of Rome (508 B.C.) Rome conquers Mediterranean world (380–202 B.C.) Golden Age of Rome (63 B.C.–14 A.D.)
A.D. 1	Seneca (c. 1 B.C.–A.D. 65) Epictetus (c. 55–135) Marcus Aurelius (121–180) Plotinus (205–c. 269) St. Augustine of Hippo (354–430)	Jesus Christ (c. 6 B.C.–A.D. 30) initiates Christianity Nero (Roman Emperor, 54–68) persecutes Christians Ptolemy envisions earth-centered universe (c. 90–168) Fall of Roman Empire to Germanic invaders (476) Dark Ages of Europe (476–800)
A.D. 500	Boethius (c. 480–524) Shankara (788–820) Al-Farabi (870–950) Avicenna (980–1037)	Muhammad (570–632) founds Islam in Arab world Arab Muslims expand, Arab empire at its height (700) Charlemagne crowned emperor of former Roman Empire (800) Classical Mayan civilization rises in Mexico (c. 250–c. 900)
A.D. 1000	Anselm (1033–1109) Abelard (1079–1142) Maimonides (1125–1204) Albert the Great (1206–1280) Roger Bacon (1214–1292) Thomas Aquinas (1225–1274) Duns Scotus (c. 1266–1308) William of Ockham (c. 1285–1349)	Sung Dynasty (960–1279) rules China, until replaced by Mongol Dynasty (1279–1368) Crusades (1096–1204) drive Muslims from Palestine Renaissance begins in Italy (1215) Dante (1265–1321) writes *Divine Comedy* (1307–1321) Black Death ravages Europe (1347) Gutenberg prints *Bible* (1453) Columbus sails to New World (1492)
A.D. 1500	D. Erasmus (1465–1536) N. Machiavelli (1469–1527) Thomas More (1478–1535) Francisco Suarez (1548–1607)	Spanish conquistadores defeat Aztecs of Mexico (1519–1524) Copernicus (1473–1543) argues Earth revolves around sun Luther (1483–1546) begins Protestant Reformation Elizabeth I crowned Queen of England (1558)

Time Period	Important Philosophers	Political, Cultural, and Scientific Events of Period
A.D. 1600	Francis Bacon (1561–1626) Thomas Hobbes (1588–1679) Rene Descartes (1596–1650) Anne Conway (1631–1679) Baruch Spinoza (1632–1677) Nicolas de Malebranche (1638–1715) Gottfried Leibniz (1646–1716) William Paley (1743–1805)	Shakespeare (1564–1616) writes plays and poems Kepler (1571–1630) discovers laws of planetary motion Galileo (1564–1642) condemned by Inquisition (1633) Age of Enlightenment begins in Europe (c. 1641) Rembrandt (1606–1669) and Velasquez (1599–1660) paint Manchu Dynasty (1644–1911) rules in China Leibniz and Newton invent the calculus (c. 1670's) Newton (1642–1727) publishes *Principia* (1687)
A.D. 1700	John Locke (1632–1704) George Berkeley (1685–1753) Voltaire (1694–1778) David Hume (1711–1776) Immanuel Kant (1724–1804) Paul d'Holbach (1723–1789) Edmund Burke (1729–1797) Jeremy Bentham (1748–1832) Mary Wollstonecraft (1759–1797) William Paley (1743–1805)	Swift (1667–1745) publishes *Gulliver's Travels* (1726) Bach (1685–1750), Handel (1685–1759) compose music American Revolution (1775–1783) Smith (1723–1790) writes *Wealth of Nations* (1776) Industrial Revolution in England (1780) French Revolution (1789–1791) Mozart (1756–1791), Beethoven (1770–1827) compose symphonies Laplace (1749–1827) writes *Celestial Mechanics* (1799) Neoclassic art of David (1748–1825) and Ingres (1780–1867)
A.D. 1800	William Whewell (1794–1866) J. G. Fichte (1762–1814) F. Schleiermacher (1768–1834) G. W. F. Hegel (1770–1831) James Mill (1773–1835) Arthur Schopenhauer (1788–1860)	Jefferson (1743–1836) is president of U.S. (1801–1809) Friedrich (1774–1840), Blake (1757–1827) paint romantic art Goethe (1749–1832) publishes *Faust* (1808) Napoleon defeated at Waterloo (1815) Revolutions in Paris, Vienna, Venice, Berlin (1848) Mendel (1822–1884) publishes laws of heredity (1866)
A.D. 1850	Ludwig Feuerbach (1804–1872) John Stuart Mill (1806–1873) Soren Kierkegaard (1813–1855) Henry David Thoreau (1817–1862) Karl Marx (1818–1883) Friedrich Engels (1820–1895) Herbert Spencer (1820–1903)	Darwin (1809–1882) writes *Origin of Species* (1859) American Civil War (1861–1865) Lincoln issues Emancipation Proclamation (1863) Tolstoy (1828–1910) publishes *War and Peace* (1863) Huxley (1825–1895) publishes *Man's Place in Nature* (1864) Brahms (1833–1897) writes his symphonies Impressionist art of Manet (1832–1883), Degas (1834–1917), Monet (1840–1926), Renoir (1841–1919), Cassatt (1844–1926) Friedrich Nietzsche (1844–1900)
A.D. 1900	Charles S. Peirce (1839–1914) William James (1842–1910) Francis Bradley (1846–1924) Edmund Husserl (1854–1938) Henri Bergson (1859–1941) John Dewey (1859–1952) J. McTaggart (1866–1925) Mahatma Gandhi (1869–1948)	Freud (1856–1939) publishes *The Interpretation of Dreams* (1900) Wright brothers fly first successful airplane (1903) Einstein (1879–1955) discovers special relativity (1905) and general relativity (1915) Quantum theory developed by Planck (1858–1947), Heisenberg, (1901–1976), Bohr (1885–1962) World War I (1914–1917) October Revolution in Russia begins communist rule (1917)

Time Period	Important Philosophers	Political, Cultural, and Scientific Events of Period
A.D. 1920	G. E. Moore (1873–1958) Bertrand Russell (1872–1970) Martin Buber (1878–1965) Moritz Schlick (1882–1936) Sarvepalli Radhakrishnan (1888–1975) Ludwig Wittgenstein (1889–1951) Martin Heidegger (1889–1976) Rudolf Carnap (1891–1970) Brand Blanshard (1892–1987) H. H. Price (1899–1984)	Joseph Stalin (1879–1953) comes to power in Russia (1922) Russian Famines, 10–13 million die (1931–1933 and 1947) Hubble (1889–1953) discovers universe is expanding (1929) Gödel (1906–1978) discovers incompleteness theorems (1931) Great Depression (1929–1939) Keynes publishes *General Theory* (1936) Hitler (1889–1945) in power in Germany (1933–1945) Hitler's Nazis murder 5 million Jews (c. 1939–1945) Anthropologists Herskovits (1895–1963), Benedict (1887–1948), and Mead (1901–1978) support moral relativism
A.D. 1940	Paul Tillich (1886–1965) Gilbert Ryle (1900–1976) Karl Popper (1902–1994) Jean-Paul Sartre (1905–1980) M. Merleau-Ponty (1907–1961) Simone de Beauvoir (1908–1986) A. J. Ayer (1910–1989) Albert Camus (1913–1960) D. M. Armstrong (1926–)	Atomic bombs dropped on Japan (1945) World War II (1939–1945) ends United Nations convenes (1946) Watson (1878–1958) and Skinner (1904–1990) develop Behaviorism; Maslow (1908–1970) and Rogers (1902–1987) develop Humanistic Psychology Mao Tse-tung's Communists take over China and establish The People's Republic (1949) Mao's purges kill 2–5 million Chinese (1949–1953)
A.D. 1950	Nelson Goodman (1906–1998) Willard V. O. Quine (1908–2000) Isaiah Berlin (1909–1997) J. L. Austin (1911–1960) Norman Malcolm (1911–1990) Roderick Chisholm (1916–1999) Kurt Baier (1917–2010) Donald Davidson (1917–2003) Richard M. Hare (1919–2002)	Korean War (1950–1953) Stalin dies (1953) after killing 4–10 million Russian "Enemies" Supreme Court makes segregation illegal (1954) European Common Market established (1958) Castro takes power in Cuba (1959) Martin Luther King Jr. begins civil rights movement (1955) Elvis Presley is "King of Rock n' Roll" (1954–1974) Mao's "Great Leap Forward" sets off famines that starve 30 million Chinese (1959–1962)
A.D. 1960	John Rawls (1921–2002) Thomas Kuhn (1922–1996) John Hick (1922–2012) Paul Feyerabend (1924–1994) Hilary Putnam (1926–) Mary Daly (1928–2010) Alasdair MacIntyre (1929–)	U.S. enters Vietnam War (1962–1973) President John F. Kennedy assassinated (1963) Beatles dominate popular music (1963–1969) Civil Rights Act passed (1964) Cultural Revolution in China (1966) Woodstock concert (1969) is icon of hippie era Apollo II lands on the moon (1969)

Time Period	Important Philosophers	Political, Cultural, and Scientific Events of Period
A.D. 1970	Jacques Derrida (1930–2004) Charles Taylor (1931–) Richard Rorty (1931–2007) John Searle (1932–) Alvin Plantinga (1932–) Richard Swinburne (1934–) Michael Walzer (1935–) Thomas Nagel (1937–) Robert Nozick (1938–2002)	Intel sells first microprocessor (1971) Supreme Court allows abortion (1972) Arab oil embargo cripples U.S. economy (1973) U.S. pulls out of Viet Nam (1973) President Nixon resigns due to Watergate scandal (1974) Mao Tse-tung dies in China (1976) Apple Computer sells first personal computer (1976) Ayatollah Khomeini overthrows Shah to rule Iran (1979) Thatcher conservative prime minister of England (1979–1990)
A.D. 1980	Saul Kripke (1940–) Stephen T. Davis (1940–) James Rachels (1941–2003) Paul Churchland (1942–) Daniel Dennett (1942–) Patricia Churchland (1943–) Peter Singer (1946–) Paul Davies (1946–) Martha Nussbaum (1947–)	Reagan conservative president of U.S. (1981–1989) O'Connor is first female Supreme Court Justice (1981) AIDS epidemic begins (1981) Michael Jackson releases *Thriller* (1982) First Space walk (1984) Hole in ozone layer over Antarctic detected (1985) Record heat and drought suggest global warming (1988) Berlin Wall falls (1989) Collapse of communism in Soviet Union (1989)
A.D. 1990	Michael J. Tye (1951–) Michael Sandel (1953–) Paul Draper (1957–) Catherine Malabou (1959–)	Persian Gulf War (1990–1991) USSR dissolves (1991) South Africa ends apartheid (1993) First animals cloned (1997)
A.D. 2000	Scott Sehon (1963–) Shaun Nicols (1964–) Mark Mercer (1965–) David Chalmers (1966–) Quentin Meillassoux (1967–) Graham Harman (1968–) Jason Stanley (1969–)	Intergovernmental Panel on Climate Change warns global warming is due to greenhouse gas emissions (2001) Terrorists blow up New York Twin Towers (2001) Afghanistan war begins (2001) Iraq war (2003–2011) Barack Obama is first African-American President (2009) Terrorist Osama Bin Laden is killed (2011) "Arab Spring" of revolutions in Tunisia, Egypt, Libya, Yemen, Syria, and Bahrain (2009–2012)